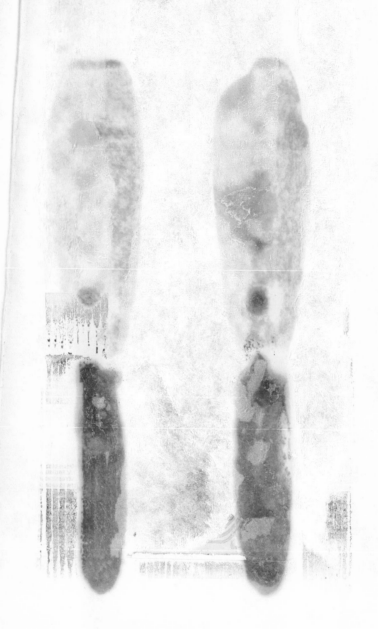

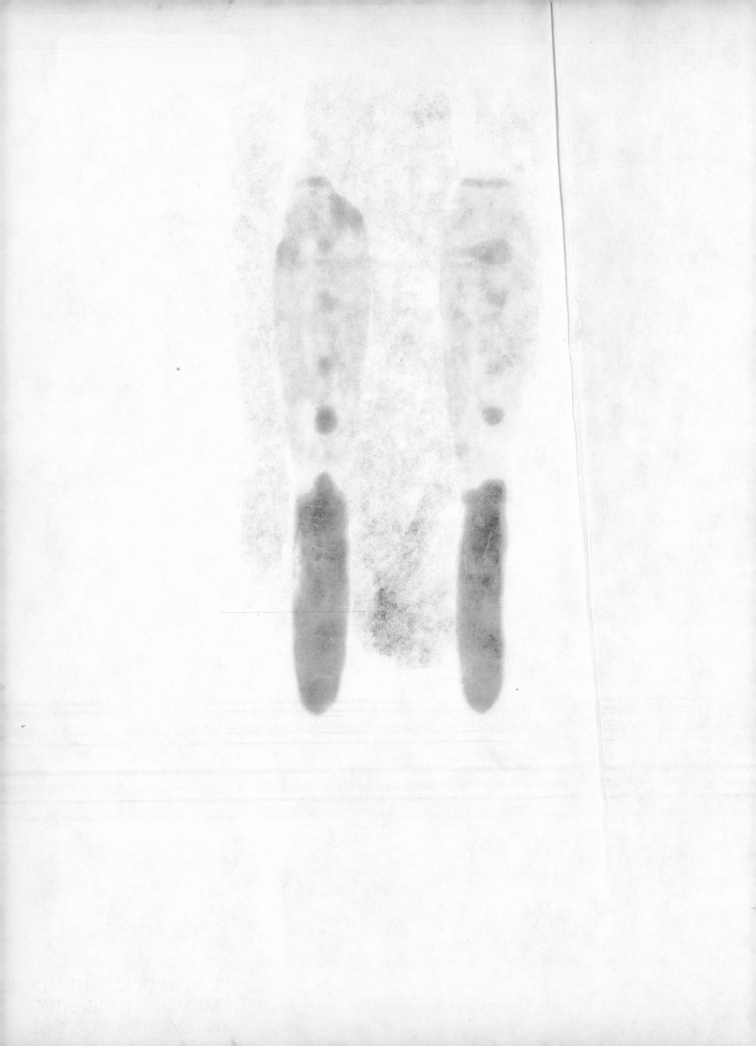

The Great American Movie Book

Paul Michael

The Academy Awards: A Pictorial History

Humphrey Bogart: The Man and His Films

The American Movies Reference Book:
The Sound Era (Editor-in-Chief)

The Great American Movie Book

PAUL MICHAEL
Editor-in-Chief

James Robert Parish
Associate Editor

John Robert Cocchi   Ray Hagen   Jack Edmund Nolan
Contributing Editors

Prentice-Hall, Inc., Englewood Cliffs, N.J.

Prentice-Hall International, Inc., London
Prentice-Hall of Australia, Pty. Ltd., Sydney
Prentice-Hall of Canada, Ltd., Toronto
Prentice-Hall of India Private Ltd., New Delhi
Prentice-Hall of Japan, Inc., Tokyo
Prentice-Hall of Southeast Asia Pte. Ltd., Singapore
Whitehall Books Limited, Wellington, New Zealand

10 9 8 7 6 5 4 3 2 1

Library of Congress Cataloging in Publication Data
    Main entry under title:

The Great American movie book.

    Bibliography: p.
    Includes indexes.
        1.   Moving-pictures—United States—Dictionaries.
I.   Michael, Paul.
PN1993.45.G7   791.43′7   79-14452
ISBN 0-13-363663-1
ISBN 0-13-363655-0 pbk.

ACKNOWLEDGMENTS

The editors wish to extend their thanks to the following for their generous help in the preparation of this volume: Entertainment Copyright Research Co., Inc., 225 West 57th Street, New York, New York, for making available their most complete files on the motion picture industry, for without the extensive library and research facilities of this organization, the book would not have been possible; Lennard DeCarl, for making available his detailed files on all available screen credits of over 1,500 performers, gathered over a period of nearly two decades; Jerry Vermilye, whose career studies of such performers as Jean Arthur, Ida Lupino and Maria Montez have appeared in *Films in Review* and *Screen Facts*, for his tremendous help in the verification of material; Ken Jones, Mrs. Peter Smith, Charles Stumpf, Charles Smith and Harry Wilkinson, for opening their superb collections of photographs; Marc Ricci, for opening the doors of The Memory Shop and allowing the selection of hundreds of photographs for use in the book.

The editors would also like to thank: William Breen, Samuel Goldwyn Productions; Ted McInerney; Martin A. Grove, American Broadcasting Company; Judith L. Bly, The Walter Reade Organization; Paul Kamey, Universal Pictures Corporation; Harvey Stewart; Leonard Brown, Collectors Book Shop; Jonas Rosenfield, Jr., and Jerry Anderson, 20th Century-Fox; Perry Mandel, Vitaprint; Michael Linden and Joseph Infantino, Motion Picture Association of America; Harold Danziger, Columbia Pictures; Charles Alicoate and Gloria Kravitz, *Film Daily*; Arthur Freed, former President of the Academy of Motion Picture Arts and Sciences; Lorraine Burdick; Mary Fiore and Mark J. Greenberg, *Photoplay* magazine; Florence Solomon; Peter Miglierini; Samuel M. Sherman; Robert Seger, Harshe-Rotman and Druck; Barney Pitkin; Phil Moshcovitz, Famous Fantasy Films; Sig Shore, Video Artists Features; David Bloom, Hollywood Television Service; Erwin Ezzes and Helen Killeen, United Artists Television; Paul Lazarus and Albert Stefanic, National Screen Service; Lou Valentino; Peter Rogers and Ruth Robinson, National Telefilm Associates; Hank Warner, CBS-TV; Marvin Korman, Screen Gems; Phil Saltman, MCA-TV; Emery Austin and Norman Kaphan, Metro-Goldwyn-Mayer; A. Morgan Maree and Earl R. Beaman, The Selznick Company; David Cantor, Magna Pictures Corporation; Lou Edelman, Embassy Film Corporation; Jack Goldstein, Allied Artists Corporation; Leonard Maltin, *Film Fan Monthly*; Albert B. Manski; Jeanne Stein; Mike Berman, Paramount Pictures; Jonas Mekas, *Film Culture* magazine; Henry Hart, *Films in Review*; Homer Dickens; William K. Everson; Jane Gordon, Seven Arts Associated Corporation; Robert W. Fouse, The American Humane Association; Mrs. Rose Cocchi; Lillian Schwartz and her staff at the Academy of Motion Pictures Arts and Sciences, Barbara Browning, Joyce Foreman, Midori Martin, Mildred Simpson; Don Koll; Hilary Knight; Victor Sanjuro; Hanna Henner; the late Walt Disney; Apco Apeda Photos; Mariana Fitzpatrick and Shirley Stein, our very patient editors, and hundreds of others in and out of the motion picture industry.

KEY TO ABBREVIATIONS

AA   Allied Artists
AIP   American International
BIP   British International Pictures
BV   Buena Vista
Col.   Columbia Pictures
DCA   Distributing Corporation of America
EL   Eagle Lion Classics
Fox   Fox Picture Corporation
GN   Grand National Pictures
Lip.   Lippert Pictures
MGM   Metro-Goldwyn-Mayer, Inc.
Mon.   Monogram Pictures
Par.   Paramount Pictures
PRC   Producers Releasing Corporation
PRO   Producers Releasing Organization
Rank   J. Arthur Rank
Rep.   Republic Pictures
RKO   RKO Radio Pictures
Tif.   Tiffany
20th   20th Century-Fox Film Corporation
UA   United Artists
Univ.   Universal Pictures, Universal-International
WB   Warner Brothers Pictures and First National Pictures

INTRODUCTION

The screen at the Warner Theatre in New York flickered. Al Jolson had just finished singing one of his numbers. "Wait a minute, wait a minute. You ain't heard nothin' yet, folks; listen to this." With these homespun phrases spoken by Jolson to a speakeasy audience in *The Jazz Singer* on October 6, 1927, a revolution started, a revolution which was to change the film industry.

Legend has it that Jolson had ad-libbed those now-famous lines during the recording of his musical number and that they had been left in the film at the insistence of Sam Warner. But, whatever the reason for the dialogue, the lines of eager people that awaited each performance of *The Jazz Singer* attested to the fact that the public was ready for sound.

It is a far cry from Jolson's simple bit of dialogue to the meticulously orchestrated Dolby Sound which reduced audiences to jelly in 1979's smash hit, *Alien*. The astonishing advances in sound technology during the last half-century are just one indication of the flexibility and vitality of a medium which has withstood the test of time and the formidable competition of television. Saturday night has meant marquees and popcorn and holding hands in the dark to generations of Americans. Movies continue to work their special magic today.

The following pages document great moments and faces in a celluloid world which at times seems as real as our own. The glamour. The nostalgia. The sheer entertainment.

Join us. Sit back and remember.

Curtain going up!

CONTENTS

THE FILMS

Abbott and Costello Meet Frankenstein with Glenn Strange, Lou Costello and Bud Abbott.

ABBOTT AND COSTELLO MEET FRANKENSTEIN (1948) Univ. Producer, Robert Arthur. Director, Charles T. Barton. Original Screenplay, Robert Lees, Frederic I. Rinaldo, John Grant. Art Directors, Bernard Herzbrun, Hilyard Brown. Music, Frank Skinner. Photography, Charles Van Enger. Editor, Frank Gross. 92 minutes

Chick: Bud Abbott, *Wilbur:* Lou Costello, *Lawrence Talbot:* Lon Chaney, *Dracula:* Bela Lugosi, *Monster:* Glenn Strange, *Sandra Mornay:* Lenore Aubert, *Joan Raymond:* Jane Randolph, *Mr. Mc-Dougal:* Frank Ferguson, *Dr. Stevens:* Charles Bradstreet, *Mr. Harris:* Howard Negley, *Man:* Joe Kirk, *Man in Armor:* Clarence Straight, *Photographer:* Harry Brown, *Woman at Baggage Counter:* Helen Spring, *Sergeant:* Paul Stader, *Voice of the Invisible Man:* Vincent Price.

ABE LINCOLN IN ILLINOIS (1940) RKO. Presented by Max Gordon Plays and Pictures Corp. Produced by Max Gordon. Directed by John Cromwell. Based on the play by Robert E. Sherwood. Screenplay, Robert E. Sherwood, Grover Jones. Music, Roy Webb. Dance Director, David Robel. Cameraman, James Wong Howe. Special Effects, Vernon Walker. Montage, Douglas Travers. 110 minutes

Abraham Lincoln: Raymond Massey, *Stephen Douglas:* Gene Lockhart, *Mary Todd Lincoln:* Ruth Gordon, *Ann Rutledge:* Mary Howard, *Elizabeth Edwards:* Dorothy Tree, *Ninian Edwards:* Harvey Stephens, *Joshua Speed:* Minor Watson, *Billy Herndon:* Alan Baxter, *Jack Armstrong:* Howard da Silva, *Judge Bowling Green:* Aldrich Bowker, *John McNeil:* Maurice Murphy, *Mentor Graham:* Louis Jean Heydt, *Ben Mattling:* Clem Bevans, *Denton Offut:* Harlan Briggs, *Sarah Lincoln:* Elisabeth Risdon, *Tom Lincoln:* Charles Middleton, *Seth Gale:* Herbert Rudley, *Mr. Crimmin:* Roger Imhof, *Stage Driver:* Andy Clyde, *Mr. Rutledge:* Edmund Elton, *Mrs. Rutledge:* Leona Roberts, *Mrs. Bowling Green:* Florence Roberts, *Dr. Chandler:*

Abe Lincoln in Illinois with Raymond Massey and Mary Howard.

1

Above and Beyond with Eleanor Parker and Robert Taylor.

George Rosener, *Mrs. Gale:* Fay Helm, *John Hanks:* Trevor Bardette, *John Johnston:* Sid Saylor, *Gobey:* Napoleon Simpson, *Trem Cogdall:* Alec Craig, *Little Girl:* Peggy Ann Garner.

ABOVE AND BEYOND (1952) MGM. Producers, Melvin Frank, Norman Panama. Directors, Melvin Frank, Norman Panama. Author, Beirne Lay, Jr. Screenplay, Melvin Frank, Norman Panama, Beirne Lay, Jr. Music, Hugo Friedhofer. Art Directors, Cedric Gibbons, Malcolm Brown. Sound, Douglas Shearer. Sets, Edwin B. Willis, Ralph Hurst. Cinematographer, Ray June. Editor, Cotton Warburton. Music conducted by Andre Previn. Montage Sequences, Peter Ballbusch. Special Effects, A. Arnold Gillespie, Warren Newcombe. 122 minutes

Colonel Paul Tibbets: Robert Taylor, *Lucey Tibbets:* Eleanor Parker, *Major Uanna:* James Whitmore, *Major Gen. Vernon C. Brent:* Larry Keating, *Captain Parsons:* Larry Gates, *Marge Bratton:* Marilyn Erskine, *Major Harry Bratton:* Stephen Dunne, *General Samuel E. Roberts:* Robert Burton, *Dr. Ramsey:* Hayden Rorke, *Dr. Van Dyke:* Larry Dobkin, *Dr. Fiske:* Jack Raine, *Dutch Van Kirk:* Jonathan Cott, *Thomas Ferebee:* Jeff Richards, *Bob Lewis:* Dick Simmons, *Wyatt Duzenbury:* John McKee, *Radio Operator:* Patrick Conway, *Paul Tibbets, Jr.:* Christie Olsen, *Driver:* William Lester, *Mary Malone:* Barbara Ruick, *General LeMay:* Jim Backus, *Major Gen. Creston:* G. Pat Collins, *Chaplain Downey:* Harlan Warde, *General Corlane:* Crane Whitley, *Dexter:* Don Gibson, *Captain:* John W. Baer, *Co-Pilot:* John Close, *General Roberts' Aide:* Lee MacGregor, *General Wolfe:* Ewing Mitchell, *General Irvine:* Mack Williams, *Captain:* Sam McKim, *M. P. Officer:* Robert Forrest, *Haddock:* Dabbs Greer, *Nurse:* Dorothy Kennedy, *Lieut. Malone:* John Hedloe, *Sergeant Wilson:* Frank Gerstle, *Miller:* John Pickard, *Burns:* Gregory Walcott, *Johnson:* Roger McGee, *Extra:* Robert Fuller.

ABRAHAM LINCOLN (1930) UA. Produced and directed by D. W. Griffith. Adapted for the screen by Stephen Vincent Benét. Screenplay, Stephen Vincent Benét, Garrit Lloyd. Art Director, William Cameron Menzies. Costumes, Walter Israel. Dialogue Director, Harry Stubbs. Photography, Karl Struss. Editors, James Smith, Hal C. Kern. Sound, Harold Witt. A Feature Production. Griffith's first sound film. 97 minutes

Abraham Lincoln: Walter Huston, *Ann Rutledge:* Una Merkel, *Mary Todd Lincoln:* Kay Hammond, *John Wilkes Booth:* Ian Keith, *D.*

Abraham Lincoln with Kay Hammond and Walter Huston.

Offut: Otto Hoffman, *General Lee:* Hobart Bosworth, *Colonel Marshall:* Henry B. Walthall, *Nancy Hanks Lincoln:* Helen Freeman, *Tom Lincoln:* W. L. Thorne, *Midwife:* Lucille La Verne, *Armstrong:* Edgar Dearing, *Stephen A. Douglas:* E. Alyn Warren, *Lincoln's Employer:* Russell Simpson, *Sheriff:* Charles Crockett, *Mrs. Edwards:* Helen Ware, *Billy Herndon:* Jason Robards, *Tad Lincoln:* Gordon Thorpe, *John Hay:* Cameron Prudhomme, *General Scott:* James Bradbury, Sr., *Young Soldier:* Jimmie Eagles, *General Grant:* Fred Warren, *Secretary of War Stanton:* Oscar Apfel, *General Philip Sheridan:* Frank Campeau, *New Englander:* Henry Kolker, *Bit:* Mary Forbes, *Man:* Robert E. Homans.

THE ABSENT-MINDED PROFESSOR (1961) BV. Producer, Walt Disney. Director, Robert Stevenson. Screenplay, Bill Walsh. Based on a story by Samuel W. Taylor. Photography, Edward Colman. Music, George Bruns. Art Direction, Carroll Clark. Editor, Cotton Warburton. Special Effects, Peter Ellenshaw and Eustace Lycett. Sound, Dean Thomas. Associate Producer, Bill Walsh. Assistant Director, Robert G. Shannon. Film debuts of Keenan Wynn's son Ned, and Steve Allen's mother Belle Montrose. 97 minutes

Ned Brainard: Fred MacMurray, *Betsy Carlisle:* Nancy Olson, *Alonzo Hawk:* Keenan Wynn, *Bill Hawk:* Tommy Kirk, *Fire Chief:* Ed Wynn, *President Rufus Daggett:* Leon Ames, *Coach Elkins:* Wally Brown, *First Referee:* Alan Carney, *Shelby Ashton:* Elliott Reid, *Defense Secretary:* Edward Andrews, *General Singer:* David Lewis, *Air Force Captain:* Jack Mullaney, *Mrs. Chatsworth:* Belle Montrose, *Officer Kelly:* Forrest Lewis, *Officer Hanson:* James Westerfield, *Youth:* Ned Wynn, *Reverend Bosworth:* Gage Clarke, *General Hotchkiss:* Alan Hewitt, *Admiral Olmstead:* Raymond Bailey, *General Poynter:* Wendell Holmes, *Lenny:* Don Ross, *Sig:* Charlie Briggs, *TV Newsman:* Wally Boag, *Basketball Player (#18):* Leon Tyler.

The Absent-Minded Professor with Fred MacMurray and Nancy Olson.

ADAM'S RIB (1949) MGM. Producer, Lawrence Weingarten. Director, George Cukor. Screenplay, Garson Kanin, Ruth Gordon. Music, Miklos Rozsa. Art Directors, Cedric Gibbons, William Ferrari. Photography, George J. Folsey. Editor, George Boemler. Song by Cole Porter: "Farewell Amanda." Film debut of Jean Hagen. 101 minutes

Adam Bonner: Spencer Tracy, *Amanda Bonner:* Katharine Hepburn, *Doris Attinger:* Judy Holliday, *Warren Attinger:* Tom Ewell, *Kip Lurie:* David Wayne, *Beryl Caighn:* Jean Hagen, *Olympia La Pere:* Hope Emerson, *Grace:* Eve March, *Judge Reiser:* Clarence Kolb, *Jules Frikke:* Emerson Treacy, *Mrs. McGrath:* Polly Moran, *Judge Marcasson:* Will Wright, *Dr. Margaret Brodeigh:* Elizabeth Flournoy, *Mary (Maid):* Janna da Loos, *Dave:* James Nolan, *Roy:* David Clarke, *Court Clerk:* John Maxwell, *Court Stenographer:* Marvin Kaplan, *Police Matron:* Gracille LaVinder, *Benjamin Klausner:* William Self, *Emerald:* Paula Raymond, *Photographer:* Ray Walker, *Reporter:* Tommy Noonan, *Adam's Assistants:* De Forrest Lawrence, John Fell, *Amanda's Assistant:* Sid Dubin, *Mr. Bonner:* Joe Bernard, *Mrs. Bonner:* Madge Blake, *Mrs. Marcasson:* Marjorie Wood, *Judge Poynter:* Lester Luther, *Mrs. Poynter:* Anna Q. Nilsson, *Hurlock:* Roger David, *Elderly Elevator Operator:* Louis Mason, *Fat Man:* Rex Evans, *Young District Attorney:* Charles Bastin.

Adam's Rib with Spencer Tracy, David Wayne, Judy Holliday and Katharine Hepburn.

THE ADVENTURES OF ROBIN HOOD (1938) WB. Producer, Hal B. Wallis. Associate Producer, Henry Blanke. Directors, Michael Curtiz, William Keighley. Color by Technicolor. Authors and Screenplay, Norman Reilly Raine, Seton I. Miller. Art Director, Carl Jules Weyl. Music, Erich Wolfgang Korngold. Musical Director, Leo F. Forbstein. Cameramen, Tony Gaudio, Sol Polito, W. Howard Green. Editor, Ralph Dawson. 105 minutes

Robin Hood: Errol Flynn, *Maid Marian:* Olivia de Havilland, *Prince John:* Claude Rains, *Sir Guy:* Basil Rathbone, *King Richard:* Ian Hunter, *Friar Tuck:* Eugene Pallette, *Little John:* Alan Hale, *High Sheriff:* Melville Cooper, *Will Scarlett:* Patric Knowles, *Much, the Miller:* Herbert Mundin, *Bess, the Maid:* Una O'Connor, *Bishop of Black Canon:* Montagu Love, *Dicken Malbott:* Harry Cording, *Sir Geoffrey:* Robert Warwick, *Sir Ralfe:* Robert Noble, *Sir Mortimer:* Kenneth Hunter, *Essex:* Leonard Willey, *Sir Ivor:* Lester Matthews, *Sir Baldwin:* Colin Kenny, *Captain of Archers:* Howard Hill, *Proprietor of Kent Road Tavern:* Ivan F. Simpson, *Crippen:* Charles McNaughton, *Humility Prin:* Lionel Belmore, *Humility's Daughter:* Janet Shaw, *Sir Nigel:* Austin Fairman, *Sir Norbett:* Craufurd Kent, *Robin's Outlaws:* Val Stanton, Ernie Stanton, Olaf Hytten, Alec Harford, Peter Hobbes, Edward Dew, *Richard's Knight:* John Sutton, *Sir Guy's Squire:* Marten Lamont, *High Sheriff's Squire:* Hal Brazeale, *Seneschal:* Herbert Evans, *Referee:* Holmes Herbert, *Norman Officer:* Leyland Hodgson.

The Adventures of Robin Hood with Basil Rathbone and Errol Flynn.

THE ADVENTURES OF THE WILDERNESS FAMILY (1975) Pacific International Enterprises. Produced by Arthur R. Dubs. Directed and Written by Stewart Raffill. Color by CFI. Associate Producer, Peter B. Good. Executive Producer and Production Manager, Joseph C. Raffill. Editor, R. Hansel Brown. Music by Gene Kauer and Douglas Lackey. Lyrics by Dennis Bachmann. Songs, "The Wilderness Family" and "To Touch the Wind," sung by Lee Dresser. Photography, Gerard Alcan. Additional Photography, Peter B. Good. Filmed in the Colorado Rockies. Rated G. 94 minutes. Sequel is *Wilderness Family Part 2* (1978) with the same leads, except Heather Rattray replaced Hollye Holmes

Skip Robinson: Robert F. Logan, *Pat Robinson:* Susan Damante Shaw, *Jenny Robinson:* Hollye Holmes, *Toby Robinson:* Ham Larsen, *Boomer (Willard Parks):* George (Buck) Flower, *Pilot:* William Cornford, *Doctor 1:* John F. Goss, *Doctor 2:* Herbert F. Nelson.

The Adventures of the Wilderness Family with Robert Logan.

AN AFFAIR TO REMEMBER (1957) 20th. Produced by Jerry Wald. Directed by Leo McCarey. Stereophonic Sound. In CinemaScope and De Luxe Color. Screenplay, Delmer Daves and Leo McCarey. Story, Leo McCarey and Mildred Cram. Art Directors, Lyle R. Wheeler and Jack Martin Smith. Music, Hugo Friedhofer. Conducted by Lionel Newman. Orchestrations, Edward B. Powell and Peter King. Title song by Harry Warren, lyrics by Leo McCarey and Harold Adamson. Sung by Vic Damone. Wardrobe Designer, Charles LeMaire. Assistant Director, Gilbert Mandelik. Cinematography, Milton Krasner. Special Photographic Effects, L. B. Abbott. Editor, James B. Clark. A remake of *Love Affair* (RKO, 1939). 119 minutes

Nickie Ferrante: Cary Grant, *Terry McKay:* Deborah Kerr, *Kenneth:*

An Affair to Remember with Deborah Kerr, Cary Grant and Cathleen Nesbitt.

Richard Denning, *Lois:* Neva Patterson, *Grandmother:* Cathleen Nesbitt, *Announcer:* Robert Q. Lewis, *Hathaway:* Charles Watts, *Courbet:* Fortunio Bonanova, *Doctor:* Walter Woolf King, *French Commentator:* Roger Til, *English TV Commentator:* Jack Raine, *Italian Commentator:* Dino Bolognese, *Painter:* Jack Lomas, *Mother:* Dorothy Adams, *Doctor:* Robert Lynn, *Blonde:* Patricia Powell, *Airline Stewardess:* Alena Murray, *Ship Passenger:* Minta Durfee, *Father McGrath:* Matt Moore, *Marius:* Louis Mercier, *Miss Webb:* Geraldine Wall, *Miss Lane:* Sarah Selby, *Gladys:* Nora Marlowe, *Bartender:* Alberto Morin, *Gabrielle:* Genevieve Aumont, *Landlady:* Jesslyn Fax, *Red-Head:* Tommy Nolan, *Orphans:* Theresa Emerson, Richard Allen, Tina Thompson, Scotty Morrow, Kathleen Charney, Terry Ross Kelman, Norman Champion, III, *Teachers:* Mary Carroll, Suzanne Ellers, Juney Ellis, *Page Boy:* Don Pietro, *Bit Man:* Paul Bradley, *Waiter:* Tony De Mario, *Waiter on Ship:* Michka Egan, *Maitre D':* Bert Stevens, *Boy, age 5:* Brian Corcoran, *French Child:* Priscilla Garcia, *Ship's Photographer:* Marc Snow, *Page Boy:* Anthony Mazzola, *Nurse:* Helen Mayon.

The African Queen with Peter Bull, Katharine Hepburn and Humphrey Bogart.

THE AFRICAN QUEEN (1951) UA. Producer, S. P. Eagle (Sam Spiegel), Director, John Huston. Color by Technicolor. Screenplay, James Agee and John Huston. Based on the novel by C. S. Forester. Music, Allan Gray. 106 minutes

Charlie Allnut: Humphrey Bogart, *Rose Sayer:* Katharine Hepburn, *Reverend Samuel Sayer:* Robert Morley, *Captain of* LOUISA: Peter Bull, *First Officer:* Theodore Bikel, *Second Officer:* Walter Gotell, *Petty Officer:* Gerald Onn, *First Officer of* SHONA: Peter Swanick, *Second Officer of* SHONA: Richard Marner.

After the Thin Man with Myrna Loy, William Powell and Sam Levene.

AFTER THE THIN MAN (1936) MGM. Produced by Hunt Stromberg. Directed by W. S. Van Dyke. Author, Dashiell Hammett. Screenplay by Frances Goodrich, Albert Hackett. Musical Score, Herbert Stothart, Edward Ward. Cameraman, Oliver T. Marsh. Editor, Robert J. Kern. Songs: "Smoke Dreams" by Arthur Freed and Nacio Herb Brown; "Blow That Horn" by Walter Donaldson, Bob Wright, and Chet Forrest. Second in the series of six pictures. 110 minutes

Nora Charles: Myrna Loy, *Nick Charles:* William Powell, *David Graham:* James Stewart, *Dancer:* Joseph Calleia, *Salma Landis:* Elissa Landi, *Aunt Katherine Forrest:* Jessie Ralph, *Robert Landis:* Alan Marshal, *Lt. Abrams:* Sam Levene, *Polly Byrnes:* Dorothy McNulty (later Penny Singleton), *Charlotte:* Dorothy Vaughn, *Helen:* Maude Turner Gordon, *Floyd Casper:* Teddy Hart, *Lum Kee:* William Law, *General:* William Burress, *William:* Thomas Pogue, *Dr. Adolph Kammer:* George Zucco, *Henry* (the Butler): Tom Ricketts, *Phil Byrnes:* Paul Fix, *Joe:* Joe Caits, *Willie:* Joe Phillips, *Hattie:* Edith Kingdon, *Jerry:* John T. Murray, *Harold:* John Kelly, *Lucius:* Clarence Kolb, *Lucy:* Zeffie Tilbury, *S. F. Police Captain:* George Guhl, *Chief of Detectives:* Guy Usher, *Bill, S. F. Policeman:* Ed Dearing, *Reporter:* Jack Norton, *S. F. Detective:* Dick Rush, *Rose* (the Cook): Mary Gordon, *Emily:* Alice H. Smith, *Eddie:* George Taylor, *Burton Forrest:* Harlan Briggs, *Kid:* Murray Alper, *Headwaiter:* Richard Loo, *Peter* (Butler): Eric Wilton, *Wrestler's Manager:* Vince Barnett, *Fingers:* Harry Tyler, *Leader of Late Crowd:* Bobby Watson.

THE AGONY AND THE ECSTASY (1965) 20th. Director, Carol Reed. Screen story and screenplay, Philip Dunne. Based on the novel by Irving Stone. Music, Alex North. Director of Photography, Leon Shamroy. Assistant Director, Gus Agosti. Costumes, Vittorio Nino Novarese. In Todd-AO and De Luxe Color. 140 minutes

Michelangelo: Charlton Heston, *Pope Julius II:* Rex Harrison, *Contessina de' Medici:* Diane Cilento, *Bramante:* Harry Andrews, *Duke of Urbino:* Alberto Lupo, *Giovanni de' Medici:* Adolfo Celi, *Paris De-Grassis:* Venantino Venantini, *Sangallo:* John Stacy, *Foreman:* Fausto Tozzi, *Woman:* Maxine Audley, *Raphael:* Tomas Milian.

The Agony and the Ecstasy with Charlton Heston and Rex Harrison.

AIR FORCE (1943) WB. Produced by Hal B. Wallis. Directed by Howard Hawks. Original Screenplay, Dudley Nichols. Music, Franz Waxman. Music Director, Leo F. Forbstein. Chief Pilot, Paul Mantz. Editor, George Amy. 124 minutes

Captain Mike (Irish) Quincannon, Pilot: John Ridgely, *Lt. Bill Williams, Copilot:* Gig Young, *Lt. Tommy McMartin, Bombardier:* Arthur Kennedy, *Lt. Munchauser, Navigator:* Charles Drake, *Sgt. Robby White, Crew Chief:* Harry Carey, *Corp. Weinberg, Assistant Crew Chief:* George Tobias, *Corp. Peterson, Radio Operator:* Ward Wood, *Pvt. Chester, Assistant Radio Operator:* Ray Montgomery, *Sgt. Joe Winocki, Aerial Gunner:* John Garfield, *Lt. Tex Rader, Pursuit Pilot:* James Brown, *Major Mallory:* Stanley Ridges, *Colonel:* Willard Robertson, *Colonel Blake, C. O.:* Moroni Olsen, *Sgt. J. J. Callahan:* Edward S. Brophy, *Major W. G. Roberts.* Richard Lane, *Lt. P. T. Moran:* Bill Crago, *Susan McMartin, Major Daniels:* Addison Richards, *Major A. M. Bagley:* James Flavin, *Mary Quincannon:* Ann Doran, *Mrs. Chester:* Dorothy Peterson, *Marine with Dog:* James Millican, *Group Cmdr. Jack Harper:* William Forrest, *Corporal, Demolition Squad:* Murray Alper, *Officer at Hickam Field:* George Neise, *Marine:* Tom Neal, *Quincannon's Son:* Henry Blair, *Control Officer:* Warren Douglas, *Nurse:* Ruth Ford, *Second Nurse:* Leah Baird, *Sergeants:* Bill Hopper and Sol Gorss, *Control Officer:* James Bush, *Ground Crew Man:* George Offerman, Jr., *Joe (Sergeant):* Walter Sande, *Nurses:* Lynne Baggett and Marjorie Hoshelle, *First Lieutenant:* Theodor von Eltz, *Second Lieutenant:* Ross Ford, *Copilot:* Rand Brooks.

Air Force with John Garfield, Harry Carey, Ray Montgomery (on ground) and Charles Drake.

AIRPORT (1970) Univ. Produced by Ross Hunter. Directed by George Seaton. Todd-AO and Technicolor. From the novel by Arthur Hailey. Screenplay, Seaton. Associate Producer, Jacque Mapes. Photography, Ernest Laszlo. Art Directors, Alexander Golitzen and E. Preston Ames. Set Decoration, Jack D. Moore and Mickey S. Michaels. Sound, Waldon O. Watson, David H. Moriarty and Ronald Pierce. Music Editor, Arnold Schwarzwald. Music composed and conducted by Alfred Newman. Costumes, Edith Head. Editor, Stuart Gilmore. Make-up, Bud Westmore. Hairstylist, Larry Germain. Technical Advisers, John N. Denend (F.A.A. Air Traffic Control) and Capt. Lee Danielson. Special Photographic Effects, Film Effects of Hollywood, Don W. Weed and James B. Gordon. Assistant Director, Donald Roberts. Locations filmed at Minneapolis-St. Paul International Airport. Rated G. 137 minutes

Mel Bakersfeld: Burt Lancaster, *Vernon Demerest:* Dean Martin, *Ada Quonsett:* Helen Hayes, *Tanya Livingston:* Jean Seberg, *Gwen Meighen:* Jacqueline Bisset, *Joe Patroni:* George Kennedy, *D. O. Guerrero:* Van Heflin, *Inez Guerrero:* Maureen Stapleton, *Lt. Anson Harris:* Barry Nelson, *Cindy Bakersfeld:* Dana Wynter, *Harry Standish:* Lloyd Nolan, *Sarah Bakersfeld Demerest:* Barbara Hale, *Harriet DuBarry Mossman:* Jessie Royce Landis, *Cy Jordan:* Gary Collins, *Peter Coakley:* John Findlater, *Commissioner Ackerman:* Larry Gates, *Marcus Rathbone:* Peter Turgeon, *Mr. Davidson:* Whit Bissell, *Mrs. Schultz:* Virginia Grey, *Judy:* Eileen Wesson, *Dr. Compagno:* Paul Picerni, *Captain Benson:* Robert Patten, *Bert Weatherby:* Clark Howat, *Reynolds:* Lew Brown, *Roberta Bakersfeld:* Ilana Dowding, *Libby Bakersfeld:* Lisa Gerritsen, *Father Steven Lonigan:* Jim Nolan, *Joan:* Patty Poulsen, *Ruth:* Ena Hartman, *Maria:* Malila Saint Duval, *Sally:* Sharon Harvey, *Lt. Ordway:* Albert Reed, *Marie Patroni:* Jodean Russo, *Bunnie:* Nancy Ann Nelson, *Mr. Schultz:* Dick Winslow, *Schuyler Schultz:* Lou Wagner, *Sister Katherine Grace:* Janis Hansen, *Sister Felice:* Mary Jackson, *Rollings:* Shelly Novack, *Parks:* Chuck Daniel, *Diller:* Charles Brewer, *Father praying:* Damian London, *Passenger:* Harry Harvey, *Cindy's Father:* Walter Woolf King.

Airport with Jean Seberg and Burt Lancaster.

AIRPORT 1975 (1974) Univ. Produced by William Frye. Directed by Jack Smight. Inspired by the film *Airport* and based on the novel by Arthur Hailey. Screenplay, Don Ingalls. Executive Producer, Jennings Lang. Photography, Philip Lathrop. Editor, J. Terry Williams. Costumes, Edith Head. Art Director, George C. Webb. Assistant Directors, Alan Crosland and Wayne Farlow. Music by John Cacavas. Song "Best Friend" by Helen Reddy and R. Burton. First sequel to *Airport*, 1970. Panavision and Technicolor. 2nd Unit Director, James Gavin. 2nd Unit Photography,

Rexford Metz. Stunt Coordinator, Joe Canutt. Rated PG. Film debut of Helen Reddy. Filmed partly at Dulles International Airport in Washington, D.C. 107 minutes

Alan Murdock: Charlton Heston, *Gloria Swanson:* Gloria Swanson, *Nancy:* Karen Black, *Joe Patroni:* George Kennedy, *Mrs. Devaney:* Myrna Loy, *Capt. Stacy:* Efrem Zimbalist, Jr., *Mrs. Patroni:* Susan Clark, *Sister Ruth:* Helen Reddy, *Janice Abbott:* Linda Blair, *Scott Freeman:* Dana Andrews, *Mrs. Freeman:* Beverly Garland, *Urias:* Roy Thinnes, *Barney:* Sid Caesar, *Maj. Alexander:* Ed Nelson, *Mrs. Abbott:* Nancy Olson, *Purcell:* Larry Storch, *Sister Beatrice:* Martha Scott, *Sam:* Jerry Stiller, *Bill:* Norman Fell, *Arnie:* Conrad Janis, *Winnie:* Augusta Summerland (Linda Harrison), *Col. Moss:* Guy Stockwell, *Julio:* Erik Estrada, *Lt. Thatcher:* Kip Niven, *Fat Man:* Charles White, *Joseph Patroni, Jr.:* Brian Morrison, *Amy:* Amy Farrell, *Carol:* Irene Tsu, *Gary:* Ken Sansom, *Danton:* Alan Fudge, *Bette:* Christopher Norris, *Air Force Sergeant:* Austin Stoker, *Oringer:* John Lupton, *First Friend:* Gene Dynarski, *Aldine:* Aldine King, *Sharon:* Sharon Gless, *Arlene:* Laurette Spang, *Themselves:* Jim Plunkett, Gene Washington, *Bit:* Ray Vitte, *Passenger:* Joan Crosby.

Airport 1975 with Augusta Summerland (Linda Harrison) and Gloria Swanson.

AIRPORT '77 (1977) Univ. Produced by William Frye. Directed by Jerry Jameson. Based on a story by H. A. L. Craig and Charles Kuenstle. Screenplay, Michael Scheff and David Spector. Executive Producer, Jennings Lang. 2nd Unit Director, Michael Moore. Photography, Philip Lathrop. 2nd Unit Photography, Rexford Metz. Editors, J. Terry Williams and Robert Watts. Production Designer, George C. Webb. Set Decoration, Mickey S. Michaels. Special Visual Effects, Albert Whitlock. Special Effects, Frank Brendel. Matte Photography, Bill Taylor and Dennis Glouner. Miniatures, Cleo E. Baker. Stunt Coordinator, Stan Barrett. Sound, Charles D. Knight, Robert Knudson and Jim Troutman. Costumes, Edith Head. Grant's Costumes, Burton Miller. Make-up, Mark Reedall. Hairstyles, Connie Nichols. Assistant Directors, Wilbur Mosier, Bob Graner and Jim Nasella. Music Composed and Conducted by John Cacavas. Song, "Beauty Is in the Eyes of the Beholder" by Tom Sullivan. Filmed in Panavision and Technicolor in California, Florida and Washington, D.C. Rated PG. 114 minutes

Don Gallagher: Jack Lemmon, *Phillip Stevens:* James Stewart, *Emily Livingston:* Olivia de Havilland, *Karen Wallace:* Lee Grant, *Eve Clayton:* Brenda Vaccaro, *Nicholas St. Downs III:* Joseph Cotten, *Martin Wallace:* Christopher Lee, *Joe Patroni:* George Kennedy, *Stan Buchek:* Darren McGavin, *Chambers:* Robert Foxworth, *Eddie:* Robert Hooks, *Banker:* Monte Markham, *Julie:* Kathleen Quinlan, *Frank Powers:* Gil Gerard, *Ralph Crawford:* James Booth, *Anne:* Monica Lewis, *Dorothy:* Maidie Norman, *Lisa:* Pamela Bellwood, *Jane Stern:* Arlene Golonka, *Steve:* Tom Sullivan, *Dr. Williams:* M. Emmet Walsh, *Walker:* Michael

Richardson, Wilson: Michael Pataki, *Gerald Lucas:* George Furth, *Commander Paul Guay:* Richard Venture, *Johnson:* Ross Bickell, *Lt. Tommy Norris:* Peter Fox, *Admiral Corrigan:* Charles Macaulay, *Hunter:* Tom Rosqui, *Commander Reed:* Arthur Davis, *Benjy:* Anthony Battaglia, *Bonnie Stern:* Elizabeth Cheshire, *Larry:* Dar Robinson, *Chef:* Ted Chapman, *Passenger:* Chuck Hayward, *Radiomen:* Chris Lemmon, William Whitaker, *Frogmen:* Peter Greene, Asa Teeter.

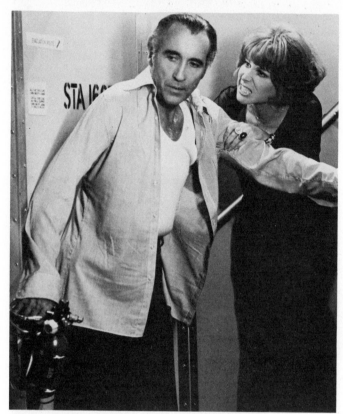

Airport '77 with Christopher Lee and Lee Grant.

The Alamo with Chill Wills and John Wayne.

THE ALAMO (1960) UA. Producer-Director, John Wayne. Todd-AO and Technicolor. Screenplay, James Edward Grant. Music, Dimitri Tiomkin. Songs, Dimitri Tiomkin and Paul Francis Webster. A Batjac Production. Second Unit Director, Cliff Lyons. Photography, William Clothier. Editor, Stuart Gilmore. Art Director, Alfred Ybarra. Sets, Victor A. Gangelin. Technical Supervision, Frank Beetson and Jack Pennick. Assistant Directors, Robert E. Relyea, Robert Saunders, John Ford. Costumes, Frank Beetson and Ann Peck. Special Effects, Lee Zavitz. Make-up, Web Overlander. Production

Manager, Nate Edwards. Assistant to the Producer, Michael Wayne. Songs, "The Green Leaves of Summer" and "Lisa." Bit player Le Jeane Guye, 27, was killed October 11, 1959. Filmed in Texas. 192 minutes

Col. David Crockett: John Wayne, *Col. James Bowie:* Richard Widmark, *Col. William Travis:* Laurence Harvey, *Gen. Sam Houston:* Richard Boone, *Lt. Reyes:* Carlos Arruza, *Smitty:* Frankie Avalon, *James Bonham:* Pat Wayne, *Flaca:* Linda Cristal, *Mrs. Dickinson:* Joan O'Brien, *Beekeeper:* Chill Wills, *Juan Seguin:* Joseph Calleia, *Capt. Dickinson:* Ken Curtis, *Parson:* Hank Worden, *Gambler Thimblerig:* Denver Pyle, *Angelina:* Aissa Wayne, *Silverio Seguin:* Julian Trevino, *Jethro:* Jester Hairston, *Blind Nell:* Veda Ann Borg, *Mrs. Dennison:* Olive Carey, *Emil:* Wesley Lau, *Bull:* Tom Hennesy, *Dr. Sutherland:* Bill Henry, *Pete:* Cy Malis, *Jocko Robertson:* John Dierkes, *Lieutenant Finn:* Guinn "Big Boy" Williams, *Sgt. Lightfoot:* Jack Pennick, *Bearded Volunteer:* Fred Graham, *Colonel Neill:* Bill Daniel, *Tennessean:* Chuck Roberson, *Woman:* Le Jeane Guye.

Alexander's Ragtime Band with Alice Faye, Tyrone Power, Jack Haley and Don Ameche.

ALEXANDER'S RAGTIME BAND (1938) 20th. Producer, Darryl F. Zanuck. Associate Producer, Harry Joe Brown. Director, Henry King. Screenplay, Kathryn Scola, Lamar Trotti, Richard Sherman. Art Directors, Bernard Herzbrun, Boris Leven. Cameraman, Peverell Marley. Editor, Barbara McLean. Songs by Irving Berlin: "Now It Can Be Told", "My Walking Stick", "Alexander's Ragtime Band", "I'm Marching Along With Time." Dances staged by Seymour Felix. 105 minutes

Alexander (Roger Grant): Tyrone Power, *Stella Kirby:* Alice Faye, *Charlie Dwyer:* Don Ameche, *Jerry Allen:* Ethel Merman, *Davey Lane:* Jack Haley, *Professor Heinrich:* Jean Hersholt, *Aunt Sophie:* Helen Westley, *Taxi Driver:* John Carradine, *Bill:* Paul Hurst, *Wally Vernon:* Himself, *Ruby:* Ruth Terry, *Snapper:* Douglas Fowley, *Louie:* Chick Chandler, *Corporal Collins:* Eddie Collins, *Dillingham's Stage Manager:* Joseph Crehan, *Dirty Eddie:* Robert Gleckler, *Specialty:* Dixie Dunbar, *Charles Dillingham:* Joe King, *Babe:* Grady Sutton, *Singer:* Donald Douglas, *Headwaiter:* Charles Coleman, *Captain:* Stanley Andrews, *Agent:* Charles Williams, *Trio:* Jane Jones, Mel Kalish, Otto Fries, *Drill Sergeant:* Jack Pennick, *Member of Band:* Cully Richards, *Manager of Radio Station:* Selmer Jackson, *Dillingham's Secretary:* Charles Tannen, *Photographer:* Lon Chaney, Jr., *Assistant Stage Manager:* Arthur Rankin, *Stage Manager:* Paul McVey, *Quartette:* King's Men, *Major:* Edward Keane, *Captain:* James Flavin, *Assistant Stage Manager:* Tyler Brooke, *Captain:* Ralph Dunn, *Martha:* Eleanor Wesselhoeft, *Reporter:* Robert Lowery.

ALIBI (1929) UA. Produced and directed by Roland West. From the play *Nightstick* by John Wray, J. C. Nugent, and Elaine Sterne Car-

rington. Story and dialogue, Roland West and C. Gardner Sullivan. Music, Hugo Riesenfeld. Photography, Ray June. Editor, Hal Kern. Titles for silent version, Roland West and C. Gardner Sullivan. Shot originally as a silent, this was refilmed with sound on the *Coquette* set, at night. 90 minutes

Chick Williams (No. 1065): Chester Morris, *Danny McGann:* Regis Toomey, *Daisy Thomas:* Mae Busch, *Joan Manning:* Eleanor Griffith, *Buck Bachman:* Harry Stubbs, *Toots:* Irma Harrison, *Brown:* Al Hill, *Blake:* James Bradbury, Jr., *Soft Malone:* Elmer Ballard, *Trask:* Kernan Cripps, *Sgt. Pete Manning:* Purnell B. Pratt, *Tommy Glennon:* Pat O'Malley, *O'Brien:* DeWitt Jennings, *George Stanislaus David:* Edwin Brady, *Singers in Theater:* Virginia Flohri, Edward Jardon.

Alibi with Purnell Pratt, Pat O'Malley and Chester Morris.

Alice Adams with Katharine Hepburn and Fred Stone.

ALICE ADAMS (1935) RKO. Produced by Pandro S. Berman. Directed by George Stevens. From Booth Tarkington's 1921 Pulitzer Prize novel. Screenplay, Dorothy Yost and Mortimer Offner. Adaptation, Jane Murfin. Photography, Robert de Grasse. Song: "I Can't Waltz Alone" by Dorothy Fields and Max Steiner. 99 minutes

Alice Adams: Katharine Hepburn, *Arthur Russell:* Fred MacMurray, *Mr. Adams:* Fred Stone, *Mildred Palmer:* Evelyn Venable, *Walter Adams:* Frank Albertson, *Mrs. Adams:* Ann Shoemaker, *Mr. Lamb:*

Charles Grapewin, *Frank Dowling:* Grady Sutton, *Mrs. Palmer:* Hedda Hopper, *Mr. Palmer:* Jonathan Hale, *Henrietta Lamb:* Janet McLeod, *Mrs. Dowling:* Virginia Howell, *Mrs. Dresser:* Zeffie Tilbury, *Ella Dowling:* Ella McKenzie, *Malena:* Hattie McDaniel.

Alice Doesn't Live Here Anymore with Kris Kristofferson and Ellen Burstyn.

ALICE DOESN'T LIVE HERE ANYMORE (1974) WB. Produced by David Susskind and Audrey Maas. Directed by Martin Scorsese. Associate Producer, Sandra Weintraub. Screenplay by Robert Getchell. Photography, Kent L. Wakeford. Designer, Toby Carr Rafelson. Editor, Marcia Lucas. Sound, Don Parker. Assistant Directors, Mike Moder and Mike Kusley. Later a TV series, with Tayback repeating his role. Technicolor. Rated PG. 113 minutes

Alice Hyatt: Ellen Burstyn, *David:* Kris Kristofferson, *Flo:* Diane Ladd, *Ben:* Harvey Keitel, *Audrey:* Jodie Foster, *Mel:* Vic Tayback, *Vera:* Valerie Curtin, *Tommy Hyatt:* Alfred Lutter, *Donald Hyatt:* Billy Green Bush, *Bea:* Lelia Goldoni, *Rita:* Lane Bradbury, *Jacobs:* Murray Moston, *Bartender:* Harry Northup, *Alice at 8:* Mia Bendixsen, *Old Woman:* Ola Moore, *Lenny:* Martin Brinton, *Chicken:* Dean Casper.

All About Eve with Celeste Holm, Hugh Marlowe, Bette Davis and Anne Baxter.

ALL ABOUT EVE (1950) 20th. Producer, Darryl F. Zanuck. Director-Screenplay, Joseph Mankiewicz. Author, Mary Orr from *The Wisdom of Eve*. Music, Alfred Newman. Art Directors, Lyle Wheeler, George W. Davis. Photography, Milton Krasner. Editor, Barbara

McLean. Scenes filmed at the Curran Theatre, San Francisco. Later a Broadway musical, *Applause, Applause*. 138 minutes

Margo Channing: Bette Davis, *Eve Harrington:* Anne Baxter, *Addison De Witt (Narrator):* George Sanders, *Karen Richards:* Celeste Holm, *Bill Sampson:* Gary Merrill, *Lloyd Richards:* Hugh Marlowe, *Birdie:* Thelma Ritter, *Miss Caswell:* Marilyn Monroe, *Max Fabian:* Gregory Ratoff, *Phoebe:* Barbara Bates, *Speaker at Dinner:* Walter Hampden, *Girl:* Randy Stuart, *Leading Man:* Craig Hill, *Doorman:* Leland Harris, *Autograph Seeker:* Barbara White, *Stage Manager:* Eddie Fisher, *Clerk:* William Pullen, *Pianist:* Claude Stroud, *Frenchman:* Eugene Borden, *Reporter:* Helen Mowery, *Captain of Waiters:* Steven Geray, *Well-Wisher:* Bess Flowers.

All Quiet on the Western Front with Lew Ayres and Raymond Griffith.

ALL QUIET ON THE WESTERN FRONT (1930) Univ. Directed by Lewis Milestone. Based on the novel by Erich Maria Remarque. Screenplay, Dell Andrews, Maxwell Anderson and George Abbott. Art Directors, Charles D. Hall and W. R. Schmitt. Synchronization and Score, David Broekman. Assistant Director, Nate Watt. Photography, Arthur Edeson. Editors, Edgar Adams and Milton Carruth. Sound, C. Roy Hunter. Titles (Silent Version), Walter Anthony. Filmed at Universal City, Balboa, the Irving Ranch. The European version featured ZaSu Pitts as Mrs. Baumer (she was in the original film, before being replaced by Beryl Mercer). Reissued in 1939 with a narrator telling of the horrors of war. 140 minutes

Paul Baumer: Lew Ayres, *Katczinsky:* Louis Wolheim, *Himmelstoss:* John Wray, *Gerard Duval:* Raymond Griffith, *Tjaden:* George (Slim) Summerville, *Muller:* Russell Gleason, *Albert:* William Bakewell, *Leer:* Scott Kolk, *Behm:* Walter Browne Rogers, *Kemmerick:* Ben Alexander, *Peter:* Owen Davis, Jr., *Mrs. Baumer:* Beryl Mercer, *Mr. Baumer:* Edwin Maxwell, *Detering:* Harold Goodwin, *Miss Baumer:* Marion Clayton, *Westhus:* Richard Alexander, *Lieutenant Bertinck:* G. Pat Collins, *Suzanne:* Yola D'Avril, *French Girls:* Renée Damonde, Poupée Androit, *Kantorek:* Arnold Lucy, *Ginger:* Bill Irving, *Herr Meyer:* Edmund Breese, *Hammacher:* Heinie Conklin, *Sister Libertine:* Bertha Mann, *Watcher:* Bodil Rosing, *Poster Girl:* Joan Marsh, *Orderly:* Tom London, *Cook:* Vince Barnett, *Man:* Fred Zinnemann. Lewis Milestone's hand was used for Ayres' at the end when Paul reaches for a butterfly.

ALL THE KING'S MEN (1949) Col. Producer, Robert Rossen. Director, Robert Rossen. Based on the novel by Robert Penn Warren. Screenplay, Robert Rossen. Musical Director, Morris Stoloff. Art Director, Sturges Carne. Photography, Burnett Guffey. Editor, Al Clark. 109 minutes

All the King's Men with Mercedes McCambridge, John Ireland, Broderick Crawford and Walter Burke.

Willie Stark: Broderick Crawford, *Tom Stark:* John Derek, *Anne Stanton:* Joanne Dru, *Jack Burden:* John Ireland, *Sadie Burke:* Mercedes McCambridge, *Adam Stanton:* Shepperd Strudwick, *Tiny Duffy:* Ralph Dumke, *Lucy Stark:* Ann Seymour, *Mrs. Burden:* Katharine Warren, *Judge Stanton:* Raymond Greenleaf, *Sugar Boy:* Walter Burke, *Dolph Pillsbury:* Will Wright, *Floyd McEvoy:* Grandon Rhodes, *Pa Stark:* H. C. Miller, *Hale:* Richard Hale, *Commissioner:* William Bruce, *Sheriff:* A. C. Tillman, *Madison:* Houseley Stevenson, *Minister:* Truett Myers, *Football Coach:* Phil Tully, *Helene Hale:* Helene Stanley, *Politician:* Judd Holdren, *Receptionist:* Reba Watterson, *Man:* Paul Ford, *Dance Caller:* Ted French, *Local Chairman:* Paul Maxey, *Doctor:* Frank McLure, *Man:* Frank Wilcox, *Butler:* Irving Smith, *Minister:* Louis Mason, *Drunk:* John Skins Miller, *Radio Announcer:* Edwin Chandler, *Reporter:* King Donovan, *Politician:* Pat O'Malley.

All the President's Men with Dustin Hoffman and Robert Redford.

ALL THE PRESIDENT'S MEN (1976) WB. A Wildwood Enterprises Production of A Robert Redford-Alan J. Pakula Film. Produced by Walter Coblenz. Directed by Alan J. Pakula. Based on the book by Carl Bernstein and Bob Woodward. Screenplay, William Goldman and Alvin Sargent. Panavision and Technicolor. Music by David Shire. Photography, Gordon Willis. Production Designer, George Jenkins. Editor, Robert L. Wolfe. Associate Producers, Michael Britton and Jon Boorstin. Executive Production Manager, E. Darrell Hallenbeck. 1st Assistant Directors, Bill Green and Art Levinson. 2nd Assistant Directors, Charles Ziarko and Kim Kurumada. Set Decorator, George Gaines. Costume Supervisor, Bernie Pollack. Key Make-up Artist, Gary Liddiard. Make-up Artists, Fern Buchner and Don Cash. Hairdressers, Romaine Greene and Lynda Gurasich. Production Publicist, Jack Hirshberg. Unit Publicist, Joanna Ney. Publicity Consultant, Lois Smith. Filmed in Washington, D.C., and at The Burbank Studios. Rated PG. 138 minutes

Bob Woodward: Robert Redford, *Carl Bernstein:* Dustin Hoffman, *Ben Bradlee:* Jason Robards, *Howard Simons:* Martin Balsam, *Harry M. Rosenfeld:* Jack Warden, *Deep Throat:* Hal Holbrook, *Bookkeeper:* Jane Alexander, *Debbie Sloan:* Meredith Baxter, *Dardis:* Ned Beatty, *Hugh W. Sloan, Jr.:* Stephen Collins, *Sally Aiken:* Penny Fuller, *Foreign Editor:* John McMartin, *Donald Segretti:* Robert Walden, *Frank Wills:* Frank Wills, *Sgt. Leeper:* F. Murray Abraham, *Bachinski:* David Arkin, *Bernard L. Barker:* Henry Calvert, *Eugenio R. Martinez:* Dominic Chianese, *Arguing Attorney:* Bryan E. Clark, *Markham:* Nicolas Coster, *Kay Eddy:* Lindsay Ann Crouse, *Miss Milland:* Valerie Curtin, *Court Clerk:* Gene Dynarski, *Virgilio R. Gonzales:* Nate Esformes, *Frank A. Sturgis:* Ron Hale, *James W. McCord, Jr.:* Richard Herd, *Dardis' Secretary:* Polly Holliday, *Sloan's Lawyer:* James Karen, *National Editor:* Paul Lambert, *Judge:* Frank Latimore, *Baldwin, Binoculars Lookout:* Gene Lindsey, *Arresting Officer #2:* Anthony Mannino, *Carolyn Abbott:* Allyn Ann McLerie, *Congress Library Clerk:* James Murtaugh, *Joe, FBI Man:* Jess Osuna, *Angry CRP Woman:* Neva Patterson, *George:* George Pentecost, *Sharon Lyons:* Penny Peyser, *Al Lewis:* Joshua Shelley, *Bookkeeper's Sister:* Sloane Shelton, *Ray Steuben:* Ralph Williams, *Post Librarian:* Jamie Smith Jackson, *Salesman:* Louis Quinn, *Bradlee's Secretary:* Carol Trost, *CIA Men:* Del Rager, Rick O'Donnell, *John Mitchell:* Voice of John Randolph.

American Graffiti with Cindy Williams and Ron Howard.

AMERICAN GRAFFITI (1973) Univ. A Lucasfilm Ltd./Coppola Co. Production. Produced by Francis Ford Coppola. Directed by George Lucas. Coproduced by Gary Kurtz. Screenplay by George Lucas, Gloria Katz and Willard Huyck. Photography, Ron Eveslage and Jan D'Alquen. Visual Consultant, Haskell Wexler. Editors, Verna Fields and Marcia Lucas. Assistant to the Producer, Beverly Walker. Art Director, Dennis Clark. Costume Designer, Aggie Guerard Rodgers. Assistant Directors, Ned Kopp and Charles Myers. Production Associates, Nancy Giebink and Jim Bloom. Choreographer, Toni Basil. Sound Editing, James Nelson. Music Coordinator, Karin Green. Titles and Optical Effects, Universal Title. Music Recorded and Produced by Kim Fowley. Songs and Artists: "At the Hop," "She's So Fine" and "Louie Louie," Flash Cadillac and the Continental Kids; "A Thousand Miles Away," the Heartbeats; "Barbara

Anne," the Regents; "Fannie Mae," Buster Brown; "Gee," the Crows; "Heart and Soul," the Cleftones; "I Only Have Eyes for You," the Flamingos; "Party Doll," Buddy Knox; "Peppermint Twist," Joey Dee and the Starlighters; "See You in September," the Tempos; "Why Do Fools Fall in Love?" Frankie Lymon; "Ya Ya," Lee Dorsey; "Chantilly Lace," the Big Bopper; "The Great Pretender," "Only You" and "Smoke Gets in Your Eyes," the Platters; "Little Darlin' " and "The Stroll," the Diamonds; "Almost Grown" and "Johnny B. Goode," Chuck Berry; "Book of Love," the Monotones; "Goodnight Sweetheart Goodnight," the Spaniels; "Ain't That a Shame," Fats Domino; "He's the Great Imposter," the Fleetwoods; "Love Potion #9," the Clovers; "You're Sixteen," Johnny Burnette; "Maybe Baby" and "That'll Be the Day," Buddy Holly; "Rock Around the Clock," Bill Haley and His Comets; "All Summer Long" and "Surfin' Safari," the Beach Boys; "Get a Job," the Silhouettes; "To the Aisle," the Five Satins; "Crying in the Chapel," Sonny Till and the Orioles; "Do You Wanna Dance," Bobby Freeman; "Green Onions," Booker T and the M.G.'s; "Runaway," Del Shannon; "Teen Angel," Mark Dinning; "Since I Don't Have You," the Skyliners; "Come Go with Me," the Del Vikings; "Sixteen Candles," the Crests. Harrison Ford sings "Some Enchanted Evening" by Richard Rodgers and Oscar Hammerstein II. Film debuts of Paul Le Mat, Mackenzie Phillips and Suzanne Somers. Filmed in Marin and Sonoma counties (principally Petaluma, San Rafael and San Francisco), California, and at American Zoetrope Studios, San Francisco. Technicolor. Rated PG. 110 minutes. Reissued in 1978 with Dolby Sound, 112 minutes (reedited)

Curt Henderson: Richard Dreyfuss, *Steve Bolander:* Ronny Howard, *Big John Milner:* Paul Le Mat, *Terry the Toad Fields:* Charlie Martin Smith, *Laurie Henderson:* Cindy Williams, *Debbie:* Candy Clark, *Carol Morrison:* Mackenzie Phillips, *Disc Jockey:* Wolfman Jack, *Bob Falfa:* Harrison Ford, *Joe:* Bo Hopkins, *Carlos:* Manuel Padilla, Jr., *Ants:* Beau Gentry, *Herby and the Heartbeats:* Flash Cadillac and the Continental Kids, *Peg:* Kathy (Kathleen) Quinlan, *Eddie:* Tim Crowley, *Mr. Wolfe:* Terry McGovern, *Girl at Dance:* Jan Wilson, *Announcer:* Caprice Schmidt, *Budda:* Jana Bellan, *Vic:* Joe Spano, *Al:* Chris Pray, *Judy:* Susan Richardson, *Carhop:* Donna Wehr.

An American in Paris with Gene Kelly and Leslie Caron.

AN AMERICAN IN PARIS (1951) MGM. Producer, Arthur Freed. Director, Vincente Minnelli. Color by Technicolor. Art Directors, Cedric Gibbons, Preston Ames. Musical Directors, Johnny Green and Saul Chapell. Story and Screenplay, Alan Jay Lerner. Photography, Alfred Gilks, John Alton. Editor, Adrienne Fazan. Songs by Ira and George Gershwin: "I Got Rhythm," "Embraceable You," " 'S Wonderful," "By Strauss," "Tra-La-La-La," "Our Love Is Here to Stay," "I'll Build a Stairway to Paradise" (lyrics by E. Ray Goetz and B. G. DeSylva), "Concerto in F" and "An American in Paris" (both instrumental numbers). 113 minutes

Jerry Mulligan: Gene Kelly, *Lise Bourvier:* Leslie Caron, *Adam Cook:*

Oscar Levant, *Henri Baurel:* Georges Guetary, *Milo Roberts:* Nina Foch, *Georges Mattieu:* Eugene Borden, *Mathilde Mattieu:* Martha Bamattre, *Old Woman Dancer:* Mary Young, *Therese:* Ann Codee, *Francois:* George Davis, *Tommy Baldwin:* Hayden Rorke, *John Mc-Dowd:* Paul Maxey, *Ben Macrow:* Dick Wessel, *Honeymoon Couple:* Don Quinn, Adele Coray, *Boys with Bubble Gum:* Lucian Planzoles, Christian Pasques, Anthony Mazola, *Nuns:* Jeanne Lafayette, Louise Laureau, *Postman:* Alfred Paix, *American Girl:* Noel Neill, *Maid:* Nan Boardman, *Jack Jansen:* John Eldredge, *Kay Jansen:* Anna Q. Nilsson, *Edna Mae Bestram (Customer):* Madge Blake, *Driver:* Art Dupuis, *Artist:* Greg McClure, *Dancing Partner:* Andre Charisse, *News Vendor:* Marie Antoinette Andrews.

Anastasia with Ingrid Bergman and Helen Hayes.

ANASTASIA (1956) 20th. Producer, Buddy Adler. Director, Anatole Litvak. CinemaScope, De Luxe Color. From the play by Marcelle Maurette as adapted by Guy Bolton. Screenplay, Arthur Laurents. Art Directors, Andrei Andrejew, Bill Andrews. Music, Alfred Newman. Orchestration, Edward B. Powell. Cinematographer, Jack Hildyard. Editor, Bert Bates. 105 minutes.

Anastasia: Ingrid Bergman, *Prince:* Yul Brynner, *Dowager Empress:* Helen Hayes, *Chernov:* Akim Tamiroff, *Livenbaum:* Martita Hunt, *Chamberlain:* Felix Aylmer, *Petrovin:* Sacha Piteoff, *Prince Paul:* Ivan Desny, *Lissemskaia:* Natalie Schafer, *Stepan:* Gregoire Gromoff, *Vlados:* Karel Stepanek, *Marusia:* Ina De La Haye, *Maxime:* Katherine Kath, *Zhadanov:* Olaf Pooley, *Older Man:* Andre Mickhelson, *Countess Baranova:* Olga Valery, *Von Drivnitz:* Eric Pohlmann, *Bechmetieff:* Alexis Bobrinskoy, *Footman:* Edward Forsyth, *Empress' Cossack:* Stanley Zevick, *Kasbek Dancers:* Tutte Lemkow and Anatole Smirnoff, *Grischa:* Peter Sallis, *Zenia:* Tamara Shane, *Blonde Man:* Alan Cuthbertson, *Prince Bolkonoski:* Henry Vidon, *Blonde Lady:* Hy Hazell, *Schiskin:* Mr. Pavlov, *Jean:* Paula Catton, *Marguerite:* Marguerite Brennan.

ANATOMY OF A MURDER (1959) Col. Producer-Director, Otto Preminger. Screenplay, Wendell Mayes. Music by Duke Ellington, Assistant Director, David Silver. Art Director, Boris Leven. Cinematographer, Sam Leavitt. Editor, Louis R. Loeffler. A Carlyle Production. Based on the novel by Robert Traver (Michigan Supreme Court Justice John D. Voelker). Filmed in Ishpeming, Michigan. Film debut of Boston lawyer Joseph N. Welch. 160 minutes

Paul Biegler: James Stewart, *Laura Manion:* Lee Remick, *Lt. Manion:* Ben Gazzara, *Parnell McCarthy:* Arthur O'Connell, *Maida:* Eve Arden, *Mary Pilant:* Kathryn Grant, *Claude Dancer:* George C. Scott, *Dr. Smith:* Orson Bean, *Mr. Lemon:* Russ Brown, *Paquette:* Murray Hamilton, *Mitch Lodwick:* Brooks West, *Sgt. Durgo:* Ken Lynch, *Sulo:* John Qualen, *Pie Eye:* Duke Ellington, *Judge Weaver:* Joseph N. Welch, *Sheriff Battisfore:* Royal Beal, *Dr. Dompierre:* Howard McNear, *Dr. Raschid:* Ned Wever, *Madigan:* Jimmy Conlin, *Mr. Burke:* Joseph Kearns, *Duane Miller:* Don Russ, *Court Clerk:* Lloyd LeVasseur, *An Army Sergeant:* James Waters, *Dr. Harcourt:* Alexander Campbell, *Distinguished Gentleman:* Irv Kupcinet, *Juror:* Mrs. Joseph Welch.

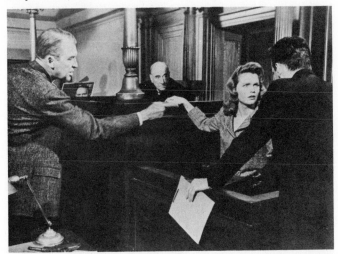

Anatomy of a Murder with James Stewart, Joseph N. Welch, Lee Remick and George C. Scott.

ANCHORS AWEIGH (1945) MGM. Producer, Joe Pasternak. Director, George Sidney. Color by Technicolor. Author, Natalie Marcin. Screenplay, Isobel Lennart. Musical Director, Georgie Stoll. Art Directors, Cedric Gibbons, Randall Duell. Cameramen, Robert Planck, Charles Boyle. Editor, Adrienne Fazan. Songs: "All of a Sudden My Heart Sings," "We Hate to Leave," "What Makes the Sun Set?," "The Charm of You," "I Begged Her" and "I Fall in Love Too Easily" by Sammy Cahn and Jule Styne; "The Worry Song" by Ralph Freed and Sammy Fain. Choreography, Gene Kelly. Cartoon sequence, William Hanna and Joseph Barbera. 140 minutes

Anchors Aweigh with William "Bill" Phillips, Gene Kelly, Frank Sinatra, Douglas Cowan and Henry Armetta.

Joseph Brady: Gene Kelly, *Clarence Doolittle:* Frank Sinatra, *Susan Abbott:* Kathryn Grayson, *Jose Iturbi:* Himself, *Donald Martin:*

Dean Stockwell, *Carlos:* Carlos Ramirez, *Admiral Hammond:* Henry O'Neill, *Commander:* Leon Ames, *Police Sergeant:* Rags Ragland, *Police Captain:* Edgar Kennedy, *Girl from Brooklyn:* Pamela Britton, *Hamburger Man:* Henry Armetta, *Cafe Manager:* Billy Gilbert, *Little Girl Beggar:* Sharon McManus, *Studio Cop:* James Burke, *Radio Cop:* James Flavin, *Iturbi's Assistant:* Chester Clute, *Bertram Kramer:* Grady Sutton, *Specialty (cartoon):* Tom and Jerry, *Lana Turner Double:* Peggy Maley, *Iturbi Secretary:* Sondra Rodgers, *Soldiers:* Garry Owen, Steve Brodie, *Butler:* Charles Coleman, *Bearded Man:* Milton Parsons, *Waitress:* Renie Riano, *Commander:* Alex Callam. *Sailors:* Harry Barris, John James, Wally Cassell, Douglas Cowan, Henry Daniels, Jr., Phil Hanna, William "Bill" Phillips, Tom Trout, *Hamburger Woman:* Esther Michelson, *Movie Director:* William Forrest, *Asst. Movie Director:* Ray Teal, *Bartender:* Milton Kibbee.

ANGELS WITH DIRTY FACES (1938) WB. Producer, Sam Bischoff. Director, Michael Curtiz. Original Story, Rowland Brown. Screenplay, John Wexley, Warren Duff. Cameraman, Sol Polito. Editor, Owen Marks. Song by Fred Fisher and Maurice Spitalny: "Angels With Dirty Faces." 97 minutes

Rocky Sullivan: James Cagney, *Jerry Connelly:* Pat O'Brien, *James Frazier:* Humphrey Bogart, *Laury Ferguson:* Ann Sheridan, *Mac Keefer:* George Bancroft, *Soapy:* Billy Halop, *Swing:* Bobby Jordan, *Bim:* Leo Gorcey, *Hunky:* Bernard Punsley, *Pasty:* Gabriel Dell, *Crab:* Huntz Hall, *Rocky (as a boy):* Frankie Burke, *Jerry (as a boy):* William Tracy, *Laury (as a girl):* Marilyn Knowlden, *Steve:* Joe Downing, *Blackie:* Adrian Morris, *Guard Kennedy:* Oscar O'Shea, *Guard Edwards:* Edward Pawley, *Bugs, Gunman:* William Pawley, *Police Captain:* John Hamilton, *Priest:* Earl Dwire, *Death Row Guard:* Jack Perrin, *Mrs. Patrick:* Mary Gordon, *Soapy's Mother:* Vera Lewis, *Warden:* William Worthington, *R. R. Yard Watchman:* James Farley, *Red:* Chuck Stubbs, *Maggione Boy:* Eddie Syracuse, *Policeman:* Robert Homans, *Basketball Captain:* Harris Berger, *Pharmacist:* Harry Hayden, *Gangsters:* Dick Rich, Stevan Darrell, Joe A. Devlin, *Italian:* William Edmunds, *Buckley:* Charles Wilson, *Boys:* Frank Coghlan Jr., David Durand.

Angels With Dirty Faces with Humphrey Bogart and James Cagney.

ANIMAL CRACKERS (1930) Par. Directed by Victor Heerman. Based on the Marx Brothers musical by George S. Kaufman, Bert Kalmar, Morrie Ryskind, and Harry Ruby. Screenplay, Morrie Ryskind and Pierre Collings. Photography, George Folsey. Sound, Ernest F. Zatorsky. Songs: "Why Am I So Romantic?", "Hooray for Captain Spaulding" by Kalmar and Ruby; "Collegiate" by Moe Jaffe and Nat Bonx; "Some of These Days" by Shelton Brooks. Filmed in Long Island, N. Y. Studios. Ann Roth is Lillian Roth's sister. 100 minutes

Captain Geoffrey T. Spaulding: Groucho Marx, *The Professor:* Harpo Marx, *Emanuel Ravelli:* Chico Marx, *Horatio W. Jamison:* Zeppo Marx, *Arabella Rittenhouse:* Lillian Roth, *Mrs. Rittenhouse:* Margaret Dumont, *Roscoe Chandler:* Louis Sorin, *John Parker:* Hal Thompson, *Mrs. Whitehead:* Margaret Irving, *Grace Carpenter:* Kathryn Reece, *Hives:* Robert Greig, *Hennessey:* Edward Metcalf, *Footmen:* The Music Masters, *Girl:* Ann Roth, *Guest:* Donald MacBride.

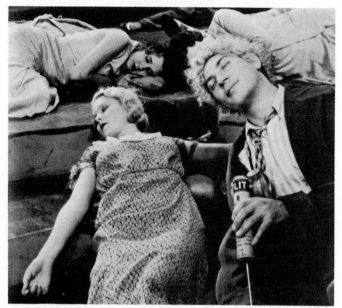

Animal Crackers: Harpo Marx gasses the cast and self with his Flit at end.

THE ANIMAL KINGDOM (1932) RKO. Produced by David O. Selznick. Directed by Edward H. Griffith. Based on the play by Philip Barry. Adaptation, Horace Jackson. Photography, George Folsey. Editor, Daniel Mandell. Sound, Daniel Cutler. The first feature to play the Roxy Theatre, New York. Remade as *One More Tomorrow* (WB, 1946). 90 minutes

Daisy Sage: Ann Harding, *Tom Collier:* Leslie Howard, *Cecelia Henry:* Myrna Loy, *Owen:* Neil Hamilton, *Regan:* William Gargan, *Rufus Collier:* Henry Stephenson, *Grace:* Ilka Chase, *Franc:* Leni Stengel, *Joe:* Donald Dillaway.

The Animal Kingdom with Leslie Howard and Myrna Loy.

ANNA AND THE KING OF SIAM (1946) 20th. Producer, Louis D. Lighton. Director, John Cromwell. Based on the book by Margaret Landon. Screenplay, Talbot Jennings, Sally Benson. Musical Score, Bernard Herrman. Art Directors, Lyle Wheeler, William Darl-

ing. Cameraman, Arthur Miller. Special Effects, Fred Sersen. Editor, Harmon Jones. Remade as *The King and I* (20th, 1956). 128 minutes

Anna: Irene Dunne, *The King:* Rex Harrison, *Tuptim:* Linda Darnell, *Kralahome:* Lee J. Cobb, *Lady Thiang:* Gale Sondergaard, *Alak:* Mikhail Rasumny, *Sir Edward:* Dennis Hoey, *Prince (grown up):* Tito Renaldo, *Louis Owens:* Richard Lyon, *Moonshee:* William Edmunds, *Phya Phrom:* John Abbott, *Interpreter:* Leonard Strong, *Prince:* Mickey Roth, *Beebe:* Connie Leon, *Princess Fa-Ying:* Diana Van den Ecker, *Dancer:* Si-lan Chen, *Miss MacFarlane:* Marjorie Eaton, *Mrs. Cortwright:* Helena Grant, *Mr. Cortwright:* Stanley Mann, *Captain Orton:* Addison Richards, *Phra Palat:* Neyle Morrow, *Government Clerk:* Julian Rivero, *Lady Sno Klin:* Yvonne Rob, *Wives of King:* Loretta Luiz, Chabing, Marianne Quon, Lillian Molieri, Buff Cobb, Sydney Logan, *Old Woman:* Oie Chan, *Judge:* Ted Hecht, *Third Judge:* Ben Welden, *Guard:* Aram Katcher, *Guide:* Pedro Regas, *Guard:* Rico DeMontes, *Slave:* Hazel Shon.

Anna and the King of Siam with Irene Dunne and Rex Harrison.

ANNA CHRISTIE (1930) MGM. Directed by Clarence Brown. Based on the play by Eugene O'Neill. Screenplay, Frances Marion. Art Director, Cedric Gibbons. Photography, William Daniels. Editor, Hugh Wynn. Sound, Douglas Shearer. Titles (silent version), Madeleine Ruthven. Garbo's first talkie; she also starred in a German version for MGM. Remake of 1923 First National film, in which George Marion also played Chris. 86 minutes

Anna Gustafson (Anna Christie): Greta Garbo, *Matt Burke:* Charles Bickford, *Chris Gustafson:* George F. Marion, *Marthy Owens:* Marie Dressler, *Larry, the Bartender:* Lee Phelps, *Johnny the Harp:* James T. Mack.

Anna Christie with Charles Bickford and Greta Garbo.

Anna Karenina with Basil Rathbone, Greta Garbo, Ethel Griffies, Fredric March and Constance Collier.

ANNA KARENINA (1935) MGM. Produced by David O. Selznick. Directed by Clarence Brown. From Count Leo Tolstoy's novel. Screenplay, Clemence Dane, Salka Viertel. Adaptation and Dialogue, S. N. Behrman. Collaborator, Erich von Stroheim. Art Director, Cedric Gibbons. Costumes, Adrian. Music, Herbert Stothart. Ballet staged by Margarete Wallmann. Mazurka staged by Chester Hale. Consultant, Count Andrey Tolstoy. Associate Art Directors, Fredric Hope and Edwin B. Willis. Technical Adviser, Erich von Stroheim. Assistant Director, Charlie Dorian. Photography, William Daniels. Sound, Douglas Shearer. Editor, Robert J. Kern. Vocal and choral effects by Russian Symphony Choir. Other versions: *Love* (MGM, 1927), *Anna Karenina* (20th Century-Fox [British], 1948). 95 minutes

Anna Karenina: Greta Garbo, *Count Alexei Vronsky:* Fredric March, *Kitty:* Maureen O'Sullivan, *Countess Vronsky:* May Robson, *Countess Lidia:* Constance Collier, *Stiva:* Reginald Owen, *Sergei Karenin:* Freddie Bartholomew, *Alexei Karenin:* Basil Rathbone, *Dolly:* Phoebe Foster, *Capt. Nicki Yashvin:* Reginald Denny, *Levin:* Gyles Isham, *Grisha:* Buster Phelps, *Anna's Maid:* Ella Ethridge, *Vronsky's Valet:* Sidney Bracy, *Tania:* Cora Sue Collins, *Butler:* Olaf Hytten, *Butler:* Joseph E. Tozer, *Tutor, Ivanovich:* Guy D'Ennery, *Cord:* Harry Allen, *Princess Sorokino:* Mary Forbes, *Barbara:* Helen Freeman, *Mme. Kartasoff:* Ethel Griffies, *Matve:* Harry Beresford, *Governess:* Sarah Padden, *Lily:* Joan Marsh, *Best Man:* Dennis O'Keefe, *Mahotin:* Mischa Auer, *Woman:* Betty Blythe, *Colonel:* Robert Warwick, *Mr. Kartasoff:* Keith Kenneth, *Colonel:* Mahlon Hamilton, *Officer:* Pat Somerset, *Officers at Banquet:* Harry Cording, Francis McDonald, Larry Steers, *Waiter:* Gino Corrado, *Waitress:* Antoinette Lees (Andrea Leeds).

Annie Get Your Gun with J. Carrol Naish and Betty Hutton.

ANNIE GET YOUR GUN (1950) MGM. Producer, Arthur Freed. Director, George Sidney. Color by Technicolor. Based on the musical by Dorothy Fields and Herbert Fields. Screenplay, Sidney Sheldon. Musical Director, Adolph Deutsch. Art Directors, Cedric Gibbons, Paul Groesse. Photography, Charles Rosher. Editor, James E. Newcom. Songs by Irving Berlin: "Colonel Buffalo Bill," "Doin' What Comes Naturally," "The Girl That I Marry," "You Can't Get a Man With a Gun," "There's No Business Like Show Business," "My Defenses Are Down," "I'm an Indian Too," "I Got the Sun in the Morning," "Anything You Can Do," and "They Say It's Wonderful." Hutton replaced Judy Garland. 107 minutes

Annie Oakley: Betty Hutton, *Frank Butler:* Howard Keel, *Buffalo Bill:* Louis Calhern, *Sitting Bull:* J. Carrol Naish, *Pawnee Bill:* Edward Arnold, *Charlie Davenport:* Keenan Wynn, *Dolly Tate:* Benay Venuta, *Foster Wilson:* Clinton Sundberg, *Mac:* James H. Harrison, *Little Jake:* Bradley Mora, *Nellie:* Diana Dick, *Jessie:* Susan Odin, *Minnie:* Eleanor Brown, *Little Horse:* Chief Yowlachie, *Conductor:* Robert Malcolm, *Waiter:* Lee Tung Foo, *Barker:* William Tannen, *Miss Willoughby:* Anne O'Neal, *Queen Victoria:* Evelyn Beresford, *Ship Captain:* John Hamilton, *Tall Man:* William Bill Hall, *Footman:* Edward Earle, *Constance:* Marjorie Wood, *Helen:* Elizabeth Flournoy, *Mrs. Adams:* Mae Clarke Langdon, *Mr. Clay:* Frank Wilcox, *President Loubet of France:* Andre Charlot, *King Victor Emmanuel:* Nino Pipitone, *Kaiser Wilhelm II:* John Mylong, *Cowboys:* Carl Sepulveda, Carol Henry, Fred Gilman.

Annie Hall with Woody Allen, Tony Roberts and Diane Keaton.

ANNIE HALL (1977) UA. A Jack Rollins–Charles H. Joffe Production. Produced by Joffe. Directed by Woody Allen. Screenplay, Woody Allen and Marshall Brickman. Executive Producer and Production Manager, Robert Greenhut. Photography, Gordon Willis. Editor, Ralph Rosenblum. Art Direction, Mel Bourne. Set Decorations, Robert Drumheller and Justin Scoppa, Jr. Sound, James Sabat, Jack Higgens and Dan Sable. Costumes by Ruth Morley. Make-up, Fern Buchner. Hairstyles, Romaine Green. Animation Sequence, Chris Ishii. Unit Publicist, Scott MacDonough. Associate Producer, Fred T. Gallo. Assistant Directors, Gallo and Fred Blankfein. Sound (Los Angeles), James Pilcher. Set Decorations (L.A.), Barbara Krieger. Wardrobe (L.A.), Nancy McArdle. Make-up (L.A.), John Inzerella. Hairstyles (L.A.), Vivienne Walker. Songs, "Seems Like Old Times" by Carmen Lombardo and John Jacob Loeb, "It Had to Be You" by Isham Jones and Gus Kahn, sung by Keaton, accompanied by Artie Butler. Color by DeLuxe. Filmed in New York, New Jersey and California. Rated PG. 93 minutes

Alvy Singer: Woody Allen, *Annie Hall:* Diane Keaton, *Rob:* Tony Roberts, *Allison Porchnik Singer:* Carol Kane, *Tony Lacey:* Paul Simon, *Mom Hall:* Colleen Dewhurst, *Pam:* Shelley Duvall, *Robin Singer:* Janet Margolin, *Duane Hall:* Christopher Walken, *Dad Hall:* Donald Symington, *Grammy Hall:* Helen Ludlam, *Leo Singer:* Mordecai Lawner, *Mrs. Singer:* Joan Newman, *Alvy at 9:* Jonathan Munk, *Alvy's Aunt:* Ruth

Volner, *Alvy's Uncle:* Martin Rosenblatt, *Joey Nichols:* Hy Ansel, *Aunt Tessie Moskowitz:* Rashel Novikoff, *Man in Theater Line:* Russell Horton, *Himself:* Marshall McLuhan, *Dorrie:* Christine Jones, *Miss Reed, Teacher:* Mary Boylan, *Janet:* Wendy Gerard, *Coke Fiend:* John Doumanian, *Doctor:* Chris Gampel, *Himself:* Dick Cavett, *Navy Officer:* Mark Lenard, *Comedian at Rally:* Dan Ruskin, *Actor Boyfriend:* John Glover, *Comic's Agent:* Bernie Styles, *Comic:* Johnny Haymer, *Maharishi:* Ved Bandhu, *Tony's Girl Friend:* Lauri Bird, *Mantra Man:* Jeff Goldblum, *Dr. Flicker, Psychiatrist:* Humphrey Davis, *Annie's Psychiatrist:* Veronica Radburn, *Petronia:* Petronia Johnson, *Sean:* Sean Casey, *Street Strangers:* Lou Pisetta, Lucille Tupper, James Burge, Shelly Hack, Albert Ottenheimer, Paula Trueman, *TV Actors:* Beverly D'Angelo and Tracy Walter, *Waitress at Health Food Restaurant:* Lucy Lee Flippen, *Man at Health Food Restaurant:* Gary Muledeer, *Alvy's Date Outside Theater:* Sigourney Weaver, *Annie's Date Outside Theater:* Walter Bernstein, *Kitchen Worker at Stevenson Rally:* Renee Semes, *Yankee Stadium Policeman:* Bob Dahdah.

Anthony Adverse with Fredric March and Gale Sondergaard.

ANTHONY ADVERSE (1936) WB. Produced by Jack L. Warner. Associate Executive in charge of Production, Hal B. Wallis. Directed by Mervyn LeRoy. Supervisor, Henry Blanke. From the novel by Hervey Allen. Screenplay by Sheridan Gibney. Cinematographer, Tony Gaudio. Director of Recording, Major Nathan Levinson. Film Editor, Ralph Dawson. Art Director, Anton Grot. Costumer, Milo Anderson. Original Musical Score, Erich Wolfgang Korngold. Operatic Sequences, Aldo Franchetti. Assistant Director, Bill Cannon. Film debut of Gale Sondergaard. 136 minutes

Anthony Adverse: Fredric March, *Angela Guisseppi:* Olivia De Havilland, *Maria:* Anita Louise, *John Bonnyfeather:* Edmund Gwenn, *Don Luis:* Claude Rains, *Vincente Nolte:* Donald Woods, *Dennis Moore:* Louis Hayward, *Faith:* Gale Sondergaard, *Carlo Cibo:* Akim Tamiroff, *Neleta:* Steffi Duna, *Anthony (age 10):* Billy Mauch, *Father Xavier:* Henry O'Neill, *De Bruille:* Ralph Morgan, *Ouvrard:* Fritz Leiber, *Tony Guisseppi:* Luis Alberni, *Florence Udney (age 10):* Marilyn Knowlden, *Angela (as a child):* Ann Howard, *Napoleon Bonaparte:* Rollo Lloyd, *Sancho:* George E. Stone, *Captain Elisha Jorham:* Joseph Crehan, *Mrs. Jorham:* Clara Blandick, *Little Boy Anthony:* Scotty Beckett, *Captain Matanze:* Addison Richards, *Major Doumet:* J. Carrol Naish, *Brother Francois:* Pedro de Cordoba, *Lucia:* Grace Stafford, *Captain, Boat to America:* Joseph King, *Mother Superior:* Eily Malyon, *De Bourrienne:* Leonard Mudie, *Senora Bovina:* Rafaela Ottiano, *Cook Guisseppi:* Mathilde Comont, *Driver, Coach to Paris:* Frank Reicher, *Ferdinando:* Paul Sotoff, *Half-caste Dancer:* Joan Woodbury, *Arabs:* Frank Lackteen, Martin Garralaga, *Old Woman at Chalet:* Zeffie Tilbury, *Sister Ursula:* Tola Nesmith, *Second Nun:* Myra Marsh, *Third Nun:* Bess Flowers.

APACHE (1954) UA. Producer, Harold Hecht. Director, Robert Aldrich. Color by Technicolor. Assistant Director, Sid Sidman. Screenplay by James R. Webb. Based on novel by Paul I. Wellman. Music by David Raksin. Cinematographer, Ernest Laszlo. Editor, Alan Crosland, Jr. 91 minutes

Massai: Burt Lancaster, *Nalinle:* Jean Peters, *Al Sieber:* John McIntire, *Hondo:* Charles Buchinsky (Charles Bronson), *Weddle:* John Dehner, *Santos:* Paul Guilfoyle, *Glagg:* Ian MacDonald, *Lt. Col. Beck:* Walter Sande, *Dawson:* Morris Ankrum, *Geronimo:* Monte Blue.

Apache with Burt Lancaster and Jean Peters.

THE APARTMENT (1960) UA. Producer-Director, Billy Wilder. Screenplay, Billy Wilder and I. A. L. Diamond. Associate Producers, Doane Harrison and I. A. L. Diamond. Music, Adolph Deutsch. Assistant Director, Hal Polaire. A Mirisch Company Production in Panavision. Art Director, Alexander Trauner. Sets, Edward G. Boyle. Sound, Gordon E. Sawyer. Cinematography, Joseph LaShelle. Editor, Daniel Mandell. Songs: "Lonely Room" (Theme from *The Apartment*) by Adolph Deutsch, "Jealous Lover" by Charles Williams. Locations filmed in New York. Includes scenes from *Stagecoach* (UA, 1939). Film debut of Edie Adams. 125 minutes

C. C. (Bud) Baxter: Jack Lemmon, *Fran Kubelik:* Shirley MacLaine, *Jeff D. Sheldrake:* Fred MacMurray, *Joe Dobisch:* Ray Walston, *Al Kirkeby:* David Lewis, *Dr. Dreyfuss:* Jack Kruschen, *Sylvia:* Joan Shawlee, *Miss Olsen:* Edie Adams, *Margie MacDougall:* Hope Holiday, *Karl Matuschka:* Johnny Seven, *Mrs. Dreyfuss:* Naomi Stevens, *Mrs. Lieberman:* Frances Weintraub Lax, *The Blonde:* Joyce Jameson, *Mr. Vanderhof:* Willard Waterman, *Mr. Eichelberger:* David White, *Bartender:* Benny Burt, *Santa Claus:* Hal Smith, *Office Worker:* Dorothy Abbott.

The Apartment with Jack Lemmon and Shirley MacLaine.

APARTMENT FOR PEGGY (1948) 20th. Producer, William Perlberg. Directors, Henry Koster, George Seaton. Color by Technicolor. From a story by Faith Baldwin. Screenplay, George Seaton. Art Directors, Lyle Wheeler, Richard Irvine. Musical Director, Lionel Newman. Photography, Harry Jackson. Editor, Robert Simpson. Technicolor Director, Natalie Kalmus. Associate, Clemens Finley. 98 minutes

Peggy: Jeanne Crain, *Jason:* William Holden, *Prof. Henry Barnes:* Edmund Gwenn, *Prof. Edward Bell:* Gene Lockhart, *Dr. Conway:* Griff Barnett, *Dorothy:* Randy Stuart, *Ruth:* Marion Marshall, *Jeanne:* Pati Behrs, *Prof. Roland Pavin:* Henri Letondal, *Prof. T. J. Beck:* Houseley Stevenson, *Della:* Helen Ford, *Mrs. Landon:* Almira Sessions, *Prof. Collins:* Charles Lane, *Delivery Boy:* Ronnald Burns, *Jerry:* Gene Nelson, *Student:* Bob Patten, *Wife:* Betty Lynn, *Nurse:* Theresa Lyon, *Nurse:* Ann Staunton, *Salesmen:* Hal K. Dawson, Robert Williams, *Mailman:* Robert Adler.

Apartment for Peggy with Edmund Gwenn, Jeanne Crain and William Holden.

APPLAUSE (1929) Par. Directed by Rouben Mamoulian. From the novel by Beth Brown. Adaptation, Garrett Fort. Photography, George Folsey. Editor, John Bassler. Filmed at Paramount's Astoria, Long Island, Studios and in New York City: Grand Central Station, the Battery, Brooklyn Bridge. Songs: "What Wouldn't I Do for That Man" by E. Y. Harburg and Jay Gorney; "Everybody's Doing It," "Doing the New Raccoon," "Give Your Little Baby Lots of Lovin'" by Dolly Morse and Joe Burke. Also silent version. First film directed by Mamoulian. Film debut of Helen Morgan. 87 minutes

Kitty Darling: Helen Morgan, *April Darling:* Joan Peers, *Hitch Nelson:* Fuller Melish, Jr., *Tony:* Henry Wadsworth, *Joe King:* Jack Cameron, *Mother Superior:* Dorothy Cumming, *Producer:* Jack Singer, *Slim Lamont:* Paul Barrett.

Applause with Joan Peers and Fuller Mellish, Jr.

Around the World in 80 Days with Buster Keaton, Cantinflas, David Niven and Shirley MacLaine.

AROUND THE WORLD IN 80 DAYS (1956) UA. Producer, Michael Todd. Associate Producer, William Cameron Menzies. Director, Michael Anderson. Screenplay by S. J. Perelman. Based on Jules Verne's novel. Music by Victor Young. Costumes by Miles White. Choreography by Paul Godkin. In Todd-AO Process and Eastman Color. Locations: London; Southern France; on the Mediterranean; India; Hong Kong; Pakistan; Siam; Yokohama, Japan; Durango, Colorado; San Francisco; Mexico; Spain; Egypt; Chatsworth, California. Prologue includes the Melies version of Verne's *A Trip to the Moon*, 1902. 168 minutes

Phileas Fogg: David Niven, *Passepartout:* Cantinflas, *Mr. Fix:* Robert Newton, *Aouda:* Shirley MacLaine, *Monsieur Gasse:* Charles Boyer, *Stationmaster:* Joe E. Brown, *Tourist:* Martine Carol, *Colonel Proctor Stamp:* John Carradine, *Clerk:* Charles Coburn, *Official of Railway:* Ronald Colman, *Steward:* Melville Cooper, *Hesketh-Baggott:* Noel Coward, *Whist Partner:* Finlay Currie, *Police Chief:* Reginald Denny, *First Mate:* Andy Devine, *Hostess:* Marlene Dietrich, *Bullfighter:* Luis Miguel Dominguin, *Coachman:* Fernandel, *Foster:* Sir John Gielgud, *Sportin' Lady:* Hermione Gingold, *Dancer:* Jose Greco, *Sir Francis Gromarty:* Sir Cedric Hardwicke, *Fallentin:* Trevor Howard, *Companion:* Glynis Johns, *Conductor:* Buster Keaton, *Flirt:* Evelyn Keyes, *Revivalist:* Beatrice Lillie, *Steward:* Peter Lorre, *Engineer:* Edmund Lowe, *Helmsman:* Victor McLaglen, *Commander:* Colonel Tim McCoy, *Club Member:* A. E. Mathews, *Character:* Mike Mazurki, *Cabby:* John Mills, *Consul:* Alan Mowbray, *Ralph:* Robert Morley, *Narrator:* Edward R. Murrow, *Captain:* Jack Oakie, *Bouncer:* George Raft, *Achmed Abdullah:* Gilbert Roland, *Henchman:* Cesar Romero, *Pianist:* Frank Sinatra, *Drunk:* Red Skelton, *Member:* Ronald Squire, *Member:* Basil Sydney, *Hinshaw:* Harcourt Williams, *Spectator:* Ava Gardner.

ARROWSMITH (1931) UA. Produced by Samuel Goldwyn. Directed by John Ford. Based on the novel by Sinclair Lewis. Scenario and Dialogue, Sidney Howard. Photography, Ray June. Editor, Hugh Bennett. Sound, Jack Noyes. Music Score, Alfred Newman. Settings, Richard Day. 108 minutes

Martin Arrowsmith: Ronald Colman, *Leora Tozer:* Helen Hayes, *Dr. Gustav Sondelius:* Richard Bennett, *Professor Max Gottlieb:* A. E. Anson, *Doctor Tubbs:* Claude King, *Terry Wickett:* Russell Hopton, *Joyce Lanyon:* Myrna Loy, *Bert Tozer:* Bert Roach, *The Pioneer Girl:* Charlotte Henry, *The Old Doctor:* James Marcus, *Mr. Tozer:* DeWitt Jennings, *Mrs. Tozer:* Beulah Bondi, *Henry Novak:* John M. Qualen, *Mrs. Novak:* Adele Watson, *Doctor Hesselink:* Sidney DeGrey, *State Veterinary:* David Landau, *Twyford:* Alec B. Francis, *Miss Twyford:* Florence Britton, *Sir Robert Fairland:* Lumsden Hare, *Oliver Marchand:* Clarence Brooks, *Cop:* Ward Bond, *Ship's Officers:* Pat Somerset, Eric Wilton, *Pioneer:* Erville Alderson, *Italian Uncle:* George Humbert, *Drunk:* Raymond Hatton, *Native Mother:* Theresa Harris.

Arrowsmith with Alec B. Francis, Myrna Loy and Ronald Colman.

ARSENIC AND OLD LACE (1944) WB. Produced by Howard Lindsay and Russell Crouse. Directed by Frank Capra. Based on the play by Joseph Kesselring, which closed in 1944 after a 3½-year run. Screenplay, Julius J. and Philip G. Epstein. Music, Max Steiner. Music Director, Leo F. Forbstein. Orchestral Arrangements, Hugo Friedhofer. Editor, Daniel Mandell. Josephine Hull, Jean Adair, John Alexander repeat their Broadway roles. 118 minutes

Mortimer Brewster: Cary Grant, *Elaine Harper:* Priscilla Lane, *Jonathan Brewster:* Raymond Massey, *O'Hara:* Jack Carson, *Mr. Witherspoon:* Edward Everett Horton, *Doctor Einstein:* Peter Lorre, *Lieutenant Rooney:* James Gleason, *Abby Brewster:* Josephine Hull, *Martha Brewster:* Jean Adair, *Teddy "Roosevelt" Brewster:* John Alexander, *Reverend Harper:* Grant Mitchell, *Brophy:* Edward McNamara, *Taxi Driver:* Garry Owen, *Saunders:* John Ridgely, *Judge Cullman:* Vaughan Glaser, *Doctor Gilchrist:* Chester Clute, *Reporter:* Charles Lane, *Gibbs:* Edward McWade, *Man in Phone Booth:* Leo White, *Marriage License Clerk:* Spencer Charters, *Photographer:* Hank Mann, *Umpire:* Lee Phelps.

Arsenic and Old Lace with Cary Grant, Leo White and Priscilla Lane.

THE ASPHALT JUNGLE (1950) MGM. Producer, Arthur Hornblow, Jr. Director, John Huston. Author, W. R. Burnett. Screenplay, Ben Maddow, John Huston. Art Directors, Cedric Gibbons, Randall Duell. Photography, Harold Rosson. Editor, George Boemler. Sound, Douglas Shearer. Make-up, Sydney Guilaroff. Remade as *Cairo* (MGM-British, 1963), *The Badlanders* (1958) and *Cool Breeze* (1972). 112 minutes

The Asphalt Jungle with Sterling Hayden, Brad Dexter, Louis Calhern and Sam Jaffe.

Dix Handley: Sterling Hayden, *Alonzo D. Emmerich:* Louis Calhern, *Doll Conovan:* Jean Hagen, *Gus Minissi:* James Whitmore, *Doc Erwin Riedenschneider:* Sam Jaffe, *Police Commissioner Hardy:* John McIntire, *Cobby:* Marc Lawrence, *Lieut. Ditrich:* Barry Kelley, *Louis Ciavelli:* Anthony Caruso, *Maria Ciavelli:* Teresa Celli, *Angela Phinlay:* Marilyn Monroe, *Timmons:* William Davis, *May Emmerich:* Dorothy Tree, *Bob Brannon:* Brad Dexter, *Maxwell:* Alex Gerry, *James X. Connery:* Thomas Browne Henry, *Janocek:* James Seay, *Andrews:* Don Haggerty, *Franz Schurz:* Henry Rowland, *Jeannie:* Helene Stanley, *Tallboy:* Raymond Roe, *Red:* Charles (Chuck) Courtney, *Woman:* Jean Carter, *Older Officer:* Ralph Dunn, *Younger Officer:* Pat Flaherty, *Jack (Police Clerk):* Tim Ryan, *Karl Anton Smith:* Henry Corden, *William Doldy:* Strother Martin, *Night Clerk:* Frank Cady, *Driver:* Benny Burt, *Truck Driver:* Fred Graham, *Evans:* David Hydes, *Private Policeman:* Saul Gorss, *Man:* Wilson Wood, *Suspect:* William Washington, *Vivian:* Eloise Hardt, *Eddie Donato:* Albert Morin.

At War With the Army with Jerry Lewis and Dean Martin.

AT WAR WITH THE ARMY (1950) Par. Produced by Fred F. Finklehoffe. Executive Producer, Abner J. Greshler. Directed by Hal Walker. Based on a play by James B. Allardice. Screenplay, Fred F. Finklehoffe. A York Pictures Corporation and Screen Associates Production. Songs by Mack David and Jerry Livingston: "The Navy Gets the Gravy But the Army Gets the Beans," "Tonda Wanda Hoy," "You and Your Beautiful Eyes." Martin and Lewis' first starring film. 93 minutes

Sergeant Vic Puccinelli: Dean Martin, *Pfc. Korwin:* Jerry Lewis, *Ser-*

geant McVey: Mike Kellin, Eddie: Jimmy Dundee, Pokey: Dick Stabile, Corporal Clark: Tommy Farrell, Corporal Shaughnessy: Frank Hyers, Sergeant Miller: Dan Dayton, Captain Caldwell: William Mendrek, Lieutenant Davenport: Kenneth Forbes, Private Edwards: Paul Livermore, Lieutenant Terray: Ty Perry, Millie: Jean Ruth, Mrs. Caldwell: Angela Greene, Helen Palmer: Polly Bergen, Colonel: Douglas Evans, Doctor: Steven Roberts, Orderly: Al Negbo, Bartender: Dewey Robinson, Soldier: Lee Bennett.

Auntie Mame with Peggy Cass and Rosalind Russell.

AUNTIE MAME (1958) WB. Directed by Morton DaCosta. In Technirama and Technicolor. Screenplay, Betty Comden and Adolph Green. From the novel by Patrick Dennis, and the play as adapted by Jerome Lawrence and Robert E. Lee, which evolved into the musical *Mame*. Music, Bronislau Kaper. Costumes, Orry-Kelly. Assistant Director, Don Page. Art Director, Malcolm Bert. Musical Director, Ray Heindorf. Cinematographer, Harry Stradling. Editor, William Ziegler. Sound, M. A. Merrick. Russell, Smith, Cass, Handzlik, Shimoda and Alexander repeat their original stage roles. Film debut of Jan Handzlik, 11. Remade as *Mame* (1974). 143 minutes

Auntie Mame Dennis: Rosalind Russell, *Beauregard Burnside:* Forrest Tucker, *Vera Charles:* Coral Browne, *Mr. Babcock:* Fred Clark, *Patrick Dennis:* Roger Smith, *Lindsay Woolsey:* Patric Knowles, *Agnes Gooch:* Peggy Cass, *Patrick as a boy:* Jan Handzlik, *Gloria Upson:* Joanna Barnes, *Pegeen Ryan:* Pippa Scott, *Mrs. Upson:* Lee Patrick, *Mr. Upson:* Willard Waterman, *Brian O'Bannion:* Robin Hughes, *Norah Muldoon:* Connie Gilchrist, *Ito:* Yuki Shimoda, *Sally Cato:* Brook Byron, *Mrs. Burnside:* Carol Veazie, *Acacius Page:* Henry Brandon, *Emory:* Butch Hengen, *Veterinarian:* Dub Taylor, *Woman in White:* Evelyn Ceder, *Cousin Jeff:* Doye O'Dell, *Michael:* Terry Kelman, *Edwin Dennis:* Morton DaCosta, *Pianist:* Rand Harper, *Vladimir Klinkoff:* Gregory Gay, *Mrs. Klinkoff:* Gladys Roach, *Perry:* Booth Colman, *Dr. Feuchtwanger:* Charles Heard, *Stage Manager:* Paul Davis, *Dowager-type Lady:* Olive Blakeney, *Noblewoman:* Margaret Dumont, *Man with Monocle:* Owen McGiveney, *Lord Dudley:* Robert Gates, *Reginald:* Mark Dana, *Mr. Krantz:* Dick Reeves, *Mrs. Krantz:* Barbara Pepper, *Mr. Loomis:* Chris Alexander, *Mrs. Jennings:* Ruth Warren.

THE AWFUL TRUTH (1937) Col. Produced by Leo McCarey. Associate Producer, Everett Riskin. Directed by Leo McCarey. Based on the 1922 play by Arthur Richman. Screenplay, Viña Delmar. Assistant Director, William Mull. Art Directors, Stephen Goosson and Lionel Banks. Music Director, Morris Stoloff. Interior Decorations, Babs Johnstone. Gowns, Kalloch. Photography, Joseph Walker. Editor, Al Clark. Sound, Edward Bernds. Songs by Ben Oakland and Milton Drake: "My Dreams Have Gone With the Wind" and "I

Don't Like Music." Remade by Columbia as *Let's Do It Again*, 1953. 90 minutes

Lucy Warriner: Irene Dunne, *Jerry Warriner:* Cary Grant, *Daniel Leeson:* Ralph Bellamy, *Armand Duvalle:* Alexander D'Arcy, *Aunt Patsy:* Cecil Cunningham, *Barbara Vance:* Molly Lamont, *Mrs. Leeson:* Esther Dale, *Dixie Belle Lee (Toots Binswanger):* Joyce Compton, *Frank Randall:* Robert Allen, *Mr. Vance:* Robert Warwick, *Mrs. Vance:* Mary Forbes, *Lord Fabian:* Claud Allister, *Lady Fabian:* Zita Moulton, *Motor Cop:* Edgar Dearing, *Mr. Barnsley:* Scott Colton, *Mrs. Barnsley:* Wyn Cahoon, *Judge:* Paul Stanton, *Jerry's Attorney:* Mitchell Harris, *Motor Cop:* Alan Bridge, *Butler:* Leonard Carey, *Japanese Servant:* Miki Morita, *M.C.:* Frank Wilson, *Police Sergeant:* Vernon Dent, *Caretaker:* George C. Pearce, *Hotel Clerk:* Bobby Watson, *Secretary:* Byron Foulger, *Celeste:* Kathryn Curry, *Bailiff:* Edward Peil, Sr., *Viola Heath:* Bess Flowers, *Hank:* John Tyrrell, *Lucy's Attorney:* Edward Mortimer.

The Awful Truth with Cary Grant and Irene Dunne.

Babes in Arms with Mickey Rooney and Judy Garland.

17

BABES IN ARMS (1939) MGM. Produced by Arthur Freed. Directed by Busby Berkeley. Based on the musical by Richard Rodgers and Lorenz Hart. Screenplay by Jack MacGowan and Kay Van Riper. Art Director, Cedric Gibbons. Associate, Merrill Pye. Wardrobe, Dolly Tree. Photography, Ray June. Editor, Frank Sullivan. Songs: "Babes in Arms," "Where or When," "The Lady Is a Tramp" by Rodgers and Hart; "You Are My Lucky Star," "Good Morning" by Arthur Freed and Nacio Herb Brown; "I Cried for You" by Arthur Freed, Gus Arnheim, and Abe Lyman; "God's Country" by E. Y. Harburg and Harold Arlen. Music Director, George Stoll. 97 minutes.

Mickey Moran: Mickey Rooney, *Patsy Barton:* Judy Garland, *Joe Moran:* Charles Winninger, *Judge Black:* Guy Kibbee, *Rosalie Essex:* June Preisser, *Florrie Moran:* Grace Hayes, *Molly Moran:* Betty Jaynes, *Don Brice:* Douglas McPhail, *Jeff Steele:* Rand Brooks, *Dody Martini:* Leni Lynn, *Bobs:* John Sheffield, *Madox:* Henry Hull, *William:* Barnett Parker, *Mrs. Barton:* Ann Shoemaker, *Martha Steele:* Margaret Hamilton, *Mr. Essex:* Joseph Crehan, *Brice:* George McKay, *Shaw:* Henry Roquemore, *Mrs. Brice:* Lelah Tyler, *Boy:* Lon McCallister, *Agent:* Robert Emmett Keane, *Larry Randall:* Charles D. Brown, *Sid:* Sid Miller, *Receptionist:* Mary Treen.

The Bachelor and the Bobby-Soxer with Myrna Loy, Cary Grant, Harry Davenport, Shirley Temple and Ray Collins.

THE BACHELOR AND THE BOBBY-SOXER (1947) RKO. Producer, Dore Schary. Director, Irving Reis. Author, I. Sidney Sheldon. Screenplay, I. Sidney Sheldon. Art Directors, Albert D'Agostino, Carroll Clark. Music, Leigh Harline. Music Director, C. Bakaleinikoff. Cameraman, Robert De Grasse. Editor, Frederick Knudtson. 95 minutes

Dick: Cary Grant, *Margaret:* Myrna Loy, *Susan:* Shirley Temple, *Tommy:* Rudy Vallee, *Beemish:* Ray Collins, *Thaddeus:* Harry Davenport, *Jerry:* Johnny Sands, *Tony:* Don Beddoe, *Bessie:* Lillian Randolph, *Agnes Prescott:* Veda Ann Borg, *Walters:* Dan Tobin, *Judge Treadwell:* Ransom Sherman, *Winters:* William Bakewell, *Melvin:* Irving Bacon, *Perry:* Ian Bernard, *Florence:* Carol Hughes, *Anthony Herman:* William Hall, *Maitre d'Hotel:* Gregory Gay, *Mr. Mittwick:* Charles Halton, *Miss Wells:* Myra Marsh, *Mr. Roberts:* Charles Marsh, *Bailiff:* J. Farrell MacDonald, *Woman:* Ellen Corby, *Cops in Courtroom:* Jack Gargan, Mickey Simpson, *Mrs. Baldwin:* Elena Warren, *Mr. Baldwin:* William Forrest, *Doris Baldwin:* Carlotta Jelm, *Cab Driver:* Ned Roberts, *Coach:* Pat Flaherty, *Man at Gate:* Robert Bray.

BACK STREET (1932) Univ. Produced by Carl Laemmle, Jr. Associate Producer, E. M. Asher. Directed by John M. Stahl. From the novel by Fannie Hurst. Screenplay and Continuity, Gladys Lehman. Dialogue, Lynn Starling. Art Director, Charles D. Hall. Costumes, Vera West. Assistant Director, Scott R. Beal. Photography, Karl Freund.

Editor, Milton Carruth. Sound, C. Roy Hunter. Remade by Universal in 1941 and 1961. 93 minutes

Ray Schmidt: Irene Dunne, *Walter Saxel:* John Boles, *Freda Schmidt:* June Clyde, *Kurt Shendler:* George Meeker, *Mrs. Dole:* ZaSu Pitts, *Francine:* Shirley Grey, *Mrs. Saxel:* Doris Lloyd, *Richard:* William Bakewell, *Beth:* Arletta Duncan, *Mrs. Saxel, Sr.:* Maude Turner Gordon, *Bakeless:* Walter Catlett, *Profhero:* James Donlan, *Mr. Schmidt:* Paul Weigel, *Mrs. Schmidt:* Jane Darwell, *Hugo:* Paul Fix, *Uncle Felix:* Robert McWade.

Back Street with George Meeker and Irene Dunne.

THE BAD AND THE BEAUTIFUL (1952) MGM. Producer, John Houseman. Director, Vincente Minnelli. Author, George Bradshaw. Screenplay, Charles Schnee. Music, David Raksin. Art Directors, Cedric Gibbons, Edward Carfagno. Sound, Douglas Shearer. Sets, Edwin B. Willis, Keough Gleason. Cinematographer, Robert Surtees. Editor, Conrad A. Nervig. 118 minutes

Georgia Lorrison: Lana Turner, *Jonathan Shields:* Kirk Douglas, *Harry Pebbel:* Walter Pidgeon, *James Lee Bartlow:* Dick Powell, *Fred Amiel:* Barry Sullivan, *Rosemary Bartlow:* Gloria Grahame, *Victor "Gaucho" Ribera:* Gilbert Roland, *Henry Whitfield:* Leo G. Carroll, *Kay Amiel:* Vanessa Brown, *Syd Murphy:* Paul Stewart, *Gus:* Sammy White, *Lila:* Elaine Stewart, *Assistant Director:* Jonathan Cott, *Von Ellstein:* Ivan Triesault, *Miss March:* Kathleen Freeman, *Ida:* Marietta Canty, *Blonde:* Lucille Knoch, *Leading Man:* Steve Forrest, *Secretary:* Perry Sheehan, *McDill:* Robert Burton, *Eulogist:* Francis X. Bushman, *Wardrobe Man:* Ned Glass, *Little Girl:* Sandy Descher, *Lionel Donovan:* George Lewis, *Linda Ronley:* Dee Turnell, *Casting Director:* Bob Carson, *Lucien:* Barbara Billingsley, *Priest:* Alex Davidoff, *Mrs. Rosser:* Madge Blake, *Amiel's Boy:* Chris Olsen, *Rosa:* Kaaren Verne, *Joe:* Ben Astar, *Arlene:* Dorothy Patrick, *Mr. Z:* Jay Adler, *Joe's Friend:* Bess Flowers, *Singer:* Peggy King, *Sheriff:* Stanley Andrews, *Ferraday:* John Bishop, *Hugo Shields:* William E. Green, *Assistant Director:* William "Bill" Phillips.

The Bad and the Beautiful with Kirk Douglas, Paul Stewart and Barry Sullivan.

BAD DAY AT BLACK ROCK (1954) MGM. Producer, Dore Schary. Associate Producer, Herman Hoffman. Director, John Sturges. Screenplay, Millard Kaufman. Art Directors, Cedric Gibbons, Malcolm Brown. Editor, Newell P. Kimlin. CinemaScope-Eastman Color. Adaptation, Don McGuire. Based on a story by Howard Breslin. Music, Andre Previn. Assistant Director, Joel Freeman. Photography, William C. Mellor. Remade as *Platinum High School* (1960). 81 minutes

John J. MacReedy: Spencer Tracy, *Reno Smith:* Robert Ryan, *Liz Wirth:* Anne Francis, *Tim Horn:* Dean Jagger, *Doc Velie:* Walter Brennan, *Pete Wirth:* John Ericson, *Coley Trimble:* Ernest Borgnine, *Hector David:* Lee Marvin, *Mr. Hastings:* Russell Collins, *Sam:* Walter Sande.

Bad Day at Black Rock with Anne Francis and Spencer Tracy.

THE BAD NEWS BEARS (1976) Par. Produced by Stanley R. Jaffe. Directed by Michael Ritchie. Written by Bill Lancaster. Photography, John A. Alonzo. Music adapted and conducted by Jerry Fielding. Editor, Richard A. Harris. Production Design, Polly Platt. Music themes from *Carmen* by Georges Bizet. Unit Production Manager and Assistant Director, Jack Roe. Second Assistant Director, Blair Robertson. Set Decorator, Cheryal Kearney. Sound Mixer, Gene Cantamessa. Men's Costumer, Tommy Dawson. Women's Costumer, Nancy Martinelli. Make-up, Jack Obringer. Hairstylist, Caryl Codon. Lenses and Panaflex Camera by Panavision. Color by Movielab. Locations filmed in Chatsworth, California. First of the series. Rated PG. 102 minutes

Morris Buttermaker: Walter Matthau, *Amanda Whurlizer:* Tatum O'Neal, *Roy Turner:* Vic Morrow, *Cleveland:* Joyce Van Patten, *Bob*

Whitewood: Ben Piazza, *Kelly Leak:* Jackie Earle Haley, *Albert Ogilvie:* Alfred W. Lutter, *Joey Turner:* Brandon Cruz, *Tanner Boyle:* Chris Barnes, *Ahmad Abdul Rahim:* Erin Blunt, *Engelberg:* Gary Lee Cavagnaro, *Regi Tower:* Scott Firestone, *Jose Agilar:* Jaime Escobedo, *Miguel Agilar:* George Gonzales, *Jimmy Feldman:* Brett Marx, *Rudi Stein:* David Pollock, *Timmy Lupus:* Quinn Smith, *Toby Whitewood:* David Stambaugh, *Mrs. Lupus:* Timothy Blake, *Mr. Tower:* Bill Sorrells, *Mrs. Turner:* Shari Summers, *Umpire:* Joe Brooks, *White Sox Manager:* George Wyner, *Yankee:* David Lazarus, *Athletic:* Charles Matthau, *Announcer:* Maurice Marks.

The Bad News Bears with Tatum O'Neal and Walter Matthau.

THE BAD SEED (1956) WB. Director, Mervyn LeRoy. Screenplay by John Lee Mahin. Based on play by Maxwell Anderson, and novel by William March. Music by Alex North. Costumes by Moss Mabry. Assistant Director, Mel Mellar. 129 minutes

Christine: Nancy Kelly, *Rhoda:* Patty McCormack, *LeRoy:* Henry Jones, *Mrs. Daigle:* Eileen Heckart, *Monica:* Evelyn Varden, *Kenneth:* William Hopper, *Bravo:* Paul Fix, *Emory:* Jesse White, *Tasker:* Gage Clarke, *Miss Fern:* Joan Croydon, *Mr. Daigle:* Frank Cady.

The Bad Seed with Nancy Kelly and Joan Croydon.

The Bank Dick with Pierre Watkin, W. C. Fields and Franklin Pangborn.

THE BANK DICK (1940) Univ. Directed by Edward Cline. Original Story and Screenplay, Mahatma Kane Jeeves (W. C. Fields). Photography, Milton Krasner. Musical Director, Charles Previn. Art Director, Jack Otterson. Editor, Arthur Hilton. 74 minutes

Egbert Sousé: W. C. Fields, *Agatha Sousé:* Cora Witherspoon, *Myrtle Sousé:* Una Merkel, *Elsie Mae Adele Brunch Sousé:* Evelyn Del Rio, *Mrs. Hermisillo Brunch:* Jessie Ralph, *J. Pinkerton Snoopington:* Franklin Pangborn, *Joe Guelpe:* Shemp Howard, *Mackley Q. Greene:* Dick Purcell, *Og Oggilby:* Grady Sutton, *J. Frothingham Waterbury:* Russell Hicks, *Skinner, Bank President:* Pierre Watkin, *Repulsive Rogan:* Al Hill, *Loudmouth McNasty:* George Moran, *Otis:* Bill Wolfe, *A. Pismo Clam:* Jack Norton, *Assistant Director:* Pat West, *Francois:* Reed Hadley, *Miss Plupp:* Heather Wilde, *Dr. Stall:* Harlan Briggs, *Mr. Cheek, Bank Teller:* Bill Alston, *Mrs. Muckle:* Jan Duggan, *Clifford Muckle:* Bobby Larson, *Skinner's Secretary:* Fay Adler, *Teller in Straw Hat:* David Oliver, *Cops:* Jack Clifford, Pat O'Malley, *Cabdriver:* Charles Sullivan, *Script Girl:* Dorothy Haas, *Old Lady in Car:* Margaret Seddon, *Reporter:* Eddie Acuff, *Girl on Bench:* Kay Sutton, *Desk Clerk:* Emmett Vogan, *Hotel Guest:* Nora Cecil, *James, Chauffeur:* Eddie Dunn, *Woman:* Mary Field, *Man:* John Rawlings, *Francois' Valet:* Lowden Adams, *Plupp's Maid:* Bonnie Washington, *Old Lady with Dog:* Vangie Beilby, *Depositor:* Billy Mitchell.

The Barefoot Contessa with Ava Gardner and Humphrey Bogart.

THE BAREFOOT CONTESSA (1954) UA. A Figaro Inc. Production. Written and directed by Joseph L. Mankiewicz. Assistant Director, Pietro Mussetta. Music by Mario Nascimbene. Color by Technicolor. Photography, Jack Cardiff. Editor, William Hornbeck. Art Director, Arrigo Equini. Gowns by Fontana. Filmed in Italy. 128 minutes

Harry Dawes: Humphrey Bogart, *Maria Vargas:* Ava Gardner, *Oscar Muldoon:* Edmond O'Brien, *Alberto Bravano:* Marius Goring, *Eleanora Torlato-Favrini:* Valentina Cortesa, *Vincenzo Torlato-Favrini:* Rossano Brazzi, *Jerry:* Elizabeth Sellars, *Kirk Edwards:* Warren Stevens, *Pedro:* Franco Interlenghi, *Myrna:* Mari Aldon, *Nightclub Proprietor:* Alberto Rabagliati, *The Pretender:* Tonio Selwart, *The Pretender's Wife:* Margaret Anderson, *Mrs. Eubanks:* Bessie Love, *Busboy:* Enzo Staiola, *Maria's Mother:* Maria Zanoli, *Maria's Father:* Renato Chiantoni, *J. Montague Brown:* Bill Fraser, *Mr. Black:* John Parrish, *Mr. Blue:* Jim Gerald, *Drunken Blonde:* Diana Decker, *Gypsy Dancer:* Riccardi Rioli, *Lulu McGee:* Gertrude Flynn, *Hector Eubanks:* John Horne, *Eddie Blake:* Robert Christopher.

BAREFOOT IN THE PARK (1967) Par. Produced by Hal Wallis. Directed by Gene Saks. Color by Technicolor. Based on the play by Neil Simon. Screenplay by Neil Simon. Produced in association with Nancy Productions. Associate Producers, Paul Nathan and Neil Simon. Assistant Director, Bud Grace. Music by Neal Hefti. Title song by Neal Hefti and Johnny Mercer. Costumes by Edith Head. Art Direction, Hal Pereira and Walter Tyler. Sets, Arthur Krams. Production Manager, Frank Caffey. Photography, Joseph La Shelle. Editor, William A. Lyon. Sound, Harold Lewis. Backgrounds filmed in New York. Redford and Natwick repeat their stage roles. 104 minutes

Paul Bratter: Robert Redford, *Corie Bratter:* Jane Fonda, *Victor Velasco:* Charles Boyer, *Ethel Banks:* Mildred Natwick, *Harry Pepper:* Herbert Edelman, *Aunt Harriet:* Mabel Albertson, *Restaurant Owner:* Fritz Feld, *Delivery Man:* James Stone, *Frank:* Ted Hartley, *Cop:* John Indrisano, *Bum in Park:* Paul E. Burns.

Barefoot in the Park with Jane Fonda and Robert Redford.

THE BARKLEYS OF BROADWAY (1949) MGM. Produced by Arthur Freed. Directed by Charles Walters. Color by Technicolor. Original screenplay by Betty Comden and Adolph Green. Art Directors, Cedric Gibbons and Edward Carfagno. Photography, Harry Stradling. Editor, Albert Akst. Music, Harry Warren. Music Director, Lennie Hayton. Songs: "You'd Be Hard to Replace," "Week-End in the Country," "Manhattan Downbeat," "Shoes With Wings On," "My One and Only Highland Fling" by Ira Gershwin and Harry Warren; "They

Can't Take That Away From Me" by Ira and George Gershwin (from *Shall We Dance*, 1937). The last Astaire-Rogers film (and the first since *The Story of Vernon and Irene Castle* in 1939) and the only one in color. 109 minutes

Josh Barkley: Fred Astaire, *Dinah Barkley:* Ginger Rogers, *Ezra Miller:* Oscar Levant, *Mrs. Belney:* Billie Burke, *Shirlene May:* Gale Robbins, *Jacques Barredout:* Jacques Francois, *The Judge:* George Zucco, *Bert Felsher:* Clinton Sundberg, *Pamela Driscoll:* Inez Cooper, *Gloria Amboy:* Carol Brewster, *Larry:* Wilson Wood, *First Woman:* Jean Andren, *Second Woman:* Laura Treadwell, *Mary (Maid):* Margaret Bert, *Taxi Driver:* Allen Wood, *Guests in Theater Lobby:* Forbes Murray, Bess Flowers, Lois Austin, Betty Blythe, *Doorman at Theater:* Bill Tannen, *Apartment Doorman:* Mahlon Hamilton, *Cleo Fernby:* Lorraine Crawford, *Blonde:* Dee Turnell, *Husband:* Reginald Simpson, *Ladislaus Ladi:* Hans Conried, *Chauffeur:* Sherry Hall, *Mr. Perkins:* Frank Ferguson, *Stage Doorman:* Nolan Leary, *Duke de Morny:* Joe Granby, *Sarah's Mother:* Esther Somers, *Sarah's Aunt:* Helen Eby-Rock, *Genevieve:* Joyce Mathews, *Henrietta:* Roberta Johnson, *Clementine:* Mary Jo Ellis, *Ticket Man:* Jack Rice.

The Barkleys of Broadway with Fred Astaire and Ginger Rogers.

The Barretts of Wimpole Street with Fredric March and Norma Shearer.

THE BARRETTS OF WIMPOLE STREET (1934) MGM. Produced by Irving G. Thalberg. Directed by Sidney Franklin. Author, Rudolf Besier. Screenplay by Ernst Vajda, Claudine West, Donald Ogden Stewart. Film Editor, Margaret Booth. Photographer, William Daniels. Recording Engineer, Douglas Shearer. Assistant Director, Hugh Boswell. Art Director, Cedric Gibbons. Associate Art Directors, Harry McAffe, Edwin B. Willis. Costumes, Adrian. Musical Numbers,

Herbert Stothart. TV title: *Forbidden Alliance*. Remade by MGM, 1957. 110 minutes

Elizabeth Barrett: Norma Shearer, *Robert Browning:* Fredric March, *Barrett:* Charles Laughton, *Henrietta Barrett:* Maureen O'Sullivan, *Arabel:* Katharine Alexander, *Captain Cook:* Ralph Forbes, *Wilson:* Una O'Connor, *Bella:* Marion Clayton, *Bevan:* Ian Wolfe, *Dr. Chambers:* Ferdinand Munier, *Dr. Waterloo:* Leo G. Carroll, *Brothers:* Alan Conrad, Neville Clark, Peter Hobbes, Mathew Smith, *Octavius:* Vernon P. Downing, *Butler:* Lowden Adams, *Clergyman:* Winter Hall, *Coachman:* George Kirby, *Brother:* Robert Carleton.

Bataan with Robert Walker, Robert Taylor, Kenneth Spencer and Phillip Terry.

BATAAN (1943) MGM. Producer, Irving Starr. Director, Tay Garnett. Screenplay, Robert D. Andrews. Musical Score, Bronislau Kaper. Art Director, Cedric Gibbons. Cameraman, Sidney Wagner. Special Effects, Arnold Gillespie, Warren Newcombe. Editor, George White. "Unofficial" remake of *The Lost Patrol* (RKO, 1934). 114 minutes

Sergeant Bill Dane: Robert Taylor, *Lt. Steve Bentley:* George Murphy, *Corp. Jake Feingold:* Thomas Mitchell, *Corp. Barney Todd:* Lloyd Nolan, *Capt. Lassiter:* Lee Bowman, *Leonard Purckett:* Robert Walker, *Felix Ramirez:* Desi Arnaz, *F. X. Matowski:* Barry Nelson, *Gilbert Hardy:* Phillip Terry, *Corp. Jesus Katigbay:* Roque Espiritu, *Wesley Epps:* Kenneth Spencer, *Yankee Salazar:* J. Alex Havier, *Sam Malloy:* Tom Dugan, *Lieutenant:* Donald Curtis, *Nurses:* Lynne Carver, Mary McLeod, Dorothy Morris, *Infantry Officer:* Bud Geary, *Wounded Soldier:* Ernie Alexander, *Machine Gunner:* Phil Schumacher.

Battle Cry with Tab Hunter, Aldo Ray and William Campbell.

21

BATTLE CRY (1955) WB. Director, Raoul Walsh. CinemaScope, WarnerColor. Based on Leon Uris' novel. Screenplay, Leon M. Uris. Art Director, John Beckman. Musical Director, Max Steiner. Cinematographer, Sid Hickox. Editor, William Ziegler. 149 minutes

Colonel Huxley: Van Heflin, *Andy:* Aldo Ray, *Kathy:* Mona Freeman, *Pat:* Nancy Olson, *Mac:* James Whitmore, *General Snipes:* Raymond Massey, *Danny:* Tab Hunter, *Elaine Yarborough:* Dorothy Malone, *Rae:* Anne Francis, *Ski:* Bill Campbell, *Marion:* John Lupton, *L. Q.:* Justus Mc Queen (L. Q. Jones), *Spanish Joe:* Perry Lopez, *Speedy:* Fess Parker, *Lightower:* Jonas Applegarth, *Ziltch:* Tommy Cook, *Indian Marine:* Felix Noriego, *Susan:* Susan Morrow, *Major Wellman:* Carleton Young, *Pedro:* Victor Millan, *Seabags:* Glenn Denning, *Sgt. Beller:* Gregory Walcott, *Enoch Rogers:* Rhys Williams, *Chaplain Petersen:* Chick Chandler, *Mr. Forrester:* Willis Bouchey, *Mrs. Forrester:* Sarah Selby, *Bud Forrester:* Harold Knudsen, *Mr. Walker:* Frank Ferguson, *Mrs. Walker:* Kay Stewart, *Waitress:* Allyn McLerie, *First New Zealander:* Lumsden Hare, *Second New Zealander:* Carl Harbaugh, *Mrs. Rogers:* Hilda Plowright, *Old Man:* George Selk.

BATTLEGROUND (1949) MGM. Producer, Dore Schary. Director, William Wellman. Author-Screenplay, Robert Pirosh. Art Directors, Cedric Gibbons, Hans Peters. Music Score, Lennie Hayton. Photography, Paul C. Vogel. Editor, John Dunning. 118 minutes

Holley: Van Johnson, *Jarvess:* John Hodiak, *Roderiguez:* Ricardo Montalban, *"Pop" Ernest Stazak:* George Murphy, *Jim Layton:* Marshall Thompson, *Abner Spudler:* Jerome Courtland, *Standiferd:* Don Taylor, *Wolowicz:* Bruce Cowling, *Kinnie:* James Whitmore, *"Kipp" Kippton:* Douglas Fowley, *Chaplain:* Leon Ames, *Hansan:* Guy Anderson, *Doc "Medic":* Thomas E. Breen, *Denise:* Denise Darcel, *Bettis:* Richard Jaeckel, *Garby:* Jim Arness, *William J. Hooper:* Scotty Beckett, *Lt. Teiss:* Brett King, *German Lieutenant:* Roland Varno, *Major:* Edmon Ryan, *Levenstein:* Michael Browne, *Supply Sergeant:* Jim Drum, *G. I. Stragglers:* Dewey Martin, Tom Noonan, David Holt, *G.I.'s:* George Offerman, Jr., William Self, *Sergeant:* Steve Pendleton, *German Sergeant:* Jerry Paris, *Runner:* Tommy Bond, *Belgian Woman Volunteer:* Nan Boardman, *German Captain:* Ivan Triesault, *German:* Henry Rowland, *German Major:* John Mylong, *American Colonel:* Ian MacDonald, *Tank Destroyer Man:* William Leicester (Lester), *Mess Sergeant:* George Chandler, *Tanker:* Dick Jones, *Medic Private:* Chris Drake, *Casualty:* Tommy Kelly.

Battleground with Ricardo Montalban, John Hodiak and Van Johnson.

BEAT THE DEVIL (1954) UA. A Santana-Romulus Production. Director, John Huston. Associate Producer, Jack Clayton. Screenplay by John Huston and Truman Capote. Based on novel by James Helvick. Art Director, Wilfred Shingleton. Cinematographers, Oswald Morris, Freddie Francis. Editor, Ralph Kemplen. Music, Franco Mannino. Filmed in Italy. 92 minutes

Billy Dannreuther: Humphrey Bogart, *Gwendolen Chelm:* Jennifer Jones, *Maria Dannreuther:* Gina Lollobrigida, *Petersen:* Robert Morley, *O'Hara:* Peter Lorre, *Harry Chelm:* Edward Underdown, *Major Ross:* Ivor Barnard, *C.I.D. Inspector:* Bernard Lee, *Ravello:* Marco Tulli, *Purser:* Marrio Perroni, *Hotel Manager:* Alex Pochet, *Charles:* Aldo Silvani.

Beat the Devil with Humphrey Bogart and Jennifer Jones.

Beau Geste with Robert Preston, Ray Milland and Gary Cooper.

BEAU GESTE (1939) Par. Produced and Directed by William A. Wellman. Based on the novel by Percival Christopher Wren. Screenplay, Robert Carson. Music, Alfred Newman. Orchestrations, Edward Powell. Photography, Theodor Sparkuhl and Archie Stout. Editor, Thomas Scott. Art Directors, Hans Dreier and Robert Odell. Sound, Hugo Grenzbach and Walter Oberst. Technical Adviser, Louis Van Der Ecker. 114 minutes. Other versions: Par., 1926; Univ., 1966; *The Last Remake of Beau Geste*, Univ., 1977

Beau (Michael) Geste: Gary Cooper, *John Geste:* Ray Milland, *Digby Geste:* Robert Preston, *Sgt. Markoff:* Brian Donlevy, *Isobel Rivers:* Susan Hayward, *Rasinoff:* J. Carrol Naish, *Schwartz:* Albert Dekker, *Hank Miller:* Broderick Crawford, *Buddy McMonigal:* Charles Barton, *Maj. Henri de Beaujolais:* James Stephenson, *Lady Patricia Brandon:* Heather Thatcher, *Lt. Dufour:* James Burke, *Augustus Brandon:* George P. Huntley, Jr., *Voisin:* Harold Huber, *Beau as a boy:* Donald O'Connor, *John as a boy:* Billy Cook, *Digby as a boy:* Martin Spellman, *Isobel as a girl:* Ann Gillis, *Augustus as a boy:* David Holt, *Lt. Martin:* Harvey

Stephens, *Maris*: Stanley Andrews, *Renoir*: Harry Woods, *Renault*: Arthur Aylsworth, *Renouf*: Henry Brandon, *Krenke*: Barry Macollum, *A Bugler*: Ronnie Rondell, *Burdon, Butler*: Frank Dawson, *Cordier*: George Chandler, *Glock*: Duke Green, *Colonel in Recruiting Office*: Thomas Jackson, *Sergeant Major*: Jerome Storm, *Sergeant*: Joe Whitehead, *Corporal*: Harry Worth, *Corp. Golas*: Nestor Paiva, *Arab Scouts*: George Regas, Francis McDonald, *Legionnaire Roberts*: Carl Voss, *Legionnaire Williams*: Joe Bernard, *Legionnaire Paul*: Robert Perry, *Legionnaire Fenton*: Larry Lawson, *Legionnaire Clements*: Henry Sylvester, *Legionnaire Virginia*: Joseph William Cody, *Trumpeter Leo*: Joe Colling, *Girl in Port Said Cafe*: Gladys Jeans.

BELLE OF THE NINETIES (1934) Par. Produced by William Le Baron. Director, Leo McCarey. Author, Mae West. Cameraman, Karl Struss. Editor, LeRoy Stone. New songs by Arthur Johnston and Sam Coslow: "When a St. Louis Woman Goes Down to New Orleans," "My Old Flame," "My American Beauty," "Troubled Waters." 75 minutes

Ruby Carter: Mae West, *Tiger Kid*: Roger Pryor, *Brooks Claybourne*: John Mack Brown, *Molly Brant*: Katherine De Mille, *Ace Lamont*: John Miljan, *Kirby*: James Donlan, *Gilbert*: Tom Herbert, *Dirk*: Stuart Holmes, *Slade*: Harry Woods, *Stogie*: Edward Gargan, *Jasmine*: Libby Taylor, *Colonel Claybourne*: Frederick Burton, *Mrs. Claybourne*: Augusta Anderson, *Blackie*: Benny Baker, *Butch*: Morrie Cohan, *St. Louis Fighter*: Warren Hymer, *Editor*: Wade Boteler, *Leading Man*: George Walsh, *Comedians*: Eddie Borden, Fuzzy Knight, Tyler Brooke, *Beef Trust Chorus Girl*: Kay Deslys, *Extra*: Mike Mazurki. Duke Ellington and Orchestra.

Belle of the Nineties with John Miljan and Mae West.

THE BELLS OF ST. MARY'S (1945) RKO. Producer and Director, Leo McCarey. Author, Leo McCarey. Screenplay, Dudley Nichols. Musical Score, Robert Emmett Dolan. Art Director, William Flannery. Cameraman, George Barnes. Special Effects, Vernon L. Walker. Editor, Harry Marker. Songs: "Aren't You Glad You're You?" by Johnny Burke and Jimmy Van Heusen; "In the Land of Beginning Again" by Grant Clarke and George W. Meyer; "The Bells of St. Mary's" by Douglas Furber and A. Emmett Adams; "Ave Maria." A Rainbow Production. 126 minutes

Father O'Malley: Bing Crosby, *Sister Benedict*: Ingrid Bergman, *Bogardus*: Henry Travers, *Patsy's Father*: William Gargan, *Sister Michael*: Ruth Donnelly, *Patsy*: Joan Carroll, *Patsy's Mother*: Martha Sleeper, *Dr. McKay*: Rhys Williams, *Eddie*: Dickie Tyler, *Mrs. Breen*: Una O'Connor, *Tommy*: Bobby Frasco, *Nuns*: Aina Constant, Gwen Crawford, Eva Novak, *Clerk in Store*: Matt McHugh, *Delphine*:

Edna Wonacott, *Luther*: Jimmy Crane, *Truck Driver*: Dewey Robinson, *Taxi Driver*: Jimmy Dundee, *Workman*: Joseph Palma, *Landlady*: Minerva Urecal, *Blind Man*: Peter Sasso, *Old Lady*: Cora Shannon.

The Bells of St. Mary's with Ingrid Bergman and Bing Crosby.

BEND OF THE RIVER (1952) Univ. Producer, Aaron Rosenberg. Director, Anthony Mann. Color by Technicolor. From William Gulick's *Bend of the Snake*. Screenplay, Borden Chase. Art Directors, Bernard Herzbrun, Nathan Juran. Music, Hans J. Salter. Cinematographer, Irving Glassberg. Editor, Russell Schoengarth. 91 minutes

Glyn McLyntock: James Stewart, *Cole Garett*: J. Arthur Kennedy, *Laura Baile*: Julia Adams, *Trey Wilson*: Rock Hudson, *Marjie Baile*: Lori Nelson, *Jeremy Baile*: Jay C. Flippen, *Shorty*: Harry Morgan, *Captain Mello*: Chubby Johnson, *Long Tom*: Royal Dano, *Tom Hendricks*: Howard Petrie, *Adam*: Stepin' Fetchit, *Red*: Jack Lambert, *Don Grundy*: Frank Ferguson, *Mrs. Prentiss*: Frances Bavier, *Wullie*: Cliff Lyons, *Lock*: Jennings Miles, *Wasco*: Frank Chase, *Aunt Tildy*: Lillian Randolph, *Roustabout*: Britt Wood, *Miner*: Gregg Barton, *Johnson*: Hugh Prosser, *Barkers*: Donald Kerr, Harry Arnie.

Bend of the River with Rock Hudson, Jay C. Flippen, Julie Adams and James Stewart.

BEN-HUR (1959) MGM. Producer, Sam Zimbalist. Director, William Wyler. Screenplay, Karl Tunberg. Based on novel by Lew Wallace. Music by Miklos Rozsa. Associated Directors, Andrew Marton, Yakima Canutt and Mario Soldati. Assistant Directors, Gus Agosti and Alberto Cardone. Costumes by Elizabeth Haffenden. Art Directors, William A. Horning, Edward Carfagno. Cinematographer, Robert L. Surtees. Additional Photography, Harold E. Wellman, Pietro Portalupi. Editors, Ralph E. Winters, John D. Dunning. Technicolor, Camera 65. Produced in Italy. Photographed in Panavision. 217 minutes

Judah Ben-Hur: Charlton Heston, *Quintus Arrius:* Jack Hawkins, *Messala:* Stephen Boyd, *Ester:* Haya Harareet, *Skeik Ilderim:* Hugh Griffith, *Miriam:* Martha Scott, *Simonides:* Sam Jaffe, *Tirzah:* Cathy O'Donnell, *Balthasar:* Finlay Currie, *Pontius Pilate:* Frank Thring, *Drusus:* Terence Longden, *Sextus:* Andre Morell, *Flavia:* Marina Berti, *Tiberius:* George Relph, *Malluch:* Adi Berber, *Amrah:* Stella Vitelleschi, *Mary:* Jose Greci, *Joseph:* Laurence Payne, *Spintho:* John Horsley, *Metellus:* Richard Coleman, *Marius:* Duncan Lamont, *Aide to Tiberius:* Ralph Truman, *Gaspar:* Richard Hale, *Melchior:* Reginald Lal Singh, *Quaestor:* David Davies, *Jailer:* Dervis Ward, *The Christ:* Claude Heater, *Gratus:* Mino Doro, *Chief of Rowers:* Robert Brown, *Leper:* Tutte Lemkow, *Hortator:* Howard Lang, *Captain, Rescue Ship:* Ferdy Mayne, *Doctor:* John Le Mesurier, *Blind Man:* Stevenson Lang, *Barca:* Aldo Mozele, *Marcello:* Dino Fazio, *Raimondo:* Michael Cosmo, *Decurian:* Remington Olmstead, *Mario:* Hugh Billingsley, *Man in Nazareth:* Aldo Silvani, *The Lubian:* Cliff Lyons, *The Egyptian:* Joe Yrigoyen, *Sportsman:* Joe Canutt.

Ben-Hur with Charlton Heston.

Benji with Cynthia Smith, Patsy Garrett, Higgins as Benji, and Allen Fiuzat.

BENJI (1974) Mulberry Square Productions. Produced, Directed and Written by Joe Camp. Color by CFI. Executive Producer, Ed Vanston. Associate Producer, Erwin Hearne and Ben Vaughn. Production Manager, Neil Roach. Photography, Don Reddy. Editor, Leon Seith. Production Designer, Harland Wright. Music, Euel Box. Sound, Bruce Shearin. Animal Trainers, Mr. and Mrs. Frank Inn. Song, "I Feel Love" by Euel and Betty Box, sung by Charlie Rich. Filmed in Denton and McKinney, Texas. Rated G. 85 minutes. Sequel was *For the Love of Benji* (1977)

Benji: Higgins, *Dr. Chapman:* Peter Breck, *Bill:* Edgar Buchanan, *Officer Tuttle:* Terry Carter, *Henry:* Christopher Connelly, *Mary:* Patsy Garrett, *Riley:* Tom Lester, *Mitch:* Mark Slade, *Lt. Samuels:* Herb Vigran, *Linda:*

Deborah Walley, *Lady with the Cat:* Frances Bavier, *Cindy Chapman:* Cynthia Smith, *Paul Chapman:* Allen Fiuzat, *Payton Murrah:* Victor Raider-Wexler, *Custodian:* Charles Starkey, *Floyd:* Larry Swartz, *Plainclothesman:* Don Puckett, *Mr. Harvey:* Erwin Hearne, *Mrs. Harvey:* Katie Hearne, *Policeman:* J. D. Young, *Man:* Ben Vaughn, *Bob:* Ed DeLatte, *Boy:* Joey Camp.

The Best of Everything with Stephen Boyd and Hope Lange.

THE BEST OF EVERYTHING (1959) 20th. Producer, Jerry Wald. Director, Jean Negulesco. Screenplay by Edith Sommer and Mann Rubin. Based on novel by Rona Jaffe. Music by Alfred Newman. Title song by Sammy Cahn and Alfred Newman, sung by Johnny Mathis. Costumes by Adele Palmer. Assistant Director, Eli Dunn. In CinemaScope and De Luxe Color. Art Directors, Lyle R. Wheeler, Jack Martin Smith, Mark-Lee Kirk. Orchestration, Herbert Spencer and Earle Hagen. Photography, William C. Mellor. Editor, Robert Simpson. Locations filmed in New York City. Film debut of Donald Harron, stage actor. 127 minutes

Caroline Bender: Hope Lange, *Mike Rice:* Stephen Boyd, *Gregg Adams:* Suzy Parker, *Barbara Lemont:* Martha Hyer, *April Morrison:* Diane Baker, *Fred Shalimar:* Brian Aherne, *Dexter Key:* Robert Evans, *Eddie Harris:* Brett Halsey, *Sidney Carter:* Donald Harron, *Mary Agnes:* Sue Carson, *Jane:* Linda Hutchings, *Paul Landis:* Lionel Kane, *Dr. Ronnie Wood:* Ted Otis, *David Savage:* Louis Jourdan, *Amanda Farrow:* Joan Crawford, *Brenda:* June Blair, *Judy Masson:* Myrna Hansen, *Scrubwoman:* Nora O'Mahoney, *Joe:* David Hoffman, *Margo Stewart:* Theodora Davitt, *Girls in Typing Pool:* Alena Murray, Rachel Stephens, Julie Payne, *Drunk:* Wally Brown, *Man:* Al Austin.

THE BEST YEARS OF OUR LIVES (1946) RKO. Producer, Samuel Goldwyn. Director, William Wyler. From the novel *Glory For Me* by MacKinlay Kantor. Screenplay, Robert E. Sherwood. Art Directors, George Jenkins, Perry Ferguson. Cameraman, Gregg Toland. Editor, Daniel Mandell. Song by Sidney Arodin and Hoagy Carmichael, "Lazy River." Only professional film of amputee Harold Russell. Remade as a TV movie, *Returning Home* (1975). 172 minutes

Milly Stephenson: Myrna Loy, *Al Stephenson:* Fredric March, *Fred Derry:* Dana Andrews, *Peggy Stephenson:* Teresa Wright, *Marie Derry:* Virginia Mayo, *Wilma Cameron:* Cathy O'Donnell, *Butch Engle:* Hoagy Carmichael, *Homer Parrish:* Harold Russell, *Hortense Derry:* Gladys George, *Pat Derry:* Roman Bohnen, *Mr. Milton:* Ray Collins, *Mrs. Parrish:* Minna Gombell, *Mr. Parrish:* Walter Baldwin, *Cliff:* Steve Cochran, *Mrs. Cameron:* Dorothy Adams, *Mr. Cameron:* Don Beddoe, *Woody:* Victor Cutler, *Luella Parrish:* Marlene Aames, *Prew:* Charles Halton, *Mr. Mollett:* Ray Teal, *Thorpe:* Howland Chamberlin, *Novak:* Dean White, *Bullard:* Erskine Sanford, *Rob Stephenson:* Michael Hall, *Merkle:* Norman Phillips, *Dexter:* Teddy Infuhr, *Taxi Driver:* Clancy Cooper, *Mr. Gibbons:* Ralph

Sanford, *Tech. Sergeant:* Robert Karnes, *ATC Sergeant:* Bert Conway, *Corporal:* Blake Edwards, *Gus (Waiter):* John Tyrrell, *Steve (Bartender):* Donald Kerr, *Desk Clerk:* Jack Rice, *Miss Garrett:* Ruth Sanderson, *Latham:* Ben Erway, *Mrs. Talburt:* Claire Dubrey, *Minister:* Harry Cheshire, *Karney:* Pat Flaherty, *Jackie:* James Ames.

The Best Years of Our Lives with Dana Andrews, Myrna Loy, Donald Kerr (bartender), Fredric March, Hoagy Carmichael and Harold Russell.

THE BIG COUNTRY (1958) UA. Producers, William Wyler and Gregory Peck. Director, William Wyler. Screenplay by James R. Webb, Sy Bartlett and Robert Wilder. Adaptation by Jessamyn West and Robert Wyler. From the novel by Donald Hamilton. Costumes by Emile Santiago and Yvonne Wood. Assistant Directors, Ivan Volkman, Ray Gosnell and Henry Hartman. Music by Jerome Moross. An Anthony-Worldwide Production in Technirama and Technicolor. Gregory Peck's three sons make their film debuts. Filmed on the Drais Ranch, near Stockton, California. 165 minutes

James McKay: Gregory Peck, *Julie Maragon:* Jean Simmons, *Patricia Terrill:* Carroll Baker, *Steve Leech:* Charlton Heston, *Rufus Hannassey:* Burl Ives, *Major Henry Terrill:* Charles Bickford, *Ramon:* Alfonso Bedoya, *Buck Hannassey:* Chuck Connors, *Rafe Hannassey:* Chuck Hayward, *Dude Hannassey:* Buff Brady, *Blackie Hannassey:* Jim Burk, *Hannassey Woman:* Dorothy Adams, *Terrill Cowboys:* Chuck Roberson, Bob Morgan, John McKee, Jay Slim Talbot, *Liveryman:* Donald Kerr, *Guests:* Ralph Sanford, Harry V. Cheshire, Dick Alexander, *Boys:* Jonathan, Stephen, Carey Paul Peck.

The Big Country with Charlton Heston and Gregory Peck.

THE BIG HOUSE (1930) MGM. Produced by Irving Thalberg. Directed by George Hill. Story, Frances Marion. Screenplay, Frances Marion, Joe Farnham, and Martin Flavin. Art Director, Cedric Gibbons. Photography,

Harold Wenstrom. Editor, Blanche Sewell. Sound, Douglas Shearer. Jute mill scenes filmed at the Pacific Woolen and Blanket Works, Long Beach. A Cosmopolitan Production. Also French, German, Italian and Spanish versions. 88 minutes

John Morgan: Chester Morris, *Butch Schmidt:* Wallace Beery, *Warden James Adams:* Lewis Stone, *Kent Marlowe:* Robert Montgomery, *Anne Marlowe:* Leila Hyams, *Pop Riker:* George F. Marion, *Mr. Marlowe:* J. C. Nugent, *Olsen:* Karl Dane, *Captain Wallace:* DeWitt Jennings, *Gopher:* Mathew Betz, *Mrs. Marlowe:* Claire McDowell, *Sergeant Donlin:* Robert Emmet O'Connor, *Uncle Jed:* Tom Kennedy, *Sandy, a Guard:* Tom Wilson, *Dopey:* Eddie Foyer, *Putnam:* Rosco Ates, *Oliver:* Fletcher Norton, *Prison Barber:* Adolph Seidel, *Bits:* Eddie Lambert, Michael Vavitch.

The Big House with Chester Morris and Wallace Beery.

THE BIG SLEEP (1946) WB. Producer and Director, Howard Hawks. From the novel by Raymond Chandler. Screenplay, William Faulkner, Leigh Brackett, Jules Furthman. Art Director, Carl Jules Weyl. Music, Leo F. Forbstein. Cameraman, Sid Hickox. Special Effects, E. Roy Davidson. Editor, Christian Nyby. Song, "Her Tears Flowed Like Wine." Footage from *Case of the Stuttering Bishop* (WB, 1937). Remade in England (UA, 1978) with Robert Mitchum and Sarah Miles. 114 minutes

The Big Sleep with Humphrey Bogart and Lauren Bacall.

Phil Marlowe: Humphrey Bogart, *Vivian Sternwood Rutledge:* Lauren Bacall, *Eddie Mars:* John Ridgely, *Carmen Sternwood:* Martha Vickers, *Proprietress:* Dorothy Malone, *Mona Mars:* Peggy Knudsen, *Bernie Ohls:* Regis Toomey, *General Sternwood:* Charles Waldron, *Norris, the Butler:* Charles D. Brown, *Canino:* Bob Steele, *Harry Jones:* Elisha Cook, Jr., *Joe Brody:* Louis Jean Heydt, *Agnes Lowzier:* Sonia Darrin, *Captain Cronjager:* James Flavin, *Medical Examiner:* Joseph Crehan, *Carol Lundgren:* Tom Rafferty, *Arthur Gwynne Geiger:* Theodor Von Eltz, *Taxicab Driver:* Joy Barlowe, *Sidney:* Tom Fadden, *Pete:* Ben Welden, *Art Huck:* Trevor Bardette, *Ed, Deputy:* Emmett Vogan, *Furtive Man:* Forbes Murray, *Motorcycle Officer:* Pete Kooy, *Librarian:* Carole Douglas, *Croupier:* Jack Chefe, *Mars' Thugs:* Paul Weber, Jack Perry, Wally Walker, *Hatcheck Girl:* Lorraine Miller, *Cigarette Girl:* Shelby Payne, *Waitresses:* Tanis Chandler, Deannie Bert. Cut are: Thomas Jackson as District Attorney Wilde, Dan Wallace as Owen Taylor.

A Bill of Divorcement with Katharine Hepburn, Billie Burke and John Barrymore.

A BILL OF DIVORCEMENT (1932) RKO. Executive Producer, David O. Selznick. Directed by George Cukor. Assistant Director, Dewey Starkey. From the play by Clemence Dane. Screenplay, Howard Estabrook and Harry Wagstaff Gribble. Art Director, Carroll Clark. Costume Design, Josette De Lima. Photography, Sid Hickox. Editor, Arthur Roberts. Sound, George Ells. Film debut of Katharine Hepburn. Remade by RKO in 1940. 76 minutes

Hillary Fairfield: John Barrymore, *Sydney Fairfield:* Katharine Hepburn, *Margeret Fairfield:* Billie Burke, *Kit Humphrey:* David Manners, *Gray Meredith:* Paul Cavanagh, *Doctor Alliot:* Henry Stephenson, *Aunt Hester:* Elizabeth Patterson, *Bassett:* Gayle Evers.

Billy Jack with Tom Laughlin.

BILLY JACK (1971) WB., later a Warners-Taylor/Laughlin Distribution Co. release. Produced by Mary Rose Solti. A National Student Film Corp. Presentation. Directed by T. C. Frank (Tom Laughlin). Screenplay by Frank and Teresa Christina (Tom Laughlin and Delores Taylor Laughlin). Technicolor. Associate Producers, Ed Haldeman and Earl D. Elliott. Assistant Directors, Mike Dmytryk and Joseph E. Rickards. Photography, Fred Koenekamp and John Stephens. Editors, Larry Heath and Marion Rothman. Sound Effects, Edit International Ltd. Titles and Opticals, Pacific Title. Production Supervisor, Linda Morrow. Music composed and conducted by Mundell Lowe. Songs: "One Tin Soldier" (Dennis Lambert and Brian Potter), sung by Jinx Dawson of Coven; "Johnnie" and "Look, Look to the Mountain" (Teresa Kelly), sung by Kelly; "When Will Billy Love Me?" and "A Rainbow Made of Children" (Lynn Baker), sung by Baker; "Freedom over Men," sung by Gwen Smith; "The Ring Song" (Katy Moffatt), sung by Moffatt; "Mary and the Jesus Babe," sung by Robbyn Etelson. Filmed in New Mexico and Arizona. Rated GP. 112 minutes. Others in the series: *Born Losers* (AIP, 1967), *The Trial of Billy Jack* (Taylor-Laughlin, 1974), *Billy Jack Goes to Washington* (unreleased, 1976)

Billy Jack: Tom Laughlin, *Jean Roberts:* Delores Taylor, *Sheriff Cole:* Clark Howat, *Stuart Posner:* Bert Freed, *Barbara:* Julie Webb, *Deputy:* Kenneth Tobey, *Doctor:* Victor Izay, *Kit:* Debbie Schock, *Martin:* Stan Rice, *Carol:* Teresa Kelly, *Maria:* Katy Moffatt, *Cindy:* Susan Foster, *Councilman:* Paul Bruce, *Sarah:* Lynn Baker, *Sunshine:* Susan Sosa, *Bernard Posner:* David Roya, *Angela:* Gwen Smith, *Dinosaur:* John McClure, *Miss Eyelashes:* Cissie Colpitts, *Council Chairman:* Richard Stahl, *O. K. Corrales:* Allan Meyerson, *Drama Teachers:* Ed Greenberg and Don Sturdy, *Student:* Dan Barrows, *Other Ways Demolition Squad Codirector:* Herb Kohl, *Members of the Committee.*

Billy the Kid with Brian Donlevy and Robert Taylor.

BILLY THE KID (1941) MGM. Produced by Irving Asher. Directed by David Miller. Color by Technicolor. Suggested by the book *The Saga of Billy The Kid* by Walter Noble Burns. Screenplay, Gene Fowler. Story, Howard Emmett Rogers and Bradbury Foote. Music, David Snell. Photography, Leonard Smith and William V. Skall. Editor, Robert J. Kern. Remake of the 1930 MGM film. 95 minutes

Billy Bonney: Robert Taylor, *Jim Sherwood:* Brian Donlevy, *Eric Keating:* Ian Hunter, *Edith Keating:* Mary Howard, *Dan Hickey:* Gene Lockhart, *Tim Ward:* Henry O'Neill, *Pedro Gonzales:* Frank Puglia, *Cass McAndrews (Sheriff):* Cy Kendall, *Mildred:* Connie Gilchrist, *Mrs. Hanky:* Ethel Griffies, *Tom Patterson:* Chill Wills, *Ed Bronson:* Guinn Williams, *Mrs. Patterson:* Olive Blakeney, *Spike Hudson:* Lon Chaney, Jr., *Judge Blake:* Frank Conlan, *Bart Hodges:* Mitchell Lewis, *Kirby Claxton:* Dick Curtis, *Bill Cobb:* Ted Adams, *Jesse Martin:* Earl Gunn, *Pat Shanahan:* Eddie Dunn, *Ed Shanahan:* Grant Withers, *Milton:* Joe Yule, *"Bat" Smithers:* Carl Pitti, *Drunk:*

Arthur Housman, *The Duke:* Lew Harvey, *Bessie:* Priscilla Lawson, *Thad Decker:* Kermit Maynard, *Butch:* Slim Whitaker, *Axel:* Ray Teal, *Bud:* Wesley White, *Hickey Gang Members:* Ben Pitti, George Chesebro, Jack L. King, *Vagrant #1:* Jules Cowles, *Vagrant #2:* Edwin J. Brady, *Man in Saloon:* Frank Hagney, *Gambler:* Buck Mack, *Leader:* Tom London.

Bird Man of Alcatraz with Burt Lancaster and Neville Brand.

BIRD MAN OF ALCATRAZ (1962) UA. Executive Producer, Harold Hecht. Producers, Stuart Millar, Guy Trosper. Director, John Frankenheimer. Screenplay, Guy Trosper. Based on the book by Thomas E. Gaddis. Art Director, Ferdie Carrere. Music, Elmer Bernstein. Cinematographer, Burnett Guffey. Editor, Edward Mann. A Norma Production. 147 minutes

Robert Stroud: Burt Lancaster, *Harvey Shoemaker:* Karl Malden, *Elizabeth Stroud:* Thelma Ritter, *Stella Johnson:* Betty Field, *Bull Ransom:* Neville Brand, *Tom Gaddis:* Edmond O'Brien, *Roy Comstock:* Hugh Marlowe, *Feto Gomez:* Telly Savalas, *Kramer:* Crahan Denton, *Jess Younger:* James Westerfield, *Logue:* Chris Robinson, *Dr. Ellis:* Whit Bissell, *Eddie Kassellis:* Leo Penn, *Chaplain Wentzel:* Lewis Charles, *Guard Captain:* Art Stewart, *Judge:* Raymond Greenleaf, *Crazed Prisoner:* Nick Dennis, *Fred Daw:* William Hansen, *City Editor:* Harry Holcombe, *Senator Ham Lewis:* Robert Burton, *Burns:* Len Lesser, *Father Matthieu:* George Mitchell, *John Clary:* Ed Mallory, *Mrs. Woodrow Wilson:* Adrienne Marden, *Reporter:* Harry Jackson.

The Birds with Rod Taylor, Jessica Tandy, Tippi Hedren and Veronica Cartwright.

THE BIRDS (1963) Univ. Producer-Director, Alfred Hitchcock. Screenplay, Evan Hunter. From the story by Daphne du Maurier.

Assistant Director, James H. Brown. Costumes, Edith Head. In Technicolor. Backgrounds filmed in San Francisco. Cinematographer, Robert Burks. Editor, George Tomasini. 120 minutes

Mitch Brenner: Rod Taylor, *Melanie Daniels:* Tippi Hedren, *Lydia Brenner:* Jessica Tandy, *Annie Hayworth:* Suzanne Pleshette, *Cathy Brenner:* Veronica Cartwright, *Mrs. Bundy:* Ethel Griffies, *Sebastian Sholes:* Charles McGraw, *Mrs. MacGruder:* Ruth McDevitt, *Travelling Salesman:* Joe Mantell, *Deputy Al Malone:* Malcolm Atterbury, *Drunk:* Karl Swenson, *Helen Carter:* Elizabeth Wilson, *Deke Carter:* Lonny Chapman, *Fisherman:* Doodles Weaver, *Postal Clerk:* John McGovern, *Man in Elevator:* Richard Deacon, *Man:* William Quinn, *Man Leaving Pet Shop with White Poodles:* Alfred Hitchcock, *Hysterical Woman:* Doreen Lang.

The Bishop's Wife with David Niven and Cary Grant.

THE BISHOP'S WIFE (1947) RKO. Producer, Samuel Goldwyn. Director, Henry Koster. From the novel by Robert Nathan. Screenplay, Robert E. Sherwood, Leonardo Bercovici. Music, Hugo Friedhofer. Musical Director, Emil Newman. Art Directors, George Jenkins, Perry Ferguson. Cameraman, Gregg Toland. Editor, Monica Collingswood. Song by Edgar DeLange, Emile Newman and Herbert Spencer: "Lost April." 108 minutes

Dudley: Cary Grant, *Julia Brougham:* Loretta Young, *Henry Brougham:* David Niven, *Professor Wutheridge:* Monty Woolley, *Sylvester:* James Gleason, *Mrs. Hamilton:* Gladys Cooper, *Matilda:* Elsa Lanchester, *Mildred Cassaway:* Sara Haden, *Debby Brougham:* Karolyn Grimes, *Maggenti:* Tito Vuolo, *Mr. Miller:* Regis Toomey, *Mrs. Duffy:* Sarah Edwards, *Miss Trumbull:* Margaret McWade, *Mrs. Ward:* Anne O'Neal, *Mr. Perry:* Ben Erway, *Stevens:* Erville Alderson, *Defense Captain:* Bobby Anderson, *Attack Captain:* Teddy Infuhr, *Michel:* Eugene Borden, *First Lady in Michel's:* Almira Sessions, *Second Lady:* Claire DuBrey, *Third Lady:* Florence Auer, *Hat Shop Proprietress:* Margaret Wells, *Hat Shop Customer:* Kitty O'Neill, *Hysterical Mother:* Isabel Jewell, *Blind Man:* David Leonard, *Delia:* Dorothy Vaughan, *Cop:* Edgar Dearing, *Saleslady:* Edythe Elliott, *Santa Claus:* Joseph J. Greene.

THE BLACKBOARD JUNGLE (1955) MGM. Producer, Pandro Berman. Director, Richard Brooks. Screenplay, Richard Brooks. Art Directors, Cedric Gibbons, Randall Duell. Musical Adaptation, Charles Wolcott. Cinematographer, Russell Harlan. Editor, Ferris Webster. Music, Bill Haley and the Comets. Includes "Rock Around the Clock." 101 minutes

Richard Dadier: Glenn Ford, *Anne Dadier:* Anne Francis, *Jim Murdock:* Louis Calhern, *Lois Judby Hammond:* Margaret Hayes, *Mr. Warneke:* John Hoyt, *Joshua Edwards:* Richard Kiley, *Mr. Halloran:* Emile Meyer, *Dr. Bradley:* Warner Anderson, *Prof. A. R. Kraal:* Basil Ruysdael, *Gregory Miller:* Sidney Poitier, *Artie West:* Vic Morrow, *Belazi:* Dan Terranova, *Pete V. Morales:* Rafael Campos, *Emmanuel*

Stoker: Paul Mazursky, *Detective:* Horace McMahon, *Santini:* Jameel Farah (Jamie Farr), *De Lica:* Danny Dennis, *Lou Savoldi:* David Alpert, *Levy:* Chris Randall, *Tomita:* Yoshi Tomita, *Carter:* Gerald Phillips, *Miss Panucci:* Dorothy Neumann, *Miss Brady:* Henny Backus, *Mr. Lefkowitz:* Paul Hoffman, *Manners:* Tom McKee, *Mr. Katz:* Robert Foulk, *Italian Proprietor:* Manuel Paris.

The Blackboard Jungle with Paul Mazursky, Chris Randall, John Erman, Vic Morrow, Sidney Poitier and Glenn Ford.

BLACK LEGION (1936) WB. Directed by Archie Mayo. Original Story, Robert Lord. Screenplay by William Wister Haines, Abem Finkel. Cameraman, George Barnes. Editor, Owen Marks. 83 minutes.

Frank Taylor: Humphrey Bogart, *Ed Jackson:* Richard (Dick) Foran, *Betty Grogan:* Ann Sheridan, *Ruth Taylor:* Erin O'Brien Moore, *Pearl Davis:* Helen Flint, *Billings:* Paul Harvey, *Osgood:* Charles Halton, *Cliff Moore:* Joseph Sawyer, *Judge:* Samuel S. Hinds, *Prosecuting Attorney:* Addison Richards, *Alexander Hargrave:* Alonzo Price, *Mike Grogan:* Clifford Soubier, *Mrs. Grogan:* Dorothy Vaughan, *Bud Taylor:* Dickie Jones, *Sam Dombrowsky:* Henry Brandon, *Old Man Dombrowsky:* Egon Brecher, *Nick Strumpas:* Pat C. Flick, *Tommy Smith:* John Litel, *Metcalf:* Eddie Acuff, *Dr. Barkham:* Paul Stanton, *Jones:* Harry Hayden; *Charlie:* Francis Sayles, *Drunken Member:* Don Barclay, *News Commentator:* Emmett Vogan, *Counterman:* Billy Wayne, *Helper:* Frank Sully, *First Cop:* Eddy Chandler, *Second Cop:* Robert E. Homans, *Truck Driver:* Max Wagner, *March of Time Voice:* Fredrich Lindsley, *Reporters:* Carlyle Moore, Jr., Dennis Moore, Milt Kibbee, *Guard:* Lee Phelps, *Bailiff:* Wilfred Lucas, *County Clerk:* Jack Mower.

Black Legion with Humphrey Bogart, Robert E. Homans, Eddy Chandler and Billy Wayne.

Blazing Saddles with Mel Brooks.

BLAZING SADDLES (1974) WB. Produced by Michael Hertzberg. Directed by Mel Brooks. A Crossbow Production in Panavision and Technicolor. Story by Andrew Bergman. Screenplay, Mel Brooks, Norman Steinberg, Andrew Bergman, Richard Pryor and Alan Uger. Photography, Joseph Biroc. Production Designer, Peter Wooley. Editors, John C. Howard and Danford Greene. Sound, Gene S. Cantamessa. Set Decorator, Morey Hoffman. Choreography, Alan Johnson. Orchestrations, Jonathan Tunick and John Morris. Special Costumes Designed by Nino Novarese. Special Effects, Douglas Pettibone. 1st Assistant Director, John C. Chulay. Music composed and conducted by John Morris. "I'm Tired," "The French Mistake" and "The Ballad of Rock Ridge" by Mel Brooks; "Blazing Saddles" by Morris and Brooks, sung by Frankie Laine. Rated R. 94 minutes

Bart: Cleavon Little, *Jim:* Gene Wilder, *Gov. William J. Le Petomane, Indian Chief, Cycle Hood:* Mel Brooks, *Lili Von Shtupp:* Madeline Kahn, *Hedley Lamarr:* Harvey Korman, *Taggart:* Slim Pickens, *Olson Johnson:* David Huddleston, *Reverend Johnson:* Liam Dunn, *Mongo:* Alex Karras, *Howard Johnson:* John Hillerman, *Van Johnson:* George Furth, *Gabby Johnson:* Claude Ennis Starrett, Jr., *Harriett Van Johnson:* Carol Arthur, *Charlie:* Charles McGregor, *Miss Stein:* Robyn Hilton, *Buddy Bizarre:* Dom LeLuise, *Dr. Sam Johnson:* Richard Collier, *Rowdy:* Don Megowan, *Gum Chewer:* John Alderson, *Cut Throat #1:* Karl Lukas, *Lyle:* Burton Gilliam, *Themselves:* Count Basie and His Orchestra.

BLOOD AND SAND (1941) 20th. Producer, Darryl F. Zanuck. Associated Producer, Robert T. Kane. Director, Rouben Mamoulian. Color by Technicolor. Based on the novel by Vicente Blasco Ibañez. Screenplay, Jo Swerling. Technicolor Director, Natalie Kalmus. Musical Director, Alfred Newman. Art Directors, Richard Day, Joseph C. Wright. Cameramen, Ernest Palmer, Ray Rennahan.

Juan: Tyrone Power, *Carmen Espinosa:* Linda Darnell, *Doña Sol:* Rita Hayworth, *Señora Augustias:* Nazimova, *Manola de Palma:* Anthony Quinn, *Garabato:* J. Carrol Naish, *Nacional:* John Carradine, *Encarnacion:* Lynn Bari, *Natalio Curro:* Laird Cregar, *Antonio:* William Montague (Monty Banks), *Captain Pierre Laurel:* George Reeves, *Guitarist:* Vicente Gomez, *Don Jose:* Pedro de Cordoba, *Pedro Espinosa:* Fortunio Bonanova, *Priest:* Victor Kilian, *La Pulga:*

Michael Morris (Adrian Morris), *Pablo:* Charles Stevens, *Carmen as a child:* Ann Todd, *Encarnacion as a child:* Cora Sue Collins, *Marquis:* Russell Hicks, *Juan as a Boy:* Rex Downing, *El Milquetoast:* Maurice Cass, *Francisco:* John Wallace, *Gachi:* Jacqueline Dalya, *Manola as a boy:* Cullen Johnson, *La Pulga as a boy:* Ted Frye, *Pablo as a boy:* Larry Harris, *Nacional as a boy:* Schuyler Standish, *Specialty Dancers:* Elena Verdugo, Mariquita Flores, *Singer:* Rosita Granada, *Woman:* Kay Linaker, *Friend:* Francis McDonald, *Ortega:* Paul Ellis.

Blue Hawaii with Elvis Presley.

BLUE HAWAII (1961) Par. Producer, Hal Wallis. Director, Norman Taurog. Panavision and Technicolor. Screenplay, Hal Kanter. Associate Producer, Paul Nathan. Assistant Director, Mickey Moore. Based on Allan Weiss' story "Beach Boy." Photography, Charles Lang, Jr. Art Direction, Hal Pereira and Walter Tyler. Sets, Sam Comer and Frank McKelvy. Editors, Warren Low and Terry Morse. Technical Advisor, Colonel Tom Parker. Costumes, Edith Head. Make-up, Wally Westmore. Color Consultant, Richard Mueller. Sound, Philip Mitchell, Charles Grenzbach. Music, Joseph J. Lilley. Numbers staged by Charles O'Curran. Songs. "Blue Hawaii," "Aloha Oe," "Rock-a-Hula Blues," "Can't Help Falling in Love," "Almost Always True," "Hawaiian Wedding Song," "Calypso Chant," "Slicin' Sand," "Moonlight Swim," "You're Stepping Out of Line," "Island Of Love," "I Love You More Today," "Ito Eat," "Please Come Back to My Heart," "Sleep, Hawaii Sleep." Locations filmed in Hawaii. 101 minutes

Chad Gates: Elvis Presley, *Maile Duval:* Joan Blackman, *Abigail Prentace:* Nancy Walters, *Fred Gates:* Roland Winters, *Sarah Lee Gates:* Angela Lansbury, *Jack Kelman:* John Archer, *Mr. Chapman:* Howard McNear, *Mrs. Manaka:* Flora Hayes, *Mr. Duval:* Gregory Gay, *Tucker Garvey:* Steve Brodie, *Enid Garvey:* Iris Adrian, *Patsy:* Darlene Tompkins, *Sandy:* Pamela Akert, *Beverly:* Christian Kay, *Ellie Corbett:* Jenny Maxwell, *Ito O'Hara:* Frank Atienza, *Carl:* Lani Kai, *Ernie:* Jose De Varga, *Wes:* Ralph Hanalie, *Waihila:* Hilo Hattie, *Accompanists:* The Jordanaires, *Bit:* Tiki Hanalie, *Harmonica-Playing Convict:* Richard Reeves, *Lt. Grey:* Michael Ross.

Blood and Sand with Rita Hayworth and Tyrone Power.

BLOSSOMS IN THE DUST (1941) MGM. Produced by Irving Asher. Directed by Mervyn LeRoy. Color by Technicolor. Based on a story by Ralph Wheelwright. Art Director, Cedric Gibbons. Associate, Urie McCleary. Gowns, Adrian. Men's Costumes, Gile Steele. Screenplay, Anita Loos. Hair Styles, Sydney Guilaroff. Photography, Karl Freund, W. Howard Green. Color Director, Natalie Kalmus. Color Associate, Henri Jaffa. Score, Herbert Stothart. Sound, Douglas Shearer. Sets, Edwin B. Willis. Special Effects, Warren Newcombe. Editor, George Boemler. Make-up, Jack Dawn. 100 minutes

Edna Gladney: Greer Garson, *Sam Gladney:* Walter Pidgeon, *Dr. Max Breslar:* Felix Bressart, *Charlotte:* Marsha Hunt, *Mrs. Kahly:* Fay Holden, *Mr. Kahly:* Samuel S. Hinds, *Mrs. Keats:* Kathleen Howard, *Mr. Keats:* George Lessey, *Allan Keats:* William Henry, *Judge:* Henry O'Neill, *Damon:* John Eldredge, *Zeke:* Clinton Rosemond, *Cleo:* Theresa Harris, *G. Harrington Hedger:* Charlie Arnt, *Mrs. Gilworth:* Cecil Cunningham, *Mrs. Loring:* Ann Morriss, *Sammy:* Richard Nichols, *Tony:* Pat Barker, *Helen:* Mary Taylor, *La Verne:* Marc Lawrence.

The Blue Max with Ursula Andress and George Peppard.

THE BLUE MAX (1966) 20th. Executive Producer, Elmo Williams. Producer, Christian Ferry. Director, John Guillermin. Adaptation by Ben

Blossoms in the Dust with Greer Garson, Walter Pidgeon and Charles Arnt.

Barzman and Basilio Franchina. Screenplay, David Pursall, Jack Seddon, Gerald Hanley. Based on the novel by Jack Hunter. Director of Photography, Douglas Slocombe. Music composed and conducted by Jerry Goldsmith. Filmed in Ireland. Color by De Luxe and CinemaScope. 156 minutes

Bruno Stachel: George Peppard, *Count von Klugermann:* James Mason, *Countess Kaeti von Klugermann:* Ursula Andress, *Willi von Klugermann:* Jeremy Kemp, *Heidemann:* Karl Michael Vogler, *Elfi Heidemann:* Loni Von Friedl, *Holbach:* Anton Diffring, *Rupp:* Peter Woodthorpe, *Fabian:* Derren Nesbitt, *Von Richthofen:* Carl Schell, *Ziegel:* Derek Newark, *Kettering:* Harry Towb, *Field Marshal Von Lenndorf:* Friedrich Ledebur, *Crown Prince:* Roger Ostime, *Hans:* Hugo Schuster, *Pilots:* Tim Parkes, Ian Kingsley, Ray Browne.

Bob & Carol & Ted & Alice with Natalie Wood, Robert Culp, Dyan Cannon and Elliott Gould.

BOB & CAROL & TED & ALICE (1969) Col. Produced by Larry Tucker. Directed by Paul Mazursky. Executive Producer, Mike J. Frankovich. A Frankovich/Coriander Production. Technicolor. Screenplay, Mazursky and Tucker. Photography, Charles E. Lang. Music by Quincy Jones. Editor, Stuart H. Pappe. Art Director, Pato Guzman. Choreography, Miriam Nelson. Costumes, Moss Mabry. Assistant Director, Anthony Ray. Songs: "What the World Needs Now Is Love" by Hal David and Burt Bacharach, sung by Jackie DeShannon; "I Needs to Be Be'd With" by Ernie Shelby and Quincy Jones, sung by Johnnie Wesley. Rated R. 105 minutes

Bob Sanders: Robert Culp, *Carol Sanders:* Natalie Wood, *Ted Henderson:* Elliott Gould, *Alice Henderson:* Dyan Cannon, *Horst:* Horst Ebersberg, *Emelio:* Lee Bergere, *Psychiatrist:* Donald F. Muhich, *Sean Sanders:* Noble Lee Holderread, Jr., *Phyllis:* K. T. Stevens, *Susan:* Celeste Yarnall, *Institute Group Leader:* Greg Mullavey, *Oscar:* Andre Philippe, *Myrna:* Diane Berghoff, *Conrad:* John Halloran, *Toby:* Susan Merin, *Roger:* Jeffrey Walker, *Jane:* Vicki Thal, *Wendy:* Joyce Easton, *Howard:* Howard Dayton, *Alida:* Alida Ihle, *Dave:* John Brent, *Bert:* Garry Goodrow, *Sue:* Carol O'Leary, *Norma:* Constance Egan.

BONNIE AND CLYDE (1967) WB-7 Arts Produced by Warren Beatty. Associate Producer, Elaine Michael. Directed by Arthur Penn. Color by Technicolor. A Tatira-Hiller Production. Original screenplay by David Newman and Robert Benton. Music by Charles Strouse includes Flatt and Scruggs' "Foggy Mountain Breakdown." Assistant Director, Jack N. Reddish. Production Manager, Russ Saunders. Costumes, Theadora Van Runkle. Art Director, Dean Tavoularis. Sets, Raymond Paul. Special Effects, Danny Lee. Photography, Burnett Guffey. Editor, Dede Allen. Sound, Francis E. Stahl. Includes a scene from *Gold Diggers of 1933* with Charles C. Wilson, Ned Sparks, and with Ginger Rogers singing "We're in the Money." Other songs heard include: "Deep Night," "The Shadow Waltz," "One Hour With You." Filmed mainly in Dallas, Texas. 111 minutes

Clyde Barrow: Warren Beatty, *Bonnie Parker:* Faye Dunaway, *C. W. Moss:* Michael J. Pollard, *Buck Barrow:* Gene Hackman, *Blanche Barrow:* Estelle Parsons, *Malcolm Moss:* Dub Taylor, *Captain Frank Hamer:* Denver Pyle, *Velma Davis:* Evans Evans, *Eugene Grizzard:* Gene Wilder, *Bonnie's Mother:* Mabel Cavitt, *Butcher:* James Stivers.

Bonnie and Clyde with Warren Beatty and Faye Dunaway.

Bon Voyage with Fred MacMurray and Jane Wyman.

BON VOYAGE (1962) BV. Producer, Walt Disney. Associate Producers, Bill Walsh. Ron Miller. Director, James Neilson. Screenplay, Bill Walsh. Based on the novel by Marrijane and Joseph Hayes. Music, Paul Smith. Title Song, Richard M. and Robert B. Sherman. Costumes, Bill Thomas. Assistant Director, Joseph L. McEveety. In Technicolor. French Production Supervisor, Sacha Kamenka. Filmed in New York, Paris, Cannes. Cinematographer, William Snyder. Editor, Cotton Warburton. 133 minutes

Harry Willard: Fred MacMurray, *Katie Willard:* Jane Wyman, *Nick O'Mara:* Michael Callan, *Amy Willard:* Deborah Walley, *Countessa DuFresne:* Jessie Royce Landis, *Elliott Willard:* Tommy Kirk, *Skipper Willard:* Kevin Corcoran, *Rudolph Hunschak:* Ivan Desny, *The Girl:* Francoise Prevost, *Madame Clebert:* Georgette Anys, *Judge Henderson:* Howard I. Smith, *Passport Clerk:* Philip Coolidge, *Penelope Walthorne:* Carol White, *Florelle Clebert:* Marie Sirago, *Horace Bidwell:* Alex Gerry, *The Tight Suit:* Casey Adams, *Ship's Librarian:* James Milhollin, *Sewer Guide:* Marcel Hillaire, *Englishman:* Richard Wattis, *Mrs. Henderson:* Doris Packer, *Shamra:* Ana Maria Majalca, *Shamra's Father:* Hassan Khayyam.

Boomerang! with Dana Andrews.

BOOMERANG! (1947) 20th. Producer, Louis de Rochemont. Director, Elia Kazan. Based on a *Reader's Digest* article by Anthony Abbott. Screenplay, Richard Murphy. Art Directors, Richard Day, Chester Gore. Music, David Buttolph. Music Director, Alfred Newman. Cameraman, Norbert Brodine. Editor, Harmon Jones. Filmed in Connecticut. 88 minutes

Henry L. Harvey: Dana Andrews, *Mrs. Harvey:* Jane Wyatt, *Chief Robinson:* Lee J. Cobb, *Irene Nelson:* Cara Williams, *John Waldron:* Arthur Kennedy, *Woods:* Sam Levene, *Wade:* Taylor Holmes, *McCreery:* Robert Keith, *Harris:* Ed Begley, *Crossman:* Philip Coolidge, *Whitney:* Lewis Leverett, *Sgt. Dugan:* Barry Kelley, *Mr. Rogers:* Richard Garrick, *Lieut. White:* Karl Malden, *James:* Ben Lackland, *Annie:* Helen Carew, *Father Lambert:* Wyrley Birch, *Rev. Gardiner:* Johnny Stearns, *Dr. Rainsford:* Dudley Sadler, *Mayor Swayze:* Walter Greaza, *Miss Manion:* Helen Hatch, *Cartucci:* Guy Thomajan, *Mrs. Lukash:* Lucia Seger, *Mr. Lukash:* Joe Kazan, *Miss Roberts:* Ida McGuire, *Callahan:* John Carmody, *Cary:* Lester Lonergan, *Mr. Rogers:* Richard Garrick, *O'Shea:* George Petrie, *Judge Tate:* Clay Clement, *McDonald:* E. G. Ballantine, *Stone:* William Challee, *Coroner:* Edgar Stehli, *Bill (Reporter):* Jimmy Dobson, *Man:* Robert Keith, Jr. (Brian Keith), *Mrs. Crossman:* Leona Roberts, *Tom:* Bernard Hoffman, *Graham:* Fred Stewart, *Warren:* Anthony Ross, *Man:* Bert Freed.

BOOM TOWN (1940) MGM. Produced by Sam Zimbalist. Directed by Jack Conway. Based on the short story "A Lady Comes to Burknurnet" by James Edward Grant. Screenplay by John Lee Mahin. Art Director, Cedric Gibbons. Musical Score, Franz Waxman. Cameraman, Elwood Bredell. Special Effects, Arnold Gillespie. Montage, John Hoffman. Editor, Paul Landres. 116 minutes

Big John McMasters: Clark Gable, *Square John Sand:* Spencer Tracy, *Betsy Bartlett:* Claudette Colbert, *Karen Vanmeer:* Hedy Lamarr, *Luther Aldrich:* Frank Morgan, *Harry Compton:* Lionel Atwill, *Harmony Jones:* Chill Wills, *Whitey:* Marion Martin, *Spanish Eva:* Minna

Gombell, *Ed Murphy:* Joe Yule, *Tom Murphy:* Horace Murphy, *McCreery:* Roy Gordon, *Assistant District Attorney:* Richard Lane, *Little Jack:* Casey Johnson, *Baby Jack:* Baby Quintanilla, *Judge:* George Lessey, *Miss Barnes:* Sara Haden, *Barber:* Frank Orth, *Deacon:* Frank McGlynn, Jr., *Ferdie:* Curt Bois, *Hiring Boss:* Dick Curtis.

Boom Town with Hedy Lamarr and Clark Gable.

BORN TO DANCE (1936) MGM. Assistant Producer, Jack Cummings. Directed by Roy Del Ruth. Authors, Jack McGowan, Sid Silvers, B. G. DeSylva. Screenplay by Jack McGowan, Sid Silvers. Musical Director, Alfred Newman. Musical Arrangements, Roger Edens. Dances, Dave Gould. Cameraman, Ray June. Editor, Blanche Sewell. Songs by Cole Porter: "I've Got You Under My Skin," "Easy to Love," "Love Me, Love My Pekinese," "I'm Nuts About You," "Rap-Tap on Wood," "Swingin' the Jinx Away," "Rolling Home," "Hey, Babe, Hey." American debut of Reginald Gardiner. 108 minutes

Nora Paige: Eleanor Powell, *Ted Barker:* James Stewart, *Lucy James:* Virginia Bruce, *Jenny Saks:* Una Merkel, *Gunny Saks:* Sid Silvers, *Peggy Turner:* Frances Langford, *Captain Dingby:* Raymond Walburn, *McKay:* Alan Dinehart, *Mush Tracy:* Buddy Ebsen, *Sally Saks:* Juanita Quigley, *Georges & Jalna:* Themselves, *Policeman:* Reginald Gardiner, *Floorwalker:* Barnett Parker, *The Foursome:* J. Marshall Smith, L. Dwight Snyder, Jay Johnson, Del Porter, *Girl:* Mary Dees, *Recruiter:* John Kelly, *Telephone Operator:* Helen Troy, *Acrobats:* William and Joe Mandel, *Maid:* Anita Brown, *Acrobats:* Leona and Naomi Keene, *Stage Manager:* Charles (Levison) Lane, *Assistant Stage Manager:* Bobby Watson, *Waiter:* Charles Coleman, *Ship's Officer:* James Flavin, *Hector:* Jonathan Hale, *Newsboy:* Billy Watson, *Pianist:* Fuzzy Knight, *Cameraman:* Sherry Hall, *Extra:* Dennis O'Keefe, *Man:* David Horsley.

Born to Dance with Frances Langford, Buddy Ebsen, Eleanor Powell, James Stewart, Una Merkel and Sid Silvers.

Born Yesterday with Judy Holliday and William Holden.

BORN YESTERDAY (1950) Col. Producer, S. Sylvan Simon. Director, George Cukor. Based on the play by Garson Kanin. Screenplay, Albert Mannheimer. Art Director, Harry Horner. Musical Director, Morris Stoloff. Photography, Joseph Walker. Editor, Charles Nelson. 103 minutes

Billie Dawn: Judy Holliday, *Harry Brock:* Broderick Crawford, *Paul Verrall:* William Holden, *Jim Devery:* Howard St. John, *Eddie:* Frank Otto, *Norval Hedges:* Larry Oliver, *Mrs. Hedges:* Barbara Brown, *Sanborn:* Grandon Rhodes, *Helen:* Claire Carleton, *Bootblack:* Smoki Whitfield, *Manicurist:* Helyn Eby Rock, *Bellboy:* William Mays, *Barber:* David Pardoll, *Elevator Operator:* Mike Mahoney, *Interpreter:* Paul Marion, *Native:* John L. Morley, *Native:* Ram Singh, *Policeman:* Charles Cane.

Boys Town with Frankie Thomas, Spencer Tracy and Mickey Rooney.

BOYS TOWN (1938) MGM.   Producer, John W. Considine, Jr. Director, Norman Taurog. Authors, Dore Schary, Eleanore Griffin. Screenplay, John Meehan, Dore Schary. Cameraman, Sidney Wagner. Editor, Elmo Vernon. Sequel was *Men of Boys Town*, 1941. 90 minutes

Father Flanagan: Spencer Tracy, *Whitey Marsh:* Mickey Rooney, *Davie Morris:* Henry Hull, *Tony Ponessa:* Gene Reynolds, *Mo Kahn:* Sidney Miller, *Freddie Fuller:* Frankie Thomas, *Pee Wee:* Bobs Watson, *Hillbilly:* Murray Harris, *Paul Ferguson:* Jimmy Butler, *Red:* Tom Noonan, *Apples:* Al Hill, Jr., *Butch:* Wesley Giraud, *Dan Farrow:*

Leslie Fenton, *Hargraves:* Jonathan Hale, *Judge:* Addison Richards, *Alabama:* Donald Haines, *Young Thunder:* Bennie Chorre, *Weasel:* John Wray, *Warden:* John Hamilton, *Bishop:* Minor Watson, *Jimmy:* Ronald Paige, *Tommy Anderson:* Mickey Rentschler, *Skinny:* Martin Spellman, *Mr. Reynolds:* Robert Gleckler, *Warden:* Orville Caldwell, *Burton:* Robert Emmett Keane, *Sheriff:* Victor Kilian, *Tim:* Arthur Aylsworth, *Rod:* Al Hill, *Lane (Reporter):* Roger Converse, *Judge:* Walter Young, *Governor:* William Worthington, *Joe Marsh:* Edward Norris, *Calateri:* George Humbert, *Jackson (Reporter):* Kane Richmond *Sister (Nun):* Barbara Bedford, *Doctor:* Gladden James, *Reporter:* Phillip Terry, *Gangster (with Marsh):* Jay Novello, *Charley Haines:* Johnny Walsh.

Branded with Charles Bickford and Alan Ladd.

BRANDED (1950) Par. Producer, Mel Epstein. Director, Rudolph Mate. Color by Technicolor. Based on novel *Montana Rides* by Evan Evans. Screenplay, Sydney Boehm, Cyril Hume. Art Directors, Hans Dreier, Roland Anderson. Music, Roy Webb. Photography, Charles B. Lang, Jr. Editor, Alma Macrorie. Filmed in Arizona. 104 minutes

Choya: Alan Ladd, *Ruth Lavery:* Mona Freeman, *Mr. Lavery:* Charles Bickford, *Leffingwell:* Robert Keith, *Rubriz:* Joseph Calleia, *Tonio:* Peter Hansen, *Mrs. Lavery:* Selena Royle, *Ransome:* Tom Tully, *Andy:* George Lewis, *Hank:* Robert Kortman, *Tatto:* John Berkes, *Jake:* Pat Lane, *Peon:* Natividad Vacio, *Hernandez:* Martin Garralaga, *Dad Travis:* Edward Clark, *Joe's Wife:* Julia Montoya, *Spig (Lavery Cook):* John Butler, *Link:* Jimmie Dundee, *Roberto:* Salvador Baguez, *Burly Fellow:* Frank McCarroll, *Second Man:* Len Hendry, *Dawson:* Milburn Stone, *Tully:* Ed Peil, *Bank Clerk:* Olan Soule.

BREAKFAST AT TIFFANY'S (1961) Par. Producers, Martin Jurow, Richard Shepherd. Director, Blake Edwards. Technicolor. Based on the novel by Truman Capote. Screenplay, George Axelrod. Art Directors, Hal Pereira, Roland Anderson. Music, Henry Mancini. Song, "Moon River" by Johnny Mercer, Henry Mancini. Cinematographer, Franz Planer. Process Photography, Farciot Edouart. Special Photographic Effects, John P. Fulton. Editor, Howard Smith. 115 minutes

Holly Golightly: Audrey Hepburn, *Paul Varjak:* George Peppard, *2-E:* Patricia Neal, *Doc Golightly:* Buddy Ebsen, *O.J. Berman:* Martin Balsam, *José:* Villalonga, *Tiffany's Salesman:* John McGiver, *Sally Tomato:* Alan Reed, *Mag Wildwood:* Dorothy Whitney, *Stripper:* Miss Beverly Hills, *Rusty Trawler:* Stanley Adams, *Sid Arbuck:* Claude Stroud, *Librarian:* Elvia Allman, *Mr. Yunioshi:* Mickey Rooney, *Girl in Low-cut Dress:* Joan Staley, *Taxi Driver:* Dick Crockett, *The Cousin:* James Lanphier, *Man at Party:* Gil Lamb, *Chinese Girl at Party:* Annabella Soong, *Man at Party:* Wilson Wood, *Hindu at Party:* William Benegal Rav, *Man at Party:* Tommy Farrell, *Delivery Boy:* Kip King, *Woman at Party:* Hanna Landy, *Woman at Party:* Fay McKenzie, *Woman at Party:* Helen Spring.

Breakfast at Tiffany's with Audrey Hepburn.

BRIDE OF FRANKENSTEIN (1935) Univ. Produced by Carl Laemmle, Jr. Directed by James Whale. Story and Screenplay, John L. Balderston and William Hurlbut. Music, Franz Waxman. Photography, John Mescall. Editor, Ted Kent. A sequel to 1931's *Frankenstein*, based on Mary Shelley's book. 80 minutes

The Monster: Boris Karloff, *Henry Frankenstein:* Colin Clive, *Elizabeth:* Valerie Hobson, *The Bride/Mary Shelley:* Elsa Lanchester, *Doctor Pretorious:* Ernest Thesiger, *The Hermit:* O. P. Heggie, *Karl:* Dwight Frye, *Rudy:* Ted Billings, *Burgomaster:* E. E. Clive, *Minnie:* Una O'Connor, *Shepherdess:* Anne Darling, *Percy Shelley:* Douglas Walton, *Lord Byron:* Gavin Gordon, *Ludwig:* Neil Fitzgerald, *Hans:* Reginald Barlow, *Hans' Wife:* Mary Gordon, *Uncle Glutz:* Gunnis Davis, *Aunt Glutz:* Tempe Pigott, *Albert the Butler:* Lucien Prival, *A Hunter:* John Carradine, *Neighbor:* Rollo Lloyd, *Baby:* Billy Barty, *Neighbor:* Walter Brennan, *A Hunter:* Robert Adair, *Priest:* Lucio Villegas, *A Mother:* Brenda Fowler, *The Coroner:* Edwin Mordant, *Marta:* Sarah Schwartz, *A Hunter:* John Curtis, *A Neighbor:* Mary Stewart, *Little Archbishop:* Norman Ainsley, *Little Queen:* Joan Woodbury, *Henry VIII (Little King):* Arthur S. Byron, *Communion Girl:* Helen Parrish, *A Hunter:* Frank Terry, *Mermaid:* Josephine McKim, *Ballerina:* Kansas DeForrest, *Villagers:* Ed Peil, Sr., Anders Van Haden, John George.

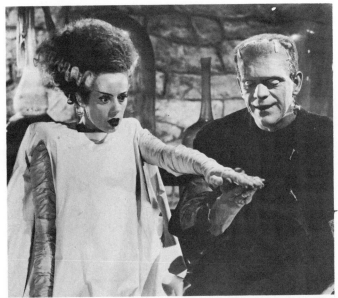

Bride of Frankenstein with Elsa Lanchester and Boris Karloff.

THE BRIDGE ON THE RIVER KWAI (1957) Col. Producer, Sam Spiegel. Director, David Lean. Screenplay by Pierre Boulle based on his novel. Assistant Directors, Gus Agosti and Ted Sturgis. Music by Malcolm Arnold. In CinemaScope and Technicolor. A Horizon Picture. Filmed in Ceylon. 161 minutes

Shears: William Holden, *Colonel Nicholson:* Alec Guinness, *Major Warden:* Jack Hawkins, *Colonel Saito:* Sessue Hayakawa, *Major Clipton:* James Donald, *Lieutenant Joyce:* Geoffrey Horne, *Colonel Green:* Andre Morell, *Major Reeves:* Peter Williams, *Major Hughes:* John Boxer, *Grogan:* Percy Herbert, *Baker:* Harold Goodwin, *Nurse:* Ann Sears, *Captain Kanematsu:* Henry Okawa, *Lieutenant Miura:* Keiichiro Katsumoto, *Yai:* M. R. B. Chakrabandhu, *Siamese Girls:* Vilaiwan Seeboonreaung, Ngamta Suphaphongs, Javanart Punychoti, Kannikar Bowklee.

The Bridge on the River Kwai with Sessue Hayakawa and Alec Guinness.

A Bridge Too Far with Anthony Hopkins (right).

A BRIDGE TOO FAR (1977) UA. Produced by Joseph E. and Richard P. Levine. Directed by Richard Attenborough. Based on the book by Cornelius Ryan. Screenplay, William Goldman. 2nd Unit Director, Sidney Hayers. Panavision and Technicolor. Photography, Geoffrey Unsworth. 2nd Unit Photography, Harry Waxman. Aerial Photography, Robin Browne. Parachute Photography, Dave Waterman and John Partington-Smith. Special Photographic Effects, Wally Veevers. Music composed and conducted by John Addison. Editor, Anthony Gibbs. Production Designer, Terence Marsh. Art Direction, Roy Stannard, Stuart Craig and Alan Tomkins. Set Decoration, Peter Howitt. Special Effects, John Richardson. Stunt Arranger, Alf Joint. Titles, Joe Caroff. Sound, Simon Kaye, Les

Wiggins, Peter Horrocks, Gerry Humphreys and Robin O'Donoghue. Costumes, Anthony Mendleson. Make-up, Tom Smith. Hairstyles, Ronnie Cogan. Technical Adviser, Kathryn Morgan Ryan. Military Advisers/Consultants, Col. J. L. Waddy, Col. Frank A. Gregg, Maj.-Gen. J. D. Frost, Gen. James H. Gavin, Lt.-Gen. Sir Brian Horrocks, Maj.-Gen. Robert Urquhart and Brig. J. O. E. Vandeleur. Assistant Directors, David Tomblin, Steve Lanning, Roy Button, Peter Waller, Geoffrey Ryan and Bert Batt. Coproduced by Michael Stanley-Evans. Associate Producer, John Palmer. Filmed in the Netherlands. Rated PG. 176 minutes

Maj. Julian Cook: Robert Redford, *Lt. Gen. Frederick "Boy" Browning:* Dirk Bogarde, *Lt. Col. Joe Vandeleur:* Michael Caine, *Maj. Gen. Robert Urquhart:* Sean Connery, *Lt. Gen. Brian Horrocks:* Edward Fox, *Lt. Col. John Frost:* Anthony Hopkins, *Staff Sgt. Eddie Dohun:* James Caan, *Col. Bobby Stout:* Elliott Gould, *Brig. Gen. James M. Gavin:* Ryan O'Neal, *Maj. Gen. Stanislaw Sosabowski:* Gene Hackman, *Maj. Gen. Ludwig:* Hardy Kruger, *Lt. Gen. Wilhelm Bittrich:* Maximilian Schell, *Dr. Spaander:* Laurence Olivier, *Kate ter Horst:* Liv Ullmann, *Jan ter Horst:* Tom Van Beek, *Medical Colonel:* Arthur Hill, *Field Marshal Gerd von Rundstedt:* Wolfgang Preiss, *Underground Leader:* Siem Vroom, *Leader's Wife:* Marlies Van Alcmaer, *Leader's Son:* Eric Van't Wout, *Old Dutch Lady:* Mary Smithuysen, *Old Lady's Son:* Hans Croiset, *Capt. Glass:* Nicholas Campbell, *Maj. Carlyle:* Christopher Good, *Lt. Cornish:* Keith Drinkel, *Capt. Bestebreurtje:* Peter Faber, *Gen. Blumentritt:* Hans Von Borsody, *Cafe Waitress:* Josephine Peeper, *Maj. Gen. Maxwell Taylor:* Paul Maxwell, *Field Marshal Model:* Walter Kohut, *Maj. Fuller:* Frank Grimes, *RAF Meteorological Briefing Officer:* Jeremy Kemp, *RAF Meteorological Officer:* Denholm Elliott, *Lt. Col. Mackenzie:* Donald Pickering, *Brig. Lathbury:* Donald Douglas, *Lt. Cole:* Peter Settelen, *Maj. Steele:* Stephen Moore, *Lt. Col. Vandeleur:* Michael Byrne, *Pvt. Wicks:* Paul Copley, *Col. Sims:* Gerald Sim, *Organist:* Erik Chitty, *Vicar:* Brian Hawksley, *Corp. Hancock:* Colin Farrell, *Pvt. Morgan:* Norman Gregory, *Corp. Davies:* Alun Armstrong, *Pvt. Dodds:* Anthony Milner, *Pvt. Clark:* Barry McCarthy, *Sgt. Matthias:* Lex Van Delden, *Capt. Grabner:* Fred Williams, *Sgt. Clegg:* John Judd, *Trooper Binns:* Ben Cross, *British Medical Officer:* Hilary Minster, *Pvt. Andrews:* David English, *Sgt. Towns:* Ben Howard, *Capt. Cleminson:* Michael Graham Cox, *Lt. Rafferty:* Garrick Hagon, *Pvt. Gibbs:* James Wardroper, *Col. Barker:* Neil Kennedy, *Pvt. Ginger Marsh:* John Salthouse, *Glider Pilot:* Jonathan Hackett, *Taffy Brace:* David Auker, *Col. Weaver:* Richard Kane, *Capt. Krafft:* Dick Rienstra, *Flute Player:* Andrew Branch, *Dutch Priest:* Feliks Arons.

The Bridges at Toko-Ri with Mickey Rooney and William Holden.

THE BRIDGES AT TOKO-RI (1954) Par. Producers, William Perlberg, George Seaton. Director, Mark Robson. Technicolor, VistaVision. Based on the novel by James Michener. Screenplay, Valentine Davies. Art Directors, Hal Pereira, Henry Bumstead. Cameramen, Loyal Griggs, Charles G. Clarke. Editor, Alma Macorrie. 103 minutes.

Lt. Harry Brubaker (USNR): William Holden, *Nancy Brubaker:* Grace Kelly, *Rear Admiral George Tarrant:* Fredric March, *Mike Forney:* Mickey Rooney, *Beer Barrel:* Robert Strauss, *Commander*

Wayne Lee: Charles McGraw, *Kimiko:* Keiki Awaji, *Nestor Gamidge:* Earl Holliman, *Lt. (S. G.) Olds:* Richard Shannon, *Capt. Evans:* Willis B. Bouchey, *Kathey Brubaker:* Nadene Ashdown, *Susie Brubaker:* Cheryl Lynn Callaway, *Asst. C.I.C. Officer:* James Jenkins, *Pilot:* Marshall V. Beebe, *M.P. Major:* Charles Tannen, *Japanese Father:* Teru Shimada, *Air Intelligence Officer:* Dennis Weaver, *C.I.C. Officer:* Gene Reynolds, *Officer of the Day:* James Hyland, *Flight Surgeon:* Robert A. Sherry, *C.P.O. 2nd Class:* Gene Hardy, *Quartermaster:* Jack Roberts, *Bellboy:* Rollin Moriyama, *Bartender:* Robert Kino, *Captain Parker:* Paul Kruger.

Bright Victory with Peggy Dow and Arthur Kennedy.

BRIGHT VICTORY (1951) Univ. Producer, Robert Buckner. Director, Mark Robson. Based on a novel by Bayard Kendrick (*Lights Out*). Screenplay, Robert Buckner. Art Directors, Bernard Herzbrun, Nathan Juran. Music, Frank Skinner. Photography, William Daniels. Editor, Russell Schoengarth. 97 minutes

Larry Nevins: Arthur Kennedy, *Judy Greene:* Peggy Dow, *Chris Paterson:* Julia Adams, *Joe Morgan:* James Edwards, *Mr. Nevins:* Will Geer, *Mr. Paterson:* Minor Watson, *Bill Grayson:* Jim Backus, *Janet Grayson:* Joan Banks, *Mrs. Nevins:* Nana Bryant, *Mrs. Paterson:* Marjorie Crossland, *Sergeant John Masterson:* Richard Egan, *Private Fred Tyler:* Russell Dennis, *Corporal John Flagg:* John Hudson, *Pete Hamilton:* Murray Hamilton, *"Moose" Garvey:* Donald Miele, *Jess Coe:* Larry Keating, *Captain Phelan:* Hugh Reilly, *Nurse Bailey:* Mary Cooper, *Dudek:* Rock Hudson, *Scanlon:* Ken Harvey, *Lt. Atkins:* Phil Faversham, *Psychiatrist:* Robert F. Simon, *Reynolds:* Jerry Paris, *Nurse:* Ruth Esherick, *Negro Soldier:* Bernard Hamilton, *M. P.:* Robert Anderson, *Nurse at Oran:* June Whitley, *Dr. Bannerman:* Sydney Mason, *Bartenders:* Richard Karlan, Billy Newell, *Mrs. Coe:* Virginia Mullen, *Lt. Conklin:* Glen Charles Gordon.

THE BROADWAY MELODY (1929) MGM. Directed by Harry Beaumont. Scenes in Technicolor. Story, Edmund Goulding. Continuity, Sarah Y. Mason. Dialogue, Norman Houston and James Gleason. Photography, John Arnold. Musical Director, Nacio Herb Brown. Titles, Earl Baldwin. Art Director, Cedric Gibbons. Costumes, David Cox. Songs by Arthur Freed and Nacio Herb Brown: "The Broadway Melody," "You Were Meant For Me," "Wedding of the Painted Doll," "Boy Friend," "Love Boat," "Harmony Babies From Melody Lane," "Give My Regards to Broadway" by George M. Cohan; "Truthful Deacon Brown" by Willard Robison. Sound, Douglas Shearer. Editors, Sam S. Zimbalist (sound), William Levanway (silent version). The first of a series of "Broadway Melody" films; other editions: 1936, 1938, and 1940. Remade by MGM as *Two Girls On Broadway*, 1940. 110 minutes

Hank Mahoney: Bessie Love, *Queenie Mahoney:* Anita Page, *Eddie Kearns:* Charles King, *Uncle Jed:* Jed Prouty, *Jack Warriner:* Kenneth Thomson, *Flo:* Mary Doran, *Francis Zanfield:* Eddie Kane, *Dillon, Stage Manager:* Edward Dillon, *Babe Hatrick:* J. Emmett Beck, *Stew:* Marshall Ruth, *Turpe:* Drew Demarest, *Singer:* James Burrows,

The Broadway Melody with Mary Doran, Anita Page, Bessie Love and Charles King.

BROADWAY MELODY OF 1936 (1935) MGM.

Produced by John W. Considine, Jr. Directed by Roy Del Ruth. Original Story, Moss Hart. Screenplay, Jack McGowan, Sid Silvers. Art Director, Cedric Gibbons. Costumes, Adrian. Dances created and staged by Dave Gould. "Lucky Star" ballet staged by Albertina Rasch. Assistant Director, Bill Scully. Photography, Charles Rosher. Sound, Douglas Shearer. Editor, Blanche Sewell. Songs by Nacio Herb Brown and Arthur Freed: "Broadway Rhythm," "You Are My Lucky Star," "I Gotta Feelin' You're Foolin'," "On a Sunday Afternoon," "Sing Before Breakfast." Additional Dialogue, Harry Conn. 103 minutes.

Bert Keeler: Jack Benny, *George Brown:* Robert Taylor, *Kitty Corbett:* Una Merkel, *Irene (Mlle. Arlette):* Eleanor Powell, *Lillian:* June Knight, *Sally:* Vilma Ebsen, *Buddy Burke:* Buddy Ebsen, *Basil Newcombe:* Nick Long, Jr., *Hornblow:* Robert Wildhack, *Snoop Blue:* Sid Silvers, *Singers:* Frances Langford, Harry Stockwell, *Show Girls:* Irene Coleman, Beatrice Coleman, Georgina Gray, Mary Jane Halsey, Lucille Lund, Ada Ford, *Managing Editor:* Paul Harvey, *Maid:* Theresa Harris, *Headwaiter:* Max Barwyn, *Waitresses:* Bernadene Hayes, Treva Lawler, *Pullman Porter:* Bud Williams, *Conductor:* Lee Phelps, *Hotel Manager:* Andre Cheron, *Assistant Hotel Manager:* Rolfe Sedan, *Bellhop:* Eddie Tamblyn, *Hotel Clerk:* Bert Moorhouse, *Character Man:* Neely Edwards, *Copy Boy:* Bobby Gordon, *Chorus Girls:* Anya Teranda, Luana Walters, Patricia Gregory.

Broadway Melody of 1936 with June Knight and Robert Taylor.

Broken Arrow with Jeff Chandler and James Stewart.

BROKEN ARROW (1950) 20th.

Produced by Julian Blaustein. Directed by Delmer Daves. Color by Technicolor. Based on the novel *Blood Brother* by Elliott Arnold. Screenplay, Michael Blankfort. Music Director, Alfred Newman. Art Directors, Lyle Wheeler and Arthur Hogsett. Photography, Ernest Palmer. Editor, J. Watson Webb, Jr. Later the basis for a TV series, the initial episode (in 1956) being an adaptation of the feature. 93 minutes

Tom Jeffords: James Stewart, *Cochise:* Jeff Chandler, *Sonseeahray:* Debra Paget, *General Howard:* Basil Ruysdael, *Ben Slade:* Will Geer, *Terry:* Joyce MacKenzie, *Duffield:* Arthur Hunnicutt, *Colonel Bernall:* Raymond Bramley, *Goklia:* Jay Silverheels, *Nalikadeya:* Argentina Brunetti, *Boucher:* Jack Lee, *Lonergan:* Robert Adler, *Miner:* Harry Carter, *Lowrie:* Robert Griffin, *Juan:* Billy Wilkerson, *Chip Slade:* Mickey Kuhn, *Nochalo:* Chris Willow Bird, *Pionsenay:* J. W. Cody, *Nahilzay:* John War Eagle, *Skinyea:* Charles Soldani, *Teese:* Iron Eyes Cody, *Machogee:* Robert Foster Dover, *Maury:* John Marston, *Sergeant:* Edward Rand, *Mule Driver:* John Doucette, *Adjutant:* Richard Van Opel, *Barber:* Nacho Galindo, *Stage Passenger:* Trevor Bardette.

The Buccaneer with Fredric March and Franciska Gaal.

THE BUCCANEER (1938) Par.

Producer, Cecil B. De Mille. Associate Producer, William H. Pine. Director, Cecil B. De Mille. Author, Lyle Saxon (from *Lafitte, the Pirate*). Screenplay, Jeanie MacPherson, Edwin Justus Mayer, Harold Lamb, C. Gardner Sullivan. Musical Director, Boris Morros. Cameraman, Victor Milner. Editor, Anne Bauchens. Technical Assistance, Louisiana State Museum. Remade under DeMille's supervision in 1958, with Quinn as director. 90 minutes

Jean Lafitte: Fredric March, *Gretchen:* Franciska Gaal, *Dominique You:* Akim Tamiroff, *Annette de Remy:* Margot Grahame, *Ezra Peavey:* Walter Brennan, *Crawford:* Ian Keith, *Dolly Madison:* Spring Byington, *Governor Claiborne:* Douglass Dumbrille, *Captain Brown:* Robert Barrat, *Andrew Jackson:* Hugh Sothern, *Aunt Charlotte:* Beulah Bondi, *Beluche:* Anthony Quinn, *Marie de Remy:* Louise Campbell, *Admiral Cockburn:* Montagu Love, *General Ross:* Eric Stanley, *Gramby:* Fred Kohler, *Captain Lockyer:* Gilbert Emery, *Captain McWilliams:* Holmes Herbert, *Mouse:* John Rogers, *Tarsus:* Hans Steinke, *Collector of Port:* Stanley Andrews, *Sir Harry Smith:* Evan Thomas, *John Freeman:* Thaddeus Jones, *Ship's Surgeon:* Reginald Sheffield, *James Smith:* Eugene Jackson, *Colonel Butler:* Davison Clark, *Creole:* James Craig, *Lieutenant Reed:* Richard Denning, *Dying Pirate:* Paul Fix, *Charles:* Jack Hubbard, *Madeleine:* Evelyn Keyes, *Roxanne:* Lina Basquette, *Suzette:* Luana Walters, *Jailer:* J. P. McGowan, *Villere:* Barry Norton, *Daniel Carrol:* Charles Trowbridge, *Scipio:* Alex Hill, *Girl:* Terry Ray (Ellen Drew), *Vincent Nolte:* Charles Brokaw, *Major Latour:* Alphonse Martell, *Woman:* Mae Busch.

BULLDOG DRUMMOND (1929) UA. Produced by Samuel Goldwyn. Directed by F. Richard Jones. Based on the British play by Sapper (Herman Cyril McNeile). Dialogue, Sidney Howard. Photography, George Barnes and Gregg Toland. Editors, Frank and Viola Lawrence. Song by Jack Yellen and Harry Akst, "(I Says to Myself Says I) There's the One for Me." Art Director, William Cameron Menzies. Assistant Director, Paul Jones. Scenario, Wallace Smith and Sidney Howard. Talkie debuts of Ronald Colman and Joan Bennett. 90 minutes

Bulldog Drummond: Ronald Colman, *Phyllis Clavering:* Joan Bennett, *Erma:* Lilyan Tashman, *Peterson:* Montagu Love, *Doctor Lakington:* Lawrence Grant, *Danny:* Wilson Benge, *Algy Longworth:* Claud Allister, *Marcovitch:* Adolph Milar, *Travers:* Charles Sellon, *Chong:* Tetsu Komai.

Bulldog Drummond with Lawrence Grant, Ronald Colman and Joan Bennett.

BULLETS OR BALLOTS (1936) WB. Produced by Lou Edelman. Directed by William Keighley. Authors, Martin Mooney, Seton I. Miller. Screenplay by Seton I. Miller. Cameraman, Hal Mohr. Editor, Jack Killifer. 77 minutes

Johnny Blake: Edward G. Robinson, *Lee Morgan:* Joan Blondell, *Al Kruger:* Barton MacLane, *Nick Fenner:* Humphrey Bogart, *Herman:* Frank McHugh, *Captain Dan MacLaren:* Joseph King, *Ed Driscoll:* Richard Purcell, *Wires:* George E. Stone, *Nellie LaFleur:* Louise Beavers, *Grand Jury Spokesman:* Joseph Crehan, *Bryant:* Henry O'Neill, *Thorndyke:* Gilbert Emery, *Hollister:* Henry Kolker, *Caldwell:* Herbert Rawlinson, *Specialty:* Rosalind Marquis, *Vinci:* Norman Willis, *Gatley:* Frank Faylen, *Announcer's Voice:* Addison Richards, *Proprietor:* Ray Brown, *Actor Impersonating Kruger:* Max Wagner, *Judge:* Ed Stanley, *Jury Foreman:* Milton Kibbee, *Chauffeur:* Frank Marlowe, *Eddie:* Joe Connors,

Mary: Virginia Dabney, *Crail:* William Pawley, *Kruger's Secretary:* Carlyle Moore, Jr. *Bank Secretaries:* Gordon Elliott, Anne Nagel, *Garber:* Ed Butler, *Kelly:* Ralph M. Ramley, *Rose (Maid):* Edna Mae Harris, *Lambert:* Wallace Gregory, *Ben:* Chic Bruno, *Jail Keeper:* Tom Wilson, *Timothy:* John Lester Johnson, *Police Captain:* Tom Brower, *Policeman:* Ralph Dunn.

Bullets or Ballots with Humphrey Bogart, Barton MacLane and Edward G. Robinson.

BULLITT (1968) WB.–Seven Arts. A production of Steve McQueen's Solar company. Produced by Philip D'Antoni. Directed by Peter Yates. Executive Producer, Robert E. Relyea. Based on the novel *Mute Witness* by Robert L. Pike. Screenplay, Alan R. Trustman and Harry Kleiner. In Technicolor. Assistant Director, Tim Zinnemann and Daisy Gerber. Music by Lalo Schifrin. Photography, William A. Fraker. Editor, Frank P. Keller. Art Director, Albert Brenner. Set Decorations, Ralph S. Hurst and Philip Abramson. Special Effects, Sass Bedig. Titles, Pablo Ferro Films. Stunt Coordinator, Carey Loftin. Sound, John K. Kean. Costumes, Theadora Van Runkle. Make-up, Emile La Vigne. Hairstyles, Pat Davey. Filmed in San Francisco. 114 minutes

Lt. Frank Bullitt: Steve McQueen, *Walter Chalmers:* Robert Vaughn, *Cathy:* Jacqueline Bisset, *Detective Delgetti:* Don Gordon, *Weissberg:* Robert Duvall, *Capt. Bennett:* Simon Oakland, *Capt. Baker:* Norman Fell, *Dr. Willard:* Georg Stanford Brown, *Eddy:* Justin Tarr, *Detective Stanton:* Carl Reindel, *Ross, Decoy:* Felice Orlandi, *Pete Ross:* Vic Tayback, *1st Aide:* Robert Lipton, *Wescott:* Ed Peck, *Johnny Ross (Albert Renick):* Pat Renella, *Mike, Hired Killer:* Paul Genge, *Killer:* John Aprea, *Desk Clerk:* Al Checco, *Phil:* Bill Hickman.

Bullitt with Steve McQueen and Robert Vaughn.

Bus Stop with Marilyn Monroe and Eileen Heckart.

BUS STOP (1956) 20th. Producer, Buddy Adler. Director, Joshua Logan. CinemaScope, De Luxe Color. Based on the play by William Inge. Screenplay, George Axelrod. Art Directors, Lyle R. Wheeler, Mark-Lee Kirk. Musical Director, Alfred Newman. Music, Alfred Newman, Cyril J. Mockridge. Orchestration, Edward B. Powell. Song, Ken Darby. Cinematographer, Milton Krasner. Editor, William Reynolds. Later a TV series. 96 minutes

Cherie: Marilyn Monroe, *Bo:* Don Murray, *Virgil:* Arthur O'Connell, *Grace:* Betty Field, *Vera:* Eileen Heckart, *Carl:* Robert Bray, *Elma:* Hope Lange, LIFE *Photographer:* Hans Conreid, LIFE *Reporter:* Casey Adams, *Manager of Nightclub:* Henry Slate, *Gerald:* Terry Kelman, *Landlady:* Helen Mayon, *Blonde on Street:* Lucille Knox, *Elderly Passengers:* Kate Mac Kenna, George Selk, *Cashier:* Mary Carroll, *Preacher:* Phil J. Munch, *Usher:* Fay L. Ivor, *Announcer:* G. E. "Pete" Logan, *Orville:* J. M. Dunlap, *Japanese Cook:* Jim Katugi Noda.

Butch Cassidy and the Sundance Kid with Robert Redford, Katharine Ross and Paul Newman.

BUTCH CASSIDY AND THE SUNDANCE KID (1969) 20th. Produced by John Foreman. Directed by George Roy Hill. Presented by Campanile Productions/Newman-Foreman/George Roy Hill–Paul Monash Productions. Panavision and DeLuxe Color. Original Screenplay, William Goldman. Executive Producer, Paul Monash. Photography, Conrad Hall. 2nd Unit Director, Michael Moore. Music composed and conducted by Burt Bacharach. Song, "Raindrops Keep Fallin' on My

Head" by Bacharach and Hal David, sung by B. J. Thomas. Art Directors, Jack Martin Smith and Philip Jefferies. Editors, John C. Howard and Richard C. Meyer. Sound, William E. Edmondson and David E. Dockendorf. Costumes, Edith Head. Assistant Director, Steven Bernhardt. Filmed in Utah, Colorado, Wyoming and Mexico. Rated M. 110 minutes. Sequels: *Mrs. Sundance* (ABC-TV, 1974) with Elizabeth Montgomery and *Wanted: The Sundance Woman* (later called *Mrs. Sundance Rides Again*, ABC-TV, 1976) with Katharine Ross, both made by Fox. Prequel is *Butch and Sundance: The Early Days* (20th, 1979) with Tom Berenger, William Katt and Jill Eikenberry

Butch Cassidy: Paul Newman, *The Sundance Kid:* Robert Redford, *Etta Place:* Katharine Ross, *Agnes:* Cloris Leachman, *Sheriff Brady Bledsoe:* Jeff Corey, *Percy Garris:* Strother Martin, *Bike Salesman:* Henry Jones, *Woodcock:* George Furth, *Harvey Logan:* Ted Cassidy, *Marshal:* Kenneth Mars, *Macon:* Donnelly Rhodes, *Large Woman Passenger:* Jody Gilbert, *News Carver:* Timothy Scott, *Fireman:* Don Keefer, *Flat Nose Curry:* Charles Dierkop, *Bank Manager:* Francisco Cordova, *Photographer:* Nelson Olmstead, *Card Players:* Paul Bryar and Sam Elliott, *Bank Teller:* Charles Akins, *Tiffany's Salesman:* Eric Sinclair, *Sweet Face:* Percy Helton.

BUTTERFIELD 8 (1960) MGM. Produced by Pandro S. Berman. Directed by Daniel Mann. CinemaScope and MetroColor. Based on the novel by John O'Hara. Screenplay, Charles Schnee and John Michael Hayes. Music, Bronislau Kaper. Costumes, Helen Rose. Associate Producer, Kathryn Hereford. Assistant Directors, Hank Moonjean and John Clarke Bowman. Art Directors, George W. Davis and Urie McCleary. Cinematography, Joseph Ruttenberg, Charles Harten. Editor, Ralph E. Winters. An Afton-Lindbrook Production. 109 minutes

Gloria Wandrous: Elizabeth Taylor, *Weston Liggett:* Laurence Harvey, *Steve Carpenter:* Eddie Fisher, *Emily Liggett:* Dina Merrill, *Mrs. Wandrous:* Mildred Dunnock, *Mrs. Fanny Thurber:* Betty Field, *Bingham Smith:* Jeffrey Lynn, *Happy:* Kay Medford, *Norma:* Susan Oliver, *Dr. Tredman:* George Voskovec, *Clerk:* Virginia Downing, *Mrs. Jescott:* Carmen Matthews, *Anderson:* Whitfield Connor, *Elevator Man:* Dan Bergin, *Cabbie:* Vernon Dowling, *Doorman:* Samuel Schwartz, *Tipsy Man:* Robert Pastene, *Doorman:* John Armstrong, *Policeman:* Leon B. Stevens, *Bartender:* Tom Ahearne, *Big Man:* Rudy Bond, *Irate Man:* Victor Harrison, *Chauffeur:* Beau Tilden, *Irate Woman:* Marion Leeds, *Gossip:* Helen Stevens, *Photographer:* Don Burns, *Man:* Philip Faversham, *Messenger:* Joseph Boley, *State Trooper:* Richard X. Slattery.

Butterfield 8 with Elizabeth Taylor and Eddie Fisher.

BWANA DEVIL (1952) UA. Producer and Director, Arch Oboler. Ansco Color, 3-Dimension. Screenplay, Arch Oboler. Natural Vision Supervision, M.L. Gunzberg. Music composed and directed by Gordon Jenkins. Orchestrations, Fred Neff. Three Dimension Technician, O. S. Bryhn. Sound, Con McKay. Technical Consultants, Major

Ramsay Hill, Bhogwam Singh. Special Effects, Russell Shearman, Henry Maak. Cinematographer, Joseph F. Biroc. Editor, John Hoffman. 79 minutes

Bob Hayward: Robert Stack, *Alice Hayward:* Barbara Britton, *Dr. Ross:* Nigel Bruce, *Major Parkhurst:* Ramsay Hill, *Commissioner:* Paul McVey, *Portuguese Girl:* Hope Miller, *Drayton:* John Dodsworth, *Indian Dancer:* Bhupesh Guha.

Bwana Devil with Nigel Bruce and Robert Stack.

Bye Bye Birdie with Ann-Margret, Trudi Ames, Jesse Pearson, Janet Leigh, Dick Van Dyke, Frank Albertson and Beverly Yates.

BYE BYE BIRDIE (1963) Col. Producer, Fred Kohlmar. Director, George Sidney. Panavision, Technicolor. Based on the musical by Michael Stewart. Screenplay, Irving Brecher. Music supervised, arranged and conducted by Johnny Green. Orchestration, Johnny Green, Al Woodbury. Cinematographer, Joseph Biroc. Editor, Charles Nelson. Songs by Charles Strouse and Lee Adams: "Bye Bye Birdie," "Kids," "Honestly Sincere," "Put on a Happy Face," "Telephone Hour," "A Lot of Living to Do," "Rosie," "One Last Kiss," "One Boy," "Hymn for a Sunday Evening," "How Lovely to Be a Woman," "The Shriners Ballet." Dick Van Dyke and Paul Lynde repeat their 1960 stage roles. 111 minutes

Rosie DeLeon: Janet Leigh, *Albert Peterson:* Dick Van Dyke, *Kim McAfee:* Ann-Margret, *Mama Peterson:* Maureen Stapleton, *Hugo Peabody:* Bobby Rydell, *Conrad Birdie:* Jesse Pearson, *Ed Sullivan:* Ed Sullivan, *Mr. McAfee:* Paul Lynde, *Mrs. McAfee:* Mary LaRoche, *Claude Paisley:* Michael Evans, *Bob Precht:* Robert Paige, *Borov:*

Gregory Morton, *Randolph:* Bryan Russell, *Mr. Maude:* Milton Frome, *Ballet Manager:* Ben Astar, *Ursula:* Trudi Ames, *Mr. Nebbitt:* Cyril Delevanti, *Mayor:* Frank Albertson, *Mayor's Wife:* Beverly Yates, *Bartender:* Frank Sully, *Ursula's Mother:* Bo Peep Karlin, *Teenager:* Melinda Marx, *Shriner:* Mell Turner, *Shriner:* Gil Lamb, *Leader:* Lee Aaker, *Prima Ballerina:* Karel Shimoff, *Russian Consul:* Donald Lawton, *Telephone Operator:* Yvonne White, *Debbie:* Debbie Stern, *Sheila:* Sheila Denner, *Harvey:* Pete Menefee, *Tommy:* George Spicer, *Leader, Fireman's Band:* Dick Winslow, *Marge, Birdie's Secretary:* Hazel Shermet.

Cabaret with Liza Minnelli.

CABARET (1972) AA. Produced by Cy Feuer. Directed and Choreographed by Bob Fosse. An ABC Pictures presentation of a Cy Feuer–Ernest Martin Production. Based on the musical play by Joe Masteroff (Grey repeats his stage role), the 1951 play *I Am a Camera* by John Van Druten and the 1939 book *Goodbye to Berlin* by Christopher Isherwood. Screenplay, Jay Presson Allen. Photography, Geoffrey Unsworth. Production Designer, Rolf Zehetbauer. Art Director, Jurgen Kiebach. Set Decorations, Herbert Strabl. Assistant Choreographer, John Sharpe. Editor, David Bretherton. Titles, Modern Film Effects. Sound, David Hildyard, Robert Knudson and Arthur Piantadosi. Costumes, Charlotte Flemming. Make-up and Hairstyles, Raimund Stangl and Susi Krause. Minnelli's Hairstyles, Gus Le Pre. Associate Producer, Harold Nebenzal. Assistant Directors, Douglas Green and Wolfgang Glattes. Musical Direction and Orchestrations, Ralph Burns. Music Coordinator, Raoul Kraushaar. Songs by John Kander and Fred Ebb: "Cabaret," "Willkommen," "Maybe This Time (I'll Be Lucky)," "Money, Money, Money," "Mein Herr," "Two Ladies," "Tiller Girls," "Heiraten" (Married), "If You Could See Her Through My Eyes," "Tomorrow Belongs to Me," "Finale." Filmed in Technicolor at West Germany's Bavaria Atelier Gesellschaft. Rated PG. 118 minutes

Sally Bowles: Liza Minnelli, *Brian Roberts:* Michael York, *Master of Ceremonies:* Joel Grey, *Baron Maximilian von Heune:* Helmut Griem, *Fritz Wendel:* Fritz Wepper, *Natalia Landauer:* Marisa Berenson, *Fraulein Schneider:* Elisabeth Neumann-Viertel, *Fraulein Mayr:* Sigrid von Richthofen, *Fraulein Kost:* Helen Vita, *Bobby:* Gerd Vespermann, *Herr Ludwig:* Ralf Wolter, *Willi:* Georg Hartmann, *Elke:* Ricky Renee, *Cantor:* Estrongo Nachama, *Kit-Kat Dancers:* Louise Quick (Gorilla), Kathryn Doby, Inge Jaeger, Angelika Koch, Helen Velkovorska and Gitta Schmidt.

CACTUS FLOWER (1969) Col. Produced by Mike J. Frankovich. Directed by Gene Saks. Technicolor. From the play by Abe Burrows, based on the French play by Barillet and Gredy. Screenplay by I. A. L. Diamond. Photography, Charles E. Lang. Music, Quincy Jones. Choreography, Miriam Nelson. Costumes, Moss Mabry. Assistant Director, Anthony Ray. Sarah Vaughan sings "A Time for Love Is Anytime." Editor, Maury Winetrobe. 103 minutes

Dr. Julian Winston: Walter Matthau, *Stephanie Dickinson:* Ingrid Bergman, *Toni Simmons:* Goldie Hawn, *Harvey Greenfield:* Jack Weston, *Igor Sullivan:* Rick Lenz, *Señor Sanchez:* Vito Scotti, *Mrs. Durant:* Irene Hervey, *Georgia:* Eve Bruce, *Store Manager:* Irwin Charone, *Nephew:* Matthew Saks.

Cactus Flower with Walter Matthau and Goldie Hawn.

THE CAINE MUTINY (1954) Col. Producer, Stanley Kramer. Director, Edward Dmytryk. Technicolor. Based on the novel by Herman Wouk. Screenplay, Stanley Roberts. Art Director, Cary Odell. Cinematographer, Franz Planer. Editor, William A. Lyon. 125 minutes

Captain Queeg: Humphrey Bogart, *Lt. Barney Greenwald:* José Ferrer, *Lt. Steve Maryk:* Van Johnson, *Lt. Tom Keefer:* Fred MacMurray, *Ensign Willie Keith:* Robert Francis, *May Wynn:* May Wynn, *Captain DeVriess:* Tom Tully, *Lt. Cdr. Challee:* E. G. Marshall, *Lt. Paynter:* Arthur Franz, *Meatball:* Lee Marvin, *Captain Blakely:* Warner Anderson, *Horrible:* Claude Akins, *Mrs. Keith:* Katharine Warren, *Ensign Harding:* Jerry Paris, *Chief Budge:* Steve Brodie, *Stilwell:* Todd Karns, *Lt. Cdr. Dickson:* Whit Bissell, *Lt. Jorgensen:* James Best, *Ensign Carmody:* Joe Haworth, *Ensign Rabbit:* Guy Anderson, *Whittaker:* James Edwards, *Urban:* Don Dubbins, *Engstrand:* David Alpert, *Uncle Lloyd:* Dayton Lummis, *Commodore Kelvey:* James Todd, *Court Stenographer:* Don Keefer, *Movie Operator:* Patrick Miller, *Sgt.-at-Arms:* Ted Cooper, *Chauffeur:* Don Dillaway, *Winston:* Eddie Laguna.

The Caine Mutiny with Van Johnson, Humphrey Bogart, Fred MacMurray, Arthur Franz and Jerry Paris.

Camelot with Franco Nero, Richard Harris and Vanessa Redgrave.

CAMELOT (1967) WB-7 Arts. Produced by Jack L. Warner. Directed by Joshua Logan. Panavision and Technicolor. Based on the musical by Frederick Loewe, Alan Jay Lerner, and Moss Hart, from the novel *The Once and Future King* by T. H. White. Screenplay, Alan Jay Lerner. Music by Frederick Loewe. Music supervised and conducted by Alfred Newman. Associate musical supervision by Ken Darby. Costumes, scenery and production design by John Truscott. Art direction and sets by Edward Carrere. Assistant Producer, Joel Freeman. Assistant Director, Arthur Jacobson. Second Unit directed by Tap and Joe Canutt. Photography, Richard H. Kline. Editor, Folmer Blangsted. Sound, M. A. Merrick and Dan Wallin. Songs, Alan Jay Lerner and Frederick Loewe: "I Wonder What the King Is Doing Tonight," "The Simple Joys of Maidenhood," "Camelot," "C'est Moi," "The Lusty Month of May," "Follow Me," "How to Handle a Woman," "Take Me to the Fair," "If Ever I Would Leave You," "What Do the Simple Folk Do?", "I Loved You Once in Silence," "Guinevere." 179 minutes

King Arthur: Richard Harris, *Guinevere:* Vanessa Redgrave, *Lancelot du Lac:* Franco Nero, *Mordred:* David Hemmings, *King Pellinore:* Lionel Jeffries, *Merlin:* Laurence Naismith, *Dap:* Pierre Olaf, *Lady Clarinda:* Estelle Winwood, *Sir Lionel:* Gary Marshal, *Sir Dinadan:* Anthony Rogers, *Sir Sagramore:* Peter Bromilow, *Lady Sybil:* Sue Casey, *Tom:* Gary Marsh, *Arthur as a boy:* Nicholas Beauvy.

Camille with Robert Taylor, Greta Garbo, Laura Hope Crews and Rex O'Malley.

CAMILLE (1936) MGM. Produced by Irving Thalberg and Bernard Hyman. Directed by George Cukor. Author, Alexandre Dumas. Screenplay by Zoe Akins, Frances Marion, James Hilton. Musical Score, Herbert Stothart. Dances, Val Raset. Cameraman, William Daniels. Editor, Margaret Booth. 108 minutes

Marguerite Gautier: Greta Garbo, *Armand:* Robert Taylor, *General Duval:* Lionel Barrymore, *Baron de Varville:* Henry Daniell, *Nichette:* Elizabeth Allan, *Olympe:* Lenore Ulric, *Prudence:* Laura Hope Crews, *Nanine:* Jessie Ralph, *Gaston:* Rex O'Malley, *Gustave:* Russell Hardie, *St. Gadeau:* E. E. Clive, *Henri:* Douglas Walton, *Corinne:* Marion Ballou, *Marie Jeanette:* Joan Brodel (Joan Leslie), *Louise:* June Wilkins, *Madame Duval:* Elsie Esmond, *Valentine:* Fritz Leiber, Jr, *Doctor:* Edwin Maxwell, *Therese:* Eily Malyon, *Friend of Camille:* Mariska Aldrich, *DeMusset:* John Bryan, *Companion:* Rex Evans, *Gypsy Leader:* Eugene King, *Singer:* Adrienne Matzenauer, *Streetwalker:* Georgia Caine, *Madame Barjon:* Mabel Colcord, *Priest:* Chappel Dossett, *Attendant:* Elspeth Dudgeon, *Grandma Duval:* Effie Ellsler, *Georges Sand:* Sibyl Harris, *Aunt Henriette:* Maude Hume, *Croupier:* Olaf Hytten, *Governess:* Gwendolyn Logan, *Priest:* Ferdinand Munier, *Emille:* Barry Norton, *Orchestra Leader:* John Picorri, *Auctioneer:* Guy Bates Post, *Old Duchess:* Zeffie Tilbury.

CAPTAIN BLOOD (1935) WB. Produced by Harry Joe Brown. Directed by Michael Curtiz. From the novel by Rafael Sabatini. Screenplay, Casey Robinson. Photography, Hal Mohr. Editor, George Amy. Locations: Corona, Laguna Beach, Palm Canyon near Palm Springs, California. A Cosmopolitan Production. 119 minutes

Dr. Peter Blood: Errol Flynn, *Arabella Bishop:* Olivia De Havilland, *Colonel Bishop:* Lionel Atwill, *Captain Levasseur:* Basil Rathbone, *Jeremy Pitt:* Ross Alexander, *Hagthorpe:* Guy Kibbee, *Lord Willoughby:* Henry Stephenson, *Governor Steed:* George Hassell, *Honesty Nuthall:* Forrester Harvey, *Wolverstone:* Robert Barrat, *Dr. Bronson:* Hobart Cavanaugh, *Dr. Whacker:* Donald Meek, *Reverend Ogle:* Frank McGlynn, Sr., *Andrew Baynes:* David Torrence, *Cahusac:* J. Carrol Naish, *Don Diego:* Pedro de Cordoba, *Lord Jeffries:* Leonard Mudie, *Mrs. Barlowe:* Jessie Ralph, *Captain Hobart:* Stuart Casey, *Lord Sunderland:* Halliwell Hobbes, *Lord Chester Dyke:* Colin Kenny, *Court Clerk:* E. E. Clive, *Captain Gardiner:* Holmes Herbert, *Mrs. Steed:* Mary Forbes, *Dixon:* Reginald Barlow, *Prosecutor:* Ivan F. Simpson, *Lord Gildoy:* Denis d'Auburn, *King James II:* Vernon Steele, *French Captain:* Georges Renavent, *Clerk in Governor Steed's Court:* Murray Kinnell, *Kent:* Harry Cording, *Baynes' Wife:* Maude Leslie, *Governor's Attendant:* Stymie Beard, *Judge Advocate:* Ivan F. Simpson, *Slave:* Gardner James, *Gunner:* Sam Appel, *Sentry:* Chris-Pin Martin, *Girls in Tavern:* Yola D'Avril, Tina Menard, *French Officer:* Frank Puglia, *Pirates:* Artie Ortego, Gene Alsace, Kansas Moehring, Tom Steele, Blackie Whiteford, Jim Thorpe, William Yetter, Buddy Roosevelt, Jimmy Mason.

Captain Blood with Guy Kibbee, Robert Barrat, Frank McGlynn, Sr., and Errol Flynn.

CAPTAIN NEWMAN, M.D. (1963) Univ. Produced by Robert Arthur. Directed by David Miller. In Eastman Color by Pathé. A Brentwood-Reynard Production. Screenplay, Richard L. Breen and Phoebe and Henry Ephron. From the novel by Leo Rosten. Photography, Russell Metty. Music, Frank Skinner. Costumes, Rosemary Odell. Assistant Director, Phil Bowles. Art Directors, Alexander

Golitzen and Alfred Sweeney. Music Supervisor, Joseph Gershenson. Editor, Alma Macrorie. 126 minutes

Captain Josiah Newman: Gregory Peck, *Corporal Jackson Laibowitz:* Tony Curtis, *Lt. Francie Corum:* Angie Dickinson, *Col. Norval Algate Bliss:* Eddie Albert, *Corporal Jim Tompkins:* Bobby Darin, *Col. Edgar Pyser:* James Gregory, *Lt. Grace Blodgett:* Jane Withers, *Helene Winston:* Bethel Leslie, *Capt. Paul Cabot Winston:* Robert Duvall, *Lt. Alderson:* Dick Sargent, *Corporal Gavoni:* Larry Storch, *Lt. Colonel Larrabee:* Robert F. Simon, *Major General Snowden:* Crahan Denton, *Captain Howard:* Gregory Walcott, *Patient:* Martin West, *Master Sgt. Arkie Kopp:* Syl Lamont, *Major Alfredo Fortuno:* Vito Scottl, *Waitress at Blue Grotto:* Penny Santon, *Kathie:* Amzie Strickland, *Major Dawes:* Barry Atwater, *Mrs. Pyser:* Ann Doran, *Maccarades:* Joey Walsh, *Patient:* David Winters, *Hollingshead:* Byron Morrow, *Corporal:* David Landfield, *Chaplain (Priest):* Ron Brogan, *Chaplain (Rabbi):* Robert Strong, *Officer:* John Hart, *Gorkow:* Charles Briggs, *Arthur Werbel:* Paul Carr, *Haskell:* Sam Reese, *Carrozzo:* Ted Bessell, *Patients:* Marc Cavell, Seamon Glass, Jack Grinnage.

Captain Newman, M.D. with Robert F. Simon, Gregory Peck and Angie Dickinson.

Captains Courageous with Spencer Tracy, Freddie Bartholomew and Lionel Barrymore.

CAPTAINS COURAGEOUS (1937) MGM. Produced by Louis D. Lighton. Directed by Victor Fleming. Based on the novel by Rudyard Kipling. Screenplay, John Lee Mahin, Marc Connelly, Dale Van Every. Music Score, Franz Waxman. Marine Director, James Havens. Art Director, Cedric Gibbons. Associate Art Directors, Arnold Gillespie and Edwin B. Willis. Photography, Harold Rosson. Editor, Elmo Vernon. Sound, Douglas Shearer. Songs, "Don't Cry Little Fish" and "Ooh, What a Terrible Man!" by Franz Waxman and Gus Kahn. 116 minutes

Harvey: Freddie Bartholomew, *Manuel:* Spencer Tracy, *Disko:*

Lionel Barrymore, *Father:* Melvyn Douglas, *Dan:* Mickey Rooney, *Uncle Salters:* Charley Grapewin, *Old Clemant:* Christian Rub, *Dr. Finley:* Walter Kingsford, *Tyler:* Donald Briggs, *Doc:* Sam McDaniel, *Tom:* Dave Thursby, *Long Jack:* John Carradine, *Elliott:* William Stack, *Burns:* Leo G. Carroll, *Dr. Walsh:* Charles Trowbridge, *First Steward:* Richard Powell, *Charles:* Billy Burrud, *Pogey:* Jay Ward, *Alvin:* Kenneth Wilson, *Nate Rogers:* Roger Gray, *Priest:* Jack La Rue, *Cushman:* Oscar O'Shea, *Reporter:* Bobby Watson, *Soda Steward:* Billy Gilbert, *Robbins:* Norman Ainsley, *Secretary Cobb:* Gladden James, *Boys:* Tommy Bupp, Wally Albright, *Mrs. Disko:* Katherine Kenworthy, *Lars:* Dave Wengren, *Minister:* Murray Kinnell, *Appleton's Wife:* Dora Early, *Nate's Wife:* Gertrude Sutton.

Carmen Jones with Harry Belafonte and Dorothy Dandridge.

CARMEN JONES (1954) 20th. Producer-Director, Otto Preminger. Assistant Director, David Silver. Book and lyrics by Oscar Hammerstein II. Screenplay by Harry Kleiner. Music by Georges Bizet. Art Director, Edward L. Ilou. Cinematographer, Sam Leavitt. A CinemaScope Production in De Luxe Color. Stereophonic sound. Songs by Oscar Hammerstein II, based on the music of Georges Bizet: "Stand Up and Fight," "Beat Out That Rhythm on a Drum," "Dere's a Cafe on de Corner," "Lift 'em Up and Put 'em Down," "Dat's love (I Go For You, But You're Taboo)," "You Talk Just Like My Maw," "Dis Flower," "De Cards Don't Lie," "My Joe," "Dat's Our Man," "Whizzin' Away Along de Track." 105 minutes

Carmen: Dorothy Dandridge, *Joe:* Harry Belafonte, *Cindy Lou:* Olga James, *Frankie:* Pearl Bailey, *Myrt:* Diahann Carroll, *Rum:* Roy Glenn, *Dink:* Nick Stewart, *Husky:* Joe Adams, *Sgt. Brown:* Brock Peters, *T-Bone:* Sandy Lewis, *Sally:* Mauri Lynn, *Trainer:* DeForest Covan. Marilyn Horne sings for Dorothy Dandridge, LeVern Hutcherson for Harry Belafonte, and Marvin Hayes for Joe Adams.

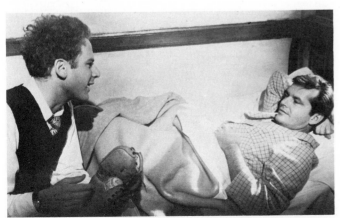

Carnal Knowledge with Art Garfunkel and Jack Nicholson.

CARNAL KNOWLEDGE (1971) Avco Embassy. Produced and Directed by Mike Nichols. Executive Producer, Joseph E. Levine. Written by Jules Feiffer. Associate Producer, Clive Reed. Photography, Giuseppe Rotunno. Editor, Sam O'Steen. Production Designer, Richard Sylbert. Costume Designer, Anthea Sylbert. Sound, Lawrence O. Jost. Assistant Director, Tim Zinnemann. Set Decorator, George R. Nelson. Hairstyles, Sydney Guilaroff. Art Director, Robert Luthardt. Panavision and Technicolor. Filmed in New York City and Vancouver, B.C. Rated R. 100 minutes

Jonathan Fuerst: Jack Nicholson, *Bobbie:* Ann-Margret, *Sandy:* Art Garfunkel, *Susan:* Candice Bergen, *Louise:* Rita Moreno, *Cindy:* Cynthia O'Neal, *Jennifer:* Carol Kane.

THE CARPETBAGGERS (1964) Par. Producer, Joseph E. Levine. Director, Edward Dmytryk. Technicolor. Based on the novel by Harold Robbins. Screenplay, John Michael Hayes. Art Directors, Hal Pereira, Walter Tyler. Music, Elmer Bernstein. Cinematographer, Joseph MacDonald. Special Photographic Effects, Paul K. Lerpae. Editor, Frank Bracht. Last film of Alan Ladd. Sequel was *Nevada Smith* (1966). 150 minutes

Jonas Cord: George Peppard, *Nevada Smith:* Alan Ladd, *Dan Pierce:* Bob Cummings, *Jennie Denton:* Martha Hyer, *Monica:* Elizabeth Ashley, *McAllister:* Lew Ayres, *Bernard Norman:* Martin Balsam, *Buzz Dalton:* Ralph Taeger, *Jedediah:* Archie Moore, *Jonas Cord, Sr.:* Leif Erickson, *Rina Marlowe Cord:* Carroll Baker, *Morrissey:* Arthur Franz, *Amos Winthrop:* Tom Tully, *Woman:* Audrey Totter, *Moroni:* Anthony Warde, *Denby:* Charles Lane, *David Woolf:* Tom Lowell, *Ed Ellis:* John Conte, *Doctor:* Vaughn Taylor, *Cynthia Randall:* Francesca Bellini, *Jo-Ann Cord:* Victoria Jean, *Bellboy:* Frankie Darro, *Moroni's Secretary:* Lisa Seagram, *Woman Reporter:* Ann Doran, *Reporter:* Joseph Turkel, *Sound Man:* Donald Barry, *Asst. Director:* Peter Duryea.

The Carpetbaggers with Carroll Baker and George Peppard.

CARRIE (1976) UA. Produced by Paul Monash. Directed by Brian De Palma. Based on the novel by Stephen King. Screenplay, Lawrence D. Cohen. Editor, Paul Hirsch. Associate Producer, Louis Stroller. Photography, Mario Tosi. Music, Pino Donaggio. Music Supervisor, Michael Arciaga. Songs, "Carrie" and "Born to Have It All." Stunt Coordinator, Dick Ziker. Special Effects, Gregory M. Auer. Sets, "Get Set." Assistant Directors, Donald Heitzer and William Scott. Make-up, Wesley Dawn. Hairstylist, Adele Taylor. Costumer, Agnes Lyon. Assistant Special Effects, Kenneth Pepiot. Set Decorator, Robert Gould. Laboratory, MGM. Release prints by DeLuxe General. Film debuts of Nancy Allen and Betty Buckley. Amy Irving is Priscilla Pointer's daughter. Rated R. 98 minutes

Carrie White: Sissy Spacek, *Margaret White:* Piper Laurie, *Sue Snell:* Amy Irving, *Tommy Ross:* William Katt, *Billy Nolan:* John Travolta, *Chris Hargenson:* Nancy Allen, *Miss Collins:* Betty Buckley, *Norma*

41

Watson: P. J. Soles, *Mr. Fromm:* Sydney Lassick, *Mr. Morton:* Stefan Gierasch, *Mrs. Snell:* Priscilla Pointer, *Freddy:* Michael Talbot, *The Beak:* Doug Cox, *George:* Harry Gold, *Frieda:* Noelle North, *Cora:* Cindy Daly, *Rhonda:* Dierdre Berthrong, *Ernest:* Anson Downes, *Boy on Bicycle:* Cameron De Palma, *Kenny:* Rory Stevens, *Helen:* Edie McClurg.

Carrie with Sissy Spacek and William Katt.

CAR WASH (1976) Univ. Produced by Art Linson and Gary Stromberg. Directed by Michael Schultz. Written by Joel Schumacher. Photography, Frank Stanley. Associate Producer/Casting, Don Phillips. Music composed and produced by Norman Whitfield. Songs Performed by Rose Royce. Art Director, Robert Clatworthy. Editor, Christopher Holmes. Set Decorations, A. C. Montenaro. Sound, Willie D. Burton and Robert L. Hoyt. Costume Designer, Daniel Paredes. 1st Assistant Director, Phil Bowles. 2nd Assistant Directors, Richard Hashimoto and Dan Franklin. Make-up, Chuck Crafts. Hairstylist, Robert Stevenson. Technicolor. Film debuts of Richard Brestoff, Michael Fennell, 13, comedian George Carlin and Oakland Raiders football star Otis Sistrunk. Rated PG. 97 minutes

T.C., "The Fly": Franklin Ajaye, *Leon, Mr. B:* Sully Boyar, *Irwin:* Richard Brestoff, *Taxi Driver:* George Carlin, *Mad Bomber:* Professor Irwin Corey, *Lonnie:* Ivan Dixon, *Duane (Abdullah):* Bill Duke, *Lindy:* Antonio Fargas, *Calvin:* Michael Fennell, *Charlie:* Arthur French, *Hysterical Lady:* Lorraine Gary, *Floyd:* Darrow Igus, *Earl:* Leonard Jackson, *Lloyd:* DeWayne Jessie, *Marleen, Hooker:* Lauren Jones, *Scruggs:* Jack Kehoe, *Goody:* Henry Kingi, *Marsha:* Melanie Mayron, *Slide:* Garrett Morris, *Snapper:* Clarence Muse, *Justin:* Leon Pinkney, *The Wilson Sisters:* The Pointer Sisters, *Daddy Rich:* Richard Pryor, *Mona:* Tracy Reed, *Chuco:* Pepe Serna, *Hippo:* James Spinks, *Geronimo:* Ray Vitte, *Loretta:* Ren Woods, *Foolish Father:* Carmine Caridi, *Charlene:* Antonie Becker, *Lonnie's Son:* Erin Blunt, *Daddy Rich's Chauffeur:* Reginald Farmer, *Hysterical Lady's Son:* Ricky Fellen, *Man Behind:* Ben Fromer, *Bandaged Man's Wife:* Cynthia Hamowy, *Foolish Father's Son:* John Linson, *Arresting Cop:* Ed Metzger, *Sonny Fredericks:* Antar Mubarak, *Foolish Father's Son:* Derek Schultz, *Harold, Bandaged Man:* Mike Slaney, *Oldsmobile Owner:* Al Stellone, *Calvin's Mother:* Jackie Toles, *Lonnie's Daughter:* Janine Williams, *Otis:* Otis Sistrunk, *Kenny:* Timothy Thomerson, *Parole Officer:* Jason Bernard, *Voice of AM Disc Jockey:* Jay Butler, *Voices of PM Disc Jockeys:* Rod McGrew, J. J. Jackson, *Voices of Newscasters:* Sarina C. Grant, Billy Bass. Cut from release print were: Brooke Adams as *Terry G.*, Danny De Vito as *Joe Graziano*, Benny Baker as *Barney Zalinsky*, *Mailman*, and Barbara Walden as *Saleswoman*.

Car Wash with Darrow Igus and DeWayne Jessie.

Casablanca with Dooley Wilson, Humphrey Bogart and Ingrid Bergman.

CASABLANCA (1942) WB. Produced by Hal B. Wallis. Directed by Michael Curtiz. Based on *Everybody Comes to Rick's*, an unproduced play by Murray Burnett and Joan Alison. Screenplay, Julius J. Epstein, Philip G. Epstein, Howard Koch. Music, Max Steiner. Music Director, Leo F. Forbstein. Orchestral Arrangements, Hugo Friedhofer. Editor, Owen Marks. Photography, Arthur Edeson. Sound, Francis J. Scheid. Art Director, Carl Jules Weyl. Sets, George James Hopkins. Special Effects, Lawrence Butler. Songs by M. K. Jerome and Jack Scholl: "Knock on Wood," "That's What Noah Done," "Muse's Call"; "As Time Goes By" by Herman Hupfeld. Montages, Don Siegel and James Leicester. Special Effects Director, Willard Van Enger. Gowns, Orry-Kelly. Assistant Director, Lee Katz. Make-up, Perc Westmore. Dialogue Director, Hugh MacMullan. Technical Advisor, Robert Aisner. Filmed near Palm Springs. Originally named for the leads were Ann Sheridan, Ronald Reagan, and Dennis Morgan. Elliott Carpenter played the piano for Dooley Wilson, who, in his film debut, sang "As Time Goes By" and "It Had to Be You." 102 minutes

Rick Blaine: Humphrey Bogart, *Ilsa Lund Laszlo:* Ingrid Bergman, *Victor Laszlo:* Paul Henreid, *Captain Louis Renault:* Claude Rains, *Maj. Heinrich Strasser:* Conrad Veidt, *Senor Ferrari:* Sydney Greenstreet, *Ugarte:* Peter Lorre, *Carl:* S. Z. Sakall, *Yvonne:* Madeleine LeBeau, *Sam:* Dooley Wilson, *Annina Brandel:* Joy Page, *Berger:* John Qualen, *Sascha:* Leonid Kinskey, *Jan Brandel:* Helmut Dantine, *Dark European:* Curt Bois, *Croupier:* Marcel Dalio, *Singer:* Corinna Mura, *Mr. Leuchtag:* Ludwig Stossel, *Mrs. Leuchtag:* Ilka Gruning, *Senor Martinez:* Charles La Torre, *Arab Vendor:* Frank Puglia, *Abdul:* Dan Seymour, *Blue Parrot Waiter:* Oliver Prickett (Oliver Blake), *German Banker:* Gregory Gay, *Friend:* George Meeker, *Contact:* William Edmunds, *Banker:* Torben Meyer, *Waiter:* Gino Corrado, *Casselle:* George Dee, *Englishwoman:* Norma Varden, *Fydor:* Leo Mostovoy, *Heinz:* Richard Ryen, *Headwaiter:* Martin Garralaga, *Prosperous Man:* Olaf Hytten, *American:* Monte Blue, *Vendor:* Michael Mark, *Dealer:* Leon Belasco, *Native:* Paul Porcasi, *German Officer:* Hans Twardowski, *French Officer:* Albert Morin, *Customer:* Creighton Hale, *German Officer:* Henry Rowland.

Cass Timberlane with Spencer Tracy, Cameron Mitchell and Lana Turner.

CASS TIMBERLANE (1947) MGM. Producer, Arthur Hornblow, Jr. Director, George Sidney. Based on the novel by Sinclair Lewis. Screenplay, Donald Ogden Stewart. Art Directors, Cedric Gibbons, Daniel B. Cathcart. Music Score, Roy Webb. Musical Director, Constantin Bakaleinikoff. Cameraman, Robert Planck. Editor, John Dunning. Locations: Minnesota, Idaho, Florida, Los Angeles. 119 minutes

Cass Timberlane: Spencer Tracy, *Virginia Marshland:* Lana Turner, *Brad Criley:* Zachary Scott, *Jamie Wargate:* Tom Drake, *Queenie Havock:* Mary Astor, *Boone Havock:* Albert Dekker, *Louise Wargate:* Selena Royle, *Lillian Drover:* Josephine Hutchinson, *Chris Gray:* Margaret Lindsay, *Diantha Marl:* Rose Hobart, *Webb Wargate:* John Litel, *Mrs. Avis Elderman:* Mona Barrie, *Roy Drover:* John Alexander, *Gregg Marl:* Frank Wilcox, *Alice:* Pat Clark, *Dennis Thayne:* Richard Gaines, *John Prutt:* Willis Claire, *Henrietta Prutt:* Winnona Walthal, *Eino Rochinan:* Cameron Mitchell, *Mrs. Higbie:* Jessie Grayson, *Herman:* Griff Barnett, *Harvey Plint:* Howard Freeman, *George Hame:* Guy Beach, *Humbert Bellile:* Cliff Clark, *Himself:* Walter Pidgeon, *Sheriff Alex Carlson:* Ken Christy, *Dr. Leskett:* Selmer Jackson, *Court Clerk:* Frank Ferguson, *Nestor Purdwin:* Milburn Stone, *Zilda Hatter:* Almira Sessions, *Vincent Osprey:* Jack Rice, *Ellen Olliford:* Mimi Doyle, *Arthur Olliford:* Bill Conselman, *Charles Sayward:* Sam Flint, *Dagmar:* Greta Granstedt, *Policeman:* Robert Williams, *Chauffeur:* William Tannen, *Charlie Ellis:* Tim Ryan, *Mary Ann Milligan:* Bess Flowers, *Raveau:* William Trenk.

CAT BALLOU (1965) Col. Producer, Harold Hecht. Associate Producer, Mitch Lindemann. Director, Elliott Silverstein. Technicolor. Based on the novel by Roy Chanslor. Screenplay, Walter Newman, Frank R. Pierson. Art Director, Malcolm Brown. Music, De Vol. Songs, Mack David, Jerry Livingston. Cinematographer, Jack Marta. Editor, Charles Nelson. 96 minutes

Cat Ballou: Jane Fonda, *Kid Shelleen/Strawn:* Lee Marvin, *Clay Boone:* Michael Callan, *Jed:* Dwayne Hickman, *Shouter:* Nat King Cole, *Shouter:* Stubby Kaye, *Jackson Two-Bears:* Tom Nardini, *Frankie Ballou:* John Marley, *Sir Harry Percival:* Reginald Denny, *Sheriff Cardigan:* Jay C. Flippen, *Butch Cassidy:* Arthur Hunnicutt, *Sheriff Maledon:* Bruce Cabot, *Accuser:* Burt Mustin, *Train Messenger:* Paul Gilbert, *Klem:* Robert Phillips, *James:* Charles Wagenheim, *Homer:* Duke Hobbie, *Hedda:* Ayllene Gibbons, *Train Engineer:* Everett L. Rohrer, *Train Conductor:* Harry Harvey, Sr., *Honey Girl:* Hallene Hill, *Mabel Bentley:* Gail Bonney, *Frenchie:* Joseph Hamilton, *Singing Tart:* Dorothy Claire, *Hardcase:* Charles Horvath, *Armed Guard:* Chuck Roberson, *Ad-Lib:* Nick Cravat, *Gunslinger:* Ted White, *Valet:* Erik Sorensen, *Train Fireman:* Ivan L. Middleton, *Mrs. Parker:* Carol Veazie.

Cat Ballou with Lee Marvin (dual role).

CAT ON A HOT TIN ROOF (1958) MGM. An Avon Production. Producer, Lawrence Weingarten. Director, Richard Brooks. Color by MetroColor. Screenplay by Richard Brooks and James Poe. Based on the play by Tennessee Williams. Assistant Director, William Shanks. Wardrobe by Helen Rose. Art Directors, William A. Horning and Urie McCleary. Film Editor, Ferris Webster. Cinematography by William Daniels. 108 minutes

Maggie: Elizabeth Taylor, *Brick:* Paul Newman, *Big Daddy:* Burl Ives, *Gooper:* Jack Carson, *Big Mama:* Judith Anderson, *Mae:* Madeleine Sherwood, *Dr. Baugh:* Larry Gates, *Deacon Davis:* Vaughn Taylor, *Lacy:* Vince Townsend, Jr., *Sookey:* Zelda Cleaver, *Boy:* Brian Corcoran, *Buster:* Hugh Corcoran, *Sonny:* Rusty Stevens, *Dixie:* Patty Ann Gerrity, *Trixie:* Deborah Miller, *Party Guests:* Tony Merrill, Jeane Wood, *Groom:* Bobby Johnson.

Cat on a Hot Tin Roof with Paul Newman and Elizabeth Taylor.

CAT PEOPLE (1942) RKO. Producer, Val Lewton. Director, Jacques Tourneur. Screenplay, DeWitt Bodeen. Musical Director, C. Bakaleinikoff. Score, Roy Webb. Art Directors, Albert d'Agostino, Walter E. Keller. Cameraman, Nicholas Musuraca. Editor, Mark Robson. Sequel was *The Curse of the Cat People* (RKO, 1944). 73 minutes

Irena Dubrovna: Simone Simon, *Oliver Reed:* Kent Smith, *Doctor Judd:* Tom Conway, *Alice Moore:* Jane Randolph, *The Commodore:* Jack Holt, *Carver:* Alan Napier, *Miss Plunkett:* Elizabeth Dunne, *The Cat Woman:* Elizabeth Russell, *Blondie:* Mary Halsey, *Zookeeper:* Alec Craig, *Minnie:* Theresa Harris, *The Organ Grinder:* Steve Soldi, *Bus Driver:* Charles Jordan, *Whistling Cop:* George Ford, *Mrs. Hansen:* Betty Roadman, *Mrs. Agnew:* Dot Farley, *Taxi Driver:* Don Kerr, *Women:* Connie Leon, Henrietta Burnside, *Patient:* Leda Nicova, *Cafe Proprietor:* John Piffl, *Sheep Caretaker:* Murdock MacQuarrie, *Mounted Cop:* Bud Geary, *Street Cop:* Eddie Dew.

The Cat People with Elizabeth Dunne, Kent Smith, Jane Randolph and Mary Halsey.

Cavalcade with Herbert Mundin, Diana Wynyard, Clive Brook and Una O'Connor.

CAVALCADE (1933) Fox. Produced by Winfield Sheehan. Directed by Frank Lloyd. Based on the play by Noel Coward. Adaptation and Dialogue, Reginald Berkeley. Continuity Editor, Sonya Levien. Art Director, William Darling. Ladies' Costumes, Earl Luick. Men's Costumes, A. McDonald. War Scenes, William Cameron Menzies. Technical Advisor, Lance Baxter. Dialogue Director, George Hadden. Unit Manager, Charles Woolstenhulme. Assistant Director, William Tummel. Photography, Ernest Palmer. Editor, Margaret Clancy. Sound, Joseph E. Aiken. Dances, Sammy Lee. Filmed entirely at Movietone City, Westwood, Cal. Song by Noel Coward: "Twentieth Century Blues." 109 minutes

Robert Marryot: Clive Brook, *Jane Marryot:* Diana Wynyard, *Fanny Bridges:* Ursula Jeans, *Alfred Bridges:* Herbert Mundin, *Ellen Bridges:* Una O'Connor, *Annie:* Merle Tottenham, *Margaret Harris:* Irene Browne, *Cook:* Beryl Mercer, *Joe Marryot:* Frank Lawton, *Edward Marryot:* John Warburton, *Edith Harris:* Margaret Lindsay, *Mrs. Snapper:* Tempe Piggott, *George Grainger:* Billy Bevan, *Ronnie James:* Desmond Roberts, *Uncle Dick:* Frank Atkinson, *Mirabelle:* Ann Shaw, *Ada:* Adele Crane, *Tommy Jolly:* Will Stanton, *Lieutenant Edgar:* Stuart Hall, *Duchess of Churt:* Mary Forbes, *Major Domo:* C. Montague Shaw, *Uncle George:* Lionel Belmore, *Edward, age 12:* Dick Henderson, Jr., *Joey, age 8:* Douglas Scott, *Edith, age 10:* Sheila MacGill, *Fanny at 7-12:* Bonita Granville, *Agitator:* Howard Davies, *Man at Disarmament Conference:* David Torrence, *Man at Microphone:* Lawrence Grant, *Minister:* Winter Hall, *Speaker (Officer):* Claude King, *Ringsider:* Pat Somerset, *Soldier (Friend):* Douglas Walton, *Waiter:* Tom Ricketts, *Girl on Couch:* Betty Grable, *Buskers:* Harry Allen, John Rogers, *Gilbert & Sullivan Actor:* Brandon Hurst.

Ceiling Zero with James Cagney, June Travis and Pat O'Brien.

CEILING ZERO (1935) WB. Produced by Harry Joe Brown. Directed by Howard Hawks. Based on the play by Frank Wead. Screenplay, Frank Wead. Photography, Arthur Edeson. Editor, William Holmes. A Cosmopolitan Production. 95 minutes

Dizzy Davis: James Cagney, *Jake Lee:* Pat O'Brien, *Tommy Thomas:* June Travis, *Texas Clark:* Stuart Erwin, *Tay Lawson:* Henry Wadsworth, *Lou Clark:* Isabel Jewell, *Al Stone:* Barton MacLane, *Mary Lee:* Martha Tibbetts, *Joe Allen:* Craig Reynolds, *Buzz Gordon:* James H. Bush, *Les Bogan:* Robert Light, *Fred Adams:* Addison Richards, *Eddie Payson:* Carlyle Moore, Jr., *Smiley Johnson:* Richard Purcell, *Transportation Agent:* (Bill) Gordon Elliott, *Baldy Wright:* Pat West, *Doc Wilson:* Edward Gargan, *Mike Owens:* Garry Owen, *Mama Gini:* Mathilde Comont, *Birdie:* Carol Hughes, *Stunt Fliers:* Frank Tomick, Paul Mantz.

The Champ with Wallace Beery, Ed Brophy, Jackie Cooper and Roscoe Ates.

THE CHAMP (1931) MGM. Directed by King Vidor. Original story by Frances Marion. Scenario and Dialogue, Leonard Praskins. Photography, Gordon Avil. Editor, Hugh Wynn. Scenes filmed in Mexico and at the Caliente race track. 86 minutes. Remade as *The Clown* (MGM, 1953) with Red Skelton and as *The Champ* (MGM-UA, 1979) with Jon Voight.

Champ: Wallace Beery, *Dink:* Jackie Cooper, *Linda Carson:* Irene Rich, *Sponge:* Roscoe Ates, *Tim:* Edward Brophy, *Tony:* Hale Hamilton, *Jonah:* Jesse Scott, *Mary Lou:* Marcia Mae Jones, *Louie (Bartender):* Lee Phelps, *Manuel:* Frank Hagney.

CHAMPION (1949) UA. Producer, Stanley Kramer. Associate Producer, Robert Stillman. Director, Mark Robson. From the story by Ring Lardner. Screenplay, Carl Foreman. Art Director, Rudolph Sternad. Musical Director, Dimitri Tiomkin. Photography, Franz Planer. Editor, Harry Gerstad. A Screen Plays Corporation Production. Polly Bergen's voice is heard on a juke box. 99 minutes

Midge Kelly: Kirk Douglas, *Grace Diamond:* Marilyn Maxwell, *Connie Kelly:* Arthur Kennedy, *Tommy Haley:* Paul Stewart, *Emma Bryce:* Ruth Roman, *Mrs. Harris:* Lola Albright, *Jerome Harris:* Luis Van Rooten, *Johnny Dunne:* John Day, *Lew Bryce:* Harry Shannon.

Champion with Arthur Kennedy, Kirk Douglas and Paul Stewart.

Charade with Cary Grant and Audrey Hepburn.

CHARADE (1963) Univ. Producer, Stanley Donen. Associate Producer, James Ware. Director, Stanley Donen. Technicolor. Authors, Peter Stone, Marc Behm. Screenplay, Peter Stone. Art Director, Jean D'Eaubonne. Music, Henry Mancini. "Charade," lyric, Johnny Mercer; music, Henry Mancini. Cinematographer, Charles Lang,

Jr. Editor, James Clark. Filmed in Paris, Megve, the French Alps. 114 minutes

Alexander Dyle, or Adam Canfield, or Peter Joshua, or Bryan Cruikshank: Cary Grant, *Reggie Lampert (Vass):* Audrey Hepburn, *Hamilton Bartholomew:* Walter Matthau, *Tex:* James Coburn, *Herman Scobie:* George Kennedy, *Leopold Gideon:* Ned Glass, *Insp. Grandpierre:* Jacques Marin, *Felix:* Paul Bonifas, *Sylvie:* Dominique Minot, *Jean-Louis:* Thomas Chelimsky.

The Charge at Feather River with Henry Kulky, Vera Miles, Lane Chandler, Neville Brand and Guy Madison.

THE CHARGE AT FEATHER RIVER (1953) WB. Producer, David Weisbart. Director, Gordon Douglas. 3-Dimension and Warner-Color. Author, James R. Webb. Screenplay, James R. Webb. Art Director, Stanley Fleischer. Cinematographer, Peverell Marley. Editor, Folmar Blangsted. 96 minutes

Miles Archer: Guy Madison, *Sgt. Baker:* Frank Lovejoy, *Anne McKeever:* Helen Westcott, *Jennie McKeever:* Vera Miles, *Cullen:* Dick Wesson, *Grover Johnson:* Onslow Stevens, *Johnny McKeever:* Ron Hagerthy, *Ryan:* Steve Brodie, *Morgan:* Neville Brand, *Smiley:* Henry Kulky, *Lieutenant Colonel Kilrain:* Fay Roope, *Poinsett:* Lane Chandler, *Conner:* James Brown, *Adams:* Rand Brooks, *Carver:* Ben Corbett, *Dabney:* John Damler, *Curry:* Louis Tomei, *Hudkins:* Carl Andre, *Leech:* Fred Kennedy, *Danowicz:* Dub Taylor, *Wilhelm:* Ralph Brooke, *Griffin:* David Alpert, *Chief Thunder Hawk:* Fred Carson, *Signal Private:* Wayne Taylor, *Sentry:* Richard Bartlett, *Quartermaster Sergeant:* Joe Bassett, *Ordinance Sergeant:* Dennis Dengate, *Mamie:* Vivian Mason, *Officer:* John Pickard.

THE CHARGE OF THE LIGHT BRIGADE (1936) WB. Produced by Hal B. Wallis. Directed by Michael Curtiz. Assistant Producer, Sam Bischoff. Based on the poem by Alfred Tennyson. Story, Michel Jacoby. Screenplay by Michel Jacoby and Rowland Leigh. Musical Director, Leo F. Forbstein. Music, Max Steiner. Art Director, Jack Hughes. Cameramen, Sol Polito, Fred Jackman. Editor, George Amy. Photographic Effects, Fred Jackman. Technical Advisor, Captain E. Rochfort-John. Tactical and Military Drills, Major Sam Harris. 116 minutes

Captain Geoffrey Vickers: Errol Flynn, *Elsa Campbell:* Olivia de Havilland, *Captain Perry Vickers:* Patric Knowles, *Colonel Campbell:* Donald Crisp, *Sir Charles Macefield:* Henry Stephenson, *Sir Benjamin Warrenton:* Nigel Bruce, *Captain James Randall:* David Niven, *Major Jowett:* G. P. Huntley, Jr., *Lady Octavia Warrenton:* Spring Byington, *Surat Khan:* C. Henry Gordon, *Sir Humphrey Harcourt:* E. E. Clive, *Colonel Woodward:* Lumsden Hare, *Count Igor Volonoff:* Robert Barrat, *Cornet Barclay:* Walter Holbrook, *Cornet Pearson:* Charles Sedgwick, *Subahdar Major Puran Singh:* J. Carrol Naish, *Prema Singh:* Scotty Beckett, *Prema's Mother:* Princess Beigum, *Wazir:* George Regas, *Mrs. Jowett:* Helen Sanborn, *Captain Brown:*

Craufurd Kent, *Suristani:* George David, *Court Interpreter:* Carlos San Martin, *Orderly:* Jimmy Aubrey, *Major Domo:* Herbert Evans, *Sepoy Chief:* Harry Semels, *Russian General:* Michael Visaroff, *Panjari:* Frank Lackteen, *Panjari:* Martin Garralaga, *Bentham:* Reginald Sheffield, *General Canrobert:* Georges Renavent, *Lord Cardigan:* Charles Croker King, *Lord Raglan:* Brandon Hurst: *Captain:* Wilfred Lucas, *General Dunbar:* Boyd Irwin, *Colonel Coventry:* Gordon Hart, *General O'Neill:* Holmes Herbert; Stunts: Yakima Canutt.

The Charge of the Light Brigade with Errol Flynn.

Charley Varrick with Sheree North and Walter Matthau.

CHARLEY VARRICK (1973) Univ. Produced and Directed by Don Siegel. Executive Producer, Jennings Lang. Technicolor and Panavision. From the novel *The Looters* by John Reese. Screenplay, Howard Rodman and Dean Riesner. Photography, Michael Butler. Art Director, Fernando Carrere. Set Decorator, Darrell Silvera. Sound, John K. Kean, Waldon O. Watson, Robert Hoyt and Bill Stuart. Music by Lalo Schifrin. Editor, Frank Morriss. Assistant Directors, Joe Cavalier and Ron Satlof. Dialogue Coach, Scott Hale. Stunt Coordinator, Paul Baxley. Flying Sequences, Frank Tallman/Tallmantz Aviation. Costumes, Helen Colvig. Cosmetics,

Cinematique. Make-up, Gene Hibbs. Titles and Optical Effects, Universal Title. Filmed in Nevada. Rated PG. 111 minutes

Charley Varrick: Walter Matthau, *Molly:* Joe Don Baker, *Sybil Fort:* Felicia Farr, *Harman Sullivan:* Andy Robinson, *Maynard Boyle:* John Vernon, *Jewell Everett:* Sheree North, *District Attorney Garfinkle:* Norman Fell, *Honest John:* Benson Fong, *Young:* Woodrow Parfrey, *Sheriff Bill Horton:* William Schallert, *Nadine Varrick:* Jacqueline Scott, *Mrs. Taff:* Marjorie Bennett, *Deputy Rudy Sanchez:* Rudy Diaz, *Deputy Theron "Stainless" Steele:* Colby Chester, *Deputy Blaine:* Charlie Briggs, *Miss Ambar:* Priscilla Garcia, *Mr. Scott:* Scott Hale, *Little Boy,* Charles Matthau, *Miss Vesta:* Hope Summers, *Beverly:* Monica Lewis, *Dynamite Salesman (Hardware Clerk):* Jim Nolan, *Tom:* Tom Tully, *Randolph Percy:* Albert Popwell, *Jessie:* Kathleen O'Malley, *Jana:* Christina Hart, *Van Sickle:* Craig Baxley, *Taxi Driver:* Al Dunlap, *Chinese Hostess:* Virginia Wing, *Murph:* Don Siegel, *Brindle, Bank Guard:* Bob Steele, *Al:* Fred Scheiwiller, *Doorman:* Art Cribbs, *Store Proprietor:* Guy Way, *Indian Girl:* Carol Daniels DeMent, *TV News Reporter:* Carlos Velasquez, *Announcer:* Thomas Dunbar, *Man:* Richard R. Hogan, *Doorman/Attendant:* Fred Little, *Flower Delivery Boy:* Walt Wallace, *Little Girl on Swing:* Holly Nutter, *Bartender:* Robert D. Carver, *Stunt Pilot:* Frank Tallman, *Stunts:* Paul Baxley, Jerry Summers, Fred Stromsoe, Maurice Marks, Dean Jeffries, Max Klevin, George Robotham, *Prostitutes:* Mustang Ranch madame and girls.

The Cheap Detective with Peter Falk.

THE CHEAP DETECTIVE (1978) Col. A Rastar Production. An EMI Presentation. Produced by Ray Stark. Directed by Robert Moore. Original Screenplay by Neil Simon, a spoof of *The Maltese Falcon* and *Casablanca*. Panavision and Color. Music, Dave Grusin. Photography, John A. Alonzo. Editor, Sidney Levin. Assistant Editors, David Garfield and John Brice. 1st Assistant Director, John Chulay. 2nd Assistant Director, Steve Perry. Production Designer, Robert Luthardt. Art Director, Phillip Bennett. Set Decorator, Chuck Pierce. Costume Designer, Theoni V. Aldredge, assisted by Donna Thomas. Men's Costumer, John Anderson. Women's Costumer, Agnes Henry. Illustrator, Nikita Knatz. Special Effects, Augie Lohman. Sound Mixer, Al Overton, Jr. Make-up, Charlie Schram, assisted by Joe DeBella. Hairdresser, Kathryn Blondell. Rated PG. 92 minutes

Lou Peckinpaugh: Peter Falk, *Jezebel Dezire:* Ann-Margret, *Betty De-Boop:* Eileen Brennan, *Ezra C. V. Mildew Dezire, Jr.:* Sid Caesar, *Bess Duffy:* Stockard Channing, *Marcel:* James Coco, *Pepe Damascus:* Dom DeLuise, *Marlene DuChard:* Louise Fletcher, *Jasper Blubber:* John Houseman, *Paul DuChard:* Fernando Lamas, *Georgia Merkle:* Marsha Mason, *Hoppy, Cabby:* Phil Silvers, *Sgt. Rizzuto:* Abe Vigoda, *Boy:* Paul Williams, *Col. Schlissel:* Nicol Williamson, *Butler:* Emory Bass, *Sgt. Crosseti:* Carmine Caridi, *Lt. Frank DiMaggio:* Vic Tayback, *Tinker:* Scatman Crothers, *Captain of Waiters:* David Ogden Stiers, *Schnell:* James Cromwell, *Qvicker:* John Calvin, *Floyd Merkle:* Wally Berns, *Hat*

Check Girl: Carole Wells, *Cop:* Lew Gallo, *Military Man:* David Matthau, *Scrub Woman:* Bella Bruck, *Bits:* Carmen Montenegro alias Denise Manderley, Wanda Coleman, Gilda Dabney, Chloe La Marr, Natasha Oublenskaya, Alison Parker, Diane Glucksman, Alma Chalmers, Sophia DeVega, Vivien Purcell, Lady Edwina Morgan St. Paul, Mary Jones. Norma Shearer, Barbara Stanwyck: Madeline Kahn.

Cheaper by the Dozen with Clifton Webb, Myrna Loy, Jimmy Hunt, Jeanne Crain, Betty Lynn and Carole Nugent (second from right).

CHEAPER BY THE DOZEN (1950) 20th. Producer, Lamar Trotti. Director, Walter Lang. Color by Technicolor. Based on the novel by Frank B. Gilbreth, Jr. and Ernestine Gilbreth Carey. Screenplay, Lamar Trotti. Musical Director, Lionel Newman. Art Directors, Lyle Wheeler, Leland Fuller. Photography, Leon Shamroy. Editor, J. Watson Webb, Jr. Sequel was *Belles on Their Toes*, 20th, 1952. 85 minutes

Frank Bunker Gilbreth: Clifton Webb, *Ann Gilbreth:* Jeanne Crain, *Mrs. Lillian Gilbreth:* Myrna Loy, *Libby Lancaster:* Betty Lynn, *Dr. Burton:* Edgar Buchanan, *Ernestine:* Barbara Bates, *Mrs. Mebane:* Mildred Natwick, *Mrs. Monahan:* Sara Allgood, *Fred Gilbreth:* Anthony Sydes, *Jack Gilbreth:* Roddy McCaskill, *Frank Gilbreth, Jr.:* Norman Ollestad, *Martha Gilbreth:* Patti Brady, *Lillie Gilbreth:* Carole Nugent, *William Gilbreth:* Jimmy Hunt, *Dan Gilbreth:* Teddy Driver, *Mary Gilbreth:* Betty Barker, *School Principal:* Evelyn Varden, *Mr. Higgins:* Frank Orth, *Tom Black:* Craig Hill, *Mrs. Benson:* Virginia Brissac, *Jim Bracken:* Walter Baldwin, *Joe Scales:* Bennie Bartlett, *Plumber:* Syd Saylor, *Mailman:* Ken Christy, *Music Teacher:* Mary Field, *Jane, age 1:* Denise Courtemarche, *Jane, age 2:* Tina Thompson, *Messenger Boy:* Vincent Graeff, *Assistant Principal:* Anita Gegna, *Baby Denise:* Judy Ann Whaley.

China Seas with Clark Gable, Jean Harlow, Wallace Beery and C. Aubrey Smith.

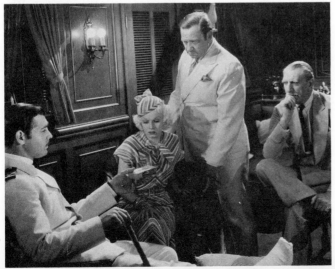

CHINA SEAS (1935) MGM. Produced by Albert Lewin. Directed by Tay Garnett. Based on the 1931 novel by the late Crosbie Garstin. Screenplay, Jules Furthman and James Keven McGuinness. Photography, Ray June. Editor, William Levanway. Song: "China Seas" by Arthur Freed and Nacio Herb Brown. 89 minutes

Captain Alan Gaskell: Clark Gable, *China Doll (Dolly Portland):* Jean Harlow, *Jamesy MacArdle:* Wallace Beery, *Tom Davids:* Lewis Stone, *Sybil Barclay:* Rosalind Russell, *Dawson:* Dudley Digges, *Sir Guy Wilmerding:* C. Aubrey Smith, *Charlie McCaleb:* Robert Benchley, *Rockwell:* William Henry, *Mrs. Vollberg:* Live Demaigret, *Mrs. Timmons:* Lilian Bond, *Wilbur Timmons:* Edward Brophy, *Yu-Lan:* Soo Yong, *Carol Ann:* Carol Ann Beery, *Romanoff:* Akim Tamiroff, *Ngah:* Ivan Lebedeff, *Isabel McCarthy:* Hattie McDaniel, *Chess Player:* Donald Meek, *Lady:* Emily Fitzroy, *Second Officer Kingston:* Pat Flaherty, *Ship's Officer:* Tom Gubbins, *Steward:* Forrester Harvey, *Purser, Bertie:* Charles Irwin, *Cabin Boy:* Willie Fung, *Police Superintendent:* Ferdinand Munier, *Rickshaw Boy:* Chester Gan, *Pilot:* John Ince.

Chinatown with Faye Dunaway.

CHINATOWN (1974) Par. Produced by Robert Evans. Directed by Roman Polanski. Panavision and Technicolor. Written by Robert Towne. A Long Road Production. Photography, John A. Alonzo. Associate Producer/Unit Production Manager, C. O. Erickson. Music, Jerry Goldsmith. Costume Designer, Anthea Sylbert. Editor, Sam O'Steen. Production Designer, Richard Sylbert. Assistant Directors, Howard W. Koch, Jr., and Michele Ader. Art Director, W. Stewart Campbell. Sound Mixer, Larry Jost. Set Designers, Gabe and Robert Resh. Set Decorator, Ruby Levitt. Make-up, Hank Edds and Lee Harmon. Hairstylists, Susan Germaine and Vivienne Walker. Wardrobe, Richard Bruno and Jean Merrick. Jewels by The Family Jewels. Rated R. 131 minutes

J. J. Gittes: Jack Nicholson, *Evelyn Cross Mulwray:* Faye Dunaway, *Noah Cross:* John Huston, *Lt. Lou Escobar:* Perry Lopez, *Yelburton:* John Hillerman, *Hollis Mulwray:* Darrell Zwerling, *Ida Sessions:* Diane Ladd, *Mulvihill:* Roy Jenson, *Man with Knife:* Roman Polanski, *Loach:* Dick Bakalyan, *Walsh:* Joe Mantell, *Duffy:* Bruce Glover, *Sophie:* Nandu Hinds, *Lawyer:* James O'Reare, *Evelyn's Butler:* James Hong, *Maid:* Beulah Quo, *Gardener:* Jerry Fujikawa, *Katherine:* Belinda Palmer, *Mayor Bagby:* Roy Roberts, *Irate Farmer:* Rance Howard, *Councilmen:* Noble Willingham and Elliott Montgomery, *Barber:* George Justin, *Customer:* Doc Erickson, *Mulwray's Secretary:* Fritzi Burr, *Mortician:* Charles Knapp, *Boy on Horseback:* Claudio Martinez, *Cross' Butler:* Federico Roberto, *Clerk:* Allan Warnick, *Valley Farmers:* John Holland,

Jesse Vint, Jim Burke, Denny Arnold, *Curly:* Burt Young, *Curly's Wife:* Elizabeth Harding, *Mr. Palmer:* John Rogers, *Emma Dill:* Cecil Elliott, *Policemen:* Paul Jenkins, Lee De Broux, Bob Golden.

Cimarron with Richard Dix, Douglas Scott and Irene Dunne.

CIMARRON (1931) RKO. Associate Producer, Louis Sarecky. Directed by Wesley Ruggles. Based on the novel by Edna Ferber. Scenario and Dialogue, Howard Estabrook. Assistant Directors, Doran Cox and Dewey Starkey. Art Director and Costumes, Max Ree. Photography, Edward Cronjager. Editor, William Hamilton. Sound, Clem Portman. Remade by MGM in 1961. 130 minutes

Yancey Cravat: Richard Dix, *Sabra Cravat:* Irene Dunne, *Dixie Lee:* Estelle Taylor, *Felice Venable:* Nance O'Neil, *The Kid:* William Collier, Jr., *Jess Rickey:* Roscoe Ates, *Sol Levy:* George E. Stone, *Lon Yountis:* Stanley Fields, *Louie Heffner:* Robert McWade, *Mrs. Tracy Wyatt:* Edna May Oliver, *Mr. Bixley:* Frank Darien, *Isaiah:* Eugene Jackson, *Ruby Big Elk (elder):* Dolores Brown, *Ruby (younger):* Gloria Vonic, *Murch Rankin:* Otto Hoffman, *Grat Gotch:* William Orlamond, *Louis Venable:* Frank Beal, *Donna Cravat (elder):* Nancy Dover, *Donna (younger):* Helen Parrish, *Cim (elder):* Donald Dillaway, *Cim (younger):* Junior Johnson, *Cim (youngest):* Douglas Scott, *Yancey, Jr.:* Reginald Streeter, *Felice, Jr.:* Lois Jane Campbell, *Aunt Cassandra:* Ann Lee, *Sabney Venable:* Tyrone Brereton, *Cousin Bella:* Lillian Lane, *Jouett Goforth:* Henry Roquemore, *Arminta Greenwood:* Nell Craig, *Pat Leary:* Robert McKenzie, *Indian Girl:* Clara Hunt, *Bits:* Bob Kortman, Dennis O'Keefe.

Citizen Kane with Ray Collins, Dorothy Comingore, Orson Welles and Ruth Warrick.

CITIZEN KANE (1941) RKO. Produced and directed by Orson Welles. A Mercury Theatre Production. Original Screenplay, Herman J. Mankiewicz and Orson Welles. Photography, Gregg Toland. Music composed and conducted by Bernard Herrmann. Art Director, Van Nest Polglase. Associate, Perry Ferguson. Sets, Darrell Silvera. Special Effects, Vernon L. Walker. Costumes, Edward Stevenson. Sound, Bailey Fesler and James G. Stewart. Editor, Robert Wise. Film debuts of Orson Welles, Joseph Cotten, Agnes Moorehead, Ruth Warrick, Paul Stewart, Ray Collins; Dorothy Comingore formerly acted as Linda Winters. 119 minutes

Charles Foster Kane: Orson Welles, *Susan Alexander:* Dorothy Comingore, *Jedediah Leland:* Joseph Cotten, *Bernstein:* Everett Sloane, *Walter Parks Thatcher:* George Coulouris, *James W. Gettys:* Ray Collins, *Emily Norton:* Ruth Warrick, *Herbert Carter:* Erskine Sanford, *Thompson (Narrator):* William Alland, *Mrs. Kane:* Agnes Moorehead, *Hillman:* Richard Baer, *Raymond:* Paul Stewart, *Matiste:* Fortunio Bonanova, *Georgia:* Joan Blair, *Kane at 8:* Buddy Swan, *Kane, Sr.:* Harry Shannon, *Bertha:* Georgia Backus, *Mike:* Al Eben, *Entertainer:* Charles Bennett, *Rawlston:* Philip Van Zandt, *Reporter:* Milt Kibbee, *Teddy Roosevelt:* Tom Curran, *Kane III:* Sonny Bupp, *Dr. Corey:* Irving Mitchell, *Nurse:* Edith Evanson, *Orchestra Leader:* Arthur Kay, *Chorus Master:* Tudor Williams, *City Editor:* Herbert Corthell, *Reporters:* Alan Ladd, Louise Currie, Eddie Coke, Walter Sande, Arthur O'Connell, Richard Wilson, Katherine Trosper, *Smather:* Benny Rubin, ENQUIRER *Reporter:* Edmund Cobb, *Ethel:* Frances Neal, *Photographer:* Robert Dudley, *Miss Townsend:* Ellen Lowe, *Headwaiter:* Gus Schilling, *Gino, Waiter:* Gino Corrado.

City Streets with Gary Cooper and Sylvia Sidney.

CITY STREETS (1931) Par. Directed by Rouben Mamoulian. Story, Dashiell Hammett. Screenplay, Max Marcin and Oliver H. P. Garrett. Photography, Lee Garmes. Sound, J. A. Goodrich and M. M. Paggi. Terry Carroll is Nancy's sister. Clara Bow was replaced by Sylvia Sidney as Nan. 82 minutes

The Kid: Gary Cooper, *Nan:* Sylvia Sidney, *Big Fellow Maskal:* Paul Lukas, *McCoy:* William (Stage) Boyd, *Pop Cooley:* Guy Kibbee,

Blackie: Stanley Fields, *Aggie:* Wynne Gibson, *Pansy:* Betty Sinclair, *Woman:* Barbara Leonard, *Esther March:* Terry Carroll, *Inspector:* Robert E. Homans, *Detective:* Willard Robertson, *Cop:* Allan Cavan, *Baldy, a Henchman:* Bert Hanlon, *Man Who's Stabbed with a Fork:* Matty Kemp, *Shooting Gallery Patrons:* Edward Le Saint, Hal Price, *Killer at Prison:* Ethan Laidlaw, *Machine-Gunner:* George Regas, *Servant:* Bob Kortman, *Henchman:* Leo Willis, *Dance Extra:* Bill Elliott.

CLASH BY NIGHT (1952) RKO. Producer, Harriet Parsons. Director, Fritz Lang. Based on the play by Clifford Odets. Screenplay, Alfred Hayes. Art Directors: Albert S. D'Agostino, Carroll Clark. Music Director, C. Bakaleinikoff. Cinematographer, Nicholas Musuraca. Editor, George J. Amy. Song by Dick Gasparre, Jack Baker and George Fragos: "I Hear a Rhapsody." A Wald-Krasna Production. 105 minutes

Mae: Barbara Stanwyck, *Jerry:* Paul Douglas, *Earl:* Robert Ryan, *Peggy:* Marilyn Monroe, *Uncle Vince:* J. Carrol Naish, *Joe Doyle:* Keith Andes, *Papa:* Silvio Minciotti, *Twin Baby:* Diane Stewart, *Twin Baby:* Deborah Stewart, *Sad-eyed Waiter:* Julius Tannen, *Bartender:* Bert Stevens, *Waiter:* William Bailey, *Bartender:* Mario Siletti, *Customer:* Bill Slack, *Customer:* Art Dupuis, *Art:* Frank Kreig, *Fisherman at Pier:* Tony Dante.

Clash by Night with Paul Douglas, Barbara Stanwyck and Robert Ryan.

Claudia with Robert Young, Ina Claire and Dorothy McGuire.

CLAUDIA (1943) 20th. Producer, William Perlberg. Director, Edmund Goulding. Based on the play by Rose Franken. Screenplay, Morrie Ryskind. Musical Score, Alfred Newman. Art Directors, James Basevi, Albert Hogsett. Cameraman, Leon Shamroy. Special Effects, Fred Sersen. Editor, Robert Simpson. Song by Alfred Newman and Charles Henderson: "From Yesterday to Tomorrow." Film debut of Dorothy

McGuire, 24, repeating her stage role. 91 minutes. Sequel was *Claudia and David* (1946)

Claudia Naughton: Dorothy McGuire, *David Naughton:* Robert Young, *Mrs. Brown:* Ina Claire, *Jerry Seymour:* Reginald Gardiner, *Madame Daruschka:* Olga Baclanova, *Julia:* Jean Howard, *Fritz:* Frank Tweddell, *Bertha:* Elsa Janssen, *Carl:* John Royce.

Cleopatra with Henry Wilcoxon and Claudette Colbert.

CLEOPATRA (1934) Par. Produced and directed by Cecil B. De Mille, Screenplay, Waldemar Young and Vincent Lawrence. Adaptation. Bartlett Cormack. Music, Rudolph Kopp. Photography, Victor Milner. U. S. film debut of Henry Wilcoxon. Other versions of *Cleopatra:* Helen Gardner Pictures, 1912; Fox, 1917; MGM, 1928 short; 20th Century-Fox, 1963. 101 minutes

Cleopatra: Claudette Colbert, *Julius Caesar:* Warren William, *Marc Antony:* Henry Wilcoxon, *Calpurnia:* Gertrude Michael, *Herod:* Joseph Schildkraut, *Octavian:* Ian Keith, *Enobarbus:* C. Aubrey Smith, *Cassius:* Ian Maclaren, *Brutus:* Arthur Hohl, *Pothinos:* Leonard Mudie, *Apollodorus:* Irving Pichel, *Octavia:* Claudia Dell, *Charmian:* Eleanor Phelps, *Drussus:* John Rutherford, *Iras:* Grace Durkin, *Achillas:* Robert Warwick, *Casca:* Edwin Maxwell, *Cicero:* Charles Morris, *The Soothsayer:* Harry Beresford, *Slave Girl:* Olga Celeste, *Leopard:* Ecki, *Glabrio:* Ferdinand Gottschalk, *Senator:* William Farnum, *Flora:* Florence Roberts, *Scribes:* Kenneth Gibson, Wedgwood Nowell, *Romans:* John Peter Richmond (John Carradine), Jayne Regan, Celia Rylan, Robert Manning, *Party Guest:* Lionel Belmore, *Egyptian Messenger:* Dick Alexander, *Romans Greeting Antony:* Jack Mulhall, Wilfred Lucas, *Onlooker at Procession:* Hal Price, *Murderer:* Edgar Dearing.

CLEOPATRA (1963) 20th. Producer, Walter Wanger. Director, Joseph L. Mankiewicz. Based upon histories by Plutarch, Suetonius, Appian, other ancient sources and *The Life and Times of Cleopatra* by C. M. Franzero. Screenplay, Joseph L. Mankiewicz, Ranald MacDougall, Sidney Buchman. Art Directors, John De Cuir, Jack Martin Smith, Hilyard Brown, Herman Blumenthal, Elven Webb, Maurice Pelling, Boris Juraga. Music composed and conducted by Alex North. Associate Music Conductor, Lionel Newman. Cinematographer, Leon Shamroy. Special Photographic Effects, L. B. Abbott, Emil Kosa, Jr. Editor, Dorothy Spencer. 243 minutes

Cleopatra: Elizabeth Taylor, *Mark Antony:* Richard Burton, *Julius Caesar:* Rex Harrison, *High Priestess:* Pamela Brown, *Flavius:* George Cole, *Sosigenes:* Hume Cronyn, *Apollodorus:* Cesare Danova, *Brutus:* Kenneth Haigh, *Agrippa:* Andrew Keir, *Rufio:* Martin Landau, *Octavio:* Roddy McDowall, *Germanicus:* Robert Stephens, *Eiras:* Francesca Annis, *Pothinus:* Gregoire Aslan, *Ramos:* Martin Benson,

Cleopatra with Rex Harrison and Elizabeth Taylor.

Theodotus: Herbert Berghof, *Phoebus:* John Cairney, *Lotus:* Jacqui Chan, *Charmian:* Isabelle Cooley, *Achilles:* John Doucette, *Canidius:* Andrew Faulds, *Metullus Cimber:* Michael Gwynne, *Cicero:* Michael Hordern, *Cassius:* John Hoyt, *Euphranor:* Marne Maitland, *Casca:* Carroll O'Connor, *Ptolemy:* Richard O'Sullivan, *Calpurnia:* Gwen Watford, *Decimus:* Douglas Wilmer, *Titus:* Finlay Currie, *Queen at Tarsus:* Marina Berti, *High Priest:* John Carlson, *Caesarion at 4:* Loris Loddy, *Caesarion at 7:* Del Russell, *Caesarion at 12:* Kenneth Nash, *Octavia:* Jean Marsh, *Marcellus:* Gin Mart, *Mithridates:* Furio Meniconi, *Vallus:* John Valva, *Archesilaus:* Laurence Naismith, *First Officer:* John Alderson, *Second Officer:* Peter Forster.

The Clock with Robert Walker and Judy Garland.

THE CLOCK (1945) MGM. Producer, Arthur Freed. Director, Vincente Minnelli. Based on a story by Paul and Pauline Gallico. Screenplay, Robert Nathan, Joseph Schrank. Score, George Bassman. Art Directors, Cedric Gibbons, William Ferrari. Cameraman, George Folsey. Special Effects, A. Arnold Gillespie. Editor, George White. 90 minutes

Alice Mayberry: Judy Garland, *Corporal Joe Allen:* Robert Walker, *Al Henry:* James Gleason, *The Drunk:* Keenan Wynn, *Bill:* Marshall Thompson, *Mrs. Al Henry:* Lucile Gleason, *Helen:* Ruth Brady, *Michael Henry:* Chester Clute, *Friendly Man:* Dick Elliott, *Official:* Robert E. Homans, *Blood Tester:* Arthur Space, *Cop:* Ray Teal, *Bartender:* Paul E. Burns, *Extra:* Major Sam Harris.

CLOSE ENCOUNTERS OF THE THIRD KIND (1977) Col. Produced by Michael and Julia Phillips. A Columbia/EMI Presentation. Directed and Written by Steven Spielberg. Music by John Williams. Photography, Vilmos Zsigmond. Special Photographic Effects, Douglas Trumbull. Additional American Scenes Photography Director, William A. Fraker. India Sequence Photography Director, Douglas Slocombe. Pro-

duction Designer, Joe Alves. Editor, Michael Kahn. Associate Producer/Unit Production Manager, Clark Paylow. Visual Effects Concepts, Spielberg. Additional Photography Directors, John Alonzo, Laszlo Kovacs and Frank W. Stanley. Technical Adviser, Dr. J. Allen Hynek. Set Decoration, Phil Abramson. Realization of "Extraterrestrial," Carlo Rambaldi. Art Director, Dan Lomino. Assistant Directors, Chuck Myers and Jim Bloom. Make-up Supervisor, Bob Westmoreland. Hairdresser, Edie Panda. Stunt Coordinator, Buddy Joe Hooker. Title Design, Dan Perri. 2nd Unit Director of Photography, Steve Poster. Director of Photography for Photographic Effects, Richard Yuricich. Matte Artist, Matthew Yuricich. Effects Unit Project Manager, Robert Shepherd. Special Visual Effects Coordinator, Larry Robinson. UFO Photography, Dave Stewart. Animation Supervision, Robert Swarthe. Animator, Harry Moreau. Film debuts of Cary Guffey, 4, and Dreyfuss' nephew Justin, 8. Dolby Sound. Filmed in Panavision and Metrocolor in Mobile, Alabama; Gillette, Wyoming; India; California; The Burbank Studios. Rated PG. 135 minutes

Roy Neary: Richard Dreyfuss, *Claude Lacombe:* Francois Truffaut, *Ronnie Neary:* Teri Garr, *Jillian Guiler:* Melinda Dillon, *Barry Guiler:* Cary Guffey, *David Laughlin:* Bob Balaban, *Project Leader:* J. Patrick McNamara, *Wild Bill:* Warren Kemmerling, *Farmer:* Roberts Blossom, *Jean Claude:* Philip Dodds, *Brad Neary:* Shawn Bishop, *Silvia Neary:* Adrienne Campbell, *Toby Neary:* Justin Dreyfuss, *Robert:* Lance Henriksen, *Team Leader:* Merrill Connally, *Maj. Benchley:* George DiCenzo.

Close Encounters of the Third Kind with Richard Dreyfuss.

The Cock-eyed World with Victor McLaglen and Edmund Lowe.

THE COCK-EYED WORLD (1929) Fox. Directed by Raoul Walsh. Story, Laurence Stallings, Maxwell Anderson, Wilson Mizner, Tom Barry. Dialogue, William K. Wells. Photography, Arthur Edeson. Assistant Director, Archie Buchanan. Technical Advisers, Captain Ross Adams and Lt. Commander Cheadle of U. S. S. *Henderson;* Colonel Rhea, Marine Commander at Mare Island; Captain Kearney, Mare Island Commandant. Filmed at Mare Island Navy Yard, Vallejo, Cal.: U. S. Marine Base at San Diego; aboard U. S. S. *Henderson* in San Francisco Bay; Fox Hollywood Studios and Fox-Movietone City, Westwood Hills, Cal. Songs by Con Conrad, Sidney Mitchell, and Archie Gottler: "So Long," "Elenita," and "So Dear to Me." Scenario, Raoul Walsh. Chief Sound Man, Edmund H. Hansen. Titles (silent version), Wilbur Morse Jr. Editor, Jack Dennis. Sequel to *What Price Glory* (Fox, 1921). 115 minutes

Top Sergeant Flagg: Victor McLaglen, *Sergeant Harry Quirt:* Edmund Lowe, *Mariana Elenita:* Lily Damita, *Olga:* Lelia Karnelly, *Olson:* El Brendel, *Connors:* Bobby Burns, *Fanny:* Jean Bary, *Brownie:* Joe Brown, *Buckley:* Stuart Erwin, *Sanovich:* Ivan Linow, *Innkeeper:* Soledad Jiminez, *O'Sullivan:* Albert "Curley" Dresden, *Jacobs:* Joe Rochay, *Katinka:* Jeanette Dagna, *Scout:* Warren Hymer, *Conductor:* Con Conrad, *Bit:* William K. Wells, *Brawlers:* "Sugar" Willie Keeler, Joe Herrick, Leo Houck, Charlie Sullivan. Navy Bands from Mare Island and San Diego Marine Base. Mexican Marimba Band of Agua Caliente. Jose Arias Spanish String Band Serenaders. Kamerko Balalaika Orchestra.

Come and Get It with Walter Brennan, Edward Arnold, Mady Christians and Frances Farmer.

COME AND GET IT (1936) UA. A Samuel Goldwyn Production. Produced by Merritt Hulburd. Directed by Howard Hawks and William Wyler. Logging scenes by Richard Rosson. From Edna Ferber's novel. Adapted by Jules Furthman and Jane Murfin. Editor, Edward Curtiss. Camera, Gregg Toland and Rudolph Mate. Film debuts of Robert Lowery and tennis player Frank Shields. Reissued as *Roaring Timber.* 99 minutes

Barney Glasgow: Edward Arnold, *Richard Glasgow:* Joel McCrea, *Lotta Morgan/Lotta Bostrom:* Frances Farmer, *Swan Bostrom:* Walter Brennan, *Evvie Glasgow:* Andrea Leeds, *Tony Schwerke:* Frank Shields, *Karie:* Mady Christians, *Emma Louise Glasgow:* Mary Nash, *Gunnar Gallagher:* Clem Bevans, *Sid Le Maire:* Edwin Maxwell, *Josie:* Cecil Cunningham, *Gubbins:* Harry Bradley, *Steward:* Rollo Lloyd, *Hewitt:* Charles Halton, *Chore Boy:* Phillip Cooper, *Goodnow:* Al K. Hall, *Young Man:* Robert Lowery.

COME BACK, LITTLE SHEBA (1952) Par. Producer, Hal B. Wallis. Director, Daniel Mann. Based on the play by William Inge. Screenplay, Ketti Frings. Art Directors, Hal Pereira, Henry Bumstead. Sets, Sam Comer, Russ Dowd. Sound, Walter Oberst, Don McKay. Musical Score, Franz Waxman. Cinematographer, James Wong Howe. Editor, Warren Low. Film debut of Shirley Booth. 99 minutes

Doc Delaney: Burt Lancaster, *Lola Delaney:* Shirley Booth, *Marie Loring:* Terry Moore, *Turk Fisher:* Richard Jaeckel, *Ed Anderson:* Philip Ober, *Elmo Huston:* Edwin Max, *Mrs. Coffman:* Lisa Golm, *Bruce:* Walter Kelley, *Postman:* Paul McVey, *Milkman:* Peter Leeds, *Mr. Cruthers:* Anthony Jochim, *Pearl Stinson:* Kitty McHugh, *Parent:* Ned Glass, **Girl:** Susan Odin, **Western Union Boy:** Henry Blair, *Henrietta:* Virginia Mullen, *Blonde:* Virginia Hall, *Judy Coffman:* Beverly Mook, *Interne:* William Haade.

Come Back, Little Sheba with Burt Lancaster and Shirley Booth.

COME SEPTEMBER (1961) Univ. Producer, Robert Arthur. Associate Producer, Henry Wilson. Director, Robert Mulligan. Technicolor. Screenplay, Stanley Shapiro, Maurice Richlin. Art Director, Henry Bumstead. Music Supervision, Joseph Gershenson. Music, Hans J. Salter. Songs: "Multiplication," words and music by Bobby Darin; "Come September," music by Bobby Darin. Cinematographer, William Daniels. Editor, Russell F. Schoengarth. Filmed in Italy. 112 minutes

Robert Talbot: Rock Hudson, *Lisa:* Gina Lollobrigida, *Sandy:* Sandra Dee, *Tony:* Bobby Darin, *Maurice:* Walter Slezak, *Margaret:* Brenda De Banzie, *Spencer:* Ronald Howard, *Anna:* Rosanna Rory, *Beagle:* Joel Grey, *Sparrow:* Ronnie Haran, *Larry:* Chris Seitz, *Julia:* Cindy Conroy, *Linda:* Joan Freeman, *Patricia:* Nancy Anderson, *Ron:* Michael Eden, *Carol:* Claudia Brack, *Marie, Maid:* Anna Maestri, *Teresa, Maid:* Stella Vitelleschi, *Melina, Maid:* Melina Vukotic, *Warren:* Charles Fawcett, *Douglas:* John Stacy, *Claire:* Katherine Guildford, *Lisa's Maid:* Edy Nogara, *Seamstress:* Liliana Celli, *Robert's Secretary:* Franco Tensi, *Elena:* Betty Foa, *Mother Superior:* Liliana Del Balzo, *Katherine:* Helen Stirling.

Come September with Rock Hudson and Walter Slezak.

Come to the Stable with Celeste Holm and Loretta Young.

COME TO THE STABLE (1949) 20th. Producer, Samuel G. Engel. Director, Henry Koster. Based on a story by Clare Boothe Luce. Screenplay, Oscar Millard, Sally Benson. Musical Director, Lionel Newman. Art Directors, Lyle Wheeler, Joseph C. Wright. Photography, Joseph La Shelle. Editor, William Reynolds. Songs: "My Bolero" by James Kennedy and Nat Simon; "Through a Long and Sleepless Night" by Mack Gordon and Alfred Newman. 94 minutes

Sister Margaret: Loretta Young, *Sister Scholastica:* Celeste Holm, *Robert Mason:* Hugh Marlowe, *Miss Potts:* Elsa Lanchester, *Luigi Rossi:* Thomas Gomez, *Kitty:* Dorothy Patrick, *Bishop:* Basil Ruysdael, *Anthony James:* Dooley Wilson, *Monsignor:* Regis Toomey, *Father Barraud:* Henri Letondal, *Jarman:* Walter Baldwin, *Heavy Man:* Mike Mazurki, *Mr. Thompson:* Tim Huntley, *Mrs. Thompson:* Virginia Keiley, *Mr. Newman:* Louis Jean Heydt, *Nuns:* Pati Behrs, Nan Boardman, Louise Colombet, Georgette Duane, Yvette Reynard, Loulette Sablon, *Mr. Matthews:* Ian MacDonald, *Mrs. Matthews:* Jean Prescott, *Willie:* Gordon Gebert, *Johnnie:* Gary Pagett, *Station Master:* Nolan Leary, *Sheldon:* Wallace Brown, *George:* Danny Jackson, *Whitey:* Edwin Max, *Policeman:* Russ Clark, *Policeman:* Robert Foulk, *Manicurist:* Marion Martin.

Coming Home with Jane Fonda and Jon Voight.

COMING HOME (1978) UA. Produced by Jerome Hellman. Directed by Hal Ashby. Story by Nancy Dowd, based on an idea by Jane Fonda and Bruce Gilbert. Screenplay, Waldo Salt and Robert C. Jones. In Color. Photography, Haskell Wexler. Associate Producer, Gilbert. Production Designer, Mike Haller. 1st Assistant Director, Chuck Myers. 2nd Assistant Director/Location Manager, Jim Bloom. Costume Designer, Ann Roth. Men's Costumers, Mike Hoffman and Silvio Scarano. Women's

Costumer, Jennifer Parson. Set Decorator, George Gaines. Hairstylists, Lola (Skip) McNally and Lynda Gurasich. Make-up, Bernadine Anderson and Gary Liddiard. Editor, Don Zimmerman. Assistant Editor, Elayne Bretherton. Technical Adviser, Mike Jacobs. Voight was originally cast as Hyde. Filmed in Hong Kong and Southern California. Rated R. 127 minutes

Sally Hyde: Jane Fonda, *Luke Martin:* Jon Voight, *Capt. Bob Hyde:* Bruce Dern, *Sgt. Dink Mobley:* Robert Ginty, *Viola Munson:* Penelope Milford, *Bill Munson:* Robert Carradine, *Virgil Hunt:* Willie Tyler, *Corney:* Cornelius H. Austin, Jr., *Nurse Degroot:* Tresa Hughes, *Corrine:* Olivia Cole, *Pee Wee:* Charles Cyphers, *Dr. Lincoln:* Bruce French, *Fleta Wilson:* Mary Jackson, *Jason:* Jim Pelt, *Pat:* Richard Lawson, *Harris:* Pat Corley, *Mrs. Harris:* Gwen Van Dam, *Johnson:* Rita Taggart, *Willie Malone:* Jim Klein, *Ed, Hell's Angel:* Ed Lang, *Benny:* Marc McClure, *Ronnie:* Mark Vahanian, *Marine Recruiter:* Gary Lee Davis, *Rusty:* Dennis Rucker, *FBI Agents:* George Roberts, Bob Ott, *Maj. Hustedt:* Gary Downey, *Lt. Roscoe:* Jan Michel Shultz, *Western Band in Kowloon:* Tokyo Ernie, *Connie:* Sally Frei, *Kathy Delise:* Kathleen Miller, *Capt. Earl Delise:* Beeson Carroll, *Martha Vickery:* Mary Gregory.

COMMAND DECISION (1948) MGM. Producer, Sidney Franklin. Director, Sam Wood. Based on the play by William Wister Haines. Screenplay, William R. Laidlaw, George Froeschel. Art Directors, Cedric Gibbons, Urie McCleary. Music Score, Miklos Rozsa. Photography, Harold Rosson. Editor, Harold F. Kress. 112 minutes

Brigadier General K.C. "Casey" Dennis: Clark Gable, *Major General Roland Goodlow Kane:* Walter Pidgeon, *Technical Sergeant Immanuel T. Evans:* Van Johnson, *Brigadier General Clifton I. Garnet:* Brian Donlevy, *Colonel Edward Rayton Martin:* John Hodiak, *Elmer Brockhurst:* Charles Bickford, *Congressman Arthur Malcolm:* Edward Arnold, *Captain George Washington Bellpepper Lee:* Marshall Thompson, *Major George Rockton:* Richard Quine, *Lieutenant Ansel Goldberg:* Cameron Mitchell, *Major Homer V. Prescott:* Clinton Sundberg, *Major Desmond Lansing:* Ray Collins, *Colonel Earnest Haley:* Warner Anderson, *Major Belding Davis:* John McIntire, *Captain Incius Malcolm Jenks:* Michael Steele, *Lieutenant Colonel Virgil Jackson:* Mack Williams, *Congressman Stone:* Moroni Olsen, *James Carwood:* John Ridgely, *Congressman Watson:* Edward Earle, *Major Garrett Davenport:* James Millican, *Parker, the Chauffeur:* William Leicester (William Lester), *Congressmen:* Henry Hall, Sam Flint, *R.A.F. Officer:* Marten Lamont, *Chairman:* Holmes Herbert, *Jeep Driver:* William "Bill" Phillips, *Sergeant:* Gregg Barton, *Sergeant Cahill:* Alvin Hammer, *Command Officer:* Don Haggerty, *Operations Officer:* Bruce Cowling, *Loudspeaker Voice:* Barry Nelson, *G.I. Waiter:* George Offerman, Jr., *Officer:* John James, *Command Sgt.:* Pete Martin.

Command Decision with Clark Gable and John Hodiak.

Commandos Strike at Dawn with Paul Muni and Robert Coote.

COMMANDOS STRIKE AT DAWN (1942) Col. Produced by Lester Cowan. Directed by John Farrow. Based on the *Cosmopolitan* magazine story by C. S. Forester. Screenplay, Irwin Shaw. Art Direction, Edward Jewell. Music Score, Louis Gruenberg. Music Director, M. W. Stoloff. Photography, William C. Mellor. Sound, John Goodrich. Editor, Anne Bauchens. Songs: "Commandos March" by Ann Ronell and Louis Gruenberg; "Out to Pick the Berries" by Ann Ronell. 98 minutes

Erik Toresen: Paul Muni, *Judith Bowen:* Anna Lee, *Mrs. Bergesen:* Lillian Gish, *Admiral Bowen:* Sir Cedric Hardwicke, *Robert Bowen:* Robert Coote, *Bergesen:* Ray Collins, *Hilma Arnesen:* Rosemary De Camp, *Gunner Korstad:* Richard Derr, *German Captain:* Alexander Knox, *Pastor:* Rod Cameron, *Lars Arnesen:* Louis Jean Heydt, *Anna Korstad:* Elisabeth Fraser, *Johan Garmo:* Erville Alderson, *Schoolteacher:* George Macready, *Mrs. Olav:* Barbara Everest, *German Colonel:* Arthur Margetson, *Solveig Toresen:* Ann Carter, *Mrs. Korstad:* Elsa Janssen, *Mr. Korstad:* Ferdinand Munier, *Alfred Korstad:* John Arthur Stockton, *Young Soldier:* Lloyd Bridges, *Otto:* Walter Sande, *Thirsty Soldier:* Philip Van Zandt.

Compulsion with Dean Stockwell, Bradford Dillman and Orson Welles.

COMPULSION (1959) 20th. Producer, Richard D. Zanuck. Director, Richard Fleischer. Screenplay by Richard Murphy. Based on the novel and play by Meyer Levin. Music by Lionel Newman. Wardrobe, Charles LeMaire. Assistant Director, Ben Kadish. Art Directors, Lyle R. Wheeler, Mark-Lee Kirk. Orchestration, Earle Hagen. Cinematographer, William C. Mellor. Editor, William Reynolds. A Darryl F. Zanuck Production in CinemaScope and High Fidelity Stereophonic Sound. Straus and Steiner are based on the real-life Leopold and Loeb, who murdered young Bobby Franks in Chicago in 1924 and were defended by Clarence Darrow. Dean Stockwell repeats his role from the 1957 play. 103 minutes

Jonathan Wilk: Orson Welles, *Ruth Evans:* Diane Varsi, *Judd Steiner:* Dean Stockwell, *Artie Straus:* Bradford Dillman, *D. A. Horn:* E. G. Marshall, *Sid Brooks:* Martin Milner, *Max Steiner:* Richard Anderson, *Lieutenant Johnson:* Robert Simon, *Tom Daly:* Edward Binns, *Mr. Straus:* Robert Burton, *Mrs. Straus:* Louise Lorimer, *Mr. Steiner:* Wilton Graff, *Padua:* Gavin MacLeod, *Benson:* Terry Becker, *Edgar Llewellyn:* Russ Bender, *Emma:* Gerry Lock, *Detective Davis:* Harry Carter, *Detective Brown:* Simon Scott, *Judge:* Voltaire Perkins, *Albert:* Peter Brocco, *Coroner:* Jack Lomas, *Jonas Kessler:* Wendell Holmes, *Waiter:* Henry Kulky, *Doctor:* Dayton Lummis.

Confessions of a Nazi Spy with Edward G. Robinson and Francis Lederer.

CONFESSIONS OF A NAZI SPY (1939) WB. Directed by Anatole Litvak. Screenplay, Milton Krims and John Wexley. Based on materials gathered by Leon G. Turrou, former FBI agent. Camera, Sol Polito. 102 minutes

Ed Renard: Edward G. Robinson, *Schneider:* Francis Lederer, *Schlager:* George Sanders, *Dr. Kassel:* Paul Lukas, *D. A. Kellogg:* Henry O'Neill, *Erika Wolff:* Lya Lys, *Mrs. Schneider:* Grace Stafford, *Scotland Yard Man:* James Stephenson, *Krogman:* Sig Rumann, *Phillips:* Fred Tozere, *Hilda:* Dorothy Tree, *Mrs. Kassel:* Celia Sibelius, *Renz:* Joe Sawyer, *Hintze:* Lionel Royce, *Wildebrandt:* Hans von Twardowski, *Helldorf:* Henry Victor, *Captain Richter:* Frederik Vogeding, *Klauber:* George Rosener, *Straubel:* Robert Davis (Rudolph Anders), *Westphal:* John Voigt, *Gruetzwald:* Willy Kaufman, *Captain Von Eichen:* William Vaughn (Von Brincken), *McDonald:* Jack Mower, *Harrison:* Robert Emmett Keane, *Mrs. MacLaughlin:* Eily Malyon, *Staunton:* Frank Mayo, *Postman:* Alec Craig, *Kassel's Nurse:* Jean Brook, *Kranz:* Lucien Prival, *A Man:* Niccolai Yoshkin, *Anna:* Bodil Rosing, *Young:* Charles Sherlock, *U.S. District Court Judge:* Frederick Burton, *Narrator:* John Deering, *American Legionnaire:* Ward Bond, *Goebbels:* Martin Kosleck.

A Connecticut Yankee with Will Rogers and Myrna Loy.

A CONNECTICUT YANKEE (1931) Fox. Directed by David Butler. Based on Mark Twain's story *A Connecticut Yankee at King Arthur's Court.* Adaptation and Dialogue, William Conselman. Photography, Ernest Palmer. Editor, Irene Morra. Sound, Joseph E. Aiken. Other versions of *A Connecticut Yankee at King Arthur's Court:* Fox, 1921; Paramount, 1949. 96 minutes

Hank (Sir Boss): Will Rogers, *Alisande:* Maureen O'Sullivan, *Queen Morgan Le Fay:* Myrna Loy, *Clarence:* Frank Albertson, *King Arthur:* William Farnum, *Merlin:* Mitchell Harris, *Sagramor:* Brandon Hurst.

Coogan's Bluff with Tisha Sterling and Clint Eastwood.

COOGAN'S BLUFF (1968) Univ. Produced and Directed by Don Siegel. Executive Producer, Richard E. Lyons. Associate Producer, Irving Leonard. Based on a story by Herman Miller. Screenplay by Herman Miller, Dean Reisner and Howard Rodman. Music by Lalo Schifrin. Photography, Bud Thackery. Art Direction, Alexander Golitzen and Robert C. MacKichan. Set Decorations, John McCarthy and John Austin. Editor, Sam E. Waxman. Sound by Waldon O. Watson, Lyle Cain and Jack Bolger. Costumes, Helen Colvig. Make-up by Bud Westmore. Hairstyles, Larry Germain. Assistant Director, Joe Cavalier. Dialogue Director, Scott Hale. Color by Technicolor. A Universal-Malpaso Production. Songs sung by Pigeon-Toed Orange Peel, "Pigeon-Toed Orange Peel" and "Everybody." Locations filmed in New York. Interiors shot at Biltmore East Studios. 94 minutes

Walt Coogan: Clint Eastwood, *Lt. McElroy:* Lee J. Cobb, *Julie Roth:* Susan Clark, *Linny Raven:* Tisha Sterling, *James Ringerman:* Don Stroud, *Ellen Ringerman:* Betty Field, *Sheriff McCrea:* Tom Tully, *Millie:* Melodie Johnson, *Sergeant Wallace:* James Edwards, *Running Bear:* Rudy Diaz, *Pushie:* David Doyle, *Taxi Driver:* Louis Zorich, *Big Red:* Meg Myles, *Mrs. Fowler:* Marjorie Bennett, *Joe, Young Hood:* Seymour Cassel, *Bellboy:* John Coe, *Omega:* Skip Battyn, *Wonderful Digby:* Albert Popwell, *Madison Avenue Man:* Conrad Bain, *Ferguson:* James Gavin, *Desk Sergeant:* Albert Henderson, *Room Clerk:* James McCallion, *Apartment Manager:* Syl Lamont, *Prison Hospital Guards:* Jess Osuna, Doug Reid, *Good Eyes:* Jerry Summers, *Mrs. Amador:* Antonia Rey, *Go-Go Dancer:* Marya Henriques, *Prison Hospital Doctor:* Jim Dukas, *Deputy:* Robert Osterloh, *Whippy:* Allen Pinson, *Zig Zag:* Larry Duran, *Hooker:* Eve Brent, *Mother:* Constance Davis, *Negro:* James McEachin, *Gay Boys:* George Fargo, Diki Lerner, *Plainclothesman:* Clark Warren, *Waiter:* Cliff Pellow, *Woman:* Kathleen O'Malley, *Detectives:* Ted Jacques, Al Ruban, *Hip Type:* James Oliver, *Man in Discotheque:* James Joyce, *Hippie Boy:* David Brandon, *Psychedelic Paint Girl:* Diana Rose, *Hippie Twins:* Colleen and Morreen Thornton, *Stuntmen:* Clyde Howdy, Dave Ekins, *Dr. Scott:* Scott (Roy) Hale.

COOL HAND LUKE (1967) WB. Produced by Gordon Carroll. Directed by Stuart Rosenberg. Panavision and Technicolor. A Jalem Production. Based on the novel by Donn Pearce. Screenplay, Donn Pearce and Frank R. Pierson. Music, Lalo Schifrin. Assistant Director, Hank Moonjean. Associate Producer, Carter DeHaven, Jr. Photography, Conrad Hall. Editor, Sam O'Steen. Filmed near Stockton, California. 126 minutes

Luke: Paul Newman, *Dragline:* George Kennedy, *Society Red:* J. D. Cannon, *Koko:* Lou Antonio, *Loudmouth Steve:* Robert Drivas, *The Captain:* Strother Martin, *Arletta:* Jo Van Fleet, *Carr:* Clifton James, *Boss Godfrey:* Morgan Woodward, *Boss Paul:* Luke Askew, *Rabbitt:* Marc Cavell, *Tattoo:* Warren Finnerty, *Babalugats:* Dennis Hopper, *Boss Kean:* John McLiam, *Gambler:* Wayne Rogers, *Boss Higgins:* Charles Tyner, *Alibi:* Ralph Waite, *Dog Boy:* Anthony Zerbe, *Dynamite:* Buck Kartalian, *The Girl:* Joy Harmon, *Sleepy:* Jim Gammon, *Fixer:* Joe Don Baker, *Sailor:* Donn Pearce, *Stupid Blondie:* Norman Goodwins, *Chief:* Chuck Hicks, *John, Sr.* John Pearce, *John, Jr.* Eddie Rosson, *Patrolman:* Rush Williams, *Wickerman:* James Jeter, *Jabo:* Robert Luster, *Negro Boys:* James Bradley, Jr., Cyril "Chips" Robinson, *Sheriff:* Rance Howard, *Tramp:* Dean Stanton, *Blind Dick:* Richard Davalos, *Boss Shorty:* Robert Donner.

Cool Hand Luke with Paul Newman and Robert Drivas.

The Corn Is Green with Bette Davis.

THE CORN IS GREEN (1945) WB. Producer, Jack Chertok. Director, Irving Rapper. Screenplay, Casey Robinson and Frank Cavett. Based on the play by Emlyn Williams. Score, Max Steiner. Art Director, Carl Jules Weyl. Musical Director, Leo F. Forbstein. Cameraman,

54

Sol Polito. Editor, Frederick Richards. Film debut of John Dall. 114 minutes. Later the musical play *Miss Moffat* with Davis.

Miss Moffat: Bette Davis, *Morgan Evans:* John Dall, *Bessie Watty:* Joan Lorring, *The Squire:* Nigel Bruce, *Mr. Jones:* Rhys Williams, *Mrs. Watty:* Rosalind Ivan, *Miss Ronberry:* Mildred Dunnock, *Sarah Pugh:* Gwyneth Hughes, *Idwal Morris:* Billy Roy, *Old Tom:* Thomas Louden, *William Davis:* Arthur Shields, *John Owen:* Leslie Vincent, *Rhys Norman:* Robert Regent, *Will Hughes:* Tony Ellis, *Glyn Thomas:* Elliott Dare, *Dai Evans:* Robert Cherry, *Gwilym Jones:* Gene Ross, *Trap Driver:* George Mathews, *Squire's Groom:* Jock Watt, *Tudor:* Jack Owen, *Welshman:* John Dehner, *Lewellyn Powell:* Brandon Hurst, *Wylodine:* Rhoda Williams, *Old Woman Reading:* Adeline De Walt Reynolds, *Militant Corps Woman:* Margaret Hoffman, *Mrs. Watty's Friend:* Sarah Edwards, *Station Master:* Leonard Mudie.

THE COUNT OF MONTE CRISTO (1934) UA. A Reliance Pictures Production. Supervision, Edward Small. Director, Rowland V. Lee. Based on the novel by Alexandre Dumas. Screenplay, Philip Dunne, Dan Totheroh, Rowland V. Lee. Cameraman, Peverell Marley. Editor, Grant Whytock. Music Director, Alfred Newman. Song, "The World Is Mine" by E. Y. Harburg and Johnny Green. 113 minutes

Edmond Dantes: Robert Donat, *Mercedes de Rosas:* Elissa Landi, *Raymond De Villefort, Jr.:* Louis Calhern, *Fernand de Mondego:* Sidney Blackmer, *Danglars:* Raymond Walburn, *Abbe Faria:* O. P. Heggie, *Captain Leclere:* William Farnum, *Madame de Rosas:* Georgia Caine, *Morrel:* Walter Walker, *De Villefort, Sr.:* Lawrence Grant, *Jacopo:* Luis Alberni, *Valentine De Villefort:* Irene Hervey, *Albert de Mondego:* Douglas Walton, *Clothilde:* Juliette Compton, *Fouquet:* Clarence Wilson, *Haydee:* Eleanor Phelps, *Louis XVIII:* Ferdinand Munier, *Judge:* Holmes Herbert, *Napoleon:* Paul Irving, *Captain Vampa:* Mitchell Lewis, *Ali:* Clarence Muse, *Prison Governor:* Lionel Belmore, *Detective:* Wilfred Lucas, *Cockeye:* Tom Ricketts, *Bertrand:* Edward Keane, *Ali Pasha:* Sydney Jarvis, *Blacas:* Desmond Roberts, *Pellerin:* John Marsden, *Batistino:* Alphonse Martell, *Manouse:* Russell Powell, *Albert, age 8:* Wallace Albright, *Beauchamp:* Leon Waycoff (Ames), *Angry Man:* Paul Fix, *Fencing Master:* Fred Cavens.

The Count of Monte Cristo with Luis Alberni, Robert Donat and Clarence Muse.

THE COUNTRY DOCTOR (1936) 20th. Produced by Darryl F. Zanuck. Directed by Henry King. Author, Charles E. Blake. Screenplay, Sonya Levien. Cameramen, John Seitz, Daniel B. Clark. Editor, Barbara McLean. 110 minutes

Quintuplets: The Dionne Quintuplets, *Dr. Roy Luke:* Jean Hersholt, *Nurse Andrews:* Dorothy Peterson, *Mary:* June Lang, *Ogden:* Slim Summerville, *Tony:* Michael Whalen, *Mac Kenzie:* Robert Barrat,

Mike: J. Anthony Hughes, *Asa Wyatt:* John M. Qualen, *Greasy:* George Chandler, *Sir Basil:* Montagu Love, *Dr. Paul Luke:* Frank Reicher, *Dr. Wilson:* George Meeker, *Nurse:* Jane Darwell, *Governor General:* David Torrence, *Peg-leg Walter:* William Conlon, *Gawker:* William Benedict, *Joe:* Joseph Sawyer, *Lumberjack:* Harry Cording, *Editor:* Edward McWade, *Mrs. Ogden:* Helen Jerome Eddy, *Young Logger:* Kane Richmond, *Jerry:* Garry Owen, *Mack:* Paul McVey, *Minister:* Harry C. Bradley, *Women:* Mary Carr, Cecil Weston, *Proprietor:* Wilfred Lucas, *Piano Player:* Dillon Ober, *Mrs. Wyatt:* Aileen Carlyle, *Bishop:* Richard Carlyle, *Secretary:* Margaret Fielding, *Toastmaster:* Claude King, *City Editor:* John Dilson, *Grandmother:* Florence Roberts, *Boy:* Delmar Watson.

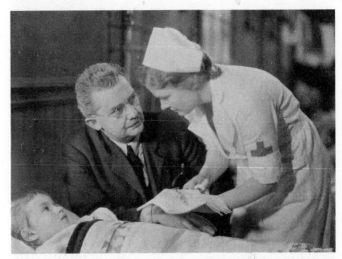

The Country Doctor with Delmar Watson, Jean Hersholt and Dorothy Peterson.

THE COUNTRY GIRL (1954) Par. Producers, William Perlberg, George Seaton. Director-Screenplay, George Seaton. Based on the play by Clifford Odets. Art Director, Hal Pereira. Cameraman, John F. Warren. Editor, Ellsworth Hoagland. Musical numbers staged by Robert Alton. Songs by Ira Gershwin and Harold Arlen: "Live and Learn," "The Pitchman," "The Search Is Through." 104 minutes

Frank Elgin: Bing Crosby, *Georgie Elgin:* Grace Kelly, *Bernie Dodd:* William Holden, *Phil Cook:* Anthony Ross, *Larry:* Gene Reynolds, *Singer-Actress:* Jacqueline Fontaine, *Ed:* Eddie Ryder, *Paul Unger:* Robert Kent, *Henry Johnson:* John W. Reynolds, *First Woman:* Ida Moore, *Bartender:* Frank Scannell, *Second Woman:* Ruth Rickaby, *Actor:* Hal K. Dawson, *Actor:* Howard Joslin, *Photographer:* Charles Tannen, *Jimmie:* Jonathan Provost, *Bellboy:* Bob Alden, *Ralph (Dresser):* Chester Jones.

The Country Girl with Bing Crosby and William Holden.

Cover Girl with Leslie Brooks (second left), Rita Hayworth and Gene Kelly.

COVER GIRL (1944) Col. Directed by Charles Vidor. Color by Technicolor. Story, Erwin Gelsey. Screenplay, Virginia Van Upp. Adaptation, Marion Parsonnet and Paul Gangelin. Music Director, M. W. Stoloff. Orchestrations, Carmen Dragon. Editor, Viola Lawrence. Songs by Jerome Kern and Ira Gershwin: "Long Ago and Far Away," "Cover Girl," "Sure Thing," "The Show Must Go On," "Who's Complaining?", "Put Me to the Test," "Make Way for Tomorrow." Gene Kelly dances the Alter Ego ballet. Film debut of Shelley Winters, 20, although released after several succeeding films. 107 minutes

Rusty Parker/Maribelle Hicks: Rita Hayworth, *Danny McGuire:* Gene Kelly, *Noel Wheaton:* Lee Bowman, *Genius:* Phil Silvers, *Jinx:* Jinx Falkenburg, *Maurine Martin:* Leslie Brooks, *Cornelia (Stonewall) Jackson:* Eve Arden, *John Coudair:* Otto Kruger, *Coudair as a young man:* Jess Barker, *Anita:* Anita Colby, *Chem:* Curt Bois, *Joe:* Ed Brophy, *Tony Pastor:* Thurston Hall, *Harry (Drunk):* Jack Norton, *Pop: (Doorman):* Robert Homans, *Mac (Cop):* Eddie Dunn, *Autograph Hound:* Ilene (Betty) Brewer, *Pianist:* Johnny Mitchell, *"Who's Complaining?" Dancer:* Virginia Wilson (Virginia de Luce), *Girl:* Shelley Winters, *Cover Girls:* AMERICAN MAGAZINE: Jean Colleran, AMERICAN HOME: Francine Counihan, COLLIER'S MAGAZINE: Helen Mueller, CORONET: Cecilia Meagher, COSMOPOLITAN: Betty Jane Hess, FARM JOURNAL: Dusty Anderson, GLAMOUR: Eileen McClory, HARPER'S BAZAAR: Cornelia B. Von Hessert, LIBERTY: Karen X. Gaylord, LOOK: Cheryl Archer, MADEMOISELLE: Peggy Lloyd, MC CALLS: Betty Jane Graham, REDBOOK: Martha Outlaw, VOGUE: Susann Shaw, WOMEN'S HOME COMPANION: Rose May Robson, *Chorus Girl:* Barbara Pepper, *Elevator Boy:* Stanley Clements, *Receptionist:* Constance Worth, *Coudair's Secretary:* Frances Morris, *Naval Officer:* William Sloan, *Florist Boy:* Billy Benedict.

Crime Without Passion with Claude Rains and Margo.

CRIME WITHOUT PASSION (1934) Par. Directors, Ben Hecht and Charles MacArthur. From *Caballero of The Law* by Ben Hecht and Charles MacArthur, who also adapted it. Special Effects, Slavko Vorkapich. Photography and Codirector, Lee Garmes. Filmed in Paramount's Astoria, Long Island, Studios. Film debuts of Esther Dale and Margo. 80 minutes

Lee Gentry: Claude Rains, *Carmen Brown:* Margo, *Katy Costello:* Whitney Bourne, *Eddie White:* Stanley Ridges, *Buster Malloy:* Paula Trueman, *O'Brien:* Leslie Adams, *Della:* Greta Granstedt, *Miss Keeley:* Esther Dale, *Lieutenant Norton:* Charles Kennedy, *Judge:* Fuller Mellis, *Reporters:* Charles MacArthur, Ben Hecht, *Extras in Hotel Lobby:* Helen Hayes, Fanny Brice.

CROSSFIRE (1947) RKO. Producer, Adrian Scott. Director, Edward Dmytryk. From a novel by Richard Brooks (*The Brick Foxhole*). Screenplay, John Paxton. Art Directors, Albert S. D'Agostino, Alfred Herman. Musical Director, C. Bakaleinikoff. Cameraman, J. Roy Hunt. Editor, Harry Gerstad. 86 minutes

Captain Finlay: Robert Young, *Sgt. Peter Keeley:* Robert Mitchum, *Montgomery:* Robert Ryan, *Ginny Tremaine:* Gloria Grahame, *The Man:* Paul Kelly, *Joseph Samuels:* Sam Levene, *Mary Mitchell:* Jacqueline White, *Floyd Bowers:* Steve Brodie, *Arthur Mitchell:* George Cooper, *Bill Williams:* Richard Benedict, *Detective:* Richard Powers (Tom Keene), *Leroy:* William Phipps, *Harry:* Lex Barker, *Miss Lewis:* Marlo Dwyer, *Tenant:* Harry Harvey, *Deputy:* Carl Faulkner, *M. P.:* Jay Norris, *M. P.:* Robert Bray, *Police Sergeant:* Philip Morris, *Major:* Kenneth McDonald, *M. P.:* George Turner, *Soldier:* Allen Ray, *M. P.:* Don Cadell, *Waiter:* Bill Nind, *Police Surgeon:* George Meader.

Crossfire with Robert Ryan and Sam Levene.

THE CRUSADES (1935) Par. Produced and directed by Cecil B. De Mille. Story and Screenplay, Harold Lamb, Waldemar Young, and Dudley Nichols. Camera, Victor Milner. "Song of the Crusades" by Leo Robin, Richard Whiting, and Rudolph Kopp. Technical Effects, Gordon Jennings. 123 minutes

Berengaria, Princess of Navarre: Loretta Young, *King Richard:* Henry Wilcoxon, *Saladin, Sultan of Islam:* Ian Keith, *The Hermit:* C. Aubrey Smith, *Princess Alice:* Katherine De Mille, *Conrad, Marquis of Montferrat:* Joseph Schildkraut, *Blondel:* Alan Hale, *King Philip II:* C. Henry Gordon, *Sancho, King of Navarre:* George Barbier, *The Blacksmith:* Montagu Love, *Robert, Earl of Leicester:* Lumsden Hare, *Duke Hugo of Burgundy:* William Farnum, *Duke Frederick:* Hobart Bosworth, *Karakush:* Pedro de Cordoba, *Prince John:* Ramsay Hill, *Monk:* Mischa Auer, *Alan:* Maurice Murphy, *Duke Leopold of Austria:* Albert Conti, *Sverre, the Norse King:* Sven-Hugo Borg, *Prince Michael of Russia:* Paul Satoff, *King William of Sicily:* Fred W. Malatesta,

Count Nicholas of Hungary: Hans Von Twardowski, *Duenna:* Anna Demetrio, *Soldier:* Perry Askam, *Ship's Master:* Edwin Maxwell, *Archbishop:* Winter Hall, *Alan's Mother:* Emma Dunn, *Amir/Slave in Saladin's Garden:* Jason Robards, *Nun:* Georgia Caine, *Arab Slave Dealer:* J. Carrol Naish, *Christian Girl:* Ann Sheridan, *Buyer:* Josef Swickard, *Christian Girl:* Jean Fenwick, *Priest:* Alphonz Ethier, *Knight:* Jack Rutherford, *Stranger (Messenger):* Colin Tapley, *Amir:* Harry Cording, *Amir:* Stanley Andrews, *Sentry:* Addison Richards, *Amir:* Maurice Black, *Amir:* William B. Davidson, *Greybeard/Templar:* Guy Usher, *Templar:* Boyd Irwin, Sr., *Templar:* Gordon Griffith, *Captain of Hospitalers:* Sam Flint, *King/Wise Man:* John Carradine, *Whipping Master:* Dewey Robinson.

The Crusades with Loretta Young and Ian Keith.

Cyrano De Bergerac with Mala Powers and José Ferrer.

CYRANO DE BERGERAC (1950) UA. Produced by Stanley Kramer. Directed by Michael Gordon. Filmed with the Garutso Lens. From the Brian Hooker translation of the play by Edmond Rostand. Screenplay, Carl Foreman. Music composed and directed by Dimitri Tiomkin. Production Design, Rudolph Sternad. Photography, Franz Planer. Editor, Harry Gerstad. Fencing Master, Fred Cavens. 112 minutes

Cyrano: José Ferrer, *Roxane Robin:* Mala Powers, *Baron Christian de Neuvillette:* William Prince, *Captain Le Bret:* Morris Carnovsky, *Count Antoine de Guiche:* Ralph Clanton, *Ragueneau:* Lloyd Corrigan, *Duenna:* Virginia Farmer, *Cardinal:* Edgar Barrier, *Orange Girl:* Elena Verdugo, *Viscount Valvert:* Albert Cavens, *Montfleury:* Arthur Blake, *The Meddler:* Don Beddoe, *Bellerose:* Percy Helton, *Sister Marthe:* Virginia Christine, *Doctor:* Gil Warren, *Man with Gazette:* Philip Van Zandt, *Guardsman:* Eric Sinclair, *Marquis:* Richard Avonde, *Cadets:* Paul Dubov, John Crawford, Jerry Paris, Robin Hughes, *Monk:* Francis Pierlot, *Lackey (Assassin):* John Harmon.

Daddy Long Legs with Una Merkel, Janet Gaynor, John Arledge, Sheila Bromley, Warner Baxter and Kathlyn Williams.

DADDY LONG LEGS (1931) Fox. Directed by Alfred Santell. From the play and novel by Jean Webster. Scenario, Sonya Levien. Dialogue, Sonya Levien and S. N. Behrman. Photography, Lucien Andriot. Editor, Ralph Dietrich. Other versions: First National, 1919; 20th Century-Fox, 1955. 73 minutes

Judy Abbott: Janet Gaynor, *Jervis Pendleton:* Warner Baxter, *Sally McBride:* Una Merkel, *Jimmy McBride:* John Arledge, *Riggs:* Claude Gillingwater, Sr., *Mrs. Pendleton:* Kathlyn Williams, *Miss Pritchard:* Louise Closser Hale, *Mrs. Lippett:* Elizabeth Patterson, *Freddie Perkins:* Kendall McComas, *Gloria Pendleton:* Sheila Mannors (Bromley), *Wykoff:* Edwin Maxwell, *Mrs. Semple:* Effie Ellsler, *Katie:* Martha Lee Sparks, *Billy:* Billy Barty.

DANGEROUS (1935) WB. Produced by Harry Joe Brown. Directed by Alfred E. Green. Original Story and Screenplay, Laird Doyle. Photography, Ernest Haller. Assistant Director, Russ Saunders. Art Director, Hugo Reticker. Editor, Thomas Richards. Unit Manager, Lee Huginin. Remade by WB as *Singapore Woman* (WB, 1941). 78 minutes

Joyce Heath: Bette Davis, *Don Bellows:* Franchot Tone, *Gail Armitage:* Margaret Lindsay, *Mrs. Williams:* Alison Skipworth, *Gordon Heath:* John Eldredge, *Teddy:* Richard (Dick) Foran, *George Sheffield:* Pierre Watkin, *Roger Farnsworth:* Walter Walker, *Charles Melton:* George Irving, *Reed Walsh:* William B. Davidson, *Elmont:* Douglas Wood, *Pitt Hanly:* Richard Carle, *Roger's Chauffeur, Williams:* Milton Kibbee, *Waiter:* George Andre Beranger, *Bartender:* Frank O'Connor, *Cato:* Miki Morita, *Waiter:* Larry McGrath, *Foreman:* Eddie Shubert, *Secretary:* Florence Fair, *Gail's Maid, Betty:* Pauline Garon, *Male Lead:* (Bill) Gordon Elliott, *Beulah:* Libby Taylor, *Reporter:* Craig Reynolds, *Nurse:* Mary Treen, *Doctor:* Edward Keane, *Passerby (Extra):* Eddie Foster, *Teddy's Chauffeur:* Billy Wayne.

Dangerous with Alison Skipworth and Bette Davis.

Dark Victory with Bette Davis, Dorothy Peterson and George Brent.

DARK VICTORY (1939) WB. Associate Producer, David Lewis. Director, Edmund Goulding. From the play by George Brewer, Jr. and Bertram Bloch. Screenplay, Casey Robinson. Cameraman, Ernest Haller. Editor, William Holmes. Song by Elsie Janis and Edmund Goulding: "Oh Give Me Time for Tenderness." Remade as *Stolen Hours* (UA, 1963). 106 minutes

Judith Traherne: Bette Davis, *Dr. Frederick Steele:* George Brent, *Michael O'Leary:* Humphrey Bogart, *Ann King:* Geraldine Fitzgerald, *Alec Hamin:* Ronald Reagan, *Dr. Parsons:* Henry Travers, *Carrie Spottswood:* Cora Witherspoon, *Martha:* Virginia Brissac, *Miss Wainwright:* Dorothy Peterson, *Colonel Mantle:* Charles Richman, *Dr. Carter:* Herbert Rawlinson, *Dr. Driscoll:* Leonard Mudie, *Miss Dodd:* Fay Helm, *Lucy:* Lottie Williams, *Agatha:* Diane Bernard, *Veterinarian:* Jack Mower, *First Specialist:* William Worthington, *Second Specialist:* Alexander Leftwich, *Secretary:* Ila Rhodes, *Doctor:* Stuart Holmes, *Anxious Little Man:* Frank Darien, *First Man:* John Harron, *Second Man:* John Ridgely, *Bartender:* Sidney Bracy, *Girl in Box:* Rosella Towne, *Trainer:* Edgar Edwards.

A Date With Judy with Carmen Miranda, Xavier Cugat, Jane Powell and Elizabeth Taylor.

A DATE WITH JUDY (1948) MGM. Producer, Joe Pasternak. Director, Richard Thorpe. Color by Technicolor. Screenplay, Dorothy Cooper, Dorothy Kingsley. Musical Director, Georgie Stoll. Art

Directors, Cedric Gibbons, Paul Groesse. Photography, Robert Surtees. Editor, Harold F. Kress. Based on the characters created by Aleen Leslie. Songs: "Judaline" by Don Raye and Gene DePaul; "It's a Most Unusual Day" by Harold Adamson and Jimmy McHugh; "I'm Strictly on the Corny Side" by Stella Unger and Alec Templeton; "I've Got a Date With Judy" and "I'm Gonna Meet My Mary" by Bill Katz and Calvin Jackson. 113 minutes

Melvin R. Foster: Wallace Beery, *Judy Foster:* Jane Powell, *Carol Foster:* Elizabeth Taylor, *Rosita Conchellas:* Carmen Miranda, *Cugat:* Xavier Cugat, *Stephen Andrews:* Robert Stack, *Mrs. Foster:* Selena Royle, *Ogden "Oogie" Pringle:* Scotty Beckett, *Lucien T. Pringle:* Leon Ames, *Gramps:* George Cleveland, *Pop Scully:* Lloyd Corrigan, *Jameson:* Clinton Sundberg, *Mitzie:* Jean McLaren, *Randolph Foster:* Jerry Hunter, *Jo-Jo Hoffenpepper:* Buddy Howard, *Nightingale:* Lillian Yarbo, *Miss Clarke:* Eula Guy, *Prof. Green:* Francis Pierlot, *Olga:* Rena Lenart, *Little Girl in Drugstore:* Sheila Stein, *Girl:* Alice Kelley, *Elderly Woman:* Polly Bailey, *Miss Sampson:* Fern Eggen, *Headwaiter:* Paul Bradley.

DAVID AND LISA (1963) Continental. Producer, Paul M. Heller. Director, Frank Perry. Screenplay, Eleanor Perry. Based on book by Theodore Isaac Rubin. Music, Mark Lawrence. Costumes, Anna Hill Johnstone. Associate Producer, Vision Associates. Art Director, Paul M. Heller. Music arranged and conducted by Norman Paris. Cinematographer, Leonard Hirschfield. Editor, Irving Oshman. Film debut of Karen Gorney. 94 minutes

David: Keir Dullea, *Lisa:* Janet Margolin, *Dr. Swinford:* Howard da Silva, *Mrs. Clemens:* Neva Patterson, *John:* Clifton James, *Mr. Clemens:* Richard McMurray, *Maureen:* Nancy Nutter, *Simon:* Mathew Anden, *Kate:* Coni Hudak, *Carlos:* Jaime Sanchez, *Sandra:* Janet Lee Parker, *Josette:* Karen Gorney.

David and Lisa with Janet Margolin and Keir Dullea.

DAVID COPPERFIELD (1935) MGM. Produced by David O. Selznick. Directed by George Cukor. Based on the novel by Charles Dickens. Adaptation, Hugh Walpole. Screenplay, Howard Estabrook. Special Effects, Slavko Vorkapich. Art Director, Cedric Gibbons. Costumes, Dolly Tree. Musical Numbers, Herbert Stothart. Assistant Director, Joe Newman. Photography, Oliver T. Marsh. Editor, Robert J. Kern. Sound, Douglas Shearer. American film debut of Freddie Bartholomew. Other version: Associated Exhibitors, 1923. 133 minutes

Mr. Micawber: W. C. Fields, *Dan Peggotty:* Lionel Barrymore, *Dora:* Maureen O'Sullivan, *Agnes:* Madge Evans, *Aunt Betsey:* Edna May Oliver, *Mr. Wickfield:* Lewis Stone, *David, the man:* Frank Lawton, *David, the child:* Freddie Bartholomew, *Mrs. Copperfield:* Elizabeth Allan, *Uriah Heep:* Roland Young, *Mr. Murdstone:* Basil Rathbone, *Clickett:* Elsa Lanchester, *Mrs. Micawber:* Jean Cadell, *Nurse Peggotty:* Jessie Ralph, *Mr. Dick:* Lennox Pawle,

Jane Murdstone: Violet Kemble-Cooper, *Mrs. Gummidge:* Una O'Connor, *Ham:* John Buckler, *Steerforth:* Hugh Williams, *Limmiter:* Ivan Simpson, *Barkis:* Herbert Mundin, *Little Em'ly, the child:* Fay Chaldecott, *Little Em'ly, the woman:* Florine McKinney, *Agnes, the child:* Marilyn Knowlden, *Dr. Chillip:* Harry Beresford, *Mary Ann:* Mabel Colcord, *The Vicar:* Hugh Walpole, *Janet:* Renee Gadd, *Donkey Man:* Arthur Treacher.

David Copperfield with Frank Lawton, W.C. Fields and Roland Young.

A Day at the Races with Maureen O'Sullivan, Allan Jones, Groucho, Chico and Harpo Marx.

A DAY AT THE RACES (1937) MGM. Associate Producer, Max Siegel. Directed by Sam Wood. Story, Robert Pirosh and George Seaton. Screenplay, Robert Pirosh, George Seaton, George Oppenheimer. Art Director, Cedric Gibbons. Music Director, Franz Waxman. Dances, Dave Gould. Choral arrangements, Leo Arnaud. Photography, Joseph Ruttenberg. Editor, Frank E. Hull. Songs by Bronislau Kaper, Walter Jurmann, and Gus Kahn: "A Message From the Man in the Moon," "On Blue Venetian Waters," "Tomorrow Is Another Day," "All God's Chillun Got Rhythm." 111 minutes

Dr. Hugo Z. Hackenbush: Groucho Marx, *Tony:* Chico Marx, *Stuffy:* Harpo Marx, *Gil Stewart:* Allan Jones, *Judy Standish:* Maureen O'Sullivan, *Emily Upjohn:* Margaret Dumont, *Whitmore:* Leonard Ceeley, *Morgan:* Douglass Dumbrille, *Flo Marlowe:* Esther Muir, *Dr. Leopold X. Steinberg:* Sig Rumann, *Sheriff:* Robert Middlemass, *Solo Dancer:* Vivien Fay, *Dr. Wilmerding:* Charles Trowbridge, *Doctors:* Frank Dawson, Max Lucke, *Morgan's Jockey:* Frankie Darro, *Detective:* Pat Flaherty, *Messenger:* Si Jenks, *Race Judge:* Hooper Atchley, *Judges:* John Hyams, Wilbur Mack, *Nurse:* Mary MacLaren, *Doctor:* Edward LeSaint, *Drunk:* Jack Norton, *Extra:* Carole Landis. And Ivie Anderson and the Crinoline Choir.

Days of Heaven with Linda Manz.

DAYS OF HEAVEN (1978) Par. Produced by Bert and Harold Schneider. Directed and Written by Terrence Malick. Music Composed and Conducted by Ennio Morricone. Costumes Designed by Patricia Norris. Photography, Nestor Almendros. Additional Photography, Haskell Wexler. Executive Producer/2nd Unit Director, Jacob Brackman. Art Director, Jack Fisk. Editor, Billy Weber. Additional Music, Leo Kottke. Color Consultant, Bob McMillian. 1st Assistant Director, Skip Cosper. Technical Adviser, Clenton Owensby. Title Design, Dan Perri. Additional Editors, Caroline Ferriol, Marion Segal and Susan Martin. Special Sound Effects, James Cox. Special Effects, John Thomas and Mel Merrells. Set Decorator, Robert Gould. 2nd Assistant Directors, Rob Lockwood and Martin Walters. 2nd Unit Photography, Paul Ryan. Special Environmental Sound Recordings, Syntonic Research, Inc. Sound Effects, Neiman-Tillar Associates. Assistant Editors, Roberta Friedman and George Trirogoff. Hairstylist, Bertine Taylor. Make-up, Jamie Brown. Men's Wardrobe, Gerad Green. Time Lapse Photography, Ken Middleham. Harmonica, Rick Smith. Stunt Flying, Erin Talbott and Joe Watts. An O. P. Production. Title Sequence Photographs by Lewis Hine, Henry Hamilton Bennett, Frances Benjamin Johnston, Chansonetta Emmons, William Notman and Edie Baskin. Music: "Enderlin," written and performed by Leo Kottke, "Swamp Dance," written and performed by Doug Kershaw, "Carnival of the Animals—The Aquarium" by Camille Saint-Saens, performed by the Vienna Philharmonic Orchestra. Metrocolor. Lenses and Panaflex Camera by Panavision. 70 mm. Sound by Dolby System. Rerecording by Glen Glenn Sound. Filmed near Calgary, Alberta, Canada. Film debuts of Manz and Shepard. Rated PG. 95 minutes

Bill: Richard Gere, *Abby:* Brooke Adams, *The Farmer:* Sam Shepard, *Linda, Narrator:* Linda Manz, *Farm Foreman:* Robert Wilke, *Linda's Friend:* Jackie Shultis, *Mill Foreman:* Stuart Margolin, *Harvest Hand:* Tim Scott, *Dancer:* Gene Bell, *Fiddler:* Doug Kershaw, *Vaudeville Leader:* Richard Libertini, *Vaudeville Wrestler:* Frenchie Lemond, *Vaudeville Dancer:* Sahbra Markus, *Accountant:* Bob Wilson, *Headmistress:* Muriel Jolliffe, *Preacher:* John Wilkinson, *Farm Worker:* King Cole.

DAYS OF WINE AND ROSES (1962) WB. Producer, Martin Manulis. Director, Blake Edwards. Screenplay, J. P. Miller. Art Director, Joseph Wright. Music, Henry Mancini. "Days of Wine and Roses": lyric, Johnny Mercer, music, Henry Mancini. Cinematographer, Phil Lathrop. Editor, Patrick McCormack. Martin Manulis-Salem Production. 117 minutes

Joe Clay: Jack Lemmon, *Kirsten Arnesen:* Lee Remick, *Ellis Arnesen:* Charles Bickford, *Jim Hungerford:* Jack Klugman, *Radford Leland:* Alan Hewitt, *Debbie Clay:* Debbie Megowan, *Mrs. Nolan:* Katherine Squire, *Dottie:* Maxine Stuart, *Trayner:* Jack Albertson, *Proprietor, Liquor Store:* Ken Lynch, *Ballefoy:* Tom Palmer, *Gladys:* Gail Bonney, *Tenants:* Mary Benoit, Ella Ethridge, Rita Kenaston, Pat O'Malley, Robert "Buddy" Shaw, Al Paige, *Boors:* Doc Stortt, Russ Bennett, Dick Crockett, *Abe:* Roger Barrett, *Waiter:* Jack Railey, *Belly Dancer:* Lisa Guiraut, *Loud Man:* Carl Arnold, *Bettor:* Tom Rosqui, *Guests:* Barbara Hines, Charlene Holt.

Days of Wine and Roses with Lee Remick, Charles Bickford and Debbie Megowan.

DEAD END (1937) UA. Produced by Samuel Goldwyn. Associate Producer, Merritt Hulburd. Directed by William Wyler. Based on the play by Sidney Kingsley. Screenplay, Lillian Hellman. Cinematography, Gregg Toland. Art Director, Richard Day. Musical Director, Alfred Newman. Editor, Daniel Mandell. Costumes, Omar Kiam. Assistant Director, Eddie Bernoudy. Set Director, Julie Heron. Sound, Frank Maher. 93 minutes

Drina: Sylvia Sidney, *Dave:* Joel McCrea, *Baby Face Martin:* Humphrey Bogart, *Kay:* Wendy Barrie, *Francie:* Claire Trevor, *Hunk:* Allen Jenkins, *Mrs. Martin:* Marjorie Main, *Tommy:* Billy Halop, *Dippy:* Huntz Hall, *Angel:* Bobby Jordan, *Spit:* Leo Gorcey, *T.B.:* Gabriel Dell, *Milty:* Bernard Punsley, *Philip Griswold:* Charles Peck, *Mr. Griswold:* Minor Watson, *Mulligan:* James Burke, *Doorman:* Ward Bond, *Mrs. Connell:* Elisabeth Risdon, *Janitress, Mrs. Fenner:* Esther Dale, *Pascagli:* George Humbert, *Governess:* Marcelle Corday, *Whitey:* Charles Halton, *Cop:* Robert E. Homans, *Drunk:* Bill Dagwell, *Milty's Brother:* Jerry Cooper, *Milty's Sister:* Kath Ann Lujan, *Old Lady:* Gertrude Valerie, *Old Man:* Tom Ricketts, *Women with Poodle:* Charlotte Treadway, Maude Lambert, *Kay's Chauffeur:* Bud Geary, *Well-dressed Couple:* Frank Shields, Lucille Browne, *Tough Boys:* Micky Martin, Wesley Girard, *Woman with Coarse Voice:* Esther Howard, *Man with Weak Voice:* Gilbert Clayton, *Griswold Chauffeur:* Earl Askam, *Nurse:* Mona Monet, *Interne:* Don Barry.

Dead End with Billy Halop, Leo Gorcey and Joel McCrea.

DEAR RUTH (1947) Par. Producer, Paul Jones. Director, William D. Russell. Based on the play by Norman Krasna. Screenplay, Arthur Sheekman. Art Directors, Hans Dreier, Earl Hedrick. Musical Score, Robert Emmett Dolan. Cameraman, Ernest Laszlo. Editor, Archie Marshek. Song by Johnny Mercer and Robert Emmett Dolan: "Fine Things." Sequels: *Dear Wife* (1949), *Dear Brat* (1951) 95 minutes

Ruth Wilkins: Joan Caulfield, *Lieut. William Seacroft:* William Holden, *Miriam Wilkins:* Mona Freeman, *Judge Harry Wilkins:* Edward Arnold, *Albert Kummer:* Billy De Wolfe, *Mrs. Wilkins:* Mary Philips, *Martha Seacroft:* Virginia Welles, *Sergeant Chuck Vincent:* Kenny O'Morrison, *Dora, the Maid:* Marietta Canty, *Delivery Man:* Irving Bacon, *Harold Klobbermeyer:* Jimmie Dundee, *Cab Driver:* Jay Gerard, *Woman:* Isabel Randolph, *Headwaiter:* Erno Verebes.

Dear Ruth with William Holden, Joan Caulfield and Edward Arnold.

DEATH OF A SALESMAN (1951) Col. Producer, Stanley Kramer. Director, Laslo Benedek. From the play by Arthur Miller. Screenplay, Stanley Roberts. Musical Director, Morris Stoloff. Art Director, Cary Odell. Photography, Franz F. Planer. Editor, William Lyon. 115 minutes

Willy Loman: Fredric March, *Linda Loman:* Mildred Dunnock, *Biff:* Kevin McCarthy, *Happy:* Cameron Mitchell, *Charley:* Howard Smith, *Ben:* Royal Beal, *Bernard:* Don Keefer, *Stanley:* Jesse White, *Miss Francis:* Claire Carleton, *Howard Wagner:* David Alpert, *Miss Forsythe:* Elizabeth Fraser, *Letta:* Patricia Walker, *Mother:* Gail Bonney, *Boy:* Roger Broaddus, *Girl:* Beverly Aadland, *Girl:* Wanda Perry, *Girl:* Christa Gail Walker, *Mother:* Jeanne Bates, *Subway Guard:* Paul Bryar.

Death of a Salesman with Fredric March.

Death Wish with Charles Bronson and Stuart Margolin.

DEATH WISH (1974) Par. Produced by Hal Landers, Bobby Roberts and Michael Winner. Directed by Michael Winner. From the novel by Brian Garfield. Screenplay, Wendell Mayes. Music composed, orchestrated and performed by Herbie Hancock. Photography, Arthur J. Ornitz. Editor, Bernard Gribble. Production Manager, Stanley Neufeld. Assistant Director, Charles Okun. Production Designer, Robert Gundlach. Sound Recordist, James Sabat. Make-up, Phillip Rhodes. Costume Designer, Joseph G. Aulisi. Assistant Directors, Larry Albucher and Ralph Singleton. Filmed in New York City; Tucson, Arizona; and Turtle Bay on Oahu, Hawaii, in Technicolor. Film debut of Kathleen Tolan. Rated R. 93 minutes

Paul Kersey: Charles Bronson, *Joanna Kersey:* Hope Lange, *Inspector Frank Ochoa:* Vincent Gardenia, *Jack Toby:* Steven Keats, *Sam Kreutzer:* William Redfield, *Aimes Jainchill:* Stuart Margolin, *Police Commissioner:* Stephen Elliott, *Carol Kersey Toby:* Kathleen Tolan, *Hank:* Jack Wallace, *District Attorney:* Fred Scollay, *Ives:* Chris Gampel, *Joe Charles:* Robert Kya-Hill, *Lt. Briggs:* Ed Grover, *Freak 1:* Jeff Goldberg, *Freak 2:* Christopher Logan, *Spraycan:* Gregory Rozakis, *Desk Sergeant:* Floyd Levine, *Alma Lee Brown:* Helen Martin, *Andrew McCabe:* Hank Garrett, *Patrolman Reilly:* Christopher Guest.

The Deep with Nick Nolte, Robert Shaw and Jacqueline Bisset.

THE DEEP (1977) Col. A Columbia/EMI Presentation of a Casablanca FilmWorks Production. Produced by Peter Guber. Directed by Peter Yates. Based on the novel by Peter Benchley. Screenplay, Peter Benchley and Tracy Keenan Wynn. Music, John Barry. Production Design, Tony Masters. Photography, Christopher Challis. Supervising Editor, Robert L.

Wolfe. Editor, David Berlatsky. Assistant Editors, Mike Klein and Marilyn Madderom. Associate Producer/Production Manager, George Justin. 2nd Unit Underwater Cinematographers and Directors, Al Giddings and Stan Waterman. Costume Designer, Ron Talsky. Production Executive, Peter A. Lake. Special Consultant, Teddy Tucker. Art Director, Jack Maxsted. Set Decorator, Vernon Dixon. Underwater Art Director, Terry Ackland-Snow. Assistant Director, Derek Cracknell. 2nd Assistant Directors, Richard Jenkins and Raymond Becket. Marine Biologists, Kym Murphy and John Hart. Marine Environments, Carlos Machado. Underwater 3rd Cameraman/Lighting, Chuck Nicklin. Sound, Robin Gregory. Special Effects by Ira Anderson, Sr., Ira Anderson, Jr., Walter Stones, Gene Cornelius and Don Puck. Stunt Coordinators, Max Kleven, Howard Curtis, Bob Minor, Jim Nickerson and Richard Washington. Wardrobe, Tom Bronson. Hairdresser, Pat McDermott. Make-up, Robert Dawn and Ed Henriques. Assistant to the Producer, Bill Rudin. Assistant to Director, Mike Nathanson. Assistant Associate Producer, Sam Gellis. Special Assistants, Lynda Guber and Missy Alpern. Titles Designed by Anthony Goldschmidt. Dive Master, Dennis Breese. Filmed in Panavision and Metrocolor in the British Virgin Islands, Bermuda and Australia's Great Barrier Reef. "Calypso Disco" sung by Bennett; theme from *The Deep* sung by Donna Summer. Rated PG. 123 minutes

Romer Treece: Robert Shaw, *Gail Berke:* Jacqueline Bisset, *David Sanders:* Nick Nolte, *Adam Coffin:* Eli Wallach, *Cloche (Henri Bondurant):* Louis Gossett, *Kevin:* Robert Tessier, *Ronald:* Earl Maynard, *Slake:* Dick Anthony Williams, *Wiley:* Bob Minor, *The Harbor Master:* Teddy Tucker, *Johnson:* Lee McClain. Cut were Peter Benchley as The First Mate, Peter Wallach (Eli's son, in his film debut) as The Young Coffin, Colin Shaw (Robert's son, 14, in his film debut) as Treece as a boy.

The Deer Hunter with John Cazale, Chuck Aspegren, Robert De Niro, John Savage, Rutanya Alda, Christopher Walken and Meryl Streep.

THE DEER HUNTER (1978) Univ. An EMI Films Presentation. Produced by Barry Spikings, Michael Deeley, Michael Cimino and John Peverall. Directed by Michael Cimino. Story by Cimino, Deric Washburn, Louis Garfinkle and Quinn K. Redeker. Screenplay, Washburn. Photography, Vilmos Zsigmond. Production Consultant, Joann Carelli. Associate Producers, Marion Rosenberg and Carelli. Executive in Charge of Production, Elliot Schick. Art Directors, Ron Hobbs and Kim Swados. Editor, Peter Zinner. Music, Stanley Myers. Main Title Theme performed by John Williams. Speical Make-up in Thailand, Dick Smith and Daniel Striepeke. Hairstylist, Mary Keats. Assistant Editors, Flo Williamson, Thomas K. Avildsen and Penelope Shaw. Assistant Director, Charles Okun. Second Assistant Director, Mike Grillo. Military Technical Adviser, Richard Dioguardi. Costume Supervisor, Eric Seelig. Men's Costumer, Laurie Riley. Women's Costumer, Sandy Berke. Make-up, Del Acevedo and Ed Butterworth. Special Effects, Fred Cramer. Assistant Special Effects, Gary Elmendorf. Assistant Special Effects in Thailand, Jay King. Sound Mixer, Darrin Knight. Stunt Coordinator in U.S.A., Carey Loftin. Stunt Coordinator in Thailand, Buddy Van Horn. Vietnamese Adviser, Eleanor Dawson. Title Design, Wayne Fitzgerald. Post Production Sound, MGM Studios. Filmed in Technicolor, Panavision and Dolby Stereo in Pennsylvania; West Virginia; Thailand; Cleveland and Mingo Junction, Ohio; Mount Baker, Bellingham, Washington. Film debut of steelworker Aspegren of Gary, Indiana. Last film of Cazale, who died March 12, 1978, at 42. Rated R. 183 minutes

Michael: Robert De Niro, *Stan:* John Cazale, *Steven:* John Savage, *Nick:* Christopher Walken, *Linda:* Meryl Streep, *John Welch:* George Dzundza, *Axel:* Chuck Aspegren, *Steven's Mother:* Shirley Stoler, *Angela:* Rutanya Alda, *Julien:* Pierre Segui, *Axel's Girl:* Mady Kaplan, *Bridesmaid:* Amy Wright, *Stan's Girl:* Mary Ann Haenel, *Linda's Father:* Richard Kuss, *Bandleader:* Joe Grifasi, *Wedding Man:* Christopher Colombi, Jr., *Sad-Looking Girl:* Victoria Karnafel, *Cold Old Man:* Jack Scardino, *Bingo Caller:* Joe Strnad, *Helen:* Helen Tomko, *Sergeant:* Paul D'Amato, *Cab Driver:* Dennis Watlington, *Redhead:* Charlene Darrow, *Girl Checker:* Jane Colette Disko, *Stock Boy:* Michael Wollet, *World War Veterans:* Robert Beard and Joe Dzizmba, *Priest:* Father Stephen Kopestonsky, *Barman:* Frank Devore, *Doctor:* Tom Becker, *Nurse:* Lynn Kongkham, *Sergeant:* Parris Hicks, *NVA Officer:* Vitoon Winwitoon, *Chinese Boss:* Charan Nusvanon, *Woman in Village:* Phip Manee, *VC Guards:* Ding Santos, Krieng Chaiyapuk, Ot Palapoo and Chok Chai Mahasoke, *Stuntmen:* Max Balchowsky, Jerry Brutsche, Howard Curtis, Ted Duncan, Bob Harris, Troy Melton, Jack Verbois and Chuck Waters.

THE DEFIANT ONES (1958) UA. Producer-Director, Stanley Kramer. Screenplay by Nathan E. Douglas and Harold Jacob Smith. Music by Ernest Gold. Assistant Director, Paul Helmick. Song "Long Gone" by W. C. Handy and Chris Smith. A Lomitas-Curtleigh Production. Filmed in Georgia. Last film of Carl "Alfalfa" Switzer, one of Our Gang. 97 minutes

John "Joker" Jackson: Tony Curtis, *Noah Cullen:* Sidney Poitier, *Sheriff Max Muller:* Theodore Bikel, *Captain Frank Gibbons:* Charles McGraw, *Big Sam:* Lon Chaney, Jr., *Solly:* King Donovan, *Mac:* Claude Akins, *Editor:* Lawrence Dobkin, *Lou Gans:* Whit Bissell, *Angus:* Carl Switzer, *The Kid:* Kevin Coughlin, *The Woman:* Cara Williams, *Joe:* Boyd (Red) Morgan, *Wilson, Posseman:* Robert Hoy, *State Trooper:* Don Brodie.

The Defiant Ones with Tony Curtis and Sidney Poitier.

DELIVERANCE (1972) WB. Produced and Directed by John Boorman. An Elmer Enterprises Film. Panavision and Technicolor. Screenplay by James Dickey, based on his novel. Photography, Vilmos Zsigmond. 2nd Unit Photography, Bill Butler. Editor, Tom Priestley. Art Director, Fred Harpman. Special Effects, Marcel Vercouters. Creative Associate, Rospo Pallenberg. Sound, Jim Atkinson, Walter Goss and Doug Turner. Wardrobe, Bucky Rous. Make-up, Michael Hancock, Hairstyles, Donoene McKay. Assistant Directors, Al Jennings and Miles Middough. "Duelling Banjos" arranged and played by Eric Weissberg, with Steve Mandel. Filmed along the Chattooga River, Georgia. Rated R. 109 minutes

Ed Gentry: Jon Voight, *Lewis Medlock:* Burt Reynolds, *Bobby Trippe:* Ned Beatty, *Drew Ballinger:* Ronny Cox, *Mountain Man:* Billy McKinney, *Toothless Man:* Herbert "Cowboy" Coward, *Sheriff Bullard:* James Dickey, *Old Man:* Ed Ramey, *Lonny:* Billy Redden, *Griners:* Seamon Glass and Randall Deal, *Deputies:* Lewis Crone and Ken Keener, *Ambulance Driver:* Johnny Popwell, *Doctor:* John Fowler, *Nurse:* Kathy Rickman, *Mrs. Biddiford:* Louise Coldren, *Taxi Driver:* Pete Ware, *Boy at Gas Station:* Hoyt J. Pollard, *Martha Gentry:* Belinha Beatty, *Ed's Boy:* Charlie Boorman.

Deliverance with Jon Voight and Burt Reynolds.

DESTINATION TOKYO (1943) WB. Producer, Jerry Wald. Director, Delmer Daves. Author, Steve Fisher. Screenplay, Delmer Daves, Albert Maltz. Musical Score, Franz Waxman. Art Director, Leo K. Kuter. Musical Director, Leo F. Forbstein. Cameraman, Bert Glennon. Special Effects, Lawrence Butler, Willard Van Enger. Editor, Chris Nyby. Narrated by Lou Marcelle. 135 minutes

Captain Cassidy: Cary Grant, *Wolf:* John Garfield, *Cookie:* Alan Hale, *Reserve:* John Ridgely, *Tin Can:* Dane Clark, *Executive:* Warner Anderson, *Pills:* William Prince, *Tommy:* Bob Hutton, *Mike:* Tom Tully, *Mrs. Cassidy:* Faye Emerson, *Dakota:* Peter Whitney, *English Officer:* Warren Douglas, *Sparks:* John Forsythe, *Sound Man:* John Alvin, *Torpedo Officer:* Bill Kennedy, *Commanding Officer:* John Whitney, *Quartermaster:* William Challee, *Yo Yo:* Whitner Bissell, *Chief of Boat:* George Lloyd, *Toscanini:* Maurice Murphy, *Admiral:* Pierre Watkin, *Admiral's Aide:* Stephen Richards (Mark Stevens), HORNET's *Admiral:* Cliff Clark, *Debby Cassidy:* Deborah Daves, *Michael Cassidy:* Michael Daves, *Admiral's Aide:* Jack Mower, *Tin Can's Girl:* Mary Landa, *Man on Phone:* Carlyle Blackwell, *Captain:* Kirby Grant, *C.P.O.:* Lane Chandler, *Wolf's Girl:* Joy Barlowe, *Market St. "Commando":* Bill Hunter, *Crewmen:* George Robotham, Dan Borzage, William Hudson, Charles Sullivan, Duke York, Harry Bartell, Jay Ward, Paul Langton.

Destination Tokyo with Cary Grant, William Prince, Peter Whitney, Maurice Murphy, Bob Hutton, John Garfield, Alan Hale, Warner Anderson, John Ridgely and Bill Kennedy.

Destry Rides Again with Marlene Dietrich and Lillian Yarbo.

DESTRY RIDES AGAIN (1939) Univ. Producer, Joseph Pasternak. Director, George Marshall. Based on the novel by Max Brand. Screenplay, Felix Jackson, Gertrude Purcell, Henry Myers. Cameraman, Hal Mohr. Editor, Milton Carruth. Songs by Frank Loesser and Frederick Hollander: "Little Joe, The Wrangler," "You've Got That Look That Leaves Me Weak" and "(See What) The Boys In the Back Room (Will Have)." Assistant Director, Vernon Keays. Other Universal versions: *Destry Rides Again* (1932); *Frenchie* (1950); *Destry* (1954). 94 minutes

Tom Destry: James Stewart, *Frenchy:* Marlene Dietrich, *Boris Callahan:* Mischa Auer, *"Wash" Dimsdale:* Charles Winninger, *Kent:* Brian Donlevy, *Gyp Watson:* Allen Jenkins, *Bugs Watson:* Warren Hymer, *Janice Tyndall:* Irene Hervey, *Lily Belle Callahan:* Una Merkel, *Lem Claggett:* Tom Fadden, *Judge Slade:* Samuel S. Hinds, *Clara:* Lillian Yarbo, *Rockwell:* Edmund MacDonald, *Bartender, Loupgerou:* Billy Gilbert, *Sophie Claggett:* Virginia Brissac, *Claggett Girl:* Ann Todd, *Eli Whitney Claggett:* Dickie Jones, *Jack Tyndall:* Jack Carson, *Dancer:* Carmen D'Antonio, *Sheriff Keogh:* Joe King, *Rowdy:* Harry Cording, *Cowboy:* Dick Alexander, *Mrs. DeWitt:* Minerva Urecal, *Doctor:* Bob McKenzie, *Pianist:* Billy Bletcher, *Turner, Express Agent:* Lloyd Ingraham, *Small Boy:* Bill Cody, Jr., *Jugglers:* Loren Brown, Harold DeGarro, *Cowboy:* Bill Steele Gettinger, *Stage Rider:* Harry Tenbrook, *Stage Driver:* Bud McClure, *Asst. Bartender:* Alex Voloshin, *Indian:* Chief John Big Tree.

Detective Story with Luis Van Rooten, Kirk Douglas and William Bendix.

DETECTIVE STORY (1951) Par. Producer-Director, William Wyler. Based on the play by Sidney Kingsley. Screenplay, Philip Yordan, Robert Wyler. Art Directors, Hal Pereira, Earl Hedrick. Photography, Lee Garmes. Editor, Robert Swink. Film debuts of Lee Grant and Joseph Wiseman. 103 minutes

Jim McLeod: Kirk Douglas, *Mary McLeod:* Eleanor Parker, *Lou Brody:* William Bendix, *Susan:* Cathy O'Donnell, *Karl Schneider:* George Macready, *Lieutenant Monahan:* Horace McMahon, *Miss Hatch:* Gladys George, *First Burglar:* Joseph Wiseman, *Shoplifter:* Lee Grant, *Tami Giacoppetti:* Gerald Mohr, *Gallagher:* Frank Faylen, *Arthur:* Craig Hill, *Lewis Abbott:* Michael Strong, *Joe Feinson:* Luis Van Rooten, *Dakis:* Bert Freed, *Sims:* Warner Anderson, *O'Brien:* Grandon Rhodes, *Callahan:* William (Bill) Phillips, *Barnes:* Russell Evens, *Detective Ed:* Edmund F. Cobb, *Willie (Janitor):* Burt Mustin, *Mr. Pritchett:* James Maloney, *Gus Keogh:* Howard Joslin, *Coleman:* Mike Mahoney, *Mrs. Farragut:* Catharine Doucet, *Frenchwoman:* Ann Codee, *Finney:* Ralph Montgomery, *Desk Sgt.:* Pat Flaherty, *Mulvey:* Bob Scott, *Gallants:* Harper Goff, *Taxi Driver:* Donald Kerr.

Dial "M" for Murder with John Williams, Grace Kelly and Ray Milland.

DIAL M FOR MURDER (1954) WB. Producer and Director, Alfred Hitchcock. Assistant Director, Mel Dellar. Screenplay by Frederick Knott as adapted from his play. Music by Dimitri Tiomkin. Art Director, Edward Carrere. Cinematographer, Robert Burks. Editor, Rudi Fehr. Color by WarnerColor, 3-Dimension. 105 minutes

Tony: Ray Milland, *Margot:* Grace Kelly, *Mark:* Robert Cummings, *Inspector Hubbard:* John Williams, *Captain Lesgate:* Anthony Dawson, *The Storyteller:* Leo Britt, *Pearson:* Patrick Allen, *Williams:* George Leigh, *First Detective:* George Alderson, *Police Sergeant:* Robin Hughes, *Man in Photo:* Alfred Hitchcock, *Detectives:* Guy Doleman, Thayer Roberts, Sanders Clark, *Police Photographer:* Robert Dobson, *Man in Phone Booth:* Major Sam Harris, *Bobby:* Jack Cunningham.

DIAMONDS ARE FOREVER (1971) UA. An Eon-Danjaq Production. Produced by Albert R. Broccoli and Harry Saltzman. Directed by Guy Hamilton. Panavision and Technicolor. Based on Ian Fleming's novel. Screenplay, Richard Maibaum and Tom Mankiewicz. Production Designed by Ken Adam. Music by John Barry. Lyrics, Don Black. Title song sung by Shirley Bassey. Associate Producer, Stanley Sopel. Photography, Ted Moore. Editors, Bert Bates and John W. Holmes. Main Title, Maurice Binder. Wardrobe Supervisors, Elsa Fennell and Ted Tetrick. St. John's Costumes by Donfeld. Sound, John Mitchell and Al Overton. Location Managers, Bernard Hanson and Eddie Saeta. Stunt Arrangers, Bob Simmons and Paul Baxley. 2nd Unit Cameraman, Harold Wellman. Special Photographic Effects, Albert Whitlock and Wally Veevers. Special

Effects, Leslie Hillman and Whitney McMahon. Set Decorators, Peter Lamont and John Austin. Art Direction, Jack Maxsted and Bill Kenney. Assistant Directors, Derek Cracknell and Jerome M. Siegel. James Bond Theme by Monty Norman. Film debuts of Jay Sarno, president of Circus Circus and a founder of Caesar's Palace; and Putter (Patrick) Smith, bass player with Thelonius Monk's group. Last film of Bruce Cabot, 67, who died May 3, 1972. Eighth James Bond film, first made in the United States. Locations: Los Angeles International Airport, Los Angeles, Palm Springs and an oil rig four miles off Oceanside, California; Reno and Las Vegas, Nevada; Frankfurt, Germany; Nice, France; Amsterdam, Holland; Southampton, Dover and London, England; interiors made at Pinewood Studios, London. Rated GP. 119 minutes

James Bond: Sean Connery, *Tiffany Case:* Jill St. John, *Ernst Stavros Blofeld:* Charles Gray, *Plenty O'Toole:* Lana Wood, *Willard Whyte:* Jimmy Dean, *Saxby:* Bruce Cabot, *Wint:* Bruce Glover, *Kidd:* Putter Smith, *Felix Leiter:* Norman Burton, *Dr. Metz:* Joseph Furst, *M:* Bernard Lee, *Q:* Desmond Llewelyn, *Moneypenny:* Lois Maxwell, *Sir Donald Monger:* Laurence Naismith, *Maxwell:* Burt Metcalf, *Shady Tree:* Leonard Barr, *Mrs. Whistler:* Margaret Lacey, *Peter Franks:* Joe Robinson, *Bambi:* Donna Garratt, *Thumper:* Trina Parks, *Klaus Hergersheimer:* Edward Bishop, *Barker:* Larry Blake, *Dentist:* Henry Rowland, *Doorman, Trop:* Nicky Blair, *Metz's Aides:* Constantin De Goguel, Janos Kurucz, *Tom:* Shane Rimmer, *Immigration Officer:* Clifford Earl, *Doctor:* David De Keyser, *Agent:* Karl Held, *Airline Representative:* John Abineri, *Blofeld's Double:* Max Latimer, *Moon Crater Controller:* Bill Hutchinson, *Moon Crater Guard:* Frank Mann, *Slumber:* David Bauer, *Sir Donald's Secretary:* Mark Elwes, *Man in Fez:* Frank Olegario, *Vandenburg Launch Director:* David Healy, *Vandenburg Aide:* Gordon Ruttan, *Houseboy:* Brinsley Forde, *Attendants:* Marc Lawrence, Sid Haig, Michael Valente, *Maxie:* Ed Call, *Helicopter Pilot:* Raymond Baker, *Boy:* Gary Dubin, *Welfare Worker:* Catherine Deeney, *Sideshow Barker:* Jay Sarno, *Marie:* Denise Perrier, *Guard:* Tom Steele, *SPECTRE Agent (steel finger trap):* George Cooper, *Crane Operator:* Dick Crockett.

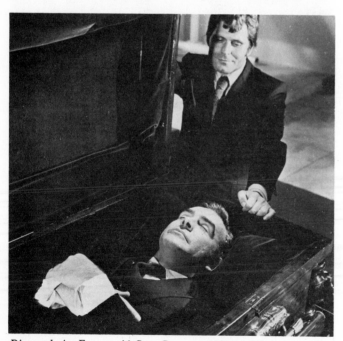

Diamonds Are Forever with Sean Connery and Bruce Glover.

THE DIARY OF ANNE FRANK (1959) 20th. Producer, George Stevens. Associate Producer, George Stevens, Jr. Director, George Stevens. CinemaScope. Authors, Frances Goodrich, Albert Hackett (from *Anne Frank: The Diary of a Young Girl*). Screenplay, Frances Goodrich, Albert Hackett. Art Directors, Lyle R. Wheeler, George W. Davis. Music, Alfred Newman. Orchestration, Edward B. Powell. Cinematographer, William C. Mellor. Special Photographic Effects, L. B. Abbott. Editors, Robert Swink, David Brotherton, William Mace. Film debut of Millie Perkins. 170 minutes

Anne Frank: Millie Perkins, *Otto Frank:* Joseph Schildkraut, *Mrs. Van Daan:* Shelley Winters, *Mr. Dussell:* Ed Wynn, *Peter Van Daan:* Richard Beymer, *Mrs. Frank:* Gusti Huber, *Mr. Van Daan:* Lou Jacobi, *Margot Frank:* Diane Baker, *Kraler:* Douglas Spencer, *Miep:* Dody Heath, *Sneak Thief:* Charles Wagenheim, *Night Watchman:* Frank Tweddell, *SS Men:* Delmar Erickson, Robert Boon, *Dutch Girl:* Gretchen Goertz, *Workman in Shop:* William Kirschner.

The Diary of Anne Frank with Millie Perkins and Joseph Schildkraut.

DINNER AT EIGHT (1933) MGM. Directed by George Cukor. Based on the 1932 play by George S. Kaufman and Edna Ferber. Adaptation, Frances Marion and Herman J. Mankiewicz. Photography, William Daniels. Editor, Ben Lewis. 113 minutes

Carlotta Vance: Marie Dressler, *Larry Renault:* John Barrymore, *Dan Packard:* Wallace Beery, *Kitty Packard:* Jean Harlow, *Oliver Jordan:* Lionel Barrymore, *Max Kane:* Lee Tracy, *Dr. Wayne Talbot:* Edmund Lowe, *Millicent Jordan:* Billie Burke, *Paula Jordan:* Madge Evans, *Jo Stengel:* Jean Hersholt, *Lucy Talbot:* Karen Morley, *Hattie Loomis:* Louise Closser Hale, *Ernest De Graff:* Phillips Holmes, *Mrs. Wendel, the Cook:* May Robson, *Ed Loomis:* Grant Mitchell, *Miss Alden:* Phoebe Foster, *Miss Copeland:* Elizabeth Patterson, *Tina, Kitty's Maid:* Hilda Vaughn, *Fosdick:* Harry Beresford, *Mr. Fitch, Hotel Manager:* Edwin Maxwell, *Mr. Hatfield, Assistant Manager:* John Davidson, *Eddie:* Edward Woods, *Gustave, the Butler:* George Baxter, *The Waiter:* Herman Bing, *Dora, Maid:* Anna Duncan.

Dinner at Eight with Madge Evans and John Barrymore.

The Dirty Dozen with John Cassavetes, Lee Marvin and Richard Jaeckel.

THE DIRTY DOZEN (1967) MGM. Produced by Kenneth Hyman. Directed by Robert Aldrich. 70mm and MetroColor. An M. K. H. Production. Associate Producer, Raymond Anzarut. Based on the novel by E. M. Nathanson. Screenplay, Nunnally Johnson and Lukas Heller. Music by Frank DeVol. Assistant Director, Bart Batt. Production Manager, Julian Mackintosh. Art Director, W. E. Hutchinson. Photography, Edward Scaife. Editor, Michael Luciano. Special Effects, Cliff Richardson. Sound, Franklin Milton and Claude Hitchcock. Songs: "The Bramble Bush" by Frank DeVol and Mack David; "Einsam" by Frank DeVol and Sibylle Siegfried. Filmed in England. 149 minutes

Major Reisman: Lee Marvin, *General Worden:* Ernest Borgnine, *Joseph Wladislaw:* Charles Bronson, *Robert Jefferson:* Jim Brown, *Victor Franko:* John Cassavetes, *Sergeant Bowren:* Richard Jaeckel, *Major Max Armbruster:* George Kennedy, *Pedro Jiminez:* Trini Lopez, *Captain Stuart Kinder:* Ralph Meeker, *Colonel Everett Dasher-Breed:* Robert Ryan, *Archer Maggott:* Telly Savalas, *Samson Posey:* Clint Walker, *General Denton:* Robert Webber, *Vernon Pinkley:* Donald Sutherland, *Milo Vladek:* Tom Busby, *Glenn Gilpin:* Ben Carruthers, *Roscoe Lever:* Stuart Cooper, *Corporal Morgan:* Robert Phillips, *Seth Sawyer:* Colin Maitland, *Tassos Bravos:* Al Mancini, *Private Gardner:* George Roubicek, *Worden's Aide:* Thick Wilson, *German Girl:* Dora Reisser.

DIRTY HARRY (1971) WB. A Malpaso Company Production. Produced and Directed by Don Siegel. Panavision and Technicolor. Story by Harry Julian Fink and R. M. Fink. Screenplay, the Finks and Dean Riesner. Executive Producer, Robert Daley. Photography, Bruce Surtees. Art Director, Dale Hennesy. Set Decorator, Robert DeVestel. Associate Producer and Film Editor, Carl Pingitore. Sound, William Randall. Make-up Supervisor, Gordon Bau. Music by Lalo Schifrin. Assistant to the Producer, George Fargo. Dialogue Supervisor, Scott Hale. Wardrobe, Glenn Wright. Supervising Hairstylist, Jean Burt Reilly. Assistant Director, Robert Rubin. Film debut of Andy Robinson. Others in the series: *Magnum Force* (1973) and *The Enforcer* (1976). Filmed in San Francisco. Rated R. 103 minutes

Detective Harry Callahan: Clint Eastwood, *Lt. Bressler:* Harry Guardino, *Chico:* Reni Santoni, *Scorpio:* Andy Robinson, *Police Chief:* John Larch, *Mayor:* John Vernon, *DeGeorgio:* John Mitchum, *Mrs. Russell:* Mae Mercer, *Norma:* Lyn Edgington, *Bus Driver:* Ruth Kobart, *Mr. Jaffe:* Woodrow Parfrey, *Rothko:* Josef Sommer, *Bannerman:* William Paterson, *Liquor Proprietor:* James Nolan, *Sid Kleinman:* Maurice S. Argent, *Miss Willis:* Jo De Winter, *Sgt. Reineke:* Craig G. Kelly, *Girl Swimmer:* Diana Davidson, *Big Black Man:* Raymond Johnson, *Mayor's Secretary:* Diane Darnell, *Thug:* James Joyce, *Building Jumper:* William T. Couch, *Ann Mary Deacon:* Debbi Scott, *Ann Mary in photo:* Melody Thomas, *Robbers:* Albert Popwell, Ernest Robinson, *Black Queen:* Richard Lawson, *Homicide Detective:* George Fargo, *Homicide Secretary:* Angela Paton, *Walkie-Talkie Policeman:* John W. Peebles, *Taxi Driver:* George R.

Burrafato, *Underwear Chick:* Kathleen Harper, *Black Queen's Friend:* John Tracy, *Hippie Guy:* Kristoffer Tabori, *Hippie Chick:* Diann Henrichsen, *Newsmen:* Dean Webber, Scott Hale, *Communications Secretary:* Joy Carlin, *Nudes:* Janet Wisely, Laury Monk, Juana D'Amico, *Bed Nude:* Lolita Rios, *Hospital Orderly:* Allen Seaman, *Policemen:* Stuart P. Klitsner, Eddie Garrett, *Hippie Guy:* Frederic D. Ross, *Hippie Girl:* Ann Noland, *Doctor:* Marc Hertsens, *Hot Mary:* Lois Foraker, *Gay Cat:* David Gilliam, *Fire Chief:* John F. Vick, *Police Sergeant:* Tony Dario, *Interne:* Charles C. Washburn, *Miss Van Sachs:* Mary Ann Neis, *Cafe Customers:* Kathleen O'Malley, Al Dunlap, *Pedestrian:* Vincent P. Deadrick, *Flower Vendor:* Chuck Hicks, *Voices:* Joanne Moore Jordan, Don Haggerty, *Stunts:* Wayne Van Horn, Robert J. Miles, Jr., Jerry Maren, Bennie Dobbins, Raylene Holliday, Paula Martin, Emory Souza, Carl Rizzo, Billy Curtis, Regina Parton, John Hudkins, Everett Creach, Fred Lerner, Julie Ann Johnson, George Sawaya, Larry Duran, Dick Crockett, Boyd "Red" Morgan, Walter Scott, Mark Thomas, Alex A. Brown, Richard A. Washington, Bill Lane, Fred Stromsoe, Alex Sharp, Willie Harris, Eddie Smith, Jane Aull.

Dirty Harry with Clint Eastwood.

Dirty Mary Crazy Larry with Susan George and Peter Fonda.

DIRTY MARY CRAZY LARRY (1974) 20th. Produced by Norman T. Herman. Directed by John Hough. An Academy Pictures Corp. Production. Associate Producer, Mickey Zide. Based on the novel *The Chase* by Richard Unekis. Screenplay, Leigh Chapman and Antonio Santean. Assistant Director, Ronald L. Schwary. Editor, Christopher Holmes. Photography, Mike Margulies. Special Effects, Greg Auer. Make-up Artist, Wes Dawn. 2nd Assistant Director, Steve Lim. Stunt Coordinator, Al Wyatt. Hairdresser, Charlene Johnson. Production Executive, James Boyd. Music by Jimmy Haskell. Song, "Time (Is Such a Funny Thing)" by Danny Janssen and Bobby Hart, sung by Marjorie McCoy. DeLuxe Color. California locations: Stockton, Sonora, Clements, Linden and Jamestown. Rated PG. 93 minutes

Larry Rayder: Peter Fonda, *Mary Coombs:* Susan George, *Deke Sommers:* Adam Roarke, *George Stanton:* Roddy McDowall, *Capt. Everett Franklin:* Vic Morrow, *Sheriff Carl Donahue:* Kenneth Tobey, *Evelyn Stanton:* Lynn Borden, *Hank:* Eugene Daniels, *Millie:* Janear Hines, *Dispatcher:* Elizabeth James, *Cindy Stanton:* Adrianne Herman, *Steve:* Tom Castranova, *Helicopter Pilot:* James Gavin, *Surl:* Al Rossi, *Police Chief Markey:* Ben Niems, *Bridge Operator:* George Westcott, *Farmer:* Tom O'Neill, *Seller at Swampmeet:* Edna MacAfee, *Swampmeet Characters:* Don Coughlin, Sonny Dukes, Beau Gentry, Bob Hirshfield, *Roy:* William Catching, *Police Operator:* Judy Carlson, *Trooper Who Drives Through Billboard:* Bob Minor, *Troopers:* Jerry Wills, Ted White, Al Wyatt, Jr., Jerry Summers.

Disraeli with Joan Bennett, Anthony Bushell and George Arliss.

DISRAELI (1929) WB. Directed by Alfred E. Green. From the play by Louis N. Parker. Adaptation, Julian Josephson. Orchestra Conductor, Louis Silvers. Hughenden (Disraeli's estate) scenes filmed at Busch Gardens, Pasadena. Photography, Lee Garmes. Editor, Owen Marks. Titles (silent version), DeLeon Anthony. Other versions of *Disraeli:* Paul Cromelin, 1917; United Artists, 1921 (also starring George Arliss). Film debut of Anthony Bushell. 89 minutes

Disraeli: George Arliss, *Lady Clarissa Pevensey of Glastonbury:* Joan Bennett, *Lady Mary Beaconsfield:* Florence Arliss, *Charles, Lord Deeford:* Anthony Bushell, *Sir Michael, Lord Probert:* David Torrence, *Hugh Myers:* Ivan Simpson, *Mrs. Agatha Travers:* Doris Lloyd, *Duchess of Glastonbury:* Gwendolen Logan, *Duke of Glastonbury:* Henry Carvill, *Potter:* Charles E. Evans, *Mr. Terle:* Kyrle Bellew, *Bascot:* Jack Deery, *Count Bosrinov:* Michael Visaroff, *Foljambe:* Norman Cannon, *Dr. Williams:* Shayle Gardner, *Flookes:* Powell York, *Queen Victoria:* Margaret Mann, *Bit:* George Atkinson.

DIVE BOMBER (1941) WB. Producer, Hal B. Wallis. Associate Producer, Robert Lord. Technicolor. Director, Michael Curtiz. Author, Frank Wead. Screenplay, Frank Wead, Robert Buckner. Art Director, Robert Haas. Musical Director, Leo F. Forbstein. Cameramen, Bert Glennon, Winton C. Hoch. Aerial Photography, Elmer Dyer, Charles Marshall. Editor, George Amy. 133 minutes

Doug Lee: Errol Flynn, *Joe Blake:* Fred MacMurray, *Dr. Lance Rogers:* Ralph Bellamy, *Linda Fisher:* Alexis Smith, *Tim Griffin:* Regis Toomey, *Art Lyons:* Robert Armstrong, *Lucky Dice:* Allen Jenkins, *John Thomas Anthony:* Craig Stevens, *Chubby:* Herbert Anderson, *Senior Flight Surgeon:* Moroni Olsen, *Swede:* Louis Jean Heydt, *Mrs. James:* Dennie Moore, *Corpsman:* Cliff Nazarro, *Helen:* Ann Doran, *Senior Flight Surgeon:* Addison Richards, *Admiral:* Russell Hicks, *Admiral:* Howard Hickman, *Pilot:* De Wolfe Hopper (William Hopper), *Pilot:* Charles Drake, *Pilot:* Byron Barr (Gig Young), *Squadron Commander:* Alexander Lockwood, *Commander:* George Meeker, *General:* Wedgwood Nowell, *Hospital Attendant:* Creighton Hale, *Hostess:* Charlotte Wynters, *Singer:* Jane Randolph, *Cigarette Girl:* Juanita Stark, *Girl at Newsstand:* Alice Talton, *Squadron C.O.:* Max Hoffman, Jr., *Pilot:* Alan Hale, Jr., *Pilot:* Sol Gorss, *Blue Jacket:* Walter Sande, *Telephone Man:* Michael Ames (Tod Andrews), *Flag Man:* Harry Lewis.

Dive Bomber with Errol Flynn and Fred MacMurray.

The Divorcee with Chester Morris and Norma Shearer.

THE DIVORCEE (1930) MGM. Produced and Directed by Robert Z. Leonard. Based on Ursula Parrott's novel *Ex-Wife*. Adapted by Nick Grinde and Zelda Sears. Continuity and Dialogue, John Meehan. Costumes, Adrian. Art Director, Cedric Gibbons. Photography, Norbert Brodine. Editors, Hugh Wynn and Truman K. Wood. Sound, Douglas Shearer. 80 minutes

Jerry: Norma Shearer, *Ted:* Chester Morris, *Paul:* Conrad Nagel, *Don:* Robert Montgomery, *Helen:* Florence Eldridge, *Mary:* Helene Millard, *Bill:* Robert Elliott, *Janice:* Mary Doran, *Hank:* Tyler Brooke, *Hannah:* Zelda Sears, *Dr. Bernard:* George Irving, *Dorothy:* Helen Johnson (Judith Wood).

Dr. Jekyll and Mr. Hyde with Fredric March and Miriam Hopkins.

DR. JEKYLL AND MR. HYDE (1932) Par. Directed by Rouben Mamoulian. Based on Robert Louis Stevenson's story. Adaptation and Dialogue, Samuel Hoffenstein and Percy Heath. Assistant Director, Bob Lee. Art Director, Hans Dreier. Costume Design, Travis Banton. Photography, Karl Struss. Editor, William Shea. Sound, Martin Paggi. The book was published in London in 1885; the first stage version starred Richard Mansfield at the Boston Museum in 1887. Other film versions: Paramount, 1920; Pioneer Film Corp., 1920; MGM, 1941; *Two Faces of Dr. Jekyll* ("House of Fright"—British, 1961). Robert Louis Stevenson, a nephew of the author, has a bit. Miriam Hopkins sings "Champagne Ivy Is My Name." 90 minutes

Dr. Henry Jekyll/Mr. Hyde: Fredric March, *Ivy Pearson:* Miriam Hopkins, *Muriel Carew:* Rose Hobart, *Dr. Lanyan:* Holmes Herbert, *Brig. Gen. Sir Danvers Carew:* Halliwell Hobbes, *Poole, Jekyll's Butler:* Edgar Norton, *Utterson:* Arnold Lucy, *Hobson, Carew's Butler:* Colonel MacDonnell, *Mrs. Hawkins:* Tempe Pigott, *Briggs, Lanyan's Butler:* Eric Wilton, *Student:* Douglas Walton, *Waiter:* John Rogers, *Doctor:* Murdock MacQuarrie, *Dance Extra:* Major Sam Harris.

DR. NO (1963) UA. Producers, Harry Saltzman, Albert R. Broccoli. Director, Terence Young. Screenplay, Richard Maibaum, Johanna Harwood, Berkley Mather. Based on novel by Ian Fleming. Music, Monty Norman. Art Director, Syd Cain. Editor, Peter Hunt. Filmed in Jamaica in Technicolor. 111 minutes

James Bond: Sean Connery, *Felix Leiter:* Jack Lord, *Dr. No:* Joseph Wiseman, *Honey Ryder:* Ursula Andress, *Miss Taro:* Zena Marshall, *Sylvia:* Eunice Gayson, *Moneypenny:* Lois Maxwell, *Photographer:* Margaret LeWars, *Quarrel:* John Kitzmiller, *"M":* Bernard Lee, *Professor Dent:* Anthony Dawson, *Puss Feller:* Lester Prendergast, *Strangways:* Tim Moxon, *Jones:* Reggie Carter, *Major Boothroyd:* Peter Burton, *Duff:* William Foster-Davis, *Playdell-Smith:* Louis Blaazer, *Sister Rose:* Michele Mok, *Mary:* Dolores Keator.

Doctor No with Sean Connery and Ursula Andress.

DR. STRANGELOVE: OR HOW I LEARNED TO STOP WORRYING AND LOVE THE BOMB (1964) Col. Producer-Director, Stanley Kubrick. Screenplay, Stanley Kubrick, Terry Southern, Peter George. Based on book *Red Alert* by Peter George. Associate Producer, Victor Lyndon. Director of Photography, Gilbert Taylor. Music, Laurie Johnson. Assistant Director, Eric Rattray. Filmed in England. 93 minutes

Group Captain Lionel Mandrake/President Muffley/Dr. Strangelove: Peter Sellers, *General "Buck" Turgidson:* George C. Scott, *General Jack D. Ripper:* Sterling Hayden, *Colonel "Bat" Guano:* Keenan Wynn, *Major T. J. "King" Kong:* Slim Pickens, *Ambassador de Sadesky:* Peter Bull, *Miss Scott:* Tracy Reed, *Lt. Lothar Zogg:* James Earl Jones, *Mr. Staines:* Jack Creley, *Lt. H. R. Dietrich:* Frank Berry, *Lt. W. D. Kivel:* Glenn Beck, *Capt. G. A. "Ace" Owens:* Shane Rimmer, *Lt. B. Goldberg:* Paul Tamarin, *General Faceman:* Gordon Tanner, *Admiral Randolph:* Robert O'Neil, *Frank:* Roy Stephens, *Members of Defense Team:* Laurence Herder, John McCarthy, Hal Galili.

Dr. Strangelove with George C. Scott, Peter Bull and Peter Sellers.

DOCTOR ZHIVAGO (1965) MGM. Producer, Carlo Ponti. Director, David Lean. Screenplay, Robert Bolt. From the novel by Boris Pasternak. Director of Photography, Fred A. Young. Music, Maurice Jarre. Executive Producer, Arvid L. Griffen. Assistant Directors, Roy Stevens, Pedro Vidal, Jose Maria Ochoa. Costumes, Phyllis Dalton. In Panavision and Color. 197 minutes

Tonya: Geraldine Chaplin, *Lara:* Julie Christie, *Pasha:* Tom Courtenay, *Yevgraf:* Alec Guinness, *Anna:* Siobhan McKenna, *Alexander:*

Ralph Richardson, *Yuri:* Omar Sharif, *Komarovsky:* Rod Steiger, *The Girl:* Rita Tushingham, *Amelia:* Adrienne Corri, *Prof. Kurt:* Geoffrey Keen, *Sasha:* Jeffrey Rockland, *Katya:* Lucy Westmore, *Razin:* Noel Willman, *Liberius:* Gerard Tichy, *Kostoyed:* Klaus Kinski, *Petya:* Jack MacGowran, *Gentlewoman:* Maria Martin, *Yuri (at 8):* Tarek Sharif, *Tonya (at 7):* Mercedes Ruiz, *Colonel:* Roger Maxwell, *Major:* Inigo Jackson, *Captain:* Virgilio Texeira, *Bolshevik:* Bernard Kay, *Old Soldier:* Eric Chitty, *Priest:* Jose Nieto, *Young Engineer:* Mark Eden, *Mr. Sventytski:* Emilio Carrer, *David:* Gerhard Jersch, *Comrade Yelkin:* Wolf Frees, *Comrade Kaprugina:* Gwen Nelson, *Militiaman:* Jose Caffarel, *Streetwalker:* Brigitte Trace, *Mrs. Sventytski:* Luana Alcaniz, *Raddled Woman:* Lili Murati, *Raped Woman:* Catherine Ellison, *Demented Woman:* Maria Vico, *Dragoon Colonel:* Dodo Assad Bahador.

Doctor Zhivago with Tom Courtenay and Julie Christie.

Dodge City with Alan Hale and Errol Flynn.

DODGE CITY (1939) WB. Produced by Robert Lord. Directed by Michael Curtiz. Original Screenplay, Robert Buckner. Color by Technicolor. Music, Max Steiner. Photography, Sol Polito. Technicolor Cameraman, Ray Rennahan. Editor, George Amy. Georgia Caine replaced Elisabeth Risdon. 105 minutes

Wade Hatton: Errol Flynn, *Abbie Irving:* Olivia De Havilland, *Ruby Gilman:* Ann Sheridan, *Jeff Surrett:* Bruce Cabot, *Joe Clemens:* Frank McHugh, *Rusty Hart:* Alan Hale, *Matt Cole:* John Litel, *Yancy:* Victor Jory, *Lee Irving:* William Lundigan, *Dr. Irving:* Henry Travers, *Colonel Dodge:* Henry O'Neill, *Tex Baird:* Guinn "Big Boy" Williams,

Mrs. Cole: Gloria Holden, *Munger:* Douglas Fowley, *Mrs. Irving:* Georgia Caine, *Surrett's Lawyer:* Charles Halton, *Bud Taylor:* Ward Bond, *Harry Cole:* Bobs Watson, *Crocker:* Nat Carr, *Orth:* Russell Simpson, *Charlie, Barber:* Clem Bevans, *Mrs. McCoy:* Cora Witherspoon, *Hammond:* Joseph Crehan, *Twitchell:* Thurston Hall, *Coggins:* Chester Clute, *Barlow, Indian Agent:* Monte Blue, *Cattle Auctioneer:* James Burke, *Mail Clerk:* Robert Homans, *Marshal Jason:* George Guhl, *Minister:* Spencer Charters, *Stagecoach Driver/Waiter:* Bud Osborne, *Bartender:* Wilfred Lucas, *Clerk:* Richard Cramer, *Printer:* Milton Kibbee, *Woman:* Vera Lewis, *Spieler:* Earle Hodgins, *Al:* Fred Graham, *Passenger:* Tom Chatterton, *Conductor:* Pat O'Malley, *Cowhand:* Pat Flaherty.

Dodsworth with Ruth Chatterton and Walter Huston.

DODSWORTH (1936) UA. Produced by Samuel Goldwyn. Directed by William Wyler. Based on the novel by Sinclair Lewis. Screenplay by Sidney Howard. Associate Producer, Merritt Hulburd. Art Director, Richard Day. Music, Alfred Newman. Costumes, Omar Kiam. Photography, Rudolph Mate. Editor, Daniel Mandell. Assistant Director, Eddie Bernoudy. Sound, Oscar Lagerstrom. Special Effects, Ray Binger. Film debut of John Payne. 90 minutes

Sam Dodsworth: Walter Huston, *Fran Dodsworth:* Ruth Chatterton, *Arnold Iselin:* Paul Lukas, *Edith Cortright:* Mary Astor, *Lockert:* David Niven, *Kurt von Obersdorf:* Gregory Gaye, *Baroness von Obersdorf:* Maria Ouspenskaya, *Madame de Penable:* Odette Myrtil, *Emily:* Kathryn Marlowe, *Harry:* John Payne, *Matey Pearson:* Spring Byington, *Tubby Pearson:* Harlan Briggs.

Dog Day Afternoon with Al Pacino and Penny Allen.

68

DOG DAY AFTERNOON (1975) WB. Produced by Martin Bregman and Martin Elfand. Directed by Sidney Lumet. An Artists Entertainment Complex Production, in Technicolor. Screenplay by Frank Pierson, based on a true incident. Associate Producer, Robert Greenhut. Editor, Dede Allen. Photography, Victor J. Kemper. Assistant Director, Burtt Harris. 2nd Assistant Director, Alan Hopkins. Based on a magazine article by P. F. Kluge and Thomas Moore. Production Designer, Charles Bailey. Costume Designer, Anna Hill Johnstone. Set Decorator, Robert Drumheller. Art Director, Doug Higgins. Wardrobe Supervisors, Cliff Capone and Peggy Farrell. Make-up Artist, Reginald Tackley. Hairdresser, Philip Leto. Sound Mixer, James Sabat. Filmed in Brooklyn's Park Slope and at Kennedy Airport, New York. Rated R. 130 minutes

Sonny: Al Pacino, *Sal:* John Cazale, *Sheldon:* James Broderick, *Jenny:* Carol Kane, *Moretti:* Charles Durning, *Sylvia:* Penny Allen, *Mulvaney:* Sully Boyar, *Margaret:* Beulah Garrick, *Deborah:* Sandra Kazan, *Miriam:* Marcia Jean Kurtz, *Maria:* Amy Levitt, *Howard:* John Marriott, *Edna:* Estelle Omens, *Bobby:* Gary Springer, *Leon:* Chris Sarandon, *Carmine:* Carmine Foresta, *Murphy:* Lance Henriksen, *Phone Cop:* Floyd Levine, *Angie:* Susan Peretz, *Policeman with Angie:* Thomas Murphy, *Vi:* Judith Malina, *Vi's Husband:* Dominic Chianese, *Vi's Friend:* Marcia Haufrecht, *TV Studio Anchorman:* William Bogert, *TV Reporter:* Ron Cummins, *Sam:* Jay Gerber, *Doctor:* Philip Charles Mackenzie, *Maria's Boyfriend:* Chu Chu Malave, *Pizza Boy:* Lionel Pina, *Limo Driver:* Dick Anthony Williams.

The Dolly Sisters with Betty Grable, June Haver and S.Z. Sakall.

THE DOLLY SISTERS (1945) 20th. Producer, George Jessel. Director, Irving Cummings. Color by Technicolor. Screenplay, John Larkin, Marian Spitzer. Dance Director, Seymour Felix. Musical Directors, Alfred Newman, Charles Henderson. Art Directors, Lyle Wheeler, Leland Fuller. Cameraman, Ernest Palmer. Special Effects, Fred Sersen. Editor, Barbara McLean. Technicolor Director, Natalie Kalmus. Associate, Richard Mueller. Songs: "I Can't Begin to Tell You" and "Don't Be Too Old-Fashioned (Old-Fashioned Girl)" by Mack Gordon and Jimmy Monaco; "Give Me the Moonlight, Give Me the Girl" by Lew Brown and Albert Von Tilzer; "We Have Been Around" by Mack Gordon and Charles Henderson; "Carolina in the Morning" by Walter Donaldson; "Powder, Lipstick and Rouge" by Mack Gordon and Harry Revel; "Darktown Strutters' Ball" by Shelton Brooks; "Smiles" by Lee Roberts; "Arrah Go on I'm Gonna Go Back to Oregon" by Joe Yound, Sam Lewis and Bert Grant; "Oh, Frenchie" by Sam Ehrlich and Con Conrad; "I'm Always Chasing Rainbows" by Joseph McCarthy and Harry Carroll; "On the Mississippi" by Ballard MacDonald, Buddy Fields and Harry Carroll. 114 minutes

Jenny Dolly: Betty Grable, *Harry Fox:* John Payne, *Rosie Dolly:* June Haver, *Uncle Latsie:* S. Z. Sakall, *Duke:* Reginald Gardiner,

Irving Netcher: Frank Latimore, *Professor Winnup:* Gene Sheldon, *Tsimmis:* Sig Rumann, *Lenore:* Trudy Marshall, *Flo Daly:* Collette Lyons, *Jenny, as a child:* Evon Thomas, *Rosie, as a child:* Donna Jo Gribble, *Hammerstein:* Robert Middlemass, *Dowling:* Paul Hurst, *Morrie Keno:* Lester Allen, *Stage Manager:* Frank Orth, *Will Rogers:* Sam Garrett, *Al Smith:* J. C. Fowler, *Mrs. Al Smith:* Betty Farrington, *Nun:* Virginia Brissac, *Man:* Charles Evans, *Frank Tinney:* George O'Hara, *Madame Polaire:* Ricki Van Dusen, *Doorman:* J. Farrell MacDonald, *Fields (Weber & Fields):* Herbert Ashley, *Bartender:* William Nye, *Man:* Julius Tannen, *Conductor:* Walter Soderling, *Pianist:* Harry Seymour, *French Juggler:* George Davis, *German Actress:* Trudy Berliner, *Russian Actor:* Igor Dolgoruki, *French Actor:* Nino Bellini, *Ellabelle:* Theresa Harris, *Hammerstein's Secretary:* Mary Currier, *Phillipe:* Andre Charlot, *Harris:* Edward Kane, *Flower Lady:* Mae Marsh, *Kathi:* Else Janssen.

Don't Go Near the Water with Fred Clark, Russ Tamblyn and Glenn Ford.

DON'T GO NEAR THE WATER (1957) MGM. Producer, Lawrence Weingarten. Director, Charles Walters. CinemaScope, MetroColor. Screenplay by Dorothy Kingsley and George Wells. Based on novel by William Brinkley. Music by Bronislau Kaper. Lyrics for song by Sammy Cahn, sung by the Lancers. Assistant Director, Al Jennings. Costumes by Helen Rose. An Avon Production. Photography, Robert Bronner. 107 minutes

Lt. Max Siegel: Glenn Ford, *Melora:* Gia Scala, *Adam Garrett:* Earl Holliman, *Lt. Alice Tomlen:* Anne Francis, *Gordon Ripwell:* Keenan Wynn, *Lt. Comdr. Clinton Nash:* Fred Clark, *Deborah Aldrich:* Eva Gabor, *Ensign Tyson:* Russ Tamblyn, *Lt. Ross Pendleton:* Jeff Richards, *Farragut Jones:* Mickey Shaughnessy, *Admiral Boatwright:* Howard Smith, *Mr. Alba:* Romney Brent, *Janie:* Mary Wickes, *Lt. Comdr. Gladstone:* Jack Straw, *Lt. Comdr. Hereford:* Robert Nichols, *Lt. Comdr. Diplock:* John Alderson, *Rep. George Jansen:* Jack Albertson, *Rep. Arthur Smithfield:* Charles Watts, *Mr. Seguro:* Julian Rivero, *Lt. Comdr. Pratt:* Ike Gibson, *Lt. Hepburn:* Don Burnett, *Jerry Wakely:* Hugh Boswell, *Yeoman:* Wilson Wood, *Corp. Donohue:* John Dennis, *Seaman Flaherty:* Steve Warren, *Lt. Boone:* William Ogden Joyce, *Boatswain:* Gregg Martell, *Seabee Metkoff:* John L. Cason, *Lt. Comdr. Flaherty:* Paul Bryar.

DOUBLE INDEMNITY (1944) Par. Produced by Joseph Sistrom. Directed by Billy Wilder. From the novel by James M. Cain, also presented in *Liberty* magazine. Screenplay, Billy Wilder and Raymond Chandler. Musical Score, Miklos Rozsa. Art Directors, Hans Dreier and Hal Pereira. Camera, John Seitz. Process Photography, Farciot Edouart. Editor, Doane Harrison. Based on the 1927 slaying of Albert Snyder in Queens Village, New York, by his wife Ruth and her lover Judd Gray, for his insurance. Cut from the release print were scenes dealing with MacMurray's execution. Bits in these sequences included:

Alan Bridge (Execution Chamber Guard), Edward Hearn (Warden's Secretary), George Anderson (Warden), Boyd Irwin and George Melford (Doctors), Lee Shumway (Door Guard), and William O'Leary (Chaplain). 106 minutes. Later a 1973 TV film

Walter Neff: Fred MacMurray, *Phyllis Dietrichson:* Barbara Stanwyck, *Barton Keyes:* Edward G. Robinson, *Mr. Jackson:* Porter Hall, *Lola Dietrichson:* Jean Heather, *Mr. Dietrichson:* Tom Powers, *Nino Zachetti:* Byron Barr, *Edward S. Norton:* Richard Gaines, *Sam Gorlopis:* Fortunio Bonanova, *Joe Peters:* John Philliber, *Bit:* George Magrill, *Norton's Secretary:* Bess Flowers, *Conductor:* Kernan Cripps, *Redcap:* Harold Garrison, *Pullman Porter:* Oscar Smith, *Nettie, the Maid:* Betty Farrington, *Woman:* Constance Purdy, *Pullman Conductor:* Dick Rush, *Pullman Porter:* Frank Billy Mitchell, *Train Conductor:* Edmund Cobb, *Pullman Porter:* Floyd Shackelford, *Pullman Porter:* James Adamson, *Garage Attendant, Charlie:* Sam McDaniel, *Man:* Clarence Muse, *Telephone Operator:* Judith Gibson, *Keyes' Secretary:* Miriam Franklin, *Lou Schwartz:* Douglas Spencer.

Double Indemnity with Richard Gaines, Bess Flowers, Edward G. Robinson and Fred MacMurray.

DRACULA (1931) Univ. Directed by Tod Browning. From the novel by Bram Stoker and the play by Hamilton Deane and John Balderston. Scenario, Garrett Fort. Photography, Karl Freund. Editor, Milton Carruth. Sound, C. Roy Hunter. Bela Lugosi repeats his 1927 stage role, which was to have been played in the film by Lon Chaney, Sr. 84 minutes

Count Dracula: Bela Lugosi, *Mina Seward:* Helen Chandler, *John Harker:* David Manners, *Renfield:* Dwight Frye, *Professor Van Helsing:* Edward Van Sloan, *Doctor Seward:* Herbert Bunston, *Lucy Weston:* Frances Dade, *Martin:* Charles Gerrard, *Maid:* Joan Standing, *Briggs:* Moon Carroll, *English Nurse:* Josephine Velez, *Innkeeper:* Michael Visaroff.

Dracula with Bela Lugosi and Helen Chandler.

Dragnet with Ben Alexander, Jack Webb and Georgia Ellis.

DRAGNET (1954) WB. Producer, Stanley Meyer. Director, Jack Webb. Color by WarnerColor. A Mark VII Production. Art Director, Feild Gray. Cinematographer, Edward Colman. Editor, Robert M. Leeds. 89 minutes

Joe Friday: Jack Webb, *Frank Smith:* Ben Alexander, *Captain Hamilton:* Richard Boone, *Max Troy:* Stacy Harris, *Grace Downey:* Ann Robinson, *Mrs. Starkie:* Virginia Gregg, *Miller Starkie:* Dub Taylor, *Belle Davitt:* Georgia Ellis, *Chester Davitt:* Willard Sage, *Jesse Quinn:* Jim Griffith, *Adolph Alexander:* Vic Perrin, *Lee Reinhard:* Malcolm Atterbury, *Charlie Weaver:* Cliff Arquette, *Captain Lohrman:* Dennis Weaver, *Fred Kemp:* James Anderson, *Fabian Gerard:* Monte Masters, *Ray Pinker:* Olan Soule, *Roy Cleaver:* Dick Cathcart, *Cuban Singer:* Meg Myles, *Mrs. Caldwell:* Virginia Christine, *Mr. Archer:* Herb Vigran, *Officer Tilden:* Fred Dale, *Sergeant McCreadie:* Roy Whaley, *Ken, Stenotypist:* Charles Hibbs, *Walker Scott:* Guy Hamilton, *McQueen:* George Sawaya, *Eddy King:* Eddy King, *Pat, Script Secretary:* Jean Dean, *Lieutenant Stevens:* Harry Bartell, *Booking Sergeant:* Herb Ellis, *Jailer:* Mauritz Hugo, *Hank Wild:* Bill Brundidge, *Doctor:* Art Gilmore, *Hotel Clerk:* Dick Paxton, *Intelligence Officer:* Ross Elliott, *Wesley Cannon:* Ramsay Williams, *Interne:* Harlan Warde, *Officer Keeler:* Gayle Kellogg, *Officer Gene James:* Ken Peters, *Officer Greeley:* Harry Lauter.

Drums Along the Mohawk with Henry Fonda and Claudette Colbert.

DRUMS ALONG THE MOHAWK (1939) 20th. Associate Producer, Raymond Griffith. Directed by John Ford. Color by Technicolor. Based on the novel by Walter D. Edmonds. Screenplay, Lamar Trotti and Sonya Levien. Director of Photography, Bert Glennon. Technicolor Director of Photography, Ray Rennahan. Technicolor Director, Natalie Kalmus. Associate, Henri Jaffa. Editor, Robert Simpson. 103 minutes

Lana (Magdalena) Martin: Claudette Colbert, *Gil Martin:* Henry Fonda, *Sarah McKlennar:* Edna May Oliver, *Christian Reall:* Eddie Collins, *Caldwell:* John Carradine, *Mary Reall:* Dorris Bowdon, *Mrs. Weaver:* Jessie Ralph, *Reverend Rosenkrantz:* Arthur Shields, *John Weaver:* Robert Lowery, *General Nicholas Herkimer:* Roger Imhof, *Joe Boleo:* Francis Ford, *Adam Helmer:* Ward Bond, *Mrs. Demooth:* Kay Linaker, *Dr. Petry:* Russell Simpson, *Landlord:* Spencer Charters, *Jacob Small:* Si Jenks, *Amos Hartman:* Jack Pennick, *George Weaver:* Arthur Aylesworth, *Blue Back:* Chief Big Tree, *Dr. Robert Johnson:* Charles Tannen, *Captain Mark Demooth:* Paul McVey, *Mrs. Reall:* Elizabeth (Tiny) Jones, *Daisy:* Beulah Hall Jones, *Reverend Daniel Gros:* Edwin Maxwell, *Mr. Borst:* Robert Greig, *Mrs. Borst:* Clara Blandick, *Morgan:* Tom Tyler, *General:* Lionel Pape, *Indian:* Noble Johnson, *Paymaster:* Clarence H. Wilson, *Pioneer Woman:* Mae Marsh.

DUEL IN THE SUN (1946) Selznick Releasing Organization. Produced by David O. Selznick. Directed by King Vidor. Second Units directed by Otto Brower and Reaves Eason. Color by Technicolor. A Vanguard Production. Suggested by the novel by Niven Busch. Screenplay, David O. Selznick. Adaptation, Oliver H. P. Garrett. Art Director, James Basevi. Associate, John Ewing. Production Design, J. Mc-Millan Johnson. Technical Director, Natalie Kalmus. Solo Dances, Tilly Losch. Group Dances, Lloyd Shaw. Music, Dimitri Tiomkin. Song, "Gotta Get Me Somebody to Love" by Allie Wrubel. Narrated by Orson Welles. Costumes, Walter Plunkett. Photography, Lee Garmes, Hal Rosson, Ray Rennahan. Special Effects, Clarence Slifer and Jack Cosgrove. Supervising Editor, Hal C. Kern. Editors, William Ziegler, John Saure. Film debut of Joan Tetzel, 22. 138 minutes

Pearl Chavez: Jennifer Jones, *Jesse McCanles:* Joseph Cotten, *Lewt McCanles:* Gregory Peck, *Senator McCanles:* Lionel Barrymore, *Laura Belle McCanles:* Lillian Gish, *The Sinkiller:* Walter Huston, *Scott Chavez:* Herbert Marshall, *Sam Pierce:* Charles Bickford, *Helen Langford:* Joan Tetzel, *Lem Smoot:* Harry Carey, *Mr. Langford:* Otto Kruger, *The Lover:* Sidney Blackmer, *Mrs. Chavez:* Tilly Losch, *Sid:* Scott McKay, *Vashti:* Butterfly McQueen, *Gambler:* Francis McDonald, *Gambler:* Victor Kilian, *The Jailer:* Griff Barnett, *Ken:* Frank Cordell, *Ed:* Dan White, *Jake:* Steve Dunhill, *Captain of U.S. Cavalry:* Lane Chandler, *Caller at Barbecue:* Lloyd Shaw, *Engineer:* Thomas Dillon, *Bartender:* Robert McKenzie, *Sheriff Thomson:* Charles Dingle, *Barfly, Presidio Bar:* Kermit Maynard, *Ranch Hand:* Hank Bell, *Hand at Barbecue:* Johnny Bond, *An Eater:* Bert Roach, *Dancers at Barbecue:* Si Jenks, Hank Worden, Rose Plummer, *Barfly:* Guy Wilkerson, *Engineer:* Lee Phelps.

Duel in the Sun with Jennifer Jones and Lionel Barrymore.

DUFFY'S TAVERN (1945) Par. Associate Producer, Danny Dare. Directed by Hal Walker. Based on characters created by Ed Gardner. Original Screenplay, Melvin Frank and Norman Panama. Sketches, Norman Panama and Melvin Frank, Abram S. Burrows, Barney Dean, George White, Eddie Davis and Matt Brooks. Music Director,

Robert Emmett Dolan. Photography, Lionel Lindon. Songs: "The Hard Way" by Johnny Burke and Jimmy Van Heusen; "You Can't Blame a Girl for Tryin' " by Ben Raleigh and Bernie Wayne. Bing's sons Dennis and Phillip, 10, and Lindsay, 6, make their film debuts. 97 minutes

Themselves: Bing Crosby, Betty Hutton, Paulette Goddard, Alan Ladd, Dorothy Lamour, Eddie Bracken, Brian Donlevy, Sonny Tufts, Veronica Lake, Arturo De Cordova, William Bendix, Joan Caulfield, Gail Russell, *Bing's Father:* Barry Fitzgerald, *Archie:* Ed Gardner, *Michael O'Malley:* Victor Moore, *Peggy O'Malley:* Marjorie Reynolds, *Danny Murphy:* Barry Sullivan, *Finnegan:* Charles Cantor, *Eddie, the Waiter:* Eddie Green, *Miss Duffy:* Ann Thomas, *Heavy:* Howard da Silva, *Doctor:* Billy De Wolfe, *Director:* Walter Abel, *Dancer-Waiter:* Johnny Coy, *Ronald:* Charles Quigley, *Gloria:* Olga San Juan, *Dancer:* Miriam Franklin, *Piano Specialty:* Maurice Rocco, *Themselves:* Cass Daley, Diana Lynn, Robert Benchley, William Demarest, James Brown, Helen Walker, Gary, Phillip, Dennis, and Lin Crosby, Jean Heather, Barney Dean, *Masseur:* Bobby Watson, *Customer:* Frank Faylen, *Mr. Richardson:* George M. Carleton, *Mr. Smith:* Addison Richards, *Regan:* George McKay, *Assistant Director:* James Millican, *Make-up Man:* Emmett Vogan, *Nurse:* Catherine Craig, *School Kid:* Noel Neill.

Duffy's Tavern with Jean Heather, Bing Crosby, Helen Walker and Gail Russell.

Earthquake with Charlton Heston and Ava Gardner.

EARTHQUAKE (1974) Univ. Produced and Directed by Mark Robson. A Mark Robson-Filmmakers Group Production. An MCA Presentation. Screenplay, George Fox and Mario Puzo. Executive Producer, Jennings

71

Lang. In Panavision, Technicolor and Sensurround. Photography, Philip Lathrop. Editor, Dorothy Spencer. Music by John Williams. Production Designer, Alexander Golitzen. Art Director, E. Preston Ames. Costumes, Burton Miller. Assistant Directors, Fred R. Simpsom and Murray Schwartz. Rated PG. 129 minutes

Stewart Graff: Charlton Heston, *Remy Graff:* Ava Gardner, *Slade:* George Kennedy, *Royce:* Lorne Greene, *Denise:* Genevieve Bujold, *Miles:* Richard Roundtree, *Jody:* Marjoe Gortner, *Stockle:* Barry Sullivan, *Dr. Vance:* Lloyd Nolan, *Rosa:* Victoria Principal, *Drunk:* Walter Matuschanskayasky (Matthau), *Barbara:* Monica Lewis, *Sal:* Gabriel Dell, *Chavez:* Pedro Armendariz, Jr., *Cameron:* Lloyd Gough, *Mayor:* John Randolph, *Walter Russell:* Kip Niven, *Assistant Caretaker:* Scott Hylands, *Dam Caretaker:* Gene Dynarski, *Corry:* Tiger Williams, *Dr. Harvey Johnson:* Donald Moffat, *Buck:* Jesse Vint, *Ralph:* Alan Vint, *Hank:* Lionel Johnston, *Carl Leeds:* John Elerick, *Chief Inspector:* John S. Ragin, *Colonel:* George Murdock, *Sid:* Donald Mantooth, *Sandy:* Michael Richardson, *Pool Players:* Alex A. Brown, H. B. Haggerty, *Dr. Frank Ames:* Bob Cunningham, *Brawny Foreman:* John Dennis, *Farmer Griggs:* Bob Gravage, *Technician:* Dave Morick, *Laura:* Inez Pedroza.

EASTER PARADE (1948) MGM. Producer, Arthur Freed. Director, Charles Walters. Color by Technicolor. Original Story, Frances Goodrich, Albert Hackett. Screenplay, Sidney Sheldon, Frances Goodrich, Albert Hackett. Art Directors, Cedric Gibbons, Jack Martin Smith. Musical Director, Johnny Green. Orchestration, Conrad Salinger, Van Cleave, Leo Arnaud. Editor, Albert Akst. Photography by Harry Stradling. Songs by Irving Berlin: "Happy Easter," "Drum Crazy," "It Only Happens When I Dance With You," "Everybody's Doing It," "I Wanna Go Back to Michigan," "A Fella With an Umbrella," "I Love a Piano," "Snooky Ookums," "Ragtime Violin", "When the Midnight Choo Choo Leaves for Alabam," "Shaking the Blues Away," "Stepping Out With My Baby," "A Couple of Swells," "Beautiful Faces Need Beautiful Clothes," "The Girl on the Magazine Cover," "Better Luck Next Time," "Easter Parade." 103 minutes

Don Hewes: Fred Astaire, *Hannah Brown:* Judy Garland, *Jonathan Harrow III:* Peter Lawford, *Nadine Hale:* Ann Miller, *Mike, the Bartender:* Clinton Sundberg, *Francois:* Jules Munshin, *Essie:* Jeni LeGon, *Singer:* Richard Beavers, *Al, Stage Manager for Ziegfeld:* Dick Simmons, *Boy in "Drum Crazy":* Jimmy Bates, *Cabby:* Jimmy Dodd, *Cop Who Gives Johnny a Ticket:* Robert Emmet O'Connor, *Specialty Dancers:* Patricia Jackson, Bobbie Priest, Dee Turnell, *Hat Models:* Lola Albright, Joi Lansing, *"Delineator" Twins:* Lynn and Jean Romer, *Modiste:* Helene Heigh, *Marty:* Wilson Wood, *Dog Act:* Hector and His Pals (Carmi Tryon), *Sam, Valet:* Peter Chong, *Drug Clerk:* Nolan Leary, *Mary:* Doris Kemper, *Headwaiter:* Frank Mayo, *Bar Patron:* Benay Venuta.

Easter Parade with Peter Lawford, Judy Garland and Fred Astaire.

East of Eden with Jo Van Fleet and James Dean.

EAST OF EDEN (1955) WB. Producer, Elia Kazan. Director, Elia Kazan. CinemaScope and WarnerColor. Screenplay, Paul Osborn. Art Directors, James Basevi, Malcolm Bert. Musical Director, Leonard Rosenman. Cinematographer, Ted McCord. Editor, Owen Marks. 115 minutes

Cal: James Dean, *Abra:* Julie Harris, *Adam:* Raymond Massey, *Sam:* Burl Ives, *Kate:* Jo Van Fleet, *Aron:* Richard Davalos, *Will:* Albert Dekker, *Anne:* Lois Smith, *Mr. Albecht:* Harold Gordon, *Dr. Edwards:* Richard Garrick, *Joe:* Timothy Carey, *Rantini:* Nick Dennis, *Roy:* Lonnie Chapman, *Nurse:* Barbara Baxley, *Madame:* Bette Treadville, *Bartender:* Tex Mooney, *Bouncer:* Harry Cording, *Card Dealer:* Loretta Rush, *Coalman:* Bill Phillips, *Piscora:* Mario Siletti, *Piscora's Son:* Jonathan Haze, *Carnival People:* Jack Carr, Roger Creed, Effie Laird, Wheaton Chambers, Ed Clark, Al Ferguson, Franklyn Farnum, Rose Plummer, *Photographer:* John George, *Shooting Gallery Attendant:* Earle Hodgins, *English Officer:* C. Ramsay Hill, *Soldier:* Edward McNally.

Easy Rider with Dennis Hopper and Peter Fonda.

EASY RIDER (1969) Col. Produced by Peter Fonda. Directed by Dennis Hopper. Technicolor. A Pando Company/Raybert Production. Executive Producer, Bert Schneider. Screenplay, Fonda, Hopper and Terry Southern. Photography, Laszlo Kovacs. Art Direction, Jerry Kay. Editor, Donn Cambern. Associate Producer, William L. Hayward. Assistant Director and Production Manager, Paul Lewis. "Ballad of Easy Rider" by Bob Dylan and Roger McGuinn, performed by McGuinn. Other songs by Hoyt Axton, Mars Bonfire, Gerry Goffin, Carole King, Jaime Robbie Robertson, Antonia Duren, Elliott Ingber, Larry Wagner, Jimi Hendrix, Jack Keller, David Axelrod, Mike Bloomfield. Filmed between California and Louisiana. Rated R. 94 minutes

Wyatt (Captain America): Peter Fonda, Billy: Dennis Hopper, George Hanson: Jack Nicholson, Lisa: Luana Anders, Stranger on Highway: Luke Askew, Mary: Toni Basil, Karen: Karen Black, Rancher: Warren Finnerty, Sarah: Sabrina Scharf, Jack: Robert Walker (Jr.), Jesus: Antonio Mendoza, Connection: Phil Spector, Bodyguard: Mac Mashourian, Rancher's Wife: Tita Colorado, Joanne: Sandy Wyeth, Mimes: Robert Ball, Carmen Phillips, Ellie Walker, Michael Pataki, Guard: George Fowler, Jr., Sheriff: Keith Green, Cat Man: Hayward Robillard, Deputy: Arnold Hess, Jr., Customers: Buddy Causey, Jr., Duffy Lafont, Blase M. Dawson, Paul Guedry, Jr., Girls: Suzie Ramagos, Elida Ann Hebert, Rose Le Blanc, Mary Kaye Hebert, Cynthia Grezaffi, Colette Purpera, Madame: Lea Marmer, Dancing Girl: Cathé Cozzi, Hookers: Thea Salerno, Anne McClain, Beatriz Montelli, Marcia Bowman, Men in Pickup Truck: David C. Billodeau, Johnny David.

Easy to Wed with Lucille Ball and Keenan Wynn.

EASY TO WED (1946) MGM. Producer, Jack Cummings. Director, Edward Buzzell. Color by Technicolor. Authors, Maurine Watkins, Howard Emmett Rogers, George Oppenheimer (from *Libeled Lady*). Screenplay, Dorothy Kingsley. Musical Score Supervision and Direction, Johnny Green. Technicolor Director, Natalie Kalmus. Art Director, Cedric Gibbons. Photography, Harry Stradling, Editor, Blanche Sewell. Songs: "Easy to Wed" by Ted Duncan and Johnny Green; "Goosey-Lucy" and "It Shouldn't Happen to a Duck" by Robert Franklin and Johnny Green; "Continental Polka" and "(Tell You What I'm Gonna Do) Gonna Fall in Love With You" by Ralph Blane and Johnny Green; "Come Closer to Me" by Osvaldo Farres. Remake of MGM's *Libeled Lady*, 1936. 110 minutes

Bill Chandler: Van Johnson, *Connie Allenbury:* Esther Williams, *Gladys Benton:* Lucille Ball, *Warren Haggerty:* Keenan Wynn, *J. B. Allenbury:* Cecil Kellaway, *Carlos:* Carlos Ramirez, *Spike Dolan:* Ben Blue, *Ethel:* Ethel Smith, *Babs Norvell:* June Lockhart, *Homer Henshaw:* Grant Mitchell, *Mrs. Burns Norvell:* Josephine Whittell, *Frances:* Jean Porter, *Farwood:* Paul Harvey, *Boswell:* Jonathan Hale, *Joe:* James Flavin, *Farwood's Secretary:* Celia Travers, *Taxi Driver:* Robert Emmet O'Connor, *Truck Drivers:* Charles Sullivan, Frank Hagney, *Receptionist:* Sybil Merritt, *Orchestra Leader:* Dick Winslow, *Justice of the Peace:* Joel Friedkin, *Private Detective:* Milton Kibbee, *Waiter:* Tom Dugan, *Masseuse:* Katherine Black, *Butler:* Guy Bates Post, *Mr. Dibson:* Walter Soderling, *Mrs. Dibson:* Sarah Edwards, *Lifeguard:* Jack Shea.

THE EDDY DUCHIN STORY (1956) Col. Producer, Jerry Wald. Associate Producer, Jonie Taps. Director, George Sidney. CinemaScope, Technicolor. Author, Leo Katcher. Screenplay, Samuel Taylor. Art Director, Walter Holscher. Music supervised and conducted by Morris Stoloff. Piano recordings by Carmen Cavallaro. Incidental music, George Duning. Cinematographer, Harry Stradling. Editors, Viola Lawrence, Jack W. Ogilvie. 123 minutes

Eddy Duchin: Tyrone Power, *Marjorie Oelrichs:* Kim Novak, *Chiquita:* Victoria Shaw, *Lou Sherwood:* James Whitmore, *Peter Duchin at 12:* Rex Thompson, *Peter at 5:* Mickey Maga, *Mr. Wadsworth:* Shepperd Strudwick, *Mrs. Wadsworth:* Frieda Inescort, *Mrs. Duchin:* Gloria Holden, *Leo Reisman:* Larry Keating, *Mr. Duchin:* John Mylong, *Philip:* Gregory Gay, *Native Boy:* Warren Hsieh, *Piano Tuner:* Jack Albertson, *Doctor:* Carlyle Mitchell, *Nurse:* Lois Kimbrell, *Mayor Walker:* Ralph Gamble, *Captain:* Richard Cutting, *Seaman:* Richard Crane, *Seaman:* Brad Trumbull, *Mrs. Rutledge:* Gloria Ann Simpson, *Bit Man:* Rick Person, *Bit Man:* Michael Legend, *Girl:* Betsy Jones Moreland, *Young Man:* Kirk Alyn.

The Eddy Duchin Story with Kim Novak, James Whitmore and Tyrone Power.

El Cid with Raf Vallone, Charlton Heston and Douglas Wilmer.

EL CID (1961) AA. Producer, Samuel Bronston. Director, Anthony Mann. Associate Producers, Michael Waszynski, Jaime Prades. Screenplay, Fredric M. Frank, Philip Yordan. Music, Miklos Rozsa. Assistant Directors, Yakima Canutt, Luciano Sacripanti, Jose Maria Ochoa, Jose Lopez Rodero. Produced in association with Dear Film Productions in 70-mm Super Technirama and Technicolor. Filmed in Madrid and Rome. 184 minutes

El Cid (Rodrigo Diaz): Charlton Heston, *Chimene:* Sophia Loren, *Ordonez:* Raf Vallone, *Urraca:* Genevieve Page, *Alfonso:* John Fraser, *Sancho:* Gary Raymond, *Arias:* Hurd Hatfield, *Fanez:* Massimo Serato, *Ben Yussuf:* Herbert Lom, *Gormaz:* Andrew Cruickshank, *Don Martin:* Christopher Rhodes, *Don Diego:* Michael Hordern, *King Ferdinand:* Ralph Truman, *Don Pedro:* Tullio Carminati, *King Ramiro:* Gerard Tichy, *Bermudez:* Carlo Giustini, *Moutamin:* Douglas Wilmer, *Al Kadir:* Frank Thring.

ELMER GANTRY (1960) UA. Producer, Bernard Smith. Director, Richard Brooks. Assistant Directors, Tom Shaw, Rowe Wallerstein, Carl Beringer. Costumes, Dorothy Jeakins. Screenplay, Richard Brooks. Based on the novel by Sinclair Lewis. Art Director, Ed Carrere. Music, Andre Previn. Cinematography, John Alton. Editor, Marge Fowler. Color by Eastman Color. 146 minutes

Elmer Gantry: Burt Lancaster, *Sister Sharon Falconer:* Jean Simmons, *Jim Lefferts:* Arthur Kennedy, *Lulu Bains:* Shirley Jones, *William L. Morgan:* Dean Jagger, *Sister Rachel:* Patti Page, *George Babbitt:* Edward Andrews, *Rev. Pengilly:* John McIntire, *Pete:* Joe Maross, *Rev. Brown:* Everett Glass, *Rev. Phillips:* Michael Whalen, *Rev. Garrison:* Hugh Marlowe, *Rev. Planck:* Philip Ober, *Rev. Ulrich:* Wendell Holmes, *Captain Holt:* Barry Kelley, *Preacher:* Rex Ingram, *Publisher Eddington:* Dayton Lummis, *Friends:* Ray Walker, Ralph Dumke, George Cisar, Norman Leavitt, *Mac, Bartender:* Larry J. Blake, *Sam, Storekeeper:* John Qualen, *Valet:* George Selk (Budd Buster), *Clean-up Man:* Guy Wilkerson, *Revivalist:* Milton Parsons, *Speaker:* Dan Riss, *Prostitutes:* Jean Willes and Sally Fraser, *Benny, Photographer:* Peter Brocco, *Deaf Man:* Casey Adams, *Cheerleader:* George (Buck) Flower.

Elmer Gantry with Burt Lancaster.

Emma with Marie Dressler and Myrna Loy.

EMMA (1932) MGM. Directed by Clarence Brown. Story, Frances Marion. Adaptation and Dialogue, Leonard Praskins. Additional Dialogue, Zelda Sears. Art Director, Cedric Gibbons. Gowns, Adrian. Photography, Oliver T. Marsh. Assistant Director, Charles Dorian. Editor, William Levanway. Recording Engineer, A. MacDonald. 73 minutes

Emma: Marie Dressler, *Ronnie Smith:* Richard Cromwell, *Mr. Smith:* Jean Hersholt, *Isabelle:* Myrna Loy, *District Attorney:* John Miljan, *Haskins:* Purnell B. Pratt, *Matilda:* Leila Bennett, *Gypsy:* Barbara Kent, *Sue:* Kathryn Crawford, *Bill:* George Meeker, *Maid:* Dale Fuller, *Drake:* Wilfred Noy, *Count Pierre:* Andre Cheron.

The Enforcer with Tom O'Neil and Clint Eastwood.

THE ENFORCER (1976) WB. A Malpaso Company Film. Produced by Robert Daley. Directed by James Fargo. Based on the story "Moving Target" by Gail Morgan Hickman and S. W. Schurr. Screenplay, Stirling Silliphant and Dean Reisner. Based on characters created by Harry Julian Fink and R. M. Fink. Art Director, Allen E. Smith. Editors, Ferris Webster and Joel Cox. Music by Jerry Fielding. Photography, Charles W. Short. Assistant to the Producer, Fritz Manes. Assistant Director, Joe Cavalier. 2nd Assistant Directors, Joe Florence and Billy Ray Smith. Set Decoration, Ira Bates. Stunt Coordinator, Wayne Van Horn. Sound, Bert Hallberg. Make-up Supervision, Joe McKinney. Special Effects, Joe Unsinn. Hairstylist, Lorraine Roberson. Costume Supervisor, Glenn Wright. Panavision, Color by DeLuxe, Prints by Technicolor. San Francisco locations include Alcatraz Island. Third "Dirty Harry" film and Fargo's directorial debut. Rated R. 97 minutes

Harry Callahan: Clint Eastwood, *Lt. Bressler:* Harry Guardino, *Kate Moore:* Tyne Daly, *Capt. McKay:* Bradford Dillman, *Lt. Frank Di-Georgio:* John Mitchum, *Bobby Maxwell:* DeVeren Bookwalter, *The Mayor:* John Crawford, *Police Sergeant:* Tom O'Neil, *Wanda:* Samantha Doane, *Buchinski:* Robert Hoy, *Big Ed:* Albert Popwell, *Henry Lee Caldwell:* Tim Burrus, *Stunt Double:* Wayne (Buddy) Van Horn.

Enter the Dragon with Bruce Lee.

ENTER THE DRAGON (1973) WB. Produced by Fred Weintraub and Paul Heller. Associate Producer, Raymond Chow. Directed by Robert Clouse. A Concord Production, in Panavision and Technicolor. Screenplay by Michael Allin. Music by Lalo Schifrin. Photography, Gilbert Hubbs. Editors, Kurt Hirshler and George Watters. Art Director, James Wong Sun. Assistant Director, Chaplin Chang. 2nd Unit Photography, Charles Low. Sound, Zee Shao Lin. Fight Arranger, Bruce Lee. Rated R. 98 minutes

Lee: Bruce Lee, *Roper:* John Saxon, *Williams:* Jim Kelly, *Han:* Shih Kien, *Oharra:* Bob Wall, *Tania:* Ahna Capri, *Su-Lin:* Angela Mao Ying, *Mei Ling:* Betty Chung, *Braithwaite:* Geoffrey Weeks, *Bolo:* Yang Sze, *Parsons:* Peter Archer, *Old Man:* Ho Lee Wan, *Secretary:* Marlene Clark, *Golfer:* Allan Kent, *L.A. Cops:* William Keller and Mickey Caruso, *Hoods:* Pat Johnson, Darnell Garcia, Mike Bissell.

Every Which Way But Loose with Clint Eastwood and Sondra Locke.

EVERY WHICH WAY BUT LOOSE (1978) WB. A Malpaso Company Film. Produced by Robert Daley. Directed by James Fargo. Written by Jeremy Joe Kronsberg. Panavision equipment, DeLuxe Color. Photography, Rexford Metz. Art Director, Elayne Ceder. Editors, Ferris Webster and Joel Cox. Associate Producers, Fritz Manes and Kronsberg. Music Supervision, Snuff Garrett. Music conducted by Steve Dorff. Assistant Director, Larry Powell. 2nd Assistant Directors, Wendy Shear, Al Silvani and Alain J. Silver. Set Decoration, Robert De Vestel. Stunt Coordinator, Wayne Van Horn. Sound, Bert Hallberg. Special Effects, Chuck Gaspar. Make-up Artist, Don Schoenfeld. Hairstylist, Dorothie J. Long. Costume Supervisor, Glenn Wright. Technical Adviser, Al Silvani. Songs: "Every Which Way But Loose" by Steve Dorff, M. Brown and T. Garrett, sung by Eddie Rabbitt; "I'll Wake You Up When I Get Home" by Dorff and Brown, sung by Charlie Rich; "Behind Closed Doors" by K. O'Dell, sung by Rich; "Coca-Cola Cowboy" by S. Pinkard, I. Dain, Dorff and S. Atchley, sung by Mel Tillis; "Send Me Down to Tucson" by Cliff Crofford and T. Garrett, sung by Tillis; "Ain't Love Good Tonight" by G. Sklerov, R. Cate and G. Howe, sung by Wayne Parker; "Don't Say You Don't Love Me No More" by Phil Everly and J. Paige, sung by Sondra Locke and Everly; "Honky Tonk Fever" by Crofford and T. Garrett, sung by Crofford; "Monkey See, Monkey Do" by Crofford and T. Garrett, sung by Crofford; "I Can't Say No to a Truck Drivin' Man" by Crofford, sung by Carol Chase; "I Seek the Night," sung by Locke; "Red Eye Special" by S. Collins, Pinkard and T. Garrett, sung by Larry Collins; "Salty Dog Blues," adapted by Dorff and T. Garrett; "Under the Double Eagle," adapted by Dorff and T. Garrett; "Six Pack to Go," by Hank Thompson, Lowe and Hart, sung by Hank Thompson. Rated PG. 115 minutes

Philo Beddoe: Clint Eastwood, *Lynn Halsey-Taylor:* Sondra Locke, *Orville Boggs:* Geoffrey Lewis, *Ma Boggs:* Ruth Gordon, *Echo:* Beverly D'Angelo, *Themselves:* Phil Everly, Mel Tillis, Charlie Rich, *Cholly:* John Quade, *Putnam:* Gregory Walcott, *Herb:* James McEachin, *Woody:* Roy Jenson, *Frank:* William O'Connell, *Tank Murdock:* Walter Barnes, *Church:* George Wilbur, *Trailer Camp Owner:* Hank Worden, *Department of Motor Vehicles Clerk:* George Chandler, *Waitress:* Joyce Jameson, *Fruit Customer:* Thelma Pelish, *Bartender:* Guy Way, *Oiler:* Jerry Wills, *Clyde the Orangutan:* Manis (trained by Bobby and Joan Berosini). Cut was Doug McGrath as the Albuquerque Zoo Keeper.

EXECUTIVE SUITE (1954) MGM. Producer, John Houseman. Director, Robert Wise. Based on the novel by Cameron Hawley. Screenplay, Ernest Lehman. Art Directors, Cedric Gibbons, Edward Carfango. Cinematographer, George Folsey. Editor, Ralph E. Winters. 104 minutes

McDonald Walling: William Holden, *Mary Blemond Walling:* June Allyson, *Julia O. Tredway:* Barbara Stanwyck, *Loren Phineas Shaw:* Fredric March, *Frederick Alderson:* Walter Pidgeon, *Eva Bardeman:* Shelley Winters, *Josiah Dudley:* Paul Douglas, *George Nyle Caswell:* Mike Walling:* Tim Considine, *Bill Lundeen:* William Phipps, *Mrs. Caswell:* Lucille Knoch, *Sara Grimm:* Mary Adams, *Edith Alderson:* Virginia Brissac, *Julius Steigel:* Edgar Stehli, *Ed Benedeck:* Harry Shannon, *Grimm's Secretary:* May McAvoy, *Luigi Cassoni:* Charles Wagenheim, *Cop:* Jonathan Cott, *Morgue Officials:* Willis Bouchey, John Doucette, *News Dealers:* Esther Michelson, Gus Schilling, *Stork Club Waiter:* Paul Bryar, *Enrique, Waiter Captain at Stork Club:* John Banner, *Jimmy Farrell:* Roy Engel, *Wailing Housekeeper:* Maidie Norman, *City Editor:* Dan Riss, *Avery Bullard:* Raoul Freeman, *Lee Ormond:* Bob Carson, *Shaw's Secretary:* Ann Tyrrell, *Alderson's Secretary:* Ray Mansfield, *Liz:* Kazia Orzazewski, *Sam Teal:* Burt Mustin, *Miss Clark:* Helen Brown, *Airport Clerk:* Wilson Wood, *Servant:* Matt Moore.

Executive Suite with Nina Foch, Barbara Stanwyck, Walter Pidgeon, William Holden, Dean Jagger, Louis Calhern and Fredric March.

Exodus with Sal Mineo and Paul Newman.

EXODUS (1960) UA. Producer-Director, Otto Preminger. Screenplay, Dalton Trumbo. From the novel by Leon Uris. Music, Ernest Gold. Costumes, Rudi Gernreich, Hope Bryce. Assistant Directors, Otto Plaschkes, Gerry O'Hara, Yoel Silberg, Larry Frisch, Christopher Trumbo. In Super-Panavision 70 and Technicolor. Art Director, Richard Day. Cinematography, Sam Leavitt. Editor, Louis R. Loeffler. Produced in Israel. 213 minutes

Ari Ben Canaan: Paul Newman, *Kitty Fremont:* Eva Marie Saint, *General Sutherland:* Ralph Richardson, *Major Caldwell:* Peter Lawford, *Barak Ben Canaan:* Lee J. Cobb, *Dov Landau:* Sal Mineo, *Taha:* John Derek, *Mandria:* Hugh Griffith, *Lakavitch:* Gregory Ratoff, *Dr. Lieberman:* Felix Aylmer, *Akiva:* David Opatoshu, *Karen:* Jill

Haworth, *Von Storch:* Marius Goring, *Jordana:* Alexandra Stewart, *David:* Michael Wager, *Mordekai:* Martin Benson, *Reuben:* Paul Stevens, *Sarah:* Betty Walker, *Dr. Odenheim:* Martin Miller, *Sergeant:* Victor Maddern, *Yaov:* George Maharis, *Hank:* John Crawford, *Proprietor:* Samuel Segal, *Uzi:* Dahn Ben Amotz, *Colonel:* Ralph Truman, *Dr. Clement:* Peter Madden, *Avidan:* Joseph Furst, *Driver:* Paul Stassino, *Lieutenant O'Hara:* Marc Burns, *Mrs. Hirshberg:* Esther Reichstadt, *Mrs. Frankel:* Zeporah Peled, *Novak:* Philo Hauser.

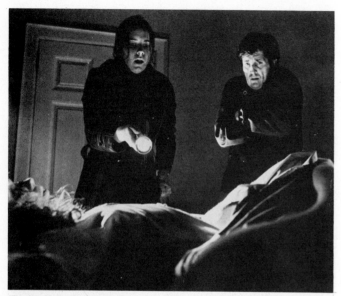

The Exorcist with Linda Blair, Ellen Burstyn and Jason Miller.

THE EXORCIST (1973) WB. A Hoya Production. Produced by William Peter Blatty. Executive Producer, Noel Marshall. Directed by William Friedkin. Screenplay by Blatty, based on his 1971 novel. Photography, Owen Roizman. Iraq Photography, Billy Williams. Production Designer, Bill Malley. Supervising Film Editor, Jordan Leondopoulos. Editors, Evan Lottman and Norman Gay. Iraq Editor, Bud Smith. Sound, Chris Newman. Iraq Sound, Jean-Louis Ducarme. Set Decorator, Jerry Wunderlich. Special Effects, Marcel Vercoutere. Costume Designer, Joseph Fretwell. Make-up, Dick Smith. Associate Producer, David Salven. Technical Advisers: Rev. John Nicola, S.J.; Rev. Thomas V. Bermingham, S.J.; Rev. William J. O'Malley, S.J.; Dr. Norman E. Chase, Professor of Radiology, New York University Medical Center; Dr. Herbert E. Walker; and Dr. Arthur I. Snyder. Assistant Directors, Terence A. Donnelly and Alan Green. Publicist, Howard Newman. Last film of Jack MacGowran, 54, who had replaced J. Lee Thompson and died January 30, 1973. Metrocolor. Photographic Equipment by Panavision. Filmed in Iraq, New York City and Washington, D.C.'s Georgetown section. Music by Jack Nitzsche, originally assigned to Lalo Schifrin. Burstyn's part was originally designed for (but not about) Shirley MacLaine. Rated R. 121 minutes. Sequel was *Exorcist II: The Heretic* (1977), also with Blair, Von Sydow and Winn

Chris MacNeil: Ellen Burstyn, *Father Merrin:* Max von Sydow, *Lt. Kinderman:* Lee J. Cobb, *Father Damian Karras:* Jason Miller, *Regan Teresa MacNeil:* Linda Blair, *Sharon Spencer:* Kitty Winn, *Burke Dennings:* Jack MacGowran, *Father Dyer:* Rev. William J. O'Malley, *Dr. Klein:* Barton Heyman, *Clinic Director:* Peter Masterson, *Karl:* Rudolf Schundler, *Willie:* Gina Petrushka, *Dr. Tanney:* Robert Symonds, *Psychiatrist:* Arthur Storch, *Georgetown University President:* Rev. Thomas V. Bermingham, *Mary Karras:* Vasiliki Maliaros, *Karras' Uncle:* Titos Vandis, *Bishop:* Wallace Rooney, *Assistant Director:* Ron Faber, *Jesuit Dean:* Roy Cooper, *Senator:* Robert Gerringer, *Senator's Wife:* Joanne Dusseau, *Mary Joe Perrin:* Donna Mitchell, *Language Lab Director:* John Mahon, *Astronaut:* Richard Callinan, *Nurse:* Yvonne M. Jones, *Derelict in Subway:* Vincent Russell, *Woman:* Beatrice Hunter, *Priest:* Rev. John Nicola, *1st Mental Patient:* Mary Boylan, *Interne:* Bob Dahdah, *Regan's Demon:* Voice of Mercedes McCambridge, *Other Voices:* Kitty Malone, Michael Cristofer, Liam Dunn, Phillippa Harris, Maidie Norman, Victor Argo, Mason Curry, Claudia Lennear, *Stunts:* Eileen Dietz, Ann Miles, Chuck Waters.

A FACE IN THE CROWD (1957) WB. A Newton Production. Director, Elia Kazan. Story and screenplay by Budd Schulberg. Score by Tom Glazer. Songs by Tom Glazer and Budd Schulberg. Costumes by Anna Hill Johnstone. Wardrobe by Florence Transfield. Assistant Director, Charles H. Maguire. From the short story "Your Arkansas Traveler" by Budd Schulberg. James G. McGhee plays the guitar for Andy Griffith. Songs: "Mama Git-tar," "Free Man in the Morning." Film debuts of Andy Griffith, 30 and Lee Remick, 21. 125 minutes

Lonesome Rhodes: Andy Griffith, *Marcia Jeffries:* Patricia Neal, *Joey Kiely:* Anthony Franciosa, *Mel Miller:* Walter Matthau, *Betty Lou Fleckum:* Lee Remick, *Col. Hollister:* Percy Waram, *Beanie:* Rod Brasfield, *Mr. Luffler:* Charles Irving, *J. B. Jeffries:* Howard Smith, *Macey:* Paul McGrath, *First Mrs. Rhodes:* Kay Medford, *Jim Collier:* Alexander Kirkland, *Senator Fuller:* Marshall Nielan, *Sheriff Hosmer:* Big Jeff Bess, *Abe Steiner:* Henry Sharp, *Themselves:* Bennett Cerf, Faye Emerson, Betty Furness, Virginia Graham, Burl Ives, Sam Levenson, John Cameron Swayze, Mike Wallace, Earl Wilson, Walter Winchell.

A Face in the Crowd with Walter Matthau, Patricia Neal and Andy Griffith.

Fancy Pants with Bob Hope and Lucille Ball.

FANCY PANTS (1950) Par. Produced by Robert Welch. Directed by George Marshall. Color by Technicolor. Based on the story *Ruggles of Red Gap* by Harry Leon Wilson. Screenplay, Edmund Hartman and Robert O'Brien. Art Directors, Hans Dreier and Earl Hedrick. Music, Van Cleave. Photography, Charles B. Lang, Jr. Editor, Archie Marshek. Songs by Ray Evans and Jay Livingston: "Fancy Pants," "Home Cookin'" and "Yes, M'Lord." Remake of *Ruggles of Red Gap* (Paramount, 1935) 92 minutes

Humphrey: Bob Hope, *Aggie Floud:* Lucille Ball, *Cart Belknap:* Bruce Cabot, *Mike Floud:* Jack Kirkwood, *Effie Floud:* Lea Penman, *George Van Basingwell:* Hugh French, *Sir Wimbley:* Eric Blore, *Wampum:*

Joseph Vitale, *Teddy Roosevelt:* John Alexander, *Lady Maude:* Norma Varden, *Rosalind:* Virginia Kelley, *Twombley:* Colin Keith-Johnston, *Wong:* Joe Wong, *Cyril:* Robin Hughes, *Mayor Fogarty:* Percy Helton, *Millie:* Hope Sansberry, *Dolly:* Grace Gillern Albertson, *Mr. Andrews:* Oliver Blake, *Guest:* Chester Conklin, *Mr. Jones:* Edgar Dearing, *Daisy:* Alva Marie Lacy, *Betsy and Bessie:* Ida Moore, *Mrs. Wilkins:* Ethel Wales, *Miss Wilkins:* Jean Ruth, *First Henchman:* Jimmie Dundee, *Second Henchman:* Bob Kortman, *Umpire:* Major Sam Harris, *Wicket Keeper:* Gilchrist Stuart, *Man:* Charley Cooley, *Stage Manager:* Olaf Hytten, *Stagehand:* Alex Frazer, *First Secret Service Man:* Howard Petrie, *Second Secret Service Man:* Ray Bennett, *Belle:* Almira Sessions.

Fantasia.

FANTASIA (1940) Walt Disney-RKO. Produced by Walt Disney. Production Supervisor, Ben Sharpsteen. In Wide Screen, Multiplane Technicolor, and Fantasound (later Stereoponic Sound). Story Directors, Joe Grant and Dick Huemer. Directors of individual numbers: Samuel Armstrong, James Algar, Bill Roberts, Paul Satterfield, Hamilton Luske, Jim Handley, Ford Beebe, T. Hee, Norm Ferguson, Wilfred Jackson. Music Director, Edward H. Plumb. Music Film Editor, Stephen Csillag. Fantasound recorded by RCA, developed in collaboration with Walt Disney Studio. Recording, William E. Garity, C. O. Slyfield, J. N. A. Hawkins. Selections: "Toccata and Fugue in D Minor" by Bach, "The Nutcracker Suite" by Tchaikovsky, "The Sorcerer's Apprentice" by Dukas, "The Pastoral Symphony" by Beethoven, "Rite of Spring" by Stravinsky, "Dance of the Hours" by Ponchielli, "Night on Bald Mountain" by Moussorgsky, "Ave Maria" by Franz Schubert. 135 minutes

Leopold Stokowski conducts the Philadelphia Orchestra. Deems Taylor does the narrative introductions. Mickey Mouse is featured in "The Sorcerer's Apprentice." Bela Lugosi was the model for Tchernabog.

Fantastic Voyage with Raquel Welch, Arthur Kennedy, William Redfield, Donald **Pleasence** and Stephen Boyd.

FANTASTIC VOYAGE (1966) 20th. Saul David Production. Directed by Richard Fleischer. CinemaScope and De Luxe Color. Screenplay, Harry Kleiner. Based on a story by Otto Klement and Jay Lewis Bixby, as adapted by David Duncan. Camera, Ernest Laszlo. Editor, William B. Murphy. Music, Leonard Rosenman. Assistant Director, Ad Schaumer. 100 minutes

Grant: Stephen Boyd, *Cora:* Raquel Welch, *Gen. Carter:* Edmond O'Brien, *Dr. Michaels:* Donald Pleasence, *Colonel Reid:* Arthur O'Connell, *Captain Owens:* William Redfield, *Dr. Duval:* Arthur Kennedy, *Jan Benes:* Jean Del Val, *Communications Aide:* Barry Coe, *Secret Service:* Ken Scott, *Nurse:* Shelby Grant, *Technician:* James Brolin, *Wireless Operator:* Brendan Fitzgerald.

A FAREWELL TO ARMS (1932) Par. Directed by Frank Borzage. Assistant Directors, Lou Borzage and Art Jacobson. Based on the novel by Ernest Hemingway. Adapted by Benjamin Glazer, Oliver H. P. Garrett. Photography, Charles Lang. Sound, Harold C. Lewis. Art Director, Roland Anderson. Costumes, Travis Banton. Technical Director of war sequences, Charles Griffin. Technical Director of hospital sequences, Dr. Jardini. Editor, Otho Lovering. Remade as *Force of Arms* (Warners, 1951), *A Farewell to Arms* (20th Century-Fox, 1957). 78 minutes

Catherine Barkley: Helen Hayes, *Frederic Henry:* Gary Cooper, *Major Rinaldi:* Adolphe Menjou, *Helen Ferguson:* Mary Philips, *The Priest:* Jack La Rue, *Head Nurse:* Blanche Frederici, *Bonello:* Henry Armetta, *Piani:* George Humbert, *Manera:* Fred Malatesta, *Miss Van Campen:* Mary Forbes, *Count Greffi:* Tom Ricketts, *Gordoni:* Robert Cauterio, *British Major:* Gilbert Emery.

A Farewell to Arms with Gary Cooper, Helen Hayes and Jack La Rue.

THE FARMER'S DAUGHTER (1947) RKO. Producer, Dore Schary. Director, H.C. Potter. Suggested by a play by Juhni Tervataa. Screenplay, Allen Rivkin, Laura Kerr. Art Directors, Albert S. D'Agostino, Feild Gray. Music, Leigh Harline. Musical Director, C. Bakaleinikoff. Cameraman, Milton Krasner. Editor, Harry Marker. Song by Frank Loesser and Frederick Hollander, "Jungle Jingle." Later the basis for a TV series. 97 minutes

Katrin Holstrom: Loretta Young, *Glenn Morley:* Joseph Cotten, *Mrs. Morley:* Ethel Barrymore, *Clancy:* Charles Bickford, *Virginia Thatcher:* Rose Hobart, *Adolph:* Rhys Williams, *Dr. Matthew Sutven:* Harry Davenport, *Hy Nordick:* Tom Powers, *Ward Hughes:* William Harrigan, *Olaf Holstrom:* Lex Barker, *Mr. Holstrom:* Harry Shannon, *Sven Holstrom:* Keith Andes, *Wilbur Johnson:* Thurston Hall, *A. J. Finley:* Art Baker, *Einar:* Don Beddoe, *Peter Holstrom:* James Aurness (Arness), *Mrs. Holstrom:* Anna Q. Nilsson, *Dr. Mattsen:* Sven Hugo Borg, *Van:* John Gallaudet, *Eckers:* William B. Davidson, *Fisher:* Charles McGraw, *Night Editor:* Jason Robards, *Sweeney:* Cy Kendall,

Matternack: Frank Ferguson, *Windor:* William Bakewell, *Jackson, Reporter:* Charles Lane, *Silbey, Politician:* Douglas Evans, *Assistant Announcer:* Robert Clarke, *Woman:* Bess Flowers.

The *Farmer's Daughter* with Joseph Cotten, Loretta Young, Charles Bickford and Ethel Barrymore.

FATHER OF THE BRIDE (1950) MGM. Producer, Pandro S. Berman. Director, Vincente Minnelli. Author, Edward Streeter. Screenplay, Frances Goodrich, Albert Hackett. Art Directors, Cedric Gibbons, Leonid Vasian. Music, Adolph Deutsch. Photography, John Alton. Editor, Ferris Webster. Sequel was *Father's Little Dividend* (1951). 93 minutes

Stanley T. Banks: Spencer Tracy, *Ellie Banks:* Joan Bennett, *Kay Banks:* Elizabeth Taylor, *Buckley Dunstan:* Don Taylor, *Mrs. Doris Dunstan:* Billie Burke, *Mr. Massoula:* Leo G. Carroll, *Herbert Dunstan:* Moroni Olsen, *Mr. Tringle:* Melville Cooper, *Warner:* Taylor Holmes, *Rev. A. I. Galsworthy:* Paul Harvey, *Joe:* Frank Orth, *Tommy Banks:* Rusty Tamblyn, *Ben Banks:* Tom Irish, *Delilah:* Marietta Canty, *Dixon:* Willard Waterman, *Fliss:* Nancy Valentine, *Effie:* Mary Jane Smith, *Peg:* Jacqueline Duval, *Miss Bellamy:* Fay Baker, *Duffy:* Frank Hyers, *Usher:* Chris Drake, *Organist:* Douglas Spencer, *Fat Man:* Paul Maxey, *Young Man (Usher):* Peter Thompson, *Young Man With Coke (Usher):* Carleton Carpenter, *Timid Guest:* Frank Cady, *Teacher:* Lillian Bronson, *Stranger:* Thomas Browne Henry, *Movers:* Dewey Robinson, Ed Gargan, Ralph Peters, Dick Wessel, Dick Alexander, Joe Brown, Jr., Jim Hayward, Gil Perkins, *Foreman of Movers:* William "Bill" Phillips.

Father of the Bride with Spencer Tracy and Elizabeth Taylor.

FATHER'S LITTLE DIVIDEND (1951) MGM. Producer, Pandro S. Berman. Director, Vincente Minnelli. Screenplay, Albert Hackett,

Frances Goodrich. Art Directors, Cedric Gibbons, Leonid Vasian. Musical Director, Georgie Stoll. Photography, John Alton. Editor, Ferris Webster. Sequel to *Father of the Bride* (MGM, 1950). 82 minutes

Stanley Banks: Spencer Tracy, *Ellie Banks:* Joan Bennett, *Kay Dunstan:* Elizabeth Taylor, *Buckley Dunstan:* Don Taylor, *Doris Dunstan:* Billie Burke, *Herbert Dunstan:* Moroni Olsen, *Policeman:* Frank Faylen, *Delilah:* Marietta Canty, *Tommy Banks:* Rusty Tamblyn, *Ben Banks:* Tom Irish, *Dr. Andrew Nordell:* Hayden Rorke, *Reverend Galsworthy:* Paul Harvey, *Nurse:* Beverly Thompson, *Taxi Driver:* Dabbs Greer, *Officer:* Robert B. Williams, *Diaper Man:* Frank Sully, *Mike:* James Menzies, *Red:* Thomas Menzies, *Old Man:* Harry Hines, *Bridesmaids:* Nancy Valentine, Wendy Waldron, *Elderly Man on Porch:* Lon Poff, *Gym Instructor:* George Bruggeman, *The Dividend:* Donald Clark.

Father's Little Dividend with Spencer Tracy and Elizabeth Taylor.

FBI Story with Murray Hamilton and James Stewart.

THE FBI STORY (1959) WB. Producer-Director, Mervyn LeRoy. Screenplay by Robert L. Breen and John Twist. Based on the book by Don Whitehead. Music by Max Steiner. Costumes by Adele Palmer. Assistant Directors, David Silver, Gil Kissel. In Technicolor. Art Director, John Beckman. Orchestration, Murray Cutter. Photography, Joseph Biroc. Editor, Philip W. Anderson. Locations filmed in Washington, D. C., and New York City. 149 minutes

Chip Hardesty (Narrator): James Stewart, *Lucy Hardesty:* Vera Miles,

Sam Crandall: Murray Hamilton, *George Crandall:* Larry Pennell, *Jack Graham:* Nick Adams, *Jennie (adult):* Diane Jergens, *Anna Sage (The Lady In Red):* Jean Willes, *Anne (adult):* Joyce Taylor, *Mario:* Victor Millan, *Harry Dakins:* Parley Baer, *Dwight MacCutcheon:* Fay Roope, *U.S. Marshal/Radio Announcer:* Ed Prentiss, *Medicine Salesman:* Robert Gist, *Mike (adult):* Buzz Martin, *Casket Salesman:* Kenneth Mayer, *Whitey (Suspect):* Paul Genge, *Wedding Minister:* Forrest Taylor, *Mrs. Ballard:* Ann Doran, *John Dillinger:* Scott Peters, *Baby Face Nelson:* William Phipps, *Interrogator:* John Damler, *Taylor:* Paul Smith, *Mrs. Graham:* Eleanor Audley, *Neighbor:* Harry Harvey, *Doctor:* Sam Flint, *Schneider:* Burt Mustin, *Cliff:* Guy Wilkerson, *Minister:* Grandon Rhodes, *Sandy:* Nesdon Booth, *Cabby:* Ray Montgomery, *Girl:* Lori Martin, *Himself:* J. Edgar Hoover.

Fiddler on the Roof with Leonard Frey, Rosalind Harris and Topol.

FIDDLER ON THE ROOF (1971) UA. A Mirisch Company Production. Produced and Directed by Norman Jewison. Screenplay by Joseph Stein, based on his book for the 1964 musical, which was produced by Harold Prince, directed and choreographed by Jerome Robbins and which starred Zero Mostel. Adapted from the play *Tevye and His Daughters* by Sholom Aleichem. Associate Producer, Patrick Palmer. Editors, Antony Gibbs and Robert Lawrence. Violin Soloist (for fiddler), Isaac Stern. Music adapted and conducted by John Williams. Choreography adapted by Tom Abbott, assisted by Sammy Bayes. Photography, Oswald Morris. Production Designer, Robert Boyle. Art Director, Michael Stringer. Set Decorator, Peter Lamont. Costumes designed by Elizabeth Haffenden and Joan Bridge. Production Supervisor, Larry De Waay. Assistant Directors: Terry Nelson, Terry Churcher, Howard Grigsby, Paul Ibbetson and Vladimir Spindler. Asssistant to Producer, Jerry Howard. Wardrobe Supervisor, Jackie Cummins. Orchestrations, John Williams and Alexander Courage. Make-up, Del Armstrong and Wally Schneiderman. Music by Jerry Bock. Lyrics by Sheldon Harnick. Songs: "Tradition," "Matchmaker, Matchmaker," "If I Were a Rich Man," "Sabbath Prayer," "To Life," "Miracle of Miracles," "Tevye's Dream," "Sunrise, Sunset," "Bottle Dance," "Do You Love Me?" "Far from the Home I Love" and "Anatevka." Filmed in Lakenik, Yugoslavia, and at Pinewood Studios, London. In Panavision, 70mm and Technicolor. Rated G. 178 minutes

Tevye: Topol, *Golde:* Norma Crane, *Motel:* Leonard Frey, *Yente:* Molly Picon, *Lazar Wolf:* Paul Mann, *Tzeitel:* Rosalind Harris, *Hodel:* Michele Marsh, *Chava:* Neva Small, *Perchik:* (Paul) Michael Glaser, *Fyedka:* Raymond Lovelock, *Shprintze:* Elaine Edwards, *Bielke:* Candy Bonstein, *The Fiddler:* Tutte Lemkow, *Rabbi:* Zvee Scooler, *Mordcha:* Shimen Ruskin, *Constable:* Louis Zorich, *Avram:* Alfie Scopp, *Mendel:* Barry Dennen, *Nachum:* Howard Goorney, *Russian Official:* Vernon Dobtcheff, *Shandel:* Stella Courtney, *Grandma Tzeitel:* Patience Collier, *Fruma Sarah:* Ruth Madoc, *Previous Rabbi:* Alfred Maron, *Yussel:* Otto Diamant, *Sheftel:* Aharon Ipale, *Berl:* Brian Coburn, *Rifka:* Marika Rivera, *Farcel:* Stanley Fleet, *Gnessi:* Judith Harte, *Leibesh:* Harry Ditson, *Marcus:* Joel Rudnick, *Joshua:* Michael Lewis, *Hone:* George Little,

Sexton: Roger Lloyd Pack, *Rebecca:* Hazel Wright, *Isaac:* Carl Jaffe, *Yankel:* Jacob Kalich, *Russian Dancers:* Sammy Bayes, Larry Bianco, Walter Cartier, Peter Johnston, Guy Lutman, Donald MacLennan, Rene Sartoris.

THE FIGHTING 69TH (1940) In Charge of Production, Jack L. Warner. Executive Producer, Hal B. Wallis. Associate Producer, Louis F. Edelman. Directed by William Keighley. Original Screenplay, Norman Reilly Raine, Fred Niblo, Jr., and Dean Franklin. Photography, Tony Gaudio. Special Effects, Byron Haskin and Rex Wimpy. Editor, Owen Marks. Technical Advisors, Captain John T. Prout and Mark White. Battlefield scenes filmed at the Calabasas ranch. 89 minutes

Jerry Plunkett: James Cagney, *Father Duffy:* Pat O'Brien, *Wild Bill Donovan:* George Brent, *Joyce Kilmer:* Jeffrey Lynn, *Sergeant Big Mike Wynn:* Alan Hale, *"Crepe Hanger" Burke:* Frank McHugh, *Lieutenant Ames:* Dennis Morgan, *Lt. Long John Wynn:* Dick Foran, *Timmy Wynn:* William Lundigan, *Paddy Dolan:* Guinn "Big Boy" Williams, *The Colonel:* Henry O'Neill, *Captain Mangan:* John Litel, *Mike Murphy:* Sammy Cohen, *Major Anderson:* Harvey Stephens, *Private Turner:* DeWolfe (William) Hopper, *Private McManus:* Tom Dugan, *Jack O'Keefe:* George Reeves, *Moran:* John Ridgely, *Chaplain Holmes:* Charles Trowbridge, *Lt. Norman:* Frank Wilcox, *Casey:* Herbert Anderson, *Healey:* J. Anthony Hughes, *Captain Bootz:* Frank Mayo, *Carroll:* John Harron, *Ryan:* George Kilgen, *Tierney:* Richard Clayton, *Regan:* Edward Dew, *Doctors:* Wilfred Lucas, Emmett Vogan, *Sergeant:* Frank Sully, *Doctor:* Joseph Crehan, *Supply Sergeant:* James Flavin, *Jimmy:* Frank Coghlan, Jr., *Eddie:* George O'Hanlon, *Major:* Jack Perrin, *Alabama Men:* Trevor Bardette, John Arledge, Frank Melton, Edmund Glover, *Soldier:* Johnny Day, *Engineer Sergeant:* Frank Faylen, *Engineer Officer:* Edgar Edwards, *Soldier:* Sol Gorss, *Medical Captain:* Ralph Dunn.

The Fighting 69th with George Reeves and James Cagney.

THE FIREFLY (1937) MGM. Produced by Hunt Stromberg. Directed by Robert Z. Leonard. Based on the 1912 musical *The Firefly*, book and lyrics by Otto A. Harbach, music by Rudolf Friml. Screenplay, Frances Goodrich and Albert Hackett. Adaptation, Ogden Nash. Music Director, Herbert Stothart. Editor, Robert J. Kern. Filmed in Sepia. Photography, Oliver Marsh. Dances, Albertina Rasch. Pyrenees Mountains scenes shot at Lone Pine at the foot of the Sierras. Art Director, Cedric Gibbons. Song. "Donkey Serenade" by Bob Wright, Chet Forrest, and Rudolf Friml (written for the film); songs by Rudolf Friml and Otto Harbach: "Love Is Like a Firefly," "When a Maid Comes Knocking at Your Heart," "A Woman's Kiss," "Giannina Mia," "Sympathy," "When the Wine Is Full of Fire," "He Who Loves and Runs Away." Film debut of Leonard Penn, Gladys George's husband. 138 minutes

Nina Maria Azara: Jeanette MacDonald, *Don Diego Manrique de Lara/ Captain Francois DeCoucourt:* Allan Jones, *Colonel DeRougemont:* Warren William, *Innkeeper:* Billy Gilbert, *General Savary:* Henry Daniell, *Marquis DeMelito:* Douglass Dumbrille, *Etienne:* Leonard Penn, *King Ferdinand:* Tom Rutherfurd, *Lola:* Belle Mitchell, *St. Clair, Chief of French Secret Service:* George Zucco, *Duval:* Corbett Morris, *Duke of Wellington:* Matthew Boulton, *Juan:* Robert Spindola, *Izquierdo, Minister:* Ian Wolfe, *Pedro:* Manuel Alvarez Maciste, *Pablo:* Frank Puglia, *Cafe Proprietor:* John Picorri, *Smiling Waiter:* James B. Carson, *Spanish Patriot:* Jason Robards, *French Soldier:* Alan Curtis, *French Lieutenant:* Ralph Byrd, *French Soldier-Admirer:* Dennis O'Keefe, *Strawberry Vendor:* Maurice Cass, *Fruit Vendor:* Sam Appel, *Pigeon Vendor:* Maurice Black, *Hat Vendor:* Rolfe Sedan, *Flower Woman:* Inez Palange, *Secret Service Adjutant:* Harry Worth, *French Officer:* John Merton, *French Officer:* Hooper Atchley, *Joseph Bonaparte:* Stanley Price, *English General:* Brandon Hurst, *Spanish General:* Pedro de Cordoba, *Captain Pierlot:* Theodore von Eltz, *Captain of the Guard:* Lane Chandler, *Colonel (Chief of Staff):* Edward Keane, *Secretary:* Sidney Bracy, *Captain:* Eddie Phillips, *Stablehand:* Russ Powell, *Peasant:* Agostino Borgato, *Cafe Extras:* Robert Z. Leonard, Albertina Rasch.

The Firefly with Warren William and Jeanette MacDonald.

Five Easy Pieces with Karen Black and Jack Nicholson.

FIVE EASY PIECES (1970) Col. A BBS Production. Produced by Bob Rafelson and Richard Wechsler. Directed by Bob Rafelson. Color by MGM Laboratories. Screenplay, Adrien Joyce. From a story by Rafelson and Joyce. Executive Producer, Bert Schneider. Associate Producer, Harold Schneider. Photography, Laszlo Kovacs. Editors, Christopher Holmes and Gerald Sheppard. Sound by Audio Tran, mixed by Charles Knight. Interior Designer, Toby Rafelson. Assistant Director, Sheldon Schrager. Wardrobe, Bucky Rous. Assistant Editors, Pete Denenberg and Harold Hazen. Songs sung by Tammy Wynette. Piano played by Pearl Kaufman. Music includes pieces by Chopin, Bach and Mozart. Filmed mainly in Oregon. Although Challee got introductory billing, he started in films in the early forties. Rated R. 96 minutes

Robert Eroica Dupea: Jack Nicholson, *Rayette Dipesto:* Karen Black, *Catherine Van Ost:* Susan Anspach, *Partita Dupea:* Lois Smith, *Carl Fidelio Dupea:* Ralph Waite, *Elton:* Billy "Green" Bush, *Samia Glavia:* Irene Dailey, *Terry Grouse:* Toni Basil, *Waitress:* Lorna Thayer, *Recording Engineer:* Richard Stahl, *Palm Apodaca:* Helena Kallianiotes, *Nicholas Dupea:* William Challee, *Spicer:* John Ryan, *Stoney:* Fannie Flagg, *Twinky:* Marlena MacGuire, *Betty:* Sally Ann Struthers.

FIVE FINGERS (1952) 20th. Producer, Otto Lang. Director, Joseph L. Mankiewicz. From a novel by L. C. Mayzisch, *Operation Cicero.* Screenplay, Michael Wilson. Art Directors, Lyle Wheeler, George W. Davis. Music, Bernard Herrmann. Cinematographer, Norbert Brodine. Editor, James B. Clark. Filmed in Ankara and Istanbul. Narrator, John Sutton. Later a TV series. 108 minutes

Cicero: James Mason, *Anna:* Danielle Darrieux, *George Travers:* Michael Rennie, *Sir Frederic:* Walter Hampden, *Mayzisch:* Oscar Karlweis, *Col. Von Richter.* Herbert Berghof, *Von Papen:* John Wengraf, *Siebert:* Ben Astar, *Macfadden:* Roger Plowden, *Morrison:* Michael Pate, *Steuben:* Ivan Triesault, *Van Papen's Secretary:* Hannelore Axman, *Da Costa:* David Wolfe, *Santos:* Larry Dobkin, *Turkish Ambassador:* Nestor Paiva, *Japanese Ambassador:* Richard Loo, *Johnson:* Keith McConnell, *Charwoman:* Jeroma Moshan, *British Military Attaché:* Stuart Hall, *Butler:* Albert Morin, *Kaltenbrunner:* Alfred Zeisler, *Pullman Porter:* Otto Waldis, *Proprietor:* Konstantin Shayne, *Turk:* Aram Katcher, *Butler:* Martin Garralaga, *Banker:* Marc Snow, *Undersecretary:* Lester Matthews, *Ship's Captain:* Salvador Baguez, *German Singer:* Faith Kruger, *Italian Ambassador:* Antonio Filauri.

Five Fingers with James Mason and Oscar Karlweis.

THE FIVE PENNIES (1959) Par. Produced by Jack Rose. Directed by Melville Shavelson. VistaVision and Technicolor. Screenplay, Rose and Shavelson. Choreography, Earl Barton. New songs by Sylvia Fine: "The Five Pennies," "Lullaby in Ragtime," "Follow the Leader," "Good Night, Sleep Tight," "Five Pennies Saints" (special lyrics for

"When the Saints Come Marching In"). A Dena Production. Red Nichols plays the trumpet for Danny Kaye. 117 minutes

Red (Ernest Loring) Nichols: Danny Kaye, *Bobbie Meredith (Willa Stutzmeyer):* Barbara Bel Geddes, *Himself:* Louis Armstrong, *Tony Valani:* Harry Guardino, *Wil Paradise:* Bob Crosby, *Artie Shutt:* Bobby Troup, *Dorothy Nichols, ages 6 to 8:* Susan Gordon, *Dorothy Nichols at 12 to 14:* Tuesday Weld, *Jimmy Dorsey:* Ray Anthony, *Dave Tough:* Shelly Manne, *Glenn Miller:* Ray Daley, *Tommye Eden:* Valerie Allen, *Choreographer:* Earl Barton, *Murray:* Ned Glass, *Hawaiian Announcer:* Peter Potter, *Headmistress:* Blanche Sweet, *Barber:* Tito Vuolo, *Taxi Driver:* Joe McTurk, *Richard:* Paul Sullivan, *Girls at Party:* Carol Sydes (Cindy Carol), Susan Seaforth, *Boy at Party:* Richard Shavelson, *Patient:* Charles Herbert, *Rehabilitation Patient:* Babbette Bain, *Specialty Dancer:* Frank C. Radcliffe, *Himself:* Bob Hope.

The Five Pennies with Danny Kaye and Susan Gordon.

Five Star Final with Oscar Apfel, Edward G. Robinson, Anthony Bushell, Marian Marsh and Boris Karloff.

FIVE STAR FINAL (1931) WB. Directed by Mervyn LeRoy. From the play by Louis Weitzenkorn. Art Director, Jack Okey. Scenario, Robert Lord. Dialogue, Byron Morgan. Assistant Director, Gordon Hollingshead. Photography, Sol Polito. Editor, Frank Ware. Gowns, Earl Luick. Vitaphone orchestra conducted by Leo Forbstein. Remade as *Two Against the World* (Warners, 1936). 89 minutes

Joseph Randall: Edward G. Robinson, *Michael Townsend:* H. B. Warner, *Jenny Townsend:* Marian Marsh, *Phillip Weeks:* Anthony Bushell, *Ziggie Feinstein:* George E. Stone, *Nancy (Vorhees) Townsend:* Frances Starr, *Kitty Carmody:* Ona Munson, *Telephone Operator:* Polly Walters, *Brannegan:* Robert Elliott, *Miss Taylor:* Aline MacMahon, *Miss Edwards:* Gladys Lloyd, *T. Vernon Isopod:* Boris Karloff, *Mrs. Weeks:* Evelyn Hall, *Mr. Weeks:* David Torrence, *Arthur Goldberg:* Harold Waldridge, *Bernard Hinchecliffe:* Oscar Apfel, *Robert French:* Purnell Pratt, *Reporter:* James Burtis, *Schwartz, Assistant Undertaker:* Frank Darien.

The Flame and the Arrow with Nick Cravat, Virginia Mayo, Robert Douglas and Burt Lancaster.

THE FLAME AND THE ARROW (1950) WB. Produced by Harold Hecht and Frank Ross. Directed by Jacques Tourneur. Color by Technicolor. A Norma Production. Original Screenplay, Waldo Salt. Art Director, Edward Carrere. Music, Max Steiner. Photographer, Ernest Haller. Editor, Alan Crosland, Jr. 88 minutes

Dardo: Burt Lancaster, *Anne:* Virginia Mayo, *Alessandro:* Robert Douglas, *Nonna Bartoli:* Aline MacMahon, *Ulrich:* Frank Allenby, *Piccolo:* Nick Cravat, *Francesca:* Lynn Baggett, *Rudi:* Gordon Gebert, *Troubadour:* Norman Lloyd, *Apothecary:* Victor Kilian, *Papa Pietro:* Francis Pierlot, *Skinner:* Robin Hughes.

Flamingo Road with Sydney Greenstreet and Joan Crawford.

FLAMINGO ROAD (1949) WB. Producer, Jerry Wald. Director, Michael Curtiz. Based on a play by Robert Wilder and Sally Wilder. Screenplay, Robert Wilder. Musical Director, Ray Heindorf. Art Director, Leo K. Kuter. Photography, Ted McCord. Editor, Folmer Blangsted. Additional Dialogue, Edmund H. North. Song, "If I Could

Be With You" by Henry Creamer and Jimmy Johnson. Film debut of David Brian. 94 minutes

Lane Bellamy: Joan Crawford, *Fielding Carlisle:* Zachary Scott, *Titus Semple:* Sydney Greenstreet, *Dan Reynolds:* David Brian, *Lute-Mae Sanders:* Gladys George, *Annabelle Weldon:* Virginia Huston, *Doc Waterson:* Fred Clark, *Millie:* Gertrude Michael, *Gracie:* Alice White, *Boatright:* Sam McDaniel, *Pete Ladas:* Tito Vuolo, *Barker:* Dick Ryan, *Barker:* Pat Gleason, *Fire-Eater:* Louis J. Manley, *Juggler:* Duke Johnson, *Harem Girls:* Dolores Castle, Bridget Brown, *Strong Man:* Mike Carillo, *Todd:* Walter Baldwin, *Tom Coyne:* Dick Elliott, *Angry Man:* James Flavin, *Willie Weaver:* Ken Britton, *John Shelton:* William Bailey: *Ed Parker:* Tristram Coffin, *Leo Mitchell:* Frank Cady, *Tom Hill:* John Gallaudet, *Niles:* Morgan Farley, *Johnny Simms:* Merwyn Bogue (Ish Kabibble), *Tunis Simms:* Dale Robertson, *Postman:* Garry Owen, *Blanche:* Iris Adrian, *Specialty:* Raquel Flores, *Burr Lassen:* William Haade, *Bellboy:* San McKim, *Peterson:* Robert Strange, *Martin:* Larry Blake, *Sarah:* Jan Kayne, *Senators:* Pierre Watkin, Roy Gordon.

Flirtation Walk with Ross Alexander, Ruby Keeler, Dick Powell and John Arledge.

FLIRTATION WALK (1934) WB. Produced and directed by Frank Borzage. Story, Delmer Daves, Lou Edelman. Dances directed by Bobby Connolly. Photography, Sol Polito and George Barnes. Editor, William Holmes. Screenplay, Delmer Daves. Songs by Allie Wrubel and Mort Dixon: "Flirtation Walk," "Mr. and Mrs. Is the Name," "No Horse, No Wife, No Mustache," "I See Two Lovers," "Smoking in the Dark," and "When Do We Eat?" Hawaiian dances, the Luau, Hula-Kui, and Pi-ulu are performed. Scenes filmed at West Point. 97 minutes

Dick "Canary" Dorcy: Dick Powell, *Kathleen (Kit) Fitts:* Ruby Keeler, *Sergeant Scrapper Thornhill:* Pat O'Brien, *Oskie:* Ross Alexander, *Spike:* John Arledge, *Lieutenant Robert Biddle:* John Eldredge, *General John Brent Fitts:* Henry O'Neill, *Sleepy:* Guinn (Big Boy) Williams, *General Paul Landacre:* Frederick Burton, *Chase:* John Darrow, *Eight Ball:* Glen Boles, *Superintendent:* Colonel Tim Lonergan, *Dancer:* Gertrude Keeler, *Extra:* Tyrone Power, *Cadet:* Lieutenant Joe Cummins, *Soldiers:* Cliff Saum and Paul Fix, *Native Leader:* Sol Bright, *Civilian:* William J. Worthington, *Officer:* Emmett Vogan, *Dowager:* Maude Turner Gordon, *Butler:* Frank Dawson, *Blonde:* Frances Lee, *Redhead:* Avis Johnson, *Girl:* Mary Russell, *Cadets:* Carlyle Blackwell Jr., Dick Winslow. Sol Hoopii's Native Orchestra, University of Southern California and Army polo teams.

THE FLY (1958) 20th. Producer, Kurt Neumann. Director, Kurt Neumann. CinemaScope, De Luxe Color. Story, George Langelaan. Screenplay, James Clavell. Art Directors, Lyle R. Wheeler, Theobold Holsopple. Music, Paul Sawtell. Cinematographer, Karl Struss. Editor, Merrill G. White. Sequel was *Return of the Fly* (1959). 94 minutes

Andre: (David) Al Hedison, *Helene:* Patricia Owens, *Francois:* Vincent Price, *Inspector Chares:* Herbert Marshall, *Emma:* Kathleen Freeman, *Nurse Andersone:* Betty Lou Gerson, *Philippe:* Charles Herbert, *Dr. Ejoute:* Eugene Borden, *Gaston:* Torben Meyer, *Orderly:* Harry Carter, *Doctor:* Charles Tannen, *Police Doctor:* Franz Roehn, *French Waiter:* Arthur Dulac.

The Fly with Vincent Price and Herbert Marshall.

FLYING DOWN TO RIO (1933) RKO. Directed by Thornton Freeland. From a play by Anne Caldwell. Screenplay, Louis Brock. Dances, Dave Gould. Photography, J. J. Faulkner. Editor, Jack Kitchin. Scenes filmed over Malibu Beach; backgrounds shot in Rio de Janeiro. Songs by Vincent Youmans, Edward Eliscu, Gus Kahn: "Flying Down to Rio," "The Carioca," "Orchids in the Moonlight," "Music Makes Me." First film pairing Astaire and Rogers. 89 minutes

Belinha de Rezende: Dolores Del Rio, *Roger Bond:* Gene Raymond, *Julio Rubeiro:* Raul Roulien, *Honey Hale:* Ginger Rogers, *Fred Ayres:* Fred Astaire, *Dona Elena:* Blanche Frederici, *Senor de Rezende:* Walter Walker, *Negro Singer:* Etta Moten, *Greeks:* Roy D'Arcy, Maurice Black, Armand Kaliz, *Mayor:* Paul Porcasi, *Banker, Alfredo:* Reginald Barlow, *Concert Singer:* Alice Gentle, *Hammerstein, Hotel Manager:* Franklin Pangborn, *Assistant Manager:* Eric Blore, *Rio Casino Manager:* Luis Alberni, *Banjo Player:* Ray Cooke, *Pilot:* Wallace MacDonald, *Messenger:* Gino Corrado, *Blonde Friend:* Mary Kornman, *Caddy:* Clarence Muse, *Sign Poster:* Harry Semels, *Musician:* Jack Rice, *Musician:* Eddie Borden, *Bits:* Betty Furness, Lucile Browne, Julian Rivero, Pedro Regas, Movita Castaneda, *Dancer:* Martha La Venture, *Bands:* The Brazilian Turunas, The American Clippers Band, *Rodriguez, Chauffeur:* Sidney Bracey.

Flying Down to Rio with Gene Raymond, Fred Astaire and Ginger Rogers.

FOLLOW ME, BOYS! (1966) BV. Producers, Walt Disney and Winston Hibler. Technicolor. Director, Norman Tokar. Screenplay, Louis Pelletier. Based on book *God and My Country* by MacKinlay Kantor. Camera, Clifford Stine. Music, George Bruns. Editor, Robert Stafford. 131 minutes

Lemuel Siddons: Fred MacMurray, *Vida Downey:* Vera Miles, *Hetty Seibert:* Lillian Gish, *John Everett Hughes:* Charlie Ruggles, *Ralph Hastings:* Elliot Reid, *Whitey:* Kurt Russell, *Nora White:* Luana Patten, *Melody Murphy:* Ken Murray, *Edward White, Jr.:* Donald May, *Edward White, Sr.:* Sean McClory, *P.O.W. Lieutenant:* Steve Franken, *Mayor Hi Plommer:* Parley Baer, *Hoodoo Henderson (as a man):* William Reynolds, *Leo (as a man):* Craig Hill, *Doctor Ferris:* Tol Avery, *Judge:* Willis Bouchey, *Ralph's Lawyer:* John Zaremba, *Cora Anderson:* Madge Blake, *Tank Captain:* Carl Reindel, *Frankie Martin (as a man):* Hank Brandt, *Umpire:* Richard Bakalyan, *Corporal:* Tim McIntire, *Huong Lee (as a man):* Willie Soo Hoo, *Hetty's Lawyer:* Tony Regan, *Artie:* Robert B. Williams, *First P.O.W. Soldier:* Jimmy Murphy, *Hoodoo Henderson:* Dean Moray, *P.O.W. Sergeant:* Adam Williams, *Leo:* Bill Booth, *Beefy Smith:* Keith Taylor, *Frankie Martin:* Rickey Kelman, *Mickey Doyle:* Gregg Shank, *Red:* Donnie Carter, *Oliver:* Kit Lloyd, *Tiger:* Ronnie Dapo, *Jimmy:* Dennis Rush, *Eggy:* Kevin Burchett, *Duke:* David Bailey, *Harry:* Eddie Sallia, *David:* Bill "Wahoo" Mills.

Follow Me, Boys! with Fred MacMurray.

FOLLOW THE FLEET (1936) RKO. Produced by Pandro S. Berman. Directed by Mark Sandrich. Founded upon the play *Shore Leave* by Hubert Osborne and Allan Scott. Screenplay, Dwight Taylor. Music Director, Max Steiner. Cameraman, David Abel. Editor, Henry Berman. Ensembles staged by Hermes Pan. Songs by Irving Berlin: "Let Yourself Go," "Let's Face the Music and Dance," "I'm Putting All My Eggs in One Basket," "We Saw the Sea," "Here Am I, But Where Are You?" "Get Thee Behind Me, Satan," "I'd Rather Lead a Band." Film debut of Tony Martin, 20. Other versions: *Shore Leave* (First National, 1925), *Hit the Deck* (RKO, 1930). 110 minutes

Baker: Fred Astaire, *Sherry Martin:* Ginger Rogers, *Bilge Smith:* Randolph Scott, *Connie Martin:* Harriet Hilliard, *Iris Manning:* Astrid Allwyn, *Dopey:* Ray Mayer, *Captain Hickey:* Harry Beresford, *Lieutenant Williams:* Addison (Jack) Randall, *Jim Nolan:* Russell Hicks, *Sullivan:* Brooks Benedict, *Kitty Collins:* Lucille Ball, *Trio:* Betty Grable, Joy Hodges, Jennie Gray, *Sailor:* Tony Martin, *Hostess:* Maxine Jennings, *Sailor:* Edward Burns, *Waitress:* Jane Hamilton, *Sailor:* Frank Mills, *Sailor:* Frank Jenks, *Webber:* Herbert Rawlinson.

FOOTLIGHT PARADE (1933) WB. Directed by Lloyd Bacon. Dances by Busby Berkeley. Story, Manuel Seff and James Seymour. Photography, George Barnes. Editor, George Amy. Songs: "By a Waterfall," "Ah the Moon Is Here," "Sittin' on a Backyard Fence" by Sammy Fain and Irving Kahal; "Shanghai Lil" and "Honeymoon Hotel" by Harry Warren and Al Dubin. John Wayne, Frank McHugh, and Marceline Day in final scene from *Telegraph Trail* (WB, 1933). 102 minutes

Chester Kent: James Cagney, *Nan Prescott:* Joan Blondell, *Bea Thorn:* Ruby Keeler, *Scotty Blair:* Dick Powell, *Silas Gould:* Guy Kibbee, *Harriet Bowers Gould:* Ruth Donnelly, *Vivian Rich:* Claire Dodd, *Charlie Bowers:* Hugh Herbert, *Francis:* Frank McHugh, *Al Frazer:* Arthur Hohl, *Harry Thompson:* Gordon Westcott, *Cynthia Kent:* Renee Whitney, *Joe Barrington:* Philip Faversham, *Miss Smythe:* Juliet Ware, *Fralick, Music Director:* Herman Bing, *George Appolinaris:* Paul Porcasi, *Doorman:* William Granger, *Cop:* Charles C. Wilson, *Gracie:* Barbara Rogers, *Specialty Dancer:* Billy Taft, *Chorus Girls:* Marjean Rogers, Pat Wing, Donna Mae Roberts, *Chorus Boy:* Dave O'Brien, *Drugstore Attendant:* George Chandler, *Title-Thinker-Upper:* Hobart Cavanaugh, *Auditor:* William V. Mong, *Mac, Dance Director:* Lee Moran, *"Sittin' on a Backyard Fence" Mouse:* Billy Barty, *"Honeymoon Hotel" Desk Clerk:* Harry Seymour, *Porter:* Sam Mc Daniel, *Little Boy:* Billy Barty, *House Detective:* Fred Kelsey, *Uncle:* Jimmy Conlin, *"Shanghai Lil" Sailor-pal:* Roger Gray, *Joe, Assistant Dance Director:* Harry Seymour, *Chorus Girl:* Donna LaBarr.

Follow the Fleet with Fred Astaire, Ginger Rogers and Jack Randall.

Footlight Parade with Guy Kibbee, Joan Blondell, James Cagney, Arthur Hohl and Paul Porcasi.

A FOREIGN AFFAIR (1948) Par. Producer, Charles Brackett. Director, Billy Wilder. Author, David Shaw. Screenplay, Charles Brackett. Billy Wilder, Richard Breen. Art Directors, Hans Dreier, Walter Tyler. Photography, Charles B. Lang, Jr., Editor, Doane Harrison. Songs by Frederick Hollander: "Black Market," "Illusions," "Ruins of Berlin." Theme song, "Isn't It Romantic?" by Rodgers and Hart, from *Love Me Tonight* (1932). Backgrounds filmed in Berlin: Templehof Airfield, the Reichstag, Brandenburg Gate. 116 minutes

Phoebe Frost: Jean Arthur, *Erika Von Schluetow:* Marlene Dietrich, *Captain John Pringle:* John Lund, *Col. Rufus John Plummer:* Millard Mitchell, *Hans Otto Birgel:* Peter Von Zerneck, *Mike:* Stanley Prager, *Joe:* Bill Murphy, *First M.P.:* Gordon Jones, *Second M.P.:* Freddie Steele, *Pennecott:* Raymond Bond, *Giffin:* Boyd Davis, *Kraus:* Robert Malcolm, *Yandell:* Charles Meredith, *Salvatore:* Michael Raffetto, *Lt. Hornby:* James Larmore, *Lt. Colonel:* Damian O'Flynn, *Lt. Lee Thompson:* William Neff, *Major Matthews:* Frank Fenton, *Hitler:* Bobby Watson, *Russian Sergeant:* Henry Kulky, *File Room Guard:* Norman Leavitt, *General McAndrew:* Harland Tucker, *General Finney:* George Carleton, *Staff Sergeant:* Len Hendry, *German Man:* Edward Van Sloan, *German Woman:* Lisa Golm, *German Wife:* Ilka Gruning, *German Husband:* Paul Panzer, *Maier:* Richard Ryen, *Wac Tech. Sgt.:* Phyllis Kennedy, *Gerhardt (Maier, Jr.):* Ted Cottle, *Inspector:* Otto Waldis, *Accordion Player:* Frank Yaconelli, *German Policeman:* Otto Reichow, *Corporal:* Harry Lauter, *M.P. Lieutenant,* Rex Lease.

A Foreign Affair with Marlene Dietrich.

FOREIGN CORRESPONDENT (1940) UA. Produced by Walter Wanger. Directed by Alfred Hitchcock. Based on *Personal History* by Vincent Sheean. Screenplay, Charles Bennett and Joan Harrison. Dialogue, James Hilton and Robert Benchley. Music, Alfred Newman. Art Director, Alexander Golitzen. Assistant Director, Edmond Bernoudy. Special Effects, Lee Zavitz. Art Associate, Richard Irvine. Photography, Rudy Mate. Editor, Otho Lovering. 119 minutes

Johnny Jones (later Huntley Haverstock): Joel McCrea, *Carol Fisher:* Laraine Day, *Stephen Fisher:* Herbert Marshall, *Scott ffolliott:* George Sanders, *Van Meer:* Albert Bassermann, *Stebbins:* Robert Benchley, *Rowley:* Edmund Gwenn, *Krug:* Eduardo Ciannelli, *Tramp:* Martin Kosleck, *Mr. Powers:* Harry Davenport, *Doreen:* Barbara Pepper, *Latvian Diplomat:* Eddy Conrad, *Assassin:* Charles Wagenheim, *Toastmaster:* Craufurd Kent, *Mrs. Sprague:* Frances Carson, *Valet:* Alexander Granach, *Jones' Mother:* Dorothy Vaughan, *Donald:* Jack Rice, *Sophie:* (Becky) Rebecca Bohannon, *Clipper Captain:* Marten Lamont, *Miss Pimm:* Hilda Plowright, *Mrs. Benson:* Gertrude W. Hoffman, *Miss Benson:* Jane Novak, *Mr. Brood:* Roy Gordon, *Inspector McKenna:*

Leonard Mudie, *Commissioner ffolliott:* Holmes Herbert, *John Martin,* "MOHICAN" *Captain:* Emory Parnell, *Dutch Peasant:* James Finlayson, *Bradley:* Charles Halton, *Jones' Sister:* Joan Brodel (Joan Leslie), *Dr. Williamson:* Paul Irving, *Jones' Father:* Ferris Taylor, *Clark:* John T. Murray, *Stiles, the Butler:* Ian Wolfe, *Captain Lanson:* Louis Borrell, *Italian Waiter:* Gino Corrado, *English Cashier:* Eily Malyon, *English Radio Announcer:* John Burton, *Mr. Naismith:* E. E. Clive, *Man with Newspaper:* Alfred Hitchcock.

Foreign Correspondent with Eduardo Ciannelli, Herbert Marshall, Laraine Day and Joel McCrea.

FOREVER AMBER (1947) 20th. Producer, William Perlberg. Director, Otto Preminger. Color by Technicolor. From the novel by Kathleen Winsor. Screenplay, Philip Dunne, Ring Lardner, Jr. Musical Director, Alfred Newman. Art Director, Lyle Wheeler. Cameraman, Leon Shamroy. Editor, Charles Loeffler. Adaptation, Jerome Cady. Technicolor Director, Natalie Kalmus. Associate, Richard Mueller. Darnell replaced Peggy Cummins. 138 minutes

Amber: Linda Darnell, *Bruce Carlton:* Cornel Wilde, *Almsbury:* Richard Greene, *King Charles II:* George Sanders, *Rex Morgan:* Glenn Langan, *Earl of Radcliffe:* Richard Haydn, *Nan Britton:* Jessica Tandy, *Mother Red Cap:* Anne Revere, *Black Jack Mallard:* John Russell, *Corina:* Jane Ball, *Sir Thomas Dudley:* Robert Coote, *Matt Goodgroome:* Leo G. Carroll, *Countess of Castelmaine:* Natalie Draper, *Mrs. Spong:* Margaret Wycherly, *Lady Redmond:* Alma Kruger, *Lord Redmond:* Edmond Breon, *Landale:* Alan Napier, *Little Bruce:* Perry (Bill) Ward, *Mrs. Chiverton:* Ottola Nesmith, *Lord Rossmore:* Boyd Irwin, *Bob Starling:* Richard Bailey, *Mr. Starling:* Houseley Stevenson, *Queen Catherine:* Lillian Molieri, *Beck Marshall:* Susan Blanchard, *Ivers:* Tim Huntley, *Benvolio:* Robin Hughes, *Mrs. Abbott:* Norma Varden, *Killigrew:* Tom Moore, *Sarah:* Edith Evanson, *Marge:* Ellen Corby, *Bruce at 3:* Jimmy Lagano, *Jack (Wounded Cavalier):* Marten Lamont, *Blueskin:* Skelton Knaggs, *Nicks:* John Rogers, *Deacon:* Peter Shaw, *Moss Gumble:* Arthur E. Gould-Porter, *Galeazzo:* Jimmy Ames.

Forever Amber with Linda Darnell, George Sanders and Jane Ball.

Fort Apache with Henry Fonda, John Wayne, George O'Brien and Ward Bond.

FORT APACHE (1948) RKO. Producers John Ford, Merian C. Cooper. Director, John Ford. Suggested by the story "Massacre" by James Warner Bellah. Screenplay, Frank S. Nugent. Art Director, James Basevi. Photography, Archie Stout. Editor, Jack Murray. Music, Richard Hageman. An Argosy Pictures Production. Filmed in Monument Valley, Utah, and Chatsworth, California. Film debut of John Agar, 26. 127 minutes

Capt. Kirby York: John Wayne, *Col. Owen Thursday:* Henry Fonda, *Philadelphia Thursday:* Shirley Temple, *Lt. Mickey O'Rourke:* John Agar, *Sgt. Beaufort:* Pedro Armendariz, *Sgt. Major Michael O'Rourke:* Ward Bond, *Mary O'Rourke:* Irene Rich, *Capt. Sam Collingwood:* George O'Brien, *Emily Collingwood:* Anna Lee, *Sgt. Mulcahy:* Victor McLaglen, *Sgt. Quincannon:* Dick Foran, *Sgt. Shattuck:* Jack Pennick, *Doctor Wilkins:* Guy Kibbee, *Silas Meacham:* Grant Withers, *Cochise:* Miguel Inclan, *Martha:* Mae Marsh, *Ma (Barmaid):* Mary Gordon, *Guadalupe:* Movita, *Southern Rercuit:* Hank Worden, *Recruit:* Ray Hyke, *Fen (Stage Guard)* Francis Ford, *Stage Driver:* Cliff Clark, *Cavalryman:* Fred Graham, *Noncommissioned Officer:* Mickey Simpson, *Reporters:* Frank Ferguson, William Forrest, *Man:* Philip Kieffer.

FOR WHOM THE BELL TOLLS (1943) Par. Producer, Sam Wood. Director, Sam Wood. Color by Technicolor. Based on the novel by Ernest Hemingway. Screenplay, Dudley Nichols. Music Score, Victor Young. Technicolor Director, Natalie Kalmus. Art Directors, Hans Dreier, Haldane Douglas. Production Designer, William Cameron Menzies. Cameraman, Ray Rennahan. Special Effects, Gordon Jennings. Process Photography, Farciot Edouart. Editor, Sherman Todd. Songs: "A Love Like This" by Ned Washington and Victor Young; "For Whom the Bell Tolls" by Milton Drake and Walter Kent. U.S. film debut of Katina Paxinou. 170 minutes

Robert Jordan: Gary Cooper, *Maria:* Ingrid Bergman, *Pablo:* Akim Tamiroff, *Agustin:* Arturo de Cordova, *Anselmo:* Vladimir Sokoloff, *Rafael:* Mikhail Rasumny, *Fernando:* Fortunio Bonanova, *Andres:* Eric Feldary, *Primitivo:* Victor Varconi, *Pilar:* Katina Paxinou, *El Sordo:* Joseph Calleia, *Joaquin:* Lilo Yarson, *Paco:* Alexander Granach, *Gustavo:* Adia Kuznetzoff, *Ignacio:* Leonid Snegoff, *General Golz:* Leo Bulgakov, *Lieutenant Berrendo:* Duncan Renaldo, *Andre Massart:* George Coulouris, *Captain Gomez:* Frank Puglia, *Colonel Miranda:* Pedro de Cordoba, *Staff Officer:* Michael Visaroff, *Karkov:* Konstantin Shayne, *Captain Mora:* Martin Garralaga, *Sniper:* Jean Del Val, *Colonel Duval:* Jack Mylong, *Kashkin:* Feodor Chaliapin, *Don Frederico Gonzales:* Pedro de Cordoba, *Don Richardo:* Mayo

Newhall, *Don Benito Garcia, The Mayor:* Michael Dalmatoff, *Don Guillermo:* Antonio Vidal, *Don Faustino Rivero:* Robert Tafur, *Julian:* Armand Roland, *Drunkard:* Luis Rojas, *Spanish Singer:* Trini Varela, *Sergeant (Eilas Man):* Dick Botiller, *Don Guillermo's Wife:* Soledad Jiminez, *Young Cavalry Man:* Yakima Canutt, *First Sentry:* Tito Renaldo, *Girl in Cafe:* Yvonne De Carlo.

For Whom the Bell Tolls with Akim Tamiroff, Eric Feldary, Mikhail Rasumny, Katina Paxinou, Ingrid Bergman, Gary Cooper and Arturo de Cordova.

42nd Street with George Brent, Bebe Daniels, Ruby Keeler, Warner Baxter and George Irving.

42ND STREET (1933) WB. Directed by Lloyd Bacon. Dances by Busby Berkeley. From the novel of the same name by Bradford Ropes. Adaptation and Dialogue, James Seymour and Rian James. Art Director, Jack Okey. Assistant Director, Gordon Hollingshead. Costumes, Orry-Kelly. Photography, Sol Polito. Editor, Thomas Pratt. Songs by Al Dubin and Harry Warren: "42nd Street," "Shuffle off to Buffalo," "You're Getting to Be a Habit With Me," "Young and Healthy," "It Must Be June." Editor, Frank Ware. In her first leading role, Ruby Keeler appears with sisters Gertrude and Helen. Guy Kibbee's brother Milton has a bit. 98 minutes

Julian Marsh: Warner Baxter, *Dorothy Brock:* Bebe Daniels, *Pat Denning:* George Brent, *Lorraine Fleming:* Una Merkel, *Peggy Sawyer:* Ruby Keeler, *Abner Dillon:* Guy Kibbee, *Billy Lawler:* Dick Powell,

Ann Lowell (Anytime Annie): Ginger Rogers, *Andy Lee:* George E. Stone, *Al Jones:* Robert McWade, *Thomas Barry:* Ned Sparks, *Terry Neil:* Eddie Nugent, *MacElroy:* Allen Jenkins, *Jerry:* Harry Akst, *Groom,* "*Shuffle off to Buffalo*": Clarence Nordstrom, *The Actor:* Henry B. Walthall, *Songwriters:* Al Dubin, Harry Warren, "*Young and Healthy*" *Girl:* Toby Wing, *Chorus Girl:* Pat Wing, *Slim Murphy:* Tom Kennedy, *Dr. Chadwick:* Wallis Clark, *A Mug:* Jack La Rue, *Pansy:* Louise Beavers, *Chorus Boy:* Dave O'Brien, *Secretary:* Patricia Ellis, *House Doctor:* George Irving, *An Author:* Charles Lane, *News Spreader:* Milton Kibbee, *Stage Aide:* Rolfe Sedan, *Geoffrey Waring:* Lyle Talbot, *Chorus Girls:* Gertrude and Helen Keeler, Geraine Grear (Joan Barclay), Ann Hovey, Renee Whitney, Dorothy Coonan, Barbara Rogers, June Glory, Jayne Shadduck, Adele Lacy, Loretta Andrews, Margaret La Marr, Mary Jane Halsey, Ruth Eddings, Edna Callaghan, Patsy Farnum, Maxine Cantway, Lynn Browning, Donna Mae Roberts, Lorena Layson, Alice Jans.

Foul Play with Chevy Chase and Goldie Hawn.

FOUL PLAY (1978) Par. Produced by Thomas L. Miller and Edward K. Milkis. Directed and Written by Colin Higgins. Lenses and Panaflex Camera by Panavision. Color by Movielab. Music composed and conducted by Charles Fox. Associate Producer/Unit Production Manager, Peter V. Herald. Editor, Pembroke J. Herring. Sound Mixer, Jeff Wexler. Production Designer, Alfred Sweeney. Set Decorator, Robert R. Benton. Photography, David M. Walsh. Assistant Director, Gary D. Daigler. 2nd Assistant Director, Larry J. Franco. 2nd Unit Director, M. James Arnett. 2nd Unit Director of Photography, Rexford Metz. Make-up Artist, Tom Case. Hairstylist, Susan Germaine-Jeffers. Assistant Editor, Steven J. Cohen. Orchestrations, Ruby Raksin. "Ready to Take a Chance Again" by Charles Fox and Norman Gimbel, sung by Barry Manilow; "Copacabana (At the Copa)" by Jack Feldman, Bruce Sussman and Barry Manilow, sung by Manilow; "Stayin' Alive," written and sung by the Bee Gees; "I Feel the Earth Move" by Carole King; excerpts from *The Mikado* by Gilbert and Sullivan, sung by members of the New York City Opera, conducted by Julius Rudel and staged by Jack Eddleman. Filmed in San Francisco and Los Angeles. Rated PG. 116 minutes

Gloria Mundy: Goldie Hawn, *Tony Carlson:* Chevy Chase, *Mr. Hennesey:* Burgess Meredith, *Gerda Casswell:* Rachel Roberts, *Stanley Tibbets:* Dudley Moore, *Archbishop Thorncrest/Double:* Eugene Roche, *Stella:* Marilyn Sokol, *Fergie:* Brian Dennehy, *Stiltskin:* Marc Lawrence, *Theater Manager:* Chuck McCann, *J. J. MacKuen:* Billy Barty, *Scarface:* Don Calfa, *Scott:* Bruce Solomon, *Sandy:* Cooper Huckabee, *Mrs. Venus:* Pat Ast, *Mrs. Russel:* Frances Bay, *House Manager:* Lou Cutell, *Whitey Jackson (Albino):* William Frankfather, *Coleman:* John Hancock, *Sally:* Barbara Sammeth, *Elsie:* Queenie Smith, *Ethel:* Hope Summers, *Mrs. Monk:* Irene Tedrow, *Turk:* Ion Teodorescu, *Sylvia:* Janet Wood, *Theater Usher:* David Cole, *Dickinson:* Bill Gamble, *Pope Pius XIII:* Cyril Magnin, *Limo Driver:* Michael David Lee, *Luigi:* Neno Russo, *Japanese Couple:* Rollin Moriyama and Mitsu Yashima, *Truck Driver:* M. James Arnett, *Cop:* Jophery Brown, *Security Guard:* John Hatfield, *Henpecked Husband:* Garry Goodrow, *Nanki-Pooh:* Enrico Di Giuseppe, *Yum-Yum:*

Glenys Fowles, Peep-Bo: Kathleen Hegierski, *Pitti-Sing:* Sandra Walker, *Pish-Tush:* Thomas Jamerson, *Pooh-Bah:* Richard McKee, *Katisha:* Jane Shaulis, *Esme:* Shirley Python, *Stunt Players:* Craig Baxley, Hal Needham, Glynn Rubin, *Man in Phone Booth:* Joe Bellan.

Four Daughters with Eddie Acuff, Donald Kerr, Tom Dugan, John Garfield, Priscilla Lane.

FOUR DAUGHTERS (1938) WB. Producer, Hal B. Wallis. Associate Producer, Benjamin Glazer. Director, Michael Curtiz. Author, Fannie Hurst, from *Sister Act* in *Cosmopolitan* magazine. Screenplay, Julius Epstein, Lenore Coffee. Art Director, John Hughes. Musical Score, Max Steiner. Cameraman, Ernest Haller. Editor, Ralph Dawson. Assistant Director, Sherry Shourds. Dialogue Director, Irving Rapper. Unit Manager, Al Alleborn. Remade as *Young at Heart* (WB, 1954). 90 minutes

Adam Lemp: Claude Rains, *Ann Lemp:* Priscilla Lane, *Felix Deitz:* Jeffrey Lynn, *Mickey Borden:* John Garfield, *Emma Lemp:* Gale Page, *Kay Lemp:* Rosemary Lane, *Thea Lemp:* Lola Lane, *Ben Crowley:* Frank McHugh, *Aunt Etta:* May Robson, *Ernest Talbot:* Dick Foran, *Mrs. Ridgefield:* Vera Lewis, *Jake:* Tom Dugan, *Sam:* Eddie Acuff, *Earl:* Donald Kerr, *Waiter:* Joe Cunningham, *Man:* Jerry Mandy, *Doctor:* Wilfred Lucas.

Francis with Francis and Donald O'Connor.

FRANCIS (1949) Univ. Producer, Robert Arthur. Director, Arthur Lubin. Based on the novel by David Stern. Screenplay, David Stern. Art directors, Bernard Herzbrun, Richard H. Fields. Music, Frank Skinner. Photography, Irving Glassberg. Editor, Milton Carruth. First of the series of seven films, ending with *Francis in the Haunted House* (1956). 91 minutes

Peter Stirling: Donald O'Connor, *Maureen Gelder:* Patricia Medina, *Valerie Humpert:* ZaSu Pitts, *Colonel Hooker:* Ray Collins, *General Stevens:* John McIntire, *Colonel Plepper:* Eduard Franz, *Major Nadel:* Howland Chamberlin, *Colonel Saunders:* James Todd, *Carmichael:* Robert Warwick, *Sgt. Chillingbacker:* Frank Faylen, *Captain Jones:* Anthony Curtis, *Major Garber:* Mikel Conrad, *Major Richards:* Loren Tindall, *Banker Munroe:* Charles Meredith, *First Correspondent:* Harry Harvey, *Second Correspondent:* Howard Negley, *Sergeant Poor:* Duke York, *Third Correspondent:* Peter Prouse, *Japanese Lieutenant:* Joseph Kim, *Captain Grant:* Robert Anderson, *Sergeant Miller:* Jack Shutta, *First Ambulance Man:* Judd Holdren, *Lt. Bremm:* Tim Graham, *Second Ambulance Man:* Robert Blunt, *Captain Norman:* Jim Hayward, *Captain Dean:* Al Ferguson, *First M.C. Lt.:* Marvin Kaplan, *Japanese Soldier:* Harold Fong, *Captain Addison:* Mickey McCardle, and FRANCIS, The Talking Army Mule (voice of Chill Wills).

FRANKENSTEIN (1931) Univ. Directed by James Whale. Based on the novel by Mary Wollstonecraft Shelley. Scenario and Dialogue, Garrett Fort and Francis Edward Faragoh. Special Electrical Effects, Frank Graves, Kenneth Strickfadden, Raymond Lindsay. Technical Assistant, Dr. Cecil Reynolds. Photography, Arthur Edeson. Editor, Clarence Kolster. Sound, C. Roy Hunter. In a prologue, Edward Van Sloan warns the audience about what they are to see, on behalf of Mr. Carl Laemmle. 71 minutes

Henry Frankenstein: Colin Clive, *Elizabeth:* Mae Clarke, *Victor Moritz:* John Boles, *The Monster:* Boris Karloff, *Baron Frankenstein:* Frederick Kerr, *Doctor Waldman:* Edward Van Sloan, *Fritz:* Dwight Frye, *Vogel, the Burgomaster:* Lionel Belmore, *Little Maria:* Marilyn Harris, *Ludwig, Peasant Father:* Michael Mark, *Bridesmaids:* Arletta Duncan, Pauline Moore, *Extra at Lecture/Wounded Villager on the Hill:* Francis Ford, *Clive's double:* Robert Livingston.

Frankenstein with Boris Karloff and Colin Clive.

FREAKS (1932) MGM. Directed by Tod Browning. Based on "Spurs" by Tod Robbins. Screenplay, Willis Goldbeck and Leon Gordon. Dialogue, Edgar Allan Woolf and Al Boasberg. Photography, Merritt B. Gerstad. Editor, Basil Wrangell. Sound, Gavin Burns. The short story "Spurs" appeared in *Munsey's* magazine, February, 1923. Harry and Daisy Earles are brother and sister. 64 minutes

Phroso: Wallace Ford, *Venus:* Leila Hyams, *Cleopatra:* Olga Baclanova, *Roscoe:* Roscoe Ates, *Hercules:* Henry Victor, *Hans:* Harry Earles, *Frieda:* Daisy Earles, *Madame Tetrallini:* Rose Dione, *Siamese Twins:* Daisy and Violet Hilton, *Rollo Brothers:* Edward Brophy, Matt McHugh, *Bearded Lady:* Olga Roderick, *Boy with Half a Torso:* Johnny Eck, *Hindu Living Torso:* Randian, *White Pin Heads:* Schlitzie, Elvira and Jennie Lee Snow, *Living Skeleton:* Pete Robinson, *Bird Girl:* Koo Coo, *Half-Woman Half-Man:* Josephine-Joseph, *Armless Wonder:* Martha Morris, *Turtle Girl:* Frances O'Connor, *Midget:* Angelo Rossito, *Specialties:* Zip and Pip, Elizabeth Green, *Landowner:* Albert Conti, *Jean, the Caretaker:* Michael Visaroff, *Sideshow Patron:* Ernie S. Adams, *Maid:* Louise Beavers.

Freaks with Rose Dione, Harry Earles (in bed) and Olga Baclanova.

A FREE SOUL (1931) MGM. Directed by Clarence Brown. Based on the book and magazine serial by Adela Rogers St. John, and the play, dramatized by Willard Mack. Adapted by John Meehan. Art Director, Cedric Gibbons. Photography, William Daniels. Editor, Hugh Wynn. Sound, Anstruther MacDonald. Remade by MGM as *The Girl Who Had Everything*, 1953. 91 minutes

Jan Ashe: Norma Shearer, *Steve Ashe:* Lionel Barrymore, *Ace Wilfong:* Clark Gable, *Dwight Winthrop:* Leslie Howard, *Eddie:* James Gleason, *Grandmother Ashe:* Lucy Beaumont, *Aunt Helen:* Claire Whitney, *Prosecuting Attorney:* Frank Sheridan, *Bottomley, Ace's Chinese Boy:* E. Alyn Warren, *Johnson, Defense Attorney:* George Irving, *Slouch:* Edward Brophy, *Dick:* William Stacy, *Reporter:* James Donlin, *Valet:* Sam MacDaniel, *Court Clerk:* Lee Phelps, *Men's Room Patron:* Roscoe Ates, *Casino Proprietor:* Larry Steers, *Detective:* Henry Hall, *Skid Row Drunk:* Francis Ford.

A Free Soul with Norma Shearer, Lionel Barrymore and Clark Gable.

THE FRENCH CONNECTION (1971) 20th. A Philip D'Antoni Production in association with Schine-Moore Productions. Produced by Philip D'Antoni. Directed by William Friedkin. Technical Consultants, Eddie Egan and Sonny Grosso. Based on the book by Robin Moore. Screenplay by Ernest Tidyman. Executive Producer, G. David Schine. Music composed and conducted by Don Ellis. Photography, Owen Roizman. Art Director, Ben Kazaskow. Set Decorator, Ed Garzero. Sound, Chris Newman and Theodore Soderberg. Editor, Jerry Greenberg. Assistant Directors, William C. Gerrity and Terry Donnelly. Special Effects, Sass

Bedig. Stunt Coordinator, Bill Hickman. Make-up Artist, Irving Buchman. Costumes, Joseph Fretwell III. Associate Producer, Kenneth Utt. Location Consultant, Fat Thomas Rand. "Everyone's Gone to the Moon" by Jim Webb, sung by the Three Degrees. Filmed in DeLuxe Color in New York, Washington, D.C., and Marseilles, France. Rated R. 104 minutes. Sequel was *French Connection II* (1975) also with Hackman and Rey

Jimmy (Popeye) Doyle: Gene Hackman, *Alain Charnier:* Fernando Rey, *Buddy Russo:* Roy Scheider, *Sal Boca:* Tony LoBianco, *Pierre Nicoli:* Marcel Bozzuffi, *Henri Devereaux:* Frederic De Pasquale, *Mulderig:* Bill Hickman, *Marie Charnier:* Ann Rebbot, *Joel Weinstock:* Harold Gary, *Angie Boca:* Arlene Farber, *Lt. Walt Simonson:* Eddie Egan, *Officer Klein:* Sonny Grosso, *Maurice La Valle:* Andre Ernotte, *Howard, Chemist:* Pat McDermott, *Drug Pusher:* Alan Weeks, *Themselves:* The Three Degrees, *Irving, Police Mechanic:* Irving Abrahams, *Auctioneer:* Robert Weil, *Lou Boca:* Benny Marino, *Bicycle Girl:* Maureen Mooney, *Undercover Agent:* Al Fann, *Police Sergeant:* Randy Jurgenson, *Motorman:* William Coke, *Reporter:* Melba Tolliver.

The French Connection with Marcel Bozzuffi and Fernando Rey.

Friendly Persuasion with Anthony Perkins, Dorothy McGuire and Gary Cooper.

FRIENDLY PERSUASION (1956) AA. Produced and directed by William Wyler. Associate Producer, Robert Wyler. Color by De Luxe. Based on the book by Jessamyn West. Assistant Director, Austen Jewell. Costumes, Dorothy Jeakins and Bert Henrikson. A B-M Production. Songs by Paul Francis Webster and Dimitri Tiomkin: "Friendly Persuasion," sung by Pat Boone, "Mocking Bird in a Willow Tree," "Marry Me, Marry Me," "Indiana Holiday," "Coax Me a Little." 139 minutes. Remade for TV, 1975

Jess Birdwell: Gary Cooper, *Eliza Birdwell:* Dorothy McGuire, *Widow*

Hudspeth: Marjorie Main, *Josh Birdwell:* Anthony Perkins, *Little Jess:* Richard Eyer, *Sam Jordan:* Robert Middleton, *Mattie Birdwell:* Phyllis Love, *Gard Jordan:* Mark Richman, *Professor Quigley:* Walter Catlett, *Elder Purdy:* Richard Hale, *Enoch:* Joel Fluellen, *Army Major:* Theodore Newton, *Caleb:* John Smith, *Opal, Pearl, Ruby Hudspeth:* Edna Skinner, Marjorie Durant, Frances Farwell, *Elders:* Russell Simpson, Charles Halton, Everett Glass, *The Goose:* Samantha, *Shell Game Operator:* Frank Jenks, *Poor Losers:* Joe Turkel, James Anderson, *Mrs. Purdy:* Jean Inness, *Minister:* Nelson Leigh, *Old Lady:* Helen Kleeb, *Quaker Woman (Emma):* Mary Carr, *Quaker Girl (Elizabeth):* Diane Jergens, *Leader:* John Craven, *Barker:* Harry Hines, *O'Hara:* Henry Rowland, *Billy Goat:* Ivan Rasputin, *Manager:* Donald Kerr, *Haskell:* Steve Warren, *Shooting Gallery Operator:* Earle Hodgins, *Farmer:* Tom London, *Ex-Sergeant:* John Pickard, *Bushwhacker:* Richard Garland, *Clem:* Norman Leavitt, *Buster:* Don Kennedy.

From Here to Eternity with Montgomery Clift, Frank Sinatra and Robert Karnes.

FROM HERE TO ETERNITY (1953) Col. Producer, Buddy Adler. Director, Fred Zinnemann. From the novel by James Jones, Screenplay, Daniel Taradash. Art Director, Cary Odell. Cinematographer, Burnett Guffey. Editor, William Lyon. 118 minutes

Sgt. Milton Warden: Burt Lancaster, *Robert E. Lee Prewitt:* Montgomery Clift, *Karen Holmes:* Deborah Kerr, *Lorene:* Donna Reed, *Angelo Maggio:* Frank Sinatra, *Capt. Dana Holmes:* Philip Ober, *Sgt. Leva:* Mickey Shaughnessy, *Mazzioli:* Harry Bellaver, *Sgt. "Fatso" Judson:* Ernest Borgnine, *Corp. Buckley:* Jack Warden, *Sgt. Ike Galovitch:* John Dennis, *Sal Anderson:* Merle Travis, *Sgt. Pete Karelsen:* Tim Ryan, *Treadwell:* Arthur Keegan, *Mrs. Kipfer:* Barbara Morrison, *Annette:* Jean Willes, *Sgt. Baldy Dhom:* Claude Akins, *Sgt. Turp Thornhill:* Robert Karnes, *Sgt. Henderson:* Robert Wilke, *Corp. Champ Wilson:* Douglas Henderson, *Sgt. Maylon Stark:* George Reeves, *Friday Clark:* Don Dubbins, *Corp. Paluso:* John Cason, *Georgette:* Kristine Miller, *Capt. Ross:* John Bryant, *Sandra:* Joan Shawlee, *Jean:* Angela Stevens, *Nancy:* Mary Carver, *Suzanne:* Vicki Bakken, *Roxanne:* Margaret Barstow, *Billie:* Delia Salvi, *Lt. Col.:* Willis Bouchey, *Nair:* Al Sargent, *Bill:* William Lundmark, *Bartender:* Weaver Levy, *Major Stern:* Tyler McVey.

FROM RUSSIA WITH LOVE (1964) UA. Producers, Harry Saltzman, Albert R. Broccoli. Director, Terence Young. Screenplay, Richard Maibaum. Adaptation, Johanna Harwood. Based on the novel by Ian Fleming. Music, John Barry. Title song, Lionel Bart, sung by Matt Munro. Theme music, Monty Norman. Assistant Director, David Anderson. Director of Photography, Ted Moore. Costumes, Jocelyn Rickards. Eon Production in Technicolor. Filmed partly in Istanbul. 118 minutes

James Bond: Sean Connery, *Tatiana Romanova:* Daniela Bianchi,

Kerim Bey: Pedro Armendariz, *Rosa Klebb:* Lotte Lenya, *Red Grant:* Robert Shaw, *"M":* Bernard Lee, *Sylvia:* Eunice Gayson, *Morzeny:* Walter Gotell, *Vavra:* Francis de Wolff, *Train Conductor:* George Pastell, *Kerim's Girl:* Nadja Regin, *Miss Moneypenny:* Lois Maxwell, *Vida:* Aliza Gur, *Zora:* Martine Beswick, *Kronsteen:* Vladek Sheybal, *Belly Dancer:* Leila, *Foreign Agent:* Hasan Ceylan, *Krilencu:* Fred Haggerty, *Chauffeur:* Neville Jason, *Benz:* Peter Bayliss, *Tempo:* Nushet Atear, *McAdams:* Peter Madden.

From Russia With Love with Sean Connery, Daniela Bianchi and Robert Shaw.

THE FRONT PAGE (1931) UA. Produced by Howard Hughes. Directed by Lewis Milestone. Based on the 1928 play by Ben Hecht and Charles MacArthur. Scenario, Bartlett Cormack. Dialogue, Bartlett Cormack and Charles Lederer. Art Director, Richard Day. Assistant Director, Nate Watt. Photography, Glen MacWilliams. Editor, Duncan Mansfield. Sound, Frank Grenzbach. A Caddo Company Production. 101 minutes. Remade as *His Girl Friday* (Col. 1940), and by Univ. in 1974

Walter Burns: Adolphe Menjou, *Hildy Johnson:* Pat O'Brien, *Peggy Grant:* Mary Brian, *Bensinger:* Edward Everett Horton, *Murphy:* Walter Catlett, *Earl Williams:* George E. Stone, *Molly:* Mae Clarke, *Pincus:* Slim Summerville, *Kruger:* Matt Moore, *McCue:* Frank McHugh, *Sheriff Hartman:* Clarence H. Wilson, *Schwartz:* Fred Howard, *Wilson:* Phil Tead, *Endicott:* Eugene Strong, *Woodenshoe:* Spencer Charters, *Diamond Louie:* Maurice Black, *Mrs. Grant:* Effie Ellsler, *Jenny:* Dorothea Wolbert, *The Mayor:* James Gordon, *Jacobi:* Dick Alexander, *Bit:* Herman J. Mankiewicz, *Bit:* Lewis Milestone, *Reporter:* James Donlin.

The Front Page with Adolphe Menjou, Pat O'Brien and Maurice Black.

The Fuller Brush Man with Don McGuire and Red Skelton.

THE FULLER BRUSH MAN (1948) Col. Producer and Director, S. Sylvan Simon. Based on a story by Roy Huggins. Screenplay, Frank Tashlin, Devery Freeman. Art Directors, Stephen Goosson, Carl Anderson. Musical Score, Franz Roemheld. Photography, Lester White. Editor, Al Clark. An Edward Small Production. 93 minutes

Red Jones: Red Skelton, *Ann Elliot:* Janet Blair, *Keenan Wallick:* Don McGuire, *Mrs. Trist:* Hillary Brooke, *Miss Sharmley:* Adele Jergens, *Freddie Trist:* Ross Ford, *Sara Franzen:* Trudy Marshall, *Commissioner Trist:* Nicholas Joy, *Gregory Cruckston:* Donald Curtis, *Lieutenant Quint:* Arthur Space, *Henry Seward:* Selmer Jackson, *Detective Foster:* Roger Moore, *Detective Ferguson:* Stanley Andrews, *Jiggers:* Bud Wolfe, *Skitch:* David Sharpe, *Blackie:* Chick Collins, *Herman:* Billy Jones, *Chauffeur:* Jimmy Lloyd, *Butler:* Jimmy Logan, *Junior:* Jimmy Hunt, *Maid:* Ann Staunton, *Bartender:* Fred Sears, *Junior's Mother:* Verna Felton, *Milkman:* Garry Owen, *Officer #1:* Cliff Clark, *Girl:* Susan Simon, *Ranger Leader:* Mary Field, *Police Doctor:* Emmett Vogan, *Photographer:* Charles Jordan, *Plainclothesman:* Virgil Johansen, *District Attorney:* Rod O'Connor, *Policeman:* Jack Perrin, *Police Sergeant:* Dick Wessel, *Police Announcer:* William Newell.

Funny Face with Audrey Hepburn and Fred Astaire.

FUNNY FACE (1957) Par. Producer, Roger Edens. Director, Stanley Donen. VistaVision, Technicolor. Screenplay, Leonard Gershe. Art Directors, Hal Pereira, George W. Davis. Music adapted and conducted by Adolph Deutsch. Orchestral Arrangements, Conrad Salinger, Van Cleave, Alexander Courage, Skip Martin. Cinematographer, Ray June. Special Photographic Effects, John P. Fulton. Process Photography, Farciot Edouart. Editor, Frank Bracht. Songs by George and Ira Gershwin: "Funny Face," "'S Wonderful," "How Long Has This Been Going On," "Let's Kiss and Make Up," "He Loves and She Loves" and "Clap Yo' Hands"; by Roger Edens and Leonard Gershe: "Think Pink," "Bonjour Paris," "Basal Metabolism," "On How to Be Lovely" and "Marche Funebre." Dance Routines, Eugene Loring and Fred Astaire. Filmed in ·Paris, New York, and Hollywood. 103 minutes

Jo Stockton: Audrey Hepburn, *Dick Avery:* Fred Astaire, *Maggie Prescott:* Kay Thompson, *Professor Emile Flostre:* Michel Auclair, *Paul Duval:* Robert Flemyng, *Marion:* Dovima, *Babs:* Virginia Gibson, *Specialty Dancer (Pink Number):* Suzy Parker, *Laura:* Sue England, *Specialty Dancer (Pink Number):* Sunny Harnett, *Lettie:* Ruta Lee, *Hairdresser:* Jean Del Val, *Dovitch:* Alex Gerry, *Armande:* Iphigenie Castiglioni, *Beautician:* Albert D'Arno, *Assistant Hairdresser:* Nina Borget, *Receptionist:* Marilyn White, *Junior Editor:* Louise Glenn, *Junior Editor:* Heather Hopper, *Junior Editor:* Cecile Rogers, *Melissa:* Nancy Kilgas, *Assistant Beautician:* Emilie Stevens, *Specialty Dancer:* Don Powell, *Assistant Dance Director:* Bruce Hoy, *Specialty Dancer:* Carole Eastman, *Steve:* Paul Smith, *Mimi:* Diane Du Bois, *Gigi:* Karen Scott, *Madame La Farge:* Elizabeth "Lizz" Slifer, *Southern Man:* Nesdon Booth.

Funny Girl with Barbra Streisand and Kay Medford.

FUNNY GIRL (1968) Col. A Rastar Production. Produced by Ray Stark. Directed by William Wyler. Panavision, Technicolor. Musical numbers directed by Herbert Ross. Screenplay by Isobel Lennart, based on her 1964 musical play which starred Streisand. Production Designer, Gene Callahan. Photography, Harry Stradling. Art Direction, Robert Luthardt. Set Decorations, William Kiernan. Editor, Robert Swink. Sound by Charles J. Rice, Arthur Piantadosi and Jack Solomon. Titles by Lepard/-Neuhart. Costumes, Irene Sharaff. Hairstyles, Virginia Darcy and Vivienne Walker. Make-up, Ben Lane. Assistants to the Producer, David Dworski and Lorry McCauley. Production Manager, Paul Helmick. Assistant Directors, Jack Roe and Ray Gosnell. Music supervised and conducted by Walter Scharf. Vocal and Dance Arrangements, Betty Walberg. Music Editor, Ted Sebern. Orchestrations by Jack Hayes, Walter Scharf, Leo Shuken and Herbert Spencer. Songs: "Funny Girl," "People," "Sadie,

Sadie," "I'm the Greatest Star," "If a Girl Isn't Pretty," "Roller Skate Rag," "His Love Makes Me Beautiful," "You Are Woman, I Am Man," "Don't Rain on My Parade," "The Swan" by Jule Styne and Bob Merrill; "I'd Rather Be Blue" by Fred Fisher and Billy Rose; "Second Hand Rose" by James F. Hanley and Grant Clarke; "My Man" by Maurice Yvain, A. Willemetz, Jacques Charles, English adaptation by Channing Pollack. Scenes filmed in New York and New Jersey. 151 minutes

Fanny Brice: Barbra Streisand, *Nick Arnstein:* Omar Sharif, *Florenz Ziegfeld:* Walter Pidgeon, *Rose Brice:* Kay Medford, *Georgia James:* Anne Francis, *Eddie Ryan:* Lee Allen, *Mrs. Strakosh:* Mae Questel, *Tom Branca:* Gerald Mohr, *Keeney:* Frank Faylen, *Emma:* Mittie Lawrence, *Mrs. O'Malley:* Gertrude Flynn, *Mrs. Meeker:* Penny Santon, *Company Manager John:* John Harmon, *Ziegfeld Girls:* Thordis Brandt, Virginia Ann Ford, Karen Lee, Inga Neilsen, Bettina Brenna, Alena Johnston, Mary Jane Mangler, Sharon Vaughn, *Bartender:* Frank Sully, *Doorman at Keeney's:* Hal K. Dawson, *Violinist at Keeney's:* Dick Winslow, *Western Union Boy:* Billy Benedict, *Card Players:* John Warburton, Paul Bradley, George De Normand, *Bill Fallon, Lawyer:* Lloyd Gough, *Prince in Ballet:* Tommy Rall.

Funny Lady with James Caan and Barbra Streisand.

FUNNY LADY (1975) Col. A Persky-Bright/Vista Feature. Produced by Ray Stark. Director and musical numbers directed by Herbert Ross. Panavision and Technicolor. Story, Arnold Schulman. Screenplay, Jay Presson Allen and Schulman. Photography, James Wong Howe. Costumes designed by Ray Aghayan and Bob Mackie. Music arranged and conducted by Peter Matz. Production designed by George Jenkins. Editor, Marion Rothman. Ross' Assistant, Nora Kaye. Make-up, Don Cash. Hairstyles, Kaye Pownall. Associate Choreographer, Howard Jeffrey. Dance Arranger, Betty Walberg. Dance Assistant, Lester Wilson. Aquatic Sequence, Oak Park Marionettes supervised by Marion Kane. Choral Supervision, Ray Charles. Aerial Photography, Tyler Camera Systems. Assistant Directors, Jack Roe, Stu Fleming and Dodie Fawley. New songs by John Kander and Fred Ebb: "How Lucky Can You Get?" "Blind Date," "So Long, Honey Lamb," "Isn't This Better?" and "Let's Hear It for Me." "If I Love Again" by J. P. Murray and Ben Oakland. "Oh, I'm an Indian" by Leo Edwards and Blanche Merrill. Songs by Billy Rose and collaborators: "More Than You Know" (Vincent Youmans, Edward Eliscu), "It's Only a Paper Moon" (Harold Arlen, E. Y. Harburg), "I Found a Million Dollar Baby in a Five and Ten Cent Store" (Harry Warren, Mort Dixon), "Beautiful Face, Have a Heart" (James V. Monaco, Fred Fisher), "If You Want the Rainbow, You Must Have the Rain" (Oscar Levant, Mort Dixon), "I Caught a Code in My Dose" (Arthur Fields, Fred Hall), "Am I Blue?" (Harry Akst, Grant Clarke), "Clap Hands, Here Comes Charley" (Joseph Meyer, Ballard MacDonald), "Great Day" (Youmans, Eliscu), "Me and My Shadow" (Al Jolson, Dave Dreyer), "Does the Spearmint Lose Its Flavor on the Bedpost Overnight?" and "Fifty Million Frenchmen Can't Be Wrong." Film debut of Samantha Huffaker, 8, daughter of writer Clair. Rated PG. 140 minutes. Sequel to *Funny Girl* (1968)

Fanny Brice: Barbra Streisand, *Billy Rose:* James Caan, *Nick Arnstein:* Omar Sharif, *Bobby Moore:* Roddy McDowall, *Bert Robbins:* Ben Vereen, *Norma Butler:* Carole Wells, *Bernard Baruch:* Larry Gates, *Eleanor Holm:* Heidi O'Rourke, *Fran Arnstein:* Samantha Huffaker, *Buck Bolton:* Matt Emery, *Painter:* Joshua Shelley, *Conductor:* Corey Fischer, *Production Singer:* Garrett Lewis, *Buffalo Handler:* Raymond Guth, *Ned:* Gene Troobnick, *Adele:* Royce Wallace, *Crazy Quilt Director:* Byron Webster, *Mademoiselle:* Lilyan Chauvin, *Stage Manager:* Cliff Norton, *Frederick Martin (Daddy):* Ken Sansom, *Billy's Girl:* Colleen Camp, *Girl with Nick:* Alana Collins, *Mrs. Arnstein:* Jackie Stoloff, *Assistant Stage Manager:* Bert May, *Ned's Secretary:* Bea Busch, *Gossip Columnist:* Maggie Malooly, *Maître D':* Larry Arnold, *Singer:* Shirley Kirkes, *Billy's Secretary:* Deborah Sherman, *Fritz, Music Conductor:* Dick Winslow, *Choreographer:* Louis Da Pron, *Ben, Cleaning Man:* Paul Bryar, *Radio Singers:* Maralyn Thoma, Phil Gray, *Pilot:* Frank L. Pine, *Radio Announcer:* Bill Baldwin, *Paper Moon Tap Trio:* Jerry Trent, Toni Kaye, Gary Menteer.

A Funny Thing Happened on the Way to the Forum with Zero Mostel and Jack Gilford.

A FUNNY THING HAPPENED ON THE WAY TO THE FORUM (1966) UA. A Quadrangle (Melvin Frank) Production. Director, Richard Lester. De Luxe Color. Screenplay, Melvin Frank and Michael Pertwee. Musical Comedy Book, Burt Shevelove and Larry Gelbart. Camera, Nicolas Roeg. Production and Costume Design, Tony Walton. Music Director, Irwin Kostal. Editor, John Victor Smith. Choreography, Ethel and George Martin. Filmed at Bronston Studios, Spain. Songs by Stephen Sondheim: "Comedy Tonight," "Everybody Ought to Have a Maid," "Free," "Lovely," "Bring Me My Bride." Incidental Music, Ken Thorne. Assistant Director, Jos Lopez Rodero. Art Director, Syd Cain. Second Unit Director, Bob Simmons. Special Effects, Cliff Richardson. 99 minutes

Pseudolus: Zero Mostel, *Lycus:* Phil Silvers, *Erronius:* Buster Keaton, *Hysterium:* Jack Gilford, *Hero:* Michael Crawford, *Philia:* Annette Andre, *Domina:* Patricia Jessel, *Senex:* Michael Hordern, *Gymnasia:* Inga Neilsen, *Miles Gloriosus:* Leon Greene, *Vibrata:* Myrna White, *Panacea:* Lucienne Bridou, *Tintinabula:* Helen Funai, *Geminae:* Jennifer and Susan Baker, *Fertilla:* Janet Webb, *High Priestess:* Pamela Brown, *Coliseum Guard:* Alfie Bass, *Bit:* Roy Kinnear.

FUN WITH DICK AND JANE (1977) Col. Produced by Peter Bart and Max Palevsky. Directed by Ted Kotcheff. Story by Gerald Gaiser. Screenplay by David Giler, Jerry Belson, and Mordecai Richler. Photography, Fred J. Koenekamp. Music by Ernest Gold. Song, "Ahead of the Game," written and sung by the Movies. Associate Producer, Marion Segal. Editor, Danford B. Greene. Production Designer, James G. Hulsey. Additional Music, Lamont Dozier and Gene Page. Unit Production Manager, Hal W. Polaire. Assistant Directors, Charles Okun and Michael

F. Grillo. Title Design, Micheline Lanctot. Illustrations, Mary Meacham. Set Decorator, Jack Stevens. Assistant Art Director, Ronald Hobbs. Make-up, Emile La Vigne and Bernadine Anderson. Hairstylist, Lola Skip McNalley. Men's Wardrobe, Lambert E. Marks. Women's Wardrobe, Margo Baxley. Stunt Coordinator, Paul Baxley. Assistant to the Producer, Eric A. Sears. Panavision and Metrocolor. Rated PG. 95 minutes

Dick Harper: George Segal, *Jane Harper:* Jane Fonda, *Charlie Blanchard:* Ed McMahon, *Rev. Dr. Thomas Will:* Dick Gautier, *Loan Company Manager:* Allan Miller, *Raoul Esteban:* Hank Garcia, *Jane's Father:* John Dehner, *Jane's Mother:* Mary Jackson, *Jim Weeks:* Walter Brooke, *Billy Harper:* Sean Frye, *Johnson, Food Stamp Man:* Thalmus Rasulala, *Mildred Blanchard:* Gloria Stroock, *Immigration Officer:* James Jeter, *Charlie's Secretary:* Maxine Stuart, *Bob:* Fred Willard, *Robbers:* Darrow Igus, DeWayne Jessie, *Unemployment Clerk:* Robert Lussier, *Pete Winston:* John Brandon, *Roger:* Burke Byrnes, *Paula:* Jean Carson, *Beverly Hills Matron:* Selma Archerd, *Record Store Clerk:* William Callaway, *Motel Manager:* Richard Crystal, *Guard:* Ji-Tu Cumbuka, *Deacon:* Thayer David, *Transsexual:* Jon Christian Erickson, *Landscape Man:* Richard Foronjy, *Phone Company Customer:* Louis Guss, *Phone Company Clerk:* Edward Marshall, *Pharmacist:* Harry Holcombe, *Pool Builder:* Richard Karron, *Senator:* Richard Keith, *Raoul's Friends:* Jimmy Martinez, Santos Morales, Isaac Ruiz, *Tippy:* Mickey Morton, *Restaurant Owner:* Tom Peters, *Nesbitt:* William Pierson, *Carmen:* Joan Spiga, *Carol, Babysitter:* Debi Storm. Cut were Will Geer as *Tate* and Rose Marie as a wealthy customer.

Fun with Dick and Jane with George Segal and Jane Fonda.

FURY (1936) MGM. Produced by Joseph L. Mankiewicz. Directed by Fritz Lang. Based on a story by Norman Krasna. Screenplay, Bartlett Cormack, Fritz Lang. Cameraman, Joseph Ruttenberg. Editor, Frank Sullivan. 90 minutes.

Joe Wilson: Spencer Tracy, *Katherine Grant:* Sylvia Sidney, *District Attorney:* Walter Abel, *Sheriff Hummel:* Edward Ellis, *Bugs Meyers:* Walter Brennan, *Kirby Dawson:* Bruce Cabot, *Tom Wilson:* George Walcott, *Charlie Wilson:* Frank Albertson, *Durkin:* Arthur Stone, *Fred Garrett:* Morgan Wallace, *Milton Jackson:* George Chandler, *Stranger:* Roger Gray, *Vickery:* Edwin Maxwell, *Governor:* Howard C. Hickman, *Defense Attorney:* Jonathan Hale, *Edna Hooper:* Leila Bennett, *Mrs. Whipple:* Esther Dale, *Franchette:* Helen Flint, *Judge Hopkins:* Frederick Burton, *Donelli:* Carlos Martin, *Girl in Nightclub:* Esther Muir, *Doctor:* Edward Le Saint, *Goofy:* Ben Hall, *Defendant:*

George Offerman, Jr., *Hysterical Woman:* Mira McKinney, *Dynamiter:* Frank Sully, *Assistant Defense Attorney:* Guy Usher, *Waiter:* Bert Roach, *Hector:* Raymond Hatton, *Jorgeson:* Victor Potel, *Objector:* Ward Bond, *Pippin:* Clarence Kolb, *Mrs. Tuttle:* Gertrude Sutton, *Taxi Driver:* Daniel Haynes, *Bessie:* Minerva Urecal, *Counterman:* William Newell, *Anderson:* Harry Harvey, *Peanut Vendor:* Eddie Quillan, *Uncle Billy:* Si Jenks, *Baggage Clerk:* Sid Saylor.

Fury with Esther Muir and Spencer Tracy.

The Gang's All Here with Alice Faye, Frank Faylen and James Ellison.

THE GANG'S ALL HERE (1943) 20th. Producer, William Le Baron. Director, Busby Berkeley. Color by Technicolor. Authors, Nancy Wintner, George Root, Jr., Tom Bridges. Screenplay, Walter Bullock. Dances, Busby Berkeley. Art Directors, James Basevi, Joseph C. Wright. Musical Directors, Alfred Newman, Charles Henderson. Cameraman, Edward Cronjager. Editor, Ray Curtiss. Songs by Leo Robin and Harry Warren: "No Love No Nothing," "Journey to a Star," "The Lady in the Tutti-Frutti Hat," "The Polka-Dot Polka," "You Discover You're in New York," "Paducah," "Minnie's in the Money," "Pickin' on Your Mama," "Sleepy Moon" and "Drums and Dreams." Technicolor Director, Natalie Kalmus. 103 minutes

Eadie: Alice Faye, *Rosita:* Carmen Miranda, *Phil Baker:* Himself, *Benny Goodman & Band:* Themselves, *Mr. Mason, Sr.:* Eugene Pallette, *Mrs. Peyton Potter:* Charlotte Greenwood, *Peyton Potter:* Edward

Everett Horton, *Tony DeMarco:* Himself, *Andy Mason:* James Ellison, *Vivian:* Sheila Ryan, *Sergeant Casey:* Dave Willock, *Specialty Dancer:* Miriam Lavelle, *Jitterbug Dancer:* Charles Saggau, *Jitterbug Dancer:* Deidre Gale, *Benson:* George Dobbs, *Waiter:* Leon Belasco, *Maybelle:* June Haver, *Marine:* Frank Faylen, *Sailor:* Russell Hoyt, *Secretary:* Virginia Sale, *Butler:* Leyland Hodgson, *Bit Man:* Lee Bennett, *Girl:* Jeanne Crain, *Maid:* Lillian Yarbo, *Doorman:* Frank Darien, *Stage Manager:* Al Murphy, *Old Lady:* Hallene Hill, *Organ Grinder:* Gabriel Canzona, *Newsboy:* Fred Walburn, *Dancing Partner:* Virginia Wilson (Virginia de Luce).

Gaslight with Charles Boyer and Ingrid Bergman.

GASLIGHT (1944) MGM. Producer, Arthur Hornblow, Jr. Director, George Cukor. From the play by Patrick Hamilton. Screenplay, John Van Druten, Walter Reisch, John L. Balderston. Musical Score, Bronislau Kaper. Art Director, Cedric Gibbons. Cameraman, Joseph Ruttenberg. Special Effects, Warren Newcombe. Editor, Ralph E. Winters. Remake of the 1940 British film. 114 minutes

Gregory Anton: Charles Boyer, *Paula:* Ingrid Bergman, *Brian Cameron:* Joseph Cotten, *Miss Thwaites:* Dame May Whitty, *Elizabeth Tompkins:* Barbara Everest, *Nancy Oliver:* Angela Lansbury, *Budge:* Eustace Wyatt, *Mario Guardi:* Emil Rameau, *General Huddelston:* Edmond Breon, *Mr. Mufflin:* Halliwell Hobbes, *Paula (age 14):* Judy Ford (Terry Moore), *Williams:* Tom Stevenson, *Lady Dalroy:* Heather Thatcher, *Lord Dalroy:* Lawrence Grossmith, *Wilkins:* Charles McNaughton, *Policeman:* Harry Adams, *Lamplighter:* Bobby Hale, *Young Girl:* Phyllis Yuse, *Turnkey:* Alec Craig, *Guide:* Leonard Carey, *Boy in Museum:* Simon Oliver, *Girl of 10:* Alix Terry, *Footman:* Ronald Bennett, *Butler:* Arthur Blake, *Miss Pritchard:* Joy Harrington, *Lady:* Lillian Bronson, *Valet:* Eric Wilton, *Boy:* George Nokes, *Policeman:* Pat Malone, *Lamplighter:* Frank Eldridge.

THE GAUNTLET (1977) WB. Produced by Robert Daley. Directed by Clint Eastwood. Screenplay, Michael Butler and Dennis Shryack. A Malpaso Company Film, in Panavision and DeLuxe Color. Photography, Rexford Metz. Editors, Ferris Webster and Joel Cox. Art Director, Allen E. Smith. Music, Jerry Fielding. Jazz Soloists, Art Pepper and Jon Faddis. Associate Producer, Fritz Manes. Assistant Director, Richard Hashimoto. 2nd Assistant Directors, Lynn Morgan, Peter Bergquist and Al Silvani. Make-up Artist, Don Schoenfeld. Hairstylist, Lorraine Roberson. Costume Supervisor, Glenn Wright. Set Decoration, Ira Bates. Sound, Bert Hallberg. Stunt Coordinator, Wayne Van Horn. Special Effects, Chuck Gaspar. Filmed in Arizona and Nevada. Rated R. 113 minutes

Ben Shockley: Clint Eastwood, *Gus Mally:* Sondra Locke, *Josephson:* Pat Hingle, *Commissioner Blakelock:* William Prince, *Constable:* Bill McKinney, *D. A. Feyderspiel:* Michael Cavanaugh, *Waitress:* Carole Cook, *Jail Matron:* Mara Corday, *Bookie:* Douglas McGrath, *Desk Sergeant:* Jeff Morris, *Bikers:* Samantha Doane, Roy Jenson, Dan Vadis.

The Gauntlet with Clint Eastwood and Sondra Locke.

THE GAY DIVORCEE (1934) RKO. Produced by Pandro S. Berman. Directed by Mark Sandrich. Based on the novel and the 1932 musical, *The Gay Divorce* by Dwight Taylor. Screenplay, George Marion Jr., Dorothy Yost, Edward Kaufman. Music adaptation, Kenneth Webb and Samuel Hoffenstein. Music Director, Max Steiner. Dances, Dave Gould. Songs: "Night and Day" by Cole Porter; "The Continental" and "Looking for a Needle in a Haystack" by Con Conrad and Herb Magidson; "Don't Let It Bother You" and "Let's K-nock K-neez" by Mack Gordon and Harry Revel. Photography, David Abel. Editor, William Hamilton. Astaire, Rhodes and Blore repeat their stage roles. 107 minutes

Guy Holden: Fred Astaire, *Mimi Glossop:* Ginger Rogers, *Aunt Hortense:* Alice Brady, *Egbert Fitzgerald:* Edward Everett Horton, *Rodolfo Tonetti:* Erik Rhodes, *Waiter:* Eric Blore, *Dancer:* Betty Grable, *Guy's Valet:* Charles Coleman, *Cyril Glossop:* William Austin, *Guest:* Lillian Miles, *French Waiters:* George Davis, Alphonse Martell, *French Headwaiter:* Paul Porcasi, *Call Boy at Dock:* Charles Hall, *Chief Customs Inspector:* E. E. Clive.

The Gay Divorcee with Ginger Rogers and Fred Astaire.

GENTLEMAN'S AGREEMENT (1947) 20th. Producer, Darryl F. Zanuck. Director, Elia Kazan. From the novel by Laura Z. Hobson. Screenplay, Moss Hart. Music, Alfred Newman. Art Directors, Lyle Wheeler, Mark-Lee Kirk. Cameraman, Arthur Miller. Editor, Harmon Jones. 118 minutes

Phil Green: Gregory Peck, *Kathy:* Dorothy McGuire, *Dave:* John Garfield, *Anne:* Celeste Holm, *Mrs. Green:* Anne Revere, *Miss Wales:* June Havoc, *John Minify:* Albert Dekker, *Jane:* Jane Wyatt, *Tommy:* Dean Stockwell, *Dr. Craigie:* Nicholas Joy, *Professor Lieberman:* Sam Jaffe, *Jordan:* Harold Vermilyea, *Bill Payson:* Ransom M. Sherman, *Mr. Calkins:* Roy Roberts, *Mrs. Minify:* Kathleen Lockhart, *Bert McAnny:* Curt Conway, *Bill:* John Newland, *Weisman:* Robert Warwick, *Ex-G.I.'s in Restaurant:* Robert Karnes, Gene Nelson, *Guest:* Marion Marshall, *Miss Miller:* Louise Lorimer, *Tingler:* Howard Negley, *Olsen:* Victor Kilian, *Harry:* Frank Wilcox, *Receptionist:* Marilyn Monk, *Maitre D':* Wilton Graff, *Clerk:* Morgan Farley, *Columnist:* Mauritz Hugo, *Women:* Olive Deering, Jane Green, Virginia Gregg, *Elevator Starter:* Jesse White.

Gentleman's Agreement with Gregory Peck, Celeste Holm, John Garfield, Gene Nelson and Robert Karnes.

GENTLEMEN PREFER BLONDES (1953) 20th. Producer, Sol C. Siegel. Director, Howard Hawks. Technicolor. Based on the musical by Anita Loos and Joseph Fields. Screenplay, Charles Lederer. Art Directors, Lyle Wheeler, Joseph C. Wright. Cinematographer, Harry J. Wild. Editor, Hugh S. Fowler. Music Director, Lionel Newman. Costumes, Travilla. Choreography, Jack Cole. Songs: "When Love Goes Wrong" and "Anyone Here for Love?" by Hoagy Carmichael and Harold Adamson. Songs by Jule Styne and Leo Robin: "Two Little Girls Erom Little Rock," "Diamonds Are a Girl's Best Friend," "Bye, Bye, Baby." Remake of 1928 Warners film. 91 minutes

Dorothy Shaw: Jane Russell, *Lorelei:* Marilyn Monroe, *Sir Francis Beekman:* Charles Coburn, *Malone:* Elliott Reid, *Gus Esmond:* Tommy Noonan, *Henry Spofford III:* George Winslow, *Magistrate:* Marcel Dalio, *Esmond, Sr.:* Taylor Holmes, *Lady Beekman:* Norma Varden, *Watson:* Howard Wendell, *Hotel Manager:* Steven Geray, *Grotier:* Henri Letondal, *Pritchard:* Alex Frazer, *Dancer:* George Chakiris, *Bit:* Robert Fuller, *Phillipe:* Leo Mostovoy, *Cab Driver:* George Davis, *Headwaiter:* Alphonse Martell, *Boy Dancers:* Jimmie Moultrie, Freddie Moultrie, *Winslow:* Harry Carey, Jr., *Ship's Captain:* Jean Del Val, *Peters:* Ray Montgomery, *Anderson:* Alvy Moore, *Evans:* Robert Nichols, *Ed:* Charles Tannen, *Stevens:* Jimmy Young, *Purser:* Charles De Ravenne, *Coach:* John Close, *Sims:* William Cabanne, *Steward:* Philip Sylvestre, *Pierre:* Alfred Paix, *Court Clerk:* Max Willenz, *Waiter:* Rolfe Sedan, *Passport Officials:* Robert Foulk, Ralph Peters, *Captain of Waiters:* Harry Seymour.

Gentlemen Prefer Blondes with Marilyn Monroe.

The Getaway with Ali MacGraw and Steve McQueen.

THE GETAWAY (1972) National General. Produced by David Foster and Mitchell Brower. Directed by Sam Peckinpah. A Solar/Foster-Brower Production for First Artists Production Company in Todd-AO 35 and Technicolor. Based on the novel by Jim Thompson. Screenplay, Walter Hill. Associate Producer and 2nd Unit Director, Gordon T. Dawson. Stunt Coordinator, Carey Loftin. Photography, Lucien Ballard. Editors, Roger Spottiswoode and Robert Wolfe. Art Directors, Ted Haworth and Angelo Graham. Set Decorator, George R. Nelson. Music, Quincy Jones. Harmonica Solos, Toots Thielemans. Musical Voices, Don Elliott. Titles, Latigo Productions and Pacific Title. Special Effects, Bud Hulburd. Sound, Joe Von Stroheim, Mike Colgan, Charles M. Wilborn and Richard Portman. Costumes, Ray Summers. Make-up, Al Fleming and Jack Petty. Hairstyles, Kathy Blondell. Assistant Directors, Newt Arnold and Ron Wright. Filmed in Texas. Rated PG. 122 minutes

Doc McCoy: Steve McQueen, *Carol McCoy:* Ali MacGraw, *Jack Benyon:* Ben Johnson, *Fran Clinton:* Sally Struthers, *Rudy Butler:* Al Lettieri, *Cowboy:* Slim Pickens, *Thief:* Richard Bright, *Dr. Harold Clinton:* Jack Dodson, *Laughlin:* Dub Taylor, *Frank Jackson:* Bo Hopkins, *Cully:* Roy Jenson, *Accountant:* John Bryson, *Swain:* Bill Hart, *Hayhoe:* Tom Runyon, *Soldier:* Whitney Jones, *Boys on Train:* Raymond King, Ivan Thomas, *Parole Board Chairman:* W. Dee Kutach, *Boys' Mothers:* C. W. White, Brenda W. King, *Parole Board Commissioner:* Brick Lowry, *Doc's Lawyer:* Martin Colley, *Field Captain:* O. S. Savage, *Bank Guard:* Dick Crockett, *Hardware Store Owner:* A. L. Camp, *TV Shop Proprietor:* Bob Veal, *Sporting Goods Salesman:* Bruce Bissonette, *Cannon:* Jim Kannon, *Carhop:* Maggie Gonzalez, *Max:* Doug Dudley, *Stacy:* Stacy Newton, *Cowboy's Helper:* Tom Bush.

Giant with Rock Hudson, Elizabeth Taylor and Mercedes McCambridge.

GIANT (1956) WB. Producers, George Stevens, Henry Ginsberg. Director, George Stevens. WarnerColor. Based on the novel by Edna Ferber. Screenplay, Fred Guiol, Ivan Moffat. Music composed and directed by Dimitri Tiomkin. Cinematographer, William C. Mellor. Editor, William Hornbeck. Film editor, Fred Bohanan, Phil Anderson. James Dean's last film. Filmed in Virginia and in Marfa, Texas. 198 minutes

Leslie Lynnton Benedict: Elizabeth Taylor, *Bick Benedict:* Rock Hudson, *Jett Rink:* James Dean, *Luz Benedict:* Mercedes McCambridge, *Uncle Bawley:* Chill Wills, *Vashti Snythe:* Jane Withers, *Pinky Snythe:* Robert Nichols, *Jordan Benedict III:* Dennis Hopper, *Juana:* Elsa Cardenas, *Judy Benedict:* Fran Bennett, *Luz Benedict II:* Carroll Baker, *Bob Dace:* Earl Holliman, *Dr. Horace Lynnton:* Paul Fix, *Mrs Horace Lynnton:* Judith Evelyn, *Lacey Lynnton:* Carolyn Craig, *Sir David Karfrey:* Rodney Taylor, *Old Polo:* Alexander Scourby, *Angel Obregon II:* Sal Mineo, *Bale Clinch:* Monte Hale, *Adarene Clinch:* Mary Ann Edwards, *Swazey:* Napoleon Whiting, *Whiteside:* Charles Watts, *Dr. Guerra:* Maurice Jara, *Angel Obregon I:* Victor Millan, *Mrs. Obregon:* Pilar Del Rey, *Gomez:* Felipe Turich, *Gabe Target:* Sheb Wooley, *Mexican Priest:* Francisco Villalobos, *Watts:* Ray Whitley, *Lupe:* Tina Menard, *Petra:* Ana Maria Majalca, *Sarge:* Mickey Simpson, *Lona Lane:* Noreen Nash, *Harper:* Guy Teague, *Eusubio:* Natividad Vacio, *Dr. Walker:* Max Terhune, *Dr. Borneholm:* Ray Bennett, *Mary Lou Decker:* Barbara Barie, *Vern Decker:* George Dunne, *Clay Hodgins:* Slim Talbot, *Clay Hodgins, Sr.:* Tex Driscoll, *Essie Lou Hodgins:* Juney Ellis.

G. I. BLUES (1960) Par. Producer, Hal Wallis. Associate Producer, Paul Nathan. Director, Norman Taurog. Technicolor. Screenplay, Edmund Beloin, Henry Garson. Art Director, Walter Tyler. Music scored and conducted by Joseph J. Lilley. Cinematographer, Loyal

94

Griggs. Supervising Film Editor, Warren Low. Songs: "G. I. Blues," "Tonight Is So Right for Love," "Wooden Heart," "Big Boots," "Doin' the Best I Can," "Frankfurt Special," "Pocketful of Rainbows," "Shoppin' Around," Didja Ever?," "What's She Really Like?" Locations filmed in Germany. 104 minutes

Tulsa: Elvis Presley, *Lili:* Juliet Prowse, *Cookie:* Robert Ivers, *Tina:* Leticia Roman, *Rick:* James Douglas, *Marla:* Sigrid Maier, *Sergeant McGraw:* Arch Johnson, *Jeeter:* Mickey Knox, *Captain Hobart:* John Hudson, *Mac:* Ken Becker, *Turk:* Jeremy Slate, *Warren:* Beach Dickerson, *Mickey:* Trent Dolan, *Walt:* Carl Crow, *Papa Mueller:* Fred Essler, *Harvey:* Ronald Starr, *Trudy:* Erika Peters, *Owner of Puppet Show:* Ludwig Stossel, *Guitarist-Leader:* Robert Boon, *Mrs. Hagermann:* Edit Angold, *Orchestra Leader:* Dick Winslow, *Red:* Ed Faulkner, *Band Leader:* Edward Coch, *Herr Klugmann:* Fred Kruger, *Headwaiter:* Torben Meyer, *Businessmen:* Gene Roth, Roy C. Wright, *M.P.s:* Harper Carter, Tip McClure, *Chaplain:* Walter Conrad, *Dynamite:* Edward Stroll, *Kaffeehouse Manager:* William Kaufmann, *Strolling Girl Singer:* Hannerl Melcher, *Sergeant:* Elisha Matthew (Bitsy) Mott, Jr., *Fritzie:* Judith Rawlins, *Bargirl:* Marianne Gaba.

G.I. Blues with Elvis Presley, Mickey Knox and James Douglas.

Gigi with Hermione Gingold, Louis Jourdan, and Leslie Caron.

GIGI (1958) MGM. Producer, Arthur Freed. Director, Vincente Minnelli. CinemaScope, Technicolor. Based on the novel by Colette. Screenplay, Alan Jay Lerner. Art Directors, William A. Horning, Preston Ames. Musical Director, Andre Previn. Lyrics, Alan Jay Lerner. Music, Frederick Loewe. Orchestration, Conrad Salinger. Cinematographer, Joseph Ruttenberg. Editor, Adrienne Fazan. Other versions: a French film with Danielle Delorme, and a play with Audrey Hepburn. Filmed in Hollywood, exteriors made in Paris and at Maxim's.

Betty Wand sings for Leslie Caron. Songs by Alan Jay Lerner and Frederick Loewe:
"It's a Bore," "Gigi," "The Parisians," "The Night They Invented Champagne," "Say a Prayer for Me Tonight," "Thank Heaven for Little Girls," "I Remember It Well," "I'm Glad I'm Not Young Any More," "Gossip," "Waltz at Maxim's (She's Not Thinking of Me)." 116 minutes

Gigi: Leslie Caron, *Honoré Lachaille:* Maurice Chevalier, *Gaston Lachaille:* Louis Jourdan, *Mme. Alvarez:* Hermione Gingold, *Liane d'Exelmans:* Eva Gabor, *Sandomir:* Jacques Bergerac, *Aunt Alicia:* Isabel Jeans, *Manuel:* John Abbott, *Charles (Butler):* Edwin Jerome, *Simone:* Lydia Stevens, *Prince Berensky:* Maurice Marsac, *Showgirl:* Monique Van Vooren, *Designer:* Dorothy Neumann, *Mannequin:* Maruja Plose, *Redhead:* Marilyn Sims, *Harlequin:* Richard Bean, *Blonde:* Pat Sheahan.

Gilda with Rita Hayworth and Steven Geray.

GILDA (1946) Col. Producer, Virginia Van Upp. Director, Charles Vidor. Story, E. A. Ellington. Screenplay, Marion Parsonnet. Art Directors, Stephen Goosson, Van Nest Polglase. Musical Directors, M. W. Stoloff, Marlin Skiles. Cameraman, Rudolph Maté. Editor, Charles Nelson. Adaptation, Jo Eisinger. Songs by Doris Fisher and Allan Roberts: "Amada Mio" and "Put the Blame on Mame." 110 minutes

Gilda: Rita Hayworth, *Johnny Farrell:* Glenn Ford, *Ballin Mundson:* George Macready, *Obregon:* Joseph Calleia, *Uncle Pio:* Steven Geray, *Casey:* Joe Sawyer, *Captain Delgado:* Gerald Mohr, *Gabe Evans:* Robert Scott, *German:* Ludwig Donath, *Thomas Langford:* Don Douglas, *German:* Lionel Royce, *Little Man:* S. Z. Martel; *Huerta:* George J. Lewis, *Maria:* Rosa Rey, *Girl:* Ruth Roman, *Social Citizen:* Ted Hecht, *Woman:* Argentina Brunetti, *Doorman:* Jerry DeCastro, *Man:* Robert Stevens (Robert Kellard), *Bendolin's Wife:* Fernanda Eliscu, *Argentine:* Frank Leyva, *American:* Forbes Murray, *Frenchman:* Oscar Lorraine, *American:* Sam Flint, *Italian:* George Humbert, *Englishman:* Herbert Evans, *Man:* Rodolfo Hoyos, *Bendolin:* Eduardo Ciannelli, *Clerk:* Robert Tafur, *Escort:* Russ Vincent, *Frenchman:* Jean DeBriac.

GIRL CRAZY (1943) MGM. Producer, Arthur Freed. Director, Norman Taurog. Authors, Guy Bolton, Jack McGowan. Screenplay, Fred F. Finklehoffe. Musical Adaptation, Roger Edens. Musical Director, Georgie Stoll. Dance Director, Charles Walters. Art Director, Cedric Gibbons. Cameramen, William Daniels, Robert Planck. Editor, Albert Akst. Songs by Ira and George Gershwin: "Treat Me Rough," "Sam and Delilah," "Bidin' My Time," "Embraceable You," "Fascinating Rhythm," "I Got Rhythm," "But Not for Me," "Bar-

bary Coast" and "Cactus Time in Arizona." Remade by MGM as *When the Girls Meet the Boys* (1965). 99 minutes

Danny Churchill, Jr.: Mickey Rooney, *Ginger Gray:* Judy Garland, *Bud Livermore:* Gil Stratton, *Henry Lathrop:* Robert E. Strickland, *"Rags":* Rags Ragland, *Specialty:* June Allyson, *Polly Williams:* Nancy Walker, *Dean Phineas Armour:* Guy Kibbee, *Tommy Dorsey & His Band:* Themselves, *Marjorie Tait:* Frances Rafferty, *Governor Tait:* Howard Freeman, *Mr. Churchill, Sr.:* Henry O'Neill, *Ed:* Sidney Miller, *Governor's Secretary:* Sarah Edwards, *Radio Man:* William Bishop, *Brunette:* Eve Whitney, *Blonde:* Carol Gallagher, *Buckets:* Jess Lee Brooks, *Maitre d'Hotel:* Charles Coleman, *Nervous Man:* Harry Depp, *Dignified Man:* Richard Kipling, *Fat Man:* Henry Roquemore, *Waiter:* Alphonse Martel, *Churchill's Secretary:* Barbara Bedford, *Station Master:* Victor Potel, *Tom:* William Beaudine, Jr., *Reception Clerk:* Irving Bacon, *Messenger:* George Offerman, Jr., *Blonde:* Kathleen Williams, *Southern Girl:* Mary Elliott, *Girl:* Katharine Booth, *Boy:* Don Taylor, *Showgirls:* Georgia Carroll, Noreen Roth (Noreen Nash), Hazel Brooks, Inez Cooper, *Roly-poly Man:* Frank Jaquet, *Boy:* Peter Lawford, *Committee Woman:* Bess Flowers.

Girl Crazy with Henry O'Neill, Mickey Rooney, Judy Garland and Guy Kibbee.

Girl of the Golden West with Leo Carrillo, Nelson Eddy and Jeanette MacDonald.

THE GIRL OF THE GOLDEN WEST (1938) MGM. Produced by William Anthony McGuire. Directed by Robert Z. Leonard. Based on the play by David Belasco. Screenplay, Isabel Dawn and Boyce DeGaw. Music Director, Herbert Stothart. Filmed in Sepia. Photography, Oliver Marsh. Editor, W. Donn Hayes. Dances, Albertina Rasch. Montage, Slavko Vorkapich. Songs by Sigmund Romberg and Gus Kahn: "Mariachi," "There's a Brand New Song in Town," "The Golden West," "The West Ain't Wild Anymore," "Señorita," "Soldiers of Fortune," "Who Are We to Say?," "From Sun-Up to Sundown." The fourth MacDonald-Eddy film. Previous versions of *The Girl of the Golden West:* Paramount, 1914; Warner Brothers, 1923; Warner Brothers, 1930. Cut from the release print were Ray Bolger as Happy Moore and Carol Tevis as Trixie LaVerne. 120 minutes

Mary Robbins: Jeanette MacDonald, *Ramerez (Lt. Johnson):* Nelson Eddy, *Sheriff Jack Rance:* Walter Pidgeon, *Mosquito:* Leo Carrillo, *Alabama:* Buddy Ebsen, *Pedro:* Leonard Penn, *Nina Martinez:* Priscilla Lawson, *Sonora Slim:* Bob Murphy, *Trinidad Joe:* Olin Howland, *Minstrel Joe:* Cliff Edwards, *Nick:* Billy Bevan, *The Professor:* Brandon Tynan, *Father Sienna:* H. B. Warner, *Governor:* Monty Woolley, *Uncle Davy:* Charley Grapewin, *The General:* Noah Beery, Sr., *Gringo:* Bill Cody, Jr., *The Girl Mary:* Jeanne Ellis, *Wowkle:* Ynez Seabury, *Stage Driver:* Victor Potel, *Billy Jack Rabbit:* Nick Thompson, *Handsome Charlie:* Tom Mahoney, *Long Face:* Phillip Armenta, *Indian Chief:* Chief Big Tree, *Pioneer:* Russell Simpson, *First Renegade:* Armand "Curley" Wright, *Second Renegade:* Pedro Regas, *Manuel:* Gene Coogan, *Jose:* Sergei Arabeloff, *Juan:* Alberto Morin, *Felipe:* Joe Dominguez, *Pete, a Gambler:* Frank McGlynn, *Hank, a Gambler:* Cy Kendall, *First Miner:* E. Alyn Warren, *Second Miner:* Francis Ford, *Deputy:* Hank Bell, *Lieutenant Johnson:* Walter Bonn, *Colonel:* Richard Tucker, *Governor's Wife:* Virginia Howell.

The Glenn Miller Story with The Modernaires, Frances Langford and James Stewart.

THE GLENN MILLER STORY (1954) Univ. Producer, Aaron Rosenberg. Director, Anthony Mann. Technicolor. Screenplay, Valentine Davies. Art Directors, Bernard Herzbrun, Alexander Golitzen. Cinematographer, William Daniels. Editor, Russell Schoengarth. 116 minutes

Glenn Miller: James Stewart, *Helen Burger:* June Allyson, *Don Haynes:* Charles Drake, *Chummy:* Harry Morgan, *Si Schribman:* George Tobias, *Herself:* Frances Langford, *Himself:* Louis Armstrong, *Himself:* Gene Krupa, *Himself:* Ben Pollack, *General Arnold:* Barton MacLane, *Kranz:* Sig Rumann, *Mr. Miller:* Irving Bacon, *Mr. Burger:* James Bell, *Mrs. Miller:* Kathleen Lockhart, *Mrs. Burger:* Katharine Warren, *Colonel Spaulding:* Dayton Lummis, *Polly Haynes:* Marion Ross, *Joe Becker:* Phil Garris, *Jonnie Dee:* Deborah Sydes, *Themselves:* The Modernaires, *Themselves:* The Archie Savage Dancers, *Girl Singer:* Ruth Hampton, *Colonel Baker:* Damian O'Flynn, *Adjutant General:* Carleton Young, *Sergeant:* William Challee, *Lieutenant Colonel Baessell:* Steve Pendleton, *Doctor:* Harry Harvey, Sr., *Schillinger:* Leo Mostovoy, *Garage Man:* Dick Ryan, *Used Car Salesman:*

Hal K. Dawson, *Singing Foursome:* The Mello-Men, *Skating Act:* The Rolling Robinsons, *Boy:* Robert A. Davis, *Bobby-soxer:* Lisa Gaye, *Wilbur Schwartz:* Nino Tempo, *Himself:* Babe Russin, *Music Cutter:* Carl Vernell, *Irene:* Bonnie Eddy, *Herbert:* Anthony Sydes.

"*G*" Men with Russell Hopton, James Cagney, Edward Pawley and Barton MacLane.

"G" MEN (1935) WB. Directed by William Keighley. From "Public Enemy No. 1" by Seton I. Miller. Screenplay, Seton I. Miller. Cameraman, Sol Polito. Editor, Jack Killifer. Music Director, Leo Forbstein. Song, "You Bother Me an Awful Lot" by Sammy Fain and Irving Kahal. Technical Director, Frank Gompert. Gowns, Orry-Kelly. Dance Director, Bobby Connolly. Art Director, John J. Hughes. Reissued in 1949, on the FBI's 25th anniversary, with a prologue featuring David Brian as The Chief and Douglas Kennedy as an agent. 85 minutes

James (Brick) Davis: James Cagney, *Jean Morgan:* Ann Dvorak, *Kay McCord:* Margaret Lindsay, *Jeff McCord:* Robert Armstrong, *Brad Collins:* Barton MacLane, *Hugh Farrell:* Lloyd Nolan, *McKay:* William Harrigan, *Danny Leggett:* Edward Pawley, *Gerard:* Russell Hopton, *Durfee:* Noel Madison, *Eddie Buchanan:* Regis Toomey, *Bruce J. Gregory:* Addison Richards, *Venke:* Harold Huber, *The Man:* Raymond Hatton, *Analyst:* Monte Blue, *Gregory's Secretary:* Mary Treen, *Accomplice:* Adrian Morris, *Joseph Kratz:* Edwin Maxwell, *Bill, Ballistics Expert:* Emmett Vogan, *Agent:* James Flavin, *Bank Cashier:* Ed Keane, *Cops:* Stanley Blystone, Pat Flaherty, *Agent:* James T. Mack, *Congressman:* Jonathan Hale, *Short Man:* Charles Sherlock, *Henchman at Lodge:* Wheeler Oakman, *Police Broadcaster:* Eddie Dunn, *Interne:* Gordon (Bill) Elliott, *Doctor at Store:* Perry Ivins, *Hood Shot at Lodge:* Frank Marlowe, *Collins' Moll:* Gertrude Short, *Gerard's Moll:* Marie Astaire, *Durfee's Moll:* Florence Dudley, *Moll:* Frances Morris, *Hood:* Al Hill, *Gangster:* Huey White, *Headwaiter:* Glen Cavender, *Italian, Tony:* John Impilito, *Sergeant:* Bruce Mitchell, *Deputy Sheriff:* Monte Vandergrift, *Chief:* Frank Shannon, *Announcer:* Frank Bull, *Nurse:* Martha Merrill, *Lounger:* Gene Morgan, *J. E. Blattner, Florist:* Joseph DeStefani, *Machine Gunner:* George Daly, *Machine Gunner:* Ward Bond, *Prison Guard:* Tom Wilson, *Police Driver:* Henry Hall, *McCord's Aide:* Lee Phelps, *Hood at Lodge:* Marc Lawrence, *Man:* Brooks Benedict.

THE GODFATHER (1972) Par. Produced by Albert S. Ruddy. Directed by Francis Ford Coppola. An Alfran Production in Technicolor. Based on the novel by Mario Puzo. Screenplay, Puzo and Coppola. Associate Producer, Gray Frederickson. Photography, Gordon Willis. Production Designer, Dean Tavoularis. Music composed by Nino Rota, conducted by Carlo Savina. Costume Designer, Anna Hill Johnstone. Art Director, Warren Clymer. Set Decorator, Philip Smith. Editors, William Reynolds and Peter Zinner. Editors (New York), Marc Laub and Murray Solomon. Assistant Editor (New York), Barbara Marks. Assistant Editors, Jack Wheeler and Pierre Jalbert. Stunt Coordinator, Paul Baxley. Makeup, Dick Smith and Philip Rhodes. Hairstylist, Phil Leto. Women's

Wardrobe, Marilyn Putnam. Wardrobe Supervisor, George Newman. Production Recording, Christopher Newman. Re-recording, Bud Grenzbach and Richard Portman. Special Effects, A. D. Flowers, Joe Lombardi and Sass Bedig. Executive Assistant to the Producer, Robert S. Mendelsohn. Assistant to the Producer, Gary Chazan. Assistant Director, Fred Gallo. Assistant Director, Sicilian Unit, Tony Brandt. Second Assistant Director, Steve Skloot. Assistant Art Director, Sicilian Unit, Samuel Verts. Postproduction Consultant, Walter Murch. Foreign Postproduction Supervisor, Peter Zinner. Sound Recordist, Les Lazarowitz. Unit Publicist, Howard Newman. Filmed in Hollywood, New York, Las Vegas and Sicily. Rated R. 175 minutes. Sequel was *The Godfather, Part II*, 1974

Don Vito Corleone: Marlon Brando, *Michael Corleone:* Al Pacino, *Sonny Corleone:* James Caan, *Clemenza:* Richard Castellano, *Tom Hagen:* Robert Duvall, *McCluskey:* Sterling Hayden, *Jack Woltz:* John Marley, *Barzini:* Richard Conte, *Kay Adams:* Diane Keaton, *Sollozzo:* Al Lettieri, *Tessio:* Abe Vigoda, *Connie Corleone Rizzi:* Talia Shire, *Carlo Rizzi:* Gianni Russo, *Fredo Corleone:* John Cazale, *Cuneo:* Rudy Bond, *Johnny Fontane:* Al Martino, *Mama Corleone:* Morgana King, *Luca Brasi:* Lenny Montana, *Paulie Gatto:* John Martino, *Bonasera:* Salvatore Corsitto, *Neri:* Richard Bright, *Moe Greene:* Alex Rocco, *Bruno Tattaglia:* Tony Giorgio, *Nazorine:* Vito Scotti, *Theresa Hagen:* Tere Livrano, *Phillip Tattaglia:* Victor Rendina, *Lucy Mancini:* Jeannie Linero, *Sandra Corleone:* Julie Gregg, *Mrs. Clemenza:* Ardell Sheridan, *Apollonia:* Simonetta Stefanelli, *Fabrizio:* Angelo Infanti, *Don Tommasino:* Corrado Gaipa, *Calo:* Franco Citti, *Vitelli:* Saro Urzi, *Henchman:* Tom Rosqui.

The Godfather with Al Pacino, Marlon Brando, James Caan and John Cazale.

THE GODFATHER, PART II (1974) Par. Produced and Directed by Francis Ford Coppola. Screenplay, Coppola and Mario Puzo. Based on Puzo's novel *The Godfather.* Coproduced by Gray Frederickson and Fred Roos. Associate Producer, Mona Skager. Assistant Directors, Newton Arnold, Henry J. Lange, Jr., Chuck Myers, Mike Kusley, Alan Hopkins, Burt Bluestein and Tony Brandt. Music by Nino Rota. Additional Music, Carmine Coppola. Set Decorations, George R. Nelson and Joe Chevalier. Photography, Gordon Willis. Editors, Peter Zinner, Barry Malkin and Richard Marks. Production Designer, Dean Tavoularis. Costumes, Theadora Van Runkle. Sound, Chuck Wilborn and Nathan Boxer. Art Director, Angelo Graham. Technicolor. Rated R. 200 minutes

Michael Corleone: Al Pacino, *Vito Corleone:* Robert De Niro, *Tom Hagen:* Robert Duvall, *Kay Corleone:* Diane Keaton, *Fredo Corleone:* John Cazale, *Connie Corleone:* Talia Shire, *Hyman Roth:* Lee Strasberg, *Frankie Pentangeli:* Michael V. Gazzo, *Senator Pat Geary:* G. D. Spradlin, *Al Neri:* Richard Bright, *Fanucci:* Gaston Moschin, *Rocco Lampone:* Tom Rosqui, *Young Clemenza:* B. Kirby, Jr., *Genco:* Frank Sivero, *Young Mama Corleone:* Francesca De Sapio, *Mama Corleone:* Morgana King, *Deanna Corleone:* Mariana Hill, *Signor Roberto:* Leopoldo Trieste, *Johnny Ola:* Dominic Chianese, *Michael's Bodyguard:* Amerigo Tot, *Merle Johnson:* Troy Donahue, *Tessio:* Abe Vigoda, *Young Tessio:* John Aprea, *Willie Cicci:* Joe Spinell, *Theresa Hagen:* Tere

Livrano, *Carlo:* Gianni Russo, *Vito's Mother:* Maria Carta, *Vito Andolini as a boy:* Oreste Baldini, *Don Francesco:* Giuseppe Sillato, *Don Tommasino:* Mario Cotone, *Anthony Corleone:* James Gounaris, *Marcia Roth:* Fay Spain, *FBI Men:* Harry Dean Stanton, David Baker, *Carmine Rosato:* Carmine Caridi, *Tony Rosato:* Danny Aiello, *Father Carmelo:* Father Joseph Medeglia, *Senate Committee Chairman:* William Bowers, *Impresario:* Ezio Flagello, *Tenor:* Livio Giorgi, *Girl in Senza Mamma:* Kathy Beller, *Signora Colombo:* Saveria Mazzola, *Cuban President:* Tito Alba, *Mosca:* Ignazio Pappalardo, *Strollo:* Andrea Maugeri, *Abandando:* Peter La Corte, *Vendor:* Vincent Coppola, *Questadt:* Peter Donat, *Corngold:* Tom Dahlgren, *Senator Ream:* Paul B. Brown, *Senators:* Phil Feldman, Roger Corman, *Yolanda:* Yvonne Coll, *Sonny Corleone:* James Caan.

The Godfather, Part II with John Cazale and Al Pacino.

God Is My Co-pilot with Stanley Ridges, Raymond Massey, Minor Watson and Dennis Morgan.

GOD IS MY CO-PILOT (1945) WB. Producer, Robert Buckner. Director, Robert Florey. Based on the novel by Colonel Robert L. Scott. Art Director, John Hughes. Cameraman, Sid Hickox. Editor, Folmer Blangsted. Screenplay, Peter Milne and Abem Finkel. 90 minutes

Colonel Robert L. Scott: Dennis Morgan, *Johnny Petach:* Dane Clark, *Major General Claire L. Chennault:* Raymond Massey, *"Big Mike" Harrigan:* Alan Hale, *Catherine Scott:* Andrea King, *Tex Hill:* John Ridgely, *Colonel Meriam Cooper:* Stanley Ridges, *Ed Rector:* Craig Stevens, *Bob Neale:* Warren Douglas, *Sergeant Baldridge:* Stephen Richards (Mark Stevens), *Private Motley:* Charles Smith, *Colonel Caleb V. Haynes:* Minor Watson, *"Tokyo Joe":* Richard Loo, *Sergeant Aaltonen:* Murray Alper, *Gil Bright:* Bernie Sell, *Lieutenant Doug*

Sharp: Joel Allen, *Lieutenant "Alabama" Wilson:* John Miles, *Lieutenant Jack Horner:* Paul Brooke, *"Prank":* Clarence Muse, *Doctor Reynolds:* William Forrest, *Chinese Captain:* Frank Tang, *Japanese Announcer at Hong Kong:* Philip Ahn, *Frank Schiel:* Dan Dowling, *General Kitcheburo:* Paul Fung, *Specialty Dancer:* Frances Chan, *British Officer-Prisoner:* Sanders Clark, *American Girl Prisoner:* Phyllis Adair, *American Pilots:* Dale Van Sickel, Tom Steele, Art Foster, *Scott as a boy:* Buddy Burroughs, *Catherine's Father:* George Cleveland, *Robin Lee:* Ghislaine (Gigi) Perreau, *A.V.G. Groundmen:* Don McGuire, William Challee, *Newspaper Editor:* Joel Friedkin, *Major:* James Flavin.

GOD'S LITTLE ACRE (1958) UA. Producer, Sidney Harmon. Director, Anthony Mann. Screenplay by Philip Yordan. Based on the novel by Erskine Caldwell. Music by Elmer Bernstein. Assistant Director, Louis Brandt. Costumes by Sophia Stutz. A Security Pictures Production. 110 minutes

Ty Ty Walden: Robert Ryan, *Bill Thompson:* Aldo Ray, *Griselda:* Tina Louise, *Pluto:* Buddy Hackett, *Buck Walden:* Jack Lord, *Darlin' Jill:* Fay Spain, *Shaw Walden:* Vic Morrow, *Rosamund:* Helen Westcott, *Jim Leslie:* Lance Fuller, *Uncle Felix:* Rex Ingram, *Dave Dawson:* Michael Landon.

God's Little Acre with Fay Spain, Buddy Hackett and Robert Ryan.

Going My Way with Barry Fitzgerald and Bing Crosby.

GOING MY WAY (1944) Par. Producer and director, Leo McCarey. Author, Leo McCarey. Screenplay, Frank Bulter, Frank Cavett. Art Directors, Hans Dreier, William Flannery. Musical Director, Robert Emmett Dolan. Cameraman, Lionel Lindon. Special Effects, Gordon Jennings. Editor, LeRoy Stone. Songs: "Swinging on a Star," "Day

After Forever" and "Going My Way" by Johnny Burke and Jimmy Van Heusen; "Too-Ra-Loo-Ra-Loo-Ra" by J. R. Shannon. 130 minutes

Father O'Malley: Bing Crosby, *Genevieve Linden:* Risë Stevens, *Father Fitzgibbon:* Barry Fitzgerald, *Father Timothy O'Dowd:* Frank McHugh, *Ted Haines:* James Brown, *Haines, Sr.:* Gene Lockhart, *Carol James:* Jean Heather, *Mr. Belknap:* Porter Hall, *Tomaso Bozanni:* Fortunio Bonanova, *Mrs. Carmody:* Eily Malyon, *Robert Mitchell Boychoir:* Themselves, *Pee-Wee Belknap:* George Nokes, *Officer Patrick Mc-Carthy:* Tom Dillon, *Tony Scaponi:* Stanley Clements, *Herman Langerhanke:* Carl "Alfalfa" Switzer, *Interne:* Bill Henry, *Pitch Pipe:* Hugh Maguire, *Don Jose:* Robert Tafur, *Zuniga:* Martin Garralaga, *Maid at Metropolitan Opera House:* Sybyl Lewis, *Mr. Van Heusen:* George McKay, *Max:* William Frawley, *Mr. Lilley:* Jack Norton, *Mrs. Quimp:* Anita Bolster, *Fireman:* Jimmie Dundee, *Taxi Driver:* Julie Gibson, *Mrs. Molly Fitzgibbon:* Adeline deWalt Reynolds, *Church-goer:* Gibson Gowland.

Gold Diggers of Broadway with Neely Edwards and Lee Moran.

GOLD DIGGERS OF BROADWAY (1929) WB. Directed by Roy Del Ruth. Color by Technicolor. Story, Robert Lord. From the play *The Gold Diggers* by Avery Hopwood. Numbers staged by Larry Ceballos. Sound, Western Electric Vitaphone. Songs by Al Dubin and Joe Burke: "Painting the Clouds With Sunshine," "Tip-Toe Through the Tulips," "And They Still Fall in Love," "Go to Bed," "What Will I Do Without You?", "In a Kitchenette." Editor, William Holmes. Titles, De Leon Anthony. Costumes, Earl Luick. Assistant Director, Ross Lederman. Orchestra conducted by Louis Silvers. Technicians, L. Geib, M. Parker, F. N. Murphy, and V. Vance. Photography, Barney McGill and Ray Rennahan. Also silent version. Other versions by Warner Brothers: *Gold Diggers* (1923), *Gold Diggers of 1933*, *Painting the Clouds With Sunshine* (1951). Other editions of *Gold Diggers* series 1933, 1935 and *Gold Diggers in Paris* (1938). 98 minutes

Jerry: Nancy Welford, *Stephen Lee:* Conway Tearle, *Mabel:* Winnie Lightner, *Ann Collins:* Ann Pennington, *Eleanor:* Lilyan Tashman, *Wally:* William Bakewell, *Nick:* Nick Lucas, *Violet:* Helen Foster, *Blake:* Albert Gran, *Topsy:* Gertrude Short, *Stage Manager:* Neely Edwards, *Cissy Gray:* Julia Swayne Gordon, *Dance Director:* Lee Moran, *Barney Barnett:* Armand Kaliz.

GOLD DIGGERS OF 1933 (1933) WB. Directed by Mervyn LeRoy. Based on the play *Gold Diggers* by Avery Hopwood. Adaptation, Erwin Gelsey and James Seymour. Dialogue, David Boehm and Ben Markson. Photography, Sol Polito. Editor, George Amy. Dances by Busby Berkeley. Songs by Harry Warren and Al Dubin: "The Gold Diggers' Song (We're in the Money)," "I've Got to Sing a Torch Song," "Pettin' in the Park," "The Shadow Waltz," "Remember My Forgotten Man." Remake of *Gold Diggers of Broadway*, 1929. 96 minutes

J. Lawrence Bradford: Warren William, *Carol:* Joan Blondell, *Trixie Lorraine:* Aline MacMahon, *Polly Parker:* Ruby Keeler, *Brad Roberts (Robert Treat Bradford):* Dick Powell, *Faneuil H. Peabody:* Guy Kibbee, *Barney Hopkins:* Ned Sparks, *Fay Fortune:* Ginger Rogers, *Gordon:* Clarence Nordstrom, *Dance Director:* Robert Agnew, *Gigolo Eddie:* Tammany Young, *Messenger Boy:* Sterling Holloway, *Clubman:* Ferdinand Gottschalk, *Gold Digger Girl:* Lynn Browning, *Deputy:* Charles C. Wilson, *"Pettin' in the Park" Baby:* Billy Barty, *Negro Couple:* Snowflake (Fred Toones), Theresa Harris, *Chorus Girl:* Joan Barclay, *Stage Manager:* Wallace MacDonald, *Society Reporters:* Wilbur Mack, Grace Hayle, Charles Lane, *Dog Salesman:* Hobart Cavanaugh, *Dance Extra:* Bill Elliott, *Extra during Intermission:* Dennis O'Keefe, *Call Boy:* Busby Berkeley, *"Detective Jones":* Fred Kelsey, *First Forgotten Man:* Frank Mills.

Gold Diggers of 1933 with Aline MacMahon, Guy Kibbee, Dick Powell, Tammany Young and Joan Blondell.

Gold Diggers of 1935 with Alice Brady, Adolphe Menjou and Joseph Cawthorn.

GOLD DIGGERS OF 1935 (1935) WB. Directed by Busby Berkeley. Story, Robert Lord and Peter Milne. Screenplay, Manuel Seff and Peter Milne. Dances created by Busby Berkeley. Photography, George Barnes. Editor, George Amy. Songs by Harry Warren and Al Dubin: "Lullaby of Broadway," "I'm Going Shopping With You," "The Words Are in My Heart." Film debut of Jack La Rue's sister Emily, 18. Cut from the film: Harry Holman as Mr. Higpy, Marjorie Nichols as Letitia Fry, Grace Hayle as Mrs. Fry. 95 minutes

Dick Curtis: Dick Powell, *Nikolai Nicoleff:* Adolphe Menjou, *Ann Prentiss:* Gloria Stuart, *Matilda Prentiss:* Alice Brady, *Betty Hawes:* Glenda Farrell, *Humbolt Prentiss:* Frank McHugh, *T. Mosley Thorpe:* Hugh Herbert, *August Schultz:* Joseph Cawthorn, *Louis Lampson:* Grant Mitchell, *Arline Davis:* Dorothy Dare, *Wini Shaw:* Winifred Shaw, *Haggarty:* Thomas Jackson, *Singer, "The Words Are in My Heart":* Virginia Grey, *Girl:* Emily La Rue, *Dancers:* Ramon and Rosita, *Tap Dancer:* Matty King, *Head Bellhop:* Phil Tead, *Maitre D'Hotel:* Eddie Kane, *Housekeeper:* Nora Cecil, *Head Barman:* Arthur Aylesworth, *Martin (Clerk):* Gordon (Bill) Elliott, *Bellhop:* John Quillan, *Photographer:* Don Brodie, *Reporters:* Eddie Fetherstone, Billy Newell, George Riley, Harry Seymour, *Bellhop:* Ray Cooke, *Bartender:* Franklyn Farnum, *Manders, Doorman:* Charles Coleman, *Westbrook, Chauffeur:* E. E. Clive, *Perfume Clerk:* Leo White.

Goldfinger with Gert Frobe and Sean Connery.

GOLDFINGER (1964) UA. Producers, Harry Saltzman, Albert R. Broccoli. Director, Guy Hamilton. Screenplay, Richard Maibaum, Paul Dehn. Based on the novel by Ian Fleming. Director of Photography, Ted Moore. Title song, Leslie Bricusse, Anthony Newley; sung by Shirley Bassey. Music, John Barry. Assistant Director, Frank Ernest. An Eon Production in Technicolor. Produced in England. 108 minutes

James Bond: Sean Connery, *Goldfinger:* Gert Frobe, *Pussy Galore:* Honor Blackman, *Jill Masterson:* Shirley Eaton, *Tilly Masterson:* Tania Mallett, *Oddjob:* Harold Sakata, *"M":* Bernard Lee, *Solo:* Martin Benson, *Felix Lieter:* Cec Linder, *Simmons:* Austin Willis, *Miss Moneypenny:* Lois Maxwell, *Midnight:* Bill Nagy, *Capungo:* Alf Joint, *Old Lady:* Varley Thomas, *Bonita:* Nadja Regin, *Sierra:* Raymond Young, *Smithers:* Richard Vernon, *Brunskill:* Denis Cowles, *Kisch:* Michael Mellinger, *Mr. Ling:* Bert Kwouk, *Strap:* Hal Galili, *Henchman:* Lenny Rabin.

THE GOLDWYN FOLLIES (1938) UA. Produced by Samuel Goldwyn. Directed by George Marshall. Color by Technicolor. Story and Screenplay, Ben Hecht. Associate Producer, Georgie Haight. Additional comedy sequences by Sam Perrin and Arthur Phillips. Art Director, Richard Day. Music Director, Alfred Newman. Orchestrations, Edward Powell. Ballets, George Balanchine. Photography, Gregg Toland. Editor, Sherman Todd. Assistant Director, Eddie Bernoudy. Ballet Music, Vernon Duke. Songs: "Love Walked In," "Love Is Here to Stay," "I Was Doing All Right," and "I Love to Rhyme" by George and Ira Gershwin; "Spring Again" and "I'm Not Complaining" by Ira Gershwin and Kurt Weill; "Here Pussy Pussy" by Ray Golden and Sid Kuller; arias from *La Traviata*. Film debut of Helen Jepson. Andrea Leeds replaced Virginia Verrill, who dubbed the songs for her. New York newsman Harry Selby (pseudonym) was to do the original story. Cut were dancers Olga Phillips and John Kohl. 115 minutes

Oliver Merlin: Adolphe Menjou, *Themselves:* The Ritz Brothers, *Themselves:* Edgar Bergen and Charlie McCarthy, *Olga Samara:* Vera Zorina, *Danny Beecher:* Kenny Baker, *Hazel Dawes:* Andrea Leeds, *Leona Jerome:* Helen Jepson, *Michael Day:* Phil Baker, *Glory Wood:* Ella Logan, *A. Basil Crane, Jr.:* Bobby Clark, *Director Lawrence:* Jerome Cowan, *Ada:* Nydia Westman, *Alfredo in* LA TRAVIATA: Charles Kullman, *Assistant Director:* Frank Shields, *Theater Manager:* Joseph Crehan, *Roland (Igor in "Forgotten Dance"):* Roland Drew, *Prop Man:* Frank Mills, *Auditioning Singer:* Alan Ladd, *Westinghouse, a Singer:* Walter Sande. The American Ballet of the Metropolitan Opera, under the direction of George Balanchine.

The Goldwyn Follies with Vera Zorina, Charlie McCarthy and Edgar Bergen.

Gone With the Wind with Vivien Leigh and Clark Gable.

GONE WITH THE WIND (1939) MGM. A Selznick International Picture. Producer, David O. Selznick. Directors, Victor Fleming, Sam Wood and George Cukor. Technicolor. From the novel by Margaret Mitchell. Screenplay, Sidney Howard. Art Director, Lyle Wheeler. Musical Score, Max Steiner. Dance Directors, Frank Floyd, Eddie Prinz. Cameraman, Ernest Haller. Special Effects, Jack Cosgrove, Lee Zavitz. Editors, Hal C. Kern, James E. Newcom. Costumes, Walter Plunkett. Production Designer, William Cameron Menzies. Interiors, Joseph B. Platt. Interior Decoration, Edward G. Boyle. Make-up and Hair Styling, Monty Westmore, Hazel Rogers, Ben Nye. Historian, Wilbur G. Kurtz. Technical Advisors, Susan Myrick and Will Price. Research, Lillian K. Deighton. Production Manager, Raymond A. Klune. Technicolor Supervision, Natalie Kalmus and Henri Jaffa. Assistant Directors, Eric G. Stacey and Ridgeway Callow. Reissued in 1967 with Stereophonic Sound, and in 70mm Wide Screen. 219 minutes

AT TARA *Brent Tarleton:* Fred Crane, *Stuart Tarleton:* George Reeves, *Scarlett O'Hara:* Vivien Leigh, *Mammy:* Hattie McDaniel, *Big Sam:* Everett Brown, *Elijah:* Zack Williams, *Gerald O'Hara:* Thomas Mitchell, *Pork:* Oscar Polk, *Ellen O'Hara:* Barbara O'Neil, *Jonas Wilkerson:* Victor Jory, *Suellen O'Hara:* Evelyn Keyes, *Careen O'Hara:* Ann Rutherford, *Prissy:* Butterfly McQueen.

AT TWELVE OAKS *John Wilkes:* Howard Hickman, *India Wilkes:* Alicia Rhett, *Ashley Wilkes:* Leslie Howard, *Melanie Hamilton:* Olivia de Havilland, *Charles Hamilton:* Rand Brooks, *Frank Kennedy:* Carroll Nye, *Cathleen Calvert:* Marcella Martin, *Rhett Butler:* Clark Gable, *Gentleman:* James Bush.

AT THE BAZAAR IN ATLANTA *Aunt Pittypat Hamilton:* Laura Hope Crews, *Doctor Meade:* Harry Davenport, *Caroline Meade:* Leona Roberts, *Dolly Merriwether:* Jane Darwell, *Rene Picard:* Albert Morin, *Maybelle Merriwether:* Mary Anderson, *Fanny Elsing:* Terry Shero, *Old Levi:* William McClain.

OUTSIDE THE *EXAMINER* OFFICE *Uncle Peter:* Eddie Anderson, *Phil Meade:* Jackie Moran.

AT THE HOSPITAL *Reminiscent Soldier:* Cliff Edwards, *Belle Watling:* Ona Munson, *The Sergeant:* Ed Chandler, *Wounded Soldier in Pain:* George Hackathorne, *A Convalescent Soldier:* Roscoe Ates, *A Dying Soldier:* John Arledge, *An Amputation Case:* Eric Linden, *Card player (Wounded):* Guy Wilkerson.

DURING THE EVACUATION *A Commanding Officer:* Tom Tyler, *Soldier Aiding Doctor Meade:* Frank Faylen.

DURING THE SIEGE *A Mounted Officer:* William Bakewell, *Bartender:* Lee Phelps.

GEORGIA AFTER SHERMAN *A Yankee Deserter:* Paul Hurst, *Carpetbagger's Friend:* Ernest Whitman, *A Returning Veteran:* William Stelling, *A Hungry Soldier:* Louis Jean Heydt, *Emmy Slattery:* Isabel Jewell.

DURING RECONSTRUCTION *A Yankee Major:* Robert Elliott, *His Poker-Playing Captains:* George Meeker, Wallis Clark, *The Corporal:* Irving Bacon, *A Carpetbagger Orator:* Adrian Morris, *Johnny Gallegher:* J. M. Kerrigan, *A Yankee Businessman:* Olin Howland, *A Renegade:* Yakima Canutt, *His Companion:* Blue Washington, *Tom, a Yankee Captain:* Ward Bond, *Bonnie Blue Butler:* Cammie King, *Beau Wilkes:* Mickey Kuhn, *Bonnie's Nurse:* Lillian Kemble Cooper, *Yankee on Street:* Si Jenks, *Tom's Aide:* Harry Strang.

Goodbye, Columbus with Ali MacGraw.

GOODBYE, COLUMBUS (1969) Par. Produced by Stanley R. Jaffe. Directed by Larry Peerce. Technicolor. Based on the 1959 novella by Philip Roth. Screenplay, Arnold Schulman. A Willow Tree Production. Photography, Gerald Hirschfeld. Music, Charles Fox. Editor, Ralph Rosenblum. Art Director, Manny Gerard. Associate Producer, Tony LaMarca. Assistant Director, Steve Barnett. Wardrobe, Gene Coffin. Film debuts of Benjamin and Meyers. Filmed in Westchester County and New York City. Songs composed and sung by the Association. Rated R. 105 minutes

Neil Klugman: Richard Benjamin, *Brenda Patimkin:* Ali MacGraw, *Mr. Patimkin:* Jack Klugman, *Mrs. Patimkin:* Nan Martin, *Ron Patimkin:* Michael Meyers, *Julie Patimkin:* Lori Shelle, *Carlotta:* Royce Wallace, *Aunt Gladys:* Sylvie Strauss, *Doris:* Kay Cummings, *Don Farber:* Michael Nurie, *Aunt Molly:* Betty Grayson, *Uncle Leo:* Monroe Arnold, *Busboy:* Richard Wexler, *Sarah Ehrlich:* Elaine Swann, *Uncle Max:* Rubin Schafer, *Model:* Jackie Smith, *John McKee:* Bill Derringer, *Simp:* Mari Gorman, *Harriet:* Gail Ommerle, *Wedding Guest:* Jan Peerce, *Bits:* Max Peerce, Chris Schenkel.

The Goodbye Girl with Marsha Mason, Patricia Pearcy and Richard Dreyfuss.

THE GOODBYE GIRL (1977) WB. Produced by Ray Stark. Directed by Herbert Ross. Written by Neil Simon. A Rastar Feature. Associate Producer/Unit Production Manager, Roger M. Rothstein. Photography, David M. Walsh. Production Designer, Albert Brenner. Supervising Editor, Margaret Booth. Editor, John F. Burnett. Costume Designer, Ann Roth. Assistant Director, Jack Roe. Sound, Jerry Jost and William McCaughey. Set Decorator, Jerry Wunderlich. Make-up, Allan Whitey Snyder. Hairstylist, Kaye Pownall. Mason's Hairstyle, Carrie White. Men's Wardrobe, Seth Banks. Women's Wardrobe, Shirlee Strahm. Assistant Editors, Michael A. Stevenson and Barbara Dunning. 2nd Assistant Director, Edward Markley. 2nd Assistant Director (New York), Robert P. Cohen. Special Effects, Albert Griswold. Optics by MGM. Lenses and Panaflex Camera by Panavision. Color by Metrocolor. Filmed at MGM Studios, in Los Angeles and in New York City. Film debuts of Cummings, 9, and Shawn. Music scored and adapted by Dave Grusin. Song, "Goodbye Girl," written and sung by David Gates. Mason is Mrs. Simon. Rated PG. 110 minutes

Elliot Garfield: Richard Dreyfuss, *Paula McFadden:* Marsha Mason, *Lucy McFadden:* Quinn Cummings, *Donna:* Barbara Rhoades, *Mark:* Paul Benedict, *Mrs. Crosby:* Theresa Merritt, *Ronnie:* Michael Shawn, *Rhonda:* Patricia Pearcy, *Assistant Choreographer:* Gene Castle, *Dance Instructor:* Daniel Levans, *Linda:* Marilyn Sokol, *Mrs. Morganweiss:*

Anita Dangler, *Mrs. Bodine:* Victoria Boothby, *Liquor Store Salesman:* Robert Costanzo, *Muggers:* Poncho Gonzales, Jose Machado, Hubert Kelly, *Cynthia:* Dana Laurita, *Drunk:* Dave Cass, *Strip Club Dancers:* Loyita Chapel, Caprice Clarke, *Strip Club Manager:* Esther Sutherland, *Strip Club Customers:* Joseph Carberry, Eric Uhler, *Critic:* Clarence Felder, *Japanese Salesmen:* Kensuke Haga, Ryohei Kanokogi, *Gretchen:* Kristina Hurrell, *Furniture Movers:* David Matthau, Milt Oberman, *Painter:* Eddie Villery, *Oliver Frye:* Nicol Williamson.

GOODBYE, MR. CHIPS (1939) MGM. Producer, Victor Saville. Director, Sam Wood. From the novel by James Hilton. Screenplay, R.C. Sherriff, Claudine West, Eric Maschwitz. Cameraman, F.A. Young. Editor, Charles Frend. Filmed in England. 114 minutes

Mr. Chipping: Robert Donat, *Katherine Chipping:* Greer Garson, *John Colley: Peter Colley I Peter Colley II Peter Colley III:* Terry Kilburn, *Peter Colley as a young man:* John Mills, *Staefel:* Paul Von Hernried (Henried), *Flora:* Judith Furse, *Wetherby:* Lyn Harding, *Chatteris:* Milton Rosmer, *Marsham:* Frederick Leister, *Mrs. Wickett:* Louise Hampton, *Ralston:* Austin Trevor, *Jackson:* David Tree, *Colonel Morgan:* Edmond Breon, *Helen Colley:* Jill Furse, *Sir John Colley:* Scott Sunderland.

Goodbye, Mr. Chips with Robert Donat and Greer Garson.

The Good Earth with Paul Muni and Luise Rainer.

THE GOOD EARTH (1937) MGM. Produced by Irving G. Thalberg. Associate Producer, Albert Lewin. Directed by Sidney Franklin. Based on the novel by Pearl S. Buck. Adapted for the stage by Owen and Donald Davis. Screenplay, Talbot Jennings, Tess Schlesinger,

Claudine West. Music Score, Herbert Stothart. Art Director, Cedric Gibbons. Associate Art Directors, Harry Oliver, Arnold Gillespie, Edwin B. Willis. Wardrobe, Dolly Tree. Montage, Slavko Vorkapich. Photography, Karl Freund. Editor, Basil Wrangell. Photographed in Sepia. Backgrounds filmed in China. The voice of Lotus Lui used in place of Tilly Losch's. Dedicated to Irving Grant Thalberg, his last production. 138 minutes

Wang: Paul Muni, *O-lan:* Luise Rainer, *Uncle:* Walter Connolly, *Lotus:* Tilly Losch, *Cuckoo:* Jessie Ralph, *Old Father:* Charley Grapewin, *Elder Son:* Keye Luke, *Cousin:* Harold Huber, *Younger Son:* Roland Got (Roland Lui), *Old Mistress Aunt:* Soo Young, *Ching:* Chingwah Lee, *Gateman:* William Law, *Little Bride:* Mary Wong, *Banker:* Charles Middleton, *Little Fool:* Suzanna Kim, *Dancer:* Caroline Chew, *Singer In Tea House:* Chester Gan, *Grain Merchant, Liu:* Olaf Hytten, *House Guest of Wang:* Miki Morita, *Captain:* Philip Ahn, *Chinaman:* Sammee Tong, *Farmer/Rabble-rouser/Peach Seller:* Richard Loo.

THE GRADUATE (1967) Embassy. Produced by Lawrence Turman. Directed by Mike Nichols. Panavision and Technicolor. Based on the novel by Charles Webb. Screenplay, Calder Willingham and Buck Henry. Songs by Paul Simon, sung by Simon and Garfunkel: "Mrs. Robinson," "The Sounds of Silence," "Scarborough Fair," "April Come She Will." Music by Dave Grusin. Production Design, Richard Sylbert. Assistant Director, Don Kranze. Photography, Robert Surtees. Editor, Sam O'Steen. Sound, Jack Soloman. 105 minutes

Mrs. Robinson: Anne Bancroft, *Ben Braddock:* Dustin Hoffman, *Elaine Robinson:* Katharine Ross, *Mr. Braddock:* William Daniels, *Mr. Robinson:* Murray Hamilton, *Mrs. Braddock:* Elizabeth Wilson, *Carl Smith:* Brian Avery, *Mr. Maguire:* Walter Brooke, *Mr. McCleery:* Norman Fell, *Second Lady:* Elisabeth Fraser, *Mrs. Singleman:* Alice Ghostley, *Room Clerk:* Buck Henry, *Miss De Witt:* Marion Lorne; *Berkeley Student:* Richard Dreyfuss.

The Graduate with Anne Bancroft and Dustin Hoffman.

GRAND HOTEL (1932) MGM. Directed by Edmund Goulding. From the play *Menschen im Hotel* by Vicki Baum. American version by William A. Drake. Art Director, Cedric Gibbons. Gowns, Adrian. Assistant Director, Charles Dorian. Photography, William Daniels. Editor, Blanche Sewell. Sound, Douglas Shearer. MGM financed the 1930 Broadway version. Unofficially remade many times; officially remade by MGM as *Weekend at the Waldorf,* 1945. 115 minutes

Grusinskaya: Greta Garbo, *Baron Felix von Geigern:* John Barrymore, *Flaemmchen:* Joan Crawford, *Preysing:* Wallace Beery, *Otto Kringelein:* Lionel Barrymore, *Dr. Otternschlag:* Lewis Stone, *Senf:* Jean Hersholt, *Meierheim:* Robert McWade, *Zinnowitz:* Purnell B. Pratt, *Pimenov:* Ferdinand Gottschalk, *Suzette:* Rafaela Ottiano, *Chauffeur:* Morgan Wallace, *Gerstenkorn:* Tully Marshall, *Rohna:* Frank Conroy, *Schweimann:* Murray Kinnell, *Dr. Waitz:* Edwin

Maxwell, *Honeymooner:* Mary Carlisle, *Hotel Manager:* John Davidson, *Bartender:* Sam McDaniel, *Clerk:* Rolfe Sedan, *Clerk:* Herbert Evans, *Extra in Lobby:* Lee Phelps.

Grand Hotel with Frank Conroy, Ferdinand Gottschalk, John Davidson, Greta Garbo, Robert McWade and Rafaela Ottiano.

Grand Prix with Enzo Fiermonte and Yves Montand.

GRAND PRIX (1966) MGM. Produced by Edward Lewis. Directed by John Frankenheimer. Cinerama and Super Panavision and Metro-Color. Screen story and screenplay, Robert Alan Aurthur. Music composed and conducted by Maurice Jarre. Director of Photography, Lionel Lindon. A.S.C. Production Designer, Richard Sylbert. A Joel-JFP-Cherokee Co-Production. Costumes, Make-up and Hair Supervision, Sydney Guilaroff. Assistant Director, Enrice Issace. Editors, Fredric Steinkamp, Henry Berman, Stewart Linder, Frank Santille. Special Effects, Milt Rice. Filmed in Europe and United States. 179 minutes

Pete Aron: James Garner, *Louise Frederickson:* Eva Marie Saint, *Jean-Pierre Sarti:* Yves Montand, *Izo Yamura:* Toshiro Mifune, *Scott Stoddard:* Brian Bedford, *Pat Stoddard:* Jessica Walter, *Nino Barlini:* Antonio Sabato, *Lisa:* Francoise Hardy, *Agostini Manetta:* Adolfo Celi, *Hugo Simon:* Claude Dauphin, *Monique Delvaux Sarti:* Genevieve Page, *Guido:* Enzo Fiermonte, *Jeff Jordan:* Jack Watson, *Wallace Bennett:* Donal O'Brien, *Mrs. Stoddard:* Rachel Kempson, *Mr. Stoddard:* Ralph Michael, *Mrs. Randolph:* Evans Evans, *Claude:* Arthur Howard, *Photographer, David:* John Bryson, *John Hogarth:* Richie Giuther, *Douglas McClendon:* Bruce McLaren, *Children's Father:* Jean Michaud, *Tim Randolph:* Phil Hill, *Bob Turner:* Graham Hill, *Victor, Journalist:* Bernard Cahier, *Sportscasters:* Alan Fordney, Anthony Marsh, Tommy Franklin, *Grand Prix Drivers:* Lorenzo Bandini, Bob Bondurant, Jack Brabham, *American Boy:* Alain Gerard, *Doctor at Monza:* Tiziano Feroldi, *Rafael:* Gilberto Mazzi, *BBC*

Interviewer: Raymond Baxter, *Ferrari Official:* Eugenio Dragoni, *Japanese Interpreter:* Maasaki Asukai, *Monte Carlo Doctor:* Albert Remy.

THE GRAPES OF WRATH (1940) 20th. Produced by Darryl F. Zanuck. Associate Producer, Nunnally Johnson. Directed by John Ford. Based on the novel by John Steinbeck. Screenplay, Nunnally Johnson. Music Director, Alfred Newman. Art Directors, Richard Day and Mark-Lee Kirk. Photography, Gregg Toland. Sound, George Leverett and Roger Heman. Editor, Robert Simpson. Assistant Director, Eddie O'Fearna. Theme, "Red River Valley." 128 minutes

Tom Joad: Henry Fonda, *Ma Joad:* Jane Darwell, *Casey:* John Carradine, *Grampa:* Charley Grapewin, *Rosasharn Joad Rivers:* Dorris Bowdon, *Old Tom (Pa) Joad:* Russell Simpson, *Al:* O. Z. Whitehead, *Muley:* John Qualen, *Connie Rivers:* Eddie Quillan, *Granma:* Zeffie Tilbury, *Noah:* Frank Sully, *Uncle John:* Frank Darien, *Winfield Joad:* Darryl Hickman, *Ruth Joad:* Shirley Mills, *Thomas:* Roger Imhof, *Caretaker:* Grant Mitchell, *Wilkie:* Charles D. Brown, *Davis:* John Arledge, *Policeman:* Ward Bond, *Bert:* Harry Tyler, *Bill:* William Pawley, *Father:* Arthur Aylesworth, *Joe:* Charles Tannen, *Inspection Officer:* Selmer Jackson, *Leader:* Charles Middleton, *Proprietor:* Eddy Waller, *Floyd:* Paul Guilfoyle, *Frank:* David Hughes, *City Man:* Cliff Clark, *Bookkeeper:* Joseph Sawyer, *Agent:* Adrian Morris, *Muley's Son:* Hollis Jewell, *Spencer:* Robert Homans, *Roy (a Driver):* Irving Bacon, *Mae:* Kitty McHugh, *Tim Wallace:* Frank Faylen, *Sheriff:* Tom Tyler, *Floyd's Wife:* Mae Marsh, *Joe (Deputy):* Norman Willis, *Hungry Girl:* Peggy Ryan, *Boy who Ate:* Wally Albright, *Arkansas Storekeeper:* Erville Alderson, *Fred (Truck Driver):* Harry Strang, *Cop:* Rex Lease, *Woman in Camp:* Inez Palange, *Man at Camp:* Louis Mason, *Deputy/Troublemaker:* Harry Tenbrook, *Deputy:* Frank O'Connor, *Bit Woman:* Georgia Simmons, *Deputy:* Ralph Dunn, *Gas Station Man:* Herbert Heywood, *New Mexico Border Guard:* Walter Miller, *Gas Station Attendants:* Gaylord (Steve) Pendleton, Robert Shaw, *First Deputy:* Lee Shumway, *Second Deputy:* Dick Rich, *Guard:* James Flavin, *Clerk:* George O'Hara, *Motor Cop:* Thornton Edwards, *Jule:* Trevor Bardette, *Committeeman:* Jack Pennick, *Leader of Gang:* Walter McGrail, *Boy:* George Breakstone, *Deputy Driver:* William Haade, *State Policeman:* Ted Oliver, *Gas Station Attendant:* Ben Hall, *Waitress:* Gloria Roy.

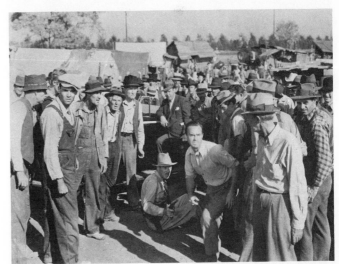

The Grapes of Wrath with Henry Fonda, John Carradine, Frank Darien, Russell Simpson, Norman Willis (with gun), Adrian Morris and Paul Guilfoyle.

GREASE (1978) Par. Produced by Robert Stigwood and Allan Carr. Directed by Randal Kleiser. Based on the 1971 musical by Jim Jacobs and Warren Casey. Screenplay, Bronte Woodard. Adaptation, Allan Carr. Dances and Musical Sequences staged and choreographed by Patricia Birch. Music Supervision, Bill Oakes. Associate Producer/Unit Production Manager, Neil A. Machlis. Photography, Bill Butler. Editor, John F.

Burnett. Production Designer, Phillip Jefferies. Special Creative Music Consultant, Louis St. Louis. Costume Designer, Albert Wolsky. Set Decorator, James Berkey. Make-up Artists, Dan Striepeke and Eddie Allen. Hairstylist, Christine George. Sound Mixer, Jerry Jost. Assistant Editor, Robert Pergament. Assistant Director, Jerry Grandley. 2nd Assistant Directors, Lynn Morgan and Paula Marcus. Stunt Coordinator, Wallace Dwight Crowder. Assistant Choreographer, Carol Culver. Dance Consultant, Tommy Smith. Women's Wardrobe, Betsy Cox, Men's Wardrobe, Bruce Walkup. Electronic Visual Effects, Ron Hays. Main Titles animated by John Wilson. New music, Charles Fox and Paul Williams. Songs by Jacobs and Casey: "Summer Nights," "Look at Me, I'm Sandra Dee," "Freddy, My Love," sung by Cindy Bullens; "Greased Lightning," "Beauty School Dropout," "Rock 'n' Roll Party Queen," sung by Louis St. Louis; "It's Raining on Prom Night," sung by Bullens; "Those Magic Changes," "Born to Hand-Jive," "Mooning," sung by St. Louis and Bullens; "There Are Worse Things I Could Do," "Alma Mater" and "We Go Together." "You're the One That I Want" and "Hopelessly Devoted to You" by John Farrar. "Sandy" by Louis St. Louis and Scott J. Simon. "Grease" by Barry Gibb. "Love Is a Many-Splendored Thing" by Sammy Fain and Paul Francis Webster. "Whole Lotta Shakin' Goin' On" by D. Williams and S. David, sung by Jerry Lee Lewis. "Rock 'n' Roll Is Here to Stay" by D. White. "Tears on My Pillow" by S. Bradford and A. Lewis. "Hound Dog" by Jerry Leiber and Mike Stoller. "Blue Moon" by Richard Rodgers and Lorenz Hart. "La Bamba," written and sung by Ritchie Valens. Film debuts of Donnelly and Ward; Kleiser's first feature. Los Angeles locations include Venice High School and Huntington Park High School. Panavision, Metrocolor and Dolby Sound. Rated PG. 110 minutes

Danny Zuko: John Travolta, *Sandy Olsson:* Olivia Newton-John, *Betty Rizzo:* Stockard Channing, *Principal McGee:* Eve Arden, *Vi:* Joan Blondell, *Coach Calhoun:* Sid Caesar, *Kenickie:* Jeff Conaway, *Frenchy:* Didi Conn, *Doody:* Barry Pearl, *Sonny:* Michael Tucci, *Putzie:* Kelly Ward, *Jan:* Jamie Donnelly, *Marty:* Dinah Manoff, *Patty Simcox:* Susan Buckner, *Tom Chisum:* Lorenzo Lamas, *Mrs. Murdock:* Alice Ghostley, *Blanche, Secretary:* Dody Goodman, *Nurse Wilkins:* Fannie Flagg, *Mr. Rudie:* Dick Patterson, *Eugene:* Eddie Deezen, *Mr. Lynch:* Darrell Zwerling, *Waitress:* Ellen Travolta, *Cha Cha:* Annette Charles, *Leo:* Dennis C. Stewart, *Teen Angel:* Frankie Avalon, *Vince Fontaine:* Edd Byrnes, *Johnny Casino and the Gamblers:* Sha-Na-Na, *Dancer:* Daniel Levans, *Face Pimple Remover Commercial:* Voice of Joe Silver.

Grease with Olivia Newton-John and John Travolta.

THE GREAT CARUSO (1951) MGM. Producer, Joe Pasternak. Director, Richard Thorpe. Color by Technicolor. Author, Dorothy Caruso. Screenplay, Sonia Levien, William Ludwig. Art Directors, Cedric Gibbons, Gabriel Scognamillo. Musical Supervision, Johnny Green. Photography, Joseph Ruttenberg. Editor, Gene Ruggiero. Song based on the melody of the Vienese waltz "Over the Waves" with lyrics by Paul Francis Webster: "The Loveliest Night of the Year." Operas: *Aida, Il Trovatore, Lucia, Martha, Rigoletto, La Tosca, Cavaliera Rusticana.* 109 minutes

Enrico Caruso: Mario Lanza, *Dorothy Benjamin:* Ann Blyth, *Louise Heggar:* Dorothy Kirsten, *Maria Selka:* Jarmila Novotna, *Carlo*

Santi: Richard Hageman, *Park Benjamin:* Carl Benton Reid, *Guilio Gatti-Casazza:* Eduard Franz, *Alfredo Brazzi:* Ludwig Donath, *Jean de Reszke:* Alan Napier, *Antonio Scotti:* Paul Javor, *Gino:* Carl Milletaire, *Fucito:* Shepard Menken, *Tullio:* Vincent Renno, *Egisto Barretto:* Nestor Paiva, *Caruso as a boy:* Peter Edward Price, *Papa Caruso:* Mario Siletti, *Mrs. Caruso:* Angela Clarke, *Hutchins:* Ian Wolfe, *Musetta:* Yvette Duguay, *Mrs. Barretto:* Argentina Brunetti, *Papa Gino:* Maurice Samuels, *Opera Stars:* Blanche Thebom, Teresa Celli, Nicolo Moscona, Guiseppe Valdengo, Marina Koshetz, Robert E. Bright, Lucine Amara, Gilbert Russell, Olive May Beach. *Hilda:* Edit Angold, *Papa Riccardo:* Antonio Filauri, *Father Bronzetti:* Peter Brocco, *Father Angelico:* David Bond, *Finch:* Charles Evans, *Max:* Matt Moore, *Musetta as a child:* Sherry Jackson, *Ottello Carmini:* Mario DeLaval, *Fucito (at 8 years):* Anthony Mazola, *Woman:* Mae Clarke.

The Great Caruso with Carl Milletaire, Vincent Renno, Shepard Menken, Mario Lanza, Ann Blyth and Ludwig Donath.

The Great Dictator with Henry Daniell, Charlie Chaplin and Jack Oakie.

THE GREAT DICTATOR (1940) UA. Produced, directed and written by Charles Chaplin. Music Director, Meredith Willson. Assistant Directors, Dan James, Wheeler Dryden and Bob Meltzer. Photography by Karl Struss and Roland Totheroh. Art Director, J. Russell Spencer. Editor, Willard Nico. Sound, Percy Townsend and Glen Rominger. 129 minutes

Hynkel (Dictator of Tomania)/A Jewish Barber: Charles Chaplin, *Hannah:* Paulette Goddard, *Napaloni (Dictator of Bacteria):* Jack

Oakie, *Schultz:* Reginald Gardiner, *Garbitsch:* Henry Daniell, *Herring:* Billy Gilbert, *Mr. Jaeckel:* Maurice Moscovich, *Mrs. Jaeckel:* Emma Dunn, *Madame Napaloni:* Grace Hayle, *Bacterian Ambassador:* Carter de Haven, *Mr. Mann:* Bernard Gorcey, *Mr. Agar:* Paul Weigel, *Bits:* Chester Conklin, Hank Mann, Esther Michelson, Florence Wright, Eddie Gribbon, Robert O. Davis (Rudolph Anders), Eddie Dunn, Nita Pike, Peter Lynn.

The Great Escape with Richard Attenborough, Donald Pleasence and James Garner.

THE GREAT ESCAPE (1963) UA. Producer-Director, John Sturges. Screenplay, James Clavell, W. R. Burnett. Based on a book by Paul Brickhill. Assistant Director, Jack Reddish. Music, Elmer Bernstein. A Mirisch-Alpha Picture in Panavision and De Luxe Color. Art Director, Fernando Carrere. Cinematographer, Daniel Fapp. Editor, Ferris Webster. Remake of *Danger Within* ("*Breakout*") British, 1958. Filmed in Germany. 168 minutes

"*Cooler King*" *Hilts:* Steve McQueen, "*The Scrounger*" *Hendley:* James Garner, "*Big X*" *Bartlett:* Richard Attenborough, *Senior Officer Ramsey:* James Donald, *Danny Velinski:* Charles Bronson, "*The Forger*" *Blythe:* Donald Pleasence, "*The Manufacturer*" *Sedgwick:* James Coburn, *Ashley-Pitt:* David McCallum, *MacDonald:* Gordon Jackson, *Willie:* John Leyton, "*The Mole*" *Ives:* Angus Lennie, *Cavendish:* Nigel Stock, *Goff:* Jud Taylor, *Sorren:* William Russell, "*The Tailor*" *Griffith:* Robert Desmond, *Nimmo:* Tom Adams, *Haynes:* Lawrence Montaigne, *Von Luger:* Hannes Messemer, *Werner:* Robert Graf, *Strachwitz:* Harry Riebauer, *Kuhn:* Hans Reiser, *Posen:* Robert Freitag, *Kramer:* Heinz Weiss, *Frick:* Til Kiwe, *Preissen:* Ulrich Beiger.

The Greatest Show on Earth with Henry Wilcoxon, James Stewart and Betty Hutton.

THE GREATEST SHOW ON EARTH (1952) Par. Producer, Cecil B. De Mille. Associate Producer, Henry Wilcoxon. Director, Cecil B. De Mille. Color by Technicolor. Authors, Fredric M. Frank, Theodore St. John, Frank Cavett. Screenplay, Fredric M. Frank, Barre Lyndon, Theodore St. John. Art Directors, Hal Pereira, Walter Tyler. Music Score, Victor Young. Cinematographers, George Barnes, J. Peverell Marley, Wallace Kelley. Editor, Anne Bauchens. Songs: "Be a Jumping Jack" and "The Greatest Show on Earth" by Ned Washington and Victor Young; "Popcorn and Lemonade," "Sing a Happy Song" and "A Picnic in the Park" by John Murray Anderson and Henry Sullivan; "Lovely Luawana Lady" by E. Ray Goetz and John Ringling North. Assistant Director, Edward Salven. Unit Director, Arthur Rosson. Costumes, Edith Head and Dorothy Jeakins. Circus Costumes, Miles White (by Brooks Costume Company, New York). Special Effects, Gordon Jennings, Devereaux Jennings, Paul Lerpae. Sets, Sam Comer and Ray Moyer. Numbers staged by John Murray Anderson. Choreography, Richard Barstow. Make-up, Wally Westmore. Sound, Harry Lindgren and John Cope. Produced with the cooperation of Ringling Brothers-Barnum & Bailey Circus. Filmed in Sarasota, Florida. 153 minutes

Holly: Betty Hutton, *Sebastian:* Cornel Wilde, *Brad:* Charlton Heston, *Phyllis:* Dorothy Lamour, *Angel:* Gloria Grahame, *Buttons:* James Stewart, *Detective:* Henry Wilcoxon, *Himself:* Emmett Kelly, *Klaus:* Lyle Bettger, *Henderson:* Lawrence Tierney, *Harry:* John Kellogg, *Jack Steelman:* John Ridgely, *Circus Doctor:* Frank Wilcox, *Ringmaster:* Bob Carson, *Buttons' Mother:* Lillian Albertson, *Birdie:* Julia Faye, *Himself:* John Ringling North, *Tuffy:* Tuffy Genders, *Jack Lawson:* John Parrish, *Keith:* Keith Richards, *Reporter:* Brad Johnson, *Mable:* Adele Cook Johnson, *Circus Girl:* Lydia Clarke, *Chuck:* John Merton, *Dave:* Lane Chandler, *Osborne:* Bradford Hatton, *Foreman:* Herbert Lytton, *Truesdale:* Norman Field, *Board Member:* Everett Glass, *Boy:* Lee Aaker, *Hank:* Ethan Laidlaw, *Spectators:* Bing Crosby, Bob Hope, Mona Freeman, Nancy Gates, Clarence Nash, Bess Flowers, *Midway Barker:* Edmond O'Brien, *Hopalong Cassidy:* William Boyd, *Circus Acts:* Lou Jacobs, Felix Adler, Liberty Horses, The Flying Concellos, Paul Jung, The Maxellos.

The Greatest Story Ever Told with Max von Sydow.

THE GREATEST STORY EVER TOLD (1965) UA. Producer-Director, George Stevens. Ultra Panavision 70, Technicolor. Screenplay, James Lee Barrett, George Stevens, in Creative Association with Carl Sandburg. Music, Alfred Newman. Executive Producer, Frank I. Davis. Associate Producers, George Stevens, Jr., Antonio Vellani. Costumes, Vittorio Nino Novarese. Screenplay based on the Bible, other ancient writings, *The Greatest Story Ever Told* by Fulton Oursler, and writings by Henry Denker. Directors of Photography, William C. Mellor, Loyal Griggs. Assistant Directors, Ridgeway Callow, John Veitch. Filmed in Utah. Choral Supervision, Ken Darby. 195 minutes

Jesus: Max von Sydow, *Mary:* Dorothy McGuire, *Joseph:* Robert Loggia, *John the Baptist:* Charlton Heston, *James the Younger:* Michael Anderson, Jr., *Simon the Zealot:* Robert Blake, *Andrew:* Burt Brinckerhoff, *John:* John Considine, *Thaddaeus:* Jamie Farr, *Philip:* David Hedison, *Nathanael:* Peter Mann, *Judas Iscariot:* David McCallum, *Matthew:* Roddy McDowall, *Peter:* Gary Raymond, *Thomas:* Tom Reese, *James the Elder:* David Sheiner, *Martha of Bethany:* Ina Balin, *Mary of Bethany:* Janet Margolin, *Lazarus:* Michael Tolan, *Simon of Cyrene:* Sidney Poitier, *Mary Magdalene:* Joanna Dunham, *Veronica:* Carroll Baker, *Young Man at the Tomb:* Pat Boone, *Bar Amand:* Van Heflin, *Uriah:* Sal Mineo, *Woman of No Name:* Shelley Winters, *Old Aram:* Ed Wynn, *The Centurion:* John Wayne, *Pontius Pilate:* Telly Savalas, *Claudia:* Angela Lansbury, *Pilate's Aide:* Johnny Seven, *Questor:* Paul Stewart, *General Varus:* Harold J. Stone, *Caiaphas:* Martin Landau, *Shemiah:* Nehemiah Persoff, *Nicodemus:* Joseph Schildkraut, *Sorak:* Victor Buono, *Emissary:* Robert Busch, *Alexander:* John Crawford, *Scribe:* Russell Johnson, *Speaker of Capernaum:* John Lupton, *Joseph of Arimathaea:* Abraham Sofaer, *Theophilus:* Chet Stratton, *Annas:* Ron Whelan, *Herod Antipas:* José Ferrer, *Herod the Great:* Claude Rains, *Aben:* John Abbott, *Captain of Lancers:* Rodolfo Acosta, *Herod's Commander:* Michael Ansara, *Chuza:* Philip Coolidge, *Philip:* Dal Jenkins, *Archelaus:* Joe Perry, *Herodias:* Marian Seldes, *Dark Hermit:* Donald Pleasence, *Barabbas:* Richard Conte, *The Tormentor:* Frank DeKova, *Dumah:* Joseph Sirola, *Melchior:* Cyril Delevanti, *Balthazar:* Mark Lenard, *Caspar:* Frank Silvera. And members of the Inbal Dance Theatre of Israel.

The Great Race with Tony Curtis, Natalie Wood and Keenan Wynn.

THE GREAT RACE (1965) WB. Producer, Martin Jurow. Associate Producer, Dick Crockett. Director, Blake Edwards. Panavision, Technicolor. Authors, Blake Edwards, Arthur Ross. Screenplay, Arthur Ross. Art Director, Fernando Carrere. Music, Henry Mancini. Songs: "The Sweetheart Tree," "He Shouldn't-a Hadn't-a, Oughtn't-a Swang on Me," words, Johnny Mercer, music, Henry Mancini. Cinematographer, Russell Harlan. Editor, Ralph E. Winters. 150 minutes

Leslie Gallant III: Tony Curtis, *Professor Fate:* Jack Lemmon, *Maggie DuBois:* Natalie Wood, *Maximillian Meen:* Peter Falk, *Hezekiah Sturdy:* Keenan Wynn, *Henry Goodbody:* Arthur O'Connell, *Hester Goodbody:* Vivian Vance, *Lilly Olay:* Dorothy Provine, *Texas Jack:* Larry Storch, *Baron Rolfe Von Stuppe:* Ross Martin, *General Kuhster:* George Macready, *Frisbee:* Marvin Kaplan, *Chairman:* J. Edward McKinley, *Vice-Chairman:* Robert Carson, *First Employee:* Paul Smith, *Starter:* Frank Kreig, *Mayor:* Hal Smith, *Sheriff:* Denver Pyle, *M.C.:* Charles Fredericks, *Man:* Clegg Hoyt, *Freight Agent:* Charles Seel, *Conductor:* Joe Palma, *Policeman:* Paul Bryar, *Man in Bear Suit:* Chester Hayes, *Soldiers:* Chuck Hayward, Greg Benedict, *First Palace Guard:* Ken Wales, *Second Palace Guard:* Robert Herron, *Guard:* Wm. Bryant, *Prison Guard:* John Truax, *Bakers:* Johnny Silver, Hal Riddle, *Stunt Double:* Dave Sharpe.

THE GREAT ZIEGFELD (1936) MGM. Produced by Hunt Stromberg. Directed by Robert Z. Leonard. Story and Screenplay by William

Anthony McGuire. Cinematographers, Oliver T. Marsh, Ray June, George Folsey, Merritt B. Gerstad. Recording Engineer, Douglas Shearer. Film Editor, William S. Gray. Art Director, Cedric Gibbons. Costumer, Adrian. Musical Director, Arthur Lange. Harriett Hoctor Ballet: Lyrics, Herb Magidson. Ballet Music, Con Conrad. Dances and Ensembles staged by Seymour Felix. Songs by Walter Donaldson and Harold Adamson: "I Wish You'd Come and Play With Me," "It's Delightful to Be Married," "A Circus Must Be Different in a Ziegfeld Show," "It's Been So Long," "You Gotta Pull Strings," "You," "Queen of the Jungle," "She's a Follies Girl," "You Never Looked So Beautiful"; and "A Pretty Girl Is Like a Melody" by Irving Berlin. Orchestrations, Frank Skinner. Allan Jones' singing voice dubbed for Dennis Morgan. 184 minutes

Flo Ziegfeld: William Powell, *Anna Held:* Luise Rainer, *Billie Burke:* Myrna Loy, *Billings:* Frank Morgan, *Sampston:* Reginald Owen, *Sandow:* Nat Pendleton, *Audrey Lane:* Virginia Bruce, *Sidney:* Ernest Cossart, *Joe:* Robert Greig, *Sage:* Raymond Walburn. *Fannie Brice:* Fannie Brice, *Mary Lou:* Jean Chatburn, *Ann Pennington:* Ann Pennington, *Ray Bolger:* Ray Bolger, *Harriett Hoctor:* Harriett Hoctor, *Julian Mitchell:* Charles Trowbridge, *Dr. Ziegfeld:* Joseph Cawthorn, *Gilda Gray:* Gilda Gray, *Will Rogers:* A. A. Trimble, *Patricia Ziegfeld:* Jean Holland, *Eddie Cantor:* Buddy Doyle, *Pierre:* Charles Judels, *Leon Errol:* Leon Errol, *Marie:* Marcelle Corday, *Prima Donna:* Esther Muir, *Customer:* Herman Bing, *Erlanger:* Paul Irving, *Gene Buck:* William Demarest, *Little Egypt:* Miss Morocco, *Miss Blair:* Suzanne Kaaren, *Telegraph Boy:* Mickey Daniels, *Customers:* Richard Tucker, Clay Clement, *Customer:* Selmer Jackson, *Alice:* Alice Keating, *Marilyn Miller:* Rosina Lawrence, *Girl with Sage:* Susan Fleming, *Charles Froman:* Edwin Maxwell, *Lillian Russell:* Ruth Gillette, *Dave Stamper:* John Hyams, *Willi Zimmerman:* Boothe Howard, *"Pretty Girl" Singer:* Stanley Morner (Dennis Morgan), *Chorus Girl:* Virginia Grey.

The Great Ziegfeld with Luise Rainer, William Powell and Marcelle Corday.

THE GREEN BERETS (1968) WB.–Seven Arts. A Batjac Production, Produced by Michael Wayne. Directed by John Wayne and Ray Kellogg, assisted by Mervyn LeRoy. 2nd Unit Director, Cliff Lyons. Based on the novel by Robin Moore. Screenplay by James Lee Barrett. Music by Miklos Rozsa. Photography, Winton C. Hoch. Production Designer, Walter M. Simonds. Set Decorations, Ray Moyer. Editor, Otho Lovering. Special Effects, Sass Bedig. Titles designed by Wayne Fitzgerald. Sound, Stanley Jones. Costumes, Jerry Alpert. Make-up, Dave Grayson. Assistant Director, Joe L. Cramer. Production Manager, Lee Lukather. Scenes filmed in Georgia and Alabama include Fort Benning, Georgia, and Fort Rucker, Alabama. In Panavision and Technicolor. 141 minutes

Col. Mike Kirby: John Wayne, *George Beckworth:* David Janssen, *Sgt.*

Petersen: Jim Hutton, *Sgt. Muldoon:* Aldo Ray, *Doc McGee:* Raymond St. Jacques, *Col. Morgan:* Bruce Cabot, *Col. Cai:* Jack Soo, *Capt. Nim:* George Takei, *Lt. Jamison (Seabee):* Patrick Wayne, *Sgt. Provo:* Luke Askew, *Lin:* Irene Tsu, *Capt. MacDaniels:* Edward Faulkner, *Capt. Coleman:* Jason Evers, *Sgt. Kowalski:* Mike Henry, *Hamchunk:* Craig Jue, *Sgt. Griffin:* Chuck Roberson, *Sgt. Watson:* Eddy Donno, *Sgt. Parks:* Rudy Robins, *Collier:* Richard "Cactus" Pryor, *Vietnamese Singer:* Bach Yen, *Lt. Sachs:* Frank Koomen, *Gen. Ti:* William Olds, *Sgt. White:* Billy Shannon, *Sgt. Lark:* Chuck Bail, *Vietcong Soldier:* Vincent Cadiente, *South Vietnamese Soldier:* Yodying Apibal. Cut was Vera Miles as *Mrs. Kirby.*

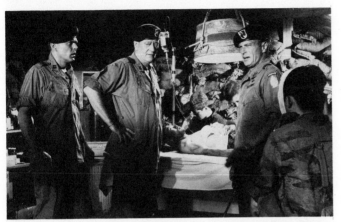

The Green Berets with Edward Faulkner, John Wayne and Jason Evers.

Green Dolphin Street with Lana Turner and Van Heflin.

GREEN DOLPHIN STREET (1947) MGM. Producer, Carey Wilson, Director, Victor Saville. Based on Elizabeth Goudge's novel. Screenplay, Samson Raphaelson. Music, Bronislau Kaper. Editor, George White. Song by Ned Washington and Bronislau Kaper: "On Green Dolphin Street." 141 minutes

Marianne Patourel: Lana Turner, *Timothy Haslam:* Van Heflin, *Marguerite Patourel:* Donna Reed, *William Ozanne:* Richard Hart, *Dr. Edmund Ozanne:* Frank Morgan, *Octavius Patourel:* Edmund Gwenn, *Mother Superior:* Dame May Whitty, *Captain O'Hara:* Reginald Owen, *Sophie Patourel:* Gladys Cooper, *Mrs. Metivier:* Moyna Macgill, *Hine-Moa:* Linda Christian, *Jacky-Pato:* Bernie Gozier, *Kapua-Manga:* Pat Aherne, *Native:* Al Kikume, *Sister Angelique:* Edith Leslie, *Veronica (4 years):* Gigi Perreau, *Sir Charles Maloney:* Douglas Walton, *Anderson:* Lumsden Hare, *Nat:* William Fawcett, *Priest:* Pedro De Cordoba, *Eurasian Girl:* Lila Leeds, *Emily:* Rhea Mitchell, *Corinne:* Ramsey Ames, *Brother:* Franco Corsaro, *Young Fisherman:* G--y Kingsford, *Government General:* Wyndham Standing, *Wife:* Florence Wix, *Commodore Hartley:* Leslie Dennison, *Niece:* Patricia Emery, *Chinaman:* Tetsu Komai, *Brown:* Michael Kirby, *Chinese Longshoreman:*

James B. Leong, *Mr. Samuel Kelly:* Murray Yeats, *Mrs. Samuel Kelly:* Lucille Curtis, *Maori Chieftain:* George Bennett, *Young Priest:* Richard Abbott, *Veronica (7 years):* Carol Nugent.

Green Pastures with Rex Ingram.

THE GREEN PASTURES (1936) WB. Produced by Jack L. Warner. Associate Executive in Charge of Production, Hal B. Wallis. Supervisor, Henry Blanke. Directed by Marc Connelly and William Keighley. Based on the play by Marc Connelly. Suggested by Roark Bradford's Southern sketches, *Ol' Man Adam An' His Chillun.* Screenplay, Marc Connelly and Sheridan Gibney. Cinematography, Hal Mohr. Sound, Major Nathan Levinson. Editor, George Amy. Art Directors, Allen Saalburg and Stanley Fleischer. Costumes, Milo Anderson. Assistant Director, Sherry Shourds. Choral music arranged and conducted by Hall Johnson. 93 minutes

De Lawd/Adam/Hezdrel: Rex Ingram, *Gabriel:* Oscar Polk, *Moses/Sexton:* Frank Wilson, *Pharaoh:* Ernest Whitman, *Noah:* Eddie Anderson, *Deshee/Isaac:* George Reed, *High Priest:* George Randol, *Abraham/King of Babylon/Head Magician:* Billy Cumby, *Zeba:* Edna M. Harris, *Master of Ceremonies/Man on Ground:* Slim Thompson, *Mrs. Noah:* Ida Forsyne, *Cain:* Al Stokes, *Eve:* Myrtle Anderson, *Joshua:* Reginald Fenderson, *Aaron:* David Bethea, *Cain the Sixth:* Jimmy Fuller, *Archangel:* Abraham Gleaves, *Dancer #1:* John Alexander, *Prophet:* Clinton Rosemond, *Zipporah:* Rosena Weston, *Mr. Randall:* William Broadus, *Mrs. Randall:* Amanda Drayton, *Zubo:* Fred (Snowflake) Toone, *Flatfoot/Gambler:* Charles Andrews, *Ham:* Dudley Dickerson, *Shem:* Ray Martin, *Japheth:* James Burruss, *Mrs. Ham:* Minnie Gray, *Mrs. Shem:* Bessie Guy, *Mrs. Japheth:* Dorothy Bishop, *Gambler:* Ben Carter, *Jacob:* Ivory Williams, *General:* Jesse Graves, *Abel/Dancer #2:* Duke Upshaw, *Mrs. Prohack:* Bessie Lyle, *Viney Prohack:* Lillian Davis, *Carlotta Prohack:* Charlotte Sneed, *Henry (Angel):* Willie Best, *Angel:* Johnny Lee, *Carlisle (Lucky) Hurlic, *Angel Chorus:* The Hall Johnson Choir.

GUADALCANAL DIARY (1943) 20th. Producer, Bryan Foy. Associate Producer, Islin Auster. Director, Lewis Seiler. Adapted by Jerry Cady from the book by Richard Tregaskis. Screenplay, Lamar Trotti. Art Directors, James Basevi, Leland Fuller. Musical Score, David Buttolph. Musical Director, Emil Newman. Cameraman, Charles Clarke. Special Effects, Fred Sersen. Editor, Fred Allen. Film debut of Richard Jaeckel. 93 minutes

Father Donnelly: Preston Foster, *Gunner O'Hara:* Lloyd Nolan, *Taxi Potts:* William Bendix, *Captain Davis:* Richard Conte, *Soose:* Anthony Quinn, *Private Johnny Anderson:* Richard Jaeckel, *Captain Cross:* Roy Roberts, *Colonel Grayson:* Minor Watson, *Ned Bowman:* Ralph Byrd, *Butch:* Lionel Stander, *Correspondent:* Reed Hadley, *Lieutenant Thurmond:* John Archer, *Tex:* Eddie Acuff, *Sammy:* Robert Rose, *Weatherby:* Miles Mander, *Dispatch Officer:* Harry Carter, *Major:*

Jack Luden, *Lieutenant:* Louis Hart, *Captain:* Tom Dawson, *Colonel Thompson:* Selmer Jackson, *Japanese Officer:* Allen Jung, *Japanese Prisoner:* Paul Fung.

Guadalcanal Diary with William Bendix, Anthony Quinn and Eddie Acuff.

The Guardsman with Alfred Lunt and Lynn Fontanne.

THE GUARDSMAN (1931) MGM. Directed by Sidney Franklin. Based on Ferenc Molnar's play. Adaptation, Ernest Vajda and Claudine West. Photography, Norbert Brodine. Editor, Conrad A. Nervig. *Elizabeth, the Queen* scene by permission of Maxwell Anderson. Lunt and Fontanne's talkie debut, repeating the roles they created on Broadway in 1924. 83 minutes. Remade as a musical, *The Chocolate Soldier* (1941)

The Actor: Alfred Lunt, *The Actress:* Lynn Fontanne, *The Critic:* Roland Young, *Liesl, the Maid:* ZaSu Pitts, *Mama:* Maude Eburne, *A Creditor:* Herman Bing, *A Fan:* Ann Dvorak.

GUESS WHO'S COMING TO DINNER (1967) Col. Produced and directed by Stanley Kramer. Associate Producer, George Glass. Color by Technicolor. Original screenplay by William Rose. Assistant Director, Ray Gosnell. Music by Frank DeVol. Title song by Billy Hill. Production Design, Robert Clatworthy. Photography, Sam Leavitt. Editor, Robert C. Jones. Sound, Charles J. Rice and Robert Martin. Last film of Spencer Tracy (released posthumously) and film debut of Katharine Houghton, 22, Hepburn's niece. 112 minutes

Matt Drayton: Spencer Tracy, *Christina Drayton:* Katharine Hepburn, *John Prentice:* Sidney Poitier, *Joey Drayton:* Katharine Houghton, *Monsignor Ryan:* Cecil Kellaway, *Mr. Prentice:* Roy E. Glenn, Sr., *Mrs. Prentice:* Beah Richards, *Tillie:* Isabell Sanford, *Hilary St. George:* Virginia Christine, *Car Hop:* Alexandra Hay, *Dorothy:* Barbara Randolph, *Frankie:* D'Urville Martin, *Peter:* Tom Heaton, *Judith:* Grace Gaynor, *Delivery Boy:* Skip Martin, *Cab Driver:* John Hudkins.

Guess Who's Coming to Dinner with Sidney Poitier, Katharine Houghton, Katharine Hepburn and Spencer Tracy.

Gunfight at the O.K. Corral with Kirk Douglas and Jo Van Fleet.

GUNFIGHT AT THE O.K. CORRAL (1957) Par. Produced by Hal B. Wallis. Directed by John Sturges. A Wallis-Hazen Production. In VistaVision and Technicolor. Screenplay, Leon Uris. Suggested by the article, "The Killer," by George Scullin. Assistant Director, Michael D. Moore. Costumes, Edith Head. Associate Producer, Paul Nathan. Music composed and conducted by Dimitri Tiomkin. Title song by Dimitri Tiomkin and Ned Washington, sung by Frankie Laine. Art Directors, Hal Pereira and Walter Tyler. Cinematographer, Charles Lang, Jr. Special Photographic Effects, John P. Fulton. Editor, Warren Low. Filmed in Arizona. 122 minutes

Wyatt Earp: Burt Lancaster, *John H. "Doc" Holliday:* Kirk Douglas, *Laura Denbow:* Rhonda Fleming, *Kate Fisher:* Jo Van Fleet, *Johnny Ringo:* John Ireland, *Ike Clanton:* Lyle Bettger, *Cotton Wilson:* Frank Faylen, *Charles Bassett:* Earl Holliman, *Shanghai Pierce:* Ted deCorsia, *Billy Clanton:* Dennis Hopper, *John P. Clum:* Whit Bissell, *John Shanssey:* George Mathews, *Virgil Earp:* John Hudson, *Morgan Earp:*

DeForest Kelley, *James Earp:* Martin Milner, *Bat Masterson:* Kenneth Tobey, *Barber:* Tony Merrill, *Cockeyed Frank Loving:* Harry B. Mendoza, *Deputy/Killer/Townsman:* Roger Creed, *Tommy Earp:* Charles Herbert, *Old Timer:* Tony Jochim, *Card Player:* James Davies, *Card Player:* Joe Forte, *Cowboy:* Gregg Martell, *Cowboy:* Dennis Moore, *Card Player:* Max Power, *Card Player:* Courtland Shepard, *Killer:* Morgan Lane, *Killer:* Paul Gary, *Ed Bailey:* Lee Van Cleef, *Betty Earp:* Joan Camden, *Mrs. Clanton:* Olive Carey, *Rick:* Brian Hutton, *Mayor Kelley:* Nelson Leigh, *Tom McLowery:* Jack Elam, *Drunken Cowboy:* Don Castle, *Stuntman:* Bill Williams, *Finn Clanton:* Lee Roberts, *Frank McLowery:* Mickey Simpson, *Hotel Clerk:* Frank Carter, *Deputy:* Edward Ingram, *Bartender:* Bing Russell, *Girl:* Dorothy Abbott, *Alby:* Henry Wills, *Wayne:* William S. Meigs, *Bartender:* Ethan Laidlaw, *Rig Driver:* John Benson, *Foreman:* Richard J. Reeves, *Bartender:* Frank Hagney, *Shaughnessy Man:* Robert C. Swan, *Bit Cowboy:* Len Hendry, *Social Hall Guest:* Trude Wyler, *Merchant:* John Maxwell.

Gunga Din with Douglas Fairbanks, Jr., Sam Jaffe and Victor McLaglen.

GUNGA DIN (1939) RKO. Pandro S. Berman in charge of production. Producer and Director, George Stevens. Based on the poem by Rudyard Kipling. Story, Ben Hecht, Charles MacArthur. Screenplay, Joel Sayre, Fred Guiol. Art Director, Van Nest Polglase. Musical Director, Alfred Newman. Cameraman, Joseph H. August. Special Effects, Vernon L. Walker. Editors, Henry Berman, John Lockert. Art Associate, Perry Ferguson. Sets, Darrell Silvera. Gowns, Edward Stevenson. Assistant Directors, Edward Killy and Dewey Starkey. Technical Advisers, Captain Clive Morgan, William Briers and Sir Robert Erskine Holland. Sound, John E. Tribby, James Stewart. Part of the Journalist (Rudyard Kipling) was deleted from American prints, has since been restored by the American Film Institute. 117 minutes

Cutter: Cary Grant, *MacChesney:* Victor McLaglen, *Ballantine:* Douglas Fairbanks, Jr., *Gunga Din:* Sam Jaffe, *Gura:* Eduardo Ciannelli, *Emmy:* Joan Fontaine, *Colonel Weed:* Montagu Love, *Higginbotham:* Robert Coote, *Chota:* Abner Biberman, *Major Mitchell:* Lumsden Hare, *Mr. Stebbins:* Cecil Kellaway, *Journalist:* Reginald Sheffield, *Girls at Party:* Ann Evers, Audrey Manners, Fay McKenzie, *Telegraph Operator:* Charles Bennett, *Corporal:* Les Sketchley, *Native Merchant:* Frank Levya, *Fulad:* Olin Francis, *Thug Chieftains:* George Ducount, Jamiel Hasson, George Regas, *Scotch Sergeant:* Bryant Fryer, *Jadoo:* Lal Chand Mehra, *Lieutenant Markham:* Roland Varno, *Lancer Captain:* Clive Morgan.

THE GUNS OF NAVARONE (1961) Col. Produced and written by Carl Foreman. Based on the novel by Alistair MacLean. Director, J. Lee Thompson. Music, Dimitri Tiomkin. Associate Producers, Cecil F. Ford, Leon Becker. Assistant Director, Peter Yates. Costumes,

Monty Berman. A Highroad Presentation in Eastman Color by Pathé and CinemaScope. Lyrics by Paul Francis Webster. Music played by Sinfonia of London. Filmed on the Island of Rhodes, Greece. Songs sung by Elga Anderson. 159 minutes

Captain Keith Mallory: Gregory Peck, *Corporal Miller:* David Niven, *Colonel Andrea Stavros:* Anthony Quinn, *CPO Brown:* Stanley Baker, *Major Roy Franklin:* Anthony Quayle, *Maria Pappadimos:* Irene Papas, *Anna:* Gia Scala, *Private Spyros Pappadimos:* James Darren, *Commander Jensen/Narrator:* James Robertson Justice, *Barnsby, Squadron Leader:* Richard Harris, *Cohn:* Bryan Forbes, *Baker:* Allan Cuthbertson, *Weaver:* Michael Trubshawe, *Sergeant Grogan:* Percy Herbert, *Sessler:* George Mikell, *Muesel:* Walter Gotell, *Nikolai:* Tutte Lemkow, *Commandant, Captain Muesel:* Albert Lieven, *Group Captain:* Norman Wooland, *Bride:* Cleo Scouloudi, *Patrol Boat Captain:* Nicholas Papakonstantinou, *German Gunnery Officer:* Christopher Rhodes.

The Guns of Navarone with Anthony Quinn and Gregory Peck.

A Guy Named Joe with Van Johnson, Spencer Tracy, James Gleason and Ward Bond.

A GUY NAMED JOE (1943) MGM. Producer, Everett Riskin. Director, Victor Fleming. Authors, Chandler Sprague, David Boehm. Screenplay, Dalton Trumbo. Musical Score, Herbert Stothart. Art Director, Cedric Gibbons. Special Effects, Arnold Gillespie, Donald Jahraus, Warren Newcombe. Cameramen, George Folsey, Karl Freund. Editor, Frank Sullivan. Song by Roy Turk and Fred Ahlert: "I'll Get By (As Long as I Have You)". 118 minutes

Pete Sandidge: Spencer Tracy, *Dorinda Durston:* Irene Dunne, *Ted*

Randall: Van Johnson, *Al Yackey:* Ward Bond, *"Nails" Kilpatrick:* James Gleason, *The General:* Lionel Barrymore, *Dick Rumney:* Barry Nelson, *"Powerhouse" O'Rourke:* Don DeFore, *Colonel Hendricks:* Henry O'Neill, *Major Corbett:* Addison Richards, *Sanderson:* Charles Smith, *Dance Hall Girl:* Mary Elliott, *Colonel Sykes:* Earl Schenck, *Captain Robertson:* Maurice Murphy, *Old Woman:* Gertrude Hoffmann, *Lieutenant:* Mark Daniels, *Ray:* William Bishop, *Powerhouse Girl:* Eve Whitney, *Ellen Bright:* Esther Williams, *Girl At Bar:* Kay Williams, *Mess Sergeant:* Walter Sande, *Bartender:* Gibson Gowland, *Officers in Heaven:* John Whitney, Kirk Alyn, *Orderly:* James Millican, *Davy:* Ernest Severn, *George:* Edward Hardwicke, *Cyril:* Raymond Severn, *Elizabeth:* Yvonne Severn, *Peter:* Christopher Severn, *Lieutenant Ridley:* John Frederick, *Majors:* Frank Faylen, Phil Van Zandt, *Fliers:* Marshall Reed, Blake Edwards, *Corporal:* Irving Bacon, *Sergeant Hanson:* Peter Cookson, *Lieutenant Hunter:* Matt Willis, *Helen:* Jacqueline White.

GUYS AND DOLLS (1955) MGM. Produced by Samuel Goldwyn. Directed by Joseph L. Mankiewicz. CinemaScope and Eastman Color. Based on the 1950 musical by Jo Swerling and Abe Burrows, from a story by Damon Runyon. Screenplay, Joseph L. Mankiewicz. Dances and musical numbers staged by Michael Kidd. Costumes, Irene Sharaff. Art Director, Joseph Wright. Music Director, Jay Blackton. Orchestrations, Skip Martin, Nelson Riddle, Alexander Courage, Al Sendrey. Cinematography, Harry Stradling. Editor, Daniel Mandell. Make-up, Ben Lane. Production Design, Oliver Smith. Songs by Frank Loesser: "Fugue for Tinhorns," "Follow the Fold," "The Oldest Established (Permanent Floating Crap Game in New York)," "I'll Know," "Adelaide's Lament," "Guys and Dolls," "If I Were a Bell," "Take Back Your Mink," "Luck Be a Lady," "Sit Down, You're Rockin' the Boat," and "Sue Me." "Pet Me, Papa" and "A Woman in Love" were written for the film. Blaine, Kaye, Silver, Pully, repeat their original stage roles. 138 minutes

Sky Masterson: Marlon Brando, *Sarah Brown:* Jean Simmons, *Nathan Detroit:* Frank Sinatra, *Miss Adelaide:* Vivian Blaine, *Lieutenant Brannigan:* Robert Keith, *Nicely-Nicely Johnson:* Stubby Kaye, *Big Jule:* B. S. Pully, *Benny Southstreet:* Johnny Silver, *Harry the Horse:* Sheldon Leonard, *Rusty Charlie:* Danny Dayton, *Society Max:* George E. Stone, *Arvide Abernathy:* Regis Toomey, *General Cartwright:* Kathryn Givney, *Laverne:* Veda Ann Borg, *Agatha:* Mary Alan Hokanson, *Angie the Ox:* Joe McTurk, *Calvin:* Kay Kuter, *Mission Member:* Stapleton Kent, *Cuban Singer:* Renee Renor, *The Champ:* Matt Murphy, *Mug in Barber Shop:* Harry Wilson, *Pitchman:* Earle Hodgins, *Max, a Waiter:* Harry Tyler, *Ringsiders ("Pet Me, Papa" number):* Major Sam Harris, Franklyn Farnum, *Man with Packages ("Guys and Dolls" number):* Frank Richards, *Liverlips Louie:* Johnny Indrisano, *Havana Waiter:* Julian Rivero, *The Goldwyn Girls:* Larri Thomas, Jann Darlyn, June Kirby, Madelyn Darrow, Barbara Brent. Ed Sullivan appears in the trailer.

Guys and Dolls with Renee Renor, Marlon Brando and Jean Simmons.

Gypsy with Karl Malden, Natalie Wood, Rosalind Russell and Ann Jilliann.

GYPSY (1962) WB. Producer, Mervyn LeRoy. Director, Mervyn LeRoy. Technirama, Technicolor. Based on Gypsy Rose Lee's memoirs and the musical by Arthur Laurents. Screenplay, Leonard Spigelgass. Art Director, John Beckman. Music, Jule Styne. Lyrics, Stephen Sondheim. Songs: "Let Me Entertain You," "Small World," "Baby June and Her Newsboys," "Some People," "Mr. Goldstone," "Little Lamb," "You'll Never Get Away From Me," "If Momma Was Married," "All I Need is the Girl," "Wherever We Go," "You Gotta Get a Gimmick," "Rose's Turn." Music composed and conducted by Frank Perkins. Orchestration, Frank Perkins, Carl Brandt. Cinematographer, Harry Stradling, Sr. Editor, Philip W. Anderson. 149 minutes

Rose: Rosalind Russell, *Louise:* Natalie Wood, *Herbie Sommers:* Karl Malden, *Tulsa:* Paul Wallace, *Tessie Tura:* Betty Bruce, *Mr. Kringelein:* Parley Baer, *Grandpa:* Harry Shannon, *"Baby" June:* Suzanne Cupito, *"Dainty" June:* Ann Jilliann, *"Baby" Louise:* Diane Pace, *Mazeppa:* Faith Dane, *Electra:* Roxanne Arlen, *George:* George Petrie, *Mr. Beckman:* James Millhollin, *Mr. Willis:* William Fawcett, *Mervyn Goldstone:* Ben Lessy, *Pastey:* Guy Raymond, *Cigar:* Louis Quinn, *Yonkers:* Danny Lockin, *Angie:* Ian Tucker, *Farmboy:* Bert Michaels, *Agnes:* Lois Roberts, *Dolores:* Dina Claire, *Phil:* Harvey Korman, *Betty Cratchitt:* Jean Willes.

Hail the Conquering Hero with Franklin Pangborn, Eddie Bracken and William Demarest.

HAIL THE CONQUERING HERO (1944) Par. Director, Preston Sturges. Screenplay, Preston Sturges. Art Directors, Hans Dreier, Haldane Douglas. Musical Score, Werner Heymann. Musical Director, Sigmund Krumgold. Cameraman, John Seitz. Editor, Stuart Gilmore. Song: "Home to the Arms of Mother" by Preston Sturges. 101 minutes

Woodrow: Eddie Bracken, *Libby:* Ella Raines, *Mr. Noble:* Raymond Walburn, *Sergeant:* William Demarest, *Chairman of Reception Committee:* Franklin Pangborn, *Libby's Aunt:* Elizabeth Patterson, *Mrs. Truesmith:* Georgia Caine, *Bugsy:* Freddie Steele, *Forrest Noble:* Bill Edwards, *Doc Bissell:* Harry Hayden, *Judge Dennis:* Jimmy Conlin, *Corporal:* Jimmy Dundee, *Political Boss:* Alan Bridge, *Mrs. Noble:* Esther Howard, *Marine Colonel:* Robert Warwick, *Juke:* Len Hendry, *Jonesy:* James Damore, *Bill:* Stephen Gregory, *Progressive Band-Leader:* Victor Potel, *Alfie, Junior Bandleader:* Merrill Rodin, *Regular Band Leader:* Jack Norton, *American Legion Bandleader:* Johnny Sinclair, *Mr. Schultz:* Torben Meyer, *Western Union Man:* Chester Conklin, *Reverend Upperman:* Arthur Hoyt, *Sheriff:* George Melford, *Town Painter:* Frank Moran, *Town Councilmen:* Tom McGuire, Philo McCullough, Franklyn Farnum, Kenneth Gibson, *Manager of Cafe:* Paul Porcasi, *Bartender:* George Anderson, *Singer:* Julie Gibson, *Marine Colonel's Wife:* Mildred Harris, *Mamie's Mother:* Dot Farley, *Mamie:* Marjean Neville, *Colonel's Daughter:* Maxine Fife, *Telephone Operator:* Pauline Drake.

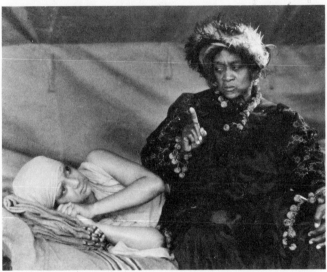

Hallelujah! with Nina Mae McKinney and Fannie Belle de Knight.

HALLELUJAH! (1929) MGM. Produced and directed by King Vidor. Story, King Vidor. Scenario, Wanda Tuchock. Dialogue, Ransom Rideout. Photography, Gordon Avil. Editor, Hugh Wynn. Sound, Western Electric Sound (on disk). Titles for silent version, Marian Ainslee. Editor of silent version, Anson Stevenson. Adaptation, Richard Schayer. Music Supervision, Eva Jessye. Wardrobe, Henriette Frazer. Assistant Director, Robert A. Golden. Second Assistant Director, William Allen Garrison. Filmed in Memphis, along the Mississippi, and in Culver City, Hollywood. Songs by Irving Berlin: "The End of the Road," "Swanee Shuffle." Nina Mae McKinney, 17, in her film debut, replaced Honey Brown. Ex-slave Harry Gray, 86, also made his film debut. 109 minutes

Zeke: Daniel L. Haynes, *Chick:* Nina Mae McKinney, *Hot Shot:* William Fountaine, *Parson:* Harry Gray, *Mammy:* Fannie Belle de Knight, *Spunk:* Everett McGarrity, *Missy Rose:* Victoria Spivey, *Johnson Kids:* Milton Dickerson, Robert Couch, Walter Tait, *Singer:* Evelyn Pope Burwell, *Singer and Bit:* Eddie Connors, *Heavy:* William Allen Garrison ("Slickem"); and The Dixie Jubilee Singers, directed by Eva Jessye.

HALLS OF MONTEZUMA (1950) 20th. Producer, Robert Bassler. Director, Lewis Milestone. Color by Technicolor. Author-Screenplay, Michael Blankfort. Art Directors, Lyle Wheeler and Albert Hogstett. Music, Lionel Newman. Photography, Winton C. Hoch, Harry Jackson. Editor, Charles LeMaire. Technicolor Consultant, Leonard Doss. 113 minutes

Lieutenant Anderson: Richard Widmark, *Pigeon Lane:* Walter (Jack) Palance, *Sergeant Johnson:* Reginald Gardiner, *Coffman:* Robert Wagner, *Doc:* Karl Malden, *Corporal Conroy:* Richard Hylton, *Lieutenant Colonel Gilfillan:* Richard Boone, *Pretty Boy:* Skip Homeier, *Lieutenant Butterfield:* Don Hicks, *Correspondent Dickerman:* Jack Webb, *Slattery:* Bert Freed, *Sergeant Zelenko:* Neville Brand, *Private Whitney:* Martin Milner, *Nomura:* Philip Ahn, *Captain Makino:* Howard Chuman, *Romeo:* Frank Kumagai, *Captain McCreavy:* Fred Coby, *Captain Seaman:* Paul Lees, *Pharmacist's Mate:* Fred Dale, *Frank:* Chris Drake, *Corpsman:* George Conrad, *Radioman:* Harry McKim, *Paskowicz:* William Hawes, *Davis:* Roger McGee, *Aunt Emma:* Helen Hatch, *Ship's Captain:* Michael Road, *Fukado:* Rollin Moriyama, *Willie:* Ralph Nagai, *Nurse:* Marion Marshall, *Bos'n Mate:* Harry Carter, *Private Stewart:* Richard Allan.

Halls of Montezuma with Richard Widmark, Richard Boone and Reginald Gardiner.

HANS CHRISTIAN ANDERSEN (1952) RKO. Producer, Samuel Goldwyn. Director, Charles Vidor. Color by Technicolor. Screenplay, Moss Hart. Based on a story by Myles Connolly. Words and music by Frank Loesser. Choreography by Roland Petit. 120 minutes

Hans Christian Andersen: Danny Kaye, *Niels:* Farley Granger, *Doro:* Jeanmaire, *Peter:* Joey Walsh, *Otto:* Philip Tonge, *The Hussar:* Erik Bruhn, *The Prince in the Ballet:* Roland Petit, *Schoolmaster:* John Brown, *Burgomaster:* Jehn Qualen, *Celine:* Jeanne Lafayette, *Stage Doorman:* Robert Malcolm, *Farmer:* George Chandler, *First Gendarme:* Fred Kelsey, *Second Gendarme:* Gil Perkins, *Lars:* Peter Votrian.

Hans Christian Andersen with Jeanmaire, Farley Granger and Danny Kaye.

HAPPY LANDING (1938) 20th. Associate Producer, David Hempstead. Director, Roy Del Ruth. Authors, Milton Sperling, Boris Ingster. Screenplay, Milton Sperling, Boris Ingster. Cameraman, John Mescal. Editor, Louis Loeffler. Songs by Jack Yellen and Samuel Pokrass: "Hot and Happy," "Yonny and His Oompah," "You Are

The Words to the Music in My Heart" and "A Gypsy Told Me."
"You Appeal to Me" by Walter Bullock and Harold Spina. Dances,
Harry Losee. Assistant Director, Booth McCracken. Music Director,
Louis Silvers. 102 minutes

Trudy Erickson: Sonja Henie, *Jimmy Hall:* Don Ameche, *Flo Kelly:*
Ethel Merman, *Sargent:* Cesar Romero, *Herr Erickson:* Jean Hersholt,
Counter Man: Billy Gilbert, *Specialty:* Raymond Scott and His Quintet,
Al Mahoney: Wally Vernon, *Specialty Song with Orchestra:* Leah Ray,
Specialty: Condos Brothers, *Yonnie:* El Brendel, *Agent:* Joseph Crehan,
Count: Alex Novinsky, *Manager:* William B. Davidson, *Rajah:* Marcel
de Labrosse, *Justice of the Peace:* William Wagner, *Manager, Madison
Square Garden:* Ben Welden, *Tuba Player:* Sid Saylor, *Hecklers:*
Harvey Parry, Matt McHugh, *Olaf:* Louis Adlon, Jr. *Gypsy:* Marcelle
Corday, *Waiter:* Eddy Conrad, *Turnkey:* Fred Kelsey, *Stewardess:*
June Storey, *Reporters:* Robert Lowery and Lon Chaney, Jr., *Specialty:* The Peters Sisters.

Happy Landing with Sonja Henie, Cesar Romero and Don Ameche.

The Hard Way with Jack Carson, Ida Lupino, Thurston Hall and
Joan Leslie.

THE HARD WAY (1942) WB. Producer, Jerry Wald. Director, Vincent
Sherman. Screenplay, Daniel Fuchs, Peter Viertel. Art Director, Max
Parker. Dance Director, LeRoy Prinz. Musical Director, Leo F. Forb-
stein. Cameraman, James Wong Howe. Special Effects, Willard Van
Enger. Editor, Thomas Pratt. Songs: "Am I Blue" by Grant Clarke
and Harry Akst; "Youth Must Have Its Fling," "Good Night Oh My
Darling" by Jack Scholl and M. K. Jerome. 109 minutes

Helen Chernen: Ida Lupino, *Paul Collins:* Dennis Morgan, *Katherine
Chernen:* Joan Leslie, *Albert Runkel:* Jack Carson, *Lily Emery:* Gladys
George, *Blonde Waitress:* Faye Emerson, *John Shagrue:* Paul Cavanagh,
Laura Bithorn: Leona Maricle, *Sam Chernen:* Roman Bohnen, *Johnny*

Gilpin: Ray Montgomery, *Chorine:* Julie Bishop, *Max Wade:* Nestor
Paiva, *Maria:* Joan Woodbury, *Dorshka:* Ann Doran, *Motion Picture
Executive:* Thurston Hall, *Frenchy:* Lou Lubin, *Anderson:* Jody Gil-
bert, *Duglatz:* Murray Alper, *Policemen:* Frank Faylen, Emory Parnell,
Edgar Dearing, *Interne:* Bill Edwards, *Police Officer:* Eddy Chandler,
Bum: Wallace Scott, *Pudgy Girl:* Jean Ames, *Serious Young Man:*
Harry Lewis, *Second Young Girl:* Dolores Moran, *Janitor:* Hank Mann,
Midget: Mary Curtis, *Midget:* Billy Curtis, *Radio Announcer:* Bill
Kennedy, *Stage Manager:* Philip Van Zandt, *Essie:* Libby Taylor,
Call Boy: Bud (Lon) McCallister, *Flora Ames:* Jean Inness, *Jimmy at 6:*
Joel Davis.

Harold and Maude with Bud Cort and Ruth Gordon.

HAROLD AND MAUDE (1971) Par. Produced by Colin Higgins and
Charles Mulvehill. Directed by Hal Ashby. Executive Producer, Mildred
Lewis. Screenplay, Colin Higgins. Photography, John A. Alonzo. Art
Director, Michael Haller. Editors, William A. Sawyer and Edward
Warschilka. Camera Operator, Joe Marquette, Jr. Production Assistant,
Jeff Wexler. Costume Designer, Bill Theiss. Wardrobe Supervisor, Andrea
Weaver. Make-up, Robert Stein. Hairstylist, Cathy Blondell. Production
Associate, Steve Silver. Assistant Directors, Michael Dmytryk and Robert
Enrietto. Special Visual Effects, A. D. Flowers. Sound, William Randall.
Re-recording, Richard Portman. Music Editor, Kenneth Johnson. Sound
Editor, James A. Richards. Editorial Consultant, Don Zimmerman. Music
composed and conducted by Cat Stevens including "If You Want to Sing."
Filmed in and around San Mateo, San Francisco and the George T.
Cameron estate in Hillsborough (San Francisco suburb), California. Film
debut of Henry W. Von Dieckoff, who was the Camerons' butler. In
Technicolor. Rated GP. 91 minutes

Harold Chasen: Bud Cort, *Maude:* Ruth Gordon, *Mrs. Chasen:* Vivian
Pickles, *Glaucus:* Cyril Cusack, *Uncle Victor:* Charles Tyner, *Sunshine
Doré:* Ellen Geer, *Priest:* Eric Christmas, *Psychiatrist:* G. Wood, *Candy
Gulf:* Judy Engles, *Edith Fern:* Shari Summers, *Police Officers:* Ray
Goman, Gordon Devol, *Cop:* Harvey Brumfield, *Motorcycle Policeman:*
William Lucking, *Butler:* Henry Dieckoff, *Doctor:* Philip Schultz, *Head
Nurse:* Sonia Sorrell, *Student Nurse:* Margot Jones, *Intern:* Barry Thomas
Higgins, *Stunt Doubles:* Pam Bebermeyer, Joe Hooker, *Bits:* Susan
Madigan, Jerry Randall, *Hairdresser:* Robert Stein, *Truck Driver:* Ed
Barrett. Cut was Marjorie Morley Eaton as *Madame Arouet.*

HARPER (1966) WB. A Jerry Gershwin-Elliott Kastner production.
Director, Jack Smight. Technicolor. Screenplay, William Goldman. Based
on Ross MacDonald's novel, *The Moving Target.* Camera, Conrad Hall.
Editor, Stefan Arnsten. Music, Johnny Mandel. Song, Dory and Andre
Previn, "Livin' Alone." 121 minutes. Sequel was *The Drowning Pool*
(1974)

Lew Harper: Paul Newman, *Mrs. Simpson:* Lauren Bacall, *Betty Fraley:* Julie Harris, *Albert Graves:* Arthur Hill, *Susan Harper:* Janet Leigh, *Miranda Sampson:* Pamela Tiffin, *Alan Traggert:* Robert Wagner, *Dwight Troy:* Robert Webber, *Fay Estabrook:* Shelley Winters, *Sheriff:* Harold Gould, *Claude:* Strother Martin, *Puddler:* Roy Jensen, *Deputy:* Martin West, *Mrs. Kronberg:* Jacqueline de Wit, *Felix:* Eugene Iglesias, *Fred Platt:* Richard Carlyle, *Eddie Fraley:* Tom Steele, *Telephone Operator:* Kathryn Janssen, *Albino Waiter:* Herbert Sullivan, Jr., *Bunny Dancer:* China Lee.

Harper with Paul Newman.

HARVEY (1950) Univ. Producer, John Beck. Director, Henry Koster. From the play by Mary C. Chase. Screenplay, Mary C. Chase, Oscar Brodney. Art Directors, Bernard Herzbrun, Nathan Juran. Music, Frank Skinner. Photography, William Daniels. Editor, Ralph Dawson. 104 minutes

Elwood P. Dowd: James Stewart, *Veta Louise Simmons:* Josephine Hull, *Miss Kelly:* Peggy Dow, *Doctor Sanderson:* Charles Drake, *Doctor Chumley:* Cecil Kellaway, *Myrtle Mae:* Victoria Horne, *Wilson:* Jesse White, *Judge Gaffney:* William Lynn, *Lofgren:* Wallace Ford, *Mrs. Chumley:* Nana Bryant, *Mrs. Chauvenet:* Grace Mills, *Herman:* Clem Bevans, *Mrs. McGiff:* Ida Moore, *Cracker:* Richard Wessel, *Policeman:* Pat Flaherty, *Cab Driver:* Norman Leavitt, *Elvira:* Maudie Prickett, *Salesman:* Ed Max, *Mrs. Strickleberger:* Grace Hampton, *Nurse Dunphy:* Minerva Urecal, *Miss LaFay:* Ruthelma Stevens, *Mrs. Halsey:* Almira Sessions, *Nurse:* Anne O'Neal, *Mrs. Johnson:* Eula Guy, *Minninger:* Sam Wolfe, *Chauffeur:* William Val, *Eccentric Man:* Gino Corrado, *Mrs. Krausmeyer:* Polly Bailey, *Mailman:* Don Brodie, *Meegles:* Harry Hines, *Mrs. Tewksbury:* Aileen Carlyle, *Mrs. Cummings:* Sally Corner.

Harvey with Peggy Dow, Charles Drake and James Stewart.

The Harvey Girls with Virginia O'Brien, Judy Garland and Cyd Charisse.

THE HARVEY GIRLS (1946) MGM. Producer, Arthur Freed. Associate Producer, Roger Edens. Director, George Sidney. Color by Technicolor. Based on the book by Samuel Hopkins Adams. Original Story, Eleanore Griffin, William Rankin. Screenplay, Edmund Beloin, Nathaniel Curtis. Musical Director, Lennie Hayton. Art Directors, Cedric Gibbons, William Ferrari. Cameraman, George Folsey. Special Effects, Warren Newcombe. Editor, Albert Akst. Songs by Johnny Mercer and Harry Warren: "On the Atchinson, Topeka and the Santa Fe,""In the Valley When the Evening Sun Goes Down," "Wait and See," "Swing Your Partner Round and Round," "The Wild Wild West" and "It's a Great Big World." 104 minutes

Susan Bradley: Judy Garland, *Ned Trent:* John Hodiak, *Chris Maule:* Ray Bolger, *Judge Sam Purvis:* Preston Foster, *Alma:* Virginia O'Brien, *Em:* Angela Lansbury, *Sonora Cassidy:* Marjorie Main, *H. H. Hartsey:* Chill Wills, *Terry O'Halloran:* Kenny Baker, *Miss Bliss:* Selena Royle, *Deborah:* Cyd Charisse, *Ethel:* Ruth Brady, *Louise:* Catherine McLeod, *Marty Peters:* Jack Lambert, *Jed Adams:* Edward Earle, *Jane:* Virginia Hunter, *First Cowboy:* William "Bill" Phillips, *Second Cowboy:* Norman Leavitt, *Reverend Claggett:* Morris Ankrum, *John Henry:* Ben Carter, *Sandy:* Mitchell Lewis, *Goldust McClean:* Horace McNally (Stephen McNally), *Big Joe:* Bill Hall, *Conductor:* Ray Teal, *Mule Skinner:* Jim Toney, *Fireman:* Jack Clifford, *Engineer:* Vernon Dent, *Conductor:* Robert Emmet O'Connor, *Station Agent:* Paul Newlan, *Trick Roper:* Sam Garrett.

Hatari! with Red Buttons and Elsa Martinelli.

113

HATARI! (1962) Par. Producer, Howard Hawks. Associate Producer, Paul Helmick. Director, Howard Hawks. Technicolor. Author, Harry Kurnitz. Screenplay, Leigh Brackett. Art Directors, Hal Pereira, Carl Anderson. Music Score, Henry Mancini. "Just for Tonight," lyrics, Johnny Mercer; music, Hoagy Carmichael. Cinematographer, Russell Harlan. Special Photographic Effects, John P. Fulton. Editor, Stuart Gilmore. A Malabar Production. Assistant Directors, Tom Connors and Russ Saunders. Filmed in Tanganyika. 159 minutes

Sean: John Wayne, *Kurt:* Hardy Kruger, *Dallas:* Elsa Martinelli, *Pockets:* Red Buttons, *Chips:* Gerard Blain, *Indian:* Bruce Cabot, *Brandy:* Michele Girardon, *Luis:* Valentine de Vargas, *Doctor:* Eduard Franz, *Joseph:* Jon Chevron, *Nurse:* Queenie Leonard, *Bartender:* Emmett E. Smith, *Man:* Jack Williams, *Sikh Clerk:* Henry Scott, *Masai Warrior:* Jack Williams, *Native Boy:* Jack Williams.

A Hatful of Rain with Don Murray and Lloyd Nolan.

A HATFUL OF RAIN (1957) 20th. Producer, Buddy Adler. Director, Fred Zinnemann. CinemaScope. Based on the play by Michael Vincente Gazzo. Screenplay, Michael Vincente Gazzo, Alfred Hayes. Art Directors, Lyle R. Wheeler, Leland Fuller. Music, Bernard Herrmann. Cinematographer, Joe MacDonald. Editor, Dorothy Spencer. 109 minutes

Celia Pope: Eva Marie Saint, *Johnny Pope:* Don Murray, *Polo:* Anthony Franciosa, *John Pope, Sr.:* Lloyd Nolan, *Mother:* Henry Silva, *Chuch:* Gerald O'Loughlin, *Apples:* William Hickey, *Cab Driver:* Michael Vale, *Mounted Cop:* Art Fleming, *Bartender:* Tom Ahearne, *Middle-aged Man:* Gordon B. Clark, *John:* Norman Willis, *Boss:* Jason Johnson, *Bartender:* Paul Kruger, *Man:* Rex Lease, *Man:* William Bailey, *Wiry Man:* Herb Vigran, *Doctor:* Jay Jostyn, *Spectator:* Ralph Montgomery, *Executive:* William Tannen, *Office Manager:* Emerson Treacy.

Hawaii with Max von Sydow and Julie Andrews.

HAWAII (1966) UA. Release of a Mirisch Corp. presentation. Produced by Walter Mirisch. Director, George Roy Hill. Panavision, De Luxe Color. Screenplay, Dalton Trumbo, Daniel Taradash. Based on James A. Michener's novel. Camera, Russell Harlan. Choreography, Miriam Nelson. Costumes, Dorothy Jeakins. Editor, Stuart Gilmore. Music, Elmer Bernstein. Song, "My Wishing Doll," Bernstein, Mack David. Filmed in Norway, New England, Hollywood, Tahiti, Hawaii. 186 minutes

Jerusha Bromley: Julie Andrews, *Abner Hale:* Max Von Sydow, *Rafer Hoxworth:* Richard Harris, *Charles Bromley:* Carroll O'Connor, *Abigail Bromley:* Elizabeth Cole, *Charity Bromley:* Diane Sherry, *Mercy Bromley:* Heather Menzies, *Reverend Thorn:* Torin Thatcher, *Reverend John Whipple:* Gene Hackman, *Reverend Immanuel Quigley:* John Cullum, *Reverend Abraham Hewlett:* Lou Antonio, *Malama:* Jocelyne La Garde, *Keoki:* Manu Tupou, *Kelolo:* Ted Nobriga, *Noelani:* Elizabeth Logue, *Iliki:* Lokelani S. Chicarell, *Gideon Hale:* Malcolm Atterbury, *Hepzibah Hale:* Dorothy Jeakins, *Captain Janders:* George Rose, *Mason:* Michael Constantine, *Collins:* John Harding, *Cridland:* Robert Crawford, *Micah (18):* Bertil Werjefelt, *Micah (4):* Robert Oakley, *Micah (7):* Henrik von Sydow, *Micah (12):* Clas von Sydow.

HEAVEN CAN WAIT (1943) 20th. Produced and directed by Ernst Lubitsch. Color by Technicolor. Based on the play *Birthday* by Lazlo Bush-Fekete. Screenplay, Samson Raphaelson. Score, Alfred Newman. Art Directors, James Basevi and Leland Fuller. Technicolor Director, Natalie Kalmus. Photography, Edward Cronjager. Editor, Dorothy Spencer. 113 minutes

Martha: Gene Tierney, *Henry Van Cleve:* Don Ameche, *Grandfather (Hugo Van Cleve):* Charles Coburn, *Mrs. Strabel:* Marjorie Main, *His Excellency:* Laird Cregar, *Bertha Van Cleve:* Spring Byington, *Albert Van Cleve:* Allyn Joslyn, *Mr. Strabel:* Eugene Pallette, *Mademoiselle:* Signe Hasso, *Randolph Van Cleve:* Louis Calhern, *Peggy Nash:* Helene Reynolds, *James:* Aubrey Mather, *Jack Van Cleve:* Michael Ames (Tod Andrews), *Flogdell:* Leonard Carey, *Jasper:* Clarence Muse, *Henry (age 15):* Dickie Moore, *Albert (age 15):* Dickie Jones, *Jane:* Trudy Marshall, *Mrs. Craig:* Florence Bates, *Grandmother:* Clara Blandick, *Mrs. Cooper-Cooper:* Anita Bolster, *Albert's Father:* Alfred Hall, *Albert's Mother:* Grayce Hampton, *Smith:* Gerald Oliver Smith, *Jack as a child:* Nino Pipitone, Jr., *Miss Ralston:* Claire DuBrey, *Clerk in Britano's:* Charles Halton, *Policeman:* James Flavin, *Henry age 15 months:* Michael McLean, *Doctor:* Edwin Maxwell, *Henry age 9:* Scotty Beckett, *Mary:* Marlene Mains, *Nurse:* Doris Merrick.

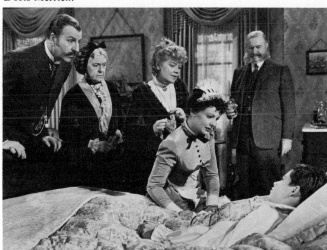

Heaven Can Wait with Louis Calhern, Clara Blandick, Spring Byington, Signe Hasso, Charles Coburn and Dickie Moore.

HEAVEN CAN WAIT (1978) Par. Produced by Warren Beatty. Directed by Warren Beatty and Buck Henry. Screenplay, Elaine May and Beatty. Based on the play *Heaven Can Wait* by Harry Segall. Executive Producers,

Howard W. Koch, Jr., and Charles H. Maguire. Photography, William A. Fraker. Production Designer, Paul Sylbert. Set Decorator, George Gaines. Editors, Robert C. Jones and Don Zimmerman. Music by Dave Grusin. Costume designs for Christie and Cannon by Theadora Van Runkle. Costume Design, Richard Bruno. Make-up Artist, Lee Harmon. Hairstylist, Lynda Gurasich. Unit Production Manager, Charles H. Maguire. Assistant Directors, Howard W. Koch, Jr., and Craig Huston. Art Director, Edwin O'Donovan. Sound Mixer, Tommy Overton. Technical Consultants, Les Josephson and Frank O'Neill. Special Effects, Robert MacDonald. Filmed in Los Angeles and at Filoli Estate near San Jose, California. Lenses and Panaflex Camera by Panavision. Color by Movielab. Rated PG. 101 minutes. A remake of *Here Comes Mr. Jordan* (Col., 1941)

Joe Pendleton (alias Leo Farnsworth and Tom Jarrett): Warren Beatty, *Betty Logan:* Julie Christie, *Mr. Jordan:* James Mason, *Julia Farnsworth:* Dyan Cannon, *Tony Abbott:* Charles Grodin, *Max Corkle:* Jack Warden, *The Escort:* Buck Henry, *Lt. Krim:* Vincent Gardenia, *Sisk:* Joseph Maher, *Bentley:* Hamilton Camp, *Everett:* Arthur Malet, *Corinne:* Stephanie Faracy, *Lavinia:* Jeannie Linero, *Gardener:* Harry D. K. Wong, *Security Guard:* George J. Manos, *Peters:* Larry Block, *Conway:* Frank Campanella, *Tomarken:* Bill Sorrells, *TV Interviewer:* Dick Enberg, *Head Coach:* Dolph Sweet, *General Manager:* R. G. Armstrong, *Trainer:* Ed V. Peck, *Former Owner:* John Randolph, *Former Owner's Adviser:* Richard O'Brien, *Haitian Ambassador:* Joseph F. Makel, *Team Doctor:* Will Hare, *Way Station Attendant:* Lee Weaver, *Newspaperman:* Roger Bowen, *Oppenheim:* Keene Curtis, *Renfield:* William Larsen, *Middleton:* Morgan Farley, *Lawson:* William Bogert, *Board Members:* Robert E. Leonard, Joel Marston, Earl Montgomery, Robert C. Stevens, *Coliseum Security Guard:* Bernie Massa, *Reporters:* Peter Tomarken, Lisa Blake Richards, *Nuclear Reporter:* William Sylvester, *High-wire Performer:* Charlie Charles, *Chauffeur:* Nick Outin, *Hodges:* Jerry Scanlan, *Kowalsky:* Jim Boeke, *Gudnitz:* Marvin Fleming, *Gorman:* Deacon Jones, *Owens:* Les Josephson, *Cassidy:* Jack T. Snow, *Football Players:* Charlie Cowan, Joe Corolla, *TV Sportscasters:* Bryant Gumbel, Jim Healy, *TV Commentator:* Curt Gowdy, *TV Color Analyst:* Al DeRogatis, *Waiters:* Elliott Reid, Bryon Webster, *Swimmer:* Garrett Craig, *Swimmer's Friend:* Paul D'Amato, *Wealthy Man in Restaurant:* Robert Fortier.

Heaven Can Wait with James Mason and Warren Beatty.

Heaven Knows, Mr. Allison with Deborah Kerr and Robert Mitchum.

HEAVEN KNOWS, MR. ALLISON (1957) 20th. Producers, Buddy Adler and Eugene Frenke. Director, John Huston. Screenplay by John Lee Mahin and John Huston. Based on the novel by Charles Shaw. Music by Georges Auric. Costumes by Elizabeth Haffenden. Assistant Director, Adrian Pryco-Jones. In CinemaScope and De Luxe Color. Filmed on the Island of Tobago, British West Indies. 107 minutes

Sister Angela: Deborah Kerr, *Corporal Allison, USMC:* Robert Mitchum.

THE HEIRESS (1949) Par. Produced and directed by William Wyler. Screenplay, Ruth and Augustus Goetz. Based on the play *The Heiress* by the Goetzes. Suggested by the novel *Washington Square* by Henry James. Art Director, John Meehan. Music, Aaron Copland. Photography, Leo Tover. Editor, William Hornbeck. Song by Ray Evans and Jay Livingston, "My Love Loves Me." 115 minutes

Catherine Sloper: Olivia de Havilland, *Morris Townsend:* Montgomery Clift, *Doctor Austin Sloper:* Ralph Richardson, *Lavinia Penniman:* Miriam Hopkins, *Maria:* Vanessa Brown, *Marian Almond:* Mona Freeman, *Jefferson Almond:* Ray Collins, *Mrs. Montgomery:* Betty Linley, *Elizabeth Almond:* Selena Royle, *Arthur Townsend:* Paul Lees, *Mr. Abeel:* Harry Antrim, *Quintus:* Russ Conway, *Geier:* David Thursby.

The Heiress with Olivia de Havilland and Montgomery Clift.

HELL DIVERS (1931) MGM. Directed by George Hill. Story by Lieutenant Commander Frank Wead. Adaptation, Harvey Gates and Malcolm Stuart Boylan. Photography, Harold Wenstrom. Editor, Blanche Sewell. Filmed at North Island, Panama, aboard the aircraft carrier *Saratoga*, during naval maneuvers. 113 minutes

Windy: Wallace Beery, *Steve:* Clark Gable, *Duke:* Conrad Nagel, *Ann:* Dorothy Jordan, *Mame Kelsey:* Marjorie Rambeau, *Lulu:* Marie Prevost, *Baldy:* Cliff Edwards, *Griffin:* John Miljan, *Admiral:* Landers Stevens, *Lieutenant Fisher:* Reed Howes, *Captain:* Alan Roscoe, *Chaplain:* Frank Conroy, *Young Officer:* Robert Young, *Trainee:* Jack Pennick, *Sailor:* John Kelly.

Hell Divers with John Kelly (rear), Clark Gable and Wallace Beery.

Hello, Dolly! with Walter Matthau and Barbra Streisand.

HELLO, DOLLY! (1969) 20th. Produced by Ernest Lehman. Directed by Gene Kelly. Todd-AO and DeLuxe Color. Based on the Broadway musical *Hello, Dolly!* by Michael Stewart and the play *The Matchmaker* by Thornton Wilder. Screenplay by Ernest Lehman. Staging by Michael Kidd. Photography, Harry Stradling. Musical scoring and conducting by Lennie Hayton and Lionel Newman. Production Design, John DeCuir. Costumes, Irene Sharaff. Special Effects, L. B. Abbott and Art Cruickshank. Art Directors, Jack Martin Smith and Herman Blumenthal. Set Decorations, Walter M. Scott, George Hopkins and Raphael Bretton. Editor, William Reynolds. Sound, Jack Solomon and Murray Spivak. Orchestrations by Philip J. Lang, Lennie Hayton, Joseph Lipman, Don Costa, Alexander Courage, Warren Barker, Frank Comstock and Herbert Spencer. Songs by Jerry Herman: "Hello, Dolly!" "Before the Parade Passes By," "It Takes a Woman," "So Long, Dearie." Locations filmed in Garrison, New York. 148 minutes. Previous nonmusical version, *The Matchmaker* (Par., 1958), Shirley Booth

Dolly Levi: Barbra Streisand, *Horace Vandergelder:* Walter Matthau, *Cornelius Hackl:* Michael Crawford, *Irene Molloy:* Marianne McAndrew, *Louis, Orchestra Leader:* Louis Armstrong, *Minnie Fay:* E. J. Peaker, *Barnaby Tucker:* Danny Lockin, *Ermengarde Vandergelder:* Joyce Ames, *Gussie Granger:* Judy Knaiz, *Rudolph Reisenweber:* David Hurst, *Fritz, German Waiter:* Fritz Feld, *Joe, Barber:* Richard Collier, *Policeman in Park:* J. Pat O'Malley, *Mr. Jones, Redcap:* Scatman Crothers, *Mr. Cassidy:* Eddie Quillan, *Rhine Maiden:* Lisa Todd, *Workman/Onlooker:* Morgan Farley, *Drunk:* Jimmy Cross, *Woman with Groceries:* Jessie Garnier, *Onlooker:* Ross Kimbrough, *Keystone Kop:* Hubie Kerns, *Officer Gogarty:* Patrick O'Moore, *Pushcart Men:* Michael Mark, Charles Wagenheim, *Policeman:* Ralph Roberts, *Sullivan, Ticket Seller:* James Chandler, *News Vendor:* Billy Benedict, *Laborers-singers:* James McEachin, Sam Edwards, Ralph Montgomery, Clay Tanner, Charles Lampkin, Guy Wilkerson, Tyler McVey, Jerry James, Ken Hooker, David Ahdar, *Patron in Harmonia Gardens:* Bern Hoffman.

HELLO, FRISCO, HELLO (1943) 20th. Producer, Milton Sperling. Director, Bruce Humberstone. Color by Technicolor. Screenplay, Robert Ellis, Helen Logan, Richard Macauley. Dance Directors, Hermes Pan, Val Raset. Art Directors, James Basevi, Boris Leven. Musical Directors, Charles Henderson, Emil Newman. Cameramen, Charles Clarke, Allen Davey. Editor, Barbara McLean. Technical Director, Natalie Kalmus. Songs: "You'll Never Know" and "I Gotta Have You" by Mack Gordon and Harry Warren; "Ragtime Cowboy Joe" by Grant Clarke, Maurice Abrahams and Lewis E. Muir; "Hello, Frisco, Hello" by Louis A. Hirsch and Gene Buck; "San Francisco" by Bronislau Kaper, Walter Jurmann and Gus Kahn. 98 minutes

Trudy Evans: Alice Faye, *Johnnie Cornell:* John Payne, *Dan Daley:* Jack Oakie, *Bernice:* Lynn Bari, *Sam Weaver:* Laird Creger, *Beulah:*

June Havoc, *Sharkey:* Ward Bond, *Cochran:* Aubrey Mather, *Colonel Weatherby:* George Barbier, *Ned:* John Archer, *Lou, the Bartender:* Frank Orth, *Proprietor:* George Lloyd, *Missionary:* Frank Darien, *Burkham:* Harry Hayden, *Foreman:* Eddie Dunn, *O'Reilly:* Charles Cane, *Auctioneer:* Frank Thomas, *Cockney Maid:* Mary Field, *Bit:* Ted (Michael) North, *Roller Skating Specialty:* James Sills and Marie Brown, *Specialty Singer:* Kirby Grant, *Waiter:* Ralph Dunn, *Aunt Harriet:* Esther Dale, *Doorman:* Edward Clark, *Opera Singers:* Gino Corrado, Adia Kuznetzoff, Fortunio Bonanova, *Singer:* Lorraine Elliott, *Stage Manager:* Edward Earle, *Headwaiters:* Ken Christy, James Flavin, *Child Dancers:* Jackie Averill, Jimmie Clemens, Jr., *Singer:* Ruth Gillette.

Hello, Frisco, Hello with John Payne and Alice Faye.

Hell's Angels with Jean Harlow and Ben Lyon.

HELL'S ANGELS (1930) UA. Produced and Directed by Howard Hughes. Red tints, ball sequence in Technicolor. Story, Marshall Neilan and Joseph Moncure March. Dialogue Director, James Whale. Scenario, Howard Estabrook and Harry Behn. Photography, Tony Gaudio, Harry Perry, E. Burton Steene. Art Directors, J. Boone Fleming and Carroll Clarke. Orchestra conducted by Hugo Riesenfeld. Assistant Directors, Reginald Callow, William J. Scully, Fred A. Fleck. Editors, Frank Lawrence, Douglas Biggs, Perry Hollingsworth. Sound, Lodge Cunningham. A Caddo Company Production, filmed at Metropolitan Studios, Caddo Field in Van Nuys, Inglewood, Chatsworth, Santa Cruz, Encino, Ryan Field in San Diego, March Field in Riverside, Oakland Airport. Started in 1927 as a silent; Jean Harlow replaced Greta Nissen when the sound version was made. Shot silent, the air scenes were later dubbed.

Wide screen was used twice during the film. 87 planes and 137 pilots were used on the production; killed were fliers Al Johnson and Phil Jones; cameraman Steene died of a stroke. English titles translate the German dialogue. 135 minutes

Monte Rutledge: Ben Lyon, *Roy Rutledge:* James Hall, *Helen:* Jean Harlow, *Karl Arnstedt:* John Darrow, *Baron von Kranz:* Lucien Prival, *Lieutenant von Bruen:* Frank Clarke, *Baldy Maloney:* Roy Wilson, *Captain Redfield:* Douglas Gilmore, *Baroness von Kranz:* Jane Winton, *Lady Randolph:* Evelyn Hall, *Staff Major:* William B. Davidson, *Squadron Commander, Royal Flying Corps:* Wyndham Standing, *Zeppelin Commander:* Carl Von Haartman, *First Officer of Zeppelin:* F. Schumann-Heink, *Elliott:* Stephen Carr, *Marryat:* Pat Somerset, *Von Richthofen:* William Von Brincken, *Von Schlieben:* Hans Joby, *Gretchen, German Waitress:* Lena Malena, *Anarchist:* Harry Semels, *Girl Selling Kisses:* Marilyn Morgan (Marian Marsh), *Pilots:* Stewart Murphy, Ira Reed, Maurice "Loop the Loop" Murphy, Leo Nomis, Frank Tomick, Al Wilson, Roscoe Turner.

Herbie Rides Again with Ken Berry and Helen Hayes.

HERBIE RIDES AGAIN (1974) BV. A Walt Disney Production. Produced by Bill Walsh. Directed by Robert Stevenson. Based on a story by Gordon Buford. Screenplay by Walsh. Music by George Bruns. Photography, Frank Phillips. Editor, Cotton Warburton. Art Directors, John B. Mansbridge and Walter Tyler. 2nd Unit Director, Arthur J. Vitarelli. Set Decorator, Hal Gausman. Assistant Directors, Ronald R. Grow and Dorothy Kieffer. Costumes, Chuck Keehne and Emily Sundby. Technicolor. Rated G. 88 minutes. Sequel to *The Love Bug* (1969) followed by *Herbie Goes to Monte Carlo* (1977)

Mrs. Steinmetz: Helen Hayes, *Willoughby Whitfield:* Ken Berry, *Nicole Harris:* Stefanie Powers, *Mr. Judson:* John McIntire, *Alonzo Hawk:* Keenan Wynn, *Judge:* Huntz Hall, *Chauffeur:* Ivor Barry, *Lawyers:* Dan Tobin, Raymond Bailey, Bob Carson, John Zaremba, *Taxi Driver:* Vito Scotti, *Doctor:* Liam Dunn, *Secretary:* Elaine Devry, *Loostgarten:* Chuck McCann, *Traffic Commissioner:* Richard X. Slattery, *Sir Lancelot:* Hank Jones, *Red Knight:* Rod McCary, *Bits:* Larry J. Blake, Don Pedro Colley, Iggie Wolfington, Hal Baylor, Herb Vigran, Candy Candido, Edward Ashley, Norman Grabowski, Gail Bonney, Burt Mustin, John Myhers, John Stephenson, Arthur Space, John Hubbard, Fritz Feld, Alvy Moore, Alan Carney, Maurice Marsac, Martin Braddock.

HERE COMES MR. JORDAN (1941) Col. Producer, Everett Riskin. Director, Alexander Hall. Based on a play by Harry Segall. Screenplay, Seton I. Miller, Sidney Buchman. Art Director, Lionel Banks. Music, M. W. Stoloff. Cameraman. Joseph Walker. Editor, Viola

Lawrence. Sequel was *Down to Earth* (1947). 93 minutes. Remade as *Heaven Can Wait* (Par., 1978)

Joe Pendleton: Robert Montgomery, *Bette Logan:* Evelyn Keyes, *Mr. Jordan:* Claude Rains, *Julia Farnsworth:* Rita Johnson, *Messenger 7013:* Edward Everett Horton, *Max Corkle:* James Gleason, *Tony Abbott:* John Emery, *Inspector Williams:* Donald MacBride, *Lefty:* Don Costello, *Sisk:* Halliwell Hobbes, *Bugs:* Benny Rubin, *Plainclothesman:* Ken Christy, *Doctor:* Joseph Crehan, *Handler:* Billy Newell, *Announcer:* Tom Hanlon, *Gilbert:* Joe Hickey, *Charlie:* Warren Ashe, *Johnny:* Billy Dawson, *Chips:* Bobby Larson, *Sparring Partner:* John Kerns, *Secretary:* Mary Currier, *Newsboy:* Chester Conklin, *Copilot:* Lloyd Bridges, *Elderly Man:* Edmund Elton.

Here Comes Mr. Jordan with Robert Montgomery and James Gleason.

Here Come the Waves with Bing Crosby, Betty Hutton (dual role) and Sonny Tufts.

HERE COME THE WAVES (1944) Par. Producer and Director, Mark Sandrich. Original Screenplay, Allan Scott, Ken Englund, Zion Myers. Musical Director, Robert Emmett Dolan. Art Directors, Hans Dreier, Roland Anderson. Process Photography, Farciot Edouart. Special Effects, Gordon Jennings, Paul Lerpae. Cameraman, Charles Lang. Editor, Ellsworth Hoagland. Songs by Johnny Mercer and Harold Arlen: "I Promise You," "There's a Fellow Waiting in Poughkeepsie," "My Mama Thinks I'm a Star," "Let's Take the Long Way Home," "Here Come the Waves" and "Accent-Chu-Ate the Positive." 99 minutes

Johnny Cabot: Bing Crosby, *Susie and Rosemary Allison:* Betty Hutton, *Windy:* Sonny Tufts, *Ruth:* Ann Doran, *Tex:* Gwen Crawford, *Dorothy:* Noel Neill, *Lieutenant Townsend:* Catherine Craig, *Isabel:* Marjorie Henshaw, *Bandleader:* Harry Barris, *Ensign Kirk:* Mae Clarke, *High-Ranking Officer:* Minor Watson, *Specialty Dancers:* Dorothy Jarnac and Joel Friend, *The Commodore:* Oscar O'Shea, *Miles &*

Kover Trio: Don Kramer, Eddie Kover, Ruth Miles, *Specialty Dancers:* Roberta Jonay, Guy Zanett, *First Fainting Girl:* Mona Freeman, *Second Fainting Girl:* Carlotta Jelm, *Waiter (Cabana Club):* Jack Norton, *Chief Petty Officer:* Jimmie Dundee, *Cabot Fan:* Lillian Bronson, *Girl:* Jean Willes, *Waiter:* Alex Havier, *Shore Patrolman:* James Flavin, *First Civilian:* Weldon Heyburn, *Second Civilian:* Edward Emerson, *Yellow Cab Driver:* Kit Guard, *First Pretty Girl:* Kay Linaker, *Second Pretty Girl:* Terry Adams, *Girl Window Washer:* Babe London, *Wave Control Tower Operator:* Greta Granstedt, *Girl:* Yvonne de Carlo, *Recruit:* George Turner, *C.P.O.:* William Haade, *Lieutenant Commander:* William Forrest, *Lieutenant Colonel:* Cyril Ring, *Captain Johnson:* Charles D. Brown.

Dan Roman: John Wayne, *May Holst:* Claire Trevor, *Lydia Rice:* Laraine Day, *Sullivan:* Robert Stack, *Sally McKee:* Jan Sterling, *Ed Joseph:* Phil Harris, *Gustave Pardee:* Robert Newton, *Ken Childs:* David Brian, *Flaherty:* Paul Kelly, *Humphrey Agnew:* Sidney Blackmer, *Spalding:* Doe Avedon, *Nell Buck:* Karen Sharpe, *Milo Buck:* John Smith, *Lillian Pardee:* Julie Bishop, *Gonzalez:* Gonzalez-Gonzalez, *Howard Rice:* John Howard, *Wilby:* Wally Brown, *Hobie Wheeler:* William Campbell, *Mrs. Joseph:* Ann Doran, *Jose Locota:* John Qualen, *Frank Briscoe:* Paul Fix, *Ben Sneed:* George Chandler, *Dorothy Chen:* Joy Kim, *Toby Field:* Michael Wellman, *Alsop:* Douglas Fowley, *Garfield:* Regis Toomey, *Ensign Keim:* Carl Switzer, *Lieutenant Mowbray:* Robert Keys, *Roy:* William DeWolf Hopper, *Dispatcher:* William Schallert.

Hers to Hold with Deanna Durbin and Joseph Cotten.

The High and the Mighty with John Qualen, Sidney Blackmer, Robert Newton, John Wayne, John Howard, Julie Bishop, Laraine Day and Jan Sterling.

HERS TO HOLD (1943) Univ. Produced by Felix Jackson. Associate Producer, Frank Shaw. Directed by Frank Ryan. Based on a story by John D. Klorer. Screenplay, Lewis R. Foster. Music Director, Charles Previn. Art Director, John B. Goodman. Photography, Woody Bredell. Editor, Ted Kent. Songs: "Begin the Beguine" by Cole Porter; "Say A Prayer for the Boys Over There" by Jimmy McHugh and Herb Magidson; "Seguidilla" aria from Georges Bizet's *Carmen*, "Kashmiri Song." Filmed at Vega Aircraft in Burbank and at Lockheed Air Terminal. Sequel to *Three Smart Girls*, 1936, *Three Smart Girls Grow Up*, 1939, incorporating scenes from them and from *Mad About Music*, 1938. 94 minutes

Penny Craig: Deanna Durbin, *Bill Morley:* Joseph Cotten, *Judson Craig:* Charles Winninger, *Dorothy Craig:* Nella Walker, *Rosey Blake:* Gus Schilling, *Binns:* Ludwig Stossel, *Doctor Bacon:* Irving Bacon, *Nurse Willing:* Nydia Westman, *Smiley, Foreman:* Murray Alper, *Doctor Crane:* Samuel S. Hinds, *Arlene:* Iris Adrian, *Hannah Gordon:* Fay Helm, *Peter Cartwright:* Douglas Wood, *Mrs. Cartwright:* Minna Phillips, *Flo Simpson:* Evelyn Ankers, *Reporters:* Eddie Acuff, Eddie Dunn, *Doctor:* Harry Holman, *Guests:* Henry Roquemore, Brooks Benedict, *Al, a Guest:* William B. Davidson, *Aircraft Worker at Inn:* Billy Nelson, *Joe, Coast Guardsman:* Billy Wayne, *Coast Guardsman with Tommy Gun:* George O'Hanlon, *Orchestra Leader:* Leon Belasco, *Miss Crawford:* Ruth Lee, *Babe:* Jody Gilbert, *Guest Eating Sandwich:* Eddie Borden, *Flier's Father:* Ernie S. Adams, *Enlisted Man:* George Chandler, *Hazel:* Alice Talton, *Ella Mae:* Marie Harmon, *Personnel Woman:* Virginia Sale, *Bomber Captain:* James Bush, *Jeanne:* Evelyn Wahle, *William Morley:* Spec O'Donnell, *Joey:* Teddy Infuhr, *Girl:* Jennifer Holt.

THE HIGH AND THE MIGHTY (1954) WB. A Wayne-Fellows Production. Director, William A. Wellman. Screenplay by Ernest K. Gann from his novel. Music by Dimitri Tiomkin. Assistant Director, Andrew McLaglen. Art Director, Al Ybarra. Cinematographer, Archie Stout. Editor, Ralph Dawson. CinemaScope, Stereophonic Sound and Warner Color. 147 minutes

High Anxiety with Madeline Kahn, Howard Morris (rear), Ron Carey and Mel Brooks.

HIGH ANXIETY (1977) 20th. Produced and Directed by Mel Brooks. Written by Brooks, Ron Clark, Rudy DeLuca and Barry Levinson. Dedicated to the master of suspense, Alfred Hitchcock. Photography, Paul Lohmann. Production Designer, Peter Wooley. Editor, John C. Howard, Special Visual Effects, Albert J. Whitlock. Costumes designed by Patricia Norris. Assistant Director, Jonathan Sanger. 2nd Assistant Directors, Mark Johnson and David Sosna. Assistant to Producer, Stuart Cornfeld. Production Consultant, Ron Clark. Continuity sequences by Harold Michelson. Set Decorators, Richard Kent and Anna MacCauley. Costumers, Jered Green, Nancy Martinelli and Wally Harton. Make-up, Tom Tuttle and Terry Miles. Hairdressers, Sugar Blymyer and Linda Trainoff. Production Mixer, Gene Cantamessa. Special Effects, Jack Monroe. Music composed and conducted by John Morris. Song, "High Anxiety," written and sung by Brooks. Panavision and DeLuxe Color. Rated PG. 94 minutes

Dr. Richard Harpo Thorndyke/Assassin Double: Mel Brooks, *Victoria Brisbane:* Madeline Kahn, *Nurse Diesel:* Cloris Leachman, *Dr. Charles Montague:* Harvey Korman, *Brophy:* Ron Carey, *Dr. Vicktor Lillolman:* Howard Morris, *Dr. Wentworth:* Dick Van Patten, *Desk Clerk:* Jack Riley, *Cocker Spaniel:* Charlie Callas, *Zachary Cartwright:* Ron Clark, *Killer:* Rudy DeLuca, *Bellboy:* Barry Levinson, *Norton:* Lee Delano, *Dr. Baxter:* Richard Stahl, *Dr. Eckhardt:* Darrell Zwerling, *Piano Player:* Murphy Dunne, *Man Who Is Shot:* Al Hopson, *Flasher:* Bob Ridgely, *Arthur Brisbane:* Albert J. Whitlock, *Screaming Woman at Airport:* Pearl Shear, *Dr. Colburn:* Arnold Soboloff, *Doctor at Convention:* Eddie Ryder, *Airport Attendant:* Sandy Helberg, *Man:* Frederic Franklyn, *Stewardess:* Deborah Dawes, *Dr. Wilson:* Bernie Kuby, *Customer:* Billy Sands, *Psychiatrist with Children:* Ira Miller, *Waiter:* Jimmy Martinez, *Policemen at Airport:* Robert Manuel, Hunter Von Leer, *Maid:* Beatrice Colen, *Orderly:* John Dennis, *Cocktail Waitress:* Robin Menken, *Bartender:* Frank Campanella, *New Groom:* Henry Kaiser, *Man in Phone Booth:* Bullets Durgom, *Attendant:* Joe Bellan, *Bar Patron:* Mitchell Bock, *Patient:* Jay Burton, *2nd Orderly:* Bryan Englund, *Screaming Woman:* Anne Macey, *Psychiatrist:* Alan U. Schwartz.

High Noon with Lon Chaney, Jr., Thomas Mitchell, Henry (Harry) Morgan, Eve McVeagh, Otto Kruger, Grace Kelly and Gary Cooper.

HIGH NOON (1952) UA. Producer, Stanley Kramer. Director, Fred Zinnemann. Music by Dimitri Tiomkin. Screenplay, Carl Foreman. Based on story "The Tin Star" by John W. Cunningham. Title Song "High Noon (Do Not Forsake Me, Oh My Darlin)" by Johnny Mercer and Dimitri Tiomkin, sung by Tex Ritter. 85 minutes

Will Kane: Gary Cooper, *Jonas Henderson:* Thomas Mitchell, *Harvey Pell:* Lloyd Bridges, *Helen Ramirez:* Katy Jurado, *Amy Kane:* Grace Kelly, *Percy Mettrick:* Otto Kruger, *Martin Howe:* Lon Chaney, Jr., *William Fuller:* Henry Morgan, *Frank Fuller:* Ian MacDonald, *Mildred Fuller:* Eve McVeagh, *Cooper:* Harry Shannon, *Jack Colby:* Lee Van Cleef, *James Pierce:* Bob Wilke, *Ben Miller:* Sheb Woolley, *Sam:* Tom London.

HIGH SIERRA (1941) WB. Producers, Jack L. Warner, Hal B. Wallis. Associate Producer, Mark Hellinger. Director, Raoul Walsh. Screenplay, John Huston, W. R. Burnett. Cameraman, Tony Gaudio. Editor, Jack Killifer. From the novel by W. R. Burnett. Remade by Warner Brothers as *Colorado Territory*, 1949; *I Died a Thousand Times*, 1955. 100 minutes

Roy Earle: Humphrey Bogart, *Marie:* Ida Lupino, *Babe:* Alan Curtis, *Red:* Arthur Kennedy, *Velma:* Joan Leslie, *"Doc" Banton:* Henry Hull, *Jake Kranmer:* Barton MacLane, *Pa:* Henry Travers, *Ma:* Elisabeth Risdon, *Louis Mendoza:* Cornel Wilde, *Mrs. Baughman:* Minna Gombell, *Mr. Baugham:* Paul Harvey, *Big Mac:* Donald MacBride, *Healy:* Jerome Cowan, *Lou Preiser:* John Eldredge, *Blonde:* Isabel Jewell, *Algernon:* Willie Best, *Auto Court Owner:* Arthur Aylesworth, *Art:* Robert Strange, *Sheriff:* Wade Boteler, *Radio Commen-*

tater: Sam Hayes, *Gangster:* George Lloyd, *Farmer:* Erville Alderson, *Ed:* Spencer Charters, *Fisherman:* Carl Harbaugh, *Shaw:* Cliff Saum, *Pfiffer:* George Meeker, *Policeman:* Eddy Chandler, *Woman:* Charlette Wynters, *Man:* Louis Jean Heydt, *Watchman:* William Gould, *Blonde:* Maris Wrixon, *Brunette:* Lucia Carroll, *Margie:* Dorothy Appleby, *Joe:* Garry Owen, *Bus Driver:* Eddie Acuff, *Druggist:* Harry Hayden.

High Sierra with Humphrey Bogart and Ida Lupino.

High Society with Frank Sinatra and Grace Kelly.

HIGH SOCIETY (1956) MGM. Producer, Sol C. Siegel. Director, Charles Walters. VistaVision, Technicolor. Based on the play *The Philadelphia Story* by Philip Barry. Screenplay, John Patrick. Art Directors, Cedric Gibbons, Hans Peters. Music supervised and adapted by Johnny Green, Saul Chaplin. Music, Lyrics, Cole Porter. Orchestration, Conrad Salinger, Nelson Riddle. Cinematographer, Paul A. Vogel. Editor, Ralph E. Winters. Remake of *The Philadelphia Story* (MGM, 1940). Locations filmed in Newport, Rhode Island. Last film of Louis Calhern, whe died at 61 on May 12, 1956. Songs by Cole Porter: "True Love," "High Society," "Well, Did You Evah?," "You're Sensational," "Who Wants to Be a Millionaire," "Little One," "Now You Has Jazz," "Mind If I Make Love to You," "I Love You, Samantha." 107 minutes

C. K. Dexter-Haven: Bing Crosby, *Tracy Lord:* Grace Kelly, *Mike Connor:* Frank Sinatra, *Liz Imbrie:* Celeste Holm, *George Kittredge:* John Lund, *Uncle Willie:* Louis Calhern, *Seth Lord:* Sidney Blackmer, *Himself:* Louis Armstrong, *Mrs. Seth Lord:* Margalo Gillmore, *Caro-*

line *Lord:* Lydia Reed, *Dexter-Haven's Butler:* Gordon Richards, *Lord's Butler:* Richard Garrick, *Mac:* Richard Keene, *Matrons:* Ruth Lee, Helen Spring, *Editor:* Paul Keast, *Uncle Willie's Butler:* Reginald Simpson, *Parson:* Hugh Boswell.

Hitler's Children with Bonita Granville, Kent Smith and Tim Holt.

HITLER'S CHILDREN (1943) RKO. Produced by Edward A. Golden. Directed by Edward Dmytryk. Based on the book *Education For Death* by Gregor Ziemer. Screenplay, Emmet Lavery. Music, Roy Webb. Music Director, C. Bakaleinikoff. Editor, Joseph Noriega. Film debut of Orley Lindgren, 3. 83 minutes

Karl Bruner: Tim Holt, *Anna Muller:* Bonita Granville, *Professor Nichols (Narrator):* Kent Smith, *Colonel Henkel:* Otto Kruger, *The Bishop:* H. B. Warner, *Franz Erhart:* Lloyd Corrigan, *Doctor Schmidt:* Erford Gage, *Doctor Graf:* Hans Conreid, *Brenda:* Nancy Gates, *Nazi Major:* Gavin Muir, *Murph:* Bill Burrud, *Irwin:* Jimmy Zaner, *Gestapo Man:* Richard Martin, *Arresting Sergeant:* Goetz Van Eyck (Peter Van Eyck), *Gestapo Officer:* John Merton, *Plane Dispatcher:* Max Lucke, *N.S.V. Worker:* Anna Loos, *Mother:* Bessie Wade, *Boys:* Orley Lindgren, Billy Brow, Chris Wren, *Mr. Muller:* Egon Brecher, *Mrs. Muller:* Elsa Janssen, *American Vice Consul:* William Forrest, *Young Matrons:* Ariel Heath and Rita Corday, *Bit:* Mary Stuart, *Lieutenant S.A.:* Roland Varno, *Whipping Sergeant:* Crane Whitley, *Chief Trial Judge:* Edward Van Sloan, *Radio Announcer:* Douglas Evans, *Magda:* Carla Boehm, *Storm Trooper:* Bruce Cameron, *First Matron:* Betty Roadman, *Chief Matron:* Kathleen Wilson, *Bit (Labor Camp):* Joey Ray, *Bit Boy:* Harry McKim, *Gestapo Officer:* John Stockton.

Hold Back the Dawn with Charles Boyer and Olivia de Havilland.

HOLD BACK THE DAWN (1941) Par. Producer, Arthur Hornblow. Director, Mitchell Leisen. Author, Ketti Frings. Screenplay, Charles

Brackett, Billy Wilder. Art Directors, Hans Dreier, Robert Usher. Cameraman, Leo Tover. Editor, Doane Harrison. Song, "My Boy, My Boy" by Frank Loesser, Jimmy Berg, Fred Spielman and Fred Jacobson. 155 minutes

Georges Iscoveseu: Charles Boyer, *Emmy Brown:* Olivia de Havilland, *Anita Dixon:* Paulette Goddard, *Van Den Luecken:* Victor Francen, *Inspector Hammock:* Walter Abel, *Bonbois:* Curt Bois, *Berta Kurz:* Rosemary De Camp, *Josef Kurz:* Eric Feldary, *Flores:* Nestor Paiva, *Lupita:* Eva Puig, *Christine:* Micheline Cheirel, *Anni:* Madeleine LeBeau, *Tony:* Billy Lee, *Mechanic:* Mikhail Rasumny, *Mr. Saxon:* Mitchell Leisen, *Actor:* Brian Donlevy, *Actor:* Richard Webb, *Actress:* Veronica Lake, *Mac:* John Hamilton, *Mr. Spitzer:* Leon Belasco, *Vivienne Worthington:* June Wilkins, *Sam:* Sonny Boy Williams, *American Consul:* Edward Fielding, *Joe:* Don Douglas, *Young Woman at Climax Bar:* Gertrude Astor, *Mexican Doctor:* Francisco Maran, *Mexican Judge:* Carlos Villarias, *Hollander Planter (Mr. Elvestad):* Arthur Loft, *Mr. MacAdams:* Charles Arnt, *American Immigration Official:* Harry T. Shannon, *Assistant Director:* William Faralla, *Bride:* Ella Neal, *Mexican Priest:* Antonio Filauri, *Old Peon:* Placido Sigueiros, *Mexican Bridegroom:* Ray Mala, *Old Peon's Wife:* Soledad Jimenez.

Hold That Ghost with Joan Davis, Evelyn Ankers, Bud Abbott, Richard Carlson and Lou Costello.

HOLD THAT GHOST (1941) Univ. Associate Producers, Burt Kelly, Glenn Tryon. Director, Arthur Lubin. Authors, Robert Lees, Fred Rinaldo. Screenplay, Robert Lees, Fred Rinaldo, John Grant. Art Director, Jack Otterson. Musical Director, H. J. Salter. Musical Numbers, Nick Castle. Cameramen, Elwood Bredell, Joseph Valentine. Editor, Philip Cahn. Songs: "Sleepy Serenade" by Mort Greene and Lou Singer; "Aurora" by Harold Adamson, Maria Logo and Roberto Roberti, "When My Baby Smiles at Me," "Me and My Shadow." 86 minutes

Chuck Murray: Bud Abbott, *Ferdinand Jones:* Lou Costello, *Doctor Jackson:* Richard Carlson, *Norma Lind:* Evelyn Ankers, *Camille Brewster:* Joan Davis, *Charlie Smith:* Marc Lawrence, *Harry Hoskins:* Milton Parsons, *Snake-Eyes:* Frank Penny, *Irondome:* Edgar Dearing, *High Collar:* Edward Pawley, *Glum:* Nestor Paiva, *Gregory:* Mischa Auer, *Soda Jerk:* Shemp Howard, *Lawyer Bannister:* Russell Hicks, *Moose Matson:* William Davidson, *Jenkins:* Harry Hayden; The Andrews Sisters, Ted Lewis and Band; *Alderman:* Thurston Hall, *Alderman's Girl:* Janet Shaw, *Gunman:* Frank Richards, *Customer:* William Ruhl.

A HOLE IN THE HEAD (1959) UA. Producer-Director, Frank Capra. Panavision, De Luxe Color. Screenplay by Arnold Shulman. Based on the TV play *The Heart's a Lonely Hotel*, and the 1957 stage play by Arnold Shulman. Filmed in Cypress Gardens, Florida. Film debut of Eddie Hodges, 11. Main titles on a banner carried by Goodyear blimp.

Music by Nelson Riddle. Costumes by Edith Head. Assistant Directors, Arthur S. Black, Jr. and Jack R. Berne. Art Director, Eddie Imazu. Cinematographer, William H. Daniels. Editor, William Hornbeck. A SinCap Production. Songs by Sammy Cahn and Jimmy Van Heusen: "High Hopes" and "All My Tomorrows." 120 minutes

Tony Manetta (Narrator): Frank Sinatra, *Mario Manetta:* Edward G. Robinson, *Eloise Rogers:* Eleanor Parker, *Ally Manetta:* Eddie Hodges, *Shirl:* Carolyn Jones, *Sophie Manetta:* Thelma Ritter, *Jerry Marks:* Keenan Wynn, *Dorine:* Joi Lansing, *Mendy:* George DeWitt, *Julius Manetta:* Jimmy Komack, *Fred:* Dub Taylor, *Miss Wexler:* Connie Sawyer, *Abe Diamond:* Benny Rubin, *Sally:* Ruby Dandridge, *Hood No. 1:* B. S. Pully, *Alice:* Joyce Nizzari, *Master of Ceremonies:* Pupi Campo, *Cabby:* Robert B. Williams, *Sheriff:* Emory Parnell, *Andy:* Bill Walker.

A Hole in the Head with Carolyn Jones and Frank Sinatra.

Holiday with Ann Harding and Mary Astor.

HOLIDAY (1930) RKO-Pathé. Produced by E. B. Derr. Directed by Edward H. Griffith. Based on the play by Philip Barry. Scenario, Horace Jackson. Art Director, Carroll Clark. Assistant Director, Paul Jones. Orchestra conducted by Josiah Zuro. Costumes, Gwen Wakeling. Photography, Norbert Brodine. Editor, Daniel Mandell. Sound, D. A. Cutler and Harold Stine. Remade by Columbia in 1938. The William Holden is not the same Holden of today. 89 minutes

Linda Seton: Ann Harding, *Julia Seton:* Mary Astor, *Nick Potter:*

Edward Everett Horton, *John Case:* Robert Ames, *Susan Potter:* Hedda Hopper, *Ned Seton:* Monroe Owsley, *Edward Seton:* William Holden, *Seton Cram:* Hallam Cooley, *Mary Jessup:* Mabel Forrest, *Laura:* Elizabeth Forrester, *Pete Hedges:* Creighton Hale, *Mrs. Pritchard Ames:* Mary Elizabeth Forbes.

Holiday with Katharine Hepburn, Cary Grant and Henry Kolker.

HOLIDAY (1938) Col. Associate Producer, Everett Riskin. Director, George Cukor. From the play by Philip Barry. Screenplay, Donald Ogden Stewart, Sidney Buchman. Art Directors, Stephen Goosson, Lionel Banks. Musical Director, Morris Stoloff. Cameraman, Franz Planer. Editors, Otto Meyer, Al Clark. Remake of the 1930 Pathé film. 93 minutes

Linda Seton: Katharine Hepburn, *Johnny Case:* Cary Grant, *Julia Seton:* Doris Nolan, *Ned Seton:* Lew Ayres, *Nick Potter:* Edward Everett Horton, *Edward Seton:* Henry Kolker, *Laura Cram:* Binnie Barnes, *Susan Potter:* Jean Dixon, *Seton Cram:* Henry Daniell, *Banker:* Charles Trowbridge, *Henry:* George Pauncefort, *Thayer:* Charles Richman, *Jennings:* Mitchell Harris, *Edgar:* Neil Fitzgerald, *Grandmother:* Marion Ballou, *Man in Church:* Howard Hickman, *Woman in Church:* Hilda Plowright, *Cook:* Mabel Colcord, *Countess:* Bess Flowers *Scotchmen:* Harry Allen, Edward Cooper, *Farmer's Wife:* Margaret McWade, *Farmer:* Frank Shannon, *Farm Girl:* Aileen Carlyle, *Taxi Driver:* Matt McHugh, *Steward:* Maurice Brierre, *Mrs. Jennings:* Esther Peck, *Mrs. Thayer:* Lillian West, *Grandfather:* Luke Cosgrave.

Holiday Inn With Bing Crosby and Marjorie Reynolds.

HOLIDAY INN (1942) Par. Producer and Director, Mark Sandrich. Screenplay, Claude Binyon. Musical Director, Robert Emmett Dolan.

Adapted by Elmer Rice from an original idea by Irving Berlin. Dance Director, Danny Dare. Art Directors, Hans Dreier, Roland Anderson. Cameraman, David Abel. Editor, Ellsworth Hoagland. Songs by Irving Berlin: "Be Careful It's My Heart," "White Christmas," "Abraham," "You're Easy to Dance With," "Let's Start the New Year Right," "Plenty to Be Thankful For," "I'll Capture Your Heart Singing" and "Happy Holiday." 101 minutes

Jim Hardy: Bing Crosby, *Ted Hanover:* Fred Astaire, *Linda Mason:* Marjorie Reynolds, *Lila Dixon:* Virginia Dale, *Danny Reed:* Walter Abel, *Mamie:* Louise Beavers, *Gus:* Irving Bacon, *Francois:* Marek Windheim, *Dunbar:* James Bell, *Parker:* John Gallaudet, *Vanderbilt:* Shelby Bacon, *Daphne:* Joan Arnold, *Specialty Dancer:* June Ealey, *Specialty Dancer:* David Tihmar, *Man at Holiday Inn:* Edward Emerson, *Proprietor in Flower Shop:* Leon Belasco, *Orchestra Leader:* Harry Barris, *Assistant Headwaiter:* Jacques Vanaire, *Orchestra Leader:* Ronnie Rondell, *Assistant Director:* Keith Richards, *Assistant Director:* Reed Porter, *Doorman:* Oscar G. Hendrian, *Doorman:* Bob Homans, *Hatcheck Girl:* Katharine Booth, *Cigarette Girl:* Judith Gibson, *Dancing Girl:* Lynda Grey, *Woman:* Kitty Kelly, *Man:* Edward Arnold, Jr., *Man:* Mel Ruick, *Santa Claus:* Bud Jamison.

Hollywood Canteen with Joan Crawford, Dane Clark and Robert Hutton.

HOLLYWOOD CANTEEN (1944) WB. Producer, Alex Gottlieb. Director, Delmer Daves. Original Screenplay, Delmer Daves. Musical Numbers, LeRoy Prinz. Art Director, Leo Kuter. Musical Director, Leo F. Forbstein. Music Adaptation, Ray Heindorf. Cameraman, Bert Glennon. Editor, Christian Nyby. Musical numbers: "Don't Fence Me In" by Cole Porter; "You Can Always Tell a Yank" by E. Y. Harburg and Burton Lane; "What Are You Doin' the Rest of Your Life?" by Ted Koehler and Burton Lane; "We're Having a Baby (My Baby and Me)" by Harold Adamson and Vernon Duke; "Sweet Dreams Sweetheart" by Ted Koehler and M. K. Jerome; "Voodoo Moon" by Marian Sunshine, Julio Blanco and Obdulio Morales; "The General Jumped at Dawn" by Larry Neal and Jimmy Mundy; "Tumblin' Tumbleweeds" by Bob Nolan; "Ballet In Jive" by Ray Heindorf; "Hollywood Canteen" by Ted Koehler, Ray Heindorf and M. K. Jerome; "Gettin' Corns for My Country" by Jean Barry, Leah Worth, Dick Charles; "Once to Every Heart"; violin numbers, "The Bee" and "Slavonic Dance." Sets, Casey Roberts. Assistant Director, Art Lueker. Make-up, Perc Westmore. Wardrobe, Milo Anderson. Unit Manager, Chuck Hansen. Sound, Oliver S. Garretson and Charles David Forrest. 124 minutes

Joan Leslie: Joan Leslie, *Slim:* Robert Hutton, *Sergeant:* Dane Clark, *Angela:* Janis Paige, *Themselves:* Andrews Sisters, Jack Benny, Joe E. Brown, Eddie Cantor, Kitty Carlisle, Jack Carson, Joan Crawford, Helmut Dantine, Bette Davis, Faye Emerson, Victor Francen, John

Garfield, Sydney Greenstreet, Alan Hale, Paul Henreid, Andrea King, Peter Lorre, Ida Lupino, Irene Manning, Nora Martin, Joan McCracken, Dolores Moran, Dennis Morgan, Eleanor Parker, William Prince, Joyce Reynolds, John Ridgely, Roy Rogers and Trigger, S. Z. Sakall, Alexis Smith, Zachary Scott, Barbara Stanwyck, Craig Stevens, Joseph Szigeti, Donald Woods, Jane Wyman, Jimmy Dorsey and his Band, Carmen Cavallaro and his Orchestra, Golden Gate Quartet, Rosario and Antonio, Sons of the Pioneers, Virginia Patton, Lynne Baggett, Betty Alexander, Julie Bishop, Robert Shayne, Johnny Mitchell, John Sheridan, Colleen Townsend, Angela Green, Paul Brooke, Marianne O'Brien, Dorothy Malone, Bill Kennedy, Mary Gordon, Chef Joseph Milani, *Mr. Brodel:* Jonathan Hale, *Mrs. Brodel:* Barbara Brown, *Betty Brodel:* Betty Brodel, *Soldiers on Deck:* Steve Richards (Mark Stevens), Dick Erdman, *Marine Sergeant:* James Flavin, *Dance Director:* Eddie Marr, *Director:* Theodore von Eltz, *Captain:* Ray Teal, *Orchestra Leader:* Rudolph Friml, Jr., *Dance Specialty:* Betty Bryson, Willard Van Simons, William Alcorn, Jack Mattis, Jack Coffey, *Tough Marine:* George Turner.

Hollywood Cavalcade with Don Ameche and Donald Meek.

HOLLYWOOD CAVALCADE (1939) 20th. Executive Producer, Darryl F. Zanuck. Directed by Irving Cummings. Associate Producer, Harry Joe Brown. Color by Technicolor. Authors, Hilary Lynn, Brown Holmes. Screenplay, Ernest Pascal. Art Directors, Richard Day, Wiard B. Ihnen. Musical Director, Louis Silvers. Cameramen, Allen M. Davey, Ernest Palmer. Editor, Walter Thompson. 96 minutes

Molly Adair: Alice Faye, *Michael Linnett Connors:* Don Ameche, *Dave Spingold:* J. Edward Bromberg, *Nicky Hayden:* Alan Curtis, *Pete Tinney:* Stuart Erwin, *Chief of Police:* Jed Prouty, *Buster Keaton:* Himself, *Lyle P. Stout:* Donald Meek, *Claude (Actor):* George Givot, *Keystone Cops:* Eddie Collins, Hank Mann, Heinie Conklin, James Finlayson, *Assistant Director, Chick:* Chick Chandler, *Henry Potter:* Robert Lowery, *Roberts:* Russell Hicks, *Agent:* Ben Welden, *Willie:* Willie Fung, *Lawyer:* Paul Stanton, *Mrs. Gaynes:* Mary Forbes, *Attorney, Bill:* Joseph Crehan, *Clerk:* Irving Bacon, *Bartender:* Ben Turpin, *Sheriff:* Chester Conklin, *Telephone Operator:* Marjorie Beebe, *Thomas:* Frederick Burton, *Themselves:* Lee Duncan, Mack Sennett, Al Jolson, *Rin-Tin-Tin:* Rin-Tin-Tin, Jr., *Porter:* Snowflake, *Prop Boy:* Harold Goodwin, *Slim, Counterman:* Victor Potel, *Actor:* Edward Earle, *Court Officer:* John Ince, *Well-Wisher:* Franklyn Farnum, *Motorcycle Cop:* J. Anthony Hughes, *Actress in The Man Who Came Back:* Lynn Bari, *Roscoe (Fatty Arbuckle):* Marshall Ruth.

THE HOLLYWOOD REVUE OF 1929 MGM. Produced by Harry Rapf. Directed by Charles F. Reisner. Dialogue, Al Boasberg and Robert E. Hopkins. Dances and Ensembles, Sammy Lee, assisted by George Cunningham. Orchestral Arrangements, Arthur Lange. Skit, Joe Farnham. Photography, John Arnold, Irving G. Ries, and Maximilian Fabian. Settings, Cedric Gibbons and Richard Day. Costumes, David Cox. Editor, William Gray. Sound, Douglas Shearer. With

Technicolor sequences. Songs: "Singin' In the Rain," "You Were Meant for Me," and "Tommy Atkins on Parade" by Arthur Freed and Nacio Herb Brown; "Low-Down Rhythm" by Raymond Klages and Jesse Greer; "For I'm the Queen" by Andy Rice and Martin Broones; "Gotta Feelin' For You," by Jo Trent and Louis Alter; "Bones and Tambourines," "Strike Up the Band," "Tableaux of Jewels" by Fred Fisher; "Lon Chaney Will Get You If You Don't Watch Out," "Strolling Through the Park One Day," "Your Mother and Mine," "Orange Blossom Time," "Minstrel Days," "Nobody But You," "I Never Knew I Could Do a Thing Like That" by Joe Goodwin and Gus Edwards. 130 minutes

Specialties: Jack Benny (M.C.), Buster Keaton, Joan Crawford, John Gilbert, Norma Shearer, Laurel and Hardy, Marion Davies, Marie Dressler, William Haines, Lionel Barrymore, Anita Page, Conrad Nagel (M.C.), Polly Moran, Bessie Love, Charles King, Cliff Edwards, Gus Edwards, Karl Dane, George K. Arthur, Nils Asther, The Brox Sisters, Albertina Rasch, Gwen Lee, Natacha Natova and Company, The Rounders, The Biltmore Quartet, Ernest Belcher's Dancing Tots, *Chorus Girl:* Ann Dvorak.

Hollywood Revue of 1929 with The Brox Sisters.

Home From the Hill with George Peppard and Luana Patten.

HOME FROM THE HILL (1960) MGM. Produced by Edmund Grainger. Directed by Vincente Minnelli. CinemaScope and Metro-Color. Based on the novel by William Humphrey. Screenplay, Harriet Frank Jr. and Irving Ravetch. Music, Bronislau Kaper. Costumes, Walter Plunkett. Art Directors, George W. Davis and Preston Ames. Music conducted by Charles Wolcott. Assistant Director, William McGarry. Cinematography, Milton Krasner. Editor, Harold F. Kress. A Sol C. Siegel Production. 150 minutes

Capt. Wade Hunnicutt: Robert Mitchum, *Hannah Hunnicutt:* Eleanor Parker, *Rafe Copley:* George Peppard, *Theron Hunnicutt:*

George Hamilton, *Albert Halstead:* Everett Sloane, *Libby Halstead:* Luana Patten, *Sarah Halstead:* Anne Seymour, *Opal Bixby:* Constance Ford, *Chauncey:* Ken Renard, *Dr. Reuben Carson:* Ray Teal, *Melba:* Hilda Haynes, *Dick Gibbons:* Charlie Briggs, *Hugh Macauley:* Guinn "Big Boy" Williams, *Marshall Bradley:* Denver Pyle, *Peyton Stiles:* Dan Sheridan, *Ed Dinwoodie:* Orville Sherman, *Bob Skaggs:* Dub Taylor, *Ramsey:* Stuart Randall, *John Ellis:* Tom Gilson, *Minister:* Rev. Duncan Gray, Jr., *Foreman:* Joe Ed Russell, *Gas Station Attendant:* Burt Mustin.

Home of the Brave with Lloyd Bridges and Steve Brodie.

HOME OF THE BRAVE (1949) UA. Produced by Stanley Kramer. Directed by Mark Robson. A Screen Plays Corporation Production. Screenplay, Carl Foreman. Based on the play by Arthur Laurents. Music, Dimitri Tiomkin. Art Director, Rudolph Sternad. Photography, Robert De Grasse. Editor, Harry Gerstad. Film debut of James Edwards. 85 minutes

Major Robinson: Douglas Dick, *T. J.:* Steve Brodie, *The Doctor:* Jeff Corey, *Finch:* Lloyd Bridges, *Mingo:* Frank Lovejoy, *Moss:* James Edwards, *Colonel:* Cliff Clark.

Hondo with John Wayne and Geraldine Page.

HONDO (1953) WB. Produced by Robert Fellows. Directed by John Farrow. In 3-Dimension and WarnerColor. A Wayne-Fellows Production. From the *Collier's* magazine story by Louis L'Amour. Screenplay, James Edward Grant. Music, Emil Newman and Hugo Friedhofer. Art Director, Al Ybarra. Cinematographers, Robert Burks, Archie Stout. Filmed in Camargo, Mexico. 93 minutes

Hondo: John Wayne, *Angie Lowe:* Geraldine Page, *Buffalo:* Ward Bond, *Vittorio:* Michael Pate, *Lennie:* James Arness, *Silva:* Rodolfo Acosta, *Ed Lowe:* Leo Gordon, *Lieutenant McKay:* Tom Irish, *Johnny:* Lee Aaker, *Major Sherry:* Paul Fix, *Pete:* Rayford Barnes.

Honky Tonk with Clark Gable, Chill Wills, Lana Turner and Frank Morgan.

HONKY TONK (1941) MGM. Producer, Pandro S. Berman. Director, Jack Conway. Screenplay, Marguerite Roberts, John Sanford. Music Score, Franz Waxman. Art Director, Cedric Gibbons. Cameraman, Harold Rosson. Editor, Blanche Sewell. 105 minutes

Candy Johnson: Clark Gable, *Elizabeth Cotton:* Lana Turner, *Judge Cotton:* Frank Morgan, *"Gold Dust" Nelson:* Claire Trevor, *Reverend Mrs. Varner:* Marjorie Main, *Brazos Hearn:* Albert Dekker, *The Sniper:* Chill Wills, *Daniel Wells:* Henry O'Neill, *Kendall:* John Maxwell, *Adams:* Morgan Wallace, *Governor Wilson:* Douglas Wood, *Mrs. Wilson:* Betty Blythe, *Senator Ford:* Hooper Atchley, *Harry Gates:* Harry Worth, *Eleanore:* Veda Ann Borg, *Pearl:* Dorothy Granger, *Louise:* Sheila Darcy, *Man With Tar:* Cy Kendall, *Man with Rail:* Erville Alderson, *Man with Feathers:* John Farrell, *Man with Gun:* Don Barclay, *Poker Player:* Ray Teal, *Prostitute:* Esther Muir, *Dealer:* Ralph Bushman (Francis X. Bushman Jr.), *Dealer:* Art Miles, *Tug:* Demetrius Alexis, *Nurse:* Anne O'Neal, *Dr. Otis:* Russell Hicks, *Butcher:* Henry Roquemore, *Blackie:* Lew Harvey, *Brazos' Henchman:* John (Jack) Carr.

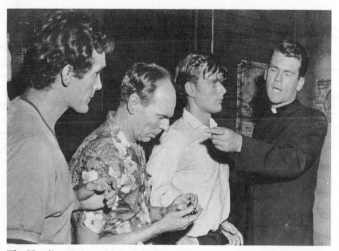

The Hoodlum Priest with Keir Dullea (third from left) and Don Murray.

THE HOODLUM PRIEST (1961) UA. Producers, Don Murray and Walter Wood. Director, Irvin Kershner. Screenplay, Don Deer and Joseph Landon. Music, Richard Markowitz. Assistant Directors, George Batcheller and Eddie Bernoudy. Art director, Jack Poplin. Cinematographer, Haskell Wexler. Editor, Maurice Wright. Filmed in St. Louis, Missouri. 101 minutes

Rev. Charles Dismas Clark: Don Murray, *Louis Rosen:* Larry Gates, *Ellen Henley:* Cindi Wood, *Billy Lee Jackson:* Keir Dullea, *George Hale:* Logan Ramsey, *Pio Gentile:* Don Joslyn, *Mario Mazziotti:* Sam Capuano, *Asst. District Attorney:* Vince O'Brien, *Judge Garrity:* Al Mack, *Angelo Mazziotti:* Lou Martini, *Father Dunne:* Norman KacKaye, *Hector Sterne:* Joseph Cusanelli, *Weasel:* Bill Atwood, *Detective Shattuck:* Roger Ray, *Genny:* Kelley Stephens, *Governor:* Ralph Petersen, *Prisoner:* Jack Eigen, *Father David Michaels:* Walter L. Wiedmer, *Warden:* Warren Parker, *Prison Chaplain:* Joseph Hamilton.

Hooper with Sally Field, Burt Reynolds, Jan-Michael Vincent and Robert Klein.

HOOPER (1978) WB. A Burt Reynolds-Lawrence Gordon Production. Produced by Hank Moonjean. Executive Producer, Lawrence Gordon. Directed by Hal Needham. Story, Walt Green and Walter S. Herndon. Screenplay, Thomas Rickman and Bill Kerby. Photography, Bobby Byrne. Stunt Coordinator, Bobby Bass. Art Director, Hilyard Brown. Editor, Donn Cambern. Assistant Director, David Hamburger. 2nd Assistant Director, Bill Scott. Sound, Jack Solomon. Set Decorator, Ira Bates. Costume Supervisor, Norman Salling. Men's Costumers, Gene Deardorff and Mike Balker. Women's Costumer, Paula Kaatz. Makeup, Tom Ellingwood and William Turner. Hairstylist, Dorothy Byrne. Special Effects, Cliff Wenger, Sr., and Cliff Wenger, Jr. Music, Bill Justis. "A Player, a Pawn, a Hero, a King" sung by Tammy Wynette. "Hooper," written and sung by Bent Myggen. Film debut of Pittsburgh Steelers quarterback Terry Bradshaw. Filmed at Burbank Studios, in Los Angeles and at Tuscaloosa, Alabama, where the Northington Campus of the University of Alabama was demolished. Reynolds is seen in the rapids from *Deliverance*, 1972. Panaflex camera by Panavision. Metrocolor. Rated PG. 97 minutes

Sonny Hooper: Burt Reynolds, *Ski Chinski:* Jan-Michael Vincent, *Gwen Doyle:* Sally Field, *Jocko Doyle:* Brian Keith, *Roger Deal:* Robert Klein, *Himself:* Adam West, *Max Berns:* John Marley, *Cully:* James Best, *Tony:* Alfie Wise, *SWAT Commander:* Terry Bradshaw, *Sheriff:* Don "Red" Barry, *Amtrac, SWAT man:* Robert Tessier, *Hammerhead:* Norman Grabowski, *Doctor:* Richard Tyler, *George, Humane Society Representative:* George Furth, *Cliff, Special Effects Man:* Hal Floyd, *Kent:* Kent Lane, *Pete:* Peter Craig, *Reynolds' Helicopter Fall:* A. J. Bakunas, *Helicopter Pilot:* Chuck Tamburro, *Vincent's Building Descent:* Buddy Joe Hooker, *Stunts:* Carter Alsop, Jerry Barrett, Stan Barrett, Pam Bebermeyer, Janet Brady, Greg Brickman, Alex Brown, Jophery Brown, Blair Burrows, Bill Burton, Gary Combs, Gilbert Combs, Jim Connors, Evelyn Cuffee, Jade David, Sam Davis, Patti Elder, Tom Elliott, David Ellis, Gary Epper, Tony Epper, John Escobar, Lawrence E. Fatino, Mickey Gilbert, Len Glascow, Don Fox Green, Stefan Gudju, Clifford Happy, Fred Hice, Hank Hooker, Hugh Hooker, Tom Huff, Louise Johnson, Harold Jones, Ed Lang, Thomas Lee Lupo, Sam Melville, Ace

Moore, Bennie Moore, Dave Mungenast, Mike McGaughy, Gary McLarty, Bonnie McPherson, Alan Oliney, Bob Orrison, Reg Parton, Regina Parton, Mary Peters, Sorin Pricopie, J. N. Roberts, R. A. Rondell, Jr., Reid Rondell, Ronnie Rondell, Tim Rossovich, Fred Scheiwiller, Sammy Thurman, Loyal Truesdale, Glenn R. Wilder, Walter Wyatt, Dick Ziker. Cut was Soupy Sales as Himself.

THE HORSE SOLDIERS (1959) UA. Produced by John Lee Mahin and Martin Rackin. Directed by John Ford. Color by De Luxe. Screenplay by John Lee Mahin and Martin Rackin. Based on the novel by Harold Sinclair. Art Director, Frank Hotaling. Assistant Directors, Wingate Smith and Ray Gosnell Jr. Music, David Buttolph. Song, "I Left My Love," by Stan Jones. Cinematography, William Clothier. Editor, Jack Murray. A Mirisch Production. Special Effects, Augie Lohman. Make-up, Webb Overlander. Filmed in Louisiana and Mississippi. Based on the Civil War exploits of Union Col. Benjamin Grierson, who destroyed Confederacy's supply route in Tennessee. Film debut of tennis star Althea Gibson. Stuntman Fred Kennedy died as the result of a horse fall. Production Manager, Allen K. Wood. Sound, Jack Solomon. Editor, Jack Murray. Wardrobe, Frank Bretson and Ann Peck. 119 minutes

Colonel John Marlowe: John Wayne, *Major Henry Kendall:* William Holden, *Hannah Hunter:* Constance Towers, *Lukey:* Althea Gibson, *Brown:* Hoot Gibson, *Mrs. Buford:* Anna Lee, *Sheriff:* Russell Simpson, *General Ulysses S. Grant:* Stan Jones, *Colonel Jonathan Miles:* Carleton Young, *Commandant:* Basil Ruysdael, *Sergeant Kirby:* Judson Pratt, *Colonel Phil Seacord:* Willis Bouchey, *Major Richard Gray:* William Leslie, *Wilkie:* Ken Curtis, *Dunker:* Bing Russell, *Union Officer:* Walter Reed, *Deacon:* Hank Worden, *Bugler:* Ron Hagerthy, *Dr. Marvin:* Donald Foster, *Bartender:* Charles Seel, *Confederate Lieutenant:* Bill Henry, *Sergeant-Major Mitchell:* Jack Pennick, *General Sherman:* Richard Cutting, *Hopkins:* O. Z. Whitehead, *General Steve Hurlburt:* William Forrest, *Woodward:* Chuck Hayward, *Virgil:* Strother Martin, *Joe:* Denver Pyle, *Union Scout:* Fred Graham, *Southern Major:* Major Sam Harris, *Sergeant:* Cliff Lyons, *Cavalryman:* Fred Kennedy, *Bugler:* William Wellman, Jr., *Dying Man:* Jan Stine.

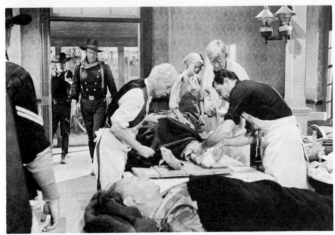

The Horse Soldiers with Cliff Lyons, John Wayne, Donald Foster, Constance Towers, O.Z. Whitehead and William Holden.

HOUSEBOAT (1958) Par. Produced by Jack Rose. Directed by Mel Shavelson. VistaVision and Technicolor. Screenplay, Jack Rose and Mel Shavelson. A Scribe Production. Songs by Jay Livingston and Ray Evans: "Almost in Your Arms," sung by Sam Cooke; and "Bing! Bang! Bong!" Scenes filmed in Washington, D.C. 110 minutes

Tom Winters: Cary Grant, *Cinzia Zaccardi:* Sophia Loren, *Carolyn Gibson:* Martha Hyer, *Angelo Donatello:* Harry Guardino, *Arturo Zaccardi:* Eduardo Ciannelli, *Alan Wilson:* Murray Hamilton, *Elizabeth Winters:* Mimi Gibson, *David Winters:* Paul Petersen, *Robert Winters:* Charles Herbert, *Mrs. Farnsworth:* Madge Kennedy, *Mr. Farnsworth:* John Litel, *Harold Messner:* Werner Klemperer, *Elizabeth*

Wilson: Peggy Connelly, *Women in Laundromat:* Kathleen Freeman, Helen Brown, *Laundromat Attendant:* Florence MacAfee, *Spanish Diplomat:* Julian Rivero, *French Diplomat:* Ernst Brengk, *British Society Woman:* Mary Forbes, *Justice of the Peace:* William R. Remick, *Pitchmen:* Wally Walker, Brooks Benedict, Joe McTurk, *Pizza Saleswoman:* Gilda Oliva, *Clown:* Pat Moran, *Specialty Dancer:* Marc Wilder.

Houseboat with Mimi Gibson, Charles Herbert, Sophia Loren and Cary Grant.

The House of Rothschild with Florence Arliss, George Arliss, Loretta Young, Robert Young and C. Aubrey Smith.

THE HOUSE OF ROTHSCHILD (1934) UA. A 20th Century Picture. Produced by Darryl F. Zanuck. Associate Producers, William Goetz and Raymond Griffith. Presented by Joseph M. Schenck. Directed by Alfred Werker. From an unproduced play by George Hembert Westley. Last sequence in Technicolor. Screenplay, Nunnally Johnson. Music, Alfred Newman. Photography, Peverell Marley. Editors, Alan McNeil and Barbara McLean. 86 minutes

Mayer Rothschild/Nathan Rothschild: George Arliss, *Count Ledrantz:* Boris Karloff, *Julie Rothschild:* Loretta Young, *Captain Fitzroy:* Robert Young, *Duke of Wellington:* C. Aubrey Smith, *Baring:* Arthur Byron, *Gudula Rothschild:* Helen Westley, *Herries:* Reginald Owen, *Hannah Rothschild:* Florence Arliss, *Metternich:* Alan Mowbray, *Rowerth:* Holmes Herbert, *Solomon Rothschild:* Paul Harvey, *Amschel Rothschild:* Ivan Simpson, *Carl Rothschild:* Noel Madison, *James Rothschild:* Murray Kinnell, *Talleyrand:* Georges Renavent, *Prussian Officer:* Oscar Apfel, *Prince Regent:* Lumsden Hare, *Amschel's Secretary:* Leo McCabe, *Prime Minister:* Gilbert Emery, *Nesselrode:*

Charles Evans, *Guest at Hall of Reception:* Desmond Roberts, *Messenger in Stock Exchange:* Earl McDonald, *Woman Guest at Hall of Reception:* Ethel Griffies, *Doctor:* Lee Kohlmar, *Messenger:* William Strauss, *Prussian Guard:* Mathew Betz, *Stock Traders:* Reginald Sheffield, Brandon Hurst, Harold Minjir, Horace Claude Cooper, Craufurd Kent, *Rothschild Children:* Gerald Pierce, Milton Kahn, George Offerman, Jr., Cullen Johnson, Bobbie La Manche, *Tax Collector:* Leonard Mudie, *Prussian Soldier:* Walter Long, *Page:* Wilfred Lucas.

House of Wax with Paul Cavanagh, Phyllis Kirk, Paul Picerni and Vincent Price.

HOUSE OF WAX (1953) WB. Producer, Bryan Foy. Director, Andre de Toth. 3-Dimension, WarnerColor. Author, Charles Belden. Screenplay, Crane Wilbur. Art Director, Stanley Fleischer. Cinematographer, Bert Glennon. Editor, Rudi Fehr. Remake of Warners' *Mystery of the Wax Museum* (1933). 88 minutes

Professor Henry Jarrod: Vincent Price, *Matthew Burke:* Roy Roberts, *Sidney Wallace:* Paul Cavanagh, *Cathy Gray:* Carolyn Jones, *Sue Allen:* Phyllis Kirk, *Scott Andrews:* Paul Picerni, *Mrs. Andrews:* Angela Clarke, *Lieutenant Tom Brennan:* Frank Lovejoy, *Sergeant Jim Shane:* Dabbs Greer, *Igor:* Charles Buchinsky (Charles Bronson), *Leon Averill:* Ned Young, *Barker:* Reggie Rymal, *Bruce Alison:* Philip Tonge, *Ma Flanagan:* Riza Royce, *Scrubwoman:* Ruth Warren, *First Detective:* Richard Benjamin, *Second Detective:* Jack Mower, *Surgeon:* Grandon Rhodes, *Medical Examiner:* Frank Ferguson, *Pompous Man:* Oliver Blake, *Portly Man:* Leo Curley, *Millie:* Mary Lou Holloway, *Ticket Taker:* Merry Townsend, *Waiter:* Lyle Latell.

THE HOUSE ON 92ND STREET (1945) 20th. Produced by Louis de Rochemont. Directed by Henry Hathaway. Story by Charles G. Booth. Screenplay, Barre Lyndon, Charles G. Booth, and John Monks, Jr. Art Directors, Lyle Wheeler and Lewis Creber. Score, David Buttolph. Music Director, Emil Newman. Cameraman, Norbert Brodine. Special Effects, Fred Sersen. Editor, Harmon Jones. Filmed with the cooperation of the Federal Bureau of Investigation, and comprised, in part, of prewar and wartime footage taken by the FBI. Shot on location in Washington, D.C., and New York City. 88 minutes.

Bill Dietrich: William Eythe, *Inspector George A. Briggs:* Lloyd Nolan, *Elsa Gebhardt:* Signe Hasso, *Charles Ogden Roper:* Gene Lockhart, *Colonel Hammersohn:* Leo G. Carroll, *Johanna Schmedt:* Lydia St. Clair, *Walker:* William Post, Jr., *Max Cobura:* Harry Bellaver, *Adolphe Lange:* Bruno Wick, *Conrad Arnulf:* Harro Meller, *Gus Huzmann:* Charles Wagenheim, *Klaen:* Alfred Linder, *Luise Vadja:* Renee Carson, *Dr. Arthur C. Appleton:* John McKee, *Major General:* Edwin Jerome, *Freda Kassel:* Elisabeth Neumann, *Frank Jackson:* George Shelton, *Colonel Strassen:* Alfred Zeisler, *Admiral:* Rusty Lane, *Franz Von Wirt:* Salo Douday, *Sergeant:* Paul Ford, *Customs Officer:* William Adams, *Policeman:* Lew Eckles, *Interne:* Tom Brown, *Narrator:* Reed Hadley, *F. B. I. Man:* Bruce Fernald, *Aide:* Benjamin Burroughs,

Colonel: Douglas Rutherford, *Customer:* Sheila Bromley, *Toll Guard:* Victor Sutherland, *Instructor:* Stanley Tackney, *Trainees:* Vincent Gardenia, Frank Richards, *Policeman:* Fred Hillebrand, *Attendant at Morgue:* Edward (E.G.) Marshall, *Travel Agent:* Frank Kreig.

The House on 92nd Street with William Eythe and Leo G. Carroll

How Green Was My Valley with Walter Pidgeon and Roddy McDowall.

HOW GREEN WAS MY VALLEY (1941) 20th. Producer, Darryl F. Zanuck. Director, John Ford. Based on the novel by Richard Llewellyn. Screenplay, Philip Dunne. Cameraman, Arthur Miller. Editor, James B. Clark. Song by Alfred Newman: "How Green Was My Valley." 118 minutes. Remade as a British TV film (1977)

Mr. Gruffydd: Walter Pidgeon, *Angharad:* Maureen O'Hara, *Mr. Morgan:* Donald Crisp, *Bronwyn:* Anna Lee, *Huw:* Roddy McDowall, *Ianto:* John Loder, *Mrs. Morgan:* Sara Allgood, *Cyfartha:* Barry Fitzgerald, *Ivor:* Patric Knowles, *Mr. Jonas:* Morton Lowry, *Mr. Parry:* Arthur Shields, *Cienwen:* Ann Todd, *Dr. Richards:* Frederic Worlock, *Davy:* Richard Fraser, *Gwilym:* Evan S. Evans, *Owen:* James Monks, *Dai Bando:* Rhys Williams, *Mervyn:* Clifford Severn, *Mr. Evans:* Lionel Pape, *Mrs. Nicholas:* Ethel Griffies, *Meillyn Lewis:* Eve March, *Iestyn Evans:* Marten Lamont, *Narrator:* Irving Pichel, *Welsh Singers:* Themselves, *Ensemble Singer:* Tudor Williams, *Postman:* Herbert Evans, *Eve:* Mary Field, *Woman:* Mae Marsh.

HOW THE WEST WAS WON (1962)* MGM. Producer, Bernard Smith. Directors, John Ford, Henry Hathaway, George Marshall.

Cinerama and Technicolor. Screenplay, James R. Webb. Art Directors, George W. Davis, William Ferrari, Addison Hehr. Music, Alfred Newman. "How the West Was Won," music by Alfred Newman, lyrics by Ken Darby; "Home in the Meadow," lyrics by Sammy Cahn; "Raise a Ruckus," "Wait for the Hoedown," "What Was Your Name in the States," lyrics by Johnny Mercer. Cinematographers, William H. Daniels, Milton Krasner, Charles Lang, Jr., Joseph LaShelle. Editor, Harold F. Kress. 165 minutes. Later a TV series

Eve Prescott: Carroll Baker, *Marshal:* Lee J. Cobb, *Jethro Stuart:* Henry Fonda, *Julie Rawlings:* Carolyn Jones, *Zebulon Prescott:* Karl Malden, *Cleve Van Valen:* Gregory Peck, *Zeb Rawlings:* George Peppard, *Roger Morgan:* Robert Preston, *Lilith Prescott:* Debbie Reynolds, *Linus Rawlings:* James Stewart, *Charlie Gant:* Eli Wallach, *General Sherman:* John Wayne, *Mike King:* Richard Widmark, *Dora:* Brigid Bazlen, *Colonel Hawkins:* Walter Brennan, *Attorney:* David Brian, *Peterson:* Andy Devine, *Abraham Lincoln:* Raymond Massey, *Rebecca Prescott:* Agnes Moorehead, *General Grant:* Henry (Harry) Morgan, *Agatha Clegg:* Thelma Ritter, *Deputy:* Mickey Shaughnessy, *Reb Soldier:* Russ Tamblyn, *Narrator:* Spencer Tracy, *Sam Prescott:* Kim Charney, *Zeke Prescott:* Bryan Russell, *Harvey:* Tudor Owen, *Angus:* Barry Harvey, *Bruce:* Jamie Ross, *Colin:* Mark Allen, *Marty:* Lee Van Cleef, *Barker:* Charles Briggs, *Huggins:* Jay C. Flippen, *Hylan Seabury:* Clinton Sundberg, *Gamblers:* James Griffith, Walter Burke, *Ship's Officer:* Joe Sawyer, *Grimes:* John Larch, *Corporal Murphy:* Jack Pennick, *James Marshall:* Craig Duncan, *Jeremiah:* Claude Johnson, *Henchman:* Rodolfo Acosta.

*U.S. release: 1963

How the West Was Won with James Stewart, Barry Harvey, Carroll Baker, Kim Charney, Brian Russell and Karl Malden.

How to Marry a Millionaire with Marilyn Monroe, William Powell and Lauren Bacall.

HOW TO MARRY A MILLIONAIRE (1953) 20th. Producer, Nunnally Johnson. Director, Jean Negulesco. CinemaScope, Technicolor. Based on plays by Zoe Akins, Dale Eunson, Katherine Albert. Screenplay, Nunnally Johnson. Art Directors, Lyle Wheeler, Leland Fuller. Cinematographer, Joe MacDonald. Editor, Louis Loeffler. "Street Scene" composed and conducted by Alfred Newman. Remake of *The Greeks Had a Word for Them* (UA, 1932). 95 minutes. Later a TV series

Loco: Betty Grable, *Pola:* Marilyn Monroe, *Schatze Page:* Lauren Bacall, *Freddie Denmark:* David Wayne, *Eben:* Rory Calhoun, *Tom Brookman:* Cameron Mitchell, *J. Stewart Merrill:* Alex D'Arcy, *Waldo Brewster:* Fred Clark, *J. D. Hanley:* William Powell, *Mike (Elevator Man):* George Dunn, *Elevator Operator:* Harry Carter, *Cab Driver:* Robert Adler, *Mr. Otis:* Tudor Owen, *Antoine:* Maurice Marsac, *Man at Bridge:* Emmett Vogan, *Madame:* Hermine Sterler, *Secretary:* Abney Mott, *Bennett:* Rankin Mansfield, *Jewelry Salesman:* Ralph Reid, *Tony:* Jan Arvan, *Maid:* Ivis Goulding, *Justice:* Dayton Lummis, *Butler:* Eric Wilton, *Captain of Waiters:* Ivan Triesault, *Emir:* George Saurel, *Mrs. Salem:* Hope Landin, *Motorcycle Cop:* Tom Greenway, *Models:* Charlotte Austin, Merry Anders.

The Hucksters with Clark Gable and Sydney Greenstreet.

THE HUCKSTERS (1947) MGM. Producer, Arthur Hornblow, Jr. Director, Jack Conway. Based on the novel by Frederic Wakeman. Screenplay, Luther Davis. Art Directors, Cedric Gibbons, Urie McCleary. Musical Score, Lennie Hayton. Cameraman, Harold Rosson. Editor, Frank Sullivan. Song by Buddy Pepper: "Don't Tell Me." 115 minutes

Victor Albee Norman: Clark Gable, *Kay Dorrance:* Deborah Kerr, *Evan Llewellyn Evans:* Sydney Greenstreet, *Mr. Kimberly:* Adolphe Menjou, *Jean Ogilvie:* Ava Gardner, *Buddy Hare:* Keenan Wynn, *Dave Lash:* Edward Arnold, *Valet:* Aubrey Mather, *Cooke:* Richard Gaines, *Max Herman:* Frank Albertson, *Michael Michaelson:* Clinton Sundberg, *Georgie Gaver:* Douglas Fowley, *Mrs. Kimberly:* Gloria Holden, *Betty:* Connie Gilchrist, *Regina Kennedy:* Kathryn Card, *Miss Hammer:* Lillian Bronson, *Secretary:* Vera Marshe, *Allison:* Ralph Bunker, *Kimberly Receptionist:* Virginia Dale, *Blake:* Jimmy Conlin, *Freddie Callahan:* George O'Hanlon, *George Rockton:* Ransom Sherman, *Paul Evans:* Tom Stevenson, *Teletypist:* Anne Nagel, *Radio Announcer:* John Hiestand, *Clerk:* Jack Rice, *Doorman:* Robert Emmet O'Connor, *Ellen Dorrance:* Dianne Perine, *Cab Driver:* Johnny Day, *Hal Dorrance:* Eugene Baxtor Day, *Secretary:* Florence Stephens, *Kimberly Butler:* Gordon Richards, *Taxi Driver:* Fred Sherman, *First Girl:* Marie Windsor, *Western Union Messenger:* Sammy McKim, *Indian:* Chief Yowlachie, *Harry Spooner:* Edwin Cooper, *Joe Lorrison:* Harry V. Cheshire, *Bellboy:* Billy Benedict, *Businessman:* Mahlon Hamilton.

Hud with Paul Newman, Melvyn Douglas and Brandon de Wilde.

HUD (1963) Par. Producers, Martin Ritt, Irving Ravetch. Director, Martin Ritt. Based on the novel *Horseman, Pass By* by Larry McMurtry. Screenplay, Irving Ravetch, Harriet Frank, Jr. Art Directors, Hal Pereira, Tambi Larsen. Music Score, Elmer Bernstein. Cinematographer, James Wong Howe. Special Photographic Effects, Paul K. Lerpae. Editor, Frank Bracht. A Salem-Dover Production. 112 minutes

Hud Bannon: Paul Newman, *Homer Bannon:* Melvyn Douglas, *Alma Brown:* Patricia Neal, *Lon Bannon:* Brandon de Wilde, *Burris:* Whit Bissell, *Hermy:* John Ashley, *Joe Scanlon:* George Petrie, *Thompson:* Sheldon Allman, *Kirby:* Carl Low, *Charlie Tucker:* Don Kennedy, *Jesse:* Crahan Denton, *Jose:* Val Avery, *Truman Peters:* Curt Conway, *Larker:* Pitt Herbert, *Announcer:* Robert Hinkle, *Myra:* Sharyn Hillyer, *Lilly Peters:* Yvette Vickers, *Cowboy:* John Indrisano, *Proprietor:* Carl Saxe, *Cowboy:* Monty Montana, *George:* Peter Brooks, *Donald:* David Kent, *Dumb Billy:* Frank Killmond.

The Human Comedy with John Craven and Van Johnson.

THE HUMAN COMEDY (1943) MGM. Producer and Director, Clarence Brown. From the novel by William Saroyan. Screenplay, Howard Estabrook. Dance Director, Ernst Matray. Musical Score, Herbert Stothart. Art Director, Cedric Gibbons. Cameraman, Harry Stradling. Editor, Conrad A. Nervig. 118 minutes.

Homer Macauley: Mickey Rooney, *Tom Spangler:* James Craig, *Willie Grogan:* Frank Morgan, *Mrs. Macauley:* Fay Bainter, *Diana Steed:* Marsha Hunt, *Marcus Macauley:* Van Johnson, *Bess Macauley:* Donna Reed, *Tobey George:* John Craven, *Mary Arena:* Dorothy

Morris, *Ulysses Macauley:* Jackie (Butch) Jenkins, *Miss Hicks:* Mary Nash, *Mrs. Steed:* Katharine Alexander, *Matthew:* Ray Collins, *Charles Steed:* Henry O'Neill, *Lionel:* Darryl Hickman, *Mr. Ara:* S. Z. Sakall, *Brad Stickman:* Alan Baxter, *Fat:* Barry Nelson, *Texas:* Don DeFore, *Horse:* Bob Mitchum, *Mrs. Sandoval:* Ann Ayars, *Negro:* Ernest Whitman, *Soldier:* Mark Daniels, *Librarian:* Adeline de Walt Reynolds, *Helen Elliott:* Rita Quigley, *Hubert Ackley:* David Holt, *Dolly:* Connie Gilchrist, *Mr. Mechano:* Howard J. Stevenson, *Larry:* Frank Jenks, *Rev. Holly:* Howard Freeman, *Felix:* Jay Ward, *Leonine Type Man:* Gibson Gowland, *Soldier:* Don Taylor, *Blenton:* Byron Foulger, *Principal:* Wallis Clark, *Mrs. Beaufrere:* Mary Servoss, *Mr. Beaufrere:* Morris Ankrum, *Daughter:* Lynne Carver, *Auggie:* Carl "Alfalfa" Switzer, *Henderson:* Clem Bevans.

The Hunchback of Notre Dame with Charles Laughton and Maureen O'Hara.

THE HUNCHBACK OF NOTRE DAME (1939) RKO. Producer, Pandro S. Berman. Director, William Dieterle. From the novel by Victor Hugo. Screenplay, Sonya Levien, Bruno Frank. Musical Adaptor, Alfred Newman. Art Director, Van Nest Polglase. Dance Director, Ernst Matray. Cameraman, Joseph H. August. Special Effects, Vernon L. Walker. Editors, William Hamilton, Robert Wise. American film debut of Maureen O'Hara. Film debut of Edmond O'Brien, 23. 117 minutes. Other versions: Univ., 1923, Lon Chaney; AA, 1957, Anthony Quinn. Also a Broadway musical, *Quasimodo* (1979)

Quasimodo: Charles Laughton, *Frollo:* Sir Cedric Hardwicke, *Clopin:* Thomas Mitchell, *Esmeralda:* Maureen O'Hara, *Gringoire:* Edmond O'Brien, *Phoebus:* Alan Marshal, *Archbishop:* Walter Hampden, *King Louis XI:* Harry Davenport, *Fleur's Mother:* Katharine Alexander, *Procurator:* George Zucco, *Fleur:* Helene Whitney, *Queen of Beggars:* Minna Gombell, *Old Nobleman:* Fritz Leiber, *Doctor:* Etienne Girardot, *Olivier:* Arthur Hohl, *Beggar:* George Tobias, *Phillipo:* Rod La Rocque, *Court Clerk:* Spencer Charters.

THE HURRICANE (1937) UA. Produced by Samuel Goldwyn. Directed by John Ford and Stuart Heisler. From the novel by Charles Nordhoff and James Norman Hall. Adaptation, Dudley Nichols and Oliver H. P. Garrett. Score, Alfred Newman. Associate Producer, Merritt Hulburd. Photography, Bert Glennon. Editor, Lloyd Nosler. Sound, Jack Noyes. Song by Frank Loesser and Alfred Newman, "Moon of Manakoora." 110 minutes. Remade in 1979

Marama: Dorothy Lamour, *Terangi:* Jon Hall, *Madame De Laage:* Mary Astor, *Father Paul:* C. Aubrey Smith, *Doctor Kersaint:* Thomas Mitchell, *Governor De Laage:* Raymond Massey, *Warden:* John Carradine, *Captain Nagle:* Jerome Cowan, *Chief Mehevi:* Al Kikume, *Tita:* Kuulei De Clercq, *Mako:* Layne Tom, Jr., *Hitia:* Mamo Clark, *Aral:* Movita Castenada, *Reri:* Reri, *Tavi:* Francis Kaai, *Mata:* Pauline Steele, *Mama Rua:* Flora Hayes, *Marunga:* Mary Shaw, *Judge:* Spencer Charters, *Captain of Guards:* Roger Drake, *Girl On Ship:* Inez Courtney, *Stuntman:* Paul Stader, *Man Who's Injured:* William B. Davidson.

The *Hurricane* with Dorothy Lamour and Jon Hall.

Hush... Hush, Sweet Charlotte with Olivia de Havilland and Bette Davis.

HUSH...HUSH, SWEET CHARLOTTE (1965) 20th. Producer-Director, Robert Aldrich. Screenplay, Henry Farrell, Lukas Heller. Story by Henry Farrell. Associate Producer, Walter Blake. Director of Photography, Joseph Biroc. Music, Frank DeVol. Title Song Lyrics, Mack David. Assistant Directors, William McGarry, Sam Strangis. Costumes, Norma Koch. Choreography, Alex Ruiz. An Associates

and Aldrich Production. Art Director, William Glasgow. Editor, Michael Luciano. Sound, Bernard Freericks. Production Supervisor, Jack R. Berne. 133 minutes

Charlotte Hollis: Bette Davis, *Miriam Deering:* Olivia de Havilland, *Dr. Drew Bayliss:* Joseph Cotten, *Velma Cruther:* Agnes Moorehead, *Harry Willis:* Cecil Kellaway, *Big Sam Hollis:* Victor Buono, *Mrs. Jewel Mayhew:* Mary Astor, *Paul Marchand:* William Campbell, *Sheriff Luke Standish:* Wesley Addy, *John Mayhew:* Bruce Dern, *Foreman:* George Kennedy, *Taxi Driver:* Dave Willock, *Boy:* John Megna, *Gossips:* Ellen Corby, Helen Kleeb, Marianne Stewart, *Newspaper Editor:* Frank Ferguson.

The *Hustler* with Paul Newman and Myron McCormick.

THE HUSTLER (1961) 20th. Producer, Robert Rossen. Director, Robert Rossen. CinemaScope. Based on the novel by Walter Tevis. Screenplay, Robert Rossen, Sidney Carroll. Art Directors, Harry Horner, Albert Brenner. Cinematographer, Gene Shufton. Editor, Dede Allen. Filmed in New York City. 135 minutes

Eddie Felson: Paul Newman, *Sarah Packard:* Piper Laurie, *Bert Gordon:* George C. Scott, *Minnesota Fats:* Jackie Gleason, *Charlie Burns:* Myron McCormick, *Oames Findley:* Murray Hamilton, *Big John:* Michael Constantine, *Preacher:* Stefan Gierasch, *Bartender:* Jake LaMotta, *Cashier-Bennington's:* Gordon B. Clarke, *Scorekeeper:* Alexander Rose, *Waitress:* Carolyn Coates, *Young Man:* Carl York, *Bartender:* Vincent Gardenia, *Willie:* Willie Mosconi, *Old Man Attendant:* Art Smith, *Another Player:* Don De Leo, *Bartender:* Tom Aherne, *Player:* Brendan Fay, *Turk:* Cliff Pellow, *Waiter:* Charles Andre, *First Man:* Sid Raymond, *Second Man:* Charles Mosconi, *Old Doctor:* Wm. P. Adams, *Reservation Clerk:* Charles McDaniel, *Hotel Proprietor:* Jack Healy, *Racetrack Ticket Clerk:* Don Koll, *Kibitzer:* Jim Dukas.

I AM A FUGITIVE FROM A CHAIN GANG (1932) WB. Directed by Mervyn LeRoy. Based on a story by Robert E. Burns, "I Am a Fugitive From a Georgia Chain Gang." Screenplay, Howard J. Green and Brown Holmes. Art Director, Jack Okey. Photography, Sol Polito. Editor, William Holmes. Gowns, Orry-Kelly. Technical Advisers, S. H. Sullivan and Jack Miller. Cut from existing prints: Spencer Charters (C. K. Hobb), Roscoe Karns (Steve), William Janney (Sheriff's Son), Harry Holman (Sheriff of Monroe). Actors replaced during production: Oscar Apfel by Edward Le Saint, C. Henry Gordon by Douglass Dumbrille, John Marston by Willard Robertson, Russell Simpson by Erville Alderson, Sam Baker by Everett Brown, Dewey Robinson by Walter Long, Edward Arnold by Wallis Clark, Morgan Wallace by Robert McWade. 93 minutes

James Allen: Paul Muni, *Marie Woods:* Glenda Farrell, *Helen:* Helen Vinson, *Pete:* Preston Foster, *Barney Sykes:* Allen Jenkins, *Bomber Wells:* Edward Ellis, *Nordine:* John Wray, *Reverend Robert Clinton Allen:* Hale Hamilton, *Guard:* Harry Woods, *Warden:* David Landau, *Second Warden:* Edward J. McNamara, *Ramsey:* Robert McWade, *Prison Commissioner:* Willard Robertson, *Linda:* Noel Francis, *Mrs. Allen:* Louise Carter, *The Judge:* Berton Churchill, *Allen's Secretary:* Sheila Terry, *Alice:* Sally Blane, *Red:* James Bell, *Chairman of Chamber of Commerce:* Edward Le Saint, *District Attorney:* Douglass Dumbrille, *Fuller:* Robert Warwick, *Train Conductor:* Charles Middleton, *Parker:* Reginald Barlow, *Ackerman:* Jack La Rue, *Owner of Hot Dog Stand:* Charles Sellon, *Chief of Police:* Erville Alderson, *Wilson:* George Pat Collins, *Doggy:* William Pawley, *Mike, Proprietor of Diner:* Lew Kelly, *Sebastian T. Yale:* Everett Brown, *Texas:* William LeMaire, *Vaudevillian:* George Cooper, *Lawyer:* Wallis Clark, *Blacksmith:* Walter Long, *Georgia Prison Official:* Frederick Burton, *Barber, Bill:* Irving Bacon, *Arresting Officers:* Lee Shumway, J. Frank Glendon, *Dance Extra:* Dennis O'Keefe.

I Am a Fugitive From a Chain Gang with Glenda Farrell and Paul Muni.

I'LL BE SEEING YOU (1944) UA. Producer, Dore Schary. Director, William Dieterle. Author, Charles Martin. Screenplay, Marion Parsonnet. Musical Score, Daniele Amfitheatrof. Art Director, Mark-Lee Kirk. Cameraman, Tony Gaudio. Editor, William H. Ziegler. Song by Irving Kahal and Sammy Fain: "I'll Be Seeing You." 85 minutes

Mary Marshall: Ginger Rogers, *Zachary Morgan:* Joseph Cotten, *Barbara Marshall:* Shirley Temple, *Mrs. Marshall:* Spring Byington, *Mr. Marshall:* Tom Tully, *Swanson:* Chill Wills, *Lieutenant Bruce:* Dare Harris (John Derek), *Sailor on Train:* Kenny Bowers.

I'll Be Seeing You with Chill Wills, Joseph Cotten and Ginger Rogers.

I'll Cry Tomorrow with Richard Conte and Susan Hayward.

I'LL CRY TOMORROW (1955) MGM. Producer, Lawrence Weingarten. Director, Daniel Mann. Based on the book by Lillian Roth, Mike Connolly and Gerold Frank. Screenplay, Helen Deutsch, Jay Richard Kennedy. Art Directors, Cedric Gibbons, Malcolm Brown. Musical Director, Charles Henderson. Music, Alex North. Cinematographer, Arthur E. Arlings. Editor, Harold F. Kress. 117 minutes.

Lillian Roth: Susan Hayward, *Tony Bardeman:* Richard Conte, *Burt McGuire:* Eddie Albert, *Katie:* Jo Van Fleet, *Wallie:* Don Taylor, *David Tredman:* Ray Danton, *Selma:* Margo, *Ellen:* Virginia Gregg, *Jerry:* Don Barry, *David as a child:* David Kasday, *Lillian as a child:* Carole Ann Campbell, *Richard:* Peter Leeds, *Fat Man:* Tol Avery, *Man:* Guy Wilkerson, *Derelict:* Tim Carey, *Stage Manager:* Charles Tannen, *Director:* Ken Patterson, *Mr. Byrd:* Voltaire Perkins, *Messenger:* George Lloyd, *Nurse:* Nora Marlowe, *Director:* Stanley Farrar, *Stage Manager:* Harlan Warde, *Doctor:* Peter Brocco, *Henry:* Bob Dix, *Paul, the Butler:* Anthony Jochim, *Dress Designer:* Kay English, *Ethel:* Eve McVeagh, *Waitress:* Veda Ann Borg, *Lillian (age 15):* Gail Ganley, *Stagehand:* Robert B. Williams, *M. C.:* Bob Hopkins, *Club Manager:* Vernon Rich, *Conductor:* Herbert C. Lytton, *Switchman:* George Selk, *Elderly Lady:* Cheerio Meredith.

I Met Him in Paris with Melvyn Douglas, Claudette Colbert and Robert Young.

I MET HIM IN PARIS (1937) Par. Produced and directed by Wesley Ruggles. Based on a story by Helen Meinardi. Screenplay, Claude Binyon. Art Directors, Hans Dreier and Ernst Fegte. Musical Director, Boris Morros. Special Effects, Farciot Edouart. Camera, Leo

Tover. Editor, Otho Lovering. Interior Decorator, A. E. Freudeman. Technical Adviser, D'Arcy Rutherford. Title song, Helen Meinardi and Hoagy Carmichael. Costumes, Travis Banton. Sound, Earl Hayman and Don Johnson. 86 minutes

Kay Denham: Claudette Colbert, *George Potter:* Melvyn Douglas, *Gene Anders:* Robert Young, *Berk Sutter:* Lee Bowman, *Helen Anders:* Mona Barrie, *Cutter Driver:* George Davis, *Swiss Hotel Clerk:* Fritz Feld, *Romantic Waiter:* Rudolph Amendt (Rudolph Anders), *John Hadley:* Alexander Cross, *Hotel Clerk:* George Sorel, *Bartender:* Louis La Bey, *Upper Tower Man (Emile):* Egon Brecher, *Lower Tower Man:* Hans Joby, *Frenchman (Flirt):* Jacques Vanaire, *Double Talk Waiter:* Gennaro Curci, *Headwaiter:* Eugene Borden, *Elevator Operator:* Captain Fernando Garcia, *Headwaiter:* Albert Morin, *Hotel Clerk:* Arthur Hurni, *Conductor:* Albert Pollet, *Bartender:* Jacques Lory, *Couple in Apartment:* Francesco Maran, Yola d'Avril, *Steward:* Jean De Briec, *Waiters:* Charles Haas, Otto Jehly, Paco Moreno, Roman Novins, *Bartender:* Joe Ploski, *Porter:* Alexander Schonberg, *Assistant Bartender:* Joe Thoben, *Women:* Gloria Williams, Priscilla Moran.

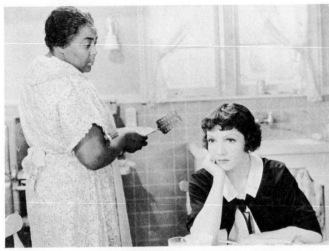
Imitation of Life with Louise Beavers and Claudette Colbert.

IMITATION OF LIFE (1934) Univ. Directed by John Stahl. Based on the novel by Fannie Hurst. Screenplay, William Hurlbut. Cameraman, Merritt Gerstad. Editor, Phil Cahn. Remade by Universal, 1959. 106 minutes

Beatrice (Bea) Pullman: Claudette Colbert, *Stephen Archer:* Warren William, *Elmer:* Ned Sparks, *Delilah Johnson:* Louise Beavers, *Jessie Pullman at 3:* Baby Jane, *Jessie at 8:* Marilyn Knowlden, *Jessie at 18:* Rochelle Hudson, *Peola Johnson at 4:* Sebie Hendricks, *Peola at 9:* Dorothy Black, *Peola at 19:* Fredi Washington, *Martin (Furniture Man):* Alan Hale, *Landlord:* Clarence Hummel Wilson, *Painter:* Henry Armetta, *Dr. Preston:* Henry Kolker, *Butler:* Wyndham Standing, *French Maid:* Alice Ardell, *Restaurant Manager:* Paul Porcasi, *Man:* William B. Davidson, *Man at Party:* G. P. Huntley, Jr., *Hugh:* Walter Walker, *Mrs. Eden:* Noel Francis, *Mr. Carven:* Franklin Pangborn, *Tipsy Man:* Tyler Brooke, *Englishman:* William Austin, *Butler:* Edgar Norton, *Maid:* Hazel Washington, *Mrs. Carven:* Alma Tell, *Mrs. Dale:* Lenita Lane, *Young Man:* Barry Norton, *Woman:* Joyce Compton, *Minister:* Reverend Gregg, *Chauffeur:* Curry Lee, *Teacher:* Claire McDowell, *Cook:* Madame Sul-Te-Wan, *Undertaker:* Stuart Johnston, *Bits at Funeral:* Fred (Snowflake) Toone, Hattie McDaniel, *Dance Extra:* Dennis O'Keefe.

I'M NO ANGEL (1933) Par. Directed by Wesley Ruggles. Story, Mae West and Lowell Brentano. Adaptation, Harlan Thompson. Dialogue, Mae West. Photography, Leo Tover. Editor, Otho Lovering. Sound, Phil S. Wisdon and F. E. Dine. Songs by Harvey Brooks, Gladys du Bois, Ben Ellison: "They Call Me Sister Honky Tonk," "No One Loves Me Like That Dallas Man," "I Found a New Way

to Go to Town," "I Want You, I Need You," "I'm No Angel." Mae dances the Mid-way. 87 minutes

Tira: Mae West, *Jack Clayton:* Cary Grant, *Bill Barton:* Edward Arnold, *Slick Wiley:* Ralf Harolde, *Flea Madigan:* Russell Hopton, *Alicia Hatton:* Gertrude Michael, *Kirk Lawrence:* Kent Taylor, *Thelma:* Dorothy Peterson, *Benny Pinkowitz:* Gregory Ratoff, *Beulah Thorndyke:* Gertrude Howard, *The Chump (Ernest Brown):* William Davidson, *Rajah:* Nigel de Brulier, *Bob, the Attorney:* Irving Pichel, *Omnes:* George Bruggeman, *Harry:* Nat Pendleton, *Chauffeur:* Morrie Cohen, *Judge:* Walter Walker, *Sailor:* Monte Collins, *Sailor:* Ray Cooke, *Maid:* Hattie McDaniel, *Libby (Maid):* Libby Taylor, *Reporter:* Dennis O'Keefe.

I'm No Angel with Mae West.

INCENDIARY BLONDE (1945) Par. Director, George Marshall. Screenplay, Claude Binyon, Frank Butler. Musical Director, Robert Emmett Dolan. Dance Director, Danny Dare. Art Directors, Hans Dreier, William Flannery. Cameraman, Ray Rennahan. Special Effects, Farciot Edouart. Editor, Archie Marshek. Authors, Thomas and W. D. Guinan (from *Life of Texas Guinan*). Songs: "Ragtime Cowboy Joe" by Maurice Abrahams and Lewis F. Muir; "Ida" by Eddie Leonard; "Oh By Jingo Oh By Gee" by Lew Brown and Albert Von Tilzer; "What Do You Want to Make Those Eyes at Me For?" by Howard Johnson, Joseph McCarthy and Jimmy Monaco; "Row, Row, Row" by William Jerome and Jimmy Monaco; "Darktown Strutters' Ball" by Shelton Brooks; "It Had to Be You" by Gus Kahn and Isham Jones; "Sweet Genevieve" by Henry Tucker and George Cooper. 113 minutes

Texas Guinan: Betty Hutton, *Bill Kilgannon:* Arturo de Cordova, *Cherokee Jim:* Charlie Ruggles, *Cadden:* Albert Dekker, *Mike Guinan:* Barry Fitzgerald, *Bessie Guinan:* Mary Phillips, *Tim Callahan:* Bill Goodwin, *Nick, The Greek:* Eduardo Ciannelli, *The Maxellos:* Themselves, *Maurice Rocco:* Himself, *Waco Smith:* Ted Mapes, *Mr. Ballinger:* Charles C. Wilson, *Pearl Guinan, 21 years:* Maxine Fife, *Pearl Guinan, 17 years:* Carlotta Jelm, *Pearl Guinan, 7 years:* Ann Carter, *Tommy Guinan, 19 years:* Billy Lechner, *Tommy Guinan, 15 years:* Eddie Nichols, *Tommy Guinan, 5 years:* George Nokes, *Willie Guinan:* Robert Winkler, *Texas Guinan, 9 years:* Patricia Prest, *Baby Joe:* Billy Curtis, *Charley Rinaldo:* Edmund MacDonald, *Gus Rinaldo:*

131

Don Costello, *Louella Parsons:* Catherine Craig, *Singer:* Johnnie Johnston, *Specialty Singer:* Jane Jones, *Woman:* Ruth Roman, *Hatcheck Girl:* Betty Walker, *Master of Ceremonies:* George McKay, *George, a cop:* Harry Shannon, *O'Keefe:* Matt McHugh, *Jenkins:* Russell Simpson, *McKee:* Arthur Loft, *Hadley:* Andrew Tombes, *Otto Hammel:* Pierre Watkin, *Hector:* James Millican, *Mr. Zweigler:* Edwin Stanley, *Gus, Stage Manager:* Ray Walker, *Horace Biggs:* Harry Hayden, *Hotel Clerk:* Frank Faylen.

Incendiary Blonde with Betty Hutton.

In Cold Blood with Robert Blake and Scott Wilson.

IN COLD BLOOD (1967) Col. Produced and directed by Richard Brooks. Panavision. Based on the book by Truman Capote. Adapted by Richard Brooks. Assistant Director, Tom Shaw. Music, Quincy Jones. Art Direction, Robert Boyle. Sets, Jack Ahern. Photography, Conrad Hall. Sound, William Randall Jr., Jack Haynes, A. Piantadosi, Richard Tyler. Editor, Peter Zinner. Filmed in Kansas, Missouri, Nevada, Colorado, Texas, Mexico. 134 minutes

Perry Smith: Robert Blake,* *Dick Hickock:* Scott Wilson, *Alvin Dewey:* John Forsythe, *Reporter:* Paul Stewart, *Harold Nye:* Gerald S. O'Loughlin, *Mr. Hickock:* Jeff Corey, *Roy Church:* John Gallaudet, *Clarence Duntz:* James Flavin, *Mr. Smith:* Charles McGraw, *Officer Rohleder:* James Lantz, *Prosecutor:* Will Geer, *Herbert Clutter:* John McLiam, *Bonnie Clutter:* Ruth Storey, *Nancy Clutter:* Brenda C. Currin, *Kenyon Clutter:* Paul Hough, *Good Samaritan:* Vaughn Taylor, *Young Reporter:* Duke Hobbie, *Reverend Post:* Sheldon Allman, *Mrs. Smith:* Sammy Thurman, *Herself:* Mrs. Sadie Truitt, *Herself:* Myrtle Clare, *Young Hitchhiker:* Teddy Eccles, *Old Hitchhiker:*

Raymond Hatton, *Susan Kidwell:* Mary-Linda Rapelye, *Nancy's Friend:* Ronda Fultz, *Sheriff:* Al Christy, *Salesman:* Don Sollars, *Mrs. Hartman:* Harriet Levitt, *Insurance Man:* Stan Levitt.

*Inasmuch as most of the critics identified Robert Blake as a newcomer, the following footnote is in order: Far from being a newcomer, Robert Blake started out with Our Gang at MGM in 1939 under his real name, Michael Gubitosi. Later, as Bobby Blake, he played Little Beaver in all the Red Ryder Western features at Republic. As an adult, he co-starred in "Revolt in the Big House" (1958) and "The Purple Gang" (1960), and was one of Richard Boone's repertory company on his TV series.

Indiscreet with Cary Grant and Ingrid Bergman.

INDISCREET (1958) WB. Producer-Director, Stanley Donen. Screenplay by Norman Krasna, from his play *Kind Sir.* Associate Producer, Sydney Streeter. Music by Richard Bennett and Ken Jones. Song by Sammy Cahn and James Van Heusen. Assistant Director, Tom Pevsner. A Grandon Production in Technicolor. 100 minutes

Philip Adams: Cary Grant, *Ann Kalman:* Ingrid Bergman, *Alfred Munson:* Cecil Parker, *Margaret Munson:* Phyllis Calvert, *Carl Banks:* David Kossoff, *Doris Banks:* Megs Jenkins, *Finleigh:* Oliver Johnston, *Finleigh's Clerk:* Middleton Woods.

The Informer with Clyde Cook, Victor McLaglen and J.M. Kerrigan.

THE INFORMER (1935) RKO. Produced by Cliff Reid. Directed by John Ford. From the book by Liam O'Flaherty, first published in London in 1925. Screenplay, Dudley Nichols. Music, Max Steiner. Art Director, Van Nest Polglase. Art Associate, Charles Kirk. Photography, Joseph H. August. Editor, George Hively. Sound, Hugh McDowell, Jr. American film debut of English actress Margot Grahame. 91 minutes. Other version: British, 1929, with Lars Hanson.

132

Gypo Nolan: Victor McLaglen, *Mary McPhillip:* Heather Angel, *Dan Gallagher:* Preston Foster, *Katie Madden:* Margot Grahame, *Frankie McPhillip:* Wallace Ford, *Mrs. McPhillip:* Una O'Connor, *Terry:* J. M. Kerrigan, *Bartly Mulholland:* Joseph Sauers (Joe Sawyer), *Tommy Connor:* Neil Fitzgerald, *Peter Mulligan:* Donald Meek, *The Blind Man:* D'Arcy Corrigan, *Donahue:* Leo McCabe, *Dennis Daly:* Gaylord (Steve) Pendleton, *Flynn:* Francis Ford, *"Aunt" Betty:* May Boley, *The Lady:* Grizelda Harvey, *Street Singer:* Dennis O'Dea, *Man at Wake:* Jack Mulhall, *Young Soldier:* Bob Parrish, *Singer:* Anne O'Neal, *McCabe, Bouncer in House:* Frank Moran, *House Patrons:* Cornelius Keefe, Eddy Chandler, *Admirers:* Pat Moriarity, Frank Marlowe, Harry Tenbrook, *Detractor:* Robert E. Homans, *Policeman:* Frank Hagney, *Bartender:* Bob Perry, *British Officer:* Pat Somerset, *Patron:* Clyde Cook.

Inherit the Wind with Fredric March and Spencer Tracy.

INHERIT THE WIND (1960) UA. Producer-Director, Stanley Kramer. Screenplay, Nathan E. Douglas and Harold Jacob Smith. Based on the play by Jerome Lawrence and Robert E. Lee. Music, Ernest Gold. Assistant Director, Ivan Volkman. Wardrobe, Joe King.

Henry Drummond: Spencer Tracy, *Matthew Harrison Brady:* Fredric March, *E. K. Hornbeck:* Gene Kelly, *Mrs. Brady:* Florence Eldridge, *Bertram T. Cates:* Dick York, *Rachel Brown:* Donna Anderson, *Judge:* Harry Morgan, *Davenport:* Elliott Reid, *Mayor:* Philip Coolidge, *Rev. Brown:* Claude Akins, *Meeker:* Paul Hartman, *Howard:* Jimmy Boyd, *Stebbins:* Noah Beery, Jr., *Sillers:* Gordon Polk, *Dunlap:* Ray Teal, *Radio Announcer:* Norman Fell, *Mrs. Krebs:* Hope Summers, *Mrs. Stebbins:* Renee Godfrey.

The Inn of the Sixth Happiness with Robert Donat, Ingrid Bergman and Curt Jurgens.

THE INN OF THE SIXTH HAPPINESS (1958) 20th. Producer, Buddy Adler. Director, Mark Robson. CinemaScope and De Luxe Color. Screenplay by Isobel Lennart. Based on the novel *The Small Woman* by Alan Burgess. Music by Malcolm Arnold. Costumes by Margaret Furse. Assistant Director, David Middlemas. Photography, F. A. Young. Filmed in Wales and England. Last film of Robert Donat. 158 minutes

Gladys: Ingrid Bergman, *Linnan:* Curt Jurgens, *The Mandarin:* Robert Donat, *Hok-A:* Michael David, *Mrs. Lawson:* Athene Seyler, *Sir Francis:* Ronald Squire, *Dr. Robinson:* Moultrie Kelsall, *Mr. Murfin:* Richard Wattis, *Yang:* Peter Chong, *Sui Lan:* Tsai Chin, *Secretary:* Edith Sharpe, *Cook:* Joan Young, *Miss Thompson:* Noel Hood, *Li:* Burt Kwouk, *Woman with Baby:* Lian Shin Yang, *Young Lin:* Ronald Kyaing, *Bai Boa:* Ye Min, *Mai Da:* Louise Lin, *Sixpense:* Judith Lai, *Timothy:* Frank Goh, *Russian Commissar:* Andre Mikhelson, *Russian Conductor:* Stanislaw Mikula, *Innkeeper's Wife:* Lin Chen, *Chief Muleteer:* Ronald Lee, *Mandarin's Aide:* Michael Wee, *Tax Collector:* Christopher Chen, *Buddhist Priest:* Aung Min, *Madman:* Frank Blaine.

In Old Arizona with Warner Baxter and Dorothy Burgess.

IN OLD ARIZONA (1929) Fox. Directed by Raoul Walsh and Irving Cummings. Based on the character created by O. Henry. Scenario, adaptation, and dialogue, Tom Barry. Photography, Arthur Edeson. Sound, Edmund H. Hansen. Editor, Louis Loeffler. Assistant Directors, Archie Buchanan and Charles Woolstenhulme. The first Fox Movietone feature. Filmed in Zion National Park and Bryce Canyon, Utah; the Mohave Desert at Victorville, Cal.; San Fernando's old mission; Cedar City, Utah; San Juan Capistrano mission. Theme, "My Tonia," by DeSylva, Brown, and Henderson. Film debut of Dorothy Burgess. Talkie debuts of Warner Baxter, Roy Stewart. 95 minutes

Sergeant Mickey Dunn: Edmund Lowe, *The Cisco Kid:* Warner Baxter, *Tonia Maria:* Dorothy Burgess, *Tad:* J. Farrell MacDonald, *Russian Immigrant:* Ivan Linow, *Cook:* Soledad Jiminez, *Piano Player:* Fred Warren, *Barber:* Henry Armetta, *Cowpunchers:* Frank Campeau, Frank Nelson, Tom Santschi, Duke Martin, Pat Hartigan, *Blacksmith:* James Marcus, *Commandant:* Roy Stewart, *Sheriff:* Alphonse Ethier, *Soldier:* James Bradbury, Jr., *Second Soldier:* John Dillon, *Bartender:* Joe Brown, *Italian Girl:* Lola Salvi, *Man:* Edward Piel, Sr., *Woman:* Helen Lynch.

IN OLD CHICAGO (1938) 20th. Produced by Darryl F. Zanuck. Associate Producer, Kenneth Macgowan. Directed by Henry King. Screenplay, Lamar Trotti and Sonya Levien. Research, Chicago Historical Society. Editor, Barbara McLean. Based on the story "We the O'Learys" by Niven Busch. Photography, Peverell Marley. Art Director, William Darling. Associate, Rudolph Sternad. Sets, Thomas Little. Unit Manager, Booth McCracken. Assistant Director, Robert

Webb. Costumes, Royer. Music Direction, Louis Silvers. Songs: "In Old Chicago" by Mack Gordon and Harry Revel; "I've Taken a Fancy to You," "I'll Never Let You Cry," "Take a Dip in the Sea" by Sidney Mitchell and Lew Pollack; "Carry Me Back to Old Virginny." Special Effects Director, H. Bruce Humberstone. Special Effects Photography, Daniel B. Clark. Special Effects Staged by Fred Sersen, Ralph Hammeras, Louis J. Witte. Sound, Eugene Grossman. 110 minutes

Dion O'Leary: Tyrone Power, *Belle Fawcett:* Alice Faye, *Jack O'Leary:* Don Ameche, *Molly O'Leary:* Alice Brady, *Pickle Bixby:* Andy Devine, *Gil Warren:* Brian Donlevy, *Ann Colby:* Phyllis Brooks, *Bob O'Leary:* Tom Brown, *General Phil Sheridan:* Sidney Blackmer, *Senator Colby:* Berton Churchill, *Gretchen O'Leary:* June Storey, *Mitch:* Paul Hurst, *Specialty Singer:* Tyler Brooke, *Patrick O'Leary:* J. Anthony Hughes, *Dion as a boy:* Gene Reynolds, *Bob as a boy:* Bobs Watson, *Jack as a boy:* Billy Watson, *Hattie:* Madame Sul-Te-Wan, *Beavers:* Spencer Charters, *Rondo, Bodyguard:* Rondo Hatton, *Carrie Donahue:* Thelma Manning, *Miss Lou:* Ruth Gillette, *Drunk:* Eddie Collins, *Beef King:* Scotty Mattraw, *Stuttering Clerk:* Joe Twerp, *Booking Agent:* Charles Lane, *Lawyer:* Clarence Hummel Wilson, *Judge:* Frank Dae, *Fire Commissioner:* Harry Stubbs, *Ship's Captain:* Joe King, *Driver:* Francis Ford, *Police Officers:* Robert Murphy, Wade Boteler, *Men in Jack's Office:* Gustav von Seyffertitz, Russell Hicks, *Specialty:* Rice and Cady, *Johnson, Secretary:* Harry Hayden, *Witness:* Vera Lewis, *Wagon Driver:* Ed Brady, *Frantic Mother:* Minerva Urecal.

In Old Chicago with Alice Faye and Tyrone Power.

In Old Kentucky with Will Rogers and Bill Robinson.

IN OLD KENTUCKY (1935) Fox. Produced by Edward Butcher. Directed by George Marshall. Story, Charles T. Dazey. Screenplay, Sam Hellman and Gladys Lehman. Photography, L. W. O'Connell. 86 minutes

Steve Tapley: Will Rogers, *Nancy Martingale:* Dorothy Wilson, *Lee Andrews:* Russell Hardie, *Wash Jackson:* Bill Robinson, *Arlene Shattuck:* Louise Henry, *Slick Doherty:* Alan Dinehart, *Ezra Martingale:* Charles Sellon, *Pole Shattuck:* Charles Richman, *Dolly Breckenridge:* Esther Dale, *The Rain Maker:* Etienne Girardot, *The Sheriff:* John Ince, *Jockey:* Fritz Johannet, *Jailer:* Everett Sullivan, *Deputy Officer:* G. Raymond (Bill) Nye, *Bit:* William J. Worthington, *Steward:* Edward Le Saint, *Jockey:* Bobby Rose, *Saleslady:* Dora Clemant, *Bookie:* Ned Norton, *Jockey:* Eddie Tamblyn, *Stewards:* Allen Cavan, Stanley Andrews.

Interiors with Marybeth Hurt and Diane Keaton.

INTERIORS (1978) UA. Produced by Charles H. Joffe. A Jack Rollins–Charles H. Joffe Production. Directed and Written by Woody Allen. Executive Producer, Robert Greenhut. Photography, Gordon Willis. Editor, Ralph Rosenblum. Production Designer, Mel Bourne. Costume Designer, Joel Schumacher. Casting, Juliet Taylor. Production Supervisor, John Nicolella. 1st Assistant Director, Martin Berman. Unit Publicist, Scott McDonough. Heard is "Keepin' out of Mischief Now" by the Tommy Dorsey Orchestra. Filmed in New York in Panavision and Technicolor. Rated PG. 99 minutes

Renata: Diane Keaton, *Arthur:* E. G. Marshall, *Eve:* Geraldine Page, *Pearl:* Maureen Stapleton, *Joey:* Marybeth Hurt, *Mike:* Sam Waterston, *Frederick:* Richard Jordan, *Flyn:* Kristin Griffith, *Judge Bartel:* Henderson Forsythe.

INTERRUPTED MELODY (1955) MGM. Producer, Jack Cummings. Director, Curtis Bernhardt. CinemaScope, Eastman Color. Based on her life story by Marjorie Lawrence. Screenplay, William Ludwig, Sonya Levien. Art Directors, Cedric Gibbons, Daniel B. Cathcart. Operatic recordings supervised and conducted by Walter Du Cloux. Musical Supervision, Saul Chaplin. Music Adviser, Harold Gelman. Dramatic music score adapted and conducted by Adolph Deutsch. Cinematographers, Joseph Ruttenberg, Paul C. Vogel. Editor, John Dunning. Eileen Farrell sings for Eleanor Parker. 106 minutes

Dr. Thomas King: Glenn Ford, *Marjorie Lawrence:* Eleanor Parker, *Cyril Lawrence:* Roger Moore, *Bill Lawrence:* Cecil Kellaway, *Dr. Ed Ryson:* Peter Leeds, *Clara:* Evelyn Ellis, *Jim Owens:* Walter Baldwin, *Madame Gilly:* Ann Codee, *Himself:* Leopold Sachse, *Comte Claude des Vigneux:* Stephen Bekassy, *Ted Lawrence:* Charles R. Keane, *Eileen Lawrence:* Fiona Hale, *Tenors:* Rudolf Petrak, William Olvis, *Volunteer Worker:* Doris Lloyd, *Adjudicator:* Alex Frazer, *Gilly Secretary:* Penny Santon, *Louise:* Phyllis Altivo, *Tenor's Manager:*

Gabor Curtiz, *Tenor:* Claude Stroud, *Monsieur Bertrand:* Andre Charlot, *Metropolitan Cashier:* Paul McGuire, *Nurse:* Doris Merrick, *Suzie:* Sandra Descher, *Mr. Norson:* Jack Raine, *Accompanist:* Freda Stoll, *Mrs. Schultz:* Gloria Rhods, *Man on Beach:* Stuart Whitman, *Vocal Student:* Eileen Farrell.

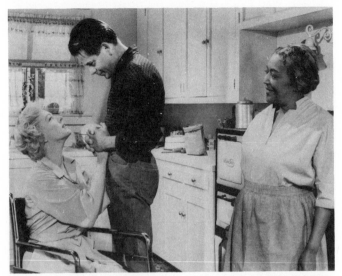

Interrupted Melody with Eleanor Parker, Glenn Ford and Evelyn Ellis.

In the Heat of the Night with Sidney Poitier and Rod Steiger.

IN THE HEAT OF THE NIGHT (1967) UA. Produced by Walter Mirisch. Directed by Norman Jewison. A Mirisch Corporation Presentation. In De Luxe Color. Based on the novel by John Ball. Screenplay, Stirling Silliphant. Supervision, Allan K. Wood. Production Manager, James E. Henderling. Art Director, Paul Groesse. Sets, Bob Priestley. Music, Quincy Jones. Title song by Quincy Jones, Marilyn and Alan Bergman, sung by The Ray Charles Singers. Assistant Directors, Newton Arnold and Terry Morse, Jr. Titles, Murray Naidich. Photography, Haskell Wexler. Editor, Hal Ashby. Sound, Walter Goss. Filmed in Sparta, Ill. 109 minutes. First Mr. Tibbs movie; others: *They Call Me MISTER Tibbs* (1970); *The Organization* (1971), both with Poitier.

Virgil Tibbs: Sidney Poitier, *Police Chief Bill Gillespie:* Rod Steiger, *Deputy Sam Wood:* Warren Oates, *Mrs. Leslie Colbert:* Lee Grant, *Purdy:* James Patterson, *Delores Purdy:* Quentin Dean, *Eric Endicott:* Larry Gates, *Webb Schubert:* William Schallert, *Mama Caleba (Mrs. Bellamy):* Beah Richards, *Harvey Oberst:* Scott Wilson, *Philip Colbert:* Jack Teter, *Packy Harrison:* Matt Clark, *Ralph Henshaw:* Anthony James, *H. E. Henderson:* Kermit Murdock, *Jess:* Khalil Bezaleel, *George Courtney:* Peter Whitney, *Harold Courtney:* William

Watson, *Shagbag Martin:* Timothy Scott, *City Council:* Michael LeGlaire, Larry D. Mann, Stewart Nisbet, *Charlie Hawthorne:* Eldon Quick, *Dr. Stuart:* Fred Stewart, *Ted Ulam:* Arthur Malet, *Arnold Fryer:* Peter Masterson, *Engineers:* Alan Oppenheimer, Philip Garris, *Henry:* Jester Hairston, *Deputy:* Clegg Hoyt, *Young Toughs:* Phil Adams Nikita Knatz, *Baggage Master:* David Stinehart, *Conductor:* Buzz Barton.

Intruder in the Dust with Elizabeth Patterson, Elzie Emanuel and Claude Jarman, Jr.

INTRUDER IN THE DUST (1949) MGM. Producer, Clarence Brown. Director, Clarence Brown. Based on the novel by William Faulkner. Screenplay, Ben Maddow. Music Score, Adolph Deutsch. Art Directors, Cedric Gibbons, Randell Duell. Photography, Robert Surtees. Editor, Robert J. Kern. 89 minutes

John Gavin Stevens: David Brian, *Chick Mallison:* Claude Jarman Jr., *Lucas Beauchamp:* Juano Hernandez, *Nub Gowrie:* Porter Hall, *Miss Habersham:* Elizabeth Patterson, *Crawford Gowrie:* Charles Kemper, *Sheriff Hampton:* Will Geer, *Vinson Gowrie:* David Clarke, *Aleck:* Elzie Emanuel, *Mrs. Mallison:* Lela Bliss, *Mr. Mallison:* Harry Hayden, *Mr. Tubbs:* Harry Antrim, *Will Legate:* Dan White, *Paralee:* Alberta Dishmon, *Mr. Lilley:* R. X. Williams, *Gowrie Twins:* Ephraim Lowe, Edmund Lowe, *Molly Beauchamp:* Julia S. Marshbanks, *Truck Driver:* Jack Odom, *Barber:* Freddie B. Patton, *Deputy:* W. G. Kimmons, *Fraser's Son:* Eugene Roper, *Negro Convicts:* John Morgan, James Kirkwood, *Girl:* Ann Hartsfield, *Attendant:* Ben H. Hilbun.

I Remember Mama with Philip Dorn, Irene Dunne, Barbara Bel Geddes, Steve Brown and June Hedin.

135

I REMEMBER MAMA (1948) RKO. Producers, George Stevens, Harriet Parsons. Director, George Stevens. Based on the 1944 play by John Van Druten and Kathryn Forbes' novel, *Mama's Bank Account*. Screenplay, DeWitt Bodeen. Art Directors, Albert S. D'Agostino, Carroll Clark. Music, Roy Webb. Music Director, C. Bakaleinikoff. Photography, Nick Musuraca. Editor, Robert Swink. Later the basis for a TV series. 134 minutes

Mama: Irene Dunne, *Katrin:* Barbara Bel Geddes, *Uncle Chris:* Oscar Homolka, *Papa:* Philip Dorn, *Mr. Hyde:* Sir Cedric Hardwicke, *Peter Thorkelsen:* Edgar Bergen, *Dr. Johnson:* Rudy Vallee, *Jessie Brown:* Barbara O'Neil, *Florence Dana Moorehead:* Florence Bates, *Christine:* Peggy McIntyre, *Dagmar:* June Hedin, *Nels:* Steve Brown, *Aunt Trina:* Ellen Corby, *Aunt Jenny:* Hope Landin, *Aunt Sigrid:* Edith Evanson, *Cousin Arne:* Tommy Ivo, *Nurse:* Lela Bliss, *Nurse:* Constance Purdy, *Minister:* Stanley Andrews, *Man:* Franklyn Farnum, *Schoolteacher:* Cleo Ridgley, *Postman:* George Atkinson.

Island in the Sun with Harry Belafonte and Dorothy Dandridge.

ISLAND IN THE SUN (1957) 20th. Producer, Darryl F. Zanuck. Director, Robert Rossen. Screenplay by Alfred Hayes. Based on the novel by Alec Waugh. Music by Malcolm Arnold. Assistant Director, Gerry O'Hara. Costumes by David Ffolkes. In CinemaScope and De Luxe Color. Filmed in Granada and the Barbados. 119 minutes

Maxwell Fleury: James Mason, *Mavis:* Joan Fontaine, *Margot Seaton:* Dorothy Dandridge, *Jocelyn:* Joan Collins, *Hilary Carson:* Michael Rennie, *Mrs. Fleury:* Diana Wynyard, *Col. Whittingham:* John Williams, *Euan Templeton:* Stephen Boyd, *Sylvia:* Patricia Owens, *Julian Fleury:* Basil Sydney, *David Archer:* John Justin, *The Governor:* Ronald Squire, *Bradshaw:* Hartley Power, *David Boyeur:* Harry Belafonte.

IT HAPPENED ONE NIGHT (1934) Col. Produced by Harry Cohn. Directed by Frank Capra. Based on the *Cosmopolitan* magazine short story "Night Bus" by Samuel Hopkins Adams. Screenplay, Robert Riskin. Art Director, Stephen Goosson. Assistant Director, C.C. Coleman. Photography, Joseph Walker. Editor, Gene Havlick. Sound, E. E. Bernds. Costumes, Robert Kalloch. Music Director, Louis Silvers. Remade as *You Can't Run Away From It* (Columbia, 1956), *Eve Knew Her Apples* (Columbia, 1945). 105 minutes

Peter Warne: Clark Gable, *Ellie Andrews:* Claudette Colbert, *Oscar Shapeley:* Roscoe Karns, *Alexander Andrews:* Walter Connolly, *Danker:* Alan Hale, *Bus Driver:* Ward Bond, *Bus Driver:* Eddy Chandler, *King Westley:* Jameson Thomas, *Lovington:* Wallis Clark, *Zeke:* Arthur Hoyt, *Zeke's Wife:* Blanche Frederici, *Joe Gordon:* Charles C. Wilson, *Reporter:* Charles D. Brown, *Henderson:* Harry C. Bradley, *Auto Camp Manager:* Harry Holman, *Manager's Wife:* Maidel Turner, *Station Attendant:* Irving Bacon, *Flag Man:* Harry Todd, *Tony:*

Frank Yaconelli, *Drunken Boy:* Henry Wadsworth, *Mother:* Claire McDowell, *Detectives:* Ky Robinson, Frank Holliday, James Burke, Joseph Crehan, *Drunk:* Milton Kibbee, *Vender:* Mickey Daniels, *Dykes:* Oliver Eckhardt, *Boy:* George Breakston, *Secretary:* Bess Flowers, *Minister:* Father Dodd, *Best Man:* Edmund Burns, *Maid of Honor:* Ethel Sykes, *Old Man:* Tom Ricketts, *Radio Announcer:* Eddie Kane, *Bus Passengers:* Ernie Adams, Kit Guard, Billy Engle, Allen Fox, Marvin Loback, Dave Wengren, Bert Starkey, Rita Ross, *Reporter:* Hal Price.

It Happened One Night with Clark Gable and Claudette Colbert.

It's a Mad, Mad, Mad, Mad World with Sid Caesar and Edie Adams.

IT'S A MAD, MAD, MAD, MAD WORLD (1963) UA. Producer-Director, Stanley Kramer. Screenplay, William and Tania Rose. Music, Ernest Gold. In Ultra Panavision and Technicolor. A Casey Production. Title song by Ernest Gold and Mack David. Cinematography, Ernest Laszlo. Editors, Frederic Knudson, Robert C. Jones, and Gene Fowler Jr. Sound Director, Gordon E. Sawyer. Sound Effects, Walter G. Elliott. Stunt Supervisor, Carey Loftin. Dance sequence played by The Shirelles, sung by The Four Mads. Filmed at Santa Rosita Beach State Park. 190 minutes (cut to 153 minutes)

Captain C. G. Culpeper: Spencer Tracy, *J. Russell Finch:* Milton Berle, *Melville Crump:* Sid Caesar, *Benjy Benjamin:* Buddy Hackett, *Mrs. Marcus:* Ethel Merman, *Ding Bell:* Mickey Rooney, *Sylvester Marcus:* Dick Shawn, *Otto Meyer:* Phil Silvers, *Lientenant Colonel J. Algernon Hawthorne:* Terry-Thomas, *Lennie Pike:* Jonathan Winters, *Monica Crump:* Edie Adams, *Emmeline Finch:* Dorothy Provine,

First Cab Driver: Eddie "Rochester" Anderson, *Tyler Fitzgerald:* Jim Backus, *Airplane Pilot:* Ben Blue, *Police Sergeant:* Alan Carney, *Mrs. Halliburton:* Barrie Chase, *Chief of Police:* William Demarest, *Second Cab Driver:* Peter Falk, *Col. Wilberforce:* Paul Ford, *Third Cab Driver:* Leo Gorcey, *Dinckler:* Edward Everett Horton, *Jimmy, the Crook:* Buster Keaton, *Nervous Man:* Don Knotts, *Tower Control:* Carl Reiner, *Firemen:* Moe Howard, Larry Fine, Joe DeRita (The Three Stooges), *Union Official:* Joe E. Brown, *Sheriff Mason:* Andy Devine, *Fire Chief:* Sterling Holloway, *Irwin:* Marvin Kaplan, *Airport Manager:* Charles Lane, *Lieutenant Matthews:* Charles McGraw, *Switchboard Operator:* ZaSu Pitts, *Police Secretary Schwartz:* Madlyn Rhue, *Ray:* Arnold Stang, *Radio Tower Operator:* Jesse White, *Mayor:* Lloyd Corrigan, *Culpeper's Wife:* Voice of Selma Diamond, *Deputy Sheriff:* Stan Freberg, *Billie Sue:* Voice of Louise Glenn, *George, the Steward:* Ben Lessy, *Pilot's Wife:* Bobo Lewis, *Miner:* Mike Mazurki, *Truck Driver:* Nick Stewart, *Chinese Laundryman:* Sammee Tong, *Detectives:* Norman Fell, Nicholas Georgiade, *Smiler Grogan:* Jimmy Durante, *Police Officer:* Allen Jenkins, *Detective:* Stanley Clements, *Radio Operator:* Harry Lauter, *Salesman:* Doodles Weaver, *Traffic Cop:* Tom Kennedy, *Bits:* Chick Chandler, Barbara Pepper, Cliff Norton, Roy Roberts, *Tower Radioman:* Eddie Ryder, *Helicopter Observer:* Don C. Harvey, *Patrolmen:* Roy Engel, Paul Birch, *Stuntman:* Dale Van Sickel, *Man on Road:* Jack Benny, *Mad Driver:* Jerry Lewis.

It's a Wonderful Life with William Edmunds, James Stewart and Stanley Andrews.

IT'S A WONDERFUL LIFE (1946) RKO. Produced and directed by Frank Capra. A Liberty Films Production. Based on the short story "The Greatest Gift" by Philip Van Doren Stern. Screenplay, Frances Goodrich, Albert Hackett, and Frank Capra. Additional Scenes, Jo Swerling. Music composed and directed by Dimitri Tiomkin. Art Director, Jack Okey. Photography, Joseph Walker and Joseph Biroc. Editor, William Hornbeck. 129 minutes. TV remake: *It Happened One Christmas* (1977) with Marlo Thomas in Stewart's role

George Bailey: James Stewart, *Mary Hatch:* Donna Reed, *Mr. Potter:* Lionel Barrymore, *Uncle Billy:* Thomas Mitchell, *Clarence:* Henry Travers, *Mrs. Bailey:* Beulah Bondi, *Ernie:* Frank Faylen, *Bert:* Ward Bond, *Violet Bick:* Gloria Grahame, *Mr. Gower:* H. B. Warner, *Sam Wainwright:* Frank Albertson, *Harry Bailey:* Todd Karns, *Pa Bailey:* Samuel S. Hinds, *Cousin Tilly:* Mary Treen, *Ruth Dakin:* Virginia Patton, *Cousin Eustace:* Charles Williams, *Mrs. Hatch:* Sarah Edwards. *Mr. Martini:* Bill Edmunds, *Annie:* Lillian Randolph, *Mrs. Martini:* Argentina Brunetti, *Little George:* Bobby Anderson, *Little Sam:* Ronnie Ralph, *Little Mary:* Jean Gale, *Little Violet:* Jeanine Anne Roose, *Little Marty Hatch:* Danny Mummert, *Little Harry Bailey:* Georgie Nokes, *Nick:* Sheldon Leonard, *Potter's Bodyguard:* Frank Hagney, *Joe (Luggage Shop):* Ray Walker, *Real Estate Salesman:* Charlie Lane, *The Bailey Children: Janie:* Carol Coomes, *Zuzu:* Karolyn Grimes, *Pete:* Larry Sims, *Tommy:* Jimmy Hawkins, *High School Principal:* Harry Holman, *Marty Hatch:* Hal Landon, *Freddie:* Alfalfa Switzer, *Mickey:* Bobby Scott, *Dr. Campbell:* Harry Cheshire, *Bit:* Ellen Corby, *Drinker:* Stanley Andrews.

IVANHOE (1952) MGM. Producer, Pandro S. Berman. Director, Richard Thorpe. Technicolor. Screenplay, Noel Langley. Adaptation by Aeneas MacKenzie. Based on the novel by Sir Walter Scott. Music, Miklos Rozsa. Filmed in England. 106 minutes

Ivanhoe: Robert Taylor, *Rebecca:* Elizabeth Taylor, *Rowena:* Joan Fontaine, *De Bois-Guilbert:* George Sanders, *Wamba:* Emlyn Williams, *Sir Hugh De Bracy:* Robert Douglas, *Cedric:* Finlay Currie, *Isaac:* Felix Aylmer, *Font De Boeuf:* Francis DeWolff, *Prince John:* Guy Rolfe, *King Richard:* Norman Wooland, *Waldemar Fitzurse:* Basil Sydney, *Locksley:* Harold Warrender.

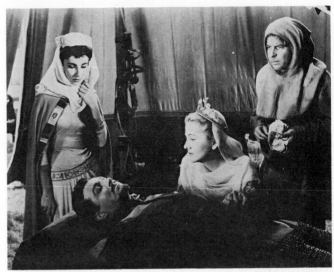

Ivanhoe with Elizabeth Taylor, Robert Taylor, Joan Fontaine and Emlyn Williams.

I Wake Up Screaming with Alan Mowbray, Carole Landis, Allyn Joslyn and Victor Mature.

I WAKE UP SCREAMING (1941) 20th. Produced by Milton Sperling. Directed by H. Bruce Humberstone. Based on the novel by Steve Fisher. Screenplay, Dwight Taylor. Photography, Edward Cronjager. Music Director, Cyril J. Mockridge. Editor, Robert Simpson. Song, "The Things I Love" by Harold Barlow and Lewis Harris. Themes, "Street Scene Theme" and "Over the Rainbow." Locations filmed in New York. 81 minutes. Remade as *Vicki* (20th, 1953)

Jill Lynn: Betty Grable, *Frankie Christopher (Botticelli):* Victor Mature, *Vicky Lynn:* Carole Landis, *Ed Cornell:* Laird Cregar, *Jerry McDonald:* William Gargan, *Robin Ray:* Alan Mowbray, *Larry Evans:* Allyn

Joslyn, *Harry Williams:* Elisha Cook, Jr., *Reporter:* Chick Chandler, *Assistant D. A.:* Morris Ankrum, *Mrs. Handel:* May Beatty, *Reporter:* Cyril Ring, *Florist Keating:* Charles Lane, *Caretaker:* Frank Orth, *Headwaiter:* Gregory Gaye, *Newsboy:* Stanley Clements, *Detectives:* Dick Rich, James Flavin, Tim Ryan, *Detective-partners:* Ralph Dunn, Wade Boteler, *Police Matron:* Cecil Weston, *Cop:* Stanley Blystone, *Officer Murphy:* Harry Strang, *Old Man:* Edward McWade, *Bartender:* Harry Seymour, *Newsman:* Pat McKee, *Waiter:* Albert Pollet, *Girl at Table:* Dorothy Dearing, *Mr. Handel:* Forbes Murray, *Extra:* Brooks Benedict.

I Wanted Wings with Wayne Morris, William Holden and Brian Donlevy.

I WANTED WINGS (1941) Par. Produced by Arthur Hornblow, Sr. Directed by Mitchell Leisen. Screenplay by Richard Maibaum, Lieut. Beirne Lay, Jr. and Sig Herzig. Based on a story by Eleanore Griffin and Frank Wead. From the book *I Wanted Wings* by Lieut. Beirne Lay, Jr. Art Directors, Hans Dreier and Robert Usher. Editor, Hugh Bennett. Director of Photography: Leo Tover. Aerial photography by Elmer Dyer. Song, "Born to Love," by Ned Washington and Victor Young. 131 minutes

Jeff Young: Ray Milland, *Al Ludlow:* William Holden, *Tom Cassidy:* Wayne Morris, *Capt. Mercer:* Brian Donlevy, *Carolyn Bartlett:* Constance Moore, *Sally Vaughn:* Veronica Lake, *"Sandbags" Riley:* Harry Davenport, *Jimmy Masters:* Phil Brown, *President of the Court:* Edward Fielding, *Judge Advocate:* Willard Robertson, *Flight Commander:* Richard Lane, *Flight Surgeon:* Addison Richards, *Mickey:* Hobart Cavanaugh, *Lieut. Hopkins:* Douglas Aylesworth, *Lieut. Ronson:* John Trent, *Lieut. Clankton:* Archie Twitchell, *Cadet Captain:* Richard Webb, *Radio Announcer:* John Hiestand, *Montgomery (copilot):* Harlan Warde, *Ranger:* Lane Chandler, *Cadet:* Charles Drake, *Cadet:* Alan Hale, Jr., *Cadet:* Renny McEvoy, *Detective:* Ed Peil, Sr., *Detective:* Frank O'Connor, *Corporal:* James Millican, *Sergeant:* Emory Johnson, *Supply Sergeant:* Russ Clark, *Private:* George Turner, *Private:* Hal Brazeale, *Cadet Adjutant:* Warren Ashe, *Meteorology Instructor:* Charles A. Hughes, *Buzzer Class Instructor:* George Lollier, *Mrs. Young:* Hedda Hopper, *Mr. Young:* Herbert Rawlinson.

I WANT TO LIVE! (1958) UA. Producer, Walter Wanger. Director, Robert Wise. Screenplay, Nelson Gidding and Don Mankiewicz. Based on newspaper articles by Ed Montgomery and letters of Barbara Graham. Music by John Mandel. Assistant Director, George Vieira. A Figaro Production. Jazz played by Gerry Mulligan, Shelly Manne, Art Farmer, Bud Shank, Red Mitchell, Frank Rosolino, Pete Jolly. 120 minutes

Barbara Graham: Susan Hayward, *Ed Montgomery:* Simon Oakland, *Peg:* Virginia Vincent, *Carl Palmberg:* Theodore Bikel, *Henry Graham:* Wesley Lau, *Emmett Perkins:* Philip Coolidge, *Jack Santo:* Lou Krugman, *Bruce King:* James Philbrook, *District Attorney:* Bartlett Robinson, *Richard Tibrow:* Gage Clark, *Al Matthews:* Joe De Santis, *Father Devers:* John Marley, *San Quentin Captain:* Dabbs Greer,

Warden: Raymond Bailey, *Nurse:* Alice Backes, *Matron:* Gertrude Flynn, *San Quentin Sergeant:* Russell Thorson, *Detective Sergeant:* Stafford Repp, *Lieutenant:* Gavin MacLeod, *Ben Miranda:* Peter Breck, *Rita:* Marion Marshall, *Corona Warden:* Olive Blakeney, *Corona Guard:* Lorna Thayer, *Personal Effects Clerk:* Evelyn Scott, *NCO:* Jack Weston, *San Francisco Hood:* Leonard Bell, *Himself:* George Putnam, *Newsman:* Bill Stout, *Bixel:* Jason Johnson, *Judge:* Rusty Lane, *San Quentin Officer:* S. John Launer, *Police Broadcaster:* Dan Sheridan, *Detective:* Wendell Holmes.

I Want to Live! with Susan Hayward.

I Was a Male War Bride with Ann Sheridan and Cary Grant.

I WAS A MALE WAR BRIDE (1949) 20th. Producer, Sol C. Siegel. Director, Howard Hawks. From a story by Henri Rochard. Screenplay, Charles Lederer, Leonard Spigelgass, Hagar Wilde. Musical Director, Lionel Newman. Art Directors, Thomas Little, Walter M. Scott. Photography, Norbert Brodine, O. Borrodaile. Editor, James B. Clark. 105 minutes

Henri Rochard: Cary Grant, *Lieutenant Catherine Gates:* Ann Sheridan, *WACS:* Marion Marshall, Randy Stuart, *Captain Jack Rumsey:* William Neff, *Tony Jewitt:* Eugene Gericke, *Innkeeper's Assistant:*

Ruben Wendorf, *Waiter:* Lester Sharpe, *Trumble:* John Whitney, *Seaman:* Ken Tobey, *Shore Patrol:* Joe Haworth, *Sergeants:* William Pullen, William Self, *Sergeant:* Bill Murphy, *Lieutenant:* Robert Stevenson, *Bartender:* Alfred Linder, *Chaplain:* David McMahon, *First German Policeman:* Otto Reichow, *Second German Policeman:* William Yetter, *French Minister:* Andre Charlot, *Waiter:* Alex Gerry, *Commander Willis:* Russ Conway, *Lieutenant:* Harry Lauter, *Major Prendergast:* Kay Young, *Innkeeper's Wife:* Lillie Kann, *Jail Officer:* Carl Jaffe, *Schindler:* Martin Miller, *Burgermeister:* Paul Hardmuth, *French Notary:* John Serrett.

JAILHOUSE ROCK (1957) MGM. Produced by Pandro S. Berman. Directed by Richard Thorpe. Panavision. Associate Producer, Kathryn Hereford. Based on a story by Ned Young. Screenplay, Guy Trosper. Assistant Director, Robert E. Relyea. An Avon Production. Songs by Mike Stoller and Jerry Leiber, and Roy C. Bennett, Aaron Schroeder, Abner Silver, Sid Tepper, Ben Weisman: "One More Day," "Young and Beautiful," "I Wanna Be Free," "Don't Leave Me Now," "Treat Me Nice," "Jailhouse Rock," "Baby, I Don't Care." Last film of Judy Tyler, 24, who was killed July 3, 1957. 96 minutes

Vince Everett: Elvis Presley, *Peggy Van Alden:* Judy Tyler, *Hunk Houghton:* Mickey Shaughnessy, *Mr. Shores (Narrator):* Vaughn Taylor, *Sherry Wilson:* Jennifer Holden, *Teddy Talbot:* Dean Jones, *Laury Jackson:* Anne Neyland, *Prof. August Van Alden:* Grandon Rhodes, *Mrs. Van Alden:* Katharine Warren, *Mickey Alba:* Don Burnett, *Musicians:* The Jordanaires, *Jake, Bartender:* George Cisar, *Simpson, Convict:* Glenn Strange, *Convict:* John Indrisano, *Extra in Cafe:* Dorothy Abbott, *Bardeman, TV Studio Manager:* Robert Bice, *Warden:* Hugh Sanders, *Sam Brewster:* Percy Helton, *Jack Lease:* Peter Adams, *Studio Head:* William Forrest, *Paymaster:* Dan White, *Dotty:* Robin Raymond, *Ken:* John Day, *Judge:* S. John Launer, *Guard:* Dick Rich, *Cleaning Woman:* Elizabeth Slifer, *Striptease:* Gloria Pall, *Bartender:* Fred Coby, *Shorty:* Walter Johnson, *Drunk:* Frank Kreig, *Record Distributor:* William Tannen, *Record Engineer:* Wilson Wood, TV *Director:* Tom McKee, *Photographer:* Donald Kerr, *Drummond:* Carl Milletaire, *Surgeon:* Francis DeSales, *Hotel Clerk:* Harry Hines.

Jailhouse Rock with Elvis Presley.

JAWS (1975) Univ. Produced by Richard D. Zanuck and David Brown. Directed by Steven Spielberg. Based on the novel by Peter Benchley. Screenplay, Benchley and Carl Gottlieb and Howard Sackler, uncredited. Photography, Bill Butler. Production Designer, Joseph Alves, Jr. Production Manager, Jim Fargo. Production Executive, William S. Gilmore, Jr. Editor, Verna Fields. Music by John Williams. Underwater Photography, Rexford Metz. Assistant Directors, Tom Joyner and Barbara Bass. Panavision and Technicolor. Film debut of Lorraine Gary. Filmed at Martha's Vineyard, Massachusetts. Live shark footage, Ron and Valerie Taylor. Set Decorator, John M. Dwyer. Special Effects, Robert A. Mattey. Sound, John R. Carter and Robert Hoyt. Technical Adviser, Manfred Zendar. Stunt Coordinator, Ted Grossman. Rated PG. 124 minutes

Martin Brody, Police Chief: Roy Scheider, *Quint:* Robert Shaw, *Matt Hooper:* Richard Dreyfuss, *Ellen Brody:* Lorraine Gary, *Larry Vaughn, Mayor:* Murray Hamilton, *Meadows:* Carl Gottlieb, *TV Interviewer:* Peter Benchley, *Deputy Hendricks:* Jeffrey C. Kramer, *Chrissie Watkins:* Susan Backlinie, *Estuary Victim:* Ted Grossman, *Michael Brody:* Chris Rebello, *Sean Brody:* Jay Mello, *Mrs. Kintner:* Lee Fierro, *Alex Kintner:* Jeffrey Voorhees, *Ben Gardner:* Craig Kingsbury, *Medical Examiner:* Dr. Robert Nevin, *Cassidy:* Jonathan Filley, *Charlie:* Robert Chambers, *Denherder:* Edward Chalmers, Jr., *Posner:* Cyprien P. R. Dube, *Polk:* Robert Carroll, *Harbor Master:* Donald Poole, *Iteisel/Mr. Wiseman:* Alfred Wilde.

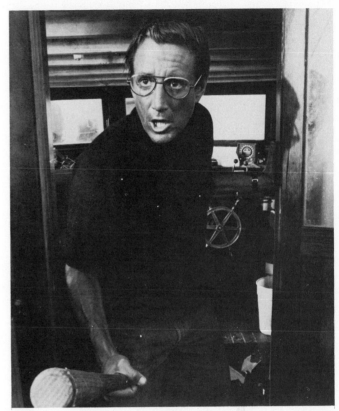

Jaws with Roy Scheider.

JAWS 2 (1978) Univ. Produced by Richard D. Zanuck and David Brown. Directed by Jeannot Szwarc, replacing John Hancock. Panavision and Technicolor. Based on characters created by Peter Benchley. Written by Carl Gottlieb, Howard Sackler and, uncredited, Dorothy Tristan. Photography, Michael Butler. Editor, Neil Travis. Music, John Williams. Production Designer/Associate Producer/2nd Unit Director, Joe Alves. Art Directors, Gene Johnson and Stu Campbell. 2nd Unit Assistant Director, Wilbur Mosier. 2nd Unit Cameramen, David Butler and Michael McGowan. Special Mechanical Effects, Robert A. Mattey and Roy Arbogast. Live shark photography, Ron and Valerie Taylor. Set Decorations, Philip Abramson. Sound, Jim Alexander. 1st Assistant Directors, Scott Maitland and Don Zepfel. 2nd Assistant Directors, Kathy Marie Emde and Beau Marks. Technical Adviser, Manfred Zendar. Marine Coordinator, Philip Kingry. Underwater Cameraman, Michael Dugan. Stunt Coordinator, Ted Grossman. Costume Designer, Bill Jobe. Make-up, Ron Snyder, Rick Sharp and Bob Jiras. Hairstylist, Phil Leto. Editors, Steve Potter and Arthur Schmidt, assisted by Freeman Davies, Jr., Michael T. Elias, Robert Hernandez and Sherrie Sanet Jacobson. Special Photographer, Susan Ford. Filmed in Martha's Vineyard, Massachusetts, and Navarre Beach, Florida. Rated PG. 118 minutes

Chief Martin Brody: Roy Scheider, *Ellen Brody:* Lorraine Gary, *Mayor Larry Vaughan:* Murray Hamilton, *Len Peterson:* Joseph Mascolo, *Deputy Jeff Hendricks:* Jeffrey Kramer, *Dr. Lureen Elkins:* Collin Wilcox, *Tina Wilcox, Miss Amity:* Ann Dusenberry, *Mike Brody:* Mark Gruner, *Andrews:* Barry Coe, *Old Lady:* Susan French, *Andy:* Gary Springer, *Jackie:* Donna Wilkes, *Ed:* Gary Dubin, *Polo:* John Dukakis, *Timmy:* G. Thomas Dunlop, *Larry Vaughan, Jr.:* David Elliott, *Sean Brody:* Marc

Gilpin, *Doug:* Keith Gordon, *Lucy:* Cynthia Grover, *Patrick:* Ben Marley, *Marge:* Martha Swatek, *Bob Burnside:* Billy Van Zandt, *Brooke Peters:* Gigi Vorgan, *Helicopter Pilot:* Jerry M. Baxter, *Ski Boat Driver:* Jean Coulter, *Swimmer #1:* Daphne Dibble, *Swimmer #2:* David Tintle, *Swimmer with Child:* Jim Wilson, *Water Skier:* Christine Freeman, *Renee:* April Gilpin, *Lifeguard:* William Griffith, *Diver #1:* Frank Sparks, *Diver #2:* Greg Harris, *Red:* Coll Red McLean, *Denise, Girl Sailor:* Susan O. McMillan, *Donnie, Boy Sailor:* David Owsley, *Crosby:* Allan L. Paddack, *Ambulance Driver:* Oneida Rollins, *Assistant Dive Master:* Thomas A. Stewart, *Mrs. Bryant:* Kathy Wilson, *Phil Fogarty:* Herb Muller, *Irate Man:* William (Bill) Green.

Jaws 2 with David Elliott, Billy Van Zandt and Gary Springer.

The Jazz Singer with Al Jolson.

THE JAZZ SINGER (1927) WB. Directed by Alan Crosland. Based on the 1925 play by Samson Raphaelson. Adaptation, Alfred A. Cohn. Titles, Jack Jarmuth. Songs: "Blue Skies" by Irving Berlin; "Mammy" by Sam Lewis, Joe Young, Walter Donaldson; "Toot Toot Tootsie, Goodbye" by Gus Kahn, Ernie Erdman, Dan Russo; "Dirty Hands, Dirty Face" by Edgar Leslie, Grant Clarke, Al Jolson, Jimmy Monaco; "Mother I Still Have You" by Al Jolson and Louis Silvers; "Kol Nidre," "Yahrzeit." A part-talking film, considered the first sound movie. Film debut of Al Jolson, 44. Remade by Warners in 1952. 88 minutes

Jakie Rabinowitz (Jack Robin): Al Jolson, *Mary Dale:* May McAvoy, *Cantor Rabinowitz:* Warner Oland, *Sara Rabinowitz:* Eugenie Besserer, *Moisha Yudleson:* Otto Lederer, *Jakie at 13:* Bobbie Gordon, *Harry Lee:* Richard Tucker, *Himself:* Cantor Josef Rosenblatt, *Levi:* Nat Carr, *Buster Billings:* William Demarest, *Dillings:* Anders Randolf, *Doctor:* Will Walling, *The Agent:* Roscoe Karns, *Chorus Girl:* Myrna Loy.

Jeremiah Johnson with Robert Redford and Stefan Gierasch.

JEREMIAH JOHNSON (1972) WB. Produced by Joe Wizan. Directed by Sydney Pollack. A Wizan-Sanford Production, in Panavision and Technicolor. Based on the novel *Mountain Man* by Vardis Fisher and the story "Crow Killer" by Raymond W. Thorp and Robert Bunker. Screenplay, John Milius, Edward Anhalt and David Rayfiel (uncredited). 2nd Unit and Assistant Director, Mike Moder. Associate Producers, John R. Coonan and Mike Moder. Photography, Andrew (Duke) Callaghan. Music, John Rubinstein and Tim McIntire. Editor, Thomas Stanford. Art Director, Ted Haworth. Set Decorations, Raymond Molyneaux. Titles, Phill Norman. Sound, Charles Wilborn, J. Von Stroheim and Mike Colgan. Make-up, Gary Liddiard and Ken Chase. Hairstyles, Lynn Del Kail. Animal Supervision, Kenneth Lee. Production Manager, John R. Coonan. Filmed in Utah. Rated PG. 108 minutes

Jeremiah Johnson: Robert Redford, *Bear Claw:* Will Geer, *Del Gue:* Stefan Gierasch, *Caleb's Mother:* Allyn Ann McLerie, *Robidoux:* Charles Tyner, *Swan:* Delle Bolton, *Caleb:* Josh Albee, *Paints His Shirt Red:* Joaquin Martinez, *Reverend:* Paul Benedict, *Qualen:* Matt Clark, *Lebeaux:* Richard Angarola, *Lt. Mulvey:* Jack Colvin.

Jesse James with Tyrone Power and Nancy Kelly.

140

JESSE JAMES (1939) 20th. Producer, Darryl F. Zanuck. Associate Producer, Nunnally Johnson. Director, Henry King. Technicolor. Original Screenplay, Nunnally Johnson. Technicolor Director, Natalie Kalmus. Art Directors, William Darling, George Dudley. Musical Director, Louis Silvers. Cameraman, George Barnes. Technicolor Photography, W. H. Greene. Editor, Barbara McLean. 105 minutes. Sequel was *The Return of Frank James* (1940) with Fonda.

Jesse James: Tyrone Power, *Frank James:* Henry Fonda, *Zee:* Nancy Kelly, *Will Wright:* Randolph Scott, *Major:* Henry Hull, *Jailer:* Slim Summerville, *Runyon, Pinkerton Man:* J. Edward Bromberg, *Barshee:* Brian Donlevy, *The Killer:* John Carradine, *Mc Coy:* Donald Meek, *Jesse James, Jr.:* John Russell, *Mrs. Samuels:* Jane Darwell, *Charles Ford:* Charles Tannen, *Mrs. Ford:* Claire Du Brey, *Clark:* Willard Robertson, *Lynch:* Paul Sutton, *Pinky:* Ernest Whitman, *Bill:* Paul Burns, *Preacher:* Spencer Charters, *Tom:* Arthur Aylsworth, *Heywood:* Charles Halton, *Roy:* George Chandler, *Old Marshall:* Erville Alderson, *Farmer:* Harry Tyler, *Farmer Boy:* George Breakston, *Boy's Mother:* Virginia Brissac, *Judge Rankin:* Edward J. Le Saint, *Judge Matthews:* John Elliott, *One of Jesse's Gang:* Lon Chaney, Jr., *Engineer:* Harry Holman, *Barshee's Henchmen:* Wylie Grant, Ethan Laidlaw, *Infantry Captain:* Don Douglas, *Cavalry Captain:* James Flavin, *Teller:* George O'Hara, *Doctor:* Charles Middleton.

Jezebel with Bette Davis, Henry Fonda and Jac George.

JEZEBEL (1938) WB. Associate Producer, Henry Blanke. Directed by William Wyler. From the play by Owen Davis, Sr. Screenplay, Clements Ripley, Abem Finkel, and John Huston. Art Director, Robert Haas. Music Score, Max Steiner. Camera, Ernest Haller. Editor, Warren Low. Songs, "Jezebel," by Johnny Mercer and Harry Warren; "Raise a Ruckus" by Warren and Dubin. 104 minutes

Julie Morrison: Bette Davis, *Preston Dillard:* Henry Fonda, *Buck Cantrell:* George Brent, *Amy Bradford Dillard:* Margaret Lindsay, *Aunt/Belle Massey:* Fay Bainter, *Ted Dillard:* Richard Cromwell, *Dr. Livingstone:* Donald Crisp, *General Bogardus:* Henry O'Neill, *Jean La Cour:* John Litel, *Dick Allen:* Gordon Oliver, *Molly Allen:* Janet Shaw, *Mrs. Kendrick:* Spring Byington, *Stephanie Kendrick:* Margaret Early, *Huger:* Irving Pichel, *De Lautrec:* Georges Renavent, *Uncle Cato:* Lew Payton, *Gros Bat:* Eddie Anderson, *Zette:* Theresa Harris, *Ti Bat:* Stymie Beard, *Mrs. Petion:* Georgia Caine, *Bob:* Fred Lawrence, *Madame Poulard, Dressmaker:* Ann Codee, *Durette:* Jacques Vanaire, *Negro Flower Girl:* Daisy Bufford, *Negro Servant:* Jesse A. Graves, *First Director:* Frederick Burton, *Second Director:* Edward McWade, *Bookkeeper:* Frank Darien, *Midinette:* Suzanne Dulier, *Jenkins:* John Harron, *Erronens:* Phillip "Lucky" Hurlic, *Errata:* Dolores Hurlic, *Deputy Sheriff:* Davison Clark, *Sheriff at Plantation:* Trevor Bardette, *Fugitive Planter:* George Guhl, *Drunk:*

Jack Norton, *Bar Companion:* Louis Mercier, *New Orleans Sheriff:* Alan Bridge, *Customer:* Charles Wagenheim, *Orchestra Leader:* Jac George.

Joan of Arc with Herbert Rudley, Shepperd Strudwick, Ingrid Bergman and Aubrey Mather.

JOAN OF ARC (1948) RKO-Sierra. Producer, Walter Wanger. Director, Victor Fleming. Color by Technicolor. Adapted from Maxwell Anderson's play *Joan of Lorraine.* Screenplay, Maxwell Anderson, Andrew Solt. Musical Director, Emil Newman. Art Director, Richard Day. Photography, Joe Valentine, Editor, Frank Sullivan. Film debut of José Ferrer. 145 minutes

Joan of Arc: Ingrid Bergman, *Dauphin:* José Ferrer, *Robert De Baudricourt:* George Coulouris, *Jean De Metz:* Richard Derr, *Bertrand De Poulengy:* Ray Teal, *Durand Laxart:* Roman Bohnen, *Jacques D'Arc:* Robert Barrat, *Pierre D'Arc:* Jimmy Lydon, *Jean D'Arc:* Rand Brooks, *Isabelle D'Arc:* Selene Royle, *Pierre Cauchon:* Francis L. Sullivan, *Catherine Le Royer:* Irene Rich, *Henry Le Royer:* Nestor Paiva, *George De La Tremoille:* Gene Lockhart, *Archbishop of Theims:* Nicholas Joy, *Duke of Bedford:* Frederic Worlock, *Raoul De Gaucourt:* Tom Browne Henry, *Duke of Burgundy:* Colin Keith-Johnson, *Alain Chartier:* Vincent Donahue, *Duke of Claremont:* Richard Ney, *Jean Dunois:* Leif Erickson, *Duke of Alencon:* John Emery, *La Hire:* Ward Bond, *St. Severe:* John Ireland, *Giles De Raiz:* Henry Brandon, *Admiral De Culan:* Gregg Barton, *John of Luxembourg:* J. Carrol Naish, *William Glasdale:* Dennis Hoey, *Jean D'Aulon:* Ethan Laidlaw, *Father Pasquerel:* Hurd Hatfield, *Jean Le Maistre:* Cecil Kellaway, *Poton De Xantrailles:* Morris Ankrum, *Jean D'Estivet:* Philip Bourneuf, *Jean Massieu:* Shepperd Strudwick, *Thomas De Courcelles:* Stephen Roberts, *Avranches:* Taylor Holmes, *Nicholas De Houppeville:* Frank Puglia, *Winchester:* Houseley Stevenson, *Nicholas Midi:* Victor Wood, *Earl of Warwick:* Alan Napier, *Thirache (Executioner):* Bill Kennedy, *Jean Fournier:* David Bond, *Constable of Clervaux:* George Zucco, *Isombard De La Pierre:* Herbert Rudley, *La Fontaine:* Aubrey Mather, *Judge Mortemer:* James Kirkwood, *Judge Marguerie:* Herbert Rawlinson, *Judge Courneille:* Matt Moore.

JOE (1970) Cannon. Produced by David Gil. Directed by John G. Avildsen. Color by DeLuxe. Executive Producers, Dennis Friedland and Christopher C. Dewey. Screenplay, Norman Wexler. Music composed and conducted by Bobby Scott. Editor, George T. Norris. Associate Producer/Production Manager, George Manasse. Assistant Directors, Harvey Vincent and Michael Lerner. Photography, John G. Avildsen. Production Assistants, Tom Feledy, Ken Robertson and Lloyd Kaufman. Musical Supervisor, Gene Orloff. Songs: "Hey Joe," lyrics by Danny Meehan, sung by Dean Michaels; "You Don't Know What's Going On," written and sung by Exuma; "Where Are You Going?" and "You Can

Fly," sung by Jerry Butler. Filmed in New York City. Film debut of Sarandon. Rated R. 107 minutes

Joe Curran: Peter Boyle, *Bill Compton:* Dennis Patrick, *Melissa Compton:* Susan Sarandon, *Joan Compton:* Audrey Caire, *Frank Russo:* Patrick McDermott, *Mary Lou Curran:* K. Callan, *Bellevue Nurse:* Marlene Warfield, *Bargain Store Customers:* Estelle Omens, Bob O'Connell, *Teeny Boppers:* Mary Case, Jenny Paine, *American Bartender:* Reid Cruickshanks, *TV Newscaster:* Robert Emerick, *Janine:* Gloria Hoye, *Sam:* Bo Enivel, *Bartender at Ginger Man:* Patrick O'Neil, *Gil Richards:* Frank Moon, *Phyllis:* Jeanne M. Lange, *Poster Shop Proprietor:* Al Sentesy, *Nancy:* Patti Caton, *Gail:* Francine Middleton.

Joe with Dennis Patrick and Peter Boyle.

JOHNNY BELINDA (1948) WB. Producer, Jerry Wald. Director, Jean Negulesco. Based on the play by Elmer Harris. Screenplay, Irmgard Von Cube, Allen Vincent. Art Director, Robert Haas. Musical Director, Leo F. Forbstein. Photography, Ted McCord. Editor, David Weisbart. Film debut of Jan Sterling. 102 minutes

Belinda McDonald: Jane Wyman, *Dr. Robert Richardson:* Lew Ayres, *Black McDonald:* Charles Bickford, *Aggie McDonald:* Agnes Moorehead, *Locky McCormick:* Stephen McNally, *Stella Maguire:* Jan Sterling, *Mrs. Poggety:* Rosalind Ivan, *Pacquet:* Dan Seymour, *Mrs. Lutz:* Mabel Paige, *Mrs. McKee:* Ida Moore, *Defense Attorney:* Alan Napier, *Ben:* Monte Blue, *Mountie:* Douglas Kennedy, *Interpreter:* James Craven, *Floyd McQuiggen:* Richard Taylor (Jeff Richards), *Fergus McQuiggen:* Richard Walsh, *Mrs. Tim Moore:* Joan Winfield, *Rector:* Ian Wolfe, *Judge:* Holmes Herbert, *Dr. Gray:* Jonathan Hale, *Tim Moore:* Ray Montgomery, *Dan'l:* Blayney Lewis, *Gracie Anderson:* Barbara Bates, *Prosecutor:* Fred Worlock, *Bailiff:* Creighton Hale.

Johnny Eager with Joseph Downing, Robert Taylor and Cy Kendall.

JOHNNY EAGER (1941) MGM. Producer, John W. Considine, Jr. Director, Mervyn LeRoy. Author, James Edward Grant. Screenplay, John Lee Mahin, James Edward Grant. Cameraman, Harold Rosson. Editor, Albert Akst. 107 minutes

Johnny Eager: Robert Taylor, *Lisbeth Bard:* Lana Turner, *John Benson Farrell:* Edward Arnold, *Jeff Hartnett:* Van Heflin, *Jimmy Courtney:* Robert Sterling, *Garnet:* Patricia Dane, *Mae Blythe:* Glenda Farrell, *Mr. Verne:* Henry O'Neill, *Judy Sanford:* Diana Lewis, *Lew Rankin:* Barry Nelson, *Marco:* Charles Dingle, *Julio:* Paul Stewart, *Halligan:* Cy Kendall, *Billiken:* Don Costello, *Benjy:* Lou Lubin, *Ryan:* Joseph Downing, *Peg:* Connie Gilchrist, *Matilda:* Robin Raymond, *Miss Mines:* Leona Maricle, *Officer No. 711:* Byron Shores.

JOHNNY GUITAR (1954) Rep. Produced by Herbert J. Yates. Director, Nicholas Ray. Trucolor. Based on Roy Chanslor's novel. Screenplay, Philip Yordan. Art Director, James Sullivan. Cinematographer, Harry Stradling. Editor, Richard L. Van Enger. 110 minutes

Vienna: Joan Crawford, *Johnny Guitar:* Sterling Hayden, *Emma Small:* Mercedes McCambridge, *Dancin' Kid:* Scott Brady, *John McIvers:* Ward Bond, *Turkey Ralston:* Ben Cooper, *Bart Lonergan:* Ernest Borgnine, *Old Tom:* John Carradine, *Corey:* Royal Dano, *Marshall Williams:* Frank Ferguson, *Eddie:* Paul Fix, *Mr. Andrews:* Rhys Williams, *Pete:* Ian MacDonald, *Ned:* Will Wright, *Jake:* John Maxwell, *Sam:* Robert Osterloh, *Frank:* Frank Marlowe, *Jenks:* Trevor Bardette, *Possemen:* Sumner Williams, Sheb Woolley, Denver Pyle, Clem Harvey.

Johnny Belinda with Charles Bickford, Jane Wyman and Lew Ayres.

Johnny Guitar with Ben Cooper, Joan Crawford, Frank Marlowe, Sterling Hayden and Scott Brady.

The Joker Is Wild with Eddie Albert and Frank Sinatra.

THE JOKER IS WILD (1957) Par. Produced by Samuel J. Briskin. Directed by Charles Vidor. In VistaVision. From the book by Art Cohn, based on the life of Joe E. Lewis. Screenplay, Oscar Saul. Art Directors, Hal Pereira and Roland Anderson. Music scored and conducted by Walter Scharf. Assistant Director, C. C. Coleman, Jr. Costumes, Edith Head. Dances staged by Josephine Earl. Photography, Daniel L. Fapp. Special Effects, John P. Fulton. Editor, Everett Douglas. An A. M. B. L. Production. Song by Sammy Cahn and James Van Heusen, "All the Way." Reissued as *All the Way*, 1966. 126 minutes

Joe E. Lewis: Frank Sinatra, *Letty Page:* Jeanne Crain, *Martha Stewart:* Mitzi Gaynor, *Austin Mack:* Eddie Albert, *Cassie Mack:* Beverly Garland, *Swifty Morgan:* Jackie Coogan, *Captain Hugh McCarthy:* Barry Kelley, *Georgie Parker:* Ted de Corsia, *Tim Coogan:* Leonard Graves, *Flora:* Valerie Allen, *Burlesque Comedian:* Hank Henry, *Photographer:* Dennis McMullen, *Heckler:* Wally Brown, *Harry Bliss:* Harold Huber, *Johnson:* Ned Glass, *Dr. Pierson:* Ned (Ed H.) Wever, *Mr. Page:* Walter Woolf King, *Hecklers:* Don Beddoe, Mary Treen, Paul Bryar, *Runner:* Sid Melton, *Man Shaving:* Dick Elliott, *Allen:* John Harding, *Girl:* Lucy Knoch, *Letty's Husband:* William Pullen, *Judge:* Oliver McGowan, *Burlesque Straight Man:* James J. Cavanaugh, *Burlesque Girls:* Harriette Tarler, Paula Hill, *Elevator Starter:* George Offerman, *Jack:* James Cross, *Butler:* Eric Wilton, *Doorman of The Valencia:* Kit Guard, *Mugs:* Paul T. Salata, Bill Hickman, John D. Benson.

JOLSON SINGS AGAIN (1949) Col. Produced by Sidney Buchman. Directed by Henry Levin. Color by Technicolor. Story, Sidney Buchman. Music, George Duning. Music Director, Morris Stoloff. Art Director, Walter Holscher. Photography, William Snyder. Editor, William Lyon. A sequel to 1946's *The Jolson Story*, this was based on the later life and career of Al Jolson, and featured many of his songs. Evelyn Keyes as Julie Benson (based on Ruby Keeler) was seen only in a newspaper photograph. Songs: "I Only Have Eyes For You" by Al Dubin and Harry Warren; "I'm Just Wild About Harry" by Noble Sissle and Eubie Blake; "Ma Blushin' Rosie" by Edgar Smith and John Stromberg; "April Showers" by B. G. DeSylva, and Louis Silvers; "Swanee" by Irving Caesar and George Gershwin; "I'm

Looking Over a Four-Leaf Clover" by Mort Dixon and Harry M. Woods; "California Here I Come" by B. G. DeSylva, Al Jolson and Joseph Meyer; "Chinatown My Chinatown" by Joe Young, Sam Lewis and Jean Schwartz; "Carolina In the Morning" by Gus Kahn and Walter Donaldson; "Pretty Baby" by Gus Kahn, Tony Jackson and Egbert Van Alstyne; "Baby Face" by Benny Davis and Harry Akst. 96 minutes

Al Jolson: Larry Parks, The singing voice of Al Jolson, *Larry Parks:* Larry Parks, *Ellen Clark:* Barbara Hale, *Steve Martin:* William Demarest, *Cantor Yoelson:* Ludwig Donath, *Tom Baron:* Bill Goodwin, *Ralph Bryant:* Myron McCormick, *Mama Yoelson:* Tamara Shayne, *Henry:* Eric Wilton, *Charlie:* Robert Emmett Keane, *Man:* Jock O'Mahoney (Jock Mahoney), *Woman:* Gertrude Astor, *Captain of Waiters:* Peter Brocco, *Soldier:* Dick Cogan, *Mr. Estrada:* Martin Garralaga, *Writer:* Michael Cisney, *Writer:* Ben Erway, *Script Girl:* Helen Mowery, *Orchestra Leader:* Morris Stoloff, *Sound Mixer:* Philip Faulkner, Jr., *Theater Manager:* Nelson Leigh, *Mrs. Bryant:* Virginia Mullen, *Nurse:* Margie Stapp.

Jolson Sings Again with Larry Parks.

THE JOLSON STORY (1946) Col. Produced by Sidney Skolsky. Associate Producer, Gordon Griffith. Directed by Alfred E. Green. Color by Technicolor. Assistant Director, Wilbur McGaugh. Montage Director, Lawrence W. Butler. Screenplay, Stephen Longstreet. Adaptation, Harry Chandlee and Andrew Solt. Dances, Jack Cole. Production Numbers, Joseph H. Lewis. Gowns, Jean Louis. Musical Director, M. W. Stoloff. Photography, Joseph Walker. Technicolor Color Director, Natalie Kalmus. Associate, Morgan Padelford. Editor, William Lyon. Art Directors, Stephen Goosson and Walter Holscher. Sets, William Kiernan and Louis Diage. Make-up, Clay Campbell. Hair Styles, Helen Hunt. Sound, Hugh McDowell. Vocal Arrangements, Saul Chaplin. Orchestral Arrangements, Martin Fried. Music Recording, Edwin Wetzel. Re-recording, Richard Olson. Songs: "By the Light of the Silvery Moon" by Edward Madden and Gus Edwards; "You Made Me Love You" by Joseph McCarthy and Jimmy Monaco; "I'm Sitting on Top of the World" by Sam Lewis, Joe Young and Ray Henderson; "There's a Rainbow 'Round My Shoulder" by Al Jolson, Billy Rose and Dave Dreyer; "My Mammy" by Sam Lewis, Joe Young and Walter Donaldson; "Rock-a-bye Your Baby to a Dixie Melody" by Sam Lewis, Joe Young and Jean Schwartz; "Liza" by Ira and George Gershwin; "Waiting for the Robert E. Lee" by L. Wolfe Gilbert and Lewis E. Muir; "April Showers" by B. G. DeSylva and Louis Silvers; "About a Quarter to Nine" by Al Dubin and Harry Warren; "I Want a Girl Just Like the Girl That Married Dear Old Dad" by Will Dillon and Harry Von Tilzer; "Anniversary Song" by Al Jolson; "The Spaniard Who Blighted My Life" by Billy Merson. Based on the career of Al Jolson, and featuring his songs. A sequel, *Jolson Sings Again* (1949), traced Jolson's later life. Julie Benson is based on Ruby Keeler. 128 minutes

Songs sung by Al Jolson. *Al Jolson:* Larry Parks, *Julie Benson:* Evelyn Keyes, *Steve Martin:* William Demarest, *Tom Baron:* Bill Goodwin, *Cantor Yoelson:* Ludwig Donath, *Mrs. Yoelson:* Tamara Shayne, *Lew Dockstader:* John Alexander, *Ann Murray:* Jo-Carroll Dennison, *Father McGee:* Ernest Cossart, *Al as a boy:* Scotty Beckett, *Dick Glenn:* William Forrest, *Ann as a girl:* Ann E. Todd, *Oscar Hammerstein:* Edwin Maxwell, *Jonsey:* Emmett Vogan, *Ziegfeld:* Eddie Kane, *Roy Anderson:* Jimmy Lloyd, *Young Priest:* Coulter Irwin, *Ingenue:* Adele Roberts, *Henry:* Bob Stevens, *Policeman, Riley:* Harry Shannon, *Call Boy:* Bud Gorman, *Assistant Stage Manager:* Charles Jordan, *Architect:* Pierre Watkin, *Woman:* Lillian Bond, *Headwaiter:* Eugene Borden, *Master of Ceremonies:* Eddie Rio, *Sourpuss Movie Patron:* Will Wright, *Stage Manager:* Arthur Loft, *Director:* Edward Keane, *Assistant Stage Manager:* Eddie Fetherstone, *Orchestra Leader:* Bill Brandt, *Cameraman:* Pat Lane, *Lab Manager:* Mike Lally, *Gaffer:* George Magrill, *Dancer-Actress:* Helen O'Hara, *Wardrobe Woman:* Jessie Arnold, *Girl Publicist:* Donna Dax, *Cutter:* Fred Sears, *Harry, the Butler:* Eric Wilton, *Choir:* The Robert Mitchell Boy Choir, *Extra in Audience:* Franklyn Farnum, *Nightclubber:* Major Sam Harris.

The Jolson Story with John Alexander, Larry Parks and William Demarest.

Journey for Margaret with Laraine Day, Billy Severn, Robert Young and Margaret O'Brien.

JOURNEY FOR MARGARET (1942) MGM. Producer, B. P. Fineman. Director, Major W. S. Van Dyke. Author, William L. White. Screenplay, David Hertz, William Ludwig. Art Director, Cedric Gibbons. Cameraman, Ray June. Editor, George White. 81 minutes

John Davis: Robert Young, *Nora Davis:* Laraine Day, *Trudy Strauss:* Fay Bainter, *Anya:* Signe Hasso, *Margaret:* Margaret O'Brien, *Herbert V. Allison:* Nigel Bruce, *Peter Humphreys:* William Severn,

Rugged: G. P. Huntley, Jr., *Mrs. Barrie:* Doris Lloyd, *Mr. Barrie:* Halliwell Hobbes, *Susan Fleming:* Jill Esmond, *Fairoaks:* Charles Irwin, *Mrs. Bailey:* Elisabeth Risdon, *Frau Weber:* Lisa Golm, *Man:* Herbert Evans, *Child:* Clare Sandars, *Censor:* Leyland Hodgson, *Woman:* Anita Bolster, *Warden:* Matthew Boulton, *Nurse:* Lilyan Irene, *Manager:* Olaf Hytten, *Nurse:* Ottola Nesmith, *Surgeon:* John Burton, *Steward:* Colin Kenny, *Porter:* Jimmy Aubrey, *Mrs. Harris:* Heather Thatcher, *Isabel:* Joan Kemp, *Hans:* Norbert Muller, *Policeman:* Al Ferguson, *Nora's Mother:* Bea Nigro, *Stage Manager:* Cyril Delevanti, *Mme. Bornholm:* Jody Gilbert, *Everton:* Craufurd Kent, *Japanese Statesman:* Keye Luke, *Air Raid Warden:* David Thursby, *Polish Captain:* Henry Guttman.

Journey's End with Billy Bevan and David Manners.

JOURNEY'S END (1930) Tiffany. Directed by James Whale. Supervised by George Pearson. Based on the play by R. C. Sheriff. Scenario, Joseph Moncure March. Art Director, Hervey Libbert. Photography, Benjamin Kline. Editor, Claude Berkeley. Sound, Bud Myers. A Gainsborough Production. Colin Clive repeats his role from the London stage. 130 minutes. Remake as *Aces High* (British, 1976)

Captain Stanhope: Colin Clive, *Lieutenant Osborne:* Ian MacLaren, *Second Lieutenant Raleigh:* David Manners, *Second Lieutenant Hibbert:* Anthony Bushell, *Second Lieutenant Trotter:* Billy Bevan, *Private Mason:* Charles Gerrard, *Captain Hardy:* Robert A'Dair, *Company Sergeant Major:* Thomas Whiteley, *The Colonel:* Jack Pitcairn, *German Soldier:* Werner Klinger.

JUAREZ (1939) WB. Produced by Hal B. Wallis. Directed by William Dieterle. Based on the play *Maximilian and Carlotta* by Franz Werfel and the novel *The Phantom Crown* by Bertita Harding. Associate Producer, Henry Blanke. Screenplay, John Huston, Wolfgang Reinhardt, Aeneas MacKenzie. Art Director, Anton Grot. Music, Erich Wolfgang Korngold. Musical Director, Leo F. Forbstein. Cameraman, Tony Gaudio. Editor, Warren Low. Bette Davis recites an English translation of the Mexican love song "La Paloma." Mexico City sequences filmed at Calabasas, Cal. 132 minutes

Benito Pablo Juarez: Paul Muni, *Empress Carlotta von Habsburg:*

Bette Davis, *Emperor Maximilian von Habsburg:* Brian Aherne, *Louis Napoleon:* Claude Rains, *Porfirio Diaz:* John Garfield, *Marechal Bazaine:* Donald Crisp, *Empress Eugenie:* Gale Sondergaard, *Alejandro Uradi:* Joseph Calleia, *Colonel Miguel Lopez:* Gilbert Roland, *Miguel Miramon:* Henry O'Neill, *Riva Palacio:* Pedro de Cordoba, *Jose de Montares:* Montagu Love, *Dr. Samuel Basch:* Harry Davenport, *Achille Fould:* Walter Fenner, *Drouyn de Lhuys:* Alex Leftwich, *Countess Battenberg:* Georgia Caine, *Major DuPont:* Robert Warwick, *Senor de Leon:* Gennaro Curci, *Tomás Mejía:* Bill Wilkerson, *Mariano Escobedo:* John Miljan, *John Bigelow:* Hugh Sothern, *Senor Salas:* Fred Malatesta, *Tailor:* Carlos de Valdez, *Carbajal:* Irving Pichel, *Coachman:* Frank Lackteen, *Senator del Valle:* Walter O. Stahl, *Duc de Morny:* Frank Reicher, *Marshall Randon:* Holmes Herbert, *Prince Metternich:* Walter Kingsford, *Baron von Magnus:* Egon Brecher, *Lerdo de Tajada:* Monte Blue, *LeMarc:* Louis Calhern, *Pepe:* Manuel Diaz, *Augustin Iturbide:* Mickey Kuhn, *Josefa Iturbide:* Lillian Nicholson, *Regules:* Noble Johnson, *Negroni:* Martin Garralaga, *Camilo:* Vladimir Sokoloff, *Mr. Harris:* Grant Mitchell, *Mr. Roberts:* Charles Halton.

Juarez with Paul Muni.

Judgment at Nuremberg with Spencer Tracy and Marlene Dietrich.

JUDGMENT AT NUREMBERG (1961) UA.

Producer-Director, Stanley Kramer. Associate Producer, Philip Langner. Screenplay, Abby Mann. Music, Ernest Gold. A Roxlom Production. Production Designer, Rudolph Sternad. Cinematographer, Ernest Laszlo. Editor, Fred Knudtson. 178 minutes

Judge Dan Haywood: Spencer Tracy, *Ernst Janning:* Burt Lancaster,

Colonel Tad Lawson: Richard Widmark, *Mme. Bertholt:* Marlene Dietrich, *Hans Rolfe:* Maximilian Schell, *Irene Hoffman:* Judy Garland, *Rudolph Petersen:* Montgomery Clift, *Captain Byers:* William Shatner, *Senator Burkette:* Edward Binns, *Judge Kenneth Norris:* Kenneth MacKenna, *Emil Hahn:* Werner Klemperer, *General Merrin:* Alan Baxter, *Werner Lammpe:* Torben Meyer, *Judge Curtiss Ives:* Ray Teal, *Friedrich Hofstetter:* Martin Brandt, *Mrs. Halbestadt:* Virginia Christine, *Major Abe Radnitz:* Joseph Bernard, *Halbestadt:* Ben Wright, *Dr. Wieck:* John Wengraf, *Dr. Geuter:* Karl Swenson, *Wallner:* Howard Caine, *Pohl:* Otto Waldis, *Mrs. Lindnow:* Olga Fabian, *Mrs. Ives:* Sheilia Bromley, *Perkins:* Bernard Kates, *Elsa Scheffler:* Jana Taylor, *Schmidt:* Paul Busch, *Spectator:* Joseph Crehan.

Julia with Jane Fonda and Jason Robards.

JULIA (1977) 20th.

Produced by Richard Roth. Directed by Fred Zinnemann (who replaced Sydney Pollack). Based on a story in the book *Pentimento* by Lillian Hellman. Screenplay, Alvin Sargent. Executive Producer, Julien Derode. Associate Producer, Tom Pevsner. Photography, Douglas Slocombe. Production designed by Gene Callahan, Willy Holt and Carmen Dillon. Editor, Walter Murch. Music composed and conducted by Georges Delerue. Principals' Costumes designed by Anthea Sylbert. Wardrobe Design, Joan Bridge and Annalisa Nasalli Rocca. Assistant Directors, Alain Bonnot and Anthony Waye. Make-up, George Frost. Fonda's Make-up, Bernadine Anderson. Hairdresser, Ramon Gow. Editor, Marcel Durham. Set Dressers, Pierre Charron and Tessa Davies. 2nd Unit Photography, Paddy Carey and Guy Delattre. Costume Supervision, John Apperson and Colette Baudot. Sound Mixer, Derek Ball. Film debut of Streep. Filmed in England and France; Shepperton Studios, EMI, Elstree, England; Studios de Boulogne, France; beach scenes filmed on the Isle of Wight. Panavision. Technicolor, prints by DeLuxe. Rated PG. 118 minutes

Lillian Hellman: Jane Fonda, *Julia:* Vanessa Redgrave, *Dashiell Hammett:* Jason Robards, *Johann:* Maximilian Schell, *Alan Campbell:* Hal Holbrook, *Dottie Parker:* Rosemary Murphy, *Anne Marie:* Meryl Streep, *Young Julia:* Lisa Pelikan, *Young Lillian:* Susan Jones, *Woman Passenger:* Dora Doll, *Girl Passenger:* Elisabeth Mortensen, *Sammy:* John Glover, *Grandmother:* Cathleen Nesbitt, *Undertaker:* Maurice Denham, *Passport Officer:* Gerard Buhr, *Hamlet:* Stefan Gryff, *Little Boy:* Phillip Siegel, *Woman:* Molly Urquhart, *Butler:* Antony Carrick, *Woman in Berlin Station:* Ann Queensberry, *Man in Berlin Station:* Edmond Bernard, *Fat Man:* Jacques David, *Woman in Green Hat:* Jacqueline Staup, *Vienna Concierge:* Hans Verner, *Paris Concierge:* Christian De Tiliere, *Pratt:* Mark Metcalf, *Customs Officer, New York Port Authority:* Shane Rimmer, *First-Nighter at Sardi's:* Don Koll, *Sardi:* Jim Kane, *Sardi Customer (Extra):* Dick Marr, *Extra:* Vincent Sardi, Jr.

Julius Caesar with Louis Calhern and James Mason.

JULIUS CAESAR (1953) MGM. Producer, John Houseman. Director, Joseph Mankiewicz. Based on the play by William Shakespeare. Art Directors, Cedric Gibbons, Edward Carfagno. Cinematographer, Joseph Ruttenberg. Editor, John Dunning. 120 minutes

Mark Antony: Marlon Brando, *Brutus:* James Mason, *Cassius:* John Gielgud, *Julius Caesar:* Louis Calhern, *Casca:* Edmond O'Brien, *Calpurnia:* Greer Garson, *Portia:* Deborah Kerr, *Marullus:* George Macready, *Flavius.* Michael Pate, *Soothsayer:* Richard Hale, *Cicero:* Alan Napier, *Decius Brutus:* John Hoyt, *Metellus Cimber:* Tom Powers, *Cinna:* William Cottrell, *Trebonius:* Jack Raine, *Casius Ligarius:* Ian Wolfe, *Lucius:* John Hardy, *Artemidorus:* Morgan Farley, *Antony's Servant:* Bill Phipps, *Octavius Caesar:* Douglas Watson, *Lepidus:* Douglass Dumbrille, *Lucillus:* Rhys Williams, *Pindarus:* Michael Ansara, *Messala:* Dayton Lummis, *Volumnius:* Thomas Browne Henry, *Strato:* Edmund Purdom, *Citizens of Rome:* Paul Guilfoyle, John Doucette, Lawrence Dobkin, *Caesar's Servant:* Chester Stratton, *Publius:* Lumsden Hare, *Popilius Lena:* Victor Perry, *Officer:* Michael Tolan, *Varro:* John Lupton, *Claudius:* Preston Hanson, *Titinius:* John Parrish, *Clitus:* Joe Waring, *Dardanius:* Stephen Roberts, *Cinna, Poet:* O. Z. Whitehead, *Cobbler:* Ned Glass.

Keeper of the Flame with Spencer Tracy, Darryl Hickman and Katharine Hepburn.

KEEPER OF THE FLAME (1942) MGM. Produced by Victor Saville. Associate Producer, Leon Gordon. Directed by George Cukor. Based on the novel by I. A. R. Wylie. Screenplay, Donald Ogden Stewart. Art Director, Cedric Gibbons. Score, Bronislau Kaper. Camera, William Daniels. Editor, James E. Newcom. 100 minutes

Steven O'Malley: Spencer Tracy, *Christine Forrest:* Katharine Hepburn, *Clive Spencer:* Richard Whorf, *Mrs. Forrest:* Margaret Wycherly, *Mr. Arbuthnot:* Donald Meek, *Freddie Ridges:* Horace (Stephen) McNally, *Jane Harding:* Audrey Christie, *Dr. Fielding:* Frank Craven, *Geoffrey Midford:* Forrest Tucker, *Orion:* Percy Kilbride, *Jason Rickards:* Howard da Silva, *Jeb Rickards:* Darryl Hickman, *Piggot:* William Newell, *John:* Rex Evans, *Anna:* Blanche Yurka, *Janet:* Mary McLeod, *William:* Clifford Brooke, *Ambassador:* Craufurd Kent, *Messenger Boy:* Mickey Martin, *Reporters:* Manart Kippen, Donald Gallaher, Cliff Danielson, *Men:* Major Sam Harris, Art Howard, Harold Miller, *Pete:* Jay Ward, *Susan:* Rita Quigley, *Auctioneer:* Dick Elliott, *Lawyer:* Edward McWade, *Boy Reporter:* Irvin Lee, *Girls:* Diana Dill (Diana Douglas), Gloria Tucker, *Minister's Voice:* Dr. Charles Frederick Lindsley, *Tim:* Robert Pittard, *Gardener:* Louis Mason.

Key Largo with Humphrey Bogart, Claire Trevor and Lauren Bacall.

KEY LARGO (1948) WB. Producer, Jerry Wald. Director, John Huston. Based on the play by Maxwell Anderson. Screenplay, Richard Brooks, John Huston. Art Director, Leo K. Kuter. Music, Max Steiner. Photography, Karl Freund. Editor, Rudi Fehr. Song by Howard Dietz and Ralph Rainger: "Moanin' Low." 101 minutes

Frank McCloud: Humphrey Bogart, *Johnny Rocco:* Edward G. Robinson, *Nora Temple:* Lauren Bacall, *James Temple:* Lionel Barrymore, *Gaye:* Claire Trevor, *Curley:* Thomas Gomez, *Toots:* Harry Lewis, *Deputy Sawyer:* John Rodney, *Ziggy:* Marc Lawrence, *Angel:* Dan Seymour, *Ben Wade:* Monte Blue, *Osceola Brothers:* Jay Silverheels, Rodric Redwing, *Bus Driver:* Joe P. Smith, *Skipper:* Albert Morin, *Man:* Pat Flaherty, *Ziggy's Henchmen:* Jerry Jerome, John Phillips, Lute Crockett, *Old Indian Woman:* Felipa Gomez.

KEYS OF THE KINGDOM (1944) 20th. Producer, Joseph L. Mankiewicz. Director, John M. Stahl. Based on the novel by A. J. Cronin. Screenplay, Joseph L. Mankiewicz, Nunnally Johnson. Musical Score, Alfred Newman. Art Directors, James Basevi, William Darling. Cameraman, Arthur Miller. Special Effects, Fred Sersen. Editor, James B. Clark. 137 minutes

Father Francis Chisholm: Gregory Peck, *Dr. Willie Tullock:* Thomas Mitchell, *Rev. Angus Mealy:* Vincent Price, *Mother Maria Veronica:* Rose Stradner, *Francis as a boy:* Roddy McDowall, *Rev. Hamish MacNabb:* Edmund Gwenn, *Monsignor Sleeth:* Sir Cedric Hardwicke, *Nora as a child:* Peggy Ann Garner, *Nora:* Jane Ball, *Dr. Wilbur Fiske:* James Gleason, *Agnes Fiske:* Anne Revere, *Lisbeth Chisholm:* Ruth Nelson, *Joseph:* Benson Fong, *Mr. Chia:* Leonard Strong, *Mr. Pao:* Philip Ahn, *Father Tarrant:* Arthur Shields, *Aunt Polly:* Edith Barrett, *Sister Martha:* Sara Allgood, *Lieutenant*

Shon: Richard Loo, *Sister Clotilde:* Ruth Ford, *Father Craig:* Kevin O'Shea, *Hosannah Wang:* H. T. Tsiang, *Philomena Wang:* Si-Lan Chen, *Anna:* Eunice Soo Hoo, *Alex Chisholm:* Dennis Hoey, *Bandit Captain:* Abner Biberman, *Ned Bannon:* J. Anthony Hughes, *Andrew:* George Nokes, *Chia-Yu:* Hayward Soo Hoo, *Taoist Priest:* James Leong, *Chinese Physician:* Moy Ming, *Father Chou:* Frank Eng, *Grandmother:* Oie Chan, *Captain:* Beal Wong, *Joshua:* Eugene Louie, *Sister Mercy Mary:* Ruth Clifford.

The Keys of the Kingdom with Arthur Shields, Vincent Price and Gregory Peck.

The Kid From Brooklyn with Ralph Dunn, Danny Kaye, Clarence Kolb and Billy Nelson.

THE KID FROM BROOKLYN (1946) RKO. Producer, Samuel Goldwyn. Director, Norman Z. McLeod. Color by Technicolor. Based on a play by Lynn Root and Harry Clork (*The Milky Way*). Screenplay, Grover Jones, Frank Butler, Richard Connell. Adaptation, Don Hartman, Melville Shavelson. Art Directors, Peggy Ferguson, Stewart Chaney. Musical Director, Carmen Dragon. Musical Supervisor, Louis Forbes. Cameraman, Gregg Toland. Editor, Daniel Mandell. Songs: "I Love an Old-Fashioned Song," "You're the Cause of It All," "Hey, What's Your Name?," "Josie" and "Sunflower Song" by Sammy Cahn and Jule Styne. "Pavlova" by Sylvia Fine. Dorothy Ellers sings for Vera-Ellen, Betty Russell for Virginia Mayo. Remake of *The Milky Way* (Paramount, 1936). 114 minutes

Burleigh Sullivan: Danny Kaye, *Polly Pringle:* Virginia Mayo, *Susie Sullivan:* Vera-Ellen, *Speed McFarlane:* Steve Cochran, *Ann Westley:* Eve Arden, *Gabby Sloan:* Walter Abel, *Spider Schultz:* Lionel Stander, *Mrs. E. Winthrop LeMoyne:* Fay Bainter, *Mr. Austin:* Clarence Kolb,

Photographer: Victor Cutler, *Willard:* Charles Cane, *Fight Announcer:* Jerome Cowan, *Radio Announcer:* Don Wilson, *Radio Announcer:* Knox Manning, *Matron:* Kay Thompson, *Master of Ceremonies:* Johnny Downs, *Guests:* Torben Meyer, Jack Norton, William Forrest, *Seconds:* Ralph Dunn, Billy Nelson, *The Goldwyn Girls:* Karen X. Gaylord, Ruth Valmy, Shirley Ballard, Virginia Belmont, Betty Cargyle, Jean Cronin, Vonne Lester, Diana Mumby, Mary Simpson, Virginia Thorpe, Tyra Vaughn, Kismi Stefan, Betty Alexander, Martha Montgomery, Joyce MacKenzie, Helen Kimball, Donna Hamilton, Jan Bryant, *Specialty Dancer in "What's Your Name":* Jimmy Kelly, *Specialty Dancers in "Old Fashioned":* Eddie Cutler, Harvey Karels, Al Ruiz, *Technical Man and Boxing Instructor:* John Indrisano.

THE KID FROM SPAIN (1932) UA. Produced by Samuel Goldwyn. Directed by Leo McCarey. Dances by Busby Berkeley. Story and Screenplay, William Anthony McGuire, Bert Kalmar, Harry Ruby. Photography, Gregg Toland. Editor, Stuart Heisler. Sound, Vinton Vernon. Songs by Bert Kalmar and Harry Ruby: "Look What You've Done," "In the Moonlight," and "What a Perfect Combination" by Kalmar, Ruby and Harry Akst. 90 minutes

Eddie Williams: Eddie Cantor, *Rosalie:* Lyda Roberti, *Ricardo:* Robert Young, *Anita Gomez:* Ruth Hall, *Pancho:* John Miljan, *Alonza Gomez:* Noah Beery, *Pedro:* J. Carroll Naish, *Crawford:* Robert Emmet O'Connor, *Jose:* Stanley Fields, *Gonzales, Border Guard:* Paul Porcasi, *Dalmores:* Julian Rivero, *Martha Oliver:* Theresa Maxwell Conover, *The Dean:* Walter Walker, *Red:* Ben Hendricks, Jr., *The American Matador (Himself):* Sidney Franklin, *Goldwyn Girls:* Betty Grable, Paulette Goddard, Toby Wing, *Negro Bull Handler:* Edgar Connor, *Robber:* Leo Willis, *Traffic Cop:* Harry Gribbon, *Patron:* Eddie Foster, *Man on Line:* Harry C. Bradley.

The Kid From Spain with John Miljan, Eddie Cantor and J. Carroll Naish.

THE KILLERS (1946) Univ. Producer, Mark Hellinger. Director, Robert Siodmak. From the short story by Ernest Hemingway. Screenplay by Anthony Veiller. Music by Miklos Rozsa. Film Editor, Arthur Hilton. Photographed by Woody Bredell. Film debuts of Burt Lancaster, 32, and William Conrad. Song, "The More I Know of Love," music by Miklos Rozsa, lyrics by Jack Brooks. Art directors, Jack Otterson and Martin Obzina. Remade by Universal, 1964. 105 minutes

Jim Reardon: Edmond O'Brien, *Kitty Collins:* Ava Gardner, *Big Jim Colfax:* Albert Dekker, *Lt. Sam Lubinsky:* Sam Levene, *Jake:* John Miljan, *Lilly:* Virginia Christine, *Charleston:* Vince Barnett, *Swede (Pete Lunn/Ole Anderson):* Burt Lancaster, *Packy Robinson:* Charles D. Brown, *Kenyon:* Donald MacBride, *Nick Adams:* Phil Brown, *Al:* Charles McGraw, *Max:* William Conrad, *Queenie:* Queenie Smith, *Joe:* Garry Owen, *George:* Harry Hayden, *Sam:* Bill

Walker, *Dum Dum:* Jack Lambert, *Blinky:* Jeff Corey, *Charlie:* Wally Scott, *Ginny:* Gabrielle Windsor, *Man:* Rex Dale, *Paymaster:* Harry Brown, *Nurse:* Beatrice Roberts, *Police Chief:* Howard Freeman, *Plunther:* John Berkes, *Doctor:* John Sheehan, *Farmer Brown:* Charles Middleton, *Customer:* Al Hill, *Lou Tingle:* Noel Cravat, *Minister:* Rev. Neal Dodd, *Doctor:* George Anderson, *Mrs. Hirsch:* Vera Lewis, *Policeman:* Howard Negley, *Waiter:* Milton Wallace, *Stella:* Ann Staunton, *Motorman:* William Ruhl, *Housekeeper:* Therese Lyon, *Policeman:* Perc Launders, *Gimp:* Ernie Adams, *Police Driver:* Jack Cheatham, *Conductor:* Ethan Laidlaw, *Policeman:* Geoffrey Ingham, *Pete:* Michael Hale, *Bartender:* Wally Rose, *Waiters:* Nolan Leary, John Trebach, *Assistant Paymaster:* Audley Anderson, *Timekeeper:* Mike Donovan.

The Killers with Ava Gardner and Burt Lancaster.

Kim with Paul Lukas and Dean Stockwell.

KIM (1950) MGM. Produced by Leon Gordon. Directed by Victor Saville. Color by Technicolor. Based on the novel by Rudyard Kipling. Screenplay, Leon Gordon, Helen Deutsch, and Richard Schayer. Art Directors, Cedric Gibbons and Hans Peters. Music, Andre Previn. Photography, William Skall. Editor, George Boemler. Filmed in India. 113 minutes

Mahbub Ali, the Red Beard: Errol Flynn, *Kim:* Dean Stockwell, *Lama:* Paul Lukas, *Colonel Creighton:* Robert Douglas, *Emissary:* Thomas Gomez, *Hurree Chunder:* Cecil Kellaway, *Lurgan Sahib:* Arnold Moss, *Father Victor:* Reginald Owen, *Laluli:* Laurette Luez, *Hassan Bey:* Richard Hale, *The Russians:* Roman Toporow, Ivan Triesault, *Major Ainsley:* Hayden Rorke, *Dr. Bronson:* Walter Kingsford, *Wanna:* Henry Mirelez, *Shadow:* Frank Lackteen, *Abul:* Frank Richards, *Conspirators:* Henry Corden, Peter Mamakos, *Haikun:* Donna Martell, *Foster Mother:* Jeanette Nolan, *Servant:* Rod Red-

wing, *Guard:* Michael Ansara, *Policeman:* Lal Chand Mehra, *Water Carrier:* Stanley Price, *Woman with Baby:* Movita Castenada, *British General:* Wallis Clark, *Guard:* Lou Krugman, *Old Maharanee:* Adeline deWalt Reynolds, *Letter Writer:* Francis McDonald, *Biggs:* Danny Rees, *Thorpe:* Robin Camp, *Master:* Keith McConnell, *Miss Manners:* Betty Daniels, *Gerald:* Wilson Wood, *Mr. Fairlee:* Olaf Hytten, *Cart Driver:* Bobby Barber, *Farmer:* Mitchell Lewis.

The King and I with Deborah Kerr, Yul Brynner and (at left) Martin Benson.

THE KING AND I (1956) 20th. Producer, Charles Brackett. Director, Walter Lang. CinemaScope, De Luxe Color. From Margaret Landon's book *Anna and the King of Siam.* Screenplay, Ernest Lehman. Book and Lyrics, Oscar Hammerstein II. Music, Richard Rodgers. Music supervised and conducted by Alfred Newman. Orchestration, Edward B. Powell, Gus Levene, Bernard Mayers, Robert Russell Bennett. Art Directors, Lyle R. Wheeler, John De Cuir. Cinematographer, Leon Shamroy. Editor, Robert Simpson. Choreography by Jerome Robbins. Marni Nixon sings for Deborah Kerr. Songs by Richard Rodgers and Oscar Hammerstein II: "The Small House of Uncle Thomas," "March of the Siamese Children," "Getting to Know You," "Whistle a Happy Tune," "Hello, Young Lovers," "I Have Dreamed," "Shall We Dance?" "Something Wonderful," "Is a Puzzlement," "Shall I Tell You What I Think of You?" "We Kiss in a Shadow." Remake of 20th's *Anna and the King of Siam* (1946). 133 minutes

Anna: Deborah Kerr, *The King:* Yul Brynner, *Tuptim:* Rita Moreno, *Kralahome:* Martin Benson, *Lady Thiang:* Terry Saunders, *Louis Leonowens:* Rex Thompson, *Lun Tha:* Carlos Rivas, *Prince Chulalongkorn:* Patrick Adiarte, *British Ambassador:* Alan Mowbray, *Ramsey:* Geoffrey Toone, *Eliza (in Ballet):* Yuriko, *Simon Legree (in Ballet):* Marion Jim, *Keeper of the Dogs:* Robert Banas, *Uncle Thomas (in Ballet):* Dusty Worrall, *Specialty Dancer:* Gemze de Lappe, *Twins:* Thomas Bonilla, Dennis Bonilla, *Angel (in Ballet):* Michiki Iseri, *Ship's Captain:* Charles Irwin, *Interpreter:* Leonard Strong, *Whipping Guards:* Fuji, Weaver Levy, *High Priest:* William Yip, *Messenger:* Eddie Luke, *Princess Ying Yoowalak:* Jocelyn Lew.

KING KONG (1933) RKO. Executive Producer, David O. Selznick. Directed by Merian C. Cooper and Ernest B. Schoedsack. Story, Edgar Wallace and Merian C. Cooper. Adaptation, James Creelman and Ruth Rose. Chief Technician, Willis O'Brien. Editor, Ted Cheeseman. Sound, E. A. Wolcott. Music, Max Steiner. Idea created by Merian C. Cooper. Technical Staff, E. B. Gibson, Marcel Delgado, Fred Reefe, Orville Goldner, Carol Shepphird. Art Directors, Carroll Clark and Al Herman. Photography, Edward Linden, Verne Walker, J. O. Taylor. Sound Effects, Murray Spivak. Production Assistants, Archie S. Marshek and Walter Daniels. Art Technicians, Mario Larrinaga and Byron L. Crabbe. Sets also used in RKO's *The Most Dangerous Game,* 1932. 100 minutes

Ann Darrow: Fay Wray, *Carl Denham:* Robert Armstrong, *John Driscoll:* Bruce Cabot, *Captain Englehorn:* Frank Reicher, *Weston:* Sam Hardy, *Native Chief:* Noble Johnson, *Briggs, Second Mate:* James Flavin, *Witch King:* Steve Clemento, *Cook:* Victor Wong, *Mate:* Ethan Laidlaw, *Sailor:* Dick Curtis, *Sailor:* Charlie Sullivan, *Theater Patron:* Vera Lewis, *Theater Patron:* LeRoy Mason, *Apple Vendor:* Paul Porcasi, *Reporters:* Lynton Brent, Frank Mills, and King Kong, the Eighth Wonder of the World.

King Kong with Fay Wray.

King Kong with Kong and Jessica Lange.

KING KONG (1976) Par. Produced by Dino De Laurentiis. Directed by John Guillermin. Screenplay, Lorenzo Semple, Jr. Executive Producers, Federico De Laurentiis and Christian Ferry. Photography, Richard H. Kline. In Charge of Production, Jack Grossberg. Music composed and conducted by John Barry. Editor, Ralph E. Winters. Production designed by Mario Chiari and Dale Hennesy. Set Decorator, John Franco, Jr. Assistant Directors, David McGiffert and Kurt Neumann. 2nd Assistant Director, Pat Kehoe. 2nd Unit Director, William Kronick. 2nd Unit Assistant Director, Nate Haggard. Additional Photographic Effects, Harold E. Wellman. Art Directors, Archie J. Bacon, David A. Constable and Robert Gundlach. Sound Mixer, Jack Solomon. Make-up Artist, Del Acevedo. Hairstylist, Jo McCarthy. Costume Designer, Moss Mabry. Gowns and Native Costumes, Anthea Sylbert. Wardrobe, Army Lipin and Fern Weber. Special Effects, Glen Robinson and Joe Day. Hair Design for Kong, Michaeldino. Make-up for Kong, John Truwe. Sculptor of Kong, Don Chandler. Kong Mechanical Coordinator, Eddie Surkin. Miniature Coordinator, Aldo Puccini. Stunt Coordinator, Bill Couch. Supervisor of

Photographic Effects, Frank Van Der Veer. Matte Artist, Lou Lichtenfield. Native Dance Choreography, Claude Thompson. Kong designed and engineered by Carlo Rambaldi, constructed by Carlo Rambaldi and Glen Robinson, with Rick Baker's special contributions. Filmed in New York City and Hawaii in Panavision and Color. Rated PG. 134 minutes

Jack Prescott: Jeff Bridges, *Fred Wilson:* Charles Grodin, *Dwan:* Jessica Lange, *Capt. Ross:* John Randolph, *Bagley:* Rene Auberjonois, *Boan:* Julius Harris, *Joe Perko:* Jack O'Halloran, *Sunfish:* Dennis Fimple, *Carnahan:* Ed Lauter, *City Official:* John Agar, *Garcia:* Jorge Moreno, *Timmons:* Mario Gallo, *Chinese Cook:* John Lone, *Army General:* Garry Halberg, *Ape Masked Man:* Keny Long, *Petrox Chairman:* Sid Conrad, *Army Helicopter Pilot:* George Whiteman, *Air Force Colonel:* Wayne Heffley.

King of Kings with Jeffrey Hunter and Siobhan McKenna.

KING OF KINGS (1961) MGM. Producer, Samuel Bronston. Director, Nicholas Ray. Screenplay, Philip Yordan. Music, Miklos Rozsa. Costumes, George Wakhevitch. Filmed in Technirama 70 and Technicolor. Associate Producers, Alan Brown, Jaime Prades. Cinematographers, Franz F. Planer, Milton Krasner, Manuel Berenguer. Special Photographic Effects, Lee LeBlanc. Editors, Harold Kress, Renee Lichtig. Filmed in Spain. 168 minutes

Jesus Christ: Jeffrey Hunter, *Mary:* Siobhan McKenna, *Pontius Pilate:* Hurd Hatfield, *Lucius:* Ron Randell, *Claudia:* Viveca Lindfors, *Herodias:* Rita Gam, *Mary Magdalene:* Carmen Sevilla, *Salome:* Brigid Bazlen, *Barabbas:* Harry Guardino, *Judas:* Rip Torn, *Herod Antipas:* Frank Thring, *Caiphas:* Guy Rolfe, *Nicodemus:* Maurice Marsac, *Herod:* Gregoire Aslan, *Peter:* Royal Dano, *Balthazar:* Edric Connor, *John The Baptist:* Robert Ryan, *Camel Driver:* George Coulouris, *General Pompey:* Conrado San Martin, *Joseph:* Gerard Tichy, *Young John:* Jose Antonio, *Good Thief:* Luis Prendes, *Burly Man:* David Davies, *Caspar:* Jose Nieto, *Matthew:* Ruben Rojo, *Madman:* Fernando Sancho, *Thomas:* Michael Wager, *Joseph of Arimathea:* Felix de Pomes, *Melchior:* Adriano Rimoldi, *Bad Thief:* Barry Keegan, *Simon of Cyrene:* Rafael Luis Calvo, *Andrew:* Tino Barrero, *Blind Man:* Franisco Moran.

KING SOLOMON'S MINES (1950) MGM. Produced by Sam Zimbalist. Directed by Compton Bennett and Andrew Marton. Color by Technicolor. Based on the novel by H. Rider Haggard. Screenplay, Helen Deutsch. Art Directors, Cedric Gibbons and Conrad A. Nervig. Photography, Robert Surtees. Editors, Ralph E. Winters and Conrad A. Nervig. Produced in Africa: Belgian Congo, Tanganyika, Uganda, Kenya. Songs by Eric Maschwitz and Mischa Spoliansky: "Climbing Up, Climbing Up" and "Ho! Ho!" Other versions: *King Solomon's Mines* (Gaumont-British, 1937), *Watusi* (MGM, 1959). 102 minutes

Elizabeth Curtis: Deborah Kerr, *Allan Quartermain:* Stewart Granger,

149

John Goode: Richard Carlson, *Van Brun:* Hugo Haas, *Eric Masters:* Lowell Gilmore, *Khiva:* Kimursi, *Umbopa:* Siriaque, *Chief Gagool:* Sekaryongo, *King Twala:* Baziga, *Chief Bilu:* Corp. Munto Anampio, *Kafa:* Gutare, *Blue Star:* Ivargwema, *Black Circle:* Benempinga, *Austin:* John Banner, *Traum:* Henry Rowland, *Double for "Umbopa":* Gutare.

King Solomon's Mines with Stewart Granger, Deborah Kerr and Richard Carlson.

Kings Row with Ronald Reagan and Ann Sheridan.

KINGS ROW (1941) WB. Producer, Hal B. Wallis. Associate Producer, David Lewis. Director, Sam Wood. Based on the novel by Henry Bellamann. Screenplay by Casey Robinson. Film Editor, Ralph Dawson. Photographed by James Wong Howe. Music by Erich Wolfgang Korngold. Art Director, Carl Jules Weyl. 127 minutes

Randy Monoghan: Ann Sheridan, *Parris Mitchell:* Robert Cummings, *Drake McHugh:* Ronald Reagan, *Cassandra Tower:* Betty Field, *Dr. Henry Gordon:* Charles Coburn, *Dr. Alexander Tower:* Claude Rains, *Mrs. Harriet Gordon:* Judith Anderson, *Louise Gordon:* Nancy Coleman, *Elise Sandor:* Kaaren Verne, *Madame Von Eln:* Maria Ouspenskaya, *Colonel Skeffington:* Harry Davenport, *Pa Monoghan:* Ernest Cossart, *Tom Monoghan:* Pat Moriarty, *Ann, the Maid:* Ilka Gruning, *Sam Winters:* Minor Watson, *Dr. Berdoff:* Ludwig Stossel, *Mr. Sandor:* Erwin Kalser, *Dr. Candell:* Egon Brecher, *Randy, as child:* Ann Todd, *Parris, as child:* Scotty Beckett, *Drake, as child:* Douglas Croft, *Cassandra, as child:* Mary Thomas, *Louise, as child:* Joan Du Valle, *Benny Singer:* Danny Jackson, *Willie:* Henry Blair, *Aunt Mamie:* Leah Baird, *Mrs. Tower:* Eden Gray, *Poppy Ross:* Julie Warren, *Ginny Ross:* Mary Scott, *Esther:* Bertha Powell, *Deputy Constable:* Walter Baldwin, *Conductor:* Frank Mayo, *Freight Conductor:* Jack Mower, *Patterson Lawes:* Thomas W. Ross, *Teller:*

Frank Milan, *Livery Stable Keeper:* Hank Mann, *Bill Hockinson:* Fred Kelsey, *Arnold Kelly:* Herbert Heywood, *Harley Davis:* Emory Parnell, *Nurse:* Elizabeth Valentine, *Porter:* Ludwig Hardt, *Secretary:* Hermine Sterler, *Gordons' Maid:* Hattie Noel.

KITTY FOYLE (1940) RKO. Produced by Harry E. Edington and David Hempstead. Directed by Sam Wood. From the novel by Christopher Morley. Screenplay, Dalton Trumbo. Additional Dialogue, Donald Ogden Stewart. Art Director, Van Nest Polglase. Music, Roy Webb. Photography, Robert De Grasse. Editor, Henry Berman. Special Effects, Vernon L. Walker. Art Director's Associate, Mark-Lee Kirk. Gowns, Renie. Sets, Darrell Silvera. Sound, John L. Cass. Assistant Director, Argyle Nelson. 108 minutes

Kitty Foyle: Ginger Rogers, *Wyn Strafford:* Dennis Morgan, *Mark:* James Craig, *Giono:* Eduardo Ciannelli, *Pop:* Ernest Cossart, *Mrs. Strafford:* Gladys Cooper, *Delphine Detaille:* Odette Myrtil, *Pat:* Mary Treen, *Molly:* Katharine Stevens, *Mr. Kennett:* Walter Kingsford, *Grandmother:* Cecil Cunningham, *Aunt Jessica:* Nella Walker, *Uncle Edgar:* Edward Fielding, *Wyn's Wife:* Kay Linaker, *Wyn's Boy:* Richard Nichols, *Customer:* Florence Bates, *Girl in Prologue:* Heather Angel, *Boy in Prologue:* Tyler Brooke, *Negro Woman:* Hattie Noel, *Parry:* Frank Milan, *Bill:* Charles Quigley, *Miss Bala:* Harriett Brandon, *Butler:* Howard Entwistle, *Neway:* Billy Elmer, *Trumpeter:* Walter Sande, *Saxaphonist:* Ray Teal, *Drummer:* Joey Ray, *Violinist-Leader:* Mel Ruick, *Pianist:* Doodles Weaver, *Hotel Clerk:* Theodor Von Eltz, *Flower Man:* Max Davidson, *Doctor:* Charles Miller, *Charwoman:* Mary Gordon, *Prim Girl:* Fay Helm, *Girl in Elevator:* Helen Lynd, *Charwoman:* Dorothy Vaughan, *Jane:* Mimi Doyle, *Nurse:* Hilda Plowright, *Father:* Spencer Charters, *Guest:* Gino Corrado.

Kitty Foyle with Ginger Rogers, Dennis Morgan, Eduardo Ciannelli and Gino Corrado.

KLUTE (1971) WB. Produced and Directed by Alan J. Pakula. Panavision and Technicolor. Coproducer, David Lange. Written by Andy K. and Dave Lewis. Photography, Gordon Willis. Art Director, George Jenkins. Editor, Carl Lerner. Sound, Chris Newman. Set Decorator, John Mortensen. Titles designed by Arthur Eckstein. Fashion photographs courtesy of *Harper's Bazaar.* Executive Associate Producer, C. Kenneth Deland. Music composed and conducted by Michael Small. Costumes designed by Ann Roth. Fonda's hairstyles, Paul Macgregor. Make-up, Irving Buckman. Hairdresser, Bob Grimaldi. Assistant Director, William Gerrity. Filmed at Filmways, Inc., and New York City. Rated R. 114 minutes

Bree Daniels: Jane Fonda, *John Klute:* Donald Sutherland, *Peter Cable:* Charles Cioffi, *Frank Ligourin:* Roy Scheider, *Arlyn Page:* Dorothy Tristan, *Trina:* Rita Gam, *Psychiatrist:* Vivian Nathan, *Lt. Trask:* Nathan George, *Mama Reese:* Shirley Stoler, *Janie Dale:* Jane White, *Mr.*

Goldfarb: Morris Strassberg, *Berger:* Barry Snider, *Actor's Agent:* Anthony Holland, *Sugarman:* Richard Shull, *Holly Gruneman:* Betty Murray, *Man in Chicago Hotel:* Fred Burrell, *Goldfarb's Secretary:* Jean Stapleton, *Tom Gruneman:* Robert Milli, *Custodian:* Jerome Collamore, *Off-Broadway Director:* Robert Ronan, *Stage Manager:* Richard Ramos, *Mrs. Vasek, Landlady:* Antonia Rey, *Psychiatrist's Secretary:* Jan Fielding, *Evie:* Margaret Linn, *Pat:* Rosalind Cash, *Nate Goldfarb:* Lee Wallace, *Ad Agency Secretary:* Mary Louise Wilson, *Dr. Spangler:* Joe Silver, *Bill Azure:* Tony Major.

Klute with Donald Sutherland and Jane Fonda.

The Lady Eve with Charles Coburn, Barbara Stanwyck and Henry Fonda.

THE LADY EVE (1941) Par. Produced by Paul Jones. Directed by Preston Sturges. Based on a story by Monckton Hoffe. Screenplay, Preston Sturges. Photography, Victor Milner. Editor, Stuart Gilmore. Remade as *The Birds and the Bees* (Paramount, 1956). 97 minutes

Jean: Barbara Stanwyck, *Charles:* Henry Fonda, *"Colonel" Harrington:* Charles Coburn, *Mr. Pike:* Eugene Pallette, *Muggsy:* William Demarest, *Sir Alfred McGlennan Keith:* Eric Blore, *Gerald:* Melville Cooper, *Martha:* Martha O'Driscoll, *Mrs. Pike:* Janet Beecher, *Burrows:* Robert Greig, *Gertrude:* Dora Clemant, *Pike's Chef:* Luis Alberni,

Stewards: Jimmy Conlin, Alan Bridge, Victor Potel, *Bartender at Party:* Frank C. Moran, *Social Secretary:* Pauline Drake, *Piano Tuner:* Harry Rosenthal, *Man with Potted Palm:* Abdullah Abbas, *Sir Alfred's Servant:* Norman Ainsley, *Lawyers:* Julius Tannen, J. W. Johnston, Ray Flynn, Harry A. Bailey, Arthur Hoyt, *Sparky:* Wally Walker, *Purser:* Torben Meyer, *Bank Manager:* Robert Warwick, *Mac:* Ambrose Barker, *Professor Jones:* Reginald Sheffield, *Sweetie:* Jean Phillips, *Bartender:* Pat West, *Daughters on Boat:* Ella Neal, Wanda McKay, Marcelle Christopher, *Young Man on Boat:* John Hartley, *Husbands on Boat:* Cyril Ring, Sam Ash, Robert Dudley.

LADY FOR A DAY (1933) Col. Directed by Frank Capra. Based on the story "Madame La Gimp" by Damon Runyon. Adaptation, Robert Riskin. Art Director, Stephen Goosson. Costumes, Robert Kalloch. Assistant Director, Charles C. Coleman. Photography, Joseph Walker. Editor, Gene Havlick. Sound, E. L. Bernds. A blind man, Dad Mills, portrays a blind man in the film. Remade as *Pocketful of Miracles* (United Artists, 1961). 95 minutes

Dave the Dude: Warren William, *Apple Annie:* May Robson, *Judge Blake:* Guy Kibbee, *Missouri Martin:* Glenda Farrell, *Happy:* Ned Sparks, *Louise:* Jean Parker, *Count Romero:* Walter Connolly, *Shakespeare:* Nat Pendleton, *Inspector:* Robert Emmet O'Connor, *Commissioner:* Wallis Clark, *Governor:* Hobart Bosworth, *Blind Man:* Dad Mills, *Carlos:* Barry Norton.

Lady for a Day with Hobart Bosworth, Jean Parker, May Robson, Barry Norton, Walter Connolly, Samuel S. Hinds.

LADY IN THE DARK (1944) Par. Associate Producer, Richard Blumenthal. Directed by Mitchell Leisen. Color by Technicolor. Based on the play by Moss Hart with music by Kurt Weill and lyrics by Ira Gershwin. Screenplay, Frances Goodrich and Albert Hackett. Music scored and directed by Robert Emmett Dolan. Orchestral Arrangements, Robert Russell Bennett. Art Director, Hans Dreier. Photography, Ray Rennahan. Editor, Alma Macrorie. Special Effects, Gordon Jennings. Songs: "One Life to Live," "Girl of the Moment," "It Looks Like Liza," "This Is New," "My Ship," and "Jenny" by Ira Gershwin and Kurt Weill; "Artist's Waltz" by Robert Emmett Dolan; "Suddenly It's Spring" by Johnny Burke and Jimmy Van Heusen; and "Dream Lover" by Clifford Grey and Victor Schertzinger. 100 minutes

Liza Elliott: Ginger Rogers, *Charley Johnson:* Ray Milland, *Kendall Nesbitt:* Warner Baxter, *Randy Curtis:* Jon Hall, *Doctor Brooks:* Barry Sullivan, *Russell Paxton:* Mischa Auer, *Allison DuBois:* Phyllis Brooks, *Maggie Grant:* Mary Phillips, *Doctor Carlton:* Edward Fielding, *Adams:* Don Loper, *Miss Parker:* Mary Parker, *Miss Foster:* Catherine Craig, *Martha:* Marietta Canty, *Miss Edwards:* Virginia Farmer, *Miss Bowers:* Fay Helm, *Barbara:* Gail Russell, *Miss Stevens:* Marian Hall, *Liza's Mother:* Kay Linaker, *Liza's Father:* Harvey Stephens, *Office Boy:* Billy Daniels, *Miss Sullivan:* Georgia Backus,

Ben: Rand Brooks, *Clown:* Pepito Perez, *Barbara's Boy Friend:* Charles Smith, *Librarian:* Mary MacLaren, *Jack Goddard:* Paul McVey, *Specialty Dancers:* Paul Pierce, George Mayon, *Men:* Tristram Coffin, Dennis Moore, Jack Luden, *Captain of Waiters:* George Calliga, *Girl with Randy:* Frances Robinson, *Miss Shawn:* Jan Buckingham, *Photographer:* Jack Mulhall, *Miss Barr:* Hillary Brooke, *Dancer:* Miriam Franklin, *Autograph Hunter:* Dorothy Granger, *Butler:* Charles Coleman, *Pianist:* Lester Sharpe, *Charley as a boy:* Bobby Beers, *Barbara at 7:* Phyllis M. Brooks, *Liza at 5 and 7:* Marjean Neville, *David:* Charles Bates.

Lady in the Dark with Ray Milland and Ginger Rogers.

Lady Sings the Blues with Diana Ross and Billy Dee Williams.

LADY SINGS THE BLUES (1972) Par. Produced by Jay Weston and James S. White. Executive Producer, Berry Gordy. Directed by Sidney J. Furie. A Motown-Weston-Furie Production in Eastman Color and Panavision. Based on the 1956 autobiography by Billie Holiday (1915–59) and William Dufty. Screenplay by Terence McCloy, Chris Clark and Suzanne de Passe. Associate Producer, Eddie Saeta. Photography, John Alonzo. Editor, Argyle Nelson. Production Designer, Carl Anderson. Assistant Director, Charles Washburn. Set Decorator, Reg Allen. Dialogue Coach, Terence McCloy. Sound Recording, William Ford and David Dockendorf. Music by Michel Legrand. Musical Supervisor, Gil Askey. Hairstyles, Cherie (Huffman). Ross' costumes executed by Elizabeth Courtney. Costumes, Norma Koch. Ross' costumes designed by Bob Mackie and Ray Aghayan. Furs, Frank Somper. Creative Consultant, Judy St. Gerard. Research, Janet Hubbard. Postproduction Supervisor, Millie Moore. Make-up Supervisor, Don Schoenfeld. Technical Adviser, Louis McKay. Associate Editor, Roberta Adye. Titles and Montages conceived and

executed by Lawrence Schiller. Songs: "Lover Man," "Don't Explain," "I Cried for You," "All of Me," "Strange Fruit," "My Man," "God Bless the Child," "You've Changed," "Them There Eyes," "The Man I Love," "Mean to Me," "Fine and Mellow," "What a Little Moonlight Can Do," "Lady Sings the Blues," "T'ain't Nobody's Biz'ness If I Do," "Our Love Is Here to Stay," "Gimme a Pigfoot and a Bottle of Beer," "Good Morning Heartache." Musicians heard include Holiday accompanists Harry "Sweets" Edison, trumpet; Red Holloway, bass; and John Collins, guitar. Filmed in Los Angeles' Echo Park and Union Station and elsewhere; Alhambra, Pasadena, Rancho Sierra Vista in Thousand Oaks, Lincoln Heights jail, California. Rated R. 144 minutes

Billie Holiday: Diana Ross, *Louis McKay:* Billy Dee Williams, *Piano Man:* Richard Pryor, *Reg Hanley:* James Callahan, *Harry:* Paul Hampton, *Jerry:* Sid Melton, *Mama Holiday:* Virginia Capers, *Yvonne:* Yvonne Fair, *Big Ben:* Scatman Crothers, *Hawk:* Robert L. Gordy, *Rapist:* Harry Caesar, *Doctor:* Milton Selzer, *Agent:* Ned Glass, *Mrs. Edson:* Paulene Myers, *First Madame:* Isabel Sanford, *Whore:* Tracee Lyles, *Detective:* Norman Bartold, *Bits:* Jester Hairston, Clay Tanner, Bert Kramer, Paul Micale, Byron Kane, Barbara Minkus, George Wyner, Shirley Melline, Larry Duran, Ernie Robinson, Charles Woolf, Lynn Hamilton, Denise Denise, Victor Morosco.

LASSIE COME HOME (1943) MGM. Producer, Samuel Marx. Director, Fred M. Wilcox. From the novel by Eric Knight. Screenplay, Hugo Butler. Musical Score, Daniele Amfitheatrof. Art Director, Cedric Gibbons. Cameraman, Leonard Smith. Special Effects, Warren Newcombe. Editor, Ben Lewis. 88 minutes. Remade as *Gypsy Colt* (1954)

Joe Carraclough: Roddy McDowall, *Sam Carraclough:* Donald Crisp, *Rowlie:* Edmund Gwenn, *Dolly:* Dame May Whitty, *Duke of Rudling:* Nigel Bruce, *Mrs. Carraclough:* Elsa Lanchester, *Priscilla:* Elizabeth Taylor, *Hynes:* J. Patrick O'Malley, *Dan'l Fadden:* Ben Webster, *Snickers:* Alec Craig, *Buckles:* John Rogers, *Jock:* Arthur Shields, *Andrew:* Alan Napier, *Butcher:* Roy Parry, *Allen:* George Broughton, *Cobbler:* Howard Davies, *Miner:* John Power, *Teacher:* Nelson Leigh, *Fat Woman:* May Beatty, *Tom:* Charles Irwin, *Teacher:* Hugh Harrison.

Lassie Come Home with Elsa Lanchester, Roddy McDowall, Lassie and Donald Crisp.

THE LAST HURRAH (1958) Col. Produced and directed by John Ford. Based on the novel by Edwin O'Connor. Screenplay, Frank Nugent. Assistant Directors, Wingate Smith and Sam Nelson. Art Director, Robert Peterson. Photography, Charles Lawton, Jr. Editor, Jack Murray. Cut from release print was Edmund Lowe as Johnny Byrne. Last film of Ed Brophy, who died at 65, May 27, 1960. 121 minutes. TV version (1978) with Carroll O'Connor

Frank Skeffington: Spencer Tracy, *Adam Caulfield:* Jeffrey Hunter,

Maeve Caulfield: Dianne Foster, *John Gorman:* Pat O'Brien, *Norman Cass, Sr.:* Basil Rathbone, *The Cardinal:* Donald Crisp, *Cuke Gillen:* James Gleason, *Ditto Boland:* Edward Brophy, *Amos Force:* John Carradine, *Roger Sugrue:* Willis Bouchey, *Bishop Gardner:* Basil Ruysdael, *Sam Weinberg:* Ricardo Cortez, *Hennessey:* Wallace Ford, *Festus Garvey:* Frank McHugh, *Mr. Winslow:* Carleton Young, *Jack Mangan:* Frank Albertson, *Degnan:* Bob Sweeney, *Dan Herlihy:* William Leslie, *Gert:* Anna Lee, *Monsignor Killian:* Ken Curtis, *Delia:* Jane Darwell, *Norman Cass, Jr.:* O. Z. Whitehead, *Frank Skeffington, Jr.:* Arthur Walsh, *Ellen Davin:* Ruth Warren, *Kevin McCluskey:* Charles Fitzsimons, *Mrs. McCluskey:* Helen Westcott, *Mamie Burns:* Mimi Doyle, *Pete:* Dan Borzage, *Police Captain:* James Flavin, *Doctor:* William Forrest, *Fire Captain:* Frank Sully, *Chauffeur:* Charlie Sullivan, *Young Politicians:* Bill Henry, Rand Brooks. Harry Lauter, *Riley:* Jack Pennick, *Nurse:* Ruth Clifford, *Club Secretary:* Richard Deacon, *Retainer:* Harry Tyler, *Jules Kowalsky:* Robert Levin, *Mr. Kowalsky:* Julius Tannen, *Managing Editor:* Hal K. Dawson, *Footsie:* Harry Tenbrook, *News Commentator:* Clete Roberts, *Man:* Edmund Cobb, *Man:* Charles Trowbridge, *Gregory McClusky:* Tommy Earwood, *Man:* Tommy Jackson.

The Last Hurrah with Spencer Tracy and Jeffrey Hunter.

THE LAST PICTURE SHOW (1971) Col. A BBS Production. Produced by Stephen J. Friedman. Directed by Peter Bogdanovich. Based on the novel by Larry McMurtry. Screenplay, McMurtry and Bogdanovich. Executive Producer, Bert Schneider. Design by Polly Platt. Photography, Robert Surtees. Associate Producer, Harold Schneider. Art Director, Walter Scott Herndon. Editor, Donn Cambern. Assistant Directors, Robert Rubin and William Morrison. Assistant to the Director, Gary Chason. Sound Mixer, Tom Overton. Production Assistant, Mae Woods. Wardrobe, Nancy McArdle and Mickey Sherrard. Sound Effects, Edit-Rite, Inc. Rerecording, Producers Sound Service, Inc. Songs sung by Hank Williams, Bob Wills and His Texas Playboys, Tony Bennett, Lefty Frizzell, Frankie Laine, Johnnie Ray, Eddy Arnold, Eddie Fisher, Phil Harris, Pee Wee King, Hank Snow, Johnny Standley, Kay Starr, Hank Thompson, Webb Price, Jo Stafford. Scenes from *Father of the Bride* (MGM, 1950) and *Red River* (UA, 1948) and the TV shows *Strike It Rich* and *Your Show of Shows.* Film debut of model Cybill Shepherd, 21. Filmed in Archer City, Texas. Rated R. 118 minutes

Sonny Crawford: Timothy Bottoms, *Duane Jackson:* Jeff Bridges, *Jacy Farrow:* Cybill Shepherd, *Sam the Lion:* Ben Johnson, *Ruth Popper:* Cloris Leachman, *Lois Farrow:* Ellen Burstyn, *Genevieve:* Eileen Brennan, *Abilene:* Clu Gulager, *Billy:* Sam Bottoms, *Charlene Duggs:* Sharon Taggart, *Lester Marlow:* Randy Quaid, *Sheriff:* Joe Heathcock, *Coach Popper:* Bill Thurman, *Joe Bob Blanton:* Barc Doyle, *Miss Mosey:* Jessie Lee Fulton, *Bobby Sheen:* Gary Brockette, *Jimmie Sue:* Helena Humann, *Leroy:* Loyd Catlett, *Gene Farrow:* Robert Glenn, *Teacher:* John Hillerman, *Mrs. Clarg:* Janice O'Malley, *Oklahoma Patrolman:* Floyd Mahaney, *Annie-Annie Martin:* Kimberly Hyde, *Chester:* Noble Willingham, *Winnie Snips:* Marjory Jay, *Mrs. Jackson:* Joye Hash, *Jackie Lee French:* Pamela Kelier, *Monroe:* Gordon Hurst, *Johnny:* Mike Hosford, *Nurse:*

Faye Jordan, Andy Fanner: Charlie Seybert, *Mr. Crawford:* Grover Lewis, *Marlene:* Rebecca Ulrick, *Agnes:* Merrill Shepherd, *Bud:* Buddy Wood, *Ken:* Kenny Wood, *Cowboy in Cafe:* Leon Brown, *Cowboy:* George Gaulden, *Truck Driver:* Bobby McGriff, *Oil Pumper:* Jack Mueller, *Brother Blanton:* Robert Arnold, *Tommy Logan:* Frank Marshall, *1st Mechanic:* Otis Elmore, *Roughneck Driver:* Charles Salmon, *Gas Station Man:* Will Morris Hannis, *Band:* The Leon Miller Band.

The Last Picture Show with Cybill Shepherd and Jeff Bridges.

Laura with Vincent Price, Judith Anderson, Gene Tierney and Clifton Webb.

LAURA (1944) 20th. Producer and Director, Otto Preminger. From the novel by Vera Caspary. Screenplay, Jay Dratler, Samuel Hoffenstein, Betty Reinhardt. Art Directors, Lyle Wheeler, Leland Fuller. Musical Score, David Raksin. Musical Director, Emil Newman. Cameraman, Joseph La Shelle. Editor, Louis Loeffler. Song by Johnny Mercer and David Raksin, "Laura." 88 minutes

Laura: Gene Tierney, *Mark McPherson:* Dana Andrews, *Waldo Lydecker:* Clifton Webb, *Shelby Carpenter:* Vincent Price, *Ann Treadwell:* Judith Anderson, *Bessie Clary:* Dorothy Adams, *McAvity:* James Flavin, *Bullitt:* Clyde Fillmore, *Fred Callahan:* Ralph Dunn, *Corey:* Grant Mitchell, *Louise:* Kathleen Howard, *Detectives:* Harold Schlickenmayer, Harry Strang, Lane Chandler, *Hairdresser:* Frank La Rue, *Bits:* Dorothy Christy, Aileen Pringle, Forbes Murray, Cyril Ring, *Girls:* Kay Linaker, Cara Williams, *Office Boy:* Buster Miles, *Secretary:* Jane Nigh, *Man:* William Forrest, *Jacoby:* John Dexter.

LAWRENCE OF ARABIA (1962) Col. Producer, Sam Spiegel. Director, David Lean. Screenplay, Robert Bolt. Music, Maurice Jarre. Filmed in Super Panavision 70 and Technicolor. Music played by the London Symphony Orchestra. A Horizon Pictures Production. Art Director, John Box. Cinematographer, F. A. Young. 221 minutes

T. E. Lawrence: Peter O'Toole, *Prince Feisal:* Alec Guinness, *Auda abu Tayi:* Anthony Quinn, *General Allenby:* Jack Hawkins, *Dryden:* Claude Rains, *Colonel Harry Brighton:* Anthony Quayle, *Jackson Bentley:* Arthur Kennedy, *The Bey:* José Ferrer, *Sherif Ali ibn el Kharish:* Omar Sharif, *Farraj:* Michel Ray, *Daud:* John Dimech, *Gasim:* I. S. Johar, *General Murray:* Donald Wolfit, *Majid:* Gamil Ratib, *Tafas:* Zia Mohyeddin, *Corporal Jenkins:* Norman Rossington, *Elder Harith:* John Ruddock, *Medical Officer:* Howard Marion Crawford, *Club Secretary:* Jack Gwillim, *R.A.M.C. Colonel:* Hugh Miller, *Allenby's Aide:* Kenneth Fortescue, *Regimental Sergeant Major:* Stuart Saunders, *Turkish Sergeant:* Fernando Sancho, *Reciter:* Henry Oscar.

Lawrence of Arabia with Anthony Quayle, Omar Sharif and Peter O'Toole.

Leave Her to Heaven with Vincent Price, Gene Tierney and Cornel Wilde.

LEAVE HER TO HEAVEN (1945) 20th. Producer, William A. Bacher. Director, John M. Stahl. Color by Technicolor. Based on the novel by Ben Ames Williams. Screenplay, Jo Swerling. Musical Score, Alfred Newman. Art Directors, Lyle Wheeler, Maurice Ransford. Cameraman, Leon Shamroy. Special Effects, Fred Sersen. Editor, James B. Clark. Technicolor Director, Natalie Kalmus. Associate, Richard Mueller. Locations filmed in Wyoming. 111 minutes

Ellen Berent: Gene Tierney, *Richard Harland:* Cornel Wilde, *Ruth Berent:* Jeanne Crain, *Russell Quinton:* Vincent Price, *Mrs. Berent:*

Mary Philips, *Glen Robie:* Ray Collins, *Dr. Saunders:* Gene Lockhart, *Dr. Mason:* Reed Hadley, *Danny Harland:* Darryl Hickman, *Leick Thorne:* Chill Wills, *Judge:* Paul Everton, *Mrs. Robie:* Olive Blakeney, *Bedford:* Addison Richards, *Catterson:* Harry Depp, *Carlson:* Grant Mitchell, *Medcraft (Mortician):* Milton Parsons, *Norton:* Earl Schenck, *Lin Robie:* Hugh Maguire, *Tess Robie:* Betty Hannon, *Nurse:* Kay Riley, *Sheriff:* Guy Beach, *Cook at Robie's Ranch:* Audrey Betz, *Conductor:* Jim Farley, *Man:* Charles Tannen, *Fisherwoman:* Mae Marsh.

Lenny with Dustin Hoffman and Valerie Perrine.

LENNY (1974) UA. Produced by Marvin Worth. Directed by Bob Fosse. Executive Producer, David V. Picker. Screenplay by Julian Barry, based on his play. Production Manager and Associate Producer, Robert Greenhut. Photography, Bruce Surtees. Editor, Alan Heim. Designer, Joel Schiller. Costumes, Albert Wolsky. Assistant Directors, Ted Zachary, Douglas Green and Tommy Lofaro. Set Decorations, Nicholas Romanac. Music supervised by Ralph Burns and performed by the Miles Davis Quintet. Sound, Dennis Maitland. Technical Advisers, Honey Bruce, Sally Marr and Kitty Bruce. Rated R. 112 minutes

Lenny Bruce: Dustin Hoffman, *Honey Bruce:* Valerie Perrine, *Sally Marr:* Jan Miner, *Artie Silver:* Stanley Beck, *Sherman Hart:* Gary Morton, *Aunt Mema:* Rashel Novikoff, *Jack Goldstein:* Guy Rennie, *Baltimore Strip Club MC:* Frankie Man, *San Francisco Defense Attorney:* Mark Harris, *San Francisco Judge:* Lee Sandman, *Kitty Bruce at 11:* Susan Malnick, *San Francisco Judge:* Martin Begley, *New York Cop:* Phil Philbin, *New York Attorneys:* Ted Sorrell and Clarence Thomas, *New York District Attorney:* Mike Murphy, *Marty:* Buddy Boylan, *San Francisco Fingerprint Officer:* Mickey Gatlin, *Comic:* George DeWitt, *Chorus Girl:* Judy LaScala, *Hunters:* Glen Wilder and Frank Orsatti, *Nurse's Aide:* Michelle Young, *Kitty at 1:* Allison Goldstein, *Kitty at 2:* Bridghid Glass, *Rev. Mooney:* Jack Nagle.

LES GIRLS (1957) MGM. Producer, Sol C. Siegel. Associate Producer, Saul Chaplin. Director, George Cukor. CinemaScope, MetroColor. Author, Vera Caspary. Screenplay, John Patrick. Art Directors, William A. Horning, Gene Allen. Music adapted and conducted by Adolph Deutsch. Orchestration, Alexander Courage, Skip Martin. Songs by Cole Porter: "Ladies in Waiting," "Les Girls," "Flower Song," "Ça, C'est L'Amour," "You're Just Too, Too," "Why Am I So Gone About That Gal?" Cinematographer, Robert Surtees. Editor, Ferris Webster. Choreography, Jack Cole. 114 minutes

Barry Nichols: Gene Kelly, *Joy Henderson:* Mitzi Gaynor, *Lady Wren:* Kay Kendall, *Angele Ducros:* Taina Elg, *Pierre Ducros:* Jacques Bergerac, *Sir Gerald Wren:* Leslie Phillips, *Judge:* Henry Daniell, *Sir Percy:* Patrick Macnee, *Mr. Outward:* Stephen Vercoe, *Associate*

Judge: Philip Tonge, *Court Usher:* Owen McGiveney, *French Stage Manager:* Francis Ravel, *Wardrobe Woman:* Adrienne d'Ambricourt, *French House Manager:* Maurice Marsac, *English Photographer:* Gil Stuart, *Fanatic:* Cyril Delevanti, *Waiter:* George Navarro, *Headwaiter:* Marcel de la Brosse, *Spanish Peasant Man:* Nestor Paiva, *Stage Manager:* Alberto Morin, *Stout French Woman:* Maya van Horn, *Sleepy Frenchman:* George Davis, *Flamenco Dancer:* Louisa Triana, *Shopkeeper:* Genevieve Pasques, *Dancer:* Lilyan Chauvin, *Stagehand:* Dick Alexander.

Les Girls with Kay Kendall, Mitzi Gaynor, Gene Kelly and Taina Elg.

Les Miserables with Frances Drake, John Beal and Rochelle Hudson.

LES MISERABLES (1935) UA. A 20th Century Pictures Production. Produced by Darryl F. Zanuck. Associate Producers, William Goetz and Raymond Griffith. Directed by Richard Boleslawski. Based on the novel by Victor Hugo. Screenplay, W. P. Lipscomb. Art Director, Richard Day. Costumes, Omar Kiam. Musical Numbers, Alfred Newman. Assistant Director, Eric Stacey. Cinematography, Gregg Toland. Editor, Barbara McLean. Sound, Frank Maher and Roger Heman. 108 minutes. Other versions include 20th, 1952

Jean Valjean: Fredric March, *Inspector Javert:* Charles Laughton, *Cosette:* Rochelle Hudson, *Little Cosette:* Marilyn Knowlden, *Eponine Thernardier:* Frances Drake, *Marius:* John Beal, *Bishop Bienvenu:* Sir Cedric Hardwicke, *Madame Magloire:* Jessie Ralph, *Mlle. Baptieme:* Mary Forbes, *Fantine:* Florence Eldridge, *M. Thernardier:* Ferdinand Gottschalk, *Madame Thernardier:* Jane Kerr, *Mother Superior:* Eily Malyon, *Brissac:* Vernon Downing, *LeMarque:* Lyons Wickland, *Enjolras:* John Carradine, *Brevet:* Charles Jockey Haefeli, *Genflou:* Leonid Kinskey, *Chenildieu:* John M. Bleifer, *Cochepaille:* Harry Semels, *Toussaint:* Florence Roberts, *Valsin (Dog Fancier):* Lorin Raker, *Inspector Devereury:* Perry Ivins, *Francois:* Pat Somer-

set, *Judge at Favorelles:* Herbert Bunston, *Senior Prefect:* Keith Kenneth Jacques: G. Raymond (Bill) Nye, *Prison Governor:* Robert Greig, *Old Beggarwoman:* Virginia Howell, *Beam Warder:* Harry Cording, *Innkeeper:* Paul Irving, *Duval:* Lowell Drew, *L'Estrange:* Thomas R. Mills, *Marcin:* Davison Clark, *Factory Foreman:* Montague Shaw, *Factory Forewoman:* Margaret Bloodgood, *Mayor's Clerk:* Sidney Bracy, *Lodging Housekeeper:* Cecil Weston, *Head Gardener at Convent:* Ian Maclaren, *Duchaine:* Gilbert Clayton, *Priest:* Leonard Mudie, *Pierre:* Olaf Hytten.

The Letter with Gale Sondergaard, Bette Davis and Tetsu Komai.

THE LETTER (1940) WB. In Charge of Production, Jack L. Warner. Executive Producer, Hal B. Wallis. Producers, Jack L. Warner, Hal B. Wallis. Associate Producer, Robert Lord. Director, William Wyler. From the story by W. Somerset Maugham. Screenplay, Howard Koch. Cameraman, Tony Gaudio. Editor, George Amy. Orchestral Arrangements, Hugo Friedhofer. Technical Advisers, Louis Vincenot and John Vallasin. Other versions: *The Letter* (Paramount, 1929), *The Unfaithful* (WB, 1947). 97 minutes

Leslie Crosbie: Bette Davis, *Robert Crosbie:* Herbert Marshall, *Howard Joyce:* James Stephenson, *Dorothy Joyce:* Frieda Inescort, *Mrs. Hammond:* Gale Sondergaard, *John Withers:* Bruce Lester, *Adele Ainsworth:* Elizabeth Earl, *Prescott:* Cecil Kellaway, *Ong Chi Seng:* (Victor) Sen Yung, *Mrs. Cooper:* Doris Lloyd, *Chung Hi:* Willie Fung, *Head Boy:* Tetsu Komai, *Fred:* Leonard Mudie, *Driver:* John Ridgely, *Bob's Friends:* Charles Irwin, Holmes Herbert, *Well-Wisher:* Douglas Walton.

A Letter to Three Wives with Ann Sothern, Linda Darnell and Jeanne Crain.

155

A LETTER TO THREE WIVES (1948) 20th. Producer, Sol C. Siegel. Director-Screenplay, Joseph L. Mankiewicz. Adapted by Vera Caspary, from a *Cosmopolitan* magazine novel by John Klempner. Art Directors, Lyle Wheeler, J. Russell Spencer. Music, Alfred Newman. Photography, Arthur Miller. Editor, J. Watson Webb, Jr. 103 minutes

Deborah Bishop: Jeanne Crain, *Lora May Hollingsway:* Linda Darnell, *Rita Phipps:* Ann Sothern, *George Phipps:* Kirk Douglas, *Porter Hollingsway:* Paul Douglas, *Babe:* Barbara Lawrence, *Brad Bishop:* Jeffrey Lynn, *Mrs. Finney:* Connie Gilchrist, *Mrs. Manleigh:* Florence Bates, *Mr. Manleigh:* Hobart Cavanaugh, *Kathleen:* Patti Brady, *Miss Hawkins:* Ruth Vivian, *Sadie:* Thelma Ritter, *Old Man:* Stuart Holmes, *Nick:* George Offerman, Jr., *Character:* Ralph Brooks, *Thomasino:* Joe Bautista, *Butler:* James Adamson, *Waiter:* John Davidson, *Messengers:* Carl Switzer, John Venn, *Waiter:* Sammy Finn.

LIBELED LADY (1936) MGM. Produced by Lawrence Weingarten. Directed by Jack Conway. Story, Wallace Sullivan. Screenplay, Maurine Watkins, Howard Emmett Rogers, and George Oppenheimer. Camera, Norbert Brodine. Editor, Frederick Y. Smith. Score, William Axt. Remade as *Easy to Wed* (MGM, 1946). 98 minutes

Bill Chandler: William Powell, *Gladys:* Jean Harlow, *Connie Allenbury:* Myrna Loy, *Haggerty:* Spencer Tracy, *Mr. Allenbury:* Walter Connolly, *Mr. Bane:* Charley Grapewin, *Mrs. Burns-Norvell:* Cora Witherspoon, *Fishing Instructor:* E. E. Clive, *Babs:* Bunny Lauri Beatty, *Ching:* Otto Yamaoka, *Graham:* Charles Trowbridge, *Magistrate:* Spencer Charters, *Bellhop:* George Chandler, *Connie's Maid:* Greta Meyer, *Johnny:* Billy Benedict, *Harvey Allen:* Hal K. Dawson, *Divorce Detective:* William Newell, *Taxi Driver:* Duke York, *Jacques:* Harry Allen, *Detective:* Pat West, *Clerk:* Edwin Stanley, *Photographer:* Wally Maher, *Alex:* Tom Mahoney, *Photographer:* Pat Somerset, *Barker:* Richard Tucker, *Maid:* Libby Taylor, *Dickson:* Jed Prouty, *Barker:* Jack Mulhall, *Steward:* Charles Irwin, *Moe:* Eddie Shubert, *Waiter:* George Davis, *Minister:* Thomas Pogue, *Maid in Hall:* Hattie McDaniel, *Cable Editor:* Howard C. Hickman, *Barker:* Charles King, *Archibald:* Charles Croker King, *Fortune Teller:* Ines Palange, *Justice of the Peace:* Harry C. Bradley, *Justice's Wife:* Bodil Ann Rosing, *Butler:* Barnett Parker, *Palmer:* Robin Adair, *Ragamuffins:* Buster Phelps, Bobby (Bobs) Watson, Tommy Bond.

Libeled Lady with Jean Harlow, William Powell and Spencer Tracy.

LIFE BEGINS FOR ANDY HARDY (1941) MGM. Directed by George Seitz. Based on the characters created by Aurania Rouverol. Screenplay, Agnes Christine Johnston. Art Director, Cedric Gibbons. Music Director, Georgie Stoll. Photography, Lester White. Editor, Elmo Veron. 100 minutes

Andy Hardy: Mickey Rooney, *Judge Hardy:* Lewis Stone, *Betsy Booth:* Judy Garland, *Mrs. Hardy:* Fay Holden, *Polly Benedict:* Ann Ruther-

ford, *Aunt Milly:* Sara Haden, *Jennitt Hicks:* Patricia Dane, *Jimmy Frobisher:* Ray McDonald, *Beezy:* George Breakston, *Father Gallagher:* Ralph Byrd, *Rabbi Strauss:* Manart Kippen, *Dr. Griffin:* William J. Holmes, *Dr. Storfen:* Purnell Pratt, *Dr. Waggoner:* Pierre Watkin, *Operator:* Frances Morris, *Chuck:* Tommy Kelly, *Private:* Robert Winkler, *Commandant:* William Forrest, *Jackson:* Byron Shores, *Ted:* Hollis Jewell, *Boys:* Sidney Miller, Roger Daniel, *Policemen:* Arthur Loft, James Flavin, *Elizabeth Norton:* Charlotte Wynters, *Delivery Boy:* Bob Pittard, *Mr. Maddox:* Lester Mathews, *Clerk:* Don Brodie, *Taxi Driver:* John Harmon, *Stationer:* Frank Ferguson, *Boy "Kelly":* Leonard Sues, *Florist:* George Carleton, *Janitor:* George Ovey, *Watchman:* Robert Homans, *Miss Dean:* Ann Morriss, *Miss Gomez:* Mira McKinney, *Miss Howard:* Nora Lane, *Paul McWilliams:* John Eldredge, *Peter Dugan:* Joseph Crehan, *Secretary:* Bess Flowers, *Truckmen:* Paul Newlan, Duke York.

Life Begins for Andy Hardy with Judy Garland and Lewis Stone.

LIFEBOAT (1944) 20th. Producer, Kenneth Macgowan. Director, Alfred Hitchcock. Author, John Steinbeck. Screenplay, Jo Swerling. Art Directors, James Basevi, Maurice Ransford. Musical Score, Hugo W. Friedhofer. Musical Director, Emil Newman. Cameraman, Glen MacWilliams. Special Effects, Fred Sersen. Editor, Dorothy Spencer. 96 minutes

Connie Porter: Tallulah Bankhead, *Gus:* William Bendix, *The German:* Walter Slezak, *Alice:* Mary Anderson, *Kovak:* John Hodiak, *Rittenhouse:* Henry Hull, *Mrs. Higgins:* Heather Angel, *Stanley Garrett:* Hume Cronyn, *Joe:* Canada Lee, *German Sailor:* William Yetter, Jr., *Man in Before and After Ad:* Alfred Hitchcock.

Lifeboat with Hume Cronyn, Henry Hull, Tallulah Bankhead, John Hodiak, Mary Anderson and Canada Lee.

Life of Emile Zola with Vladimir Sokoloff, Paul Muni and Erin O'Brien-Moore.

THE LIFE OF EMILE ZOLA (1937) WB. Vice-President in Charge of Production, Jack L. Warner. Associate Executive in Charge of Production, Hal B. Wallis. Supervisor, Henry Blanke. Directed by William Dieterle. Story, Heinz Herald and Geza Herczeg. Screenplay, Heinz Herald, Geza Herczeg, and Norman Reilly Raine. Music, Max Steiner. Orchestra Direction, Leo Forbstein. Assistant Director, Russ Saunders. Cinematography, Tony Gaudio. Editor, Warren Lowe. Art Director, Anton Grot. Make-up, Perc Westmore. Dialogue Director, Irving Rapper. Gowns, Milo Anderson and Ali Hubert. Interior Decorator, Albert C. Wilson. 116 minutes

Emile Zola: Paul Muni, *Lucie Dreyfus:* Gale Sondergaard, *Captain Alfred Dreyfus:* Joseph Schildkraut, *Alexandrine Zola:* Gloria Holden, *Maitre Labori:* Donald Crisp, *Nana:* Erin O'Brien-Moore, *Charpentier:* John Litel, *Colonel Picquart:* Henry O'Neill, *Anatole France:* Morris Carnovsky, *Major Dort:* Louis Calhern, *Commander of Paris:* Ralph Morgan, *Major Walsin-Esterhazy:* Robert Barrat, *Paul Cezanne:* Vladimir Sokoloff, *Chief of Staff:* Harry Davenport, *Major Henry:* Robert Warwick, *M. Delagorgue:* Charles Richman, *Pierre Dreyfus:* Dickie Moore, *Jeanne Dreyfus:* Rolla Gourvitch, *Minister of War:* Gilbert Emery, *Colonel Sandherr:* Walter Kingsford, *Assistant Chief of Staff:* Paul Everton, *Cavaignac:* Montagu Love, *Van Cassell:* Frank Sheridan, *Mr. Richards:* Lumsden Hare, *Helen Richards:* Marcia Mae Jones, *Madame Zola:* Florence Roberts, *Georges Clemenceau:* Grant Mitchell, *Captain Guignet:* Moroni Olsen, *Brucker:* Egon Brecher, *M. Perrenx:* Frank Reicher, *Senator Scheurer-Kestner:* Walter O. Stahl, *Albert:* Frank Darien, *Madame Charpentier:* Countess Iphigenie Castiglioni, *Chief Censor:* Arthur Aylesworth, *Mathieu Dreyfus:* Frank Mayo, *Major D'Aboville:* Alexander Leftwich, *La Rue:* Paul Irving, *Prefect of Police:* Pierre Watkin, *Commander of Paris:* Holmes Herbert, *General Gillian:* Robert Cummings, Sr., *Lieutenant:* Harry Worth, *Swartzkoppen:* William von Brincken.

LIFE WITH FATHER (1947) WB. Produced by Robert Buckner. Directed by Michael Curtiz. Color by Technicolor. From Oscar Serlin's stage production of the play by Howard Lindsay and Russell Crouse. Screenplay, Donald Ogden Stewart. Art Director, Robert Haas. Technicolor Color Director, Natalie Kalmus. Associate, Monroe W. Burbank. Photography, Peverell Marley and William V. Skall. Music Director, Leo F. Forbstein. Assistant Director, Robert Vreeland. Editor, George Amy. Sound, C. A. Riggs. Dialogue Director, Herschel Daugherty. Montages, James Leicester. Special Effects, William McGann. Special Effects Director, Ray Foster. Technical Advisor, Mrs. Clarence Day. Sets, George James Hopkins. Wardrobe, Milo Anderson. Make-up, Perc Westmore. Music, Max Steiner. Orchestral Arrangements, Murray Cutter. The play ran from 1939 to 1947, inspiring a sequel, *Life With Mother* (1948-9), and a TV series (1955). 118 minutes

Father Clarence: William Powell, *Vinnie:* Irene Dunne, *Mary:* Eliza-beth Taylor, *Reverend Dr. Lloyd:* Edmund Gwenn, *Cora:* ZaSu Pitts, *Clarence:* Jimmy Lydon, *Margaret:* Emma Dunn, *Dr. Humphries:* Moroni Olsen, *Mrs. Whitehead:* Elisabeth Risdon, *Harlan:* Derek Scott, *Whitney:* Johnny Calkins, *John:* Martin Milner, *Annie:* Heather Wilde, *The Policeman:* Monte Blue, *Nora:* Mary Field, *Maggie:* Queenie Leonard, *Delia:* Nancy Evans, *Miss Wiggins:* Clara Blandick, *Dr. Somers:* Frank Elliott, *Scrub Woman:* Clara Reid, *Milk Man:* Philo McCullough, *Corsetierre:* Loie Bridge, *Salesman:* George Meader, *Mr. Morley:* Douglas Kennedy, *Clerk:* Phil Van Zandt, *Stock Quotation Operator:* Russell Arms, *Hilda:* Faith Kruger, *Francois:* Jean Del Val, *Twins:* Michael and Ralph Mineo, *Father of Twins:* Creighton Hale, *Mother of Twins:* Jean Andren, *Ellen:* Elaine Lange, *Perkins (Clerk):* John Beck, *Chef:* Jack Martin, *Girl in Delmonico's:* Arlene Dahl.

Life With Father with William Powell, Irene Dunne, Derek Scott, James Lydon, Johnny Calkins and Martin Milner.

LIGHTS OF NEW YORK (1928) WB. Directed by Bryan Foy. Story and Scenario, F. Hugh Herbert and Murray Roth. Cameraman, E. B. Dupar. Editor, Jack Killifer. The first all-talking film, this also had titles in the silent tradition. 57 minutes

Kitty Lewis: Helene Costello, *Eddie Morgan:* Cullen Landis, *Hawk Miller:* Wheeler Oakman, *Gene:* Eugene Pallette, *Molly Thompson:* Gladys Brockwell, *Mrs. Morgan:* Mary Carr, *Detective Crosby:* Robert Elliott, *Sam:* Tom Dugan, *Police Chief Collins:* Tom McGuire, *Tommy:* Guy D'Ennery, *Jake Jackson:* Walter Percival, *Dan Dickson:* Jere Delaney.

Lights of New York with Cullen Landis and Helene Costello.

LILI (1953) MGM. Producer, Edwin H. Knopf. Director, Charles Walters. Technicolor. From a story by Paul Gallico. Screenplay, Helen Deutsch. Art Directors, Cedric Gibbons, Paul Groesse. Cinematographer, Robert Planck. Editor, Ferris Webster. Choreography, Charles

Walters and Dorothy Jarnac. Music, Bronislau Kaper. Costumes, Mary Anne Nyberg. Puppets created by Paul B. Walton and Michael O'Rourke. Song, "Hi-Lili, Hi-Lo" by Helen Deutsch and Bronislau Kaper. 81 minutes

Lili Daurier: Leslie Caron, *Paul Berthalet:* Mel Ferrer, *Marc:* Jean Pierre Aumont, *Rosalie:* Zsa Zsa Gabor, *Jacquot:* Kurt Kasznar, *Peach Lips:* Amanda Blake, *Proprietor:* Alex Gerry, *Monsieur Corvier:* Ralph Dumke, *Monsieur Tonit:* Wilton Graff, *Monsieur Erique:* George Baxter, *Fruit Peddler:* Eda Reiss Merin, *Workman:* George Davis, *Second Workman:* Reginald Simpson, *Concessionaire:* Mitchell Lewis, *Whistler:* Fred Walton, *Flirting Vendor:* Richard Grayson, *Specialty Dancer:* Dorothy Jarnac, *Specialty Dancers:* Arthur Mendez, Dick Lerner, Frank Radcliffe, Lars Hensen.

Lili with Leslie Caron.

Lilies of the Field with Isa Crino, Pamela Branch, Lilia Skala, Francesca Jarvis, Lisa Mann and Sidney Poitier.

LILIES OF THE FIELD (1963) UA. Producer-Director, Ralph Nelson. Screenplay, James Poe. Based on a novel by William E. Barrett.

Associate Producer, J. Paul Popkin. Music, Jerry Goldsmith. A Rainbow Production. Cinematographer, Ernest Haller. Editor, John McCafferty. 94 minutes

Homer Smith: Sidney Poitier, *Mother Maria:* Lilia Skala, *Sister Gertrude:* Lisa Mann, *Sister Agnes:* Isa Crino, *Sister Albertine:* Francesca Jarvis, *Sister Elizabeth:* Pamela Branch, *Juan Acalito:* Stanley Adams, *Father Murphy:* Dan Frazer, *Ashton, the Contractor:* Ralph Nelson.

Limelight with Claire Bloom and Charlie Chaplin.

LIMELIGHT (1952) UA. Producer-Director, Charles Chaplin. Screenplay by Charles Chaplin. Music by Charles Chaplin. Assistant Director, Robert Aldrich. 114 minutes

Calvero: Charles Chaplin, *Terry:* Claire Bloom, *Neville:* Sydney Chaplin, *Harlequin:* Andre Eglevsky, *Columbine:* Melissa Hayden, *Clowns:* Charles Chaplin, Jr., Wheeler Dryden, *Children:* Geraldine, Michael and Victoria Chaplin, *Postant:* Nigel Bruce, *Accompanist:* Norman Lloyd, *Partner:* Buster Keaton, *Landlady:* Marjorie Bennett.

LITTLE BIG MAN (1970) National General. A Cinema Center Films presentation. Produced by Stuart Millar. Directed by Arthur Penn. Panavision and Technicolor. Based on the novel by Thomas Berger. Screenplay, Calder Willingham. A Stockbridge-Hiller Production. Music, John Hammond. Associate Producer, Gene Lasko. Editor, Dede Allen. Photography, Harry Stradling, Jr. Production designed by Dean Tavoularis. Costumes designed by Dorothy Jeakins. Assistant Director, Mike Moder. Sound, Al Overton, Jr., and Bud Alper. Art Director, Angelo Graham. Set Decorator, George R. Nelson. Hoffman's Make-up by Dick Smith. Hairstylist, Lynn del Kail. Make-up, Terry Miles. Wardrobe, Frank Delmar. Cavalry Adviser, Jerry Gatlin. Stunt-Gaffer, Hal Needham. Filmed in Montana, California and Alberta, Canada, with the assistance of the Crow, Cheyenne and Stony Nations. Rated GP. 150 minutes

Jack Crabb: Dustin Hoffman, *Louise Pendrake (Lulu Kane):* Faye Dunaway, *Allardyce T. Merriweather:* Martin Balsam, *Gen. George A. Custer:* Richard Mulligan, *Old Lodge Skins:* Chief Dan George, *Wild Bill Hickok:* Jeff Corey, *Sunshine:* Amy Eccles, *Olga:* Kelly Jean Peters, *Caroline Crabb:* Carole Androsky, *Little Horse:* Robert Little Star, *Younger Bear:* Cal Bellini, *Shadow That Comes in Sight:* Ruben Moreno, *Burns Red in the Sun:* Steve Shemayne, *Historian:* William Hickey, *Sergeant:* James Anderson, *Lieutenant:* Jesse Vint, *Major:* Alan Oppenheimer, *Rev. Silas Pendrake:* Thayer David, *Mr. Kane:* Philip Kenneally, *Captain:* Jack Bannon, *Young Jack:* Ray Dimas, *Adolescent Jack:* Alan Howard, *Card Player:* Jack Mullaney, *Younger Bear as youth:* Steve Miranda, *Deacon:* Lou Cutell, *Shotgun Guard:* M. Emmet Walsh, *Digging Bear:* Emily Cho, *Little Elk:* Cecelia Kootenay, *Corn Woman:* Linda Dyer, *Buffalo Wallow Woman:* Dessie Bad Bear, *Crow Scout:* Len George, *Pawnee:* Norman Nathan, *Madame:* Helen Verbit, *Bartender:*

Bert Conway, *Giant Trooper:* Earl Rosell, *Sergeant:* Ken Mayer, *Man at Bar:* Bud Cokes, *Assassin:* Rory O'Brien, *Flirt:* Tracy Hotchner, *Bit:* Herb Nelson, *Stage Passenger:* Don Brodie.

Little Big Man with Dustin Hoffman and Faye Dunaway.

Little Caesar with Edward G. Robinson and Douglas Fairbanks, Jr.

LITTLE CAESAR (1930) WB. Directed by Mervyn LeRoy. Based on the novel by W. R. Burnett. Scenario and Dialogue, Francis Faragoh. Photography, Tony Gaudio. Art Director, Anton Grot. Editor, Ray Curtiss. General Music Director, Erno Rapee. Vitaphone. 77 minutes

Caesar Enrico Bandello: Edward G. Robinson, *Joe Massara:* Douglas Fairbanks, Jr., *Olga Strassoff:* Glenda Farrell, *Tony Passa:* William Collier, Jr., *Diamond Pete Montana:* Ralph Ince, *Otero:* George E. Stone, *Lt. Tom Flaherty:* Thomas Jackson, *Sam Vettori:* Stanley Fields, *DeVoss:* Armand Kaliz, *The Big Boy:* Sidney Blackmer, *Commissioner McClure:* Landers Stevens, *Little Arnie Lorch:* Maurice Black, *Peppi:* Noel Madison, *Ritz Colonna:* Nick Bela, *Ma Magdalena:* Lucille La Verne, *Kid Bean:* Ben Hendricks, Jr., *Waiter:* Al Hill, *Cashier:* Ernie S. Adams, *Cafe Guest:* Larry Steers, *Machine Gunner:* George Daly.

THE LITTLE FOXES (1941) RKO. Produced by Samuel Goldwyn. Directed by William Wyler. Based on the play by Lillian Hellman. Music, Meredith Willson. Screenplay, Lillian Hellman. Art Director, Stephen Goosson. Assistant Director, William Tummel. Costumes, Orry-Kelly. Sets, Howard Bristol. Miss Davis' make-up, Perc Westmore. Photography, Gregg Toland. Editor, Daniel Mandell. Sound, Frank Maher. Sequel was *Another Part of the Forest* (Univ., 1948), which was set 20 years earlier. 116 minutes

Regina Hubbard Giddens: Bette Davis, *Horace Giddens:* Herbert Marshall, *Alexandra Giddens:* Teresa Wright, *David Hewitt:* Richard Carlson, *Birdie Hubbard:* Patricia Collinge, *Leo Hubbard:* Dan Duryea, *Ben Hubbard:* Charles Dingle, *Oscar Hubbard:* Carl Benton Reid, *Addie:* Jessica Grayson, *Cal:* John Marriott, *William Marshall:* Russell Hicks, *Sam Manders:* Lucien Littlefield, *Lucy Hewitt:* Virginia Brissac, *Julia:* Terry Nibert, *Dawson, Hotel Manager:* Alan Bridge, *Simon:* Charles R. Moore, *Servant:* Kenny Washington, *Bit:* Henry "Hot Shot" Thomas, *Train Companion:* Lew Kelly, *Guest:* Hooper Atchley, *Depositor:* Henry Roquemore.

The Little Foxes with Herbert Marshall and Bette Davis.

Little Miss Marker with Dorothy Dell, John Kelly, Adolphe Menjou and Shirley Temple.

LITTLE MISS MARKER (1934) Par. Produced by B. P. Schulberg. Directed by Alexander Hall. From a story by Damon Runyon. Screenplay, William R. Lipman, Sam Hellman, Gladys Lehman. Photography, Alfred Gilks. Editor, William Shea. Songs by Ralph Rainger and Leo Robin: "I'm a Black Sheep Who Is Blue," "Low Down Lul-

159

laby," "Laugh You Son-of-a-Gun." 80 minutes. Remade as *Sorrowful Jones* (Par., 1949), *Forty Pounds of Trouble* (Univ., 1963) and *Little Miss Marker* (Univ., 1979)

Sorrowful Jones: Adolphe Menjou, *Bangles Carson:* Dorothy Dell, *Big Steve Halloway:* Charles Bickford, *Marthy Jane, Miss Marker:* Shirley Temple, *Regret:* Lynne Overman, *Doc Chesley:* Frank McGlynn, Sr., *Sun Rise:* Jack Sheehan, *Grinder:* Gary Owen, *Dizzy Memphis:* Sleep 'n Eat (Willie Best), *Eddie:* Puggy White, *Buggs:* Tammany Young, *Bennie The Gouge:* Sam Hardy, *Marky's Father:* Edward Earle, *Sore Toe:* Warren Hymer, *Canvas Back:* John Kelly, *Doctor Ingalls:* Frank Conroy, *Detective Reardon:* James Burke, *Bookie:* Stanley Price, *Bettors:* Ernie Adams, Don Brodie.

LITTLE WOMEN (1933) RKO. Executive Producer, Merian C. Cooper. Supervised by Kenneth Macgowan. Directed by George Cukor. From the novel by Louisa May Alcott. Screenplay, Sarah Y. Mason and Victor Heerman. Music, Max Steiner. Photography, Henry Gerrard. Editor, Jack Kitchin. Sound, Frank H. Harris. Remade by MGM, 1949. 107 minutes (originally 115 mins.)

Jo: Katharine Hepburn, *Amy:* Joan Bennett, *Fritz Bhaor:* Paul Lukas, *Meg:* Frances Dee, *Beth:* Jean Parker, *Aunt March:* Edna May Oliver, *Laurie:* Douglass Montgomery, *Mr. Laurence:* Henry Stephenson, *Marmee:* Spring Byington, *Mr. March:* Samuel Hinds, *Hannah:* Mabel Colcord, *Brooks:* John Davis Lodge, *Mamie:* Nydia Westman.

The Littlest Rebel with James Flavin, John Boles and Shirley Temple.

Live and Let Die with Roger Moore and Gloria Hendry.

THE LITTLEST REBEL (1935) 20th. Produced by Darryl F. Zanuck. Associate Producer, B. G. DeSylva. Directed by David Butler. Screenplay, Edwin Burke. Musical Arrangement, Cyril Mockridge. Photography, John Seitz. Editor, Irene Morra. From the play by Edward Peple. Assistant Director, Booth McCracken. Art Director, William Darling. Settings, Thomas K. Little. Costumes, Gwen Wakeling. Sound, S. C. Chapman and Roger Heman. 70 minutes

Virgie Cary: Shirley Temple, *Captain Herbert Cary:* John Boles, *Colonel Morrison:* Jack Holt, *Mrs. Cary:* Karen Morley, *Uncle Billy:* Bill Robinson, *Sergeant Dudley:* Guinn (Big Boy) Williams, *James Henry:* Willie Best, *Abraham Lincoln:* Frank McGlynn, Sr., *Mammy:* Bessie Lyle, *Sally Ann:* Hannah Washington, *Guard:* James Flavin.

LIVE AND LET DIE (1973) UA. Produced by Albert R. Broccoli and Harry Saltzman. Directed by Guy Hamilton. Screenplay by Tom Mankiewicz, based on Ian Fleming's characters. Photography, Ted Moore. Choreography, Geoffrey Holder. Music by George Martin. Title song by Paul and Linda McCartney, performed by Paul McCartney and Wings. Supervising Art Director, Syd Cain. Costumes, Julie Harris. Assistant Director, Derek Cracknell and Alan Hopkins. Editors, Bert Bates, Raymond Poulton and John Shirley. Shark scenes directed by William Grefe. 2nd Unit Photography, John Harris. Special Effects, Derek Meddings. Titles, Maurice Binder. Stunt Coordinators, Bob Simmons, Jerry Comeaux, Ross Kananga, Bill Bennot, Eddie Smith and Joie Chitwood. An Eon Production in Eastman Color. Produced in England. Roger Moore's first 007 film. Rated PG. 121 minutes

James Bond: Roger Moore, *Dr. Kananga (Mr. Big):* Yaphet Kotto, *Solitaire:* Jane Seymour, *Sheriff Pepper:* Clifton James, *Tee Hee:* Julius W. Harris, *Baron Samedi:* Geoffrey Holder, *Felix Leiter:* David Hedison, *Rosie:* Gloria Hendry, *M:* Bernard Lee, *Moneypenny:* Lois Maxwell, *Adam:* Tommy Lane, *Whisper:* Earl Jolly Brown, *Quarrel:* Roy Stewart, *Strutter:* Lon Satton, *Cabdriver:* Arnold Williams, *Mrs. Bell:* Ruth Kempf, *Charlie;* Joie Chitwood, *Beautiful Girl:* Madeline Smith, *Dambala:* Michael Ebbin, *Salesgirl:* Kubi Chaza, *Singer:* B. J. Arnau, *Hungarian Delegate:* Gabor Vernon.

Little Women with Katharine Hepburn and Edna May Oliver.

LIVES OF A BENGAL LANCER (1935) Par. Produced by Louis D. Lighton. Directed by Henry Hathaway. From the book by Francis Yeats-Brown. Screenplay, Waldemar Young, John L. Balderston, Achmed Abdullah, Grover Jones, William Slavens McNutt. Assistant Directors, Paul Wing and Clem Beauchamp. Editor, Ellsworth Hoagland. Cinematography, Charles Lang. Recording Engineer, Harold Lewis. Art Directors, Hans Dreier and Roland Anderson. Costumes, Travis Banton. 109 minutes

Captain McGregor: Gary Cooper, *Lieutenant Fortesque:* Franchot Tone, *Lieutenant Stone:* Richard Cromwell, *Colonel Stone:* Sir Guy

Standing, *Major Hamilton:* C. Aubrey Smith, *Hamzulla Kahn:* Monte Blue, *Tania Volkanskaya:* Kathleen Burke, *Lieutenant Barrett:* Colin Tapley, *Mohammed Khan:* Douglass R. Dumbrille, *Emir:* Akim Tamiroff, *Hendrickson:* Jameson Thomas, *Ram Singh:* Noble Johnson, *Major General Woodley:* Lumsden Hare, *Grand Vizier:* J. Carrol Naish, *The Ghazi:* Rollo Lloyd, *McGregor's Servant:* Charles Stevens, *Afridi:* Mischa Auer, *Solo Dancer:* Myra Kinch, *Shah:* Boghwan Singh, *Ali Hamdi:* Abdul Hassan, *Lieutenant Norton:* Clive Morgan, *Servant:* Eddie Das, *Snake Charmer:* Leonid Kinskey, *Muezzin:* Hussain Nasri, *Lieutenant Gilhooley:* James Warwick, *Kushal Khan:* George Regas, *British Officer:* Major Sam Harris, *Indian Officers:* Ram Singh, Jamiel Hasson, James Bell, General Ikonnikoff, F. A. Armenta, *Experienced Clerk:* Claude King, *Novice:* Reginald Sheffield, *Girl on Train:* Lya Lys.

Lives of a Bengal Lancer with Franchot Tone and Gary Cooper.

Lloyds of London with Tyrone Power and Madeleine Carroll.

LLOYDS OF LONDON (1936) 20th. Associate Producer, Kenneth Macgowan. Directed by Henry King. Author, Curtis Kenyon. Screenplay by Ernest Pascal, Walter Ferris. Musical Director, Louis Silvers. Cameraman, Bert Glennon. Editor, Barbara McLean. 115 minutes.

Young Jonathan: Freddie Bartholomew, *Clementine:* Madeleine Carroll, *Angerstein:* Sir Guy Standing, *Jonathan:* Tyrone Power, *Old "Q":* C. Aubrey Smith, *Polly:* Virginia Field, *Hawkins:* Montagu Love, *Gavin Gore:* Gavin Muir, *First Captain:* Arthur Hohl, *Watson:* J. M. Kerrigan, *Young Nelson:* Douglas Scott, *Captain Suckling:* Lumsden Hare, *Waiter at Lloyd's:* Charles Coleman, *Waiter at Lloyd's:* Charles McNaughton, *Jukes:* Miles Mander, *Waiter at Lloyd's:* Leonard Mudie, *Reverend Nelson:* Murray Kinnell, *Widow Blake:* Una O'Con-

nor, *Smutt:* Will Stanton, *Potts:* Forrester Harvey, *Lord Stacy:* George Sanders, *Magistrate:* E. E. Clive, *Lord Drayton:* Robert Greig, *Lord Nelson:* John Burton, *Old Man:* Ivan F. Simpson, *Spokesman:* Holmes Herbert, *Lady Masham:* May Beatty, *Prince of Wales:* Hugh Huntley, *Willoughby:* Charles Croker-King, *French Lieutenant:* Georges Renavent, *Captain Hardy:* Lester Mathews, *Joshua Lamb:* Barlowe Borand, *Sir Thomas Lawrence:* Vernon Steele, *Dr. Beatty:* Winter Hall, *Catherine:* Ann Howard, *Susannah:* Fay Chaldecott, *Ann:* Yvonne Severn, *Benjamin Franklin:* Thomas Pogue, *Dr. Johnson:* Yorke Sherwood, *Boswell:* William Wagner, *Singer:* Constance Purdy.

LONG DAY'S JOURNEY INTO NIGHT (1962) Embassy. Producer, Ely Landau. Director, Sidney Lumet. Based on the play by Eugene O'Neill. Music, Andre Previn. Costumes, Motley. Cinematographer, Boris Kaufman. 180 minutes

Mary Tyrone: Katharine Hepburn, *James Tyrone, Sr.:* Ralph Richardson, *James Tyrone, Jr.:* Jason Robards, Jr., *Edmund Tyrone:* Dean Stockwell, *Cathleen:* Jeanne Barr.

Long Day's Journey Into Night with Jason Robards, Jr., Dean Stockwell, Katharine Hepburn and Sir Ralph Richardson.

THE LONGEST DAY (1962) 20th. Produced by Darryl F. Zanuck. Associate Producer, Elmo Williams. Directors, (American episodes) Andrew Marton, (British episodes) Ken Annakin, (German episodes) Bernhard Wicki. Based on the book by Cornelius Ryan, who also did the screenplay. Additional episodes written by Romain Gary, James Jones, David Pursall, Jack Seddon. Art Directors, Ted Haworth, Leon Barsacq, Vincent Korda. Thematic music by Paul Anka. Music composed and conducted by Maurice Jarre. Arrangements, Mitch Miller. Assistant Directors, Bernard Farrel, Louis Pitzele, Gerard Renateau, Henri Sokal. Cinematography, Henri Persin, Walter Wottitz, Pierre Levent, Jean Bourgoin. Editor, Samuel E. Beetley. Filmed in France. 180 minutes

Lt. Colonel Benjamin Vandervoort: John Wayne, *Brig. General Norman Cota:* Robert Mitchum, *Brig. General Theodore Roosevelt:* Henry Fonda, *Brig. General James M. Gavin:* Robert Ryan, *Destroyer Commander:* Rod Steiger, *U.S. Rangers:* Robert Wagner, Paul Anka, Fabian, Tommy Sands, *Private Dutch Schultz:* Richard Beymer, *Major General Robert Haines:* Mel Ferrer, *Sergeant Fuller:* Jeffrey Hunter, *Private Martini:* Sal Mineo, *Private Morris:* Roddy McDowall, *Lieutenant Sheen:* Stuart Whitman, *Captain Harding:* Steve Forrest, *Colonel Tom Newton:* Eddie Albert, *General Raymond O. Barton:* Edmond O'Brien, *Private John Steele:* Red Buttons, *Lieutenant Wilson:* Tom Tryon, *Major Gen. Walter Bedell Smith:* Alexander Knox, *Captain Frank:* Ray Danton, *General Dwight D. Eisenhower:* Henry Grace, *Private Harris:* Mark Damon, *Private Wilder:* Dewey Martin,

Colonel Caffey: John Crawford, *Joe Williams:* Ron Randell, *Lt. General Omar N. Bradley:* Nicholas Stuart, *Rear-Admiral Alan G. Kirk:* John Meillon, *Major of the Rangers:* Fred Dur, *R.A.F. Pilots:* Richard Burton, Donald Houston, *Captain Colin Maud:* Kenneth More, *Lord Lovat:* Peter Lawford, *Major John Howard:* Richard Todd, *Brig. General Parker:* Leo Genn, *British Padre:* John Gregson, *Private Flanagan:* Sean Connery, *Private Watney:* Michael Medwin, *R.A.F. Officer:* Leslie Phillips, *Janine Boitard:* Irina Demich, *Mayor of Colleville:* Bourvil, *Father Roulland:* Jean-Louis Barrault, *Commander Philippe Kieffer:* Christian Marquand, *Madame Barrault:* Arletty, *Maj. General Gunther Blumentritt:* Curt Jurgens, *Field Marshal Erwin Rommel:* Werner Hinz, *Field Marshal Gerd von Rundstedt:* Paul Hartmann, *Sergeant Kaffeeklatsch:* Gerd Froebe, *Major General Max Pemsel:* Wolfgang Preiss, *Lt. Colonel Ocker:* Peter Van Eyck, *Col. General Alfred Jodl:* Wolfgang Luckschy, *Several Bits:* Christopher Lee, *General Sir Bernard L. Montgomery:* Trevor Reid, *Nazi Soldier:* Eugene Deckers, *British Soldier:* Richard Wattis.

The Longest Day with Steve Forrest and John Wayne.

The Longest Yard with Burt Reynolds and Eddie Albert.

THE LONGEST YARD (1974) Par. Produced by Albert S. Ruddy. Directed by Robert Aldrich. Technicolor. Screenplay by Tracy Keenan Wynn. Based on the story by Ruddy. Photography, Joseph Biroc. Asso-

ciate Producer, Alan P. Horowitz. Music by Frank DeVol. Production Design, James S. Vance. Editor, Michael Luciano. Wardrobe, Charles James. Make-up, Tom Ellingwood. 2nd Unit Director for car chase, Hal Needham. Production Manager, Russell Saunders. Assistant Directors, Clifford Coleman and Ron Wright. Technical Adviser, Patrick Studstill. Script Supervisor, Alvin Greenman. Glen Glenn Recording. "Saturday Night Special" by Ronnie Van Zant and Edward Calhoun King, sung by Lynyrd Skynyrd; "Teach Me to Cheat," sung by Judy Kester; "Roadside Roses," sung by Jack Barlow. Filmed in Georgia and at Georgia State Prison, Reidsville, with the cooperation of Governor Jimmy Carter and Warden Joe Hopper. Rated R. 120 minutes

Paul Crewe: Burt Reynolds, *Warden Hazen:* Eddie Albert, *Capt. Knauer:* Ed Lauter, *Nate Scarboro:* Michael Conrad, *Caretaker:* James Hampton, *Granville:* Harry Caesar, *Pop:* John Steadman, *Unger:* Charles Tyner, *Rassmeusen:* Mike Henry, *Warden's Secretary:* Bernadette Peters, *Mawabe:* Pervis Atkins, *Rotka:* Tony Cacciotti, *Melissa Gaines:* Anitra Ford, *Walking Boss:* Joe Kapp, *Samson:* Richard Kiel, *Shop Steward:* Pepper Martin, *Assistant Warden:* Mort Marshall, *Bogdanski:* Ray Nitschke, *The Indian:* Sonny Sixkiller, *Mason:* Dino Washington, *Schokner:* Robert Tessier, *Spooner:* Ernie Wheelwright, *Bartender:* Joseph Dorsey, *Team Doctor:* Dr. Gus Carlucci, *Trainer:* Jack Rockwell, *Tannen:* Sonny Shroyer, *Schmidt:* Ray Ogden, *Referee:* Don Ferguson, *Troopers:* Chuck Hayward, Alfie Wise, *Levitt:* Tony Reese, *J.J.:* Steve Wilder, *Big George:* George Jones, *Big Wilbur:* Wilbur Gillan, *Buttercup:* Wilson Warren, *Little Joe:* Joe Jackson, *Howie:* Howard Silverstein, *Donny:* Donald Hixon, *Ice Man:* Jim Nicholson, *Prison Announcer:* Michael Fox, *Hampton's Fire Stunt:* Frank Orsatti, *Prison Band:* The Soul Touchers Band and Chorus.

The Long Gray Line with Tyrone Power and Peter Graves.

THE LONG GRAY LINE (1955) Col. Produced by Robert Arthur. Directed by John Ford. In CinemaScope and Technicolor. Based on *Bringing Up the Brass* by Marty Maher and Nardi Reeder Campion. Screenplay, Edward Hope. Art Director, Robert Peterson, Music Director, Morris Stoloff. Musical Adaptation, George Duning. Gowns, Jean Louis. Assistant Directors, Wingate Smith and Jack Corrick. Cinematography, Charles Lawton, Jr., Editor, William Lyon. 138 minutes

Marty Maher: Tyrone Power, *Mary O'Donnell:* Maureen O'Hara, *James Sundstrom, Jr.:* Robert Francis, *Old Martin:* Donald Crisp, *Captain Herman J. Koehler:* Ward Bond, *Kitty Carter:* Betsy Palmer, *Charles Dotson:* Phil Carey, *Red Sundstrom:* William Leslie, *Dwight Eisenhower:* Harry Carey, Jr., *Cherub Overton:* Patrick Wayne, *Dinny Maher:* Sean McClory, *Corporal Rudolph Heinz:* Peter Graves, *Captain John Pershing:* Milburn Stone, *Mike Shannon:* Walter D. Ehlers, *Major Thomas:* Willis Bouchey, *McDonald:* Don Barclay, *Jim O'Carberry:* Martin Milner, *Whitey Larson:* Chuck Courtney, *Superintendent:* Major Philip Kieffer, *Gus Dorais:* Norman Van Brocklin, *The President:* Elbert Steele, *Nurse:* Diane DeLaire, *Army Captain:* Donald Murphy, *Eleanor:* Lisa Davis, *Girl:* Jean Moorhead, *Peggy:* Dona Cole, *Priest:* Pat O'Malley, *Priest:* Harry Denny, *Lieutenant:* Robert

Knapp, *Cadet Pirelli:* Robert Roark, *Cadet Kennedy:* Robert Hoy, *Cadet Short:* Robert Ellis, *Cadet Curly Stern:* Mickey Roth, *Peter Dotson:* Tom Hennesy, *Cadet Ramsey:* John Herrin, *Cadet Thorne:* James Lilburn, *Specialty:* Ken Curtis, *Recruiting Sergeant:* Jack Pennick, *Knute Rockne:* James Sears, *New York Policeman:* Mickey Simpson, *Mrs. Koehler:* Erin O'Brien-Moore.

The Long Hot Summer with Anthony Franciosa, Lee Remick, Paul Newman and Orson Welles.

THE LONG HOT SUMMER (1958) 20th. Produced by Jerry Wald. Directed by Martin Ritt. Based on William Faulkner's novel *The Hamlet* and his short stories "Barn Burning" and "The Spotted Horses." Screenplay, Irving Ravetch and Harriet Frank, Jr. CinemaScope, De Luxe Color and Stereophonic Sound. Song, "The Long Hot Summer" by Sammy Cahn and Alex North, sung by Jimmie Rodgers. Photography, Joseph La Shelle. Film debut of Sarah Marshall. Filmed in Baton Rouge, Louisiana. Later the basis for a TV series. 115 minutes

Ben Quick: Paul Newman, *Clara Varner:* Joanne Woodward, *Jody Varner:* Anthony Franciosa, *Will Varner:* Orson Welles, *Eula Varner:* Lee Remick, *Minnie Littlejohn:* Angela Lansbury, *Agnes Stewart:* Sarah Marshall, *Alan Stewart:* Richard Anderson, *Mrs. Stewart:* Mabel Albertson, *Ratliff:* J. Pat O'Malley, *Lucius:* William Walker, *Peabody:* George Dunn, *Armistead:* Jess Kirkpatrick, *Wilk:* Val Avery, *Houstin:* I. Stanford Jolley, *Mrs. Houstin:* Helen Wallace, *Harris:* Byron Foulger, *Justice of the Peace:* Victor Rodman, *Pete Armistead:* Terry Rangno, *Ambulance Driver:* Bob Adler, *Negro Girl:* Pat Rosemond, *John Fisher:* Nicholas King, *Tom Shortly:* Lee Erickson, *J.V. Bookright:* Ralph Reed, *Buddy Peabody:* Steve Widders, *Linus Olds:* Jim Brandt, *Harry Peabody:* Brian Corcoran, *Waiter:* Eugene Jackson.

THE LONG, LONG TRAILER (1954) MGM. Produced by Pandro S. Berman. Directed by Vincente Minnelli. Based on a novel by Clinton Twiss. Screenplay, Albert Hackett and Frances Goodrich. Art Directors, Cedric Gibbons and Edward Carfagno. Music, Adolph Deutsch. Cinematography, Robert Surtees. Editor, Ferris Webster. Photographed in Ansco Color, print by Technicolor. Theme, "Breezin' Along With the Breeze" by Haven Gillespie, Seymour Simmons, and Richard A. Whiting. 96 minutes

Tacy Collini: Lucille Ball, *Nicky Collini:* Desi Arnaz, *Mrs. Hittaway:* Marjorie Main, *Policeman:* Keenan Wynn, *Mrs. Bolton:* Gladys Hurlbut, *Mr. Tewitt:* Moroni Olsen, *Foreman:* Bert Freed, *Aunt Anastacia:* Madge Blake, *Uncle Edgar:* Walter Baldwin, *Mr. Judlow:* Oliver Blake, *Bridesmaid:* Perry Sheehan, *Little Boy:* Charles Herbert, *Trailer Salesman:* Herb Vigran, *Mr. Bolton:* Emmett Vogan, *Manager:* Edgar Dearing, *Inspector:* Karl Lukas, *Mr. Hittaway:* Howard McNear, *Mechanic:* Jack Kruschen, *Girl Friends:* Geraldine Carr, Sarah Spencer, *Minister:* Dallas Boyd, *Mrs. Dudley:* Ruth Warren, *Mrs. Barrett:*

Edna Skinner, *Mr. Elliott:* Alan Lee, *Carl Barrett:* Robert Anderson, *Mr. Dudley:* Phil Rich, *Shorty:* John Call, *Garage Owner:* Wilson Wood, *Aunt Ellen:* Dorothy Neumann, *Uncle Bill:* Howard Wright, *Grace:* Connie Van, *Jody:* Dennis Ross, *Tom:* Christopher Olsen, *Candy Store Clerk:* Ida Moore, *Officer:* Emory Parnell, *Judge:* Fay Roope, *Garage Manager:* Peter Leeds, *Mrs. Tewitt:* Ruth Lee, *Father:* Dick Alexander, *Bettie:* Judy Sackett, *Kay:* Janet Sackett, *Driver:* Norman Leavitt, *Waitress:* Juney Ellis, *Attendant:* Frank Gerstle.

The Long, Long Trailer with Frank Gerstle, Desi Arnaz and Lucille Ball.

THE LONG VOYAGE HOME (1940) UA. Produced by Walter Wanger. Directed by John Ford. An Argosy Production. Based on four one-act plays by Eugene O'Neill: *The Moon of the Caribbees, Bound East for Cardiff, In the Zone* and *The Long Voyage Home*, performed under the unifying title, *S. S. Glencairn.* Screenplay, Dudley Nichols. Music, Richard Hageman. Music Director, Edward Paul. Art Director, James Basevi. Photography, Gregg Toland. Editor, Sherman Todd. Special Effects, R. T. Layton and R. O. Binger. Interior Decorations, Julia Heron. Film debut of Baltimore stage actress Mildred Natwick. 104 minutes

Ole Olson: John Wayne, *Driscoll:* Thomas Mitchell, *Smitty:* Ian Hunter, *Cocky:* Barry Fitzgerald, *The Captain:* Wilfrid Lawson, *Freda:* Mildred Natwick, *Axel Swanson:* John Qualen, *Yank:* Ward Bond, *Donkey Man:* Arthur Shields, *Davis:* Joseph Sawyer, *Crimp (Nick):* J. M. Kerrigan, *Tropical Woman:* Rafaela Ottiano, *Bumboat Girls:* Carmen Morales, Carmen D'Antonio, Tina Menard, Judith Linden, Elena Martinez, Lita Cortez, Soledad Gonzales, *Scotty:* David Hughes, *Joe, Proprietor:* Billy Bevan, *First Mate:* Cyril McLaglen, *Second Mate:* Douglas Walton, *Frank:* Constantine Romanoff, *Cook:* Edgar "Blue" Washington, *Mr. Clifton:* Lionel Pape, *Kate:* Jane Crowley, *Mag:* Maureen Roden-Ryan, *Paddy:* Bob Perry, *Norway:* Constant Franke, *Max:* Harry Tenbrook, *Tim:* Dan Borzage, *Captain of the* AMINDRA: Arthur Miles, *First Mate of* AMINDRA: Harry Woods, *Dock Policemen:* James Flavin, Lee Shumway, *British Naval Officer:* Wyndham Standing, *Bald Man:* Lowell Drew, *Seaman:* Sammy Stein, *Bergman:* Jack Pennick.

The Long Voyage Home with Ward Bond and Thomas Mitchell.

Looking for Mr. Goodbar with Richard Gere and Diane Keaton.

LOOKING FOR MR. GOODBAR (1977) Par. Produced by Freddie Fields. Directed and Written for the Screen by Richard Brooks. Based on the novel by Judith Rossner. Photography, William A. Fraker. Art Director, Edward Carfagno. Editor, George Grenville. Title Montage Photographs by Kathy Fields. Music, Artie Kane. Unit Production Manager/Assistant Director, David Silver. 2nd Assistant Director, Alan Brimfield. Set Decorator, Ruby Levitt. Sound, Al Overton, Jr. Costume Supervisor, Jodie Lynn Tillen. Make-up, Charles Schram. Hairstylists, Susan Germaine and Judith Corey. Optical Effects, Westheimer Co. "Don't Ask to Stay Until Tomorrow" by Artie Kane and Carol Connors, sung by Marlena Shaw. Lenses and Panaflex Camera by Panavision. Metrocolor. Rated R. 136 minutes

Theresa Dunn: Diane Keaton, *Katherine Dunn:* Tuesday Weld, *James Morrissey:* William Atherton, *Mr. Dunn:* Richard Kiley, *Tony Lopanto:* Richard Gere, *Prof. Martin Engle:* Alan Feinstein, *Gary Cooper White:* Tom Berenger, *Mrs. Dunn:* Priscilla Pointer, *Brigid:* Laurie Prange, *Barney:* Joel Fabiani, *Black Cat:* Julius Harris, *George:* Richard Bright, *Cap Jackson:* LeVar Burton, *Mrs. Jackson:* Marilyn Coleman, *Marvella:* Carole Mallory, *Principal:* Mary Ann Mallis, *Teachers:* Jolene Dellenbach, Louie Fant, *Bartender:* Eddie Garrett, *Arthur:* Alexander Courtney, *Surgeon:* Brian Dennehy, *Doctor:* Richard Venture, *Patrick:* Robert Burke, *Rafe:* Robert Fields, *Father Timothy:* Richard O'Brien, *Chuck:* Tony Hawkins, *Rhoda:* Caren Kaye, *TV Announcer:* Richard Spangler, *Little Theresa:* Elizabeth Cheshire, *Woman in Bar:* Marilyn Roberts.

LOST HORIZON (1937) Col. Produced and directed by Frank Capra. Based on the novel by James Hilton. Screenplay, Robert Riskin. Art Director, Stephen Goosson. Musical Score, Dimitri Tiomkin. Musical Director, Max Steiner. Assistant Director, C. C. Coleman. Cinematography, Joseph Walker. Aerial Photography, Elmer Dyer. Editors, Gene Havlick and Gene Milford. Costumes, Ernst Dryden. Technical Advisor, Harrison Forman. Special Camera Effects, E. Roy Davidson and Ganahl Carson. Interior Decorations, Babs Johnstone. Voices, Hall Johnson Choir. Henry B. Walthall and Walter Connolly were replaced by Sam Jaffe in the part of the High Lama. 118 minutes. Remade as a musical, 1973.

Robert Conway: Ronald Colman, *Sondra:* Jane Wyatt, *Alexander P. Lovett:* Edward Everett Horton, *George Conway:* John Howard, *Henry Barnard:* Thomas Mitchell, *Maria:* Margo, *Gloria Stone:* Isabel Jewell, *Chang:* H. B. Warner, *High Lama:* Sam Jaffe, *Lord Gainsford:* Hugh Buckler, *Carstairs:* John Miltern, *First Man:* Lawrence Grant, *Wynant:* John Burton, *Meeker:* John T. Murray, *Seiveking:* Max Rabinowitz, *Bandit Leader:* Willie Fung, *Missionary:* Wyrley Birch, *Montaigne:* John Tettener, *Assistant Foreign Secretary:* Boyd Irwin, Sr. *Foreign Secretary:* Leonard Mudie, *Steward:* David Clyde, *Radio Operator:* Neil Fitzgerald, *Talu:* Val Durand, *Missionaries:* Ruth Robinson, Margaret McWade, *Leader of Porters:* Noble

Johnson, *Aviator:* Dennis D'Auburn, *Fenner:* Milton Owen, *Bandit Leader:* Victor Wong, *Missionary:* Carl Stockdale, *Passengers:* Beatrice Curtis, Mary Lou Dix, Beatrice Blinn, Arthur Rankin, *Radio Operator:* Darby Clark, *Chinese Priest:* George Chan, *Englishman:* Eric Wilton, *Porter:* Chief Big Tree, *Shanghai Airport Official:* Richard Loo.

Lost Horizon with John Howard (lower left), Edward Everett Horton and Ronald Colman.

THE LOST PATROL (1934) RKO. Associate Producer, Cliff Reid. Directed by John Ford. From the story "Patrol" by Philip MacDonald. Screenplay, Dudley Nichols. Adaptation, Garrett Fort. Music, Max Steiner. Photography, Harold Wenstrom. Editor, Paul Weatherwax. Remakes: *Bad Lands* (RKO, 1939), *Bataan* (MGM, 1943) (Partial remake). 74 minutes

Sergeant: Victor McLaglen, *Sanders:* Boris Karloff, *Morelli:* Wallace Ford, *Brown:* Reginald Denny, *Quincannon:* J. M. Kerrigan, *Hale:* Billy Bevan, *Abelson:* Sammy Stein, *Cook:* Alan Hale, *Pearson:* Douglas Walton, *Corporal Bell:* Brandon Hurst, *Mackay:* Paul Hanson, *Lieutenant Hawkins:* Neville Clark, *Aviator:* Howard Wilson.

The Lost Patrol with Brandon Hurst and Victor McLaglen.

THE LOST WEEKEND (1945) Par. Produced by Charles Brackett. Directed by Billy Wilder. From the novel by Charles R. Jackson. Screenplay, Charles Brackett and Billy Wilder. Art Direction, Hans Dreier and Earl Hedrick. Music, Miklos Rozsa. Photography, John F. Seitz. Editor, Doane Harrison. Special Effects, Gordon Jennings. Process Photography, Farciot Edouart. Costumes, Edith Head. Make-up, Wally Westmore. Sound, Stanley Cooley and Joel Moss. Sets, Bertram Granger. Film debut of Lilian Fontaine, mother of Joan Fontaine and Olivia de Havilland. Filmed in New York City, including Bellevue's alcoholic ward. 101 minutes

Don Birnam: Ray Milland, *Helen St. James:* Jane Wyman, *Wick Birnam:* Phillip Terry, *Nat:* Howard da Silva, *Gloria:* Doris Dowling, *Bim:* Frank Faylen, *Mrs. Deveridge:* Mary Young, *Mrs. Foley:* Anita Bolster, *Mrs. St. James:* Lilian Fontaine, *Mr. St. James:* Lewis L. Russell, *Attendant at Opera:* Frank Orth, *Mrs. Wertheim:* Gisela Werbisek, *Mr. Brophy:* Eddie Laughton, *Piano Player:* Harry Barris, *M.M.:* Jayne Hazard, *M.M.'s Escort:* Craig Reynolds, *Dave (Janitor):* David Clyde, *Hardware Man:* William Meader, *Albany:* Walter Baldwin, *Waiter:* Crane Whitley, *Mike (Bouncer):* Max Wagner, *Little Girl:* Bunny Sunshine, *Washroom Attendants:* Fred "Snowflake" Toones, Clarence Muse, *Fruit Clerk:* Stanley Price, *Mrs. Frink:* Helen Dickson, *Mrs. Wertheim's Assistant:* Willa Pearl Curtis, *Man with Ear in Bandage:* Ted Hecht, *Mattress Man:* Al Stewart, *Shaky and Sweaty:* Peter Potter, *Beetle:* Douglas Spencer, *Doctor:* Emmett Vogan, *Male Nurse:* James Millican, *Negro Man Talking to Himself:* Ernest Whitman, *Guard:* Lee Shumway, *Liquor Store Proprietor:* William Newell, *Irishman:* Pat Moriarity.

The Lost Weekend with Howard da Silva and Ray Milland.

Love Affair with Irene Dunne, Maria Ouspenskaya and Charles Boyer.

LOVE AFFAIR (1939) RKO. Produced and directed by Leo Mc-Carey. Screenplay, Delmer Daves and Donald Ogden Stewart. Story by Mildred Cram and Leo McCarey. Camera, Rudolph Mate. Editors, Edward Dmytryk and George Hiveley, Special Effects, Vernon Walker. Assistant Director, James Anderson. Montage, Douglas Travers. Songs: "Wishing" by B. G. DeSylva; "Sing My Heart" by Harold

Arlen and Ted Koehler. Remade as *An Affair to Remember* (20th, 1957). 87 minutes

Terry McKay: Irene Dunne, *Michel Marnet:* Charles Boyer, *Grandmother:* Maria Ouspenskaya, *Ken Bradley:* Lee Bowman, *Lois Clarke:* Astrid Allwyn, *Maurice Cobert:* Maurice Moscovich, *Boy on Ship:* Scotty Beckett, *Couple on Deck:* Bess Flowers, and Harold Miller, *Autograph Seeker:* Joan Brodel (Joan Leslie), *Cafe Manager:* Dell Henderson, *Nightclub patron:* Carol Hughes, *Doctor:* Leyland Hodgson, *Boarding House Keeper:* Ferike Boros, *Orphanage Superintendent "Picklepuss":* Frank McGlynn, Sr., *Priest:* Oscar O'Shea, *Drunk with Christmas Tree:* Tom Dugan, *Doctor:* Lloyd Ingraham, *Maid:* Phyllis Kennedy, *Extra:* Gerald Mohr.

Love and Death with Diane Keaton and Woody Allen.

LOVE AND DEATH (1975) UA. A Jack Rollins–Charles H. Joffe Production. Produced by Joffe. Directed and Written by Woody Allen. Executive Producer, Martin Poll. Music by S. Prokofiev. Associate Producer, Fred T. Gallo. Photography, Ghislain Cloquet. Art Director, Willy Holt. Editor, Ralph Rosenblum. Costume Designer, Gladys De Segonzac. Editor, Ron Kalish. Assistant Directors, Paul Feyder and Bernard Cohn. Make-up, Marie-Madeleine Paris and Anatole Paris. Hairdresser, Renee Guidet. Wardrobe, Andree Demarez. Panavision and Color by DeLuxe General. Filmed in Paris and Budapest. Rated PG. 89 minutes

Boris Dimitrovich Grushenko: Woody Allen, *Sonja:* Diane Keaton, *Countess Alexandrovna:* Olga Georges-Picot, *Anton Ivanovitch:* Harold Gould, *Mother:* Despo Diamantidou, *Natasha Petrovna:* Jessica Harper, *Young Boris:* Alfred Lutter III, *Napoleon/Soldier Double:* James Tolkan, *Krapotkin:* Jack Lenoir, *Old Nehamkin:* Georges Adet, *Mikhail:* Feodor Atkine, *Rimsky:* Yves Barsacq, *Don Francisco:* Lloyd Battista, *General Lecoq:* Jack Berard, *Andre:* Yves Brainville, *Dimitri:* Brian Coburn, *Sergei Minskov:* Henry Coutet, *Cheerleaders:* Patricia Crown, Narcissa McKinley, *Ivan Grushenko:* Henry Czarniak, *Grandmother:* Luce Fabiole, *Uncle Nikolai:* Florian, *Ludmilla:* Jacqueline Fogt, *Leonid Voscovec:* Sol L. Frieder, *Uncle Sasha:* Harry Hankin, *Vladimir Maximovitch:* Tony Jay, *Pierre:* Tutte Lemkow, *Father Andre:* Leib Lensky, *Olga:* Ann Lonnberg, *Raskov:* Ed Marcus, *Spanish Countess:* Denise Peron, *Anna:* Beth Porter, *Borslov:* Shimen Ruskin, *Berdykov:* Persival Russel, *Joseph:* Chris Sanders, *Father:* Zvee Scooler, *Father Nikolai:* C. A. R. Smith, *Jacques:* Clement-Thierry, *Sergeant:* Alan Tilvern, *Madame Wolfe:* Helene Vallier, *Gen. Leveque:* Howard Vernon, *Sushkin:* Jacob Witkin. *Musicians:* Members of the Dimtrievitch Gypsy Orchestra.

THE LOVE BUG (1969) BV. A Walt Disney Production. Produced by Bill Walsh. Directed by Robert Stevenson. Technicolor. Based on the story "Car-Boy-Girl" by Gordon Buford. Screenplay, Bill Walsh and Don DaGradi. Photography, Edward Colman. Special Effects, Robert A. Mattey, Howard Jensen, Dan Lee, Eustace Lycett, Alan Maley and Peter

Ellenshaw. Music, George Bruns. Orchestration, Walter Sheets. Art Direction, Carroll Clark and John B. Mansbridge. Editor, Cotton Warburton. Driving Sequence Supervisor, Carey Loftin. 2nd Unit Director, Arthur J. Vitarelli. Assistant Director, Christopher Hibley. 107 minutes. Sequels: *Herbie Rides Again* (1974); *Herbie Goes to Monte Carlo* (1977)

Jim Douglas: Dean Jones, *Carole Bennett:* Michele Lee, *Tennessee Steinmetz:* Buddy Hackett, *Peter Thorndyke:* David Tomlinson, *Havershaw:* Joe Flynn, *Mr. Wu:* Benson Fong, *Detective:* Joe E. Ross, *Police Sergeant:* Barry Kelley, *Carhop:* Iris Adrian, *Association President:* Andy Granatelli, *Bits:* Gary Owens, Ned Glass, Robert Foulk, Gil Lamb, Pedro Gonzalez-Gonzalez, Nicole Jaffe, Wally Boag, Russ Caldwell, Max Balchowksy, P. L. Renoudet, Brian Fong, Alan Fordney, Stan Duke, Chick Hearn.

The Love Bug with Iris Adrian, Michele Lee and Dean Jones.

Love Finds Andy Hardy with Cecilia Parker, Lewis Stone, Fay Holden, Mickey Rooney and Judy Garland.

LOVE FINDS ANDY HARDY (1938) MGM. Directed by George B. Seitz. From the stories by Vivien R. Bretherton, based on the characters created by Aurania Rouverol. Screenplay, William Ludwig. Music, David Snell. Photography, Lester White. Editor, Ben Lewis. Songs: "In Between" by Roger Edens; "What Do You Know About Love?" "Meet the Beat of My Heart" and "It Never Rains But It Pours" by Mack Gordon and Harry Revel. 90 minutes

Judge James Hardy: Lewis Stone, *Andy Hardy:* Mickey Rooney, *Betsy Booth:* Judy Garland, *Marian Hardy:* Cecilia Parker, *Mrs. Hardy:* Fay Holden, *Polly Benedict:* Ann Rutherford, *Aunt Milly:* Betty Ross Clarke, *Cynthia Potter:* Lana Turner, *Augusta:* Marie

Blake, *Dennis Hunt:* Don Castle, *Jimmy MacMahon:* Gene Reynolds, *Mrs. Tompkins:* Mary Howard, *Beezy:* George Breakston, *Peter Dugan:* Raymond Hatton, *Bill Collector:* Frank Darien, *Judge:* Rand Brooks, *Court Attendant:* Erville Alderson.

Love Is a Many Splendored Thing with Jennifer Jones and William Holden.

LOVE IS A MANY SPLENDORED THING (1955) 20th. Producer, Buddy Adler. Director, Henry King. CinemaScope, De Luxe Color. Author, Han Suyin (from *A Many Splendored Thing*). Screenplay, John Patrick. Art Directors, Lyle R. Wheeler, George W. Davis. Music, Alfred Newman. Orchestration, Edward B. Powell. Cinematographer, Leon Shamroy. Editor, William Reynolds. Title song, Sammy Fain and Paul Francis Webster. 102 minutes

Mark Elliott: William Holden, *Han Suyin:* Jennifer Jones, *Mr. Palmer-Jones:* Torin Thatcher, *Adeline Palmer-Jones:* Isobel Elsom, *Dr. Tam:* Murray Matheson, *Ann Richards:* Virginia Gregg, *Robert Hung:* Richard Loo, *Nora Hung:* Soo Yong, *Third Uncle:* Philip Ahn, *Suzanne:* Jorja Curtright, *Suchen:* Donna Martell, *Oh-No:* Candace Lee, *Dr. Sen:* Kam Tong, *Fifth Brother:* James Hong, *Father Low:* Herbert Heyes, *Mei Loo:* Angela Loo, *Rosie Wu:* Marie Tsien, *British Sailor:* Ashley Cowan, *Nurse:* Jean Wong, *General Song:* Joseph Kim, *Wine Steward:* Marc Krah, *Hotel Manager:* Salvador Baguez, *Dining Room Captain:* Edward Colmans, *Fortune Teller:* Leonard Strong, *Second Brother:* Howard Soo Hoo, *Third Brother:* Walter Soo Hoo, *Elder Brother:* Keye Luke, *Old Loo:* Lee Tung Foo.

Love Me or Leave Me with Dale Van Sickel, James Cagney and Johnny Day.

LOVE ME OR LEAVE ME (1955) MGM. Producer, Joe Pasternak. Director, Charles Vidor. CinemaScope, Eastman Color. Author, Daniel Fuchs. Screenplay, Daniel Fuchs, Isobel Lennart. Art Directors, Cedric Gibbons, Urie McCleary. Musical Director, George Stoll. Cinematographer, Arthur E. Arling. Editor, Ralph E. Winters. Dances, Alex Romero. 122 minutes

Ruth Etting: Doris Day, *Martin Snyder:* James Cagney, *Johnny Alderman:* Cameron Mitchell, *Bernard V. Loomis:* Robert Keith, *Frobisher:* Tom Tully, *Georgie:* Harry Bellaver, *Paul Hunter:* Richard Gaines, *Fred Taylor:* Peter Leeds, *Eddie Fulton:* Claude Stroud, *Jingle Girl:* Audrey Young, *Greg Trent:* John Harding, *Dancer:* Dorothy Abbott, *Bouncer:* Phil Schumacher, *Bouncer:* Henry Kulky, *Second Bouncer:* Otto Reichow, *Orry:* Jay Adler, *Irate Customer:* Mauritz Hugo, *Hostess:* Veda Ann Borg, *Claire:* Claire Carleton, *Stage Manager:* Benny Burt, *Mr. Brelston, Radio Station Manager:* Robert B. Carson, *Assistant Director:* James Drury, *Dance Director:* Richard Simmons, *Assistant Director:* Michael Kostrick, *First Reporter:* Roy Engel, *Second Reporter:* John Damler, *Woman:* Genevieve Aumont, *Prop Man:* Roy Engel, *Stagehands:* Dale Van Sickel, Johnny Day.

Love Me Tender with Richard Egan, Debra Paget and Elvis Presley.

LOVE ME TENDER (1956) 20th. Producer, David Weisbart. Director, Robert D. Webb. CinemaScope. Based on a story by Maurice Geraghty. Screenplay, Robert Buckner. Art Directors, Lyle R. Wheeler, Maurice Ransford. Music, Lionel Newman. Songs, Elvis Presley, Vera Matson. Orchestration, Edward B. Powell. Cinematographer, Leo Tover. Special Photographic Effects, Ray Kellogg. Editor, Hugh S. Fowler. Film debut of Elvis Presley, 21. 89 minutes

Vance: Richard Egan, *Cathy:* Debra Paget, *Clint:* Elvis Presley, *Siringo:* Robert Middleton, *Brett Reno:* William Campbell, *Mike Gavin:* Neville Brand, *The Mother:* Mildred Dunnock, *Major Kincaid:* Bruce Bennett, *Ray Reno:* James Drury, *Ed Galt:* Russ Conway, *Kelso:* Ken Clark, *Davis:* Barry Coe, *Fleming:* L. Q. Jones, *Jethro:* Paul Burns, *Train Conductor:* Jerry Sheldon, *Storekeeper:* James Stone, *Auctioneer:* Ed Mundy, *First Soldier:* Joe Di Reda, *Station Agent:* Bobby Rose, *Paymaster:* Tom Greenway, *Major Harris:* Jay Jostyn, *Train Conductor:* Steve Darrell.

LOVE ME TONIGHT (1932) Par. Produced and directed by Rouben Mamoulian. Story, Leopold Marchand and Paul Arment. Screenplay, Samuel Hoffenstein, Waldemar Young, George Marion, Jr. Photography, Victor Milner. Songs by Richard Rodgers and Lorenz Hart: "The Song of Paree," "How Are You?", "Isn't It Romantic?", "Lover," "Mimi," "Poor Apache," "Love Me Tonight," "A Woman Needs Something Like That," "The Son of a Gun Is Nothing But a Tailor." 104 minutes

Maurice Courtelin: Maurice Chevalier, *Princess Jeanette:* Jeanette

MacDonald, *Vicomte Gilbert de Vareze:* Charlie Ruggles, *Count de Savignac:* Charles Butterworth, *Countess Valentine:* Myrna Loy, *The Duke:* C. Aubrey Smith, *First Aunt:* Elizabeth Patterson, *Second Aunt:* Ethel Griffies, *Third Aunt:* Blanche Frederici, *Bridge Player:* Major Sam Harris, *The Doctor:* Joseph Cawthorn, *Major-Domo, Flamond:* Robert Greig, *Madame Dutoit, Dressmaker:* Ethel Wales, *Bakery Girl:* Marion "Peanuts" Byron, *Madame Dupont:* Mary Doran, *Emile:* Bert Roach, *Laundress:* Cecil Cunningham, *Composer:* Tyler Brooke, *Valet:* Edgar Norton, *Groom:* Herbert Mundin, *Chambermaid:* Rita Owin, *Shirtmaker:* Clarence Wilson, *Collector:* Gordon Westcott, *Pierre Dupont:* George Davis, *Taxi Driver:* Rolfe Sedan, *Hat Maker:* Tony Merlo, *Boot Maker:* William H. Turner, *Grocer:* George (Gabby) Hayes, *Bit:* Tom Ricketts.

Love Me Tonight with Myrna Loy and Maurice Chevalier.

THE LOVE PARADE (1929) Par. Produced and directed by Ernst Lubitsch. From the play *The Prince Consort* by Leon Xanrof and Jules Chancel. Story, Ernst Vajda and Guy Bolton. Editor, Merrill White. Photography, Victor Milner. Songs by Victor Schertzinger and Clifford Grey: "My Love Parade," "Dream Lover," "Let's Be Common," "Anything to Please the Queen," "March of the Grenadiers," "Paris Stays the Same," "Nobody's Using It Now," "Oo La La La," "The Queen Is Always Right." Film debut of Jeanette MacDonald. 110 minutes

Count Alfred Renard: Maurice Chevalier, *Queen Louise:* Jeanette MacDonald, *Jacques:* Lupino Lane, *Lulu:* Lillian Roth, *Master of Ceremonies:* Edgar Norton, *Prime Minister:* Lionel Belmore, *Foreign Minister:* Albert Roccardi, *Admiral:* Carl Stockdale, *Minister of War:* Eugene Pallette, *Sylvanian Ambassador:* E. H. Calvert, *Afghan Ambassador:* Russell Powell, *First Lady-in-Waiting:* Margaret Fealy, *Second Lady-in-Waiting:* Virginia Bruce, *Paulette:* Yola d'Avril, *Paulette's Husband:* Andre Cheron, *Priest:* Winter Hall, *Cross-eyed Lackey:* Ben Turpin, *Extra in Theater Audience and to the Left of Theater Box:* Jean Harlow.

The Love Parade with Jeanette MacDonald and Maurice Chevalier.

LOVE STORY (1970) Par. Produced by Howard G. Minsky. Directed by Arthur Hiller. Color. Executive Producer, David Golden. Screenplay by Erich Segal. Music by Francis Lai. Photography, Dick Kratina. Assistant Director, Peter Scoppa. Costumes, Alice Manougian Martin and Pearl Somner. Art Director, Robert Gundlach. Sound, Jack Jackson. Hairstylist, William Farley. Make-up, Martin Bell. Editor, Robert C. Jones. Film debut of Gil Gerard (1979's Buck Rogers). Filmed in Cambridge and Boston, Massachusetts, and New York City. Rated GP. 99 minutes. Sequel is *Oliver's Story* (1978) with O'Neal and Milland.

Oliver Barrett IV: Ryan O'Neal, *Jenny Cavilleri:* Ali MacGraw, *Oliver Barrett III:* Ray Milland, *Phil Cavilleri:* John Marley, *Mrs. Barrett:* Katherine Balfour, *Dean Thompson:* Russell Nype, *Dr. Shapely:* Sydney Walker, *Dr. Addison:* Robert Modica, *Ray Stratton:* Walker Daniels, *Hank:* Tommy Lee Jones, *Steve:* John Merensky, *Rev. Blauvelt:* Andrew Duncan, *Doorman:* Bob O'Connell, *Clerk, Mount Sinai Hospital:* Charlotte Ford Niarchos, *Extra:* Gil Gerard.

Love Story with Ali MacGraw and Ryan O'Neal.

Love With the Proper Stranger with Steve McQueen and Natalie Wood.

LOVE WITH THE PROPER STRANGER (1963) Par. Produced by Alan J. Pakula. Directed by Robert Mulligan. A Pakula-Mulligan and Rona Production. Screenplay, Arnold Schulman. Music, Elmer Bernstein. Costumes, Edith Head. Art Directors, Hal Pereira and Roland Anderson. Cinematography, Milt Krasner. Editor, Aaron Stell. Title song by Johnny Mercer and Elmer Bernstein, sung by Jack Jones. Scenes filmed in New York City. 100 minutes

Angie Rossini: Natalie Wood, *Rocky Papasano:* Steve McQueen,

Barbie (Barbara of Seville): Edie Adams, *Dominick Rossini:* Herschel Bernardi, *Anthony Columbo:* Tom Bosley, *Julio Rossini:* Harvey Lembeck, *Mama Rossini:* Penny Santon, *Anna:* Virginia Vincent, *Guido Rossini:* Nick Alexander, *Mrs. Papasano:* Augusta Ciolli, *Beetie:* Anne Hegira, *Lou:* Henry Howard, *Elio Papasano:* Mario Badolati, *Woman Doctor:* Elena Karam, *Mrs. Columbo:* Nina Varela, *Gina:* Marilyn Chris, *Priest:* Wolfe Barzell, *Little Boy:* Keith Worthey, *Carlos:* Frank Marth, *Flower Vendor:* Richard Bowler, *Truck Driver:* Lennie Bremen, *Yuki:* Nobu McCarthy, *Charlene:* Jean Shulman, *Harold:* Lou Herbert, *Moish:* M. Enserro, *Sidney:* Barney Martin, *Flooey:* Louis Guss, *Fat:* Tony Mordente, *Stein:* Val Avery, *Louie:* Dick Mulligan, *Klepp:* Paul Price, *Marge:* Arlene Golonka, *Accountant:* Richard Dysart, *Maria:* Loraine Abate, *Call Boy:* Vincent Deadrick, *Cye:* Victor Tayback.

Lust for Life with Anthony Quinn and Kirk Douglas.

LUST FOR LIFE (1956) MGM. Producer, John Houseman. Associated Producer, Jud Kinberg. Director, Vincente Minnelli. CinemaScope, MetroColor. Based on the novel by Irving Stone. Screenplay, Norman Corwin. Art Directors, Cedric Gibbons, Hans Peters, Preston Ames. Musical Director, Miklos Rozsa. Cinematographers, F. A. Young, Russell Harlan. Editor, Adrienne Fazan. 122 minutes

Vincent Van Gogh: Kirk Douglas, *Paul Gauguin:* Anthony Quinn, *Theo Van Gogh:* James Donald, *Christine:* Pamela Brown, *Dr. Gachet:* Everett Sloane, *Roulin:* Niall MacGinnis, *Anton Mauve:* Noel Purcell, *Theodorus Van Gogh:* Henry Daniell, *Anna Cornelia Van Gogh:* Madge Kennedy, *Willemien:* Jill Bennett, *Dr. Peyron:* Lionel Jeffries, *Dr. Bosman:* Laurence Naismith, *Colbert:* Eric Pohlmann, *Kay:* Jeanette Sterke, *Johanna:* Toni Gerry, *Rev. Stricker:* Wilton Graff, *Mrs. Stricker:* Isobel Elsom, *Rev. Peeters:* David Horne, *Commissioner Van Den Berghe:* Noel Howlett, *Commissioner De Smet:* Ronald Adam, *Ducrucq:* John Ruddock, *Rachel:* Julie Robinson, *Camille Pissarro:* David Leonard, *Emile Bernard:* William Phipps, *Seurat:* David Bond, *Pere Tanguy:* Frank Perls, *Waiter:* Jay Adler, *Adeline Ravoux:* Laurence Badie, *Durand-Ruel:* Rex Evans, *Sister Clothilde:* Marion Ross, *Elizabeth:* Mitzi Blake, *Cor:* Anthony Sydes, *Tersteeg:* Anthony Eustrel, *Jet:* Ernestine Barrier, *Lautrec:* Jerry Bergen, *Mme. Tanguy:* Belle Mitchell, *Dr. Rey:* Alec Mango, *Cordan:* Fred Johnson, *Pier:* Norman MacCowan, *Jan:* Mickey Maga.

MADAME CURIE (1943) MGM. Produced by Sidney Franklin. Directed by Mervyn LeRoy. Based on the book by Eve Curie. Screenplay, Paul Osborn and Paul H. Rameau. Art Director, Cedric Gibbons. Associate, Paul Groesse. Set Decorations, Edwin B. Willis. Associate, Hugh Hunt. Music, Herbert Stothart. Photography, Joseph Ruttenberg. Special Effects, Warren Newcombe. Costume Supervision, Irene Sharaff. Men's Costumes, Giles Steele. Make-up, Jack Dawn. Editor, Harold F. Kress. Sound, Douglas Shearer. Narrated by James Hilton. Film debut of Gigi Perreau, 2. 124 minutes

Madame Marie Curie: Greer Garson, *Pierre Curie:* Walter Pidgeon, *Eugene Curie:* Henry Travers, *Professor Perot:* Albert Basserman, *David LeGros:* Robert Walker, *Lord Kelvin:* C. Aubrey Smith, *Madame Eugene Curie:* Dame May Whitty, *University President:* Victor Francen, *Madame Perot:* Elsa Basserman, *Doctor Becquerel:* Reginald Owen, *Reporter:* Van Johnson, *Irene, age 5:* Margaret O'Brien, *Eve, 18 months:* Ghislaine (Gigi) Perreau, *Professor Roget:* Lumsden Hare, *President of Businessmen's Board:* Moroni Olsen, *Businessmen:* Miles Mander, Arthur Shields, Frederic Worlock, *Doctor:* Eustace Wyatt, *Jewelry Salesman:* Marek Windheim, *Lucille:* Lisa Golm, *Doctor Bladh:* Alan Napier, *Lecturer's Voice:* Ray Collins, *Professor Constant's Voice:* Howard Freeman, *Monsieur Michaud:* Francis Pierlot, *Madame Michaud:* Almira Sessions, *Master Michaud:* Dickie Meyers, *Photographer:* Leo Mostovoy, *Singing Professor:* George Meader, *King Oscar:* Wyndham Standing, *Swedish Queen:* Ruty Cherrington, *Driver:* Ray Teal, *Seamstress:* Ilka Gruning.

Madame Curie with Greer Garson and Walter Pidgeon.

Madame X with Ruth Chatterton and Mary Gordon.

MADAME X (1929) MGM. Directed by Lionel Barrymore. From the play by Alexandre Bisson. Scenario and Dialogue, Willard Mack. Photography, Arthur Reed. Editor, William S. Gray. Sound, Western Electric Movietone (Fox-Case) Process. Recording Engineer, Douglas Shearer. Art Director, Cedric Gibbons. Wardrobe, David Cox. Other versions of *Madame X:* Pathé, 1915; Goldwyn, 1920; MGM, 1937; Universal, 1966; *The Trial of Madame X* (British, 1955). 95 minutes

Floriot: Lewis Stone, *Jacqueline:* Ruth Chatterton, *Raymond:* Ray-

mond Hackett, *Noel:* Holmes Herbert, *Rose:* Eugenie Besserer, *Doctor:* John P. Edington, *Colonel Hamby:* Mitchell Lewis, *Larocque:* Ullrich Haupt, *Merivel:* Sidney Toler, *Perissard:* Richard Carle, *Darrell:* Carroll Nye, *Valmorin:* Claude King, *Judge:* Chappell Dossett, *Baby's Nurse:* Mary Gordon.

Magic with Fats and Anthony Hopkins.

MAGIC (1978) 20th. Produced by Joseph E. and Richard P. Levine. Directed by Richard Attenborough. Screenplay by William Goldman, based on his novel. Executive Producer/Production Manager, C. O. Erickson. Photography, Victor J. Kemper. Production Designer, Terence Marsh. Music, Jerry Goldsmith. Editor, John Bloom. 1st Assistant Director, Arne Schmidt. 2nd Assistant Director, Jerald Sobul. Art Director, Richard Lawrence. Set Decorator, John Franco, Jr. Costumes, Ruth Myers. Assistant to the Director, Michael White. Sound Mixer, Larry Jost. Special Effects, Robert MacDonald, Jr. Make-up Artists, Lee Harman and Hallie Smith-Simmons. Hairstyles, Cherie. Men's Costumer, Michael Harte. Women's Costumer, Shirlee Strahm. Consultant Ventriloquist, Dennis Alwood. Consultant Magicians, Michael Bailey and Lewis Horwitz. Dialect Adviser, Patrick Watkins. Accent Consultant, Robert Easton. 1st Assistant Director (New York), Mike Haley. 2nd Assistant Director (New York), Francois Moullin. Sound Mixer (New York), John Bolz. Men's Costumer (New York), Al Craine. Make-up Artist (New York), Robert Laden. Hairstylist (New York), Mona Orr. Lenses and Panaflex Camera by Panavision. Color by Technicolor, prints by DeLuxe. Filmed in New York and at Fox Studios, California. Rated R. 106 minutes

Corky Withers/Voice of Fats: Anthony Hopkins, *Peggy Ann Snow:* Ann-Margret, *Ben Greene ("Gangrene"):* Burgess Meredith, *Duke:* Ed Lauter, *Merlin, Jr.:* E. J. Andre, *Cabdriver:* Jerry Houser, *George Hudson Todson:* David Ogden Stiers, *Sadie:* Lillian Randolph, *Club M.C.:* Joe Lowry, *Laughing Lady:* Beverly Sanders, *Maître D':* I. W. Klein, *Captain:* Stephen Hart, *Zachary, Doorman:* Patrick McCullough, *Father:* Bob Hackman, *Mother:* Mary Munday, *Corky's Brother:* Scott Garrett, *Young Corky:* Brad Beesley, *Minister:* Michael Harte.

THE MAGNIFICENT AMBERSONS (1942) RKO. Produced and directed by Orson Welles. A Mercury Production. Based on the novel by Booth Tarkington. Screenplay, Orson Welles. Art Director, Mark-Lee Kirk. Music, Bernard Herrmann. Cameraman, Stanley Cortez. Special Effects, Vernon L. Walker. Editor, Robert Wise. Remake of *Pampered Youth* (Vitagraph, 1925). 88 minutes

Eugene: Joseph Cotten, *Isabel:* Dolores Costello, *Lucy:* Anne Baxter, *George:* Tim Holt, *Fanny:* Agnes Moorehead, *Jack:* Ray Collins, *Major Amberson:* Richard Bennett, *Benson:* Erskine Sanford, *Wilbur Minafer:* Don Dillaway, *Sam, the Butler:* J. Louis Johnson, *Uncle John:* Charles Phipps, *Spectators at Funeral:* Dorothy Vaughan, Elmer Jerome, *Mary:* Olive Ball, *Guests:* Nina Guilbert, John Elliott, *Mrs. Foster:* Anne O'Neal, *Matrons:* Kathryn Sheldon, Georgia Backus, *Hardware Man:* Henry Roquemore, *Nurse:* Hilda Plowright, *Fred Kinney:* Mel Ford, *Charles Johnson:* Bob Pittard, *Landlady:* Lillian Nicholson, *House Servant:* Billy Elmer, *Citizens:* Lew Kelly, Maynard Holmes, *Drug Clerk:* Gus Schilling, *George as a boy:* Bobby Cooper, *Elijah:* Drew Roddy, *Reverend Smith:* Jack Baxley, *Laborer:* Heenan Elliott, *Girl:* Nancy Gates, *Young Man:* John Maguire, *Chauffeur/Citizen:* Ed Howard, *Youth at Accident:* William Blees, *Cop at Accident:* James Westerfield, *Cop:* Philip Morris, *Barber:* Jack Santoro, *Ballroom Extra (cut from featured role):* Louis Hayward.

The Magnificent Ambersons with Tim Holt and Dolores Costello.

Magnificent Obsession with Jane Wyman and Rock Hudson.

MAGNIFICENT OBSESSION (1954) Univ. Producer, Ross Hunter. Director, Douglas Sirk. Technicolor. Based on the novel by Lloyd C. Douglas and screenplay by Sarah Y. Mason, Victor Heerman. Adaptation, Wells Root. Screenplay, Robert Blees. Art Directors, Bernard Herzbrun, Emrich Nicolson. Cinematographer, Russell Metty. Editor, Milton Carruth. Music, Frank Skinner. Remake of Universal's 1935 film. 108 minutes

Helen Phillips: Jane Wyman, *Bob Merrick:* Rock Hudson, *Nancy*

Ashford: Agnes Moorehead, *Joyce Phillips:* Barbara Rush, *Tom Masterson:* Gregg Palmer, *Randolph:* Otto Kruger, *Dr. Giraud:* Paul Cavanagh, *Valerie:* Sara Shane, *Dr. Dodge:* Richard H. Cutting, *Judy:* Judy Nugent, *Mrs. Eden:* Helen Kleeb, *Sgt. Burnham:* Robert B. Williams, *Sgt. Ames:* Will White, *Williams:* George Lynn, *First Mechanic:* Jack Kelly, *Switchboard Girl:* Lisa Gaye, *Customers:* William Leslie, Lance Fuller, Brad Jackson, Myrna Hansen, *Dr. Allan:* Alexander Campbell, *Dr. Fuss:* Rudolph Anders, *Dr. Laradetti:* Fred Nurney, *Dr. Hofer:* John Mylong, *Dan:* Joe Mell, *Mr. Jouvet:* Harold Dyrenforth, *Mr. Long:* Norbert Schiller, *Mrs. Miller:* Mae Clarke, *Switchboard Girl:* Kathleen O'Malley, *Maid:* Joy Hallward, *Second Mechanic:* Lee Roberts, *Chris:* Harvey Grant.

Magnum Force with Clint Eastwood.

MAGNUM FORCE (1973) WB. Produced by Robert Daley. Directed by Ted Post. Technicolor. Based on a story by John Milius, from original material by Harry Julian Fink and R. M. Fink. Screenplay, John Milius and Michael Cimino. Photography, Frank Stanley. Editor, Ferris Webster. Music by Lalo Schifrin. Art Director, Jack Collis. Assistant Director, Wes McAfee. Rated R. The second *Dirty Harry* film. 124 minutes

Harry Callahan: Clint Eastwood, *Lt. Briggs:* Hal Holbrook, *Early Smith:* Felton Perry, *Charlie McCoy:* Mitchell Ryan, *Davis:* David Soul, *Sweet:* Tim Matheson, *Grimes:* Robert Urich, *Astrachan:* Kip Niven, *Carol McCoy:* Christine White, *Sunny:* Adele Yoshioka.

THE MAJOR AND THE MINOR (1942) Par. Produced by Arthur Hornblow, Jr. Directed by Billy Wilder. Suggested by the play *Connie Goes Home* by Edward Childs Carpenter, and the *Saturday Evening Post* story "Sunny Goes Home" by Fannie Kilbourne. Screenplay, Charles Brackett and Billy Wilder. Art Directors, Hans Dreier and Roland Anderson. Music Score, Robert Emmett Dolan. Cameraman, Leo Tover. Editor, Doane Harrison. Remade as *You're Never Too Young* (Paramount, 1955) with Martin and Lewis. Lela Rogers is Ginger's mother. 100 minutes

Susan Applegate: Ginger Rogers, *Major Kirby:* Ray Milland, *Pamela Hill:* Rita Johnson, *Mr. Osborne:* Robert Benchley, *Lucy Hill:* Diana Lynn, *Colonel Hill:* Edward Fielding, *Cadet Osborne:* Frankie Thomas, Jr., *Cadet Wigton:* Raymond Roe, *Cadet Korner:* Charles Smith,

Cadet Babcock: Larry Nunn, Cadet Miller: Billy Dawson, Cadet Summerville: Billy Ray, Shumaker: Stanley Desmond, Bertha: Marie Blake, Mrs. Applegate: Lela Rogers, Mrs. Osborne: Norma Varden, Mrs. Shackleford: Gretl Sherk, Mother in Railroad Station: Mary Field, Reverend Doyle: Aldrich Bowker, Major Griscom: Boyd Irwin, Captain Durand: Byron Shores, Will Duffy: Richard Fiske, Doorman: Dell Henderson, Station Master: Ed Peil, Sr., Elevator Boy: Ken Lundy.

The Major and the Minor with Ray Milland, Ginger Rogers, Edward Fielding and Rita Johnson.

Make Way for Tomorrow with Thomas Mitchell, Beulah Bondi and Victor Moore.

MAKE WAY FOR TOMORROW (1937) Par. Produced and directed by Leo McCarey. Based on the novel *The Years Are So Long* by Josephine Lawrence, and a play by Helen and Nolan Leary. Screenplay, Vina Delmar. Art Directors, Hans Dreier and Bernard Herzbrun. Music, George Antheil. Arrangements, Victor Young. Musical Director, Boris Morros. Title song by Leo Robin, Sam Coslow, and Jean Schwartz. Camera, William C. Mellor. Editor, LeRoy Stone. Special Effects, Gordon Jennings. Assistant Director, Harry Scott. Sound, Walter Oberst and Don Johnson. Minna Gombell and Ray Mayer replaced Margaret Hamilton and Charles Arnt. 92 minutes

Barkley Cooper: Victor Moore, Lucy Cooper: Beulah Bondi, Anita Cooper: Fay Bainter, George Cooper: Thomas Mitchell, Harvey Chase: Porter Hall, Rhoda Cooper: Barbara Read, Max Rubens: Maurice Moscovich, Cora Payne: Elisabeth Risdon, Mr. Henning: Gene Lockhart, Bill Payne: Ralph M. Remley, Mamie: Louise Beavers, Doctor: Louis Jean Heydt, Carlton Gorman: Gene Morgan, Auto Salesman: Dell Henderson, Nellie Chase: Minna Gombell, Robert Cooper: Ray Mayer, Secretary: Ruth Warren, Hotel Manager: Paul Stanton, Richard Payne: George Offerman, Jr., Jack Payne: Tommy Bupp, Mrs. Rubens: Ferike Boros, Mr. Hunter: Granville Bates, Mr. Dale: Byron Foulger, Mrs. McKenzie: Averil Cameron, Boy

Friend: Nick Lukats, Head Usherette: Kitty McHugh, Usherette: Terry Ray (Ellen Drew), Doorman: Ralph Brooks, Woman Customer: Ethel Clayton, Businessmen: Ralph Lewis, Phillips Smalley, Letter Carrier: Howard Mitchell, Man: Don Brodie, Ticket Seller: William Newell, Woman: Rosemary Theby, Man: Richard R. Neill, Bridge Player: Helen Dickson, Passerby/Man in Overcoat/Carpet Sweeper: Leo McCarey.

THE MALE ANIMAL (1942) WB. Producer, Hal B. Wallis. Associate Producer, Wolfgang Reinhardt. Directed by Elliott Nugent. From the play by James Thurber and Elliott Nugent. Screenplay, Julius J. and Philip G. Epstein and Stephen Morehouse Avery. Photography, Arthur Edeson. Editor, Thomas Richards. Remade as *She's Working Her Way Through College* (WB, 1952), which also featured Don DeFore. 101 minutes

Tommy Turner: Henry Fonda, Ellen Turner: Olivia de Havilland, Joe Ferguson: Jack Carson, Patricia Stanley: Joan Leslie, Ed Keller: Eugene Pallette, Michael Barnes: Herbert Anderson, Cleota: Hattie McDaniel, Dr. Damon: Ivan Simpson, Wally: Don DeFore, Hot Garters Garner: Jean Ames, Blanche Damon: Minna Phillips, Myrtle Keller: Regina Wallace, Coach Sprague: Frank Mayo, Alumnus: William B. Davidson, Nutsy Miller: Bobby Barnes, Boy: Albert Faulkner, Secretary: Jane Randolph, Faculty Member: Howard Hickman, Editor: John Maxwell, News Dealer: Edward Clark, Newspapermen: George Meeker, Will Morgan, Raymond Bailey, Trustee: Arthur Loft, Trustee's Wife: Leah Baird, Students: Spec O'Donnell, Ray Montgomery, David Willock, Byron Barr (Gig Young), Michael Ames (Tod Andrews), Audrey Long, Charles Drake, Joan Winfield, Reporters: Walter Brooke, Hank Mann, De Wolfe Hopper (William Hopper), Creighton Hale.

The Male Animal with Henry Fonda and Olivia de Havilland.

THE MALTESE FALCON (1941) WB. Executive Producer, Hal B. Wallis. Associate Producer, Henry Blanke. Directed by John Huston. Based on the novel by Dashiell Hammett. Screenplay, John Huston. Art Director, Robert Haas. Music, Adolph Deutsch. Photography, Arthur Edeson. Editor, Thomas Richards. Assistant Director, Claude Archer. Dialogue Director, Robert Foulk. Sound, Oliver S. Garretson. Orchestrations, Arthur Lange. Make-up, Perc Westmore. Gowns, Orry-Kelly. Film debut of Sydney Greenstreet, 61; John Huston's first film as a director. Previous Warner Brothers versions: *The Maltese Falcon* (also, *Dangerous Female*, 1931), and *Satan Met a Lady* (1936). 100 minutes

Sam Spade: Humphrey Bogart, Brigid O'Shaughnessy: Mary Astor, Iva Archer: Gladys George, Joel Cairo: Peter Lorre, Detective Lt. Dundy: Barton MacLane, Effie Perine: Lee Patrick, Kasper Gutman: Sydney Greenstreet, Detective Tom Polhaus: Ward Bond, Miles Archer: Jerome Cowan, Wilmer Cook: Elisha Cook, Jr., Luke: James

Burke, *Frank Richman:* Murray Alper, *District Attorney Bryan:* John Hamilton, *Mate of the* LA PALOMA: Emory Parnell, *Policeman:* Robert E. Homans, *Stenographer:* Creighton Hale, *Reporters:* Charles Drake, William Hopper, Hank Mann, *Announcer:* Jack Mower, *Captain Jacobi:* Walter Huston.

The Maltese Falcon with Humphrey Bogart, Mary Astor and Jerome Cowan.

A Man Called Peter with Jean Peters and Richard Todd.

A MAN CALLED PETER (1955) 20th. Producer, Samuel G. Engel. Director, Henry Koster. CinemaScope, De Luxe Color. Based on the novel by Catherine Marshall. Screenplay, Eleanore Griffin. Art Directors, Lyle Wheeler, Maurice Ransford. Musical Director, Alfred Newman. Cinematographer, Harold Lipstein. Special Photographic Effects, Ray Kellogg. Editor, Robert Simpson. 119 minutes

Peter Marshall: Richard Todd, *Catherine Marshall:* Jean Peters, *Mrs. Fowler:* Marjorie Rambeau, *Mrs. Findlay:* Jill Esmond, *Senator Harvey:* Les Tremaine, *Mr. Peyton:* Robert Burton, *Mrs. Peyton:* Gladys Hurlbut, *Col. Tremayne:* Richard Garrick, *Barbara Tremaine:* Gloria Gordon, *Peter John Marshall:* Billy Chapin, *Mrs. Tremaine:* Sally Corner, *Senator Wiley:* Voltaire Perkins, *Emma:* Marietta Canty, *Senator Prescott:* Edward Earle, *Peter Marshall (ages 7 and 14):* Peter Votrian, *Maitre 'D:* Sam McDaniel, *Miss Crilly:* Dorothy Neumann, *Miss Hopkins:* Doris Lloyd, *President:* William Forrest, *Miss Standish:* Barbara Morrison, *Dr. Black:* Carlyle Mitchell, *Willie:* Amanda Randolph, *Mr. Briscoe:* Emmett Lynn, *Butler:* William Walker, *President of Senate:* Charles Evans, *Chaplain Thomas:* Larry Kent, *Holden:* Roy Glenn, Sr., *Nurse:* Ruth Clifford, *Mr. Findlay:* Ben Wright, *Mrs. Ferguson:* Florence MacAfee.

THE MANCHURIAN CANDIDATE (1962) UA. Producers, George Axelrod, John Frankenheimer. Director, John Frankenheimer. Screenplay, George Axelrod. Based on the novel by Richard Condon. Executive Producer, Howard W. Koch. Music, David Amram. Assistant Director, Joseph Behm. Costumes, Moss Mabry. An M. C. Production. Executive Producer, Howard W. Koch. Art Director, Richard Sylbert. Cinematographer, Lionel Lindon. Editor, Ferris Webster. 126 minutes

Bennett Marco: Frank Sinatra, *Raymond Shaw:* Laurence Harvey, *Rosie:* Janet Leigh, *Raymond's mother:* Angela Lansbury, *Chunjin:* Henry Silva, *Senator John Iselin:* James Gregory, *Jocie Jordon:* Leslie Parrish, *Senator Thomas Jordon:* John McGiver, *Yen Lo:* Khigh Dhiegh, *Cpl. Melvin:* James Edwards, *Colonel:* Douglas Henderson, *Zilkov:* Albert Paulsen, *Secretary of Defense:* Barry Kelley, *Holborn Gaines:* Lloyd Corrigan, *Berezovo:* Madame Spivy.

The Manchurian Candidate with Frank Sinatra and Janet Leigh.

THE MAN FROM LARAMIE (1955) Col. Producer, William Goetz. Director, Anthony Mann. CinemaScope, Technicolor. Based on a story by Thomas T. Flynn. Screenplay, Philip Yordan, Frank Burt. Art Director, Cary Odell. Musical Director, Morris Stoloff. Cinematographer, Charles Lang, Jr. Editor, William Lyon. 104 minutes

Will Lockhart: James Stewart, *Vic Hansbro:* Arthur Kennedy, *Alec Waggoman:* Donald Crisp, *Barbara Waggoman:* Cathy O'Donnell, *Dave Waggoman:* Alex Nicol, *Kate Canaday:* Aline MacMahon, *Charley O'Leary:* Wallace Ford, *Chris Boldt:* Jack Elam, *Frank Darrah:* John War Eagle, *Tom Quigby:* James Millican, *Fritz:* Gregg Barton, *Spud Oxton:* Boyd Stockman, *Padre:* Frank de Kova, *Dr. Selden:* Eddy Waller.

The Man From Laramie with Aline MacMahon and James Stewart.

172

Manhattan Melodrama with Clark Gable, Nat Pendleton and John Marston.

MANHATTAN MELODRAMA (1934) MGM.

Produced by David O. Selznick. Directed by W. S. Van Dyke. Original Story, Arthur Caesar. A Cosmopolitan Production. Screenplay, Oliver H. P. Garrett and Joseph L. Mankiewicz. Photography, James Wong Howe. Editor, Ben Lewis. Song by Richard Rodgers and Lorenz Hart, "The Bad in Every Man," later became "Blue Moon." 93 minutes

(Edward) Blackie Gallagher: Clark Gable, *Jim Wade:* William Powell, *Eleanor Packer:* Myrna Loy, *Father Joe:* Leo Carrillo, *Spud:* Nat Pendleton, *Poppa Rosen:* George Sidney, *Annabelle:* Isabel Jewell, *Tootsie Malone:* Muriel Evans, *Richard Snow:* Thomas Jackson, *Miss Adams:* Claudelle Kaye, *Blackie's Attorney:* Frank Conroy, *Mannie Arnold:* Noel Madison, *Blackie at 12:* Mickey Rooney, *Jim at 12:* Jimmy Butler, *Dancer on Boat:* Vernon Dent, *Heckler:* Pat Moriarity, *Trotskyite:* Leonid Kinskey, *Yacht Captain Swenson:* Edward Van Sloan, *Politician:* George Irving, *Assistant Prosecutor:* Emmett Vogan, *Bailiff* (Extra): Lee Phelps, *Negro Con:* Sam McDaniel, *Warden:* Samuel S. Hinds, *Guard:* Wade Boteler, *Cotton Club Singer:* Shirley Ross, *Coates:* John Marston.

The Man in the Gray Flannel Suit with Sandy Descher, Jennifer Jones, Gregory Peck, Portland Mason.

THE MAN IN THE GRAY FLANNEL SUIT (1956) 20th.

Producer, Darryl F. Zanuck. Director, Nunnally Johnson. CinemaScope, De Luxe Color. Based on the novel by Sloan Wilson. Screenplay, Nunnally Johnson. Art Directors, Lyle R. Wheeler, Jack Martin Smith. Music, Bernard Herrmann. Cinematographer, Charles G. Clarke. Editor, Dorothy Spencer. 153 minutes

Tom Rath: Gregory Peck, *Betsy Rath:* Jennifer Jones, *Hopkins:*

Fredric March, *Maria:* Marisa Pavan, *Judge Bernstein:* Lee J. Cobb, *Mrs. Hopkins:* Ann Harding, *Caesar Gardella:* Keenan Wynn, *Hawthorne:* Gene Lockhart, *Susan Hopkins:* Gigi Perreau, *Janie:* Portland Mason, *Walker:* Arthur O'Connell, *Bill Ogden:* Henry Daniell, *Mrs. Manter:* Connie Gilchrist, *Edward Schultz:* Joseph Sweeney, *Barbara:* Sandy Descher, *Pete:* Mickey Maga, *Mahoney:* Kenneth Tobey, *Miriam:* Geraldine Wall, *Police Sergeant:* Jack Mather, *Dr. Pearce:* Frank Wilcox, *Miss Lawrence:* Nan Martin, *Gina:* Phyllis Graffeo, *Mrs. Hopkins'* Maid: Dorothy Adams, *Maid:* Dorothy Phillips, *Waiter:* John Breen, *Carriage Driver:* Mario Siletti, *Master Sergeant Mathews:* Roy Glenn, *First German Soldier:* Robert Boon, *Second German Soldier:* Jim Brandt, *Third German Soldier:* Otto Reichow, *Soldier:* Harry Lauter, *Soldier:* William Phipps, *Medic:* De Forrest Kelley.

THE MAN WHO CAME TO DINNER (1941) WB.

Vice-president in Charge of Production, Jack L. Warner. Executive Producer, Hal B. Wallis. Associate Producers, Jack Saper and Jerry Wald. Directed by William Keighley. Based on the play by George S. Kaufman and Moss Hart (which evolved into the musical *Sherry*, 1967). Screenplay, Julius J. and Philip G. Epstein. Art Director, Robert Haas. Music, Frederick Hollander. Music Director, Leo F. Forbstein. Photography, Tony Gaudio. Editor, Jack Killifer. Assistant Director, Dick Mayberry. Sound, Charles Long. Gowns, Orry-Kelly. Make-up, Perc Westmore. Monty Woolley repeats his stage role, a caricature of Alexander Woollcott. 112 minutes

Sheridan Whiteside: Monty Woolley, *Maggie Cutler:* Bette Davis, *Lorraine Sheldon:* Ann Sheridan, *Bert Jefferson:* Richard Travis, *Banjo:* Jimmy Durante, *Beverly Carlton:* Reginald Gardiner, *Mrs. Stanley:* Billie Burke, *June Stanley:* Elisabeth Fraser, *Ernest Stanley:* Grant Mitchell, *Dr. Bradley:* George Barbier, *Miss Preen:* Mary Wickes, *Richard Stanley:* Russell Arms, *Harriett Stanley:* Ruth Vivian, *John:* Edwin Stanley, *Sarah:* Betty Roadman, *Mrs. Gibbons:* Laura Hope Crews, *Mr. Gibbons:* Chester Clute, *Sandy:* Charles Drake, *Cosette:* Nanette Vallon, *Radio Man:* John Ridgely, *Harry:* Pat McVey, *Telegraph Boy:* Frank Coghlan, Jr., *Newspaperman:* Roland Drew, *Announcer:* Sam Hayes, *Guard:* Eddy Chandler, *Michaelson:* Frank Moran, *Haggerty:* Ernie Adams, *Expressmen:* Hank Mann, Cliff Saum, *Vendor:* Billy Wayne, *Porter:* Dudley Dickerson, *Radio Men:* Herbert Gunn, Creighton Hale, *Plainclothesmen:* Jack Mower, Frank Mayo, *Man:* Fred Kelsey, *Girls:* Georgia Carroll, Lorraine Gettman (Leslie Brooks), Peggy Diggins, Alix Talton.

The Man Who Came to Dinner with Junior Coghlan, Bette Davis and Monty Woolley.

THE MAN WHO KNEW TOO MUCH (1956) Par.

Producer, Alfred Hitchcock. Associate Producer, Herbert Coleman. Director, Alfred Hitchcock. VistaVision, Technicolor. Authors, Charles Bennett, D. B. Wyndham-Lewis. Screenplay, John Michael Hayes, Angus Mac-

Phail. Art Directors, Hal Pereira, Henry Bumstead. Musical Director, Bernard Herrmann. Cinematographer, Robert Burks. Editor, George Tomasini. Songs: "Que Sera Sera" by Livingston and Evans; "Storm Cloud Cantata" by Arthur Benjamin and D. B. Wyndham-Lewis. Remake of the 1934 Gaumont-British Hitchcock film. 120 minutes

Ben McKenna: James Stewart, *Jo McKenna:* Doris Day, *Mrs. Drayton:* Brenda de Banzie, *Mr. Drayton:* Bernard Miles, *Buchanan:* Ralph Truman, *Louis Bernard:* Daniel Gelin, *Ambassador:* Mogens Wieth, *Val Parnell:* Alan Mowbray, *Jan Peterson:* Hillary Brooke, *Hank McKenna:* Christopher Olsen, *Rien-Assassin:* Reggie Nalder, *Asst. Mgr.:* Richard Wattis, *Woburn:* Noel Willman, *Helen Parnell:* Alix Talton, *Police Inspector:* Yves Brainville, *Cindy Fontaine:* Carolyn Jones, *Foreign Prime Minister:* Alexis Bobrinskoy, *Arab:* Abdelhaq Chraibi, *Edna:* Betty Baskcomb, *Chauffeur:* Leo Gordon, *English Handyman:* Patrick Aherne, *French Police:* Louis Mercier, Anthony Warde, *Detective:* Lewis Martin, *Bernard's Girl Friend:* Gladys Holland, *Headwaiter:* Peter Camlin, *Henchman:* Ralph Neff, *Butler:* John Marshall, *Special Branch Officer:* Eric Snowden, *Arab:* Lou Krugman, *Guard:* Milton Frome.

The Man Who Knew Too Much with Doris Day and James Stewart.

The Man Who Played God with Bette Davis and George Arliss.

THE MAN WHO PLAYED GOD (1932) WB. Directed by John G. Adolfi. Based on the short story by Gouverneur Morris, and the play *The Silent Voice* by Jules Eckert Goodman. Scenario and Dialogue, Julian Josephson and Maude Howell. Photography, James Van Trees. Editor, William Holmes. George Arliss starred in the play and the 1922 silent version. Other versions: *The Man Who Played God* (United Artists, 1922), *Sincerely Yours* (Warners, 1955) with Liberace. 81 minutes

Montgomery Royle: George Arliss, *Mildred Miller:* Violet Heming,

Battle: Ivan Simpson, *Florence Royle:* Louise Closser Hale, *Grace Blair:* Bette Davis, *The King:* Andre Luguet, *Harold Van Adam:* Donald Cook, *Doctor:* Charles E. Evans, *Lip Reader:* Oscar Apfel, *French Concert Manager:* Paul Porcasi, *Eddie:* Ray Milland, *Jenny:* Dorothy Libaire, *First Boy:* William Janney, *First Girl:* Grace Durkin, *Reporter:* Russell Hopton, *King's Aide:* Murray Kinnell, *Chittendon:* Harry Stubbs, *Alice Chittendon:* Hedda Hopper, *Detective:* Wade Boteler, *Russian Officers:* Alex Ikonikoff, Michael Visaroff, Paul Panzer, *Man:* Fred Howard.

The Man With the Golden Arm with Frank Sinatra and Kim Novak.

THE MAN WITH THE GOLDEN ARM (1955) UA. Produced and directed by Otto Preminger. From the novel by Nelson Algren. Screenplay, Walter Newman and Lewis Meltzer. Music, Elmer Bernstein. Jazz by Shorty Rogers and his Giants with Shelly Manne. Assistant to the Producer, Maximilian Slater. Designed by Joe Wright. Assistant Directors, Horace Hough and James Engle. Costume Superviser, Mary Ann Nyberg. Music Editor, Leon Birnbaum. Photography, Sam Leavitt. Editor, Louis R. Loeffler. 119 minutes

Frankie: Frank Sinatra, *Zosh:* Eleanor Parker, *Molly:* Kim Novak, *Sparrow:* Arnold Stang, *Louie:* Darren McGavin, *Schwiefka:* Robert Strauss, *Drunky:* John Conte, *Vi:* Doro Merande, *Markette:* George E. Stone, *Williams:* George Mathews, *Dominowski:* Leonid Kinskey, *Bednar:* Emile Meyer, *Shorty Rogers:* Himself, *Shelly Manne:* Himself, *Piggy:* Frank Richards, *Lane:* Will Wright, *Kvorka:* Tommy Hart, *Antek:* Frank Marlowe, *Chester:* Ralph Neff, *Vangie:* Martha Wentworth.

THE MAN WITH THE GOLDEN GUN (1974) UA. Produced by Albert R. Broccoli and Harry Saltzman. Directed by Guy Hamilton. Screenplay by Richard Maibaum and Tom Mankiewicz, based on Ian Fleming's novel. Associate Producer, Charles Orme. Photography, Ted Moore and Ossie Morris. Designer, Peter Murton. Art Directors, John Graysmark and Peter Lamont. Editor, Ray Poulton. Music by John Barry. Lyrics by Don Black. Title song sung by Lulu. Assistant Director, Derek Cracknell. 2nd Unit Photography, John Harris. Special Effects, John Stears. Miniatures, Derek Meddings. Titles, Maurice Binder. Stunt Coordinator, W. J. Milligan, Jr. An Eon Production, in Eastman Color. Produced in England. rated PG. 125 minutes

James Bond: Roger Moore, *Scaramanga:* Christopher Lee, *Mary Goodnight:* Britt Ekland, *Andrea:* Maud Adams, *Nick Nack:* Herve Villechaize, *J. W. Pepper:* Clifton James, *Hip:* Soon Taik Oh, *Hai Fat:* Richard Loo, *Rodney:* Marc Lawrence, *M:* Bernard Lee, *Moneypenny:* Lois Maxwell, *Lazar:* Marne Maitland, *Q:* Desmond Llewelyn, *Colthorpe:* James Cossins, *Chula*: Chan Yiu Lam, *Saida*: Carmen Sautoy, *Frazier*: Gerald James, *Naval Lieutenant*: Michael Osborne, *Communications Officer*: Michael Fleming.

The Man with the Golden Gun with Christopher Lee and Roger Moore.

Marathon Man with Dustin Hoffman and Marthe Keller.

MARATHON MAN (1976) Par. Produced by Robert Evans and Sidney Beckerman. Directed by John Schlesinger. Screenplay by William Goldman, based on his novel. Photography, Conrad Hall. Associate Producer, George Justin. Production Designer, Richard MacDonald. Editor, Jim Clark. Music composed and conducted by Michael Small. Art Director, Jack De Shields. Associate Editor, Arthur Schmidt. Assistant Directors, Howard W. Koch, Jr., and Burtt Harris. Set Decorator, George Gaines. Stunt Coordinator and 2nd Unit Director, Everett Creach. Costumes, Robert De Mora. Special Effects, Richard E. Johnson and Charles Spurgeon. Makeup Artist, Ben Nye. Special Make-up Consultant, Dick Smith. Hairstylist, Barbara Lorenz. Wardrobe, Bernie Pollack and Robert M. Moore. 2nd Assistant Director, William Saint John. Scheider's clothes, Roland Meledandri. Title Design, Dan Perri. Special Photography, Garrett Brown. Panavision and MetroColor. Filmed in New York, Paris and Paramount Studio, Hollywood. Rated R. 125 minutes. American film debut of Keller.

Babe: Dustin Hoffman, *Szell*: Laurence Olivier, *Doc*: Roy Scheider, *Janeway*: William Devane, *Elsa*: Marthe Keller, *Prof. Biesenthal*: Fritz Weaver, *Karl*: Richard Bright, *Erhard*: Marc Lawrence, *The Father*: Allen Joseph, *Melendez*: Tito Goya, *Szell's Brother*: Ben Dova, *Rosenbaum*: Lou Gilbert, *LeClerk*: Jacques Marin, *Chen*: James Wing Woo, *Nicole*: Nicole Deslauriers, *Old Lady*: Lotta Andor-Palfi, *Jewelry Salesmen*: Harry Goz, Michael Vale, Fred Stuthman, Lee Steele, *Bank Guard*:

William Martel, *Plainclothesmen*: Glenn Robards, Ric Carrott, *Laundress*: Alma Beltran, *Tourists*: Billy Kearns, Sally Wilson, *TV Announcer*: Tom Ellis, *Young Photographer*: Bryant Fraser, *Hotel Valet*: George Dega, *French Doctor*: Gene Bori, *Nurse*: Annette Claudier, *Headwaiter*: Roger Etienne, *Truck Driver*: Ray Serra, *Lady in Bank*: Madge Kennedy, *Young Babe*: Jeff Palladini, *Young Doc*: Scott Price.

MARIE ANTOINETTE (1938) MGM. Producer, Hunt Stromberg. Director, W. S. Van Dyke. Based on the book by Stephan Zweig. Screenplay, Claudine West, Donald Ogden Stewart, Ernst Vajda. Art Director, Cedric Gibbons. Montage, Slavko Vorkapich. Score, Herbert Stothart. Dances, Albertina Rasch. Cameraman, William Daniels. Editor, Robert J. Kern. Song by Bob Wright, Chet Forrest and Herbert Stothart: "Amour Eternal Amour." 160 minutes

Marie Antoinette: Norma Shearer, *Count Axel de Fersen*: Tyrone Power, *King Louis XV*: John Barrymore, *Mme. DuBarry*: Gladys George, *King Louis XVI*: Robert Morley, *Princess DeLamballe*: Anita Louise, *Duke of Orleans*: Joseph Schildkraut, *Count Mercy*: Henry Stephenson, *Artois*: Reginald Gardiner, *Gamin*: Peter Bull, *Provence*: Albert Van Dekker, *Prince DeRohan*: Barnett Parker, *Mme. De-Noailles*: Cora Witherspoon, *Drouet*: Joseph Calleia, *Court Aide*: Henry Kolker, *Rabblerouser*: Horace McMahon, *Citizen-Officer*: Robert Barrat, *Sauce*: Ivan F. Simpson, *Robespierre*: George Meeker, *Princess Theresa*: Marilyn Knowlden, *Dauphin*: Scotty Beckett, *La Motte*: Henry Daniell, *Empress Marie Theresa*: Alma Kruger, *Toulan*: Leonard Penn, *Gov. of Conciergerie*: George Zucco, *Herbert (Jailer)*: Ian Wolfe, *LaFayette*: John Burton, *Mme. La Motte*: Mae Busch, *Mme. DeLerchenfeld*: Cecil Cunningham, *Mme. LePolignac*: Ruth Hussey, *Benjamin Franklin*: Walter Walker, *Choisell*: Claude King, *Goguelot*: Herbert Rawlinson, *Danton*: Wade Crosby, *Marquis De St. Priest*: George Houston, *Bearded Man, a Leader of the People*: Moroni Olsen, *Peddler*: Barry Fitzgerald, *M. de Cosse*: Harry Davenport, *Boehmer (Jeweler)*: Olaf Hytten, *Marat*: Anthony Warde, *Louise*: Rafaela Ottiano.

Marie Antoinette with Mae Busch, Anita Louise, Olaf Hytten and Norma Shearer.

MARJORIE MORNINGSTAR (1958) WB. Producer, Milton Sperling. Director, Irving Rapper. WarnerColor. Screenplay by Everett Freeman. Based on novel by Herman Wouk. Costumes by Howard Shoup. Assistant Director, Don Page. Music by Max Steiner. "A Very Precious Love," song by Sammy Fain and Paul Francis Webster. Dances and musical numbers staged by Jack Baker. A Beachwold Picture. Photography, Harry Stradling. 123 minutes

Noel Airman: Gene Kelly, *Marjorie Morgenstern*: Natalie Wood, *Uncle Samson*: Ed Wynn, *Rose Morgenstern*: Claire Trevor, *Arnold Morgenstern*: Everett Sloane, *Wally*: Marty Milner, *Marsha Zelenko*: Carolyn Jones, *Greech*: George Tobias, *Lou Michaelson*: Jesse White,

Doctor David Harris: Martin Balsam, *Puddles Podell:* Alan Reed, *Sandy Lamm:* Edward Byrnes, *Seth:* Howard Bert, *Philip Berman:* Paul Picerni, *Imogene:* Ruta Lee, *Karen:* Patricia Denise, *Elevator Operator:* Lester Dorr, *Leon Lamm:* Carl Sklover, *Mary Lamm:* Jean Vachon, *Miss Kimble:* Elizabeth Harrower, *Mr. Klabber:* Guy Raymond, *Carlos:* Edward (Eddie) Foster, *Blair:* Leslie Bradley, *Tonia Zelenko:* Maida Severn, *Helen Harris:* Fay Nuell, *Nate:* Fred Rapport, *Frank:* Harry Seymour, *Seth's Girl Friend:* Shelly Fabares, *Mr. Zelenko:* Walter Clinton, *Civil Official:* Pierre Watkin, *Clerk:* Reginald Sheffield, *Betsy:* Sandy Livingston, *Alec:* Peter Brown, *Wally's Girl Friend:* Gail Ganley, *Harry Morgenstern:* Russell Ash, *Romeo:* Rad Fulton.

Marjorie Morningstar with Everett Sloane, Natalie Wood and Ed Wynn.

Marked Woman with Ralph Dunn, Humphrey Bogart, Gordon Hart and Bette Davis.

MARKED WOMAN (1937) WB. Executive Producer, Hal B. Wallis. Associate Producer, Lou Edelman. Directed by Lloyd Bacon. Original Screenplay, Robert Rossen and Abem Finkel. Art Director, Max Parker. Music Director, Leo F. Forbstein. Photography, George Barnes. Editor, Jack Killifer. Song by Harry Warren and Al Dubin, "My Silver Dollar Man." 96 minutes

Mary Dwight (Strauber): Bette Davis, *David Graham:* Humphrey Bogart, *Betty Strauber:* Jane Bryan, *Johnny Vanning:* Eduardo Ciannelli, *Emmy Lou Egan:* Isabel Jewell, *Louie:* Allen Jenkins, *Estelle Porter:* Mayo Methot, *Gabby Marvin:* Lola Lane, *Charley Delaney:* Ben Welden, *D. A. Arthur Sheldon:* Henry O'Neill, *Florrie Liggett:* Rosalind Marquis, *Gordon:* John Litel, *Ralph Krawford:* Damian O'Flynn, *George Beler:* Robert Strange, *Bell Captain:* James (Archie) Robbins, *Bob Crandall:* William B. Davidson, *Vincent, Sugar Daddy:* John Sheehan, *Mac:* Sam Wren, *Eddie, Sugar Daddy:* Kenneth Harlan, *Lawyer at Jail:* Raymond Hatton, *Henchmen:* Alan Davis, Allen Matthews, *Taxi Driver:* John Harron, *Taxi Driver:* Frank Faylen, *Mug:* Norman Willis, *Detectives: Ferguson,* Guy Usher, *Casey,* Ed Stanley, *Judge:* Gordon Hart, *Sheriff John Truble:* Arthur Aylesworth, *Court Clerk:* Ralph Dunn, *Foreman of Jury:* Wilfred Lucas, *Drunk:* Jack Norton, *Elevator Boy:* Carlyle Moore, Jr., *Court Clerk:* Emmett

Vogan, *Foreman:* Jack Mower, *Judge:* Pierre Watkin, *Little Joe:* Herman Marks.

THE MARK OF ZORRO (1940) 20th. Director, Rouben Mamoulian. Based on the story "The Curse of Capistrano" by Johnston McCulley. Adaptation, Garrett Fort, Bess Meredyth. Cameraman. Arthur Miller. Editor, Robert Bischoff. Remake of 1920 UA film. 93 minutes

Diego Vega: Tyrone Power, *Lolita Quintero:* Linda Darnell, *Captain Esteban Pasquale:* Basil Rathbone, *Inez Quintero:* Gale Sondergaard, *Fray Felipe:* Eugene Pallette, *Don Luis Quintero:* J. Edward Bromberg, *Don Alejandro Vega:* Montagu Love, *Senora Isabella Vega:* Janet Beecher, *Rodrigo:* Robert Lowery, *Turnkey:* Chris-Pin Martin, *Sgt. Gonzales:* George Regas, *Maria:* Belle Mitchell, *Pedro:* John Bleifer, *Proprietor:* Frank Puglia, *Don Miguel:* Pedro de Cordoba, *Don Jose:* Guy D'Ennery, *Officer of Day:* Eugene Borden, *First Sentry:* Fred Malatesta, *Sentry:* Fortunio Bonanova, *Caballeros:* Harry Worth, Lucio Villegas, *Soldier:* Paul Sutton, *Officer-Student:* Ralph Byrd, *Bit:* (Michael) Ted North, *Manservant:* Rafael Corio, *Orderly:* Franco Corsaro, *Peon Selling Cocks:* William Edmunds, *Peon at Inn:* Hector Sarno, *Jose, a Peon:* Charles Stevens, *Commanding Officer:* Stanley Andreuh, *Boatman:* Victor Kilian, *Caballero:* Gino Corrado.

The Mark of Zorro with Tyrone Power and Basil Rathbone.

MARTY (1955) UA. Producer, Harold Hecht. Director, Delbert Mann. Story and screenplay by Paddy Chayefsky. Costumes by Norma. Music by Roy Webb. Assistant Directors, Paul Helmick and Mark Sandrich, Jr. A Hecht-Lancaster-Steven Production. Title song by Harry Warren. Originally presented as a drama on TV Playhouse. Filmed in the Bronx. Ed Sullivan is seen in a TV kinescope. 99 minutes

Marty Pilletti: Ernest Borgnine, *Clara Snyder:* Betsy Blair, *Mrs. Pilletti:* Esther Minciotti, *Catherine:* Augusta Ciolli, *Angie:* Joe Mantell, *Virginia:* Karen Steele, *Thomas:* Jerry Paris, *Ralph:* Frank Sutton,

The Kid: Walter Kelley, *Joe:* Robin Morse, *Lou, Bartender:* Charles Cane, *A Bachelor:* Nick Brkich, *Herb:* Alan Wells, *Mrs. Rosari:* Minerva Urecal, *Mr. Snyder,* James Bell.

Marty with Ernest Borgnine and Betsy Blair.

Mary Poppins with Dick Van Dyke, Julie Andrews, Matthew Garber and Karen Dotrice.

MARY POPPINS (1964) BV. Producer, Walt Disney. Directed by Robert Stevenson. Technicolor. Co-produced and written by Bill Walsh. Based on Mary Poppins books by P. L. Travers. Music, Irwin Kostal. Songs by Richard M. and Robert B. Sherman: "Chim-Chim-Cheree," "Spoonful of Sugar," "Jolly Holiday," "Supercalifragilisticexpialidocious," "The Life I Lead," "Sister Suffragette," "Step in Time," "Stay Awake," "A Man Has Dreams," "Feed the Birds (Tuppence a Bag)," "I Love to Laugh." Choreography, Marc Breaux and Dee Dee Wood. Costume and Design Consultant, Tony Walton. Photography, Edward Colman. Art Directors, Carroll Clark and William H. Tuntke. Editor, Cotton Warburton. Sets, Emile Kuri and Hal Gausman. Costumes, Bill Thomas. Sound, Robert O. Cook. Costumes, Chuck Keehne and Gertrude Casey. Assistant Directors, Joseph L. McEveety and Paul Feiner. Animation Director, Hamilton Luske. 140 minutes

Mary Poppins: Julie Andrews, *Bert/Old Dawes:* Dick Van Dyke, *Mr. Banks:* David Tomlinson, *Mrs. Banks:* Glynis Johns, *Ellen:* Hermione Baddeley, *Jane Banks:* Karen Dotrice, *Michael Banks:* Matthew Garber, *Katie Nanna:* Elsa Lanchester, *Uncle Albert:* Ed Wynn, *Bird Woman:* Jane Darwell, *Constable Jones:* Arthur Treacher, *Admiral Boom:* Reginald Owen, *Mrs. Brill:* Reta Shaw, *Mr. Dawes, Jr.:* Arthur Malet, *Mr. Binnacle:* Don Barclay, *Miss Lark:* Marjorie Bennett, *Miss Persimmon:* Marjorie Eaton, *Citizen:* Major Sam Harris, *Depositor:* Doris Lloyd, *Bank Directors: Mr. Grubbs,* Cyril Delevanti, *Mr. Tomes,* Lester Mathews, *Mr. Mousley,* Clive L. Halliday, *Mrs. Corry:* Alma Lawton.

M*A*S*H with Tom Skerritt and Donald Sutherland.

M*A*S*H (1970) 20th. An Aspen Production. Produced by Ingo Preminger. Directed by Robert Altman. Panavision and DeLuxe Color. From the novel by Richard Hooker. Screenplay, Ring Lardner, Jr. Photography, Harold E. Stine. Associate Producer, Leon Ericksen. Assistant Director, Ray Taylor, Jr. Music by Johnny Mandel. Song, "Suicide Is Painless," lyrics by Mike Altman. Art Directors, Jack Martin Smith and Arthur Lonergan. Set Decoration, Walter M. Scott and Stuart A. Reiss. Orchestration, Herbert Spencer. Medical Adviser, Dr. David Sachs. Editor, Danford B. Greene. Sound, Bernard Freericks and John Stack. Make-up Supervision, Dan Striepeke. Make-up Artist, Lester Beins. Hairstyling, Edith Lindon. Rated R. 116 minutes. Later a TV series

Hawkeye: Donald Sutherland, *Trapper John:* Elliott Gould, *Duke:* Tom Skerritt, *Maj. Hot Lips Houlihan:* Sally Kellerman, *Maj. Frank Burns:* Robert Duvall, *Lt. Dish:* Jo An Pflug, *Dago Red:* Rene Auberjonois, *Col. Henry Blake:* Roger Bowen, *Radar O'Reilly:* Gary Burghoff, *Sgt. Major Vollmer:* David Arkin, *Spearchucker:* Fred Williamson, *Me Lay:* Michael Murphy, *Ho-Jon:* Kim Atwood, *Corp. Judson:* Tim Brown, *Lt. Leslie:* Indus Arthur, *Painless Pole:* John Schuck, *PFC Seidman:* Ken Prymus, *Capt. Scorch:* Dawne Damon, *Ugly John:* Carl Gottlieb, *Capt. Knocko:* Tamara Horrocks, *Gen. Hammond:* G. Wood, *Sgt. Gorman:* Bobby Troup, *Private Boone:* Bud Cort, *Capt. Murrhardt:* Danny Goldman, *Captain Bandini:* Corey Fischer, *Pretty WAC:* Monica Peterson, *Nurse Corps Captain:* Cathleen Cordell, *Japanese Nurse:* Sumi Haru, *Japanese Caddies:* Susan Ikeda, Masami Saito, *Japanese Golf Pro:* John Mamo, *Michiko:* Yoko Young, *Nurse/"Pin-up Model":* Samantha Scott, *Col. Merrill:* J. B. Douglas, *Corporal:* Tom Falk, *Second Lieutenant:* Harvey Levine, *Correspondent:* Dianne Turley, *Korean Doctors:* Weaver Levy, Dale Ishimoto, *Motor Pool Sergeant:* Jerry Jones, *Hawkeye's 5-year-old son:* Stephen Altman, *Korean Prostitute:* Hiroko Watanabe, *Offstage Dialogue:* H. Lloyd Nelson, Ted Knight, Marvin Miller.

Mata Hari with Greta Garbo and Ramon Novarro.

MATA HARI (1931) MGM. Directed by George Fitzmaurice. Story by Benjamin Glazer and Leo Birinski. Dialogue, Doris Anderson and Gilbert Emery. Photography, William Daniels. Editor, Frank Sullivan. Sound, J. K. Brock. 91 minutes

Mata Hari: Greta Garbo, *Lieutenant Alexis Rosanoff:* Ramon Novarro, *General Serge Shubin:* Lionel Barrymore, *Andriani:* Lewis Stone, *Dubois:* C. Henry Gordon, *Carlotta:* Karen Morley, *Major Caron:* Alec B. Francis, *Sister Angelica:* Blanche Frederici, *Warden:* Edmund Breese, *Sister Genevieve:* Helen Jerome Eddy, *The Cook-Spy:* Frank Reicher, *Sister Teresa:* Sarah Padden, *Ivan:* Harry Cording, *Aide:* Gordon De Main, *Condemned Man:* Mischa Auer, *Gambler:* Cecil Cunningham, *Orderly:* Michael Visaroff.

Maytime with Nelson Eddy and Jeanette MacDonald.

MAYTIME (1937) MGM. Produced by Hunt Stromberg. Directed by Robert Z. Leonard. Based on the 1917 operetta; book and lyrics by Rida Johnson Young, score by Sigmund Romberg. Screenplay, Noel Langley. Music adapted and directed by Herbert Stothart. Photography, Oliver T. Marsh. Editor, Conrad A. Nervig. Songs: "Sweetheart (Will You Remember?)," "Maytime Finale" by Romberg and Young; "Virginia Ham and Eggs," "Vive L'Opera" by Herbert Stothart, Bob Wright, and Chet Forrest: "Student Drinking Song" by Stothart; "Carry Me Back to Old Virginny" by James A. Bland; "Czaritza," based on Tchaikovsky's Fifth Symphony, libretto by Wright and Forrest; "Reverie," based on Romberg airs. "Jump Jim Crow," "Road to Paradise" and "Dancing Will Keep You Young" by Rida Johnson Young, Cyrus Wood and Sigmund Romberg; "Maypole" by Ed Ward. "Street Singer" by Bob Wright, Chet Forrest and Herbert Stothart. Adaptation of French libretto, Gilles Guilbert. Vocal arrangements, Leo Arnaud. Opera sequences, William Von Wymetal. Associate Art Directors, Fredric Hope and Edwin B. Willis. Gowns, Adrian. Sound, Douglas Shearer. Film debuts of Lynne Carver, 19, and Joan Crawford's niece Joan Le Sueur, 3. 132 minutes

Marcia Mornay (Miss Morrison): Jeanette MacDonald, *Paul Allison:* Nelson Eddy, *Nicolai Nazaroff:* John Barrymore, *August Archipenko:* Herman Bing, *Kip:* Tom Brown, *Barbara Roberts:* Lynne Carver, *Ellen:* Rafaela Ottiano, *Cabby:* Charles Judels, *Composer Trentini:* Paul Porcasi, *Fanchon:* Sig Rumann, *Rudyard:* Walter Kingsford, *Secretary:* Edgar Norton, *Emperor Louis Napoleon:* Guy Bates Post, *Empress Eugenie:* Iphigenie Castiglioni, *Madame Fanchon:* Anna Demetrio, *Orchestra Conductor:* Frank Puglia, *Dubrovsky, Czaritza's Minister/Student at Cafe:* Adia Kuznetzoff, *Maypole Dancer:* Joan Le Sueur, *M. Bulliet, Voice Coach:* Russell Hicks, *Opera Directors:* Harry Davenport, Harry Hayden, Howard Hickman, Robert C. Fischer, *Bearded Director:* Harlan Briggs, *O'Brien, a Director:* Frank Sheridan, *Drunk:* Billy Gilbert, *Empress' Dinner Companion:* Ivan Lebedeff, *Student in Bar:* Leonid Kinskey, *Waiter:* Clarence Wilson, *Opera House Manager:* Maurice Cass, *Massilon, Hotel Manager:* Douglas Wood, *Assistant Manager:* Bernard Suss, *Publicity Man:* Henry Roquemore, *French Proprietor:* Alexander Schonberg, *Opera Singer:* Mariska Aldrich, *Singers:* The Don Cossack Chorus.

MEET JOHN DOE (1941) WB. Produced and directed by Frank Capra. Based on a story by Richard Connell and Robert Presnell. Screenplay, Robert Riskin. Art Director, Stephen Goosson. Music, Dimitri Tiomkin. Choral Arrangements, Hall Johnson. Music Director, Leo F. Forbstein. Assistant Director, Arthur S. Black. Photography, George Barnes. Sound, C. A. Riggs. Editor, Daniel Mandell. Gowns, Natalie Visart. Special Effects, Jack Cosgrove. Montage Effects, Slavko Vorkapich. 135 minutes

Long John Willoughby (John Doe): Gary Cooper, *Ann Mitchell:* Barbara Stanwyck, *D. B. Norton:* Edward Arnold, *The Colonel:* Walter Brennan, *Mrs. Mitchell:* Spring Byington, *Henry Connell:* James Gleason, *Mayor Lovett:* Gene Lockhart, *Ted Sheldon:* Rod La Rocque, *Beany:* Irving Bacon, *Bert Hansen:* Regis Toomey, *Mrs. Hansen:* Ann Doran, *Sourpuss Smithers:* J. Farrell MacDonald, *Angelface:* Warren Hymer, *Mayor Hawkins:* Harry Holman, *Spencer:* Andrew Tombes, *Hammett:* Pierre Watkin, *Weston:* Stanley Andrews, *Bennett:* Mitchell Lewis, *Charlie Dawson:* Charles C. Wilson, *Governor:* Vaughan Glaser, *Dan:* Sterling Holloway, *Radio Announcer:* Mike Frankovich, *Radio Announcers at Convention:* Knox Manning, Selmer Jackson, John B. Hughes, *Pop Dwyer:* Aldrich Bowker, *Mrs. Brewster:* Mrs. Gardner Crane, *Mike:* Pat Flaherty, *Ann's Sisters:* Carlotta Jelm, Tina Thayer, *Red, Office Boy:* Bennie Bartlett, *Mrs. Hawkins:* Sarah Edwards, *Radio M.C.:* Edward Earle, *Sheriff:* James McNamara, *Mrs. Delaney:* Emma Tansey, *Grubbel:* Frank Austin, *Relief Administrator:* Edward Keane, *Mr. Delaney:* Lafe McKee, *Joe, Newsman:* Edward McWade, *Bixler:* Guy Usher, *Barrington:* Walter Soderling, *Policeman:* Edmund Cobb, *Midget:* Billy Curtis, *Lady Midget:* Johnny Fern, *Jim, Governor's Associate:* John Hamilton, *Governor's Associate:* William Forrest, *Fired Reporter:* Charles K. French, *Mayor's Secretary:* Edward Hearn, *Newspaper Secretary:* Bess Flowers, *Ed, a Photographer:* Hank Mann, *Photographer:* James Millican. And The Hall Johnson Choir.

Meet John Doe with Barbara Stanwyck, Gary Cooper and James Gleason.

MEET ME IN ST. LOUIS (1944) MGM. Producer, Arthur Freed. Director, Vincente Minnelli. Color by Technicolor. Screenplay by Irving Brecher and Fred F. Finklehoffe. Based on the *New Yorker* stories and the novel by Sally Benson. Title song by Andrew B. Sterling and Kerry Mills. New songs by Hugh Martin and Ralph Blane: "The

Boy Next Door," "The Trolley Song," "Have Yourself a Merry Little Christmas," "Skip to My Lou." Dances by Paul Jones. Music adapted by Roger Edens. Music Director, Georgie Stoll. Orchestrations by Conrad Salinger. Film Editor, Albert Akst. Photographed by George Folsey. Dance Director, Charles Walters. Art Directors, Cedric Gibbons and Lemuel Ayers. 113 minutes

Esther Smith: Judy Garland, *"Tootie" Smith:* Margaret O'Brien, *Mrs. Anne Smith:* Mary Astor, *Rose Smith:* Lucille Bremer, *Lucille Ballard:* June Lockhart, *John Truett:* Tom Drake, *Katie (Maid):* Marjorie Main, *Grandpa:* Harry Davenport, *Mr. Alonzo Smith:* Leon Ames, *Lon Smith, Jr.:* Henry H. Daniels, Jr. (Hank Daniels), *Agnes Smith:* Joan Carroll, *Colonel Darly:* Hugh Marlowe, *Warren Sheffield:* Robert Sully, *Mr. Neely:* Chill Wills, *Doctor Terry:* Donald Curtis, *Ida Boothby:* Mary Jo Ellis, *Quentin:* Ken Wilson, *Motorman:* Robert Emmet O'Connor, *Johnny Tevis:* Darryl Hickman, *Conductor:* Leonard Walker, *Baggage Man:* Victor Kilian, *Mailman:* John Phipps, *Mr. March:* Major Sam Harris, *Mr. Braukoff:* Mayo Newhall, *Mrs. Braukoff:* Belle Mitchell, *Hugo Borvis:* Sidney Barnes, *George:* Myron Tobias, *Driver:* Victor Cox, *Clinton Badgers:* Kenneth Donner, Buddy Gorman, Joe Cobb.

Meet Me in St. Louis with Leon Ames, Judy Garland, Harry Davenport, Lucille Bremer, Hank Daniels, Joan Carroll and Mary Astor.

The Men with Marlon Brando and Teresa Wright.

THE MEN (1950) UA. Produced by Stanley Kramer. Directed by Fred Zinnemann. Story and Screenplay, Carl Foreman. Music composed and directed by Dimitri Tiomkin. Photography, Robert De

Grasse. Editor, Harry Gerstad. Filmed at Birmingham Veterans Administration Hospital. Film debut of Marlon Brando, 25. Reissued as *Battle Stripe* (NTA, 1957). 86 minutes

Ken: Marlon Brando, *Ellen:* Teresa Wright, *Doctor Brock:* Everett Sloane, *Norm:* Jack Webb, *Leo:* Richard Erdman, *Angel:* Arthur Jurado, *Nurse Robbins:* Virginia Farmer, *Ellen's Mother:* Dorothy Tree, *Ellen's Father:* Howard St. John, *Dolores:* Nita Hunter, *Laverne:* Patricia Joiner, *Mr. Doolin:* John Miller, *Dr. Kameran:* Cliff Clark, *Man at Bar:* Ray Teal, *Angel's Mother:* Marguerita Martin, *The Lookout:* Obie Parker, *Thompson:* Ray Mitchell, *Mullin:* Pete Simon, *Hopkins:* Paul Peltz, *Fine:* Tom Gillick, *Baker:* Randall Updyke III, *Romano:* Marshall Ball, *Gunderson:* Carlo Lewis, *Walter:* William Lea, Jr.

Middle of the Night with Fredric March and Kim Novak.

MIDDLE OF THE NIGHT (1959) Col. Producer, George Justin. Director, Delbert Mann. Screenplay by Paddy Chayefsky, originally a TV play. Music by George Bassman. Gowns by Jean Louis. Costumes by Frank L. Thompson. Assistant Director, Charles H. Maguire. Art Director, Edward S. Haworth. Cinematographer, Joseph Brun. Editor, Carl Lerner. A Sudan Production. Filmed in New York City. 118 minutes

Jerry Kingsley: Fredric March, *Betty Preisser:* Kim Novak, *Mrs. Mueller:* Glenda Farrell, *Alice:* Jan Norris, *Marilyn:* Lee Grant, *The Neighbor, Mrs. Herbert:* Effie Afton, *George:* Lee Philips, *Evelyn Kingsley:* Edith Meiser, *Lillian:* Joan Copeland, *Jack:* Martin Balsam, *Paul Kingsley:* David Ford, *Elizabeth Kingsley:* Audrey Peters, *The Widow, Rosalind Neiman:* Betty Walker, *Walter Lockman:* Albert Dekker, *Gould:* Rudy Bond, *Sherman:* Lou Gilbert, *Lucy Lockman:* Dora Weissman, *Joey Lockman:* Lee Richardson, *Caroline:* Anna Berger, *Ellman:* Alfred Leberfeld, *Erskine:* Nelson Olmsted.

MIDNIGHT COWBOY (1969) UA. Produced by Jerome Hellman. Directed by John Schlesinger. DeLuxe Color. Based on the novel by James Leo Herlihy. Screenplay, Waldo Salt. Photography, Adam Holender. 2nd Unit Director, Burtt Harris. Production Designer, John Robert Lloyd. Set Decorations, Phil Smith. Editor, Hugh A. Robertson. Creative Consultant, Jim Clark. Musical Supervision, John Barry. Musical Production, Toxey French. Special Lighting Effects, Joshua Light Show. Titles and Graphic Effects, Pablo Ferro. Sound, Jack Fitzstephens, Vincent Connolly, Richard Vorisek and Abe Seidman. Costumes, Ann Roth. Make-up, Dick Smith and Irving Buchman. Hairstyles, Bob Grimaldi. Assistant Director, Michael Childers. "Everybody's Talkin'" by Fred Neil, sung by Nilsson. Harmonica Accompaniment, Toots Thielemans. Electronic Music by Sear Electronic Music Production. Filmed in New York, Florida and Texas. Rated X. 113 minutes

Ratso Rizzo: Dustin Hoffman, *Joe Buck:* Jon Voight, *Cass:* Sylvia Miles,

Mr. O'Daniel: John McGiver, *Shirley:* Brenda Vaccaro, *Towny:* Barnard Hughes, *Sally Buck:* Ruth White, *Annie:* Jennifer Salt, *Woodsay Niles:* Gil Rankin, *Little Joe:* Gary Owens, T. Tom Marlow, *Ralph:* George Eppersen, *Cafeteria Manager:* Al Scott, *Mother on Bus:* Linda Davis, *Old Cowhand:* J. T. Masters, *Old Lady:* Arlene Reader, *Rich Lady:* Georgann Johnson, *Jackie:* Jonathan Kramer, *TV Bishop:* Anthony Holland, *Young Student:* Bob Balaban, *Freaked-out Lady:* Jan Tice, *Bartender:* Paul Benjamin, *Vegetable Grocers:* Peter Scalia, Vito Siracusa, *Hat Shop Owner:* Peter Zamagias, *Hotel Clerk:* Arthur Anderson, *Laundromat Ladies:* Tina Scala, Alma Felix, *Escort Service Man:* Richard Clarke, *Frantic Lady:* Ann Thomas, *Waitress:* Joan Murphy, *Bus Driver:* Al Stetson, *Gretel McAlbertson:* Viva, *Hansel McAlbertson:* Gastone Rossilli, *Party Guests:* Ultra Violet, Paul Jahara, International Velvet, William Door, Cecelia Lipson, Taylor Mead, Paul Morrissey, Paul Jasmin.

Midnight Cowboy with Dustin Hoffman.

Midnight Express with Irene Miracle and Brad Davis.

MIDNIGHT EXPRESS (1978) Col. A Casablanca FilmWorks Production. Produced by Alan Marshall and David Puttnam. Directed by Alan Parker. Based on the book "Midnight Express" by Billy Hayes and William Hoffer. Screenplay, Oliver Stone. Executive Producer, Peter Guber. Music, Giorgio Moroder. Song, "Istanbul Blues" by David Castle.

Production Designer, Geoffrey Kirkland. Editor, Gerry Hambling. Costume Designer, Milena Canonero. Make-Up, Mary Hillman and Penny Steyne. Hairdressing, Sarah Monzani and Pat Hay. Art Director, Evan Hercules. Wardrobe, Bobby Lavender. Sound Mixer, Clive Winter. 1st Assistant Director, Ray Corbett. 2nd Assistant Director, David Wimbury. 3rd Assistant Director, Kieron Phipps. Assistant Editors, Eddy Joseph, Tony Orton and Richard Taylor. Fight Arranger, Roy Scammell. Film debuts of Brad Davis and Irene Miracle. Color. Processing by Rank Film Laboratories. Filmed in Malta, including Fort St. Elmo, and in Greece. Rated R. 123 minutes

Billy Hayes: Brad Davis, *Jimmy Booth:* Randy Quaid, *Max:* John Hurt, *Hamidou:* Paul Smith, *Mr. Hayes:* Mike Kellin, *Erich:* Norbert Weisser, *Susan:* Irene Miracle, *Tex:* Bo Hopkins, *Rifki:* Paolo Bonacelli, *Yesil:* Franco Diogene, *Stanley Daniels:* Michael Ensign, *Chief Judge:* Gigi Ballista, *Prosecutor:* Kevork Malikyan, *Ahmet:* Peter Jeffrey.

A MIDSUMMER NIGHT'S DREAM (1935) WB. Produced by Max Reinhardt. Directed by Max Reinhardt and William Dieterle. From William Shakespeare's play, with Felix Mendelssohn's *A Midsummer Night's Dream* music. Screenplay, Charles Kenyon and Mary McCall, Jr. Musical Arrangement, Erich Wolfgang Korngold. Dance Ensembles, Bronislawa Nijinska. Photography, Hal Mohr, Fred Jackman, Byron Haskin, H. F. Koenekamp. Editor, Ralph Dawson. Film debut of Olivia de Havilland. 132 minutes

Bottom: James Cagney, *Lysander:* Dick Powell, *Flute:* Joe E. Brown, *Helena:* Jean Muir, *Snout:* Hugh Herbert, *Theseus:* Ian Hunter, *Quince:* Frank McHugh, *Oberon:* Victor Jory, *Hermia:* Olivia de Havilland, *Demetrius:* Ross Alexander, *Egeus:* Grant Mitchell, *First Fairy:* Nini Theilade, *Hippolyta, Queen of Amazons:* Verree Teasdale, *Titania:* Anita Louise, *Puck:* Mickey Rooney, *Snug:* Dewey Robinson, *Philostrate:* Hobart Cavanaugh, *Starveling:* Otis Harlan, *Ninny's Tomb:* Arthur Treacher, *Mustardseed:* Billy Barty.

A Midsummer Night's Dream with Hugh Herbert, Frank McHugh, Arthur Treacher, Otis Harlan, Dewey Robinson, James Cagney and Joe E. Brown.

MILDRED PIERCE (1945) WB. Producer, Jerry Wald. Director, Michael Curtiz. From a novel by James M. Cain. Screenplay, Ranald MacDougall, Catherine Turney. Musical Score, Max Steiner. Art Director, Anton Grot. Cameraman, Ernest Haller. Special Effects, Willard Van Enger. Editor, David Weisbart. 113 minutes

Mildred Pierce: Joan Crawford, *Wally Fay:* Jack Carson, *Monte Beragon:* Zachary Scott, *Ida:* Eve Arden, *Veda Pierce:* Ann Blyth, *Bert Pierce:* Bruce Bennett, *Mr. Chris:* George Tobias, *Maggie Binderhof:* Lee Patrick, *Inspector Peterson:* Moroni Olsen, *Kay Pierce:* Jo Ann Marlowe, *Mrs. Forrester:* Barbara Brown, *Mr. Williams:*

Charles Trowbridge, *Ted Forrester:* John Compton, *Lottie:* Butterfly McQueen, *Policeman on Pier:* Garry Owen, *Policemen:* Clancy Cooper, Tom Dillon, *Two Detectives:* James Flavin, Jack O'Connor, *Policeman:* Charles Jordan, *High School Boy:* Robert Arthur, *Waitresses:* Joyce Compton, Lynne Baggett, *Party Guest:* Ramsay Ames, *Police Matron:* Leah Baird, *Singing Teacher:* John Christian, *Piano Teacher:* Joan Winfield, *Houseboy:* Jimmy Lono, *Nurse:* Mary Servoss, *Doctor Gale:* Manart Kippen, *Pancho:* David Cota, *Mr. Jones:* Chester Clute, *Wally's Lawyer:* Wallis Clark.

Mildred Pierce with Garry Owen and Joan Crawford.

Million Dollar Mermaid with Victor Mature, Esther Williams and Jesse White.

MILLION DOLLAR MERMAID (1952) MGM. Producer, Arthur Hornblow, Jr. Director, Mervyn LeRoy. Technicolor, partly in Wide Screen. Screenplay, Everett Freeman. Sound, Douglas Shearer. Musical Director, Adolph Deutsch. Orchestrations, Alexander Courage. Production numbers staged by Busby Berkeley. Art Director, Cedric Gibbons. Sets, Edwin B. Willis, Richard Pefferee. Cinematographer, George J. Folsey. Editor, John McSweeney, Jr. 115 minutes

Annette Kellerman: Esther Williams, *James Sullivan:* Victor Mature, *Frederick Kellerman:* Walter Pidgeon, *Alfred Harper:* David Brian, *Annette, 10 years:* Donna Corcoran, *Doc Cronnol:* Jesse White, *Pavlova Maria Tallchief, Aldrich:* Howard Freeman, *Policeman:* Charles Watts, *Garvey:* Wilton Graff, *Prosecutor:* Frank Ferguson, *Judge:* James Bell, *Conductor:* James Flavin, *Director:* Willis Bouchey, *Marie, Housekeeper:* Adrienne d'Ambricourt, *Judge:* Clive Morgan, *Mrs Graves:* Queenie Leonard, *Son:* Stuart Torres, *Pawnbroker:* James Aubrey, *Master of Ceremonies:* Patrick O'Moore, *Soprano:* Elizabeth

Slifer, *Casey:* Gordon Richards, *London Bobby:* Al Ferguson, *Bum:* Benny Burt, *Marcellino, the Clown:* Rod Rogers, *Bud Williams:* George Wallace, *Watchman:* Harry Hines, *Newsboy:* Clarence Hennecke, *Maid:* Genevive Pasques, *Policeman:* Pat Flaherty, *Second Policeman:* James L. "Tiny" Kelly, *Process Server:* Thomas Dillon, *Band Leader:* Paul Frees, *Nurse:* Louise Lorimer, *Robbie, Prop Man:* Mack Chandler, *Bit:* Rosemarie Bowe.

Min and Bill with Wallace Beery and Marie Dressler.

MIN AND BILL (1930) MGM. Directed by George Hill. From the book *Dark Star* by Lorna Moon. Scenario and Dialogue, Frances Marion and Marion Jackson. Photography, Harold Wenstrom. Editor, Basil Wrangell. Sound, Douglas Shearer. Art Director, Cedric Gibbons. Film debut of Don Dillaway. 69 minutes

Min Divot: Marie Dressler, *Bill:* Wallace Beery, *Nancy Smith:* Dorothy Jordan, *Bella Pringle:* Marjorie Rambeau, *Dick Cameron:* Donald Dillaway, *Groot:* DeWitt Jennings, *Alec Johnson:* Russell Hopton, *Mr. Southard:* Frank McGlynn, *Mrs. Southard:* Gretta Gould, *Woman:* Miss Vanessi, *Merchant Seaman:* Jack Pennick, *Bella's Stateroom Lover:* Henry Roquemore, *Sailor:* Hank Bell.

The Miracle of Morgan's Creek with Betty Hutton, William Demarest and Diana Lynn.

THE MIRACLE OF MORGAN'S CREEK (1944) Par. Directed by Preston Sturges. Screenplay, Preston Sturges. Music, Leo Shuken and Charles Bradshaw. Art Directors, Hans Dreier and Ernest Fegte. Photography, John Seitz. Editor, Stuart Gilmore. Remade as *Rock-A-Bye Baby* (Paramount, 1958). 99 minutes

Norval Jones: Eddie Bracken, *Trudy Kockenlocker:* Betty Hutton,

Emmy Kockenlocker: Diana Lynn, *McGinty:* Brian Donlevy, *The Boss:* Akim Tamiroff, *Justice of the Peace:* Porter Hall, *Mr. Tuerck:* Emory Parnell, *Mr. Johnson:* Alan Bridge, *Mr. Rafferty:* Julius Tannen, *Newspaper Editor:* Victor Potel, *Justice's Wife:* Almira Sessions, *Sally:* Esther Howard, *Sheriff:* J. Farrell MacDonald, *Cecilia:* Connie Tompkins, *Mrs. Johnson:* Georgia Caine, *Doctor:* Torben Meyer, *U. S. Marshal:* George Melford, *The Mayor:* Jimmy Conlin, *Mr. Schwartz:* Harry Rosenthal, *Pete:* Chester Conklin, *First M. P.:* Frank Moran, *Second M. P.:* Budd Fine, *McGinty's Secretary:* Byron Foulger, *McGinty's Secretary:* Arthur Hoyt, *Head Nurse:* Nora Cecil, *Man Opening Champagne:* Jack Norton, *Mussolini:* Joe Devlin, *Hitler:* Bobby Watson, *Officer Kockenlocker:* William Demarest.

Miracle on 34th Street with Natalie Wood and Edmund Gwenn.

MIRACLE ON 34th STREET (1947) 20th. Producer, William Perlberg. Director, George Seaton. Story, Valentine Davies. Screenplay, George Seaton. Art Directors, Richard Day, Richard Irvine. Musical Director, Alfred Newman. Music, Cyril Mockridge. Cameramen, Charles Clarke, Lloyd Ahern. Editor, Robert Simpson. Filmed in New York City. Film debut of Thelma Ritter. 96 minutes. **Later a 1973 TV movie**

Doris Walker: Maureen O'Hara, *Fred Gailey:* John Payne, *Kris Kringle:* Edmund Gwenn, *Judge Henry X. Harper:* Gene Lockhart, *Susan Walker:* Natalie Wood, *Mr. Sawyer:* Porter Hall, *Charles Halloran:* William Frawley, *D. A. Thomas Mara:* Jerome Cowan, *Mr. Shellhammer:* Philip Tonge, *Doctor Pierce:* James Seay, *Mr. Macy:* Harry Antrim, *Peter's Mother:* Thelma Ritter, *Girl's Mother:* Mary Field, *Cleo:* Theresa Harris, *Alfred:* Alvin Greenman, *Mrs. Mara:* Anne Staunton, *Thomas Mara, Jr.:* Robert Hyatt, *Reporters:* Richard Irving, Jeff Corey, *Sawyer's Secretary:* Anne O'Neal, *Mrs. Shellhammer:* Lela Bliss, *Peter:* Anthony Sydes, *Dr. Rogers:* William Forrest, *Mara's Assistant:* Alvin Hammer, *Bailiff:* Joseph McInerney, *Drum Majorette:* Ida McGuire, *Santa Claus:* Percy Helton, *Mrs. Harper:* Jane Green, *Dutch Girl:* Marlene Lyden, *Post Office Employees:* Guy Thomajan, Jack Albertson, *Mr. Gimbel:* Herbert H. Heyes, *Guard:* Stephen Roberts, *Salesman (Macy's):* Robert Lynn, *Window Dresser:* Robert Gist, *Terry:* Teddy Driver, *Alice:* Patty Smith, *Interne:* Robert Karnes, *Mail-bearing Court Officer:* Snub Pollard.

THE MIRACLE WORKER (1962) UA. Producer, Fred Coe. Director, Arthur Penn. Screenplay, William Gibson. Music, Laurence Rosenthal. Costumes, Ruth Morley. A Playfilms' Production. Based on Helen Keller's *The Story of My Life.* William Gibson's "The Miracle Worker" was originally an unproduced ballet in 1953, then a Playhouse 90 TV presentation in 1957, and a play in 1959, in which Anne Bancroft and Patty Duke originated their roles. Exteriors filmed in New Jersey, interiors in New York City. 106 minutes

Annie Sullivan: Anne Bancroft, *Helen Keller:* Patty Duke, *Captain Keller:* Victor Jory, *Kate Keller:* Inga Swenson, *James Keller:* Andrew Prine, *Aunt Ev:* Kathleen Comegys, *Viney:* Beah Richards, *Mr. Anagnos:* Jack Hollander, *Percy (10 years):* Michael Darden, *Helen at 7:* Peggy Burke, *Martha at 10:* Dale Ellen Bethea, *Percy at 8:* Walter Wright, Jr., *Martha at 7:* Donna Bryan, *Helen at 5:* Mindy Sherwood, *Martha at 5:* Diane Bryan, *Percy at 6:* Keith Moore, *Young Annie:* Michele Farr, *Young Jimmie:* Allan Howard, *Crones:* Judith Lowry, William F. Haddock, Helen Ludlum.

The Miracle Worker with Patty Duke and Anne Bancroft.

THE MISFITS (1961) UA. Producer, Frank E. Taylor. Director, John Huston. Screenplay, Arthur Miller. Music, Alex North. Assistant Director, Carl Beringer. A Seven Arts Production. Art Directors, Stephen Grimes, William Newberry. Music composed and conducted by Alex North. Cinematographer, Russell Metty. Editor, George Tomasini. 124 minutes

Gay Langland: Clark Gable, *Roslyn Taber:* Marilyn Monroe, *Perce Howland:* Montgomery Clift, *Isabelle Steers:* Thelma Ritter, *Guido:* Eli Wallach, *Old Man in Bar:* James Barton, *Church Lady:* Estelle Winwood, *Raymond Taber:* Kevin McCarthy, *Young Boy in Bar:* Dennis Shaw, *Charles Steers:* Philip Mitchell, *Old Groom:* Walter Ramage, *Young Bride:* Peggy Barton, *Fresh Cowboy in Bar:* J. Lewis Smith, *Susan:* Marietta Tree, *Bartender:* Bobby La Salle, *Man in Bar:* Ryall Bowker, *Ambulance Driver:* Ralph Roberts.

The Misfits with Eli Wallach, Thelma Ritter, Clark Gable and Marilyn Monroe.

Mister Roberts with William Powell, Jack Lemmon and Henry Fonda.

MISTER ROBERTS (1955) WB. Producer, Leland Hayward. Directors, John Ford, Mervyn LeRoy. Screenplay by Frank Nugent and Joshua Logan. Based on the play by Thomas Heggen and Joshua Logan, from the novel by Thomas Heggen. Music by Franz Waxman. Assistant Director, Wingate Smith. An Orange Production in Cinema-Scope and WarnerColor, Stereophonic Sound. Filmed in Hawaii. 123 minutes. Sequel was *Ensign Pulver* (1964) with Robert Walker, Jr.

Lieutenant (jg) Doug Roberts: Henry Fonda, *The Captain:* James Cagney, *Doc:* William Powell, *Ensign Pulver:* Jack Lemmon, *Lieutenant Ann Girard:* Betsy Palmer, *C.P.O. Dowdy:* Ward Bond, *Mannion:* Phil Carey, *Shore Patrol Officer:* Martin Milner, *Shore Patrolman:* Gregory Walcott, *Military Policeman:* James Flavin, *Marine Sergeant:* Jack Pennick, *Native Chief:* Duke Kahanamoko, *Reber:* Nick Adams, *Dolan:* Ken Curtis, *Stefanowski:* Harry Carey, Jr., *Gerhart:* Frank Aletter, *Lindstrom:* Fritz Ford, *Mason:* Buck Kartalian, *Lieutenant Billings:* William Henry, *Olson:* William Hudson, *Schlemmer:* Stubby Kruger, *Cookie:* Harry Tenbrook, *Rodrigues:* Perry Lopez, *Insigna:* Robert Roark, *Bookser:* Pat Wayne, *Wiley:* Tiger Andrews, *Kennedy:* Jim Moloney, *Gilbert:* Denny Niles, *Cochran:* Francis Connor, *Johnson:* Shug Fisher, *Jonesy:* Danny Borzage, *Taylor:* Jim Murphy, *Nurses:* Kathleen O'Malley, Jeanne Murray, Maura Murphy, Lonnie Pierce, Mimi Doyle.

Moby Dick with Gregory Peck.

MOBY DICK (1956) WB. Producer, John Huston. Associate Producer, Lehman Katz. Director, John Huston. Technicolor. Based on the novel by Herman Melville. Screenplay, Ray Bradbury, John Huston. Art Director, Ralph Brinton. Music composed by Philip Stainton. Musical Director, Louis Levy. Cinematographer, Oswald Morris. Editor, Russell Lloyd. A Moulin Picture. Filmed in Youghal, Ireland, in Wales, and off the coasts of Madeira and the Canary Islands. The vessel *Pequod* was actually a ship called the *Hispanola*. Narrated by Richard Basehart. Remake of *The Sea Beast* (1926), *Moby Dick* (1930). 116 minutes

Captain Ahab: Gregory Peck, *Ishmael:* Richard Basehart, *Starbuck:* Leo Genn, *Father Mapple:* Orson Welles, *Captain Boomer:* James Robertson Justice, *Stubb:* Harry Andrews, *Manxman:* Bernard Miles, *Carpenter:* Noel Purcell, *Daggoo:* Edric Connor, *Peleg:* Mervyn Johns, *Peter Coffin:* Joseph Tomelty, *Captain Gardiner:* Francis De Wolff, *Bildad:* Philip Stainton, *Elijah:* Royal Dano, *Flask:* Seamus Kelly, *Queequeg:* Friedrich Ledebur, *Blacksmith:* Ted Howard, *Pip:* Tamba Alleney, *Tashtego:* Tom Clegg, *Lady with Bibles:* Iris Tree, *Blacksmith:* Ted Howard.

Mogambo with Ava Gardner, Grace Kelly and Clark Gable.

MOGAMBO (1953) MGM. Produced by Sam Zimbalist. Directed by John Ford. Based on a play by Wilson Collison. Color by Technicolor. Screenplay, John Lee Mahin. Art Director, Alfred Junge. Cinematographers, Robert Surtees, F. A. Young. Editor, Frank Clarke. Filmed in Africa. Remake of MGM's *Red Dust*, 1932; and *Congo Maisie*, 1940. 115 minutes

Victor Marswell: Clark Gable, *Eloise Kelly:* Ava Gardner, *Linda Nordley:* Grace Kelly, *Donald Nordley:* Donald Sinden, *John Brown-Pryce:* Philip Stainton, *Leon Boltchak:* Eric Pohlmann, *Skipper:* Laurence Naismith, *Father Josef:* Denis O'Dea.

THE MONKEY'S UNCLE (1965) BV. Producer, Walt Disney. Co-producer, Ron Miller. Director, Robert Stevenson. Technicolor. Screenplay, Tom and Helen August. Music, Buddy Baker. Title Song, Richard M. Sherman, Robert B. Sherman. Sung by The Beach Boys. Director of Photography, Edward Colman. Assistant Director, Joseph L. McEveety. Costumes, Chuck Keehne, Gertrude Casey. 87 minutes. Sequel to *The Misadventures of Merlin Jones* (1964)

Merlin Jones: Tommy Kirk, *Jennifer:* Annette Funicello, *Judge Holmsby:* Leon Ames, *Mr. Dearborne:* Frank Faylen, *Darius Green III:* Arthur O'Connell, *Leon:* Leon Tyler, *Norman:* Norman Grabowski, *Prof. Shattuck:* Alan Hewitt, *Housekeeper:* Connie Gilchrist, *Lisa:* Cheryl Miller, *College President:* Gage Clarke, *Haywood:* Mark Goddard, *Board of Regents:* Harry Holcombe, Alexander Lockwood, Harry Antrim.

The Monkey's Uncle with Annette Funicello and Tommy Kirk.

THE MOON IS BLUE (1953) UA. Produced and directed by Otto Preminger. Screenplay by F. Hugh Herbert, from his play. Song by Herschel Burke Gilbert and Sylvia Fine: "The Moon Is Blue." Cinematographer, Ernest Laszlo. Editor, Otto Ludwig. Film debut of Maggie McNamara. 99 minutes

Donald Gresham: William Holden, *David Slater:* David Niven, *Patty O'Neill:* Maggie McNamara, *Michael O'Neill:* Tom Tully, *Cynthia Slater:* Dawn Addams, *Television Announcer:* Fortunio Bonanova.

The Moon Is Blue with William Holden and Maggie McNamara.

THE MORE THE MERRIER (1943) Col. Produced and directed by George Stevens. Associate Producer, Fred Guiol. Story, Robert Russell and Frank Ross. Screenplay, Robert Russell, Frank Ross, Richard Flournoy, Lewis R. Foster. Art Directors, Lionel Banks and Rudolph Sternad. Music, Leigh Harline. Music Director, Morris W. Stoloff. Photography, Ted Tetzlaff. Editor, Otto Meyer. Song, "Damn the Torpedos (Full Speed Ahead)" by Henry Meyers, Edward Eliscu and Jay Gorney. Remade by Columbia as *Walk, Don't Run* (1966). 104 minutes

Connie Milligan: Jean Arthur, *Joe Carter:* Joel McCrea, *Benjamin Dingle:* Charles Coburn, *Charles J. Pendergast:* Richard Gaines, *Evans:* Bruce Bennett, *Pike:* Frank Sully, *Senator Noonan:* Clyde Fillmore, *Morton Rodakiewicz:* Stanley Clements, *Harding:* Don Douglas, *Miss Dalton:* Ann Savage, *Waiter:* Grady Sutton, *Dancer:* Sugar Geise, *Drunk:* Don Barclay, *Drunk:* Frank Sully, *Girl:* Shirley Patterson, *Miss Bilby:* Ann Doran, *Waitress:* Mary Treen, *Barmaid:* Gladys Blake, *Miss Allen:* Kay Linaker, *Miss Chasen:* Nancy Gay,

Air Corps Captain: Byron Shores, *Miss Finch:* Betzi Beaton, *Texan:* Harrison Greene, *Southerner:* Robert McKenzie, *Cattleman:* Vic Potel, *Character:* Lon Poff, *Senator:* Frank La Rue, *Senator:* Douglas Wood, *Minister:* Harry Bradley, *Miss Geeskin:* Betty McMahan, *Dumpy Woman:* Helen Holmes, *Fat Statistician:* Marshall Ruth, *Second Statistician:* Hal Gerard, *Reporter:* Henry Roquemore, *Taxi Driver:* Jack Carr, *Hotel Clerk:* Chester Clute, *Head Waiter:* Robert F. Hill, *Police Captain:* Eddy Chandler, *Dancer:* Peggy Carroll, *Caretaker:* George Reed, *Taxi Driver:* Kitty McHugh.

The More the Merrier with Jean Arthur, Joel McCrea and Charles Coburn.

MORNING GLORY (1933) RKO. Produced by Pandro S. Berman. Directed by Lowell Sherman. Story, Zoe Akins. Adaptation, Howard J. Green. Photography, Bert Glennon. Editor, George Nicholls, Jr. Sound, Hugh McDowell. Remade as *Stage Struck* (Buena Vista, 1958). 74 minutes

Eva Lovelace (Ada Love): Katharine Hepburn, *Joseph Sheridan:* Douglas Fairbanks, Jr., *Louis Easton:* Adolphe Menjou, *Rita Vernon:* Mary Duncan, *Robert Harley Hedges:* C. Aubrey Smith, *Pepe Velez:* Don Alvarado, *Will Seymour:* Frederic Santley, *Henry Lawrence:* Richard Carle, *Charles Van Dusen:* Tyler Brooke, *Gwendolyn Hall:* Geneva Mitchell.

Morning Glory with Katharine Hepburn, Douglas Fairbanks, Jr., Frederic Santley and Adolphe Menjou.

MOROCCO (1930) Par. Directed by Josef von Sternberg. From the play *Amy Jolly* by Benno Vigny. Scenario and Dialogue, Jules Furthman. Photography, Lee Garmes. Editor, Sam Winston. 90 minutes

Tom Brown: Gary Cooper, *Amy Jolly:* Marlene Dietrich, *Labessier:* Adolphe Menjou, *Adjutant Caesar:* Ulrich Haupt, *Anna Dolores:*

Juliette Compton, *Sergeant Barney Latoche:* Francis McDonald, *Colonel Quinnovieres:* Albert Conti, *Madame Caesar:* Eve Southern, *Barrative:* Michael Visaroff, *Lo Tinto:* Paul Porcasi, *Camp Follower:* Theresa Harris.

Morocco with Gary Cooper, Marlene Dietrich and Adolphe Menjou.

The Mortal Storm with Margaret Sullavan, William Edmunds and Irene Rich.

THE MORTAL STORM (1940) MGM. Produced by Sidney Franklin. Directed by Frank Borzage. Based on the novel by Phyllis Bottome. Screenplay, Claudine West, Andersen Ellis and George Froeschel. Art Director, Cedric Gibbons. Associate, Wade Rubottom. Music, Edward Kane. Assistant Director, Lew Borzage. Photography, William Daniels. Sound, Douglas Shearer. Editor, Elmo Veron. Gowns, Adrian. Men's Wardrobe, Gile Steele. Make-up, Jack Dawn. Hair Styles, Sydney Guilaroff. 100 minutes

Freya Roth: Margaret Sullavan, *Martin Brietner:* James Stewart, *Fritz Marberg:* Robert Young, *Professor Roth:* Frank Morgan, *Otto Von Rohn:* Robert Stack, *Elsa:* Bonita Granville, *Mrs. Roth:* Irene Rich, *Erich Von Rohn:* William T. Orr, *Mrs. Brietner:* Maria Ouspenskaya, *Rudi:* Gene Reynolds, *Rector:* Russell Hicks, *Lehman:* William Edmunds, *Marta:* Esther Dale, *Holl:* Dan Dailey, Jr., *Berg:* Granville Bates, *Professor Werner:* Thomas Ross, *Franz:* Ward Bond, *Theresa:* Sue Moore, *Second Colleague:* Harry Depp, *Third Colleague:* Julius Tannen, *Fourth Colleague:* Gus Glassmire, *Guard:* Dick Rich, *Guard:* Ted Oliver, *Man:* Howard Lang, *Woman:* Bodil Rosing, *Passport Officials:* Lucien Prival, Dick Elliott, *Gestapo Official:* Henry Victor, *Waiter:* William Irving, *Fat Man in Cafe:* Bert Roach, *Gestapo Guard:* Bob Stevenson, *Old Man:* Max Davidson, *Gestapo Official:* John Stark, *Oppenheim:* Fritz Leiber, *Hartman:* Robert O. Davis (Rudolph Anders).

Mother Wore Tights with Betty Grable and Dan Dailey.

MOTHER WORE TIGHTS (1947) 20th. Produced by Lamar Trotti. Directed by Walter Lang. Color by Technicolor. Based on the book by Miriam Young. Screenplay, Lamar Trotti. Art Directors, Richard Day and Joseph C. Wright. Dances staged by Seymour Felix and Kenny Williams. Music Direction, Alfred Newman. Vocal Arrangements, Charles Henderson. Orchestral Arrangements, Gene Rose. Photography, Harry Jackson. Technicolor Director, Natalie Kalmus. Associate, Leonard Doss. Sets, Thomas Little. Editor, J. Watson Webb Jr. Songs: "Tra-La-La-La" by Mack Gordon and Harry Warren; "Kokomo, Indiana," "You Do," "There's Nothing Like a Song," "This Is My Favorite City," "Fare-Thee-Well Dear Alma Mater," "On a Little Two-Seat Tandem," and "Rolling Down to Bowling Green" by Mack Gordon and Josef Myrow. Filmed partly in San Francisco. 107 minutes

Myrtle McKinley Burt: Betty Grable, *Frank Burt:* Dan Dailey, *Iris Burt:* Mona Freeman, *Mikie Burt:* Connie Marshall, *Bessie:* Vanessa Brown, *Bob Clarkman:* Robert Arthur, *Grandmother McKinley:* Sara Allgood, *Mr. Schneider:* William Frawley, *Miss Ridgeway:* Ruth Nelson, *Alice Flemmerhammer:* Anabel Shaw, *Roy Bivins:* Michael (Stephen) Dunne, *Grandfather McKinley:* George Cleveland, *Rosemary Olcott:* Veda Ann Borg, *Papa:* Sig Rumann, *Lil:* Lee Patrick, *Specialty:* Señor Wences with Johnny, *Mrs. Muggins:* Maude Eburne, *Papa Capucci:* Antonio Filauri, *Stage Doorman:* Frank Orth, *Mama:* Lotte Stein, *Mr. Clarkman:* William Forrest, *Mrs. Clarkman:* Kathleen Lockhart, *Ed:* Chick Chandler, *Dance Director:* Kenny Williams, *Withers:* Will Wright, *Opera Singer:* Eula Morgan, *Man:* Tom Moore, *Man:* Harry Seymour, *Boy:* Lee MacGregor, *Myrtle's Dancing Partner:* Stephen Kirchner, *Clarence:* Alvin Hammer, *Minister:* Harry Cheshire, *Sailor:* Brad Slaven, *Sailor:* Ted Jordan, *Waiter:* George Davis, *Mikie at 3:* Ann Gowland, *Iris at 6:* Karolyn Grimes, *Narrator:* Anne Baxter.

MOULIN ROUGE (1952) UA. Produced and directed by John Huston. Associate Producer, Jack Clayton. A Romulus Films Production. Color by Technicolor. From the novel by Pierre LaMure. Screenplay, Anthony Veiller and John Huston. Music composed by Georges Auric. Production Manager, Leigh Aman. Art Director, Paul Sheriff. Photography, Ossie Morris. Editor, Ralph Kemplin. Costumes, Marcel Vértés. Filmed in France and England. 123 minutes

Toulouse-Lautrec and The Comte de Toulouse-Lautrec: José Ferrer, *Marie Charlet:* Colette Marchand, *Myriamme:* Suzanne Flon, *Jane Avril:* Zsa Zsa Gabor, *La Goulue:* Katherine Kath, *Countess de Toulouse-Lautrec:* Claude Nollier, *Aicha:* Muriel Smith, *Patou:* Georges Lannes, *Aicha's Partner:* Tutte Lemkow, *Chocolat:* Rupert

John, *Bar Proprietor:* Eric Pohlmann, *Valentin Dessosse:* Walter Crisham, *Madame Loubet:* Mary Clare, *Maurice Joyant:* Lee Montague, *Denise:* Maureen Swanson, *Pere Cotelle:* Jim Gerald, *Zidler:* Harold Gasket, *Sarah:* Jill Bennett, *Racing Fan:* Peter Cushing.

Moulin Rouge with Suzanne Flon and José Ferrer.

MR. BLANDINGS BUILDS HIS DREAM HOUSE (1948) RKO.
Selznick Releasing Organization. Producers, Norman Panama, Melvin Frank. Director, H. C. Potter. Based on the novel by Eric Hodgins. Screenplay, Norman Panama, Melvin Frank. Art Directors, Albert D'Agostino, Carroll Clark. Music, C. Bakaleinikoff. Photography, James Wong Howe. Editor, Harry Marker. 94 minutes

Jim Blandings: Cary Grant, *Muriel Blandings:* Myrna Loy, *Bill Cole:* Melvyn Douglas, *Henry Simms:* Reginald Denny, *Joan Blandings:* Sharyn Moffett, *Betsy Blandings:* Connie Marshall, *Gussie:* Louise Beavers, *Smith:* Ian Wolfe, *W. D. Tesander:* Harry Shannon, *Mr. Zucca:* Tito Vuolo, *Joe Appollonio:* Nestor Paiva, *John Retch:* Jason Robards, *Mary:* Lurene Tuttle, *Carpenter Foreman:* Lex Barker, *Mr. Pe Delford:* Emory Parnell, *Bunny Funkhauser:* Dan Tobin, *Eph Hackett:* Will Wright, *Judge Quarles:* Frank Darien, *Murphy:* Stanley Andrews, *Jones:* Cliff Clark, *Simpson:* Franklin Parker, *Wrecker:* Charles Middleton, *Workman:* Robert Bray, *Workman:* Frederick Ledebur, *Charlie:* Don Brodie, *Mr. Selby:* Hal K. Dawson, *Cop:* Kernan Cripps, *Customer:* Bud Wiser.

Mr. Blandings Builds His Dream House with Cary Grant, Myrna Loy, Sharyn Moffett and Connie Marshall.

MR. DEEDS GOES TO TOWN (1936) Col. Produced and directed by
Frank Capra. Author, Clarence Budington Kelland (from the story "Opera Hat"). Cinematographer, Robert Riskin. Recording Engineer, Edward Bernds. Film Editor, Gene Havlick. Art Director, Stephen Goosson. Costumer, Samuel Lange. Musical Director, Howard Jackson. Assistant Director, C. C. Coleman. 115 minutes

Longfellow Deeds: Gary Cooper, *Babe Bennett:* Jean Arthur, *MacWade:* George Bancroft, *Cornelius Cobb:* Lionel Stander, *John Cedar:* Douglass Dumbrille, *Walter:* Raymond Walburn, *Madame Pomponi:* Margaret Matzenauer, *Judge Walker:* H. B. Warner, *Bodyguard:* Warren Hymer, *Theresa:* Muriel Evans, *Mabel Dawson:* Ruth Donnelly, *Mal:* Spencer Charters, *Mrs. Meredith:* Emma Dunn, *Psychiatrist:* Wryley Birch, *Budington:* Arthur Hoyt, *James Cedar:* Stanley Andrews, *Arthur Cedar:* Pierre Watkin, *Farmer:* John Wray, *Swenson:* Christian Rub, *Mr. Semple:* Jameson Thomas, *Mrs. Semple:* Mayo Methot, *Doctor Malcolm:* Russell Hicks, *Dr. Frazier:* Gustav Von Seyffertitz, *Dr. Fosdick:* Edward Le Saint, *Hallor:* Charles (Levison) Lane, *Frank:* Irving Bacon, *Bob:* George Cooper, *Waiter:* Gene Morgan, *Morrow:* Walter Catlett, *The Butler:* Barnett Parker, *Jane Faulkner:* Margaret Seddon, *Amy Faulkner:* Margaret McWade, *Anderson:* Harry C. Bradley, *Second Bodyguard:* Edward Gargan, *Douglas:* Edwin Maxwell, *First Deputy:* Paul Hurst, *Italian:* Paul Porcasi, *Tailor:* Franklin Pangborn, *Farmers' Spokesman:* George F. Hayes, *Cabby:* Billy Bevan, *Reporter:* Dennis O'Keefe, *Brookfield:* George Meeker, *Lawyer:* Dale Van Sickel.

Mr. Deeds Goes to Town with Walter Catlett, Gary Cooper and Jean Arthur.

Mr. Lucky with Cary Grant.

MR. LUCKY (1943) RKO. Produced by David Hempstead. Directed
by H. C. Potter. Based on the story *Bundles for Freedom* by Milton Holmes. Screenplay, Milton Holmes and Adrian Scott. Music, Roy Webb, Music Director, C. Bakaleinikoff. Art Directors, Albert S.

D'Agostino and Mark-Lee Kirk. Photography, George Barnes. Special Effects, Vernon L. Walker. Editor, Theron Warth. 98 minutes. Remade by RKO as *Gambling House* (1950). Later a TV series

Joe Adams: Cary Grant, *Dorothy Bryant:* Laraine Day, *Swede:* Charles Bickford, *Captain Steadman:* Gladys Cooper, *Crunk:* Alan Carney, *Mr. Bryant:* Henry Stephenson, *Zepp:* Paul Stewart, *Mrs. Ostrander:* Kay Johnson, *Gaffer:* Erford Gage, *Commissioner Hargraves:* Walter Kingsford, *McDougal:* J. M. Kerrigan, *Foster:* Edward Fielding, *Greek Priest:* Vladimir Sokoloff, *Siga:* John Bleifer, *Joe Bascopolus:* Juan Varro, *Dealer (Gaffer):* Don Brodie, *Workman at Slot Machine:* Frank Mills, *Dowager:* Mary Forbes, *Girls:* Mary Stuart, Rita Corday, Ariel Heath, *Plainclothesman:* Joseph Crehan, *Plainclothesman:* Kernan Cripps, *Draft Board Director:* Hal K. Dawson, *Captain Costello:* Robert Strange, *Reporter on Street:* Frank Henry, *Comstock:* Charles Cane, *Stevedore:* Budd Fine, *Maid:* Hilda Plowright, *Taxi Driver:* Lloyd Ingraham, *Dock Watchman:* Emory Parnell, *Gambler (Extra):* Major Sam Harris, *Mrs. Van Every:* Florence Bates.

MR. SKEFFINGTON (1944) WB. Produced by Philip G. and Julius J. Epstein. Directed by Vincent Sherman. Based on the story by "Elizabeth." Screenplay, Philip G. and Julius J. Epstein. Photography, Ernest Haller. Score, Franz Waxman. Music Direction, Leo F. Forbstein. Orchestral Arrangements, Leonid Raab. Art Director, Robert Haas. Editor, Ralph Dawson. Costumes, Orry-Kelly. 146 minutes

Fanny Trellis Skeffington: Bette Davis, *Job Skeffington:* Claude Rains, *George Trellis:* Walter Abel, *Trippy Trellis:* Richard Waring, *Doctor Byles:* George Coulouris, *Young Fanny:* Marjorie Riordan, *MacMahon:* Robert Shayne, *Jim Conderley:* John Alexander, *Edward Morrison:* Jerome Cowan, *Johnny Mitchell:* Johnny Mitchell, *Manby:* Dorothy Peterson, *Chester Forbish:* Peter Whitney, *Thatcher:* Bill Kennedy, *Reverend Hyslup:* Tom Stevenson, *Soames:* Halliwell Hobbes, *Doctor Melton:* Walter Kingsford, *Young Fanny at 2–5:* Gigi Perreau, *Young Fanny at 5:* Bunny Sunshine, *Singer:* Dolores Gray, *Miss Morris:* Molly Lamont, *Young Fanny at 10:* Sylvia Arslan, *The Rector:* Harry Bradley, *Casey, Employee:* Creighton Hale, *Nursemaid:* Ann Doran, *Mrs. Newton:* Georgia Caine, *Mrs. Forbish:* Lelah Tyler, *Mrs. Hyslup:* Mary Field, *Mrs. Conderley:* Regina Wallace, *Mrs. Thatcher:* Bess Flowers, *Justice of the Peace:* Edward Fielding, *Justice's Wife:* Vera Lewis, *Doctor Fawcette:* Erskine Sanford, *Perry Lanks:* Cyril Ring, *"Louie":* Crane Whitley, *Drunks:* Matt McHugh, Will Stanton, *Plainclothesman:* Saul Gorss, *French Modiste:* Ann Codee, *Henri:* Jac George, *Woman:* Dagmar Oakland, *Clinton:* William Forrest.

Music Score, Herbert Stothart. Photography, Joseph Ruttenberg. Sound, Douglas Shearer. Art Director, Cedric Gibbons. Associate, Urie McCleary. Set Decorations, Edwin B. Willis. Special Effects, Arnold Gillespie and Warren Newcombe. Gowns, Kalloch. Men's Wardrobe, Gile Steele. Miss Garson's Hair Styles, Sydney Guilaroff. Editor, Harold F. Kress. Song, "Midsummer's Day" by Gene Lockhart. The sequel was *The Miniver Story* (1950). 134 minutes

Kay Miniver: Greer Garson, *Clem Miniver:* Walter Pidgeon, *Carol Beldon:* Teresa Wright, *Lady Beldon:* Dame May Whitty, *Mr. Ballard:* Henry Travers, *Foley:* Reginald Owen, *Vicar:* Henry Wilcoxon, *Vin Miniver:* Richard Ney, *Toby Miniver:* Christopher Severn, *Gladys:* Brenda Forbes, *Judy Miniver:* Clare Sandars, *Horace:* Rhys Williams, *Ada:* Marie De Becker, *German Flyer:* Helmut Dantine, *Miss Spriggins:* Mary Field, *Nobby:* Paul Scardon, *Ginger:* Ben Webster, *George (Innkeeper):* Aubrey Mather, *Huggins:* Forrester Harvey, *Fred (Porter):* John Abbott, *Simpson:* Connie Leon, *Conductor:* Billy Bevan, *Saleslady:* Ottola Nesmith, *Car Dealer:* Gerald Oliver Smith, *Joe:* Alec Craig, *Mrs. Huggins:* Clara Reid, *William:* Harry Allen, *Halliday:* John Burton, *Beldon's Butler:* Leonard Carey, *Marston:* Eric Lonsdale, *Mac:* Charles Irwin, *Dentist:* Ian Wolfe, *Sir Henry:* Arthur Wimperis, *Carruthers:* David Clyde, *Bickles:* Colin Campbell, *Doctor:* Herbert Clifton, *Man in Tavern:* Walter Byron, *Mr. Verger:* Thomas Louden, *Pilot:* Peter Lawford, *German Agent's Voice:* Miles Mander. St. Luke's Choristers.

Mrs. Miniver with Teresa Wright, Walter Pidgeon, Greer Garson and Richard Ney.

Mr. Skeffington with Walter Abel, Richard Waring, Bette Davis and Claude Rains.

Mr. Smith Goes to Washington with Eugene Pallette, James Stewart, Edward Arnold, Allan Cavan, Maurice Costello and Lloyd Whitlock.

MRS. MINIVER (1942) MGM. Produced by Sidney Franklin. Directed by William Wyler. Based on the novel by Jan Struther. Screenplay, Arthur Wimperis, George Froeschel, James Hilton, Claudine West.

MR. SMITH GOES TO WASHINGTON (1939) Col. Producer and Director, Frank Capra. Author, Lewis R. Foster. Screenplay, Sidney Buchman. Art Director, Lionel Banks. Musical Director, M. W.

Stoloff. Score, Dimitri Tiomkin. Cameraman, Joseph Walker. Montage Effects, Slavko Vorkapich. Editors, Gene Havlick, Al Clark. 125 minutes

Saunders: Jean Arthur, *Jefferson Smith:* James Stewart, *Senator Joseph Paine:* Claude Rains, *Jim Taylor:* Edward Arnold, *Governor Hubert Hopper:* Guy Kibbee, *Diz Moore:* Thomas Mitchell, *Chick McCann:* Eugene Pallette, *Ma Smith:* Beulah Bondi, *Senator Agnew:* H. B. Warner, *President of the Senate:* Harry Carey, *Susan Paine:* Astrid Allwyn, *Emma Hopper:* Ruth Donnelly, *Senator MacPherson:* Grant Mitchell, *Senator Monroe:* Porter Hall, *Senator Barnes:* Pierre Watkin, *Nosey:* Charles Lane, *Bill Griffith:* William Demarest, *Carl Cook:* Dick Elliott. *The Hopper Boys:* Billy and Delmar Watson, John Russell, Harry and Garry Watson, Baby Dumpling (Larry Simms), *Broadcaster:* H. V. Kaltenborn, *Announcer:* Kenneth Carpenter, *Sweeney:* Jack Carson, *Summers:* Joe King, *Flood:* Paul Stanton, *Allen:* Russell Simpson, *Senator Hodges:* Stanley Andrews, *Senator Pickett:* Walter Soderling, *Senator Byron:* Frank Jaquet, *Senator Carlisle:* Ferris Taylor, *Senator Burdette:* Carl Stockdale, *Senator Dwight:* Alan Bridge, *Senator Gower:* Edmund Cobb, *Senator Dearhorn:* Frederick Burton, *Mrs. Edwards:* Vera Lewis, *Mrs. McGann:* Dora Clemant, *Mrs. Taylor:* Laura Treadwell, *Paine's Secretary:* Ann Doran, *Francis Scott Key:* Douglas Evans, *Ragner:* Allan Cavan, *Diggs:* Maurice Costello, *Schultz:* Lloyd Whitlock, *Jane Hopper:* Myonne

Murder by Death with Peter Sellers, Maggie Smith and David Niven, with dog Myron.

MURDER BY DEATH (1976) Col. A Rastar Feature. Produced by Ray Stark. Directed by Robert Moore. Written by Neil Simon. Music, Dave Grusin. Photography, David M. Walsh. Associate Producer, Roger M. Rothstein. Supervising Editor, Margaret Booth. Production Designer, Stephen Grimes. Costumes designed by Ann Roth. Editor, John F. Burnett. Art Director, Harry Kemm. Set Decorator, Marvin March. Make-up Supervision, Charles Schram. Make-up, Joseph De Bella. Hairstylist, Vivienne Walker. Men's Costumer, Tony Faso. Women's Costumer, Agnes G. Henry. Assistant to the Producer, Frank Bueno. Assistant Director, Fred T. Gallo. 2nd Assistant Director, David O. Sosna. Special Effects, Augie Lohman. Title Design by Wayne Fitzgerald. Title Drawings by Charles Addams. Film debut of Truman Capote and feature directing debut of Robert Moore. Filmed at the Burbank Studios in Panavision and Color. Rated PG. 96 minutes

Dick Charleston: David Niven, *Dora Charleston:* Maggie Smith, *Bensonmum:* Alec Guinness, *Sidney Wang:* Peter Sellers, *Willie Wang:* Richard Narita, *Sam Diamond:* Peter Falk, *Tess Skeffington:* Eileen Brennan, *Jessica Marbles:* Elsa Lanchester, *Miss Withers:* Estelle Winwood, *Milo Perrier:* James Coco, *Marcel, Chauffeur:* James Cromwell, *Yetta:* Nancy Walker, *Lionel Twain:* Truman Capote.

MURDER ON THE ORIENT EXPRESS (1974) Par. Produced by John Brabourne and Richard Goodwin. Directed by Sidney Lumet. From the novel by Agatha Christie. Screenplay, Paul Dehn. Photography, Geoffrey Unsworth. Editor, Anne V. Coates. Music, Richard Rodney Bennett. Production Design and Costumes, Tony Walton. Art Director, Jack Stephens. Assistant Director, Ted Sturgis. Presented by EMI Film Distributors Ltd. Produced in England in Panavision and Technicolor. Rated PG. 128 minutes

Hercule Poirot: Albert Finney, *Mrs. Hubbard:* Lauren Bacall, *Bianchi:* Martin Balsam, *Greta Ohlsson:* Ingrid Bergman, *Countess Andrenyi:* Jacqueline Bisset, *Pierre Paul Michel:* Jean-Pierre Cassel, *Col. Arbuthnot:* Sean Connery, *Beddoes:* John Gielgud, *Princess Dragomiroff:* Wendy Hiller, *Hector McQueen:* Anthony Perkins, *Mary Debenham:* Vanessa Redgrave, *Hildegarde Schmidt:* Rachel Roberts, *Ratchett:* Richard Widmark, *Count Andrenyi:* Michael York, *Hardman:* Colin Blakely, *Dr. Constantine:* George Coulouris, *Foscarelli:* Denis Quilley, *Concierge:* Vernon Dobtcheff, *A.D.C.:* Jeremy Lloyd, *Chief Attendant:* John Moffatt.

Murder on the Orient Express with Albert Finney, George Coulouris, John Gielgud, Colin Blakely, Rachel Roberts and Wendy Hiller.

The Music Man with Buddy Hackett and Robert Preston.

THE MUSIC MAN (1962) WB. Producer, Morton DaCosta. Director, Morton DaCosta. Technirama, Technicolor. Based on the musical by Meredith Willson. Screenplay, Marion Hargrove. Art Director, Paul Groesse. Music Supervisor and Conductor, Ray Heindorf. Orchestration, Ray Heindorf, Frank Comstock, Gus Levene. Cinematographer, Robert Burks. Editor, William Ziegler. Songs by Meredith Willson: "Rock Island," "Iowa Stubborn," "Trouble," "Piano Lesson," "Goodnight My Someone," "76 Trombones," "Sincere," "The Sadder-But-Wiser Girl," "Pickilittle," "Goodnight My Ladies," "Marian the Librarian," "Being in Love," "Wells Fargo Wagon," "It's You," "Shipoopi," "Lida Rose," "Will I Ever Tell You," "Gary, Indiana,"

"Till There Was You." Choreography, Onna White, Tom Panko. 151 minutes

Harold Hill: Robert Preston, *Marian Paroo:* Shirley Jones, *Mayor Shinn:* Paul Ford, *Marcellus Washburn:* Buddy Hackett, *Eulalie Mackechnie Shinn:* Hermione Gingold, *Amaryllis:* Monique Vermont, *Winthrop Paroo:* Ronny Howard, *Mrs. Paroo:* Pert Kelton, *Norbert Smith:* Ronnie Dapo, *Jacey Squires, Olin Britt, Ewart Dunlop, Oliver Hix:* The Buffalo Bills, *Constable Locke:* Charles Lane, *Tommy Djilas:* Timmy Everett, *Zaneeta Shinn:* Susan Luckey, *Charlie Cowell:* Harry Hickox, *Mrs. Squires:* Mary Wickes, *Avis Grubb:* Jesslyn Fax, *Gracie Shinn:* Patty Lee Hilka, *Dewey:* Garry Potter, *Harley MacCauley:* J. Delos Jewkes, *Harry Joseph:* Ray Kellogg, *Lester Lonnergan:* William Fawcett, *Oscar Jackson:* Rance Howard, *Gilbert Hawthorne:* Roy Dean, *Chet Glanville:* David Swain, *Herbert Malthouse:* Arthur Mills, *Duncan Shyball:* Rand Barker, *Jessie Shyball:* Jeannine Burnier, *Amy Dakin:* Shirley Claire, *Truthful Smith:* Natalie Core, *Dolly Higgins:* Therese Lyon, *Lila O'Brink:* Penelope Martin, *Feril Hawkes:* Barbara Pepper, *Stella Jackson:* Anne Loos, *Ada Nutting:* Peggy Wynne, *Undertaker:* Hank Worden, *Farmer:* Milton Parsons, *Farmer's Wife:* Natalie Masters.

Mutiny on the Bounty with Franchot Tone and Charles Laughton.

MUTINY ON THE BOUNTY (1935) MGM. Produced by Irving Thalberg. Associate Producer, Albert Lewin. Directed by Frank Lloyd. Based on the novel by Charles Nordhoff and James Norman Hall. Art Director, Cedric Gibbons. Musical Score, Herbert Stothart. Cinematographer, Arthur Edeson. Recording Engineer, Douglas Shearer. Editor, Margaret Booth. Screenplay by Talbot Jennings, Jules Furthman, Carey Wilson. Song, "Love Song of Tahiti," by Gus Kahn, Bronislau Kaper, and Walter Jurmann. Remade by MGM in 1962. 132 minutes

Fletcher Christian: Clark Gable, *Captain Bligh:* Charles Laughton, *Byam:* Franchot Tone, *Bachus:* Dudley Digges, *Sir Joseph Banks:* Henry Stephenson, *Burkitt:* Donald Crisp, *Ellison:* Eddie Quillan, *Captain Nelson:* Francis Lister, *Mrs. Byam:* Spring Byington, *Tehani:* Maria Castaneda (Movita), *Maimiti:* Mamo Clark, *Young:* Robert Livingston, *Stewart:* Douglas Walton, *Samuel:* Ian Wolfe, *Fryer:* DeWitt C. Jennings, *Morgan:* Ivan Simpson, *Hayward:* Vernon Downing, *Muspratt:* Stanley Fields, *Morrison:* Wallis Clark, *Tinkler:* Dick Winslow, *Quintal:* Byron Russell, *Coleman:* Percy Waram, *Lord Hood:* David Torrence, *Mr. Purcell:* John Harrington, *Mary Ellison:* Marion Clayton, *Millard:* Hal LeSueur, *Hitihiti:* William Bainbridge, *McIntosh:* David Thursby, *Lieutenant Edwards:* Craufurd Kent, *Churchill:* Pat Flaherty, *McCoy:* Alec Craig, *Byrne:* Charles Irwin, *Hillebrandt:* John Powers, *Richard Skinner:* King Mojave, *Cockney Moll:* Doris Lloyd, *Judge Advocate:* William Stack, *Captain Colpoys:* Harold Entwhistle, *Portsmouth Joe:* Will Stanton, *Innkeeper:* Lionel Belmore, *Soldier:* Harry Cording, *Peddler:* Mary Gordon, *Smith:* Herbert Mundin, *Captain of Board:* Eric Wilton.

Mutiny on the Bounty with Marlon Brando and Trevor Howard.

MUTINY ON THE BOUNTY (1962) MGM. Producer, Aaron Rosenberg. Director, Lewis Milestone. Screenplay, Charles Lederer. Based on the novel by Charles Nordhoff and James Norman Hall. Music, Bronislau Kaper. Assistant Director, Ridgeway Callow. Costumes, Moss Mabry. Choreographer, Hamil Petroff. An Arcola Picture in Ultra Panavision and Technicolor. Art Directors, George W. Davis, J. McMillan Johnson. Cinematographer, Robert L. Surtees. Editor, John McSweeney, Jr. Previous versions: *In the Wake of the Bounty* (Australian, 1933), *Mutiny on the Bounty* (MGM. 1935). 179 minutes

Fletcher Christian: Marlon Brando, *Captain Bligh:* Trevor Howard, *John Mills:* Richard Harris, *Smith:* Hugh Griffith, *Brown:* Richard Haydn, *Maimiti:* Tarita, *Quintal:* Percy Herbert, *Williams:* Duncan Lamont, *Birkett:* Gordon Jackson, *Byrne:* Chips Rafferty, *McCoy:* Noel Purcell, *Mack:* Ashley Cowan, *Fryer:* Eddie Byrne, *Minarii:* Frank Silvera, *Young:* Tim Seely, *Morrison:* Keith McConnell.

My Darling Clementine with Henry Fonda and Cathy Downs.

MY DARLING CLEMENTINE (1946) 20th. Producer, Samuel G. Engel. Director, John Ford. Authors, Sam Hellman, Stuart N. Lake (from *Wyatt Earp, Frontier Marshall*). Screenplay, Samuel G. Engel, Winston Miller. Music, Alfred Newman. Art Directors, James Basevi, Lyle Wheeler. Cameraman, Joe MacDonald. Editor, Dorothy Spencer. Remake of *Frontier Marshal* (Fox, 1939). 97 minutes

Wyatt Earp: Henry Fonda, *Chihuahua:* Linda Darnell, *Doc Holliday:* Victor Mature, *Old Man Clanton:* Walter Brennan, *Virgil Earp:* Tim Holt, *Clementine:* Cathy Downs, *Morgan Earp:* Ward Bond, *Thorndyke:* Alan Mowbray, *Billy Clanton:* John Ireland, *Mayor:* Roy Roberts, *Kate:* Jane Darwell, *Ike Clanton:* Grant Withers, *Bartender:* J. Farrell MacDonald, *John Simpson:* Russell Simpson, *James Earp:* Don Garner, *Town Drunk:* Francis Ford, *Barber:* Ben Hall, *Hotel Clerk:* Arthur Walsh, *Francois:* Louis Mercier, *Sam Clanton:* Mickey Simpson, *Phin Clanton:* Fred Libby, *Owner of Oriental Saloon:* William B. Davidson, *Gambler:* Earle Foxe, *Townsman and Guitar Player:* Aleth (Speed) Hansen, *Townsman and Accordion Player:* Dan Borzage, *Opera House Owner:* Don Barclay, *Marshal:* Harry Woods, *Indian Charlie:* Charles Stevens, *Piano Player:* Frank Conlan, *Stagecoach Driver:* Robert Adler.

My Fair Lady with Rex Harrison, Audrey Hepburn and Wilfrid Hyde-White.

MY FAIR LADY (1964) WB. Produced by Jack L. Warner. Directed by George Cukor. Technicolor and Super Panavision 70. Based on the musical play *My Fair Lady* by Alan Jay Lerner and Frederick Loewe, and the play *Pygmalion* by George Bernard Shaw. Screenplay, Alan Jay Lerner. Art Director, Gene Allen. Music supervised and conducted by Andre Previn. Orchestration, Alexander Courage, Robert Franklyn, Al Woodbury. Choreography, Hermes Pan. Costumes, Cecil Beaton. Assistant Director, David Hall. Photography, Harry Stradling. Editor, William Ziegler. Songs by Lerner and Loewe: "Why Can't the English," "Wouldn't It Be Lovely?" "I'm an Ordinary Man," "With a Little Bit of Luck," "Just You Wait," "The Servants' Chorus," "The Rain in Spain," "I Could Have Danced All Night," "Ascot Gavotte," "On the Street Where You Live," "The Embassy Waltz," "You Did It," "Show Me," "The Flower Market," "Get Me to the Church on Time," "A Hymn to Him," "Without You," "I've Grown Accustomed to Her Face." Remake of *Pygmalion* (MGM, 1938). The musical, *My Fair Lady*, ran on Broadway from 1956 to 1962, and was originally called *Lady Liza*. Rex Harrison, Wilfrid Hyde-White, and Olive Reeves-Smith repeated their original roles in the film. Last film of Henry Daniell, 69, who died October 31, 1963. 170 minutes

Professor Henry Higgins: Rex Harrison, *Eliza Doolittle:* Audrey Hepburn, *Alfred P. Doolittle:* Stanley Holloway, *Colonel Hugh Pickering:* Wilfrid Hyde-White, *Mrs. Higgins:* Gladys Cooper, *Freddy Eynsford-Hill:* Jeremy Brett, *Zoltan Karpathy:* Theodore Bikel, *Mrs. Eynsford-Hill:* Isobel Elsom, *Mrs. Pearce:* Mona Washbourne, *Butler:* John Holland, *Jamie:* John Alderson, *Harry:* John McLiam, *Bystander (Warns Eliza):* Walter Burke, *Man at Coffee Stand:* Owen McGiveney, *Cockney with Pipe:* Marjorie Bennett, *George:* Jack Greening, *Algernon/Bartender:* Ron Whelan, *First Maid:* Dinah Anne Rogers, *Second Maid:* Lois Battle, *Parlor Maid:* Jacquire Squire, *Cook:* Gwen Watts, *King:* Charles Fredericks, *Lady Ambassador:* Lily Kemble-Cooper, *Lady Boxington:* Moyna MacGill, *Prince Gregor of Transylvania:* Henry Daniell, *Queen of Transylvania:* Baroness Rothschild, *Footman at Ball:* Ben Wright, *Greek Ambassador:* Oscar Beregi, *Ad-lib at Ball:* Betty Blythe, *Prince:* Buddy Bryan, *Dancer:* Nick Navarro, *Ambassador:* Alan Napier, *Mrs. Higgins' Maid:* Jennifer Crier, *Mrs. Hopkins:* Olive Reeves-Smith, *Landlady:* Miriam Schiller, *Fat Woman at Pub:* Ayllene Gibbons, *Doolittle's Dance Partner:* Barbara Pepper, *Ascot Extra/Guest at Ball:* Grady Sutton, *Guest at Ball:* Major Sam Harris.

My Favorite Blonde with Isabel Randolph, Carl "Alfalfa" Switzer, Bob Hope and Madeleine Carroll.

MY FAVORITE BLONDE (1942) Par. Associate Producer, Paul Jones. Directed by Sidney Lanfield. Story, Melvin Frank and Norman Panama. Screenplay, Don Hartman and Frank Butler. Art Directors, Hans Dreier and Robert Usher. Music Score, David Buttolph. Photography, William Mellor. Editor, William Shea. 78 minutes

Larry Haines: Bob Hope, *Karen Bentley:* Madeleine Carroll, *Madame Stephanie Runick:* Gale Sondergaard, *Dr. Hugo Streger:* George Zucco, *Karl:* Lionel Royce, *Dr. Faber:* Walter Kingsford, *Miller:* Victor Varconi, *Lanz:* Otto Reichow, *Turk O'Flaherty:* Charles Cane, *Ulrich:* Crane Whitley, *Sheriff:* Erville Alderson, *Mrs. Topley:* Esther Howard, *Mulrooney:* Ed Gargan, *Union Secretary:* James Burke, *Porter:* Dooley Wilson, *Mortician:* Milton Parsons, *Tom Douglas:* Tom Fadden, *Sam:* Fred Kelsey, *Joe:* Edgar Dearing, *Elvan:* Leslie Denison, *Burton:* Robert Emmett Keane, *Herbert Wilson:* Addison Richards, *Colonel Ashmont:* Matthew Boulton, *Conductor:* Wade Boteler, *Colonel Raeburn:* William Forrest, *Frederick:* Carl "Alfalfa" Switzer, *Frederick's Mother:* Isabel Randolph, *Train Official:* Edward Hearn, *English Driver:* Leyland Hodgson, *Spectator:* Jack Luden, *Cop at Union Hall:* Monte Blue, *Backstage Doorman:* Dick Elliott, *Male Nurse:* Arno Frey, *Apartment Manager:* Lloyd Whitlock, *Ole, Bartender:* Vernon Dent, *Mrs. Weatherwax:* Sarah Edwards, *Dr. Higby:* Paul Scardon, *Telegraph Operator:* Bill Lally, *Frozen-faced Woman:* Minerva Urecal, *Truck Driver:* James Millican, *Yard Man:* Edmund Cobb, *Stuttering Boy:* Jimmy Dodd, *Pilots:* Eddie Dew, George Turner, Kirby Grant, William Cabanne.

My Favorite Brunette with Bob Hope and Dorothy Lamour.

MY FAVORITE BRUNETTE (1947) Par. Producer, Daniel Dare. Director, Elliott Nugent. Screenplay, Edmund Beloin, Jack Rose. Art Directors, Hans Dreier, Earl Hedrick. Musical Score, Robert Emmett

Dolan. Cameraman, Lionel Lindon. Editor, Ellsworth Hoagland. Songs by Ray Evans and Jay Livingston: "Beside You" and "My Favorite Brunette." 87 minutes

Ronnie Jackson: Bob Hope, *Carlotta Montay:* Dorothy Lamour, *Kismet:* Peter Lorre, *Willie:* Lon Chaney, Jr., *Dr. Lundau:* John Hoyt, *Major Simon Montague:* Charles Dingle, *James Collins:* Reginald Denny, *Baron Montay:* Frank Puglia, *Miss Rogers:* Ann Doran, *Prison Warden:* Willard Robertson, *Tony:* Jack La Rue, *Crawford:* Charles Arnt, *Reporter:* Garry Owen, *Reporter:* Richard Keene, *"Raft" Character:* Tony Caruso, *"Cagney" Character:* Matt McHugh, *Prison Guard:* George Lloyd, *Prison Guard:* Jack Clifford, *State Trooper:* Ray Teal, *State Trooper:* Al Hill, *Caddy:* Eddie Johnson, *Mr. Dawsen:* Boyd Davis, *Man in Condemned Row:* Clarence Muse, *Mabel:* Helena Evans, *Baby Fong:* Roland Soo Hoo, *Doctor:* John Westley, *Waiter:* Charley Cooley, *Mrs. Fong:* Jean Wong, *Matron:* Betty Farrington, *Butler:* Brandon Hurst, *Henri (Waiter):* Jack Chefe, *Asst. Manager:* Reginald Simpson, *Mac (Detective):* James Flavin, *Second Detective:* Jim Pierce, *Third Detective:* Budd Fine, *Guest Star:* Bing Crosby, *Detective:* Alan Ladd.

My Favorite Wife with Gail Patrick, Ann Shoemaker, Irene Dunne, Cary Grant, Scotty Beckett and Mary Lou Harrington.

MY FAVORITE WIFE (1940) RKO. Producer, Leo McCarey. Director, Garson Kanin. Authors, Sam and Bella Spewack, Leo McCarey. Screenplay, Sam and Bella Spewack. Cameraman, Rudolph Mate. Editor, Robert Wise. Remade as *Move Over, Darling* (Fox, 1963). 88 minutes

Ellen: Irene Dunne, *Nick:* Cary Grant, *Burkett:* Randolph Scott, *Bianca:* Gail Patrick, *Ma:* Ann Shoemaker, *Tim:* Scotty Beckett, *Chinch:* Mary Lou Harrington, *Hotel Clerk:* Donald MacBride, *Johnson:* Hugh O'Connell, *Judge:* Granville Bates, *Dr. Kohlmar:* Pedro de Cordoba, *Dr. Manning:* Brandon Tynan, *Henri:* Leon Belasco, *Assistant Clerk:* Harold Gerard, *Bartender:* Murray Alper, *Clerk of Court:* Earle Hodgins, *Lawyer:* Clive Morgan, *Witness:* Florence Dudley, *Contestant:* Cy Ring, *Witness:* Jean Acker, *Lawyer:* Bert Moorhouse, *Phillip:* Joe Cabrillas, *Photographer:* Frank Marlowe, *Miss Rosenthal:* Thelma Joel, *Truck Driver:* Horace McMahon, *Little Man:* Chester Clute, *Janitor:* Eli Schmudkler, *Waiter:* Franco Corsaro, *Caretaker:* Pat West, *Detective:* Cy Kendall.

MY GAL SAL (1942) 20th. Directed by Irving Cummings. Produced by Robert Bassler. Color by Technicolor. Screenplay by Seton I. Miller, Darrell Ware and Karl Tunberg. Based on Theodore Dreiser's *My Brother Paul.* Songs: "Come Tell Me What's Your Answer, Yes or No," "I'se Your Honey If You Wants Me, Liza Jane," "On the Banks of the Wabash," "The Convict and the Bird," "My Gal Sal," "Mr. Volunteer" (or "You Don't Belong to the Regulars, You're Just a Volunteer"), by Paul Dreiser. Additional songs: "Me and My Fella and a

Big Umbrella, "On the Gay White Way," "Oh the Pity of It All," "Here You Are," "Midnight at the Masquerade," by Leo Robin and Ralph Rainger. Dances staged by Hermes Pan and Val Raset. Director of Photography, Ernest Palmer. Technicolor Director, Natalie Kalmus. Associate, Henri Jaffa. Musical Direction, Alfred Newman. Art Direction, Richard Day. Set Decorations, Thomas Little. Film Editor, Robert Simpson. Costumes, Gwen Wakeling. Make-up Artist, Guy Pearce. Sound, Alfred Bruzlin, Roger Heman. 103 minutes

Sally Elliott: Rita Hayworth, *Paul Dreiser:* Victor Mature, *Fred Haviland:* John Sutton, *Mae Collins:* Carole Landis, *Pat Hawley:* James Gleason, *Wiley:* Phil Silvers, *Colonel Truckee:* Walter Catlett, *Countess Rossini:* Mona Maris, *McGuinness:* Frank Orth, *Mr. Dreiser:* Stanley Andrews, *Mrs. Dreiser:* Margaret Moffat, *Ida:* Libby Taylor, *John L. Sullivan:* John Kelly, *De Rochement:* Curt Bois, *Garnier:* Gregory Gaye, *Corbin:* Andrew Tombes, *Henri:* Albert Conti, *Tailor:* Charles Arnt, *Quartette:* Clarence Badger, Kenneth Rundquist, Gene Ramey, Delos Jewkes, *Murphy:* Chief Thundercloud, *Specialty Dancer:* Hermes Pan, *Sally's Friends:* Robert Lowery, Dorothy Dearing, (Michael) Ted North, Roseanne Murray, *Carrie:* Judy Ford (Terry Moore), *Theodore:* Barry Downing, *Usher:* Tommy Seide, *Men:* Gus Glassmire, Tom O'Grady, Frank Ferguson, John "Skins" Miller, Cyril Ring, *Midget Driver:* Billy Curtis, *Midget Footman:* Tommy Cotton.

My Gal Sal with John Sutton, Phil Silvers and Rita Hayworth.

My Little Chickadee with Mae West and W. C. Fields.

MY LITTLE CHICKADEE (1940) Univ. Produced by Lester Cowan. Directed by Edward Cline. Original Screenplay, Mae West and W. C. Fields. Music by Frank Skinner, directed by Charles Previn. Photography, Joseph Valentine. Art Director, Jack Otterson. Editor, Edward Curtiss. Assistant Director, Joe McDonough. Gowns by Vera West. Sound

Supervision, Bernard B. Brown. Song, "Willie of the Valley" by Ben Oakland and Milton Drake. 84 minutes

Cuthbert J. Twillie: W. C. Fields, *Flower Belle Lee:* Mae West, *Wayne Carter:* Dick Foran, *Jeff Badger (The Masked Bandit):* Joseph Calleia, *Amos Budge:* Donald Meek, *Ermingarde Foster:* Anne Nagel, *Mrs. Gideon:* Margaret Hamilton, *Aunt Lou:* Ruth Donnelly, *Cousin Zeb:* Fuzzy Knight, *Hotel Clerk:* Harlan Briggs, *Milton:* George Moran, *Uncle John:* Willard Robertson, *Squawk Mulligan, Bartender:* Jimmy Conlin, *Deputy:* Si Jenks, *Candy:* Russell Hall, *Coco:* Otto Heimel, *Henchmen:* Eddie Butler, Bing Conley, John Kelly, Jack Roper, *Sheriff:* William B. Davidson, *Judge:* Addison Richards, *Woman:* Jan Duggan, *Mrs. Pygmy Allen:* Fay Adler, *Pete, Printer:* Otto Hoffman, *Chinaman:* Chester Gan, *Sheriff:* George Melford, *Schoolboys:* Jackie Searle, Delmar Watson, Ben Hall, *Lem, Schoolboy:* Billy Benedict, *Boys:* Buster Slaven, Danny Jackson, Charles Hart, George Billings, *Gambler:* Morgan Wallace, *Gambler/Townsman:* Vester Pegg, *Leading Citizens:* Wade Boteler, Lloyd Ingraham, *Men:* Jeff Conlon, Walter McGrail, Bob McKenzie, Dick Rush, James C. Morton, Joe Whitehead, Charles McMurphy, Hank Bell, *Porter:* Bud Harris, *Bowlegged Man:* Slim Gant, *Barflies:* Alan Bridge, Edward Hearn, Bill Wolfe, *Barfly-dandies:* Bob Burns and Bob Reeves, *Train Passenger:* Al Ferguson, *Townsmen:* Mark Anthony and Frank Ellis, *Diner:* Dorothy Vernon. Cut were Gene Austin as himself, Lita Chevret as Indian Squaw, Lane Chandler as a Porter.

My Man Godfrey with Carole Lombard and William Powell.

MY MAN GODFREY (1936) Univ. Produced and directed by Gregory LaCava. Author, Eric Hatch. Screenplay by Morrie Ryskind, Eric Hatch, Gregory LaCava. Cameraman, Ted Tetzlaff. Editor, Ted Kent. Film debut of Jane Wyman, 22. Remade by Universal, 1957. 95 minutes

Godfrey: William Powell, *Irene Bullock:* Carole Lombard, *Angelica Bullock:* Alice Brady, *Alexander Bullock:* Eugene Pallette, *Cornelia Bullock:* Gail Patrick, *Tommy Gray:* Alan Mowbray, *Molly:* Jean Dixon, *Carlo:* Mischa Auer, *George:* Robert Light, *Mike:* Pat Flaherty, *Hobo:* Robert Perry, *Scorekeeper:* Franklin Pangborn, *Guest (Blake):* Selmer Jackson, *Forgotten Man:* Ernie Adams, *Party Guest:* Phyllis Crane, *Von Ronkel:* Grady Sutton, *Headwaiter:* Jack Chefe, *Process Server:* Eddie Fetherston, *Detectives:* Edward Gargan, James Flavin, *Chauffeur:* Art Singley, *Mayor:* Reginald Mason, *Girl at Party:* Jane Wyman, *Guest:* Bess Flowers.

MY SON JOHN (1952) Par. Producer, Leo McCarey. Director, Leo McCarey. Story, Leo McCarey. Screenplay, Myles Connolly, Leo McCarey. Art Directors, Hal Pereira, William Flannery. Music Score, Robert Emmett Dolan. Cinematographer, Henry Stradling. Editor,

Marvin Coil. Adaptation, John Lee Mahin. Used Robert Walker's outtakes from *Strangers on a Train.* 122 minutes

Lucille Jefferson: Helen Hayes, *Stedman:* Van Heflin, *John Jefferson:* Robert Walker, *Dan Jefferson:* Dean Jagger, *Dr. Carver:* Minor Watson, *Father O'Dowd:* Frank McHugh, *Chuck Jefferson:* Richard Jaeckel, *Ben Jefferson:* James Young, *Nurse:* Nancy Hale, *Bedford:* Todd Karns, *Secretary:* Frances Morris, *Parcel Post Man:* William McLean, *Cleaner:* Fred Sweeney, *FBI Agent:* Russell Conway, *Boy:* Lee William Aaker, *Secretary:* Vera Stokes, *Government Employee:* Douglas Evans, *Jail Matron:* Gail Bonney, *Ruth Carlin:* Irene Winston, *FBI Agent:* David Newell, *Professor:* Erskine Sanford, *Nurse:* Margaret Wells, *College Professor:* David Bond, *College Professor:* Eghiche Harout, *Taxi Driver:* Jimmie Dundee.

My Son John with Robert Walker, Helen Hayes and Dean Jagger.

The Naked City with Barry Fitzgerald, Dorothy Hart, Enid Markey and Don Taylor.

THE NAKED CITY (1948) Univ. Producer, Mark Hellinger. Director, Jules Dassin. Author, Malvin Wald. Screenplay, Albert Maltz, Malvin Wald. Art Director, John F. De Cuir. Musical Supervisor, Milton Schwarzwald. Photography, William Daniels. Editor, Paul Weatherwax. Associate Producer, Jules Buck. Filmed in New York City. 96 minutes

Lieutenant Dan Muldoon: Barry Fitzgerald, *Frank Niles:* Howard Duff, *Ruth Morrison:* Dorothy Hart, *Jimmy Halloran:* Don Taylor, *Garzah:* Ted deCorsia, *Little Old Lady:* Jean Adair, *McCormick:* Nicholas Joy, *Dr. Stoneman:* House Jameson, *Mrs. Halloran:* Anne Sargent, *Mrs. Batory:* Adelaide Klein, *Mr. Batory:* Grover Burgess, *Detective Perelli:* Tom Pedi, *Mrs. Hylton:* Enid Markey, *Captain Donahue:* Frank Conroy, *Backalis:* Walter Burke, *Ben Miller:* David Opatoshu, *Constentino:* John McQuade, *Nurse:* Hester Sondergaard, *Henry Fowler:* Paul Ford, *Dr. Hoffman:* Ralph Bunker,

Nick: Curt Conway, *Qualen:* Kermit Kegley, *Fredericks:* George Lynn, *Shaeffer:* Arthur O'Connell, *Martha:* Virginia Mullen, *Mrs. Stoneman:* Beverly Bayne, *Proprietress:* Celia Adler, *Miss Livingston:* Grace Coppin, *Druggist:* Robert Harris, *Hicks:* James Gregory, *Publisher:* Edwin Jerome, *Ed Garzah:* Anthony Rivers, *Wrestler:* Bernard Hoffman, *Freed:* G. Pat Collins, *Ned Harvey:* Joe Kerr, *Mr. Stillman:* Johnny Dale, *Publisher:* Judson Laire, *Stout Girl:* Kathleen Freeman, *City Editor:* Raymond Greenleaf.

Nashville with Ronee Blakley, Henry Gibson and Barbara Baxley.

NASHVILLE (1975) Par. Produced and Directed by Robert Altman. An ABC Entertainment presentation. A Jerry Weintraub Production. Executive Producers, Martin Starger and Jerry Weintraub. Written by Joan Tewkesbury. Photography, Paul Lohmann. Music arranged and supervised by Richard Baskin. Editors, Sidney Levin and Dennis Hill. Political Campaign, Thomas Hal Phillips. Associate Producers, Robert Eggenweiler and Scott Bushnell. Assistant Directors, Tommy Thompson and Alan Rudolph. Assistant to the Producer, Jac Cashin. Sound, Jim Webb and Chris McLaughlin. Sound System, Lion's Gate 8 Track Sound. Music recorded live on Fanta 16-track by Gene Eichelberger and Johnny Rosen. Assistant Editors, Tony Lombardo and Tom Walls. Hairstylist, Ann Wadlington. Make-up, Tommy Thompson. Wardrobe, Jules Melillo. Filmed in Nashville, Tennessee, in Panavision and Color by MGM Film Laboratories. Chem-Tone Process by TCV Lab. Songs: "Keep a' Goin'" and "200 Years" by Henry Gibson and Richard Baskin: "I'm Easy," "It Don't Worry Me" and "Honey" by Keith Carradine; "Down to the River," "Bluebird," "Tapedeck in His Tractor (The Cowboy Song)," "Dues" and "My Idaho Home" by Ronee Blakley: "Yes, I Do" by Baskin and Lily Tomlin: "Let Me Be the One" and "One, I Love You" by Baskin; "Sing a Song" by Joe Raposo; "The Heart of a Gentle Woman" by Dave Peel; "The Day I Looked Jesus in the Eye" by Baskin and Altman; "Memphis," "I Don't Know If I Found It in You" and "Rolling Stone" by Karen Black; "For the Sake of the Children" by Baskin and Richard Reicheg; "Swing Low, Sweet Chariot" arrangements by Millie Clements; "I Never Get Enough" by Baskin and Ben Raleigh; "Rose's Cafe" by Allan Nicolls; "Old Man Mississippi" by Juan Grizzle; "My Baby's Cookin' in Another's Man's Pan" by Jonnie Barnett; "Since You've Gone" by Gary Busey; and "Trouble in the U.S.A." by Arlene Barnett. Film debuts of Blakley, Hayward and Peel. Rated R. 159 minutes

Haven Hamilton: Henry Gibson, *Linnea Reese:* Lily Tomlin, *Tom Frank:* Keith Carradine, *Albuquerque:* Barbara Harris, *Opal:* Geraldine Chaplin, *Barbara Jean:* Ronee Blakley, *Connie White:* Karen Black, *Delbert Reese:* Ned Beatty, *Lady Pearl:* Barbara Baxley, *Norman:* David Arkin, *Tommy Brown:* Timothy Brown, *Wade:* Robert Doqui, *L.A. Joan:* Shelley Duvall, *Barnett:* Allen Garfield, *PFC Glenn Kelly:* Scott Glenn, *Tricycle Man:* Jeff Goldblum, *Kenny Fraiser:* David Hayward, *John Triplette:* Michael Murphy, *Bill:* Allan Nicholls, *Bud Hamilton:* Dave Peel, *Mary:* Cristina

Raines, *Star:* Bert Remsen, *Sueleen Gay:* Gwen Welles, *Mr. Green:* Keenan Wynn, *Frog:* Richard Baskin, *Jimmy Reese:* James Dan Calvert, *Donna Reese:* Donna Denton, *Trout:* Merle Kilgore, *Jewel:* Carol McGinnis, *Smokey Mountain Laurel:* Sheila Bailey, Patti Bryant. *Themselves:* Jonnie Barnett, Vassar Clements, Misty Mountain Boys, Sue Barton, Elliot Gould, Julie Christie.

National Lampoon's Animal House with James Daughton, Mary Louise Weller, Tim Matheson and John Belushi.

NATIONAL LAMPOON'S ANIMAL HOUSE (1978) Univ. Produced by Matty Simmons and Ivan Reitman. Directed by John Landis. Written by Harold Ramis, Douglas Kenney and Chris Miller. Photography, Charles Correll. Editor, George Folsey, Jr. Music, Elmer Bernstein. Art Director, John J. Lloyd. Set Decorations, Hal Gausman. Stunt Coordinator and 2nd Unit Director, Gary R. McLarty. Costumes, Deborah Nadoolman. Wardrobe, Dan Chichester and Gene Deardorff. Assistant Directors, Cliff Coleman and Ed Milkovich. Sound, William B. Kaplan. Special Effects, Henry Millar. Make-up, Lynn Brooks and Gerald Soucie. Hairstylist, Marilyn Phillips. Songs: "Animal House" and "Dream Girl," composed and performed by Stephen Bishop; "Money," sung by John Belushi; "Shout"; "Shama Lama Ding Dong"; "Louie Louie," sung by the Kingsmen; "Tossin' and Turnin'," sung by Bobby Lewis; "Wonderful World" and "Twistin' the Night Away," sung by Sam Cooke; "Let's Dance," sung by Chris Montez; "Who's Sorry Now," sung by Connie Francis; "Hey Paula," sung by Paul and Paula. Filmed in Eugene and Cottage Grove, Oregon, Panaflex lenses by Panavision. Technicolor. Rated R. 109 minutes. Later a TV series, *Delta House*, debuting in 1979

John Blutarsky (Bluto): John Belushi, *Dave Jennings:* Donald Sutherland, *Eric Stratton (Otter):* Tim Matheson, *Dean Vernon Wormer:* John Vernon, *Marion Wormer:* Verna Bloom, *Larry Kroger (Pinto):* Thomas Hulce, *Mayor Carmine DePasto:* Cesare Danova, *Donald Schoenstein:* Peter Riegert, *Mandy Pepperidge:* Mary Louise Weller, *Kent Dorfman (Flounder):* Stephen Furst, *Greg Marmalard:* James Daughton, *Daniel Simpson Day (D-Day):* Bruce McGill, *Doug Neidermeyer:* Mark Metcalf, *Otis Day:* DeWayne Jessie, *Katy:* Karen Allen, *Robert Hoover:* James Widdoes, *Babs Jansen:* Martha Smith, *Clorette DePasto:* Sarah Holcomb, *Shelly:* Lisa Baur, *Chip Diller:* Kevin Bacon, *Stork:* Douglas Kenney, *Hardbar:* Christian Miller, *B.B.:* Bruce Bonnheim, *Mothball:* Joshua Daniel, *Trooper:* Junior, *Otter's Co-ed:* Sunny Johnson, *Sissy:* Stacy Grooman, *Charming Guy with Guitar:* Stephen Bishop, *Brunella:* Eliza Garrett, *Beth:* Aseneth Jurgenson, *Noreen:* Katherine Denning, *Mean Dude:* Raymone Robinson, *Meaner Dude:* Robert Elliott, *Meanest Dude:* Reginald H. Farmer, *Gigantic Dude:* Jebidiah R. Dumas, *Dean's Secretary:* Priscilla Lauris, *Omega:* Rick Eby, *Man on Street:* John Freeman, *Lucky Boy:* Sean McCartin, *Sorority Girl:* Helen Vick, *Mongol:* Rick Greenough, *Stunt People:* Gary McLarty, Albert M. Mauro, Karen Werner, Fred Hice, Bill Hooker, Clifford Happy, Pam Bebermeyer, Bud Ekins, Jim Halty, R. A. Rondell, Walter Wyatt, Gilbert Combs.

National Velvet with Mickey Rooney and Elizabeth Taylor.

NATIONAL VELVET (1944) MGM. Producer, Pandro S. Berman. Director, Clarence Brown. Color by Technicolor. Based on the novel by Enid Bagnold. Screenplay by Theodore Reeves and Helen Deutsch. Music score by Herbert Stothart. Film Editor, Robert J. Kern. Photographed by Leonard Smith. Art Directors, Cedric Gibbons and Urie McCleary. Special effects by Warren Newcombe. 125 minutes. Sequel was *International Velvet* (MGM-UA, 1978) with Tatum O'Neal.

Mi Taylor: Mickey Rooney, *Mr. Brown:* Donald Crisp, *Velvet Brown:* Elizabeth Taylor, *Mrs. Brown:* Anne Revere, *Edwina Brown:* Angela Lansbury, *Malvolia Brown:* Juanita Quigley, *Donald Brown:* Jack (Butch) Jenkins, *Farmer Ede:* Reginald Owen, *Ted:* Terry Kilburn, *Tim:* Alec Craig, *Mr. Taski:* Eugene Loring, *Miss Sims:* Norma Varden, *Mr. Hallam:* Arthur Shields, *Mr. Greenford:* Dennis Hoey, *Entry Official:* Aubrey Mather, *Stewart:* Frederic Worlock, *Man with Umbrella:* Arthur Treacher, *Van Driver:* Harry Allen, *Constable:* Billy Bevan, *Townsman:* Barry Macollum, *Entry Clerk:* Matthew Boulton, *First Pressman:* Leyland Hodgson, *Second Pressman:* Leonard Carey, *Cockney:* Colin Campbell, *Englishman:* Frank Benson, *Jockey:* Wally Cassell, *Valet:* Alec Harford, *Reporter:* William Austin, *Cameraman:* Gerald Oliver Smith, *First Villager:* Olaf Hytten, *Second Villager:* George Kirby, *Woman:* Moyna MacGill, *American:* Donald Curtis, *Schoolboy:* Howard Taylor.

Naughty Marietta with Jeanette MacDonald, Cecilia Parker and Douglass Dumbrille.

NAUGHTY MARIETTA (1935) MGM. Produced by Hunt Stromberg. Directed by W. S. Van Dyke. Based on the 1910 operetta by Victor Herbert, book by Rida Johnson Young. Screenplay, John Lee Mahin,

Frances Goodrich, Albert Hackett. Musical Adaptation, Herbert Stothart. Art Director, Cedric Gibbons. Sound, Douglas Shearer. Costumes, Adrian. Assistant Director, Eddie Woehler. Photography, William Daniels. Editor, Blanche Sewell. Violin obligato by Jan Rubini. Songs by Victor Herbert, Rida Johnson Young, Gus Kahn: "I'm Falling in Love With Some One," "Chansonette," "The Owl and the Polecat," "Antoinette and Anatole," "Live for Today," "Tramp, Tramp, Tramp Along the Highway," "Dance of the Marionettes," "Italian Street Song," "Neath the Southern Moon," "Ah Sweet Mystery of Life," "Students' Song." Dr. Lippe is Nelson Eddy's coach. The first MacDonald-Eddy musical. 106 minutes

Princess Marie (*Marietta*): Jeanette MacDonald, *Captain Warrington:* Nelson Eddy, *Governor d'Annard:* Frank Morgan, *Madame d'Annard:* Elsa Lanchester, *Uncle:* Douglass Dumbrille, *Herr Schuman:* Joseph Cawthorn, *Julie:* Cecilia Parker, *Don Carlos:* Walter Kingsford, *Frau Schuman:* Greta Meyer, *Rudolpho:* Akim Tamiroff, *Abe:* Harold Huber, *Zeke:* Edward Brophy, *Casquette Girls:* Mary Doran, Jean Chatburn, Pat Farley, Jane Barnes, Kay English, Linda Parker, Jane Mercer, *Bit:* Dr. Edouard Lippe, *Pirate Leader:* Walter Long, *Madame Renavant:* Olive Carey. *Gendarme Chief:* William Desmond, *Felice:* Cora Sue Collins, *Ship's Captain:* Guy Usher, *Duelist:* Louis Mercier, *Town Crier:* Robert McKenzie, *Mama's Boy:* Ben Hall, *Prospective Groom:* Harry Tenbrook, *Major Bonnell:* Edward Keane, *Suitors:* Edward Norris, Ralph Brooks, *Messenger:* Richard Powell, *Announcer:* Wilfred Lucas, *Scouts:* Arthur Belasco, Tex Driscoll, Edward Hearn, Edmund Cobb, Charles Dunbar, Frank Hagney, Ed Brady.

Neptune's Daughter with Keenan Wynn, Esther Williams and Ricardo Montalban.

NEPTUNE'S DAUGHTER (1949) MGM. Producer, Jack Cummings. Director, Edward Buzzell. Color by Technicolor. Screenplay, Dorothy Kingsley. Musical Director, Georgie Stoll. Art Directors, Cedric Gibbons, Edward Carfagno. Photography, Charles Rosher. Editor, Irvine Warburton. Songs by Frank Loesser: "My Heart Beats Faster," "Baby, It's Cold Outside" and "I Love Those Men." 93 minutes

Eve Barrett: Esther Williams, *Jack Spratt:* Red Skelton, *Jose O'Rourke:* Ricardo Montalban, *Betty Barrett:* Betty Garrett, *Joe Beckett:* Keenan Wynn, *Xavier Cugat and His Orchestra:* Themselves, *Lukie Luzette:* Ted de Corsia, *Mac Mazolla:* Mike Mazurki, *Julio:* Mel Blanc, *Second Groom:* Juan Duval, *Tall Wrangler:* George Mann, *Little Wrangler:* Frank Mitchell, *Coach:* Harold S. Kruger, *Official:* Matt Moore, *Linda:* Joi Lansing, *Announcer:* Carl Saxe, *Matilda:* Theresa Harris, *Voice of Record:* Juan Duval, *Miss Pratt:* Elaine Sterling, *Headwaiter:* Henry Sylvester, *Cigarette Girl:* Lillian Molieri, *First Henchman:* Dewey Robinson, *Second Henchman:* Michael Jordon, *Mr. Magoo:* Dick Simmons, *Models:* Bette Arlen, Jonnie Pierce, Dorothy Abbott, *Mr. Canford:* Pierre Watkin, *Man:* Dell Henderson, *Woman:* Kay Mansfield, *Gardner:* Clarence Hennecke, *Groom:* Heinie Conklin.

Network with Peter Finch.

Cops: Henry Beckman and Willard Sage, *Young Men:* Bill Foster and Robert Ellis, *Cab Driver:* Harry Carey, Jr., *Dancer:* Gloria Gordon.

Niagara with Marilyn Monroe.

NETWORK (1976) UA. Produced by Howard Gottfried. Directed by Sidney Lumet. Original Story and Screenplay, Paddy Chayefsky. Presented by MGM. A Howard Gottfried/Paddy Chayefsky Production, in Panavision and MetroColor. Photography, Owen Roizman. Production Designer, Philip Rosenberg. Costume Designer, Theoni V. Aldredge. Editor, Alan Heim. Associate Producer, Fred Caruso. Original music composed and conducted by Elliot Lawrence. Assistant Directors, Jay Allan Hopkins and Ralph Singleton. Set Decorator, Edward Stewart. Dunaway's Make-up, Lee Harman. Dunaway's Hair, Susan Germaine. Make-up Artist, John Alese. Hairstylist, Phil Leto. Costumers, George Newman and Marilyn Putnam. UBS Video Logeo by Steve Rutt/ EUE Video Services. Last film of Peter Finch. Rated R. 120 minutes

Diana Christensen: Faye Dunaway, *Max Schumacher:* William Holden, *Howard Beale:* Peter Finch, *Frank Hackett:* Robert Duvall, *Louise Schumacher:* Beatrice Straight, *Arthur Jensen:* Ned Beatty, *Nelson Chaney:* Wesley Addy, *Bill Herron:* Darryl Hickman, *Laureen Hobbs:* Marlene Warfield, *Barbara Scheslinger:* Conchata Ferrell, *Great Ahmed Kahn:* Arthur Burghardt, *TV Director:* Bill Burrows, *George Bosch:* John Carpenter, *Harry Hunter:* Jordan Charney, *Mary Ann Gifford:* Kathy Cronkite, *Joe Donnelly:* Ed Crowley, *Walter C. Amundsen:* Jerome Dempsey, *Milton K. Steinman:* Gene Gross, *Jack Snowden:* Stanley Grover, *Caroline Schumacher:* Cindy Grover, *Arthur Zangwill:* Mitchell Jason, *TV Stage Manager:* Paul Jenkins, *Merrill Grant:* Ken Kercheval, *Associate Producer:* Kenneth Kimmins, *TV Production Assistant:* Lynn Klugman, *Max's Secretary:* Carolyn Krigbaum, *Audio Man:* Zane Lasky, *Tommy Pellegrino:* Michael Lipton, *Willie Stein:* Michael Lombard, *Herb Thackeray:* Pirie MacDonald, *TV Associate Director:* Russ Petranto, *Lou:* Bernard Pollock, *Sam Haywood:* Roy Poole, *Edward George Ruddy:* William Prince, *Helen Miggs:* Sasha von Scherler, *Robert McDonough:* Lane Smith, *Giannini:* Theodore Sorel, *Mosaic Figure:* Fred Stuthman, *TV Technical Director:* Cameron Thomas, *Hunter's Secretary:* Lydia Wilen, *Narrator:* Lee Richardson.

NIAGARA (1953) 20th. Produced by Charles Brackett. Directed by Henry Hathaway. Color by Technicolor. Story by Charles Brackett, Walter Reisch, Richard Breen. Music, Sol Kaplan. Art Directors, Lyle Wheeler and Maurice Ransford. Photography, Joe MacDonald. Editor, Barbara McLean. Filmed at Niagara Falls. 89 minutes

Rose Loomis: Marilyn Monroe, *George Loomis:* Joseph Cotten, *Polly Cutler:* Jean Peters, *Ray Cutler:* Casey Adams, *Inspector Starkey:* Denis O'Dea, *Patrick:* Richard Allan, *Mr. Kettering:* Don Wilson, *Mrs. Kettering:* Lurene Tuttle, *Mr. Qua:* Russell Collins, *Boatman:* Will Wright, *Doctor:* Lester Mathews, *Policeman:* Carleton Young, *Sam:* Sean McClory, *Landlady:* Minerva Urecal, *Wife:* Nina Varela, *Husband:* Tom Reynolds, *Straw Boss:* Winfield Hoeny, *Canadian Customs Officer:* Neil Fitzgerald, *Morris:* Norman McKay, *American Guide:* Gene (Baxter) Wesson, *Carillon Tower Guide:* George Ives, *Detective:* Patrick O'Moore, *Cab Driver:* Arch Johnson, *Motorcycle*

Night and Day with Cary Grant and Alexis Smith.

NIGHT AND DAY (1946) WB. Produced by Arthur Schwartz. Directed by Michael Curtiz. Based on the career and featuring the songs of Cole Porter (1891–1964). Color by Technicolor. Screenplay, Charles Hoffman, Leo Townsend, and William Bowers. Adaptation, Jack Moffitt. Art Director, John Hughes. Music Director, Leo F. Forbstein. Orchestral Arrangements, Ray Heindorf. Photography, Peverell Marley and William V. Skall. Technicolor Director, Natalie Kalmus. Production numbers orchestrated and conducted by Ray Heindorf. Dance Numbers, LeRoy Prinz. Additional Music, Max Steiner. Vocal Arrangements, Dudley Chambers. Montages, James Leicester. Sets, Armor Marlowe. Special Effects, Robert Burks. Editor, David Weisbart. Sound, Everett A. Brown and David Forrest. Songs by Cole Porter: "In the Still of the Night," "Old-Fashioned Garden," "Let's Do It," "You Do Something to Me," "Miss Otis Regrets," "What Is This Thing Called Love?", "I've Got You Under My Skin," "Just One of Those Things," "You're the Top," "I Get a Kick Out of You," "Easy to Love", "My Heart Belongs to Daddy," "Begin the Beguine" and "Night and Day." Film debut of Joe Kirkwood, Jr., later "Joe Palooka." 128 minutes

Cole Porter: Cary Grant, *Linda Lee Porter:* Alexis Smith, *Monty Woolley:* Monty Woolley, *Carole Hill:* Ginny Simms, *Gracie Harris:* Jane Wyman, *Gabrielle:* Eve Arden, *Anatole Giron:* Victor Francen, *Leon Dowling:* Alan Hale, *Nancy:* Dorothy Malone, *Bernie:* Tom D'Andrea, *Kate Porter:* Selena Royle, *Ward Blackburn:* Donald Woods, *Omer Cole:* Henry Stephenson, *Bart McClelland:* Paul

Cavanagh, *Willowsky*: Sig Rumann, *Specialty Singer*: Carlos Ramirez, *Specialty Dancer*: Milada Mladova, *Specialty Dancer*: George Zoritch, *Specialty Team*: Adam and Jayne DeGatano, *Specialty Dancer*: Estelle Sloan, *Mary Martin*: Mary Martin, *Petey*: John Alvin, *Caleb*: Clarence Muse, *O'Halloran*: George Riley, *Producer*: Howard Freeman, *Director*: Bobby Watson, *First "Peaches"*: John "Red" Pierson, *Second "Peaches"*: Herman Bing, *Classmate*: Joe Kirkwood, Jr., *Dean*: Boyd Davis, *Clarence, Piano Player*: Harry Seymour, *Tina*: JoAnn Marlowe, *Tina's Mother*: Regina Wallace, *Tina's Father*: Frank Ferguson, *Sexboat*: Lynne Baggett, *Chorus Girl*: Rebel Randall, *Red*: James Dodd, *Orchestra Leader*: Emile Hilb, *Customer*: Richard Erdman, *Customer*: Robert Arthur, *Wayne Blackburn as a boy*: George Nokes, *Cochran*: Gordon Richards, *Librettist*: Philip Van Zandt, *Chorine*: Joyce Compton, *Headwaiter*: Eddie Kane.

A Night At the Opera with Allan Jones, Sig Rumann, Harpo, Chico and Groucho Marx.

A NIGHT AT THE OPERA (1935) MGM. Produced by Irving Thalberg. Directed by Sam Wood. Story, James Kevin McGuinness. Screenplay, George S. Kaufman and Morrie Ryskind. Music Score, Herbert Stothart. Editor, William Levanway. Dances, Chester Hale. Photography, Merritt B. Gerstad. Songs: "Alone" by Nacio Herb Brown and Arthur Freed; "Cosi-Cosa" by Bronislau Kaper, Walter Jurmann, Ned Washington. The show was tested on the stage before filming. The first Marx Brothers film without Zeppo. 96 minutes

Otis B. Driftwood: Groucho Marx, *Fiorello*: Chico Marx, *Tomasso*: Harpo Marx, *Rosa Castaldi*: Kitty Carlisle, *Riccardo Baroni*: Allan Jones, *Rodolfo Lassparri*: Walter Woolf King, *Herman Gottlieb*: Sig Rumann, *Mrs. Claypool*: Margaret Dumont, *Captain*: Edward Keane, *Detective Henderson*: Robert Emmet O'Connor, *Steward*: Gino Corrado, *Mayor*: Purnell Pratt, *Engineer*: Frank Yaconelli, *Peasant*: Billy Gilbert, *Extra on Ship and at Dock*: Sam Marx, *Police Captain*: Claude Peyton, *Dancers*: Rita and Rubin, *Ruiz*: Luther Hoobyar, *Count di Luna*: Rodolfo Hoyos, *Azucena*: Olga Dane, *Ferrando*: James J. Wolf, *Maid*: Ines Palange, *Stage Manager*: Jonathan Hale, *Elevator Man*: Otto Fries, *Captain of Police*: William Gould, *Aviators*: Leo White, Jay Eaton, Rolfe Sedan, *Committee*: Wilbur Mack, George Irving, *Policeman*: George Guhl, *Sign Painter*: Harry Tyler, *Committee*: Phillips Smalley, Selmer Jackson, *Immigration Inspector*: Alan Bridge, *Doorman*: Harry Allen, *Louisa*: Lorraine Bridges, *Engineer's Assistant*: Jack Lipson.

NIGHT MUST FALL (1937) MGM. Produced by Hunt Stromberg. Directed by Richard Thorpe. From the play by Emlyn Williams. Screenplay, John Van Druten. Art Director, Cedric Gibbons. Music, Edward Ward. Photography, Ray June. Editor, Robert J. Kern. Remade by MGM as a British film in 1964. 117 minutes.

Danny: Robert Montgomery, *Olivia*: Rosalind Russell, *Mrs. Bramson*:

Dame May Whitty, *Justin*: Alan Marshal, *Dora*: Merle Tottenham, *Mrs. Terence*: Kathleen Harrison, *Belsize*: Matthew Boulton, *Nurse*: Eily Malyon, *Guide*: E. E. Clive, *Saleslady*: Beryl Mercer, *Mrs. Laurie*: Winifred Harris.

Night Must Fall with Robert Montgomery, Dame May Whitty and Rosalind Russell.

THE NIGHT OF THE IGUANA (1964) MGM. Producer, Ray Stark. Director, John Huston. Screenplay, Anthony Veiller, John Huston. Based on the play by Tennessee Williams. Director of Photography, Gabriel Figueroa. Music, Benjamin Frankel. An MGM Seven Arts Presentation. Assistant Director, Tom Shaw. 125 minutes

Reverend T. Lawrence Shannon: Richard Burton, *Maxine Faulk*: Ava Gardner, *Hannah Jelkes*: Deborah Kerr, *Charlotte Goodall*: Sue Lyon, *Hank Prosner*: James Ward, *Judith Fellowes*: Grayson Hall, *Nonno*: Cyril Delevanti, *Miss Peebles*: Mary Boylan, *Miss Dexter*: Gladys Hill, *Miss Throxton*: Billie Matticks, *Pepe*: Fidelmar Duran, *Pedro*: Roberto Leyva, *Chang*: C. G. Kim, *Teachers*: Eloise Hardt, Thelda Victor, Betty Proctor, Dorothy Vance, Liz Rubey, Bernice Starr, Barbara Joyce.

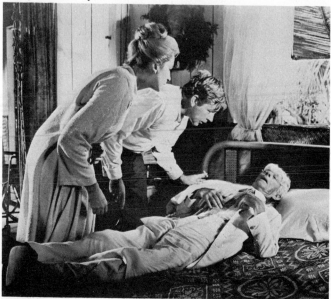

The Night of the Iguana with Deborah Kerr, Richard Burton and Cyril Delevanti.

NINOTCHKA (1939) MGM. Produced and directed by Ernst Lubitsch. Based on an original story by Melchior Lengyel. Screenplay, Charles Brackett, Billy Wilder, and Walter Reisch. Art Director, Cedric Gibbons. Associate, Randall Duell. Music, Werner R. Heymann. Photography, William Daniels. Editor, Gene Ruggiero. Sound,

Douglas Shearer. Make-up, Jack Dawn. Assistant Director, Horace Hough. Remade by MGM as *The Iron Petticoat* (1956) and *Silk Stockings* (1957). 110 minutes

Ninotchka (Lena Yakushova): Greta Garbo, *Count Leon Dalga*: Melvyn Douglas, *Grand Duchess Swana*: Ina Claire, *Michael Iranoff*: Sig Rumann, *Buljanoff*: Felix Bressart, *Kopalski*: Alexander Granach, *Commissar Razinin*: Bela Lugosi, *Count Alexis Rakonin*: Gregory Gaye, *Gaston*: Richard Carle, *Mercier*: Edwin Maxwell, *Hotel Manager*: Rolfe Sedan, *Russian Visa Official*: George Tobias, *Swana's Maid, Jacqueline*: Dorothy Adams, *General Savitsky*: Lawrence Grant, *Pere Mathieu, Cafe Owner*: Charles Judels, *Lawyer*: Frank Reicher, *Lawyer*: Edwin Stanley, *French Maid*: Peggy Moran, *Manager*: Marek Windheim, *Lady Lavenham*: Mary Forbes, *Bearded Man*: Alexander Schonberg, *Porter*: George Davis, *Louis (Headwaiter)*: Armand Kaliz, *Taxi Driver*: Wolfgang Zilzer, *Anna*: Tamara Shayne, *Bartender*: William Irving, *Gossip*: Bess Flowers, *Indignant Woman*: Elizabeth Williams, *Vladimir*: Paul Weigel, *Neighbor-Spy*: Harry Semels, *Streetcar Conductress*: Jody Gilbert, *Marianne*: Florence Shirley.

Ninotchka with Greta Garbo and Melvyn Douglas.

None But the Lonely Heart with Cary Grant and Ethel Barrymore.

NONE BUT THE LONELY HEART (1944) RKO. Producer, David Hempstead. Associate Producer, Sherman Todd. Director, Clifford Odets. From the novel by Richard Llewellyn. Screenplay, Clifford Odets. Art Directors, Albert S. D'Agostino, Jack Okey. Musical Score, Hanns Eisler. Musical Director, C. Bakaleinikoff. Cameraman, George Barnes. Special Effects, Vernon L. Walker. Editor, Roland Gross. 113 minutes

Ernie Mott: Cary Grant, *Ma Mott*: Ethel Barrymore, *Twite*: Barry Fitzgerald, *Ada*: June Duprez, *Aggie Hunter*: Jane Wyatt, *Jim Mordinoy*: George Coulouris, *Lew Tate*: Dan Duryea, *Ike Weber*: Konstantin Shayne, *Ma Chalmers*: Eva Leonard Boyne, *Taz*: Morton Lowry, *Sister Nurse*: Helene Thimig, *Knocker*: William Challee, *Blake*: Forrester Harvey, *Rossi*: Chef Milani, *Madam La Vaka*: Marie De Becker, *Cash*: Joseph Vitale, *Dad Pettyjohn*: Roman Bohnen, *Flo*: Renie Riano, *Percy*: Marcel Dill, *Lame Girl*: Amelia Romano, *Ma Snowden*: Queenie Vassar, *Mrs. Tate*: Rosalind Ivan, *Marjoriebanks*: Art Smith, *Barmaid*: Claire Verdera, *Millie Wilson*: Katherine Allen, *Defeated Man*: Charles Thompson, *Miss Tate*: Diedra Vale, *Dad Fitchitt*: Herbert Heywood, *Ma Segwiss*: Virginia Farmer, *Pa Floom*: Walter Soderling, *Ma Floom*: Polly Bailey, *Blind Man*: Bill Wolfe, *Dancer*: Barry Regan, *Ike Lesser*: Milton Wallace, *Dancer*: Rosemary Blong, *Dancer*: Jack Jackson, *Dancer*: Rosemary La Planche, *Slush*: Skelton Knaggs.

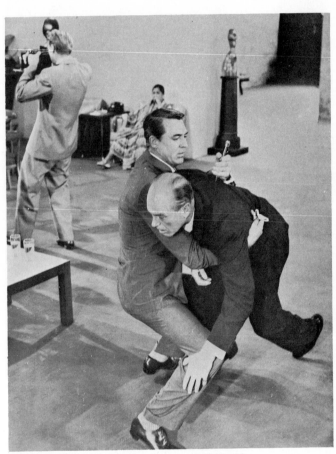

North by Northwest with Cary Grant and Philip Ober.

NORTH BY NORTHWEST (1959) MGM. Produced and directed by Alfred Hitchcock. Associate Producer, Herbert Coleman. Technicolor and VistaVision. Screenplay, Ernest Lehman. Music, Bernard Herrmann. Art Directors, William A. Horning and Merrill Pye. Assistant Director, Robert Saunders. Photography, Robert Burks. Editor, George Tomasini. Filmed on location: Plaza Hotel Oak Room, N.Y.C.; UN Building; Grand Central Station; Long Island; Chicago's Ambassador East; Indiana plains; Mount Rushmore, South Dakota. 136 minutes

Roger Thornhill: Cary Grant, *Eve Kendall*: Eva Marie Saint, *Phillip Vandamm*: James Mason, *Clara Thornhill*: Jessie Royce Landis, *Professor*: Leo G. Carroll, *Lester Townsend*: Philip Ober, *Handsome Woman*: Josephine Hutchinson, *Leonard*: Martin Landau, *Valerian*: Adam Williams, *Victor Larrabee*: Edward Platt, *Licht*: Robert Ellenstein, *Auctioneer:* Les Tremayne, *Dr. Cross:* Philip Coolidge, *Captain Junket:* Edward Binns, *Chicago Policemen:* Pat McVey, Ken Lynch, *Sergeant Emile Klinger:* John Beradino, *Housekeeper, Anna:* Nora Marlowe, *Maggie:* Doreen Lang, *Judge Anson B. Flynn:* Alexander Lockwood, *Lieutenant Harding:* Stanley Adams, *Cartoonist:* Larry Dobkin, *Stock Broker:* Harvey Stephens, *Reporter:* Walter Coy, *Housewife:* Madge Kennedy, *Elevator Starter:* Tommy Farrell, *Captain of Waiters:* Harry Seymour, *Weltner:* Frank Wilcox, *Larry Wade:* Robert Shayne, *Fanning Nelson:* Carleton Young, *Lieutenant Hagerman:* Paul Genge, *Patrolman Waggoner:* Robert B. Williams, *Maid, Elsie:* Maudie Prickett, *Valet:* James McCallion, *Taxi Driver:* Baynes Barron, *Indian Girl:* Doris Singh, *Girl Attendants:* Sally Fraser, Susan Whitney, Maura McGiveney, *Ticket Agent:* Ned Glass, *Conductor:* Howard Negley, *Woman:* Jesslyn Fax, *Steward:* Jack Daly, *Man on Road:* Malcolm Atterbury, *Assistant Auctioneer:* Olan Soule, *Woman Bidder:* Helen Spring, *Bit:* Patricia Cutts, *Ranger:* Dale Van Sickel, *Cab Driver, Dakota:* Frank Marlowe, *Assistant Conductor:* Harry Strang, *Telephone Operator:* Sara Berner, *Man Who Misses Bus:* Alfred Hitchcock.

North to Alaska with Fabian, Stewart Granger, John Wayne and Mickey Shaughnessy.

NORTH TO ALASKA (1960) 20th. Produced and directed by Henry Hathaway. CinemaScope and De Luxe Color. Based on the play *Birthday Gift* by Laszlo Fodor, from an idea by John Kafka. Screenplay, John Lee Mahin, Martin Rackin, and Claude Binyon. Music, Lionel Newman. Orchestration, Urban Thielmann and Bernard Mayers. Costumes, Bill Thomas. Choreography, Josephine Earl. Assistant Director, Stanley Hough. Art Directors, Duncan Cramer and Jack Martin Smith. Cinematography, Leon Shamroy. Special Effects, L. B. Abbott and Emil Kosa, Jr. Editor, Dorothy Spencer. Song by Russell Faith, Robert P. Marcucci and Peter DeAngelis: "If You Knew." 122 minutes

Sam McCord: John Wayne, *George Pratt:* Stewart Granger, *Frankie Canon:* Ernie Kovacs, *Billy Pratt:* Fabian, *Michelle:* Capucine, *Boggs:* Mickey Shaughnessy, *Lars:* Karl Swenson, *Commissioner:* Joe Sawyer, *Lena:* Kathleen Freeman, *Lumberjack:* John Qualen, *Breezy:* Stanley Adams, *Duggan:* Stephen Courtleigh, *Lieutenant:* Douglas Dick, *Sergeant:* Jerry O'Sullivan, *Mack:* Ollie O'Toole, *Arnie:* Frank Faylen, *Ole:* Fred Graham, *Bartender:* Alan Carney, *Olaf:* Peter Bourne, *Gold Buyers:* Charles Seel, Rayford Barnes, *Lumberjacks:* Fortune Gordien, Roy Jenson, *Sourdough:* Joey Faye, *Woman at Picnic:* Esther Dale, *Captain:* Oscar Beregi, *Skinny Sourdough:* Richard Collier, *Desk Clerk:* Richard Deacon, *Bish, the Waiter:* Max Mellinger, *Queen Lil:* Arlene Harris, *Pony Dancer:* Pamela Raymond, *Butler:* Marcel Hillaire, *Jenny:* Lilyan Chauvin, *Bartender:* Maurice Delamore, *Specialty Dancer:* Patty Wharton, *Coachman:* Johnny Lee, *Barber:* Tom Dillon, *Speaker:* James Griffith, *Purser:* Tudor Owen, *Townsman (Extra):* Kermit Maynard.

NORTH WEST MOUNTED POLICE (1940) Par. Producer, Cecil B. De Mille. Associate Producer, William H. Pine. Director, Cecil

B. De Mille. Author, R. C. Fetherstonhaugh (from *Royal Canadian Mounted Police*). Screenplay, Alan Le May, Jesse Lasky, Jr., C. Gardner Sullivan. Cameramen, Victor Milner, Duke Green. Song by Frank Loesser and Victor Young: "Does the Moon Shine Through the Tall Pine?" Associate Director, Arthur Rosson. Assistant Director, Eric Stacey. Second Unit Camera, Dewey Wrigley. 125 minutes

Dusty Rivers: Gary Cooper, *April Logan:* Madeleine Carroll, *Louvette Corbeau:* Paulette Goddard, *Sergeant Jim Brett:* Preston Foster, *Ronnie Logan:* Robert Preston, *Jacques Corbeau:* George Bancroft, *Tod McDuff:* Lynne Overman, *Dan Duroc:* Akim Tamiroff, *Big Bear:* Walter Hampden, *Shorty:* Lon Chaney, Jr., *Inspector Cabot:* Montagu Love, *Louis Riel:* Francis McDonald, *Johnny Pelang:* George E. Stone, *Supt. Harrington:* Willard Robertson, *Constable Jerry Moore:* Regis Toomey, *Constable Thornton:* Richard Denning, *Constable Carter:* Douglas Kennedy, *Constable Dumont:* Robert Ryan, *Constable Fenton:* James Seay, *Constable Fyffe:* Lane Chandler, *Constable Ackroyd:* Ralph Byrd, *Constable Kent:* Eric Alden, *Constable Rankin:* Wallace Reid, Jr., *Constable Herrick:* Bud Geary, *Captain Gower:* Evan Thomas, *Sergeant Field:* Jack Pennick, *Corporal Underhill:* Rod Cameron, *Surgeon Roberts:* Davison Clark, *Bugler:* Jack Chapin, *Wandering Spirit:* Chief Thundercloud, *The Crow:* Harry Burns, *Lesur:* Lou Merrill, *Mrs. Burns:* Clara Blandick, *Mrs. Shorty:* Ynez Seabury, *Ekawo:* Eva Puig, *Wapiskau:* Julia Faye, *Freddie:* George Regas, *Niska:* Norma Nelson, *Corporal:* John Laird, *Constable Grove:* James Dundee, *Constable Cameron:* Weldon Heyburn, *Constable Judson:* Phillip Terry, *Constable Porter:* Kermit Maynard, *George Higgins:* Emory Parnell.

North West Mounted Police with Preston Foster, Gary Cooper and Lynne Overman.

NORTHWEST PASSAGE (1940) MGM. Produced by Hunt Stromberg. Directed by King Vidor. Color by Technicolor. Based on the novel *Northwest Passage*, Book I, "Rogers' Rangers," by Kenneth Roberts. Screenplay, Laurence Stallings and Talbot Jennings. Technicolor Director, Natalie Kalmus. Art Director, Cedric Gibbons. Associate, Malcolm Brown. Music, Herbert Stothart. Photography, Sidney Wagner and William V. Skall. Sound, Douglas Shearer. Editor, Conrad A. Nervig. Make-up, Jack Dawn. Assistant Director, Robert Golden. Later the basis for a TV series. 126 minutes

Major Robert Rogers: Spencer Tracy, *Langdon Towne:* Robert Young, *Hunk Marriner:* Walter Brennan, *Elizabeth Browne:* Ruth Hussey, *Cap Huff:* Nat Pendleton, *Reverend Browne:* Louis Hector, *Humphrey Towne:* Robert Barrat, *General Amherst:* Lumsden Hare, *Sergeant McNott:* Donald MacBride, *Jennie Coit:* Isabel Jewell, *Lieutenant Avery:* Douglas Walton, *Lieutenant Crofton:* Addison Richards, *Jesse Beacham:* Hugh Sothern, *Webster:* Regis Toomey, *Wiseman Clagett:* Montagu Love, *Sam Livermore:* Lester Mathews, *Captain Ogden:* Truman Bradley, *Konkapot:* Andrew Pena, *A Ranger:* Tom London, *A Ranger:* Eddie Parker, *Richard Towne:* Don Castle, *Eben Towne:* Rand Brooks, *Odiorne Towne:* Kent Rogers, *Mrs. Towne:*

Verna Felton, *Sheriff Packer:* Richard Cramer, *Bradley McNeil:* Ray Teal, *Captain Butterfield:* Edward Gargan, *Lieutenant Dunbar:* John Merton, *MacPherson:* Gibson Gowland, *Captain Grant:* Frank Hagney, *Mrs. Brown:* Gwendolen Logan, *Jane Browne:* Addie McPhail, *Sarah Hadden:* Helen MacKellar, *Flint, Innkeeper:* Arthur Aylesworth, *Farrington:* Ted Oliver, *Billy, Indian Boy:* Lawrence Porter, *Captain Jacobs:* Tony Guerrero, *Stoodley:* Ferdinand Munier, *McMullen:* George Eldredge, *Solomon:* Robert St. Angelo, *Captain Williams:* Denis Green, *Turner:* Peter George Lynn, *Sir William Johnson:* Frederic Worlock, *A Ranger:* Hank Worden.

Northwest Passage with Truman Bradley, Spencer Tracy and Robert Young.

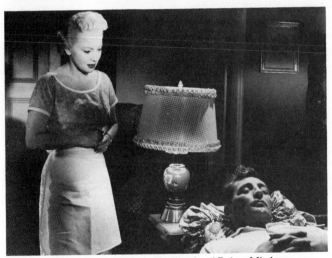

Not As a Stranger with Olivia de Havilland and Robert Mitchum.

NOT AS A STRANGER (1955) UA. Producer-Director, Stanley Kramer. Screenplay by Edna and Edward Anhalt. Based on the novel by Morton Thompson. Music by George Antheil. Song by Jimmy Van Heusen and Buddy Kaye. Assistant Director, Carter DeHaven, Jr. Gowns by Don Loper. 135 minutes

Kristina Hedvigson: Olivia de Havilland, *Lucas Marsh:* Robert Mitchum, *Alfred Boone:* Frank Sinatra, *Harriet Lang:* Gloria Grahame, *Dr. Aarons:* Broderick Crawford, *Dr. Runkleman:* Charles Bickford, *Dr. Snider:* Myron McCormick, *Job Marsh:* Lon Chaney, *Ben Cosgrove:* Jesse White, *Oley:* Harry Morgan, *Brundage:* Lee Marvin, *Bruni:* Virginia Christine, *Dr. Dietrich:* Whit Bissell, *Dr. Lettering:* Jack Raine, *Miss O'Dell:* Mae Clarke.

NO TIME FOR SERGEANTS (1958) WB. Produced and directed by Mervyn LeRoy. From the TV and Broadway play by Ira Levin, based on the novel by Mac Hyman. Screenplay, John Lee Mahin. Music,

Ray Heindorf. Assistant Director, Dick Moder. Photography, Harold Rosson. Art Director, Malcolm Brown. Editor, William Ziegler. Sound, Stanley Jones. Sammy Jackson starred as Will on the 1964–65 TV series of the same name. Griffith starred in the stage and TV versions; McCormick repeats his stage role. Film debut of Don Knotts. 111 minutes.

Will Stockdale (Narrator): Andy Griffith, *Sergeant King:* Myron McCormick, *Ben Whitledge:* Nick Adams, *Irvin Blanchard:* Murray Hamilton, *General Bush:* Howard Smith, *Lieutenant Bridges:* Will Hutchins, *General Pollard:* Sydney Smith, *Psychiatrist:* James Milhollin, *Corporal Brown:* Don Knotts, *W. A. F. Captain:* Jean Willes, *Captain:* Bartlett Robinson, *Lieutenant Cover:* Henry McCann, *Draft Board Man:* Dub Taylor, *Pa Stockdale:* William Fawcett, *Colonel:* Raymond Bailey, *Lieutenant Gardella:* Jameel Farah (Jamie Farr), *Lieutenant Kendall:* Bob Stratton, *Sheriff:* Jack Mower, *Man with Applications:* Malcolm Atterbury, *Rosabelle:* Peggy Hallack, *Inductees:* Sammy Jackson, Rad Fulton, *Tiger:* Dan Barton, *Supervising Sergeant:* Francis De Sales, *Oculist:* Robert Sherman, *Infantryman:* Dick Wessel, *Senator:* Tom Browne Henry, *Charles, Aide:* Tom McKee, *Baker:* George Neise, *Abel:* Benny Baker, *Sentry:* Fred Coby, *M.P.:* John Close, *Announcer's Voice:* Verne Smith.

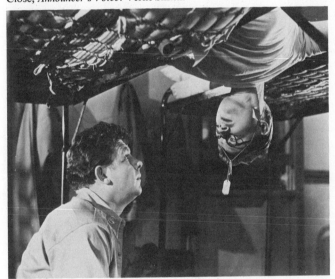

No Time for Sergeants with Andy Griffith and Nick Adams.

Notorious with Ingrid Bergman and Cary Grant.

NOTORIOUS (1946) RKO. Producer-Director, Alfred Hitchcock. Screenplay, Ben Hecht. Art Directors, Albert S. D'Agostino, Carroll Clark. Musical Score, Roy Webb. Musical Director, C. Bakaleinikoff. Cameraman, Ted Tetzlaff. Special Effects, Vernon L. Walker, Paul Eagler. Editor, Theron Warth. 103 minutes

Devlin: Cary Grant, *Alicia Huberman:* Ingrid Bergman, *Alexander Sebastian:* Claude Rains, *Paul Prescott:* Louis Calhern, *Mme. Sebastian:* Madame Konstantin, *"Dr. Anderson":* Reinhold Schunzel, *Walter Beardsley:* Moroni Olsen, *Eric Mathis:* Ivan Triesault, *Joseph:* Alex Minotis, *Mr. Hopkins:* Wally Brown, *Ernest Weylin:* Gavin Gordon, *Commodore:* Sir Charles Mendl, *Dr. Barbosa:* Ricardo Costa, *Hupka:* Eberhard Krumschmidt, *Ethel:* Fay Baker, *Señor Ortiza:* Antonio Moreno, *Knerr:* Frederick Ledebur, *Dr. Silva:* Luis Serrano, *Adams:* William Gordon, *Judge:* Charles D. Brown, *Dr. Silva:* Ramon Nomar, *Rossner:* Peter Von Zerneck, *Huberman:* Fred Nurney, *Mr. Cook:* Herbert Wyndham, *Defense Counsel:* Harry Hayden, *Clerk of Court:* Dink Trout, *District Attorney:* Warren Jackson, *Bailiff:* Howard Mitchell, *Motor Cop:* Garry Owen, *Mrs. Jackson:* Patricia Smart, *Motor Cop:* Lester Dorr, *Maid:* Tina Menard, *Ribero:* Alfredo DeSa, *File Clerks:* Bea Benaderet, Virginia Gregg, Bernice Barrett.

No Way Out with Sidney Poitier and Richard Widmark.

NO WAY OUT (1950) 20th. Producer, Darryl F. Zanuck. Director, Joseph Mankiewicz. Authors-Screenplay, Joseph Mankiewicz, Lesser Samuels. Music, Alfred Newman. Art Directors, Lyle Wheeler, George W. Davis. Photography, Milton Krasner. Editor, Barbara McLean. Film debut of Sidney Poitier. 106 minutes

Ray Biddle: Richard Widmark, *Edie:* Linda Darnell, *Dr. Wharton:* Stephen McNally, *Dr. Luther Brooks:* Sidney Poitier, *Cora:* Mildred Joanne Smith, *George Biddle:* Harry Bellaver, *Dr. Moreland:* Stanley Ridges, *Lefty:* Dots Johnson, *Gladys:* Amanda Randolph, *Connie:* Ruby Dee, *John:* Ossie Davis, *Whitey:* George Tyne, *Rocky:* Bert Freed, *Luther's Mother:* Maude Simmons, *Kowalsky:* Ken Christy, *Mac:* Frank Richards, *Assistant Deputy:* Robert Adler, *Deputy Sheriff:* Jim Toney, *Day Deputy:* Ray Teal, *Dr. Cheney:* Will Wright, *Jonah:* Wade Dumas, *Ambulance Driver:* Fred Graham, *Ambulance Doctor:* William Pullen, *Henry:* Jasper Weldon, *Polish Husband:* Ruben Wendorf, *Polish Wife:* Laiola Wendorf, *Johnny Biddle:* Dick Paxton, *Internes:* Stan Johnson, Frank Overton, *Landlady:* Kitty O'Neil, *Joe:* Emmett Smith, *Terry:* Ralph Hodges, *Priest:* Thomas Ingersoll, *Man:* Jack Kruschen.

NOW, VOYAGER (1942) WB. Producer, Hal B. Wallis. Director, Irving Rapper. From the novel by Olive Higgins Prouty. Screenplay, Casey Robinson. Art Director, Robert Haas. Cameraman, Sol Polito. Editor, Warren Low. Song: "It Can't Be Wrong" by Kim Gannon and Max Steiner. 117 minutes

Charlotte Vale: Bette Davis, *Jerry (J. D.) Durrence:* Paul Henreid, *Dr. Jaquith:* Claude Rains, *Mrs. Vale:* Gladys Cooper, *June Vale:* Bonita Granville, *Elliott Livingston:* John Loder, *Lisa Vale:* Ilka Chase, *"Deb" McIntyre:* Lee Patrick, *Frank McIntyre:* James Rennie, *Leslie Trotter:* Charles Drake, *Miss Trask:* Katharine Alexander,

Tina: Janis Wilson, *Dora Pickford:* Mary Wickes, *Dr. Dan Regan:* Michael Ames (Tod Andrews), *Mr. Thompson:* Franklin Pangborn, *William:* David Clyde, *Hilda:* Claire du Brey, *George Weston:* Don Douglas, *Grace Weston:* Charlotte Wynters, *Manoel:* Frank Puglia, *Captain:* Lester Mathews, *Katie:* Sheila Hayward, *Passenger:* Mary Field, *Celestine:* Yola d'Avril, *M. Henri:* Georges Renavent, *Hamilton Hunneker:* Bill Kennedy, *Henry Montague:* Reed Hadley, *Woman:* Dorothy Vaughan, *Aunt Hester:* Elspeth Dudgeon, *Uncle Herbert:* George Lessey, *Lloyd:* Ian Wolfe, *Rosa:* Constance Purdy, *Hilary:* Corbett Morris, *Justine:* Hilda Plowright, *Mrs. Smith:* Tempe Pigott.

Now, Voyager with Bette Davis, Ilka Chase and John Loder.

THE NUN'S STORY (1959) WB. Producer, Henry Blanke. Director, Fred Zinnemann. Technicolor. From the book by Kathryn C. Hulme. Screenplay, Robert Anderson. Art Director, Alexander Trauner. Music composed and conducted by Franz Waxman. Cinematographer, Franz Planer. Editor, Walter Thompson. Filmed in Rome, Belgium, the Belgian Congo. 149 minutes

Sister Luke: Audrey Hepburn, *Dr. Fortunati:* Peter Finch, *Mother Emmanuel:* Edith Evans, *Mother Mathilde:* Peggy Ashcroft, *Dr. Van Der Mal:* Dean Jagger, *Sister Margharita:* Mildred Dunnock, *Mother Christophe:* Beatrice Straight, *Sister William:* Patricia Collinge, *Simone:* Patricia Bosworth, *Mother Marcella:* Ruth White, *Mother Katherine:* Barbara O'Neil, *Sister Pauline:* Margaret Phillips, *Archangel:* Colleen Dewhurst, *Sister Augustine:* Molly Urquhart, *Sister Aurelie:* Dorothy Alison, *Father Vermeuhlen:* Niall MacGinnis, *Sister Eleanor:* Rosalie Crutchley, *Kalulu:* Orlando Martins, *Sister Marie:* Eva Kotthaus, *Illunga:* Errol John, *Louise:* Jeannette Sterke, *Pierre:* Richard O'Sullivan, *Marie:* Marina Wolkonsky, *Jeannette Milonet:* Penelope Horner, *Pascin:* Charles Lamb, *Sister Bernard:* Ave Ninchi, *Bishop:* Ludovice Bonhomme, *Doctor Coovaerts:* Lionel Jeffries, *Sister Ellen:* Dara Gavin, *Sister Timothy:* Elfrida Simbari.

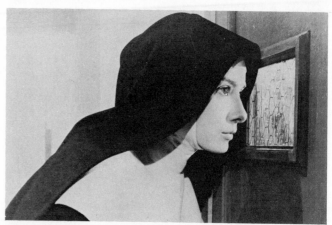

The Nun's Story with Audrey Hepburn.

The Nutty Professor with Jerry Lewis.

THE NUTTY PROFESSOR (1963) Par. Producer, Ernest D. Glucksman. Associate Producer, Arthur P. Schmidt. Director, Jerry Lewis. Technicolor. Screenplay, Jerry Lewis, Bill Richmond. Art Directors, Hal Pereira, Walter Tyler. Music scored and conducted by Walter Scharf. "We've Got a World That Swings," lyrics, Lil Mattis, music, Yule Brown. "Stella by Starlight," "That Old Black Magic." Cinematographer, Wallace Kelley. Special Photographic Effects, Paul K. Lerpae. Editor, John Woodcock. 107 minutes

Professor Julius Ferris Kelp/Buddy Love: Jerry Lewis, *Stella Purdy:* Stella Stevens, *Dr. Warfield:* Del Moore, *Millie Lemmon:* Kathleen Freeman, *College Student:* Med Flory, *College Student:* Norman Alden, *Kelp's Father:* Howard Morris, *Kelp's Mother:* Elvia Allman, *Dr. Leevee:* Milton Frome, *Bartender:* Buddy Lester, *English Boy:* Marvin Kaplan, *College Student:* David Landfield, *College Student:* Skip Ward, *College Student:* Julie Parrish, *College Student:* Henry Gibson, *Boy:* Gary Lewis, *Bartender:* Dave Willock, *Rube:* Doodles Weaver, *Cab Driver:* Mushy Callahan, *Salesman Clothier:* Gavin Gordon, *College Student:* Celeste Yarnall, *Girl Student:* Francine York, *Faculty Member:* Joe Forte, *Cigarette Girl:* Terry Higgins, *Judo Instructor:* Murray Alper.

Ocean's 11 with Frank Sinatra, Peter Lawford and Richard Conte.

OCEAN'S 11 (1960) WB. Produced and directed by Lewis Milestone. Associate Producers, Henry W. Sanicola and Milton Ebbins. Assistant Director, Ray Gosnell, Jr. In Technicolor and Panavision. Screenplay, Harry Brown and Charles Lederer. Story, George Clayton Johnson and Jack Golden Russell. Music composed and conducted by Nelson Riddle. Orchestration, Arthur Morton. Art Director, Nicolai Remisoff. Costumes, Howard Shoup. Cinematography, William H. Daniels. Editor,

Philip W. Anderson. A Dorchester Production. Songs by Sammy Cahn and James Van Heusen: "Ain't That a Kick in the Head," "Ee-O-Leven." Filmed in Las Vegas. 127 minutes

Danny Ocean: Frank Sinatra, *Sam Harmon:* Dean Martin, *Josh Howard:* Sammy Davis, Jr., *Jimmy Foster:* Peter Lawford, *Beatrice Ocean:* Angie Dickinson, *Anthony Bergdorf:* Richard Conte, *Duke Santos:* Cesar Romero, *Adele Ekstrom:* Patrice Wymore, *Mushy O'Conners:* Joey Bishop, *Spyros Acebos:* Akim Tamiroff, *Roger Corneal:* Henry Silva, *Mrs. Restes:* Ilka Chase, *Vincent Massler:* Buddy Lester, *Rheimer:* Norman Fell, *Louis Jackson:* Clem Harvey, *Mr. Kelly:* Hank Henry, *Mr. Cohen:* Charles Meredith, *Delores:* Anne Neyland, *Helen:* Joan Staley, *Proprietor:* George E. Stone, *Customer:* Marjorie Bennett, *De Wolfe:* Louis Quinn, *Sugarface:* Laura Cornell, *Texan:* John Indrisano, *Snake Dancer:* Shiva, *Major Taylor:* Steve Pendleton, *Timmy:* Ronnie Dapo, *Hungry Girl:* Carmen Phillips, *Police Officer:* Paul Bryar, *Client:* Red Skelton, *Cashier:* John Craven, *Jealous Young Man:* Lew Gallo, *Man:* John Holland, *First Girl:* Shirley MacLaine, *Second Girl:* Barbara Sterling, *Deputy:* Murray Alper, *TV Newscaster:* Tom Middleton, *Roadblock Deputy:* Hoot Gibson, *Riviera Manager:* Sparky Kaye, *Sands Manager:* Forrest Lederer, *Jack Strager:* George Raft, *Castleman:* Rummy Bishop, *Freeman:* Gregory Gay, *McCoy:* Don "Red" Barry, *Parelli:* William Justine.

The Odd Couple with Walter Matthau and Jack Lemmon.

THE ODD COUPLE (1968) Par. Produced by Howard W. Koch. Directed by Gene Saks. Screenplay by Neil Simon, based on his 1965 play which starred Art Carney and Walter Matthau; later a TV series with Tony Randall and Jack Klugman. Music by Neal Hefti. Art Direction, Hal Pereira and Walter Tyler. Set Decorations, Robert Benton and Ray Moyer. Photography, Robert A. Hauser. Editor, Frank Bracht. Sound, John Carter and Charles Grenzbach. Costumes, Jack Bear. Make-up, Wally Westmore. Hairstyles, Nellie Manley. Production Manager, William C. Davidson. Assistant Director, Hank Moonjean. In Panavision and Technicolor. Scenes filmed in New York. 105 minutes

Felix Ungar: Jack Lemmon, *Oscar Madison:* Walter Matthau, *Vinnie:* John Fiedler, *Murray:* Herb Edelman, *Roy:* David Sheiner, *Speed:* Larry Haines, *Cecily Pigeon:* Monica Evans, *Gwendolyn Pigeon:* Carole Shelley, *Waitress:* Iris Adrian, *Sportswriter:* Heywood Hale Broun, *Hotel Clerk:* John C. Becher.

OF HUMAN BONDAGE (1934) RKO. Produced by Pandro S. Berman. Directed by John Cromwell. Based on the novel by Somerset Maugham. Screenplay, Lester Cohen. Photography, Henry W. Gerrard. Editor, William Morgan. Remakes: Warner Brothers, 1946; MGM, 1964. 83 minutes

Philip Carey: Leslie Howard, *Mildred Rogers:* Bette Davis, *Sally Athelny:* Frances Dee, *Athelny:* Reginald Owen, *Harry Griffiths:* Reginald Denny, *Norah:* Kay Johnson, *Emil:* Alan Hale, *Dunsford:* Reginald Sheffield, *Dr. Jacobs:* Desmond Roberts, *Landlady:* Tempe Pigott.

Of Human Bondage with Reginald Owen and Leslie Howard.

Of Mice and Men with Burgess Meredith and Lon Chaney, Jr.

OF MICE AND MEN (1939) UA. Producer, Lewis Milestone. Associate Producer, Frank Ross. Director, Lewis Milestone. Based on the novel by John Steinbeck. Screenplay, Eugene Solow. Art Director, Nicolai Remisoff. Musical Score, Aaron Copland. Cameraman, Norbert Brodine. Photographic Effects, Roy Seawright. Editor, Bert Jordan. Also produced on the stage by Sam H. Harris, staged by George S. Kaufman. 107 minutes

George: Burgess Meredith, *Mae:* Betty Field, *Lennie:* Lon Chaney, Jr., *Slim:* Charles Bickford, *Candy:* Roman Bohnen, *Curley:* Bob Steele, *Whit:* Noah Beery, Jr., *Jackson:* Oscar O'Shea, *Carlson:* Granville Bates, *Crooks:* Leigh Whipper, *Aunt Clara:* Leona Roberts, *Susie:* Helen Lynd, *Second Girl:* Barbara Pepper, *Third Girl:* Henriette Kaye, *Bus Driver:* Eddie Dunn, *Sheriff:* Howard Mitchell, *Ranch Hands:* Whitney de Rhan, Baldy Cooke, Charles Watt, Jack Lawrence, Carl Pitti, John Beach.

OH, GOD! (1977) WB. Produced by Jerry Weintraub. Directed by Carl Reiner. Based on the novel by Avery Corman. Screenplay, Larry Gelbart. Technicolor. Photography, Victor Kemper. Editor, Bud Molin. Art

Director, Jack Senter. Music by Jack Elliott. Assistant Director, Bob Birnbaum. 2nd Assistant Directors, Victor Hsu and David Nicksay. Make-up, Leo Lotito. Hairdresser, Ruby Ford. Assistant Editor, Ron Spang. Set Decorator, Stuart Reiss. Production Mixer, Richard Wagner. Wardrobe, Michael J. Harte and Nancy McArdle. Denver's film debut. Rated PG. 104 minutes

God: George Burns, *Jerry Landers:* John Denver, *Bobbie Landers:* Teri Garr, *Sam Raven:* Ralph Bellamy, *Herself:* Dinah Shore, *Bishop Reardon:* Barry Sullivan, *Dr. Harmon:* Donald Pleasence, *George Summers:* William Daniels, *Judge Baker:* Barnard Hughes, *Rev. Willie Williams:* Paul Sorvino, *Rabbi Silverstein:* Jeff Corey, *Briggs:* George Furth, *Mr. McCarthy:* David Ogden Stiers, *Bishop Makros:* Titos Vandis, *Adam Landers:* Moosie Drier, *Becky Landers:* Rachel Longacker, *Interview Guest:* Carl Reiner, *Girl:* Zane Buzby.

Oh, God! with John Denver and Teri Garr.

Oklahoma! with Gordon MacRae and Shirley Jones.

OKLAHOMA! (1955) Magna. Producer, Arthur Hornblow, Jr. Director, Fred Zinnemann. Music by Richard Rodgers. Book and lyrics by Oscar Hammerstein II. Screenplay by Sonya Levien and William Ludwig. Choreography by Agnes De Mille. Costumes by Orry-Kelly and Motley. Adapted from Rodgers and Hammerstein's musical which was based on a play, *Green Grow the Lilacs,* by Lynn Riggs. Assistant Director, Arthur Black, Jr. Production designed by Oliver Smith. Music conducted and supervised by Jay Blackton. Editor, Gene Ruggiero. Songs: "Oklahoma!" "Oh What a Beautiful Mornin," "The Surrey With the Fringe on Top," "Everything's Up-to-Date in Kansas City," "Many a New Day," "People Will Say We're in Love," "The Farmer and the Cowman," "I Can't Say No," "All Er Nuthin,"

202

"Pore Jud." A Rodgers and Hammerstein Production filmed in Eastman Color and Todd-AO. Film debut of Shirley Jones. 145 minutes

Curly: Gordon MacRae, *Ado Annie:* Gloria Grahame, *Will Parker:* Gene Nelson, *Aunt Eller:* Charlotte Greenwood, *Laurey:* Shirley Jones, *Ali Hakim:* Eddie Albert, *Carnes:* James Whitmore, *Jud Fry:* Rod Steiger, *Gertie:* Barbara Lawrence, *Skidmore:* Jay C. Flippen, *Marshal:* Roy Barcroft, *Dream Curly:* James Mitchell, *Dream Laurey:* Bambi Linn, *Dancers:* James Mitchell, Bambi Linn, Jennie Workman, Kelly Brown, Marc Platt, Lizanne Truex, Virginia Bosler, Evelyn Taylor, Jane Fischer, *Cowboy at Train Depot:* Ben Johnson.

The Old Maid with Bette Davis and Miriam Hopkins.

THE OLD MAID (1939) WB. Producer, Hal B. Wallis. Associate Producer, Henry Blanke. Director, Edmund Goulding. Authors, Zoe Akins, Edith Wharton. Screenplay, Casey Robinson. Art Director, Robert Haas. Music, Max Steiner. Orchestral Arrangements, Hugo Freidhofer. Musical Director, Leo F. Forbstein. Cameraman, Tony Gaudio. Editor, George Amy. 95 minutes

Charlotte Lovell: Bette Davis, *Delia Lovell:* Miriam Hopkins, *Clem Spender:* George Brent, *Tina:* Jane Bryan, *Doctor Lanskell:* Donald Crisp, *Dora:* Louise Fazenda, *Jim Ralston:* James Stephenson, *Joe Ralston:* Jerome Cowan, *Lanning Halsey:* William Lundigan, *Grandmother Lovell:* Cecilia Loftus, *Jim:* Rand Brooks, *Dee:* Janet Shaw, *John:* DeWolf Hopper, *Tina as a child:* Marlene Burnett, *Man:* Rod Cameron, *Aristocratic Maid:* Doris Lloyd, *Mr. Halsey:* Frederick Burton.

THE OMEN (1976) 20th. Produced by Harvey Bernhard. Directed by Richard Donner. Written by David Seltzer. Executive Producer, Mace Neufeld. Associate Producer, Charles Orme. Music by Jerry Goldsmith. Assistant Director, David Tomblin. Photography, Gilbert Taylor. Sound Recordist, Gordon Everett. Art Director, Carmen Dillon. Assistant Art Director, George Richardson. Set Dresser, Tessa Davies. Special Effects, John Richardson. Editor, Stuart Baird. Wardrobe Supervisor, G. W. Nicholls. Chief Make-up, Stuart Freeborn. Hairdresser, Pat McDermott. Religious Advisers, Rev. Don Williams, Ph.D., and Robert L. Munger. Filmed in Rome, Jerusalem, England and at Pyrford Court near Ripley, England, and Shepperton Studio Center near London. DeLuxe Color. Rated R. 111 minutes. Sequel was *Damien—Omen II* (1978)

Robert Thorn: Gregory Peck, *Katherine Thorn:* Lee Remick, *Jennings:* David Warner, *Mrs. Baylock:* Billie Whitelaw, *Damien:* Harvey Stevens, *Father Brennan:* Patrick Troughton, *Father Spiletto:* Martin Benson, *Monk:* Robert Rietty, *Priest:* Tommy Duggan, *Dr. Becker:* Anthony Nicholls, *Nanny:* Holly Palance, *Reporter:* Roy Boyd, *Nun:* Freda Dowie, *Psychiatrist:* John Stride, *Mrs. Horton:* Sheila Raynor, *Horton:* Robert

MacLeod, *Themselves:* The Officers and Men of U. S. Marine Barracks, London, England, *Archaeologist:* Leo McKern.

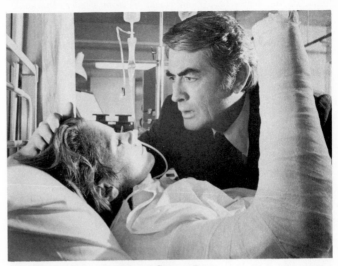

The Omen with Lee Remick and Gregory Peck.

One-Eyed Jacks with Mickey Finn, Karl Malden, Marlon Brando and Slim Pickens.

ONE-EYED JACKS (1961) Par. Producer, Frank P. Rosenberg. Executive Producers, George Glass and Walter Seltzer. Directed by Marlon Brando. In VistaVision and Technicolor. Based on the novel *The Authentic Death of Hendry Jones* by Charles Neider. Screenplay, Guy Trosper, Calder Willingham. Art Directors, Hal Pereira and J. McMillan Johnson. Music, Hugo Friedhofer. Assistant Directors, Francisco Day and Harry Caplan. Costumes, Yvonne Wood. Dances, Josephine Earl. Cinematography, Charles Lang, Jr. Special Effects, John P. Fulton. Editor, Archie Marshek. A Pennebaker Production. Stanley Kubrick was replaced as the director by Brando (his first effort) before filming began at Monterey Beach in 1958. More than a million feet were shot, and the film was cut from an original running time of 4 hours, 42 minutes. Brando's stand-in (since *Viva Zapata!*) Larry Duran made his acting debut. The only American film of Pina Pellicer, who killed herself at 24, on December 10, 1964, after a brief Mexican career. 141 minutes

Rio: Marlon Brando, *Dad Longworth:* Karl Malden, *Maria:* Katy Jurado, *Louisa:* Pina Pellicer, *Lon:* Slim Pickens, *Bob Amory:* Ben Johnson, *Harvey:* Sam Gilman, *Modesto:* Larry Duran, *Howard Tetley:* Timothy Carey, *Redhead:* Miriam Colon, *Bank Teller:* Elisha Cook, Jr., *Rurales Officer:* Rudolph Acosta, *Bartender:* Ray Teal, *Barber-Photographer:* John Dierkes, *Nika, Flamenco Dancer:* Margarita Cordova, *Doc:* Hank Worden, *Margarita, Castilian Girl:* Nina Martinez, *Uncle:* Philip Ahn, *Tim:* Clem Harvey, *Banker:*

William Forrest, *Owner of Cantina:* Shichizo Takeda, *Posseman:* Henry Wills, *Blacksmith:* Mickey Finn, *Squaredance Caller:* Fenton Jones, *Corral Keeper:* Joe Dominguez, *Mexican Vendor:* Margarita Martin, *Rurales Sergeant:* John Michael Quijada, *Cantina Girl:* Francy Scott, *Card Sharp:* Felipe Turich, *Townsman:* Nesdon Booth, *Mexican Townsman:* Nacho Galindo, *Bouncer in Shack:* Jorge Moreno.

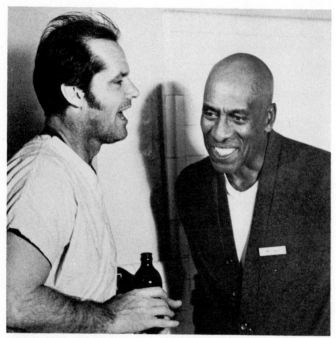

One Flew Over the Cuckoo's Nest with Jack Nicholson and Scatman Crothers.

ONE FLEW OVER THE CUCKOO'S NEST (1975) UA. Produced by Saul Zaentz and Michael Douglas. Directed by Milos Forman. A Fantasy Film in color. Based on the 1962 novel by Ken Kesey and the 1963 play by Dale Wasserman, which starred Kirk Douglas. Screenplay, Lawrence Hauben and Bo Goldman. Photography, Haskell Wexler. Additional Photography, William Fraker and Bill Butler. Original music composed by Jack Nitzsche. Supervising Film Editor, Richard Chew. Editors, Lynzee Klingman and Sheldon Kahn. Sound, Lawrence Jost. Associate Producer, Martin Fink. Production Designer, Paul Sylbert. Art Director, Edwin O'Donovan. Assistant Directors, Irby Smith and William St. John. Costumer, Agnes Rodgers. Make-up, Fred Phillips. Hairdresser, Gerry Leetch. Film debuts of Sampson, 6'6" Creek Indian painter: Dourif; Lloyd; Dr. Brooks, Oregon State Hospital superintendent. Filmed at the Oregon State Hospital at Salem. Rated R. 129 minutes

Randle Patrick McMurphy: Jack Nicholson, *Nurse Mildred Ratched:* Louise Fletcher, *Harding:* William Redfield, *Chief Bromden:* Will Sampson, *Turkle:* Scatman Crothers, *Billy Bibbit:* Brad Dourif, *Dr. John Spivey:* Dr. Dean R. Brooks, *Ellis:* Michael Berryman, *Gen. Matterson:* Peter Brocco, *Miller:* Alonzo Brown, *Warren:* Mwako Cumbuka, *Martini:* Danny De Vito, *Jim Sefelt:* William Duell, *Bancini:* Josip Elic, *Nurse Itsu:* Lan Fendors, *Washington:* Nathan George, *Beans Garfield:* Ken Kenny, *Harbor Master:* Mel Lambert, *Charlie Cheswick:* Sydney Lassick, *Night Supervisor:* Kay Lee, *Taber:* Christopher Lloyd, *Ellsworth:* Dwight Marfield, *Hap Arlich:* Ted Markland, *Rose:* Louisa Moritz, *Woolsey:* Phil Roth, *Nurse Pilbow:* Mimi Sarkisian, *Fredrickson:* Vincent Schiavelli, *Candy:* Marya Small, *Scanlon:* Delos V. Smith, Jr., *Ruckley:* Tim Welch, *News Commentator:* Tim McCall (former governor of Oregon).

ONE FOOT IN HEAVEN (1941) WB. Producers, Jack L. Warner, Hal B. Wallis. Associate Producers, Robert Lord, Irving Rapper. Directed by Irving Rapper. Screenplay, Casey Robinson. Cameraman, Charles Rosher. Editor, Warren Low. From the novel by Hartzell Spence. Scenes from William S. Hart's *The Silent Man,* 1916. 108 minutes

William Spence: Fredric March, *Mother:* Martha Scott, *Mrs. Lydia Sandow:* Beulah Bondi, *Preston Thurston:* Gene Lockhart, *Clayton Potter:* Grant Mitchell, *Dr. John Romer:* Moroni Olsen, *Samson:* Harry Davenport, *Eileen (18 years old):* Elisabeth Fraser, *Hartzell (17 years old):* Frankie Thomas, *Mrs. Thurston:* Laura Hope Crews, *Dr. Horrigan:* Jerome Cowan, *John E. Morris:* Ernest Cossart, *Mrs. Morris:* Nana Bryant, *Louella Digby:* Mary Field, *Case:* Hobart Bosworth, *George Reynolds:* Roscoe Ates, *Mrs. Watkins:* Clara Blandick, *Haskins:* Charles Halton, *Miss Peabody:* Paula Trueman, *Mrs. Jellison:* Virginia Brissac, *Fraser Spence:* Casey Johnson, *Eileen (11 years old):* Carlotta Jelm, *Hartzell (10 years old):* Peter Caldwell, *Alf McAfee:* Milt Kibbee, *Druggist MacFarlan:* Harlan Briggs, *Zeke:* Olin Howland, *Drummer:* Frank Mayo, *Conductor:* Fred Kelsey, *Mrs. Simpson:* Vera Lewis, *Mrs. Ehrlich:* Dorothy Vaughan, *Mrs. Dibble:* Tempe Pigott, *Mrs. Spicer:* Sarah Edwards, *Storekeeper:* Herbert Heywood, *Casper Cullenbaugh:* Dick Elliott, *Ella Hodges:* Charlotte Treadway *Bride:* Ann Edmonds, *Groom:* Byron Barr (Gig Young).

One Foot in Heaven with Nana Bryant, Martha Scott and Ernest Cossart.

One Hour With You with Genevieve Tobin and Maurice Chevalier.

ONE HOUR WITH YOU (1932) Par. Produced by Ernst Lubitsch. Directed by George Cukor. From the play *Only a Dream* by Lothar Schmidt. Screenplay, Samson Raphaelson. Photography, Victor Milner. Songs by Leo Robin, Oscar Straus, Richard Whiting: "One Hour With You," "Oh, That Mitzi," "We Will Always Be Sweethearts," "Three Times a Day," "What Would You Do?" Film debut of Florine McKinney. Remake of *The Marriage Circle* (Warners, 1924). 80 minutes

Dr. Andre Bertier: Maurice Chevalier, *Colette Bertier:* Jeanette MacDonald, *Mitzi Olivier:* Genevieve Tobin, *Adolph:* Charles Ruggles,

204

Professor Olivier: Roland Young, *Police Commissioner:* George Barbier, *Mademoiselle Martel:* Josephine Dunn, *Detective:* Richard Carle, *Policeman:* Charles Judels, *Mitzi's Maid:* Barbara Leonard, *Girl:* Florine McKinney, *Singer:* Donald Novis, *Marcel, Butler:* Charles Coleman, *Butler:* Eric Wilton, *Cabby:* George Davis, *Dance Extra:* Bill Elliott.

100 Men and a Girl with Mischa Auer and Deanna Durbin.

100 MEN AND A GIRL (1937) Univ. Produced by Charles R. Rogers. Associate Producer, Joseph Pasternak. Directed by Henry Koster. Screenplay, Bruce Manning, Charles Kenyon, and Hans Kraly. Photography, Joseph Valentine. Editor, Bernard W. Burton. Songs: "It's Raining Sunbeams" by Frederick Hollander and Sam Coslow; "A Heart That's Free" by Alfred G. Robyn and Thomas T. Railey. 84 minutes

Patricia Cardwell: Deanna Durbin, *Leopold Stokowski:* Leopold Stokowski, *John Cardwell:* Adolphe Menjou, *Mrs. Frost:* Alice Brady, *John R. Frost:* Eugene Pallette, *Michael Borodoff:* Mischa Auer, *Garage Owner:* Billy Gilbert, *Mrs. Tyler:* Alma Kruger, *Doorman, Marshall:* Jack (J. Scott) Smart, *Tommy Bitters:* Jed Prouty, *Russell:* Jameson Thomas, *Johnson:* Howard Hickman, *Taxi Driver:* Frank Jenks, *Gustave Brandstetter:* Christian Rub, *Stevens, Butler:* Gerald Oliver Smith, *Rudolph, a Bearded Musician/A Boarder:* Jack Mulhall, *Music Lover:* James Bush, *Manager:* John Hamilton, *Butler:* Eric Wilton, *Theater Patron:* Mary Forbes, *Guests:* Rolfe Sedan, Charles Coleman, Hooper Atchley, *Pianist:* Leonid Kinskey, *Ira Westing, Music Editor:* Edwin Maxwell.

ONE IN A MILLION (1936) 20th. Produced by Darryl F. Zanuck. Directed by Sidney Lanfield. Associate Producer, Raymond Griffith. Authors, Leonare Praskins, Mark Kelly. Musical Director, Louis Silvers. Skating Ensembles, Jack Haskell. Cameraman, Edward Cronjager. Editor, Robert Simpson. Songs by Sidney D. Mitchell and Lew Pollack: "One in a Million," "Who's Afraid of Love?", "The Moonlight Waltz," "Lovely Lady in White," "We're Back in Circulation Again." 95 minutes

Greta Muller: Sonja Henie, *Tad:* Adolphe Menjou, *Heinrich Muller:* Jean Hersholt, *Photographer:* Ned Sparks, *Ritz Brothers:* Themselves, *Billie:* Arline Judge, *Goldie:* Dixie Dunbar, *Bob:* Don Ameche, *Adolph:* Borrah Minevitch, *Ratoffsky:* Montagu Love, *Leah:* Leah Ray, *Members of Girls' Band:* Shirley Deane, June Gale, Lillian Porter, Diana Cook, Bonnie Bannon, June Wilkins, Clarice Sherry, Pauline Craig, *Manager of St. Moritz Hotel:* Albert Conti, *Chapelle:* Julius Tannen, *French Skater:* Margo Webster, *German Announcer:* Frederic Gierman, *Woman in Box:* Bess Flowers, *Chairman:* Egon Brecher, *Announcer, Madison Square Garden:* Paul McVey, *Adolph's Gang:* Borrah Minevitch's Gang.

One in a Million with Jean Hersholt and Sonja Henie.

One Night of Love with Lyle Talbot and Grace Moore.

ONE NIGHT OF LOVE (1934) Col. Produced by Harry Cohn. Directed by Victor Schertzinger. Story, Dorothy Speare and Charles Beahan. Screenplay, S. K. Lauren, James Gow, and Edmund North. Art Director, Stephen Goosson. Photography, Joseph Walker. Editor, Gene Milford. Sound, Paul Neal. Assistant Director, Arthur Balch. Costumes, Robert Kalloch. Music Director, Dr. Pietro Cimini. Special Effects, John Hoffman. Song, "One Night of Love," by Gus Kahn and Victor Schertzinger. Music, Louis Silvers. 82 minutes

Mary: Grace Moore, *Monteverdi:* Tullio Carminati, *Bill Houston:* Lyle Talbot, *Lally:* Mona Barrie, *Muriel:* Nydia Westman, *Angelina:* Jessie Ralph, *Giovanni:* Luis Alberni, *Frappazini:* Rosemary Glosz, *Mary's Mother:* Jane Darwell, *Mary's Father:* William Burress, *Impresario:* Frederick Burton, *Cafe Proprietor:* Henry Armetta, *Caluppi:* Andres De Segurola, *Radio Announcer:* Sam Hayes, *Stage Manager:* Reginald Barlow, *First Doctor:* Fredrik Vogeding, *Second Doctor:*

Arno Johnson, *Viennese Valet:* Olaf Hytten, *Florist:* Leo White, *Vegetable Man:* Herman Bing, *Stage Director:* Edward Keane, *Opera Director:* Reginald Le Borg, *Men:* Wilfred Lucas, Edmund Burns, *Pinkerton:* Paul Ellis, *Captain of Italian Yacht:* Joseph Mack, *German Girl:* Marion Lessing, *Taxi Driver:* Hans Joby, *Man:* Rafael Storm, *Cora Florida:* Victoria Stuart, *Radio Judge:* John Ardizoni, *Viennese Stage Manager:* Kurt Furberg, *Call Boy:* Spec O'Donnell, *Flower Store Man:* Michael Mark, *Steward:* Richard La Marr, *Judge:* Wadsworth Harris, *Sugar Daddy:* Arthur Stuart Hull.

One, Two, Three with Arlene Francis, James Cagney and Pamela Tiffin.

ONE, TWO, THREE (1961) UA. Producer-Director, Billy Wilder. Screenplay, Billy Wilder, I. A. L. Diamond. Based on play by Ferenc Molnar. Music, Andre Previn. Associate Producers, I. A. L. Diamond, Doane Harrison. Assistant Director, Tom Pevsner. Presented by Mirisch Company in association with Pyramid Productions. Filmed in Panavision. Second Unit Director, Andre Smagghe. Art Director, Alex Trauner. Cinematographer, Daniel Fapp. Editor, Daniel Mandell. 108 minutes

MacNamara: James Cagney, *Otto:* Horst Buchholz, *Scarlett:* Pamela Tiffin, *Phylis:* Arlene Francis, *Ingeborg:* Lilo Pulver, *Hazeltine:* Howard St. John, *Schlemmer:* Hanns Lothar, *Mrs. Hazeltine:* Lois Bolton, *Peripetchikoff:* Leon Askin, *Mishkin:* Peter Capell, *Borodenko:* Ralf Wolter, *Fritz:* Karl Lieffen, *Dr. Bauer:* Henning Schluter, *M. P. Sergeant:* Red Buttons, *Tommy MacNamara:* John Allen, *Cindy MacNamara:* Christine Allen, *Count von Droste-Schattenburg:* Hubert Von Meyerinck, *Newspaperman:* Tile Kiwe, *Zeidlitz:* Karl Ludwig Lindt, *Bertha:* Rose Renee Roth, *M. P. Corporal:* Ivan Arnold, *Pierre:* Jacques Chevalier, *Krause:* Paul Bos.

One Way Passage with William Powell and Kay Francis.

ONE WAY PASSAGE (1932) WB. Directed by Tay Garnett. Original Story, Robert Lord. Screenplay, Wilson Mizner and Joseph Jackson. Editor, Ralph Dawson. Camera, Robert Kurrle. Filmed aboard the Pacific liner S. S. *Calawaii.* Theme, "Where Was I." Remade as *Till We Meet Again* (1940). 69 minutes

Dan Hardesty: William Powell, *Joan Ames:* Kay Francis, *Skippy:* Frank McHugh, *Countess Barilhaus* (*Barrel House Betty*): Aline MacMahon, *Steve Burke:* Warren Hymer, *Doctor:* Frederick Burton, *Sir Harold:* Douglas Gerrard, *Steward:* Herbert Mundin, *Ship's Bartender:* Roscoe Karns, *Singing Drunk:* Wilson Mizner, *Singer* ("*If I Had My Way*"): Heinie Conklin, *Hong Kong Bartender:* Mike Donlin, *Honolulu Contact:* Dewey Robinson, *Agua Caliente Bartender:* William Halligan, *Captain:* Stanley Fields, *Curio Dealer:* Willie Fung, *Ship's Officer:* Harry Seymour, *Joan's Friends:* Ruth Hall, Allan Lane.

On Her Majesty's Secret Service with George Lazenby.

ON HER MAJESTY'S SECRET SERVICE (1969) UA. Produced by Albert R. Broccoli and Harry Saltzman. Directed by Peter Hunt. An Eon-Danilaq Production in Panavision and Technicolor. Based on Ian Fleming's novel. Screenplay, Richard Maibaum. Photography, Michael Reed. Associate Producer, Stanley Sopel. Costumes, Marjorie Cornelius. Assistant Director, Frank Ernst. Art Director, Bob Laing. Music, John Barry. Editor, John Glen. Produced in England. 140 minutes

James Bond: George Lazenby, *Tracy Draco:* Diana Rigg, *Ernst Stavros Blofeld:* Telly Savalas, *Irma Bunt;* Ilse Steppat, *Marc Ange Draco:* Gabriele Ferzetti, *Grunther:* Yuri Borienko, *Campbell:* Bernard Horsfall, *Sir Hilary Bray:* George Baker, *M:* Bernard Lee, *Miss Moneypenny:* Lois Maxwell, *Q:* Desmond Llewelyn, *Ruby:* Angela Scoular, *Nancy:* Catherina Von Schell, *Casino Guest:* Bessie Love, *Toussaint:* Geoffrey Cheshire, *Che Che:* Irvin Allen, *Raphael:* Terry Mountain, *Klett:* Bill Morgan, *Felsen:* Less Crawford, *Braun:* George Cooper, *Gumpold:* James Bree, *Olympe:* Virginia North, *Manuel:* Brian Worth, *American Girl:* Dani Sheridan, *Scandinavian Girl:* Julie Ege, *English Girl:* Joanna Lumley, *Chinese Girl:* Mona Chong, *Australian Girl:* Anoushka Hempel, *German Girl:* Ingrit Back, *Italian Girl:* Jenny Hanley, *Indian Girl:* Zara, *Jamaican Girl:* Sylvana Henriques, *Israeli Girl:* Helena Ronee.

On the Avenue with Dick Powell (in photo) and Madeleine Carroll.

ON THE AVENUE (1937) 20th. Associate Producer, Gene Markey. Directed by Roy Del Ruth. Screenplay, Gene Markey and William Conselman. Music Director, Arthur Lange. Dance Director, Seymour Felix. Orchestrations, Herbert Spencer. Art Director, Mark-Lee Kirk. Associate Art Director, Haldane Douglas. Set Decoration, Thomas Little. Assistant Director, William J. Scully. Costumes, Gwen Wakeling. Photography, Lucien Andriot. Editor, Allen McNeil. Sound, Joseph Aiken and Roger Heman. Songs by Irving Berlin: "Slumming on Park Avenue," "I've Got My Love to Keep Me Warm," "This Year's Kisses," "You're Laughing at Me," "He Ain't Got Rhythm," "The Girl on the Police Gazette." 89 minutes

Gary Blake: Dick Powell, *Mimi Caraway:* Madeleine Carroll, *Mona Merrick:* Alice Faye, *Themselves:* The Ritz Brothers, *Commodore Caraway:* George Barbier, *Frederick Sims:* Alan Mowbray, *Aunt Fritz Peters:* Cora Witherspoon, *Jake Dibble:* Walter Catlett, *Eddie Eads:* Douglas Fowley, *Miss Katz:* Joan Davis, *Step:* Stepin Fetchit, *Herr Hanfstangel:* Sig Rumann, *Joe Papaloupas:* Billy Gilbert, *Binns, the Cabby:* E. E. Clive, *Mr. Trivet:* Douglas Wood, *Stage Manager:* John Sheehan, *Harry Morris:* Paul Irving, *Kelly:* Harry Stubbs, *Luigi:* Ricardo Mandia, *Chorus Girl* ("*I've Got My Love to Keep Me Warm*"): Lynn Bari, *Chorine:* Geneva Sawyer, *Footman in Sketch:* Hank Mann.

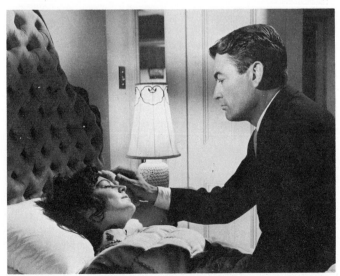

On the Beach with Ava Gardner and Gregory Peck.

ON THE BEACH (1959) UA. Producer-Director, Stanley Kramer. A Lomitas Production. Screenplay by John Paxton and James Lee Barrett. Based on the novel by Nevil Shute. Music by Ernest Gold. Song by Marie Cowan and A. B. Patterson, "Waltzing Matilda."

Costumes, Joe King. Assistant Director, Ivan Volkman. Art Director, Fernando Carrere. Cinematographer, Giuseppe Rotunno. Auto Race Photography, Daniel Fapp. Editor, Frederic Knudtson. Produced in Australia. Production Design, Rudolph Sternad. Production Manager, Clem Beauchamp. Special Effects, Lee Zavitz. Sound, Hans Wetzel. Make-up, John O'Gorman and Frank Prehoda. Hairstyles, Jane Shugrue. Technical Advisor, Admiral Charles A. Lockwood. Film debut of Donna Anderson, 19. 133 minutes

Dwight Towers: Gregory Peck, *Moira Davidson:* Ava Gardner, *Julian Osborn:* Fred Astaire, *Peter Holmes:* Anthony Perkins, *Mary Holmes:* Donna Anderson, *Admiral Bridie:* John Tate, *Lieutenant Hosgood:* Lola Brooks, *Davidson:* Lou Vernon, *Farrel:* Guy Doleman, *Benson:* Ken Wayne, *Swain:* John Meillon, *Davis:* Richard Meikle, *Sundstrom:* Harp McGuire, *Chrysler:* Jim Barrett, *Sir Douglas Froude:* Basil Buller Murphy, *Dr. Fletcher:* Keith Eden, *Senior Officer:* John Royle, *Radio Officer:* Frank Gatcliff, *Port Man:* Paddy Moran, *Salvation Army Captain:* John Casson, *Dr. King:* Kevin Brennan, *Dykers:* C. Harding Brown, *Morgan:* Grant Taylor, *Professor Jorgenson:* Peter Williams, *Sykes:* Harvey Adams, *Jones:* Stuart Finch, *Ackerman:* Joe McCormick, *Betty:* Audine Leith, *Fogarty, Sonar Operator:* Jerry Ian Seals, *Boy:* Carey Paul Peck, *Jennifer Holmes:* Katherine Hill.

On the Town with Jules Munshin, Ann Miller, Gene Kelly, Betty Garrett and Frank Sinatra.

ON THE TOWN (1949) MGM. Produced by Arthur Freed. Directed by Gene Kelly and Stanley Donen. Color by Technicolor. Screenplay, Adolph Green and Betty Comden. Based on the musical; book and lyrics by Comden and Green, music by Leonard Bernstein, from an idea by Jerome Robbins. New songs by Roger Edens, Comden and Green. Songs: "New York, New York," "Miss Turnstiles," "Prehistoric Man," "Come Up to My Place," "Main Street," "You're Awful," "On the Town," "Count on Me," "A Day in New York." Score, Roger Edens and Lennie Hayton. Musical Director, Lennie Hayton. Art Directors, Cedric Gibbons and Jack Martin Smith. Photography, Harold Rosson. Editor, Ralph E. Winters. Filmed in New York City. Alice Pearce repeats her role from the 1944 musical. 98 minutes

Gabey: Gene Kelly, *Chip:* Frank Sinatra, *Brunhilde Esterhazy:* Betty Garrett, *Claire Huddesen:* Ann Miller, *Ozzie:* Jules Munshin, *Ivy Smith:* Vera-Ellen, *Madame Dilyovska:* Florence Bates, *Lucy Shmeeler:* Alice Pearce, *Professor:* George Meader, *Worker* ("*New York, New York*"): Bern Hoffman, *Subway Passenger:* Lester Dorr, *Working Girl:* Bea Benaderet, *Sign Poster:* Walter Baldwin, *Photo Layout Man:* Don Brodie, *Spud:* Sid Melton, *Officer, Car 44:* Robert B. Williams, *Officer Tracy, Car 44:* Tom Dugan, *Cab Company Owner:* Murray Alper, *François, Headwaiter:* Hans Conreid, *Redhead:* Claire Carleton, *Sailor Simpkins:* Dick Wessel, *Sailor:* William "Bill" Phillips, *Cop:* Frank Hagney, *Dancer in Green* ("*A Day in New York*"): Carol Haney.

On the Waterfront with Lee J. Cobb and Marlon Brando.

ON THE WATERFRONT (1954) Col. Producer, Sam Spiegel. Director, Elia Kazan. Screenplay, Budd Schulberg, from his story based on articles by Malcolm Johnson. Music by Leonard Bernstein. Photography, Boris Kaufman. Editor, Gene Milford. Art Director, Richard Day. Filmed in New York City and Hoboken, New Jersey. Eva Marie Saint's film debut. 108 minutes

Terry Malloy: Marlon Brando, *Father Barry:* Karl Malden, *Johnny Friendly:* Lee J. Cobb, *Charles Malloy:* Rod Steiger, *"Kayo" Dugan:* Pat Henning, *Edie Doyle:* Eva Marie Saint, *Glover:* Leif Erickson, *Big Mac:* James Westerfield, *Truck:* Tony Galento, *Tillio:* Tami Mauriello, *"Pop" Doyle:* John Hamilton, *Mott:* John Heldabrand, *Moose:* Rudy Bond, *Luke:* Don Blackman, *Jimmy:* Arthur Keegan, *Barney:* Abe Simon, *J. P.:* Barry Macollum, *Specs:* Mike O'Dowd, *Gillette:* Marty Balsam, *Slim:* Fred Gwynne, *Tommy:* Thomas Handley, *Mrs. Collins:* Anne Hegira, *Cab Driver:* Nehemiah Persoff.

Operation Pacific with John Wayne and Ward Bond.

OPERATION PACIFIC (1951) WB. Produced by Louis F. Edelman. Director, George Waggner. Story and Screenplay, George Waggner. Art Director, Leo K. Kuter. Music, Max Steiner. Photography, Bert Glennon. Editor, Alan Crosland, Jr. Filmed partly in Honolulu. Cary Grant is seen in a clip from *Destination Tokyo* (1943). 111 minutes

Commander Duke Gifford: John Wayne, *Mary Stuart:* Patricia Neal, *Captain Pop Perry:* Ward Bond, *Larry:* Scott Forbes, *Bob Perry:* Philip Carey, *Jonesy:* Paul Picerni, *The Talker:* Bill Campbell, *Commander Steele:* Kathryn Givney, *Caldwell:* Martin Milner, *Comsubpac:* Cliff Clark, *The Chief:* Jack Pennick, *Sister Anna:* Virginia Brissac, *Soundman:* Vincent Fotre, *Squad Commander:* Lewis Martin, *Junior:* Sam Edwards, *Radarman:* Louis Mosconi, *Herbie:* Gayle Kellogg,

Rafferty: Steve Wayne, *Quartermaster:* Bob Nash, *Helmsman:* William Self, *Shore Patrolman:* Carl Saxe, *Shore Patrol Chief, Mick:* James Flavin, *Hawaiian:* Al Kikume, *Torpedo Officer:* Bob Carson, *Talker:* Ray Hyke, *Radioman, Sparks:* Chris Drake, *Sub Commander, Freddie:* Harry Lauter, *Briefing Officer, USAF:* Carleton Young, *Commander:* Harlan Warde, *Fighter Pilot:* John Baer, *Japanese Flyer:* Richard Loo.

Operation Petticoat with Tony Curtis and Dina Merrill.

OPERATION PETTICOAT (1959) Univ. Produced by Robert Arthur. Directed by Blake Edwards. In Eastman Color. Story, Paul King and Joseph Stone. Screenplay, Stanley Shapiro and Maurice Richlin. Music, David Rose. Art Directors, Alexander Golitzen and Robert E. Smith. Gowns, Bill Thomas. Assistant Directors, Frank Shaw, Wilson Shyer, and Charles Scott. Photography, Russell Harlan. Special Photography, Clifford Stine. Editors, Ted J. Kent and Frank Gross. A Granart Production. Filmed at Key West, Florida, and on the submarine *Balboa*. 124 minutes. Later a TV series

Admiral Matt Sherman: Cary Grant, *Lieutenant Nick Holden:* Tony Curtis, *Lieutenant Dolores Crandall:* Joan O'Brien, *Lieutenant Barbara Duran:* Dina Merrill, *Sam Tostin:* Arthur O'Connell, *Molumphrey:* Gene Evans, *Stovall:* Richard Sargent, *Major Edna Hayward:* Virginia Gregg, *Captain J. B. Henderson:* Robert F. Simon, *Watson:* Robert Gist, *Ernest Hunkle:* Gavin MacLeod, *The Prophet:* George Dunn, *Harmon:* Dick Crockett, *Lieutenant Claire Reid:* Madlyn Rhue, *Lieutenant Ruth Colfax:* Marion Ross, *Ramon:* Clarence E. Lung, *Dooley:* Frankie Darro, *Fox:* Tony Pastor, Jr., *Kraus:* Nicky Blair, *Williams:* John Morley, *Reiner:* Robert Hoy, *Control Talker:* Glenn Jacobson, *Crewman:* Nino Tempo, *Filipino Farmer:* Leon Lontoc, *Lieutenant Commander Daly:* James F. Lanphier, *Navy Chief:* Alan Dexter, *Admiral Koenig:* Nelson Leigh, *Captain Kress:* Francis De Sales, *Lieutenant Colonel Simpson:* Preston Hanson, *M.P. Sergeant:* Hal Baylor, *Marine Lieutenant:* Bob Stratton, *Soldier:* Harry Harvey, Jr., *Pregnant Filipino Woman:* Vi Ingraham, *Chief of Demolition Crew:* Alan Scott, *Third Class Petty Officer:* Francis L. Ward, *Lieutenant Morrison:* William R. Callinan, *Colonel Higginson:* Gordon Casell, *Witch Doctor:* Tusi Faiivae.

THE OTHER SIDE OF MIDNIGHT (1977) 20th. Produced by Frank Yablans. A Martin Ransohoff-Frank Yablans Production. Directed by Charles Jarrott. Based on the novel by Sidney Sheldon. Screenplay, Herman Raucher and Daniel Taradash. Executive Producer, Howard W. Koch, Jr. Associate Producer/Production Manager, Jack B. Bernstein. Music by Michel Legrand. Production Designer, John DeCuir. Editor, Donn Cambern and Harold F. Kress. Costumes designed by Irene Sharaff. Photography, Fred J. Koenekamp. 2nd Unit Director, Donn Cambern. 2nd Unit Photography, Robert Huke. Aerial Sequences, Tallmantz Aviation. Assistant Director, Fred Brost. 2nd Assistant Directors, Craig Huston and Jerram Swartz. Assistant Directors (Paris), Louis Pitzele and Christian Fuin. Set Decorators, Raphael Bretton and Tony Mondell. Make-up, Lee Harman. Hairdressers, Sugar Blymyer and Kaye Pownall. Recording Mixer, Larry Jost. Jewels by Cartier. Furs by Ben Thylan Corp.

Filmed in Panavision and DeLuxe Color in Virginia's Luray Caverns, Greece, Paris, Washington, D.C., and the Fox Studio. Rated R. 165 minutes

Noelle Page: Marie-France Pisier, *Larry Douglas:* John Beck, *Catherine Alexander Douglas:* Susan Sarandon, *Constantin Demeris:* Raf Vallone, *Bill Fraser:* Clu Gulager, *Armand Gautier:* Christian Marquand, *Barbet:* Michael Lerner, *Lanchon:* Sorrell Booke, *Paul Metaxas:* Antony Ponzini, *Demonides:* Louis Zorich, *Chotas:* Charles Cioffi, *Sister Theresa:* Dimitra Arliss, *Warden:* Jan Arvan, *Madame Rose:* Josette Banzet, *Doc Peterson:* John Chappell, *Female Guard:* Eunice Christopher, *Jacques Page:* Roger Etienne, *O'Brien:* Howard Hesseman, *Susie:* Garrie Kelly, *Henri Corveger:* Curt Lowens, *Cocyannis:* Peter Mamakos, *Philippe Sorel:* Jacques Maury, *Paris Cabdriver:* Louis Mercier, *Sultry Girl:* Lina Raymond, *Steve Whitney:* Charles Siebert, *Doctor:* George Skaff, *Spyros:* George Sperdakos, *Hotel Detective:* Roger Til, *President of Council:* Titos Vandis, *Greek Priest:* Than Wyenn, *Beverly Hills Bellhop:* John Blackwell, *Mrs. Page:* Lilyan Chauvin, *Dr. K.:* George Keymas, *Housekeeper:* Lidia Kristen, *Nun:* Denise DeMirjian, *Old Dressmaker:* Matilda Calnan, *Actor (extra):* George DeNormand, *Man in Restaurant:* Harry Holcombe.

The Other Side of Midnight with John Beck, Charles Cioffi and Marie-France Pisier.

The Other Side of the Mountain with Dabney Coleman and Marilyn Hassett.

THE OTHER SIDE OF THE MOUNTAIN (1975) Univ. A Filmways-Larry Peerce Production. Produced by Edward S. Feldman. Directed by Larry Peerce. Technicolor. Based on the book *A Long Way Up* by E. G. Valens. Screenplay, David Seltzer. Photography, David M. Walsh. Editor, Eve Newman. Set Decorations, Philip Abramson. Sound, Richard

Overton and Robert Knudsen. Second Unit Director and Stunt Coordinator, Max Kleven. Second Unit Photography, John Morley Stephens. Assistant Directors, Ken Swor and Henry Lange. Assistant to the Producer, Judi Rosner. Costumes, Grady Hunt. Ski Coordinator, Dennis Agee. Technical Advisers, Jill and Jerry Kinmont and Dr. Theodore A. Lynn. Music, Charles Fox. Song, "Richard's Window" by Norman Gimbel and Charles Fox, sung by Olivia Newton-John. California locations: Los Angeles, Mammoth, Bishop, Paiute Indian Reservation near Bishop, Inyo National Forest, the Veterans Administration at Long Beach. Film debut of Bill Vint. Rated PG. 103 minutes. Sequel was *The Other Side of the Mountain Part II* (1977)

Jill Kinmont: Marilyn Hassett, *Dick (Mad Dog) Buek:* Beau Bridges, *Audra-Jo:* Belinda J. Montgomery, *June Kinmont:* Nan Martin, *Bill Kinmonth:* William Bryant, *Dave McCoy:* Dabney Coleman, *Buddy Werner:* Bill Vint, *Lee Zadroga:* Hampton Fancher, *Dr. Pittman:* William Roerick, *Cookie:* Dori Brenner, *Dean:* Walter Brooke, *Linda Meyers:* Jocelyn Jones, *Bob Kinmont:* Greg Mabrey, *Jerry Kinmont:* Jerry Kinmont, *Jerry as a boy:* Tony Becker, *Herbie Johnson:* Griffin Dunne, *Dr. Enders:* Warren Miller, *Skeeter Werner:* Robin Pepper, *Boy in Wheelchair:* Brad Savage, *CRC Patient:* John David Garfield, *Ambulance Driver:* John Perell, *Ambulance Attendant:* Terry Hall, *Head of Ski Patrol:* Bruce Dennis Cosbey, *Nurse:* Sharri Zak, *Man in Car:* Dick Winslow, *Himself:* Lee Baumgarth, *Andrea Mead Lawrence:* Candy McCoy Bartlett.

OUR MAN FLINT (1966) 20th. Saul David production. Director, Daniel Mann. CinemaScope, De Luxe Color. Screenplay, Hal Fimberg, Ben Starr. Based on story by Fimberg. Camera, Daniel L. Fapp. Music, Jerry Goldsmith. Editor, William Reynolds. Art Direction, Jack Martin Smith and Ed Graves. Special action scenes by Buzz Henry. 107 minutes

Derek Flint: James Coburn, *Cramden:* Lee J. Cobb, *Gila:* Gila Golan, *Malcolm Rodney:* Edward Mulhare, *Dr. Schneider:* Benson Fong, *Leslie:* Shelby Grant, *Anna:* Sigrid Valdis, *Gina:* Gianna Serra, *Sakito:* Helen Funai, *Gruber:* Michael St. Clair, *Dr. Krupov:* Rhys Williams, *American General:* Russ Conway, *Wac:* Ena Hartman, *American Diplomat:* William Walker, *Dr. Wu:* Peter Brocco, *Technician:* James Brolin.

Our Man Flint with Lee J. Cobb and James Coburn.

OUR TOWN (1940) UA. Produced by Sol Lesser. Directed by Sam Wood. A Principal Artists Production. From the Pulitzer Prize play by Thornton Wilder. Screenplay, Thornton Wilder, Frank Craven, and Harry Chandlee. Music, Aaron Copland. Orchestra Director, Irvin Talbot. Production Designer, William Cameron Menzies. Associate, Harry Horner. Photography, Bert Glennon. Editor, Sherman Todd. Craven and Scott repeat their stage roles. Scott in film debut. 90 minutes

Mr. Morgan, *The Narrator:* Frank Craven, *George Gibbs:* William Holden, *Emily Webb:* Martha Scott, *Dr. Gibbs:* Thomas Mitchell, *Mrs. Gibbs:* Fay Bainter, *Editor Webb:* Guy Kibbee, *Mrs. Webb:* Beulah Bondi, *Howie Newsome:* Stuart Erwin, *Simon Stimson:* Phillip Wood, *Rebecca Gibbs:* Ruth Toby, *Wally Webb:* Douglas Gardiner, *Constable:* Spencer Charters, *Mrs. Soames:* Doro Merande, *Professor Willett:* Arthur Allen, *Reverend:* Charles Trowbridge, *Joe Crowell:* Tim Davis, *Si Crowell:* Dix Davis, *Wedding Guest:* Dan White.

Our Town with Martha Scott and William Holden.

OUR VERY OWN (1950) RKO. Producer, Samuel Goldwyn. Director, Dave Miller. Author-Screenplay, F. Hugh Herbert. Music, Victor Young. Art Director, Richard Day. Photography, Lee Garmes. Editor, Sherman Todd. 93 minutes

Gail: Ann Blyth, *Chuck:* Farley Granger, *Joan:* Joan Evans, *Lois Macaulay:* Jane Wyatt, *Mrs. Lynch:* Ann Dvorak, *Fred Macaulay:* Donald Cook, *Penny:* Natalie Wood, *Frank:* Gus Schilling, *Zaza:* Phyllis Kirk, *Violet:* Jessie Grayson, *Bert:* Martin Milner, *Gwendolyn:* Rita Hamilton, *Mr. Lynch:* Ray Teal.

Our Very Own with Jane Wyatt and Ann Blyth.

THE OUTLAW (1943) RKO. Produced and directed by Howard Hughes. Screenplay, Jules Furthman. Music Director, Victor Young. Photography, Gregg Toland. Editor, Wallace Grissell. Photographic Effects, Roy Davidson. Originally scheduled for United Artists release in 1941, this was officially distributed in 1950. Film debuts of Jane Russell and Jack Buetel. 123 minutes

Rio: Jane Russell, *Billy the Kid:* Jack Buetel, *Pat Garrett:* Thomas Mitchell, *Doc Holliday:* Walter Huston, *Aunt Guadalupe:* Mimi Aguglia, *Woodruff:* Joe Sawyer, *Dolan:* Emory Parnell, *Waiter:* Martin Garralaga, *Pablo:* Julian Rivero.

The Outlaw with Thomas Mitchell, Walter Huston, Jane Russell and Jack Buetel.

Outward Bound with Alec B. Francis, Helen Chandler and Douglas Fairbanks, Jr.

OUTWARD BOUND (1930) WB. Directed by Robert Milton. Based on the play by Sutton Vane, first produced in London in 1923. Scenario, J. Grubb Alexander. Photography, Hal Mohr. Editor, Ralph Dawson. American film debut of Leslie Howard, who was Henry in the play. Remade as *Between Two Worlds* (Warners, 1944), *The Flight That Disappeared* (United Artists, 1961). 82 minutes

Tom Prior: Leslie Howard, *Henry:* Douglas Fairbanks, Jr., *Ann:* Helen Chandler, *Mrs. Midget:* Beryl Mercer, *Scrubby:* Alec B. Francis, *Mrs. Cliveden-Banks:* Alison Skipworth, *Reverend William Duke:* Lyonel Watts, *Mr. Lingley:* Montagu Love, *Thompson, The Examiner:* Dudley Digges, *The Policeman:* Walter Kingsford, *Dog:* Laddie.

THE OX-BOW INCIDENT (1943) 20th. Produced by Lamar Trotti. Directed by William A. Wellman. Based on the novel by Walter Van Tilburg Clark. Screenplay, Lamar Trotti. Art Directors, Richard Day and James Basevi. Photography, Arthur Miller. Music, Cyril J. Mockridge. Editor, Allen McNeil. Adapted for TV's 20th Century-Fox Hour in 1956. 75 minutes

Gil Carter: Henry Fonda, *Martin:* Dana Andrews, *Rose Mapen:* Mary Beth Hughes, *Mexican:* Anthony Quinn, *Gerald:* William Eythe, *Art Croft:* Henry Morgan, *Ma Grier:* Jane Darwell, *Judge Tyler:* Matt Briggs, *Davies:* Harry Davenport, *Major Tetley:* Frank Conroy, *Farnley:* Marc Lawrence, *Darby:* Victor Kilian, *Monty Smith:* Paul Hurst, *Poncho:* Chris-Pin Martin, *Joyce:* Ted (Michael) North,

Mr. Swanson: George Meeker, *Mrs. Swanson:* Almira Sessions, *Mrs. Larch:* Margaret Hamilton, *Mapes:* Dick Rich, *Old Man:* Francis Ford, *Bartlett:* Stanley Andrews, *Greene:* Billy Benedict, *Hart:* Rondo Hatton, *Winder:* Paul Burns, *Sparks:* Leigh Whipper, *Moore:* George Lloyd, *Jimmy Cairnes:* George Chandler, *Red:* Hank Bell, *Mark:* Forrest Dillon, *Alec Small:* George Plues, *Sheriff:* Willard Robertson, *Deputy:* Tom London.

The Ox-Bow Incident with Anthony Quinn, Dick Rich, Francis Ford, Dana Andrews, George Lloyd, Henry Fonda, Rondo Hatton, Frank Conroy and Jane Darwell.

The Pajama Game with John Raitt and Doris Day.

THE PAJAMA GAME (1957) WB. Produced by George Abbott and Stanley Donen. Associate Producers, Frederick Brisson, Robert E. Griffith, and Harold S. Prince. Directed by George Abbott and Stanley Donen. WarnerColor. Screenplay by George Abbott and Richard Bissell, from their musical based on Richard Bissell's novel *7.5 Cents.* Choreography, Bob Fosse. Art Director, Malcolm Bert. Orchestral Arrangements, Nelson Riddle and Buddy Bregman. Photography, Harry Stradling. Editor, William Ziegler. Costumes, William and Jean Eckart, assisted by Frank Thompson. Assistant Director, Russ Llewellyn. Sound, M. A. Merrick and Dolph Thomas. Songs by Richard Adler and Jerry Ross: "The Pajama Game," "I'm Not at All in Love," "Hey There," "Once-a-Year-Day," "Small Talk," "There Once Was a Man," "Steam Heat," "Hernando's Hideaway," "Seven and a Half Cents," "Her Is," "Racing With the Clock," "I'll Never Be Jealous Again." Technical Adviser, Weldon Pajama Company. Filmed in part at Hollenbeck Park, L. A. Repeating their roles from the 1954 musical: Raitt, Foy, Haney, Shaw, Dunn, Chambers, Miller, Pelish, Waldron, Gennaro, LeRoy. 101 minutes

(Katie) Babe Williams: Doris Day, *Sid Sorokin:* John Raitt, *Gladys Hotchkiss:* Carol Haney, *Vernon Hines:* Eddie Foy, Jr., *Mabel:* Reta Shaw, *Poopsie:* Barbara Nichols, *Mae:* Thelma Pelish, *Prez:* Jack Straw, *Hasler:* Ralph Dunn, *Max:* Owen Martin, *First Helper:* Jackie Kelk, *Charlie:* Ralph Chambers, *Brenda:* Mary Stanton, *Dancers:* Buzz Miller, Kenneth LeRoy, *Salesman:* Jack Waldron, *Second Helper:* Ralph Volkie, *Pop Williams:* Franklyn Fox, *Joe:* William A. Forester, *Dancer:* Peter Gennaro, *Waiter:* Elmore Henderson, *Tony, Headwaiter:* Fred Villani, *Holly:* Kathy Marlowe, *Otis:* Otis Griffith.

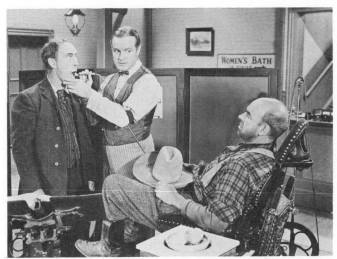

The Paleface with George Chandler, Bob Hope and Nestor Paiva.

THE PALEFACE (1948) Par. Produced by Robert L. Welch. Directed by Norman Z. McLeod. Color by Technicolor. Original Screenplay, Edmund Hartmann and Frank Tashlin. Additional Dialogue, Jack Rose. Art Directors, Hans Dreier and Earl Hedrick. Music, Victor Young. Dances, Billy Daniel. Photography, Ray Rennahan. Technicolor Director, Natalie Kalmus. Editor, Ellsworth Hoagland. Songs: "Buttons and Bows" and "Meetcha 'Round the Corner" by Jay Livingston and Ray Evans, and "Get a Man" by Joseph J. Lilley. The sequel was *Son of Paleface* (1952). 91 minutes

Painless Peter Potter: Bob Hope, *Calamity Jane:* Jane Russell, *Terris:* Robert Armstrong, *Pepper:* Iris Adrian, *Toby Preston:* Robert (Bobby) Watson, *Jasper Martin:* Jackie Searl, *Indian Scout:* Joseph Vitale, *Wapato, Medicine Man:* Henry Brandon, *Governor Johnson:* Charles Trowbridge, *Hank Billings:* Clem Bevans, *Joe:* Jeff York, *Commissioner Emerson:* Stanley Andrews, *Jeb:* Wade Crosby, *Chief Yellow Feather:* Chief Yowlachie, *Chief Iron Eyes:* Iron Eyes Cody, *Village Gossip:* John Maxwell, *Bartender:* Tom Kennedy, *Lance:* Francis J. McDonald, *Greg:* Frank Hagney, *Pete:* Skelton Knaggs, *Undertaker:* Olin Howlin, *First Patient:* George Chandler, *Second Patient:* Nestor Paiva, *Clem:* Earle Hodgins, *Zach:* Arthur Space, *Sheriff:* Edgar Dearing, *Bath House Attendant:* Dorothy Granger, *Mr. X:* Charles Cooley, *Bob:* Eric Alden, *Woman in Bath House:* Jody Gilbert, *Pioneer:* Al M. Hill, *Justice of the Peace:* Harry Harvey, *Handsome Cowboy:* Hall Bartlett, *Onlooker:* Stanley Blystone, *Onlooker:* Bob Kortman, *Character:* Oliver Blake, *Tough Galoot:* Lane Chandler, *Cowboy:* Syd Saylor, *Justice of the Peace:* Paul E. Burns, *The Mayor:* Dick Elliott, *Child:* Sharon McManus.

PAL JOEY (1957) Col. Produced by Fred Kohlmar. Directed by George Sidney. Color by Technicolor. From the musical play and book by John O'Hara. Screenplay, Dorothy Kingsley. Music Adaptation, George Duning and Nelson Riddle. Choreography, Hermes Pan. Gowns, Jean Louis. Assistant Director, Art Black. Music supervised and conducted by Morris Stoloff. Art Director, Walter Holscher. Orchestration, Arthur Morton. Photography, Harold Lipstein. Editors, Viola Lawrence and Jerome Thoms. An Essex-George Sidney Production. Songs by Richard Rodgers and Lorenz Hart: "The Lady Is a Tramp," "I Didn't Know What Time It Was," "There's a Small

Hotel," "My Funny Valentine," "Bewitched, Bothered and Bewildered," "Zip," "What Do I Care for a Dame?", "I Could Write a Book," "Do It the Hard Way," "Big Town," "What Is a Man?" The 1941 play and 1952 revival had Joey as a dancer; the film changes him into a singer. 111 minutes

Joey Evans: Frank Sinatra, *Vera Simpson:* Rita Hayworth, *Linda English:* Kim Novak, *Gladys:* Barbara Nichols, *Ned Galvin:* Bobby Sherwood, *Mike Miggins:* Hank Henry, *Mrs. Casey:* Elizabeth Patterson, *Bartender:* Robin Morse, *Colonel Langley:* Frank Wilcox, *Mr. Forsythe:* Pierre Watkin, *Anderson:* Barry Bernard, *Carol:* Ellie Kent, *Sabrina:* Mara McAfee, *Patsy:* Betty Utey, *Lola:* Bek Nelson, *Specialty Dance Double:* Jean Corbett, *Detective:* Tol Avery, *Stanley:* John Hubbard, *Livingstone:* James Seay, *Policeman:* Robert Anderson, *Pet Store Owner:* Everett Glass, *Barker:* Frank Sully, *Shorty:* Henry McCann, *Chef Tony:* Ernesto Molinari, *Headwaiter:* George Nardelli, *Vera's Maid:* Giselle D'Arc, *Bit:* Bess Flowers, *Bit:* Franklyn Farnum, *Choreographer:* Hermes Pan.

Pal Joey with Frank Sinatra and Kim Novak.

Panic in the Streets with Richard Widmark and Paul Douglas.

PANIC IN THE STREETS (1950) 20th. Producer, Sol C. Siegel. Director, Elia Kazan. Authors, Edna Anhalt, Edward Anhalt (from *Quarantine* and *Some Like 'em Cold*). Screenplay, Richard Murphy. Adaptation, Daniel Fuchs. Music, Alfred Newman. Art Directors, Lyle Wheeler, Maurice Ransford. Photography, Joe MacDonald. Editor, Harmon Jones. Filmed entirely in New Orleans. 93 minutes

Clinton Reed: Richard Widmark, *Police Captain Tom Warren:* Paul Douglas, *Nancy Reed:* Barbara Bel Geddes, *Blackie:* Walter (Jack) Palance, *Raymond Fitch:* Zero Mostel, *Neff:* Dan Riss, *John Mefaris:* Alexis Minotis, *Poldi:* Guy Thomajan, *Vince Poldi:* Tommy Cook, *Jordan:* Edward Kennedy, *Cook:* H. T. Tsiang, *Kochak:* Lewis Charles, *Dubin:* Raymond Muller, *Tommy Reed:* Tommy Rettig, *Jeanette:* Lenka Peterson, *Pat:* Pat Walshe, *Dr. Paul Gafney:* Paul Hostetler, *Kleber:* George Ehmig, *Lee:* John Schilleci, *Ben:* Waldo Pitkin, *Sergeant Phelps:* Leo Zinser, *Dr. Mackey:* Beverly C. Brown, *Cortelyou:* William Dean, *Murray:* H. Waller Fowler, Jr., *Wynant:* Rex Moad, *Johnston:* Irvine Vidacovich, *Commissioner Dan Quinn:* Val Winter, *Charlie:* Wilson Bourg, Jr., *Angie Fitch:* Mary Liswood, *Rita Mefaris:* Aline Stevens, *Redfield:* Stanley J. Reyes, *Violet:* Darwin Greenfield, *Captain Beauclyde:* Emile Meyer, *Scott:* Herman Cottman, *Al:* Al Theriot, *Hotel Proprietor:* Juan Villasana, *Coast Guard Lieutenant:* Robert Dorsen, *Anson:* Henry Mamet, *Bosun:* Tiger Joe Marsh, *Lascar Boy:* Arthur Tong.

Paper Moon with Ryan and Tatum O'Neal.

PAPER MOON (1973) Par. A Directors Company presentation of a Saticoy Production. Produced and Directed by Peter Bogdanovich. Based on the novel "Addie Pray" by Joe David Brown. Screenplay by Alvin Sargent. Photography, Laszlo Kovacs. Thirties music from the collection of Rudi Fehr. Editor, Verna Fields. Production Designer, Polly Platt. Set Designer, James Spencer. Set Decorations, John Austin. Sound by Kay Rose, Frank Warner, Bill Carruth and Richard Portman. Costumes, Pat Kelly and Sandra Stewart. Make-up, Rolf Miller. Hairstyles, Dorothy Byrne. Associate Producer, Frank Marshall. Assistant Directors, Ray Gosnell and Jerry Ballew. Filmed in Hays, Kansas, and St. Joseph, Missouri. Film debut of Ryan O'Neal's daughter Tatum, 9. Rated PG. 102 minutes

Moses Pray: Ryan O'Neal, *Addie Loggins:* Tatum O'Neal, *Trixie Delight:* Madeline Kahn, *Sheriff Hardin/Jess Hardin:* John Hillerman, *Imogene:* P. J. Johnson, *Miss Ollie:* Jessie Lee Fulton, *Minister:* Jim Harrell, *Minister's Wife:* Lila Waters, *Mr. Robertson:* Noble Willingham, *Gas Station Attendant:* Bob Young, *Station Master:* Jack Saunders, *Cafe Waitress:* Jody Wilbur, *Widow Pearl Morgan:* Liz Ross, *Widow Marie Bates:* Yvonne Harrison, *Lawman at Bates' Home:* Ed Reed, *Ribbon Saleslady:* Dorothy Price, *Widow Elvira Stanley:* Eleanor Bogart, *Widow Edna Huff:* Dorothy Forster, *Moses' Girl Friend:* Lana Daniel, *Barber:* Herschel Morris, *Salesgirl:* Dejah Moore, *Store Manager:* Ralph Coder, *Store Customer:* Harriet Ketchum, *Cotton Candy Man:* Desmond Dhooge, *Harem Tent Barker:* Kenneth Hughes, *Photographer:* George Lillie, *Floyd, Desk Clerk:* Burton Gilliam, *Deputy Beau:* Floyd Mahaney, *Leroy's Father:* Gilbert Milton, *Leroy:* Randy Quaid, *Leroy's Brothers:* Tandy Arnold, Vernon Schwanke, Dennis Beden, *Deputy:* Hugh Gillin, *Silver Mine Gentleman:* Art Ellison, *Aunt Billie:* Rosemary Rumbley.

Papillon with Steve McQueen and Dustin Hoffman.

PAPILLON (1973) AA. A Corona/General Production Company Production. Produced by Robert Dorfman and Franklin J. Schaffner. Executive Producer, Ted Richmond. Directed by Franklin J. Schaffner. Based on the autobiographical novel by Henri Charriere. Screenplay by Dalton Trumbo and Lorenzo Semple, Jr. Photography, Fred Koenekamp. Music by Jerry Goldsmith. Editor, Robert Swink. Production Designer, Anthony Masters. Art Director, Jack Maxsted. Assistant Directors, Jose Lopez Rodero and Juan Lopez Rodero. In Technicolor. Panavision. Associate Producer, Robert Laffont. Assistant Producer, Robert O. Kaplan. Costume Designer, Anthony Powell. Make-up, Charles Schram. Stunt Gaffer, Joe Canutt. Technical Adviser, Lucien LaMontagne. Orchestrator, Arthur Morton. Filmed in Jamaica, Spain, Europe. Rated PG. 150 minutes

Henri Charriere, Papillon: Steve McQueen, *Louis Dega:* Dustin Hoffman, *Indian Chief:* Victor Jory, *Julot:* Don Gordon, *Toussaint:* Anthony Zerbe, *Maturette:* Robert Deman, *Clusoit:* Woodrow Parfrey, *Lariot:* Bill Mumy, *Dr. Chatal:* George Coulouris, *Zoraima:* Ratna Assan, *Warden Barrot:* William Smithers, *Antonio:* Gregory Sierra, *Mother Superior:* Barbara Morrison, *Nun:* Ellen Moss, *Butterfly Trader:* Don Hanmer, *Commandant:* Dalton Trumbo, *Pascal:* Val Avery, *Sergeant:* Victor Tayback, *McQueen's Cliff Stunt:* Dar Robinson, *Guard:* Mills Watson, *Santini:* Ron Soble, *Old Con:* E. J. Andre, *Commandant:* Richard Angarola, *Classification Officer:* Jack Denbo, *Guard:* Len Lesser, *Masked Breton:* John Quade, *Deputy Warden:* Fred Sadoff, *Turnkey:* Allen Jaffe, *Old Trustee:* Liam Dunn, *Mrs. Dega:* Anne Byrne Hoffman.

The Paradine Case with Ann Todd, Charles Coburn and Gregory Peck.

THE PARADINE CASE (1948) Selznick Releasing Organization. Produced by David O. Selznick. Directed by Alfred Hitchcock. A Vanguard Films Production. Based on the novel by Robert Hichens. Screenplay, David O. Selznick. Adaptation, Alma Reville and James Bridie. Music, Franz Waxman. Production Design, J. McMillan Johnson. Art Director, Thomas Morahan. Photography, Lee Garmes. Editor, Hal C. Kern. Associate, John Faure. American film debuts of Louis Jourdan and Alida Valli. 131 minutes

Anthony Keane: Gregory Peck, *Lord Horfield:* Charles Laughton, *Sir Simon Flaquer:* Charles Coburn, *Gay Keane:* Ann Todd, *Lady Horfield:* Ethel Barrymore, *Andre Latour:* Louis Jourdan, *Mrs. Paradine:* Valli, *Sir Joseph Farrell:* Leo G. Carroll, *Judy Flaquer:* Joan Tetzel, *Keeper at Inn:* Isobel Elsom, *Man Carrying a Cello:* Alfred Hitchcock.

Paramount on Parade with Maurice Chevalier and Evelyn Brent.

PARAMOUNT ON PARADE (1930) Par. Supervision, Elsie Janis. Directors, Dorothy Arzner, Otto Brower, Edmund Goulding, Victor Heerman, Edwin H. Knopf, Rowland V. Lee, Ernst Lubitsch, Lothar Mendes, Victor Schertzinger, Edward Sutherland, Frank Tuttle. With Technicolor sequences. Photography, Harry Fischbeck and Victor Milner. Songs: "Paramount on Parade," "I'm True to the Navy Now" and "Anytime Is the Time to Fall in Love" by Elsie Janis and Jack King; "Sweeping the Clouds Away" by Sam Coslow; "All I Want Is Just One Girl" by Leo Robin and Richard Whiting; "Dancing to Save Your Soul," "I'm in Training for You" and "Drink to the Girl of My Dreams" by L. Wolfe Gilbert and Abel Baer; "Come Back to Sorrento" by Leo Robin and Ernesto De Curtis; "My Marine" by Ray Egan and Richard Whiting, "What Did Cleopatra Say?" by Janis and King; "We're the Masters of Ceremony" by Ballard MacDonald and Dave Dreyer; "I'm Isadore the Toreador" by David Franklin. Dances directed by David Bennett. 102 minutes

Specialties: Richard Arlen, Jean Arthur, William Austin, George Bancroft, Clara Bow, Evelyn Brent, Mary Brian, Virginia Bruce, Nancy Carroll, Ruth Chatterton, Maurice Chevalier, Gary Cooper, Leon Errol, Stuart Erwin, Kay Francis, Skeets Gallagher, Harry Green, Mitzi Green, James Hall, Phillips Holmes, Helen Kane, Dennis King, Abe Lyman and his Band, Fredric March, Nino Martini, Mitzi Mayfair, David Newell, Jack Oakie, Zelma O'Neal, Joan Peers, Charles "Buddy" Rogers, Lillian Roth, Stanley Smith, Fay Wray, *Sherlock Holmes:* Clive Brook, *Dr. Fu Manchu:* Warner Oland, *Sergeant Heath:* Eugene Pallette, *Philo Vance:* William Powell, *Chorus Girl (Chevalier Number):* Iris Adrian, *Bench Sitter:* Rolfe Sedan, *Guest:* Henry Fink, The Marion Morgan Dancers, *Soldier:* Jack Pennick, *Guest:* Mischa Auer, *Egyptian:* Robert Greig, *Hostess:* Cecil Cunningham, *Himself:* Edmund Goulding.

PARRISH (1961) WB. Producer and Director, Delmer Daves. Technicolor. From the novel by Mildred Savage. Screenplay, Delmer Daves. Art Director, Leo K. Kuter. Music, Max Steiner. Songs, John Barracudo, Alfonso Marshall, Terry Carter. Orchestration, Murray Cutter. Cinematographer, Harry Stradling, Sr. Editor, Owen Marks. Locations filmed in Connecticut. 137 minutes

Parrish McLean: Troy Donahue, *Ellen McLean:* Claudette Colbert, *Judd Raike:* Karl Malden, *Sala Post:* Dean Jagger, *Alison Post:* Diane McBain, *Lucy:* Connie Stevens, *Paige Raike:* Sharon Hugueny, *Teet Howie:* Dub Taylor, *Edgar Raike:* Hampton Fancher, *Evaline:* Saundra Edwards, *Mary Howie:* Hope Summers, *Rosie:* Bibi Osterwald, *Addie:* Madeleine Sherwood, *Eileen:* Sylvia Miles, *Gladstone:* Alfonso Marshall, *Willis:* John Barracudo, *Cartwright:* Terry Carter, *John Donati:* Ford Rainey, *Tully:* Edgar Stehli, *Gramma:* Sara Taft, *Maples:* Wade Dumas, *Skipper:* John McGovern, *Tom Weldon:* Hayden Rorke, *Maizie Weldon:* Irene Windust, *Max Maine:* Don Dillaway, *Miss Daly:* Gertrude Flynn, *Oermeyer:* House Jameson, *Lemmie:* Ken Allen, *Operator:* Karen Norris, *Foreman:* Frank Campanella, *Firechief:* Carroll O'Connor, *Gas Station Attendant:* Vincent Gardenia, *Bandleader:* Bernie Richards, *Mr. Gilliam:* Martin Eric.

Parrish with Dean Jagger, Troy Donahue and Diane McBain.

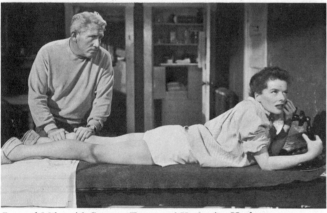

Pat and Mike with Spencer Tracy and Katharine Hepburn.

PAT AND MIKE (1952) MGM. Producer, Lawrence Weingarten. Director, George Cukor. Story and Screenplay, Ruth Gordon, Garson Kanin. Music, David Raksin. Art Directors, Cedric Gibbons, Urie McCleary. Cinematographer, William Daniels. Editor, George Boemler. 94 minutes

Mike Conovan: Spencer Tracy, *Pat Pemberton:* Katharine Hepburn, *Davie Hucko:* Aldo Ray, *Collier Weld:* William Ching, *Barney Grau:* Sammy White, *Spec Cauley:* George Mathews, *Mr. Beminger:* Loring Smith, *Mrs. Beminger:* Phyllis Povah, *Hank Tasling:* Charles Buchinski (Bronson), *Sam Garsell:* Frank Richards, *Charles Barry:* Jim Backus, *Police Captain:* Chuck Connors, *Gibby:* Joseph E. Bernard, *Harry MacWade:* Owen McGiveney, *Waiter:* Lou Lubin, *Bus Boy:* Carl Switzer, *Pat's Caddy:* William Self, *Caddies:* Billy McLean, Frankie Darro, Paul Brinegar, "Tiny" Jimmie Kelly, *Women Golfers:* Mae Clarke, Helen Eby-Rock, Elizabeth Holmes, *Commentator:* Hank Weaver, *Sportscaster:* Tom Harmon, *Themselves:* Gussie Moran, Babe Didrikson Zaharias, Don Budge, Alice Marble, Frank Parker, Betty Hicks, Beverly Hanson, Helen Dettweiler.

Patton with George C. Scott.

PATTON (1970) 20th. Produced by Frank McCarthy. Directed by Franklin J. Schaffner. In Dimension 150 and DeLuxe Color. Based on factual material from *Patton: Ordeal and Triumph* by Ladislas Farago and *A Soldier's Story* by Gen. Omar N. Bradley. Screen Story and Screenplay, Francis Ford Coppola and Edmund H. North. Music, Jerry Goldsmith. Photography, Fred Koenekamp. Assistant Directors, Eli Dunn and Jose Lopez Rodero. Associate Producer, Frank Caffey. Art Director, Urie McCleary and Gil Parrando. Set Decoration, Antonio Mateos and Pierre Louis Thevenet. Special Photographic Effects, L. B. Abbott and Art Cruickshank. Make-up Supervision, Dan Striepeke. Make-up Artist, Del Acevedo. Editor, Hugh S. Fowler. Orchestration, Arthur Morton. Technical Advisers, Gen. Paul D. Harkins, USA, Ret., and Col. Glover S. Johns, Jr., USA, Ret. Senior Military Adviser, General of the Army Omar N. Bradley, USA. Spanish Military Adviser, Lt. Col. Luis Martin Pozuelo. Filmed in Spain, Morocco, Crete, England, United States. 170 minutes

Gen. George S. Patton, Jr.: George C. Scott, *Gen. Omar N. Bradley:* Karl Malden, *Lt. Col. Charles R. Codman:* Paul Stevens, *Field Marshall Sir Bernard L. Montgomery:* Michael Bates, *Sgt. William G. Meeks:* James Edwards, *Field Marshal Erwin Rommel:* Karl Michael Vogler, *Maj. Gen. Walter Bedell Smith:* Edward Binns, *Lt. Col. Henry Davenport:* Frank Latimore, *Col. Gaston Bell:* Lawrence Dobkin, *Col. Gen. Alfred Jodl:* Richard Muench, *Capt. Chester B. Hansen:* Stephen Young, *Brig. Gen. Hobart Carver:* Michael Strong, *PFC Who Gets Slapped:* Tim Considine, *Patton's Driver:* Bill Hickman, *Bradley's Driver:* Carey Loftin, *Moroccan Minister:* Albert Dumortier, *Capt. Richard N. Jenson:* Morgan Paull, *1st Lt. Alexander Stiller:* Patrick J. Zurica, *Lt. Gen. Harry Buford:* David Bauer, *Air Vice-Marshall Sir Arthur Coningham:* John Barrie, *Capt. Oskar Steiger:* Siegfried Rauch, *Air Chief Marshal Sir Arthur Tedder:* Gerald Flood, *Gen. Sir Harold Alexander:* Jack Gwillim, *Col. John Welkin:* Peter Barkworth, *Third Army Chaplain:* Lionel Murton, *Clergyman:* David Healy, *Correspondent:* Sandy Kevin, *Maj. Gen. Francis de Guingand:* Douglas Wilmer, *Maj. Gen. Lucian K. Truscott:* John Doucette, *Willy:* Abraxas Aaran, *Tank Captain:* Clint Ritchie, *British Briefing Officer:* Alan MacNaughton.

THE PAWNBROKER (1965) Landau-Unger Allied Artists. Executive Producer, Worthington Miner. Director, Sidney Lumet. Screenplay, David Friedkin, Morton Fine. Based on novel by Edward Lewis Wallant. Producers, Roger H. Lewis, Philip Langer. Director of Photography, Boris Kaufman. Music, Quincy Jones. Associate Producer, Joseph Manduke. Costumes, Anna Hill Johnstone. Assistant Director, Dan Eriksen. 110 minutes

Sol Nazerman: Rod Steiger, *Marilyn Birchfield:* Geraldine Fitzgerald, *Rodriguez:* Brock Peters, *Jesus Ortiz:* Jaime Sanchez, *Ortiz' Girl:* Thelma Oliver, *Tessie:* Marketa Kimbrell, *Mendel:* Baruch Lumet,

Mr. Smith: Juano Hernandez, *Ruth:* Linda Geiser, *Bertha:* Nancy R. Pollock, *Tangee:* Raymond St. Jacques, *Buck:* John McCurry, *Robinson:* Ed Morehouse, *Mrs. Ortiz:* Eusebia Cosme, *Savarese:* Warren Finnerty, *Morton:* Jack Ader, *Papa:* E. M. Margolese, *Joan:* Marianne Kanter.

The Pawnbroker with Rod Steiger and Brock Peters.

Pete Kelly's Blues with Jack Webb and Peggy Lee.

PETE KELLY'S BLUES (1955) WB. Director, Jack Webb. Assistant Director, Harry D'Arcy. Screenplay by Richard L. Breen. Costumes by Howard Shoup. Music by Ray Heindorf, Sammy Cahn and Arthur Hamilton. A Mark VII Production in CinemaScope and WarnerColor. Kelly's Big 7 arrangements by Matty Matlock. Cornet solo by Ted Buckner. Plantation scene filmed in Flemming, Louisiana. 95 minutes

Pete Kelly (Narrator): Jack Webb, *Ivy Conrad:* Janet Leigh, *Fran McCarg:* Edmond O'Brien, *Rose Hopkins:* Peggy Lee, *George Tenell:* Andy Devine, *Al Gannaway:* Lee Marvin, *Maggie Jackson:* Ella Fitzgerald, *Joey Firestone:* Martin Milner, *Cigarette Girl:* Jayne Mansfield, *Rudy:* Than Wyenn, *Bedido:* Herb Ellis, *Guy Bettenhouser:* John

Dennis, *Cootie Jacobs:* Mort Marshall, *Squat Henchman:* Nesdon Booth, *Dako:* William Lazerus, *Cornetist:* Dick Cathcart, *Clarinetist:* Matty Matlock, *Trombonist:* Moe Schneider, *Saxophonist:* Eddie Miller, *Guitarist:* George Van Eps, *Drummer:* Nick Fatool, *Pianist:* Ray Sherman, *Bass Player:* Jud de Naut, *Waiter in Rudy's:* Snub Pollard. The Israelite Spiritual Church Choir of New Orleans.

THE PETRIFIED FOREST (1936) WB. Supervised by Henry Blanke. Directed by Archie L. Mayo. Based on the play by Robert Sherwood. Screenplay, Charles Kenyon and Delmer Daves. Camera, Sol Polito. Editor, Owen Marks. 83 minutes. Remade as *Escape in the Desert* (1945)

Alan Squier: Leslie Howard, *Gabrielle Maple:* Bette Davis, *Mrs. Chisholm:* Genevieve Tobin, *Boze Hertzlinger:* Dick Foran, *Duke Mantee:* Humphrey Bogart, *Jackie:* Joseph Sawyer, *Jason Maple:* Porter Hall, *Gramp Maple:* Charley Grapewin, *Mr. Chisholm:* Paul Harvey, *Lineman:* Eddie Acuff, *Ruby:* Adrian Morris, *Paula:* Nina Campana, *Slim:* Slim Thompson, *Joseph, the Chauffeur:* John Alexander, *Commander of Black Horse Troopers:* Arthur Aylesworth, *Trooper:* George Guhl, *Mantee's Girl:* Constance Bergen, *Second Lineman:* Francis Shide, *Postman:* Gus Leonard, *Sheriff:* James Farley, *Deputy:* Jack Cheatham.

The Petrified Forest with Humphrey Bogart, Leslie Howard and Bette Davis.

Peyton Place with Lana Turner and Diane Varsi.

PEYTON PLACE (1957) 20th. Producer, Jerry Wald. Director, Mark Robson. CinemaScope, De Luxe Color. Based on the novel by Grace Metalious. Screenplay, John Michael Hayes. Art Directors, Lyle R. Wheeler, Jack Martin Smith. Music, Franz Waxman. Orchestration, Edward B. Powell. Cinematographer, William Mellor. Special Photographic Effects, L. B. Abbott. Editor, David Bretherton. Later a TV series. 162 minutes

Constance MacKenzie: Lana Turner, *Selena Cross:* Hope Lange, *Michael Rossi:* Lee Philips, *Dr. Swain:* Lloyd Nolan, *Allison:* Diane Varsi, *Lucas Cross:* Arthur Kennedy, *Norman Page:* Russ Tamblyn, *Betty Anderson:* Terry Moore, *Rodney Harrington:* Barry Coe, *Ted Carter:* David Nelson, *Nellie Cross:* Betty Field, *Mrs. Thornton:* Mildred Dunnock, *Harrington:* Leon Ames, *Prosecutor:* Lorne Greene, *Seth Bushwell:* Robert H. Harris, *Margie:* Tami Connor, *Charles Partridge:* Staats Cotsworth, *Marion Partridge:* Peg Hillias, *Mrs. Page:* Erin O'Brien-Moore, *Joey Cross:* Scotty Morrow, *Paul Cross:* Bill Lundmark, *Matt:* Alan Reed, Jr., *Pee Wee:* Kip King, *Kathy:* Steffi Sidney, *Judge:* Tom Greenway, *Naval Officer:* Ray Montgomery, *Messenger:* Jim Brandt, *Miss Colton:* Edith Claire, *Army Sergeant:* John Doucette, *Bailiff:* Alfred Tonkel, *Cory Hyde:* Edwin Jerome, *Jury Foreman:* Bob Adler, *Court Clerk:* Harry Carter.

The Philadelphia Story with Katharine Hepburn, Ruth Hussey and James Stewart.

THE PHILADELPHIA STORY (1940) MGM. Produced by Joseph L. Mankiewicz. Directed by George Cukor. Based on the play by Philip Barry. Screenplay, Donald Ogden Stewart. Art Director, Cedric Gibbons. Associate, Wade B. Rubottom. Music, Franz Waxman. Photography, Joseph Ruttenberg. Editor, Frank Sullivan. Sound, Douglas Shearer. Set Decorations, Edwin B. Willis. Gowns, Adrian. Hair Styles, Sydney Guilaroff. Remade as a musical, *High Society* (MGM, 1956). 112 minutes

Dexter Haven: Cary Grant, *Tracy Lord:* Katharine Hepburn, *Mike Connor:* James Stewart, *Liz Imbrie:* Ruth Hussey, *George Kittredge:* John Howard, *Uncle Willie:* Roland Young, *Seth Lord:* John Halliday, *Dinah Lord:* Virginia Weidler, *Margaret Lord:* Mary Nash, *Sidney Kidd:* Henry Daniell, *Edward:* Lionel Pape, *Thomas:* Rex Evans, *John:* Russ Clark, *Librarian:* Hilda Plowright, *Manicurist:* Lita Chevret, *Bartender:* Lee Phelps, *Mac:* David Clyde, *Willie's Butler:* Claude King, *Dr. Parsons:* Robert de Bruce, *Elsie:* Veda Buckland, *First Mainliner:* Dorothy Fay, *Second Mainliner:* Florine McKinney, *Third Mainliner:* Helene Whitney, *Fourth Mainliner:* Hillary Brooke.

PICNIC (1955) Col. Producer, Fred Kohlmar. Director, Joshua Logan. CinemaScope, Technicolor. Based on the play by William Inge. Screenplay, Daniel Taradash. Art Director, William Flannery. Musical Director, Morris Stoloff. Music, George Duning. Orchestration, Arthur Morton. Cinematographer, James Wong Howe. Editors, Charles Nelson, William A. Lyon. Film debut of Susan Strasberg. 113 minutes. Later a musical play.

Hal Carter: William Holden, *Rosemary Sydeny:* Rosalind Russell, *Madge Owens:* Kim Novak, *Flo Owens:* Betty Field, *Millie Owens:*

Susan Strasberg, *Alan:* Cliff Robertson, *Howard Bevans:* Arthur O'Connell, *Mrs. Helen Potts:* Verna Felton, *Linde Sue Breckenridge:* Reta Shaw, *Bomber:* Nick Adams, *Mr. Benson:* Raymond Bailey, *Christine Schoenwalder:* Elizabeth W. Wilson, *Juanita Badger:* Phyllis Newman, *First Policeman:* Don C. Harvey, *Second Policeman:* Steve Benton, *President of Chamber of Commerce:* Henry P. Watson, *Trainman:* Abraham Weinlood, *Foreman:* Wayne R. Sullivan, *Stranger:* Warren Frederick Adams, *Grain Elevator Worker:* Carle E. Baker, *Mayor:* Henry Pegueo, *Committee Woman:* Flomanita Jackson, *Neighbor:* George E. Bemis.

Picnic with Arthur O'Connell, Rosalind Russell, William Holden and Susan Strasberg.

The Pied Piper with Roddy McDowall, Merrill Rodin, Fleurette Zama, Peggy Ann Garner, Monty Woolley, Anne Baxter and Maurice Tauzin.

THE PIED PIPER (1942) 20th. Produced by Nunnally Johnson. Directed by Irving Pichel. Based on the novel, which appeared in *Collier's* magazine, by Nevil Shute. Screenplay, Nunnally Johnson. Art Directors, Richard Day and Maurice Ransford. Set Decorations, Thomas Little. Costumes, Dolly Tree. Score, Alfred Newman. Photography, Edward Cronjager. Editor, Allen McNeil. Sound, E. Clayton Ward and Roger Heman. 87 minutes

Howard: Monty Woolley, *Ronnie Cavanaugh:* Roddy McDowall, *Nicole Rougeron:* Anne Baxter, *Major Diessen:* Otto Preminger, *Aristide Rougeron:* J. Carrol Naish, *Mr. Cavanaugh:* Lester Mathews, *Mrs. Cavanaugh:* Jill Esmond, *Madame:* Ferike Boros, *Sheila Cavanaugh:* Peggy Ann Garner, *Willem:* Merrill Rodin, *Pierre:* Maurice Tauzin, *Rose:* Fleurette Zama, *Frenchman:* William Edmunds, *Foquet:* Marcel Dalio, *Madame Bonne:* Marcelle Corday, *Charendon:* Edward Ashley, *Roger Dickinson:* Morton Lowry, *Madame Rougeron:* Odette

Myrtil, *Railroad Official:* Jean Del Val, *Barman:* George Davis, *Lieutenant:* Robert O. Davis (Rudolph Anders), *Military Policeman:* Henry Rowland, *Aide:* Helmut Dantine, *German Soldiers:* Otto Reichow, Henry Guttman, *Sergeants:* Hans Von Morhart, Hans Von Twardowski, *Officer at Road:* William Yetter, *Servant:* Adrienne d'Ambricourt, *Proprietress:* Mici Goty, *Fisherman:* Jean De Briac, *Soldier:* Ernst Hausman, *Anna:* Julika, *Waiter:* Wilson Benge, *Major Domo:* Brandon Hurst, *Medford:* Thomas Louden.

Pigskin Parade with Judy Garland, Patsy Kelly, Johnny Downs and Betty Grable.

PIGSKIN PARADE (1936) 20th. Associate Producer, Bogart Rogers. Directed by David Butler. Story, Arthur Sheekman, Nat Perrin, and Mark Kelly. Screenplay, Harry Tugend, Jack Yellen, and William Conselman. Music Director, David Buttolph. Camera, Arthur Miller. Editor, Irene Morra. Songs by Sidney Mitchell and Lew Pollack: "It's Love I'm After," "The Balboa," "You're Slightly Terrific," "You Do the Darndest Things, Baby," "T. S. U. Alma Mater," "Hold That Bulldog," "The Texas Tornado." By Yacht Club Boys: "We'd Rather Be in College," "Down With Everything," "Woo! Woo!" Feature film debut of Judy Garland, 14. 93 minutes

Amos Dodd: Stuart Erwin, *Bessie Winters:* Patsy Kelly, *Slug (Winston) Winters:* Jack Haley, *Chip Carson:* Johnny Downs, *Laura Watson:* Betty Grable, *Sally Saxon:* Arline Judge, *Ginger Jones:* Dixie Dunbar, *Sairy Dodd:* Judy Garland, *Tommy Barker:* Tony Martin, *Biff Bentley:* Fred Kohler, Jr., *Herbert Terwilliger Van Dyck:* Elisha Cook, Jr., *Sparks:* Eddie Nugent, *Mortimer Higgins:* Grady Sutton, *Doctor Burke:* Julius Tannen, *The Yacht Club Boys:* Themselves, *Radio Announcer (Himself):* Sam Hayes, *Country Boy:* Robert McClung, *Professor:* George Herbert, *Usher:* Jack Murphy, *Referee:* Pat Flaherty, *Messenger Boy:* Dave Sharpe, *Baggage Master:* Si Jenks, *Doctor:* John Dilson, *Policeman:* Jack Stoney, *Brakeman:* George Y. Harvey, *Boy in Stadium:* Ben Hall, *Girl in Stadium:* Lynn Bari, *Yale Coach:* Charles Wilson, *Freddy, Yale Reporter:* George Offerman, Jr., *Professor Tutweiler:* Maurice Cass, *Professor McCormick:* Jack Best, *Professor Dutton:* Douglas Wood, *Professor Pillsbury:* Charles Croker King, *Student:* Alan Ladd, *Judge:* Edward Le Saint.

PILLOW TALK (1959) Univ. Producers, Ross Hunter and Martin Melcher. Director, Michael Gordon. Screenplay by Stanley Shapiro and Maurice Richlin. Based on story by Russell Rouse and Clarence Greene. Music by Frank DeVol. Gowns by Jean Louis. Assistant Director, Phil Bowles. Art Directors, Alexander Golitzen, Richard H. Riedel. Musical Director, Joseph Gershenson. Cinematographer, Arthur E. Arling. Special Photography, Clifford Stine, Roswell Hoffman. Editor, Milton Carruth. An Arwin Production in CinemaScope and Eastman Color. Songs: "Pillow Talk" by Buddy Pepper and Inez James; "I Need No Atmosphere," "You Lied," "Possess Me" and "Inspiration" by Joe Lubin and I. J. Roth; "Roly Poly" by Elsa Doran and Sol Lake. Locations filmed in New York City. 110 minutes

Brad Allen: Rock Hudson, *Jan Morrow:* Doris Day, *Jonathan Forbes:*

Tony Randall, *Alma:* Thelma Ritter, *Tony Walters:* Nick Adams, *Marie:* Julia Meade, *Harry:* Allen Jenkins, *Pierot:* Marcel Dalio, *Mrs. Walters:* Lee Patrick, *Nurse Resnick:* Mary McCarty, *Dr. Maxwell:* Alex Gerry, *Mr. Conrad:* Hayden Rorke, *Eileen:* Valerie Allen, *Yvette:* Jacqueline Beer, *Tilda:* Arlen Stuart, *Singer:* Perry Blackwell, *Mr. Walters:* Don Beddoe, *Mr. Graham:* Robert B. Williams, *Fat Girl:* Muriel Landers, *Hotel Clerk:* William Schallert, *Miss Dickenson:* Karen Norris, *Jonathan's Secretary:* Lois Rayman, *Hansom Cabby:* Harry Tyler, *Dry Goods Man:* Joe Mell, *A Trucker:* Boyd (Red) Morgan, *A Singer:* Dorothy Abbott.

Pillow Talk with Doris Day and Tony Randall.

THE PINK PANTHER (1964) UA. Producer, Martin Jurow. Director, Blake Edwards. Technirama, Technicolor. Screenplay, Maurice Richlin, Blake Edwards. Associate Producer, Dick Crockett. Music, Henry Mancini. Director of Photography, Philip Lathrop. Assistant Director, Ottavio Oppo. Wardrobe principally by Yves St. Laurent. Presented by Mirisch Company. Song, "It Had Better Be Tonight" (Meglio Stasera) by Henry Mancini, Johnny Mercer, Franco Misliacci. 113 minutes

Sir Charles: David Niven, *Inspector Jacques Clouseau:* Peter Sellers, *George:* Robert Wagner, *Simone Clouseau:* Capucine, *Princess Dala:* Claudia Cardinale, *Angela Dunning:* Brenda De Banzie, *Greek "Cousin":* Fran Jeffries, *Tucker:* Colin Gordon, *Defense Attorney:* John LeMesurier, *Saloud:* James Lanphier, *Artoff:* Guy Thomajan, *Novelist:* Michael Trubshawe, *Greek Shipowner:* Riccardo Billi, *Hollywood Starlet:* Meri Wells, *Photographer:* Martin Miller.

The Pink Panther with Capucine, Peter Sellers and Robert Wagner.

THE PINK PANTHER STRIKES AGAIN (1976) UA. An Amjo Productions Picture. Produced and Directed by Blake Edwards. Written by Frank Waldman and Blake Edwards. Associate Producer, Tony Adams. Photography, Harry Waxman. Animation and Titles by Richard Williams Studio. Production Supervisor, Derek Kavanagh. Production

Designer, Peter Mullins. Art Director, John Siddall. Assistant Directors, Terry Marcel and David Wimbury. Sound, Peter Sutton. Editor, Alan Jones. Wardrobe, Bridget Sellers and Tiny Nicholls. Hairdresser, Barbara Ritchie. Make-up, Harry Frampton. Special Effects, Kit West. Music, Henry Mancini. Lyrics, Don Black. Song, "Come to Me," sung by Tom Jones. Produced in England in Panavision and DeLuxe Color. Sellers' fourth in the series. Rated PG. 103 minutes

Inspector Jacques Clouseau: Peter Sellers, *Ex-Chief Inspector Dreyfus:* Herbert Lom, *Alex Drummond:* Colin Blakely, *Quinlan:* Leonard Rossiter, *Olga:* Lesley-Anne Down, *Cato:* Burt Kwouk, *Francois:* Andre Maranne, *Dr. Hugo Fassbender:* Richard Vernon, *Jarvis:* Michael Robbins, *Margo Fassbender:* Briony McRoberts, *President Gerald Ford:* Dick Crockett, *Secretary of State Kissinger:* Byron Kane, *CIA Director:* Paul Maxwell, *Presidential Aide:* Jerry Stovin, *Virginia Senator:* Phil Brown, *CIA Agent:* Bob Sherman, *U. S. Admiral:* Robert Beatty, *McLaren:* Dudley Sutton, *Mrs. Leverlilly:* Vanda Godsell, *Mr. Bullock:* Norman Mitchell, *Mrs. Japonica:* Patsy Smart, *Mr. Shork:* Tony Sympson, *Mr. Stutterstut:* George Leech, *Dr. Zelmo Flek:* Murray Kash, *Pretty Lady:* April Walker, *Danny Salvo:* Hal Galili, *Marty the Mugger:* Dinny Powell, *Bruce the Knife:* Terry Richards, *Hindu Harry:* Bill Cummins, *Cairo Fred:* Terry York, *Kidnappers:* Terry Plummer and Peter Brace, *Tournier:* John Sullivan, *Bouncer:* Cyd Child, *West German Assassin:* Eddie Stacey, *Egyptian Assassin:* Rocky Taylor (Omar Sharif), *Taxi Passenger:* Fred Haggerty, *Munich Hotel Doorman:* Joe Powell, *Service Repairman:* Jackie Cooper (not the star-director), *Stewardess:* Priceless McCarthy, *Fat Lady:* Fran Fullenwider. Cut were Marne Maitland as *Deputy Commissioner* and Howard K. Smith as himself.

The Pink Panther Strikes Again with Herbert Lom and Peter Sellers.

Pinky with Arthur Hunnicutt, Jeanne Crain, Robert Osterloh, Frederick O'Neal and Nina Mae McKinney.

PINKY (1949) 20th. Producer, Darryl F. Zanuck. Director, Elia Kazan. From a novel by Cid Ricketts Sumner, *Quality.* Screenplay, Philip Dunne, Dudley Nichols. Art Directors, Lyle Wheeler, J. Russell Spencer. Photography, Joe MacDonald. Editor, Harmon Jones. Song by Harry Ruby and Alfred Newman: "Blue (With You or Without You)." 102 minutes

Pinky: Jeanne Crain, *Miss Em:* Ethel Barrymore, *Granny:* Ethel Waters, *Dr. Thomas Adams:* William Lundigan, *Judge Walker:* Basil Ruysdael, *Dr. Canady:* Kenny Washington, *Rozelia:* Nina Mae McKinney, *Dr. Joe:* Griff Barnett, *Jake Walters:* Frederick O'Neal, *Melba Wooley:* Evelyn Varden, *Judge Shoreham:* Raymond Greenleaf, *Stanley:* Dan Riss, *Mr. Goolby:* William Hansen, *Police Chief:* Arthur Hunnicutt, *Police Officer:* Robert Osterloh, *Saleslady:* Jean Inness, *Boy:* Shelby Bacon, *Mr. Wooley:* Everett Glass, *Teejore:* Rene Beard, *Nurses:* Tonya Overstreet, Juanita Moore.

A Place in the Sun with Montgomery Clift and Shelley Winters.

A PLACE IN THE SUN (1951) Par. Producer-Director, George Stevens. From a novel by Theodore Dreiser (*An American Tragedy*). Screenplay, Michael Wilson, Harry Brown. Art Directors, Hans Dreier, Walter Tyler. Music Score, Franz Waxman. Photography, William C. Mellor. Editor, William Hornbeck. Filmed at Lake Tahoe in High Sierras. Remake of Paramount's *An American Tragedy* (1931). 122 minutes

George Eastman: Montgomery Clift, *Angela Vickers:* Elizabeth Taylor, *Alice Tripp:* Shelley Winters, *Hannah Eastman:* Anne Revere, *Earl Eastman:* Keefe Brasselle, *Bellows:* Fred Clark, *Marlowe:* Raymond Burr, *Charles Eastman:* Herbert Heyes, *Anthony Vickers:* Shepperd Strudwick, *Mrs. Vickers:* Frieda Inescort, *Mrs. Louise Eastman:* Kathryn Givney, *Jansen:* Walter Sande, *Judge:* Ted de Corsia, *Coroner:* John Ridgely, *Marsha:* Lois Chartrand, *Mr. Whiting:* William R. Murphy, *Boatkeeper:* Douglas Spencer, *Kelly:* Charles Dayton, *Morrison:* Paul Frees, *Joe Parker:* John Reed, *Frances Brand:* Marilyn Dialon, *Dr. Wyeland:* Ian Wolfe, *Secy. to Charles Eastman:* Josephine Whittell, *Truck Driver:* Frank Yaconelli, *Policeman:* Ralph A. Dunn, *Eagle Scout:* Bob Anderson, *Maid:* Lisa Golm, *Mrs. Roberts (Landlady):* Mary Kent, *A Warden:* Ken Christy, *Martha:* Kathleen Freeman, *Butler at Eastman Home:* Hans Moebus, *Butler:* Eric Wilton, *Motorcycle Officer:* Mike Mahoney, *Bailiff:* Al Ferguson, *Tom Tipton:* James W. Horne, *Miss Harper:* Laura Elliot, *Miss Newton:* Pearl Miller, *Jailer:* Major Philip Kieffer, *Man:* Major Sam Harris.

THE PLAINSMAN (1936) Par. Produced and directed by Cecil B. De Mille. Based on data from stories by Courtney Ryley Cooper and *Wild Bill Hickok* by Frank Wilstach. Screenplay, Waldemar Young, Lynn Riggs, and Harold Lamb. Data compiled by Jeanie Macpherson.

Associate Director, Richard Harlan. Camera, Victor Milner and George Robinson. Editor, Anne Bauchens. Special Effects, Farciot Edouart and Gordon Jennings. Music Director, Boris Morros. Special Score, George Antheil. Dialogue Supervision, Edwin Maxwell. Remade by Universal, 1966. 113 minutes

Wild Bill Hickok: Gary Cooper, *Calamity Jane:* Jean Arthur, *Buffalo Bill Cody:* James Ellison, *John Lattimer:* Charles Bickford, *Louisa Cody:* Helen Burgess, *Jack McCall:* Porter Hall, *Yellow Hand:* Paul Harvey, *Painted Horse:* Victor Varconi, *General George A. Custer:* John Miljan, *Abraham Lincoln:* Frank McGlynn, Sr., *Van Ellyn:* Granville Bates, *Young Trooper of the Seventh Cavalry:* Frank Albertson, *Captain Wood:* Purnell Pratt, *Jake, a Teamster:* Fred Kohler, Sr., *Breezy:* George Hayes, *Sergeant McGinnis:* Patrick Moriarity, *Tony, the Barber:* Charles Judels, *Quartermaster Sergeant:* Harry Woods, *Northern Cheyenne Indian:* Anthony Quinn, *A River Gambler:* Francis McDonald, *Boy on the Dock:* George Ernest, *General Merritt:* George MacQuarrie, *Schuyler Colfax:* John Hyams, *Stanton, Secretary of War:* Edwin Maxwell, *Purser of the Lizzie Gill:* Bruce Warren, *Injun Charley:* Charlie Stevens, *Van Ellyn's Associates:* Arthur Aylesworth, Douglas Wood, George Cleveland, *Southern Girl:* Lona Andre, *Hysterical Trooper:* Irving Bacon, *Old Veteran:* Francis Ford, *Corporal Brannigan:* William Royle, *Dave, a Miner:* Fuzzy Knight, *Mary Todd Lincoln:* Leila McIntyre, *John F. Usher:* Harry Stubbs, *James Speed:* Davison Clark, *William H. Seward:* Charles W. Herzinger, *Hugh McCulloch:* William Humphries, *Giddeon Wells:* Sidney Jarvis, *Extra:* Hank Worden, *Bit Man:* Bud Flanagan (Dennis O'Keefe), *Indian:* Noble Johnson, *William Dennison:* Wadsworth Harris, *Major:* Jonathan Hale.

The Plainsman with Gary Cooper, Anthony Quinn and James Ellison.

PLANET OF THE APES (1968) 20th. An APJAC Production. Produced by Arthur P. Jacobs. Associate Producer, Mort Abrahams. Directed by Franklin J. Schaffner. Assistant Director, William Kissel. Based on the novel *Monkey Planet* by Pierre Boulle. Screenplay, Michael Wilson and Rod Serling. Music, Jerry Goldsmith. Photography, Leon Shamroy. Special Photographic Effects, L. B. Abbott, Art Cruickshank and Emil Kosa, Jr. Art Direction, Jack Martin Smith and William Creber. Set Decorations, Walter M. Scott and Norman Rockett. Editor, Hugh S. Fowler. Sound, Herman Lewis and David Dockendorf. Make-up, Ben Nye and Dan Striepeke. Special Make-up Design, John Chambers. Costumes, Morton Haack. Hairstyles, Edith Lindon. In Panavision and DeLuxe Color. Filmed partly in Utah and Arizona National Park. First of five Ape films. 112 minutes

George Taylor: Charlton Heston, *Cornelius:* Roddy McDowall, *Dr. Zira:* Kim Hunter, *Dr. Zaius:* Maurice Evans, *President of the Assembly:* James Whitmore, *Honorius:* James Daly, *Nova:* Linda Harrison, *Landon:* Robert Gunner, *Lucius:* Lou Wagner, *Maximus:* Woodrow Parfrey, *Dodge:* Jeff Burton, *Julius:* Buck Kartalian, *Hunt Leader:* Norman Burton, *Dr. Galen:* Wright King, *Minister:* Paul Lambert, *First Human:* Priscilla Boyd, *Human:* Jane Ross, *Astronaut Stewart:* Dianne Stanley, *Ape*

Photographer/Gorilla: Robert Lombardo, *Child Gorilla:* Felix Silla, *Child Apes:* Billy Curtis, Harry Monty, Frank Delfino, Jerry Maren, Emory Souza, Buddy Douglas, *Chimpanzee Woman:* Erlynn Botelho, *Chimpanzees:* Cass Martin, Smokey Roberds, George Sasaki, David Chow, Norma Jean Kron, *Gorillas:* Chuck Fisher, John Quijada, Eldon Burke, Bill Graeff, Joseph Anthony (Tornatore), Dave Rodgers, Army Archerd.

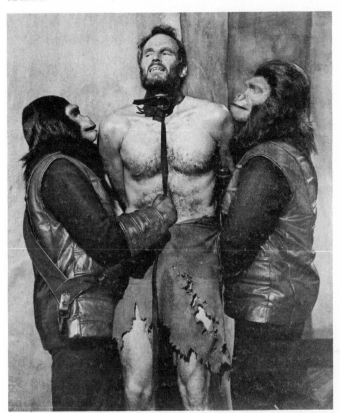

Planet of the Apes with Charlton Heston.

Play It Again, Sam with Woody Allen.

PLAY IT AGAIN, SAM (1972) Par. An Apjac/Rollins-Joffe Production. Produced by Arthur P. Jacobs. Directed by Herbert Ross. Technicolor. Screenplay by Woody Allen, based on his 1969 play which starred Allen, Keaton, Roberts and Lacy. Executive Producer, Charles Joffe. Photography, Owen Roizman. Editor, Marion Rothman. Art Director, Ed Wittstein. Set Decorations, Doug Von Koss. Sound, Richard Pietschmann and David Dockendorf. Titles, Don Record. Costumes, Anna Hill Johnstone. Make-up, Stanley R. Dufford. Hairstyles, Patricia D. Abbott. Associate Producer, Frank Capra, Jr. Assistant Director, William Gerrity. Production Supervisor, Roger M. Rothstein. Special Photographic Consultant, Keith Smith. Music by Billy Goldenberg. Songs: "Blues for Allan Felix," composed and performed by Oscar Peterson; "As Time Goes By" by Herman Hupfeld, as performed in *Casablanca* by Dooley Wilson. Filmed in and around San Francisco. Rated PG. 87 minutes

Allan Felix: Woody Allen, *Linda Christie:* Diane Keaton, *Dick Christie:* Tony Roberts, *Humphrey Bogart:* Jerry Lacy, *Nancy Felix:* Susan Anspach, *Sharon:* Jennifer Salt, *Julie:* Joy Bang, *Dream Sharon:* Mari Fletcher, *Girl in Museum:* Diana Davila, *Discotheque Girl:* Suzanne Zenor, *Hoods:* Michael Greene, Ted Markland, *Jennifer:* Viva.

Please Don't Eat the Daisies with Flip Mark, Stanley Livingston, Hobo, David Niven, Charles Herbert, Spring Byington, Doris Day, Patsy Kelly and Baby Gellert.

PLEASE DON'T EAT THE DAISIES (1960) MGM. Produced by Joe Pasternak. Associate Producer, Martin Melcher. Directed by Charles Walters. In Panavision and MetroColor. Based on the book by Jean Kerr. Screenplay, Isobel Lennart. Music, David Rose. Art Directors, George W. Davis and Hans Peters. Costumes, Morton Haack. Assistant Director, Al Jennings. Cinematography, Robert Bronner. Editor, John McSweeney, Jr. A Euterpe Production. Songs: "Please Don't Eat the Daisies" by Jay Lubin; "Any Way the Wind Blows" by Marilyn and Joe Hooven and By Dunham. Scene filmed in New York. Later a TV series. 111 minutes

Kate Mackay: Doris Day, *Larry Mackay:* David Niven, *Deborah Vaughn:* Janis Paige, *Suzie Robinson:* Spring Byington, *Alfred North:* Richard Haydn, *Maggie:* Patsy Kelly, *Joe Positano:* Jack Weston, *Reverend Dr. McQuarry:* John Harding, *Mona James:* Margaret Lindsay, *Mary Smith:* Carmen Phillips, *Mrs. Hunter:* Mary Patton, *David Mackay:* Charles Herbert, *Gabriel Mackay:* Stanley Livingston, *George Mackay:* Flip Mark, *Adam Mackay:* Baby Gellert, *Dog:* Hobo, *Jane March:* Marina Koshetz, *Dr. Sprouk:* Geraldine Wall, *Miss Yule (Principal):* Kathryn Card, *Justin Withers:* Donald Foster, *Mrs. Greenfield:* Irene Tedrow, *Paul Foster:* Anatole Winogradoff, *Young Men:* Burt Douglas, John Brennan, Guy Stockwell, *Girl:* Marianne Gaba, *Pete:* Benny Rubin, *Mrs. Kilkinny:* Madge Blake, *Waiter:* Len Lesser, *Photographer:* Wilson Wood, *Larry's Secretary:* Peter Leeds, *Pianist:* Joe Cronin, *Martha:* Amy Douglass, *Woman:* Gail Bonney, *Salesman:* Richard Collier, *Upholstery Man:* Charles Seel, *Interviewer:* Frank Wilcox, *Gus, Waiter:* Milton Frome, *Man:* Robert Darin, *Actress:* Jhean Burton.

Porgy and Bess with Sidney Poitier.

PORGY AND BESS (1959) Col. Producer, Samuel Goldwyn. Director, Otto Preminger. Screenplay by N. Richard Nash. Music by George Gershwin. Libretto by DuBose Heyward. Lyrics by DuBose Heyward and Ira Gershwin. Based on the play *Porgy* by DuBose and Dorothy Heyward. Costumes by Irene Sharaff. Choreographer, Hermes Pan. Art Directors, Serge Krizman, Joseph Wright. Musical Director, Andre Previn. Cinematographer, Leon Shamroy. Editor, Daniel Mandell. In Todd-AO and Technicolor. 138 minutes

Porgy: Sidney Poitier, *Bess:* Dorothy Dandridge, *Sportin' Life:* Sammy Davis, Jr., *Maria:* Pearl Bailey, *Crown:* Brock Peters, *Jake:* Leslie Scott, *Clara:* Diahann Carroll, *Serena:* Ruth Attaway, *Peter:* Clarence Muse, *Annie:* Everdinne Wilson, *Robbins:* Joel Fluellen, *Mingo:* Earl Jackson, *Nelson:* Moses LaMarr, *Lily:* Margaret Hairston, *Jim:* Ivan Dixon, *Scipio:* Antoine Durousseau, *Strawberry Woman:* Helen Thigpen, *Elderly Man:* Vince Townsend, Jr., *Undertaker:* William Walker, *Frazier:* Roy Glenn, *Coroner:* Maurice Manson, *Detective:* Claude Akins.

The Poseidon Adventure with Shelley Winters, Carol Lynley, Roddy McDowall and Stella Stevens.

THE POSEIDON ADVENTURE (1972) 20th. A Kent Production. Produced by Irwin Allen. Directed by Ronald Neame. Panavision, DeLuxe Color. Based on the novel by Paul Gallico. Screenplay, Stirling Silliphant and Wendell Mayes. Music by John Williams. Photography, Harold E. Stine. Orchestration, Alexander Courage. Editor, Harold F. Kress. Production Design, William Creber. Set Decorations, Raphael Bretton. Special Photographic Effects, L. B. Abbott. Special Mechanical Effects, A. D. Flowers. Stunt Coordinator, Paul Stader. Sound, Theodore

Soderberg and Herman Lewis. Costumes, Paul Zastupnevich. Make-up, Ed Butterworth, Del Acevedo and Allan Snyder. Hairstyles, Carol Pershing, Sheral Ross and Ann Wadlington. Associate Producer, Sidney Marshall. Assistant Directors, Norman Cook, Less Warner and Don White. Song, "The Morning After" by Al Kasha and Joel Hirschhorn. Filmed partly aboard the *Queen Mary* in Long Beach, California. Rated PG. 117 minutes. Sequel was *Beyond the Poseidon Adventure* (WB, 1979)

Rev. Frank Scott: Gene Hackman, *Mike Rogo:* Ernest Borgnine, *James Martin:* Red Buttons, *Belle Rosen:* Shelley Winters, *Linda Rogo:* Stella Stevens, *Manny Rosen:* Jack Albertson, *Acres:* Roddy McDowall, *Nonnie Parry:* Carol Lynley, *Susan Shelby:* Pamela Sue Martin, *Captain:* Leslie Nielsen, *Chaplain:* Arthur O'Connell, *Robin Shelby:* Eric Shea, *Linarcos:* Fred Sadoff, *Nurse:* Sheila Mathews, *Doctor:* Jan Arvan, *Purser:* Byron Webster, *M.C.:* Bob Hastings, *Chief Engineer:* John Crawford, *Tinkham:* Erik Nelson, *Passenger (Stuntman):* Dave Sharpe.

Possessed with Joan Crawford and Raymond Massey.

POSSESSED (1947) WB. Producer, Jerry Wald. Director, Curtis Bernhardt. Based on the story *One Man's Secret* by Rita Weiman. Screenplay, Silvia Richards, Ranald MacDougall. Art Director, Anton Grot. Cameraman, Joseph Valentine. Editor, Rudi Fehr. Song by Max Leif and Joseph Meyer: "How Long Will It Last?" 108 minutes

Louise Howell: Joan Crawford, *David Sutton:* Van Heflin, *Dean Graham:* Raymond Massey, *Carol Graham:* Geraldine Brooks, *Dr. Harvey Williard:* Stanley Ridges, *Harker:* John Ridgely, *Dr. Ames:* Moroni Olsen, *Dr. Max Sherman:* Erskine Sanford, *Wynn Graham:* Gerald Perreau (Peter Miles), *Nurse Rosen:* Isabel Withers, *Elsie:* Lisa Golm, *Assistant D. A.:* Douglas Kennedy, *Norris:* Monte Blue, *Dr. Craig:* Don McGuire, *Coroner's Assistant:* Rory Mallinson, *Interne:* Clifton Young, *Coroner:* Griff Barnett, *Motorman:* Ralph Dunn, *Proprietor:* Frank Marlowe, *Foreman:* James Conaty, *Secretary:* Creighton Hale, *Man at Concert:* Tristram Coffin, *Walter Sveldon:* Jacob Gimpel, *Nurse:* Nell Craig, *Dean's Secretary:* Henry Sylvester, *Caretaker's Wife:* Sarah Padden, *Waiter:* Wheaton Chambers, *Bartender:* Eddie Hart, *Nurse:* Bunty Cutler, *Butler:* Philo McCullough.

THE POSTMAN ALWAYS RINGS TWICE (1946) MGM. Producer, Carey Wilson. Director, Tay Garnett. Based on the novel by James M. Cain. Screenplay, Harry Ruskin, Niven Busch. Musical Score, George Bassman. Art Directors, Cedric Gibbons, Randall Duell. Cameraman, Sidney Wagner. Editor, George White. Song by Neil Moret and Richard Whiting: "(I Got a Woman Crazy 'Bout Me) She's Funny That Way." 113 minutes

Cora Smith: Lana Turner, *Frank Chambers:* John Garfield, *Nick

Smith: Cecil Kellaway, *Arthur Keats:* Hume Cronyn, *D. A. Kyle Sackett:* Leon Ames, *Madge Gorland:* Audrey Totter, *Ezra Liam Kennedy:* Alan Reed, *Blair:* Jeff York, *Doctor:* Charles Williams, *Willie:* Cameron Grant, *Ben:* Wally Cassell, *Judge:* William Halligan, *Judge:* Morris Ankrum, *Truck Driver:* Garry Owen, *Nurse:* Dorothy Phillips, *Doctor:* Edward Earle, *Picnic Manager:* Byron Foulger, *Matron:* Sondra Morgan, *Reporter:* Dick Crockett, *Bailiff:* Frank Mayo, *Customer:* Betty Blythe, *John X. McHugh:* Joel Friedkin, *Headwaiter:* Jack Chefe, *Telegraph Messenger:* George Noisom, *Snooty Woman:* Virginia Randolph, *Father McConnell:* Tom Dillon, *Warden:* James Farley, *Man:* Paul Bradley.

The Postman Always Rings Twice with John Garfield, Lana Turner and Alan Reed.

Pretty Poison with Tuesday Weld and Anthony Perkins.

PRETTY POISON (1968) 20th. A Lawrence Turman-Molino Production. Produced by Marshall Backlar and Noel Black. Directed by Noel Black. Executive Producer, Lawrence Turman. Color by DeLuxe. Based on the novel *She Let Him Continue* by Stephen Geller. Screenplay, Lorenzo Semple, Jr. Music by Johnny Mandel. Photography, David Quaid. Editor, William Ziegler. Art Directors, Jack Martin Smith and Harold Michelson. Sound, Dennis Maitland and David Dockendorf. Costumes by Ann Roth. Make-up, Robert Jiras. Associate Producer/Production Manager, Jack Grossberg. Filmed in Great Barrington, Massachusetts. 89 minutes

Dennis Pitt: Tony Perkins, *Sue Ann Stepanek:* Tuesday Weld, *Mrs. Stepanek:* Beverly Garland, *Azenauer:* John Randolph, *Bud Munsch:* Dick O'Neill, *Mrs. Bronson:* Clarice Blackburn, *Pete:* Joe Bova, *Harry:* Ken Kercheval, *Nightwatchman:* Parker Fennelly, *Mrs. Stepanek's Boyfriend:* Paul Larson, *Plainclothesman:* Tim Callahan, *Burly Man:* George Fisher, *Cop at Beanery:* William Sorrells, *Men in Police Station:* Dan Morgan, Mark Dawson, Gil Rogers, *Highway Patrolmen:* John Randolph

Jones, Maurice Ottinger, *Detectives:* Tom Gorman, Don Fellows, *Cops:* Bill Fort, Ed Wagner, *Themselves:* George Ryan's Winslow High-Steppers.

The Pride and the Passion with Jose Nieto and Cary Grant.

THE PRIDE AND THE PASSION (1957) UA. Producer-Director, Stanley Kramer. Story and screenplay by Edna and Edward Anhalt. Based on the novel *The Gun* by C. S. Forester. Music by George Antheil. Assistant Director, Carter DeHaven, Jr. Costumes, Joe King. Choreography, Paco Reyes. Song by Peggy Lee. In VistaVision and Technicolor. Filmed in Spain. 132 minutes

Captain Anthony Trumbull: Cary Grant, *Miguel:* Frank Sinatra, *Juana:* Sophia Loren, *General Jouvet:* Theodore Bikel, *Sermaine:* John Wengraf, *Ballinger:* Jay Novello, *Carlos:* Jose Nieto, *Vidal:* Philip Van Zandt, *Manolo:* Paco el Laberinto, *Jose:* Carlos Larranaga.

The Pride of the Yankees with Gary Cooper.

THE PRIDE OF THE YANKEES (1942) RKO. Produced by Samuel Goldwyn. Directed by Sam Wood. Assistant Director, John Sherwood. Original Story, Paul Gallico. Screenplay, Jo Swerling and Herman J. Mankiewicz. Production Design, William Cameron Menzies. Art Director, Perry Ferguson. Associate Art Director, McClure Capps. Set Decorations, Howard Bristol. Costumes, Rene Hubert. Music, Leigh Harline. Photography, Rudolph Mate. Editor, Daniel Mandell. Sound, Frank Maher. Special Effects, Jack Cosgrove. Song, "Always," by Irving Berlin. Lou Gehrig died June 2, 1941. 128 minutes

Lou Gehrig: Gary Cooper, *Eleanor Gehrig:* Teresa Wright, *Babe Ruth:* Himself, *Sam Blake:* Walter Brennan, *Hank Hanneman:* Dan Duryea, *Mom Gehrig:* Elsa Janssen, *Pop Gehrig:* Ludwig Stossel, *Myra:* Virginia Gilmore, *Bill Dickey:* Himself, *Miller Huggins:* Ernie Adams, *Mr. Twitchell:* Pierre Watkin, *Joe McCarthy:* Harry Harvey, *Robert W. Meusel:* Himself, *Mark Koenig:* Himself, *Bill Stern:* Himself, *Coach:* Addison Richards, *Van Tuyl:* Hardie Albright, *Clinic Doctor:* Edward Fielding, *Mayor of New Rochelle:* George Lessey, *Lou as a boy:* Douglas Croft, *Laddie:* Rip Russell, *Third Base Coach:* Frank Faylen, *Hammond:* Jack Shea, *Wally Pip:* George McDonald, *Billy:* Gene Collins, *Billy at 17:* David Holt, *Mayor La Guardia:* David Manley, *Colletti:* Max Willenz, *Sasha:* Jimmy Valentine, *Sasha's Mother:* Anita Bolster, *Murphy:* Robert Winkler, *Mr. Larsen:* Spencer Charters, *Mrs. Fabini:* Rosina Galli, *Joe Fabini:* Billy Roy, *Mrs. Robert:* Sarah Padden, *Tessie:* Janet Chapman, *Mrs. Worthington:* Eva Dennison, *Mr. Worthington:* Montague Shaw, *Ed Barrow:* Jack Stewart, *Christy Mathewson:* Fay Thomas, *Fraternity Boys:* Jack Arnold (Vinton Haworth), John Kellogg, Dane Clark, Tom Neal. Veloz and Yolanda. Ray Noble and his Orchestra.

The Princess and the Pirate with Walter Slezak and Bob Hope.

THE PRINCESS AND THE PIRATE (1944) RKO. Producer, Sam Goldwyn. Associate Producer, Don Hartman. Director, David Butler. Technicolor. Suggested by a story by Sy Bartlett. Screenplay, Don Hartman, Melville Shavelson, Everett Freeman. Musical Score, David Rose. Art Director, Ernst Fegte. Cameramen, Victor Milner, William Snyder. Special Effects, R. O. Binger, Clarence Slifer. Editor, Daniel Mandell. Song by Harold Adamson and Jimmy McHugh, "How Would You Like to Kiss Me in the Moonlight?" Adaptation, Allen Boretz and Curtis Kenyon. A Regent Pictures Production. 94 minutes

Sylvester: Bob Hope, *Margaret:* Virginia Mayo, *Featherhead:* Walter Brennan, *Gov. La Roche:* Walter Slezak, *The Hook:* Victor McLaglen, *Pedro:* Marc Lawrence, *Proprietor, "Bucket of Blood":* Hugo Haas, *Landlady:* Maude Eburne, *Don Jose:* Adia Kuznetzoff, *Mr. Pelly:* Brandon Hurst, *Alonzo:* Tom Kennedy, *Captain,* MARY ANN: Stanley Andrews, *The King:* Robert Warwick, *Lieutenant:* Tom Tyler, *Gorilla Man:* Rondo Hatton, *Holdup Man:* Dick Alexander, *Citizen:* Ernie Adams, *Murderous Pirate:* Ralph Dunn, *Drunken Pirate's Companion:* Bert Roach, *Drunken Pirate:* Francis Ford, *Captain, King's Ship:* Edwin Stanley, *Guard:* Ray Teal, *Palace Guard:* Weldon Heyburn, *Palace Guard:* Edward Peil, *Soldier:* Crane Whitley, *Naval Officer:* James Flavin, *Pirate:* Alan Bridge, *Pirate:* Al Hill, *Pirate:* Dick Rich, *Pirate:* Mike Mazurki, *Bartender:* Jack Carr, *First Mate* MARY ANN: Colin Kenny, *Guest Star:* Bing Crosby.

THE PRISONER OF SHARK ISLAND (1936) 20th. Produced by Darryl F. Zanuck. Directed by John Ford. Screenplay by Nunnally Johnson. Musical Director, Louis Silvers. Cameraman, Bert Glennon. Editor, Jack Murray. 95 minutes

Dr. Samuel Mudd: Warner Baxter, *Peggy Mudd:* Gloria Stuart, *Marth Mudd:* Joyce Kay, *Colonel Dyer:* Claude Gillingwater, Sr., *General Ewing:* Douglas Wood, *Sergeant Cooper:* Fred Kohler, Jr., *Commandant:* Harry Carey, *David Herold:* Paul Fix, *Sergeant Rankin:* John Carradine, *John Wilkes Booth:* Francis McDonald, *Erickson:* Arthur Byron, *Dr. McIntire:* O. P. Heggie, *Lovett:* John McGuire, *Hunter:* Paul McVey, *O'Toole:* Francis Ford, *Buck:* Ernest Whitman, *Judge Advocate Holt:* Frank Shannon, *Lincoln:* Frank McGlynn, Sr., *Carpetbagger:* Arthur Loft, *Orderly:* Maurice Murphy, *Orator:* Paul Stanton, *Signal Man:* Ronald (Jack) Pennick, *Commandant's Aide:* Merrill McCormick, *Blacksmith:* James Marcus, *Actress:* Jan Duggan, *Major Rathbone:* Lloyd Whitlock, *Mrs. Lincoln:* Leila McIntyre, *Actor:* Dick Elliott, *Spangler:* Murdock MacQuarrie, *Sergeant:* Duke Lee, *Druggist:* Robert Dudley, *Colonel:* Wilfred Lucas, *Mrs. Surratt:* Cecil Weston, *Maurice O'Laughlin:* Cyril Thornton, *Sergeant:* Robert E. Homans, *Blanche:* Beulah Hall Jones, *Judge Maiben:* J. M. Kerrigan, *Sergeant:* Bud Geary, *Rosabelle:* Etta McDaniel, *Ship's Captain:* J. P. McGowan, *Mate:* Harry Strang.

The Prisoner of Shark Island with Gloria Stuart and Warner Baxter.

The Prisoner of Zenda with C. Aubrey Smith, David Niven and Ronald Colman.

THE PRISONER OF ZENDA (1937) UA. Produced by David O. Selznick. Assistant to the Producer, William H. Wright. Directed by John Cromwell and W. S. Van Dyke. Partly in Sepiatone. Based on the novel by Anthony J. Hope and the play by Edward Rose. Screenplay, John Balderston, Wells Root, Donald Ogden Stewart. Art Director, Lyle Wheeler. Music, Alfred Newman. Costumes, Ernest Dryden. Interior Decoration, Casey Roberts. Photography, James Wong Howe. Special Effects, Jack Cosgrove. Editors, Hal C. Kern and James

E. Newcom. Assistant Director, Frederick A. Spencer. Sepia Processing, John M. Nicholaus. Recorder (Sound), Oscar Lagerlof. Technical Advisors, Prince Sigvard Bernadotte and Colonel Ivar Enhorning. Other versions made by MGM in 1922 and 1952, and Universal, 1979. 101 minutes

Rudolph Rassendyl/King Rudolf V: Ronald Colman, *Princess Flavia:* Madeleine Carroll, *Rupert of Hentzau:* Douglas Fairbanks, Jr., *Antoinette De Mauban:* Mary Astor, *Colonel Zapt:* C. Aubrey Smith, *Black Michael:* Raymond Massey, *Captain Fritz von Tarlenheim:* David Niven, *Cook:* Eleanor Wesselhoeft, *Johann:* Byron Foulger, *Detchard:* Montagu Love, *Kraftstein:* William Von Brincken, *Lauengram:* Phillip Sleeman, *Bersonin:* Ralph Faulkner, *De Gauiet:* Alexander D'Arcy, *Michael's Butler:* Torben Meyer, *Cardinal:* Ian MacLaren, *Marshal Strakencz:* Lawrence Grant, *Josef:* Howard Lang, *British Ambassador:* Ben Webster, *British Ambassador's Wife:* Evelyn Beresford, *Master of Ceremonies:* Boyd Irwin, *Von Haugwitz, Lord High Chamberlain:* Emmett King, *Bishop:* Charles K. French, *Orchestra Leader:* Al Shean, *Passport Officer:* Charles Halton, *Luggage Officer:* Otto Fries, *Duenna:* Florence Roberts, *Porter:* Spencer Charters, *Travelers:* Russ Powell, D'Arcy Corrigan, *Man:* Francis Ford.

The Professionals with Woody Strode, Lee Marvin and Burt Lancaster.

THE PROFESSIONALS (1966) Col. Produced and directed by Richard Brooks. Color by Technicolor. Based on the novel *A Mule for the Marquesa* by Frank O'Rourke. Camera, Conrad Hall. Editor, Peter Zinner. Music, Maurice Jarre. Assistant Director, Tom Shaw. Second Unit Director, Lee Lukather. Filmed in Death Valley, Nevada; along the Mexican Border. 116 minutes

Bill Dolworth: Burt Lancaster, *Rico (Henry Fardan):* Lee Marvin, *Hans Ehrengard:* Robert Ryan, *Jesus Raza:* Jack Palance, *Maria Grant:* Claudia Cardinale, *Grant:* Ralph Bellamy, *Jake Sharp:* Woody Strode, *Pascual Ortega:* Joe De Santis, *Fierro:* Rafael Bertrand, *Eduardo Padillia:* Jorge Martinez De Hoyos, *Chiquita:* Marie Gomez, *Revolutionaries:* Jose Chavez, Carlos Romero, *Banker:* Vaughn Taylor.

PSYCHO (1960) Par. Producer-Director, Alfred Hitchcock. Screenplay, Joseph Stefano. From a novel by Robert Bloch. Music, Bernard Herrmann. Art Directors, Joseph Hurley and Robert Clatworthy. Cinematography, John L. Russell. A Shamley Production. Locations: Phoenix, Arizona; Route 99 of the Fresno-Bakersfield Highway; the San Fernando Valley; a Hollywood thoroughfare. Interiors filmed at Revue Studios. 109 minutes

Norman Bates: Anthony Perkins, *Marion Crane:* Janet Leigh, *Lila Crane:* Vera Miles, *Sam Loomis:* John Gavin, *Milton Arbogast:* Martin Balsam, *Sheriff Chambers:* John McIntire, *Dr. Richmond:* Simon Oakland, *Tom Cassidy:* Frank Albertson, *Caroline:* Pat Hitchcock, *George Lowery:* Vaughn Taylor, *Mrs. Chambers:* Lurene Tuttle,

Car Salesman: John Anderson, *Policeman:* Mort Mills, *Officials:* Sam Flint, Francis De Sales, George Eldredge, *Man Outside Office in Cowboy Hat:* Alfred Hitchcock.

Psycho with Anthony Perkins and Janet Leigh.

The Public Enemy with Jean Harlow, Eddie Woods and James Cagney.

THE PUBLIC ENEMY (1931) WB. Directed by William A. Wellman. Story by Kubec Glasmon and John Bright. Adaptation by Harvey Thew. Photography, Dev Jennings. Editor, Ed McCormick. Theme, "I'm Forever Blowing Bubbles." Although billed as Bess, Louise Brooks does not appear in the film. 83 minutes

Tom Powers: James Cagney, *Gwen Allen:* Jean Harlow, *Matt Doyle:* Edward Woods, *Mame:* Joan Blondell, *Ma Powers:* Beryl Mercer, *Mike Powers:* Donald Cook, *Kitty:* Mae Clarke, *(Samuel) Nails Nathan:* Leslie Fenton, *Paddy Ryan:* Robert Emmet O'Connor, *Putty Nose:* Murray Kinnell, *Molly Doyle:* Rita Flynn, *Hack:* Snitz Edwards, *Bugs Moran:* Ben Hendricks, Jr., *Tommy as a boy:* Frank Coghlan, Jr., *Matt as a boy:* Frankie Darro, *Officer Pat Burke:* Robert E. Homans, *Nails' Girl:* Dorothy Gee, *Steve, Bartender:* Lee Phelps, *Jane:* Mia Marvin, *Dutch:* Clark Burroughs, *Mrs. Doyle:* Adele Watson, *Little Girls:* Helen Parrish, Dorothy Gray, Nancie Price, *Bugs as a boy:* Ben Hendricks III, *Machine-Gunner:* George Daly, *Joe, Headwaiter:* Eddie Kane, *Mug:* Charles Sullivan, *Assistant Tailor:* Douglas Gerrard, *Negro Headwaiter:* Sam McDaniel, *Pawnbroker:* William H. Strauss.

THE QUIET MAN (1952) Republic. Produced by Merian C. Cooper. Directed by John Ford. Color by Technicolor. An Argosy Production. Based on a story by Maurice Walsh. Screenplay, Frank S. Nugent. Music, Victor Young. Photography, Winton C. Hoch and Archie Stout. Songs: "Galway Bay" by Dr. Edward Colahan and three tradi-

tional Irish songs, "The Wild Colonial Boy," "The Humour Is on Me Now" and "Mush Mush (Tread on the Tail of Me Coat)." Filmed in Ireland. 129 minutes

Sean Thornton: John Wayne, *Mary Kate Danaher:* Maureen O'Hara, *Red Will Danaher:* Victor McLaglen, *Michaeleen Flynn:* Barry Fitzgerald, *Father Peter Lonergan, Narrator:* Ward Bond, *Sarah Tillane:* Mildred Natwick, *Dan Tobin:* Francis Ford, *Reverend Cyril "Snuffy" Playfair:* Arthur Shields, *Elizabeth Playfair:* Eileen Crowe, *The Woman:* May Craig, *Forbes:* Charles FitzSimons, *Father Paul:* James Lilburn, *Owen Glynn:* Sean McClory, *Feeney:* Jack McGowran, *Maloney, Guard:* Joseph O'Dea, *Costello, Castletown Engineer:* Eric Gorman, *Fireman:* Kevin Lawless, *Porter:* Paddy O'Donnell, *Bailey, Stationmaster:* Web Overlander, *Dermot Fahy:* Ken Curtis, *Pat Cohan:* Harry Tyler, *Father Paul's Mother:* Mae Marsh, *Second:* Bob Perry, *General:* Major Sam Harris, *Children at Race:* Melinda and Pat Wayne, *Teenagers at Race:* Mike and Toni Wayne, *Guppy:* Don Hatswell, *Sergeant Hanan:* Harry Tenbrook, *Ring Physician:* Douglas Evans, *Constable:* David H. Hughes, *Boxer:* Jack Roper, *Referee:* Al Murphy, *Man:* Pat O'Malley.

The Quiet Man with Maureen O'Hara and John Wayne.

Quo Vadis with Patricia Laffan and Peter Ustinov.

QUO VADIS (1951) MGM. Produced by Sam Zimbalist. Directed by Mervyn LeRoy. Color by Technicolor. Based on the novel by Henryk Sienkiewicz. Screenplay, John Lee Mahin, S. N. Behrman, Sonya Levien. Art Directors, William A. Horning, Cedric Gibbons, Edward Carfagno. Photography, Robert Surtees, William V. Skall. Editor, Ralph E. Winters. Filmed in Italy. 171 minutes

Marcus Vinicius: Robert Taylor, *Lygia:* Deborah Kerr, *Petronius:* Leo Genn, *Nero:* Peter Ustinov, *Poppaea:* Patricia Laffan, *Peter:*

Finlay Currie, *Paul:* Abraham Sofaer, *Eunice:* Marina Berti, *Ursus:* Buddy Baer, *Plautius:* Felix Aylmer, *Pomponia:* Nora Swinburne, *Tigellinus:* Ralph Truman, *Nerva:* Norman Wooland, *Nazarius:* Peter Miles, *Terpnos:* Geoffrey Dunn, *Seneca:* Nicholas Hannen, *Phaon:* D. A. Clarke-Smith, *Acte:* Rosalie Crutchley, *Chilo:* John Ruddock, *Croton:* Arthur Walge, *Miriam:* Elspeth March, *Rufia:* Strelsa Brown, *Lucan:* Alfredo Varelli, *Flavius:* Roberto Ottaviano, *Anaxander:* William Tubbs, *Galba:* Pietro Tordi, *Pedicurist:* Lia De Leo, *Extra:* Sophia Loren, *Extra (Guest):* Elizabeth Taylor.

Rainbow on the River with Charles Butterworth, May Robson and Bobby Breen.

RAINBOW ON THE RIVER (1936) RKO. Produced by Sol Lesser. Directed by Kurt Neumann. Associate Producer, Edward Gross. Author, Mrs. C. V. Jamison (from *Toinette's Philip*). Screenplay by Earle Snell, Harry Chandlee, William Hurlbut. Musical Settings, Hugo Riesenfeld, Abe Meyer. Cameraman, Charles Schoenbaum. Editor, Robert Crandall. Songs, "Rainbow on the River," "A Thousand Dreams of You," "You Only Live Once" by Paul Francis Webster and Louis Alter; "Waiting for the Sun to Rise" by Arthur Swanstrom and Karl Hajos. 87 minutes.

Philip: Bobby Breen, *Mrs. Ainsworth:* May Robson, *Barrett:* Charles Butterworth, *Ralph Layton:* Alan Mowbray, *Julia Layton:* Benita Hume, *Father Josef:* Henry O'Neill, *Toinette:* Louise Beavers, *Lucille Layton:* Marilyn Knowlden, *Seline:* Lillian Yarbo, *Lilybell:* Stymie Beard, *Doctor:* Eddie Anderson, *Flower Buyer:* Betty Blythe, *Mrs. Logan:* Theresa Maxwell Conover, *Pedestrian:* Clarence H. Wilson, *Cabman:* Lew Kelly, *Superintendent:* Lillian Harmer, St. Luke's Choristers and Hall Johnson Singers.

THE RAINS CAME (1939) 20th. Produced by Darryl F. Zanuck. Associate Producer, Harry Joe Brown. Directed by Clarence Brown. Based on the novel by Louis Bromfield. Screenplay, Philip Dunne and Julien Josephson. Music, Alfred Newman. Photography, Arthur Miller. Editor, Barbara McLean. Special effects scenes staged by Fred Sersen. Sets, Thomas Little. Costumes, Gwen Wakeling. Sound, Alfred Bruzlin and Roger Heman. Songs: "The Rains Came" by Mack Gordon and Harry Revel; and "Hindoo Song of Love" by Lal Chand Mehra. Remade by 20th as *The Rains of Ranchipur* (1955). 103 minutes

Lady Edwina Esketh: Myrna Loy, *Major Rama Safti:* Tyrone Power, *Tom Ransome:* George Brent, *Fern Simon:* Brenda Joyce, *Lord Albert Esketh:* Nigel Bruce, *Maharani:* Maria Ouspenskaya, *Mr. Bannerjee:* Joseph Schildkraut, *Miss MacDaid:* Mary Nash, *Aunt Phoebe Smiley:* Jane Darwell, *Mrs. Simon:* Marjorie Rambeau, *Reverend Homer Smiley:* Henry Travers, *Maharajah:* H. B. Warner, *Lily Hoggett-Egbury:* Laura Hope Crews, *Raschid Ali Khan:* William Royle, *General Keith:* Montague Shaw, *Reverend Elmer Simon:* Harry Hayden, *Bates:* Herbert Evans, *John the Baptist:* Abner Biberman, *Mrs. Bannerjee:* Mara Alexander, *Mr. Das:* William Edmunds, *Princesses:* Adele

Labansat, Sonia Charsky, *Maid:* Rita Page, *Nurse:* Rosina Galli, *Nurse:* Connie Leon, *Official:* Pedro Regas, *Bit:* Lal Chand Mehra, *Engineer:* Frank Lackteen, *Rajput:* George Regas, *Doctor:* Leyland Hodgson, *Hindu Woman:* Fern Emmett, *Mr. Durga:* Guy D'Ennery, *Aide-de-camp:* Jamiel Hasson.

The Rains Came with Maria Ouspenskaya, George Brent and Myrna Loy.

Raintree County with Montgomery Clift and Elizabeth Taylor.

RAINTREE COUNTY (1957) MGM. Produced by David Lewis. Directed by Edward Dmytryk. Technicolor and Panavision, Perspecta Sound. Based on the 1948 novel *Raintree County* by Ross Lockridge, Jr. Screenplay, Millard Kaufman. Art Direction, William A. Horning and Urie McCleary. Set Decoration, Edwin B. Willis and Hugh Hunt. Costume Design, Walter Plunkett. Score, Johnny Green. Songs by Johnny Green and Paul Francis Webster: "Never Till Now" and "Song of Raintree," the latter sung by Nat King Cole during the credits. Photography, Robert Surtees. First film made with MGM Camera 65 process, in which a 65 mm negative is reduced to 35 mm for release prints. Filmed in Danville, Kentucky; Natchez and Port Gibson, Mississippi; swamp scenes filmed at Reelfoot Lake, Tiptonville, Tennessee. Film debut of Gardner McKay, 24. 168 minutes

John Wickliff Shawnessy: Montgomery Clift, *Susanna Drake:* Elizabeth Taylor, *Nell Gaither:* Eva Marie Saint, *Professor Jerusalem Webster Stiles:* Nigel Patrick, *Orville "Flash" Perkins:* Lee Marvin, *Garwood B. Jones:* Rod Taylor, *Ellen Shawnessy:* Agnes Moorehead, *T. D. Shawnessy:* Walter Abel, *Barbara Drake:* Jarma Lewis, *Bobby Drake:* Tom Drake, *Ezra Gray:* Rhys Williams, *Niles Foster:* Russell Collins, *Southern Officer:* DeForrest Kelley, *Lydia Gray:* Myrna Hansen, *Jake, Bartender:* Oliver Blake, *Cousin Sam:* John Eldredge, *Soona:* Isabelle Cooley, *Parthenia:* Ruth Attaway, *Miss Roman:* Eileene Stevens, *Bessie:* Rosalind Hayes, *Tom Conway:* Don Burnett, *Nat Franklin:* Michael Dugan, *Jesse Gardner:* Ralph Vitti (Michael Dante), *Starter:* Phil Chambers, *Man with Gun:* James Griffith, *Granpa Peters:* Burt Mustin, *Madam Gaubert:* Dorothy Granger, *Blind Man:* Owen McGiveney, *Party Guest:* Charles Watts, *Union Lieutenant:* Stacy Harris, *Jim Shawnessy (age 2–5 Yrs):* Donald Losby, *Jim Shawnessy (age 4 Yrs.):* Mickey Maga, *Pantomimist in Blackface:* Robert Foulk, *Photographer:* Jack Daly, *Old Negro Man:* Bill Walker, *Bearded Soldier:* Gardner McKay.

Random Harvest with Greer Garson and Ronald Colman.

RANDOM HARVEST (1942) MGM. Producer, Sidney Franklin. Director, Mervyn LeRoy. From the novel by James Hilton. Screenplay, Claudine West, George Froeschel, Arthur Wimperis. Score, Herbert Stothart. Art Director, Cedric Gibbons. Cameraman, Joseph Ruttenberg. Editor, Harold F. Kress. 124 minutes

Charles Ranier: Ronald Colman, *Paula:* Greer Garson, *Dr. Jonathan Benet:* Philip Dorn, *Kitty:* Susan Peters, *"Biffer":* Reginald Owen, *Prime Minister:* Edmund Gwenn, *Dr. Sims:* Henry Travers, *Mrs. Deventer:* Margaret Wycherly, *Harrison:* Bramwell Fletcher, *Chetwynd:* Arthur Margetson, *Lydis (Chet's Wife):* Jill Esmond, *Jill (Kitty's Mother):* Marta Linden, *George:* Melville Cooper, *Julian:* Alan Napier, *Sheila:* Pax Walker, *Beddoes:* Clement May, *Chemist:* Arthur Shields, *Henry Chilcotte:* David Cavendish, *Julia:* Norma Varden, *Bridget:* Ann Richards, *Mrs. Lloyd:* Elisabeth Risdon, *Mr. Lloyd:* Charles Waldron, *The Vicar:* Ivan Simpson, *Pearson:* John Burton, *Sam:* Rhys Williams, *Comedian:* Alec Craig, *Heavy Man:* Henry Daniell, *Vicar's Wife:* Marie De Becker, *Mrs. Sims:* Mrs. Gardner Crane, *Sheldon:* Aubrey Mather, *Julia's Husband:* Montague Shaw, *Sir John:* Lumsden Hare, *Paula's Lawyer:* Frederic Worlock, *Jones:* Wallis Clark, *Badgeley:* Harry T. Shannon, *Trempitt:* Arthur Space, *Tobacconist:* Una O'Connor, *Registrar:* Ian Wolfe, *Woman:* Olive Blakeney, *Soldier:* Peter Lawford.

RASPUTIN AND THE EMPRESS (1932) MGM. Produced by Bernard Hyman. Directed by Richard Boleslavsky. Story and Screenplay, Charles MacArthur. Photography, William Daniels. Editor, Tom Held. Music, Herbert Stothart. Art Directors, Cedric Gibbons and Alexander Toluboff. Costumes, Adrian. Assistant Director, Cullen Tate. Sound, Douglas Shearer. Only film with the three Barrymores. 133 minutes

Prince Paul Chegodieff: John Barrymore, *Empress Alexandra:* Ethel Barrymore, *Rasputin:* Lionel Barrymore, *Emperor Nikolai:* Ralph Morgan, *Natasha:* Diana Wynyard, *Alexis:* Tad Alexander, *Grand Duke Igor:* C. Henry Gordon, *Doctor:* Edward Arnold, *Doctor Wolfe:* Gustav von Seyffertitz, *Anastasia:* Dawn O'Day (Anne Shirley), *Maria:* Jean Parker, *Landlady:* Sarah Padden, *Chief of Secret Police:*

Henry Kolker, *Professor Propotkin:* Frank Shannon, *German Language Teacher:* Frank Reicher, *Policeman:* Hooper Atchley, *Revelers:* Lucien Littlefield, Leo White, *Soldier:* Maurice Black, *Soldier (Extra):* Dave O'Brien, *Butler:* Mischa Auer, *Girl:* Charlotte Henry.

Rasputin and the Empress with John Barrymore, Ethel Barrymore, Tad Alexander and Lionel Barrymore.

The Razor's Edge with Tyrone Power, Gene Tierney, Louise Colombet and George Davis.

THE RAZOR'S EDGE (1946) 20th. Produced by Darryl F. Zanuck. Directed by Edmund Goulding. Based on the novel by W. Somerset Maugham. Screenplay, Lamar Trotti. Art Directors, Richard Day and Nathan Juran. Music, Alfred Newman. Photography, Arthur Miller. Editor, J. Watson Webb. Dances staged by Harry Pilcer. Gene Tierney's costumes designed by Oleg Cassini. Song, "Mam'-selle," by Mack Gordon and Edmund Goulding. Herbert Marshall repeats his Maugham characterization from *The Moon and Sixpence* (United Artists, 1942). 146 minutes

Larry Darrell: Tyrone Power, *Isabel Bradley:* Gene Tierney, *Gray Maturin:* John Payne, *Sophie:* Anne Baxter, *Elliott Templeton:* Clifton Webb, *Somerset Maugham:* Herbert Marshall, *Louisa Bradley:* Lucile Watson, *Bob MacDonald:* Frank Latimore, *Miss Keith:* Elsa Lanchester, *Kosti:* Fritz Kortner, *Joseph:* John Wengraf, *Holy Man:* Cecil Humphreys, *Specialty Dancer:* Harry Pilcer, *Princess Novemali:* Cobina Wright, Sr., *Maid:* Isabelle Lamore, *Bishop:* Andre Charlot, *Albert:* Albert Petit, *Police Inspector:* Henri Letondal, *Russian Singer:* Noel Cravat, *Specialty Dancer:* Laura Stevens, *Sea Captain:* Eugene

Borden, *Abbe:* Demetrius Alexis, *Mr. Maturin:* Forbes Murray, *Singer:* Robert Laurent, *Matron:* Bess Flowers, *Coco:* Roger Valmy, *Princess' Escort:* Barry Norton, *Sophie's Daughter:* Gale Entrekin, *Concierge:* George Davis, *Concierge's Wife:* Louise Colombet, *Show Girl:* Dorothy Abbott, *Hospital Telephone Operator:* Greta Granstedt, *Isabel's Daughters:* Susan Hartmann, Suzanne O'Connor, *Waiter:* Marek Windheim, *Guest:* Pati Behrs, *Corsican:* Bud Wolfe, *Adagio Dancers:* Ruth Miles and Edward Kover, *Adagio Dancers:* Don and Dolores Graham, *Drunk:* Saul Gorss.

Reap the Wild Wind with Martha O'Driscoll, Ray Milland and Paulette Goddard.

REAP THE WILD WIND (1942) Par. Producer, Cecil B. De Mille. Associate Producer, William Pine. Director, Cecil B. De Mille. Color by Technicolor. Screenplay, Alan LeMay, Charles Bennett, Jesse Lasky, Jr. Score, Victor Young. Art Directors, Hans Dreier, Roland Anderson. Color Cameraman, William V. Skall. Process Photography, Farciot Edouart. Special Effects, Gordon Jennings. Cameraman, Victor Milner. Editor, Anne Bauchens. Songs: "Sea Chantey" by Frank Loesser and Victor Young; "'Tis But a Little Faded Flower" by J. R. Thomas and Troy Sanders. Based on a *Saturday Evening Post* story by Thelma Strabel. Underwater Photography, Dewey Wrigley. 124 minutes

Stephen Tolliver: Ray Milland, *Captain Jack Stuart:* John Wayne, *Loxi Claiborne:* Paulette Goddard, *King Cutler:* Raymond Massey, *Dan Cutler:* Robert Preston, *Captain Phillip Philpott:* Lynne Overman, *Drusilla Alston:* Susan Hayward, *Mate of the* TYFIB: Charles Bickford, *Commodore Devereaux:* Walter Hampden, *Maum Maria:* Louise Beavers, *Ivy Devereaux:* Martha O'Driscoll, *Mrs. Claiborne:* Elisabeth Risdon, *Aunt Henrietta:* Hedda Hopper, *Widgeon:* Victor Kilian, *Salt Meat:* Oscar Polk, *Mrs. Mottram:* Janet Beecher, *Chinkapin:* Ben Carter, *The Lamb:* Wee Willie (William) Davis, *Sam:* Lane Chandler, *Judge Marvin:* Davison Clark, *Captain of the* PELICAN: Lou Merrill, *Doctor Jepson:* Frank M. Thomas, *Captain Carruthers:* Keith Richards, *Lubbock:* Victor Varconi, *Port Captain:* J. Farrell MacDonald, *Mace:* Harry Woods, *Master Shipwright:* Raymond Hatton, *Lieutenant Farragut:* Milburn Stone, *Charleston Ladies:* Barbara Britton, Julia Faye, *Pete:* Constantine Romanoff, *Jake:* Fred Graham, *Stoker Boss:* Dick Alexander, *Dancing Lady:* Mildred Harris, *Devereaux Agent:* John Saint Polis, *Dr. Jepson's Boy:* Eugene Jackson, *Girl's Father:* James Flavin, *Officer at Tea:* Monte Blue, *Ettie:* Claire McDowell, *Devereaux Secretary:* Stanhope Wheatcroft.

REAR WINDOW (1954) Par. Producer-Director, Alfred Hitchcock. Technicolor. Based on Cornell Woolrich's short story. Screenplay, John Michael Hayes. Art Director, Hal Pereira. Cinematographer, Robert Burks. Editor, George Tomasini. 122 minutes

Jeff: James Stewart, *Lisa Fremont:* Grace Kelly, *Thomas J. Doyle:* Wendell Corey, *Stella:* Thelma Ritter, *Lars Thorwald:* Raymond Burr, *Miss Lonely Hearts:* Judith Evelyn, *Song Writer:* Ross Bagdasarian

(David Seville), *Miss Torso:* Georgine Darcy, *Woman on Fire Escape:* Sara Berner, *Fire Escape Man:* Frank Cady, *Miss Hearing Aid:* Jesslyn Fax, *Honeymooner:* Rand Harper, *Mrs. Thorwald:* Irene Winston, *Newlywed:* Harris Davenport, *Party Girl:* Marla English, *Party Girl:* Kathryn Grandstaff (Kathryn Grant), *Landlord:* Alan Lee, *Detective:* Anthony Warde, *Miss Torso's Friend:* Benny Bartlett, *Stunt Detective:* Fred Graham, *Young Man:* Harry Landers, *Man:* Dick Simmons, *Bird Woman:* Iphigenie Castiglioni, *Waiter (Carl):* Ralph Smiley, *Stunt Detective:* Edwin Parker, *Woman with Poodle:* Bess Flowers, *Dancer:* Jerry Antes, *Choreographer:* Barbara Bailey, *A Butler:* Alfred Hitchcock.

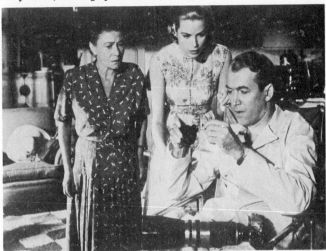

Rear Window with Thelma Ritter, Grace Kelly and James Stewart.

Rebecca with Joan Fontaine and Laurence Olivier.

REBECCA (1940) UA. Selznick International Pictures. Produced by David O. Selznick. Directed by Alfred Hitchcock. From Daphne du Maurier's novel. Screenplay by Robert E. Sherwood and Joan Harrison. Adapted by Philip MacDonald and Michael Hogan. Music by Franz Waxman. Photography by George Barnes. Hitchcock's first American film. 130 minutes

Maxim de Winter: Laurence Olivier, *Mrs. de Winter:* Joan Fontaine, *Jack Favell:* George Sanders, *Mrs. Danvers:* Judith Anderson, *Major Giles Lacy:* Nigel Bruce, *Colonel Julyan:* C. Aubrey Smith, *Frank Crawley:* Reginald Denny, *Beatrice Lacy:* Gladys Cooper, *Robert:* Philip Winter, *Frith:* Edward Fielding, *Mrs. Van Hopper:* Florence Bates, *Coroner:* Melville Cooper, *Dr. Baker:* Leo G. Carroll, *Chalcroft:* Forrester Harvey, *Tabbs:* Lumsden Hare, *Ben:* Leonard Carey, *Man Outside Phone Booth:* Alfred Hitchcock.

Rebel Without a Cause with Ann Doran, James Dean and Jim Backus.

REBEL WITHOUT A CAUSE (1955) WB. Produced by David Weisbart. Directed by Nicholas Ray. CinemaScope and WarnerColor. From a story by Nicholas Ray. Adaptation, Irving Shulman. Screenplay, Stewart Stern. Assistant Directors, Don Page and Robert Farfan. Music, Leonard Rosenman. Costumes, Moss Mabry. Art Director, Malcolm Bert. Cinematography, Ernest Haller. Editor, William Ziegler. Sound, Stanley Jones. 111 minutes

Jim: James Dean, *Judy:* Natalie Wood, *Plato:* Sal Mineo, *Jim's Father:* Jim Backus, *Jim's Mother:* Ann Doran, *Buzz:* Corey Allen, *Judy's Father:* William Hopper, *Judy's Mother:* Rochelle Hudson, *Jim's Grandma:* Virginia Brissac, *Moose:* Nick Adams, *Cookie:* Jack Simmons, *Goon:* Dennis Hopper, *Plato's Maid:* Marietta Canty, *Chick:* Jack Grinnage, *Helen:* Beverly Long, *Mil:* Steffi Sidney, *Crunch:* Frank Mazzola, *Harry:* Tom Bernard, *Cliff:* Clifford Morris, *Lecturer:* Ian Wolfe, *Ray:* Edward Platt, *Gene:* Robert Foulk, *Beau:* Jimmy Baird, *Guide:* Dick Wessel, *Sergeant:* Nelson Leigh, *Nurse:* Dorothy Abbott, *Woman Officer:* Louise Lane, *Officer:* House Peters, *Attendant:* Gus Schilling, *Monitor:* Bruce Noonan, *Old Lady Teacher:* Almira Sessions, *Hoodlum:* Peter Miller, *Desk Sergeant:* Paul Bryar, *Police Chief:* Paul Birch, *Moose's Father, Ed:* Robert B. Williams, *Crunch's Father:* David McMahon.

The Red Badge of Courage with Bill Mauldin and Audie Murphy.

THE RED BADGE OF COURAGE (1951) MGM. Producer, Gottfried Reinhardt. Director-Screenplay, John Huston. Adaptation, Albert Band. Art Directors, Cedric Gibbons, Hans Peter. Photography, Harold Rosson. Editor, Ben Lewis. 69 minutes

Youth: Audie Murphy, *Loud Soldier:* Bill Mauldin, *Lieutenant:* Douglas Dick, *Tattered Man:* Royal Dano, *Tall Soldier:* John Dierkes, *Bill Porter:* Arthur Hunnicutt, *Thompson:* Robert Easton Burke, *Captain:* Smith Ballew, *Colonel:* Glenn Strange, *Sergeant:* Dan White, *Captain:* Frank McGraw, *General:* Tim Durant, *Veterans:* Emmett Lynn, Stanford Jolley, William "Bill" Phillips, House Peters, Jr., Frank Sully, *Union Soldiers:* George Offerman, Jr., Joel Marston, Robert Nichols, *Veterans:* Lou Nova, Fred Kohler, Jr., Dick Curtis, Guy Wilkerson, Buddy Roosevelt, *Soldier:* Jim Hayward, *Southern Girl:* Gloria Eaton, *Soldier Who Sings:* Robert Cherry, *Wounded Officer:* Whit Bissell, *Officer:* William Phipps, *Corporal:* Ed Hinton, *Confederate:* Lynn Farr.

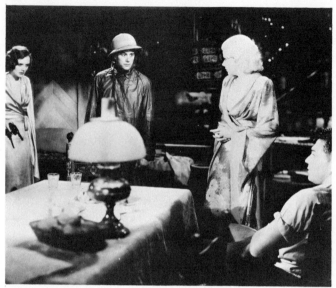

Red Dust with Mary Astor, Gene Raymond, Jean Harlow and Clark Gable.

RED DUST (1932) MGM. Produced by Hunt Stromberg. Directed by Victor Fleming. Based on the play by Wilson Collison. Screenplay, John Mahin. Photography, Harold Rosson. Editor, Blanche Sewell. Remade as *Congo Maisie* (MGM, 1940), and *Mogambo* (MGM, 1953), also with Clark Gable. 83 minutes

Dennis Carson: Clark Gable, *Vantine:* Jean Harlow, *Gary Willis:* Gene Raymond, *Barbara Willis:* Mary Astor, *Guidon:* Donald Crisp, *McQuarg:* Tully Marshall, *Limey:* Forrester Harvey, *Hoy:* Willie Fung.

Red River with John Ireland, John Wayne and Montgomery Clift.

RED RIVER (1948) United Artists-Monterey. Producer-Director, Howard Hawks. Author, Borden Chase. Screenplay, Borden Chase, Charles Schnee. Music, Dimitri Tiomkin. Art Director, John Datu Arensma. Photography, Russell Harlan. Editor, Christian Nyby. Film debut of Montgomery Clift, although his second film *The Search* was released first. 125 minutes

Tom Dunson: John Wayne, *Matthew Garth:* Montgomery Clift, *Tess Millay:* Joanne Dru, *Groot Nadine:* Walter Brennan, *Fen:* Coleen Gray, *Cherry Valance:* John Ireland, *Buster McGee:* Noah Beery, Jr., *Mr. Melville:* Harry Carey, Sr., *Dan Latimer:* Harry Carey, Jr., *Teeler Yacey:* Paul Fix, *Matt as a boy:* Mickey Kuhn, *Quo:* Chief Yowlachie, *Bunk Kenneally:* Ivan Parry, *Walt Jergens:* Ray Hyke, *Simms:* Hank Worden, *Laredo:* Dan White, *Fernandez:* Paul Fiero, *Wounded Wrangler:* William Self, *Old Leather:* Hal Taliaferro, *A Quitter:* Tom Tyler, *Colonel:* Lane Chandler, *Naylor:* Glenn Strange, *Dancehall Girl:* Shelley Winters.

Requiem for a Heavyweight with Mickey Rooney and Anthony Quinn.

REQUIEM FOR A HEAVYWEIGHT (1962) Col. Producer, David Susskind. Director, Ralph Nelson. Associate Producer, Jack Grossberg. Screenplay, Rod Serling, based on his 1956 TV play. Music, Laurence Rosenthal. Assistant Directors, Anthony LaMarca, Michael Hertzberg. Art Director, Burr Smidt. Cinematographer, Arthur J. Ornitz. Editor, Carl Lerner. 87 minutes

Mountain Rivera: Anthony Quinn, *Maish Rennick:* Jackie Gleason, *Army:* Mickey Rooney, *Grace Miller:* Julie Harris, *Perelli:* Stan Adams, *Ma Greeny:* Madame Spivy, *Bartender:* Herbie Faye, *Jack Dempsey:* Himself, *Ring Opponent:* Cassius Clay (Muhammad Ali), *Hotel Desk Clerk:* Steve Belloise, *Ring Doctor:* Lou Gilbert, *Referee:* Arthur Mercante.

THE RESCUERS (1977) BV. A Walt Disney Production. Produced by Wolfgang Reitherman. Directed by Reitherman, John Lounsbery and Art Stevens. Suggested by *The Rescuers* and *Miss Bianca* by Margery Sharp. Technicolor. Story by Larry Clemmons, Ken Anderson, Vance Gerry, David Michener, Burny Mattinson, Frank Thomas, Fred Lucky, Ted Berman and Dick Sebast. Directing Animators, Ollie Johnston, Frank Thomas, Milt Kahl and Don Bluth. Art Director, Don Griffith. Color Styling, Al Dempster. Character Animation by John Pomeroy, Andy Gaskill, Art Stevens, Chuck Harvey, Bob McCrea, Cliff Nordberg, Gary Goldman, Dale Baer, Ron Clements, Bill Hajee and Glen Keane. Layout by Joe Hale, Tom Lay, Guy Deel and Sylvia Roemer. Effects Animation by John Buckley. Dorse A. Lanpher, Ted Kierscey, James L. George and Dick Lucas. Key Assistant Animators, Stan Green, Chuck Williams, Walt Stanchfield, Dale Oliver, Harry Hester, Dave Suding and Leroy Cross. Assistant Directors, Jeff Patch and Richard Rich. Editors, James Melton and Jim Koford. Executive Producer, Ron Miller. Sound, Herb Taylor. Musical score composed and conducted by Artie Butler. Songs:

"The Journey," "Rescue Aid Society" and "Tomorrow Is Another Day" by Carol Connors and Ayn Robbins; "Someone's Waiting for You" by Sammy Fain, Connors and Robbins, sung by Shelby Flint; "The U. S. Air Force Song" by Robert Crawford. Rated G. 76 minutes

An animated feature with the following voices: *Bernard:* Bob Newhart, *Miss Bianca:* Eva Gabor, *Madame Medusa:* Geraldine Page, *Mr. Snoops:* Joe Flynn, *Penny:* Michelle Stacy, *Ellie Mae:* Jeanette Nolan, *Luke:* Pat Buttram, *Orville:* Jim Jordan, *Rufus:* John McIntire, *The Chairman:* Bernard Fox, *Gramps:* Larry Clemmons, *Evinrude:* James MacDonald, *Rabbit:* George Lindsey, *TV Announcer:* Bill McMillan, *Digger:* Dub Taylor, *Owl:* John Fiedler.

The Rescuers with Bianca, Bernard and Evinrude.

The Return of the Pink Panther with Peter Sellers, Christopher Plummer and Catherine Schell.

THE RETURN OF THE PINK PANTHER (1975) UA. An ITC, Jewel Productions Ltd. and Pimlico Films Ltd. Presentation. Produced and Directed by Blake Edwards. Screenplay, Frank Waldman and Edwards. Music, Henry Mancini. Lyrics, Hal David. Associate Producer, Tony Adams. Photography, Geoffrey Unsworth. Animation and Titles by Richard Williams Studio. Art Director, Peter Mullins. French Assistant Director, Guy Sauteret. English Assistant Director, Derek Kavanagh. Sound, Peter Sutton. Editor, Tom Priestly. Wardrobe, Bridget Sellers. Make-up, Harry Frampton. Hairdresser, Jeanette Freeman. Special Effects, John Gant. Filmed in Panavision and DeLuxe Color in Casablanca and Marrakech, Morocco; Gstaad, Switzerland; the French Riviera. Third in the Sellers series. Rated G. 113 minutes

Inspector Jacques Clouseau: Peter Sellers, *Sir Charles Litton, The Phantom:* Christopher Plummer, *Claudine Litton:* Catherine Schell, *Chief Inspector Dreyfus:* Herbert Lom, *Col. Sharki:* Peter Arne, *Cato:* Burt Kwouk, *Francois:* Andre Maranne, *Chief of Police:* Gregoire Aslan, *Gen. Wadafi:* Peter Jeffrey, *Jean Duval:* David Lodge, *The Fat Man:* Eric Pohlmann, *Beggar:* John Bluthal, *Concierge:* Victor Spinetti, *Bellboy:* Mike Grady, *Sari Lady:* Carol Cleveland, *Jealous Escort:* Jeremy Hawk, *Pepi:* Graham Stark, *Masseuse:* Claire Davenport, *Restaurant Owner:* Milton Reid. Cut was Julie Andrews as a Chambermaid.

Revenge of the Pink Panther with Peter Sellers.

REVENGE OF THE PINK PANTHER (1978) UA. Produced and Directed by Blake Edwards. A Jewel/Sellers-Edwards Production, in Panavision and Technicolor. Story, Edwards. Screenplay by Frank Waldman, Ron Clark and Edwards. Executive Producer, Tony Adams. Associate Producers, Derek Kavanagh and Ken Wales. Music, Henry Mancini. Animation by DePatie-Freleng. 2nd Unit Director, Anthony Squire. 1st Assistant Director, Terry Marcel. Photography, Ernie Day. Sound Mixer, Roy Charman. Production Designer, Peter Mullins. Art Director, John Siddall. Special Effects, Brian Johnson and Dennis Lowe. Wardrobe Supervisor, Tiny Nichols. Chief Make-up Artist, Harry Frampton. Chief Hairdresser, Bobbie Smith. Cannon's Hairdresser, Barry Richardson. Editor, Alan Jones. Stunt Arrangers, Joe Dunne and Dick Crockett. Set Decorations, Jack Stephens. Title Design, Arthur Leonardi and John Dunn. Song, "Move 'Em Out" by Mancini and Leslie Bricusse, sung by Lon Satton. Filmed in Nice, Antibes, Hong Kong, Paris and at Shepperton Studios, London. 5th Sellers-Clouseau film. Rated PG. 99 minutes

Chief Inspector Jacques Clouseau: Peter Sellers, *Former Chief Inspector Charles Dreyfus:* Herbert Lom, *Simone Legree:* Dyan Cannon, *Philippe Douvier:* Robert Webber, *Marchione:* Robert Loggia, *Julio Scallini:* Paul Stewart, *Cato Fong:* Burt Kwouk, *Therese Douvier:* Adrienne Corri, *Dr. Auguste Balls:* Graham Stark, *Francois:* Andre Maranne, *Claude Russo alias Claudine Russo:* Sue Lloyd, *Guy Algo:* Tony Beckley, *Tanya:* Valerie Leon, *Fernet:* Alfie Bass, *Cunny:* Danny Schiller, *Police Commissioner:* Douglas Wilmer, *Madame Wu:* Elisabeth Welch, *Dr. Laprone:* Ferdy Mayne, *Vic Vancouver:* Charles Augins, *Chinese Doorman:* Anthony Chinn, *Chinese Ladies:* Maureen Tann, Me Me Lai, Jacqui Simm, Fiesta Mei Ling, *President:* John Newbury, *President's Aide:* John Clive, *Police Chief:* Brian Jackson, *Police Chief's Wife:* Margaret Anderson, *Police Sergeant:* Andrew Lodge, *Officer Bardot:* Henry McGee, *Nurse:* Christine Shaw, *Hospital Clerk:* Julian Orchard, *Real Estate Agent:* Michael Ward, *Cemetery Guard:* John Bluthal, *Mr. Chow:* John A. Tinn, *Assistant Manager:* Kien Jing, *Desk Clerk:* Bernie R. Hickban, *Toledo:* John Wyman, *Haig & Haig:* Robert Labassiere, Irvin Allen, *Sam Spade and the Private Eyes:* Lon Satton, Rosita Yarboy, Keith Hodiak, Pepsi Maycock.

RHAPSODY IN BLUE (1945) WB. Produced by Jesse L. Lasky. Directed by Irving Rapper. Based on an original story by Sonya Levien. Screenplay, Howard Koch and Elliot Paul. Art Directors, John Hughes and Anton Grot. Dance Director, LeRoy Prinz. Music Director, Leo F. Forbstein. Photography, Sol Polito. Special Effects, Roy Davidson and Willard Van Enger. Editor, Folmer Blangsted. Orchestral Arrangements, Ray Heindorf and Ferde Grofe. Vocal Arrangements, Dudley Chambers. Piano Solo Recordings, Oscar Levant and Ray Turner. Based on the life of George Gershwin, and featuring his music, with lyrics by Ira Gershwin, Irving Caesar, B. G. DeSylva, Arthur Frances. Musical numbers by George Gershwin with lyrics by Ira Gershwin or those listed: "Swanee" (Irving Caesar), "'S Wonderful," "Somebody Loves Me," "The Man I Love," "Embraceable You," "Summertime," "It Ain't Necessarily So," "Oh Lady Be Good", "I Got Rhythm," "Love Walked In," "Clap Yo' Hands," "Do It Again," "I'll Build a Stairway to Paradise" (Arthur Frances and B.G. DeSylva), "Liza," "Someone to Watch Over Me," "Bidin' My Time," "Delicious," "I Got Plenty of Nuttin," "Rhapsody in Blue" and "An American in Paris." Film debut of Robert Alda. 139 minutes

George Gershwin: Robert Alda, *Julie Adams:* Joan Leslie, *Christine Gilbert:* Alexis Smith, *Max Dreyfus:* Charles Coburn, *Lee Gershwin:* Julie Bishop, *Professor Frank:* Albert Basserman, *Papa Gershwin:* Morris Carnovsky, *Mama Gershwin:* Rosemary De Camp, *Ira Gershwin:* Herbert Rudley, *Themselves:* Al Jolson, Paul Whiteman and his Orchestra, Oscar Levant, George White, Hazel Scott, Tom Patricola, *Bess:* Anne Brown, *George as a boy:* Mickey Roth, *Ira as a boy:* Darryl Hickman, *Hubert Stone:* Bill Kennedy, *Buddy De Sylva:* Eddie Marr, *Otto Kahn:* Ernest Golm, *Jascha Heifitz:* Martin Noble, *Walter Damrosch:* Hugo Kirchhoffer, *Rachmaninoff:* Will Wright, *Dancer:* Johnny Downs, *Christine's Escort:* Robert Shayne, *Mr. Million:* Andrew Tombes, *Muscatel:* Walter Soderling, *Kast:* Charles Halton, *Mr. Katzman:* Gregory Golubeff, *Commentator:* John B. Hughes, *William Foley:* Theodore Von Eltz, *Ravel:* Oscar Lorraine, *Guest in Nightclub:* Ivan Lebedeff, *Comic:* George Riley, *Cashier:* Virginia Sale, *Prima Donna:* Yola d'Avril, *Receptionist:* Claire DuBrey, *Swedish Janitor:* Christian Rub, *Madame DeBreteuil:* Odette Myrtil, *Orchestra Leader:* Jay Novello, *Sport:* Robert Johnson, *Porgy:* William Gillespie, *Singer:* Mark Stevens.

Rhapsody in Blue with Paul Whiteman, Charles Coburn, Robert Alda, Albert Basserman and Herbert Rudley.

RHYTHM ON THE RANGE (1936) Par. Produced by Benjamin Glazer. Directed by Norman Taurog. Based on a story by Mervin J. Houser. Screenplay, John C. Moffett, Sidney Salkow, Walter DeLeon, Francis Martin. Musical Director, Boris Morros. Camera, Karl Struss. Editor, Ellsworth Hoagland. Songs: "I Can't Escape From You" (Leo Robin, Richard Whiting), "I'm an Old Cowhand" (Johnny Mercer), "If You Can't Sing It You'll Have to Swing It (Mr. Paganini)" (Sam Coslow), "The House Jack Built for Jill" (Leo Robin, Frederick Hollander), "Drink It Down" (Leo Robin, Ralph Rainger), "Hang Up My Saddle" and "Rhythm on the Range" (Walter Bullock,

Richard Whiting), "Memories" (Richard Whiting, Frederick Hollander), "Roundup Lullaby" (Bager Clark, Gertrude Ross), and "Empty Saddles" (Billy Hill, J. Keirn Brennan). Feature film debut of Martha Raye, 27. 87 minutes. Remade as *Pardners* (Par., 1956) with Martin and Lewis.

Jeff Larrabee: Bing Crosby, *Doris Halliday:* Frances Farmer, *Buck Burns:* Bob Burns, *Emma:* Martha Raye, *Robert Halliday:* Samuel S. Hinds, *Big Brain:* Warren Hymer, *Penelope Ryland:* Lucille Webster Gleason, *Shorty:* George E. Stone, *Wabash:* James Burke, *Constance:* Martha Sleeper, *Gila Bend:* Clem Bevans, *Mischa:* Leonid Kinskey, *Gopher:* Charles Williams, *Cuddles:* Beau Baldwin, *Clerk:* Emmett Vogan, *Shorty:* Billy Bletcher, *Field Judge:* Eddy Waller, *Heckler:* Bud Flanagan (Dennis O'Keefe), *Officer:* Duke York, *Conductor:* James Blaine, *Brakeman:* Herbert Ashley, *Porter:* James "Slim" Thompson, *Conductor:* Robert E. Homans, *Oil Station Proprietor:* Jim Toney, *Conductor:* Edward LeSaint, *Porter:* Sam McDaniel, *Gus:* Sid Saylor, *Waiter:* Oscar Smith, *Steward:* Charles E. Arnt, *Minister:* Harry C. Bradley, *Chinese Houseboy:* Otto Yamaoka, *Farmer:* Bob McKenzie, *Announcer:* Irving Bacon, *Driver:* Heinie Conklin, *Butler:* Frank Dawson, *Singers:* Sons of the Pioneers, including Roy Rogers.

Rhythm on the Range with Martha Raye, James "Slim" Thompson, Bob Burns and Lucille Webster Gleason.

Rio Bravo with Claude Akins and John Wayne.

RIO BRAVO (1959) WB. Producer-Director, Howard Hawks. Screenplay by Jules Furthman and Leigh Brackett. From a story by B. H. McCampbell. Music by Dimitri Tiomkin. Songs by Dimitri Tiomkin and Paul Francis Webster. Costumes by Marjorie Best. Assistant Director, Paul Helmick. Art Director, Leo K. Kuter. Cinematographer, Russell Harlan. Editor, Folmer Blangsted. An Armada Production in Technicolor. Songs by Dimitri Tiomkin and Paul Francis Webster: "Rio Bravo," "My Rifle, My Pony and Me." 141 minutes

John T. Chance: John Wayne, *Dude:* Dean Martin, *Colorado Ryan:* Ricky Nelson, *Feathers:* Angie Dickinson, *Stumpy:* Walter Brennan, *Pat Wheeler:* Ward Bond, *Nathan Burdette:* John Russell, *Carlos:* Pedro Gonzalez-Gonzalez, *Joe Burdette:* Claude Akins, *Jake:* Malcolm Atterbury, *Harold:* Harry Carey, Jr., *Matt Harris:* Bob Steele, *Barfly:* Myron Healey, *Gunman:* Fred Graham, *Messenger:* Riley Hill, *Henchman:* Tom Monroe, *Consuela:* Estelita Rodriguez.

Rio Rita with Fred Burns, Georges Renavent, Bebe Daniels, John Boles and Benny Corbett.

RIO RITA (1929) RKO. Produced by William Le Baron. Directed by Luther Reed. Ballroom Scene in Technicolor. Based on the Florenz Ziegfeld musical by Guy Bolton and Fred Thompson. Adapted by Luther Reed. Dances staged by Pearl Eaton. Dialogue, Russell Mack. Sound, RCA Photophone. Songs by Harry Tierney and Joe McCarthy: "The Ranger Song," "Rio Rita," "Sweetheart, We Need Each Other," "If You're in Love You'll Waltz," "The Kinkajou," "Following the Sun Around" and "You're Always in My Arms" (But Only in My Dreams); by E. Y. Harburg and Harold Arlen: "Long Before You Came Along." Photography, Robert Kurrle and Lloyd Knetchel. Editor, William Hamilton. Art Director, Max Ree. Musical Director, Victor Baravalle. Chorus Master, Pietro Cimini. Film debut of the team of Wheeler and Woolsey. 135 minutes. Remade by MGM in 1942

Chick Bean: Bert Wheeler, *Lovett:* Robert Woolsey, *Rita Ferguson:* Bebe Daniels, *Captain Jim Stewart:* John Boles, *Dolly:* Dorothy Lee, *Roberto Ferguson:* Don Alvarado, *General Ravenoff:* Georges Renavent, *Carmen:* Eva Rosita, *McGinn:* Sam Nelson, *Wilkins:* Fred Burns, *Cafe Owner:* Sam Blum, *Padrone:* Nick De Ruiz, *Davalos:* Tiny Sandford, *Mrs. Bean:* Helen Kaiser, *Rangers:* Benny Corbett, Fred Scott.

ROAD TO BALI (1952) Par. Producer, Harry Tugend. Director, Hal Walker. Color by Technicolor. Screenplay, Frank Butler, Hal Kanter, William Morrow. Art Directors, Hal Pereira, Joseph McMillan Johnson. Sets, Sam Comer, Russ Dowd. Sound, Gene Merritt, John Cope. Musical Direction, Joseph J. Lilley. Musical numbers staged by Charles O'Curran. Orchestral Arrangements, Van Cleave. Cinematographer, George Barnes. Editor, Archie Marshek. Story, Frank Butler and Harry Tugend. Songs by Johnny Burke and James Van Heusen: "Chicago Style," "Moonflowers," "Hoot Mon," "To See You," "The Merry Go Runaround." Sixth "Road" film, last was *Road to Hong Kong* (1962). 91 minutes

Harold Gridley: Bob Hope, *George Cochran:* Bing Crosby, *Lalah:* Dorothy Lamour, *Ken Arok:* Murvyn Vye, *Gung:* Peter Coe, *Bhoma Da:* Ralph Moody, *Ramayana:* Leon Askin, *Guest Stars:* Jane Russell, Dean Martin, Jerry Lewis, *Specialty Dancer:* Jack Claus, *Bo Kassar:*

Bernie Gozier, *Priest:* Herman Cantor, *Himself:* Bob Crosby, *Guard:* Michael Ansara, *Lalah at seven:* Bunny Lewbel, *Employment Agency Clerk:* Donald Lawton, *Attendant:* Larry Chance, *Verna's Father:* Harry Cording, *Eunice's Father:* Roy Gordon, *Conductor:* Richard Keene, *Eunice:* Carolyn Jones, *Verna:* Jan Kayne, *Eunice's Brother:* Allan Nixon, *Verna's Brother:* Douglas Yorke.

Road to Bali with Bing Crosby, Dorothy Lamour and Bob Hope.

Road to Morocco with Bing Crosby and Bob Hope.

ROAD TO MOROCCO (1942) Par. Associate Producer, Paul Jones. Directed by David Butler. Original Screenplay, Frank Butler and Don Hartman. Musical Director, Victor Young. Art Directors, Hans Dreier and Robert Usher. Camera, William C. Mellor. Editor, Irene Morra. Songs by Johnny Burke and Jimmy Van Heusen: "Moonlight Becomes You," "Ain't Got a Dime to My Name," "Aladdin's Daughter," "Constantly," and "Road to Morocco" Third of the "Road" pictures. 83 minutes

Jeff Peters: Bing Crosby, *Turkey Jackson/Aunt Lucy:* Bob Hope, *Princess Shalmar:* Dorothy Lamour, *Mullay Kasim:* Anthony Quinn, *Mihirmah:* Dona Drake, *Ahmed Fey:* Mikhail Rasumny, *Hyder Khan:* Vladimir Sokoloff, *Neb Jolla:* George Givot, *Oso Bucco:* Andrew Tombes, *Yusef:* Leon Belasco, *First Aide to Mullay Kasim:* Jamiel Hasson, *Second Aid to Mullay Kasin:* Monte Blue, *Handmaidens:* Louise LaPlanche, Theo de Voe, Brooke Evans, Suzanne Ridgway, Patsy Mace, Yvonne De Carlo, Poppy Wilde, *First Guard:* George Lloyd, *Second Guard:* Sammy Stein, *Arabian Waiter:* Ralph Penney, *Arabian Buyer:* Dan Seymour, *Philippine Announcer:* Pete G. Katchenaro, *English Announcer:* Brandon Hurst, *Chinese Announcer:* Richard Loo, *Russian Announcer:* Leo Mostovoy, *Knife Dancer:* Vic Groves, *Knife Dancer:* Joe Jewett, *Arab Pottery Vendor:* Michael Mark, *Arab Sausage Vendor:* Nestor Paiva, *Idiot:* Stanley Price, *Specialty Dancer:* Rita Christiani, *Gigantic Bearded Arab:* Robert Barron, *Proprietor of Fruit Stand:* Cy Kendall, *Voice for Lady Camel:* Sara Berner, *Voice for Man Camel:* Kent Rogers, *Warrior:* Harry Cording, *Warrior:* Dick Botiller, *Bystander:* Edward Emerson, *Dancer:* Sylvia Opert.

Road to Rio with LaVerne and Maxine Andrews, Bing Crosby and Patty Andrews.

ROAD TO RIO (1947) Par. Producer, Daniel Dare. Director, Norman Z. McLeod. Authors-Screenplay, Edmund Beloin, Jack Rose. Musical Director, Robert Emmett Dolan. Art Directors, Hans Dreier, Earl Hedrick. Cameraman, Ernest Laszlo. Editor, Ellsworth Hoagland. Dances, Bernard Pearce and Billy Daniel. Songs by Johnny Burke and Jimmy Van Heusen: "But Beautiful," "Experience," "You Don't Have to Know the Language," "Apalachicola, Florida," "For What?" Fifth "Road" picture. 100 minutes

Scat Sweeney: Bing Crosby, *Hot Lips Barton:* Bob Hope, *Lucia Maria De Andrade:* Dorothy Lamour, *Catherine Vail:* Gale Sondergaard, *Harry:* Frank Faylen, *Tony:* Joseph Vitale, *Rodrigues:* Frank Puglia, *Cardoso:* Nestor Paiva, *Johnson:* Robert Barrat; The Stone-Barton Puppeteers, The Carioca Boys; *Cavalry Captain:* Jerry Colonna, *Three Musicians:* The Wiere Brothers, *The Andrews Sisters:* Themselves, *Pilot:* Tad Van Brunt, *Cavalry Officer:* Raul Roulien, *Farmer:* Charles Middleton, *Sherman Mallory:* George Meeker, *Captain Harmon:* Stanley Andrews, *Ship's Purser:* Harry Woods, *Samson:* Tor Johnson, *Specialty Dancer:* Albert Ruiz, *Specialty Dancer:* Laura Corbay, *Steward:* Donald Kerr, *Assistant Purser:* Stanley Blystone, *The Prefeito:* George Sorel, *Dancer:* John "Skins" Miller, *Ship's Officer:* Alan Bridge, *Foreman:* Ralph Dunn, *Valet:* George Chandler, *Barber:* Gino Corrado, *Mr. Stanton:* Arthur Q. Bryan, *Buck:* Ray Teal.

ROAD TO SINGAPORE (1940) Par. Produced by Harlan Thompson. Directed by Victor Schertzinger. Based on a story by Harry Hervey. Screenplay, Don Hartman and Frank Butler. Art Directors, Hans Dreier and Robert Odell. Music Director, Victor Young. Dances, LeRoy Prinz. Photography, William C. Mellor. Editor, Paul Weatherwax. Songs: "The Moon and the Willow Tree" and "Captain Custard" by Johnny Burke and Victor Schertzinger; "Sweet Potato Piper," "Too Romantic," and "Kaigoon" by Johnny Burke and James Monaco. The first "Road" picture (of seven). 84 minutes

Josh Mallon: Bing Crosby, *Mima:* Dorothy Lamour, *Ace Lannigan:* Bob Hope, *Joshua Mallon IV:* Charles Coburn, *Gloria Wycott:* Judith Barrett, *Caesar:* Anthony Quinn, *Achilles Bombanassa:* Jerry Colonna, *Timothy Willow:* Johnny Arthur, *Morgan Wycott:* Pierre Watkin, *Gordon Wycott:* Gaylord (Steve) Pendleton, *Sir Malcolm Drake:* Miles Mander, *Zato:* Pedro Regas, *Babe:* Greta Granstedt, *Bill:* Edward

Gargan, *Sailor:* John Kelly, *Sailor's Wife:* Kitty Kelly, *Father:* Roger Gray, *Native Boy:* Benny Inocencio, *Ninky Poo:* Gloria Franklin, *Native Dancing Girl:* Carmen D'Antonio, *Fred:* Don Brodie, *Secretary:* Harry C. Bradley, *Cameraman:* Richard Keene, *Columnist:* Jack Pepper, *Native Shopkeeper:* Belle Mitchell, *Native Policemen:* Fred Malatesta, Bob St. Angelo, *High Priest:* Monte Blue, *Immigration Officer:* Robert Emmet O'Connor, *Ship's Officer:* Cyril Ring, *Proprietress:* Margarita Padula, *Chaperone:* Grace Hayle, *Ship's Officer:* Richard Tucker, *Homely Girl:* Elvia Allman, *Bartender:* Arthur Q. Bryan, *Dumb-Looking Little Man:* Bobby Barber, *Society Girl:* Helen Lynd, *Girl at Party:* Claire James.

Road to Singapore with Claire James, Bob Hope and Bing Crosby.

Road to Utopia with Bob Hope, Dorothy Lamour and Bing Crosby.

ROAD TO UTOPIA (1945) Par. Produced by Paul Jones. Directed by Hal Walker. Original Screenplay, Norman Panama and Melvin Frank. Music, Leigh Harline. Music Director, Robert Emmett Dolan. Dance Director, Danny Dare. Art Directors, Hans Dreier and Roland Anderson. Animations, Jerry Fairbanks. Photography, Lionel Lindon. Process Photography, Farciot Edouart. Editor, Stuart Gilmore. Songs by Johnny Burke and Jimmy Van Heusen: "Personality," "Put It There, Pal," "Good Time Charlie," "Welcome to My Dream," "It's Anybody's Spring," "Would You?" The fourth "Road" picture. 89 minutes

Duke Johnson/Junior Hooton: Bing Crosby, *Chester Hooton:* Bob Hope, *Sal Van Hoyden:* Dorothy Lamour, *Kate:* Hillary Brooke, *Ace Larson:* Douglass Dumbrille, *Le Bec:* Jack La Rue, *Sperry:* Robert Barrat, *McGurk:* Nestor Paiva, *Narrator:* Robert Benchley, *Mr. Latimer:* Will Wright, *Ringleader of Henchmen:* Jimmy Dundee, *Newsboy:* Billy Benedict, *Purser:* Arthur Loft, *Official at Boat:* Stanley Andrews, *Boat Captain:* Alan Bridge, *Top Hat:* Romaine Callender,

Ship's Purser: Paul Newlan, *First Man:* Jack Rutherford, *Second Man:* Al Hill, *Master of Ceremonies:* Edward Emerson, *Hotel Manager:* Ronnie Rondell, *Henchmen:* Allen Pomeroy, Jack Stoney, *Waiter:* George McKay, *Ringleader:* Larry Daniels, *Bear:* Charles Gemora, *Girls:* Claire James, Maxine Fife, *Santa Claus:* Ferdinand Munier, *Officials:* Edgar Dearing, Charles C. Wilson, *Passenger:* Jim Thorpe.

Road to Zanzibar with Una Merkel, Bob Hope, Dorothy Lamour and Bing Crosby.

ROAD TO ZANZIBAR (1941) Par. Produced by Paul Jones. Directed by Victor Schertzinger. Based on the story *Find Colonel Fawcett* by Don Hartman and Sy Bartlett. Screenplay, Frank Butler and Don Hartman. Camera, Ted Tetzlaff. Editor, Alma Macrorie. Songs by Johnny Burke and Jimmy Van Heusen: "Birds of a Feather," "It's Always You," "You're Dangerous," "You Lucky People You," "African Etude," "Road to Zanzibar." Dances, LeRoy Prinz. The second "Road" film. 92 minutes

Chuck Reardon: Bing Crosby, *Fearless (Hubert) Frazier:* Bob Hope, *Donna Latour:* Dorothy Lamour, *Julia Quimby:* Una Merkel, *Charles Kimble:* Eric Blore, *Proprietor of Native Booth:* Luis Alberni, *Dimples:* Joan Marsh, *Fat Lady:* Ethel Loreen Greer, *French Soubrette:* Iris Adrian, *Saunders:* Georges Renavent, *Slave Trader:* Douglass Dumbrille, *Monsieur Lebec:* Lionel Royce, *Thonga:* Buck Woods, *Scarface:* Leigh Whipper, *Whiteface:* Ernest Whitman, *Chief:* Noble Johnson, *Boy:* Leo Gorcey, *Police Inspector:* Robert Middlemass, *Clara Kimble:* Norma Varden, *Turk at Slave Mart:* Paul Porcasi, *Solomon:* Jules Strongbow, *Curzon Sisters:* Priscilla White, LaVerne Vess, *Acrobats:* Harry C. Johnson, Harry C. Johnson, Jr., *Policeman:* Alan Bridge, *Cafe Proprietor:* Henry Roquemore, *Waiter:* James B. Carson, *Barber:* Eddy Conrad, *Clerk:* Richard Keene, *Commentator:* Ken Carpenter, *Gorilla:* Charlie Gemora.

THE ROARING TWENTIES (1939) WB. Producer, Hal B. Wallis. Directed by Raoul Walsh and Anatole Litvak. Associate Producer, Samuel Bischoff. Author, Mark Hellinger. Screenplay, Jerry Wald, Richard Macaulay, Robert Rossen. Art Director, Max Parker. Musical Director, Leo F. Forbstein. Orchestral Arrangements, Ray Heindorf. Cameraman, Ernie Haller. Special Effects, Byron Haskin, Edwin A. DuPar. Editor, Jack Killifer. Sound, E. A. Brunn. Narrator, John Deering. Themes, "Melancholy Baby" and "It Had to Be You." 104 minutes

Eddie Bartlett: James Cagney, *Jean Sherman:* Priscilla Lane, *George Hally:* Humphrey Bogart, *Lloyd Hart:* Jeffrey Lynn, *Panama Smith:* Gladys George, *Danny Green:* Frank McHugh, *Nick Brown:* Paul Kelly, *Mrs. Sherman:* Elisabeth Risdon, *Pete Henderson:* Ed Keane, *Sergeant Pete Jones:* Joseph Sawyer, *Lefty:* Abner Biberman, *Luigi,*

233

Proprietor: George Humbert, *Bramfield, Broker:* Clay Clement, *Bobby Hart:* Don Thaddeus Kerr, *Orderly:* Ray Cooke, *Mrs. Gray:* Vera Lewis, *First Mechanic:* Murray Alper, *Second Mechanic:* Dick Wessel, *Fletcher, Foreman:* Joseph Crehan, *Bootlegger:* Norman Willis, *First Officer:* Robert Elliott, *Second Officer:* Eddy Chandler, *Judge:* John Hamilton, *Man in Jail:* Elliott Sullivan, *Jailer:* Pat O'Malley, *Proprietor of Still:* Arthur Loft, *Ex-Cons: First Man:* Al Hill, *Second Man:* Raymond Bailey, *Third Man:* Lew Harvey, *Order-takers:* Joe Devlin, Jeffrey Sayre, *Mike:* Paul Phillips, *Masters:* George Meeker, *Piano Player:* Bert Hanlon, *Drunk:* Jack Norton, *Captain:* Alan Bridge, *Henchman:* Fred Graham, *Doorman:* James Blaine, *Couple:* Harry C. Bradley, Lottie Williams.

The Roaring Twenties with Gladys George, James Cagney and Humphrey Bogart.

The Robe with Emmett Lynn (second left), Richard Burton, Victor Mature, Dean Jagger and Michael Rennie.

THE ROBE (1953) 20th. Producer, Frank Ross. Director, Henry Koster. CinemaScope, Technicolor. Based on the novel by Lloyd C. Douglas. Screenplay, Philip Dunne. Adaptation, Gina Kaus. Art Directors, Lyle Wheeler, George W. Davis. Cinematographer, Leon Shamroy. Editor, Barbara McLean. The first CinemaScope film. 135 minutes

Marcellus Gallio: Richard Burton, *Diana:* Jean Simmons, *Demetrius:* Victor Mature, *Peter:* Michael Rennie, *Caligula:* Jay Robinson, *Justus:* Dean Jagger, *Senator Gallio:* Torin Thatcher, *Pilate:* Richard Boone, *Miriam:* Betta St. John, *Paulus:* Jeff Morrow, *Emperor Tiberius:* Ernest Thesiger, *Junia:* Dawn Addams, *Abidor:* Leon Askin, *Quintus:* Frank Pulaski, *Marcipor:* David Leonard, *Judas:* Michael Ansara, *Jonathan:* Nicholas Koster, *Dodinius:* Francis Pierlot, *Marius:*

Thomas Browne Henry, *Sarpedon:* Anthony Eustrel, *Lucia:* Pamela Robinson, *Voice of Christ:* Cameron Mitchell, *Ship's Captain:* Ford Rainey, *Woman:* Mae Marsh, *Rebecca:* Helen Beverly, *Tiro:* Jay Novello, *David:* Harry Shearer, *Nathan:* Emmett Lynn, *Cornelia:* Sally Corner, *Julia:* Rosalind Ivan, *Lucius:* Peter Reynolds, *Specialty Dancer:* Virginia Lee, *Shalum:* Leo Curley, *Slave Girls:* Joan & Jean Corbett, *Slave Girl:* Gloria Saunders, *Caleb:* Percy Helton, *Chamberlain:* Roy Gordon, *Gracchus:* George E. Stone, *Cleander:* Ben Astar, *Auctioneer:* Marc Snow.

Roberta with Fred Astaire, Ginger Rogers and Candy Candido (on bass).

ROBERTA (1935) RKO. Produced by Pandro S. Berman. Directed by William A. Seiter. Based on the novel by Alice Duer Miller, and the 1933 musical *Gowns by Roberta* by Jerome Kern and Otto Harbach. Adaptation, Jane Murfin and Sam Mintz. Additional Dialogue, Glenn Tryon and Allan Scott. Dances, Fred Astaire. Director of Ensembles, Hermes Pan. Music director, Max Steiner. Production Associate, Zion Myers. Art Directors, Van Nest Polglase and Carroll Clark. Costumes, Bernard Newman. Photography, Edward Cronjager. Editor, William Hamilton. Sound, John Tribby. Songs by Jerome Kern, Otto Harbach, Dorothy Fields, Jimmy McHugh, Oscar Hammerstein II: "Lovely to Look At," "I Won't Dance," "Yesterdays," "I'll Be Hard to Handle," "The Touch of Your Hand," "Let's Begin," "Smoke Gets in Your Eyes." Remade as *Lovely to Look At* (MGM, 1952). 105 minutes

Stephanie: Irene Dunne, *Huck:* Fred Astaire, *Countess Scharwenka (Lizzie Gatz):* Ginger Rogers, *John Kent:* Randolph Scott, *Roberta (Aunt Minnie):* Helen Westley, *Ladislaw:* Victor Varconi, *Sophie:* Claire Dodd, *Voyda:* Luis Alberni, *Lord Delves:* Ferdinand Munier, *Albert:* Torben Meyer, *Professor:* Adrian Rosley, *Fernando:* Bodil Rosing, *Girl:* Lucille Ball, *Cossacks:* Mike Tellegen, Sam Savitsky, *Woman:* Zena Savine, *Orchestra:* Johnny "Candy" Candido, Muzzy Marcellino, Gene Sheldon, Howard Lally, William Carey, Paul McLarind, Hal Bown, Charles Sharpe, Ivan Dow, Phil Cuthbert, Delmon Davis, William Dunn, *Mannequins:* Jane Hamilton, Margaret McChrystal, Kay Sutton, Maxine Jennings, Virginia Reid, Lorna Low, Lorraine DeSart, Wanda Perry, Diane Cook, Virginia Carroll, Betty Dumbries, Donna Roberts, *Bits:* Mary Forbes, William B. Davidson, Judith Vosselli, Rita Gould.

ROCKY (1976) UA. Produced by Irwin Winkler and Robert Chartoff. Directed by John G. Avildsen. Written by Sylvester Stallone. Executive Producer, Gene Kirkwood. Photography, James Crabe. Editor, Richard Halsey. Art Director, James H. Spencer. Executive in Charge of Production, Hal Polaire. Production Design, Bill Cassidy. Visual Consultant, David Nichols. Make-up created by Mike Westmore. Editor, Scott Conrad. Assistant Directors, Fred Gallo and Steve Perry. Preproduction Supervisor, Lloyd Kaufman. Special Camera Effects, Garrett Brown. Boxing Choreography, Sylvester Stallone. Technical Adviser, Jimmy Gambina. Stunt Coordinator, Jim Nickerson. Set Decorator, Raymond Molyneaux. Costumer, Robert Cambel. Music by Bill Conti. "Take Me Back" by Frank Stallone, Jr., performed by Valentine; "You Take My Heart Away" and "Rocky's Theme (Gonna Fly Now)" by Bill Conti, Carol Connors and Ayn Robbins. Technicolor. Prints by DeLuxe Color. Filmed in Philadelphia. Rated PG. 121 minutes. Sequel is *Rocky II—Redemption* (1979)

Rocky Balboa: Sylvester Stallone, *Adrian:* Talia Shire, *Paulie:* Burt Young, *Apollo Creed:* Carl Weathers, *Mickey:* Burgess Meredith, *Miles Jergens:* Thayer David, *Tom Gazzo:* Joe Spinell, *Mike:* Jimmy Gambina, *Fight Announcer:* Bill Baldwin, *Cut Man (Himself):* Al Silvani, *Ice Rink Attendant:* George Memmoli, *Marie:* Jodi Letizia, *TV Commentator:* Diana Lewis, *TV Commentator:* George O'Hanlon, *TV Interviewer:* Larry Carroll, *Dipper:* Stan Shaw, *Bartender:* Don Sherman, *Club Fight Announcer:* Billy Sands, *Spider Ricco:* Pedro Lovell, *Apollo's Corner:* DeForest Covan, *Club Corner Man:* Simmy Bow, *Apollo's Trainer:* Tony Burton, *Apollo Cornerman:* Hank Rolike, *Jergens' Secretary:* Shirley O'Hara, *Paulie's Date:* Kathleen Parker, *Timekeeper:* Frank Stallone, *Drunk:* Lloyd Kaufman, *Gloria, Pet Shop Owner:* Jane Marla Robbins, *Fats:* Jack Hollander, *Buddy, Bodyguard:* Joe Sorbello, *Chiptooth:* Christopher Avildsen, *Club Fight Referee:* Frankie Van, *Championship Fight Announcer:* Lou Fillipo, *Street Corner Singers:* Frank Stallone, Jr., Robert L. Tangrea, Peter Glassberg, William E. Ring, Joseph C. Giambelluca, *Butkus, Dog:* Butkus Stallone, *Himself:* Joe Frazier, *Fighter:* Paris Eagle.

Rocky with Sylvester Stallone and Talia Shire.

Roman Holiday with Audrey Hepburn, Gregory Peck and Eddie Albert.

ROMAN HOLIDAY (1953) Par. Produced and directed by William Wyler. Story, Ian McLellan Hunter. Screenplay, Ian McLellan Hunter and John Dighton. Music, Georges Auric. Art Directors, Hal Pereira and Walter Tyler. Photography, Franz F. Planer and Henri Alekan. Editor, Robert Swink. Filmed in Rome and at Cinecittà Studios. American film debut of Audrey Hepburn. 119 minutes

Joe Bradley: Gregory Peck, *Princess Anne:* Audrey Hepburn, *Irving Radovich:* Eddie Albert, *Mr. Hennessy:* Hartley Power, *Hennessy's Secretary:* Laura Solari, *Ambassador:* Harcourt Williams, *Countess Vereberg:* Margaret Rawlings, *General Provno:* Tullio Carminati, *Mario Delani:* Paolo Carlini, *Giovanni:* Claudio Ermelli, *Charwoman:* Paola Borboni, *Dr. Bonnachoven:* Heinz Hindrich, *Shoe Seller:* Gorella Gori, *Taxi Driver:* Alfredo Rizzo.

Roman Scandals with Gloria Stuart and Eddie Cantor.

ROMAN SCANDALS (1933) UA. Produced by Samuel Goldwyn. Directed by Frank Tuttle. Original Story, George S. Kaufman and Robert E. Sherwood. Adaptation, William Anthony McGuire. Additional Dialogue, George Oppenheimer, Arthur Sheekman, Nat Vinton Vernon. Songs: "Rome Wasn't Built in a Day", "Build a Little Home," "Keep Young and Beautiful," and "No More Love" by Al Dubin and Harry Warren; "Tax on Love" by L. Wolfe Gilbert and Harry Warren. Dances, Busby Berkeley. Chariot Sequence Director, Ralph Cedar. 93 minutes

Eddie: Eddie Cantor, *Olga:* Ruth Etting, *Princess Sylvia:* Gloria Stuart, *Josephus:* David Manners, *Empress Agrippa:* Verree Teasdale, *Emperor Valerius:* Edward Arnold, *Majordomo:* Alan Mowbray, *Manius:* Jack Rutherford, *Slave Dancer:* Grace Poggi, *Warren F. Cooper:* Willard Robertson, *Mayor of West Rome:* Harry Holman, *Storekeeper:* Lee Kohlmar, *Slave Auctioneer:* Stanley Fields, *Slave Market Soloists:* The Abbottiers (Florence Wilson, Rose Kirsner, Genevieve Irwin, Dolly Bell), *Police Chief Charles Pratt:* Charles C. Wilson, *Buggs, Museum Keeper:* Clarence Wilson, *Official:* Stanley Andrews, *Cop/ Roman Jailer:* Stanley Blystone, *Soldier:* Harry Cording, *Soldier:* Lane Chandler, *Slave Buyer:* William Wagner, *Lady Slave Bidder:* Louise Carver, *Citizen:* Francis Ford, *Caius, Food Tester:* Charles Arnt, *Torturer:* Leo Willis, *Soldier:* Duke York, *Lucius, Aide:* Frank Hagney, *Assistant Cook:* Michael Mark, *Guard:* Dick Alexander, *Chef:* Paul Porcasi, *Senator:* John Ince, *Manager of Beauty Salon:* Jane Darwell, *Little Eddie:* Billy Barty, *Girl:* Iris Shunn, *Slave Dancer:* Aileen Riggin, *Slave Girls:* Katharine Mauk, Rosalie Fromson, Mary Lange, Vivian Keefer, Barbara Pepper, Theo Plane, Lucille Ball.

ROMEO AND JULIET (1936) MGM. Produced by Irving Thalberg. Directed by George Cukor. Based on the play by William Shakespeare. Arranged for the screen by Talbot Jennings. Musical Score, Herbert Stothart. Art Director, Cedric Gibbons. Dance Director, Agnes De Mille. Camera, William Daniels. Editor, Margaret Booth. Settings,

Cedric Gibbons and Oliver Messel. Associates, Fredric Hope and Edwin B. Willis. Costumes, Oliver Messel and Adrian. Artistic Consultant, Oliver Messel. Literary Consultant, Prof. William Strunk, Jr. Other versions: Biograph, 1914; Metro, 1916; Fox, 1916; British-made, 1954; Russian ballet film, 1955; British ballet film, 1966; British, 1968. 127 minutes

Juliet: Norma Shearer, *Romeo:* Leslie Howard, *Nurse:* Edna May Oliver, *Mercutio:* John Barrymore, *Lord Capulet:* C. Aubrey Smith, *Tybalt:* Basil Rathbone, *Peter:* Andy Devine, *Friar Lawrence:* Henry Kolker, *Lady Capulet:* Violet Kemble-Cooper, *Paris:* Ralph Forbes, *Benvolio:* Reginald Denny, *Balthasar:* Maurice Murphy, *Prince of Verona:* Conway Tearle, *Lady Montague:* Virginia Hammond, *Lord Montague:* Robert Warwick, *Samson Capulet:* Vernon Downing, *Apothecary:* Ian Wolfe, *Gregory Capulet:* Anthony Kemble-Cooper, *Mercutio's Page:* Anthony March, *Abraham Montague:* Howard Wilson, *Tybalt's Page:* Carlyle Blackwell, Jr., *Friar John:* John Bryan, *Rosalind:* Katherine De Mille, *Town Watch:* Wallis Clark, *Bits:* Dean Richmond Bentor, Lita Chevret, Jeanne Hart, Dorothy Granger, *Noblemen:* Harold Entwistle, Charles Bancroft, Jose Rubio.

Romeo and Juliet with Norma Shearer and Ralph Forbes.

Rose Marie with Jeanette MacDonald and Nelson Eddy.

ROSE MARIE (1936) MGM. Produced by Hunt Stromberg. Directed by W. S. Van Dyke. Based on Arthur Hammerstein's production of the musical by Otto A. Harbach and Oscar Hammerstein II. Screenplay, Frances Goodrich, Albert Hackett, Alice Duer Miller. Music Director, Herbert Stothart. Camera, William Daniels. Editor, Blanche Sewell. Songs: "Rose Marie," "Song of the Mounties," "Lak Jeem," "Indian

Love Call," "Totem Tom Tom" by Otto Harbach, Oscar Hammerstein II, and Rudolf Friml; "Just for You" by Gus Kahn, Herbert Stothart, and Rudolf Friml; "Pardon Me Madame" by Gus Kahn and Herbert Stothart; "Dinah" by Sam Lewis, Joe Young, and Harry Akst; "Some of These Days" by Shelton Brooks. Totem pole dance staged by Chester Hale. Operatic episodes staged by William von Wymetal. Sound, Douglas Shearer. Art Director's Associates, Joseph Wright and Edwin B. Willis. Gowns, Adrian. TV Title: *Indian Love Call.* Other versions made by MGM as a 1928 silent and in 1954. 113 minutes

Marie de Flor: Jeanette MacDonald, *Sergeant Bruce:* Nelson Eddy, *John Flower:* James Stewart, *Meyerson:* Reginald Owen, *Romeo:* Allan Jones, *Bella:* Gilda Gray, *Boniface:* George Regas, *Cafe Manager:* Robert Greig, *Anna:* Una O'Connor, *Storekeeper:* Lucien Littlefield, *Premier:* Alan Mowbray, *Teddy:* David Niven, *Mr. Daniels:* Herman Bing, *Joe:* James Conlin, *Edith:* Dorothy Gray, *Corn Queen:* Mary Anita Loos, *Susan:* Aileen Carlyle, *Mr. Gordon:* Halliwell Hobbes, *Emil:* Paul Porcasi, *Mounted Policeman:* Ed Dearing, *Traveling Salesman:* Pat West, *Stage Manager:* Milton Owen, *Doorman:* David Clyde, *Commandant:* Russell Hicks, *Men:* Rolfe Sedan, Jack Pennick, *Louis:* Leonard Carey, *Dancers:* David Robel, Rinaldo Alacorn, *Trapper:* Bert Lindley.

Rosemary's Baby with Elisha Cook, Jr., Mia Farrow and John Cassavetes.

ROSEMARY'S BABY (1968) Par. Produced by William Castle. Directed by Roman Polanski. Based on Ira Levin's novel. Screenplay, Roman Polanski. In Technicolor. Associate Producer, Dona Holloway. Assistant Director, Daniel J. McCauley. Photography, William Fraker. Music by Christopher Komeda incorporates Beethoven's "Fuer Elise." Process Photography, Farciot Edouart. Production Designer, Richard Sylbert. Art Direction, Joel Schiller. Set Decorations, Robert Nelson. Editors, Sam O'Steen and Bob Wyman. Sound, Harold Lewis. Costumes, Anthea Sylbert. Make-up, Allan Snyder. Hairstyles by Sydney Guilaroff, Vidal Sassoon and Sherry Wilson. Production Manager, William C. Davidson. Scenes filmed in New York and in Playa Del Rey, California. 136 minutes. Sequel was *Look What's Happened to Rosemary's Baby* (ABC-TV, 1976), also with Gordon

Rosemary Woodhouse: Mia Farrow, *Guy Woodhouse:* John Cassavetes, *Minnie Castevet:* Ruth Gordon, *Roman Castevet:* Sidney Blackmer, *Hutch:* Maurice Evans, *Dr. Sapirstein:* Ralph Bellamy, *Terry Fionoffrio:* Angela Dorian, *Laura-Louise:* Patsy Kelly, *Mr. Nicklas:* Elisha Cook, Jr., *Dr. Hill:* Charles Grodin, *Elise Dunstan:* Emmaline Henry, *Joan Jellico:* Marianne Gordon, *Dr. Shand:* Phil Leeds, *Mrs. Gilmore:* Hope Summers, *Tiger:* Wendy Wagner, *Grace Cardiff:* Hanna Landy, *Guy's Agent:* Gordon Connell, *Nurse:* Janet Garland, *Pregnant Woman:* Joan T. Reilly, *Donald Baumgart:* Voice of Tony Curtis, *Mrs. John F. Kennedy:* Patricia Ann Conway, *Man at Telephone Booth:* William Castle, *Mr. Wees:* Walter Baldwin, *Mrs. Fountain:* Charlotte Boerner, *Argyron Stavropoulos:* Sebastian Brooks, *Young Japanese Man:* Ernest Kazuyoshi Harada, *Young Woman:* Natalie Park Masters, *Young Man:* Elmer

Modlin, *Mrs. Wees:* Patricia O'Neal, *Mr. Fountain:* Robert Osterloh, *Mrs. Sabatini:* Almira Sessions, *Mr. Gilmore:* Bruno (Bronislaw) Sidar, *Sun-browned Man:* Roy Barcroft, *Diego:* D'Urville Martin, *Salesman:* Bill Baldwin, *Workman:* George Savalas, *Lisa:* Viki Vigen, *Dr. Sapirstein's Receptionist:* Marilyn Harvey, *Skipper:* Paul A. Denton, *Voice of Babysitter:* Gail Bonney, *Hugh Dunstan:* Frank White, *Portia Haynes:* Mary Louise Lawson, *Rain Morgan:* Gale Peters, *Lou Comfort:* George Ross Robertson, *Claudia Comfort:* Carol Brewster: *Devil:* Clay Tanner, *Pope:* Michael Shillo, *Sister Agnes:* Jean Inness, *Sister Veronica:* Lynn Brinker, *Pedro:* Michel Gomez, *Farrow's double:* Linda Brewerton, *Mrs. Byron:* Mona Knox, *Dee Bertillon:* Joyce Davis (Smith), *Men at Party:* Floyd Mutrux, Josh Peine.

The Rose Tattoo with Anna Magnani.

THE ROSE TATTOO (1955) Par. Producer, Hal B. Wallis. Director, Daniel Mann. VistaVision. Based on the play *The Rose Tattoo* by Tennessee Williams. Screenplay, Tennessee Williams. Adaptation, Hal Kanter. Art Director, Hal Pereira, Tambi Larsen. Musical Director, Alex North. Cinematographer, James Wong Howe. Editor, Warren Low. 117 minutes

Serafina Delle Rose: Anna Magnani, *Alvaro Mangiacavallo:* Burt Lancaster, *Rosa Delle Rose:* Marisa Pavan, *Jack Hunter:* Ben Cooper, *Estelle Hohengarten:* Virginia Grey, *Bessie:* Jo Van Fleet, *Assunta:* Mimi Aguglia, *Flora:* Florence Sundstrom, *Schoolteacher:* Dorrit Kelton, *Peppina:* Rossana San Marco, *Guiseppina:* Augusta Merighi, *Mariella:* Rosa Rey, *The Strega:* Georgia Simmons, *Miss Mangiacavallo:* Zolya Talma, *Pop Mangiacavallo:* George Humbert, *Grandma Mangiacavallo:* Margherita Pasquero, *Mamma Shigura (Tattoo Artist):* May Lee, *Taxi Driver:* Lewis Charles, *Rosario Delle Rose:* Larry Chance, *Violetta:* Jean Hart, *Doctor:* Roger Gunderson, *Salvatore:* Roland Vildo, *Taxi Driver:* Virgil Osborne, *Mario:* Albert Atkins.

RUGGLES OF RED GAP (1935) Par. Produced by Arthur Hornblow, Jr. Directed by Leo McCarey. Adapted from the play and novel by Harry Leon Wilson. Screenplay, Walter De Leon, Harlan Thomson, Humphrey Pearson. Editor, Edward Dmytryk. Cinematographer, Alfred Gilks. Recording Engineer, P. G. Wisdom. Assistant Director,

A. F. Erickson. Art Directors, Hans Dreier and Robert Odell. Costumes, Travis Banton. Musical numbers by Ralph Rainger and Sam Coslow. Previous versions produced by Essanay, 1918, and Paramount, 1923. Remade as *Fancy Pants* (Paramount, 1950). 90 minutes

Ruggles: Charles Laughton, *Effie Floud:* Mary Boland, *Egbert Floud:* Charlie Ruggles, *Mrs. Judson:* ZaSu Pitts, *George Van Bassingwell:* Roland Young, *Nell Kenner:* Leila Hyams, *Ma Pettingill:* Maude Eburne, *Charles Belknap-Jackson:* Lucien Littlefield, *Mrs. Belknap-Jackson:* Leota Lorraine, *Jeff Tuttle:* James Burke, *Sam:* Dell Henderson, *Baby Judson:* Baby Ricardo Lord Cezon, *Judy Ballard:* Brenda Fowler, *Mrs. Wallaby:* Augusta Anderson, *Mrs. Myron Carey:* Sarah Edwards, *Jake Henshaw:* Clarence Hummel Wilson, *Clothing Salesman:* Rafael Storm, *Hank:* Frank Rice, *Curly:* Victor Potel, *Buck Squires:* George Burton, *Eddie:* William J. Welsh, *Red Gap Jailer:* Lee Kohlmar, *Harry,* bartender: Harry Bernard, *Lisette:* Alice Ardell, *Barber:* Rolfe Sedan, *Barfly:* Jack Norton, *Bit in Saloon:* Jim Welch, *Chinese Servant:* Willie Fung, *Negro Servant:* Libby Taylor, *Clothing Salesman:* Armand Kaliz, *Photographer:* Harry Bowen, *Frank,* patron: Henry Roquemore, *Waiter:* Heinie Conklin, *Patron:* Edward LeSaint, *Waiter in Paris Cafe:* Charles Fallon, *Frank,* Cabman: Genaro Spagnoli, *Waiter at Carousel:* Albert Petit, *Effie's Guests in Paris:* Carrie Daumery, Isabelle La Mal, *Dishwasher:* Ernest S. (Ernie) Adams, *Station Agent:* Frank O'Connor.

Ruggles of Red Gap with Charlie Ruggles, Charles Laughton and James Burke.

The Russians Are Coming with Carl Reiner, Eva Marie Saint, Sheldon Golomb, John Phillip Law and Alan Arkin.

THE RUSSIANS ARE COMING THE RUSSIANS ARE COMING (1966) UA. Produced and directed by Norman Jewison. A Mirisch Corporation Presentation. Panavision and De Luxe Color. Based on the novel *The Off-Islanders* by Nathaniel Benchley. Screenplay, William

Rose. Photography, Joseph Biroc. Music, Johnny Mandel. Art Director, Robert F. Boyle. Assistant Director, Kurt Neumann, Jr. Editors, Hal Ashby and J. Terry Williams. Production Supervisor, Allen K. Wood. Production Manager, James E. Henderling. Unit Manager, Fred Lemoine. Assistant to the Producer, Peter Nelson. Sound, Alfred J. Overton and John Romness. Wardrobe, Wesley Jeffries. Music Editor, Richard Carruth. Second Assistant Director, Les Gorall. Set Decorator, Darrell Silvera. Set Designers, James F. McGuire and Lewis E. Hurst, Jr. Script Supervisor, Betty Levin. Dialogue Director, Leon Belasco. Special Effects, Daniel W. Hays. Make-up, Del Armstrong. Sound Editor, Sidney E. Sutherland. Hair Stylist, Sydney Guilaroff. Hairdresser, Naomi Cavin. Property, Anthony N. Bavero. Sketch Artist, Thomas J. Wright, Jr. Casting, Lynn Stalmaster. Titles, Pablo Ferro, Inc. Filmed in Northern California. Film debut of Alan Arkin. U.S. debut of John Phillip Law. 126 minutes

Walt Whittaker: Carl Reiner, *Elspeth Whittaker:* Eva Marie Saint, *Rozanov:* Alan Arkin, *Link Mattocks:* Brian Keith, *Norman Jonas:* Jonathan Winters, *The Captain:* Theodore Bikel, *Fendall Hawkins:* Paul Ford, *Alice Foss:* Tessie O'Shea, *Alexei Kolchin:* John Phillip Law, *Alison Palmer:* Andrea Dromm, *Luther Grilk:* Ben Blue, *Pete Whittaker:* Sheldon Golomb, *Annie Whittaker:* Cindy Putnam, *Lester Tilly:* Guy Raymond, *Charlie Hinkson:* Cliff Norton, *Oscar Maxwell:* Dick Schaal, *Isaac Porter:* Philip Coolidge, *Irving Christiansen:* Don Keefer, *Mr. Everett:* Parker Fennelly, *Muriel Everett:* Doro Merande, *Mr. Bell:* Vaughn Taylor, *Jerry Maxwell:* Johnnie Whittaker, *Polsky:* Danny Klega, *Brodsky:* Ray Baxter, *Maliavin:* Paul Verdier, *Gromolsky:* Nikita Knatz, *Vasilov:* Constantine Baksheef, *Hrushevsky:* Alex Hassilev, *Lysenko:* Milos Milos, *Kregitkin:* Gino Gottarelli, *Stanley, Airport Worker:* Michael J. Pollard, *Reverend Hawthorne:* Peter Brocco.

Ryan's Daughter with John Mills and Trevor Howard.

RYAN'S DAUGHTER (1970) MGM. Produced by Anthony Havelock-Allan. Directed by David Lean. Super Panavision 70 and MetroColor. A Faraway Productions A. G. Gilm for EMI. Screenplay by Robert Bolt. Photography, Freddie Young. Associate Producer, Roy Stevens. Assistant Directors, Pedro Vidal and Michael Stevenson. Costumes, Jocelyn Rickards. Storm Sequence Director, Roy Stevens. 2nd Unit Director, Charles Frend. Production Design, Stephen Grimes. Art Director, Roy Walker. Special Effects, Robert MacDonald. 2nd Unit Photography, Denys Coop and Bob Huke. Editor, Norman Savage. Music, Maurice Jarre. "It Was a Good Time (Rosy's Theme)" by Jarre, lyrics by Mack David and Mike Curb. Filmed in Ireland. 206 minutes

Charles Shaughnessy: Robert Mitchum, *Rosy Ryan:* Sarah Miles, *Michael:* John Mills, *Father Collins:* Trevor Howard, *Randolph Doryan:* Christopher Jones, *Tom Ryan:* Leo McKern, *Tim O'Leary:* Barry Foster, *McCardle:* Archie O'Sullivan, *Mrs. McCardle:* Marie Kean, *Corporal:* Barry Jackson, *Driver:* Douglas Sheldon, *Bernard:* Ed O'Callaghan, *Paddy:* Philip O'Flynn, *Joseph:* Niall O'Brien, *Peter:* Owen O'Sullivan, *O'Keefe:* Niall Toibin, *Sean:* Emmet Bergin, *Storekeeper:* May Cluskey, *Old Woman:* Annie Dalton, *McCardle's Friend:* Steve Brennan, *Captain:* Gerald Sim, *Lanky Private:* Des Keogh, *Moureen:* Evin Crowley, *Moureen's Boyfriend:* Donal Neligan, *Constable O'Connor:* Brian O'Higgins, *Policeman:* Pat Layde, *Moureen's Friend:* Katherine Webb, *Bridesmaid:* Jan Cowan.

Sabrina with Humphrey Bogart and Audrey Hepburn.

SABRINA (1954) Par. Producer, Billy Wilder. Director, Billy Wilder. From Samuel Taylor's play *Sabrina Fair.* Screenplay, Billy Wilder. Art Directors, Hal Pereira, Walter Tyler. Cinematographer, Charles Lang, Jr. Editor, Doane Harrison. Filmed in Rye, New York; New York City; Glen Cove, Long Island; on the estate of Barney Balaban (President of Paramount Pictures). 113 minutes

Linus Larrabee: Humphrey Bogart, *Sabrina Fairchild:* Audrey Hepburn, *David Larrabee:* William Holden, *Oliver Larrabee:* Walter Hampden, *Thomas Fairchild:* John Williams, *Elizabeth Tyson:* Martha Hyer, *Gretchen Van Horn:* Joan Vohs, *Baron:* Marcel Dalio, *The Professor:* Marcel Hillaire, *Maude Larrabee:* Nella Walker, *Mr. Tyson:* Francis X. Bushman, *Miss McCardle:* Ellen Corby, *Margaret (Cook):* Marjorie Bennett, *Charles (Butler):* Emory Parnell, *Mrs. Tyson:* Kay Riehl, *Jenny (Maid):* Nancy Kulp, *Houseman:* Kay Kuter, *Doctor:* Paul Harvey, *Board Members:* Emmett Vogan, Colin Campbell, *Man (with Tray):* Harvey Dunn, *Spiller's Girl Friend:* Marion Ross, *Spiller:* Charles Harvey.

SAILOR BEWARE (1951) Par. Produced by Hal B. Wallis. Directed by Hal Walker. From the play *Sailor Beware* by Kenyon Nicholson and Charles Robinson. Screenplay, James Allardice and Martin Rackin. Additional Dialogue, John Grant. Adaptation, Elwood Ullman. Art Directors, Hal Pereira and Henry Bumstead. Music Director, Joseph J. Lilley. Photography, Daniel L. Fapp. Editor, Warren Low. Songs by Mack David and Jerry Livingston: "Sailors' Polka," "Never Before," "Merci Beaucoup," "The Old Calliope," and "Today, Tomorrow, Forever." Previous versions by Paramount: *Lady, Be Careful* (1936), *The Fleet's In* (1942). Bit player Duke Mitchell teamed with Sammy Petrillo to do a Martin & Lewis takeoff called *Bela Lugosi Meets a Brooklyn Gorilla* (Realart, 1952). 108 minutes

Al Crowthers: Dean Martin, *Melvin Jones:* Jerry Lewis, *Guest Star:* Corinne Calvet, *Hilda Jones:* Marion Marshall, *Lardoski:* Robert Strauss, *Commander Lane:* Leif Erickson, *Mr. Chubby:* Don Wilson, *Blayden:* Vincent Edwards, *Mac:* Skip Homeier, *'Bama:* Dan Barton, *Tiger:* Mike Mahoney, *Ginger:* Mary Treen, *Turk:* Danny Arnold, *Navy Doctor:* Louis Jean Heydt, *Lieutenant Saunders:* Elaine Stewart, *Bull:* Drew Cahill, *Petty Officer:* James Flavin, *Lt. Connors:* Don Haggerty, *Pretty Girl:* Mary Murphy, *Corpsman:* Jerry Hausner, *Jeff Spencer:* Darr Smith, *Mayo Brothers:* Bobby and Eddie Mayo, *Guard:* Richard Karlan, *Killer Jackson:* Eddie Simms, *McDurk:* Stephen Gregory, *Navy Captain:* Robert Carson, *Petty Officer:* Richard Emory, *Hospital Corpsman:* Marshall Reed, *Hospital Corpsman:* John V. Close, *Female Commentator:* Elaine Riley, *Referee:* Larry McGrath, *Second:* Duke Mitchell, *Sailor:* James Dean, *Themselves:* The Marimba Merry Makers, *Chief Bos'n Mate:* Donald MacBride, *Bandleader:* Dick Stabile, *Betty:* Betty Hutton.

Sailor Beware with Dean Martin and Jerry Lewis.

Salome with Charles Laughton and Rita Hayworth.

SALOME (1953) Col. Producer, Buddy Adler. Director, William Dieterle. Technicolor. Author, Jesse Lasky, Jr. Screenplay, Harry Kleiner. Art Director, John Meehan. Cinematographer, Charles Lang. Editor, Viola Lawrence. 103 minutes

Princess Salome: Rita Hayworth, *Commander Claudius:* Stewart Granger, *King Herod:* Charles Laughton, *Queen Herodias:* Judith Anderson, *Caesar Tiberius:* Sir Cedric Hardwicke, *John the Baptist:* Alan Badel, *Pontius Pilate:* Basil Sydney, *Ezra:* Maurice Schwartz, *Marcellus Fabius:* Rex Reason, *Micha:* Arnold Moss, *Oriental Dance Team:* Sujata and Asoka, *Courier:* Robert Warwick, *Salome's Servant:* Carmen D'Antonio, *Captain Quintus:* Michael Granger, *Slave Master:* Karl "Killer" Davis, *Simon:* Charles Wagenheim, *Guard:* Tris Coffin, *Sailor:* Rick Vallin, *Herod's Captain of the Guards:* Mickey Simpson, *Roman Guard:* Eduard Cansino, *Executioner:* Lou Nova, *Sword Dancer:* Fred Letuli, *Sword Dancer:* John Woodd, *Fire Eater:* William Spaeth, *Juggling Specialty:* Duke Johnson, *Galilean Soldier:* Earl Brown.

Samson and Delilah with Victor Mature and Hedy Lamarr.

SAMSON AND DELILAH (1949) Par. Producer-Director, Cecil B. De Mille. Color by Technicolor. Screenplay, Jesse Lasky, Jr., Frederick M. Frank. Music, Victor Young. Art Directors, Hans Dreier, Walter Tyler. Photography, George Barnes. Editor, Anne Bauchens. Song by Ray Evans, Jay Livingston and Victor Young: "Song of Delilah." From original treatments by Harold Lamb and Vladimir Jabotinsky. Based upon the history of Samson and Delilah in the Holy Bible, Judges 13-16. Choreography, Theodore Kosloff. Doubles for Victor Mature: fight sequences, Ed Hinton, lion-fighting sequence, Mel Koontz. 128 minutes

Delilah: Hedy Lamarr, *Samson:* Victor Mature, *The Saran of Gaza:* George Sanders, *Semadar:* Angela Lansbury, *Ahtur:* Henry Wilcoxon, *Miriam:* Olive Deering, *Hazel:* Fay Holden, *Hisham:* Julia Faye, *Saul:* Rusty Tamblyn, *Tubal:* William Farnum, *Teresh:* Lane Chandler, *Targil:* Moroni Olsen, *Story Teller:* Francis J. McDonald, *Garmiskar:* William Davis, *Lesh Lakish:* John Miljan, *Fat Philistine Merchant:* Arthur Q. Bryan, *Spectators:* Laura Elliot and Jeff York, *Lord of Ashdod:* Victor Varconi, *Lord of Gath:* John Parrish, *Lord of Ekron:* Frank Wilcox, *Lord of Ashkelon:* Russell Hicks, *First Priest:* Boyd Davis, *Lord Sharif:* Fritz Leiber, *Leader of Philistine Soldiers:* Mike Mazurki, *Merchant Prince:* Davison Clark, *Wounded Messenger:* George Reeves, *Bar Simon:* Pedro de Cordoba, *Village Barber:* Frank Reicher, *Princes:* Colin Tapley, Nils Asther, *Priests:* Pierre Watkin, Fred Graham, *Woman:* Karen Morley, *Danite Merchant:* Charles Judels, *Manoah, Samson's Father:* Charles Evans, *Prince:* James Craven, *Chief Scribe:* Lloyd Whitlock, *Court Astrologer:* Cranfurd Kent, *Gammad:* Harry Woods, *Bergam:* Stephen Roberts, *Makon:* Ed Hinton, *Gristmill Captain:* Tom Tyler, *Overseer at Gristmill:* Ray Bennett, *Spectators:* Margaret Field and John Kellogg, *Spectator:* Dorothy Adams, *Saran's Chariot Driver:* Henry Wills.

SAN ANTONIO (1945) WB. Produced by Robert Buckner. Directed by Robert Florey and David Butler. Color by Technicolor. Original Screenplay, Alan LeMay and W. R. Burnett. Art Director, Ted Smith. Music, Max Steiner. Music Director, Leo F. Forbstein. Orchestral Arrangements, Hugo Friedhofer. Photography, Bert Glennon. Editor, Irene Morra. Special Effects, Willard Van Enger. Songs: "Somewhere in Monterey" by Jack Scholl and Charles Kisco; "Put Your Little Foot Right Out" by Larry Spier; and "Some Sunday Morning" by Ted Koehler, M. K. Jerome, and Ray Heindorf. 111 minutes

Clay Hardin: Errol Flynn, *Jeanne Starr:* Alexis Smith, *Sacha Bozic:* S. Z. Sakall, *Legare:* Victor Francen, *Henrietta:* Florence Bates, *Charlie Bell:* John Litel, *Roy Stuart:* Paul Kelly, *Pony Smith:* John Alvin, *Cleve Andrews:* Monte Blue, *Captain Morgan:* Robert Shayne, *Colonel Johnson:* Robert Barrat, *Ricardo Torreon:* Pedro de Cordoba, *Lafe McWilliams:* Tom Tyler, *Hymie Rosas:* Chris-Pin Martin, *Sojer Harris:* Charles Stevens, *San Antonio Stage Driver:* Poodles Hanneford, *Entertainer:* Doodles Weaver, *Joey Sims:* Dan White, *Rebel White:* Ray Spiker, *Hap Winters:* Al Hill, *Tip Brice:* Wallis Clark, *Hawker:* Harry Cording, *Poker Player:* Chalky Williams, *Roper:* Bill Steele, *Clay's Henchmen:* Howard Hill, Allen E. Smith, *Dancer:* Arnold Kent, *Head Customs Officer:* Dan Seymour, *Cowboys:* John Compton, Don McGuire, Brad King, Johnny Miles, Francis Ford, Lane Chandler, Hal Taliaferro, Jack Mower, William Gould, *Bartender:* Harry Seymour, *Jay Witherspoon:* Norman Willis, *Cattlemen:* Eddy Waller, Henry Hall, James Flavin.

San Antonio with Florence Bates, S.Z. Sakall, Alexis Smith and Errol Flynn.

The Sandpiper with Elizabeth Taylor and Richard Burton.

THE SANDPIPER (1965) MGM. Producer, Martin Ransohoff. Director, Vincente Minnelli. MetroColor, Panavision. Adapted by Irene and Louis Kamp from an original by Martin Ransohoff. Screenplay, Dalton Trumbo, Michael Wilson. Art Directors, George W. Davis, Urie McCleary. Music, Johnny Mandel. Cinematographer, Milton Krasner. Editor, David Bretherton. 116 minutes

Laura Reynolds: Elizabeth Taylor, *Dr. Edward Hewitt:* Richard Burton, *Claire Hewitt:* Eva Marie Saint, *Cos Erickson:* Charles Bronson, *Ward Hendricks:* Robert Webber, *Larry Brant:* James Edwards, *Judge Thompson:* Torin Thatcher, *Walter Robinson:* Tom Drake, *Phil Suteliff:* Doug Henderson, *Danny Reynolds:* Morgan Mason, *Troopers:* Dusty Cadis, John Hart, *Trustee:* Jan Arvan, *Trustee's Wife:* Mary Benoit, *Trustee:* Tom Curtis, *Architect:* Paul Genge, *Celebrant #1:* Rex Holman, *Celebrant #2:* Kelton Garwood, *Celebrant #3:* Jimmy Murphy, *Celebrant #4:* Mel Gallagher, *Poet Celebrant #5:* Ron Whelan, *Celebrant #6:* Diane Sayer, *Celebrant #7:* Joan Connors, *Celebrant #8:* Peggy Adams Laird, *Celebrant #9:* Shirley Bonne, *Voice:* Peter O'Toole

SANDS OF IWO JIMA (1949) Rep. Associate Producer, Edmund Grainger. Director, Allan Dwan. Author, Harry Brown. Screenplay, Harry Brown, James Edward Grant. Music, Victor Young. Art Director, James Sullivan. Photography, Reggie Lanning. Editor, Richard L. Van Enger. 110 minutes

Sergeant John M. Stryker: John Wayne, *Pfc. Peter Conway:* John Agar, *Allison Bromley:* Adele Mara, *Pfc. Al Thomas:* Forrest Tucker, *Pfc. Benny Regazzi:* Wally Cassell, *Pfc. Charlie Bass:* James Brown, *Pfc. Shipley:* Richard Webb, *Corporal Robert Dunne/Narrator:* Arthur Franz, *Mary:* Julie Bishop, *Pfc. Soames:* James Holden, *Pfc. Hellenpolis:* Peter Coe, *Pfc. Frank Flynn:* Richard Jaeckel, *Pfc. Eddie Flynn:* Bill Murphy, *Pfc. Harris:* George Tyne, *Private "Ski" Choynski:* Hal Fieberling (Hal Baylor), *Captain Joyce:* John McGuire, *Private Mike McHugh:* Martin Milner, *Private Sid Stein:* Leonard Gumley, *Private L. D. Fowler, Jr.* William Self, *Grenade Instructor:* Dick Wessel, *Forrestal:* I. Stanford Jolley, *Wounded Marine:* David Clarke, *Lieutenant Baker:* Gil Herman, *Scared Marine:* Dick Jones, *Colonel:* Don Haggerty, *Marine:* Bruce Edwards, *Tall Girl:* Dorothy Ford, *Lieutenant Thompson:* John Whitney, *Themselves:* Colonel D. M. Shoup, U.S.M.C., Lieutenant Colonel H. P. Crowe, U.S.M.C., Captain Harold G. Schrier, U.S.M.C., and the three living survivors of the historic flag raising on Mount Suribachi: Pfc. Rene A. Gagnon, Pfc. Ira H. Hayes, PM 3/C John H. Bradley.

Sands of Iwo Jima with Forrest Tucker and John Wayne.

SAN FRANCISCO (1936) MGM. Produced by John Emerson, Bernard H. Hyman. Directed by W. S. Van Dyke. Story, Robert Hopkins. Screenplay by Anita Loos. Cinematographer, Oliver T. Marsh. Recording Engineer, Douglas Shearer. Film Editor, Tom Held. Art Director, Cedric Gibbons. Costumer, Adrian. Musical Director, Herbert Stothart. Songs: "San Francisco" by Gus Kahn and Bronislau Kaper; "Would

You?" by Arthur Freed and Nacio Herb Brown; "The One Love" by Gus Kahn, Bronislau Kaper, and Walter Jurmann. Dances, Val Raset. 115 minutes

Blackie: Clark Gable, *Mary:* Jeanette MacDonald, *Tim:* Spencer Tracy, *Jack Burley:* Jack Holt, *Mat:* Ted Healy, *Della:* Margaret Irving, *Mrs. Burley:* Jessie Ralph, *Babe:* Harold Huber, *Professor:* Al Shean, *Baldini:* William Ricciardi, *Chick:* Kenneth Harlan, *Alaska:* Roger Imhof, *Dealer:* Frank Mayo, *Drunk:* Tom Dugan, *Tony:* Charles Judels, *Red Kelly:* Russell Simpson, *Duane:* Bert Roach, *Hazeltine:* Warren Hymer, *Sheriff:* Edgar Kennedy, *Madame Albani:* Adrienne d'Ambricourt, *Old Man:* Nigel de Brulier, *Dancer:* Mae Digges, *Singers:* Tudor Williams, Tandy MacKenzie, *Dancer:* Nyas Berry, *Captain of Police:* Tom Mahoney, *Drunk's Girl:* Gertrude Astor, *Father:* Jason Robards, *Fat Man:* Vernon Dent, *Kinko:* Jack Baxley, *Society Man:* Anthony Jowitt, *Salvation Man:* Carl Stockdale, *Members of Founder's Club:* Richard Carle, Oscar Apfel, Frank Sheridan, Ralph Lewis, *Jowl Lee:* Chester Gan, *Old Irishman:* Jack Kennedy, *Headwaiter:* Cy Kendall, *Coast Type:* Don Rowan, *Extra New Year's Celebrant:* Dennis O'Keefe, *Trixie:* Shirley Ross.

San Francisco with Al Shean, Jeanette MacDonald and Clark Gable.

Saratoga with Lionel Barrymore, Clark Gable and Cliff Edwards.

SARATOGA (1937) MGM. Produced by Bernard H. Hyman. Associate Producer, John Emerson. Directed by Jack Conway. Original Story and Screenplay, Anita Loos and Robert Hopkins. Art Director, Cedric Gibbons. Music Score, Edward Ward. Camera, Ray June. Editor, Elmo Vernon. Songs: "The Horse With the Dreamy Eyes" and "Saratoga," music by Walter Donaldson, lyrics by Bob Wright and Chet Forrest. The last film of Jean Harlow, who died during its production, on June 7, 1937, at 26. Mary Dees replaced her and Paula Win-

slowe dubbed her voice. Seen are races at Tropical Park, Miami, and at Churchill Downs, Louisville, on Derby Day. 94 minutes

Duke Bradley: Clark Gable, *Carol Clayton:* Jean Harlow, *Grandpa Clayton:* Lionel Barrymore, *Hartley Madison:* Walter Pidgeon, *Jesse Kiffmeyer:* Frank Morgan, *Fritzi O'Malley:* Una Merkel, *Tip O'Brien:* Cliff Edwards, *Dr. Beard:* George Zucco, *Frank Clayton:* Jonathan Hale, *Rosetta:* Hattie McDaniel, *Dixie Gordon:* Frankie Darro, *Hard Riding Hurley:* Henry Stone, *Boswell:* Carl Stockdale, *Mrs. Hurley:* Ruth Gillette, *Valet:* Charley Foy, *Auctioneer:* Robert Emmett Keane, *Medbury, Trainer:* Edgar Dearing, *Kenyon:* Frank McGlynn, Sr., *Maizie:* Margaret Hamilton, *Judge:* Sam Flint, *Limpy:* Walter Robbins, *Horse Owner:* Pat West, *Clipper:* Harrison Greene, *Pullman Steward:* Forbes Murray, *Gardener:* Si Jenks, *Bartender:* Herbert Ashley, *Cameraman:* George Chandler, *Tout:* Mel Ruick, *Hurley's Kid:* Patsy O'Connor, *Bartender:* Charles R. Moore, *Porter:* Fred (Snowflake) Toones, *Bidder:* Hooper Atchley, *Steve, a Bidder:* Edward (Bud) Flanagan (Dennis O'Keefe), *Cameraman:* Drew Demarest, *Train Passengers:* Irene Franklin, Ernie Stanton, John (Skins) Miller, Hank Mann, Bert Roach.

Saratoga Trunk with John Warburton, Jerry Austin, Gary Cooper and Ingrid Bergman.

SARATOGA TRUNK (1945) WB. Executive Producer, Jack L. Warner. Produced by Hal B. Wallis. Directed by Sam Wood. From the novel by Edna Ferber. Screenplay, Casey Robinson. Music, Max Steiner. Music Director, Leo F. Forbstein. Art Director, Carl Jules Weyl. Photography, Ernie Haller. Editor, Ralph Dawson. Sound, Robert B. Lee. Technical Adviser, Dalton S. Reymond. Special Effects, Lawrence Butler. Set Decorations, Fred MacLean. Production Design, Joseph St. Amaad. Make-up, Perc Westmore. Gowns, Leah Rhodes. Assistant Director, Phil Quinn. Unit Manager, Eric Stacey. Songs by Charles Tobias and Max Steiner, "As Long as I Live" and "Goin' Home." 135 minutes

Clint Maroon: Gary Cooper, *Clio Dulane:* Ingrid Bergman, *Angelique:* Flora Robson, *Cupidon:* Jerry Austin, *Sophie Bellop:* Florence Bates, *Bart Van Steed:* John Warburton, *Roscoe Bean:* John Abbott, *Augustin Haussy:* Curt Bois, *Clarissa Van Steed:* Ethel Griffies, *Raymond Soule:* Louis Payne, *Monsieur Begue:* Fred Essler, *Mrs. Porcelain:* Marla Shelton, *Grandmother Dulane:* Adrienne D'Ambricourt, *Madame Dulane:* Helen Freeman, *Charlotte Dulane:* Sophie Huxley, *J. P. Reynolds:* Minor Watson, *Guilia Forosini:* Jacqueline de Wit, *Miss Diggs:* Sarah Edwards, *Turbaned Seller:* Ruby Dandridge, *Madame Begue:* Amelia Liggett, *Leon, the Headwaiter:* George Beranger, *McIntyre:* Edmond Breon, *Mr. Stone:* William B. Davidson, *Mr. Bowers:* Edward Fielding, *Mr. Pound:* Thurston Hall, *Woman on Piazza:* Alice Fleming, *Engineer:* Ralph Dunn, *Al:* Lane Chandler, *Politician:* Dick Elliott, *Cowboy:* Glenn Strange, *Leader of Soule's Gang:* Frank Hagney, *Hotel Clerk:* Chester Clute, *Hotel Manager:* Theodore Von Eltz, *Engineer of Soule's Gang:* Alan Bridge, *Fireman on Train:* Monte Blue, *Ship's Captain:* Georges Renavent, *Officer:* Robert Barron, *First Mate:* Louis Mercier, *Diner:* Gino Corrado, *Soule Bodyguard:* Bob Reeves, *Gamblers:* Franklyn Farnum, Major Sam Harris.

Saturday Night Fever with John Travolta and Karen Gorney.

SATURDAY NIGHT FEVER (1977) Par. Produced by Robert Stigwood. Directed by John Badham. Based on the *New York* magazine cover story "Tribal Rites of the New Saturday Night" (June 1976 issue) by Nik Cohn. Screenplay, Norman Wexler. Executive Producer, Kevin McCormick. Photography, Ralf D. Bode. Production Designer, Charles Bailey. Editor, David Rawlins. Musical numbers staged and choreographed by Lester Wilson. Assistant Choreographer, Lorraine Fields. Dance Consultant, Jo-Jo Smith. Sound Recordist, John Fundes. Associate Producer, Milt Felsen. Production Manager/Assistant Director, John Nicolella. Assistant Directors, Allan Wertheim and Joseph Ray. Location Executive, Lloyd Kaufman. Costume Designer, Patrizia Von Brandenstein. Costumer, Jennifer Nichols. Hair Designs, Joe Tubens. Make-up, Max Henriquez. Set Decorator, George Detitta. Set Decorator/Outside Props, John Godfrey. Technical Consultant, James Gambina. Stunt Coordinator, Paul Nuckles. Discotheque Lighting provided by Litelab of New York. Songs: "How Deep Is Your Love," "Night Fever," "Stayin' Alive" and "More Than a Woman," written and performed by Barry, Robin and Maurice Gibb (the Bee Gees); "If I Can't Have You," written by the Bee Gees, performed by Yvonne Elliman; "More Than a Woman," also performed by Tavares; "K-Jee," performed by M.F.S.B.; "Calypso Breakdown," performed by Ralph McDonald; "A Fifth of Beethoven," performed by Walter Murphy; "Open Sesame," performed by Kool and the Gang; "Disco Duck," performed by Rick Dees; "Disco Inferno," performed by the Trammps; "Boogie Shoes," performed by K.C. and the Sunshine Band; "You Should Be Dancing," performed by the Bee Gees; "Manhattan Skyline," "Barracuda Hangout," "Salsation" and "Night on Disco Mountain," composed and arranged by David Shire. Lenses and Panaflex Camera by Panavision. Sound by Dolby System. Color by Movielab. Filmed on Manhattan's West Side, on the Verrazano Bridge (spanning Brooklyn and Staten Island) and in Brooklyn's Bay Ridge, including 2001 Odyssey disco and Brothers Hardware & Paints store. Rated R. 118 minutes

Tony Manero: John Travolta, *Stephanie Mangano:* Karen Gorney, *Bobby C:* Barry Miller, *Annette:* Donna Pescow, *Joey:* Joseph Cali, *Double J:* Paul Pape, *Gus:* Bruce Ornstein, *Flo Manero:* Julie Bovasso, *Father Frank Manero, Jr.:* Martin Shakar, *Frank Manero, Sr.:* Val Bisoglio, *Monti, the Deejay:* Monti Rock III, *Fusco:* Sam J. Coppola, *Grandmother:* Nina Hansen, *Linda Manero:* Lisa Peluso, *Doreen:* Denny Dillon, *Pete:* Bert Michaels, *Paint Store Customer:* Robert Costanza, *Becker:* Robert Weil, *Girl in Disco:* Shelly Batt, *Connie:* Fran Drescher, *Jay Langhart:* Donald Gantry, *Haberdashery Salesman:* Murray Moston, *Detective:* William Andrews, *Pizza Girl:* Ann Travolta, *Woman in Paint Store:* Helen Travolta, *Bartender:* Ellen Marca.

Sayonara with James Garner, Reiko Kuba, Marlon Brando, Miyoshi Umeki and Red Buttons.

SAYONARA (1957) WB. Produced by William Goetz. Directed by Joshua Logan. Technirama and Technicolor. Based on the novel by James A. Michener. Screenplay, Paul Osborn. Art Direction, Ted Haworth. Sets, Robert Priestley. Music, Franz Waxman. Costumes, Norma Koch. Revue numbers staged by LeRoy Prinz. Assistant Director, Ad Schaumer. Photography, Ellsworth Fredericks. Editing, Arthur P. Schmidt and Philip W. Anderson. Sound, William H. Mueller. Song, "Sayonara" by Irving Berlin. Filmed mostly in Kobe, Japan. Film debuts of Miiko Taka and Miyoshi Umeki. A Goetz Pictures-Pennebaker Production. 147 minutes

Major Lloyd Gruver: Marlon Brando, *Joe Kelly:* Red Buttons, *Nakamura:* Ricardo Montalban, *Hana-ogi:* Miiko Taka, *Katsumi:* Miyoshi Umeki, *Eileen Webster:* Patricia Owens, *Captain Mike Bailey:* James Garner, *Mrs. Webster:* Martha Scott, *General Webster:* Kent Smith, *Colonel Craford:* Douglas Watson, *Fumiko-san:* Reiko Kuba, *Teruko-san:* Soo Yong, *Consul:* Harlan Warde. The Shochuku Kagekidan Girls Revue.

Scarface with Paul Muni and Ann Dvorak.

SCARFACE (1932) UA. Produced and supervised by Howard Hughes. Directed by Howard Hawks. Assistant Director, Richard Rosson. Based on the novel by Armitage Trail. Screenplay, Ben Hecht, Seton I. Miller, John Lee Mahin, W. R. Burnett, Fred Pasley. Photography, Lee Garmes and L. W. O'Connell. Editor, Edward Curtiss. Sound, William Snyder. 99 minutes

Tony Camonte: Paul Muni, *Cesca Camonte:* Ann Dvorak, *Poppy:* Karen Morley, *Johnny Lovo:* Osgood Perkins, *Guido Rinaldo:* George Raft, *Ben Guarino:* C. Henry Gordon, *Angelo:* Vince Barnett, *Pietro:*

Henry Armetta, *Mrs. Camonte:* Inez Palange, *Louie Costillo:* Harry J. Vejar, *Chief of Detectives:* Edwin Maxwell, *Managing Editor:* Tully Marshall, *Gaffney:* Boris Karloff, *Epstein:* Bert Starkey, *Garston:* Purnell Pratt, *Gaffney Hood:* Paul Fix, *Worker:* Hank Mann, *Bootleggers:* Charles Sullivan, Harry Tenbrook, *Hood:* Maurice Black.

The Search with Aline MacMahon, Ivan Jandl and Montgomery Clift.

THE SEARCH (1948) MGM. Produced by Lazar Wechsler. Directed by Fred Zinnemann. A Praesens-Film, Zurich, Production. Original Screenplay, Richard Schweizer in collaboration with David Wechsler. Additional Dialogue, Paul Jarrico. Music, Robert Blum. Photography, Emil Berna. Editor, Hermann Haller. Produced in Switzerland and in the U. S. Occupied Zone of Germany, through the permission of the U. S. Army and the cooperation of I. R. O. The first postwar film to be shot in the Occupied Zone. Film debut of Ivan Jandl. 105 minutes

Ralph Stevenson: Montgomery Clift, *Mrs. Murray:* Aline MacMahon, *Mrs. Malik:* Jarmila Novotna, *Jerry Fisher:* Wendell Corey, *Karel Malik:* Ivan Jandl, *Mrs. Fisher:* Mary Patton, *Mr. Crookes:* Ewart G. Morrison, *Tom Fisher:* William Rogers, *Joel Makowksy:* Leopold Borkowski, *Raoul Dubois:* Claude Gambier.

The Searchers with Ward Bond, John Wayne and Pat Wayne.

THE SEARCHERS (1956) WB. Executive Producer, Merian C. Cooper. Associate Producer, Patrick Ford. Directed by John Ford. In VistaVision and Technicolor. Based on the novel by Alan LeMay. Screenplay, Frank S. Nugent. Music, Max Steiner. Wardrobe, Frank Beetson and Ann Peck. Assistant Director, Wingate Smith. Title Song, Stan Jones. A.C.V. Whitney Pictures, Inc. Production. Art Directors, Frank Hotaling and James Basevi. Orchestration, Murray Cutter. Photography, Winton C. Hoch. Editor, Jack Murray. Locations:

Monument Valley, Utah-Arizona; Gunnison, Colorado; Alberta, Canada. 119 minutes

Ethan Edwards: John Wayne, *Martin Pawley:* Jeffrey Hunter, *Laurie Jorgensen:* Vera Miles, *Captain Rev. Clayton:* Ward Bond, *Debbie Edwards:* Natalie Wood, *Lars Jorgensen:* John Qualen, *Mrs. Jorgensen:* Olive Carey, *Chief Scar:* Henry Brandon, *Charlie McCorry:* Ken Curtis, *Brad Jorgensen:* Harry Carey, Jr., *Emilio Figueroa:* Antonio Moreno, *Lieutenant Greenhill:* Pat Wayne, *Mose Harper:* Hank Worden, *Debbie as a child:* Lana Wood, *Aaron Edwards:* Walter Coy, *Martha Edwards:* Dorothy Jordan, *Lucy Edwards:* Pippa Scott, *Look:* Beulah Archuletta, *Ranger Nesbitt:* Bill Steele, *Colonel Greenhill:* Cliff Lyons, *Texas Ranger:* Chuck Roberson, *Stuntmen:* Billy Cartledge, Chuck Hayward, Slim Hightower, Fred Kennedy, Frank McGrath, Dale Van Sickel, Henry Wills, Terry Wilson, *Comanches:* Navajo tribe, including Away Luna, Billy Yellow, Bob Many Mules, Exactley Sonnie Betsuie, Feather Hat, Jr., Harry Black Horse, Jack Tin Horn, Many Mules Son, Percy Shooting Star, Pete Gray Eyes, Pipe Line Begishe, Smile White Sheep.

The Sea Wolf with Ida Lupino and John Garfield.

THE SEA WOLF (1941) WB. Vice-president in Charge of Production, Jack L. Warner. Executive Producer, Hal B. Wallis. Directed by Michael Curtiz. Based on the novel by Jack London. Screenplay, Robert Rossen. Photography, Sol Polito. Music, Erich Wolfgang Korngold. Editor, George Amy. Associate Producer, Henry Blanke. Previous versions of *The Sea Wolf* made by: Bosworth, 1913; Par., 1920; PDC, 1925; and Fox, 1930. Remade as: *Barricade* (WB, 1950), *Wolf Larsen* (AA, 1958), and *Wolf Larsen* (Italian, 1975). 100 minutes

Wolf Larsen: Edward G. Robinson, *George Leach:* John Garfield, *Ruth Webster:* Ida Lupino, *Humphrey Van Weyden:* Alexander Knox, *Dr. Louie Prescott:* Gene Lockhart, *Cooky:* Barry Fitzgerald, *Johnson:* Stanley Ridges, *Svenson:* Francis McDonald, *Young Sailor:* David Bruce, *Harrison:* Howard da Silva, *Smoke:* Frank Lackteen, *Agent:* Ralf Harolde, *Crewman:* Louis Mason, *Crewman:* Dutch Hendrian, *First Detective:* Cliff Clark, *Second Detective:* William Gould, *First Mate:* Charles Sullivan, *Pickpocket:* Ernie Adams, *Singer:* Jeane Cowan, *Helmsman:* Wilfred Lucas.

THE SECRET LIFE OF WALTER MITTY (1947) RKO. Producer, Samuel Goldwyn. Director, Norman Z. McLeod. Color by Technicolor. From a story by James Thurber. Screenplay, Ken Englund, Everett Freeman. Art Directors, George Jenkins, Perry Ferguson. Music, David Raksin. Musical Director, Emil Newman. Cameraman, Lee Garmes. Editor, Monica Collingwood. Songs by Sylvia Fine: "Anatole of Paris" and "Symphony for Unstrung Tongues." 105 minutes

Walter Mitty: Danny Kaye, *Rosalind Van Hoorn:* Virginia Mayo,

Doctor Hugo Hollingshead: Boris Karloff, *Mrs. Mitty:* Fay Bainter, *Gertrude Griswold:* Ann Rutherford, *Bruce Pierce:* Thurston Hall, *Tubby Wadsworth:* Gordon Jones, *Mrs. Griswold:* Florence Bates, *Peter Van Hoorn:* Konstantin Shayne, *R.A.F. Colonel:* Reginald Denny, *Hendrick:* Henry Cordon, *Mrs. Follinsbee:* Doris Lloyd, *Anatole:* Fritz Feld, *Maasdam:* Frank Reicher, *Butler:* Milton Parsons, *Goldwyn Girls:* Mary Brewer, Betty Carlyle, Sue Casey, Lorraine DeRome, Karen X. Gaylord, Mary Ellen Gleason, Jackie Jordan, Georgia Lange, Michael Mauree, Martha Montgomery, Pat Patrick, Irene Vernon, Lynn Walker, *Wolf Man:* George Magrill, *Mr. Grimsby:* Joel Friedkin, *Office Boy:* Harry Harvey, Jr., *Business Manager:* Warren Jackson, *Illustrator:* Bess Flowers, *Art Editor:* Sam Ash, *Dr. Remington:* John Hamilton, *Dr. Renshaw:* Charles Trowbridge, *Vincent:* Jack Overman, *Mrs. Pierce:* Mary Forbes, *Minister:* Pierre Watkin, *Western Character:* Hank Worden, *Dr. Benbow:* Henry Kolker, *Dr. Pritchard-Mitford:* Lumsden Hare.

chell, *Private Orrin Esty:* George Offerman, Jr., *General Dillon:* Edward Fielding, *Sgt. Heldon:* Donald Curtis, *Private Bill Burk:* William "Bill" Phillips, *Captain Manville:* Douglas Fowley, *Colonel Forbes:* Morris Ankrum, *Sergeant:* Mickey Rentschler, *M.P.:* Frank Faylen, *Doctor:* Jack Luden, *Lieutenant:* Maurice Murphy, *Capt. Hamilton:* Clarence Straight, *Mr. Smith:* William Newell, *Captain:* Louis Jean Heydt, *Corporal:* Ken Scott, *Officer of Day:* Michael Owen, *Corporal:* Stephen Barclay, *Exercise Sgt.:* John Kelly, *Mess Sgt.:* Joe Devlin, *Executive Officer:* Dennis Moore, *Field Operator:* Rod Bacon, *Farmer:* Louis Mason, *Farmer's Wife:* Connie Gilchrist, *Captain:* Harry Strang, *Old Man:* Harry Tyler, *Porter:* Mantan Moreland, *Lieutenant:* Myron Healey, *Girl Clerk:* Mary McLeod, *Captain Hammond:* Eddie Acuff, *Lieutenant:* Fred Kohler, Jr., *Executive Officer:* James Warren, *Field Operator:* Blake Edwards.

The Secret Life of Walter Mitty with Danny Kaye.

Separate Tables with Deborah Kerr and David Niven.

SEPARATE TABLES (1958) UA. Producer, Harold Hecht. Director, Delbert Mann. Screenplay by Terence Rattigan and John Gay. Based on the play by Terence Rattigan. Music by David Raksin. Gowns by Edith Head. Song by Harry Warren and Harold Adamson, sung by Vic Damone. Assistant Director, Thomas F. Shaw. Costumes, Mary Grant. A Clifton Production for Hecht-Hill-Lancaster. 98 minutes

Ann Shankland: Rita Hayworth, *Sibyl Railton-Bell:* Deborah Kerr, *Major Pollock:* David Niven, *Pat Cooper:* Wendy Hiller, *John Malcolm:* Burt Lancaster, *Mrs. Railton-Bell:* Gladys Cooper, *Lady Matheson:* Cathleen Nesbitt, *Mr. Fowler:* Felix Aylmer, *Charles:* Rod Taylor, *Jean:* Audrey Dalton, *Miss Meacham:* May Hallatt, *Doreen:* Priscilla Morgan, *Mabel:* Hilda Plowright.

See Here, Private Hargrove with Stephen Barclay, Robert Walker and Donna Reed.

SEE HERE, PRIVATE HARGROVE (1944) MGM. Producer, George Haight. Director, Wesley Ruggles. Based on the book by Marion Hargrove. Screenplay, Harry Kurnitz. Musical Score, David Snell. Art Director, Cedric Gibbons. Cameraman, Charles Lawton. Editor, Frank E. Hull. Song by Frank Loesser and Ted Grouya: "In My Arms." Sequel was *What Next, Corporal Hargrove?* (MGM, 1945). 101 minutes

Marion Hargrove: Robert Walker, *Carol Halliday:* Donna Reed, *Mr. Halliday:* Robert Benchley, *Private Mulvehill:* Keenan Wynn, *Bob:* Bob Crosby, *Brody S. Griffith:* Ray Collins, *Sergt. Cramp:* Chill Wills, *Mrs. Halliday:* Marta Linden, *Uncle George:* Grant Mit-

Sergeants Three with Lindsay Crosby, Phil Crosby, Sammy Davis, Jr. and Dean Martin.

SERGEANTS 3 (1962) UA. Producer, Frank Sinatra. Director, John Sturges. Executive Producer, Howard W. Koch. Screenplay, W. R. Burnett. Assistant Director, Jack Reddish. An Essex-Claude Production in Panavision and Technicolor. Art Director, Frank Hotaling. Music, Billy May. "And the Night Wind Song," music, Johnny Rotella, lyrics, Franz Steininger. Cinematographer, Winton Hoch. Editor, Ferris Webster. Remake of *Gunga Din* (RKO, 1939). 112 minutes

First Sergeant Mike Merry: Frank Sinatra, *Sergeant Chip Deal:* Dean Martin, *Jonah Williams:* Sammy Davis, Jr., *Sergeant Larry Barrett:* Peter Lawford, *Sergeant Major Roger Boswell:* Joey Bishop, *Mountain Hawk:* Henry Silva, *Willie Sharpknife:* Buddy Lester, *Amelia Parent:* Ruta Lee, *Corporal Ellis:* Philip Crosby, *Private Page:* Dennis Crosby, *Private Wills:* Lindsay Crosby, *Blacksmith:* Hank Henry, *Colonel William Collingwood:* Richard Simmons, *Watanka:* Michael Pate, *Caleb:* Armand Alzamora, *White Eagle:* Richard Hale, *Morton:* Mickey Finn, *Corporal:* Sonny King, *Mrs. Parent:* Madge Blake, *Mrs. Collingwood:* Dorothy Abbott.

Sergeant York with Gary Cooper and Joan Leslie.

SERGEANT YORK (1941) WB. Producers, Jesse L. Lasky, Hal B. Wallis. Director, Howard Hawks. Screenplay, Abem Finkel, Harry Chandlee, Howard Koch, John Huston (from *War Diary of Sergeant York*, by Sam K. Cowan, *Sergeant York and His People* by Cowan, and *Sergeant York—Last of the Long Hunters* by Tom Skeyhill). Music, Max Steiner. Cameraman, Sol Polito. Art Director, John Hughes. Editor, William Holmes. Battle sequences photographed by Arthur Edeson. 134 minutes

Alvin York: Gary Cooper, *Pastor Rosier Pile:* Walter Brennan, *Gracie Williams:* Joan Leslie, *Pusher (Michael T. Ross):* George Tobias, *Bert Thomas:* David Bruce, *Major Buxton:* Stanley Ridges, *Ma York:* Margaret Wycherly, *George York:* Dickie Moore, *Ike Botkin:* Ward Bond, *Buck Lipscomb:* Noah Beery, Jr., *Captain Danforth:* Harvey Stephens, *Cordell Hull:* Charles Trowbridge, *German Major:* (Carl) Charles Esmond, *Zeb Andrews:* Robert Porterfield, *Lem:* Howard da Silva, *Zeke:* Clem Bevans, *Sergeant Early:* Joseph Sawyer, *Sergeant:* Frank Wilcox, *Captain Tillman:* Donald Douglas, *Sergeant Harry Parsons:* Pat Flaherty, *Corporal Savage:* Lane Chandler, *Beardsley:* Frank Marlowe, *Corporal Cutting:* Jack Pennick, *Eb:* James Anderson, *Tom:* Guy Wilkerson, *Rosie York:* June Lockhart, *Uncle Lige:* Tully Marshall, *Luke (Target Keeper):* Lee "Lasses" White, *Nate Tompkins:* Erville Alderson, *Mountaineer:* Charles Middleton, *Andrews:* Victor Kilian, *Prison Camp Commander:* Theodore Von Eltz, *Gracie's Sister:* Jane Isbell, *Drummer:* Frank Orth, *Marter, Bartender:* Arthur Aylesworth, *Piano Player:* Elisha Cook, Jr., *Card Player:* William Haade, *General Pershing:* Joseph Girard, *Marshal Foch:* Jean Del Val, *Mayor Hylan:* Douglas Wood, *Oscar of the Waldorf:* Ed Keane.

SERPICO (1973) Par. Produced by Martin Bregman. Directed by Sidney Lumet. A Dino De Laurentiis Film Produced for Produzioni De Laurentiis International Manufacturing Company S.P.A. by Artists Entertainment

Complex, Inc. Based on the book by Peter Maas. Screenplay, Waldo Salt and Norman Wexler. Editor, Dede Allen. Associate Producer, Roger M. Rothstein. Photography, Arthur J. Ornitz. Music composed by Mikis Theodorakis. Costume Designer, Anna Hill Johnstone. Production Designer, Charles Bailey. Assistant Directors, Burtt Harris and Alan Hopkins. Make-up Artist, Redge Tackley. Music arranged and conducted by Bob James. Art Director, Douglas Higgins. Sound Mixer, James J. Sabat. Filmed in New York City. Panavision equipment, Technicolor. Rated R. 130 minutes

Frank Serpico: Al Pacino, *Bob Blair:* Tony Roberts, *Chief Sidney Green:* John Randolph, *Tom Keough:* Jack Kehoe, *Capt. McClain:* Biff McGuire, *Laurie:* Barbara eda-Young, *Leslie:* Cornelia Sharpe, *Pasquale Serpico:* John Medici, *D. A. Tauber:* Allan Rich, *Rubello:* Norman Ornellas, *Lombardo:* Ed Grover, *Peluce:* Al Henderson, *Malone:* Hank Garrett, *Joey:* Damien Leake, *Potts:* Joe Bova, *Captain Tolkin:* Gene Gross, *Waterman, Arresting Officer:* John Stewart, *Larry:* Woodie King, *Steiger:* James Tolkin, *Barto:* Ed Crowley, *Palmer:* Bernard Barrow, *Mr. Serpico:* Sal Carollo, *Mrs. Serpico:* Mildred Clinton, *Detective Smith:* Nathan George, *Dr. Metz:* Gus Fleming, *Corsaro:* Richard Foronjy, *Brown:* Alan North, *Berman:* Lewis J. Stadlen, *Kellogg:* John McQuade, *Sarno:* Ted Beniades, *Gilbert:* John Lehne, *Gallagher:* M. Emmet Walsh, *Daley:* George Ede, *Black Prisoner:* Franklin Scott, *Detective Threatening Serpico:* Don Billett, *Black Hoods:* Tim Pelt and Willie Pelt, *Detective-Partner:* F. Murray Abraham, *Commissioner Delaney:* Charles White, *Girl:* Mary Louise Weller.

Serpico with Franklin Scott, John Stewart and Al Pacino.

Seven Brides for Seven Brothers with Marc Platt, Jacques D'Amboise, Matt Mattox, Jane Powell, Tommy Rall, Russ Tamblyn.

SEVEN BRIDES FOR SEVEN BROTHERS (1954) MGM. Producer, Jack Cummings. Director, Stanley Donen. CinemaScope, Ansco

Color. Screenplay, Albert Hackett, Frances Goodrich, Dorothy Kingsley. Art Director, Cedric Gibbons. Cinematographer, George Folsey. Editor, Ralph E. Winters. From Stephen Vincent Benet's story *The Sobbin' Women.* Dances, Michael Kidd. Songs by Johnny Mercer and Gene de Paul: "Bless Your Beautiful Hide," "Wonderful, Wonderful Day," "When You're in Love," "Sobbin' Women," "Goin' Courtin'," "Lament," "June Bride," "Spring, Spring, Spring." 102 minutes

Milly: Jane Powell, *Adam:* Howard Keel, *Benjamin:* Jeff Richards, *Gideon:* Russ Tamblyn, *Frank:* Tommy Rall, *Pete Perkins:* Howard Petrie, *Liza:* Virginia Gibson, *Rev. Elcott:* Ian Wolfe, *Daniel:* Marc Platt, *Caleb:* Matt Mattox, *Ephraim:* Jacques d'Amboise, *Dorcas:* Julie Newmeyer, *Alice:* Nancy Kilgas, *Sarah:* Betty Carr, *Ruth:* Ruta Kilmonis, *Martha:* Norma Doggett, *Harry:* Earl Barton, *Matt:* Dante DiPaolo, *Carl:* Kelly Brown, *Ruth's Uncle:* Matt Moore, *Dorcas' Father:* Dick Rich, *Mrs. Bixby:* Marjorie Wood, *Mr. Bixby:* Russell Simpson, *Mrs. Elcott:* Anna Q. Nilsson, *Drunk:* Larry Blake, *Prospector:* Phil Rich, *Girl:* Lois Hall, *Swains:* Russ Saunders, Terry Wilson, George Robotham, *Lem:* Walter Beaver, *Lem's Girl Friend:* Jarma Lewis, *Dorcas' Sister:* Sheila James, *Fathers:* Stan Jolley, Tim Graham.

Seven Days in May with Burt Lancaster and Fredric March (on TV).

SEVEN DAYS IN MAY (1964) Par. Producer, Edward Lewis. Director, John Frankenheimer. Screenplay, Rod Serling. Based on a novel of the same name by Fletcher Knebel and Charles W. Bailey II. Music, Jerry Goldsmith. Cinematographer, Ellsworth Fredricks. A Seven Arts-Joel Productions, Inc. Production. 120 minutes

General James M. Scott: Burt Lancaster, *Colonel Martin (Jiggs) Casey:* Kirk Douglas, *President Jordan Lyman:* Fredric March, *Eleanor Holbrook:* Ava Gardner, *Senator Raymond Clark:* Edmond O'Brien, *Paul Girard:* Martin Balsam, *Christopher Todd:* George Macready, *Senator Prentice:* Whit Bissell, *Harold McPherson:* Hugh Marlowe, *Arthur Corwin:* Bart Burns, *Colonel Murdock:* Richard Anderson, *Lieutenant Hough:* Jack Mullaney, *Colonel "Mutt" Henderson:* Andrew Duggan, *Colonel Broderick:* John Larkin, *Admiral Barnswell:* John Houseman.

THE SEVEN LITTLE FOYS (1955) Par. Producer, Jack Rose. Director, Melville Shavelson. VistaVision, Technicolor. Screenplay, Melville Shavelson, Jack Rose. Art Directors, Hal Pereira, John Goodman. Musical Director, Joseph J. Lilley. Cinematographer, John F. Warren. Editor, Ellsworth Hoagland. Choreography, Nick Castle. 95 minutes

Eddie Foy: Bob Hope, *Madeleine Morando:* Milly Vitale, *Barney Green:* George Tobias, *Clara:* Angela Clarke, *Judge:* Herbert Heyes, *Stage Manager:* Richard Shannon, *Brynie:* Billy Gray, *Charley:* Lee Erickson, *Richard Foy:* Paul De Rolf, *Mary Foy:* Lydia Reed, *Madeleine Foy:* Linda Bennett, *Eddie, Jr.,:* Jimmy Baird, *George M. Cohan:* James Cagney, *Irving:* Tommy Duran, *Father O'Casey:* Lester

Mathews, *Elephant Act:* Joe Evans, *Elephant Act:* George Boyce, *Santa Claus:* Oliver Blake, *Driscoll:* Milton Frome, *Harrison:* King Donovan, *Stage Doorman:* Jimmy Conlin, *Soubrette:* Marian Carr, *Stage Doorman at Iroquois:* Harry Cheshire, *Italian Ballerina Mistress:* Renata Vanni, *Dance Specialty Double:* Betty Uitti, *Priest:* Noel Drayton, *Theater Manager:* Jack Pepper, *Tutor:* Dabbs Greer, *Customs Inspector:* Billy Nelson, *Second Priest:* Joe Flynn, *Brynie (5 years):* Jerry Mathers, *Presbyterian Minister:* Lewis Martin.

The Seven Little Foys with Bob Hope, Billy Gray, Lee Erickson, Paul De Rolf, Lydia Reed, Linda Bennett, Jimmy Baird, Tommy Duran and Angela Clarke.

Seventh Voyage of Sinbad with Alec Mango, Harold Kasket, Kathryn Grant and Kerwin Mathews.

THE SEVENTH VOYAGE OF SINBAD (1958) Col. Producer, Charles H. Schneer. Director, Nathan Juran. Screenplay by Kenneth Kolb. Visual effects by Ray Harryhausen. Music by Bernard Herrmann. Assistant Directors, Eugenio Martin and Pedro de Juan. A Morningside Production in Dynamation and Technicolor. 89 minutes

Captain Sinbad: Kerwin Mathews, *Princess Parisa:* Kathryn Grant, *The Genie, Baronni:* Richard Eyer, *Sokurah:* Torin Thatcher, *Caliph:* Alec Mango, *Karim:* Danny *Green,* *Sultan:* Harold Kasket, *Harufa:* Alfred Brown, *Sadi:* Nana de Herrera, *Gaunt Sailor:* Nino Falanga, *Crewman:* Luis Guedes, *Ali:* Virgilio Teixeira.

THE SEVEN YEAR ITCH (1955) 20th. Producers, Charles K. Feldman, Billy Wilder. Director, Billy Wilder. CinemaScope, De Luxe Color. Based on the play by George Axelrod. Screenplay, Billy Wilder, George Axelrod. Art Directors, Lyle Wheeler, George W. Davis. Musical Director, Alfred Newman. Cinematographer, Milton Krasner. Editor, Hugh S. Fowler. 105 minutes

The Girl: Marilyn Monroe, *Richard Sherman:* Tom Ewell, *Helen Sherman:* Evelyn Keyes, *Tom MacKenzie:* Sonny Tufts, *Kruhulik:* Robert Strauss, *Dr. Brubaker:* Oscar Homolka, *Miss Morris (Secretary):* Marguerite Chapman, *Plumber:* Victor Moore, *Elaine:*

Roxanne, *Brady:* Donald MacBride, *Miss Finch (Night Nurse):* Carolyn Jones, *Ricky:* Butch Bernard, *Waitress:* Doro Merande, *Indian Girl:* Dorothy Ford, *Woman in R. R. Station:* Mary Young, *R. R. Station Gateman:* Ralph Sanford.

The Seven Year Itch with Marilyn Monroe and Tom Ewell.

Shaft with Richard Roundtree.

SHAFT (1971) MGM. A Stirling Silliphant–Roger Lewis Production. Produced by Joel Freeman. Directed by Gordon Parks. Associate Producer, David Golden. Based on the novel by Ernest Tidyman. Screenplay, Tidyman and John D. F. Black. Music by Isaac Hayes. Rhythm by the Bar-Kays and Movement. Technical Assistant to Composer, Tom McIntosh. Photography, Urs Furrer. Art Director, Emanuel Gerard. Assistant Director, Ted Zachary. Editor, Hugh A. Robertson. Costume Designer, Joe Aulisi. Set Decoration, Robert Drumheller. Sound, Lee Bost and Hal Watkins. Make-up, Martin Bell. Film debut of Drew Bundini Brown, Muhammad Ali's trainer. Filmed in New York City in MetroColor. Rated R. 98 minutes. Sequels: *Shaft's Big Score!* (1972), *Shaft in Africa* (1973)

John Shaft: Richard Roundtree, *Bumpy Jonas:* Moses Gunn, *Vic Androzzi:* Charles Cioffi, *Ben Buford:* Christopher St. John, *Ellie Moore:* Gwenn Mitchell, *Tom Hannon:* Lawrence Pressman, *Charlie:* Victor Arnold, *Marcy:* Sherri Brewer, *Rollie:* Rex Robbins, *Dina Greene:* Camille Yarbrough, *Linda:* Margaret Warncke, *Byron Leibowitz:* Joseph Leon, *Cul:* Arnold Johnson, *Patsy:* Dominic Barto, *Carmen:* George Strus, *Lee:* Edmund Hashim, *Willy:* Drew Bundini Brown, *Leroy:* Tommy Lane, *Sims:* Al Kirk, *Dr. Sam:* Shimen Ruskin, *Bunky:* Antonio Fargas, *Old Lady:* Gertrude Jeannette, *Blind Vendor:* Lee Steele, *Mal:* Damu King, *Remmy:* Donny Burks, *Davies:* Tony King, *Bey Newfield:* Benjamin R. Rixson, *Tully:* Ricardo Brown, *Gus:* Alan Weeks, *Char:* Glenn Johnson, *Dotts:* Dennis Tate, *Brothers:* Adam Wade, James Hainesworth, *Sonny:* Clee Burtonya, *Peerce:* Ed Bernard, *Tony:* Ed Barth, *Dom:* Joe Pronto, *Waitress:* Robin Nolan, *Billy:* Ron Tannas, *Mrs. Androzzi:* Betty Bresler, *Counterman:* Gonzalo Madurga, *Elevator Man:* Paul Nevens, *Elevator Starter:* Jon Richards.

The Shaggy Dog with Fred MacMurray and Jean Hagen.

THE SHAGGY DOG (1959) BV. Producer, Walt Disney. Director, Charles Barton. Associate Producer, Bill Walsh. Screenplay by Bill Walsh and Lillie Hayward. Suggested by *The Hound of Florence* by Felix Salten. Music by Paul Smith. Song by Gil George and Paul Smith. Assistant Director, Arthur Vitarelli. Art Director, Carroll Clark. Cinematographer, Edward Colman. Editor, James D. Ballas. Costumes by Chuck Keehne and Gertrude Casey. 104 minutes. Sequel was *The Shaggy D.A.* (1976)

Wilson Daniels: Fred MacMurray, *Frieda Daniels:* Jean Hagen, *Wilby Daniels:* Tommy Kirk, *Allison D'Allessio:* Annette Funicello, *Buzz Miller:* Tim Considine, *"Moochie" Daniels:* Kevin Corcoran, *Prof. Plumcutt:* Cecil Kellaway, *Dr. Mikhail Andrassy:* Alexander Scourby, *Franceska Andrassy:* Roberta Shore, *Officer Hanson:* James Westerfield, *Stefano:* Jacques Aubuchon, *Thurm:* Strother Martin, *Officer Kelly:* Forrest Lewis, and Shaggy.

SHALL WE DANCE (1937) RKO. Produced by Pandro S. Berman. Directed by Mark Sandrich. Suggested by the story *Watch Your Step* by Lee Loeb and Harold Buchman. Screenplay, Allan Scott, Ernest Pagano, P. J. Wolfson. Music Director, Nathaniel Shilkret. Ensembles staged by Hermes Pan. Ballets directed by Larry Losee. Art Director, Van Nest Polglase. Photography, David Abel. Special Effects, Vernon L. Walker. Editor, William Hamilton. Songs by George and Ira Gershwin: "Shall We Dance," "They Can't Take That Away From Me," "Let's Call the Whole Thing Off," "I've Got Beginner's Luck," "Slap That Bass," "They All Laughed," "Wake Up Brother and Dance." The seventh Astaire-Rogers teaming. 116 minutes

Petrov (Pete Peters): Fred Astaire, *Linda Keene:* Ginger Rogers, *Jeffrey Baird:* Edward Everett Horton, *Cecil Flintridge:* Eric Blore, *Arthur Miller:* Jerome Cowan, *Lady Tarrington:* Ketti Gallian, *Jim Montgom-*

ery: William Brisbane, *Harriet Hoctor:* Harriet Hoctor, *Mrs. Fitzgerald:* Ann Shoemaker, *Bandleader:* Ben Alexander, *Tai:* Emma Young, *Newsboy:* Sherwood Bailey, *Dancing Partner:* Pete Theodore, *Ballet Masters:* Marek Windheim, Rolfe Sedan, *Cop in Park:* Charles Coleman, *Big Man:* Frank Moran.

Shall We Dance with Jerome Cowan, Edward Everett Horton and Fred Astaire.

Shampoo with William Castle, Julie Christie and Warren Beatty.

SHAMPOO (1975) Col. Produced by Warren Beatty. Directed by Hal Ashby. Screenplay, Robert Towne and Beatty. A Rubeeker Production in Panavision and Technicolor. Photography, Laszlo Kovacs. Music composed by Paul Simon. Production Manager and Associate Producer, Charles H. Maguire. Assistant to the Producer, Robert Jiras. Production Designer, Richard Sylbert. Art Director, Stu Campbell. Set Director, George Gaines. Assistant Directors, Art Levinson and Ron Wright. Editor, Robert Jones. Assistant Editor, Donny Zimmerman. Costume Designer, Anthea Sylbert. Set Designers, Robert Resh and Charles Zacha. Make-up, Tom Case. Hairdresser, Kathy Blondell. Sound, Tommy Overton. Filmed in Beverly Hills and at Los Angeles' General Service Studios. Songs heard: "I Believe in You," "Born Free," "Strangers in the Night," "Pennies from Heaven," "Sgt. Pepper's Lonely Hearts Club Band," "Lucy in the Sky with Diamonds." Rated R. 112 minutes

George Roundy: Warren Beatty, *Jackie Shawn:* Julie Christie, *Jill:* Goldie Hawn, *Felicia Carr:* Lee Grant, *Lester Carr:* Jack Warden, *Johnny Pope:* Tony Bill, *Lorna Carr:* Carrie Fisher, *Norman:* Jay Robinson, *Mr. Pettis:* George Furth, *Mary:* Ann Weldon, *Dennis:* Randy Sheer, *Gloria:* Susanna Moore, *Ricci:* Mike Olton, *Devra:* Luana Anders, *Senator Joe East:* Brad Dexter, *Sid Roth:* William Castle, *Izzy:* Jack Bernardi, *Rosalind:* Doris Packer, *Kenneth:* Hal Buckley, *Red Dog:* Howard Hesseman, *Girl in Car:*

Cheri Latimer, *Younger Detective:* Richard E. Kalk, *Mona:* Brunetta Bennett, *Twins:* Melinda and Constance Smith, *Customer:* Susan McIver, *Girl at Party:* Michele Phillips, *Bits:* Kathleen Miller, Larry Bischof. Cut was Susan Blakely as *Girl on Street.*

SHANE (1953) Par. Producer, George Stevens. Associate Producer, Ivan Moffat. Director, George Stevens. Associate Director, Fred Guiol. Technicolor. Based on the novel by Jack Schaefer. Screenplay, A. B. Guthrie, Jr. Additional Dialogue, Jack Sher. Art Directors Hal Pereira, Walter Tyler. Cinematographer, Loyal Griggs. Editor, William Hornbeck, Tom McAdoo. Technicolor Consultant, Richard Mueller. 118 minutes

Shane: Alan Ladd, *Mrs. Starrett:* Jean Arthur, *Mr. Starrett:* Van Heflin, *Joey Starrett:* Brandon De Wilde, *Wilson:* Jack Palance, *Chris:* Ben Johnson, *Lewis:* Edgar Buchanan, *Ryker:* Emile Meyer, *Torrey:* Elisha Cook, Jr., *Mr. Shipstead:* Douglas Spencer, *Morgan:* John Dierkes, *Mrs. Torrey:* Ellen Corby, *Grafton:* Paul McVey, *Atkey:* John Miller, *Mrs. Shipstead:* Edith Evanson, *Wright:* Leonard Strong, *Johnson:* Ray Spiker, *Susan Lewis:* Janice Carroll, *Howells:* Martin Mason, *Mrs. Lewis:* Helen Brown, *Mrs. Howells:* Nancy Kulp, *Pete:* Howard J. Negley, *Ruth Lewis:* Beverly Washburn, *Ryker Man:* George Lewis, *Clerk:* Charles Quirk, *Ryker Men:* Jack Sterling, Henry Wills, Rex Moore, Ewing Brown.

Shane with Jean Arthur, Brandon De Wilde, Van Heflin and Alan Ladd.

Shanghai Express with Clive Brook and Marlene Dietrich.

SHANGHAI EXPRESS (1932) Par. Directed by Josef von Sternberg. Based on the story by Harry Hervey. Screenplay, Jules Furthman.

Photography, Lee Garmes. Remade by Paramount as *Peking Express*, 1951. 80 minutes

Shanghai Lilly (Madeline): Marlene Dietrich, *Captain Donald Harvey:* Clive Brook, *Hui Fei:* Anna May Wong, *Henry Chang:* Warner Oland, *Sam Salt:* Eugene Pallette, *Reverend Carmichael:* Lawrence Grant, *Mrs. Haggerty:* Louise Closser Hale, *Eric Baum:* Gustav von Seyffertitz, *Major Lenard:* Emile Chautard, *Albright:* Claude King, *Chinese Spy:* Neshida Minoru, *A Rebel:* James Leong, *Engineer:* Willie Fung, *Minister:* Leonard Carey, *Ticket Agent:* Forrester Harvey, *Officer:* Miki Morita.

She Done Him Wrong with Gilbert Roland and Mae West.

SHE DONE HIM WRONG (1933) Par. Directed by Lowell Sherman. Based on the 1928 play *Diamond Lil* by Mae West. Adaptation and Dialogue, Harvey Thew and John Bright. Assistant Director, James Dugan. Costumes, Edith Head. Art Director, Bob Usher. Photography, Charles Lang. Editor, Alexander Hall. Sound, Harry M. Lindgren. Songs by Ralph Rainger: "I Wonder Where My Easy Rider's Gone," "I Like a Man Who Takes His Time." 66 minutes

Lady Lou: Mae West, *Captain Cummings:* Cary Grant, *Serge Stanieff:* Gilbert Roland, *Gus Jordan:* Noah Beery, *Russian Rita:* Rafaela Ottiano, *Dan Flynn:* David Landau, *Sally Glynn:* Rochelle Hudson, *Chick Clark:* Owen Moore, *Rag Time Kelly:* Fuzzy Knight, *Chuck Connors:* Tammany Young, *Spider Kane:* Dewey Robinson, *Frances:* Grace La Rue, *Steak McGarry:* Harry Wallace, *Pete:* James C. Eagles, *Officer Doheney:* Robert E. Homans, *Big Bill:* Tom Kennedy, *Barfly:* Arthur Housman, *Pal:* Wade Boteler, *Mrs. Flaherty:* Aggie Herring, *Pearl:* Louise Beavers, *Jacobson:* Lee Kohlmar, *Mike:* Tom McGuire, *Janitor:* Michael Mark, *Cleaning Woman:* Mary Gordon, *Barfly:* Al Hill, *Man in Audience:* Ernie S. Adams, *Street Cleaner:* Heinie Conklin, *Patron Who Hits His Girl:* Jack Carr, *"Framed" Convict:* Frank Moran.

SHE LOVES ME NOT (1934), Par. Produced by Benjamin Glazer. Directed by Elliott Nugent. From the novel by Edward Hope and the play by Howard Lindsay. Screenplay by Benjamin Glazer. Cameraman, Charles Lang. Editor, Hugh Bennett. Songs: "Love In Bloom" by Leo Robin and Ralph Rainger; "After All You're All I'm After" by Edward Heyman and Arthur Schwartz; "Straight From the Shoulder (Right From the Heart)," "I'm Hummin', I'm Whistlin', I'm Singin'," and "Put a Little Rhythm in Everything You Do" by Mack Gordon and Harry Revel. Remade as *How to Be Very, Very Popular* (20th Century-Fox, 1955). 83 minutes

Paul Lanton: Bing Crosby, *Curly Flagg:* Miriam Hopkins, *Midge Mercer:* Kitty Carlisle, *Buzz Jones:* Edward Nugent, *Dean Mercer:* Henry Stephenson, *Mugg Schinitzel:* Warren Hymer, *Gus McNeal:* Lynne Overman, *Frances Arbuthnot:* Judith Allen, *J. Teorval Jones:*

George Barbier, *Charles M. Lanton:* Henry Kolker, *Mrs. Arbuthnot:* Maude Turner Gordon, *Martha:* Margaret Armstrong, *J. B.:* Ralf Harolde, *Andy:* Matt McHugh, *Arkle:* Franklyn Ardell, *Baldy O'Hara:* Vince Barnett.

She Loves Me Not with Miriam Hopkins and Bing Crosby.

Shenandoah with Pat Wayne, Tim McIntire, James McMullan, Glenn Corbett, James Stewart and Charles Robinson.

SHENANDOAH (1965) Univ. Producer, Robert Arthur. Director, Andrew V. McLaglen. Technirama and Technicolor. Screenplay by James Lee Barrett. Director of Photography, William H. Clothier. Music by Frank Skinner. Costumes by Rosemary Odell. Assistant Director, Terence Nelson. Art Directors, Alexander Golitzen and Alfred Sweeney. Music supervised by Joseph Gershenson. Film Editor, Otho Lovering. 105 minutes. Later a musical play

Charlie Anderson: James Stewart, *Sam:* Doug McClure, *Jacob Anderson:* Glenn Corbett, *James Anderson:* Patrick Wayne, *Jennie Anderson:* Rosemary Forsyth, *Boy Anderson:* Phillip Alford, *Ann Anderson:* Katharine Ross, *Nathan Anderson:* Charles Robinson, *Dr. Tom Witherspoon:* Paul Fix, *Pastor Bjoerling:* Denver Pyle, *Colonel Fairchild:* George Kennedy, *Henry Anderson:* Tim McIntire, *John Anderson:* James McMullan, *Carter:* James Best, *Billy Packer:* Warren Oates, *Engineer:* Strother Martin, *Abernathy:* Dabbs Greer, *Jenkins:* Harry Carey, Jr., *Mule:* Kevin Hagen, *Lt. Johnson:* Tom Simcox, *Captain Richards:* Berkeley Harris, *Union Sergeant:* Edward Faulkner, *Confederate Corporal:* Peter Wayne, *Union Guard:* Gregg Palmer, *Union Guard with beard:* Bob Steele, *First Picket:* James Heneghan, Jr., *Gabriel:* Eugene Jackson, Jr., *Negro Woman:* Pae Miller, *Horace, a Marauder:* Rayford Barnes, *Ray:* Dave Cass, *Crying Prisoner:* Hoke Howell, *Carroll:* Kelly Thordsen, *Tinkham:* Lane Bradford, *Confederate Soldier:* Shug Fisher, *Osborne:* John Daheim, *Marshall:* Joe Yrigoyen, *Rider #1:* Henry Wills, *Rider #2:* Buzz Henry, *Rider #3:* James Carter, *Rider #4:* Leroy Johnson.

She Wore a Yellow Ribbon with Harry Carey, Jr., Joanne Dru, John Wayne, John Agar and Ben Johnson.

SHE WORE A YELLOW RIBBON (1949) RKO. Produced by John Ford and Merian C. Cooper. Directed by John Ford. Color by Technicolor. An Argosy Pictures Production. From the *Saturday Evening Post* story by James Warner Bellah. Screenplay, Frank Nugent and Laurence Stallings. Score, Richard Hageman. Photography, Winton Hoch. Technical Advisers, Major Philip Kieffer, retired, and Cliff Lyons. Filmed in Monument Valley, Utah. 103 minutes

Captain Nathan Cutting Brittles: John Wayne, *Olivia Dandridge:* Joanne Dru, *Lieutenant Flint Cohill:* John Agar, *Sergeant Tyree:* Ben Johnson, *Lieutenant Ross Pennell:* Harry Carey, Jr., *Sergeant Quincannon:* Victor McLaglen, *Abby Allshard:* Mildred Natwick, *Major Mack Allshard:* George O'Brien, *Dr. O'Laughlin:* Arthur Shields, *Karl Rynders:* Harry Woods, *Pony-That-Walks:* Chief John Big Tree, *Red Shirt:* Noble Johnson, *Trooper Cliff:* Cliff Lyons, *Corp. Mike Quayne:* Tom Tyler, *Sergeant Hochbauer:* Michael Dugan, *Wagner:* Mickey Simpson, *Bugler/Indian:* Frank McGrath, *Jenkin:* Don Sommer, *Corporal Krumrein:* Fred Libbey, *Sergeant Major:* Jack Pennick, *Courier:* Billy Jones, *NCO:* Bill Goettinger, *Hench:* Fred Graham, *Badger:* Fred Kennedy, *Private Smith:* Rudy Bowman, *NCO:* Post Parks, *McCarthy:* Ray Hyke, *Interpreter:* Lee Bradley, *Indian:* Chief Sky Eagle, *Gun-runner:* Paul Fix, *Bartender:* Francis Ford, *Narrator:* Irving Pichel.

Ship of Fools with George Segal, Michael Dunn and Lee Marvin.

SHIP OF FOOLS (1965) Col. Producer, Stanley Kramer. Director, Stanley Kramer. Based on the novel by Katherine Ann Porter. Screenplay, Abby Mann. Art Director, Robert Clatworthy. Music, Ernest Gold. Songs: "Heute Abend," "Geh'n Wir Bummelin Auf Der Reeperbahn," "Irgendwie, Irgendwo, Irgenwanh"; music, Ernest Gold, lyrics, Jack Lloyd. Cinematographer, Ernest Lazlo. Special Photographic Effects, Albert Whitlock. Editor, Robert C. Jones. 149 minutes

Mary Treadwell: Vivien Leigh, *La Condesa:* Simone Signoret, *Rieber:* José Ferrer, *Tenny:* Lee Marvin, *Dr. Schumann:* Oskar Werner, *Jenny:* Elizabeth Ashley, *David:* George Segal, *Pepe:* Jose Greco, *Glocken:* Michael Dunn, *Capt. Thiele:* Charles Korvin, *Lowenthal* Heinz Ruehmann, *Frau Hutten:* Lilia Skala, *Amparo:* Barbara Luna, *Lizzi:* Christiane Schmidtmer, *Freytag:* Alf Kjellin, *Lt. Huebner:* Werner Klemperer, *Graf:* John Wengraf, *Frau Schmitt:* Olga Fabian, *Elsa:* Gila Golan, *Lutz:* Oscar Beregi, *Hutten:* Stanley Adams, *Frau Lutz:* Karen Verne, *Johann:* Charles de Vries, *Pastora:* Lydia Torea, *Fat Man:* Henry Calvin, *Carlos:* Paul Daniel, *Woodcarver:* David Renard, *Ric:* Rudy Carrella, *Rac:* Silvia Marino, *Guitarist:* Anthony Brand, *Religious Man #1:* Peter Mamakos, *Waiter:* Walter Friedel, *Second Officer:* Bert Rumsey, *Student:* Jon Alvar, *Headwaiter:* Charles Hradilac, *Steward:* Steven Geray.

A Shot in the Dark with Herbert Lom and Peter Sellers.

A SHOT IN THE DARK (1964) UA. Producer-Director, Blake Edwards. Screenplay, Blake Edwards, William Peter Blatty. Based on plays by Harry Kurnitz and Marcel Achard. Music, Henry Mancini. Song, Henry Mancini, Robert Wells. Director of Photography, Chris Challis. Associate Producer, Cecil Fors. Assistant Director, Derek Cracknell. Costumes, Margaret Furse. A Mirsch-Geoffrey Production in Panavision and De Luxe Color. 101 minutes. Sequel to *The Pink Panther* (1964). Produced in England

Inspector Jacques Clouseau: Peter Sellers, *Maria Gambrelli:* Elke Sommer, *Benjamin Ballon:* George Sanders, *Chief Inspector Charles Dreyfus:* Herbert Lom, *Dominique Ballon:* Tracy Reed, *Hercule Lajoy:* Graham Stark, *Francois:* Andre Maranne, *Henri Lafarge:* Douglas Wilmer, *Madame Lafarge:* Vanda Godsell, *Pierre:* Maurice Kaufman, *Dudu:* Ann Lynn, *Georges:* David Lodge, *Simone:* Moira Redmond, *Maurice:* Martin Benson, *Kato:* Burt Kwouk, *Receptionist at Camp:* Reginald Beckwith, *Charlie:* Turk Thrust (Bryan Forbes), *Doctor:* John Herrington, *Pschoanalyst:* Jack Melford.

SHOW BOAT (1936) Univ. Produced by Carl Laemmle, Jr. Directed by James Whale. From the novel by Edna Ferber and the musical by Oscar Hammerstein II and Jerome Kern. Music Director, Victor Baravalle. Photography, John Mescall. Editors, Ted Kent and Bernard W. Burton. Screenplay and Songs, Oscar Hammerstein II and Jerome Kern. Songs: "Ol' Man River," "Bill," "Make Believe," "Can't Help Lovin' Dat Man," "Ah Still Suits Me," "Gallivantin' Around," "I Have the Room Above," "You Are Love." Dance Director, LeRoy J. Prinz. Other versions: Universal, 1929; MGM, 1951. 110 minutes

Magnolia Hawks: Irene Dunne, *Gaylord Ravenal:* Allan Jones, *Captain Andy Hawks:* Charles Winninger, *Parthy Hawks:* Helen Westley, *Joe:* Paul Robeson, *Julie:* Helen Morgan, *Steve:* Donald Cook, *Frank:*

Sammy White, *Ellie:* Queenie Smith, *Windy:* J. Farrell MacDonald, *Pete:* Arthur Hohl, *Vallon:* Charles Middleton, *Queenie:* Hattie McDaniel, *Rubberface:* Francis X. Mahoney, *Kim (elder):* Sunnie O'Dea, *Kim (younger):* Marilyn Knowlden, *Kim as a baby:* Patricia Barry, *Chorus Girls:* Dorothy Granger, Barbara Pepper, Renee Whitney, *Jake:* Harry Barris, *Jim Green:* Charles Wilson, *Sam:* Clarence Muse, *Backwoodsman:* Stanley Fields, *Zebe:* (Tiny) Stanley J. Sandford, *Landlady:* May Beatty, *Lost Child:* Bobby Watson, *Mrs. Ewing:* Jane Keckley, *Englishman:* E. E. Clive, *Reporter:* Helen Jerome Eddy, *Press Agent:* Donald Briggs, *Dance Director:* LeRoy Prinz, *Young Negro:* Eddie Anderson, *Banjo Player:* Patti Patterson, *Simon Legree:* Theodore Lorch, *Woman:* Flora Finch, *Mrs. Brencenbridge:* Helen Hayward, *Drunk:* Arthur Housman, *Mother Superior:* Elspeth Dudgeon.

Show Boat with Irene Dunne and Allan Jones

Show Boat with Emory Parnell, Marge Champion, Kathryn Grayson and Gower Champion.

SHOW BOAT (1951) MGM. Producer, Arthur Freed. Director, George Sidney. Color by Technicolor. Based on the novel by Edna Ferber and the musical play by Jerome Kern and Oscar Hammerstein II. Screenplay, John Lee Mahin. Musical Director, Adolph Deutsch. Art Directors, Cedric Gibbons, Jack Martin Smith. Photography, Charles Rosher. Editor, John Dunning. Songs by Oscar Hammerstein II and Jerome Kern: "Why Do I Love You?", "Make Believe," "Old Man River," "Can't Help Lovin' That Man," "Bill"; with P. G. Wodehouse: "You Are Love," "Ballyhoo," "Gambler's Song," "I Fall Back on You," "After the Ball," "Life Upon the Wicked Stage." Dances, Robert Alton. Annette Warren sings for Ava Gardner. Remake of 1929 and 1936 Universal films. 108 minutes

Magnolia Hawks: Kathryn Grayson, *Julie Laverne:* Ava Gardner, *Gaylord Ravenal:* Howard Keel, *Captain Andy Hawks:* Joe E. Brown, *Ellie May Shipley:* Marge Champion, *Frank Schultz:* Gower Champion, *Stephen Baker:* Robert Sterling, *Parthy Hawks:* Agnes Moorehead, *Cameo McQueen:* Adele Jergens, *Joe:* William Warfield, *Pete:* Leif Erickson, *Windy McClain:* Owen McGiveney, *Queenie:* Frances Williams, *Sheriff (Ike Vallon):* Regis Toomey, *Mark Hallson:* Frank Wilcox, *Herman:* Chick Chandler, *Jake Green:* Emory Parnell, *Kim:* Sheila Clark, *Drunk Sport:* Ian MacDonald, *Troc Piano Player:* Fuzzy Knight, *George (Calliope Player):* Norman Leavitt, *Showboat Chorus Girls:* Lyn Wilde, Joyce Jameson, *Dabney:* Louis Mercier, *Renee:* Lisa Ferraday, *Hotel Manager:* Edward Keane, *Bellboy:* Tom Irish, *Doorman:* Jim Pierce, *Landlady:* Marjorie Wood, *Man with Julie:* William Tannen, *Seamstress:* Anna Q. Nilsson, *Drunk:* Bert Roach, *Doctor:* Frank Dae, *Piano Player:* Harry Seymour, *Bouncer:* William Hall, *Bartender:* Earle Hodgins, *Little Old Lady:* Ida Moore, *Headwaiter:* Alphonse Martell.

The Show of Shows with Louise Fazenda, Frank Fay, Beatrice Lillie and Lloyd Hamilton.

THE SHOW OF SHOWS (1929) WB. Supervising Director, Darryl F. Zanuck. Directed by John G. Adolfi. Color by Technicolor. Photography, Bernard McGill. Songs: "Military March," "What's Become of the Floradora Boys?", "Lady Luck" by Ray Perkins; "Motion Picture Pirates" by M. K. Jerome; "If I Could Learn to Love" by Herman Ruby and M. K. Jerome; "Ping Pongo" by Al Dubin and Joe Burke; "Dear Little Pup," "The Only Song I Know" by J. Kiern Brennan and Ray Perkins; "Your Mother and Mine" by Joe Goodwin and Gus Edwards; "Meet My Sister" by Brennan and Perkins; "Singin' in the Bath-Tub" by Ned Washington, Herb Magidson, Michael Cleary; "Believe Me" by Eddie Ward; "Just an Hour Of Love" by Al Bryan and Eddie Ward; "Li-Po-Li" by Bryan and Ward; "Rockabye Your Baby With a Dixie Melody" by Joe Young, Sam Lewis, Jean Schwartz; "If Your Best Friend Won't Tell You" by Dubin and Burke; "Jumping Jack" by Herman Ruby and Rube Bloom; "Your Love Is All That I Crave" by Al Dubin, Perry Bradford, Jimmy Johnson; "Stars," "You Were Meant for Me" by Arthur Freed and Nacio Herb Brown. 127 minutes

PROLOGUE UNIQUE *M. C.:* Frank Fay, *The Minister:* William Courtenay, *The Victim:* H. B. Warner, *The Executioner:* Hobart Bosworth.

MILITARY PARADE Monte Blue, 300 dancing girls, Pasadena's American Legion Fife and Drum Corps.

FLORADORA *Floradora Sextètte:* Marian Nixon, Sally O'Neil, Myrna Loy, Patsy Ruth Miller, Lila Lee, Alice Day, *Floradora Boys: Waiter,* Ben Turpin, *Ice Man,* Heinie Conklin, *Street Cleaner,* Lupino

Lane, *Plumber*, Lee Moran, *Father*, Bert Roach, *Hansom Cabby*, Lloyd Hamilton.

SKULL AND CROSSBONES Introduced by Frank Fay, Jack Mulhall, Chester Morris, Sojin. Ted Lewis and his Band, Ted Williams Adagio Dancers. *Pirates:* Noah Beery, Tully Marshall, Wheeler Oakman, Bull Montana, Kalla Pasha, Anders Randolf, Philo McCullough, Otto Matiesen, Jack Curtis, *The Hero:* Johnny Arthur, *Ladies:* Carmel Myers, Ruth Clifford, Sally Eilers, Viola Dana, Shirley Mason, Ethlyne Claire, Frances Lee, Julanne Johnston, *Dancer:* Marcelle.

EIFFEL TOWER Georges Carpentier, Patsy Ruth Miller, Alice White, chorus of 75.

RECITATIONS Beatrice Lillie, Louise Fazenda, Lloyd Hamilton, Frank Fay.

EIGHT SISTER ACTS Introduced by Richard Barthelmess: Dolores and Helene Costello, Sally O'Neil and Molly O'Day, Alice and Marceline Day, Sally Blane and Loretta Young, Lola and Armida, Marion Byron and Harriet Lake (Ann Sothern), Ada Mae and Alberta Vaughan, Shirley Mason and Viola Dana.

SINGIN' IN THE BATH-TUB Winnie Lightner, Bull Montana, male chorus of 50.

IRENE BORDONI Assisted by Eddie Ward, Lou Silvers, Ray Perkins, Harry Akst, Michael Cleary, Norman Spencer, Dave Silverman, Joe Burke, M. K. Jerome, Lester Stevens.

CHINESE FANTASY Introduced by Rin-Tin-Tin. Nick Lucas, Myrna Loy, the Jack Haskell Girls.

BICYCLE BUILT FOR TWO Introduced by Frank Fay and Sid Silvers. *Ambrose:* Douglas Fairbanks, Jr., *Traffic Cop:* Chester Conklin, *Boys:* Grant Withers, William Collier Jr., Jack Mulhall, Chester Morris, William Bakewell, *Girls:* Lois Wilson, Gertrude Olmsted, Pauline Garon, Sally Eilers, Edna Murphy, Jacqueline Logan.

BLACK AND WHITE Frank Fay, Sid Silvers, Louise Fazenda, 75 dancing girls.

YOUR LOVE IS ALL THAT I CRAVE Frank Fay, Accompanied by Harry Akst.

KING RICHARD III John Barrymore, Anthony Bushell, E. J. Ratcliffe, Reginald Sharland.

MEXICAN MOONSHINE *The General:* Frank Fay, *Condemned Man:* Monte Blue, *Soldiers:* Albert Gran, Noah Beery, Lloyd Hamilton, Tully Marshall, Kalla Pasha, Lee Moran.

LADY LUCK Betty Compson, Alexander Gray, Chorus.

STARS Members of the cast.

THE SIGN OF THE CROSS (1932) Par. Produced and directed by Cecil B. De Mille. From the play by Wilson Barrett. Screenplay, Waldemar Young and Sidney Buchman. Photography, Karl Struss. Editor, Anne Bauchens. Sound, Harry M. Lindgren. Reissued in 1944 with a prologue written by Dudley Nichols. 123 minutes

Marcus Superbus: Fredric March, *Mercia:* Elissa Landi, *Poppaea:* Claudette Colbert, *Nero:* Charles Laughton, *Tigellinus:* Ian Keith, *Dacia:* Vivian Tobin, *Flavius:* Harry Beresford, *Glabrio:* Ferdinand Gottschalk, *Titus:* Arthur Hohl, *Ancaria:* Joyzelle Joyner, *Stephan:* Tommy Conlon, *Strabo:* Nat Pendleton, *Servillus:* Clarence Burton, *Licinius:* William V. Mong, *Tibul:* Harold Healy, *Viturius:* Richard Alexander, *Philodemus:* Robert Manning, *Tyros:* Charles Middleton, *The Mute Giant:* Joe Bonomo, *A Lover:* Kent Taylor, *Leader of Gladiators/Christian:* John Carradine, *Christian in Chains:* Lane Chandler, *Complaining Wife:* Ethel Wales, *Bettor:* Lionel Belmore, *Pygmy:* Angelo Rossitto, *Bit:* Henry Kleinbach (Brandon).

1944 PROLOGUE *Chaplain James Costello:* Arthur Shields, *Chaplain Thomas Lloyd:* Stanley Ridges, *Captain Kevin Driscoll:* James Millican, *Hoboken:* Tom Tully, *Lieutenant Robert Hammond:* Oliver Thorndike, *Colonel Hugh Mason:* William Forrest, *Lieutenant Herb Hanson:* John James, *Bombardier:* Joel Allen.

The Sign of the Cross with Elissa Landi and Fredric March.

Silent Movie with Bernadette Peters, Mel Brooks, Sid Caesar and Dom DeLuise.

SILENT MOVIE (1976) 20th. Produced by Michael Hertzberg. Directed by Mel Brooks. Color by DeLuxe. Screenplay by Mel Brooks, Ron Clark, Rudy DeLuca and Barry Levinson. Story by Clark. Music by John Morris. Photography, Paul Lohmann. Editors, John C. Howard and Stanford C. Allen. Production Designer, Al Brenner. Costumes Designed by Pat Norris. Choreography, Rob Iscove. Production Consultant, Ron Clark. 2nd Unit Director/Stunt Coordinator, Max Kleven. Assistant Director, Ed Teets. 2nd Assistant Director, Richard Wells. Make-up Artist, William Tuttle. Make-up Man, Charles Schram. Assistant Art Director, Steve Berger. Men's Wardrobe, Wally Harton and Jay Caplan. Ladies' Wardrobe, Nancy Martinelli. Hairdresser, Mary Keats. Assistant Editor, David Blangsted. Special Effects, Ira Anderson, Jr. Titles, Anthony Goldschmidt. Orchestrations, Bill Byers and John Morris. Filmed without dialogue except for one word by Marceau. Rated PG. 86 minutes

Mel Funn: Mel Brooks, *Marty Eggs:* Marty Feldman, *Dom Bell:* Dom DeLuise, *Vilma Kaplan:* Bernadette Peters, *Studio Chief:* Sid Caesar, *Engulf:* Harold Gould, *Devour:* Ron Carey, *Pregnant Lady:* Carol Arthur, *News Vendor:* Liam Dunn, *Maître D':* Fritz Feld, *Studio Gate Guard:* Chuck McCann, *Intensive Care Nurse:* Valerie Curtin, *Studio Chief's Secretary:* Yvonne Wilder, *Acupuncture Man:* Arnold Soboloff, *Motel Bellhop:* Patrick Campbell, *Man Leaving Tailor Shop:* Harry Ritz, *Blindman:* Charlie Callas, *Fly in Soup Man:* Henny Youngman, *British Officer:* Eddie Ryder, *Executives:* Al Hopson, Rudy DeLuca, Barry Levinson, Howard Hesseman, Lee Delano, Jack Riley, *Beautiful Blondes:* Inga Neilsen, Sivi Aberg, Erica Hagen, *Projectionist:* Robert Lussier, *Guest Stars:* Marcel Marceau, Paul Newman, Liza Minnelli, Burt Reynolds, Anne Bancroft, James Caan.

Silver Streak with Gene Wilder and Jill Clayburgh.

SILVER STREAK (1976) 20th. Produced by Thomas L. Miller and Edward K. Milkis. Directed by Arthur Hiller. Color by DeLuxe. Written by Colin Higgins. Executive Producers, Frank Yablans and Martin Ransohoff. Music, Henry Mancini. Cinematographer, David M. Walsh. Editor, David Bretherton. Production Design, Alfred Sweeney. Set Decorator, Marvin March. Sound Mixer, Hal Etherington. Special Effects, Fred Cramer. Make-up, William Tuttle. Hairdresser, Joan Phillips. Assistant Directors, Jack Roe and Lively Andrew Stone. 2nd Unit Photography, Ralph Woolsey. Wardrobe, Phyllis Garr and Michael Harte. Rated PG. 113 minutes

George Caldwell: Gene Wilder, *Hilly Burns:* Jill Clayburgh, *Grover Muldoon:* Richard Pryor, *Roger Devereau,* Patrick McGoohan, *Sweet:* Ned Beatty, *Mr. Whiney:* Ray Walston, *Sheriff Chauncey:* Clifton James, *Johnson (Prof. Schreiner):* Stefan Gierasch, *Chief:* Len Birman, *Plain Jane:* Valerie Curtin, *Reace (Goldtooth):* Richard Kiel, *Rita Babtree:* Lucille Benson, *Ralston:* Scatman Crothers, *Jerry Jarvis:* Fred Willard, *Burt:* Delos V. Smith, *Blue-haired Lady:* Matilda Calnan, *Shoeshiner:* Nick Stewart, *Mexican Mama San:* Margarita Garcia, *Conductor:* Jack Mather, *Conventioneers:* Henry Beckman, Steve Weston, Harvey Atkin, *Porter:* Lloyd White, *Benny:* Ed McNamara, *Nightwatchman:* Raymond Guth, *Engineer:* John Day, *Fat Men:* Jack O'Leary, Lee McLaughlin, *Cabdriver:* Tom Erhart, *Moose:* Gordon Hurst.

SINCE YOU WENT AWAY (1944) UA. Produced by David O. Selznick. Directed by John Cromwell. Assistant Directors, Lowell J. Farrell, Edward F. Mull. A Selznick International Picture-Vanguard Films Production. Based on an adaptation of the book by Margaret Buell Wilder. Screenplay, David O. Selznick. Production Design, William L. Pereira. Music, Max Steiner. Associate, Louis Forbes. Settings, Mark-Lee Kirk. Special Effects, Jack Cosgrove. Associate, Clarence Slifer. Interior Decorations, Victor A. Gangelin. Technical

Adviser, Lt. Colonel J. G. Taylor, USA. Dance Director, Charles Walters. Make-up, Robert Stephanoff. Wardrobe Director, Elmer Ellsworth. Associate, Adele Sadler. Photography, Stanley Cortez and Lee Garmes. Editor, Hal C. Kern. Sound, Charles L. Freeman. Recorder, Percy Townsend. Theme, "Together," by B. G. DeSylva, Lew Brown, Ray Henderson. Other songs: "Since You Went Away" by Kermit Goell and Ted Grouya; "The Dipsy Doodle" by Larry Clinton. Neil Hamilton's photo is used for the part of Tim Hilton. 172 minutes

Anne Hilton: Claudette Colbert, *Jane Hilton:* Jennifer Jones, *Lieutenant Tony Willett:* Joseph Cotten, *Bridget "Brig" Hilton:* Shirley Temple, *Colonel Smollett:* Monty Woolley, *The Clergyman:* Lionel Barrymore, *William G. Smollett II:* Robert Walker, *Fidelia:* Hattie McDaniel, *Emily Hawkins:* Agnes Moorehead, *Harold Smith:* Guy Madison, *Danny Williams:* Craig Stevens, *Lieutenant Solomon:* Keenan Wynn, *Dr. Sigmund Gottlieb Golden:* Albert Basserman, *Zosia Koslowska, a Welder:* Nazimova, *Mr. Mahoney:* Lloyd Corrigan, *Johnny Mahoney:* Jackie Moran, *A Marine Officer:* Gordon Oliver, *Gladys Brown:* Jane Devlin, *Becky Anderson:* Ann Gillis, *Sugar:* Dorothy (Cindy) Garner, *Former Plowboy:* Andrew McLaglen, *Waitress:* Jill Warren, *Refugee Child:* Helen Koford (Terry Moore), *Negro Officer:* Robert Johnson, *Negro Officer's Wife:* Dorothy Dandridge, *AWOL:* Johnny Bond, *Bartender:* Irving Bacon, *Cabby:* George Chandler, *Major Sam Atkins:* Addison Richards, *Pin Girl:* Barbara Pepper, *Principal:* Byron Foulger, *Businessman:* Edwin Maxwell, *Hungry Woman:* Florence Bates, *Desk Clerk:* Theodore Von Eltz, *Elderly Woman:* Adeline de Walt Reynolds, *Convalescents:* Doodles Weaver, Warren Hymer, *Conductor:* Jonathan Hale, *Sergeant's Child:* Eilene Janssen, *Taxpayer:* William B. Davidson, *An Envious Girl:* Ruth Roman, *Girl:* Rhonda Fleming.

Since You Went Away with Shirley Temple, Jennifer Jones, Robert Walker, Claudette Colbert and Agnes Moorehead.

The Singing Fool with Josephine Dunn and Al Jolson.

THE SINGING FOOL (1928) WB. Directed by Lloyd Bacon. From the play by Leslie S. Barrows. Scenario, C. Graham Baker. Cameraman, Byron Haskin. Editors, Ralph Dawson and Harold McCord. Dialogue and titles, Joseph Jackson. Songs: "Sonny Boy," "I'm Sittin' on Top of the World," "It All Depends on You" by Lew Brown, B. G. DeSylva, Ray Henderson; "There's A Rainbow Round My Shoulder" by Billy Rose, Al Jolson, Dave Dreyer. 110 minutes

Al: Al Jolson, *Grace:* Betty Bronson, *Molly:* Josephine Dunn, *John Perry:* Reed Howes, *Marcus:* Edward Martindel, *Blackie Joe:* Arthur Housman, *Sonny Boy:* Davy Lee, *Cafe Manager:* Robert Emmet O'Connor.

The Singing Nun with Ricardo Montalban, Debbie Reynolds, Chad Everett, Juanita Moore and Monique Montaigne.

THE SINGING NUN (1966) Metro release of Jon Beck (Hayes Goetz) production. Director, Henry Koster. Panavision and MetroColor. Screenplay, Sally Benson, John Furia, Jr. Story, John Furia. Camera, Milton Krasner. Music, Harry Sukman. Editor, Rita Roland. Songs by Soeur Sourire, English lyrics by Randy Sparks: "Dominique," "Sister Adele," "It's a Miracle," "Beyond the Stars," "A Pied Piper's Song," "Je Voudrais," "Mets Ton Joli Jupon," "Avec Toi," "Alleluia," "Raindrops," "Brother John" and "Lovely" by Randy Sparks. 98 minutes

Sister Ann: Debbie Reynolds, *Father Clementi:* Ricardo Montalban, *Mother Prioress:* Greer Garson, *Sister Cluny:* Agnes Moorehead, *Robert Gerade:* Chad Everett, *Nicole Arlien:* Katharine Ross, *Himself:* Ed Sullivan, *Sister Mary:* Juanita Moore, *Dominic Arlien:* Ricky Cordell, *Mr. Arlien:* Michael Pate, *Fitzpatrick:* Tom Drake, *Mr. Duvries:* Larry D. Mann, *Marauder:* Charles Robinson, *Sister Michele:* Monique Montaigne, *Sister Elise:* Joyce Vanderveen, *Sister Brigitte:* Anne Wakefield, *Sister Gertude:* Pam Peterson, *Sister Marthe:* Marina Koshetz, *Sister Therese:* Nancy Walters, *Sister Elizabeth:* Violet Rensing, *Sister Consuella:* Inez Petroza.

SINGIN' IN THE RAIN (1952) MGM. Producer, Arthur Freed. Directors, Gene Kelly, Stanley Donen. Color by Technicolor. Story and screenplay, Adolph Green, Betty Comden. Musical Director, Lennie Hayton. Art Directors, Cedric Gibbons, Randall Duell. Cinematographer, Harold Rosson. Editor, Adrienne Fazan. Songs: "Would You?", "Singin' in the Rain," "All I Do Is Dream of You," "I've Got a Feeling You're Fooling," "Wedding of the Painted Doll," "Should I?", "Make 'Em Laugh," "You Were Meant For Me," "You Are My Lucky Star," "Fit As A Fiddle and Ready For Love" and "Good Morning" by Arthur Freed and Nacio Herb Brown; "Moses" by Betty Comden, Adolph Green and Roger Edens; "Beautiful Girl," "Broadway Rhythm." Russ Saunders doubles for Gene Kelly. Footage from 1948's *The Three Musketeers* (MGM). 103 minutes

Don Lockwood: Gene Kelly, *Cosmo Brown:* Donald O'Connor, *Kathy*

Selden: Debbie Reynolds, *Lina Lamont:* Jean Hagen, *R. F. Simpson:* Millard Mitchell, *Zelda Zanders:* Rita Moreno, *Roscoe Dexter:* Douglas Fowley, *Dancer:* Cyd Charisse, *Dora Bailey:* Madge Blake, *Rod:* King Donovan, *Phoebe Dinsmore, Diction Coach:* Kathleen Freeman, *Diction Coach:* Bobby Watson, *Sid Phillips, Assistant Director:* Tommy Farrell, *Male Lead in "Beautiful Girl" Number:* Jimmie Thompson, *Assistant Director:* Dan Foster, *Wardrobe Woman:* Margaret Bert, *Hairdresser:* Mae Clarke, *Olga Mara:* Judy Landon, *Baron de la May de la Toulon:* John Dodsworth, *J. C. Spendrill III:* Stuart Holmes, *Don as a boy:* Dennis Ross, *Villain in Western, Bert:* Bill Lewin, *"Phil," Cowboy Hero:* Richard Emory, *Man on Screen:* Julius Tannen, *Ladies in Waiting:* Dawn Addams, Elaine Stewart, *Villain, "Broadway Rhythm":* Carl Milletaire, *Orchestra Leader:* Jac George, *Vallee Impersonator:* Wilson Wood, *Audience:* Dorothy Patrick, William Lester, Charles Evans, Joi Lansing, *Fencers:* Dave Sharpe, Russ Saunders.

Singin' in the Rain with Donald O'Connor and Gene Kelly.

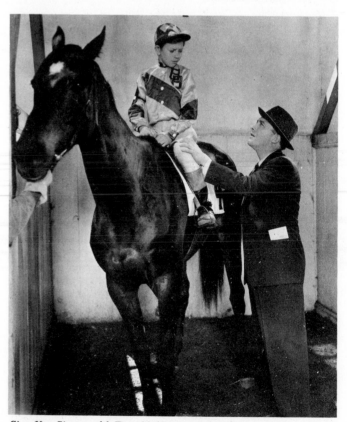

Sing You Sinners with Donald O'Connor and Bing Crosby.

SING YOU SINNERS (1938) Par. Produced and directed by Wesley Ruggles. Story and Screenplay, Claude Binyon. Music Director,

254

Boris Morros. Vocal Arrangements, Max Terr. Assistant Director, Arthur Jacobson. Editor, Alma Ruth Macrorie. Photography, Karl Struss. Art Directors, Hans Dreier and Ernst Fegte. Songs: "Small Fry" by Frank Loesser and Hoagy Carmichael; "I've Got a Pocketful of Dreams," "Laugh and Call It Love," "Don't Let the Moon Get Away," "Where Is Central Park?", by Johnny Burke and Jimmy Monaco. 88 minutes

Joe Beebe: Bing Crosby, *David Beebe:* Fred MacMurray, *Mike Beebe:* Donald O'Connor, *Mrs. Beebe:* Elizabeth Patterson, *Martha:* Ellen Drew, *Harry Ringmer:* John Gallaudet, *Pete:* William Haade, *Filter:* Paul White, *Lecturer:* Irving Bacon, *Race Fan:* Tom Dugan, *Nightclub Manager:* Herbert Corthell.

The Sin of Madelon Claudet with Helen Hayes and Neil Hamilton.

THE SIN OF MADELON CLAUDET (1931) MGM. Directed by Edgar Selwyn. From the play *The Lullaby* by Edward Knoblock. Adaptation and Dialogue, Charles MacArthur. Art Director, Cedric Gibbons. Photography, Oliver T. Marsh. Editor, Tom Held. Talkie feature debut of Helen Hayes. 74 minutes

Madelon Claudet: Helen Hayes, *Carlo Boretti:* Lewis Stone, *Larry:* Neil Hamilton, *Jacques:* Robert Young, *Victor:* Cliff Edwards, *Doctor Dulac:* Jean Hersholt, *Rosalie:* Marie Prevost, *Alice:* Karen Morley, *The Photographer:* Charles Winninger, *Hubert:* Alan Hale, *Roget:* Halliwell Hobbes, *St. Jacques:* Lennox Pawle, *Claudet:* Russ Powell, *Jacques as a boy:* Frankie Darro.

SLAP SHOT (1977) Univ. A Pan Arts Presentation. Produced by Robert J. Wunsch and Stephen Friedman. Directed by George Roy Hill. Written by Nancy Dowd. Technicolor. Associate Producer, Robert L. Crawford. Musical Supervision by Elmer Bernstein. Editor, Dede Allen. Photography, Victor Kemper. Art Director, Henry Bumstead. Song, "Right Back Where We Started From," sung by Maxine Nightingale. Set Decorations, James Payne. Associate Editor, David Howe. Sound, Don Sharpless. 1st Assistant Directors, James Westman and Tom Joyner. 2nd Assistant Directors, Wayne Farlow and Peter Burrell. Costumes, Tom Bronson. Make-up, Rick Sharp and Steve Abrams. Hairstylist, Lorraine Roberson. Stunt Coordinator and Technical Adviser, Ned Dowd. Filmed in Johnstown, Pennsylvania, and Upstate New York. Rated R. 122 minutes

Reggie Dunlop: Paul Newman, *Joe McGrath:* Strother Martin, *Ned Braden:* Michael Ontkean, *Francine Dunlop:* Jennifer Warren, *Lily Braden:* Lindsay Crouse, *Killer Carlson:* Jerry Houser, *Jim Carr:* Andrew Duncan, *Jeff Hanson:* Jeff Carlson, *Steve Hanson:* Steve Carlson, *Jack Hanson:* David Hanson, *Denis La Fleur:* Yvon Barrette, *Upton:* Allan Nicholls, *Wanchuk:* Brad Sullivan, *Jim Ahern:* Stephen Mendillo, *Drouin:* Yvan Ponton, *Charlie:* Matthew Cowles, *Anita McCambridge:* Kathryn Walker, *Suzanne Hanrahan:* Melinda Dillon, *Dickie Dunn:* M. Emmet

Walsh, *Shirley:* Swoosie Kurtz, *Tim McCracken:* Paul D'Amato, *Lebrun:* Ronald L. Docken, *Billy Charlebois:* Guido Tenesi, *Bergeron:* Jean Rosario Tetreault, *Tommy Hanrahan:* Christopher Murney, *Final Game Referee:* Myron Odegaard, *Ogilthorpe:* Ned Dowd, *Pam:* Gracie Head, *Andrea:* Nancy N. Dowd, *Bluebird:* Barbara L. Shorts, *Peterboro Referee:* Larry Block, *Hyannisport Announcer:* Paul Dooley.

Slap Shot with Michael Ontkean and Paul Newman.

Sleeper with Woody Allen.

SLEEPER (1973) UA. A Jack Rollins–Charles H. Joffe Production. Produced by Jack Grossberg. Directed by Woody Allen. Written by Woody Allen and Marshall Brickman. Executive Producer, Charles H. Joffe. Photography, David M. Walsh. Editor, Ralph Rosenblum. Assistant Directors, Fred T. Gallo and Henry J. Lange, Jr. Camera Operator, Roger Shearman. Production Designer, Dale Hennesy. Set Designer, Dianne Wager. Set Decorator, Gary Moreno. Special Effects, A. D. Flowers. Sound Mixer, Jack Solomon. Location Special Effects, Gerald Endler. Costume Designer, Joel Schumacher. Make-up, Del Acevedo. Hairstylist, Janice Brunson. Music by Woody Allen with the Preservation Hall Jazz

Band and the New Orleans Funeral and Ragtime Orchestra. In Color. Rated PG. 88 minutes

Miles Monroe: Woody Allen, *Luna Schlosser:* Diane Keaton, *Erno Windt:* John Beck, *Dr. Melik:* Mary Gregory, *Dr. Tryon:* Don Keefer, *Dr. Agon:* John McLiam, *Dr. Ovra:* Bartlett Robinson, *Rainer Krebs:* Chris Forbes, *Dr. Nero:* Marya Small, *Dr. Dean:* Peter Hobbs, *Ellen Pogrebin:* Susan Miller, *M. C.:* Lou Picetti, *Woman in the Mirror:* Jessica Rains, *Herald Cohen:* Brian Avery, *Jeb Hrmthmg:* Spencer Milligan, *Sears Swiggles:* Spencer Ross, *Janus:* Whitney Rydbeck.

The Smiling Lieutenant with Miriam Hopkins, Maurice Chevalier and George Barbier.

THE SMILING LIEUTENANT (1931) Par. Produced and directed by Ernst Lubitsch. Based on Hans Muller's novel *Nux Der Prinzgemahl* and on *The Waltz Dream* by Leopold Jacobson and Felix Dormann. Adaptation and Screenplay, Ernest Vajda, Samson Raphaelson, Ernst Lubitsch. Photography, George Folsey. Editor, Merrill White. Sound, Ernest Zatorsky. Filmed at Paramount's Astoria, Long Island, Studios. Songs by Oscar Straus and Clifford Grey: "One More Hour of Love," "Breakfast Table Love," "Toujours L'Amour in the Army," "While Hearts Are Singing," "Jazz Up Your Lingerie." 102 minutes

Lieutenant Niki: Maurice Chevalier, *Franzi:* Claudette Colbert, *Princess Anna:* Miriam Hopkins, *Max:* Charles Ruggles, *King Adolf:* George Barbier, *Orderly:* Hugh O'Connell, *Adjutant von Rockoff:* Robert Strange, *Lily:* Janet Reade, *Emperor:* Con MacSunday, *Baroness von Schwedel:* Elizabeth Patterson, *Count von Halden:* Harry C. Bradley, *Joseph:* Werner Saxtorph, *Master of Ceremonies:* Karl Stall, *Bill Collector:* Granville Bates.

Smilin' Through with Norma Shearer and Leslie Howard.

SMILIN' THROUGH (1932) MGM. Directed by Sidney Franklin. Based on the play by Jane Cowl and Jane Murfin. Screenplay, Ernest Vajda and Claudine West. Dialogue, Donald Ogden Stewart and James Bernard Fagan. Assistant Director, Harry Bucquet. Art Director, Cedric Gibbons. Gowns, Adrian. Photography, Lee Garmes. Editor, Margaret Booth. Sound, Douglas Shearer. Other versions: First National, 1922; MGM, 1941. 97 minutes

Kathleen: Norma Shearer, *Kenneth Wayne:* Fredric March, *John Carteret:* Leslie Howard, *Doctor Owen:* O. P. Heggie, *Willie Ainley:* Ralph Forbes, *Mrs. Crouch:* Beryl Mercer, *Ellen:* Margaret Seddon, *Orderly:* Forrester Harvey, *Kathleen as a child:* Cora Sue Collins.

Smokey and the Bandit with Jackie Gleason and Burt Reynolds.

SMOKEY AND THE BANDIT (1977) Univ. A Rastar Production. Produced by Mort Engleberg. Directed by Hal Needham. 2nd Unit Director and Stunt Coordinator, Alan Gibbs. Based on a story by Needham and Robert L. Levy. Screenplay by James Lee Barrett, Charles Shyer and Alan Mandel. Executive Producer, Levy. Photography, Bobby Byrne. 2nd Unit Photography, George Bouillet and Bob Jessup. Editors, Walter Hannemann and Angelo Ross. Art Direction, Mark Mansbridge. Set Decoration, Anthony C. Montenaro. Special Effects, Art Brewer. Make-up, Tom Ellingwood and Guy Del Russo. Hairstyles, Bren Plaistowe. Assistant Directors, David Hamburger, James Quinn and Toby Lovallo. Music, Bill Justis and Jerry Reed. Songs sung by Reed: "East Bound and Down" by Dick Feller and Reed, "Bandit" by Feller, "The Legend" by Reed. Technicolor. Filmed in Georgia. Rated PG. 97 minutes

Bandit: Burt Reynolds, *Sheriff Buford T. Justice:* Jackie Gleason, *Carrie:* Sally Field, *Cledus Snow:* Jerry Reed, *Junior Justice:* Mike Henry, *Little Enos Burdette:* Paul Williams, *Big Enos Burdette:* Pat McCormick, *Patrolman at Traffic Jam:* Alfie Wise, *Sheriff Branford:* George Reynolds, *Mr. B:* Macon McCalman, *Waynette Snow:* Linda McClure, *Hot Pants:* Susan McIver, *Branford's Deputy:* Michael Mann, *Sugar Bear:* Lamar Jackson, *Georgia Trooper:* Ronnie Gay, *Alabama Trooper:* Quinnon Sheffield, *Foxy Lady:* Ingeborg Kjeldsen, *Nude Smokey:* Mel Pape, *Trucker:* Hank Worden.

THE SNAKE PIT (1948) 20th. Producers, Anatole Litvak, Robert Bassler. Director, Anatole Litvak. From the novel by Mary Jane Ward. Screenplay, Frank Partos, Millen Brand. Music, Alfred Newman. Art Directors, Lyle Wheeler, Joseph C. Wright. Photography, Leo Tover. Editor, Dorothy Spencer. 108 minutes

Virginia Stuart Cunningham: Olivia de Havilland, *Robert Cunningham:* Mark Stevens, *Dr. Mark Kik:* Leo Genn, *Grace:* Celeste Holm, *Doctor Terry:* Glenn Langan, *Miss Davis:* Helen Craig, *Gordon:* Leif Erickson, *Mrs. Greer:* Beulah Bondi, *Asylum Inmate:* Lee Patrick,

Doctor Curtis: Howard Freeman, *Mrs. Stuart:* Natalie Schafer, *Ruth:* Ruth Donnelly, *Margaret:* Katherine Locke, *Doctor Gifford:* Frank Conroy, *Miss Hart:* Minna Gombell, *Miss Bixby:* June Storey, *Virginia at 6:* Lora Lee Michel, *Mr. Stuart:* Damian O'Flynn, *Valerie:* Ann Doran, *Nurse Vance:* Esther Somers, *Celia Sommerville:* Jacqueline de Wit, *Hester:* Betsy Blair, *Miss Greene:* Lela Bliss, *Lola:* Queenie Smith, *Miss Seiffert:* Virginia Brissac, *Countess:* Grayce Hampton, *Miss Neumann:* Dorothy Neumann, *Singing Inmate:* Jan Clayton, *Asylum Inmate:* Isabel Jewell, *Visor:* Syd Saylor, *Tommy's Mother:* Mae Marsh, *Young Girl:* Marion Marshall, *Tommy:* Ashley Cowan, *Patient:* Minerva Urecal, *Miss Servis:* Helen Servis, *Gertrude:* Celia Lovsky, *Doctor Somer:* Lester Sharpe, *Nurse:* Mary Treen, *Patient:* Barbara Pepper, *Virginia at 2:* Victoria Albright.

The Snake Pit with Olivia de Havilland and Leo Genn.

The Snows of Kilimanjaro with Lisa Ferraday, Hildegarde Neff and Gregory Peck.

THE SNOWS OF KILIMANJARO (1952) 20th. Producer, Darryl F. Zanuck. Director, Henry King. Color by Technicolor. From the short story by Ernest Hemingway. Screenplay, Casey Robinson. Music, Bernard Herrmann. Art Direction, Lyle Wheeler, John De Cuir. Sets, Thomas Little, Paul S. Fox. Choreography, Antonio Triana. Cinematographer, Leon Shamroy. Special Photo-effects, Ray Kellogg. Editor, Barbara McLean. 117 minutes

Harry: Gregory Peck, *Helen:* Susan Hayward, *Cynthia:* Ava Gardner, *Countess Liz:* Hildegarde Neff, *Uncle Bill:* Leo G. Carroll, *Johnson:* Torin Thatcher, *Beatrice:* Ava Norring, *Connie:* Helene Stanley, *Emile:* Marcel Dalio, *Guitarist:* Vincent Gomez, *Spanish Dancer:* Richard Allan, *Dr. Simmons:* Leonard Carey, *Witch Doctor:* Paul Thompson, *Molo:* Emmett Smith, *Charles:* Victor Wood, *American Soldier:* Bert Freed, *Margot:* Agnes Laury, *Georgette:* Monique

Chantel, *Annette:* Janine Grandel, *Compton:* John Dodsworth, *Harry (age 17):* Charles Bates, *Venduse:* Lisa Ferraday, *Princess:* Maya Van Horn, *Marquis:* Ivan Lebedeff, *Spanish Officer:* Martin Garralaga, *Servant:* George Davis, *Old Waiter:* Julian Rivero, *Clerk:* Edward Colmans, *Accordion Players:* Ernest Brunner, Arthur Brunner.

Snow White and the Seven Dwarfs.

SNOW WHITE AND THE SEVEN DWARFS (1937) RKO. Produced by Walt Disney. Supervising Director, David Hand. Color by Technicolor. Based on the Grimm's fairy tale. Story Adaptation, Ted Sears, Otto Englander, Earl Hurd, Dorothy Ann Blank, Richard Creedon, Dick Richard, Merrill de Maris, Webb Smith. Sequence Directors, Perce Pearce, Larry Morey, William Cottrell, Wilfred Jackson, Ben Sharpsteen. Art Directors, Charles Philippi, Hugh Hennesy, Terrell Stapp, McLaren Stewart, Harold Miles, Tom Codrick, Gustaf Tenggren, Kenneth Anderson, Kendall O'Connor, Hazel Sewell. Art Backgrounds, Samuel Armstrong, Mique Nelson, Merle Cox, Claude Coats, Phil Dike, Ray Lockrem, Maurice Nible. Supervising Animators, Hamilton Luske, Vladimir Tytla, Fred Moore, Herman Ferguson. Music, Frank Churchill, Leigh Harline, Paul Smith. Character Designers, Albert Hurter and Jose Grant. Animators, Frank Thomas, Duck Lundy, Arthur Babbitt, Eric Larson, Milton Kahl, Robert Stokes, James Algar, Al Eugster, Cy Young, Joshua Meader, Ugo D'Orsi, George Rowley, Les Clark, Fred Spencer, Bill Roberts, Bernard Garbutt, Grim Natwick, Jack Campbell, Marvin Woodward, James Culhane, Stan Quackenbush, Ward Kimball, Woolie Reitherman, Robert Martsch. Songs by Larry Morey and Frank Churchill: "Heigh Ho," "Just Whistle While You Work," "Some Day My Prince Will Come," "I'm Wishing," "One Song," "With a Smile and a Song," "The Washing Song," "Isn't This a Silly Song?", "Buddle-Uddle-Um-Dum," "Music in Your Soup" and "You're Never Too Old to Be Young." Adrienne Casillotti as the voice of Snow White. Margery Belcher (later Marge Champion) modeled for Snow White. 82 minutes

THE SOLID GOLD CADILLAC (1956) Col. Producer, Fred Kohlmar. Director, Richard Quine. Based on the play by George S. Kaufman and Howard Teichmann. Screenplay, Abe Burrows. Art

257

Director, Ross Bellah. Musical Director, Lionel Newman. Music composed by Cyril J. Mockridge. Orchestration, Bernard Mayers. Cinematographer, Charles Lang. Editor, Charles Nelson. 99 minutes

Laura Partridge: Judy Holliday, *Edward L. McKeever:* Paul Douglas, *Clifford Snell:* Fred Clark, *John T. Blessington:* John Williams, *Harry Harkness:* Hiram Sherman, *Amelia Shotgraven:* Neva Patterson, *Warren Gillie:* Ralph Dumke, *Alfred Metcalfe:* Ray Collins, *Jenkins:* Arthur O'Connell, *Williams:* Richard Deacon, *Miss L'Arriere:* Marilyn Hanold, *Blessington's Secretary:* Anne Loos, *Snell's Secretary:* Audrey Swanson, *Chauffeur:* Larry Hudson, *Receptionist:* Sandra White, *Senator Simpkins:* Harry Antrim, *Elevator Man:* Paul Weber, *Elderly Lady:* Emily Getchell, *First Lawyer:* Maurice Manson, *Model:* Suzanne Alexander, *Advertising Man:* Oliver Cliff, *Judge:* Voltaire Perkins, *Second Lawyer:* Joe Hamilton, *Farm Woman:* Jean G. Harvey, *Spanish-American War Veteran:* Bud Osborne, *Dowager:* Lulu Mae Bohrman, *Lady Commentator:* Madge Blake, *Bill Parker:* Jack Latham.

The Solid Gold Cadillac with Judy Holliday and Neva Patterson.

Solomon and Sheba with Gina Lollobrigida and Yul Brynner.

SOLOMON AND SHEBA (1959) UA. An Edward Small Presentation. Producer, Ted Richmond. Director, King Vidor. Screenplay by Anthony Veiller, Paul Dudley and George Bruce. From a story by Crane

Wilbur. Music by Mario Nascimbene. Art Directors, Richard Day, Alfred Sweeney. Cinematographer, Freddie Young. Editor, John Ludwig. In Technicolor and Technirama. Produced in Spain. Choreography, Jaroslav Berger. Special Effects, Alex Weldon. Sound, F. C. Hughesdon, Aubrey Lewis, and David Hildyard. Brynner replaced Tyrone Power, who died during production and is in the battle scenes. 139 minutes

Solomon: Yul Brynner, *Sheba:* Gina Lollobrigida, *Adonijah:* George Sanders, *Pharoah:* David Farrar, *Abishag:* Marisa Pavan, *Joab:* John Crawford, *Hezrai:* Laurence Naismith, *Ahab:* Jose Nieto, *Sittar:* Alejandro Rey, *Baltor:* Harry Andrews, *Zadok:* Julio Pena, *Bathsheba:* Maruchi Fresno, *Nathan:* William Devlin, *Egyptian General:* Felix De Pomes, *Takyan:* Jean Anderson, *Josiah:* Jack Gwillim, *King David:* Finlay Currie.

Somebody Up There Likes Me with Courtland Shepard and Paul Newman.

SOMEBODY UP THERE LIKES ME (1956) MGM. Produced by Charles Schnee. Directed by Robert Wise. Associate Producer, James E. Newcom. Based on the autobiography of Rocky Graziano as written by Rowland Barber. Screenplay, Ernest Lehman. Music, Bronislau Kaper. Title song by Sammy Cahn, sung by Perry Como. Assistant Director, Robert Saunders. 113 minutes

Rocky: Paul Newman, *Norma:* Pier Angeli, *Irving Cohen:* Everett Sloane, *Ma Barbella:* Eileen Heckart, *Romolo:* Sal Mineo, *Nick Barbella:* Harold J. Stone, *Benny:* Joseph Buloff, *Whitey Bimstein:* Sammy White, *Heldon:* Arch Johnson, *Questioner:* Robert Lieb, *Commissioner Eagan:* Theodore Newton, *Fidel:* Steve McQueen, *Corporal:* Robert Easton, *Ring Announcer:* Ray Walker, *Commissioner:* Billy Nelson, *Frankie Peppo:* Robert Loggia, *Lou Stillman:* Matt Crowley, *Johnny Hyland:* Judson Pratt, *Yolanda Barbella:* Donna Jo Gribble, *Colonel:* James Todd, *George:* Jack Kelk, *Captain Grifton:* Russ Conway, *Harry Wismer:* Himself, *Tony Zale:* Courtland Shepard, *Radio Announcer:* Sam Taub, *Rocky at 8:* Terry Rangno, *Yolanda at 12:* Jan Gillum, *Shorty:* Ralph Vitti (Michael Dante), *Polack:* Walter Cartier, *Warden Niles:* John Eldredge, *Captain Lancheck:* Clancy Cooper, *Private:* Dean Jones, *Bryson:* Ray Stricklyn, *Sam:* Caswell Adams, *Curtis Hughtower:* Charles Green, *Audrey at 3:* Angela Cartwright, *Mr. Mueller:* David Leonard.

SOME CAME RUNNING (1958) MGM. Producer, Sol C. Siegel. Director, Vincente Minnelli. CinemaScope, MetroColor. Based on the novel by James Jones. Screenplay, John Patrick, Arthur Sheekman. Art Directors, William A. Horning, Urie McCleary. Musical Director, Elmer Bernstein. Cinematographer, William H. Daniels. Editor, Adrienne Fazan. 127 minutes

Dave Hirsh: Frank Sinatra, *Bama Dillert:* Dean Martin, *Ginny Moor-*

head: Shirley MacLaine, *Gwen French:* Martha Hyer, *Frank Hirsh:* Arthur Kennedy, *Edith Barclay:* Nancy Gates, *Agnes Hirsh:* Leora Dana, *Dawn Hirsh:* Betty Lou Keim, *Prof. Robert Haven French:* Larry Gates, *Raymond Lanchak:* Steven Peck, *Jane Barclay:* Connie Gilchrist, *Smitty:* Ned Wever, *Rosalie:* Carmen Phillips, *Wally Dennis:* John Brennan, *Al:* William Schallert, *Sheriff:* Roy Engel, *Sister Mary Joseph:* Marion Ross, *Dewey Cole:* Denny Miller, *Hotel Clerk:* Chuck Courtney, *George Huff:* Paul Jones, *Mrs. Stevens:* Geraldine Wall, *Virginia Stevens:* Janelle Richards, *Ned Deacon:* George Brengel, *Hubie Nelson:* George Cisar, *Doc Henderson:* Donald Kerr, *Club Manager:* Jan Arvan, *Ted Harperspoon:* Don Haggerty, *Waiter:* Frank Mitchell, *Bus Driver:* Dave White, *Dealer:* Len Lesser, *Joe:* Ric Roman, *Slim:* George E. Stone, *Judge Baskin:* Anthony Jochim.

Some Came Running with Carmen Phillips, Dean Martin and Frank Sinatra.

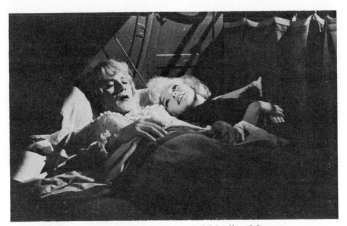

Some Like It Hot with Jack Lemmon and Marilyn Monroe.

SOME LIKE IT HOT (1959) UA. Producer-Director, Billy Wilder. Screenplay by Billy Wilder and I. A. L. Diamond. Suggested by a story by R. Thoeren and M. Logan. Associate Producers, Doane Harrison, I. A. L. Diamond. Score by Adolph Deutsch. Assistant Director, Sam Nelson. Gowns by Orry-Kelly. Art Director, Ted Haworth. Background Score, Adolph Deutsch. Cinematographer, Charles Lang, Jr. Editor, Arthur Schmidt. An Ashton Picture and Mirisch Company Presentation Songs: "Runnin' Wild," "I Wanna Be Loved by You," "I'm Through with Love." 120 minutes

Sugar Kane (Kumulchek): Marilyn Monroe, *Joe (Josephine):* Tony Curtis, *Jerry (Daphne):* Jack Lemmon, *Spats Columbo:* George Raft, *Mulligan:* Pat O'Brien, *Osgood Fielding III:* Joe E. Brown, *Bonaparte:* Nehemiah Persoff, *Sweet Sue:* Joan Shawlee, *Sig Poliakoff:* Billy Gray, *Toothpick:* George E. Stone, *Beinstock:* Dave Barry, *Spats' Henchmen:* Mike Mazurki, Harry Wilson, *Dolores:* Beverly Wills, *Nellie:* Barbara Drew, *Paradise:* Edward G. Robinson, Jr., *Bouncer:* Tom Kennedy, *Waiter:* John Indrisano.

Somewhere I'll Find You with Lee Patrick, Robert Sterling and Lana Turner.

SOMEWHERE I'LL FIND YOU (1942) MGM. Producer, Pandro S. Berman. Director, Wesley Ruggles. Author, Charles Hoffman. Screenplay, Marguerite Roberts. Art Director, Cedric Gibbons. Musical Score, Bronislau Kaper. Cameraman, Harold Rosson. 108 minutes

Jonathon Davis: Clark Gable, *Paula Lane:* Lana Turner, *Kirk Davis:* Robert Sterling, *Willie Manning:* Reginald Owen, *Eve Manning:* Lee Patrick, *George L. Stafford:* Charles Dingle, *Mama Lugovska:* Tamara Shayne, *Dorloff:* Leonid Kinskey, *Penny:* Diana Lewis, *Nurse Winifred:* Molly Lamont, *Crystal Jones:* Patricia Dane, *Miss Coulter:* Sara Haden, *Prof. Anatole:* Richard Kean, *Pearcley:* Francis Sayles, *Bartender:* Tom O'Grady, *Waiter:* Donald Kerr, *Penny's Companion:* Gayne Whitman, *Boy:* Grady Sutton, *Girl:* Dorothy Morris, *Thomas Chang:* Keye Luke, *Fred Kirsten:* Miles Mander, *Ming:* Eleanor Soohoo, *Sam Porto:* Allen Jung, *Captain:* Douglas Fowley, *Felipe Morel:* Benny Inocencio, *Lieut. Hall:* Van Johnson, *Manuel Ortega:* Angel Cruz, *Sgt. Purdy:* Keenan Wynn, *Slim:* Frank Faylen, *Pete Brady:* J. Lewis Smith, *Chinese Doctor:* Lee Tung-Foo.

The Song of Bernadette with Jennifer Jones.

THE SONG OF BERNADETTE (1943) 20th. Producer, William Perlberg. Director, Henry King. From the novel by Franz Werfel. Screenplay, George Seaton. Art Directors, James Basevi, William Darling. Music, Alfred Newman. Orchestral Arrangements, Edward Powell. Cameraman, Arthur Miller. Special Effects, Fred Sersen. Editor, Barbara McLean. 156 minutes

Bernadette: Jennifer Jones, *Antoine:* William Eythe, *Peyremaie:* Charles Bickford, *Dutour:* Vincent Price, *Dr. Dozous:* Lee Cobb, *Sister Vauzous:* Gladys Cooper, *Louise Soubirous:* Anne Revere, *Francois Soubirous:* Roman Bohnen, *Jeanne Abadie:* Mary Anderson, *Empress Eugenie:* Patricia Morison, *Lacade:* Aubrey Mather, *Jacomet:* Charles Dingle, *Croisine:* Edith Barrett, *Louis Bouriette:* Sig Rumann, *Bernarde Casterot:* Blanche Yurka, *Marie Soubirous:* Ermadean Walters, *Callet:* Marcel Dalio, *Le Crampe:* Pedro de Cordoba, *Emperor Napoleon:* Jerome Cowan, *Bishop of Tarbes:* Charles Waldron, *Chaplain:* Moroni Olsen, *Convent Mother Superior:* Nana Bryant, *Charles Bouhouhorts:* Manart Kippen, *Jean Soubirous:* Merrill Rodin, *Justin Soubirous:* Nino Pipitone, Jr., *Father Pomian:* John Maxwell Hayes, *Estrade:* Jean Del Val, *Mme. Bruat:* Tala Birell, *Mme. Nicolau:* Eula Morgan, *Dr. St. Cyr:* Frank Reicher, *Duran:* Charles La Torre, *Blessed Virgin:* Linda Darnell, *Woman:* Mae Marsh, *Adolar:* Dickie Moore, *Mother Superior:* Dorothy Shearer, *Bishop:* Andre Charlot, *Psychiatrist:* Alan Napier, *Monks:* Fritz Leiber and Arthur Hohl, *Doctor:* Edward Van Sloan.

A Song to Remember with Cornel Wilde, Merle Oberon and Paul Muni.

A SONG TO REMEMBER (1945) Col. Producer, Louis F. Edelman. Director, Charles Vidor. Color by Technicolor. From the story by Ernst Marischka. Screenplay, Sidney Buchman. Art Directors, Lionel Banks, Van Nest Polglase. Musical Supervisor, Mario Silva. Musical Director, M. W. Stoloff. Cameramen, Tony Gaudio and Allen M. Davey. Editor, Charles Nelson. Technicolor Director, Natalie Kalmus. Music Adaptation, Miklos Rozsa. 113 minutes

Professor Joseph Elsner: Paul Muni, *George Sand:* Merle Oberon, *Frederick Chopin:* Cornel Wilde, *Franz Liszt:* Stephen Bekassy, *Constantia:* Nina Foch, *Louis Pleyel:* George Coulouris, *Henri Dupont:* Sig Arno, *Kalbrenner:* Howard Freeman, *Alfred DeMusset:* George Macready, *Madame Mercier:* Claire Dubrey, *Monsieur Jollet:* Frank Puglia, *Madame Lambert:* Fern Emmett, *Isabelle Chopin:* Sybil Merritt, *Monsieur Chopin:* Ivan Triesault, *Madame Chopin:* Fay Helm, *Isabelle Chopin (age 9):* Dawn Bender, *Chopin (age 10):* Maurice Tauzin, *Paganini:* Roxy Roth, *Balzac:* Peter Cusanelli, *Titus:* William Challee, *Jan:* William Richardson, *Postman:* Charles LaTorre, *Albert:* Earl Easton, *Young Russian:* Gregory Gaye, *Major Domo:* Walter Bonn, *Russian Count:* Henry Sharp, *Countess:* Zoia Karabanova, *Russian Governor:* Michael Visaroff, *Servant:* John George, *Pleyel's Clerk:* Ian Wolfe, *Duchess of Orleans:* Norma Drury, *Duke of Orleans:* Eugene Borden, *De La Croux:* Al Luttringer; Jose Iturbi plays piano for Wilde.

SON OF FLUBBER (1963) BV. A Walt Disney presentation. Associate Producers, Bill Walsh, Ron Miller. Director, Robert Stevenson. Based on a story by Samuel W. Taylor and on the Danny Dunn books. Screenplay, Bill Walsh and Don Dagradi. Sequel to *The Absent-Minded*

Professor (1959). Art Directors, Carroll Clark, Bill Tuntke. Music, George Bruns. Orchestration, Franklyn Marks. Cinematographer, Edward Colman. Editor, Cotton Warburton. 100 minutes

Ned Brainard: Fred MacMurray, *Betsy Brainard:* Nancy Olson, *Alonzo Hawk:* Keenan Wynn, *Biff Hawk:* Tommy Kirk, *A. J. Allen:* Ed Wynn, *President Rufus Daggett:* Leon Ames, *Mr. Hurley:* Ken Murray, *Mr. Hummel:* William Demarest, *Judge Murdock:* Charlie Ruggles, *Radio Announcer:* Paul Lynde, *Mr. Harker:* Bob Sweeney, *Shelby Ashton:* Elliott Reid, *Defense Secretary:* Edward Andrews, *Desiree delaRoche:* Joanna Moore, *First Referee:* Alan Carney, *Officer Kelly:* Forrest Lewis, *Officer Hanson:* James Westerfield, *Prosecutor:* Alan Hewitt, *Coach Wilson:* Stuart Erwin, *Barley:* Jack Albertson, *Osbourne:* Eddie Ryder, *Mrs. Edna Daggett:* Harriet MacGibbon, *Humphrey Hacker:* Leon Tyler, *Assistant to Defense Secretary:* Robert Shayne, *TV Commercial Woman:* Beverly Wills, *Admiral:* Henry Hunter, *Bartender:* Hal Smith, *Sign Painter:* J. Pat O'Malley, *Rutland Football Player #33:* Norman Grabowski, *Rutland Coach:* Gordon Jones, *Newsboy (Joey Marriano):* Lindy Davis, *Secretary:* Hope Sansberry, *Proprietor:* Byron Foulger, *Second Juror:* Jack Rice, *First Juror:* Dal McKennon, *#1 Bailiff:* Burt Mustin, *Rutland Student Manager:* Ned Wynn.

Son of Flubber with Fred MacMurray, Nancy Olson and Bob Sweeney.

Son of Kong with Helen Mack and Robert Armstrong.

SON OF KONG (1933) RKO. Associate Producer, Archie Marshek. Directed by Ernest B. Schoedsack. Story, Ruth Rose. Cameramen, Eddie Linden, Vernon Walker, J. O. Taylor. Editor, Ted Cheeseman. Sound, Earl Wolcott. Sequel to *King Kong,* and one of the rare instances that a sequel was released the same year as the original film. Locations filmed on Catalina Island. Repeating their original roles are Armstrong, Reicher, Johnson, Clemento. 70 minutes

Carl Denham: Robert Armstrong, *Hilda Peterson:* Helen Mack,

260

Captain Englehorn: Frank Reicher, *Helstrom:* John Marston, *Charlie, Cook:* Victor Wong, *Mickey:* Lee Kohlmar, *Red:* Ed Brady, *Peterson:* Clarence Wilson, *Mrs. Hudson:* Katharine Ward, *Girl Reporter:* Gertrude Short, *Servant Girl:* Gertrude Sutton, *Chinese Trader:* James L. Leong, *Native Chief:* Noble Johnson, *Witch King:* Steve Clemento, *Process Server:* Frank O'Connor.

Son of Paleface with Jane Russell, Bob Hope and Bill Williams.

SON OF PALEFACE (1952) Par. Producer, Robert L. Welch. Director, Frank Tashlin. Color by Technicolor. Screenplay, Frank Tashlin, Robert L. Welch, Joseph Quillan. Cinematographer, Harry J. Wild. Special Photography, Gordon Jennings, Paul Lerpae. Process Photography, Farciot Edouart. Art, Hal Pereira, Roland Anderson. Editor, Eda Warren. Music, Lyn Murray. Dances, Josephine Earl. Songs: "Buttons and Bows (new version), "Wing Ding Tonight," "California Rose" and "What a Dirty Shame" by Ray Evans and Jay Livingston; "Am I in Love?" and "Four-Legged Friend" by Jack Brooks; "There's a Cloud in My Valley of Sunshine" by Jack Hope and Lyle Moraine. Sequel to *The Paleface* (1948). 95 minutes

Junior: Bob Hope, *Mike:* Jane Russell, *Roy Rogers:* Roy Rogers, *Kirk:* Bill Williams, *Doc Lovejoy:* Lloyd Corrigan, *Ebeneezer Hawkins:* Paul E. Burns, *Sheriff McIntyre:* Douglass Dumbrille, *Pre. Stoner:* Harry Von Zell, *Indian Chief:* Iron Eyes Cody, *Blacksmith:* Wee Willie Davis, *Charley:* Charley Cooley, *Guests:* Cecil B. De Mille, Bing Crosby, Robert L. Welch, *Ned:* Charles Morton, *Wally:* Don Dunning, *Crag:* Leo J. McMahon, *Genevieve:* Felice Richmond, *Bessie:* Charmienne Harker, *Isabel:* Isabel Cushin, *Clara:* Jane Easton, *Townsman:* Homer Dickinson, *Bank Clerk "Weaverly":* Lyle Moraine, *First Bartender:* Hank Mann, *Second Bartender "Micky":* Michael A. Cirillo, *"Becky":* Isabel Cushin, *Townsman "Chester":* Chester Conklin, *Townswoman "Flo":* Flo Stanton, *Townsman "Johnny":* John George, *Zeke:* Charles Quirk, *Dade:* Frank Cordell, *Jeb:* Willard Willingham, *Trav:* Warren Fiske, *Penelope:* Jean Willes, *Governor:* Jonathan Hale.

THE SONS OF KATIE ELDER (1965) Par. Producer, Hal Wallis. Associate Producer, Paul Nathan. Director, Henry Hathaway. Technicolor. Author, Talbot Jennings. Screenplay, William H. Wright, Allan Weiss, Harry Essex. Art Directors, Hal Pereira, Walter Tyler. Music, Elmer Bernstein. Cinematographer, Lucien Ballard. Editor, Warren Low. 122 minutes

John Elder: John Wayne, *Tom Elder:* Dean Martin, *Mary Glenney:* Martha Hyer, *Bud Elder:* Michael Anderson, Jr., *Matt Elder:* Earl Holliman, *Ben Latta:* Jeremy Slate, *Morgan Hastings:* James Gregory, *Sheriff Billy Wilson:* Paul Fix, *Curley:* George Kennedy, *Dave Hastings:* Dennis Hopper, *Deputy Harry Evers:* Sheldon Allman, *Preacher:* John Litel, *Hyselman:* John Doucette, *Banker Vennar:* James Westerfield, *Charlie Striker:* Rhys Williams, *Charlie:* John Qualen, *Bondie Adams:* Rodolfo Acosta, *Jeb Ross:* Strother Martin, *Doc Isdell/*

Bartender: Karl Swenson, *Mr. Peevey:* Percy Helton, *Jeb (Blacksmith's Son):* Harvey Grant, *Amboy:* Jerry Gatlin, *Ned Reese:* Loren Janes, *Burr Sandeman:* Red Morgan, *Townsman:* Charles Roberson, *Bit Man:* Ralph Volkie, *Andy Sharp:* Jack Williams, *Gus Dolly:* Henry Wills, *Buck Mason:* Joseph Yrigoyen.

The Sons of Katie Elder with John Wayne and Martha Hyer.

Sons of the Desert with John Merton, Stan Laurel and Oliver Hardy.

SONS OF THE DESERT (1933) MGM. Produced by Hal Roach. Original story and continuity by Frank Craven and Byron Morgan. Directed by William A. Seiter. Photography, Kenneth Peach. Editor, Bert Jordan. 68 minutes. Remake of shorts *Ambrose's First Falsehood* (Keystone, 1914), and *We Faw Down* (MGM, 1928). Songs: "Honolulu Baby," "Sons of the Desert."

Stan: Stan Laurel, *Oliver:* Oliver Hardy, *Mrs. Laurel:* Dorothy Christy, *Mrs. Hardy:* Mae Busch, *Charley:* Charley Chase, *Doc:* Lucien Littlefield, *Extra:* Hal Roach, *Bits:* John Elliott, Charles Hall, Stanley Blystone, *A Son:* John Merton, *Singer:* Ty Parvis.

SO PROUDLY WE HAIL! (1943) Par. Producer and Director, Mark Sandrich. Author, Allan Scott. Art Directors, Hans Dreier, Earl Hedrick. Cameraman, Charles Lang. Song by Edward Heyman and Miklos Rozsa, "Loved One." Film debut of Sonny Tufts. 126 minutes

Lieutenant Janet Davidson: Claudette Colbert, *Lieutenant Joan O'Doul:* Paulette Goddard, *Lieutenant Olivia D'Arcy:* Veronica Lake, *Lieutenant John Sumners:* George Reeves, *Lieutenant Rosemary Larson:* Barbara Britton, *Chaplain:* Walter Abel, *Kansas:* Sonny Tufts, *Captain "Ma" McGregor:* Mary Servoss, *Dr. Jose Bardia:* Ted Hecht,

Dr. Harrison: John Litel, *Ling Chee:* Dr. Hugh Ho Chang, *Lieutenant Sadie Schwartz:* Mary Treen, *Lieutenant Ethel Armstrong:* Kitty Kelly, *Lieutenant Elsie Bollenbacher:* Helen Lynd, *Lieutenant Toni Dacolli:* Lorna Gray, *Lieutenant Irma Emerson:* Dorothy Adams, *Lieutenant Betty Peterson:* Ann Doran, *Lieutenant Carol Johnson:* Jean Willes, *Lieutenant Fay Leonard:* Lynn Walker, *Lieutenant Margaret Stevenson:* Joan Tours, *Lieutenant Lynne Hopkins:* Jan Wiley, *Nurse:* Mimi Doyle, *Colonel White:* James Bell, *Flight Lieutenant Archie McGregor:* Dick Hogan, *Captain O'Rourke:* Bill Goodwin, *Captain O'Brien:* James Flavin, *Mr. Larson:* Byron Foulger, *Mrs. Larson:* Elsa Janssen, *Georgie Larson:* Richard Crane, *Colonel Mason:* Boyd Davis, *Colonel Clark:* Will Wright, *Nurse:* Frances Morris, *Young Ensign:* James Millican, *First Young Doctor:* Damian O'Flynn, *Ship's Captain:* Roy Gordon, *Nurse:* Julia Faye, *Steward:* Jack Luden, *Major Arthur:* Harry Strang, *Captain Lawrence:* Edward Dew, *Girl:* Yvonne De Carlo.

So Proudly We Hail! with Paulette Goddard, Mary Treen and Claudette Colbert.

Sounder with Cicely Tyson and Paul Winfield.

SOUNDER (1972) 20th. A Radnitz-Mattel Production. Producer, Robert B. Radnitz. Directed by Martin Ritt. Panavision and DeLuxe Color. Based on the 1970 Newbery Award–winning novel by William H. Armstrong. Screenplay, Lonne Elder III. Photography, John Alonzo. Editor,

Sid Levin. Art Director, Walter Herndon. Sound, Tom Overton and Jerry Rosenthal. Costumes, Nedra Watt. Assistant Directors, Charles Washburn and Donald Guest. Music by Taj Mahal. Song, "Needed Time," sung by Lightnin' Hopkins. Filmed in Louisiana. Rated G. 105 minutes. Sequel was *Sounder, Part 2* (Gamma III, 1976)

Rebecca Morgan: Cicely Tyson, *Nathan Lee Morgan:* Paul Winfield, *David Lee Morgan:* Kevin Hooks, *Mrs. Boatwright:* Carmen Mathews, *Ike:* Taj Mahal, *Sheriff Young:* James Best, *Josie Mae Morgan:* Yvonne Jarrell, *Earl Morgan:* Eric Hooks, *Harriet:* Sylvia "Kuumba" Williams, *Camille Johnson:* Janet MacLachlan, *Mr. Perkins:* Teddy Airhart, *Preacher:* Rev. Thomas N. Phillips, *Judge:* Judge William Thomas Bennett, *Court Clerk:* Inez Durham, *Clarence:* Spencer Bradford, *Mrs. Clay:* Myrl Sharkey.

THE SOUND OF MUSIC (1965) 20th. Producer-Director, Robert Wise. Todd-AO and De Luxe Color. Associate Producer, Saul Chaplin. Director of Photography, Ted McCord. Screenplay, Ernest Lehman. From the musical play by Richard Rodgers and Oscar Hammerstein II. Lyrics, Oscar Hammerstein II. Music and Additional Lyrics, Richard Rodgers. Songs: "The Sound of Music," "Overture and Preludium," "Morning Hymn," "Maria," "I Have Confidence," "Sixteen Going On Seventeen," "My Favorite Things," "Climb Every Mountain," "The Lonely Goatherd," "Do-Re-Mi," "Something Good," "Edelweiss," "So Long, Farewell." Choreography, Marc Breaux and Dee Dee Wood. Costumes, Dorothy Jeakins. Puppeteers, Bil and Cora Baird. Assistant Director, Ridgeway Callow. 171 minutes

Maria: Julie Andrews, *Captain Von Trapp:* Christopher Plummer, *The Baroness:* Eleanor Parker, *Max Detweiler:* Richard Haydn, *Mother Abbess:* Peggy Wood, *Liesl:* Charmian Carr, *Louisa:* Heather Menzies, *Friedrich:* Nicolas Hammond, *Kurt:* Duane Chase, *Brigitta:* Angela Cartwright, *Marta:* Debbie Turner, *Gretl:* Kym Karath, *Sister Margaretta:* Anna Lee, *Sister Berthe:* Portia Nelson, *Herr Zeller:* Ben Wright, *Rolfe:* Daniel Truhitte, *Frau Schmidt:* Norma Varden, *Franz:* Gil Stuart, *Sister Sophia:* Marni Nixon, *Sister Bernice:* Evadne Baker, *Baroness Ebberfeld:* Doris Lloyd.

The Sound of Music with Julie Andrews and children (Charmian Carr, Heather Menzies, Nicolas Hammond, Duane Chase, Angela Cartwright, Debbie Turner, Kym Karath).

THE SOUTHERNER (1945) UA. Produced by David Loew and Robert Hakim. Directed by Jean Renoir. Screenplay by Jean Renoir. From the novel *Hold Autumn in Your Hand* by George Sessions Perry. Music by Werner Janssen. Cameraman, Lucien Andriot. Editor, Gregg Tallas. Presented by Producing Artists, Inc. Assistant Director, Robert Aldrich. Narrated by Charles Kemper. 91 minutes

Sam Tucker: Zachary Scott, *Nona Tucker:* Betty Field, *Granny Tucker:* Beulah Bondi, *Daisy Tucker:* Bunny Sunshine (Jean Vanderwilt), *Jot Tucker:* Jay Gilpin, *Harmie:* Percy Kilbride, *Ma Tucker:* Blanche Yurka, *Tim:* Charles Kemper, *Devers:* J. Carroll Naish, *Finlay:*

Norman Lloyd, *Doc White:* Jack Norworth, *Bartender:* Nestor Paiva, *Lizzie:* Estelle Taylor, *Party Girl:* Dorothy Granger, *Becky:* Noreen Roth (Noreen Nash), *Ruston:* Paul Harvey, *Uncle Pete Tucker:* Paul E. Burns, *Wedding Guest:* Earle Hodgins.

The Southerner with Zachary Scott and J. Carroll Naish.

South Pacific with Mitzi Gaynor and Rossano Brazzi.

SOUTH PACIFIC (1958) Magna Theatre Corp. Producer, Buddy Adler. Director, Joshua Logan. Todd-AO and Technicolor. Adapted from the play *South Pacific* by Oscar Hammerstein II, Richard Rodgers, Joshua Logan, based on *Tales of the South Pacific* by James A. Michener. Book and lyrics by Oscar Hammerstein II. Music, Richard Rodgers. Screenplay, Paul Osborn. Art Directors, Lyle R. Wheeler, John De Cuir, Walter M. Scott, Paul S. Fox. Musical Director, Alfred Newman. Orchestration, Edward B. Powell, Pete King, Bernard Mayers, Robert Russell Bennett. Cinematographer, Leon Shamroy. Special Photographic Effects, L. B. Abbott. Editor, Robert Simpson. Songs by Richard Rodgers and Oscar Hammerstein II: "Some Enchanted Evening," "Younger Than Springtime," "Bali Ha'i," "Happy Talk," "A Cockeyed Optimist," "You've Got to Be Taught," "Dites-Moi Pourquoi," "Bloody Mary Is the Girl I Love," "I'm Gonna Wash That Man Right Out of My Hair," "I'm In Love With a Wonderful Guy," "Honey Bun," "Loneliness at Evening," "There Is Nothing Like a Dame," "This Nearly Was Mine," "Soliloquies," "My Girl Back Home." Giorgio Tozzi sings for Brazzi; Bill Lee for Kerr; Muriel Smith for Juanita Hall. Filmed in Kauai, Hawaii. Film debut of France Nuyen, 18. 171 minutes

Emile De Becque: Rossano Brazzi, *Nellie Forbush:* Mitzi Gaynor,

Lieutenant Cable: John Kerr, *Luther Billis:* Ray Walston, *Bloody Mary:* Juanita Hall, *Liat:* France Nuyen, *Capt. Brackett:* Russ Brown, *Professor:* Jack Mullaney, *Stewpot:* Ken Clark, *Harbison:* Floyd Simmons, *Ngana, Emile's Daughter:* Candace Lee, *Jerome, His Son:* Warren Haieh, *Buzz Adams:* Tom Laughlin, *Dancer:* Beverly Aadland, *Sub Chief:* Galvan De Leon, *Copilot:* Ron Ely, *Communications Man:* Robert Jacobs, *Native Chief:* Archie Savage, *Nurse:* Darleen Engle, *Admiral Kester:* Richard Cutting, *Radio Man:* John Gabriel, *Nurse:* Evelyn Ford, *U. S. Commander:* Joe Bailey, *Pilots:* Doug McClure, Stephen Ferry.

Spartacus with Kirk Douglas and Woody Strode.

SPARTACUS (1960) Univ. Produced by Edward Lewis. Executive Producer, Kirk Douglas. Directed by Stanley Kubrick. In Super Technirama 70 and Technicolor. Based on the novel by Howard Fast. Screenplay, Dalton Trumbo. Music composed and conducted by Alex North. Music co-conducted by Joseph Gershenson. Costumes, Bill Thomas and J. Arlington Valles. Assistant Directors, Marshall Green, Foster Phinney, Jim Welch, Joe Kenny, Charles Scott. Art Director, Eric Orbom. Cinematography, Russell Metty. Additional scenes photographed by Clifford Stine. Editor, Robert Lawrence. A Bryna Production. Filmed partly in Spain. 196 minutes

Spartacus: Kirk Douglas, *Marcus Crassus:* Laurence Olivier, *Antoninus:* Tony Curtis, *Varinia:* Jean Simmons, *Gracchus:* Charles Laughton, *Batiatus:* Peter Ustinov, *Julius Caesar:* John Gavin, *Helena Glabrus:* Nina Foch, *Tigranes:* Herbert Lom, *Crixus:* John Ireland, *Glabrus:* John Dall, *Marcellus:* Charles McGraw, *Claudia Marius:* Joanna Barnes, *Draba:* Woody Strode, *David:* Harold J. Stone, *Ramon:* Peter Brocco, *Gannicus:* Paul Lambert, *Guard Captain:* Bob Wilke, *Dionysius:* Nick Dennis, *Roman Officer, Caius:* John Hoyt, *Laelius:* Frederick Worlock, *Symmachus:* Dayton Lummis, *Old Crone:* Lili Valenty, *Julia:* Jill Jarmyn, *Slave Girl:* Jo Summers, *Otho:* James Griffith, *Marius:* Joe Haworth, *Trainer:* Dale Van Sickel, *Metallius:* Vinton Haworth, *Herald:* Carleton Young, *Beggar Woman:* Hallene Hill, *Fimbria:* Paul Burns, *Garrison Officer:* Leonard Penn, *Slaves:* Harry Harvey, Jr., Eddie Parker, Herold Goodwin, Chuck Roberson, *Slave Leaders:* Saul Gorss, Charles Horvath, Gil Perkins, *Gladiators:* Bob Morgan, Reg Parton, Tom Steele, *Ad-Libs:* Ken Terrell, Boyd Red Morgan, *Guards:* Dick Crockett, Harvey Parry, Carey Loftin, *Pirates:* Bob Burns, Seaman Glass, George Robotham, Stubby Kruger, *Soldiers:* Chuck Courtney, Russ Saunders, Valley Keene, Tap Canutt, Joe Canutt, Chuck Hayward, Buff Brady, Cliff Lyons, Rube Schaffer, *Legionaires:* Ted de Corsia, Arthur Batanides, Robert Stevenson, *Majordomo:* Terence De Marney.

SPELLBOUND (1945) UA. Produced by David O. Selznick. Directed by Alfred Hitchcock. Based on the novel *The House of Dr. Edwardes* by Francis Beeding (pseudonym of Hilary St. John Saunders and Leslie Palmer). A Selznick International Pictures-Vanguard Films Production. Screenplay, Ben Hecht. Adaptation, Angus MacPhail. Music,

Miklos Rozsa. Designer of Dream Sequence, Salvador Dali. Art Director, John Ewing. Production Designer, James Basevi. Unit Manager, Fred Aherne. Miss Bergman's Gowns, Howard Greer. Photography, George Barnes. Editor, William Ziegler. Assistant, Lowell Farrell. Sound, Richard De Weese. 111 minutes

Dr. Constance Peterson: Ingrid Bergman, *J. B.:* Gregory Peck, *Matron:* Jean Acker, *Harry:* Donald Curtis, *Miss Carmichael:* Rhonda Fleming, *Dr. Fleurot:* John Emery, *Dr. Murchison:* Leo G. Carroll, *Garmes:* Norman Lloyd, *Dr. Graff:* Steven Geray, *Dr. Hanish:* Paul Harvey, *Dr. Galt:* Erskine Sanford, *Norma:* Janet Scott, *Sheriff:* Victor Kilian, *Stranger in Hotel Lobby:* Wallace Ford, *House Detective:* Bill Goodwin, *Bellboy:* Dave Willock, *Railroad Clerk:* George Meader, *Policeman at Railroad Station:* Matt Moore, *Gateman:* Irving Bacon, *Lieutenant Cooley:* Art Baker, *Sergeant Gillespie:* Regis Toomey, *Dr. Alex Brulov:* Michael Chekhov, *Secretary at Police Station:* Clarence Straight, *J. B. as a boy:* Joel Davis, *J. B.'s Brother:* Teddy Infuhr, *Police Captain:* Addison Richards, *Ticket Taker:* Richard Bartell, *Dr. Edwardes:* Edward Fielding, *Man Carrying Violin:* Alfred Hitchcock.

Spellbound with Ingrid Bergman and Gregory Peck.

The Spirit of St. Louis with James Stewart.

THE SPIRIT OF ST. LOUIS (1957) WB. Producer, Leland Hayward. Director, Billy Wilder. CinemaScope, WarnerColor. Based on the 1953 Pulitzer Prize book by Charles A. Lindbergh. Screenplay, Billy Wilder, Wendell Mayes. Adaptation, Charles Lederer. Art Director, Art Loel. Music composed and conducted by Franz Waxman. Orchestration, Leonid Raab. Cinematographers, Robert Burks, J. Peverell Marley. Aerial Photography, Thomas Tutwiler. Editor, Arthur P. Schmidt. 138 minutes

Charles Lindbergh: James Stewart, *Bud Gurney:* Murray Hamilton, *Mirror Girl:* Patricia Smith, *B. F. Mahoney:* Bartlett Robinson, *Knight:* Robert Cornthwaite, *Model-Dancer:* Sheila Bond, *Father Hussman:* Marc Connelly, *Donald Hall:* Arthur Space, *Boedecker:* Harlan Warde,

Goldsborough: Dabbs Greer, *Blythe:* Paul Birch, *Harold Bixby:* David Orrick, *Major Lambert:* Robert Burton, *William Robertson:* James L. Robertson. Jr., *E. Lansing Ray:* Maurice Manson, *Earl Thompson:* James O'Rear, *Lane:* David McMahon, *Dad (Farmer):* Griff Barnett, *Jess, The Cook:* John Lee, *Casey Jones:* Herb Lytton, *Associate Producer:* Roy Gordon, *Director:* Nelson Leigh, *Louie:* Jack Daly, *Captain:* Carleton Young, *French Gendarme:* Eugene Borden, *Burt:* Erville Alderson, *Surplus Dealer:* Olin Howlin, *Mr. Fearless:* Aaron Spelling, *O. W. Schultz:* Charles Watts, *Secretary:* Virginia Christine, *Photographer:* Sid Saylor, *Barker:* Ray Walker, *Photographer:* Lee Roberts, *Editor, San Diego:* Robert B. Williams, *Levine:* Richard Deacon, *Mrs. Fearless:* Ann Morrison, *Professor:* Percival Vivian, *Mechanic:* George Selk, *Okie:* Paul Brinegar, *Indian:* Chief Yowlachie.

Splendor in the Grass with Pat Hingle and Warren Beatty.

SPLENDOR IN THE GRASS (1961) WB. Director, Elia Kazan. Screenplay, William Inge. Associate Producers, William Inge, Charles H. Maguire. Assistant Director, Don Kranze. Music, David Amram. Choreographer, George Tapps. Costumes, Anna Hill Johnstone. An NBI Picture in Technicolor. Art Director, Richard Sylbert. Cinematographer. Boris Kaufman. Editor, Gene Milford. 124 minutes. Filmed in Staten Island and High Falls, New York.

Wilma Dean Loomis: Natalie Wood, *Bud Stamper:* Warren Beatty, *Ace Stamper:* Pat Hingle, *Mrs. Loomis:* Audrey Christie, *Ginny Stamper:* Barbara Loden, *Angelina:* Zohra Lampert, *Del Loomis:* Fred Stewart, *Mrs. Stamper:* Joanna Roos, *Juanita Howard:* Jan Norris, *Toots:* Gary Lockwood, *Kay:* Sandy Dennis, *Hazel:* Crystal Field, *June:* Marla Adams, *Carolyn:* Lynn Loring, *Doc Smiley:* John McGovern, *Miss Metcalf:* Martine Bartlett, *Glenn:* Sean Garrison, *Rev. Whitman:* William Inge, *Texas Guinan:* Phyllis Diller.

THE SPY WHO LOVED ME (1977) UA. Produced by Albert R. Broccoli. Directed by Lewis Gilbert. Panavision, Color by Rank Labs. Original screenplay by Christopher Wood and Richard Maibaum, inspired by Ian Fleming's 1962 novel. Associate Producer, William P. Cartlidge. Production designed by Ken Adam. Main Title designed by Maurice Binder. Editor, John Glen. Photography, Claude Renoir. Assistant Director, Ariel Levy. Assistant Director, 2nd Unit, Chris Kenny. Underwater Cameraman, Lamar Boren. Ski sequence photographed and supervised by Willy Bogner. Special Assistant to Producer, Michael Wilson. Art Director, Peter Lamont, assisted by Ernie Archer. Sound Recordist, Gordon Everett. Make-up, Paul Engelen. Hairdressing, Barbara Ritchie. Fashion Consultant, Ronald Paterson. 2nd Unit Directors, Ernest Day and

John Glen. Action Arranger, Bob Simmons. Special Visual Effects, Derek Meddings. Special Optical Effects, Alan Maley. Special Studio Effects, John Evans. James Bond theme by Monty Norman. Music by Marvin Hamlisch. Theme song, "Nobody Does It Better" by Carole Bayer Sager and Hamlisch, sung by Carly Simon. Filmed in Egypt, Sardinia, Baffin Island (Canada), Malta, Scotland, Okinawa, Switzerland, London's Pinewood Studios; underwater sequence filmed in Nassau, the Bahamas. Moore's third Bond film. Rated PG. 125 minutes

James Bond: Roger Moore, *Major Anya Amasova:* Barbara Bach, *Karl Stromberg:* Curt Jurgens, *Jaws:* Richard Kiel, *Naomi:* Caroline Munro, *General Gogol:* Walter Gotell, *Minister of Defense:* Geoffrey Keen, *M:* Bernard Lee, *Capt. Benson:* George Baker, *Sergei:* Michael Billington, *Felicca:* Olga Bisera, *Q (Major Boothroyd):* Desmond Llewelyn, *Sheikh Hosein:* Edward De Souza, *Max Kalba:* Vernon Dobtcheff, *Hotel Receptionist:* Valerie Leon, *Miss Moneypenny:* Lois Maxwell, *Liparus Captain:* Sydney Tafler, *Fekkesh:* Nadim Sawalha, *Log Cabin Girl:* Sue Vanner, *Rubelvitch:* Eva Rueber-Staier, *Adm. Hargreaves:* Robert Brown, *Stromberg's Assistant:* Marilyn Galsworthy, *Sandor:* Milton Reid, *Bechmann:* Cyril Shaps, *Markovitz:* Milo Sperber, *Barman:* Albert Moses, *Cairo Club Waiter:* Rafiq Anwar, *Arab Beauties:* Felicity York, Dawn Rodrigues, Anika Pavel, Jill Goodall, *Captain of U.S.S. WAYNE:* Shane Rimmer, *Captain of H.M.S. RANGER:* Bryan Marshal, *Themselves:* The Egyptian Folklore Group, Ski Jump performed by Rick Sylvester.

The Spy Who Loved Me with Barbara Bach, Curt Jurgens and Roger Moore.

STAGECOACH (1939) UA. Produced by Walter Wanger. Directed by John Ford. From the story *Stage to Lordsburg* by Ernest Haycox. Screenplay by Dudley Nichols. Music Director, Boris Morros. Horsemen, Yakima Canutt, John Eckert, Jack Mohr. Photography, Bert Glennon and Ray Binger. Editors, Dorothy Spencer and Walter Reynolds. Produced with the cooperation of the Navajo-Apache Indian agencies and the U. S. Department of the Interior. Locations: Kernville, Dry Lake, Fremont Pass, Victorville, Calabasas, Chatsworth, California; Kayenta, Mesa, Monument Valley, Arizona. Remade by 20th Century-Fox in 1966. Themes, "Bury Me Not On The Lone Prairie" and "I Dream of Jeannie." Music Adaptation, Richard Hageman, Franke Harling, Louis Gruenberg. 96 minutes

The Ringo Kid: John Wayne, *Dallas:* Claire Trevor, *Dr. Josiah Boone:* Thomas Mitchell, *Curley Wilcox:* George Bancroft, *Buck:* Andy Devine, *Hatfield:* John Carradine, *Lucy Mallory:* Louise Platt, *Mr. Peacock:* Donald Meek, *Gatewood:* Berton Churchill, *Lieutenant Blanchard:* Tim Holt, *Chris:* Chris-Pin Martin, *Yakeema:* Elvira Rios, *Sergeant Billy Pickett:* Francis Ford, *Mrs. Pickett:* Marga Ann Daighton, *Nancy Whitney:* Florence Lake, *Captain Sickle:* Walter McGrail, *Express Agent:* Paul McVey, *Mrs. Gatewood:* Brenda Fowler, *Cheyenne Scout:* Chief Big Tree, *Cavalry Scout:* Yakima Canutt, *Indian Leader:*

Chief White Horse, Captain Simmons: Bryant Washburn, *Lordsburg Sheriff:* Duke Lee, *Luke Plummer:* Tom Tyler, *Ike Plummer:* Joe Rickson, *Captain Whitney:* Cornelius Keefe, *Telegrapher:* Harry Tenbrook, *Doc's Landlady:* Nora Cecil, *Jerry, Bartender:* Jack Pennick, *Sheriff:* Lou Mason, *Lucy's Baby (2½ days old):* Mary Kathleen Walker, *Billy, Jr.:* Kent Odell, *Cavalry Sergeant:* William Hopper, *Saloonkeeper:* Ed Brady, *Hank Plummer:* Vester Pegg, *Ranchers:* Buddy Roosevelt, Bill Cody, *Ed (Editor):* Robert Homans, *Bartender:* Si Jenks, *Jim (Expressman):* Jim Mason, *Deputy:* Franklyn Farnum, *Ogler:* Merrill McCormick, *Barfly, Lordsburg:* Artie Ortega, *Lordsburg Express Agent:* Theodore Lorch.

Stagecoach with George Bancroft, John Carradine, Donald Meek, Louise Platt, Claire Trevor and John Wayne.

Stage Door with Katharine Hepburn and Adolphe Menjou.

STAGE DOOR (1937) RKO. Associate Producer, Pandro S. Berman. Directed by Gregory La Cava. Based on the play by Edna Ferber and George S. Kaufman. Screenplay, Morrie Ryskind and Anthony Veiller. Art Director, Van Nest Polglase. Art Associate, Carroll Clark. Interior Decorations, Darrell Silvera. Music Director, Roy Webb. Costumes, Muriel King. Photography, Robert de Grasse. Editor, William Hamilton. Sound, John L. Cass. Assistant Director, James Anderson. 93 minutes

Terry Randall (Sims): Katharine Hepburn, *Jean Maitland:* Ginger Rogers, *Anthony Powell:* Adolphe Menjou, *Linda Shaw:* Gail Patrick, *Catherine Luther:* Constance Collier, *Kaye Hamilton:* Andrea Leeds,

Henry Sims: Samuel S. Hinds, *Judy Canfield:* Lucille Ball, *Milbank:* Jack Carson, *Bill:* William Corson, *Harcourt:* Franklin Pangborn, *Richard Carmichael:* Pierre Watkin, *Butcher:* Grady Sutton, *Stage Director:* Frank Reicher, *Hattie:* Phyllis Kennedy, *Eve:* Eve Arden, *Annie:* Ann Miller, *Ann Braddock:* Jane Rhodes, *Mary:* Margaret Early, *Dizzy:* Jean Rouverol, *Mrs. Orcutt:* Elizabeth Dunne, *Olga Brent:* Norma Drury, *Susan:* Peggy O'Donnell, *Madeline:* Harriett Brandon, *Cast of Play:* Katherine Alexander, Ralph Forbes, Mary Forbes, Huntley Gordon, *Aide:* Lynton Brent, *Elsworth, Critic:* Theodore Von Eltz, *Playwright:* Jack Rice, *Chauffeur:* Harry Strang, *Baggageman:* Bob Perry, *Theater Patron:* Larry Steers.

Stage Door Canteen with Otto Kruger and Ralph Morgan.

STAGE DOOR CANTEEN (1943) UA. Produced by Sol Lesser. Associate Producer, Barnett Briskin. Directed by Frank Borzage. Original Screenplay, Delmer Daves. Music Score, Freddie Rich. Music Director, C. Bakaleinikoff. Assistant Directors, Lew Borzage and Virgil Hart. Talent Co-ordinator, Radie Harris. Production Design, Harry Horner. Assistant, Clem Beauchamp. Art Director, Hans Peters. Interior Decorator, Victor Gangelin. Costumes, Albert Deano. Photography, Harry Wild. Sound, Hugh McDowell. Editor, Hal Kern. Songs: "She's A Bombshell From Brooklyn" by Sol Lesser, Al Dubin, Jimmy Monaco; "The Girl I Love to Leave Behind" by Lorenz Hart and Richard Rodgers; "We Mustn't Say Goodbye," "The Machine Gun Song," "American Boy," "Don't Worry Island," "Quick Sands," "A Rookie and His Rhythm," "Sleep Baby Sleep," "We Meet In The Funniest Places," and "You're Pretty Terrific Yourself" by Al Dubin and Jimmy Monaco; "Why Don't You Do Right?" Film debut of Sunset Carson. 132 minutes

Eileen: Cheryl Walker, *Dakota:* William Terry, *Jean:* Marjorie Riordan, *California:* Lon McCallister, *Ella Sue:* Margaret Early, *Texas:* Michael Harrison (Sunset Carson), *Mamie:* Dorothea Kent, *Jersey:* Fred Brady, *Lillian:* Marion Shockley, *The Australian:* Patrick O'Moore, *Girl:* Ruth Roman, *Stars of the Stage Door Canteen:* Judith Anderson, Tallulah Bankhead, Ray Bolger, Katharine Cornell, Jane Darwell, Dorothy Fields, Arlene Francis, Lucile Gleason, Helen Hayes, Jean Hersholt, George Jessel, Tom Kennedy, Betty Lawford, Alfred Lunt, Harpo Marx, Yehudi Menuhin, Ralph Morgan, Elliott Nugent, Helen Parrish, Lanny Ross, Cornelia Otis Skinner, Ethel Waters, Dame May Whitty, Henry Armetta, Ralph Bellamy, Helen Broderick, Lloyd Corrigan, William Demarest, Gracie Fields, Vinton Freedley, Vera Gordon, Katharine Hepburn, Sam Jaffe, Roscoe Karns, Otto Kruger, Gertrude Lawrence, Bert Lytell, Elsa Maxwell, Ethel Merman, Alan Mowbray, Merle Oberon, Brock Pemberton, Selena Royle, Ned Sparks, Johnny Weissmuller, Ed Wynn, Kenny Baker, Edgar Bergen, Ina Claire, Jane Cowl, Virginia Field, Lynn Fontanne, Billy Gilbert, Virginia Grey, Hugh Herbert, Allen Jenkins, Virginia Kaye, June Lang, Gypsy Rose Lee, Aline MacMahon, Helen Menken, Paul Muni, Franklin Pangborn, George Raft, Martha Scott, Bill Stern, Arleen Whelan, Count Basie and his Band, Xavier Cugat and his Orchestra with Lina Romay, Benny Goodman and his Orchestra with Peggy Lee, Kay Kyser and his Band, Freddy Martin and his Orchestra, Guy Lombardo and his Orchestra.

Stage Fright with Marlene Dietrich and Jane Wyman.

STAGE FRIGHT (1950) WB. Producer and Director, Alfred Hitchcock. Author, Selwyn Jepson (from *Man Running; Outrun the Constable*). Screenplay, Whitfield Cook. Art Director, Terence Verity. Sound, Harold King. Music, Leighton Lucas. Musical Director, Louis Levy. Photography, Wilkie Cooper. Editor, Edward Jarins. Song by Cole Porter: "The Laziest Gal in Town." Filmed in England. 110 minutes

Charlotte Inwood: Marlene Dietrich, *Eve Gill:* Jane Wyman, *Smith:* Michael Wilding, *Jonathan Cooper:* Richard Todd, *Commodore Gill:* Alastair Sim, *Mrs. Gill:* Dame Sybil Thorndike, *Nellie:* Kay Walsh, *Bibulous Gent:* Miles Malleson, *Freddie:* Hector MacGregor, *Shooting Gallery Attendant:* Joyce Grenfell, *Inspector Byard:* Andre Morell, *Chubby:* Patricia Hitchcock.

Stalag 17 with William Holden, Robert Strauss and Harvey Lembeck.

STALAG 17 (1953) Par. Producer and Director, Billy Wilder. Based on the play by Donald Bevan and Edmund Trzinski. Screenplay, Billy Wilder, Edwin Blum. Cinematographer, Ernest Laszlo. Editor, Doane Harrison. 120 minutes

Sefton: William Holden, *Lieutenant Dunbar:* Don Taylor, *Oberst Von Scherbach:* Otto Preminger, *Stosh (Animal):* Robert Strauss, *Harry:* Harvey Lembeck, *Hoffy:* Richard Erdman, *Price:* Peter Graves, *Duke:* Neville Brand, *Schulz:* Sig Rumann, *Manfredi:* Michael Moore, *Johnson:* Peter Baldwin, *Joey:* Robinson Stone, *Blondie:* Robert Shawley, *Marko:* William Pierson, *Cookie:* Gil Stratton, Jr., *Bagradian:* Jay Lawrence, *Geneva Man:* Erwin Kalser, *Triz:* Edmund Trzcinski, *P.O.Ws:* Ross Bagdasarian (David Seville), Robin Morse, Tommy Cook, *Barracks 1 P.O.W.:* Peter Leeds, *German Lieutenant:* Harold D. Maresh, *German Lieutenant:* Carl Forcht, *Prisoners with Beards:* Alex J. Wells, Bob Templeton, and Paul T. Salata, *The Crutch:* Jerry Singer, *German Lieutenant Supervisor:* Max Willenz.

Stanley and Livingstone with Walter Brennan and Spencer Tracy.

STANLEY AND LIVINGSTONE (1939) 20th. Associate Producer, Kenneth Macgowan. Directed by Henry King. Historical research and story outline by Hal Long and Sam Hellman. Screenplay, Philip Dunne and Julien Josephson. Sets, Thomas Little. Costumes, Royer. Photography, George Barnes. Sound, Alfred Bruzlin and Roger Heman. 101 minutes

Stanley: Spencer Tracy, *Eve:* Nancy Kelly, *Gareth Tyce:* Richard Greene, *Jeff Slocum:* Walter Brennan, *Lord Tyce:* Charles Coburn, *Dr. Livingstone:* Sir Cedric Hardwicke, *Bennett:* Henry Hull, *John Kingsley:* Henry Travers, *John Gresham:* Miles Mander, *Mr. Cranston:* David Torrence, *Frederick Holcomb:* Holmes Herbert, *Sir Oliver French:* Montague Shaw, *Sir Henry Forrester:* Brandon Hurst, *Hasson:* Hasson Said, *Col. Grimes:* Paul Harvey, *Commissioner:* Russell Hicks, *Commissioner:* Frank Dae, *Sir Francis Vane:* Clarence Derwent, *Morehead:* Joseph Crehan, *Carmichael:* Robert Middlemass, *Senator:* Frank Jaquet, *Mace:* William Williams, *Zucco:* Ernest Baskett, *Bennett's Secretary:* Emmett Vogan, *Committeeman:* James McNamara, *Chuma:* William Dunn, *Susi:* Emmett Smith, *Mombay:* Jack Clisby, *Lieutenant:* Dick Stanley, *Corporal:* Thos. A. Coleman, *Sergeant:* William E. "Red" Blair, *Man with Pills:* Frank Orth, *Copy Boy:* Billy Watson, *Man:* Harry Harvey, *Newspaperman:* Vernon Dent, *Bongo:* Everett Brown.

A STAR IS BORN (1937) UA. Produced by David O. Selznick. Directed by William A. Wellman. Color by Technicolor. A Selznick International Production. Story, William A. Wellman and Robert Carson. Screenplay, Dorothy Parker, Alan Campbell, Robert Carson. Color Design, Lansing C. Holden. Technicolor Adviser, Mrs. Natalie Kalmus. Music, Max Steiner. Settings, Lyle Wheeler. Associate, Edward Boyle. Costumes, Omar Kiam. Assistant Director, Eric Stacey. Interior Decorations, Edward G. Boyle. Special Effects, Jack Cosgrove. Property Man, Robert Lander. Construction Superintendent, Harold Fenton. Location Manager, Mason Litson. Head Grip, Fred Williams. Head Electrician, James Potevin. Photography, W. Howard Greene. Editors, Hal C. Kern and Anson Stevenson. Sound, Oscar Lagerstrom. Film debut of Lana Turner, as an extra. 111 minutes. Remade as a musical drama by WB, 1954 and 1976. Inspired by RKO's *What Price Hollywood* (1932) and the lives of John Bowers and Marguerite De La Motte.

Esther Blodgett, later Vicki Lester: Janet Gaynor, *Norman Maine (Alfred Hinkel):* Fredric March, *Oliver Niles:* Adolphe Menjou, *Danny McGuire:* Andy Devine, *Granny:* May Robson, *Libby:* Lionel Stander, *Casey Burke:* Owen Moore, *Anita Regis:* Elizabeth Jenns, *Theodore Blodgett:* J. C. Nugent, *Aunt Mattie:* Clara Blandick, *Alex:* A. W. Sweatt, *Central Casting Receptionist:* Peggy Wood, *Justice of the Peace:* Clarence Wilson, *Billy Moon:* Franklin Pangborn, *Night Court Judge:* Jonathan Hale, *Pop Randall:* Edgar Kennedy, *Cuddles:* Pat Flaherty, *Make-up Men:* Harris, Adrian Rosley, *Ward,* Arthur

Hoyt, Orchestra Leader in Hollywood Bowl: Dr. Leonard Walker, *Voice Coach:* Edwin Maxwell, *Bert (Director):* Marshall Neilan, *Posture Coach:* Guinn Williams, *Artie Carver:* Jed Prouty, *Bernie (Photographer):* Vince Barnett, *Waitress:* Trixie Friganza, *Academy Award Speaker:* Paul Stanton, *Assistant Cameraman:* Charles Williams, *Bartender at Santa Anita:* Robert Emmet O'Connor, *Rustic (Jud Baker):* Olin Howland, *Cameraman:* Carleton Griffin, *Party Guests:* Claude King, Eddie Kane and Dennis O'Keefe, *Prisoners:* Francis Ford, Kenneth Howell, Chris-Pin Martin, *Extras in Santa Anita Bar:* Carole Landis and Lana Turner, *Witness:* Snowflake.

A Star Is Born with Adolphe Menjou, Lionel Stander, Fredric March and Janet Gaynor.

A Star Is Born with Judy Garland.

A STAR IS BORN (1954) WB. Producer, Sidney Luft. Associate Producer, Vern Alves. Director, George Cukor. Authors, William A. Wellman, Robert Carson. Screenplay, Moss Hart. Art Director, Malcolm Bert. Cinematographer, Sam Leavitt. Editor, Folmer Blangsted. CinemaScope and Technicolor. Assistant Directors, Earl Bellamy, Edward Graham, and Russell Llewellyn. Dances by Richard Barstow. Songs: "Born in a Trunk," by Leonard Gershe; "The Man That Got Away," "Gotta Have Me Go With You," "It's a New World," "Here's What I'm Here For," "Someone at Last," "Lose That Long Face," by Harold Arlen and Ira Gershwin. Remake of the 1937 UA film, inspired by *What Price Hollywood* (RKO, 1932). 181 minutes.

Esther Blodgett (Vicki Lester): Judy Garland, *Norman Maine:* James Mason, *Oliver Niles:* Charles Bickford, *Libby:* Jack Carson, *Danny McGuire:* Tommy Noonan, *Lola Lavery:* Lucy Marlow, *Susan Ettinger:* Amanda Blake, *Graves:* Irving Bacon, *Libby's Secretary:* Hazel Shermet, *Glenn Williams:* James Brown, *Miss Markham:* Lotus Robb,

Announcer: Joan Shawlee, *Driver:* Dub Taylor, *Director:* Louis Jean Heydt, *Eddie:* Bob Jellison, *Man in Car:* Chick Chandler, *Landlady:* Kathryn Card, *Miss Fusselow:* Blythe Daly, *Director:* Leonard Penn, *Cameraman:* Eddie Dew, *Charley:* Olin Howland, *Justice of the Peace:* Emerson Treacy, *Director McBride:* Willis Bouchey, *Party Guest:* Mae Marsh, *Carver:* Grady Sutton, *M.C.:* Rex Evans, *Wallace:* Richard Webb, *Nigel Peters:* Steve Wyman, *Cuddles:* Henry Kulky, *Director:* Tristram Coffin, *Judge:* Frank Ferguson, *Gregory:* Percy Helton, *Reporter:* Dale Van Sickel, *Esther at 6:* Nadene Ashdown, *Esther at 3:* Heidi Meadows.

Star Spangled Rhythm with Betty Hutton, James Millican (background), Victor Moore, Gil Lamb, Eddie Bracken and Maynard Holmes.

STAR SPANGLED RHYTHM (1942) Par. Associate Producer, Joseph Sistrom. Director, George Marshall. Original screenplay by Harry Tugend. Score written and directed by Robert Emmett Dolan. Editor, Paul Weatherwax. Directors of Photography, Leo Tover and Theodor Sparkuhl. Art Directors, Hans Dreier and Ernst Fegte. Songs by Johnny Mercer and Harold Arlen: "That Old Black Magic," "Hit the Road to Dreamland," "Old Glory," "A Sweater, a Sarong and a Peekaboo Bang," "I'm Doing It for Defense," "Sharp as a Tack," "On the Swing Shift," "He Loved Me Till the All-Clear Came."

Film debut of Gary Crosby, 8. 99 minutes

Old Glory Number: Bing Crosby, *Master of Ceremonies:* Bob Hope, *Men Playing Cards Skit:* Fred MacMurray, *Men Playing Cards Skit:* Franchot Tone, *Men Playing Cards Skit:* Ray Milland, *Pop Webster:* Victor Moore, *Sweater, Sarong and Peekaboo Bang Number:* Dorothy Lamour, *Sweater, Sarong and Peekaboo Bang Number:* Paulette Goddard, *Black Magic Number:* Vera Zorina, *Dreamland Number:* Mary Martin, *Dreamland Number:* Dick Powell, *Polly Judson:* Betty Hutton, *Jimmy Webster:* Eddie Bracken, *Sweater, Sarong and Peekaboo Bang Number:* Veronica Lake, *Scarface:* Alan Ladd, *Smart as a Tack Number:* Rochester, *Husband in Bob Hope Skit:* William Bendix, *Introduces Bob Hope Skit:* Jerry Colonna, *Louie the Lug:* Macdonald Carey, *Frisbee:* Walter Abel, *Genevieve in Priorities Number:* Susan Hayward, *Swing Shift Number:* Marjorie Reynolds, *Swing Shift Number:* Betty Rhodes, *Swing Shift Number:* Dona Drake, Don Castle, *Men Playing Cards Skit:* Lynne Overman, *Himself:* Gary Crosby, *Black Magic Number:* Johnnie Johnston, *Hi-Pockets:* Gil Lamb, *Mimi:* Cass Daley, *Murgatroyd in Priorities Number:* Ernest Truex, *Smart as a Tack Number Dancers:* Katherine Dunham, Slim and Slam, *Comic in Sweater, Sarong and Peekaboo Bang Number:* Arthur Treacher, *Comic in Sweater, Sarong and Peekaboo Bang Number:* Walter Catlett, *Comic in Sweater, Sarong and Peekaboo Bang Number:* Sterling Holloway, *Sweater, Sarong and Peekaboo Bang Hitler:* Tom Dugan, *Mussolini:* Paul Porcasi, *Hirohito:* Richard Loo, *Dreamland Number:* Golden Gate Quartette, *Specialty Act:* Walter Dare Wahl and Company, *Themselves:* Cecil B. De Mille, Preston Sturges, Ralph Murphy, Barney Dean, Jack Hope, *Finale:* Veronica Lake, Dorothy Lamour, Paulette Goddard, Albert Dekker, Marjorie Reynolds, Cecil Kellaway, Lynne Overman, Alan Ladd, Ellen Drew, Jimmy Lydon, Charles Smith, Frances Gifford, Susanna Foster, Robert Preston, Louise LaPlanche, Donivee Lee, Christopher King, Alice Kirby, Marcella Phillips, *Sarah:* Anne Revere, *Mr. Freemont:* Edward Fielding, *Mac:* Edgar Dearing, *Bit Soldier in Black Magic Number:* Frank Faylen, *Duffy:* William Haade, *Sailor:* Maynard Holmes, *Sailor:* James Millican, *Tommy:* Eddie Johnson, *Casey:* Arthur Loft, *Motorcycle Chauffeur for Rochester:* Woodrow W. Strode, *Wife in Bob Hope Skit:* Marion Martin, *Air Raid Warden in Bob Hope Skit:* Chester Clute, *Captain Kingsley:* Boyd Davis, *Petty Officers:* Eddie Dew, Rod Cameron.

A Star Is Born with Kris Kristofferson.

A STAR IS BORN (1976) WB. A Barwood/Jon Peters Production. A First Artists Presentation. Produced by Jon Peters. Directed by Frank Pierson. Executive Producer, Barbra Streisand. Screenplay by John Gregory Dunne, Joan Didion and Frank Pierson. Based on a story by William Wellman and Robert Carson. Photography, Robert Surtees. Editor, Peter Zinner. Production Designer, Polly Platt. Musical Concepts, Streisand. Music and live recordings produced by Phil Ramone. Musical Underscore, Roger Kellaway. Production Manager, Howard Pine. Sound Effects Editors, Joe Von Stroheim and Marvin Kosberg. Musical Supervisor, Paul Williams. Musical Conductor, Kenny Ascher. Assistant Director, Stu Fleming. 2nd Assistant Directors, Michele Ader and Ed Ledding. Art Director, William Hiney. Set Decorator, Ruby Levitt. Choreography, David Winters. Wardrobe, Shirley Strahm and Seth Banks. Make-up, Allan Snyder and Marvin C. Thompson. Hairdresser, Barbara Lampson. Streisand's Hairdresser, Kaye Pownall. Special Effects, Chuck Gasper. Music Editor, John Caper, Jr. Streisand's Assistant, Joan Marshall Ashby. Peters' Assistant, Laura Ziskin. Panavision, Dolby System, Color by MGM, Kem Tone Scenes by TVC Labs. Song, "Evergreen" by Streisand and Paul Williams. Rated R. 140 minutes

Esther Hoffman: Barbra Streisand, *John Norman Howard:* Kris Kristofferson, *Bobby Ritchie:* Gary Busey, *Gary Danziger:* Oliver Clark, *The Oreos:* Vanetta Fields and Clydie King, *Quentin:* Marta Heflin, *Bebe Jesus:* M. G. Kelly, *Photographer:* Sally Kirkland, *Freddie:* Joanne Linville, *Mo:* Uncle Rudy, *Brian:* Paul Mazursky, *Himself:* Tony Orlando, *Patron:* Robert Englund.

Star Wars with Peter Cushing, Carrie Fisher and David Prowse.

STAR WARS (1977) 20th. A Lucasfilm Ltd. Production. Produced by Gary Kurtz. Directed and Written by George Lucas. Photography, Gilbert Taylor. 2nd Unit Photography, Carroll Ballard, Rick Clemente, Robert Dalva and Tak Fujimoto. Music by John Williams. Orchestrations, Herbert W. Spencer; performed by the London Symphony Orchestra. Editors, Paul Hirsch, Marcia Lucas and Richard Chew. Production Designer, John Barry. Art Direction, Norman Reynolds and Leslie Dilley. 2nd Unit Art Direction, Leon Erickson and Al Locatelli. Set Decoration, Roger Christian. Special Photographic Effects Supervisor, John Dykstra. Special Production and Mechanical Effects Supervisor, John Stears. Sound, Stephen Katz, Derek Ball, Don MacDougall, Bob Minkler, Ray West, Robert Litt, Michael Minkler, Les Fresholtz, Richard Portman, Sam Shaw, Robert R. Rutledge, Gordon Davidson and Gene Corso. Stunt Coordinator, Peter Diamond. Costumes, John Mollo. Make-up, Stuart Freeborn, Rick Baker and Douglas Beswick. Assistant Directors, Tony Waye, Gerry Gavigan and Terry Madden. Miniature and Optical Effects Photography, Robert Blalack. Matte Artist, P. S. Ellenshaw. Animation and Rotoscope Design, Adam Beckett. Electronics Design, Alvah J. Miller. Additional Optical Effects by Modern Film Effects, Ray Mercer Company, Van Der Veer Photo Effects, Master Film Effects and De Patie-Freleng Enterprises. Panavision and Technicolor, prints by DeLuxe. Filmed in Tunisia; Guatemala; Death Valley, California; and Elstree Studios in Borehamwood, England. Rated PG. 119 minutes. Sequel is *The Empire Strikes Back*, 1980.

Ben (Obi-Wan) Kenobi: Alec Guinness, *Luke Skywalker:* Mark Hamill, *Han Solo:* Harrison Ford, *Princess Leia Organa:* Carrie Fisher, *Grand Moff Tarkin:* Peter Cushing, *C3PO:* Anthony Daniels, *R2-D2:* Kenny Baker, *Chewbacca:* Peter Mayhew, *Lord Darth Vader:* David Prowse (voice of James Earl Jones), *Uncle Owen Lars:* Phil Brown, *Aunt Beru Lars:* Shelagh Fraser, *Chief Jawa:* Jack Purvis, *Gen. Dodonna:* Alex McCrindle, *Gen. Willard:* Eddie Byrne, *Red Leader:* Drewe Henley, *Red 2 (Wedge):* Dennis Lawson, *Red 3 (Biggs):* Garrick Hagon, *Red 4 (John D):* Jack Klaff, *Red 6 (Porkins):* William Hootkins, *Gold Leader:* Angus McInnis, *Gold 2:* Jeremy Sinden, *Gold 5:* Graham Ashley, *Gen. Taggi:* Don Henderson, *Gen. Motti:* Richard Le Parmentier, *Commander No. 1:* Leslie Schofield.

STATE FAIR (1933) Fox. Produced by Winfield Sheehan. Directed by Henry King. From the novel by Phil Stong. Screenplay, Paul Green and Sonya Levien. Assistant Director, Ray Flynn. Costume Director, Rita Kaufman. Art Director, Duncan Cramer. Photography, Hal Mohr. Editor, L. W. Bischoff. Sound, A. L. Von Kirbach. Song by Val Burton and Will Jason: "Romantic." Music Director, Louis De Francesco. 80 minutes. Remade by 20th in 1945 and 1962, as musicals, and 1976 for TV

Abel Frake: Will Rogers, *Margy Frake:* Janet Gaynor, *Pat Gilbert:* Lew Ayres, *Emily Joyce:* Sally Eilers, *Wayne Frake:* Norman Foster, *Melissa Frake:* Louise Dresser, *The Storekeeper:* Frank Craven,

The Barker: Victor Jory, *Harry Ware:* Frank Melton, *Barker at Aerial Act:* John Sheehan, *Lady at Food Contest:* Doro Merande, *Hog Owner:* Erville Alderson, *Hog Judge:* Harry Holman, *Hog Judge:* Hobart Cavanaugh.

State Fair with Norman Foster, Janet Gaynor, Louise Dresser and Will Rogers.

State of the Union with Van Johnson, Katharine Hepburn, Irving Bacon, Angela Lansbury and Adolphe Menjou.

STATE OF THE UNION (1948) MGM. Producer-Director, Frank Capra. Associate Producer, Anthony Veiller. Based on the play by Howard Lindsay and Russell Crouse. Screenplay, Anthony Veiller, Myles Connolly. Musical Score, Victor Young. Art Directors, Cedric Gibbons, Urie McCleary. Photography, George J. Folsey. Editor, William Hornbeck. A Liberty Film Production. 124 minutes

Grant Matthews: Spencer Tracy, *Mary Matthews:* Katharine Hepburn, *Spike McManus:* Van Johnson, *Kay Thorndyke:* Angela Lansbury, *Jim Conover:* Adolphe Menjou, *Sam Thorndyke:* Lewis Stone, *Sam Parrish:* Howard Smith, *Lulubelle Alexander:* Maidel Turner, *Judge Alexander:* Raymond Walburn, *Bill Hardy:* Charles Dingle, *Grace Draper:* Florence Auer, *Sen. Lauterbach:* Pierre Watkin, *Norah:* Margaret Hamilton, *Buck:* Irving Bacon, *Joyce:* Patti Brady, *Grant, Jr.:* George Nokes, *Bellboy:* Carl Switzer, *Barber:* Tom Pedi, *Waiter:* Tom Fadden, *Blink Moran:* Charles Lane, *Leith, Radio Announcer:* Art Baker, *Jenny:* Rhea Mitchell, *First Reporter:* Arthur O'Connell, *Blonde Girl:* Marion Martin, *Wrestler:* Tor Johnson, *Senator:* Stanley Andrews, *Pilot:* Dave Willock, *Politician:* Russell Meeker, *Joe Crandall:* Frank L. Clarke, *Rusty Miller:* David Clarke, *Broder:* Dell Henderson, *Bradbury:* Edwin Cooper, *Crump:* Davison Clark, *Josephs:* Francis Pierlot, *Editor:* Brandon Beach.

Steamboat 'Round The Bend with Will Rogers and Irvin S. Cobb.

STEAMBOAT 'ROUND THE BEND (1935) Fox Films. Produced by Sol M. Wurtzel. Directed by John Ford. From the novel by Ben Lucien Burman. Screenplay, Dudley Nichols and Lamar Trotti. Music, Samuel Kaylin. Photography, George Schneiderman. Editor, Al De Gaetano. The last film of Will Rogers, released posthumously. 96 minutes.

Dr. John Pearly: Will Rogers, *Fleety Belle:* Anne Shirley, *Captain Eli:* Irvin S. Cobb, *Sheriff Rufe Jetters:* Eugene Pallette, *Duke:* John McGuire, *New Moses:* Berton Churchill, *Efe:* Francis Ford, *Pappy:* Roger Imhof, *Matt Abel:* Raymond Hatton, *Chaplain:* Hobart Bosworth, *Jonah:* Stepin Fetchit, *Popkins, Fleety Belle's Suitor:* Fred Kohler, Jr., *A Listener:* Hobart Cavanaugh, *Breck:* William Benedict, *Addie May:* Lois Verner, *Uncle Jeff:* John Lester Johnson, *New Elijah:* Pardner Jones, *Fleety Belle's Father:* Charles Middleton, *Fleety Belle's Brother:* Ben Hall, *Farmer:* Si Jenks, *Race Officials:* Louis Mason, Robert E. Homans, *Character Bit:* John Wallace, *Salesman:* Dell Henderson, *Prisoner:* Otto Richards, *River Man:* Jack Pennick, *Jailer:* Captain Anderson, *Sheriff's Wife:* Grace Goodall, *Governor:* Ferdinand Munier, *Hangman:* D'Arcy Corrigan, *Warden:* James Marcus, *Labor Boss:* Luke Cosgrave, *Jailbird:* Heinie Conklin.

The Sting with Robert Shaw, Robert Redford and Paul Newman.

THE STING (1973) Univ. Produced by Tony Bill and Michael and Julia Phillips. Directed by George Roy Hill. Screenplay by David S. Ward. Music adapted by Marvin Hamlisch, from Scott Joplin's piano rags. Photography, Robert Surtees. Editor, William Reynolds. Art Director, Henry Bumstead. Assistant Director, Ray Gosnell. A Richard D. Zanuck–David Brown Production, in Technicolor. Costumes by Edith Head. Associate Producer, Robert L. Crawford. Set Decorations, James Payne. Sound, Robert Bertrand and Ronald Pierce. 2nd Assistant Director,

Charles Dismukes. Technical Consultant, John Scarne. Rated PG. 129 minutes

Henry Gondorff: Paul Newman, *Johnny Hooker:* Robert Redford, *Doyle Lonnegan:* Robert Shaw, *Lt. Snyder:* Charles Durning, *J. J. Singleton:* Ray Walston, *Billie:* Eileen Brennan, *Kid Twist:* Harold Gould, *Eddie Niles:* John Heffernan, *FBI Agent Polk:* Dana Elcar, *Erie Kid:* Jack Kehoe, *Loretta Salino:* Dimitra Arliss, *Hench, Floyd:* Charles Dierkop, *Mottola:* James Sloyan, *Luther Coleman:* Robert Earl Jones, *Crystal:* Sally Kirkland, *Benny Garfield:* Avon Long, *Combs:* Arch Johnson, *Bodyguard:* Lee Paul, *Granger:* Ed Bakey, *Cole:* Brad Sullivan, *Riley:* John Quade, *Train Conductor:* Larry D. Mann, *Burlesque Comedian:* Leonard Barr, *Alva Coleman:* Paulene Myers, *Black-gloved Gunman:* Joe Tornatore, *Duke Boudreau:* Jack Collins, *Curly Jackson:* Tom Spratley, *Greer:* Ken O'Brien, *Western Union Executive:* Ken Sansom, *Louise Coleman:* Ta-Tanisha, *Roulette Dealer:* Billy Benedict.

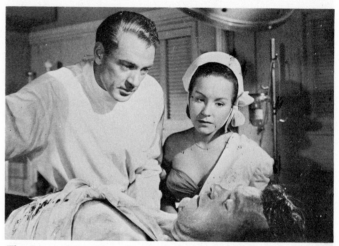

The Story of Dr. Wassell with Gary Cooper, Carol Thurston and Dennis O'Keefe.

THE STORY OF DR. WASSELL (1944) Par. Producer, Cecil B. De Mille. Associate Producer, Sidney Biddell. Director, Cecil B. De Mille. Color by Technicolor. Screenplay, Alan LeMay, Charles Bennett. Technicolor Director, Natalie Kalmus. Musical Score, Victor Young. Art Directors, Hans Dreier, Roland Anderson. Cameramen, Victor Milner, William Snyder. Process Photography, Farciot Edouart, Wallace Kelley. Based on the story of Commander Corydon M. Wassell, USN (MC), and the story by James Hilton. 140 minutes

Dr. Corydon M. Wassell: Gary Cooper, *Madeline:* Laraine Day, *Bettina:* Signe Hasso, *Hopkins (Hoppy):* Dennis O'Keefe, *Tremartini:* Carol Thurston, *Lieutenant Dirk van Daal:* Carl Esmond, *Murdock:* Paul Kelly, *Anderson (Andy):* Elliott Reid, *Commander Bill Goggins:* Stanley Ridges, *Johnny:* Renny McEvoy, *Alabam:* Oliver Thorndike, *Ping:* Philip Ahn, *Ruth:* Barbara Britton, *Francis:* Melvin Francis, *Kraus:* Joel Allen, *Whaley:* James Millican, *Borghetti:* Mike Kilian, *Hunter:* Doodles Weaver, *Dr. Ralph Wayne:* Lester Matthews, *Dr. Vranken:* Ludwig Donath, *Dr. Wei:* Richard Loo, *Dr. Holmes:* Davison Clark, *Captain Carruthers:* Richard Nugent, *Lieutenant Bainbridge:* Morton Lowry, *Captain Balen:* George Macready, *Captain Ryk:* Victor Varconi, *Admiral Hart:* Edward Fielding, *Captain in Charge of Evacuation:* Harvey Stephens, *Rear Admiral (Australia):* Minor Watson, *Little English Boy:* William Severn, *Mother of Little English Boy:* Edith Barrett, *Mrs. Wayne:* Catherine Craig, *Javanese Temple Guide:* Frank Puglia, *Missionary:* Irving Bacon, *Missionary's Wife:* Ottola Nesmith, *Admiral Hart's Aide:* Hugh Beaumont, *Lieutenant Smith:* George Lynn, *Fashta:* Linda Brent, *Praying Woman:* Ann Doran, *Anne, Dutch Nurse:* Julia Faye, *Girl:* Yvonne De Carlo.

THE STORY OF G. I. JOE (1945) UA. Producer, Lester Cowan. Associate Producer, David Hall. Director, William A. Wellman. Author, Ernie Pyle. Screenplay, Leopold Atlas, Guy Endore, Philip Stevenson. Musical Score, Ann Ronell, Louise Applebaum. Art Director, James Sullivan. Musical Director, Louis Forbes. Cameraman, Russell Metty. Editor, Otho Lovering. Musical numbers: "Linda" by Jack Lawrence and Ann Ronell; "I'm Coming Back" and "Infantry March" by Ann Ronell. 109 minutes

Ernie Pyle: Burgess Meredith, *Lieutenant Walker:* Robert Mitchum, *Sergeant Warnicki:* Freddie Steele, *Private Dondaro:* Wally Cassell, *Private Spencer:* Jimmy Lloyd, *Private Murphy:* Jack Reilly, *Private Mew:* Bill Murphy, *Cookie:* William Self, *Sergeant at Showers:* Dick Rich, *Whitey:* Billy Benedict, *Themselves:* Combat veterans of the Campaigns of Africa, Sicily, Italy.

The Story of G.I. Joe with Robert Mitchum and Burgess Meredith.

The Story of Louis Pasteur with Donald Woods and Paul Muni.

THE STORY OF LOUIS PASTEUR (1935) WB. Directed by William Dieterle. Story, Sheridan Gibney and Pierre Collins. Screenplay, Sheridan Gibney and Pierre Collins. Photography, Tony Gaudio. Editor, Ralph Dawson. 85 minutes.

Pasteur: Paul Muni, *Madame Pasteur:* Josephine Hutchinson, *Annette Pasteur:* Anita Louise, *Jean Martel:* Donald Woods, *Dr. Charbonnet:* Fritz Leiber, Sr., *Roux:* Henry O'Neill, *Dr. Rosignol:* Porter Hall, *Dr. Radisse:* Ray Brown, *Dr. Zaranoff:* Akim Tamiroff, *Napoleon III:* Walter Kingsford, *Empress Eugenie:* Iphigenie Castiglioni, *Boncourt:* Herbert Heywood, *Dr. Pheiffer:* Frank Reicher, *Dr. Lister:* Halliwell Hobbes, *Phillip Meister:* Dickie Moore, *Mrs. Meister:* Ruth Robinson, *President Thiers:* Herbert Corthell, *President Carnot:* Frank Mayo, *Doctor:* William Burress, *Magistrate:* Robert Strange, *A Lady:* Mabel Colcord, *Courier:* Niles Welch, *Coachman:* Leonard Mudie, *Midwife:* Brenda Fowler, *Lord Chamberlain:* Eric Mayne, *Finance Minister:* Alphonze Ethier, *Chairman:* Edward Van Sloan, *Assistant:* George Andre Beranger, *British Reporter:* Montague Shaw, *Farmer:* Otto Hoffman, *Woman:* Tempe Pigott, *Burly Farmer:* Richard

Alexander, *Cecile:* Lottie Williams, *Fat Doctor:* Baron Hesse, *Alsatian:* Wheaton Chambers, *Russian Ambassador:* Leonid Snegoff, *Government Inspector:* Fred Walton, *Reporters:* Wilfred Lucas, Gordon (Bill) Elliott, Jack Santoro, Ferdinand Schumann-Heink.

Strangers on a Train with Farley Granger and Robert Walker.

STRANGERS ON A TRAIN (1951) WB. Produced and directed by Alfred Hitchcock. Based on the novel by Patricia Highsmith. Screenplay, Raymond Chandler and Czenzi Ormonde. Adaptation, Whitfield Cook. Art Director, Ted Haworth. Musical Director, Ray Heindorf. Photography, Robert Burks. Editor, William H. Ziegler. 101 minutes. Remade as *Once You Kiss a Stranger* (1969)

Guy Haines: Farley Granger, *Anne Morton:* Ruth Roman, *Bruno Antony:* Robert Walker, *Senator Morton:* Leo G. Carroll, *Barbara Morton:* Patricia Hitchcock, *Miriam Joyce Haines:* Laura Elliott, *Mrs. Antony:* Marion Lorne, *Mr. Antony:* Jonathan Hale, *Captain Turley:* Howard St. John, *Professor Collins:* John Brown, *Mrs. Cunnigham:* Norma Varden, *Det. Leslie Hennessy:* Robert Gist, *Det. Hammond:* John Doucette, *Tennis Player, Fred Reynolds:* Jack Cushingham, *Bill, Cabby:* Dick Wessel, *Miller, Owner of Music Store:* Ed Clark, *"Ring-the-Gong" Concessionaire:* Al Hill, *Minister:* Dick Ryan, *Judge Donahue:* Charles Meredith, *Man Asking for a Light:* Sam Flint, *Antony's Butler:* Leonard Carey, *Mrs. Joyce:* Edna Holland, *Miriam's Boy Friends:* Tommy Farrell, Rolland Morris, *Boy:* Louis Lettieri, *Boat Man:* Murray Alper, *Blind Man:* John Butler, *Lieutenant Campbell:* Eddie Hearn, *Secretary:* Mary Alan Hokanson, *M. Darville:* George Renavent, *Mme. Darville:* Odette Myrtil, *Dowager:* Moyna Andre, *Mrs. Anderson:* Laura Treadwell, *Mortons' Butler:* J. Louis Johnson, *Dowager:* Minna Phillips, *Soda Jerk:* Joe Warfield, *Seedy Man:* Ralph Moody, *Man under Merry-Go-Round:* Harry Hines, *Man Boarding Train with Bass Fiddle:* Alfred Hitchcock.

STRATEGIC AIR COMMAND (1955) Par. Producer, Samuel J. Briskin. Director, Anthony Mann. VistaVision, Technicolor. Screenplay, Valentine Davies, Beirne Lay, Jr. Art Directors, Hal Pereira, Earl Hedrick. Musical Director, Victor Young. Cinematographer, William Daniels. Special Photographic Effects, John P. Fulton. Aerial Photography, Thomas Tutwiler. Process Photography, Farciot Edouart. Editor, Eda Warren. 114 minutes

Lieutenant Colonel Robert "Dutch" Holland: James Stewart, *Sally Holland:* June Allyson, *General Ennis C. Hawkes:* Frank Lovejoy, *Lieutenant Colonel Rocky Samford:* Barry Sullivan, *Ike Knowland:* Alex Nicol, *General Espy:* Bruce Bennett, *Doyle:* Jay C. Flippen, *General Castle:* James Millican, *Rev. Thorne:* James Bell, *Mrs. Thorne:* Rosemary De Camp, *Aircraft Commander:* Richard Shannon, *Captain Symington:* John R. McKee, *Sergeant Bible:* Henry Morgan, *Major Patrol Commander:* Don Haggerty, *Radio Operator:* Glenn Denning, *Colonel:* Anthony Warde, *Airman:* Strother Martin, *Nurse:*

Helen Brown, *Forecaster:* Wm. Hudson, *Captain Brown:* David Vaile, *Captain Johnson:* Vernon Rich, *Duty Officer:* Harlan Warde, *Air Force Captain:* Robert House Peters, Jr.

Strategic Air Command with Barry Sullivan and James Stewart.

The Stratton Story with Frank Morgan, June Allyson and James Stewart.

THE STRATTON STORY (1949) MGM. Producer, Jack Cummings. Director, Sam Wood. Author, Douglas Morrow. Screenplay, Douglas Morrow, Guy Trosper. Musical Director, Adolph Deutsch. Art Directors, Cedric Gibbons, Paul Groesse. Photography, Harold Rosson. Editor, Ben Lewis. 106 minutes

Monty Stratton: James Stewart, *Ethel:* June Allyson, *Barney Wile:* Frank Morgan, *Ma Stratton:* Agnes Moorehead, *Gene Watson:* Bill Williams, *Ted Lyons:* Bruce Cowling, *Western All-Stars Pitcher:* Eugene Bearden, *Bill Dickey:* Himself, *Jimmy Dykes:* Himself, *Higgins:* Cliff Clark, *Dot:* Mary Lawrence, *Luke Appling:* Dean White, *Larnie:* Robert Gist, *White Sox Catcher:* Mervyn Shea, *Western Manager:* Pat Flaherty, *Giants Manager:* Captain F. G. Somers, *Conductor:* Mitchell Lewis, *Pitcher:* Michael Ross, *Mrs. Appling:* Florence Lake, *Mrs. Piet:* Anne Nagel, *Mrs. Shea:* Barbara Wooddell, *Headwaiter:* Alphonse Martel, *Doctor:* Holmes Herbert, *Waiter:* Lee Tung Foo, *Theater Usher:* Charles B. Smith, *Detroit Player:* Kenneth Tobey, *Western Pitcher:* Roy Partee.

THE STRAWBERRY BLONDE (1941) WB. Producers, Jack L. Warner, Hal B. Wallis. Associate Producer, William Cagney. Director, Raoul Walsh. From a play by James Hagan (*One Sunday Afternoon*). Screenplay, Julius J. and Philip G. Epstein. Cameraman, James Wong Howe. Editor, William Holmes. Remade as *One Sunday Afternoon* (WB, 1948). Earlier version: *One Sunday Afternoon* (Par., 1933). 97 minutes

Biff Grimes: James Cagney, *Amy Lind:* Olivia de Havilland, *Virginia Brush:* Rita Hayworth, *Old Man Grimes:* Alan Hale, *Nick Pappalas:* George Tobias, *Hugo Barnstead:* Jack Carson, *Mrs. Mulcahey:* Una O'Connor, *Harold:* George Reeves, *Harold's Girl Friend:* Lucile Fairbanks, *Big Joe:* Edward McNamara, *Toby:* Herbert Heywood, *Josephine:* Helen Lynd, *Bank President:* Roy Gordon, *Street Cleaner Foreman:* Tim Ryan, *Official:* Addison Richards, *Policeman:* Frank Mayo, *Bartender:* Jack Daley, *Girl:* Suzanne Carnahan (Susan Peters), *Boy:* Herbert Anderson, *Baxter:* Frank Orth, *Inspector:* James Flavin, *Sailor:* George Campeau, *Singer:* Abe Dinovitch, *Guiseppi:* George Humbert, *Secretary:* Creighton Hale, *Treadway:* Russell Hicks, *Warden:* Wade Boteler.

The Strawberry Blonde with Rita Hayworth, Jack Carson, Olivia de Havilland and James Cagney.

A Streetcar Named Desire with Vivien Leigh and Karl Malden.

A STREETCAR NAMED DESIRE (1951) WB. Producer, Charles K. Feldman. Director-Screenplay, Elia Kazan. Based on the play by Tennessee Williams. Adaptation, Oscar Saul. Musical Director, Ray Heindorf. Art Director, Richard Day. Photography, Harry Stradling. Editor, David Weisbart. 125 minutes

Blanche DuBois: Vivien Leigh, *Stanley Kowalski:* Marlon Brando, *Stella Kowalski:* Kim Hunter, *Mitch:* Karl Malden, *Steve:* Rudy Bond, *Eunice:* Peg Hillias, *Pablo:* Nick Dennis, *Young Collector:* Wright King, *Mexican Woman:* Edna Thomas, *Strange Woman:* Ann Dere, *Strange Man:* Richard Garrick, *Sailor:* Mickey Kuhn, *Street Vendor:*

Chester Jones, *Negro Woman:* Marietta Canty, *First Passerby:* Charles Wagenheim, *Second Passerby:* Maxie Thrower, *Policeman:* Lyle Latell, *Foreman:* Mel Archer.

Street Scene with Sylvia Sidney and William Collier, Jr.

STREET SCENE (1931) UA. Produced by Samuel Goldwyn. Directed by King Vidor. Based on the play by Elmer Rice. Adaptation, Elmer Rice. Assistant Director, Lucky (Bruce) Humberstone. Art Director, Richard Day. Photography, George Barnes. Editor, Hugh Bennett. Sound, Charles Noyes. A Feature Production. Film debuts of Beulah Bondi and Eleanor Wesselhoeft. The play ran over two years, winning Elmer Rice the 1928-29 Pulitzer Prize. Repeating their stage roles: Bondi, Montor, Landau, Manning, McHugh, Wesselhoeft, Humbert, Qualen, Kostant, Washburne. 80 minutes

Rose Maurrant: Sylvia Sidney, *Sam Kaplan:* William Collier, Jr., *Anna Maurrant:* Estelle Taylor, *Emma Jones:* Beulah Bondi, *Abe Kaplan:* Max Montor, *Frank Maurrant:* David Landau, *Vincent Jones:* Matt McHugh, *Steve Sankey:* Russell Hopton, *Mae Jones:* Greta Granstedt, *George Jones:* Tom H. Manning, *Olga Olsen:* Adele Watson, *Karl Olsen:* John M. Qualen, *Shirley Kaplan:* Anna Kostant, *Filippo Fiorentino:* George Humbert, *Dick McGann:* Allan Fox, *Greta Fiorentino:* Eleanor Wesselhoeft, *Alice Simpson:* Nora Cecil, *Harry Easter:* Louis Natheaux, *Willie Maurrant:* Lambert Rogers, *Mary Hildebrand:* Virginia Davis, *Laura Hildebrand:* Helen Lovett, *Charlie Hildebrand:* Kenneth Selling, *Dan Buchanan:* Conway Washburne, *Dr. John Wilson:* Howard Russell, *Officer Harry Murphy:* Richard Powell, *Marshall James Henry:* Walter James, *Fred Cullen:* Harry Wallace, *Bits:* Monti Carter, Jane Mercer, Margaret Robertson, Walter Miller.

Sudden Fear with Joan Crawford and Jack Palance.

SUDDEN FEAR (1952) RKO. Producer, Joseph Kaufman. Director, David Miller. Screenplay by Lenore Coffee and Robert Smith. Based

on a story by Edna Sherry. Music by Elmer Bernstein. Song by Jack Brooks and Elmer Bernstein: "Afraid." 110 minutes

Myra Hudson: Joan Crawford, *Lester Blaine:* Jack Palance, *Irene Neves:* Gloria Grahame, *Steve Kearney:* Bruce Bennett, *Ann Taylor:* Virginia Huston, *Junior Kearney:* Touch (Michael) Connors.

Suddenly, Last Summer with Montgomery Clift and Elizabeth Taylor.

SUDDENLY, LAST SUMMER (1959) Col. Producer, Sam Spiegel. Director, Joseph L. Mankiewicz. Screenplay by Gore Vidal and Tennessee Williams. Adapted from Tennessee Williams play of the same name. Music by Buxton Orr and Malcolm Arnold. Assistant Director, Bluey Hill. Art Director, William Kellner. Cinematographer, Jack Hildyard. Photographic Effects, Tom Howard. Editor, Thomas G. Stanford. A Horizon Limited Production in association with Academy Pictures and Camp Films. Filmed in Great Britain. 114 minutes

Catherine Holly: Elizabeth Taylor, *Mrs. Venable:* Katharine Hepburn, *Dr. Cukrowicz:* Montgomery Clift, *Dr. Hockstader:* Albert Dekker, *Mrs. Holly:* Mercedes McCambridge, *George Holly:* Gary Raymond, *Miss Foxhill:* Mavis Villiers, *Nurse Benson:* Patricia Marmont, *Sister Felicity:* Joan Young, *Lucy:* Maria Britneva, *Dr. Hockstader's Secretary:* Sheila Robbins, *Young Blonde Interne:* David Cameron.

Summer and Smoke with Geraldine Page and Laurence Harvey.

SUMMER AND SMOKE (1961) Par. Producer, Hal B. Wallis. Director, Peter Glenville. VistaVision, Technicolor. Screenplay, James Poe, Meade Roberts. Art Director, Walter Tyler. Music, Elmer Bernstein. Cinematographer, Charles Lang, Jr. Editor, Warren Low. From Tennessee Williams' play. 118 minutes

John Buchanan: Laurence Harvey, *Alma Winemiller:* Geraldine Page,

Rosa: Rita Moreno, *Mrs. Winemiller:* Una Merkel, *Dr. Buchanan:* John McIntire, *Papa Zacharias:* Thomas Gomez, *Nellie:* Pamela Tiffin, *Rev. Winemiller:* Malcolm Atterbury, *Mrs. Ewell:* Lee Patrick, *Roger:* Casey Adams, *Archie Kramer:* Earl Holliman, *Dr. Burke:* Harry Shannon, *Cynthia:* Pattee Chapman, *Thomas:* Jester Hairston, *Nico:* Pepe Hern, *Mrs. Anderson:* Elektra Rozanska, *Dr. Hodges:* Dick Ryan, *Mrs. Bassett:* Winnie Chandler, *Twyla:* Linda Knutson, *John:* Robert Slade, *Knife Thrower:* Rico Alaniz, *Mr. Gilliam:* John Frank, *Saleslady:* Marjorie Bennett, *Betty Lou:* Susan Roberts, *Pearl:* Pamela Duncan, *Dusty:* Margaret Jane Blye, *Dignitary-Bandleader:* Charles Watts, *Alma as a girl:* Cheryl Anderson, *Woman:* Almira Sessions.

Summer of '42 with Gary Grimes and Jennifer O'Neill.

SUMMER OF '42 (1971) WB. Produced by Richard A. Roth. Directed by Robert Mulligan. Technicolor. Written by Herman Raucher (later a novel). Photography, Robert Surtees. Production Designer, Albert Brenner. Editor, Folmar Blangsted. Sound, Tom Overton. Title Design, Anthony Goldschmidt. Associate Producer, Don Kranze. Music composed and conducted by Michel Legrand. Set Decorator, Marvin March. Assistant Directors: Don Kranze, Mel Efros, Irby Smith. Paul Henried and Bette Davis are seen in a clip from *Now, Voyager* (1942). Film debut of Katherine Allentuck, 16, Maureen Stapleton's daughter. Filmed on Northern California's Mendocino Coast. Rated R. 102 minutes. Sequel was *Class of '44* (1973), also with Grimes, Houser and Conant.

Dorothy: Jennifer O'Neill, *Hermie:* Gary Grimes, *Oscy:* Jerry Houser, *Benjie:* Oliver Conant, *Aggie:* Katherine Allentuck, *Miriam:* Christopher Norris, *Druggist:* Lou Frizzell, *Dorothy's Husband:* Walter Scott, *Hermie's Mother:* Voice of Maureen Stapleton, *Narrator (Older Hermie):* Robert Mulligan.

A Summer Place with Dorothy McGuire and Richard Egan.

A SUMMER PLACE (1959) WB. Producer and Director, Delmer Daves. Technicolor. Based on the novel by Sloan Wilson. Screenplay, Delmer Daves. Art Director, Leo K. Kuter. Music, Max Steiner. Orchestration, Murray Cutter. Cinematographer, Harry Stradling. Editor, Owen Marks. 130 minutes

Ken Jorgenson: Richard Egan, *Sylvia Hunter:* Dorothy McGuire, *Molly Jorgenson:* Sandra Dee, *Bart Hunter:* Arthur Kennedy, *John Hunter:* Troy Donahue, *Helen Jorgenson:* Constance Ford, *Mrs. Hamilton Hamble:* Beulah Bondi, *Claude Andrews:* Jack Richardson, *Todd Hasper:* Martin Eric, *Captain:* Peter Constanti, *Mr. Hamble:* Junius Matthews, *Mrs. Carter:* Gertrude Flynn, *Dr. Matthias:* Marshall Bradford, *Sheriff:* Phil Chambers, *Englehardt:* Robert Griffin, *Ken's Attorney:* Arthur Space, *Bart's Attorney:* George Taylor, *Anne Talbert:* Roberta Shore, *Mrs. Talbert:* Ann Doran, *Minister:* Dale J. Nicholson, *Doctor:* Lewis Martin, *Wife:* Helen Wallace, *Dean:* Everett Glass, *Mrs. Harrington:* Eleanor Audley, *Pawnbroker:* Richard Deacon, *Alvin Frost (Justice of the Peace):* Howard Hoffman, *Young Girls in Dormitory:* Nancy Matthews, Susan Odin, Cheryl Holdridge, Bonnie Franklin.

Summer Stock with Judy Garland, Gene Kelly and Gloria De Haven.

SUMMER STOCK (1950) MGM. Producer, Joe Pasternak. Director, Charles Walters. Color by Technicolor. Author, Sy Gomberg. Screenplay, George Wells, Sy Gomberg. Musical Director, Johnny Green. Art Directors, Cedric Gibbons, Jack Martin Smith. Photography, Robert Planck. Editor, Albert Akst. Songs by Mack Gordon and Harry Warren: "Friendly Star," "Mem'ry Island," "Dig-Dig-Dig for Your Dinner," "If You Feel Like Singing, Sing," "Happy Harvest," "Blue Jean Polka" and "You Wonderful You" (lyrics by Jack Brooks and Saul Chaplin). 109 minutes

Jane Falbury: Judy Garland, *Joe D. Ross:* Gene Kelly, *Orville Wingait:* Eddie Bracken, *Abigail Falbury:* Gloria De Haven, *Esme:* Marjorie Main, *Herb Blake:* Phil Silvers, *Jasper G. Wingait:* Ray Collins, *Artie:* Carleton Carpenter, *Sarah Higgins:* Nita Bieber, *Harrison I. Keath:* Hans Conreid, *Frank:* Paul E. Burns, *Members of Stock Company:* Carole Haney, Arthur Loew, Jr., Jimmy Thompson, *Zeb:* Erville Alderson, *Show Girls:* Bette Arlen, Bunny Waters, *Clerk:* Jack Gargan, *Constance Fliggerton:* Almira Sessions, *Amy Fliggerton:* Kathryn Sheldon, *Boys:* Michael Chapin, Teddy Infuhr, *Producers:* Cameron Grant, Jack Daley, Reginald Simpson, *Sheriff:* Eddie Dunn.

SUMMERTIME (1955) UA. Producer, Ilya Lopert. Director, David Lean. Screenplay by David Lean and H. E. Bates. Based on the play *The Time of the Cuckoo* by Arthur Laurents. Music by Sandro Cicognini. Assistant Directors, Adrian Pryce-Jones and Alberto Cardone. Filmed in Venice in Eastman Color. An Alexander Korda Production for Lopert Films. 99 minutes

Jane Hudson: Katharine Hepburn, *Renato Di Rossi:* Rossano Brazzi,

Signora Fiorini: Isa Miranda, *Eddie Yaeger:* Darren McGavin, *Phyl Yaeger:* Mari Aldon, *Mrs. McIlhenny:* Jane Rose, *Mr. McIlhenny:* MacDonald Parke, *Mauro:* Gaitano Audiero, *Englishman:* Andre Morell, *Vito Di Rossi:* Jeremy Spenser, *Giovanna:* Virginia Simeon.

The Sundowners with Dina Merrill and Deborah Kerr.

THE SUNDOWNERS (1960) WB. Producer-Director, Fred Zinnemann. Screenplay, Isobel Lennart. Based on a novel by Jon Cleary. Music, Dimitri Tiomkin. Assistant Directors, Peter Bolton, Roy Stevens. Costumes, Elizabeth Haffenden. In Technicolor. Art Direction, Michael Stringer. Cinematography, Jack Hildyard. Editor, Jack Harris. Filmed in Australia. 133 minutes

Ida Carmody: Deborah Kerr, *Paddy Carmody:* Robert Mitchum, *Venneker:* Peter Ustinov, *Mrs. Firth:* Glynis Johns, *Jean Halstead:* Dina Merrill, *Quinlan:* Chips Rafferty, *Sean:* Michael Anderson, Jr., *Liz:* Lola Brooks, *Herb Johnson:* Wylie Watson, *Bluey:* John Meillon, *Ocker:* Ronald Fraser, *Jack Patchogue:* Mervyn Johns, *Mrs. Bateman:* Molly Urquhart, *Halstead:* Ewen Solon.

Summertime with Katharine Hepburn, Isa Miranda, Mari Aldon and Darren McGavin.

The Sun Also Rises with Eddie Albert, Tyrone Power, Mel Ferrer and Errol Flynn.

THE SUN ALSO RISES (1957) 20th. Producer, Darryl F. Zanuck. Director, Henry King. CinemaScope, De Luxe Color. Based on the novel by Ernest Hemingway. Screenplay, Peter Viertel. Art Directors, Lyle R. Wheeler, Mark-Lee Kirk. Music, Hugo Friedhofer, conducted by Lionel Newman. Orchestration, Edward B. Powell. Cinematographer, Leo Tover. Editor, William Mace. Filmed in Mexico City. 129 minutes

Jake Barnes: Tyrone Power, *Lady Brett Ashley:* Ava Gardner, *Robert Cohn:* Mel Ferrer, *Mike Campbell:* Errol Flynn, *Bill Gorton:* Eddie Albert, *Count Mippipopolous:* Gregory Ratoff, *Georgette:* Juliette Greco, *Zizi:* Marcel Dalio, *Doctor:* Henry Daniell, *Harris:* Bob Cummingham, *The Girl:* Danik Patisson, *Pedro Romero:* Robert J. Evans, *Frances Cohn:* Rebecca Iturbi, *Mr. Braddock:* Eduardo Noreiga, *Mrs. Braddock:* Jacqueline Evans, *Montoya:* Carlos Muzquiz, *Manager of Romero:* Carlos David Ortigos, *English Girl:* Lilia Guizar, *American at Bullfight:* Lee Morgan.

Sunrise at Campobello with Ralph Bellamy.

SUNRISE AT CAMPOBELLO (1960) WB. Produced by Dore Schary. Associate Producer, Walter Reilly. Directed by Vincent J. Donehue. In Technicolor. Screenplay by Dore Schary, based on his play *Sunrise at Campobello*. Costumes, Marjorie Best. Music, Franz Waxman. Art Director, Edward Carrere. Assistant Director, Russell Saunders. Cinematography, Russell Harlan. Editor, George Boemler. 143 minutes

Franklin D. Roosevelt: Ralph Bellamy, *Eleanor Roosevelt:* Greer Garson, *Louis Howe:* Hume Cronyn, *Missy Le Hand:* Jean Hagen, *Sara Roosevelt:* Ann Shoemaker, *Al Smith:* Alan Bunce, *James Roosevelt:* Tim Considine, *Anna Roosevelt:* Zina Bethune, *Elliot Roosevelt:* Pat Close, *Franklin, Jr.:* Robin Warga, *Johnny Roosevelt:* Tommy Carty, *Mr. Brimmer:* Lyle Talbot, *Mr. Lassiter:* David White, *Daley:* Herb Anderson, *Dr. Bennett:* Frank Ferguson, *Captain Skinner:* Walter Sande, *Marie:* Janine Grandel, *Edward:* Otis Greene, *Charles:* Ivan Browning, *Senator Walsh:* Al McGranary, *Speaker:* Jerry Crews, *Mr. Owens:* William Haddock, *Mailman:* Floyd Curtis, *Joe:* Jack Henderson, *Miss Garroway:* Ruth March, *Barker:* Ed Prentiss, *Riley:* Francis DeSales, *Newsboy:* Craig Curtis, *Sloan:* Don Dillaway, *Campaign Workers:* Fern Barry, Mary Benoit, Jack Perrin.

Sunset Boulevard with Gloria Swanson and William Holden.

SUNSET BOULEVARD (1950) Par. Produced by Charles Brackett. Directed by Billy Wilder. Based on the story *A Can of Beans* by Charles Brackett and Billy Wilder. Screenplay, Charles Brackett, Billy Wilder and D. M. Marshman, Jr. Art Directors, Hans Dreier and John Meehan. Sets, Sam Comer and Ray Moyer. Music, Franz Waxman. Photography, John F. Seitz. Editors, Doane Harrison and Arthur Schmidt. Swanson is seen in a bit from 1929's *Queen Kelly* (largely unreleased); she also does a Sennett bathing beauty routine and a takeoff on Chaplin. Among the cut footage is the song, "Paramount-Don't-Want-Me Blues" by Ray Evans and Jay Livingston: and the framing story of the coroner. De Mille is seen on the set of *Samson and Delilah*. 110 minutes

Joe Gillis: William Holden, *Norma Desmond:* Gloria Swanson, *Max Von Mayerling:* Erich Von Stroheim, *Betty Schaefer:* Nancy Olson, *Sheldrake:* Fred Clark, *Artie Green:* Jack Webb, *Morino:* Lloyd Gough, *Themselves:* Cecil B. De Mille, Hedda Hopper, Buster Keaton, Anna Q. Nilsson, H. B. Warner, Ray Evans, Jay Livingston, Sidney Skolsky, *Undertaker:* Franklyn Farnum, *First Finance Man:* Larry Blake, *Second Finance Man:* Charles Dayton, *Assistant Coroner:* Eddie Dew, *Salesman:* Michael Branden (Archie Twitchell), *Sheldrake's Secretary:* Ruth Clifford, *Gordon Cole:* Bert Moorhouse, *Doctor/Courtier:* E. Mason Hopper, *Courtier:* Virginia Randolph, *First Assistant Director:* Stan Johnson, *Second Assistant Director:* William Sheehan, *Hisham:* Julia Faye, *Courtiers:* Gertrude Astor and Frank O'Connor, *Courtier:* Eva Novak, *Herself:* Berenice Mosk, *Hairdresser:* Gertie Messinger, *Electrician (Hog Eye):* John Skins Miller, *Jonesy (Old Policeman):* Robert E. O'Connor, *Connie:* Gerry Ganzer, *Boy:* Tommy Ivo, *Man:* Emmett Smith, *Woman:* Ottola Nesmith, *Captain of Police:* Howard Negley, *Captain of Homicide:* Ken Christy, *Police Sergeant:* Len Hendry.

THE SUNSHINE BOYS (1975) UA. An MGM Presentation of A Rastar Feature. Produced by Ray Stark. Directed by Herbert Ross. Screenplay by Neil Simon, based on his 1972 play. MetroColor. Lenses and Panaflex Camera by Panavision. Associate Producer, Roger M. Rothstein. Photography, David M. Walsh. Production Designer, Albert Brenner. Supervising Film Editor, Margaret Booth. Editor, John F. Burnett. Assistant Director, Jack Roe. 2nd Assistant Director, Gary Daigler. Make-up Artist, Dick Smith. Men's Costumer, Seth Banks. Sound, Jerry Jost and Harry W. Tetrick. Set Decorator, Marvin March. Music Supervisor, Harry V. Lojewski. Costumes, Pat Norris. Assistant to the Producer, Frank Bueno. Assistant to Ross, Nora Kaye. Title Design, Wayne Fitzgerald. Filmed in Culver City, New Jersey, and New York City. Rated PG. 111 minutes

Willy Clark: Walter Matthau, *Al Lewis:* George Burns, *Ben Clark:*

Richard Benjamin, *Miss McIntosh, Nurse in Sketch:* Lee Meredith, *Doris:* Carol Arthur, *Nurse Odessa:* Rosetta LeNoire, *Mechanic:* F. Murray Abraham, *Commercial Director:* Howard Hesseman, *TV Director Schaefer:* Jim Cranna, *TV Floor Manager:* Ron Rifkin, *Helen Clark:* Jennifer Lee, *Men Auditioning:* Fritz Feld, Jack Bernardi, *Stage Manager:* Garn Stephens, *Desk Clerk (The Spanish Kid):* Santos Morales, *Assistant at Audition:* Archie Hahn, *Patient:* Sid Gould, *Card Player:* Tom Spratley, *Woman in Hotel:* Rashel Novikoff, *Man on Street:* Sammy Smith, *Mr. Ferranti:* Dan Resin, *Doctor:* Milt Kogan, *Waiter:* Bob Goldstein, *TV Executive:* Walter Stocker, *Ben's Secretary:* Duchess Dale, *Announcer:* Bill Reddick, *Delivery Boy:* Eddie Villery, *Boy:* Gary K. Steven, *Themselves:* Steve Allen, Phyllis Diller.

The Sunshine Boys with Walter Matthau and George Burns.

Super Fly with Ron O'Neal.

276

SUPER FLY (1972) WB. Produced by Sig Shore. Director and photographer of still sequence, Gordon Parks, Jr. Screenplay by Phillip Fenty. Photography, James Signorelli. Editor, Bob Brady. Sound, Harry Lapham. Script Supervisor, Naima Fuller. Associate Producer, Irving Stimler. Music composed and arranged by Curtis Mayfield, including the songs "Super Fly" and "Freddie's Dead." Music Coordinator, Marvin Stuart. Costume Designer, Nate Adams. Make-up, James Farabee. Hairstyling, Walter Fountaine and W. Knight. Assistant Director, Kurt Baker. Filmed mainly in Harlem, New York, in Technicolor. Rated R. 97 minutes. Sequel was *Super Fly T.N.T.* (Par., 1973) with O'Neal and Frazier

Youngblood Priest: Ron O'Neal, *Eddie:* Carl Lee, *Georgia:* Sheila Frazier, *Scatter:* Julius W. Harris, *Fat Freddie:* Charles MacGregor, *Dealer:* Nate Adams, *Cynthia:* Polly Niles, *Mrs. Freddie:* Yvonne Delaine, *Robbery Victim:* Henry Shapiro, *Pimp:* K.C., *Junkie:* Jim Richardson, *Capt. Reardon:* Sig Shore, *The Curtis Mayfield Experience, Stuntman:* Harry Madsen.

Superman with Christopher Reeve.

SUPERMAN (1978) WB. An International Film Production Inc. Picture, made by Dovemead Ltd. An Alexander and Ilya Salkind Production. Produced by Pierre Spengler. Directed by Richard Donner. Executive Producer, Ilya Salkind. Associate Producer, Charles F. Greenlaw. Screenplay by Mario Puzo, David Newman, Leslie Newman and Robert Benton. Story, Puzo. Based on the comic strip created by Jerry Siegel and Joe Shuster. Creative Consultant, Tom Mankiewicz. Music, John Williams, played by the London Symphony Orchestra. Editor, Stuart Baird. Photography, Geoffrey Unsworth. Production Designer, John Barry. Additional Script Material, Norman Enfield. Creative Supervisor and Director of Special Effects, Colin Chilvers. Creative Supervisor of Optical Visual Effects, Roy Field. Creative Supervisor of Mattes and Composites, Les Bowie. Creative Director of Process Photography, Denys Coop. Model Effects directed and created by Derek Meddings. Zoptic Special Effects, Zoran Perisic. Production Executive, Geoffrey Helman. 2nd Unit Direction, David Tomblin, John Glen, John Barry, David Lane and Robert Lynn. Costumes designed by Yvonne Blake. Make-up Artists, Philip Rhodes, Basil Newall, Kay and Graham Freeborn, Nick Maley, Sylvia Croft, Connie Reeve, Louis Lane and Jamie Brown. Hairdressers, Pat McDermott, Joan White, Stella Rivers, Cathy Kevany, Darby Halpin and Iloe Elliott. Stunt Coordination, Alf Joint and Vic Armstrong. New York Stunt Coordination, Alex Stevens. Additional Stunts, Paul Weston, George Cooper, Wendy Leech, Bill Weston and Stuart Fell. Canada Stunt

Coordination, Dick Butler and Richard Hackman. Filmed in New York, Alberta and New Mexico and at Pinewood Studios and Shepperton Studio Centre, England. Song, "Can You Read My Mind" by John Williams and Leslie Bricusse, sung by Margot Kidder. Main Title Credits by Steve Frankfurt Communications and R. Greenberg Associates, designed by Denis Rich. Panavision, Technicolor, Dolby Stereo. Chemtone Sequences by TVC Laboratory Inc. Alyn and Neill were the original Superman and Lois (in *Superman*, a 1948 Columbia serial) and were to play Lois' parents in this. Rated PG. 142 minutes

Superman (Clark Kent): Christopher Reeve, *Jor-El:* Marlon Brando, *Lex Luthor:* Gene Hackman, *Lois Lane:* Margot Kidder, *Eve Teschmacher:* Valerie Perrine, *Otis:* Ned Beatty, *Perry White:* Jackie Cooper, *Jonathan Kent:* Glenn Ford, *Ma Kent:* Phyllis Thaxter, *1st Elder:* Trevor Howard, *2nd Elder:* Harry Andrews, *Non:* Jack O'Halloran, *Vond-Ah:* Maria Schell, *Gen. Zod:* Terence Stamp, *Lara:* Susannah York, *Young Clark:* Jeff East, *Baby Clark:* Aaron Smolinski, *Baby Kal-El:* Lee Quigley, *Jimmy Olsen:* Marc McClure, *Ursa:* Sarah Douglas, *Lana Lang:* Diane Sherry, *Coach:* Jeff Atcheson, *Perry's Secretary:* Jill Ingham, *Himself:* Rex Reed, *Mugger:* Weston Gavin, *Patrolman Mooney:* George Harris II, *Desk Sergeant:* Rex Everhardt, *Little Girl:* Jayne Tottman, *Major:* Larry Hagman, *Sgt. Hayley:* Paul Tuerpe, *State Senators:* Phil Brown, Bill Bailey, *Indian Chief:* Chief Tug Smith, *Warden:* Roy Stevens, *Couple on Train:* Kirk Alyn, Noel Neill, *Newspaper Customer:* Bob Dahdah.

Suspicion with Joan Fontaine, Cary Grant, Nigel Bruce and Heather Angel.

SUSPICION (1941) RKO. Director, Alfred Hitchcock. Screenplay, Samson Raphaelson, Joan Harrison, Alma Reville. Music, Franz Waxman. Art Director, Van Nest Polglase. Cameraman, Harry Stradling. Special Effects, Vernon L. Walker. Editor, William Hamilton. From the novel *Before the Fact* by Francis Iles. 99 minutes

Johnnie: Cary Grant, *Lina:* Joan Fontaine, *Gen. McLaidlaw:* Sir Cedric Hardwicke, *Beaky:* Nigel Bruce, *Mrs. McLaidlaw:* Dame May Whitty, *Mrs. Newsham:* Isabel Jeans, *Ethel (Maid):* Heather Angel, *Isobel Sedbusk:* Auriol Lee, *Reggie Wetherby:* Reginald Sheffield, *Capt. Melbeck:* Leo G. Carroll, *Winnie (Maid):* Maureen Roden-Ryan, *Mrs. Fitzpatrick:* Constance Worth, *Mrs. Barham:* Violet Shelton, *Jessie Barham:* Carol Curtis-Brown, *Alice Barham:* Faith Brook, *Phoebe (Maid):* Pax Walker, *Jenner (Butler):* Leonard Carey, *Photographer:* Clyde Cook, *Sir Gerald:* Kenneth Hunter, *Mrs. Wetherby:* Gertrude Hoffmann, *Miss Wetherby:* Dorothy Lloyd, *Miss Wetherby:* Elsie Weller, *Mr. Webster:* Aubrey Mather, *Mr. Bailey:* Rex Evans, *Antique Shop Proprietor:* Edward Fielding, *Postmistress:* Hilda Plowright, *Registrar:* Ben Webster, *Bertram Sedbusk:* Gavin Gordon, *Phyllis Swinghurst:* Nondas Metcalf, *Inspector Hodgson:* Lumsden Hare, *Benson:* Vernon Downing, *Mrs. Craddock:* Clara Reid, *Ticket Taker:* Billy Bevan.

Sweet Bird of Youth with Paul Newman and Geraldine Page.

SWEET BIRD OF YOUTH (1962) MGM. Producer, Pandro S. Berman. Associate Producer, Kathryn Hereford. Director, Richard Brooks. CinemaScope, MetroColor. Based on the play by Tennessee Williams. Screenplay, Richard Brooks. Art Directors, George W. Davis, Urie McCleary. Music conducted by Robert Armbruster. Music Supervisor, Harold Gelman. Cinematographer, Milton Krasner. Editor, Henry Berman. A Roxbury Production. 120 minutes

Chance Wayne: Paul Newman, *Alexandra Del Lago:* Geraldine Page, *Heavenly Finley:* Shirley Knight, *"Boss" Finley:* Ed Begley, *Thomas J. Finley, Jr.:* Rip Torn, *Aunt Nonnie:* Mildred Dunnock, *Miss Lucy:* Madeleine Sherwood, *Dr. George Scudder:* Phillip Abbott, *Scotty:* Corey Allen, *Bud:* Barry Cahill, *Dan Hatcher:* Dub Taylor, *Leroy:* James Douglas, *Ben Jackson:* Barry Atwater, *Mayor Henricks:* Charles Arnt, *Mrs. Maribelle Norris:* Dorothy Konrad, *Professor Burtus Haven Smith:* James Chandler, *Deputy:* Mike Steen, *Sheriff Clark:* Kelly Thordsen, *Benny Taubman:* William Forrest, *Charles:* Roy Glenn, *Jackie:* Eddy Samuels, *Fly:* Davis Roberts, *Director:* Robert Burton.

Sweethearts with Douglas McPhail and Jeanette MacDonald.

SWEETHEARTS (1938) MGM. Producer, Hunt Stromberg. Director, W. S. Van Dyke. Color by Technicolor. Authors, Fred De Gresac, Harry D. Smith, Robert B. Smith. Screenplay, Dorothy Parker, Alan Campbell. Music, Victor Herbert. Cameramen, Oliver March, Allen Davey. Editor, Robert J. Kern. Songs by Chet Forrest, Bob Wright and Victor Herbert: "Angelus," "Every Lover Must Meet His Fate," "The Game of Love," "Grandmother," "Iron, Iron, Iron," "Mademoiselle on Parade," "Pretty as a Picture," "Summer Serenade," "Sweetheart," "Waiting for the Bride" and "Wooden Shoes." 120 minutes

Gwen Arden: Jeanette MacDonald, *Ernest Lane:* Nelson Eddy, *Felix Lehman:* Frank Morgan, *Fred:* Ray Bolger, *Kay Jordan:* Florence Rice, *Leo Kronk:* Mischa Auer, *Hannah:* Fay Holden, *Gwen's Brother:* Terry Kilburn, *Una Wilson:* Betty Jaynes, *Harvey Horton:* Douglas McPhail, *Norman Trumpett:* Reginald Gardiner, *Oscar Engel:* Herman Bing, *Dink Rogers:* Allyn Joslyn, *Orlando Lane:* Raymond Walburn, *Mrs. Merrill:* Lucile Watson, *Samuel Silver:* Philip Loeb, *Aunt Amelia:* Kathleen Lockhart, *Augustus:* Gene Lockhart, *Sheridan Lane:* Berton Churchill, *Appleby:* Olin Howland, *Harry:* Gerald Hamer, *Boy:* Marvin Jones, *Girl:* Dorothy Gray, *Fire Inspector:* Emory Parnell, *Dowager:* Maude Turner Gordon, *Violinist:* Jac George, *Tommy (Fighter):* Charles Sullivan, *Telephone Operators:* Mira McKinney, Grace Hayle, Barbara Pepper, *Assistant Director:* Irving Bacon, *Dance Director:* Lester Dorr, *Pianist:* Dalies Frantz.

Swing High, Swing Low with Fred MacMurray, Carole Lombard and Anthony Quinn.

SWING HIGH, SWING LOW (1937) Par. Produced by Arthur Hornblow, Jr. Directed by Mitchell Leisen. Based on the play *Burlesque* by George Manker Watters and Arthur Hopkins. Screenplay, Virginia Van Upp and Oscar Hammerstein II. Art Directors, Hans Dreier and Ernst Fegte. Music Director, Boris Morros. Arrangements, Victor Young and Phil Boutelje. Photography, Ted Tetzlaff. Special Effects, Farciot Edouart. Editor, Eda Warren. Songs: "I Hear a Call to Arms" by Sam Coslow and Al Siegel; "Panamania" by Burton Lane and Ralph Freed; "If It Isn't Pain, Then It Isn't Love," by Ralph Rainger and Leo Robin. "Swing High, Swing Low" by Ralph Freed and Burton Lane, "Spring Is in the Air" by Ralph Freed and Charles Kisco. Other versions: *Dance of Life* (Paramount, 1929), *When My Baby Smiles at Me* (20th Century-Fox, 1948). 97 minutes

Maggie King: Carole Lombard, *Skid Johnson:* Fred MacMurray, *Harry:* Charles Butterworth, *Ella:* Jean Dixon, *Anita Alvarez:* Dorothy Lamour, *Harvey Dexter:* Harvey Stephens, *Murphy:* Cecil Cunningham, *Georgie:* Charlie Arnt, *Henri:* Franklin Pangborn, *The Don:* Anthony Quinn, *The Purser:* Bud Flannigan (Dennis O'Keefe), *Tony:* Charles Judels, *Chief of Police:* Harry Semels, *Interpreter:* Ricardo Mandia, *Judge:* Enrique DeRosas, *Sleepy Servant:* Chris-Pin Martin, *Panamanian at Cockfight:* Charles Stevens, *Musselwhite:* Ralph Remley, *Men in Nightclub:* Nick Lukats, Lee Bowman, *Negro Santa Claus:* Darby Jones, *Interpreter:* Eumenio Blanco, *Justice of Peace:* George W. Jimenez, *Manager:* George Sorel, *Italian:* Gino Corrado, *Army Surgeon:* Richard Kipling, *Customer:* Esther Howard, *Cook:* Spencer Chan, *Radio Technician:* Donald Kerr, *Army Lieutenant:* P. E. (Tiny) Newland, *Attendant:* William Wright.

SWING TIME (1936) RKO. Producer, Pandro S. Berman. Director, George Stevens. Author, Erwin Gelsey. Screenplay, Howard Lindsay, Allan Scott. Musical Director, Nathaniel Shilkret. Cameraman, David Abel. Editor, Henry Berman. Ensembles staged by Hermes Pan. Songs by Jerome Kern and Dorothy Fields: "The Way You Look

Tonight," "A Fine Romance," "The Waltz in Swing Time," "Never Gonna Dance," "Pick Yourself Up," "Bojangles of Harlem." 103 minutes

John (Lucky) Garnett: Fred Astaire, *Penelope (Penny) Carrol:* Ginger Rogers, *Pop (Ed):* Victor Moore, *Mabel Anderson:* Helen Broderick, *Gordon:* Eric Blore, *Margaret Watson:* Betty Furness, *Ricardo Romero:* Georges Metaxa, *Judge Watson:* Landers Stevens, *Dice Raymond:* John Harrington, *Al Simpson:* Pierre Watkin, *Schmidt:* Abe Reynolds, *Eric:* Gerald Hamer, *Policeman:* Edgar Dearing, *Stagehands:* Harry Bowen, Harry Bernard, *Dancers:* Donald Kerr, Ted O'Shea, Frank Edmunds, Bill Brand, *Red:* Frank Jenks, *Hotel Clerk:* Ralph Byrd, *Taxi Driver:* Charles Hall, *Roulette Dealer:* Jean Perry, *Muggsy:* Olin Francis, *Romero's Butler:* Floyd Shackelford, *Minister:* Ferdinand Munier, *Announcer:* Joey Ray, *Wedding Guest:* Jack Rice, *Dancer:* Jack Good.

Swing Time with Ginger Rogers and Fred Astaire.

Take Me Out to the Ball Game with Esther Williams, Gene Kelly, Jules Munshin, Frank Sinatra, Murray Alper (short player), Richard Lane and Tom Dugan.

TAKE ME OUT TO THE BALL GAME (1949) MGM. Producer, Arthur Freed. Director, Busby Berkeley. Color by Technicolor. Authors, Gene Kelly, Stanley Donen. Screenplay, Harry Tugend, George Wells. Art Directors, Cedric Gibbons, Daniel B. Cathcart. Musical Director,

Adolph Deutsch. Photography, George Folsey. Editor, Blanche Sewell. Songs by Betty Comden, Adolph Green and Roger Edens: "The Right Girl For Me," "It's Fate Baby It's Fate," "O'Brien to Ryan to Goldberg," "Strictly U.S.A." and "Yes Indeedy." 93 minutes

Dennis Ryan: Frank Sinatra, *K. C. Higgins:* Esther Williams, *Eddie O'Brien:* Gene Kelly, *Shirley Delwyn:* Betty Garrett, *Joe Lorgan:* Edward Arnold, *Nat Goldberg:* Jules Munshin, *Michael Gilhuly:* Richard Lane, *Slappy Burke:* Tom Dugan, *Zalinka:* Murray Alper, *Nick Donford:* Wilton Graff, *Two Henchmen:* Mack Gray, Charles Regan, *Steve:* Saul Gorss, *Karl:* Douglas Fowley, *Dr. Winston:* Eddie Parkes, *Cop in Park:* James Burke, *Specialty:* The Blackburn Twins, *Senator Catcher:* Gordon Jones, *Reporter:* Frank Scannell, *Burly Acrobat:* Henry Kulky, *Girl Dancer:* Dorothy Abbott, *Two Girls on Train:* Virginia Bates, Joy Lansing, *Kid:* Jackie Jackson, *Sam:* Si Jenks, *Room Clerk:* Jack Rice, *Teddy Roosevelt:* Ed Cassidy, *Umpire:* Dick Wessel, *Dancer:* Sally Forrest.

A Tale of Two Cities with Ronald Colman, Elizabeth Allan, Edna May Oliver, Fay Chaldecott and Claude Gillingwater.

A TALE OF TWO CITIES (1935) MGM. Produced by David O. Selznick. Directed by Jack Conway. Based on the novel by Charles Dickens. Screenplay, W. P. Lipscomb and S. N. Behrman. Music, Herbert Stothart. Revolutionary sequences by Val Lewton and Jacques Tourneur. Photography, Oliver T. Marsh. Editor, Conrad A. Nervig. Christmas carols sung by Father Finn's Paulist Choristers. Other versions: *A Tale of Two Cities* (Fox, 1917), *The Only Way* (United Artists, 1926), *A Tale of Two Cities* (British: Rank, 1958). 121 minutes

Sydney Carton: Ronald Colman, *Lucie Manette:* Elizabeth Allan, *Miss Pross:* Edna May Oliver, *Madame DeFarge:* Blanche Yurka, *Stryver:* Reginald Owen, *Marquis St. Evremonde:* Basil Rathbone, *Dr. Manette:* Henry B. Walthall, *Charles Darnay:* Donald Woods, *Barsad:* Walter Catlett, *Gaspard:* Fritz Leiber, Sr., *Gabelle:* H. B. Warner, *Ernest DeFarge:* Mitchell Lewis, *Jarvis Lorry:* Claude Gillingwater, *Jerry Cruncher:* Billy Bevan, *Seamstress:* Isabel Jewell, *La Vengeance:* Lucille LaVerne, *Woodcutter:* Tully Marshall, *Lucie the Daughter:* Fay Chaldecott, *Mrs. Cruncher:* Eily Malyon, *Judge in Old Bailey:* E. E. Clive, *Prosecuting Attorney in Old Bailey:* Lawrence Grant, *Morveau:* John Davidson, *Tellson, Jr.:* Tom Ricketts, *Jerry Cruncher, Jr.:* Donald Haines, *Prosecutor:* Ralf Harolde, *Aristocrat:* Boyd Irwin, Sr., *Cartwright:* Ed Piel, Sr., *Leader:* Edward Hearn, *Executioner:* Richard Alexander, *Headsman:* Cyril McLaglen, *Jailer:* Frank Mayo, *Jacques #116:* Barlowe Borland, *Aristocrat:* Nigel DeBrulier, *Jailer, Victor:* Walter Kingsford, *Dandy Who's Condemned:* Rolfe Sedan, *Tribunal Judge:* Robert Warwick, *Old Hag:* Dale Fuller, *Chief Registrar:* Montague Shaw, *English Priest:* Chappell Dossett, *Old Hag:* Tempe Pigott, *Joe, Coach Guard:* Forrester Harvey, *Innkeeper:* Jimmy Aubrey, *Border Guard:* Billy House.

THE TALK OF THE TOWN (1942) Col. Producer, George Stevens. Associate Producer, Fred Guiol. Director, George Stevens. Author,

Sidney Harmon. Screenplay, Irwin Shaw, Sidney Buchman. Art Director, Lionel Banks. Score, Frederick Hollander. Musical Director, M. W. Stoloff. Cameraman, Ted Tetzlaff. Editor, Otto Meyer. Adaptation, Dale Van Every. 118 minutes

Leopold Dilg: Cary Grant, *Nora Shelley:* Jean Arthur, *Michael Lightcap:* Ronald Colman, *Sam Yates:* Edgar Buchanan, *Regina Bush:* Glenda Farrell, *Andrew Holmes:* Charles Dingle, *Mrs. Shelley:* Emma Dunn, *Tilney:* Rex Ingram, *Jan Pulaski:* Leonid Kinskey, *Clyde Bracken:* Tom Tyler, *Chief of Police:* Don Beddoe, *Judge Grunstadt:* George Watts, *Senator James Boyd:* Clyde Fillmore, *District Attorney:* Frank M. Thomas, *Forrester:* Lloyd Bridges, *Second Moving Man:* Max Wagner, *First Cop:* Pat McVey, *First Moving Man:* Ralph Peters, *Henry:* Eddie Laughton, *Western Union Boy:* Billy Benedict, *Ball Player:* Harold "Stubby" Kruger, *Hound Keeper:* Lee "Lasses" White, *Sheriff:* William Gould, *Sergeant:* Edward Hearn, *Mrs. Pulaski:* Ferike Boros, *Jake:* Dewey Robinson, *Operator:* Mabel Todd, *Headwaiter:* Dan Seymour, *Waiter:* Gino Corrado, *Road Cop:* Frank Sully, *Sgt. at Arms:* Lee Prather, *Doorkeeper:* Clarence Muse, *Secretary:* Leslie Brooks, *Desk Sergeant:* Alan Bridge, *McGuire:* Joe Cunningham.

Talk of the Town with Cary Grant, George Watts, Ronald Colman and Tom Tyler.

Tarzan the Ape Man with Johnny Weissmuller and Maureen O'Sullivan.

TARZAN THE APE MAN (1932) MGM. Directed by W. S. Van Dyke. Based on the character created by Edgar Rice Burroughs. Scenario, Cyril Hume. Dialogue, Ivor Novello. Cameramen, Harold Rosson and Clyde DeVinna. Editors, Ben Lewis and Tom Held. The first sound Tarzan film. 99 minutes

Tarzan: Johnny Weissmuller, *Harry Holt:* Neil Hamilton, *Jane Parker:* Maureen O'Sullivan, *James Parker:* C. Aubrey Smith, *Mrs. Cutten:* Doris Lloyd, *Beamish:* Forrester Harvey, *Riano:* Ivory Williams.

Task Force with Stanley Ridges, Jane Wyatt and Gary Cooper.

TASK FORCE (1949) WB. Producer, Jerry Wald. Director-Author-Screenplay, Delmer Daves. Art Director, Leo K. Kuter. Music, Franz Waxman. Photography, Robert Burks, Wilfrid M. Cline. Editor, Alan Crosland, Jr. Last half in Technicolor. 116 minutes

Jonathon L. Scott: Gary Cooper, *Mary Morgan:* Jane Wyatt, *McKinney:* Wayne Morris, *Pete Richard:* Walter Brennan, *Barbara McKinney:* Julie London, *McClusky:* Bruce Bennett, *Reeves:* Jack Holt, *Bently:* Stanley Ridges, *Dixie Rankin:* John Ridgely, *Jack Southern:* Richard Rober, *Senator Vincent:* Art Baker, *Ames:* Moroni Olsen, *Timmy:* Harlan Warde, *Tom Cooper:* James Holden, *Winston:* Warren Douglas, *Jennings:* John Gallaudet, *Jerry Morgan:* Rory Mallinson, *Pilot:* Ray Montgomery, *Aide:* Charles Waldron, Jr., *Lt. Kelley:* Robert Rockwell, *Mr. Secretary:* William Gould, *Mrs. Secretary:* Sally Corner, *Capt. Williamson:* Kenneth Tobey, *Japanese Representative:* Tetsu Komai, *Japanese Naval Attaché:* Beal Wong, *Mrs. Ames:* Laura Treadwell, *Ames Attache:* Roscoe J. Behan, *Admiral:* Basil Ruysdael, *Commander Price:* Edwin Fowler, *Lt. Leenhouts:* William Hudson, *Ruth Rankin:* Mary Lawrence, *Supply Officer:* John McGuire, *Capt. Wren:* Charles Sherlock, *Officer:* Reed Howes, *Jones:* Mal Merrihue, *Lindsay:* Mickey McCardell, *Harrison:* Paul McWilliams, *Chairman:* Alex Gerry, *Presidential Representative:* Joe Forte.

Taxi Driver with Cybill Shepherd, Albert Brooks and Leonard Harris (in photo).

TAXI DRIVER (1976) Col. A Bill/Phillips Production. Produced by Michael and Julia Phillips. Directed by Martin Scorsese. Written by Paul

Schrader. Music by Bernard Herrmann. Photography, Michael Chapman. Creative Consultant, Sandra Weintraub. Visual Consultant, David Nichols. Special Make-up by Dick Smith. Supervising Editor, Marcia Lucas. Editors, Tom Rolf and Melvin Shapiro. Associate Producer, Phillip M. Goldfarb. Art Director, Charles Rosen. Assistant Director, Peter R. Scoppan. 2nd Assistant Directors, Ralph Singleton and William Eustace. Set Decorator, Herbert Mulligan. Special Effects, Tony Parmelee. Costume Designer, Ruth Morley. Wardrobe, Al Craine. Make-up, Irving Buchman. Hairdresser, Mona Orr. Recorder, Roger Pietschman. Special Photography, Steve Shapiro. Publicist, Howard Newman. Special Publicity, Marion Billings. Assistant to Producers, Keith Addis. Assistant to the Director, Amy Jones. Production Assistants, Eugene Iemola, Gary Springer and Chris Soldo. Film debut of comedian Albert Brooks and critic Leonard Harris. Filmed in New York City in Panavision and Color. Rated R. 112 minutes

Travis Bickle: Robert De Niro, *Betsy:* Cybill Shepherd, *Iris Steensman:* Jodie Foster, *Wizard:* Peter Boyle, *Sport (Matthew):* Harvey Keitel, *Tom:* Albert Brooks, *Charles Palantine:* Leonard Harris, *Passenger:* Martin Scorsese, *Concession Girl:* Diahnne Abbott, *Angry Black Man:* Frank Adu, *Melio:* Vic Argo, *Policeman at Rally:* Gino Ardito, *Iris' Friend:* Garth Avery, *Cabby in Bellmore:* Harry Cohn, *Hooker in Cab:* Copper Cunningham, *Soap Opera Woman:* Brenda Dickson, *Dispatcher:* Harry Fischler, *Stick-up Man:* Nat Grant, *Tall Secret Service Man:* Richard Higgs, *Soap Opera Man:* Beau Kayser, *Secret Service Photographer:* Vic Magnotta, *Mafioso:* Robert Maroff, *Charlie T:* Norman Matlock, *Tom's Assistant:* Bill Minkin, *Iris' Time Keeper:* Murray Moston, *Doughboy:* Harry Northup, *Street Drummer:* Gene Palma, *Campaign Worker:* Carey Poe, *Easy Andy, Gun Salesman:* Steven Prince, *The John:* Peter Savage, *Palantine Aide:* Robert Shields, *TV Interviewer:* Ralph Singleton, *Personnel Officer:* Joe Spinell, *Angry Hooker on Street:* Maria Turner, *Campaign Worker:* Robin Utt, *Girl at Columbus Circle:* Devi (Debbie) Morgan.

Tea and Sympathy with Deborah Kerr and John Kerr.

TEA AND SYMPATHY (1956) MGM. Producer, Pandro S. Berman. Director, Vincente Minnelli. CinemaScope, MetroColor. Based on the play by Robert Anderson. Screenplay, Robert Anderson. Art Directors, William A. Horning, Edward Carfagno. Music, Adolph Deutsch. Cinematographer, John Alton. Editor, Ferris Webster. 122 minutes

Laura Reynolds: Deborah Kerr, *Tom Robinson Lee:* John Kerr, *Bill Reynolds:* Leif Erickson, *Herb Lee:* Edward Andrews, *Al:* Darryl Hickman, *Ellie Martin:* Norma Crane, *Ollie:* Dean Jones, *Lilly Sears:* Jacqueline de Wit, *Ralph:* Tom Laughlin, *Steve:* Ralph Votrian, *Phil:* Steven Terrell, *Ted:* Kip King, *Henry:* Jimmy Hayes, *Roger:* Richard Tyler, *Vic:* Don Burnett, *Mary Williams:* Mary Alan Hokanson, *Dick:* Ron Kennedy, *Pete:* Peter Miller, *Pat:* Bob Alexander, *Earl:* Michael Monroe, *Umpire:* Byron Kane, *Alex:* Paul Bryar, *First Boy:* Harry Harvey, Jr., *Second Boy:* Bobby Ellis, *Burly Men:* Saul Gorss, Dale Van Sickel, *Headmaster at Bonfire:* Peter Leeds, *Ferdie:* Del Erickson.

The Teahouse of the August Moon with Glenn Ford, Shichizo Takeda and Marlon Brando.

THE TEAHOUSE OF THE AUGUST MOON (1956) MGM. Producer, Jack Cummings. Director, Daniel Mann. CinemaScope, MetroColor. Based on a book by Vern J. Sneider and the play by John Patrick. Screenplay, John Patrick. Art Directors, William A. Horning, Eddie Imazu. Musical Director, Saul Chaplin. Cinematographer, John Alton. Editor, Harold F. Kress. 123 minutes

Sakini: Marlon Brando, *Captain Fisby:* Glenn Ford, *Lotus Blossom:* Machiko Kyo, *Captain McLean:* Eddie Albert, *Colonel Purdy:* Paul Ford, *Mr. Seiko:* Jun Negami, *Miss Higa Jiga:* Nijiko Kiyokawa, *Little Girl:* Mitsuko Sawamura, *Sergeant Gregovich:* Henry (Harry) Morgan, *Ancient Man:* Shichizo Takeda, *Mr. Hokaida:* Kichizaemon Saramaru, *Mr. Omura:* Frank Tokunaga, *Mr. Oshira:* Raynum K. Tsukamoto, *Mr. Sumata:* Nishida, *Sumata's Father:* Dansho Miyazaki, *Old Woman on Jeep:* Miyoshi Jingu, *Daughter on Jeep:* Aya Oyama, *Judge:* Tsuruta Yozan, *Soldiers:* John Grayson, Roger McGee, Harry Harvey, Jr., Carl Fior.

The Ten Commandments with John Derek, Debra Paget, Olive Deering, Yvonne De Carlo and Charlton Heston.

THE TEN COMMANDMENTS (1956) Par. Producer, Cecil B. De Mille. Associate Producer, Henry Wilcoxon. Director, Cecil B. De Mille. VistaVision, Technicolor. Authors, Dorothy Clarke Wilson (from *Prince of Egypt*); Rev. J. H. Ingraham (from *Pillar of Fire*);

Rev. A. E. Southon (from *On Eagle's Wings*). Screenplay, Aeneas MacKenzie, Jesse L. Lasky, Jr., Jack Gariss, Fredric M. Frank. Art Directors, Hal Pereira, Walter Tyler, Albert Nozaki. Cinematographer, Loyal Griggs. Additional Photography, J. Peverell Marley, John Warren, Wallace Kelley. Editor, Anna Bauchens. Remake of De Mille's 1923 film. 219 minutes

Moses: Charlton Heston, *Rameses:* Yul Brynner, *Nefretiri:* Anne Baxter, *Dathan:* Edward G. Robinson, *Sephora:* Yvonne De Carlo, *Lilia:* Debra Paget, *Joshua:* John Derek, *Sethi:* Sir Cedric Hardwicke, *Bithiah:* Nina Foch, *Yochabel:* Martha Scott, *Memnet:* Judith Anderson, *Baka:* Vincent Price, *Aaron:* John Carradine, *Jethro:* Eduard Franz, *Miriam:* Olive Deering, *Mered:* Donald Curtis, *Jannes:* Douglass Dumbrille, *Hur Ben Caleb:* Lawrence Dobkin, *Abiram:* Frank DeKova, *Amminadab:* H. B. Warner, *Pentaur:* Henry Wilcoxon, *Elisheba:* Julia Faye, *Jethro's Daughters:* Lisa Mitchell, Noelle Williams, Joanna Merlin, Pat Richard, Joyce Vanderveen, Diane Hall, *Rameses' Charioteer:* Abbas El Boughdadly, *The Infant Moses:* Fraser Heston, *The Blind One:* John Miljan, *Gershom:* Tommy Duran, *Simon:* Francis J. McDonald, *Rameses' Son:* Eugene Mazzola, *Rameses I:* Ian Keith, *Korah:* Ramsay Hill, *Eleazar:* Paul De Rolf, *Korah's Wife:* Joan Woodbury, *King of Ethiopia:* Woodrow Strode, *Princess Tharbis:* Esther Brown, *Amalekite Herder:* Touch (Michael) Connors, *Sardinian Captain:* Clint Walker, *Old Hebrew:* Luis Alberni, *Taskmaster:* Michael Ansara, *Slave:* Frankie Darro, *Herald:* Walter Woolf King, *Spearman Hebrew:* Robert Vaughn.

Ten North Frederick with Geraldine Fitzgerald and Gary Cooper.

TEN NORTH FREDERICK (1958) 20th. Producer, Charles Brackett. Director, Philip Dunne. CinemaScope. From the novel by John O'Hara. Screenplay, Philip Dunne. Art Directors, Lyle R. Wheeler, Addison Hehr. Music, Leigh Harline. Music conducted by Lionel Newman. Orchestration, Edward B. Powell. Cinematographer, Joe MacDonald. Special Photographic Effects, L. B. Abbott. Editor, David Bretherton. 102 minutes

Joe Chapin: Gary Cooper, *Ann Chapin:* Diane Varsi, *Kate Drummond:* Suzy Parker, *Edith Chapin:* Geraldine Fitzgerald, *Slattery:* Tom Tully, *Joby:* Ray Stricklyn, *Lloyd Williams:* Philip Ober, *Paul Donaldson:* John Emery, *Charley Bongiorno:* Stuart Whitman, *Peg Slattery:* Linda Watkins, *Stella:* Barbara Nichols, *Dr. English:* Joe McGuinn, *Arthur McHenry:* Jess Kirkpatrick, *Harry Jackson:* Nolan Leary, *Marian Jackson:* Helen Wallace, *Waitress:* Beverly Jo Morrow, *Bill:* Buck Class, *Salesgirl:* Rachel Stephens, *Farmer:* Bob Adler, *Peter:* Linc Foster, *Robert Hooker:* John Harding, *Ted Wallace:* Dudley Manlove, *General Coates:* Mack Williams, *Board Chairman:* Vernon Rich, *Nurse:* Mary Carroll, *Waiter:* George Davis, *Taxi Driver:* Joey Faye, *Hoffman:* Fred Essler, *Wife:* Irene Seidner, *Hope:* Melinda Byron, *Sax Player:* Sean Meaney.

TEST PILOT (1938) MGM. Producer, Louis D. Lighton. Director, Victor Fleming. Author, Frank Wead. Screenplay, Vincent Lawrence, Waldemar Young. Cameraman, Ray June. Editor, Tom Held. 118 minutes.

Jim Lane: Clark Gable, *Ann Barton:* Myrna Loy, *Gunner Sloane:* Spencer Tracy, *Howard B. Drake:* Lionel Barrymore, *General Ross:* Samuel S. Hinds, *Frank Barton:* Arthur Aylesworth, *Mrs. Barton:* Claudia Coleman, *Mrs. Benson:* Gloria Holden, *Benson:* Louis Jean Heydt, *Joe:* Ted Pearson, *Landlady:* Marjorie Main, *Grant:* Gregory Gaye, *Sarah:* Virginia Grey, *Mabel:* Priscilla Lawson, *Mr. Brown:* Dudley Clements, *Fat Man:* Henry Roquemore, *Designer:* Byron Foulger, *Motor Expert:* Frank Jaquet, *Advertising Man:* Roger Converse, *Photographer:* Phillip Terry, *Attendant:* Robert Fiske, *Pilot:* Garry Owen, *Fat Woman:* Dorothy Vaughan, *Little Man:* Billy Engle, *Movie Leading Man:* Brent Sargent, *Movie Leading Woman:* Mary Howard, *Interne:* Gladden James, *Singing Pilot in Cafe:* Douglas McPhail, *Pilots in Cafe:* Forbes Murray, Richard Tucker, Don Douglas, James Flavin, Hooper Atchley, Dick Winslow, Ray Walker and Frank Sully, *Saleslady:* Fay Holden, *Bartender:* Tom O'Grady, *Boss Loader:* Syd Saylor.

Test Pilot with Clark Gable, Myrna Loy and Spencer Tracy.

Thank Your Lucky Stars with Dennis Morgan, Joan Leslie and Eddie Cantor.

THANK YOUR LUCKY STARS (1943) WB. Producer, Mark Hellinger. Director, David Butler. Original Story, Everett Freeman, Arthur Schwartz. Screenplay, Norman Panama, Melvin Frank, James V. Kern. Dance Director, LeRoy Prinz. Art Directors, Anton Grot, Leo E. Kuter. Musical Director, Leo F. Forbstein. Cameraman, Arthur Edeson. Special Effects, H. F. Koenekamp. Editor, Irene Morra. Songs by Frank Loesser and Arthur Schwartz: "They're Either Too Young or Too Old," "How Sweet You Are," "The Dreamer," "I'm Riding for a Fall," "Good Night Good Neighbor," "Love Isn't Born It's Made", "Ice Cold Katie," "Thank Your Lucky Stars," "We're Staying Home Tonight," "I'm Going North," "That's What You Jolly Well Get." 127 minutes.

Assistant Photographer: Hank Mann, *Fan:* Mary Treen, *Bill:* James

Burke, *Dr. Kirby:* Paul Harvey, *Patient:* Bert Gordon, *Drunk: (Bette Davis Number):* Jack Norton, *Jitterbug: (Davis Number):* Conrad Wiedell, *Fireman:* Matt McHugh, *Sailor:* Frank Faylen, *Charlie, the Indian:* Noble Johnson, *Olaf:* Mike Mazurki, *Joe Sampson:* Eddie Cantor, *Pat Dixon:* Joan Leslie, *Tommy Randolph:* Dennis Morgan, *Dinah Shore:* Herself, *Dr. Schlenna:* S. Z. Sakall, *Farnsworth:* Edward Everett Horton, *Nurse Hamilton:* Ruth Donnelly, *Girl with Book:* Joyce Reynolds, *Barney Jackson:* Richard Lane, *Don Wilson:* Himself, *Angelo:* Henry Armetta, *Specialities:* Humphrey Bogart, Jack Carson, Bette Davis, Olivia de Havilland, Errol Flynn, John Garfield, Alan Hale, Ida Lupino, Ann Sheridan, George Tobias, and Spike Jones and His City Slickers, *Themselves:* David Butler, Mark Hellinger, *Finchley, Butler:* William Haade, *Pete:* Don Barclay, *Boy:* Stanley Clements, *Ice Cold Katie Number: Gossip,* Hattie McDaniel, *Soldier,* Willie Best, *Ice Cold Katie,* Rita Christiani, *The Justice,* Jess Lee Brooks, *The Trio:* Ford, Harris and Jones, *Good Night, Good Neighbor Number Dancer,* Alexis Smith, *Dancer:* Igor DeNavrotsky, *Dancer:* Arnold Kent, *Cab Driver:* Brandon Hurst, *Miss Latin America:* Lynne Baggett, *Miss Spain:* Mary Landa.

That Hamilton Woman with Laurence Olivier and Vivien Leigh.

THAT HAMILTON WOMAN (1941) UA. Produced and directed by Alexander Korda. Original Screenplay, Walter Reisch and R. C. Sherriff. Music, Miklos Rozsa. Photography, Rudolph Mate. Editor, William Hornbeck. Produced in Hollywood. British title: *Lady Hamilton.* 128 minutes. Previous version: *Nelson* (British, 1927). Remade as *The Nelson Affair* (Univ., 1973)

Emma Hart, Lady Hamilton: Vivien Leigh, *Lord Horatio Nelson:* Laurence Olivier, *Sir William Hamilton:* Alan Mowbray, *Mrs. Cadogan-Lyon:* Sara Allgood, *Lady Frances Nelson:* Gladys Cooper, *Captain Hardy:* Henry Wilcoxon, *Mary Smith, a Street Girl:* Heather Angel, *Reverend Nelson:* Halliwell Hobbes, *Lord Spencer:* Gilbert Emery, *Lord Keith:* Miles Mander, *Josiah:* Ronald Sinclair, *King of Naples:* Luis Alberni, *Queen of Naples:* Norma Drury, *French Ambassador:* George Renavent, *Hotel Manager:* Leonard Carey, *Orderly:* Alec Craig, *Gendarme:* George Davis.

THAT'S ENTERTAINMENT (1974) UA release of an MGM presentation. Produced, Directed and Written by Jack Haley, Jr., in MetroColor. Executive Producer, Daniel Melnick. Additional music adapted by Henry Mancini. Editors, Bud Friedgen and David E. Blewitt. Assistant Directors, Richard Bremerkamp, David Silver and Claude Binyon, Jr. Rated G. 132 minutes. Sequel was *That's Entertainment, Part 2* (1976), with Astaire and Kelly

Onscreen Narrators: Fred Astaire, Bing Crosby, Gene Kelly, Peter Lawford, Liza Minnelli, Donald O'Connor, Debbie Reynolds, Mickey Rooney, Frank Sinatra, James Stewart and Elizabeth Taylor; filmed on the MGM lot.

Numbers (in color and black and white): "Singin' in the Rain," sung by Cliff Edwards in *The Hollywood Revue of 1929;* "Singin' in the Rain," Jimmy Durante, *Speak Easily* (1932); "Singin' in the Rain," Judy Garland, *Little Nellie Kelly* (1940); "Singin' in the Rain," Kelly, O'Connor and Reynolds, *Singin' in the Rain* (1952); "The Broadway Melody," Charles King, *The Broadway Melody* (1929); "Rosalie," Eleanor Powell, *Rosalie* (1937); "Indian Love Call," Jeanette MacDonald and Nelson Eddy, *Rose Marie* (1936); "A Pretty Girl Is Like a Melody," Dennis Morgan (dubbed by Allan Jones), Virginia Bruce and chorus, *The Great Ziegfeld* (1936); "Begin the Beguine," Astaire and E. Powell, *Broadway Melody of 1940;* "The Song's Gotta Come from the Heart," Sinatra and Durante, *It Happened in Brooklyn* (1947); "Melody of Spring," Taylor, *Cynthia* (1947); "Honeysuckle Rose," Lena Horne, *Thousands Cheer* (1943); "Take Me out to the Ball Game," Sinatra and Kelly, *Take Me out to the Ball Game* (1949); "Thou Swell," June Allyson and the Blackburn Twins, *Words and Music* (1948); "Varsity Drag" and "The French Lesson," Allyson and Lawford, *Good News* (1947); "Aba Daba Honeymoon," Reynolds and Carleton Carpenter, *Two Weeks with Love* (1950); "It's a Most Unusual Day," Taylor and Jane Powell, *A Date with Judy* (1948); "On the Atchison, Topeka and the Santa Fe," Garland and Ray Bolger, *The Harvey Girls* (1946); "It Must Be You," Robert Montgomery to Lottice Howell, *Free and Easy* (1930); "I've Got a Feelin' for You," Joan Crawford, *The Hollywood Revue of 1929;* "Reckless," Jean Harlow, *Reckless* (1935); "Did I Remember," Cary Grant to Harlow, *Suzy* (1936); "Easy to Love," Stewart and E. Powell, *Born to Dance* (1936); "Puttin' on the Ritz," Clark Gable and "Les Blondes," Lorraine Kreuger, Bernadene Hayes, Joan Marsh, Paula Stone, Virginia Dale and Virginia Grey, *Idiot's Delight* (1939); Rooney dances in *Broadway to Hollywood* (1933); "You Made Me Love You (Dear Mr. Gable)," Garland, *Broadway Melody of 1938* (1937); "Babes in Arms," Douglas McPhail, *Babes in Arms* (1939); "Hoedown," Garland and Rooney, *Babes on Broadway* (1941); "Do the La Conga," Garland and Rooney, *Strike up the Band* (1940); "Waitin' for the Robert E. Lee" and "Babes on Broadway," Garland and Rooney, *Babes on Broadway;* "Strike up the Band," Garland and Rooney, *Strike up the Band;* "The Babbitt and the Bromide," Astaire and Kelly, *Ziegfeld Follies* (1946); "They Can't Take That Away from Me," Astaire and Ginger Rogers, *The Barkleys of Broadway* (1949); "Rhythm of the Day," Astaire and Crawford, *Dancing Lady* (1933); "I Guess I'll Have to Change My Plans," Astaire and Jack Buchanan, *The Band Wagon* (1953); "Sunday Jumps," Astaire and hat rack, *Royal Wedding* (1951); "Shoes with Wings On," Astaire, *The Barkleys of Broadway;* "You're All the World to Me," Astaire on wall and ceiling, *Royal Wedding;* "Dancing in the Dark," Astaire and Cyd Charisse, *The Band Wagon;* "Pagan Love Song," Esther Williams, *Pagan Love Song* (1950); Williams production number, *Bathing Beauty* (1944); Williams production number, *Million Dollar Mermaid* (1952); "I Wanna Be Loved by You," Reynolds and Carpenter, *Three Little Words* (1950); "I've Gotta Hear That Beat," Ann Miller, *Small Town Girl* (1953); "Be My Love," Mario Lanza and Kathryn Grayson, *The Toast of New Orleans* (1950); "Make 'Em Laugh," O'Connor, *Singin' in the Rain;* "Cotton Blossom" by the cast, "Make Believe" by Grayson and Howard Keel and "Ol' Man River" by William Warfield, from *Show Boat* (1951); "By Myself," Astaire, *The Band Wagon;* "Be a Clown," Kelly and the Nicholas Brothers, *The Pirate* (1948); Kelly dance from *Living in a Big Way* (1947); "Mack the Black," Kelly, *The Pirate;* "New York, New York," Kelly, Sinatra and Jules Munshin, *On the Town* (1949); "The Worry Song," Kelly and Jerry Mouse, *Anchors Aweigh* (1945); "Singin' in the Rain" and "The Broadway Melody," Kelly, *Singin' in the Rain;* "In the Good Old Summertime," Garland, Van Johnson and Minnelli, *In the Good Old Summertime* (1949); "La Cucaracha," the Gumm Sisters (with Garland), *La Fiesta de Santa Barbara* (1935 short); "Opera vs. Jazz," Garland and Deanna Durbin, *Every Sunday* (1936 short); Garland and Buddy Ebsen dance in *Broadway Melody of 1938;* "We're Off to See the Wizard," "If I Only Had a Heart" and "Over the Rainbow," Garland, with Bolger, Jack Haley and Bert Lahr, in *The Wizard of Oz* (1939); "The Trolley Song," Garland, "Under the Bamboo Tree," Garland and Margaret O'Brien and "The Boy Next Door," Garland, from *Meet Me in St. Louis* (1944); "Get Happy," Garland, *Summer Stock* (1950); "Going Hollywood," Crosby, *Going Hollywood* (1933); "Well, Did You Evah?" Crosby and Sinatra, *High Society* (1956); "Hallelujah," Kay Armen, Reynolds, J. Powell, Miller, Tony Martin, Russ Tamblyn and Vic Damone, *Hit the Deck* (1955); "Barn-Raising Ballet," cast from *Seven Brides for Seven Brothers* (1954); "Gigi," Louis Jourdan, and "Thank Heaven fro Little Girls," Maurice Chevalier, from *Gigi* (1958); and "An American in Paris," ballet by Kelly and Leslie Caron, *An American in Paris* (1951).

That's Entertainment with Elizabeth Taylor.

That Touch of Mink with Cary Grant and Billy M. Greene.

THAT TOUCH OF MINK (1962) Univ. Executive Producer, Robert Arthur. Producers, Stanley Shapiro, Martin Melcher. Director, Delbert Mann. Eastman Color, Panavision. Screenplay, Stanley Shapiro, Nate Monaster. Art Directors, Alexander Golitzen, Robert Clatworthy. Cinematographer, Russell Metty. Editor, Ted Kent. A Granley-Arwin-Nob Hill Production. 99 minutes

Philip Shayne: Cary Grant, *Cathy Timberlake:* Doris Day, *Roger:* Gig Young, *Connie:* Audrey Meadows, *Dr. Gruber:* Alan Hewitt, *Beasley:* John Astin, *Young Man:* Richard Sargent, *Short Man:* Joey Faye, *Mr. Smith:* John Fiedler, *Hodges:* Willard Sage, *Dr. Richardson:* Jack Livesey, *Collins (Chauffeur):* John McKee, *Showgirl:* Laurie Mitchell, *Millie:* June Ericson, *Mrs. Golden:* Laiola Wendorff,

Roger Maris: Roger Maris, *Mickey Mantle:* Mickey Mantle, *Yogi Berra:* Yogi Berra, *Umpire:* Art Passarella, *Stewardess:* Dorothy Abbott, *Taxi Driver:* Ralph Manza, *Leonard:* William Lanteau, *Mrs. Haskell:* Kathryn Givney, *Miriam:* Alice Backes, *Mr. Miller:* Richard Deacon, *Mr. Golden:* Fred Essler, *Mrs. Farnum:* Helen Brown, *Mr. Hackett:* Nelson Olmsted, *Truck Driver:* Clegg Hoyt, *Lisa:* Isabella Albonico, *Al:* Billy Greene, *Miss Farrell:* Melora Conway, *Fashion Consultant:* Yvonne Peattie, *Williams:* Russ Bender, *Mario:* Jon Silo, *Doorman:* Tyler McVey.

There's No Business Like Show Business with Ethel Merman, Johnny Ray, Dan Dailey, Donald O'Connor and Mitzi Gaynor.

THERE'S NO BUSINESS LIKE SHOW BUSINESS (1954) 20th. Producer, Sol C. Siegel. Director, Walter Lang. CinemaScope, De Luxe Color. Author, Lamar Trotti. Screenplay, Phoebe and Henry Ephron. Musical Supervisors, Alfred Newman, Lionel Newman. Art Directors, Lyle Wheeler, John De Cuir. Cameraman, Leon Shamroy. Editor, Robert Simpson. Songs by Irving Berlin: "You'd Be Surprised," "After You Get What You Want, You Don't Want It," "Remember," "If You Believe," "Heat Wave," "A Man Chases a Girl," "Lazy," "A Sailor's Not a Sailor Till a Sailor's Been Tattooed," "There's No Business Like Show Business," "When That Midnight Choo Choo Leaves For Alabam," "Play a Simple Melody," "A Pretty Girl," "Let's Have Another Cup of Coffee," "Alexander's Ragtime Band." 117 minutes

Molly Donahue: Ethel Merman, *Tim Donahue:* Donald O'Connor, *Vicky:* Marilyn Monroe, *Terrance Donahue:* Dan Dailey, *Steve Donahue:* Johnny Ray, *Katy Donahue:* Mitzi Gaynor, *Lew Harris:* Richard Eastham, *Charles Biggs:* Hugh O'Brian, *Eddie Duggan:* Frank McHugh, *Father Dineen:* Rhys Williams, *Marge:* Lee Patrick, *Harry:* Chick Chandler, *Hatcheck Girl:* Eve Miller, *Lillian Sawyer:* Robin Raymond, *Stage Manager:* Lyle Talbot, *Kelly, Stage Door Man:* George Melford, *Katy's Boy Friend:* Alvy Moore, *Dance Director:* Henry Slate, *Geoffrey:* Gavin Gordon, *Katy, age 4:* Mimi Gibson, *Katy, age 8:* Linda Lowell, *Steve, age 2:* John Potter, *Steve, age 6:* Jimmy Baird, *Steve, age 10:* Billy Chapin, *Tim, age 2:* Neal McCaskill, *Tim, age 6:* Donald Gamble, *Lorna:* Charlotte Austin, *Stage Manager:* John Doucette, *Sophie Tucker:* Isabelle Dwan, *Bobby Clark:* Donald Kerr.

THESE THREE (1936) UA. A Samuel Goldwyn Production. Producer, Samuel Goldwyn. Director, William Wyler. From the play *The Children's Hour* by Lillian Hellman. Screenplay, Lillian Hellman. Cameraman, Gregg Toland. Editor, Daniel Mandell. 93 minutes. Remade as *The Children's Hour* (UA, 1962), also with Hopkins

Martha Dobie: Miriam Hopkins, *Karen Wright:* Merle Oberon, *Doctor Joseph Cardin:* Joel McCrea, *Mrs. Mortar:* Catherine Doucet, *Mrs. Tilford:* Alma Kruger, *Mary Tilford:* Bonita Granville, *Rosalie:*

Marcia Mae Jones, *Evelyn:* Carmencita Johnson, *Lois:* Mary Ann Durkin, *Agatha:* Margaret Hamilton, *Helen Burton:* Mary Louise Cooper, *Taxi Driver:* Walter Brennan.

These Three with Miriam Hopkins and Merle Oberon.

They Drive by Night with Humphrey Bogart, George Raft and Ann Sheridan.

THEY DRIVE BY NIGHT (1940) WB. Producer, Hal B. Wallis. Associate Producer, Mark Hellinger. Director, Raoul Walsh. From the novel *Long Haul* by A. I. Bezzerides. Screenplay, Jerry Wald and Richard Macaulay. Musical Director, Adolph Deutsch. Art Director, John Hughes. Cameraman, Arthur Edeson. Special Effects, Byron Haskin, H. F. Koenekamp. Editor, Oliver S. Garretson. Partial remake of *Bordertown* (Warners, 1935). 93 minutes

Joe Fabrini: George Raft, *Cassie Hartley:* Ann Sheridan, *Lana Carlsen:* Ida Lupino, *Paul Fabrini:* Humphrey Bogart, *Pearl Fabrini:* Gale Page, *Ed Carlsen:* Alan Hale, *Irish McGurn:* Roscoe Karns, *Harry McNamara:* John Litel, *District Attorney:* Henry O'Neill, *George Rondolos:* George Tobias, *Farnsworth:* Charles Halton, *Sue Carter:* Joyce Compton, *Hank Dawson:* John Ridgely, *Pete Haig:* Paul Hurst, *Mike Williams:* Charles Wilson, *Neves:* Norman Willis, *Barney:* George Lloyd, *Chloe:* Lillian Yarbo, *Truck Driver:* Eddy Chandler, *Mexican Helper:* Pedro Regas, *Driver:* Frank Faylen, *Driver:* Ralph Sanford, *Drivers:* Sol Gorss, Eddie Fetherston, Dick Wessel, Al Hill, Charles Sullivan, Eddie Acuff, Pat Flaherty, *Landlady:* Vera Lewis, *Fatso:* Joe Devlin, *Tough Driver:* William Haade, *Mike:* Mack Gray, *Sweeney (Driver):* Max Wagner, *Bailiff:* Wilfred Lucas, *Defense Attorney:* John Hamilton, *Judge:* Howard Hickman.

They Shoot Horses, Don't They? with Michael Sarrazin and Jane Fonda.

THEY SHOOT HORSES, DON'T THEY? (1969) Cinerama. Produced by Irwin Winkler and Robert Chartoff. Directed by Sydney Pollack. Panavision, DeLuxe Color. An ABC Pictures/Palomar Pictures/Chartoff-Winkler/Pollack Production. Based on the 1935 novel by Horace McCoy. Screenplay, James Poe and Robert E. Thompson. Music by John Green. Orchestral Arrangements, John Green and Albert Woodbury. Photography, Philip H. Lathrop. Production Designer, Harry Horner. Editor, Fredric Steinkamp. Marathon Dances choreographed and supervised by Tom Panko. Costumes, Donfeld. Associate Producer, John Green. Production Manager, Edward Woehler. Fonda's Hairstyles, Sydney Guilaroff. Songs include "Easy Come, Easy Go" by John Green and Edward Heyman. Shot at Warner Bros.–Seven Arts Studios. Film debut of Hassett, 20. Cuts from release print were Ruby Keeler and Busby Berkeley as themselves. Rated M. 120 minutes

Gloria Beatty: Jane Fonda, *Robert Syverton:* Michael Sarrazin, *Rocky:* Gig Young, *Sailor:* Red Buttons, *Alice:* Susannah York, *James:* Bruce Dern, *Ruby:* Bonnie Bedelia, *Rollo:* Michael Conrad, *Turkey:* Al Lewis, *Joel:* Robert Fields, *Cecil:* Severn Darden, *Shirl:* Allyn Ann McLerie, *Jackie:* Jacquelyn Hyde, *Mario:* Felice Orlandi, *Max:* Art Metrano, *Lillian:* Gail Billings, *Agnes:* Maxine Greene, *Nurse:* Mary Gregory, *College Boy:* Robert Dunlap, *Jiggs:* Paul Mantee, *Mrs. Layden:* Madge Kennedy, *Doctor:* Tim Herbert, *Trainers:* Tom McFadden, Noble "Kid" Chissell, *Audience Extra:* Philo McCullough, *Girl:* Marilyn Hassett.

THEY WERE EXPENDABLE (1945) MGM. Producer, John Ford. Associate Producer, Cliff Reid. Director, John Ford. Author, William L. White. Screenplay, Lieutenant Commander Frank Wead. Musical Score, Herbert Stothart. Art Directors, Cedric Gibbons and Malcolm Browne. Cameraman, Joseph H. August. Special Effects, A. Arnold Gillespie. Editors, Frank E. Hull, Douglass Biggs. Song by Earl Brent and Herbert Stothart: "To the End of the End of the World." 135 minutes

Lieutenant John Brickley: Robert Montgomery, *Lieutenant (jg) "Rusty" Ryan:* John Wayne, *Lieutenant Sandy Davyss:* Donna Reed, *General Martin:* Jack Holt, *"Boats" Mulcahey:* Ward Bond, *Ensign Snake Gardner:* Marshall Thompson, *Ensign "Andy" Andrews:* Paul Langton, *Major James Morton:* Leon Ames, *Seaman Jones:* Arthur Walsh,

Lieutenant (jg) "Shorty" Long: Donald Curtis, Ensign George Cross: Cameron Mitchell, Ensign Tony Aiken: Jeff York, "Slug" Mahan: Murray Alper, "Squarehead" Larsen: Harry Tenbrook, "Doc" (Storekeeper): Jack Pennick, Benny Lecoco: Alex Havier, Admiral Blackwell: Charles Trowbridge, The General: Robert Barrat, Elder Tompkins: Bruce Kellogg, Engsign Brown: Tim Murdock, Ohio: Louis Jean Heydt, Dad Knowland: Russell Simpson, The Priest: Pedro de Cordoba, Army Doctor (at Corregidor): Vernon Steele, Captain at Airport: Tom Tyler, Gardner's Girl Friend: Trina Lowe, Boat Crew: Stubby Kruger, Sammy Stein, Blake Edwards, Michael Kirby, Bartender, Silver Dollar: Robert Emmet O'Connor, Army Orderly: Philip Ahn, Filipino Girl Singer: Pacita Tod-Tod, Hotel Manager: William B. Davidson, Mayor of Cebu: Max Ong, Sergeant Smith: Bill Wilkerson, Lieutenant James: John Carlyle, Officer's Wife: Betty Blythe, Officer at Airport: Kermit Maynard.

They Were Expendable with John Wayne and Jack Holt.

They Won't Forget with John Ridgely, Elisha Cook, Jr., William Moore (Peter Potter), Jerry Fletcher and Eddie Foster.

THEY WON'T FORGET (1937) WB. Produced and directed by Mervyn LeRoy. Based on the novel *Death in the Deep South* by Ward Greene. Screenplay, Robert Rossen and Aben Kandel. Music and Arrangements, Adolph Deutsch. Music Director, Leo F. Forbstein. Art Director, Robert Haas. Photography, Arthur Edeson and Warren Lynch. Film debuts of Allyn Joslyn and Gloria Dickson. 90 minutes

Andrew J. Griffin: Claude Rains, *Sybil Hale:* Gloria Dickson, *Robert Hale:* Edward Norris, *Gleason:* Otto Kruger, *Bill Brock:* Allyn Joslyn, *Mary Clay:* Lana Turner, *Imogene Mayfield:* Linda Perry, *Joe Turner:* Elisha Cook, Jr., *Det. Laneart:* Cy Kendall, *Tump Redwine:* Clinton Rosemond, *Carlisle P. Buxton:* E. Alyn Warren, *Mrs. Hale:* Elisabeth Risdon, *Jim Timberlake:* Clifford Soubier, *Det. Pindar:* Granville

Bates, *Mrs. Mountford:* Ann Shoemaker, *Governor Mountford:* Paul Everton, *Harmon Drake:* Donald Briggs, *Mrs. Clay:* Sybil Harris, *Fred, Drug Clerk:* Eddie Acuff, *Bill Price:* Frank Faylen, *Foster:* Raymond Brown, *Judge Moore:* Leonard Mudie, *Shattuck Clay:* Trevor Bardette, *Luther Clay:* Elliott Sullivan, *Ransome Clay:* Wilmer Hines, *Briggs:* John Dilson, *Tucker:* Frank Rasmussen, *First Veteran:* Harry Davenport, *Second Vetaran:* Harry Beresford, *Third Veteran:* Edward McWade, *Mrs. Timberlake:* Adele St. Maur, *First Detective:* Thomas Jackson, *Second Detective:* George Lloyd, *Dolly Holly:* Claudia Coleman, *Flannigan:* Owen King, *Stout Lady:* Maidel Turner, *Harrison (Young Juror):* Robert Porterfield, *Hazel:* Psyche Nibert, *Police Captain:* Howard Mitchell, *Pool Players:* John Ridgely, Bill Moore (Peter Potter), Jerry Fletcher, Eddie Foster.

The Thief with Ray Milland.

THE THIEF (1952) UA. Producer, Clarence Greene. Director, Russell Rouse. Screenplay by Clarence Greene and Russell Rouse. Music by Herschel Gilbert. Filmed without dialogue. 85 minutes

Allan Fields: Ray Milland, *Mr. Bleek:* Martin Gabel, *The Girl:* Rita Gam, *Harris:* Harry Bronson, *Dr. Linstrum:* John McKutcheon: *Miss Philips:* Rita Vale: *Beal:* Rex O'Malley: *Walters:* Joe Conlin.

The Thin Man with Myrna Loy, William Powell, Porter Hall and Minna Gombell.

THE THIN MAN (1934) MGM. Produced by Hunt Stromberg. Directed by W. S. Van Dyke. From the novel by Dashiell Hammett. Screenplay by Albert Hackett, Frances Goodrich. Film Editor, Robert J. Kern. Photographer, James Wong Howe. Recording Engineer, Douglas Shearer. Assistant Director, Les Selander. Art Director, Cedric Gibbons. Associate Art Directors, David Townesend, Edwin

B. Willis. Costumes, Dolly Tree. Musical Numbers, Dr. William Axt. 93 minutes

Nick: William Powell, *Nora:* Myrna Loy, *Dorothy Wynant:* Maureen O'Sullivan, *Guild:* Nat Pendleton, *Mimi:* Minna Gombell, *McCauley:* Porter Hall, *Andrew:* Henry Wadsworth, *Gilbert:* William Henry, *Nunheim:* Harold Huber, *Chris:* Cesar Romero, *Julia:* Natalie Moorhead, *Mrs. Jorgenson:* Ruth Channing, *Wynant:* Edward Ellis, *Marion:* Gertrude Short, *Quinn:* Clay Clement, *Tanner:* Cyril Thornton, *Bill:* Robert E. Homans, *Dr. Walton:* Raymond Brown, *Taxi Driver:* Douglas Fowley, *Taxi Driver:* Sherry Hall, *Headwaiter:* Fred Malatesta, *Waiters:* Rolfe Sedan, Leo White, *Stutsy:* Walter Long, *Apartment Clerk:* Kenneth Gibson, *Stenographer:* Tui Lorraine, *Foster:* Bert Roach, *Tefler:* Huey White, *Reporter:* Creighton Hale, *Police Captain:* Ben Taggart, *Fight Manager:* Charles Williams, *Detective:* Garry Owen.

Thirty Seconds Over Tokyo with Douglas Cowan, Don DeFore, Van Johnson, John R. Reilly and Robert Mitchum.

THIRTY SECONDS OVER TOKYO (1944) MGM. Produced by Sam Zimbalist. Directed by Mervyn LeRoy. Based on the book and story by Ted W. Lawson and Robert Considine. Screenplay, Dalton Trumbo. Music, Herbert Stothart. Editor, Frank Sullivan. Song by Art and Kay Fitch and Bert Lowe: "Sweetheart of All My Dreams." Film debut of Steve Brodie, 24. 138 minutes

Lieutenant Colonel James H. Doolittle: Spencer Tracy, *Ted Lawson:* Van Johnson, *David Thatcher:* Robert Walker, *Ellen Jones Lawson:* Phyllis Thaxter, *Dean Davenport:* Tim Murdock, *Davey Jones:* Scott McKay, *Bob Clever:* Gordon McDonald, *Charles McClure:* Don DeFore, *Bob Gray:* Robert Mitchum, *Shorty Manch:* John R. Reilly, *Doc White:* Horace (Stephen) McNally, *Lieutenant Randall:* Donald Curtis, *Lieutenant Miller:* Louis Jean Heydt, *Don Smith:* William "Bill" Phillips, *Brick Holstrom:* Douglas Cowan, *Captain Ski York:* Paul Langton, *Lieutenant Jurika:* Leon Ames, *General:* Moroni Olsen, *Young Chung:* Benson Fong, *Old Chung:* Dr. Hsin Kung Chuan Chi, *Girls in Officer's Club:* Myrna Dell, Peggy Maley, Hazel Brooks, Elaine Shepard, Kay Williams, *Jane:* Dorothy Ruth Morris, *Mrs. Parker:* Ann Shoemaker, *Mr. Parker:* Alan Napier, *Foo Ling:* Wah Lee, *Guerrilla Charlie:* Ching Wah Lee, *Emmy York:* Jacqueline White, *Dick Joyce:* Jack McClendon, *Pilot:* John Kellogg, *Spike Henderson:* Peter Varney, *M.P.:* Steve Brodie, *Captain Halsey:* Morris Ankrum, *Mrs. Jones:* Selena Royle, *Judge:* Harry Hayden, *Second Officer:* Blake Edwards, *Hoss Wyler:* Will Walls, *Hallmark:* Jay Norris, *Jig White:* Robert Bice, *Bud Felton:* Bill Williams, *Sailor:* Wally Cassell.

THIS GUN FOR HIRE (1942) Par. Produced by Richard M. Blumenthal. Directed by Frank Tuttle. Based on the novel by Graham Greene. Screenplay, Albert Maltz and W. R. Burnett. Photography, John Seitz. Editor, Archie Marshek. Songs by Frank Loesser and Jacques Press: "I've Got You" and "Now You See It." Cut was a dream sequence in which Dickie Jones played Raven as a boy and Hermine Sterler played his aunt. Remade by Paramount as *Short Cut to Hell*, 1957. 80 minutes

Ellen Graham: Veronica Lake, *Michael Crane:* Robert Preston, *Willard Gates:* Laird Cregar, *Raven:* Alan Ladd, *Alvin Brewster:* Tully Marshall, *Sluky:* Mikhail Rasumny, *Tommy:* Marc Lawrence, *Annie:* Pamela Blake, *Steve Finnerty:* Harry Shannon, *Albert Baker:* Frank Ferguson, *Baker's Secretary:* Bernadene Hayes, *Blair Fletcher:* Olin Howland, *Senator Burnett:* Roger Imhof, *Ruby:* Patricia Farr, *Night Watchman:* James Farley, *Crippled Girl:* Virita Campbell, *Brewster's Secretary:* Victor Kilian, *Police Captain:* Charles C. Wilson, *Salesgirl:* Mary Davenport, *Mr. Collins:* Earle Dewey, *Gates' Secretary:* Lynda Grey, *Charlie, Cop:* Emmett Vogan, *Mr. Stewart, Rooming House Manager:* Chester Clute, *Will Gates, Dressmaker:* Charles Arnt, *Lieutenant Clark:* Dick Rush, *Scissor Grinder:* Clem Bevans, *Restaurant Manager:* Harry Hayden, *Weems, Guard:* Tim Ryan, *Police Captain:* Edwin Stanley, *Officer Glennon:* Elliott Sullivan, *Mrs. Mason:* Sarah Padden, *Piano Player:* Don Barclay, *Young Man:* Richard Webb, *Keever:* John Sheehan, *Frog:* Alan Speer, *Waiter:* Cyril Ring, *Walt:* Fred Walburn, *Jimmie:* Robert Winkler, *Special Dancer at Neptune Club:* Yvonne De Carlo.

This Gun for Hire with Alan Ladd and Veronica Lake.

THIS IS THE ARMY (1943) WB. Producers, Jack L. Warner, Hal B. Wallis. Director, Michael Curtiz. Color by Technicolor. Author, Irving Berlin. Screenplay, Casey Robinson, Captain Claude Binyon. Technicolor Director, Natalie Kalmus. Art Directors, Lieutenant John Loenig, John Hughes. Musical Director, Leo F. Forbstein. Cameramen, Bert Glennon, Sol Polito. Special Effects, Jack Cosgrove. Editor, George Amy. Songs by Irving Berlin: "This Is the Army, Mr. Jones," "The Army's Made a Man Out of Me," "Mandy," "I'm Getting Tired So I Can Sleep," "What the Well-Dressed Man in Harlem Will Wear," "Give a Cheer for the Navy," "I Left My Heart at the Stage Door Canteen," "American Eagles," "Oh, How I Hate to Get Up in the Morning," "Poor Little Me I'm on K. P." and "God Bless America." 121 minutes

Himself: Irving Berlin, *Jerry Jones:* George Murphy, *Eileen Dibble:* Joan Leslie, *Maxie Stoloff:* George Tobias, *Sergeant McGee:* Alan Hale, *Eddie Dibble:* Charles Butterworth, *Ethel:* Rosemary De Camp, *Mrs. Davidson:* Dolores Costello, *Rose Dibble:* Una Merkel, *Major Davidson:* Stanley Ridges, *Mrs. O'Brien:* Ruth Donnelly, *Mrs. Nelson:* Dorothy Peterson, *Kate Smith:* Herself, *Cafe Singer:* Frances Langford, *Singer:* Gertrude Niesen, *Johnny Jones:* Lieutenant Ronald Reagan, *Joe Louis:* Sergeant Joe Louis, *Soldiers:* 1st Sergeant Allan Anderson, M/Sergeant Ezra Stone, *Tommy:* T/Sergeant Tom D'Andrea, *Soldier:* Sergeant Ross Elliott, *Ollie:* Sergeant Julie Oshins, *Ted Nelson:* Sergeant Robert Shanley, *Soldier:* Sergeant Philip Truex, *Danny Davidson:* Corporal Herbert Anderson, *Blake Nelson:* Sergeant Fisher, *Soldiers:* The Allon Trio, Corporal James MacColl, *Mrs. Twardofsky:* Ilka Gruning, *Soldier on Cot:* Doodles Weaver, *Waiter:* Irving Bacon, *Old Timer's Wife:* Leah Baird, *Sports Announcer:* Warner Anderson,

Franklin D. Roosevelt: Captain Jack Young, *Camp Cook Soldiers:* Frank Coghlan Jr., John Daheim, *Father of Soldier:* Victor Moore, *Father of Soldier:* Ernest Truex, *Mike Nelson:* Jackie Brown, *Marie Twardofsky:* Patsy Moran, *Doorman:* James Conlin.

This Is the Army with George Murphy.

The Thomas Crown Affair with Steve McQueen and Faye Dunaway.

THE THOMAS CROWN AFFAIR (1968) UA. Produced and Directed

by Norman Jewison. A Mirisch-Simcoe-Solar Production. DeLuxe Color. Screenplay by Alan R. Trustman. Photography, Haskell Wexler. Associate Producer and Supervising Film Editor, Hal Ashby. Music by Michel Legrand. Production Supervisor, Allen K. Wood. Production Manager, James E. Henderling. Multiple Screen and Titles by Pablo Ferro Films. Art Director, Robert Boyle. Set Decorator, Edward Boyle. Assistant Directors, Jack Reddish and Walter Hill. Editors, Ralph Winters and Byron Brandt. Dunaway's Wardrobe designed by Thea Van Runkle. McQueen's Wardrobe Consultant, Ron Postal. Make-up Supervisor, Del Armstrong. Wardrobe, Alan Levine. Modern Jewelry designed by Kenneth Jay Lane. Hairstylist, Lynn Del Kail. Sound, Walter Goss. Sound Editor, Jim Richard and Clem Portman. Song, "The Windmills of Your Mind" by Michel Legrand and Alan and Marilyn Bergman, sung by Noel Harrison. Filmed partly in Boston. 102 minutes

Thomas Crown: Steve McQueen, *Vicky Anderson:* Faye Dunaway, *Lt. Malone:* Paul Burke, *Erwin Weaver:* Jack Weston, *Carl:* Yaphet Kotto, *Benjy:* Todd Martin, *Dave:* Sam Melville, *Abe:* Addison Powell, *Arnie:* Sidney Armus, *Curley:* Jon Shank, *Don:* Allen Emerson, *Ernie:* Harry Cooper, *Bert (Small Robber):* Johnny Silver, *Gwen:* Astrid Heeren, *Sandy:* Biff McGuire, *Miss Sullivan:* Carol Corbett, *John:* John Orchard, *Jamie MacDonald:* Gordon Pinsent, *Danny:* Patrick Horgan, *Honey*

Weaver: Peg Shirley, *Jimmy Weaver:* Leonard Caron, *Booth Guard:* Richard Bull, *Cash Room Guards:* Paul Rhone, Victor Creatore, *Elevator Operators:* Paul Verdier, James Rawley, Charles Lampkin, *Marvin:* Ted Gehring, *Sketch Artist:* Nikita Knatz, *Marcie:* Nora Marlowe, *Motel Girl:* Carole Kelly, *Swiss Banker:* Michael Shillo, *Private Detective:* Tom Rosqui, *Pretty Girl:* Judy Pace, *Girl in Elevator:* Patty Regan.

Thoroughly Modern Millie with Julie Andrews, James Fox and Carol Channing.

THOROUGHLY MODERN MILLIE (1967) Univ. Produced by

Ross Hunter. Directed by George Roy Hill. Color by Technicolor. Original Screenplay by Richard Morris. Music composed and directed by Elmer Bernstein. Musical numbers arranged and conducted by Andre Previn, supervised by Joseph Gershenson. Choreography by Joe Layton. Costumes, Jean Louis. Art Directors, Alexander Golitzen and George Webb. Sets, Howard Bristol. Assistant Director, Douglas Green. Production Manager, Ernest B. Wehmeyer. Photography, Russell Metty. Editor, Stuart Gilmore. Sound, Waldon O. Watson, William Russell, and Ronald Pierce. Songs: "Thoroughly Modern Millie" and "Tapioca" by James Van Heusen and Sammy Cahn; "Jimmy" by Jay Thompson; "The Jewish Wedding Song" (Trinkt Le Chaim) by Sylvia Neufeld; Standards: "Baby Face," "Do It Again," "Poor Butterfly," "Stumbling," "Japanese Sandman," "Jazz Baby," "Rose of Washington Square." 138 minutes

Millie Dillmount: Julie Andrews, *Dorothy Brown:* Mary Tyler Moore, *Muzzy Van Hossmere:* Carol Channing, *Jimmy Smith:* James Fox, *Trevor Graydon:* John Gavin, *Mrs. Meers:* Beatrice Lillie, *Number One:* Jack Soo, *Number Two:* Pat Morita, *Tea:* Philip Ahn, *Miss Flannery:* Cavada Humphrey, *Juarez:* Anthony Dexter, *Cruncher:* Lou Nova, *Baron Richter:* Michael St. Clair, *Adrian:* Albert Carrier, *Gregory Huntley:* Victor Rogers, *Judith Tremaine:* Lizabeth Hush, *Taxi Driver:* Herbie Faye, *Singer:* Ann Dee, *Waiter:* Benny Rubin, *Woman in Office:* Mae Clarke.

THOSE MAGNIFICENT MEN IN THEIR FLYING MACHINES OR HOW I FLEW FROM LONDON TO PARIS IN 25 HOURS AND 11 MINUTES (1965) 20th. Producer, Stan Margulies. Associate

Producer, Jack Davies. Director, Ken Annakin. Screenplay, Jack Davies, Ken Annakin. Music, Ron Goodwin. Director of Photography, Christopher Challis. Costumes, Osbert Lancaster. Assistant Director, Clive Reed. In Todd-AO and De Luxe Color. 152 minutes

Orvil Newton: Stuart Whitman, *Patricia Rawnsley:* Sarah Miles, *Richard Mays:* James Fox, *Count Emilio Ponticelli:* Alberto Sordi, *Lord Rawnsley:* Robert Morley, *Col. Manfried Von Holstein:* Gert Frobe, *Pierre Dubois:* Jean-Pierre Cassel, *Courtney:* Eric Sykes, *Sir Percy Ware-Armitage:* Terry-Thomas, *Brigitte, Ingrid, Marlene, François, Yvette, Betty:* Irina Demich, *Fire Chief Perkins:* Benny Hill, *Yamamoto:* Yujiro Ishihara, *Mother Superior:* Flora Robson, *Capt. Rumpelstrosse:*

Karl Michael Vogler, *George Gruber:* Sam Wanamaker, *Neanderthal Man:* Red Skelton, *French Postman:* Eric Barker, *Elderly Colonel:* Fred Emney, *McDougal:* Gordon Jackson, *Jean:* Davy Kaye, *French Painter:* John LeMesurier, *Lieutenant Parsons:* Jeremy Lloyd, *Sophia Ponticelli:* Zena Marshall, *Airline Hostess:* Millicent Martin, *Italian Mayor:* Eric Pohlman, *Waitress in Old Mill:* Marjorie Rhodes, *Tremayne Gascoyne:* William Rushton, *Niven:* Michael Trubshawe, *Popperwell:* Tony Hancock.

Those Magnificent Men in Their Flying Machines with Karl Michael Vogler and Gert Frobe.

Thousands Cheer with Gene Kelly, John Boles and Kathryn Grayson.

THOUSANDS CHEER (1943) MGM. Producer, Joseph Pasternak. Director, George Sidney. Technicolor. Based on the story "Private Miss Jones" by Paul Jarrico, Richard Collins. Screenplay, Paul Jarrico, Richard Collins. Musical Director, Herbert Stothart. Art Director, Cedric Gibbons. Songs by Ferde Grofe, Harold Adamson, Lew Brown, Ralph Freed, Burton Lane, Walter Jurmann, Paul Francis Webster, Earl Brent, E. Y. Harburg, Dmitri Shostakovitch, Harold Rome. Cameraman, George Folsey. Editor, George Boemler. Musical numbers: "The Joint Is Really Jumping" by Ralph Blane and Hugh Martin; "I Dug a Ditch in Wichita" by Ralph Freed and Burton Lane; "Three Letters in the Mailbox" by Paul Francis Webster and Walter Jurmann; "Let There Be Music" by E. Y. Harburg and Earl Brent; "Daybreak" by Harold Adamson and Ferde Grofe; "Honeysuckle Rose" by Andy Razaf and Fats Waller; "United Nations on the March" by E. Y. Harburg, Harold Rome and Herbert Stothart; "Carnegie Hall" by Ralph Blane, Hugh Martin and Roger Edens; "Just as Long as I Know Katie's Waitin'" by George R. Brown and Lew Brown; "I'm Lost You're Lost" and "Why Don't We Try?" by Walter Ruick. 126 minutes

Kathryn Jones: Kathryn Grayson, *Eddie Marsh:* Gene Kelly, *Hyllary Jones:* Mary Astor, *José:* José Iturbi, *Colonel Jones:* John Boles, *Captain Avery:* Dick Simmons, *Chuck:* Ben Blue, *Sergeant Koslack:* Frank Jenks, *Alan:* Frank Sully, *Jack:* Wally Cassell, *Silent Monk:* Ben Lessy, *Marie:* Frances Rafferty, *Helen:* Mary Elliott, *Mama Corbino:* Odette Myrtil, *Papa Corbino:* Will Kaufman, *Themselves:* Kay Kyser Orchestra, *Announcer:* Lionel Barrymore, *Girl at Station:* Betty Jaynes, *Uncle Algy:* Sig Arno, *Taxicab Driver:* Connie Gilchrist, *Woman:* Bea Nigro, *Maid:* Daisy Buford, *Alex:* Pierre Watkin, *Specialty Dancer:* Paul Speer, *Soldiers:* Myron Healey, Don Taylor, *Ringmaster:* Ray Teal, *Sergeant Major:* Carl Saxe, *Lieutenant Colonel Brand:* Bryant Washburn, Jr., *Capt. Haines:* Harry Strang, *Mother at Station:* Florence Turner, *Guests:* Donna Reed, Marilyn Maxwell, Margaret O'Brien, June Allyson, Gloria DeHaven, Mickey Rooney, Judy Garland, Red Skelton, Eleanor Powell, Virginia O'Brien, José Iturbi and the MGM Orchestra and the Chorus of United Nations, Bob Crosby and His Orchestra, Lena Horne with Benny Carter and His Orchestra, and Don Loper and Maxine Barrat and *Frank Morgan Sketch: The Barber,* Frank Morgan, *First Girl,* Ann Sothern, *Second Girl,* Lucille Ball, *Third Girl,* Connie Gilchrist, *Fourth Girl,* Marsha Hunt, *New Nurse,* Sara Haden, *First Nurse,* Marta Linden, *Doctor,* John Conte.

Three Coins in the Fountain with Maggie McNamara, Louis Jourdan and Cathleen Nesbitt.

THREE COINS IN THE FOUNTAIN (1954) 20th. Producer, Sol C. Siegel. Director, Jean Negulesco. CinemaScope, De Luxe Color. From a novel by John H. Secondari. Screenplay, John Patrick. Art Directors, Lyle Wheeler, John De Cuir. Cinematographer, Milton Krasner. Editor, William Reynolds, Remade as *The Pleasure Seekers* (20th, 1964). 102 minutes

Shadwell: Clifton Webb, *Miss Francis:* Dorothy McGuire, *Anita:* Jean Peters, *Prince Dino Di Cessi:* Louis Jourdan, *Maria:* Maggie McNamara, *Georgio:* Rossano Brazzi, *Burgoyne:* Howard St. John, *Mrs. Burgoyne:* Kathryn Givney, *Principessa:* Cathleen Nesbitt, *Dr. Martinelli:* Vincent Padula, *Bartender:* Mario Siletti, *Waiter:* Alberto Morin, *Headwaiter:* Dino Bolognese, *Venice Waiter:* Tony De Mario, *Consulate Clerk:* Jack Mattis, *Mr. Hoyt:* Willard Waterman, *Ticket Agent (Theatrical):* Zachary Yaconelli, *Baroness:* Celia Lovsky, *Waiter (Select Restaurant):* Larry Arnold, *Anna:* Renata Vanni, *Maid (Louisa):* Grazia Narciso, *Butler:* Gino Corrado, *Women:* Iphigenie Castiglioni, Norma Varden, *Girl:* Merry Anders, *Chauffeur:* Charles La Torre.

THREE COMRADES (1938) MGM. Producer, Joseph L. Mankiewicz. Director, Frank Borzage. From the novel by Erich Maria Remarque. Screenplay, F. Scott Fitzgerald, Edward E. Paramore. Montage, Slavko Vorkapich. Art Director, Cedric Gibbons. Cameraman, Joseph Ruttenberg. Editor, Frank Sullivan. Songs by Chet Forrest, Bob Wright and Franz Waxman: "Yankee Ragtime College Jazz," "Comrade Song," "How Can I Leave Thee" and "Mighty Forest." 100 minutes

Erich Lohkamp: Robert Taylor, *Pat Hollmann:* Margaret Sullavan, *Otto Koster:* Franchot Tone, *Gottfried Lenz:* Robert Young, *Alfons:* Guy Kibbee, *Franz Freuer:* Lionel Atwill, *Dr. Heinrich Becker:* Henry Hull, *Dr. Plauten:* George Zucco, *Local Doctor:* Charley Grapewin, *Dr. Jaffe:* Monty Woolley, *Herr Schultz:* Spencer Charters, *Frau Schultz:* Sarah Padden, *Burgomaster:* Ferdinand Munier, *Owner of Wrecked Car:* Morgan Wallace, *Adolph:* George Offerman, Jr., *Tony:* Leonard Penn, *Frau Brunner:* Priscilla Lawson, *Frau Schmidt:* Esther Muir, *Adjutant:* Walter Bonn, *Major Domo:* Edward McWade, *Man with Patch:* Henry Brandon, *Bald-headed Man:* Harvey Clark, *Singer:* Alva Kellogg, *First Comic:* George Chandler, *Second Comic:* Ralph Bushman (Francis X. Bushman, Jr.) *Kid:* Donald Haines, *Eldest Vogt Man:* Norman Willis, *Younger Vogt Man:* William Haade, *Frau Zalewska:* Claire McDowell, *Rita:* Barbara Bedford, *Boris:* Mitchell Lewis, *Old Woman:* Marjorie Main, *Nurse:* Jessie Arnold, *Becker's Assistant:* Roger Converse, *Housekeeper:* Ricca Allen, *Bookstore Owner:* E. Alyn Warren.

Three Comrades with Robert Young, Robert Taylor, Margaret Sullavan and Franchot Tone.

3 Days of the Condor with Faye Dunaway.

3 DAYS OF THE CONDOR (1975) Par. Produced by Stanley Schneider. Directed by Sydney Pollack. A Wildwood Enterprises, Inc. Co-Production. Based on the novel *Six Days of the Condor* by James Grady. Screenplay, Lorenzo Semple, Jr., and David Rayfiel. Photography, Owen Roizman. Music, Dave Grusin. Production Design, Stephen Grimes. Art Director, Gene Rudolf. Dunaway's Clothes, Theoni V. Aldredge. 1st Assistant Director, Pete Scoppa. 2nd Assistant Directors, Mike Haley, Ralph Singleton and Kim Kurumada. Supervising Editor, Frederic Steinkamp. Editor, Don Guidice, Assistant to the Producer, Federico De

Laurentiis. Set Decorator, George De Titta. Special Effects, Augie Lohman. Costume Designer, Joseph C. Aulisi. A Dino De Laurentiis presentation, in Panavision and Technicolor. Filmed in New York City and at New York Institute of Technology, Old Westbury, New York. Rated R. 117 minutes

Joe Turner: Robert Redford, *Kathy Hale:* Faye Dunaway, *Higgins:* Cliff Robertson, *Joubert:* Max Von Sydow, *Mr. Wabash:* John Houseman, *Atwood:* Addison Powell, *Sam Barber:* Walter McGinn, *Janice:* Tina Chen, *Wicks:* Michael Kane, *Dr. Lappe:* Don McHenry, *Fowler:* Michael Miller, *Mitchell:* Jess Osuna, *Thomas:* Dino Narizzano, *Mrs. Russell:* Helen Stenborg, *Martin:* Patrick Gorman, *Hutton:* Garrison Phillips, *Heidegger:* Lee Steele, *Ordinance Man:* Ed Crowley, *Jennings:* Hansford Rowe, Jr., *Mae Barber:* Carlin Glynn, *Mailman:* Hank Garrett, *Messenger:* Arthur French, *Tall Thin Man:* Jay Devlin, *Jimmy:* Frank Savino, *Newberry:* Robert Phalen, *Beefy Man:* John Randolph Jones, *TV Reporter:* John Connell, *Alice Lieutenant:* Norman Bush, *Store Clerk:* James Keane, *Customer:* Ed Setrakian, *Landlady:* Carol Gustafson, *Locksmith:* Sal Schillizi, *CIA Agent:* Harmon Williams, *Telephone Worker:* David Bowman, *CIA Receptionist:* Eileen Gordon, *Nurses:* Marian Swan, Dorothi Fox, *Teen-ager:* Ernest Harden, Jr., *Santa Claus:* Robert Dahdah.

Three Little Words with Red Skelton, Fred Astaire and Vera-Ellen.

THREE LITTLE WORDS (1950) MGM. Producer, Jack Cummings. Director, Richard Thorpe. Color by Technicolor. Screenplay, George Wells. Musical Director, Andre Previn. Art Directors, Cedric Gibbons, Urie McCleary. Photography, Harry Jackson. Editor, Ben Lewis. Songs by Kalmar and Ruby and collaborators: "Where Did You Get That Girl?" (With Harry Puck); "Come On Papa" (Edgar Leslie); "Thinking of You"; "Nevertheless"; "She's Mine All Mine"; "My Sunny Tennessee" (with Herman Ruby); "Three Little Words"; "So Long Oo-Long"; "Who's Sorry Now?" (with Ted Snyder); "All Alone Monday"; "I Wanna Be Loved by You"; "Hooray for Captain Spaulding"; and "I Love You So Much." Choreography, Hermes Pan. Anita Ellis sings for Vera-Ellen. 102 minutes

Bert Kalmar: Fred Astaire, *Harry Ruby:* Red Skelton, *Jessie Brown Kalmar:* Vera-Ellen, *Eileen Percy:* Arlene Dahl, *Charlie Kope:* Keenan Wynn, *Terry Lordel:* Gale Robbins, *Mrs. Carter De Haven:* Gloria De Haven, *Phil Regan:* Himself, *Clanahan:* Harry Shannon, *Helen Kane:* Debbie Reynolds, *Al Masters:* Paul Harvey, *Dan Healy:* Carleton Carpenter, *Al Schacht:* George Metkovich, *Mendoza the Great:* Harry Mendoza, *Boy:* Billy Gray, *Coach:* Pat Flaherty, *Philip Goodman:* Pierre Watkin, *Barker:* Syd Saylor, *Negro Boy:* Elzie Emanuel, *Pianist:* Sherry Hall, *Assistant:* Pat Williams, *Waiter:* Charles Wagenheim, *Kid:* Tony Taylor, *Mother:* Phyllis Kennedy, *Stage Manager:* Donald Kerr, *Francesca Ladovan:* Beverly Michaels, *Photographers:* Bert Davidson, William Tannen, *Director:* George Sherwood, *Guest Piano Player:* Harry Barris, *Marty Collister:* Alex Gerry.

THE THREE MUSKETEERS (1948) MGM. Producer, Pandro S. Berman. Director, George Sidney. Color by Technicolor. Based on Alexandre Dumas' novel. Screenplay, Robert Ardrey. Musical Director, Herbert Stothart. Art Directors, Cedric Gibbons, Malcolm Brown. Photography, Robert Planck. Editor, Robert J. Kern. Songs by Walter Bullock and Samuel Pokrass: "Viola," "My Lady" and "Song of the Musketeers." 125 minutes

Milady Countess DeWinter: Lana Turner, *D'Artagnan:* Gene Kelly, *Constance Bonacieux:* June Allyson, *Athos:* Van Heflin, *Queen Anne:* Angela Lansbury, *Louis XIII:* Frank Morgan, *Richelieu:* Vincent Price, *Planchet:* Keenan Wynn, *Duke of Buckingham:* John Sutton, *Porthos:* Gig Young, *Aramis:* Robert Coote, *Treville:* Reginald Owen, *Rochefort:* Ian Keith, *Kitty:* Patricia Medina, *Albert:* Richard Stapley, *Bonacieux:* Byron Foulger, *Jussac:* Sol Gorss, *Count DeWardes:* Richard Simmons, *D'Artagnan, Sr.:* Robert Warwick, *Grimaud:* Wm. "Bill" Phillips, *Bazin:* Albert Morin, *Mousqueton:* Norman Leavitt, *Dark-eyed Girl:* Marie Windsor, *Mother:* Ruth Robinson, *First Traveler:* Tom Tyler, *First Friend:* Kirk Alyn, *Second Friend:* John Holland, *Subaltern:* Reginald Sheffield, *Landlord:* William Edmunds, *Landlord's Wife:* Irene Seidner, *Fisherman:* Francis McDonald, *Major Domo:* Paul Maxey, *Dragon Rouge Host:* Arthur Hohl, *Guard:* Gil Perkins, *Executioner:* Mickey Simpson.

The Three Musketeers *with Vincent Price, Ian Keith and Gene Kelly.*

Three Smart Girls with Deanna Durbin, Barbara Read, Charles Winninger and Nan Grey.

THREE SMART GIRLS (1936) Univ. Produced by Joseph Pasternak. Executive Producer, Charles R. Rogers. Directed by Henry Koster. Story by Adele Comandini. Camera, Joseph Valentine. Music Director, Charles Previn. Screenplay, Adele Comandini and Austin Parker. Editor, Ted Kent. Songs by Gus Kahn, Walter Jurmann, Bronislau Kaper: "My Heart Is Singing," "Someone to Care for Me." Feature

debut of Deanna Durbin. 86 minutes. Sequels: *Three Smart Girls Grow Up* (1939) and *Hers to Hold* (1943)

Donna Lyons: Binnie Barnes, *Mrs. Lyons:* Alice Brady, *Lord Michael Stuart:* Ray Milland, *Judson Craig:* Charles Winninger, *Count Arisztid:* Mischa Auer, *Joan Craig:* Nan Grey, *Kay Craig:* Barbara Read, *Penny Craig:* Deanna Durbin, *Binns:* Ernest Cossart, *Wilbur Lamb:* Hobart Cavanaugh, *Bill Evans:* John King, *Trudel:* Lucile Watson, *Dorothy Craig:* Nella Walker.

Three Smart Girls Grow Up with Helen Parrish, Robert Cummings, Deanna Durbin and Nan Grey.

THREE SMART GIRLS GROW UP (1939) Univ. Produced by Joe Pasternak. Directed by Henry Koster. Screenplay by Bruce Manning and Felix Jackson. Camera, Joe Valentine. Editor, Ted Kent. Sequel to *Three Smart Girls*, 1936. 87 minutes

Penny Craig: Deanna Durbin, *Judson Craig:* Charles Winninger, *Joan Craig:* Nan Grey, *Kay Craig:* Helen Parrish, *Harry Loren:* Robert Cummings, *Richard Watkins:* William Lundigan, *Binns:* Ernest Cossart, *Dorothy Craig:* Nella Walker.

Thunderball with Sean Connery and Claudine Auger.

THUNDERBALL (1965) UA. Producer, Kevin McClory. Director, Terence Young. Director of Photography, Ted Moore. Screenplay, Richard Maibaum, John Hopkins. Based on story by Kevin McClory, Jack Whittingham, Ian Fleming. Assistant Director, Gus Agosti. Costumes. Anthony Mendleson. Music, John Barry. Title song lyrics by Don Black. Sung by Tom Jones. Presented by Albert R. Broccoli, Harry Saltzman. In Panavision and Technicolor. 132 minutes

James Bond: Sean Connery, *Domino:* Claudine Auger, *Emilio Largo:* Adolfo Celi, *Fiona:* Luciana Paluzzi, *Felix Leiter:* Rik Van Nutter, *"M":* Bernard Lee, *Paula:* Martine Beswick, *Count Lippe:* Guy Doleman, *Patricia:* Molly Peters, *"Q":* Desmond Llewelyn, *Moneypenny:* Lois Maxwell, *Foreign Secretary:* Roland Culver, *Pinder:* Earl Cameron, *Major Derval:* Paul Stassino, *Madame Boitier:* Rose Alba, *Vargas:* Philip Locke, *Kutze:* George Pravda, *Janni:* Michael Brennan, *Group Captain:* Leonard Sachs, *Air Vice Marshal:* Edward Underdown, *Kenniston:* Reginald Beckwith, *Quist:* Bill Cummings, *Mlle. La Porte:* **Maryse Guy Mitsouko,** *Jacques Boitier:* **Bob Simmons.**

Thunderhead, Son of Flicka with Roddy McDowall and Preston Foster.

THUNDERHEAD, SON OF FLICKA (1945) 20th. Producer, Robert Bassler. Director, Louis King. Color by Technicolor. Based on a novel by Mary O'Hara. Screenplay, Dwight Cummins, Dorothy Yost. Art Directors, Lyle Little, Fred J. Rode. Musical Score, Cyril J. Mockridge. Musical Director, Emil Newman. Cameraman, Charles Clarke. Editor, Nick De Maggio. Technicolor Director, Natalie Kalmus. 78 minutes. Sequel to *My Friend Flicka* (1943)

Ken Mc Laughlin: Roddy McDowall, *Rob Mc Laughlin:* Preston Foster, *Nelle:* Rita Johnson, *Gus:* James Bell, *Hildy:* Diana Hale, *Major Harris:* Carleton Young, *Mr. Sargent:* Ralph Sanford, *Tim:* Robert Filmer, *Dr. Hicks:* Alan Bridge.

TILL THE CLOUDS ROLL BY (1946) MGM. Producer, Arthur Freed. Director, Richard Whorf. Color by Technicolor. Author, Guy Bolton, Screenplay, Myles Connoly, Jean Halloway. Adaptation, George Wells. Musical Director, Lennie Hayton. Orchestration, Conrad Salinger. Art Director, Cedric Gibbons. Cameramen, Harry Stradling, George J. Folsey. Editor, Albert Akst. Vocal Arrangements, Kay Thompson. Musical numbers staged and directed by Robert Alton. Songs by Jerome Kern (lyricists' names in parentheses): "Make Believe" (Oscar Hammerstein II); "Can't Help Lovin' That Man" (Oscar Hammerstein II); "Ol' Man River" (Oscar Hammerstein II); "Till the Clouds Roll By" (P.G. Wodehouse); "How'd You Like to Spoon With Me?" (Edward Laska); "They Didn't Believe Me" (Herbert Reynolds); "The Last Time I Saw Paris" (Oscar Hammerstein II); "I Won't Dance" (Otto Harbach and Oscar Hammerstein II); "Why Was I Born?" (Oscar Hammerstein II); "Smoke Gets in Your Eyes" (Otto Harbach); "Who?" (Otto Harbach and Oscar Hammerstein II); "Look for the Silver Lining" (B.G. DeSylva); "Sunny" (Otto Harbach and Oscar Hammerstein II); "Cleopatterer" (P. G. Wodehouse); "Leave It to Jane" (P.G. Wodehouse); "Go Little Boat" (P.G. Wodehouse); "One More Dance" (Oscar Hammerstein II); "Land Where the Good Songs Go" (P.G. Wodehouse); "Yesterdays" (Otto Harbach); "Long Ago and Far Away" (Ira Gershwin); "A

Fine Romance" (Dorothy Fields); "All the Things You Are" (Oscar Hammerstein II); "She Didn't Say Yes (She Didn't Say No)"; (Otto Harbach); and the Polka from the Mark Twain Suite. Judy Garland Numbers directed by Vincente Minnelli. Film debuts of Gower Champion and Sally Forrest. 137 minutes

Jerome Kern: Robert Walker, *Marilyn Miller:* Judy Garland, *Sally:* Lucille Bremer, *Sally as a girl:* Joan Wells, *James I. Hessler:* Van Heflin, *Oscar Hammerstein:* Paul Langton, *Mrs. Jerome Kern:* Dorothy Patrick, *Mrs. Muller:* Mary Nash, *Charles Frohman:* Harry Hayden, *Victor Herbert:* Paul Maxey, *Cecil Keller:* Rex Evans, *Hennessey:* William "Bill" Phillips, *Julie Sanderson:* Dinah Shore, *Bandleader:* Van Johnson, *Guest Stars:* June Allyson, Angela Lansbury, Ray McDonald, *Dance Specialties:* Maurice Kelly, Cyd Charisse, Gower Champion, *Orchestra Conductor:* Ray Teal, *Specialty:* Wilde Twins, *Frohman's Secretary:* Byron Foulger, *Miss Laroche:* Ann Codee, *Producer:* Russell, Hicks, *Director:* William Forest, *Dancer:* Sally Forrest.

SHOWBOAT NUMBER *Captain Andy:* William Halligan, *Ravenal:* Tony Martin, *Magnolia:* Kathryn Grayson, *Ellie:* Virginia O'Brien, *Julie:* Lena Horne, *Joe:* Caleb Peterson, *Steve:* Bruce Cowling.

FINALE Kathryn Grayson, Johnny Johnston, Lucille Bremer, Frank Sinatra, Virginia O'Brien, Lena Horne, Tony Martin.

Till the Clouds Roll By with Dorothy Patrick, Paul Langton and Robert Walker.

Titanic with Clifton Webb and Barbara Stanwyck.

TITANIC (1953). 20th. Producer, Charles Brackett. Director, Jean Negulesco. Author, Charles Brackett, Walter Reisch, Richard Breen. Screenplay, Charles Brackett, Walter Reisch, Richard Breen. Art Directors, Lyle Wheeler, Maurice Ransford. Cinematographer, Joe McDonald. Editor, Louis Loeffler. Other versions: *Titanic* (German, 1943); *A Night to Remember* (British, 1958). 98 minutes

Richard Sturgess: Clifton Webb, *Mrs. Sturgess:* Barbara Stanwyck, *Giff Rogers:* Robert Wagner, *Annette:* Audrey Dalton, *Mrs. Young:* Thelma Ritter, *Captain Smith:* Brian Aherne, *Healey:* Richard Basehart, *Earl Meeker:* Allyn Joslyn, *Sandy Comstock:* James Todd, *John Jacob Astor:* William Johnstone, *Chief Officer Wilde:* Charles FitzSimons, *First Officer Murdock:* Barry Bernard, *Norman:* Harper Carter, *Officer Lightoller:* Edmund Purdom, *Mr. Guggenheim:* Camillo Guercio, *Sanderson:* Antony Eustrel, *Quartermaster:* Alan Marston, *Devlin:* James Lilburn, *Mrs. John Jacob Astor:* Frances Westcott, *Widener:* Guy Standing, Jr., *Mrs. Straus:* Hellen Van Tuyl, *Isidor Straus:* Roy Gordon, *Mrs. Uzcadum:* Marta Mitrovich, *Emma:* Ivis Goulding, *Bride:* Dennis Fraser, *Phillips:* Ashley Cowan, *Symons:* Lehmer Graham, *College Girls:* Merry Anders, Gloria Gordon, Melinda Markey, *College Boys:* Ronald F. Hagerthy, Conrad Feia, Richard West, *Woman:* Mae Marsh, *Ship Steward:* William Cottrell, *Tailor:* David Hoffman, *Manager:* Gordon Richards, *Steward:* Owen McGiveney, *Junior Officer:* Robin Hughes.

To Catch a Thief with Grace Kelly and Cary Grant.

TO CATCH A THIEF (1955) Par. Producer, Alfred Hitchcock. Director, Alfred Hitchcock. VistaVision, Technicolor. Author, David Dodge. Screenplay, John Michael Hayes. Art Directors, Hal Pereira, Joseph MacMillan Johnson. Musical Director, Lyn Murray. Cinematographer, Robert Burks. Editor, George Tomasini. Filmed on the Riviera. 97 minutes

John Robie: Cary Grant, *Frances Stevens:* Grace Kelly, *Mrs. Stevens:* Jessie Royce Landis, *H.H. Hughson:* John Williams, *Bertani:* Charles Vanel, *Danielle:* Brigitte Auber, *Foussard:* Jean Martinelli, *Germaine:* Georgette Anys, *Claude:* Roland Lesaffre, *Mercier:* Jean Hebey, *Lepic:* Rene Blancard, *Big Man in Kitchen:* Wee Willie Davis, *Antoinette:* Dominique Davray, *Kitchen Help:* Edward Manouk, *Mr. Sanford:* Russell Gaige, *Mrs. Sanford:* Marie Stoddard, *Vegetable Man in Kitchen:* Paul "Tiny" Newlan, *Man with Milk in Kitchen:* Lewis Charles, *Woman in Kitchen:* Aimee Torriani, *Chef:* Frank Chelland, *Detective:* Don Megowan, *Detective:* John Alderson, *Chef:* Otto F. Schulze, *Monaco Policeman:* Leonard Penn, *Monaco Policeman:* Michael Hadlow, *Jewelry Clerk:* Philip Van Zandt, *Desk Clerk:* Steven Geray, *Elegant French Woman:* Gladys Holland, *Croupier:* Louis Mercier.

TO HAVE AND HAVE NOT (1944) WB. Produced and directed by Howard Hawks. Based on the novel by Ernest Hemingway. Screenplay, Jules Furthman and William Faulkner. Art Director, Charles Novi. Music Director, Leo F. Forbstein. Special Effects, Roy Davidson and Rex Wimpy. Photography, Sid Hickox. Editor, Christian Nyby. Songs by Hoagy Carmichael and Johnny Mercer: "How Little We Know" and "Hong Kong Blues"; also, "Am I Blue?" and "Limehouse Blues." Film debut of Lauren Bacall, 19. Remakes: *The Breaking Point* (WB, 1950), *The Gun Runners* (UA, 1958). 100 minutes

Harry Morgan: Humphrey Bogart, *Eddie:* Walter Brennan, *Marie Browning:* Lauren Bacall, *Hellene De Bursac:* Dolores Moran, *Cricket:* Hoagy Carmichael, *Paul De Bursac:* Walter Molnar, *Lieut. Coyo:*

Sheldon Leonard, *Gerard:* Marcel Dalio, *Johnson:* Walter Sande, *Capt. Renard:* Dan Seymour, *Bodyguard:* Aldo Nadi, *Beauclerc:* Paul Marion, *Mrs. Beauclerc:* Patricia Shay, *Rosalie:* Janette Grae, *Bartender:* Pat West, *Horatio:* Sir Lancelot, *Quartermaster:* Eugene Borden, *Negro Urchins:* Elzie Emanuel, Harold Garrison, *Civilian:* Pedro Regas, *Headwaiter:* Maj. Fred Farrell, *Cashier:* Adrienne d'Ambricourt, *Emil:* Emmett Smith, *DeGaullists:* Maurice Marsac, Fred Dosch, George Suzanne, Louis Mercier, Crane Whitley, *Detective:* Hal Kelly, *Chef:* Chef Joseph Milani, *Naval Ensign:* Ron Rondell, *Dancer:* Audrey Armstrong, *Cashier:* Marguerita Sylva.

To Have and Have Not with Humphrey Bogart and Walter Brennan.

To Hell and Back with Audie Murphy, Paul Langton and Bruce Cowling.

TO HELL AND BACK (1955) Univ. Produced by Aaron Rosenberg. Directed by Jesse Hibbs. CinemaScope and Technicolor. Based on Audie Murphy's autobiography, *To Hell and Back*. Screenplay, Gil Doud. Music Director, Joseph Gershenson. Art Directors, Alexander Golitzen and Robert Clatworthy. Photography, Maury Gertsman. Editor, Edward Curtiss. 106 minutes

Audie Murphy: Audie Murphy, *Johnson:* Marshall Thompson, *Kerrigan:* Jack Kelly, *Brandon:* Charles Drake, *Valentino:* Paul Picerni, *Lieutenant Manning:* Gregg Palmer, *Lieutenant Lee:* David Janssen, *Kovak:* Richard Castle, *Colonel Howe:* Paul Langton, *Captain Marks:* Bruce Cowling, *Steiner:* Julian Upton, *Thompson:* Denver Pyle, *Swope:* Felix Noriego, *Sanchez:* Art Aragon, *Saunders:* Brett Halsey, *Klasky:* Tommy Hart, *Lieutenant Burns:* Anthony Garcen, *Audie Murphy as a boy:* Gordon Gebert, *Mrs. Murphy:* Mary Field, *Mr. Huston:* Howard Wright, *Mrs. Huston:* Edna Holland, *Helen:* Anabel Shaw, *Maria:* Susan Kohner, *Julia:* Maria Costi, *Carla:* Didi Ramati, *Cleopatra:* Barbara James, *Vincenti:* Joey Costarella, *Lieutenant Harris:* Rand Brooks, *Maria's Mother:* Nan Boardman, *Stack:* Henry

Kulky, *M.P.*: John Pickard, *Scottish Soldier*: Ashley Cowan, *Marine Recruit Sergeant*: Don Kennedy, *Chief Petty Officer*: Ralph Sanford, *Truck Driver*: Howard Price, *Rector*: Alexander Campbell, *Dr. Snyder*: Rankin Mansfield, *Corinne*: Madge Meredith, *Soldier*: Mort Mills, *Jim*: John Brayant.

To Kill a Mockingbird with Gregory Peck, Collin Wilcox, Paul Fix and Jay Sullivan.

TO KILL A MOCKINGBIRD (1962) Univ. Producer, Alan Pakula. Director, Robert Mulligan. Screenplay, Horton Foote. Based on the novel by Harper Lee. Music, Elmer Bernstein. Costumes, Rosemary Odell. Assistant Director, Joseph Kenny. A Brentwood Productions Picture. Art Directors, Alexander Golitzen and Henry Bumstead. Photography, Russell Harlan. Editor, Aaron Stell. 129 minutes

Atticus Finch: Gregory Peck, *Scout Finch*: Mary Badham, *Jem Finch*: Philip Alford, *Dill Harris*: John Megna, *Sheriff Heck Tate*: Frank Overton, *Miss Maudie Atkinson*: Rosemary Murphy, *Mrs. Dubose*: Ruth White, *Tom Robinson*: Brock Peters, *Calpurnia*: Estelle Evans, *Judge Taylor*: Paul Fix, *Mayella Ewell*: Collin Wilcox, *Bob Ewell*: James Anderson, *Stephanie Crawford*: Alice Ghostley, *Boo Radley*: Robert Duvall, *Gilmer*: William Windom, *Walter Cunningham*: Crahan Denton, *Mr. Radley*: Richard Hale, *Walter Cunningham, Jr.*: Steve Condit, *Rev. Sykes*: Bill Walker, *Dr. Reynolds*: Hugh Sanders, *Jessie*: Pauline Myers, *Spence Robinson*: Jester Hairston, *Hiram Townsend*: Jamie Forster, *School Teacher*: Nancy Marshall, *Helen Robinson*: Kim Hamilton, *Burly Man*: Kelly Thordsen, *Men*: Dan White, Tex Armstrong, *Cecil Jacobs*: Kim Hector, *Tom Robinson, Jr.*, David Crawford, *School Boy*: Barry Seltzer, *Jury Foreman*: Guy Wilkerson, *Court Clerk*: Charles Fredericks, *Court Reporter*: Jay Sullivan.

Tom, Dick and Harry with Burgess Meredith, Ginger Rogers and Phil Silvers.

TOM, DICK AND HARRY (1941) RKO. Producer, Robert Sisk. Director, Garson Kanin. Story and Screenplay, Paul Jarrico. Cameraman, Merrit Gerstad. Special Effects, Vernon Walker. Editor, John Sturges. Song by Gene Rose and Roy Webb: "Tom Collins." Remade by RKO as *The Girl Most Likely*, 1957. 86 minutes

Janie: Ginger Rogers, *Tom*: George Murphy, *Dick Hamilton*: Alan Marshal, *Harry*: Burgess Meredith, *Pop*: Joe Cunningham, *Ma*: Jane Seymour, *Babs*: Lenore Lonergan, *Paula*: Vicki Lester, *Ice Cream Man*: Phil Silvers, *Gertrude*: Betty Breckenridge, *Announcer*: Sid Skolsky, *Miss Schlom*: Edna Holland, *Music Store Proprietor*: Gus Glassmire, *Sales Clerk*: Netta Packer, *Mrs. Burton*: Sarah Edwards, *Matron*: Ellen Lowe, *Mr. Burton*: William Halligan, *Judge*: Joe Bernard, *Bridge Matron*: Gertrude Short, *Stalled Car Driver*: Edward Colebrook, *Brenda*: Gayle Mellott, *Gypsy Oracle*: Dorothy Lloyd, *Boy Lead*: Berry Kroeger, *Girl Lead*: Lurene Tuttle, *Radio Announcer*: Knox Manning, *Newsreel Announcer*: William Alland, *Boy*: Jack Briggs.

Tommy with Oliver Reed and Ann-Margret.

TOMMY (1975) Produced by Robert Stigwood and Ken Russell. Directed and Written by Ken Russell. Inspired by the rock opera by Pete Townshend, additional material by John Entwistle and Keith Moon. Executive Producers, Beryl Vertue and Christopher Stamp. Associate Producer, Harry Benn. Photography, Dick Bush and Ronnie Taylor. Art Director, John Clark. Sets Designed by Paul Dufficey. Editor, Stuart Baird. Costume Designer, Shirley Russell. Music Director, Pete Townshend. Assistant Director, Jonathan Benson. Chief Make-up Artists, George Blackler and Peter Robb-King. Choreographer, Gillian Gregory. Chief Hairdresser, Joyce James. Songs by Townshend, Entwistle and Moon: "Underture" (with variations), "Captain Walker Didn't Come Home," "It's a Boy," " '51 Is Going to Be a Good Year," "What About the Boy?" "The Amazing Journey," "Christmas," "See Me, Feel Me," "Eyesight to the Blind," "The Acid Queen," "Do You Think It's All Right?" "Cousin Kevin," "Fiddle About," "Sparks," "Pinball Wizard," "Today It Rained Champagne," "There's a Doctor," "Go to the Mirror (The Specialist)," "Tommy Can You Hear Me?" "Smash the Mirror," "I'm Free," "Miracle Cure" (including "Extra, Extra"), "Sensation," "Sally Simpson," "Welcome," "Deceived," "Tommy's Holiday Camp," "We're Not Gonna Take It," "Listening to You." Filmed in England in MetroColor and Quintaphonic Sound. Rated PG. 110 minutes

Tommy Walker: Roger Daltrey, *Nora Walker Hobbs*: Ann-Margret, *Frank Hobbs*: Oliver Reed, *Pinball Wizard*: Elton John, *The Specialist*: Jack Nicholson, *Preacher*: Eric Clapton, *Uncle Ernie*: Keith Moon, *Group-Captain Walker*: Robert Powell, *Cousin Kevin*: Paul Nicholas, *The Acid Queen*: Tina Turner, *Young Tommy*: Barry Winch, *Priest*: Arthur Brown, *Sally Simpson*: Victoria Russell, *Rev. Simpson*: Ben Aris, *Mrs. Simpson*: Mary Holland, *Nurses*: Jennifer and Susan Baker, *Nurse*: Imogen Claire, *Handmaidens*: Juliet and Gillian King, *The Who*: Pete Townshend, John Entwistle, Daltrey and Moon.

TOMORROW IS FOREVER (1946) RKO-International. Producer, David Lewis. Director, Irving Pichel. Original, Gwen Bristow. Screenplay, Lenore Coffee. Art Director, Wiard B. Ihnen. Musical Score, Max Steiner. Associate Musical Director, Lou Forbes. Cameraman,

Joseph Valentine. Editor, Ernest Nims. Song by Charles Tobias and Max Steiner: "Tomorrow Is Forever." 105 minutes

Elizabeth (MacDonald) Hamilton: Claudette Colbert, John MacDonald (Kessler): Orson Welles, Larry Hamilton: George Brent, Aunt Jessie: Lucile Watson, Drew: Richard Long, Margaret: Natalie Wood, Brian: Sonny Howe, Dr. Ludwig: John Wengraf, Norton: Ian Wolfe, Charles Hamilton: Douglas Wood, Cherry: Joyce MacKenzie, Pudge: Tom Wirick, Butler: Henry Hastings, Hamilton's Secretary: Lane Watson, Baby Drew: Michael Ward, Servant: Jesse Graves, Receptionist: Lois Austin, Freckle-faced Nurse: Anne Loos, Commentator's Voice: Irving Pichel, Englishman on Ship: Thomas Louden, Ship's Doctor: Evan Thomas, Immigration Officer: Charles D. Brown, Postman: Milton Kibbee, Maid: Libby Taylor, Technician: Lane Chandler, Dr. Callan: Boyd Irwin.

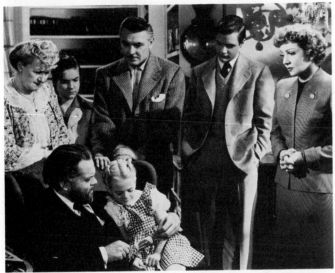

Tomorrow Is Forever with Lucile Watson, Sonny Howe, Orson Welles, Natalie Wood, George Brent, Richard Long and Claudette Colbert.

Tony Rome with Frank Sinatra and Jill St. John.

TONY ROME (1967) 20th. Produced by Aaron Rosenberg. Directed by Gordon Douglas. Panavision and De Luxe Color. An Arcola-Millfield Production. Based on the novel Miami Mayhem by Marvin H. Albert. Screenplay by Richard L. Breen. Music by Billy May. Art Direction, Jack Martin Smith and James Roth. Assistant Director, Richard Lang. Stunt Director, Buzz Henry. Photography, Joseph Biroc. Editor, Robert Simpson. Sound, Howard Warren and David Dockendorf. Song, "Tony Rome" by Lee Hazlewood, sung by Nancy Sinatra. Songs, "Something Here Inside Me" and "Hard Times" by Billy May and Randy Newman. Filmed in Miami. 109 minutes

Tony Rome: Frank Sinatra, Ann Archer: Jill St. John, Lt. Dave Santini: Richard Conte, Diana Kosterman Pines: Sue Lyon, Rita Neilson Koster-

man: Gena Rowlands, Rudy Kosterman: Simon Oakland, Adam Boyd: Jeffrey Lynn, Vic Rood: Lloyd Bochner, Ralph Turpin: Robert J. Wilke, Georgia MacKay: Deanna Lund, Irma: Elizabeth Fraser, Fat Candy: Joan Shawlee, Donald Pines: Richard Krisher, Jules Langley: Lloyd Gough, Oscar: Babe Hart, Sam Boyd: Stanley Ross, Sally Bullock: Virginia Vincent, Packy: Rocky Graziano, Sal, Maitre D'. Mike Romanoff, Catleg: Shecky Greene, Lorna: Jeanne Cooper, Ruyter: Harry Davis, Mrs. Schuyler: Templeton Fox, Bartender: Joe E. Ross, Card Player: Jilly Rizzo, Girl: Tiffany Bolling.

Top Hat with Ginger Rogers and Fred Astaire.

TOP HAT (1935) RKO. Produced by Pandro S. Berman. Directed by Mark Sandrich. Based on the musical The Gay Divorce by Dwight Taylor, and on a play by Alexander Farago and Laszlo Aladar. Screenplay, Dwight Taylor and Allan Scott. Dances, Fred Astaire. Director of Ensembles, Hermes Pan. Art Directors, Van Nest Polglase and Carroll Clark. Costumes, Bernard Newman. Photography, David Abel and Vernon Walker. Editor, William Hamilton. Sound, Hugh McDowell, Jr. Songs by Irving Berlin: "Top Hat," "Cheek to Cheek," "The Piccolino," "Isn't It a Lovely Day," "No Strings", "Get Thee Behind Me, Satan." Music Director, Max Steiner. 101 minutes

Jerry Travers: Fred Astaire, Dale Tremont: Ginger Rogers, Horace Hardwick: Edward Everett Horton, Madge Hardwick: Helen Broderick, Alberto Beddini: Erik Rhodes, Bates: Eric Blore, Bits: Ben Holmes, Nick Thompson, Tom Costello, John Impolite, Genaro Spagnoli, Rita Rozelle, Phyllis Coghlan, Charles Hall, Flower Clerk: Lucille Ball, Flower Salesman: Leonard Mudie, Curate: Donald Meek, Curate's Wife: Florence Roberts, Hotel Manager, London: Edgar Norton, Hotel Manager, Toledo: Gino Corrado, Call Boy: Peter Hobbes.

Topkapi with Maximilian Schell, Melina Mercouri, Gilles Segal, Peter Ustinov, Jess Hahn and Robert Morley.

295

TOPKAPI (1964) UA. Producer-Director, Jules Dassin. Technicolor. Screenplay, Monja Danischewsky. Based on *The Light of Day* by Eric Ambler. Music, Manos Hadjidakis. Photography, Henri Alekan. Costumes, Denny Vachlioti. Assistant Directors, Tom Pevsner, Joseph Dassin. A Filmways Presentation. Filmed in Istanbul. 120 minutes

Elizabeth Lipp: Melina Mercouri, *Arthur Simpson:* Peter Ustinov, *Walter:* Maximilian Schell, *Cedric Page:* Robert Morley, *Geven:* Akim Tamiroff, *Giulio:* Gilles Segal, *Fischer:* Jess Hahn, *Harback:* Titos Wandis, *Major Tufan:* Ege Ernart, *First Shadow:* Senih Orkan, *Second Shadow:* Ahmet Danyal Topatan, *Josef:* Joseph Dassin, *Nanny:* Amy Dalby, *Voula:* Despo Diamantidou.

To the Shores of Tripoli with Maureen O'Hara, John Payne and Randolph Scott.

TO THE SHORES OF TRIPOLI (1942) 20th. Producer, Darryl F. Zanuck. Associate Producer, Milton Sperling. Director, Bruce Humberstone. Color by Technicolor. Author, Steve Fisher. Screenplay, Lamar Trotti. Cameramen, Edward Cronjager, William Skall, Harry Jackson. Editor, Allen McNeil. Technicolor Director, Natalie Kalmus. 86 minutes

Chris Winters: John Payne, *Second Lieutenant Mary Carter:* Maureen O'Hara, *Dixie Smith:* Randolph Scott, *Helene:* Nancy Kelly, *Johnny:* William Tracy, *Okay:* Maxie Rosenbloom, *Mouthy:* Henry Morgan, *Butch:* Edmund Mac Donald, *Major Wilson:* Russell Hicks, *Captain Winters:* Minor Watson, *Bill Grady:* Ted North (Michael North), *Barber:* Frank Orth, *Blonde:* Iris Adrian, *Tom Hall:* Alan Hale, Jr., *Joe:* Basil Walker, *Swifty:* Charles Tannen, *Doctor:* Stanley Andrews, *Lieutenant:* Richard Lane, *Corporal:* Gordon Jones, *Corporal:* Gaylord (Steve) Pendleton, *Ensign:* Robert Conway, *Dancer Specialty:* Elena Verdugo, *Bartender:* James C. Morton, *Spanish Girls:* Esther Estrella, Marissa Flores, *Bellboy:* Frank Coghlan, Jr., *Truck Driver:* William Haade, *Pharmacist's Mate:* Walter Sande, *Warden:* James Flavin, *Orderly:* Hugh Beaumont, *Girl:* Hillary Brooke, *Captain:* Byron Shores, *Newscaster:* Knox Manning, *Officer:* Charles Brokaw, *C.P.O.:* Harry Strang, *Chinaman:* Chester Gan, *Radio Operator:* Pat McVey, *Truck Driver:* Frank Sully, *Officer:* Jack Anold (Vinton Haworth).

THE TOWERING INFERNO (1974) 20th and WB. Producer and Director of Action Sequences, Irwin Allen. Directed by John Guillermin. Associate Producer, Sidney Marshall. Based on the novels *The Tower* by Richard Martin Stern and *The Glass Inferno* by Thomas M. Scortia and Frank M. Robinson. Screenplay, Stirling Silliphant. Production Designer, William Creber. Photography, Fred Koenekamp and Joseph Biroc. Art Director, Ward Preston. Set Decorator, Raphael Bretton. Costume Designer, Paul Zastupnevich. 1st Assistant Directors, Wes McAfee and Newton Arnold. 2nd Assistant Directors, Don White and Bob Bender. Stunt Coordinator, Paul Stader. Aerial Sequences, Jim Freeman. Mechanical Effects, A. D. Flowers and Logan Frazee. Editors, Harold and Carl Kress. Sound, Herman Lewis. Photographic Effects, L. B. Abbott. Photographic Effects Coordinator, George Swink. 1st Assistant Director-Action Unit, Malcolm Harding. 2nd Assistant Directors-Action Unit, Phil Ball and Mike Grillo. Filmed at the Malibu Ranch, Century City and San Francisco, in Pana-

vision and DeLuxe Color. Music by John Williams. Song, "We May Never Love Like This Again" by Al Kasha and Joel Hirshborn, sung by Maureen McGovern. Rated PG. 165 minutes

Doug Roberts: Paul Newman, *Michael O'Hallorhan:* Steve McQueen, *James Duncan:* William Holden, *Susan Franklin:* Faye Dunaway, *Harlee Claiborne:* Fred Astaire, *Lisolette Mueller:* Jennifer Jones, *Patty Simmons:* Susan Blakely, *Roger Simmons:* Richard Chamberlain, *Jernigan:* O. J. Simpson, *Senator Gary Parker:* Robert Vaughn, *Dan Bigelow:* Robert Wagner, *Lorrie:* Susan Flannery, *Will Giddings:* Normann Burton, *Kappy:* Don Gordon, *Scott:* Felton Perry, *Carlos:* Gregory Sierra, *Mayor Robert Ramsay:* Jack Collins, *Paula Ramsay:* Sheila Mathews, *Mark, Fireman:* Ernie Orsatti, *Fireman:* Scott Newman, *Stunts:* Dave Sharpe, *Deaf Mute:* Carol McEvoy.

The Towering Inferno with Paul Newman and Steve McQueen.

Trader Horn with Edwina Booth, Duncan Renaldo and Harry Carey.

TRADER HORN (1931) MGM. Directed by W. S. Van Dyke. Based on the 1927 novel by Alfred Aloysius Horn and Ethelreda Lewis. Adaptation, Dale Van Every and John Thomas Neville. Screenplay, Richard Schayer. Dialogue, Cyril Hume. Production Assistant, James McKay. Camera, Clyde De Vinna, assisted by Robert Roberts and George Nogel. Sound, Andrew Anderson. African locations: Nairobi, Lake Victoria, Tanganyika, Uganda, Belgian Congo, Masdini, Butabia, Panyamur, Murchison Falls at Lake Albert, and Kenya. Completed in Hollywood. Made with the cooperation of white hunters Major W. V. D. Dickinson, A. J. Waller, J. H. Barnes, H. R. Stanton. Editor, Ben Lewis. Property Man, Harry Albiez. 123 minutes

Trader Horn: Harry Carey, *Nina Trend:* Edwina Booth, *Peru:* Duncan Renaldo, *Rencharo:* Mutia Omoolu, *Edith Trend:* Olive Fuller Golden (Olive Carey), *Trader:* C. Aubrey Smith.

TRAPEZE (1956) UA. Producer, James Hill. Director, Carol Reed. CinemaScope, De Luxe Color. Screenplay by James R. Webb. Adaptation by Liam O'Brien. Assistant Directors, Dick McWhorter, Michel

Romanoff and Robert Gendre. Music by Malcolm Arnold. Wardrobe by Frank Salvi and Gladys De Segonzac. A Susan Production. From *The Killing Frost* by Max Catto. Art Director, Rino Mondellini. Photography, Robert Krasker. Editor, Bert Bates. 105 minutes

Mike Ribble: Burt Lancaster, *Tino Orsini:* Tony Curtis, *Lola:* Gina Lollobrigida, *Rosa:* Katy Jurado, *Bouglione:* Thomas Gomez, *Max, The Dwarf:* Johnny Puleo, *John Ringling North:* Minor Watson, *Chikki:* Gerard Landry, *Otto:* J. P. Kerrien, *Snake Man:* Sidney James, *Old Woman:* Gabrielle Fontan, *Paul:* Pierre Tabard, *Stefan:* Gamil Ratab, *Ringmaster:* Michel Thomas.

Trapeze with Gina Lollobrigida, Gerard Landry, Tony Curtis, Katy Jurado, Burt Lancaster and Sidney James.

The Treasure of the Sierra Madre with Alfonso Bedoya and Humphrey Bogart.

THE TREASURE OF THE SIERRA MADRE (1948) WB. Producer, Henry Blanke. Director-Screenplay, John Huston. Based on the novel by B. Traven. Art Director, John Hughes. Musical Director, Leo F. Forbstein. Music, Max Steiner. Photography, Ted McCord. Editor, Owen Marks. Dave Sharpe doubles for Bogart. Filmed in Central Mexico and California's Mojave Desert. 126 minutes

Dobbs: Humphrey Bogart, *Howard:* Walter Huston, *Curtin:* Tim Holt, *Cody:* Bruce Bennett, *McCormick:* Barton MacLane, *Gold Hat:* Alfonso Bedoya, *Presidente:* A. Soto Rangel, *El Jefe:* Manuel Donde, *Pablo:* Jose Torvay, *Pancho:* Margarito Luna, *Flashy Girl:* Jacqueline Dalya, *Mexican Boy:* Bobby Blake, *Proprietor:* Spencer Chan, *Barber:* Julian Rivero, *White Suit:* John Huston, *Bartender:* Harry Vejar, *Customer:* Pat Flaherty, *Men:* Clifton Young, Jack Holt, Ralph Dunn, *Mexican Storekeeper:* Guillermo Calleo, *Mexican Lieutenant:* Roberto Canedo, *First Mexican Bandit:* Ernesto Escoto, *Second Mexican Bandit:* Ignacio Villalbajo, *Railroad Conductor:* Martin Garralaga, *Streetwalker:* Ann Sheridan.

A TREE GROWS IN BROOKLYN (1945) 20th. Producer, Louis D. Lighton. Director, Elia Kazan. Adapted from the novel by Betty Smith. Screenplay, Tess Slesinger, Frank Davis. Musical Score, Alfred Newman. Art Director, Lyle Wheeler. Cameraman, Leon Shamroy. Special Effects, Fred Sersen. Editor, Dorothy Spencer. 128 minutes

Katie: Dorothy McGuire, *Aunt Sissy:* Joan Blondell, *Johnny Nolan:*

James Dunn, McShane: Lloyd Nolan, *Francie Nolan:* Peggy Ann Garner, *Neeley Nolan:* Ted Donaldson, *McGarrity:* James Gleason, *Miss McDonough:* Ruth Nelson, *Steve:* John Alexander, *Christmas Tree Vendor:* B. S. Pully, *Grandma Rommely:* Ferike Boros, *Mr. Barker:* Charles Halton, *Sheila:* Patricia McFadden, *Doctor:* Robert Strange, *Street Singer:* Robert Tait, *Boys:* Teddy Infuhr, Mickey Kuhn, *Woman:* Constance Purdy, *Carney (Junk Man):* J. Farrell MacDonald, *Mrs. Waters:* Adeline deWalt Reynolds, *Mr. Spencer:* George Melford, *Tynmore Sisters:* Mae Marsh, Edna Jackson, *Henny Gaddis:* Vincent Graeff, *Flossie Gaddis:* Susan Lester, *Mr. Crackenbox:* Johnnie Berkes, *Librarian:* Lillian Bronson, *Werner:* Alec Craig, *Cheap Charlie:* Al Bridge, *Hassler:* Joseph J. Greene, *Miss Tilford:* Virginia Brissac, *Herschel:* Harry Harvey, Jr., *Augie:* Robert Anderson, *Ice Man:* Art Smith, *Undertaker:* Erskine Sanford, *Mother:* Martha Wentworth, *Priest:* Francis Pierlot, *Union Representative:* Al Eben, *Floorwalker, 5 and 10:* Harry Seymour.

A Tree Grows in Brooklyn with Adeline de Walt Reynolds and Dorothy McGuire.

Trial with John Hodiak, Glenn Ford, Robert Middleton, Rafael Campos, John Hoyt, Paul Guilfoyle and Dorothy McGuire.

TRIAL (1955) MGM. Producer, Charles Schnee. Associate Producer, James E. Newcom. Director, Mark Robson. Screenplay, Don M. Mankiewicz, from his novel. Art Directors, Cedric Gibbons, Randall Duell. Musical Director, Daniele Amfitheatrof. Cinematographer, Robert Surtees. Editor, Albert Akst. 105 minutes

David Blake: Glenn Ford, *Abbe Nyle:* Dorothy McGuire, *Barney Castle:* Arthur Kennedy, *John J. Armstrong:* John Hodiak, *Consuela Chavez:* Katy Jurado, *Angel Chavez:* Rafael Campos, *Judge Theodore Motley:* Juano Hernandez, *A.S. "Fats" Sanders:* Robert Middleton, *Ralph Castillo:* John Hoyt, *Cap Grant:* Paul Guilfoyle, *Finn:* Elisha Cook, Jr., *Gail Wiltse:* Ann Lee, *Sam Wiltse:* Whit Bissell, *Dr. Schacter:* Richard Gaines, *Jim Backett:* Barry Kelley, *Canford:* Frank Cady, *Bailiff:* Charles Tannen, *County Clerk:* David Leonard, *Assistant District Attorney:* John Rosser, *Minister:* James Todd, *Butteridge:* Sheb Wooley, *Mrs. Webson:* Charlotte Lawrence, *Youval:* Percy Helton, *Mrs. Ackerman:* Dorothy Green, *Dean:* Everett Glass, *Terry*

Bliss: Grandon Rhodes, *Lawyer #1:* Charles Evans, *Lawyer #2:* Frank Wilcox, *Checker:* Wilson Wood, *Abbott:* Robert Bice, *Benedict:* John Maxwell, *Pine:* Michael Dugan, *Dr. Abraham Tenfold:* Vince Townsend, *Kiley:* Frank Ferguson, *Reporters:* Robert Forrest, Mort Mills, *Lew Bardman:* Rodney Bell, *Johnson:* Richard Tyler, *Jury Foreman:* Mitchell Lewis.

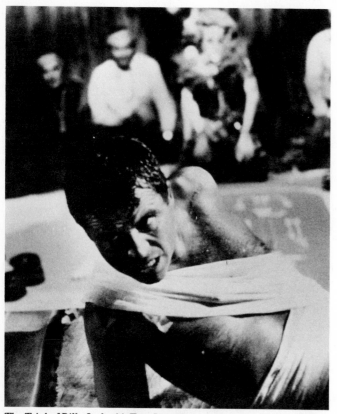

The Trial of Billy Jack with Tom Laughlin.

THE TRIAL OF BILLY JACK (1974) Taylor-Laughlin Distribution Co. Produced by Joe Cramer. Directed by Frank Laughlin. Screenplay, Frank and Teresa Christina (Tom Laughlin and Delores Taylor Laughlin). Panavision and MetroColor. Music by Elmer Bernstein. Photography, Jack A. Marta. Editors, Tom Rolf, Michael Economou, George Grenville, Michael Karr and Jules Nayfack. Associate Producers, Beverly Walker and Robert Schultz. Art Director, George W. Troast. Costumes, Moss Mabry. Assistant Directors, Jack Reddish and Thomas J. Connors III. Rated PG. 170 minutes. Others in the series: *Born Losers* (AIP, 1967), *Billy Jack* (WB, 1971), *Billy Jack Goes to Washington* (unreleased, 1975)

Billy Jack: Tom Laughlin, *Jean Roberts:* Delores Taylor, *Doc:* Victor Izay, *Carol:* Teresa Laughlin, *National Guardsman:* William Wellman, Jr., *Russell:* Russell Lane, *Michelle:* Michelle Wilson, *Joanne:* Geo Anne Sosa, *Lynn:* Lynn Baker, *Posner:* Riley Hill, *Sheriff Cole:* Sparky Watt, *Blue Elk:* Gus Greymountain, *Patsy Littlejohn:* Sacheen Littlefeather, *Danny:* Michael Bolland, *Grandfather:* Jack Stanley, *Master Han:* Bong Soo Han, *Thunder Mountain:* Rolling Thunder, *Indian Maiden:* Sandra Ego, *Vision Maiden:* Trinidad Hopkins, *Alicia:* Marianne Hall, *Turning Water:* Johnny West, *Little Bear:* Buffalo Horse, *Defense Attorney:* Dennis O'Flaherty, *Elk's Shadow:* George Aguilar, *Third Trooper:* Pepper Rogers, *Teda:* Teda Bracci, *Sunshine:* Susan Sosa, *Karate Expert:* Michael J. Shigezane, *Ken:* Ken Tealor, *Attorney:* Evans Thornton, *Bugger:* Jack White, *Militant Indian Lawyer:* Jean Newburn, *Debbie:* Debbie Hill, *Belly-Dance Teacher:* Diane Webber, *Oshannah:* Oshannah Fastwolf, *Kristen:* Kathy Cronkite, *Liz:* DeLaura Henry, *Abby:* Alexandra Nicholson.

TROUBLE IN PARADISE (1932) Par. Produced and directed by Ernst Lubitsch. From the play *The Honest Finder* by Laszlo Aladar. Screen-

play, Grover Jones and Samson Raphaelson. Photography, Victor Milner. Songs by W. Franke Harling and Leo Robin: "Trouble in Paradise," "Colet and Company." 83 minutes

Lily Vautier: Miriam Hopkins, *Mariette Colet:* Kay Francis, *Gaston Monescu (LaValle):* Herbert Marshall, *The Major:* Charlie Ruggles, *Francois Filiba:* Edward Everett Horton, *Adolph Giron:* C. Aubrey Smith, *Jacques, the Butler:* Robert Greig, *Waiter:* George Humbert, *Purse Salesman:* Rolfe Sedan, *Annoyed Opera Fan:* Luis Alberni, *Radical:* Leonid Kinsky, *Insurance Agent:* Hooper Atchley, *Madame Bouchet, Francois' Friend:* Nella Walker, *Radio Commentator:* Perry Ivins, *Singer:* Tyler Brooke, *Guest (Extra):* Larry Steers.

Trouble in Paradise with Kay Francis, Herbert Marshall and Miriam Hopkins.

True Grit with Kim Darby, Glen Campbell and John Wayne.

TRUE GRIT (1969) Par. Produced by Hal B. Wallis. Directed by Henry Hathaway. Technicolor. Based on the novel by Charles Portis. Screenplay, Marguerite Roberts. Music by Elmer Bernstein. Photography, Lucien Ballard. Production Designer, Walter Tyler. Costumes, Dorothy Jeakins. Associate Producer, Paul Nathan. Assistant Director, William W. Gray. Songs: "True Grit" by Elmer Bernstein and Don Black; "Amazing Grace," hymn, words by John Newton; "Wildwood Flower," folk song. Filmed in the Sierra Nevadas, California, and Montrose, Colorado. Rated G. 128 minutes. Sequel was *Rooster Cogburn* (Univ., 1975), with Wayne, Katharine Hepburn, Martin

Rooster Cogburn: John Wayne, *La Boeuf:* Glen Campbell, *Mattie Ross:*

298

Kim Darby, *Emmett Quincy:* Jeremy Slate, *Ned Pepper:* Robert Duvall, *Moon:* Dennis Hopper, *Goudy:* Alfred Ryder, *Col. Stonehill:* Strother Martin, *Tom Chaney:* Jeff Corey, *Capt. Boots Finch:* Ron Soble, *Lawyer Daggett:* John Fiedler, *Judge Parker:* James Westerfield, *Sheriff:* John Doucette, *Barlow:* Donald Woods, *Mrs. Floyd:* Edith Atwater, *Dirty Bob:* Carlos Rivas, *Mrs. Bagby:* Isabel Boniface, *Chen Lee:* H. W. Gim, *Frank Ross:* John Pickard, *Mrs. Ross:* Elizabeth Harrower, *Yarnell:* Ken Renard, *Harold Parmalee:* Jay Ripley, *Farrell Parmalee:* Kenneth Becker.

Tugboat Annie with Wallace Beery, Marie Dressler and Robert Young.

TUGBOAT ANNIE (1933) MGM. Produced by Harry Rapf. Directed by Mervyn LeRoy. From the *Saturday Evening Post* stories by Norman Reilly Raine. Adaptation, Zelda Sears and Eve Greene. Photography, Gregg Toland. Editor, Blanche Sewell. 88 minutes. Sequels: *Tugboat Annie Sails Again* (WB, 1940), *Captain Tugboat Annie* (Rep., 1945).

Annie Brennan: Marie Dressler, *Terry Brennan:* Wallace Beery, *Alec Brennan:* Robert Young, *Pat Severn:* Maureen O'Sullivan, *Red Severn:* Willard Robertson, *Shif'less:* Tammany Young, *Alec as a boy:* Frankie Darro, *Pete:* Jack Pennick, *Sam:* Paul Hurst, *Reynolds:* Oscar Apfel, *Mayor of Secoma:* Robert McWade, *First Mate:* Robert Barrat, *Cabby:* Vince Barnett, *Old Salt:* Robert E. Homans, *Auctioneer:* Guy Usher, *Chow, the Cook:* Willie Fung, *Mate:* Hal Price, *Sailor (Extra):* Christian Rub, *Onlooker:* Major Sam Harris.

The Turning Point with Anne Bancroft and Shirley MacLaine.

THE TURNING POINT (1977) 20th. A Hera Production. Produced by Herbert Ross and Arthur Laurents. Directed by Ross. Written by Lau-

rents. Executive Producer, Nora Kaye. Associate Producer, Roger M. Rothstein. Associate to the Producers, Howard Jeffrey. Panavision and DeLuxe Color. Cinematographer, Robert Surtees. Editor, William Reynolds. Production Designer, Albert Brenner. Costume Designer, Albert Wolsky. Theatrical Lighting Consultant, Nananne Porcher. Sound, Jerry Jost. Set Decorator, Marvin March. Assistant Directors, Jack Roe and Tony Bishop. Wardrobe, Tony Faso. Make-up Artist, Charles Schram. Hairdresser, Kathy Blondell. Produced with the participation of American Ballet Theater, Oliver Smith, artistic adviser. Music adapted and conducted by John Lanchbery. Music performed by the Los Angeles Philharmonic Orchestra, Glenn Dictorow, concertmaster. Ballets: "Legende," choreography by John Cranko, music by Wieniawsky, danced by Haydee and Cragun; "Vortex," choreography by Alvin Ailey, music by Duke Ellington, danced by Browne; "Black Swan Pas de Deux" (*Swan Lake*, Act III), choreography by Marius Petipa, music by Tchaikovsky, danced by Aldous and Bujones; "Aurora's Wedding Pas de Deux," choreography by Petipa, music by Tchaikovsky, danced by Baryshnikov and Sibley; "Le Corsaire," choreography by Petipa, music by Adam, danced by Baryshnikov; "Tchaikovsky Pas de Deux," choreography by George Balanchine, music by Tchaikovsky, danced by Farrell and Martins; "Anna Karenina," choreography by Dennis Nahat, music by Tchaikovsky, danced by Bancroft and Douglas; "La Bayadère," choreography by Alexander Minz after Petipa, music by Minkus; "Giselle," choreography by Jean Coralli and Jules Perrot, music by Adam; "Etudes," choreography by Harald Lander, music by Czerny; "Pas de Deux" (*Swan Lake*, Act II), choreography by Petipa, music by Tchaikovsky; "Romeo and Juliet," choreography by Kenneth MacMillan, music by Prokofiev; "Don Quixote Pas de Deux," choreography by Petipa, music by Minkus; "Chopin Etude," choreography by Frederick Ashton, music by Chopin. Choreography also by Michel Fokine and Lev Ivanov. Filmed in Los Angeles and New York City, including latter's Minskoff Theater, American Ballet Theater, Russian Tea Room, Carnegie Hall and Metropolitan Museum of Art. Film debuts of Baryshnikov and Browne, 19, who replaced Gelsey Kirkland. Rated PG. 119 minutes

Emma Jacklin: Anne Bancroft, *Deedee Rodgers:* Shirley MacLaine, *Yuri Kopeikine:* Mikhail Baryshnikov, *Emilia Rodgers:* Leslie Browne, *Wayne Rodgers:* Tom Skerritt, *Adelaide:* Martha Scott, *Sevilla:* Antoinette Sibley, *Dahkarova:* Alexandra Danilova, *Carolyn:* Starr Danias, *Carter:* Marshall Thompson, *Michael:* James Mitchell, *Rosie:* Anthony Zerbe, *Ethan Rodgers:* Phillip Saunders, *Janina Rodgers:* Lisa Lucas, *Freddie Ronoff:* Scott Douglas, *Arnold:* Daniel Levans, *Peter:* Jurgen Schneider, *Florence:* Saax Bradbury, *Sandra:* Hilda Morales, *Barney:* Donald Petrie, *Billy Joe:* James Crittenden, *Conductor:* David Byrd, *Boys Class Teacher:* Alexander Minz, *Dennis:* Dennis Nahat, *Ballet Master:* Enrique Martinez, *Ballet Mistress:* Anne Barlow, *Pianists:* Howard Barr and Martha Johnson, *Ballet Stars:* Lucette Aldous, Fernando Bujones, Richard Cragun, Suzanne Farrell, Marcia Haydee, Peter Martins, Clark Tippet, Marianna Tcherkassky, Martine Van Hamel, Charles Ward.

Twelve Angry Men with Henry Fonda, Edward Binns, E. G. Marshall, Jack Klugman, Jack Warden, John Fiedler, Lee J. Cobb, Ed Begley, George Voscovec and Martin Balsam.

TWELVE ANGRY MEN (1957) UA. Produced by Henry Fonda and Reginald Rose. Associate Producer, George Justin. Directed by Sidney

Lumet. Screenplay by Reginald Rose, based on his TV play. An Orion-Nova Production. 95 minutes

Juror 8: Henry Fonda, *Juror 1:* Martin Balsam, *Juror 2:* John Fiedler, *Juror 3:* Lee J. Cobb, *Juror 4:* E. G. Marshall, *Juror 5:* Jack Klugman, *Juror 6:* Edward Binns, *Juror 7:* Jack Warden, *Juror 9:* Joseph Sweeney, *Juror 10:* Ed Begley, *Juror 11:* George Voskovec, *Juror 12:* Robert Webber, *Judge:* Rudy Bond, *Guard:* James A. Kelly, *Court Clerk:* Bill Nelson, *Defendant:* John Savoca.

Twelve O'Clock High with Dean Jagger, John Kellogg and Gregory Peck.

TWELVE O'CLOCK HIGH (1949) 20th. Producer, Darryl F. Zanuck. Director, Henry King. Based on the novel and screenplay by Cy Bartlett and Beirne Lay, Jr. Art Directors, Lyle Wheeler, Maurice Ransford. Music, Alfred Newman. Photography, Leon Shamroy. Editor, Barbara McLean. Later a TV series. 132 minutes

General Savage: Gregory Peck, *Lieutenant Colonel Ben Gately:* Hugh Marlowe, *Colonel Davenport:* Gary Merrill, *General Pritchard:* Millard Mitchell, *Major Stovall:* Dean Jagger, *Sergeant McIllhenny:* Robert Arthur, *Captain "Doc" Kaiser:* Paul Stewart, *Major Cobb:* John Kellogg, *Lieutenant Bishop:* Robert Patten, *Lieutenant Zimmerman:* Lee MacGregor, *Birdwell:* Sam Edwards, *Interrogation Officer:* Roger Anderson, *Sergeant Ernie:* John Zilly, *Lieutenant Pettinghill:* William Short, *Lieutenant McKessen:* Richard Anderson, *Captain Twombley:* Lawrence Dobkin, *Sentry:* Kenneth Tobey, *Operations Officer:* John McKee, *Mr. Britton:* Campbell Copelin, *Dwight:* Don Guadagno, *Weather Observer:* Peter Ortiz, *Clerk in Antique Shop:* Steve Clark, *Nurse:* Joyce MacKenzie, *Lieutenant Wilson:* Don Hicks, *Corporal (Bartender):* Ray Hyke, *Radio Officer:* Harry Lauter, *R.A.F. Officer:* Leslie Denison, *Operations Officer:* Russ Conway.

TWENTIETH CENTURY (1934) Col. Directed by Howard Hawks. Based on the play by Ben Hecht and Charles MacArthur, which was adapted from the play *Napoleon of Broadway* by Charles Bruce Milholland. Screenplay, Ben Hecht and Charles MacArthur. Photography, Joseph August. Editor, Gene Havlick. Remade as *Streamline Express* (Mascot, 1935). 91 minutes. Later a Broadway musical, *On the Twentieth Century*

Oscar Jaffe: John Barrymore, *Lilly Garland (Mildred Plotka):* Carole Lombard, *Owen O'Malley:* Roscoe Karns, *Oliver Webb:* Walter Connolly, *George Smith:* Ralph Forbes, *Sadie:* Dale Fuller, *Matthew J. Clark:* Etienne Girardot, *First Beard:* Herman Bing, *Second Beard:* Lee Kohlmar, *Train Conductor:* James P. Burtis, *Anita:* Billie Seward, *Max Jacobs (Mandelbaum):* Charles Levison (Lane), *Emmy Lou:* Mary Jo Mathews, *Sheriff:* Ed Gargan, *McGonigle:* Edgar Kennedy, *Schultz:* Gigi Parrish, *Detective On Train:* Fred Kelsey, *Flannigan:* Pat Flaherty, *Detective:* Ky Robinson, *Lockwood:* Cliff Thompson, *Treasurer:* Nick Copeland, *Doctor Johnson:* Howard Hickman, *Stage*

Actor: Arnold Gray, *Chicago Detective:* James Burke, *Uncle Remus:* George Reed, *Stage Show Girl:* Anita Brown, *Stage Actress:* Irene Thompson, *Stage Actor:* Buddy Williams, *Southern Colonel:* Clarence Geldert, *Charwoman:* Lillian West, *Porter:* Snowflake, *Brother in play:* (Steve) Gaylord Pendleton, *Page Boy:* George Offerman, Jr., *Stage Carpenter:* Frank Marlowe, *Train Secretary:* Lynton Brent, *Artist:* Harry Semels, *McGonigle's Assistant:* King Mojave.

Twentieth Century with Carole Lombard and John Barrymore.

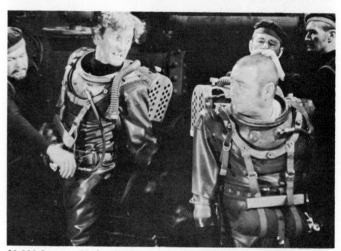

20,000 Leagues Under the Sea with Kirk Douglas and Peter Lorre.

20,000 LEAGUES UNDER THE SEA (1954) BV. Produced by Walt Disney. Directed by Richard Fleischer. CinemaScope and Technicolor. Based on the novel by Jules Verne. Screenplay, Earl Felton. Art Director, John Meehan. Camera, Franz Lehy, Ralph Hammeras, and Till Gabbani. Editor, Elmo Williams. Song, "A Whale of a Tale," by The Shermans, sung by Kirk Douglas. Filmed in New Providence, Bahamas; Long Bay, Jamaica; Disney Studios, Burbank, Cal. Stereophonic Sound. Remake of the 1916 Universal film. 122 minutes

Ned Land: Kirk Douglas, *Captain Nemo:* James Mason, *Professor Aronnax, Narrator:* Paul Lukas, *Conseil:* Peter Lorre, *First Mate of* NAUTILUS: Robert J. Wilke, *John Howard:* Carleton Young, *Captain Farragut:* Ted de Corsia, *Diver:* Percy Helton, *Mate of* LINCOLN: Ted Cooper, *Shipping Agent:* Edward Marr, *Casey Moore:* Fred Graham, *Billy:* J. M. Kerrigan, *Shipping Clerk:* Harry Harvey, *Nemo's Seal:* Esmeralda.

2001: A SPACE ODYSSEY (1968) MGM. Produced and Directed by Stanley Kubrick. Based on the 1950 short story "The Sentinel" by Arthur C. Clarke. Screenplay, Kubrick and Clarke. Filmed in Super Panavision. Presented in Cinerama, Technicolor and MetroColor. Special Photographic Effects designed and directed by Kubrick, supervised by Wally

Veevers, Douglas Trumbull, Con Pederson and Tom Howard. Production designed by Tony Masters, Harry Lange and Ernest Archer. Editor, Ray Lovejoy. Wardrobe, Hardy Amies. Photography, Geoffrey Unsworth. Additional Photography, John Alcott. Special Photographic Effects Unit: Colin J. Cantwell, Bryan Loftus, Frederick Martin, Bruce Logan, David Osborne and John Jack Malick. Art Director, John Hoesli. Sound Editor, Winston Ryder. Make-up, Stuart Freeborn. Scientific Consultant, Frederick I. Ordway III. Associate Producer, Victor Lyndon. Assistant Director, Derek Cracknell. Music: "Gayane Ballet Suite" by Aram Khatchaturian, performed by the Leningrad Philharmonic Orchestra, conducted by Gennadi Rozhdestvensky; "Atmospheres" by Gyorgy Ligeti, performed by the Southwest German Radio (Sudwestfunk) Orchestra, conducted by Ernest Bour; "Lux Aeterna" by Ligeti, performed by the Stuttgart State Orchestra (Stuttgart Schola Cantorum), conducted by Clytus Gottwald; "Requiem for Soprano, Mezzo-Soprano, Two Mixed Choirs and Orchestra" by Ligeti, performed by the Bavarian Radio Orchestra, conducted by Francis Travis; "The Blue Danube" by Johann Strauss, performed by the Berlin Philharmonic Orchestra, conducted by Herbert von Karajan; and "Thus Spake Zarathustra" by Richard Strauss, played by the Berlin Philharmonic Orchestra, conducted by Karl Boehm. Martin Balsam originally recorded the voice of HAL. Made at MGM British Studios, Boreham Wood, England. 161 minutes; cut to 142 minutes. Reissued by UA in 1978 in 70mm and Stereophonic Sound

David Bowman: Keir Dullea, *Frank Poole:* Gary Lockwood, *Dr. Heywood Floyd:* William Sylvester, *Moonwatcher (Man-Ape Leader):* Daniel Richter, *Smyslov:* Leonard Rossiter, *Elena:* Margaret Tyzack, *Halvorsen:* Robert Beatty, *Michaels:* Sean Sullivan, *Mission Controller:* Frank Miller, *Poole's Father:* Alan Gifford, *Stewardesses:* Penny Brahms, Edwina Carroll, *Astronaut:* John Ashley, *The Voice of HAL:* Douglas Rain, *Others:* Glenn Beck, Mike Lovell, Edward Bishop, Bill Weston, Ann Gillis, Heather Downham, David Hines, Jimmy Bell, Tony Jackson, David Charkham, John Jordan, Simon Davis, Scott MacKee, Jonathan Daw, Laurence Marchant, Peter Delmar, Darryl Paes, Terry Duggan, Joe Refalo, David Fleetwood, Andy Wallace, Danny Grover, Bob Wilyman, Brian Hawley, Richard Wood.

2001: A Space Odyssey with Gary Lockwood and Keir Dullea.

TWO YEARS BEFORE THE MAST (1946) Par. Associate Producer, Seton I. Miller. Director, John Farrow. Based on the book by Richard Henry Dana, Jr. Screenplay, Seton I. Miller, George Bruce. Art Directors, Hans Dreier, Franz Bachelin. Musical Score, Victor Young.

Cameraman, Ernest Laszlo. Special Effects, Gordon and J.D. Jennings. 98 minutes

Charles Stewart: Alan Ladd, *Richard Henry Dana:* Brian Donlevy, *Amazeen:* William Bendix, *Dooley:* Barry Fitzgerald, *Captain Francis Thompson:* Howard da Silva, *Maria Dominguez:* Esther Fernandez, *Brown:* Albert Dekker, *Foster:* Luis Van Rooten, *Sam Hooper:* Darryl Hickman, *Macklin:* Roman Bohnen, *Mr. Gordon Stewart:* Ray Collins, *Hayes:* Theodore Newton, *Bellamer:* Tom Powers, *Carrick:* James Burke, *Hansen:* Frank Faylen, *Mexican Captain:* Duncan Renaldo, *Mrs. Gordon Stewart:* Kathleen Lockhart, *Mercedes (Maria's Maid):* Rosa Rey, *Don Sebastian:* Pedro deCordoba, *Sailor #1:* John Roy, *Sailor #2:* Bink Hedberg, *Clark (Sailor #3):* Ethan Laidlaw, *Sailor #4:* George Bruggeman, *Sailor #5:* Clint Dorrington, *Bobson (Sailor #6):* Robert F. Kortman, *Sailor #7:* Carl Voss, *Sailor #8:* John "Blackie" Whiteford, *Sailor #9:* Mike Lally, *Sailor #10:* Joe Palma, *Sailor #11:* Dave Kashner, *Rider:* Rex Lease, *Chief Clerk:* Barry Macollum, *Blake:* Edwin Stanley, *Broker:* Crane Whitley, *Hallet:* George M. Carleton, *Crabtree:* Arthur Loft, *Staunton:* Pierre Watkin, *Crimp with Amazeen:* James Flavin, *Butler:* David Clyde, *Policeman:* Stanley Andrews.

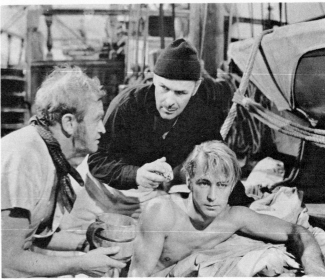

Two Years Before the Mast with Barry Fitzgerald, Brian Donlevy and Alan Ladd.

Unconquered with Howard da Silva, Paulette Goddard, Victor Varconi and Gary Cooper.

UNCONQUERED (1947) Par. Producer-Director, Cecil B. De Mille. Color by Technicolor. Based on the novel by Neil H. Swanson. Screenplay, Charles Bennett, Fredric M. Frank, Jesse Lasky, Jr. Art Directors, Hans Dreier, Walter Tyler. Cameraman, Ray Rennahan. Editor, Anne Bauchens. 146 minutes

Captain Christopher Holden: Gary Cooper, *Abby:* Paulette Goddard,

Garth: Howard da Silva, *Guyasuta, Chief of the Senecas:* Boris Karloff, *Jeremy Love:* Cecil Kellaway, *John Fraser:* Ward Bond, *Hannah:* Katherine DeMille, *Captain Steele:* Henry Wilcoxon, *Lord Chief Justice:* Sir C. Aubrey Smith, *Captain Simeon Ecuyer:* Victor Varconi, *Diana:* Virginia Grey, *Leach:* Porter Hall, *Bone:* Mike Mazurki, *Colonel George Washington:* Richard Gaines, *Mrs. John Fraser:* Virginia Campbell, *Lieutenant Fergus McKenzie:* Gavin Muir, *Sir William Johnson:* Alan Napier, *Mrs. Pruitt:* Nan Sunderland, *Sioto (Medicine Man):* Marc Lawrence, *Evelyn:* Jane Nigh, *Pontiac, Chief of the Ottawas:* Robert Warwick, *Lieutenant Hutchins:* Lloyd Bridges, *Lieutenant Baillie:* Oliver Thorndike, *Mamaultee:* Rus Conklin, *Colonel Henry Bouquet:* John Mylong, *Charles Mason:* George Kirby, *Jeremiah Dixon:* Leonard Carey, *Richard Henry Lee:* Frank R. Wilcox, *Mr. Carroll:* Davison Clark, *Brother Andrews:* Griff Barnett, *Venango Scout:* Raymond Hatton, *Widow Swivens:* Julia Faye, *Don McCoy:* Paul E. Burns, *Maggie:* Mary Field, *Jason:* Clarence Muse, *Captain Brooks:* Matthew Boulton, *Chief Killbuck:* Chief Thundercloud, *Joe Lovat:* Jack Pennick, *Royal American Officer:* Lex Barker, *Mulligan:* Charles Middleton.

Union Pacific with Joel McCrea and Barbara Stanwyck.

UNION PACIFIC (1939) Par. Producer and Director, Cecil B. De Mille. Screenplay, Walter DeLeon, C. Gardner Sullivan, Jesse Lasky, Jr. Art Directors, Hans Dreier, Roland Anderson. Musical Score, George Antheil. Cameramen, Victor Milner, Dewey Wrigley. Editor, Anne Bauchens. Based on an adaptation by Jack Cunningham of a story by Ernest Haycox. Location Director, Arthur Rosson. 133 minutes

Mollie Monahan: Barbara Stanwyck, *Jeff Butler:* Joel McCrea, *Fiesta:* Akim Tamiroff, *Dick Allen:* Robert Preston, *Leach Overmile:* Lynn Overman, *Sid Campeau:* Brian Donlevy, *Duke Ring:* Robert Barrat, *Cordray:* Anthony Quinn, *Casement:* Stanley Ridges, *Asa M. Barrows:* Henry Kolker, *Grenville M. Dodge:* Francis McDonald, *Oakes Ames:* Willard Robertson, *Calvin:* Harold Goodwin, *Mrs. Calvin:* Evelyn Keyes, *Sam Reed:* Richard Lane, *Dusky Clayton:* William Haade, *Paddy O'Rourke:* Regis Toomey, *Monahan:* J. M. Kerrigan, *Cookie:* Fuzzy Knight, *Al Brett:* Harry Woods, *Dollarhide:* Lon Chaney, Jr., *General U. S. Grant:* Joseph Crehan, *Mame:* Julia Faye, *Rose:* Sheila Darcy, *Shamus:* Joseph Sawyer, *Bluett:* Earl Askam, *Dr. Durant:* John Marston, *Andrew Whipple:* Byron Foulger, *Jerome:* Selmer Jackson, *Senator Smith:* Morgan Wallace, *Sargent:* Russell Hicks, *Mrs. Hogan:* May Beatty, *General Sheridan:* Ernie Adams, *Oliver Ames:* William J. Worthington, *Governor Stanford:* Guy Usher, *Mr. Mills:* James McNamara, *Governor Safford:* Gus Glassmire, *Dr. Harkness:* Stanley Andrews, *Rev. Dr. Tadd:* Paul Everton, *Harmonica Player:* Jack Pennick.

THE UNSINKABLE MOLLY BROWN (1964) MGM. Producer, Lawrence Weingarten. Associate Producer, Roger Edens. Director, Charles Walters. Panavision, MetroColor. Based on the musical by Richard Morris. Screenplay, Helen Deutsch. Art Directors, George W. Davis, Preston Ames. Music supervised and conducted by Robert

Armbruster. Songs, "Colorado is My Home," "I'll Never Say No," "Soliloquy," "He's My Friend," "Belly Up to the Bar, Boys," "I Ain't Down Yet." Music and Lyrics, Meredith Willson. Orchestration, Calvin Jackson, Leo Arnaud, Jack Elliott, Alexander Courage. Cinematographer, Daniel L. Fapp. Editor, Fredric Steinkamp. 128 minutes

Molly Brown: Debbie Reynolds, *Johnny Brown:* Harve Presnell, *Shamus Tobin:* Ed Begley, *Christmas Morgan:* Jack Kruschen, *Mrs Grogan:* Hermione Baddeley, *Prince Louis de Laniere:* Vassili Lambrinos, *Baron Karl Ludwig von Ettenburg:* Fred Essler, *Poluk:* Harvey Lembeck, *Mr. Fitzgerald:* Lauren Gilbert, *Mrs. Wadlington:* Kathryn Card, *Broderick:* Hayden Rorke, *Mr. Wadlington:* Harry Holcombe, *Mrs. Fitzgerald:* Amy Douglass, *Monsignor Ryan:* George Mitchell, *Grand Duchess Elise Lupovinova:* Martita Hunt, *Mr. Cartwright:* Vaughn Taylor, *Roberts:* Antony Eustrel, *Mrs. McGraw:* Audrey Christie, *Jam:* Grover Dale, *Murphy:* Brendan Dillon, *Daphne:* Maria Karnilova, *Joe:* Gus Trikonis, *Passenger:* Anna Lee, *Hotchkiss:* George Nicholson, *Lord Simon Primdale:* C. Ramsey Hill, *Lady Primdale:* Moyna Macgill, *Count Feranti:* Pat Benedetto, *Countess Feranti:* Mary Andre, *Vicar:* Pat Moran, *Spieler:* Herbert Vigran, *Mrs. Cartwright:* Eleanor Audley.

The Unsinkable Molly Brown with Vassili Lambrinos, Hayden Rorke, Audrey Christie and Debbie Reynolds.

Up in Smoke with Chong and Cheech.

UP IN SMOKE (1978) Par. Produced by Lou Adler and Lou Lombardo. Directed by Lou Adler. Written by Tommy Chong and (Richard) Cheech Marin. Panavision and MetroColor. Photography, Gene Polito. Associate Producer, John Beug. Supervising Editor, Lou Lombardo. Editor, Scott Conrad. Art Director, Leon Ericksen. Unit Production Manager/Assistant Director, Mike Moder. 2nd Assistant Director, Bill Beasley. Additional Photography, Jack Willoughby. Sound Mixer, Pat Mitchell. Special Effects, Knott Limited. Wardrobe, Ernie Misko. Make-up, Wes Dawn. Hairstylist, Lola "Skip" McNalley. Assistant Editors, Barry Leirer and Lori Jane Kranze. Title song by Cheech and Chong. New music by Danny "Kootch" Kortchmar and Waddy Wachtel. Film debuts of Cheech and Chong. Rated R. 87 minutes

Pedro De Pacas: Cheech Marin, *Man Stoner:* Tommy Chong, *Sgt. Stedenko:* Stacy Keach, *Strawberry:* Tom Skerritt, *Tempest Stoner:* Edie Adams, *Mr. Stoner:* Strother Martin, *Officer Gloria:* Louisa Moritz, *Jade East:* Zane Buzby, *Debbie:* Anne Wharton, *Harry:* Mills Watson, *Clyde:* Karl Johnson, *Murphy:* Rick Beckner, *Chauffeur:* Harold Fong, *Richard:* Richard Novo, *Jail Baits:* Jane Moder and Pam Bille, *Arresting Officer:* Arthur Roberts, *Judge Gladys Dykes:* Marian Beeler, *Bailiff:* Donald Hotton, *Prosecuting Attorney:* Jon Ian Jacobs, *Curtis:* Christopher Joy, *James, Bass Player:* Ray Vitte, *Duane, Guitarist:* Michael Caldwell, *Juan, 1st Trumpeter:* Jose Pulido, *Tom, 2nd Trumpeter:* Ruben Guevara, *Ollie, 3rd Trumpeter:* Miguel Murillo, *Ajax Lady:* June Fairchild, *Laughing Lady:* Rainbeaux Smith, *Aunt Bolita:* Angelina Estrada, *Upholstery Shop Foreman:* Ernie Fuentes, *Factory Boss:* Val Avery, *Bennie:* Ben Marino, *Toyota Kawasaki:* Akemi Kikumura, *Border Guards:* Joe Creaghe, Roy Stocking, *Sister Mary Vogue:* Marcia Wolf, *Sister Mary Secretary:* Andi Nachman, *Sister Mary Quacker:* Betty McGuire, *Sister Mary Arabian:* Cheryl Jeffrey, *Sister Mary Mary:* Gayna Shernen, *Sister Mary Yuma:* June Creaghe, *Sister Mary Indian:* Patty Proudfoot, *Motorcycle Cop:* Otto Felix, *Himself:* Rodney Bingenheimer, *The Groups:* Berlin Brats, the Dills, the Whores, *Roxy Doormen:* Durt Kaufman, David Nelson, *Tow Truck Driver:* Wayne Hazelhurst.

Up the Down Staircase with Roy Poole and Sandy Dennis.

UP THE DOWN STAIRCASE (1967) WB. A Pakula-Mulligan Production. Produced by Alan J. Pakula. Directed by Robert Mulligan. Color by Technicolor. Based on the novel by Bel Kaufman. Screenplay, Tad Mosel. Music, Fred Karlin. Art Director, George Jenkins. Assistant Director, Don Kranze. Photography, Joseph Coffey. Editor, Folmer Blangsted. Sound, Dennis Maitland. Filmed in New York City. 123 minutes

Sylvia Barrett: Sandy Dennis, *Paul Barringer:* Patrick Bedford, *Henrietta Pastorfield:* Eileen Heckart, *Beatrice Schachter:* Ruth White, *Sadie Finch:* Jean Stapleton, *Doctor Bester:* Sorrell Booke, *McHabe:* Roy Poole, *Ella Friedenberg:* Florence Stanley, *Joe Ferone:* Jeff Howard, *Alice Blake:* Ellen O'Mara, *Jose Rodriguez:* Jose Rodriguez, *Ed Williams:* John Fantauzzi, *The Mother:* Vinnette Carroll, *Miss Gordon:* Janice Mars, *Social Studies Teacher:* Loretta Leversee, *Mr. Osborne:* Robert Levine, *Nurse Eagen:* Elena Karam, *Charlotte Wolf:* Frances Sternhagen, *Linda Rosen:* Candace Culkin, *Harry A. Kagan:* Salvatore Rosa, *Lou Martin:* Lew Wallach.

UPTOWN SATURDAY NIGHT (1974) WB. Produced by Melville Tucker. Executive Producer and Director, Sidney Poitier. Associate Producer and Film Editor, Pembroke J. Herring. A First Artists and Verdon Productions presentation, in Technicolor with Panavision equipment. Screenplay, Richard Wesley. Photography, Fred J. Koenekamp. Production Designer, Alfred Sweeney. Sound, George A. Maly, Frank C. Regula and Harry W. Tetrick. Set Decoration, Robert de Vestel. Special Effects, Charles Spurgeon. Wardrobe, David Rawley and Marie V. Brown. Make-up, Monty Westmore. Hairstyles, Ann Wadlington. Assistant Directors, Charles C. Washburn and Bruce Chevillat. 2nd Unit Director, Harry F. Hogan, Sr. Filmed in Chicago and Los Angeles. Original Music Composed and Conducted by Tom Scott. "Uptown Saturday Night" by Morgan Ames and Scott, sung by Dobie Gray. Rated PG. 104 minutes

Steve Jackson: Sidney Poitier, *Wardell Franklin:* Bill Cosby, *Geechie Dan Beauford:* Harry Belafonte, *Sharp Eye Washington:* Richard Pryor, *Sarah Jackson:* Rosalind Cash, *The Reverend:* Flip Wilson, *Congressman Lincoln:* Roscoe Lee Browne, *Leggy Peggy:* Paula Kelly, *Madame Zenobia:* Lee Chamberlin, *Geechie's Henchman:* Johnny Sekka, *Irma Franklin:* Ketty Lester, *Little Seymour:* Harold Nicholas, *Silky Slim:* Calvin Lockhart, *Slim's Henchmen:* Lincoln Kilpatrick, Don Marshall, *Bit:* Henry Kingi.

Uptown Saturday Night with Sidney Poitier and Rosalind Cash.

The Valachi Papers with Charles Bronson and Jill Ireland.

THE VALACHI PAPERS (1972) Col. A Dino De Laurentiis-Euro-France Films Production. Produced by De Laurentiis. Directed by Terence Young. Based on the book by Peter Maas. Screenplay, Stephen Geller.

Executive Producer, Nino E. Krisman. Photography, Aldo Tonti. Music by Riz Ortolani. Editor, John Dwyre. Art Director, Mario Garbuglia. Set Decorations, John Godfrey and Ferdinando Ruffo. Special Effects, Eros Baciucchi. Sound, Roy Mangano. Costumes, Ann Roth and Giorgio Desideri. Make-up, Gianetto De Rossi and Mirella Sforza. Assistant Directors, Christian Raoux and Giorgio Gentili. Filmed in New York and Italy in Technicolor. Rated R. 125 minutes

Joe Valachi: Charles Bronson, *Vito Genovese:* Lino Ventura, *Salvatore Maranzano:* Joseph Wiseman, *Maria Reina Valachi:* Jill Ireland, *Dominick The Gap Petrilli:* Walter Chiari, *Ryan, FBI Agent:* Gerald S. O'Loughlin, *Gaetano Reina:* Amedeo Nazzari, *Tony Bender:* Guido Leontini, *Giuseppe Masseria:* Alessandro Sperli, *Donna Petrillo:* Maria Baxa, *Rosanna Reina:* Pupella Maggio, *Albert Anastasia:* Fausto Tozzi, *Salerto:* Mario Pilar, *Buster from Chicago:* Franco Borelli, *Charles (Lucky) Luciano:* Angelo Infanti, *Johnny Beck:* Fred Valleca, *Steven Ferrigno (Samuel Ferraro):* John Alarimo, *Warden:* Arny Freeman, *Little Augie:* Giancomino De Michelis, *Fort Monmouth Commander:* Sylvester Lamont, *Jane:* Sabine Sun, *Mary Lou:* Isabelle Marchal, *Donna's Girl Friend:* Imelde Marani, *Donald Valachi:* Jason McCallum, *Masseria:* Saro Urzi, *Frank:* Frank Gio, *Vinnie:* Steve Belouise, *Federal Investigator:* Anthony Dawson, *State Trooper:* Don Koll.

Valley of the Dolls with Barbara Parkins and Susan Hayward.

VALLEY OF THE DOLLS (1967) 20th. Produced by David Weisbart. Directed by Mark Robson. Panavision and De Luxe Color. A Red Lion Production. Based on the novel by Jacqueline Susann. Screenplay by Helen Deutsch and Dorothy Kingsley. Music by John Williams. Assistant Director, Eli Dunn. Art Direction, Jack Martin Smith and Richard Day. Sets, Walter M. Scott and Raphael G. Bretton. Photography, William Daniels. Editor, Dorothy Spencer. Sound, Don J. Bassman and David Dockendorf. Choreography, Robert Sidney. Gowns, Travilla. Production Manager, Francisco Day. Photographic Effects, L. B. Abbott, Art Cruickshank, and Emil Kosa, Jr. Orchestration, Herbert Spencer. Make-up, Ben Nye. Hair Styles, Kay Pownall. Supervised by Edith Lindon. Parkins' hair styles designed by Kenneth. Songs by Andre and Dory Previn: "Valley of the Dolls," sung by Dionne Warwick; "It's Impossible," "Come Live With Me," "Give a Little More," "I'll Plant My Own Tree." 123 minutes

Helen Lawson: Susan Hayward, *Neely O'Hara:* Patty Duke, *Anne Welles:* Barbara Parkins, *Jennifer North:* Sharon Tate, *Lyon Burke:* Paul Burke, *Tony Polar:* Tony Scotti, *Mel Anderson:* Martin Milner, *Kevin Gillmore:* Charles Drake, *Ted Casablanca:* Alex Davion, *Miriam Polar:* Lee Grant, *Miss Steinberg:* Naomi Stevens, *Henry Bellamy:* Robert H. Harris, *First Reporter:* Jacqueline Susann, *Director:* Robert Viharo, *Telethon Host:* Joey Bishop, *Host at Grammy Awards:* George Jessel, *Man:* Richard Angarola.

Variety Girl with Gary Cooper.

VARIETY GIRL (1947) Par. Producer, Daniel Dare. Director, George Marshall. Screenplay, Edmund Hartmann, Frank Tashlin, Robert Welch, Monte Brice. Musical Directors, Joseph J. Lilley, Troy Sanders. Art Directors, Hans Dreier, Robert Clatworthy. Cameramen, Lionel Lindon, Stuart Thompson. Editor, LeRoy Stone. Puppetoon sequence in Technicolor, by Thornton Hee and William Cottrell. Songs by Frank Loesser: "Tallahassee," "He Can Waltz," "Your Heart Calling Mine," "I Must Have Been Madly in Love," "I Want My Money Back," "Impossible Things" and "The French." 83 minutes

Catherine Brown: Mary Hatcher, *Amber La Vonne:* Olga San Juan, *Bob Kirby:* De Forest Kelley, *Bill Farris:* Glen Tryon, *Mrs. Webster:* Nella Walker, *Andre:* Torben Meyer, *Busboy:* Jack Norton, *Themselves:* Bing Crosby, Bob Hope, Gary Cooper, Ray Milland, Alan Ladd, Barbara Stanwyck, Paulette Goddard, Dorothy Lamour, Veronica Lake, Sonny Tufts, Joan Caulfield, William Holden, Lizabeth Scott, Burt Lancaster, Gail Russell, Diana Lynn, Sterling Hayden, Robert Preston, John Lund, William Bendix, Barry Fitzgerald, Cass Daley, Howard da Silva, Billy De Wolfe, MacDonald Carey, Arleen Whelan, Patrick Knowles, *Barker:* William Demarest, *Themselves:* Mona Freeman, Cecil Kellaway, Johnny Coy, Virginia Field, Richard Webb, Stanley Clements, *Stage Manager:* Frank Faylen, *J. R. O'Connell:* Frank Ferguson, *and* Cecil B. De Mille, Mitchell Leisen, Frank Butler, George Marshall, Roger Dann, Pearl Bailey, Jim and Mildred Mulcay, Spike Jones and his City Slickers, Mikhail Rasumny, Sally Rawlinson, Barney Dean, Mary Edwards, Virginia Welles, George Reeves, Patricia White (Barry), Wanda Hendrix, Nanette Parks.

VERA CRUZ (1954) UA. Producer, James Hill. Director, Robert Aldrich, Screenplay by Roland Kibbee and James R. Webb. Story by Bordon Chase. Presented by Harold Hecht and Burt Lancaster. Music by Hugo Friedhofer. Song "Vera Cruz" by Friedhofer and Sammy Cahn. Photography, Ernest Laszla. Editor, Alan Crosland, Jr. Color by Technicolor. Filmed in Mexico. The first film in SuperScope. 94 minutes

Benjamin Trane: Gary Cooper, *Joe Erin:* Burt Lancaster, *Countess Marie Duvarre:* Denise Darcel, *Marquis De Labordere:* Cesar Romero, *Nina:* Sarita Montiel, *Emperor Maximilian:* George Macready, *Donnegan:* Ernest Borgnine, *General Aguilar:* Morris Ankrum, *Little-Bit:* James McCallion, *Charles:* Jack Lambert, *Danette:* Henry Brandon, *Pittsburgh:* Charles (Bronson) Buchinsky, *Tex:* Jack Elam, *Abilene:* James Seay, *Ballard:* Archie Savage, *Reno:* Charles Horvath, *Pedro:* Juan Garcia.

Vera Cruz with Gary Cooper, Burt Lancaster and Cesar Romero.

The Victors with George Hamilton and Peter Fonda

THE VICTORS (1963) Col. Producer-Director-Writer, Carl Foreman. Based on a book by Alexander Baron. Music, Sol Kaplan. Associate Producer, Harold Buck. Assistant Director, Eric Rattray. A Highroad Production in Panavision. 175 minutes

Trower: George Hamilton, *Chase:* George Peppard, *Craig:* Eli Wallach, *Baker:* Vincent Edwards, *Maria:* Rosanna Schiaffino, *Grogan:* Jim Mitchum, *Sikh Soldier:* Tutte Lemkow, *French Lieutenant:* Maurice Ronet, *Jean-Pierre:* Joel Flateau, *French Woman:* Jeanne Moreau, *Regine:* Romy Schneider, *Eldridge:* Michael Callan, *Weaver:* Peter Fonda, *Madga:* Melina Mercouri, *Young British Soldier:* John Rogers, *Young French Girl:* Elizabeth Ercy, *Dennis:* Mervyn Johns, *Herr Metzger:* Albert Leiven, *Frau Metzger:* Marianne Deeming, *Trudi:* Senta Berger, *Helga:* Elke Sommer, *Russian Soldier:* Albert Finney.

The Vikings with Tony Curtis and Kirk Douglas.

THE VIKINGS (1958) UA. Producer, Jerry Bresler. Director, Richard Fleischer. Screenplay by Calder Willingham. Adaptation by Dale Wasserman. Based on a novel by Edison Marshall. Music by Mario Nascimbene. Assistant Director, Andre Smagghe. A Kirk Douglas Production in Technirama and Technicolor. 114 minutes

Einar: Kirk Douglas, *Eric:* Tony Curtis, *Ragnar:* Ernest Borgnine, *Morgana:* Janet Leigh, *Egbert:* James Donald, *Father Godwin:* Alexander Knox, *Aella:* Frank Thring, *Enid:* Maxine Audley, *Kitala:* Eileen Way, *Sandpiper:* Edric Connor, *Bridget:* Dandy Nichols, *Bjorm:* Per Buckhoj, *Pigtails:* Almut Berg.

The V.I.P.'s with Elsa Martinelli, Orson Welles, Margaret Rutherford and Martin Miller.

THE V.I.P.'S (1963) MGM. Producer, Anatole de Grunwald. Director, Anthony Asquith. Screenplay, Terence Rattigan. Music, Miklos Rozsa. Associate Producer, Roy Parkinson. Assistant Director, Kip Gowans. Gowns, Hubert de Givenchy, Pierre Cardin. In Panavision and Metro-Color. Photography, Jack Hildyard. Filmed in England. 119 minutes

Francis Andros: Elizabeth Taylor, *Paul Andros:* Richard Burton, *Marc Champselle:* Louis Jourdan, *Gloria Gritti:* Elsa Martinelli, *Duchess of Brighton:* Margaret Rutherford, *Miss Mead:* Maggie Smith, *Les Mangam:* Rod Taylor, *Miriam Marshall:* Linda Christian, *Max Buda:* Orson Welles, *Coburn:* Robert Coote, *Sanders:* Richard Wattis, *Commander Millbank:* Dennis Price, *Joslin:* Ronald Fraser, *Mr. Damer:* Peter Illing, *Airport Director:* Michael Hordern, *Waiter:* Stringer Davis, *Miss Potter:* Joan Benham, *Doctor:* Peter Sallis, *Mrs. Damer:* Joyce Carey, *Dr. Schwatzbacher:* Martin Miller.

Viva Las Vegas with Elvis Presley and Ann-Margret.

VIVA LAS VEGAS (1964) MGM. Producers, Jack Cummings, George Sidney. Director, George Sidney. MetroColor. Screenplay, Sally Benson. Art Directors, George W. Davis, Edward Carfagno. Music, George Stoll. Cinematographer, Joseph Biroc. Editor, John McSweeney, Jr. Filmed in Las Vegas. 86 minutes

Lucky Jackson: Elvis Presley, *Rusty Martin:* Ann-Margret, *Count Elmo Mancini:* Cesare Danova, *Mr. Martin:* William Demarest, *Shorty Farnsworth:* Nicky Blair, *Himself:* Jack Carter, *Swanson:* Robert B. Williams, *Big Gus Olson:* Bob Nash, *Baker:* Roy Engel, *Mechanic:* Barnaby Hale, *Driver:* Ford Dunhill, *M.C.:* Eddie Quillan, *Manager:* George Cisar, *Head Captain:* Ivan Triesault, *Francois:* Francis Raval, *Man:* Mike Ragan (Holly Bane).

Viva Villa! with Wallace Beery, Henry B. Walthall and Joseph Schildkraut.

VIVA VILLA! (1934) MGM. Produced by David O. Selznick. Directed by Jack Conway. Suggested by the book by Edgcumb Pinchon and O.B. Stade. Screenplay by Ben Hecht. Film Editor, Robert J. Kern. Photographers, James Wong Howe, Charles G. Clarke. Assistant Directors, Art Rosson, Johnny Waters. Musical Consultant, Juan Aguilar. Interior Decoration, Edwin B. Willis. Technical Advisor, Carlos Novarro. Technical Associate, Matias Santoyo. Recording Engineer, Douglas Shearer. Art Director, Harry Oliver. Costumes, Dolly Tree. Musical Numbers, Herbert Stothart. 115 minutes

Pancho Villa: Wallace Beery, *Teresa:* Fay Wray, *Diego:* Leo Carrillo, *Don Felipe:* Donald Cook, *Johnny:* Stuart Erwin, *Chavito:* George E. Stone, *Pascal:* Joseph Schildkraut, *Madero:* Henry B. Walthall, *Rosita:* Katherine DeMille, *Bugle Boy:* David Durand, *Villa as a boy:* Phillip Cooper, *Father:* Frank Puglia, *Pascal's Aide:* John Merkel, *Staff:* Charles Stevens, Steve Clemento, Pedro Regas, *Old Man:* Carlos De Valdez, *Staff:* George Regas, *Majordomo:* Harry Cording, *Prosecuting Attorney:* Sam Godfrey, *Political Judge:* Nigel De Brulier, *Grandees:* Charles Requa, Tom Ricketts, *Jail Official:* Clarence Hummel Wilson, *Mexican Officer:* James Martin, *Dancer:* Anita Gordiana, *Villa's Man:* Francis McDonald, *Soldier:* Harry Semels, *Telegraph Operator:* Julian Rivero, *Bartender:* Bob McKenzie, *Drunkard:* Dan Dix, *Newspaper Man:* Paul Stanton, *Military Attaché:* Mischa Auer, *Spanish Wife:* Belle Mitchell, *Statesmen:* John Davidson, Brandon Hurst, Leonard Mudie, *Generals:* Herbert Prior, Emile Chautard, *Mendoza Brothers:* Adrian Rosley, Hector Sarno, Henry Armetta, *Calloway:* Ralph Bushman (Francis X. Bushman, Jr.), *English Reporter:* Arthur Treacher, *German Reporter:* William Von Brincken, *French Reporter:* Andre Cheron, *Russian Reporter:* Michael Visaroff, *Wrong Girl:* Shirley Chambers, *Butcher:* Arthur Thalasso, *Peons:* Chris-Pin Martin, Nick De Ruiz.

VIVA ZAPATA! (1952) 20th. Produced by Darryl F. Zanuck. Directed by Elia Kazan. Written by John Steinbeck. Music Director, Alfred Newman. Art Directors, Lyle Wheeler and Leland Fuller. Photography, Joe MacDonald. Editor, Barbara McLean. Music, Alex North. 113 minutes

Zapata: Marlon Brando, *Josefa:* Jean Peters, *Eufemio:* Anthony Quinn, *Fernando:* Joseph Wiseman, *Don Nacio:* Arnold Moss, *Pancho Villa:* Alan Reed, *Soldadera:* Margo, *Pablo:* Lou Gilbert, *Madero:* Harold Gordon, *Senora Espejo:* Mildred Dunnock, *Huerta:* Frank Silvera, *Aunt:* Nina Varela, *Senor Espejo:* Florenz Ames, *Diaz:* Fay Roope, *Lazaro:* Will Kuluva, *Zapatista:* Bernie Gozier, *Col. Guajardo:* Frank De Kova, *Innocente:* Pedro Regas, *Old General:* Richard Garrick, *Officer:* Ross Bagdasarian, *Husband:* Leonard George, *Captain:* Abner Biberman, *C.O.:* Phil Van Zandt, *Soldier:* Henry Silva, *Eduardo:* Guy Thomajan, *Rurale:* George J. Lewis, *Soldiers:* Salvador Baquez, Peter Mamakos, *Manager:* Ric Roman, *Senior Officer:* Henry Corden, *New General:* Nester Paiva, *Captain of Rurales:* Robert Filmer, *Wife:* Julia Montoya.

Viva Zapata! with Anthony Quinn (left) and Marlon Brando (right).

Von Ryan's Express with Frank Sinatra, Vito Scotto, Sergio Fantoni and Trevor Howard.

VON RYAN'S EXPRESS (1965) 20th. Producer, Saul David. Director, Mark Robson. CinemaScope, De Luxe Color. Based on the novel by David Westheimer. Screenplay, Weldell Mayes, Joseph Landon. Art Directors, Jack Martin Smith, Hilyard Brown. Music, Jerry Goldsmith. Orchestration, Arthur Morton. Cinematographer, William A. Daniels. Special Photographic Effects, L. B. Abbott, Emil Kosa, Jr. Editor, Dorothy Spencer. 117 minutes

Colonel Joseph Ryan: Frank Sinatra, *Major Eric Fincham:* Trevor Howard, *Gabriella:* Raffaella Carra, *Sergeant Bostick:* Brad Dexter, *Captain Oriani:* Sergio Fantoni, *Orde:* John Leyton, *Constanzo:* Edward Mulhare, *Major Von Klemment:* Wolfgang Preiss, *Ames:* James Brolin, *Colonel Gortz:* John van Dreelen, *Battaglia:* Adolfo Celi, *Italian Train Engineer:* Vito Scotti, *Corporal Giannini:* Richard Bakalyan, *Captain Stein:* Michael Goodliffe, *Sergeant Dunbar:* Michael St. Clair, *Von Kleist:* Ivan Triesault, *Gortz's Aide:* Jacques Stanislavski, *American Soldiers:* Al Wyatt, Buzz Henry, John Day, James Sikking,

Ransom: Eric Micklewood, *Oriani's Aide:* John Mitory, *Italian Corporal:* Benito Prezia, *Italian Soldier:* Dominick Delgarde, *Ransom's Batman:* Barry Ford, *Gortz's Aide #2:* Gino Gottarelli, *Pilot:* Peter Hellman, *Italian Nobleman:* Mike Romanoff, *German Captain:* Walter Linden, *German Sgt:* Bard Stevens, *Italian Tailor:* Ernesto Melinari, *POW Who Opens Sweat Box:* Bob Rosen, *Extra:* Don Grant (Don Glut).

Waikiki Wedding with Bing Crosby and Shirley Ross.

WAIKIKI WEDDING (1937) Par. Produced by Arthur Hornblow, Jr. Directed by Frank Tuttle. Based on a story by Frank Butler and Don Hartman. Screenplay, Frank Butler, Don Hartman, Walter DeLeon, Francis Martin. Music Director, Boris Morros. Orchestrations, Victor Young. Arrangements, Al Siegel and Arthur Franklin. Dance Director, LeRoy Prinz. Photography, Karl Struss. Editor, Paul Weatherwax. Hawaiian lyrics, Jimmy Lovell. Costumes, Edith Head. Special Effects, Farciot Eduoart. Hawaiian Exterior, Robert C. Bruce. Sound, Gene Merritt and Louis Mesenkop. Interior Decorations, A. E. Freudeman. Songs: "Sweet Leilani" by Harry Owens; "Blue Hawaii," "In a Little Hula Heaven," "Sweet Is the Word for You," "Nani Ona Pua," "Okolehao" by Ralph Rainger and Leo Robin. 89 minutes

Tony Marvin: Bing Crosby, *Shad Buggle:* Bob Burns, *Myrtle Finch:* Martha Raye, *Georgia Smith:* Shirley Ross, *J. P. Todhunter:* George Barbier, *Dr. Victor Quimby:* Leif Erikson, *Everett Todhunter:* Grady Sutton, *Uncle Herman:* Granville Bates, *Kimo:* Anthony Quinn, *Koalani:* Mitchell Lewis, *Muamua:* George Regas, *Assistant Purser:* Nick Lukats, *Priest:* Prince Lei Lani, *Kaiaka:* Maurice Liu, *Mahina:* Raquel Echeverria, *Maile:* Nalani De Clercq, *Lani:* Kuulei De Clercq, *Specialty Dancer:* Miri Rei, *Frame:* Spencer Charters, *Harrison:* Alexander Leftwich, *Tomlin:* Ralph Remley, *Specialty Dancer:* Augie Goupil, *Keith:* Harry Stubbs, *John Durkin:* Pierre Watkin, *Secretary:* Iris Yamaoka, *Photographer:* Jack Chapin, *Cab Driver:* Pedro Regas, *Suki:* Lotus Liu, *Radio Operator:* David Newell, *Tony's Mother:* Emma Dunn, *Singer:* Ray Kinney, *First Policeman:* Robert Emmet O'Connor, *Second Policeman:* Lalo Encinas, *Bellboy:* Sojin, Jr.

Wait Until Dark with Richard Crenna and Audrey Hepburn.

WAIT UNTIL DARK (1967) WB-7 Arts. Produced by Mel Ferrer. Directed by Terence Young. Color by Technicolor. Based on the 1966 play by Frederick Knott. Screenplay, Robert and Jane-Howard Carrington. Music, Henry Mancini. Assistant Director, Jack Aldworth. Photography, Charles Lang. Editor, Gene Milford. Title song by Henry Mancini, Jay Livingston, and Ray Evans. Film debut of New York fashion model Samantha Jones. 108 minutes

Susy Hendrix: Audrey Hepburn, *Roat:* Alan Arkin, *Mike Talman:* Richard Crenna, *Carlino:* Jack Weston, *Sam Hendrix:* Efrem Zimbalist, Jr., *Lisa:* Samantha Jones, *Gloria:* Julie Herrod, *Shatner:* Frank O'Brien, *Boy:* Gary Morgan.

Wake Island with Macdonald Carey and Brian Donlevy.

WAKE ISLAND (1942) Par. Associate Producer, Joseph Sistrom. Director, John Farrow. Screenplay, W. R. Burnett, Frank Butler. Art Directors, Hans Dreier, Earl Hedrick. Cameraman, Theodor Sparkuhl. Editor, LeRoy Stone. Associate Cameraman, William C. Mellor. Filmed on the desert off Salton Sea, California. 78 minutes

Major Caton: Brian Donlevy, *Lieutenant Cameron:* Macdonald Carey, *Joe Doyle:* Robert Preston, *Smacksie Randall:* William Bendix, *Shad McCloskey:* Albert Dekker, *Commander Roberts:* Walter Abel, *Probenzki:* Mikhail Rasumny, *Private Cunkel:* Don Castle, *Captain Lewis:* Rod Cameron, *Sergeant:* Bill Goodwin, *Sally Cameron:* Barbara Britton, *Captain Patrick:* Damian O'Flynn, *Johnny Rudd:* Frank Albertson, *Private Warren:* Phillip Terry, *Corp. Goebbels:* Phillip Van Zandt, *Sparks Wilcox:* Keith Richards, *Colonel Cameron:* Willard Robertson, *Tommy:* Marvin Jones, *Squeaky Simpkins:* Jack Chapin, *Triunfo:* Rudy Robles, *Pete Hogan:* John Sheehan, *George Nielson:* Charles Trowbridge, *Cynthia Caton:* Mary Thomas, *Miss Pringle:* Mary Field, *Mr. Saburo Kurusu:* Richard Loo, *Tex Hannigan:* Earle Tex Harris, *Girl at Inn:* Hillary Brooke, *Girl at Inn:* Patti McCarty, *Major Johnson:* William Forrest, *Dr. Parkman:* Jack Mulhall, *Colonel:* Ivan Miller, *Captain:* Hugh Beaumont, *Commander:* Edward Earle, *Wounded Marine, First Lieutenant:* James Brown, *Rodrigo:* Angel Cruz, *Gordon:* Anthony Nace, *First Lieutenant:* Hollis Bane (Mike Ragan), *Wounded Marine:* Frank Faylen, *Marine:* Dane Clark, *Sight Setter:* Alan Hale, Jr.

WAKE OF THE RED WITCH (1948) Rep. Associate Producer, Edmund Grainger. Director, Edward Ludwig. Based on the novel by Garland Roark. Screenplay, Harry Brown, Kenneth Gamet. Art Director, James Sullivan. Music, Nathan Scott. Photography, Reggie Lanning. Editor, Richard L. Van Enger. 106 minutes

Captain Ralls: John Wayne, *Angelique Desaix:* Gail Russell, *Sam Rosen:* Gig Young, *Teleia Van Schreeven:* Adele Mara, *Mayrant Ruysdaal Sidneye:* Luther Adler, *Harmenszoon Van Schreeven:* Eduard Franz, *Captain Wilde Younguer:* Grant Withers, *Jacques Desaix:* Henry Daniell, *"Ripper" Arrezo:* Paul Fix, *Captain Munsey:* Dennis Hoey, *Mr. Loring:* Jeff Corey, *Dokter Van Arken:* Erskine Sanford,

Ua Nuka: Duke Kahanamoku, *Kurinua:* Henry Brandon, *Maru:* Fernando Alvarado, *Prosecuting Attorney:* John Wengraf, *Taluna:* Jose Alvarado, *Hekkim (Cabin Boy):* Carl Thompson, *Sailor:* Wallace Scott, *Young Crew Member:* Myron Healey, *Second Officer:* Mickey Simpson, *Young Sailor:* Robert Wood, *Dirk:* Grant Means, *Seaman Lookout:* Fred Libby, *Sailor (Fight Bit):* Fred Graham, *First Diver:* Jim Nolan, *Second Diver:* John Pickard, *Officer:* Rory Mallinson, *Diver's Assistant:* Harlan Warde, *Jarma:* Harry Vejar, *Lawyer:* Norman Rainey, *Mullins:* David Clarke, *Ship Surgeon:* Fred Fox, *Native Servant:* Al Kikume, *Native:* Kuka Tuitama, *Native Priest:* Leo C. Richmond, *Native:* George Piltz, *Kharma:* Harold Lishman.

Wake of the Red Witch with Kuda Tuitama, John Wayne, Henry Brandon, Gail Russell and Duke Kahanamoku.

A Walk in the Sun with Chris Drake and Richard Conte.

A WALK IN THE SUN (1945) 20th. Producer, Lewis Milestone. Production Manager, Joseph H. Nadel. Director, Lewis Milestone. From the novel by Harry Brown. Screenplay, Robert Rossen. Art Director, Max Bertisch. Musical Score, Fredric Efrem Rich. Ballads, Millard Lampell, Earl Robinson. Cameraman, Russell Harlan. Editor, Duncan Mansfield. Film debut of John Ireland. 111 minutes

Sgt. Tyne: Dana Andrews, *Rivera:* Richard Conte, *Windy:* John Ireland, *Friedman:* George Tyne, *Sgt. Ward:* Lloyd Bridges, *McWilliams:* Sterling Holloway, *Sgt. Porter:* Herbert Rudley, *Archimbeau:* Norman Lloyd, *Judson:* Steve Brodie, *Carraway:* Huntz Hall, *Sgt. Hoskins:* James Cardwell, *Rankin:* Chris Drake, *Tranella:* Richard Benedict, *Tinker:* George Offerman, Jr., *Trasker:* Danny Desmond, *Cousins:* Victor Cutler, *Giorgio:* Anthony Dante, *Cpl. Kramer:* Harry Cline, *James:* Jay Norris, *Johnson:* Al

Hammer, *Dugan:* Don Summers, *Phelps:* Malcolm O'Guinn, *Smith:* Grant Maiben, *Riddle:* John Kellogg, *Long:* Dick Daniels, *Sgt.* Matt Willis, *Reconnaissance:* George Turner.

Walking Tall with Joe Don Baker.

WALKING TALL (1973) Cinerama. A BCP Production, in color. Produced by Mort Briskin. Directed by Phil Karlson. Executive Producer, Charles A. Pratt. Written by Mort Briskin, a fictionalized account of incidents in the life of Sheriff Buford Pusser, McNairy County, Tennessee, who acted as technical consultant. Production Executive, John E. Pommer. Associate Producer, Joel Briskin. Photography, Jack A. Marta. Production Designer, Stan Jolley. Editor, Harry Gerstad. Assistant Directors: Ralph Black, David (Buck) Hall, Mark Sandrich. Special Effects, Sass Bedig. Stunt Coordinators, Gil Perkins and Carey Loftin. Make-up, Jack H. Young. Hairstylist, Virginia Jones. Costumes, Oscar Rodriguez and Phyllis Garr. Postproduction Supervisor, Houseley Stevenson. Sound Editor, James J. Klinger. Music by Walter Scharf. Song, "Walking Tall" by Walter Scharf and Don Black, sung by Johnny Mathis. Filmed entirely in Tennessee. Rated R. 125 minutes. Sequels: *Part 2 Walking Tall* (AIP, 1975) with Bo Svenson and *Final Chapter—Walking Tall* (1977) with Svenson

Buford Pusser: Joe Don Baker, *Pauline Pusser:* Elizabeth Hartman, *Sheriff Al Thurman:* Gene Evans, *Callie Hacker:* Rosemary Murphy, *Grandpa Carl Pusser:* Noah Beery, Jr., *Grandma Pusser:* Lurene Tuttle, *Luan Paxton:* Brenda Benet, *Prentiss Parley:* John Brascia, *Grady Coker:* Bruce Glover, *Obra Eaker:* Felton Perry, *Arno Purdy:* Richard X. Slattery, *Margie Ann:* Lynn Borden, *Lutie McVeigh:* Ed Call, *Sheldon Levine:* Sidney Clute, *Judge R. W. Clarke:* Douglas V. Fowley, *Dr. Lamar Stivers:* Don Keefer, *Willie Rae Lockman:* Sam Laws, *Buel Jaggers:* Arch Johnson, *Zolan Dicks:* Pepper Martin, *Lester Dickens:* John Myhers, *John Witter:* Logan Ramsey, *Augie McCullah:* Kenneth Tobey, *Singer:* Wanea Wes, *Mike Pusser:* Leif Garrett, *Dwana Pusser:* Dawn Lyn, *Bozo:* Dominick Mazzie, *Ferrin Meaks:* Russell Thorson, *Bouncers:* Gil Perkins, Gene Lebell, *Dice Player:* Carey Loftin, *Stickman:* Warner Venetz, *Otie Doss:* Del Monroe, *Prosecutor:* Lloyd Tatum, *Jury Foreman:* Vaudie Plunk, *Hassie Berlson:* Pearline Wynn, *Virgil Button:* Ted Jordan, *Sheriff Tanner:* Red West, *Prisoner:* Andrew J. Pirtle.

War and Peace with Lea Seidl, Barry Jones, Audrey Hepburn, Jeremy Brett, May Britt and Henry Fonda.

WAR AND PEACE (1956) Par. Producer, Dino De Laurentiis. Director, King Vidor. VistaVision, Technicolor. From the novel by Leo Tolstoy. Screenplay, Bridget Boland, Robert Westerby, King Vidor, Mario Camerini, Ennio De Concini, Ivo Perilli. Art Director, Mario Chiari. Musical Director, Franco Ferrara. Music Score, Nino Rota. Cinematographers, Jack Cardiff, Aldo Tonti. Supervising Editor, Stuart Gilmore. Editor, Leo Cattozzo. Assistant Directors, Piero Musetta and Guidarino Guidi. Costumes by Maria De Matteis. A Ponti-DeLaurentiis Production. Filmed in Rome. 208 minutes

Natasha: Audrey Hepburn, *Pierre:* Henry Fonda, *Andrey:* Mel Ferrer, *Anatole:* Vittorio Gassman, *Platon:* John Mills, *Napoleon:* Herbert Lom, *General Kutuzov:* Oscar Homolka, *Helene:* Anita Ekberg, *Dolokhov:* Helmut Dantine, *Count Rostov:* Barry Jones, *Mary Bolkonsky:* Anna Maria Ferrero, *Lise:* Milly Vitale, *Nicholas Rostov:* Jeremy Brett, *Countess Rostov:* Lea Seidl, *Prince Bolkonsky:* Wilfred Lawson, *Petya Rostov:* Sean Barrett, *Kuragine:* Tullio Carminati, *Sonya:* May Britt, *Denisov:* Patrick Crean, *Peronskava:* Gertrude Flynn.

The War of the Worlds.

THE WAR OF THE WORLDS (1953) Par. Producer, George Pal. Director, Byron Haskin. Technicolor. Based on the novel by H. G. Wells. Screenplay, Barre Lyndon. Art Directors, Hal Pereira, Albert Nozaki. Cinematographer, George Barnes. Editor, Everett Douglas. Technicolor Consultant, Monroe Burbank. 85 minutes

Clayton Forrester: Gene Barry, *Sylvia Van Buren:* Ann Robinson, *General Mann:* Les Tremayne, *Dr. Pryor:* Bob Cornthwaite, *Dr. Bilderbeck:* Sandro Giglio, *Pastor Matthew Collins:* Lewis Martin, *Aide to General Mann:* Houseley Stevenson, Jr., *Radio Announcer:* Paul Frees, *Wash Perry:* Bill Phipps, *Col. Ralph Heffner:* Vernon Rich, *Cop:* Henry Brandon, *Salvatore:* Jack Kruschen, *Commentary*

by: Sir Cedric Hardwicke, *Introductory Narration:* Paul Frees, *Prof. McPherson:* Edgar Barrier, *Buck Monahan:* Ralph Dumke, *Bird-Brained Blonde:* Carolyn Jones, *Man:* Pierre Cressoy, *Martian:* Charles Gemora, *Sheriff:* Walter Sande, *Dr. James:* Alex Frazer, *Dr. DuPrey:* Ann Codee, *Dr. Gratzman:* Ivan Lebedeff, *Ranger:* Robert Rockwell, *Zippy:* Alvy Moore, *Alonzo Hogue:* Paul Birch, *Fiddler Hawkins:* Frank Kreig, *Well-Dressed Man During Looting:* Ned Glass, *M. P. Driver:* Anthony Warde, *Woman News Vendor:* Gertrude Hoffman, *Secretary of Defense:* Freeman Lusk, *Fire Chief:* Sydney Mason, *Lookout:* Peter Adams, *Reporter:* Ted Hecht, *Japanese Diplomat:* Teru Shimada, *Chief of Staff, U.S.A.:* Herbert Lytton, *Staff Sergeant:* Douglas Henderson, *Looters:* Dave Sharpe, Dale Van Sickel, Fred Graham.

Watch on the Rhine with Paul Lukas, Bette Davis and George Coulouris.

WATCH ON THE RHINE (1943) WB. Producer, Hal B. Wallis. Director, Herman Schumlin. From the play by Lillian Hellman. Screenplay, Dashiell Hammett. Musical Score, Max Steiner. Art Director, Carl Jules Weyl. Musical Director, Leo F. Forbstein. Cameramen, Merritt Gerstad, Hal Mohr. Special Effects, Jack Holden, Edwin B. DuPar. Editor, Rudi Fehr. 114 minutes

Sara Muller: Bette Davis, *Kurt Muller:* Paul Lukas, *Marthe DeBrancovis:* Geraldine Fitzgerald, *Fanny Farrelly:* Lucile Watson, *Anise:* Beulah Bondi, *Teck DeBrancovis:* George Coulouris, *David Farrelly:* Donald Woods, *Phili Von Ramme:* Henry Daniell, *Joshua Muller:* Donald Buka, *Bodo Muller:* Eric Roberts, *Babette Muller:* Janis Wilson, *Young Man:* Helmut Dantine, *Mrs. Mellie Sewell:* Mary Young, *Herr Blecher:* Kurt Katch, *Dr. Klauber:* Erwin Kalser, *Overdorff:* Robert O. Davis, *Sam Chandler:* Clyde Fillmore, *Joseph:* Frank Wilson, *Horace:* Clarence Muse, *Belle:* Violett McDowell, *Chauffeur:* Creighton Hale, *Doc:* William Washington, *Italian Woman:* Elvira Curci, *Italian Man:* Anthony Caruso, *Mr. Chabeuf:* Jean DeBriac, *Miss Drake:* Leah Baird, *Cyrus Penfield:* Howard Hickman, *Admiral:* Frank Reicher, *German Ambassador:* Robert O. Fischer, *Boy:* Alan Hale, Jr., *Trainman:* Jack Mower, *Taxi Driver:* Garry Owen.

THE WAY WE WERE (1973) Col. A Rastar Production. Produced by Ray Stark. Directed by Sydney Pollack. Panavision and Color. Written by Arthur Laurents, based on his novel. (Alvin Sargent and David Rayfiel worked on the script). Photography, Harry Stradling, Jr. Production Designer, Stephen Grimes. Supervising Film Editor, Margaret Booth. Associate Producer, Richard Roth. Unit Production Manager, Russ Saunders. Costume Designers, Dorothy Jeakins and Moss Mabry. Music Editor, Ken Runyan. Assistant Directors, Howard Koch, Jr., and Jerry Ziesmer. Make-up, Donald Cash, Jr., and Gary Liddiard. Hairstyles, Kaye Pownall. Sound, Jack Solomon. Dance Director, Grover Dale. Music by Marvin Hamlisch. Song, "The Way We Were" by Hamlisch and Marilyn and Alan Bergman. Filmed in New York and California. Rated PG. 118 minutes

Katie Morosky: Barbra Streisand, *Hubbell Gardiner:* Robert Redford, *J.J.:* Bradford Dillman, *Carol Ann:* Lois Chiles, *George Bissinger:* Patrick O'Neal, *Paul Reisner:* Viveca Lindfors, *Rhea Edwards:* Allyn Ann McLerie, *Brooks Carpenter:* Murray Hamilton, *Bill Verso:* Herb Edelman, *Vicki Bissinger:* Diana Ewing, *Pony Dunbar:* Sally Kirkland, *Peggy Vanderbilt:* Marcia Mae Jones, *Radio Actor:* Don Keefer, *El Morocco Captain:* George Gaynes, *Army Corporal:* Eric Boles, *Ash Blonde:* Barbara Peterson, *Army Captain:* Roy Jenson, *Rally Speaker:* Brendan Kelly, *Frankie McVeigh:* James Woods, *Jenny:* Connie Forslund, *Dr. Short:* Robert Gerringer, *Judianne:* Susie Blakely, *Airforce:* Ed Power, *Dumb Blonde:* Suzanne Zenor, *Guest:* Dan Seymour, *Professor's Wife:* Dorian Cusick, *Officer dining:* Don Koll, *Officer passing Plaza:* Bob Dahdah.

The Way We Were with Robert Redford and Barbra Streisand.

Weekend at the Waldorf with Walter Pidgeon and Lana Turner.

WEEKEND AT THE WALDORF (1945) MGM. Producer, Arthur Hornblow, Jr., Director, Robert Z. Leonard. Author, Vicki Baum. Screenplay, Sam and Bella Spewack. Adaptation, Guy Bolton. Musical Director, Johnny Green. Dance Director, Charles Walters. Art Directors, Cedric Gibbons, Daniel B. Cathcart. Cameraman, Robert Planck. Special Effects, Warren Newcombe. Editor, Robert J. Kern. Musical numbers by Sammy Fain: "And There You Are" (lyrics by Ted Koehler) and "Guadalajara." Remake of *Grand Hotel* (MGM, 1932). 130 minutes

Irene Malvern: Ginger Rogers, *Chip Collyer:* Walter Pidgeon, *Captain*

James Hollis: Van Johnson, *Bunny Smith:* Lana Turner, *Randy Morton:* Robert Benchley, *Martin X. Edley:* Edward Arnold, *Mme. Jaleska:* Constance Collier, *Henry Burton:* Leon Ames, *Dr. Campbell:* Warner Anderson, *Cynthia Drew:* Phyllis Thaxter, *Oliver Webson:* Keenan Wynn, *Stevens:* Porter Hall, *Mr. Jessup:* Samuel S. Hinds, *Bey of Aribajan:* George Zucco, *Xavier Cugat:* Himself, *Juanita:* Lina Romay, *Singer:* Bob Graham, *Lieutenant John Rand:* Michael Kirby, *Jane Rand:* Cora Sue Collins, *Anna:* Rosemary De Camp, *Kate Douglas:* Jacqueline deWit, *Emile:* Frank Puglia, *Hi Johns:* Charles Wilson, *Sam Skelly:* Irving Bacon, *British Secretary:* Miles Mander, *Mrs. H. Davenport Drew:* Nana Bryant, *McPherson:* Russell Hicks, *Irma:* Ludmilla Pitoeff, *Night Maid:* Naomi Childers, *House Detective Blake:* Moroni Olsen, *Chief Jennings:* William Halligan, *Alix:* John Wengraf, *The Woman:* Ruth Lee, *Cassidy (Doorman):* William Hall, *Pianist:* Rex Evans, *Literary Type:* Wyndham Standing, *Anna's Boy Friend:* Harry Barris, *Barber:* Byron Foulger, *Assistant Manager:* Gladden James, *Orchestra Leader:* Carli Elinor, *Bell Captain:* Dick Crockett.

Wee Willie Winkie with Shirley Temple and C. Aubrey Smith.

WEE WILLIE WINKIE (1937) 20th. Associate Producer, Gene Markey. Directed by John Ford. Based on the story by Rudyard Kipling. Screenplay, Ernest Pascal and Julien Josephson. Photography, Arthur Miller. Editor, Walter Thompson. 99 minutes

Priscilla Williams: Shirley Temple, *Sergeant McDuff:* Victor McLaglen, *Captain Williams:* C. Aubrey Smith, *Joyce:* June Lang, *Coppy (Lieutenant Brandes):* Michael Whalen, *Khoda Khan:* Cesar Romero, *Mrs. Allardyce:* Constance Collier, *Mott:* Douglas Scott, *Captain Bibberbeigh:* Gavin Muir, *Mohammed Dihn:* Willie Fung, *Major Allardyce:* Lionel Pape, *Bagby:* Brandon Hurst, *Pipe Major:* Clyde Cook, *Elsie Allardyce:* Lauri Beatty, *Mrs. MacMonachie:* Mary Forbes, *MacMonachie:* George Hassell, *Gen. Hammond:* Lionel Braham, *Tummel:* Cyril McLaglen, *English Soldier:* Pat Somerset, *Driver:* Hector V. Sarno, *Soldier:* Jack Pennick, *Sikh Policeman:* Noble Johnson, *Merchant:* Scotty Mattraw, *African Chieftain:* Louis Vincenot.

WELCOME STRANGER (1947) Par. Producer, Sol C. Siegel. Director, Elliott Nugent. Author, Frank Butler. Screenplay, Arthur Sheekman. Art Directors, Hans Dreier, Franz Bachelin. Musical Score,

Robert Emmett Dolan. Cameraman, Lionel Lindon. Editor, Everett Douglas. Songs by Johnny Burke and Jimmy Van Heusen: "As Long as I'm Dreaming," "My Heart Is a Hobo," "Country Style," "Smile Right Back at the Sun" and "Smack in the Middle of Maine." 107 minutes

Dr. Jim Pearson: Bing Crosby, *Trudy Mason:* Joan Caulfield, *Dr. Joseph McRory:* Barry Fitzgerald, *Emily Walters:* Wanda Hendrix, *Bill Walters:* Frank Faylen, *Mrs. Gilley:* Elizabeth Patterson, *Roy Chesley:* Robert Shayne, *Dr. Ronnie Jenks:* Larry Young, *Nat Dorkas:* Percy Kilbride, *Charlie Chesley:* Charles Dingle, *Mort Elkins:* Don Beddoe, *Congressman Beeker:* Thurston Hall, *Miss Lennek:* Lillian Bronson, *Secretary, Boston:* Mary Field, *Mr. Daniels:* Paul Stanton, *Ed Chanock:* Pat McVey, *Ben, Bus Driver:* Milton Kibbee, *Clarence, Steward:* Clarence Muse, *Farmer Pinkett:* Charles Middleton, *Cousin Hattie (Photo):* Margaret Field (Maggie Mahoney), *Friends:* John Ince, Franklyn Farnum, *Train Companion:* Erville Alderson, *Mr. Cartwright:* John Westley, *Mr. Weaver:* Edward Clark, *Man:* Clarence Nordstrom, *Man:* Brandon Hurst, *Mrs. Sims:* Ethel Wales, *Mr. Crane:* Frank Ferguson, *Dr. White:* Elliott Nugent, *Telephone Operator:* Bea Allen, *Woman:* Julia Faye, *Miss Wendy:* Gertrude Hoffman, *Principal, Mr. Tilson:* Douglas Wood, *Al:* Fred Datig, Jr., *Citizen:* John "Skins" Miller.

Welcome Stranger with Elizabeth Patterson, Percy Kilbride, Charles Dingle, Barry Fitzgerald, Lillian Bronson, Clarence Nordstrom, Robert Shayne, John Westley and John "Skins" Miller.

The Westerner with Gary Cooper and Walter Brennan.

THE WESTERNER (1940) UA. Producer, Samuel Goldwyn. Director, William Wyler. Author, Stuart Lake. Screenplay, Jo Swerling, Niven Busch. Cameraman, Gregg Toland. Editor, Daniel Mandell. Film debuts of Forrest Tucker, 25, and Dana Andrews, 29. 99 minutes

Cole Hardin: Gary Cooper, *Judge Roy Bean:* Walter Brennan, *Jane-Ellen Mathews:* Doris Davenport, *Caliphet Mathews:* Fred Stone, *Chickenfoot:* Paul Hurst, *Southeast:* Chill Wills, *Mort Borrow:* Charles Halton, *Wade Harper:* Forrest Tucker, *King Evans:* Tom Tyler, *Mr. Dixon:* Arthur Aylsworth, *Teresita:* Lupita Tovar, *Juan Gomez:* Julian Rivero, *Lily Langtry:* Lilian Bond, *Bart Cobble:* Dana Andrews, *Eph Stringer:* Roger Gray, *Bantry:* Jack Pennick, *Seth Tucker:* Arthur Mix, *Janice:* Helen Foster, *Shad Wilkins:* Trevor Bardette, *Langtry Maid:* Connie Leon, *Langtry Manager:* Charles Coleman, *Ticket Man:* Lew Kelly, *Man at Window:* Heinie Conklin, *A Stranger:* Lucien Littlefield, *Orchestra Leader:* Corbet Morris, *Sheriff:* Stanley Andrews, *Stage Manager:* Henry Roquemore, *Deputy:* Hank Bell.

West Side Story with Natalie Wood, George Chakiris and Richard Beymer.

WEST SIDE STORY (1961) UA. Producer, Robert Wise. Directors, Robert Wise, Jerome Robbins. Panavision 70, Technicolor. Screenplay, Ernest Lehman. Based on stage play by Arthur Laurents, based on an idea by Jerome Robbins. Music, Leonard Bernstein. Lyrics, Stephen Sondheim. Associate Producer, Saul Chaplin. Choreography, Jerome Robbins. Assistant Director, Robert Relyea. Costumes, Irene Sharaff. Assistant Choreographers, Howard Jeffrey, Margaret Banks. A Mirisch Pictures and Seven Arts Production. Locations filmed in New York. Songs by Leonard Bernstein and Stephen Sondheim: "Jet Song," "Something's Coming," "Dance at the Gym," "Tonight," "Maria," "In America," "One Hand, One Heart," "Officer Krupke," "The Rumble," "Cool," "I Feel Pretty," "Somewhere," "A Boy Like That," "I Have a Love," "There's a Place for Us." Marni Nixon sings for Wood, Jimmy Bryant sings for Beymer. 155 minutes

Maria: Natalie Wood, *Tony:* Richard Beymer, *Riff:* Russ Tamblyn, *Anita:* Rita Moreno, *Bernardo:* George Chakiris, *The Jets: Ice,* Tucker Smith, *Action,* Tony Mordente, *Baby John,* Eliot Feld, *A-Rab,* David Winters, *Snowboy,* Burt Michaels, *Joyboy,* Robert Banas, *Big Deal,* Scooter (Anthony) Teague, *Gee-Tar,* Tommy Abbott, *Mouthpiece,* Harvey Hohnecker, *Tiger,* David Bean, *Anybodys,* Sue Oakes, *Graziella:* Gina Trikonis, *Velma:* Carole D'Andrea, *The Sharks: Chino,* Joe De Vega, *Pepe,* Jay Norman, *Indio,* Gus Trikonis, *Luis,* Robert Thompson, *Rocco,* Larry Roquemore, *Loco,* Jaime Rogers, *Juano,* Eddie Verso, *Chile,* Andre Tayir, *Toro,* Nick Covvacevich, *Del Camp,* Rudy Del Campo, *Rosalia,* Suzie Kaye, *Consuelo,* Yvonne Othon, *Francisca,* Joanne Miya, *Lieutenant Schrank:* Simon Oakland, *Officer Krupke:* Bill Bramley, *Doc:* Ned Glass, *Glad Hand, Social Worker:* John Astin, *Madame Lucia:* Penny Santon.

WESTWORLD (1973) MGM. Produced by Paul N. Lazarus III. Directed and Written by Michael Crichton. MetroColor and Panavision. Associate Producer, Michael I. Rachmil. Music by Fred Karlin. Special

Effects, Charles Schulthies. Action Coordinator, Dick Ziker. Photography, Gene Polito. Editor, David Bretherton. Art Director, Herman Blumenthal. Assistant Directors, Claude Binyon, Jr., and James Boyle. Filmed on Harold Lloyd's estate, Greenacres, in Los Angeles. Rated PG. 91 minutes. Sequel was *Futureworld* (AIP, 1976), also with Brynner

Gunslinger: Yul Brynner, *Peter Martin:* Richard Benjamin, *John Blane:* James Brolin, *Medieval Knight:* Norman Bartold, *Chief Supervisor:* Alan Oppenheimer, *Medieval Queen:* Victoria Shaw, *Banker:* Dick Van Patten, *Arlette:* Linda Scott, *Saloon Hostess:* Kevin Dignam, *Technician:* Steve Franken, *Black Knight:* Michael Mikler, *Sheriff:* Terry Wilson, *Miss Carrie:* Majel Barrett, *Servant Girl:* Anne Randall, *Girl in Dungeon:* Julie Marcus, *Apache Girl:* Sharyn Wynters, *Middle-aged Woman:* Anne Bellamy, *Stewardess:* Chris Holter, *Bellhop:* Charles Seel, *Bartender:* Wade Crosby, *Hostess:* Nora Marlowe, *Workmen:* Will J. White, Ben Young, Tom Falk, *Supervisors:* Orville Sherman, Lindsay Workman, Lauren Gilbert, Howard Platt, Davis Roberts (Robert A. Davis), *Technicians:* Jared Martin, Richard Roat, Kenneth Washington, Robert Patten, David Frank, Kip King, David Man, Larry Delaney, *Ticket Girl:* Lin Henson.

Westworld with Richard Benjamin and Linda Scott.

What Ever Happened to Baby Jane with Joan Crawford and Bette Davis.

WHAT EVER HAPPENED TO BABY JANE (1962) WB. Producer-Director, Robert Aldrich. Screenplay, Lukas Heller. Based on a novel by Henry Farrell. Executive Producer, Kenneth Hyman. Costumes, Norma Koch. Assistant Director, Tom Connors. Choreography, Alex Romero. A Seven Arts Production. Art Dic... Director, William Glasgow. Music, Frank DeVol. Cinematographer, Ernest Haller. Editor, Michael Luciano. Scenes from *Parachute Jumper* (WB, 1933), Davis; *Sadie McKee* (MGM, 1934), Crawford. 132 minutes

Blanche Hudson: Joan Crawford, *Jane Hudson:* Bette Davis, *Edwin Flagg:* Victor Buono, *Della Flagg:* Marjorie Bennett, *Elvira Stitt:* Maidie Norman, *Mrs. Bates:* Anna Lee, *Liza Bates:* Barbara Merrill, *Baby Jane:* Julie Allred, *Blanche as a child:* Gina Gillespie, *Ray Hudson:* Dave Willock, *Cora Hudson:* Ann Barton.

What's New Pussycat? with Peter Sellers and Capucine.

WHAT'S NEW PUSSYCAT? (1965) UA. Producer, Charles K. Feldman. Executive Producer, John C. Shepridge. Director, Clive Donner. Associate Producer, Richard Sylbert. Screenplay, Woody Allen. Music, Burt Bacharach. Lyrics, Hal David. Director of Photography, Jean Badal. Assistant Director, Enrico Isacco. Costumes, Mia Fonssagrives, Vicki Tiel. In Technicolor. A Production of Famous Artists Productions and Famartists Productions. Film debut of Woody Allen. 108 minutes

Fritz Fassbender: Peter Sellers, *Michael James:* Peter O'Toole, *Carol Werner:* Romy Schneider, *Renee Lefebvre:* Capucine, *Liz:* Paula Prentiss, *Victor Shakapopolis:* Woody Allen, *Rita:* Ursula Andress, *Anna Fassbender:* Edra Gale, *Jacqueline:* Catherine Schaake, *Mr. Werner:* Jess Hahn, *Mrs. Werner:* Eleanor Hirt, *Tempest O'Brien:* Nicole Karen, *Marcel:* Jean Paredes, *Philippe:* Michel Subor, *Charlotte:* Jacqueline Fogt, *Car Renter:* Robert Rollis, *Gas Station Operator:* Daniel Emilfork, *Jean:* Louis Falavigna, *Etienne:* Jacques Balutin, *Emma:* Annette Poivre, *Man in Bar:* Richard Burton.

What's Up, Doc? with Ryan O'Neal and Barbra Streisand.

WHAT'S UP, DOC? (1972) WB. Produced and Directed by Peter Bogdanovich. A Saticoy Production. Chase sequence directed by Paul Baxley. Based on a story by Bogdanovich. Screenplay by Buck Henry, David Newman and Robert Benton. Photography, Laszlo Kovacs. Music by Artie Butler. Editor, Verna Fields. Production Design, Polly Platt. Art Director, Herman A. Blumenthal. Set Decorations, John Austin. Special Effects, Robert MacDonald. Titles by the Golds West, Inc. Sound, Les Fresholtz. Costumes, Nancy McArdle and Ray Phelps. Make-up, Don Cash. Hairstyles, Lynda Gurasich. Associate Producer, Paul Lewis. Assistant to the Producer, Frank Marshall. Assistant Director, Ray Gosnell. Songs: "You're the Top" by Cole Porter, "As Time Goes By" by Herman Hupfeld. Filmed partly in San Francisco in Technicolor. Film debut of Madeline Kahn. Rated G. 94 minutes

Judy Maxwell: Barbra Streisand, *Prof. Howard Bannister:* Ryan O'Neal, *Eunice Burns:* Madeline Kahn, *Hugh Simon:* Kenneth Mars, *Frederick Larrabee:* Austin Pendleton, *Harry:* Sorrell Booke, *Fritz:* Stefan Gierasch, *Mrs. Van Hoskins:* Mabel Albertson, *Mr. Smith:* Michael Murphy, *Bailiff:* Graham Jarvis, *Judge:* Liam Dunn, *Mr. Jones:* Phil Roth, *Mr. Kaltenborn:* John Hillerman, *Rudy, The Headwaiter:* George Morfogen, *Prof. Hosquith:* Randall R. (Randy) Quaid, *Arresting Officer:* M. Emmet Walsh, *Banquet Receptionist:* Eleanor Zee, *Delivery Boy:* Kevin O'Neal, *Room Service Waiter:* Paul Condylis, *Jewel Thieves:* Fred Scheiwiller, Carl Saxe, Jack Perkins, *Druggist:* Paul B. Kipilman, *Jones' Driver:* Gil Perkins, *Mrs. Hosquith:* Christa Lang, *Musicologists:* Stan Ross, Peter Paul Eastman, *Head:* John Byner, *Larrabee's Butler:* Eric Brotherson, *Party Guest:* Elaine Partnow, *Eunice's Cabdriver:* George R. Burrafato, *Smith's Cabdriver:* Jerry Summers, *Airport Cabdriver:* Morton C. Thompson, *Airport Driver:* John Allen Vick, *Skycap:* Donald T. Bexley, *Painter on Roof:* Leonard Lookabaugh, *Ticket Seller:* Candace Brownell, *Banquet Official:* Sean Morgan, *Elderly Lady on Plane:* Patricia O'Neal, *Waiter in Hall:* Joe Alfasa, *Pizza Cook:* Chuck Hollom, *Painter:* William M. Niven, *Stunts:* Paul Baxley, Bud Walls, Glenn H. Randall, Jr., Bill Hickman, Alex Sharp, Wally Rose, Marvin James Walters, John Angelo Moio, Ernest Robinson, Ted M. Grossman, Richard E. Butler, Loren Janes, George N. Robotham, Victor Paul, Patty Elder, Paul Stader, Donna Garrett, Jack Verbois, Gerald Brutsche, Craig Baxley, Ted Duncan, Fred Stromsoe, Bob Harris, Dean Jeffries, Richard A. Washington, Joe Pronto, Joe Amsler.

When My Baby Smiles at Me with Betty Grable and Dan Dailey.

WHEN MY BABY SMILES AT ME (1948) 20th. Producer, George Jessel. Director, Walter Lang. Color by Technicolor. Based on the play *Burlesque* by George Manker Watters and Arthur Hopkins. Adaptation, Elizabeth Reinhardt. Technicolor Director, Natalie Kalmus. Screenplay, Lamar Trotti. Musical Director, Alfred Newman. Art Directors, Lyle Wheeler, Leland Fuller. Photography, Harry Jackson. Editor, Barbara McLean. Songs: "By the Way" and "What Did I Do?" by Mack Gordon and Josef Myrow; "When My Baby Smiles at Me" by Andrew B. Sterling and Harry Von Tilzer. Previous versions: *Dance of Life* (Paramount, 1929), *Swing High, Swing Low* (Paramount, 1937). 98 minutes

Bonny: Betty Grable, *Skid:* Dan Dailey, *Bozo:* Jack Oakie, *Gussie:* June Havoc, *Harvey:* Richard Arlen, *Lefty:* James Gleason, *Bubbles:* Vanita Wade, *Specialty Dancer:* Kenny Williams, *Sam Harris:* Robert

Emmett Keane, *Sylvia Marco:* Jean Wallace, *Woman in Box:* Pati Behrs, *Midget:* Jerry Maren, *Comic:* George "Beetlepuss" Lewis, *Valet:* Tom Stevenson, *Process Server:* Sam Bernard, *Stage Manager:* Mauritz Hugo, *Vendor:* Frank Scannell, *Doorman:* J. Farrell MacDonald, *Troupers:* Les Clark, Harry Seymour, *Call Boy:* Lee MacGregor, *Interne:* Charles Tannen, *Attendant:* Robert Karnes, *Conductor:* George Medford, *Girl:* Marion Marshall, *Sailor:* Robert Patten, *Man in Box:* Harry Carter, *Man:* Kit Guard, *Musician:* Tiny Timbrell, *Sailor:* Ted Jordan, *Chorus Girl:* Bee Stephens, *Tony:* Charles La Torre, *Specialty Dancers:* Dorothy Babb, Joanne Dale, Lu Anne Jones, Noel Neill.

Whispering Smith with Murvyn Vye and Alan Ladd.

WHISPERING SMITH (1948) Par. Associate Producer, Mel Epstein. Directed by Leslie Fenton. Color by Technicolor. Based on the novel by Frank H. Spearman. Screenplay, Frank Butler and Karl Kamb. Score, Adolph Deutsch. Editor, Archie Marshek. Art Directors, Hans Dreier and Walter Tyler. Photography, Ray Rennahan. Song, "Laramie" by Jay Livingston and Ray Evans. 88 minutes

Luke "Whispering" Smith: Alan Ladd, *Murray Sinclair:* Robert Preston, *Marian Sinclair:* Brenda Marshall, *Barney Rebstock:* Donald Crisp, *Bill Dansing:* William Demarest, *Emmy Dansing:* Fay Holden, *Blake Barton:* Murvyn Vye, *Whitey Du Sang:* Frank Faylen, *George McCloud:* John Eldredge, *Leroy Barton:* Robert Wood, *Bill Baggs:* J. Farrell MacDonald, *Dr. Sawbuck:* Don Barclay, *Sheriff McSwiggin:* Will Wright, *Conductor:* Eddy Waller, *Dog's Master:* Gary Gray, *Gabby Barton:* Bob Kortman.

WHITE CHRISTMAS (1954) Par. Producer, Robert Emmett Dolan. Director, Michael Curtiz. VistaVision, Technicolor. Screenplay, Norman Krasna, Norman Panama, Melvin Frank. Art Directors, Hal Pereira, Roland Anderson. Cinematographer, Loyal Griggs. Editor, Frank Bracht. The first film in VistaVision. Songs by Irving Berlin: "White Christmas," "Count Your Blessings," "Love, You Didn't Do Right by Me," "Choreography," "The Old Man," "Blue Skies," "Minstrel Show and Mandy," "Abraham," "Sisters," "Gee, I Wish I Was Back in the Army," "What Can You Do with a General," "The Best Things Happen While You're Dancing," "Snow." 120 minutes

Bob Wallace: Bing Crosby, *Phil Davis:* Danny Kaye, *Betty:* Rosemary Clooney, *Judy:* Vera-Ellen, *General Waverly:* Dean Jagger, *Emma:* Mary Wickes, *Joe:* John Brascia, *Susan:* Anne Whitfield, *Adjutant:* Richard Shannon, *General's Guest:* Grady Sutton, *Landlord:* Sig Rumann, *Albert:* Robert Crosson, *Novello:* Herb Vigran, *Asst. Stage Manager:* Dick Keene, *Ed Harrison:* Johnny Grant, *General Carlton:* Gavin Gordon, *Maître d':* Marcel De La Brosse, *Sheriff:* James Parnell, *Conductor:* Percy Helton, *Fat Lady:* Elizabeth Holmes, *Doris:* Barrie Chase, *Station Master:* I. Stanford Jolley, *Specialty Dancer:* George Chakiris.

White Christmas with Danny Kaye and Bing Crosby.

The White Cliffs of Dover with Alan Marshal, Irene Dunne and Van Johnson.

THE WHITE CLIFFS OF DOVER (1944) MGM. Producer, Sidney Franklin. Director, Clarence Brown. Screenplay, Claudine West, Jan Lustig, George Froeschel. Art Director, Cedric Gibbons. Musical Score, Herbert Stothart. Cameraman, George Folsey. Special Effects, Arnold Gillespie, Warren Newcombe. Editor, Robert J. Kern. Based on the poem "The White Cliffs" by Alice Duer Miller, with additional poetry by Robert Nathan. 126 minutes

Susan Ashwood: Irene Dunne, *Sir John Ashwood:* Alan Marshal, *Hiram Porter Dunn:* Frank Morgan, *John Ashwood II as a boy:* Roddy McDowall, *Nanny:* Dame May Whitty, *Colonel:* C. Aubrey Smith, *Lady Jean Ashwood:* Gladys Cooper, *John Ashwood II (age 24):* Peter Lawford, *Sam Bennett:* Van Johnson, *Reggie:* John Warburton, *Rosamund:* Jill Esmond, *Gwennie:* Brenda Forbes, *Mrs. Bland:* Norma Varden, *Betsy (10 years):* Elizabeth Taylor, *Betsy (18 years):* June Lockhart, *Farmer Kenney:* Charles Irwin, *Mrs. Kenney:* Jean Prescott, *American Soldier:* Tom Drake, *Mrs. Bancroft:* Isobel Elsom, *Major Bancroft:* Edmond Breon, *Major Loring:* Miles Mander, *Miss Lambert:* Ann Curzon, *Gerhard:* Steven Muller, *Dietrich:* Norbert Muller, *Helen:* Molly Lamont, *The Vicar:* Lumsden Hare, *Benson:* Arthur Shields, *Plump Lady in Boarding House:* Doris Lloyd, *Immigration Officer:* Matthew Boulton, *Woman on Train:* Ethel Griffies, *Footman:* Herbert Evans, *Duke of Waverly:* Keith Hitchcock, *Duchess:* Vera Graaff, *Miller:* Anita Bolster, *Skipper:* Ian Wolfe, *Billings:* Alec Craig, *Jennings:* Clyde Cook.

WHOOPEE (1930) UA. Produced by Samuel Goldwyn and Florenz Ziegfeld. Directed by Thornton Freeland. Color by Technicolor. Dances by Busby Berkeley. Based on the Ziegfeld musical *Whoopee*

by William Anthony McGuire, adapted from the comedy *The Nervous Wreck* by Owen Davis. Scenario, William Conselman. Photography, Lee Garmes, Ray Rennahan, Gregg Toland. Editor, Stuart Heisler. Sound, Oscar Lagerstrom. Songs: "Making Whoopee," "A Girl Friend of a Boy Friend of Mine," "My Baby Just Cares For Me," "Stetson" by Walter Donaldson and Gus Kahn; "I'll Still Belong to You" by Edward Eliscu and Nacio Herb Brown. Most of the cast of the musical is featured. Film debut of Barbara Weeks, 16. 94 minutes. Remade as Danny Kaye's *Up in Arms* (RKO, 1944)

Henry Williams: Eddie Cantor, *Sally Morgan:* Eleanor Hunt, *Wanenis:* Paul Gregory, *Sheriff Bob Wells:* Jack Rutherford, *Mary Custer:* Ethel Shutta, *Jerome Underwood:* Spencer Charters, *Black Eagle:* Chief Caupolican, *Chester Underwood:* Albert Hackett, *Andy McNabb:* Will H. Philbrick, *Judd Morgan:* Walter Law, *Harriett Underwood:* Marilyn Morgan (Marian Marsh), *Dancer:* Barbara Weeks, The George Olsen Band, *Deputy:* Dean Jagger, *Goldwyn Girls:* Betty Grable, Virginia Bruce, Claire Dodd.

Whoopee with Eleanor Hunt and Eddie Cantor.

Who's Afraid of Virginia Woolf? with Elizabeth Taylor and Richard Burton.

WHO'S AFRAID OF VIRGINIA WOOLF? (1966) WB. Produced by Ernest Lehman. Directed by Mike Nichols. Screenplay, Ernest Lehman, from the play by Edward Albee. Camera, Haskell Wexler. Editor, Sam O'Steen. Music composed and conducted by Alex North. Assistant director, Bud Grace. Sets, George James Hopkins. Costumes, Irene Sharaff. Hair Styles, Sydney Guilaroff and Jean Burt Reilly. Make-up, Gordon Bau and Ronnie Berkeley. 131 minutes

Martha: Elizabeth Taylor, *George:* Richard Burton, *Nick:* George Segal, *Honey:* Sandy Dennis.

314

The Wild Angels with Norm Alden (foreground), Bruce Dern and Peter Fonda.

THE WILD ANGELS (1966) American International. Produced and directed by Roger Corman. Panavision and Pathé Color. Screenplay, Charles B. Griffith. Camera, Richard Moore. Associate Producer, Laurence Cruikshank. Music, Mike Curb. Assistant Director, Paul Rapp. Editor, Monte Hellman. Assistant to the Director, Peter Bogdanovich. Art Director, Leon Erickson. Music produced by Group IV Productions. The last film of Art Baker. 93 minutes

Heavenly Blues: Peter Fonda, *Mike:* Nancy Sinatra, *Loser (Joey Kerns):* Bruce Dern, *Gaysh:* Diane Ladd, *Joint:* Lou Procopio, *Bull Puckey:* Coby Denton, *Frankenstein:* Marc Cavell, *Dear John:* Buck Taylor, *Medic:* Norm Alden, *Pigmy:* Michael J. Pollard, *Mama Monahan:* Joan Shawlee, *Suzie:* Gayle Hunnicutt, *Thomas, Undertaker:* Art Baker, *Preacher:* Frank Maxwell, *Hospital Policeman:* Frank Gertsle, *Nurse:* Kim Hamilton, *Mother:* Barboura Morris, *Rigger:* Dick Miller, *Bits:* Hal Bokar, Gina Grant, Jack Bernardi, Members of Hell's Angels of Venice, California.

The Wild Bunch with William Holden and Ernest Borgnine.

THE WILD BUNCH (1969) WB-Seven Arts. Produced by Phil Feldman. Directed by Sam Peckinpah. Filmed in Mexico in Panavision 70 and Technicolor. Based on a story by Walon Green and Roy N. Sickner. Screenplay, Green and Peckinpah. Associate Producer, Sickner. Photography, Lucien Ballard. Music, Jerry Fielding. Music Supervision, Sonny Burke. Art Director, Edward Carrere. Editor, Louis Lombardo. Special Effects, Bud Hulburd. Sound, Robert J. Miller. Wardrobe, Gordon Daw-

son. Assistant Directors, Cliff Coleman and Fred Gammon. 2nd Unit Director, Buzz Henry. Last film of Albert Dekker, who died May 5, 1968. Rated R. 132 minutes

Pike Bishop: William Holden, *Dutch Engstrom:* Ernest Borgnine, *Deke Thorton:* Robert Ryan, *Sykes:* Edmond O'Brien, *Lyle Gorch:* Warren Oates, *Angel:* Jaime Sanchez, *Tector Gorch:* Ben Johnson, *Mapache:* Emilio Fernandez, *Coffer:* Strother Martin, *T.C.:* L. Q. Jones, *Pat Harrigan:* Albert Dekker, *Crazy Lee:* Bo Hopkins, *Mayor Wainscoat:* Dub Taylor, *Lt. Zamorra:* Jorge Russek, *Herrera:* Alfonso Arau, *Don Jose:* Chano Urueta, *Teresa:* Sonia Amelio, *Aurora:* Aurora Clavel, *Elsa:* Elsa Cardenas, *German Army Officer:* Fernando Wagner.

Wild in the Streets with Shelley Winters.

WILD IN THE STREETS (1968) American International. Produced by James H. Nicholson and Samuel Z. Arkoff. Directed by Barry Shear. Executive Producer, Burt Topper. Screenplay by Robert Thom, based on his *Esquire* magazine story "The Day It All Happened, Baby." In Pathé Color. Photography, Richard Moore. Music by Les Baxter. Art Director, Paul Sylos. Editors, Fred Feitshans and Eve Newman. Sound, Al Overton. Costumes, Richard Bruno. Hairstyles, Myrl Stolz. Make-up, Fred Williams. Associate Producer, William J. Immerman. Assistant Director, Chuck Coleman. Songs by Barry Mann and Cynthia Weil: "The Shape of Things to Come," "52 Per Cent," "Sally LeRoy," "Listen to the Music" and "Fourteen or Fight." Vocals by Christopher Jones, Paul Wisler and the 13th Power. 97 minutes

Max Frost (Flatow): Christopher Jones, *Mrs. Flatow:* Shelley Winters, *John Fergus:* Hal Holbrook, *Mary Fergus:* Millie Perkins, *Senator Allbright:* Ed Begley, *Sally LeRoy:* Diane Varsi, *Stanley X:* Richard Pryor, *Max Flatow, Sr.:* Bert Freed, *Billy Cage:* Kevin Coughlin, *Abraham:* Larry Bishop, *Fuiji Ellie:* May Ishihara, *Jimmy Fergus:* Michael Margotta, *Joseph Fergus:* Don Wyndham, *Young Mary Fergus:* Kellie Flanagan, *Hippie Mother:* Salli Sachse, *Narrator:* Paul Frees, *Themselves:* Army Archerd, Kenneth Banghart, Melvin Belli, Dick Clark, Jack Latham, Louis Lomax, Pamela Mason, Allan J. Moll, Gene Shacove, Walter Winchell.

THE WILD ONE (1954) Col. Producer, Stanley Kramer. Director, Laslo Benedek. Author, Frank Rooney (from *The Cyclists' Raid*). Screenplay, John Paxton. Art Director, Walter Holscher. Cinematographer, Hal Mohr. Editor, Al Clark. 79 minutes

Johnny: Marlon Brando, *Kathie:* Mary Murphy, *Harry Bleeker:* Robert Keith, *Chino:* Lee Marvin, *Sheriff Singer:* Jay C. Flippen, *Mildred:* Peggy Maley, *Charlie Thomas:* Hugh Sanders, *Frank Bleeker:* Ray Teal, *Bill Hannegan:* John Brown, *Art Kleiner:* Will Wright, *Ben:* Robert Osterloh, *Wilson:* Robert Bice, *Simmy:* William Vedder, *Britches:* Yvonne Doughty, *Gringo:* Keith Clarke, *Mouse:* Gil Stratton, Jr., *Dinky:* Darren Dublin, *Red:* Johnny Tarangelo, *Dextro:*

Jerry Paris, *Crazy:* Gene Peterson, *Pigeon:* Alvy Moore, *Go Go:* Harry Landers, *Boxer:* Jim Connell, *Stinger:* Don Anderson, *Betty:* Angela Stevens, *Simmonds:* Bruno VeSoto, *Sawyer:* Pat O'Malley, *Dorothy:* Eve March, *Cyclist:* Wally Albright, *Chino Boy No. 1:* Timothy Carey, *Official:* John Doucette.

The Wild One with Ray Teal (bartender) and Marlon Brando.

Willard with Elsa Lanchester.

WILLARD (1971) Cinerama. A Bing Crosby Production, in DeLuxe Color. Produced by Mort Briskin. Directed by Daniel Mann. Based on the novel *Ratman's Notebooks* by Stephen Gilbert. Screenplay, Gilbert A. Ralston. Executive Producer, Charles A. Pratt. Music composed and conducted by Alex North. Photography, Robert B. Hauser. Art Director, Howard Hollander. Editorial Supervision, Warren Low. Assistant Director and Unit Production Manager, Robert Goodstein. Set Decorator, Ralph S. Hurst. Rats trained by Moe and Nora Di Sesso. Special Effects, Bud David. Sound, Harold Lewis. Make-up, Gus Norin. Hairstylist, Hazel Washington. Costumes, Eric Seelig and Dorothy Barkley. Postproduction Supervision, Houseley Stevenson. Rated GP. 95 minutes. Sequel was *Ben* (1972)

Willard Stiles: Bruce Davison, *Al Martin:* Ernest Borgnine, *Henrietta Stiles:* Elsa Lanchester, *Joan:* Sondra Locke, *Brandt:* Michael Dante, *Charlotte Stassen:* Jody Gilbert, *Alice Rickles:* Joan Shawlee, *Mr. Barskin:* William Hansen, *Jonathan Farley:* J. Pat. O'Malley, *Mr. Carlson:* John Myhers, *Mrs. Becker:* Helen Spring, *Ida Stassen:* Pauline Drake, *Carrie Smith:* Almira Sessions, *Walter T. Spencer:* Alan Baxter, *Mrs. Spencer:* Sherri Presnell, *Mrs. Martin:* Lola Kendrick, *Motorcycle Rider:* Robert Golden, *Extra:* Minta Durfee Arbuckle, *Guests:* Arthur Tovey, Shirley Lawrence, Louise De Carlo, *Chemist:* Paul Bradley, *Socrates and Ben.*

Wilson with Geraldine Fitzgerald, Alexander Knox and Stanley Ridges.

WILSON (1944) 20th. Producer, Darryl F. Zanuck. Director, Henry King. Color by Technicolor. Screenplay, Lamar Trotti. Director of Photography, Leon Shamroy. Technicolor Director, Natalie Kalmus. Associate, Richard Mueller. Music, Alfred Newman. Technical Advisers, Ray Stannard Baker, Miles McCahill. Orchestral Arrangements, Edward Powell. Art Direction, Wiard Ihnen, James Basevi. Set Decorations, Thomas Little. Associate, Paul S. Fox. Film Editor, Barbara McLean. Costumes, Rene Hubert. Make-up Artist, Guy Pearce. Special Photographic Effects, Fred Sersen. Sound, E. Clayton Ward, Roger Heman. 154 minutes

Woodrow Wilson: Alexander Knox, *Prof. Henry Holmes:* Charles Coburn, *Edith Wilson:* Geraldine Fitzgerald, *Joseph Tumulty:* Thomas Mitchell, *Ellen Wilson:* Ruth Nelson, *Senator Henry Cabot Lodge:* Sir Cedric Hardwicke, *William Gibbs McAdoo:* Vincent Price, *George Felton:* William Eythe, *Eleanor Wilson:* Mary Anderson, *Margaret Wilson:* Ruth Ford, *Josephus Daniels:* Sidney Blackmer, *Jessie Wilson:* Madeleine Forbes, *Admiral Grayson:* Stanley Ridges, *Eddie Foy:* Eddie Foy, Jr., *Colonel House:* Charles Halton, *Senator B. H. Jones:* Thurston Hall, *Edward Sullivan:* J. M. Kerrigan, *Jim Beeker:* James Rennie, *Helen Bones:* Katherine Locke, *Secretary Lansing:* Stanley Logan, *Clemenceau:* Marcel Dalio, *William Jennings Bryan:* Edwin Maxwell, *Lloyd George:* Clifford Brooke, *Von Bernstorff:* Tonio Selwart, *Senator Watson:* John Ince, *Senator Bromfield:* Charles Miller, *Barney Baruch:* Francis X. Bushman, *McCoombs:* George Macready, *Granddaughter:* Phyllis Brooks, *Charles F. Murphy:* Cy Kendall, *Ike Hoover:* Roy Roberts, *Jennie, the Maid:* Anne O'Neal, *Secretary Lane:* Arthur Loft, *Secretary Colby:* Russell Gaige, *Secretary Payne:* Jamesson Shade, *Secretary Baker:* Reginald Sheffield, *Secretary Garrison:* Robert Middlemass, *Secretary Burleson:* Matt Moore, *Secretary Houston:* George Anderson, *Chief Justice White:* Joseph J. Greene, *Secretary William B. Wilson:* Larry McGrath, *Senator:* Gibson Gowland, *Champ Clark:* Davison Clark, *Jeannette Rankin:* Hilda Plowright, *Usher:* Reed Hadley, *La Follette:* Ralph Dunn, *General Bliss:* Major Sam Harris.

WINCHESTER '73 (1950) Univ. Producer, Aaron Rosenberg. Director, Anthony Mann. From a story by Stuart N. Lake. Screenplay,

Robert L. Richards and Borden Chase. Art Directors, Bernard Herzbrun, Nathan Juran. Musical Director, Joseph Gershenson. Photography, William Daniels. Editor, Edward Curtiss. Filmed in Tucson. Remade by Universal as a 1967 TV feature, also with Duryea. 92 minutes

Lin McAdam: James Stewart, *Lola Manners:* Shelley Winters, *Waco Johnny Dean:* Dan Duryea, *Dutch Henry Brown:* Stephen McNally, *High Spade:* Millard Mitchell, *Steve Miller:* Charles Drake, *Joe Lamont:* John McIntire, *Wyatt Earp:* Will Geer, *Sgt. Wilkes:* Jay C. Flippen, *Young Bull:* Rock Hudson, *Jack Riker:* John Alexander, *Wesley:* Steve Brodie, *Wheeler:* James Millican, *Latigo Means:* Abner Biberman, *Doan:* Anthony Curtis, *Crater:* James Best, *Mossman:* Gregg Martell, *Cavalryman:* Frank Chase, *Long Tom:* Chuck Roberson, *Dudeen:* Carol Henry, *Marshall Noonan:* Ray Teal, *Mrs. Jameson:* Virginia Mullens, *Roan Daley:* John Doucette, *Masterson:* Steve Darrell, *Indian:* Chief Yowlachie, *Clerk:* Frank Conlan, *Charles Bender:* Ray Bennett, *Virgil:* Guy Wilkerson, *Bassett:* Bob Anderson, *Boy at Rifle Shoot:* Larry Olsen, *Target Watcher:* Edmund Cobb, *Target Clerk:* Forrest Taylor, *Station Master:* Ethan Laidlaw, *Man: Bud Osborne, *Bunny Jameson:* Gary Jackson, *Betty Jameson:* Bonnie Kay Eddy, *Stagecoach Driver:* Jennings Miles, *Indian Interpreter:* John War Eagle.

Frankie Davis: Private Lon McCallister, *Helen:* Jeanne Crain, *Irving Miller:* Sergeant Edmond O'Brien, *Jane Preston:* Jane Ball, *Alan Ross:* Sergeant Mark Daniels, *Dorothy Ross:* Jo-Carroll Dennison, *Danny "Pinky" Scariano:* Corporal Don Taylor, *Doctor:* Corporal Lee J. Cobb, *Ruth Miller:* Judy Holliday, *O'Brian:* T/Sergeant Peter Lind Hayes, *Major Halper:* Corporal Alan Baxter, *Mrs. Ross:* Geraldine Wall, *Whitey:* Corporal Red Buttons, *Mr. Scariano:* George Humbert, *Bobby Crills:* Corporal Barry Nelson, *Dave Anderson:* Sergeant Rune Hultman, *Jimmy Gardner:* Corporal Richard Hogan, *Colonel Gibney:* Corporal Phillip Bourneuf, *Captain McIntyre:* Corporal Gary Merrill, *Colonel Ross:* Corporal Damian O'Flynn, *Lieutenant Thompson:* Sergeant George Reeves, *Barker:* Private First Class George Petrie, *Milhauser:* Private First Class Alfred Ryder, *Adams:* Corporal Karl Malden, *Gleason:* Private First Class Martin Ritt, *Cadet Peter Clark:* Corporal Harry Lewis, *Officer:* Captain Ray Bidwell, *Flight Surgeon:* Corporal Henry Rowland, *Captain Speer:* Lieutenant Carroll Riddle, *Carmen Miranda:* S/Sergeant Sascha Branstoff, *Master of Ceremonies:* Corporal Archie Robbins, *Andrews Sisters:* Corporal Jack Slate, Corporal Red Buttons, Private First Class Henry Slate, *Irving Jr.:* Timmy Hawkins, *Mrs. Gardner:* Moyna Macgill, *Man:* Don Beddoe (AAF), *WAC:* Frances Gladwin, *Cigarette Girl:* Sally Yarnell.

Winterset with Burgess Meredith, Eduardo Ciannelli, Maurice Moscovich and Edward Ellis.

Winchester '73 with James Stewart, Millard Mitchell, Tony Curtis, Charles Drake and Jay C. Flippen.

WINTERSET (1936) RKO. Produced by Pandro S. Berman. Directed by Alfred Santell. From the Guthrie McClintic Production of the play by Maxwell Anderson. Screenplay, Anthony Weiler. Music Director, Nathaniel Shilkret. Music Arrangements, Maurice De Packh. Camera, Peverell Marley. Editor, William Hamilton. Film debuts of Burgess Meredith, Paul Guilfoyle, Myron McCormick. 78 minutes

Mio: Burgess Meredith, *Miriamne:* Margo, *Trock:* Eduardo Ciannelli, *Garth:* Paul Guilfoyle, *Romagna:* John Carradine, *Judge Gaunt:* Edward Ellis, *Shadow:* Stanley Ridges, *Esdras:* Maurice Moscovich, *Carr:* Myron McCormick, *A Policeman:* Willard Robertson, *A Radical:* Mischa Auer, *A Girl:* Barbara Pepper, *A Hobo:* Alec Craig, *Mrs. Romagna:* Helen Jerome Eddy, *Piny:* Fernanda Eliscu, *Lucia:* George Humbert, *Louie:* Murray Alper, *Joe:* Paul Fix, *A Sailor:* Alan Curtis, *District Attorney:* Arthur Loft, *Elderly Man:* Otto Hoffman, *Woman:* Grace Hayle, *Gangster:* Al Hill, *Girl:* Lucille Ball.

Winged Victory with Barry Nelson, Edmond O'Brien and Mark Daniels.

WINGED VICTORY (1944) 20th. Producer, Darryl F. Zanuck. Director, George Cukor. Screenplay, Moss Hart. Musical Score, David Rose. Art Directors, Lyle Wheeler, Lewis Creber. Cameraman, Glen MacWilliams. Special Effects, Fred Sersen. Editor, Barbara McLean. Song by Tod B. Galloway, Meade Minnigerode and George S. Pomeroy, "The Whiffenpoof Song." Based on the play by Moss Hart. Presented in association with the U. S. Army Air Forces. 130 minutes

WITH A SONG IN MY HEART (1952) 20th. Producer, Lamar Trotti. Director, Walter Lang. Color by Technicolor. Author, Lamar Trotti. Screenplay, Lamar Trotti. Musical Director, Alfred Newman. Art Directors, Lyle Wheeler, Earle Hagen. Cinematographer, Leon Shamroy. Editor, J. Watson Webb. Technicolor Consultant, Leonard Doss. Songs: "Blue Moon" and "With a Song in My Heart" by Lorenz Hart and Richard Rodgers; "That Old Feeling" by Lew Brown and Sammy Fain; "I've Got a Feeling You're Fooling" by Arthur Freed and Nacio Herb Brown; "Tea for Two" by Irving Caesar and Vincent Youmans; "Deep in the Heart of Texas" by June Hershey and Don Swander; "Carry Me Back to Old Virginny" by James Bland; "Dixie" by Dan Emmett; "They're Either Too Young or Too Old" by Frank Loesser and Arthur Schwartz; "It's a Good Day" by Peggy Lee and

Dave Barbour; "I'll Walk Alone" by Sammy Cahn and Jule Styne; "Give My Regards to Broadway" by George M. Cohan; "Alabamy Bound" by Bud Green, B. G. DeSylva and Ray Henderson; "California Here I Come" by B. G. DeSylva, Al Jolson and Joseph Meyer; "Chicago" by Fred Fisher; "America the Beautiful" by Katherine Lee Bates and Samuel A. Ward; "I'm Through with Love" by Gus Kahn, Fred Livingston and Matty Malneck; "Embraceable You" by Ira and George Gershwin; "On the Gay White Way" by Leo Robin and Rainger; "The Right Kind of Love" by Don George and Charles Henderson; "Montparnasse" by Alfred Newman and Eliot Daniel; "Maine Stein Song" by E. A. Fenstad and Lincoln Colcord; "(Back Home Again In) Indiana" by Ballard MacDonald and James F. Hanley; "Get Happy" by Ted Koehler and Harold Arlen; "Hoe That Corn" by Max Showalter and Jack Woodford; "Jim's Toasted Peanuts" and "Wonderful Home Sweet Home" by Ken Darby. 117 minutes

Jane Froman: Susan Hayward, *John Burn:* Rory Calhoun, *Don Ross:* David Wayne, *Clancy:* Thelma Ritter, *G. I. Paratrooper:* Robert Wagner, *Jennifer March:* Helen Westcott, *Sister Marie:* Una Merkel, *Dancer:* Richard Allan, *Guild:* Max Showalter (Casey Adams), *Radio Director:* Lyle Talbot, *General:* Leif Erickson, *Diplomat:* Stanley Logan, *Specialty:* Ernest Newton, *General:* Paul Maxey, *Kansas:* Robert Easton, *U. S. O. Man:* Eddie Firestone, *Texas:* Frank Sully, *Muleface:* George Offerman, *U. S. O. Girl:* Beverly Thompson, *Sister Margaret:* Maude Wallace, *Colonel:* Douglas Evans, *Doctors:* Carlos Molina, Nestor Paiva, Emmett Vogan.

With a Song in My Heart with Susan Hayward (center).

Without Love with Spencer Tracy and Katharine Hepburn.

WITHOUT LOVE (1945) MGM. Producer, Lawrence A. Weingarten. Director, Harold S. Bucquet. Screenplay, Donald Ogden Stewart. Score, Bronislau Kaper. Art Directors, Cedric Gibbons, Harry McAfee. Cameraman, Karl Freund. Special Effects, A. Arnold Gillespie, Danny Hall. Editor, Frank Sullivan. From Philip Barry's Theatre Guild play. 111 minutes

Pat Jamieson: Spencer Tracy, *Jamie Rowan:* Katharine Hepburn, *Kitty Trimble:* Lucille Ball, *Quentin Ladd:* Keenan Wynn, *Paul Carrell:* Carl Esmond, *Edwina Collins:* Patricia Morison, *Professor Grinza:* Felix Bressart, *Anna:* Emily Massey, *Flower Girl:* Gloria Grahame, *Caretaker:* George Davis, *Elevator Boy:* George Chandler, *Sergeant:* Clancy Cooper, *Professor Thompson:* Wallis Clark, *Professor Ellis:* Donald Curtis, *Colonel Braden:* Charles Arnt, *Driver:* Eddie Acuff, *Porter:* Clarence Muse, *Headwaiter:* Franco Corsaro, *Pageboy:* Ralph Brooks, *Doctor:* William Forrest, *Soldier:* Garry Owen, *Soldier:* Joe Devlin, *Soldier:* William Newell, *Sergeant:* James Flavin, *Girl on Elevator:* Hazel Brooks.

Witness for the Prosecution with Henry Daniell, Tyrone Power and Charles Laughton.

WITNESS FOR THE PROSECUTION (1957) UA. Produced by Arthur Hornblow. Directed by Billy Wilder. Based on the story and play by Agatha Christie. Screenplay, Billy Wilder and Harry Kurnitz. A Theme Pictures Production, presented by Edward Small. Song, "I May Never Go Home Anymore" by Ralph Arthur Roberts and Jack Brooks. Filmed at Goldwyn Studios. 114 minutes

Leonard Vole: Tyrone Power, *Christine Vole:* Marlene Dietrich, *Sir Wilfrid Robarts:* Charles Laughton, *Miss Plimsoll:* Elsa Lanchester, *Brogan-Moore:* John Williams, *Mayhew:* Henry Daniell, *Carter:* Ian Wolfe, *Janet McKenzie:* Una O'Connor, *Mr. Myers:* Torin Thatcher, *Judge:* Francis Compton, *Mrs. French:* Norma Varden, *Inspector Hearne:* Philip Tonge, *Diana:* Ruta Lee, *Miss McHugh:* Molly Roden, *Miss Johnson:* Ottola Nesmith, *Miss O'Brien:* Marjorie Eaton, *Shorts Salesman:* J. Pat O'Malley.

THE WIZARD OF OZ (1939) MGM. Produced by Mervyn LeRoy. Directed by Victor Fleming. Color by Technicolor, opening and closing scenes in Sepia. Adapted from the book by L. Frank Baum. Screenplay, Noel Langley, Florence Ryerson, Edgar Allan Woolf. Art Directors, Cedric Gibbons and William A. Horning. Sets, Edwin B. Willis. Musical numbers staged by Bobby Connolly. Music Score, Herbert Stothart. Songs by E. Y. Harburg and Harold Arlen: "Over the Rainbow," "Follow the Yellow Brick Road," "If I Only Had a Brain," "We're Off to See the Wizard," "Merry Old Land of Oz," "Laugh a Day Away," "If I Were King," "Courage," "Welcome to Munchkinland," "Ding Dong, The Witch Is Dead," "If I Only Had a Heart." Special Effects, Arnold Gillespie. Editor, Blanche Sewell. Associate Conductor, George Stoll. Orchestral and Vocal Arrangements, George Bassman, Murray Cutter, Paul Marquardt, Ken Darby. Character Makeups, Jack Dawn. Photography, Harold Rosson. Film debut of Jerry Maren, 19, 3'6". 101 minutes

Dorothy: Judy Garland, *Professor Marvel (The Wizard):* Frank Morgan, *Hunk (Scarecrow):* Ray Bolger, *Zeke (Cowardly Lion):* Bert Lahr, *Hickory (Tin Woodman):* Jack Haley, *Glinda:* Billie Burke, *Miss Gulch (The Witch):* Margaret Hamilton, *Uncle Henry:* Charley Grapewin, *Nikko:* Pat Walshe, *Auntie Em:* Clara Blandick, *Toto:* Toto, *Munchkins:* The Singer Midgets, *A Munchkin:* Jerry Marenghi (Jerry Maren).

The Wizard of Oz with Margaret Hamilton and Judy Garland.

Woman of the Year with Henry Roquemore, Katharine Hepburn, Fay Bainter and Spencer Tracy.

WOMAN OF THE YEAR (1942) MGM. Produced by Joseph L. Mankiewicz. Directed by George Stevens. Original Screenplay, Ring Lardner, Jr. and Michael Kanin. Music, Franz Waxman. Art Director, Cedric Gibbons. Associate Art Director, Randall Duell. Hair Styles, Sydney Guilaroff. Gowns, Adrian. Sets, Edwin B. Willis. Photography, Joseph Ruttenberg. Sound, Douglas Shearer. Editor, Frank Sullivan. The first Tracy–Hepburn film. Film debut of William Bendix. 112 minutes. Remade by MGM-TV, 1976, with Joseph Bologna and Renee Taylor

Sam Craig: Spencer Tracy, *Tess Harding:* Katharine Hepburn, *Ellen Whitcomb:* Fay Bainter, *Clayton:* Reginald Owen, *William Harding:* Minor Watson, *Pinkie Peters:* William Bendix, *Flo Peters:* Gladys Blake, *Gerald:* Dan Tobin, *Phil Whittaker:* Roscoe Karns, *Ellis:* William Tannen, *Dr. Martin Lubbeck:* Ludwig Stossel, *Matron at Refugee Home:* Sara Haden, *Alma:* Edith Evanson, *Chris:* George Kezas, *Radio M.C. (Voice):* Gerald Mohr, *Reporter:* Jimmy Conlin, *Justice of the Peace:* Henry Roquemore, *Harding's Chauffeur:* Cyril Ring, *Punchy:* Ben Lessy, *Pal:* Johnny Berkes, *Reporter:* Ray Teal, *Football Player:* Duke York, *Adolph:* Edward McWade.

The Women with Joan Crawford, Aileen Pringle, Beatrice Cole, Joan Fontaine, Norma Shearer, Rosalind Russell and Phyllis Povah.

THE WOMEN (1939) MGM. Producer, Hunt Stromberg. Director, George Cukor. From the play by Clare Boothe. Screenplay, Anita Loos, Jane Murfin. Art Director, Cedric Gibbons. Musical Score, Edward Ward, David Snell. Cameramen, Oliver T. Marsh, Joseph Ruttenberg. Editor, Robert J. Kerns. Song by Chet Forrest, Bob Wright and Ed Ward: "Forevermore." Fashion show sequence in Technicolor. Remade as *The Opposite Sex* (MGM, 1956). 132 minutes

Mary Haines: Norma Shearer, *Chrystal Allen:* Joan Crawford, *Sylvia Fowler:* Rosalind Russell, *Countess Delave:* Mary Boland, *Miriam Aarons:* Paulette Goddard, *Peggy Day:* Joan Fontaine, *Mrs. Moore-head:* Lucile Watson, *Edith Potter:* Phyllis Povah, *Nancy Blake:* Florence Nash, *Little Mary:* Virginia Weidler, *Miss Watts:* Ruth Hussey, *Jane:* Muriel Hutchison, *Mrs. Wagstaff:* Margaret Dumont, *Olga:* Dennie Moore, *Maggie:* Mary Cecil, *Lucy:* Marjorie Main, *Ingrid:* Esther Dale, *Dolly Dupuyster:* Hedda Hopper, *Helene (French Maid):* Mildred Shay, *First Hairdresser:* Priscilla Lawson, *Second Hairdresser:* Estelle Etterre, *Exercise Instructress:* Ann Morriss, *Miss Trimmerback:* Mary Beth Hughes, *Sadie (Old Maid In Powder Room):* Marjorie Wood, *Pat:* Virginia Grey, *Mrs. Van Adams:* Cora Witherspoon, *Olive:* Theresa Harris, *Receptionist:* Virginia Howell, *Receptionist:* Barbara Jo Allen (Vera Vague), *Saleslady:* Aileen Pringle, *Model:* Judith Allen, *Singing Teacher:* Mariska Aldrich, *Negligee Model:* Beatrice Cole.

WONDER BAR (1934) WB. Director, Lloyd Bacon. Adaptation and screenplay by Earl Baldwin. Based on the play by Geza Herczeg, Karl Farkas, and Robert Katscher. Dances by Busby Berkeley. Songs by Harry Warren and Al Dubin: "At the Wonder Bar," "I'm Going to Heaven on a Mule," "Why Do I Dream Those Dreams?" "Don't Say Goodnight" (Valse Amoureuse), "Vive La France," "Fairer on the Riviera," "Tango Del Rio," "Dark Eyes" (Ortchichorniya). Editor, George Amy. Cameraman, Sol Polito. 84 minutes

Al Wonder: Al Jolson, *Inez:* Dolores Del Rio, *Harry:* Ricardo Cortez, *Liane Renaud:* Kay Francis, *Tommy:* Dick Powell, *Henry Simpson:* Guy B. Kibbee, *Corey Pratt:* Hugh Herbert, *Captain Von Ferring:* Robert Barrat, *Ella Simpson:* Ruth Donnelly, *Pansy Pratt:* Louise Fazenda, *Mitzi:* Fifi D'Orsay, *Claire:* Merna Kennedy, *Mr. Renaud:* Henry Kolker, *Richards:* Henry O'Neill, *Ilka:* Kathryn Sergava, *First Detective:* Gordon De Main, *Second Detective:* Harry Woods, *Maid:* Marie Moreau, *Broker:* George Irving, *Concierge:* Emile Chautard, *Operator:* Pauline Garon, *Artist:* Mahlon Norvell, *Doorman:* Alphonse Martel, *Gee-Gee:* Mia Ichioka, *Bartender:* William Granger, *Waiter:* Rolfe Sedan, *Frank:* Eddie Kane, *Captain:* Edward Keane, *Baroness:* Jane Darwell, *First Young Man:* Demetrius Alexis, *Second Young Man:* John Marlow, *Call Boy:* Billy Anderson, *Bartender:* Bud Jamison, *Drunk:* Hobart Cavanaugh, *Chorus Boy:* Dave O'Brien, *Extra at*

Bar: Dennis O'Keefe, *Waiter:* Gino Corrado, *Fat Dowager:* Grace Hayle, *Norman:* Gordon Elliott (later Bill Elliott), *Chester:* Paul Power, *Page Boy:* Dick Good, *Count:* Michael Dalmatoff, *First Chorus Girl:* Renee Whitney, *Second Chorus Girl:* Amo Ingraham, *Third Chorus Girl:* Rosalie Roy, *Wardrobe Woman:* Lottie Williams, *First Businessman:* Clay Clement, *Second Businessman:* William Stack, *Pete:* Spencer Charters, *Gendarme:* Gene Perry, *Cook:* Louis Ardizoni, *Police Officer:* Robert Graves, *Night Watchman:* Alfred P. James, *Himself:* Hal LeRoy.

Wonder Bar with Al Jolson, Dick Powell and Dolores Del Rio.

Wonder Man with Vera-Ellen and Danny Kaye.

WONDER MAN (1945) RKO. Producer, Samuel Goldwyn. Director, Bruce Humberstone. Color by Technicolor. Original Story, Arthur Sheekman. Screenplay, Don Hartman, Melville Shavelson, Philip Rapp. Dances, John Wray. Art Directors, Ernest Fegte, McClure Capps. Musical Director, Louis Forbes. Technicolor Director, Natalie Kalmus. Musical Numbers, Ray Heindorf. Cameramen, Victor Milner, William Snyder. Special Effects, John Fulton. Editor, Daniel Mandell. Adaptation, Jack Jevne and Eddie Moran. Musical numbers: "So in Love" by Leo Robin and David Rose; "Bali Boogie" by Sylvia Fine. Film debut of Vera-Ellen. 98 minutes

Buzzy Bellew/Edwin Dingle: Danny Kaye, *Ellen Shanley:* Virginia Mayo, *Midge Mallon:* Vera-Ellen, *Chimp:* Allen Jenkins, *Torso:* Edward S. Brophy, *Schmidt:* S. Z. Sakall, *Ten Grand Jackson:* Steve Cochran, *Monte Rossen:* Donald Woods, *District Attorney O'Brien:* Otto Kruger, *Assistant D. A. Grosset:* Richard Lane, *Mrs. Hume:* Natalie Schafer, *The Prima Donna:* Alice Mock, *Girl on Bench (in*

Park): Virginia Gilmore, *Goldwyn Girls:* Ruth Valmy, Alma Carroll, Georgia Lange, Karen Gaylord, Mary Moore, Gloria Delson, Deannie Best, Margie Stewart, Mary Meade, Martha Montgomery, Ellen Hall, Phyllis Forbes, Mary Jane Woods, Katherine Booth, Chili Williams, *Prompter:* Luis Alberni, *Opera Conductor:* Aldo Franchetti, *Stage Manager:* Maurice Cass, *Dancer:* Carol Haney, *Customer:* Byron Foulger, *Mrs. Schmidt:* Gisela Werbiseck, *Sailor:* Huntz Hall, *Cop in the Park:* Ed Gargan, *Specialty Dancer:* Al Ruiz, *Specialty Dancer:* Willard Van Simons, *Drunk at Table:* Jack Norton, *Drunk at Bar:* Charles Irwin, *Bartender:* Frank Orth, *Barker:* Cecil Cunningham, *Meek Man on Bus:* Chester Clute, *Bus Driver:* James Flavin, *D. A.'s Secretary:* Mary Field, *Headwaiter:* Eddie Kane, *Ticket Taker:* Ray Teal, *Pianist:* Leon Belasco.

Woodstock with Joan Baez.

WOODSTOCK (1970) WB. Produced by Bob Maurice. Directed by Michael Wadleigh. 8 Track Stereo Sound. Technicolor. Assistant Directors, Martin Scorsese and Thelma Schoonmaker. Supervising Editors, Wadleigh, Schoonmaker and Scorsese. Executive in Charge of Production, Dale Bell. Principal Photography, Michael Wadleigh, David Meyers, Richard Pearce, Don Lenzer and Al Wertheimer. Additional Photography I, Michael Margetts, Ed Lynch, Richard Cheu, Charles Levey and Ted Churchill. Additional Photography II, Fred Underhill, Robert Danneman and Stan Warnow. Assistant to the Director, Larry Johnson. Documentary Unit Coordinator, John Binder. Performance Location Sound, Bill Hanley. Editors, Robert Alvarez, Yeu Bun-Yee, Bettina Kugel Hirsch, Jere Huggins, Muffie Meyer and Stan Warnow. Editing Synchronization, Mirra Bank, Ed Cariati, Ted Duffield, Barney Edmonds, Lana Jokel, Bill Lipsky, Janet Loratano, Susan Steinberg, Anita Thatcher and Winston Tucker. Editing Assistants, Jim Stark, Angela Kirby, Miriam Eger and Phyllis Altenhaus. Filmed at the Woodstock Music and Art Fair in Bethel, New York. Production Manager, Sonya Polonsky. Original 16mm processing and printing, J. & D. Labs, New York City. Rated R. 184 minutes

The Artists: Joan Baez, Joe Cocker, Country Joe and the Fish, Crosby, Stills, Nash & Young, Arlo Guthrie, Richie Havens, Jimi Hendrix, Santana, John Sebastian, Sly & the Family Stone, Ten Years After, The Who, *and a cast of 500,000.*

THE WORLD OF SUZIE WONG (1960) Par. Producer, Ray Stark. Director, Richard Quine. Screenplay, John Patrick. Adapted from the novel by Richard Mason and play by Paul Osborn. Music, George Duning. Song, James Van Heusen and Sammy Cahn. Assistant Director, Gus Agosti. In Technicolor. 129 minutes

Robert Lomax: William Holden, *Suzie Wong:* Nancy Kwan, *Kay:* Sylvia Syms, *Ben:* Michael Wilding, *O'Neill:* Laurence Naismith, *Gwenny Lee:* Jacqui Chan, *Ah Tong:* Andy Ho, *Otis:* Bernard Cribbins, *Minnie Ho:* Yvonne Shima, *Wednesday Lu:* Lier Hwang, *Dancing Sailor:* Lionel Blair, *Barman:* Robert Lee, *Waiter:* Ronald Eng.

The World of Suzie Wong with William Holden and Nancy Kwan.

Written on the Wind with Rock Hudson, Lauren Bacall, Robert Stack and Dorothy Malone.

WRITTEN ON THE WIND (1956) Univ. Producer, Albert Zugsmith. Director, Douglas Sirk. Technicolor. Based on the novel by Robert Wilder. Screenplay, George Zuckerman. Art Directors, Alexander Golitzen, Robert Clatworthy. Music, Frank Skinner. Music Supervision, Joseph Gershenson. Cinematographer, Russell Metty. Special Photography, Clifford Stine. Editor, Russell Schoengarth. Title song by Victor Young and Sammy Cahn, sung by The Four Aces. 99 minutes

Mitch Wayne: Rock Hudson, *Lucy Moore Hadley:* Lauren Bacall, *Kyle Hadley:* Robert Stack, *Marylee Hadley:* Dorothy Malone, *Jasper Hadley:* Robert Keith, *Biff Miley:* Grant Williams, *Dan Willis:* Robert J. Wilke, *Doctor Paul Cochrane:* Edward C. Platt, *Hoak Wayne:* Harry Shannon, *Roy Carter:* John Larch, *Sam:* Roy Glenn, *Bertha:* Maidie Norman, *Blonde Girl:* Dani Crayne, *Woman Beer Drinker:* Jane Howard, *Man Beer Drinker:* Floyd Simmons, *Waitress:* Cynthia Patrick, *College Girl:* Colleen McClatchey, *Brunette Girl:* Joanne Jordan, *Reporter:* William Schallert, *Hotel Manager:* Robert Brubaker, *Court Clerk:* Bert Holland, *Taxi Starter:* Don C. Harvey, *Bartender:* Carl Christian, *R. J. Courtney:* Joseph Granby, *Hotel Floorlady:* Gail Bonney, *Maitre d':* Paul Bradley, *Marylee as a girl:* Susan Odin, *Kyle as a boy:* Robert Lyden, *Mitch as a boy:* Robert Winans, *Secretary:* Dorothy Porter, *Hotel Proprietor:* Robert Malcolm.

WUTHERING HEIGHTS (1939) UA. Producer, Samuel Goldwyn. Director, William Wyler. From the novel by Emily Brönte. Screenplay, Ben Hecht, Charles MacArthur. Musical Director, Alfred Newman. Cameraman, Gregg Toland. Editor, Daniel Mandell. 103 minutes

Cathy: Merle Oberon, *Heathcliffe:* Laurence Olivier, *Edgar:* David Niven, *Dr. Kenneth:* Donald Crisp, *Nellie:* Flora Robson, *Hindley:* Hugh Williams, *Isabella:* Geraldine Fitzgerald, *Mr. Earnshaw:* Cecil Kellaway, *Joseph:* Leo G. Carroll, *Judge Linton:* Cecil Humphreys, *Lockwood:* Miles Mander, *Cathy as a child:* Sarita Wooton, *Heathcliffe as a child:* Rex Downing, *Hindley as a child:* Douglas Scott, *Robert:* Romaine Callender, *Miss Hudkins:* Helena Grant, *First Guest:* Susanne Leach, *Little Boy:* Tommy Martin, *Little Boy:* Schuyler Standish, *Little Girl:* Diane Williams, *Beadle:* Harold Entwistle, *Heathcliffe Servant:* Frank Benson, *Cathy's Partner:* Philip Winter, *Dancer:* William Stelling, *Frau Johann:* Alice Ahlers, *Giles:* Vernon Downing, *Linton Servant:* Eric Wilton.

Wuthering Heights with Merle Oberon and Laurence Olivier.

Yankee Doodle Dandy with Rosemary De Camp, Walter Huston, Jeanne Cagney, James Cagney.

YANKEE DOODLE DANDY (1942) WB. Producers, Jack L. Warner, Hal B. Wallis. Associate Producer, William Cagney. Director, Michael Curtiz. Author, Robert Buckner. Original Story, Robert Buckner. Screenplay, Robert Buckner, Edmund Joseph. Musical Director, Leo F. Forbstein. Cameraman, James Wong Howe. Montage, Don Siegel. Editor, George Amy. Songs: "I Was Born in Virginia," "The Warmest Baby in the Bunch," "Give My Regards to Broadway," "Mary's a Grand Old Name," "So Long Mary," "Yankee Doodle Boy," "Over There," "Harrigan," "Forty-Five Minutes From Broadway" and "You're a Grand Old Flag" by George M. Cohan; "All Aboard for Old Broadway" by Jack Scholl and M. K. Jerome. 126 minutes

George M. Cohan: James Cagney, *Mary:* Joan Leslie, *Jerry Cohan:*

Walter Huston, *Sam Harris:* Richard Whorf, *Dietz:* George Tobias, *Fay Templeton:* Irene Manning, *Nellie Cohan:* Rosemary De Camp, *Josie Cohan:* Jeanne Cagney, *Schwab:* S. Z. Sakall, *Erlanger:* George Barbier, *Manager:* Walter Catlett, *Singer:* Frances Langford, *Albee:* Minor Watson, *Eddie Foy:* Eddie Foy, Jr., *Goff:* Chester Clute, *George M. Cohan (age 13):* Douglas Croft, *Josie (age 12):* Patsy Lee Parsons, *Franklin D. Roosevelt:* Captain Jack Young, *Receptionists:* Audrey Long and Ann Doran, *Madame Bartholdi:* Odette Myrtil, *Butler:* Clinton Rosemond, *Stage Manager:* Spencer Charters, *Sister Act:* Dorothy Kelly and Marijo James, *George M. Cohan (age 7):* Henry Blair, *Josie Cohan (age 6):* Jo Ann Marlow, *Stage Manager:* Thomas Jackson, *Fanny:* Phyllis Kennedy, *Magician:* Leon Belasco, *Star Boarder:* Syd Saylor, *Stage Manager:* William B. Davidson, *Dr. Lewellyn:* Harry Hayden, *Dr. Anderson:* Francis Pierlot, *Teenagers:* Charles Smith, Joyce Reynolds, *Sergeant:* Frank Faylen, *Theodore Roosevelt:* Wallis Clark, *Betsy Ross:* Georgia Carroll.

The Yearling with Gregory Peck, Claude Jarman, Jr. and Jane Wyman.

THE YEARLING (1946) MGM. Producer, Sidney Franklin. Director, Clarence Brown. Color by Technicolor. Based on the novel by Marjorie Kinnan Rawlings. Art Directors, Cedric Gibbons, Paul Groesse. Music, Herbert Stothart. Cameramen, Charles Rosher, Leonard Smith. Editor, Harold F. Kress. Screenplay, Paul Osborn. Film debut of Claude Jarman, Jr. 134 minutes

Pa Baxter: Gregory Peck, *Ma Baxter:* Jane Wyman, *Jody Baxter:* Claude Jarman, Jr., *Buck Forrester:* Chill Wills, *Pa Forrester:* Clem Bevans, *Ma Forrester:* Margaret Wycherly, *Mr. Boyles:* Henry Travers, *Lem Forrester:* Forrest Tucker, *Fodderwing:* Donn Gift, *Millwheel:* Daniel White, *Gabby:* Matt Willis, *Pack:* George Mann, *Arch:* Arthur Hohl, *Twink Weatherby:* June Lockhart, *Eulalie:* Joan Wells, *Oliver:* Jeff York, *Doc Wilson:* B. M. Chick York, *Mr. Ranger:* Houseley Stevenson, *Mrs. Saunders:* Jane Green, *Captain:* Victor Kilian, *Mate:* Robert Porterfield, *Deckhand:* Frank Eldredge.

YOU CAN'T HAVE EVERYTHING (1937) 20th. Produced by Darryl F. Zanuck. Associate Producer, Laurence Schwab. Directed by Norman Taurog. Original story by Gregory Ratoff. Screenplay, Harry Tugend, Jack Yellen, and Karl Tunberg. Dances, Harry Losee. Music Director, David Buttolph. Art Director, Duncan Cramer. Photography, Lucien Andriot. Editor, Hansen Fritch. Songs by Mack Gordon and Harry Revel: "You Can't Have Everything," "Afraid to Dream," "The Loveliness of You," "Please Pardon Us We're in Love," and "Danger—Love At Work"; "Rhythm on the Radio" by Louis Prima; "It's a Southern Holiday" by Louis Prima, Jack Loman and Dave Franklin. 99 minutes

Judith Poe Wells: Alice Faye, *Ritz Brothers:* Themselves, *George McCrea:* Don Ameche, *Sam Gordon:* Charles Winninger, *Lulu Riley:* Louise Hovick (Gypsy Rose Lee), *David Rubinoff:* Himself, *Bobby Walker:* Tony Martin, *Bevins:* Arthur Treacher, *Evelyn Moore:*

Phyllis Brooks, *Orchestra Leader:* Louis Prima, *Specialty Dancing Act:* Tip, Tap and Toe (Samuel Green, Ted Fraser, Ray Winfield) *Romano:* George Humbert, *Jerry:* Wally Vernon, *Mr. Whiteman:* Jed Prouty, *Waiter:* George Davis, *Accordion Player:* Frank Yaconelli, *Guitar Player:* Nick Moro, *Waiter:* Frank Puglia, *Blonde:* Dorothy Christie, *Alderman Barney Callahan:* Robert Murphy, *Tony:* Howard Cantonwine, *Truck Driver:* Paul Hurst, *Mrs. Romano:* Inez Palange, *Lulu's Bathing Companion:* Gordon (Bill) Elliott, *Publicity Agent:* Sam Ash, *Matron in Y.W.C.A.:* Claudia Coleman, *Miss Barkow:* Margaret Fielding, *Townswoman:* Clara Blandick, *Joan:* Lynne Berkeley, *Bagpiper:* William Mathieson, *Cab Driver:* Hank Mann, *Copilot:* Robert Lowery, *Girl in Y.W.C.A.:* June Gale.

You Can't Have Everything with Alice Faye and Don Ameche.

You Can't Take It With You with Mary Forbes, James Stewart, Jean Arthur, Irving Bacon, Robert Greig and John Hamilton.

YOU CAN'T TAKE IT WITH YOU (1938) Col. Produced and directed by Frank Capra. Based on the play by George S. Kaufman and Moss Hart. Screenplay, Robert Riskin. Music Score, Dimitri Tiomkin. Music Director, Morris Stoloff. Art Director, Stephen Goosson. Associate, Lionel Banks. Miss Arthur's Gowns, Bernard Newman and Irene. Photography, Joseph Walker. Editor, Gene Havlick. Sound, Ed Bernds. Assistant Director, Arthur Black. Film debut of xylophonist Dub Taylor. 127 minutes

Alice Sycamore: Jean Arthur, *Martin Vanderhof:* Lionel Barrymore, *Tony Kirby:* James Stewart, *Anthony P. Kirby:* Edward Arnold, *Kolenkhov:* Mischa Auer, *Essie Carmichael:* Ann Miller, *Penny Sycamore:* Spring Byington, *Paul Sycamore:* Samuel S. Hinds, *Poppins:* Donald Meek, *Ramsey:* H. B. Warner, *DePinna:* Halliwell Hobbes, *Ed Carmi-*

chael: Dub Taylor, *Mrs. Anthony Kirby:* Mary Forbes, *Rheba:* Lillian Yarbo, *Donald:* Eddie Anderson, *John Blakely:* Clarence Wilson, *Professor:* Josef Swickard, *Maggie O'Neill:* Ann Doran, *Schmidt:* Christian Rub, *Mrs. Schmidt:* Bodil Rosing, *Henderson:* Charles Lane, *Judge:* Harry Davenport, *Attorneys:* Pierre Watkin, Edwin Maxwell, Russell Hicks, *Kirby's Assistant:* Byron Foulger, *Kirby's Secretary:* Ian Wolfe, *Henry:* Irving Bacon, *Hammond:* Chester Clute, *Jailer:* James Flavin, *Inmates:* Pert Kelton, Kit Guard, *Strongarm Man:* Dick Curtis, *Detectives:* James Burke, Ward Bond, *Board Member:* Edward Keane, *Court Attendant:* Edward Hearn, *Diners:* Robert Greig, John Hamilton.

You Light Up My Life with Didi Conn.

YOU LIGHT UP MY LIFE (1977) Col. Produced/Directed/Written and Music Composed/Arranged/Conducted by Joseph Brooks. Technicolor. Associate Producers, Nicholas Grippo and Edwin Morgan. Editor, Lynzee Klingman. Photography, Eric Saarinen. Production Manager/Assistant Director, Edwin Morgan. Art Director/Set Designer, Tom Rasmussen. Sound Editors, Kate Hirson and Bernard Hajdenberg. Assistant Conductor, Jeffrey Benjamin Brooks. Music performed by members of the New York Philharmonic. 2nd Assistant Director, Sandy Knoopf. Wardrobe, John Patton and Nancy Chadwick. Casting, Lynn Stalmaster. Additional Casting, Judy Novgrad. Make-up, Donna Turner. Special Comedy Material, Gerald Segal. Sound Recorder, Art Names. Assistant to the Producer, Lisa Morrison. Assistant to the Director, Gabrielle Brooks. Clam furnished by Walt Disney Productions, Inc. Recording sequences filmed at United Western Recording Studios, Hollywood. A Presentation of Mondial International Corp., Cinema Division. Songs by Brooks: "You Light Up My Life," "The Morning of My Life," "California Daydreams," "Do You Have a Piano?" and "Rollin' the Chords." Film debut of Conn. Rated PG. 90 minutes

Laurie Robinson: Didi Conn, *Laurie as a girl:* Amy Letterman, *Si Robinson:* Joe Silver, *Cris Nolan:* Michael Zaslow, *Ken Rothenberg:* Stephen Nathan, *Annie Gerrard:* Melanie Mayron, *Conductor:* Jerry Keller, *Carla Wright:* Lisa Reeves, *Charley Nelson:* John Gowans, *Mr. Granek:* Simmy Bow, *Mrs. Granek:* Bernice Nicholson, *Account Executive:* Ed Morgan, *Creative Director:* Joe Brooks, *Mr. Nussbaum:* Marty Zagon, *Harold Nussbaum:* Martin Gish, *Usher:* Arnold Weiss, *Singer:* Brian Byers, *Usher:* Terry Brannen, *Best Man:* Tom Gerrard, *Mrs. Rothenberg:* Ruth Manning, *Receptionists:* Rosemary Lovell, Judy Novgrad, *Background Singer:* Jeffrey Kramer, *Stage Manager:* Frank Conn, *Uncle Fritz:* Sparky Watts, *Aunt Emma:* Robin O'Hara, *Commercial Directors:* Ken Olfson, Richmond Shepard, *Gail Gerard:* Aurora Roland, *Rachel:* Thelma Pelish, *Studio Musician:* John Millerburg, *Producer:* Nancy Chadwick, *Engineers:* Matt Hyde, Jerry Barnes, *Assistant Engineer:* Bob Manahan, *Bridesmaid:* Kasey Ciszk.

YOUNG FRANKENSTEIN (1974) 20th. Produced by Michael Gruskoff. Directed by Mel Brooks. Based on characters in the novel *Frankenstein* by Mary Woolstonecroft Shelley. Screenplay, Gene Wilder

and Mel Brooks. Music by John Morris. Violin solo, Gerald Vinci. Photography, Gerald Hirschfeld. Editor, John Howard. Production Designer, Dale Hennesy. Assistant Directors, Marvin Miller and Barry Stern. Set Decorations, Robert DeVestel. Make-up, William Tuttle. Sound, Gene Cantamessa. Costumes, Dorothy Jeakins. Special Effects, Hal Millar and Henry Miller, Jr. Frankenstein Laboratory Equipment, Kenneth Strickfaden. A Gruskoff/Venture Films/Crossbow Productions/Jouer Presentation. Rated PG. 108 minutes.

Dr. Frederick Frankenstein: Gene Wilder, *The Monster:* Peter Boyle, *Igor:* Marty Feldman, *Elizabeth:* Madeline Kahn, *Frau Blucher:* Cloris Leachman, *Inga:* Teri Garr, *Inspector Kemp:* Kenneth Mars, *Herr Falkstein:* Richard Haydn, *Mr. Hilltop:* Liam Dunn, *Medical Student:* Danny Goldman, *Sadistic Jailer:* Oscar Beregi, *Frightened Villager:* Lou Cutell, *Village Elder:* Arthur Malet, *Kemp's Aide:* Richard Roth, *Gravediggers:* Monte Landis, Rusty Blitz, *Little Girl:* Anne Beesley, *Villagers:* Terrence Pushman, Ian Abercrombie, Randolph Dobbs, *Blindman:* Gene Hackman, *Herr Waldman:* Leon Askin.

Young Frankenstein with Gene Wilder and Peter Boyle.

THE YOUNG LIONS (1958) 20th. Producer, Al Lichtman. Director, Edward Dmytryk. CinemaScope. Based on the novel by Irwin Shaw. Screenplay, Edward Anhalt. Art Directors, Lyle R. Wheeler, Addison Hehr. Music, Hugo Friedhofer. Music conducted by Lionel Newman. Cinematographer, Joe MacDonald. Special Photographic Effects, L. B. Abbott. Editor, Dorothy Spencer. 167 minutes

Lieutenant Christian Diestl: Marlon Brando, *Noah Ackerman:* Montgomery Clift, *Michael Whiteacre:* Dean Martin, *Hope Plowman:* Hope Lange, *Margaret Freemantle:* Barbara Rush, *Gretchen Hardenberg:* May Britt, *Captain Hardenberg:* Maximilian Schell, *Simone:* Dora Doll, *Sergeant Rickett:* Lee Van Cleef, *Francoise:* Liliane Montevecchi, *Brant:* Parley Baer, *Lieutenant Green:* Arthur Franz, *Private Burnecker:* Hal Baylor, *Private Cowley:* Richard Gardner, *Captain Colclough:* Herbert Rudley, *Cafe Manager:* Gene Roth, *Colonel Mead:* Robert Burton, *General Rockland:* Harvey Stephens, *Corporal Kraus:* John Alderson, *Private Faber:* Sam Gilman, *Private Donnelly:* L. Q. Jones, *Private Brailsford:* Julian Burton, *German Major:* Stephen Bekassy, *German Colonel:* Ivan Triesault, *British Colonel:* Clive Morgan,

Maier: Ashley Cowan, *Private Abbott:* Paul Comi, *Private Hagstrom:* Michael Pataki, *Mr. Plowman:* Vaughn Taylor, *Burn:* John Gabriel, *Emerson:* Kendall Scott, *Acaro:* Stan Kamber, *Rabbi:* Robert Ellenstein, *Drunk:* Jeffrey Sayre, *Camp Commandant:* Kurt Katch, *Physician:* Milton Frome, *Bavarian:* Otto Reichow.

The Young Lions with Marlon Brando and Maximilian Schell.

Young Mr. Lincoln with Marjorie Weaver, Alice Brady, Arleen Whelan and Henry Fonda.

YOUNG MR. LINCOLN (1939) 20th. Producer, Kenneth Macgowan. Director, John Ford. Original Screenplay, Lamar Trotti. Cameraman, Bert Glennon. Editor, Walter Thompson. 100 minutes

Lincoln: Henry Fonda, *Abigail:* Alice Brady, *Mary Todd:* Marjorie Weaver, *Hannah:* Arleen Whelan, *Eph:* Eddie Collins, *Ann Rutledge:* Pauline Moore, *Matt:* Richard Cromwell, *Felder:* Donald Meek, *Carrie Sue:* Judith Dickens, *Adam:* Eddie Quillan, *Judge Bell:* Spencer Charters, *Palmer Cass:* Ward Bond, *Douglas:* Milburn Stone, *Sheriff:* Cliff Clark, *Mr. Edwards:* Charles Tannen, *Frank:* Francis Ford, *Scrub White:* Fred Kohler, Jr., *Mrs. Edwards:* Kay Linaker, *Woodridge:* Russell Simpson, *John Stuart:* Edwin Maxwell, *Hawthorne:* Charles Halton, *Mr. Clay:* Robert Homans, *Juror:* Steven Randall, *Matt as a boy:* Jack Kelly, *Adam as a boy:* Dickie Jones, *Barber:* Harry Tyler, *Court Clerk:* Louis Mason, *Buck:* Jack Pennick, *Loafers:* Paul Burns, Frank Orth, George Chandler, Dave Morris, *Women:* Dorothy Vaughan, Virginia Brissac.

YOU ONLY LIVE TWICE (1967) UA. Produced by Harry Saltzman and Albert R. Broccoli. Directed by Lewis Gilbert. Panavision and Technicolor. An Eon-Danjaq Production. Based on the novel by Ian Fleming. Screenplay by Roald Dahl. Production Design, Ken Adam. Art Director, Harry Pottle. Sets, David Ffolkes. Music by John

Barry. Title song by John Barry and Leslie Bricusse, sung by Nancy Sinatra. Second unit directed by Peter Hunt. Action scenes directed by Bob Simmons. Assistant Director, William P. Cartlidge. Production Superviser, David Middlemas. Additional Story Material, Harry Jack Bloom. Photography, Freddie Young. Second Unit Photography, Bob Huke. Aerial Photography, John Jordan. Underwater Photography, Lamar Boren. Technical Adviser, Kikumaru Okuda. Titles, Maurice Binder. Special Effects, John Stears. Editor, Peter Hunt. Sound, John Mitchell. Filmed in Japan. The sixth James Bond film, fifth with Sean Connery. 117 minutes

James Bond: Sean Connery, *Aki:* Akiko Wakabayashi, *Tiger Tanaka:* Tetsuro Tamba, *Kissy Suzuki:* Mie Hama, *Osato:* Teru Shimada, *Helga Brandt:* Karin Dor, *Miss Moneypenny:* Lois Maxwell, *Q:* Desmond Llewelyn, *M:* Bernard Lee, *Henderson:* Charles Gray, *Chinese Girl:* Tsai Chin, *Ernst Stavro Blofeld:* Donald Pleasence, *American President:* Alexander Knox, *President's Aide:* Robert Hutton, *Spectre 3:* Burt Kwouk, *Spectre 4:* Michael Chow, *Double:* Diane Cilento.

You Only Live Twice with Tetsuro Tamba and Sean Connery.

ZIEGFELD FOLLIES (1946) MGM. Producer, Arthur Freed. Director, Vincente Minnelli. Color by Technicolor. Dance Director, Robert Alton. Musical Adaptation, Roger Edens. Musical Director, Lennie Hayton. Art Directors, Cedric Gibbons, Merrill Pye, Jack Martin Smith. Cameramen, George Folsey, Charles Rosher. Editor, Albert Akst. Orchestration, Conrad Salinger and Wally Heglin. Songs: "This Heart of Mine" by Arthur Freed and Harry Warren; "There's Beauty Everywhere" by Arthur Freed and Earl Brent; "Love" by Ralph Blane and Hugh Martin; "Limehouse Blues" by Philip Braham and Douglas Furber; "Bring on the Wonderful Men" by Earl Brent and Roger Edens; "Here's to the Girls" by Ralph Freed and Roger Edens; "The Babbitt and the Bromide" by Ira and George Gershwin. 110 minutes

ZIEGFELD DAYS Fred Astaire, Bunin's Puppets.

MEET THE LADIES Fred Astaire, Lucille Ball.

DEATH AND TAXES *Jimmy Durante:* Himself, *Mr. Huggins:* Edward Arnold, *Inspector McGrath:* Horace McNally (Stephen McNally), *Inspector Ramrod:* Douglas Cowan, *Third Inspector:* Russ Clark, *Secretary:* Kay Williams.

IF SWING GOES I GO, TOO Fred Astaire.

THE BURGLAR *Baby Snooks:* Fannie Brice, *The Father:* Hanley Stafford, *The Burglar:* B. S. Pully, *Officer Todd:* Harry Shannon.

LOVE Lena Horne.

THIS HEART OF MINE *The Imposter:* Fred Astaire, *The Princess:* Lucille Bremer, *The Duke:* Count Stefenelli, *The Duchess:* Naomi Childers, *The Countess:* Helen Boice, *Retired Dyspeptic:* Robert Wayne, *The Major:* Charles Coleman, *The Lieutenant:* Feodor Chaliapin, *The Flunky:* Sam Flint.

WE WILL MEET AGAIN Esther Williams, James Melton.

THE INTERVIEW *Judy Garland:* Herself, *The Butler:* Rex Evans.

WHEN TELEVISION COMES Red Skelton.

THE BABBIT AND THE BROMIDE Fred Astaire, Gene Kelly.

TRAVIATA James Melton, Marion Bell.

LIZA Lena Horne, Avon Long.

THE SWEEPSTAKES TICKET *Norma:* Fannie Brice, *Monty:* Hume Cronyn, *Martin:* William Frawley, *Telegraph Boy:* Arthur Walsh.

LIMEHOUSE BLUES *Tai Long:* Fred Astaire, *Moy Ling:* Lucille Bremer, *Men:* Captain George Hill, Jack Deery.

PAY THE TWO DOLLARS *Victor Moore:* Himself, *Edward Arnold:* Himself, *Special Officer:* Ray Teal, *Judge:* Joseph Crehan, *Presiding Judge:* William B. Davidson, *Warden:* Harry Hayden, *Officer:* Eddie Dunn, *Second Officer:* Garry Owen.

THE PIED PIPER *Pied Piper:* Jimmy Durante, *Mailman:* Alex Pollard, *Pedestrian:* Jack Perrin, *Maitre D'Hotel:* Eddie Kane, *Waiter:* Jack Chefe.

THE COWBOY James Melton.

FINALE—There's Beauty Everywhere.

Ziegfeld Follies with Judy Garland.

ZIEGFELD GIRL (1941) MGM. Produced by Pandro S. Berman. Directed by Robert Z. Leonard. Musical numbers directed by Busby Berkeley. In Sepia. Story, William Anthony McGuire. Screenplay, Marguerite Roberts, Sonya Levien. Score, Herbert Stothart. Music Director, Georgie Stoll. Vocals and Orchestrations, Leo Arnaud, George Bassman, Conrad Salinger. Musical Presentation, Merrill Pye. Art Director, Cedric Gibbons. Art Associate, Daniel B. Cathcart. Sets, Edwin B. Willis. Gowns and Costumes, Adrian. Make-up, Jack Dawn. Photography, Ray June. Sound, Douglas Shearer. Editor, Blanche Sewell. Songs: "You Stepped Out of a Dream" by Gus Kahn and Nacio Herb Brown; "Whispering" by John Schonberger, Richard

Coburn, Vincent Rose; "Mr. Gallagher and Mr. Shean" by Edward Gallagher and Al Shean; "I'm Always Chasing Rainbows" by Joseph McCarthy and Harry Carroll; "Caribbean Love Song" by Ralph Freed and Roger Edens; "You Never Looked So Beautiful Before" by Walter Donaldson; (from *The Great Ziegfeld,* 1936) "Minnie from Trinidad," "Ziegfeld Girls," and "Laugh? I Thought I'd Split My Sides" by Roger Edens: "You Gotta Pull Strings" (from *The Great Ziegfeld,* 1936) by Harold Adamson and Walter Donaldson. 131 minutes

Gilbert Young: James Stewart, *Susan Gallagher:* Judy Garland, *Sandra Kolter:* Hedy Lamarr, *Sheila Regan:* Lana Turner, *Frank Merton:* Tony Martin, *Jerry Regan:* Jackie Cooper, *Geoffrey Collis:* Ian Hunter, *Pop Gallagher:* Charles Winninger, *Noble Sage:* Edward Everett Horton, *Franz Kolter:* Philip Dorn, *John Slayton:* Paul Kelly, *Patsy Dixon:* Eve Arden, *Jimmy Walters:* Dan Dailey, Jr., *Al:* Al Shean, *Mrs. Regan:* Fay Holden, *Mischa:* Felix Bressart, *Mrs. Merton:* Rose Hobart, *Nick Capalini:* Bernard Nedell, *Mr. Regan:* Ed McNamara, *Jenny:* Mae Busch, *Annie:* Renie Riano, *Perkins:* Josephine Whittell, *Native Dancer:* Sergio Orta, *Ziegfeld Girls:* Jean Wallace, Myrna Dell, Lorraine Gettman (Leslie Brooks), Georgia Carroll, Louise La Planche, Nina Bissell, Virginia Cruzon, Alaine Brandes, Frances Gladwin, Patricia Dane, Irma Wilson, Anya Tarana, Madeline Martin, Vivien Mason.

Ziegfeld Girl with Lana Turner and Judy Garland.

Zorba the Greek with Anthony Quinn and Alan Bates.

ZORBA THE GREEK (1964) International Classics. Produced, directed and written by Michael Cacoyannis. Based on the novel by Nikos Kazantzakis. Camera, Walter Lassaly. Music, Mikis Theodorakis. 142 minutes.

Alexis Zorba: Anthony Quinn, *Basil:* Alan Bates, *The Widow:* Irene Papas, *Madame Hortense:* Lila Kedrova, *Mavrandoni:* George Foundas, *Lola:* Eleni Anousaki, *Mimithos:* Sotiris Moustakas, *Manolakas:* Takis Emmanuel, *Pavlo:* George Voyadjis, *Soul:* Anna Kyriakou.

THE AWARDS

FIRST YEAR   1927–1928

Best Picture: *Wings.* **Best Actor:** Emil Jannings in *The Way of All Flesh* and *The Last Command.* **Best Actress:** Janet Gaynor in *Seventh Heaven, Street Angel* and *Sunrise.* **Best Directors:** Frank Borzage for *Seventh Heaven*, Lewis Milestone for *Two Arabian Knights.*

SECOND YEAR   1928–1929

Best Picture: *Broadway Melody.* **Best Actor:** Warner Baxter in *In Old Arizona.* **Best Actress:** Mary Pickford in *Coquette.* **Best Director:** Frank Lloyd for *The Divine Lady.*

THIRD YEAR   1929–1930

Best Picture: *All Quiet on the Western Front.* **Best Actor:** George Arliss in *Disraeli.* **Best Actress:** Norma Shearer in *The Divorcee.* **Best Director:** Lewis Milestone for *All Quiet on the Western Front.*

FOURTH YEAR   1930–1931

Best Picture: *Cimarron.* **Best Actor:** Lionel Barrymore in *A Free Soul.* **Best Actress:** Marie Dressler in *Min and Bill.* **Best Director:** Norman Taurog for *Skippy.*

FIFTH YEAR   1931–1932

Best Picture: *Grand Hotel.* **Best Actors:** Fredric March in *Dr. Jekyll and Mr. Hyde*, Wallace Beery in *The Champ.* **Best Actress:** Helen Hayes in *The Sin of Madelon Claudet.* **Best Director:** Frank Borzage for *Bad Girl.*

SIXTH YEAR   1932–1933

Best Picture: *Cavalcade.* **Best Actor:** Charles Laughton in *The Private Life of Henry VIII.* **Best Actress:** Katharine Hepburn in *Morning Glory.* **Best Director:** Frank Lloyd for *Cavalcade.*

SEVENTH YEAR   1934

Best Picture: *It Happened One Night.* **Best Actor:** Clark Gable in *It Happened One Night.* **Best Actress:** Claudette Colbert in *It Happened One Night.* **Best Director:** Frank Capra for *It Happened One Night.*

EIGHTH YEAR   1935

Best Picture: *Mutiny on the Bounty.* **Best Actor:** Victor McLaglen in *The Informer.* **Best Actress:** Bette Davis in *Dangerous.* **Best Director:** John Ford for *The Informer.*

NINTH YEAR   1936

Best Picture: *The Great Ziegfeld*. **Best Actor:** Paul Muni in *The Story of Louis Pasteur*. **Best Actress:** Luise Rainer in *The Great Ziegfeld*. **Best Supporting Actor:** Walter Brennan in *Come and Get It*. **Best Supporting Actress:** Gale Sondergaard in *Anthony Adverse*. **Best Director:** Frank Capra for *Mr. Deeds Goes to Town*.

TENTH YEAR   1937

Best Picture: *The Life of Emile Zola*. **Best Actor:** Spencer Tracy in *Captains Courageous*. **Best Actress:** Luise Rainer in *The Good Earth*. **Best Supporting Actor:** Joseph Schildkraut in *The Life of Emile Zola*. **Best Supporting Actress:** Alice Brady in *In Old Chicago*. **Best Director:** Leo McCarey for *The Awful Truth*.

ELEVENTH YEAR   1938

Best Picture: *You Can't Take It With You*. **Best Actor:** Spencer Tracy in *Boys' Town*. **Best Actress:** Bette Davis in *Jezebel*. **Best Supporting Actor:** Walter Brennan in *Kentucky*. **Best Supporting Actress:** Fay Bainter in *Jezebel*. **Best Director:** Frank Capra for *You Can't Take It With You*.

TWELFTH YEAR   1939

Best Picture: *Gone With the Wind*. **Best Actor:** Robert Donat in *Goodbye, Mr. Chips*. **Best Actress:** Vivien Leigh in *Gone With the Wind*. **Best Supporting Actor:** Thomas Mitchell in *Gone With the Wind*. **Best Supporting Actress:** Hattie McDaniel in *Gone With the Wind*. **Best Director:** Victor Fleming for *Gone With the Wind*.

THIRTEENTH YEAR   1940

Best Picture: *Rebecca*. **Best Actor:** James Stewart in *The Philadelphia Story*. **Best Actress:** Ginger Rogers in *Kitty Foyle*. **Best Supporting Actor:** Walter Brennan in *The Westerner*. **Best Supporting Actress:** Jane Darwell in *The Grapes of Wrath*. **Best Director:** John Ford for *The Grapes of Wrath*.

FOURTEENTH YEAR   1941

Best Picture: *How Green Was My Valley*. **Best Actor:** Gary Cooper in *Sergeant York*. **Best Actress:** Joan Fontaine in *Suspicion*. **Best Supporting Actor:** Donald Crisp in *How Green Was My Valley*. **Best Supporting Actress:** Mary Astor in *The Great Lie*. **Best Director:** John Ford for *How Green Was My Valley*.

FIFTEENTH YEAR   1942

Best Picture: *Mrs. Miniver*. **Best Actor:** James Cagney in *Yankee Doodle Dandy*. **Best Actress:** Greer Garson in *Mrs. Miniver*. **Best Supporting Actor:** Van Heflin in *Johnny Eager*. **Best Supporting Actress:** Teresa Wright in *Mrs. Miniver*. **Best Director:** William Wyler for *Mrs. Miniver*.

SIXTEENTH YEAR   1943

Best Picture: *Casablanca*. **Best Actor:** Paul Lukas in *Watch on the Rhine*. **Best Actress:** Jennifer Jones in *The Song of Bernadette*. **Best Supporting Actor:** Charles Coburn in *The More the Merrier*. **Best Supporting Actress:** Katina Paxinou in *For Whom the Bell Tolls*. **Best Director:** Michael Curtiz for *Casablanca*.

SEVENTEENTH YEAR   1944

Best Picture: *Going My Way*. **Best Actor:** Bing Crosby in *Going My Way*. **Best Actress:** Ingrid Bergman in *Gaslight*. **Best Supporting Actor:** Barry Fitzgerald in *Going My Way*. **Best Supporting Actress:** Ethel Barrymore in *None But the Lonely Heart*. **Best Director:** Leo McCarey for *Going My Way*.

EIGHTEENTH YEAR   1945

Best Picture: *The Lost Weekend*. **Best Actor:** Ray Milland in *The Lost Weekend*. **Best Actress:** Joan Crawford in *Mildred Pierce*. **Best Supporting Actor:** James Dunn in *A Tree Grows in Brooklyn*. **Best Supporting Actress:** Anne Revere in *National Velvet*. **Best Director:** Billy Wilder for *The Lost Weekend*.

NINETEENTH YEAR   1946

Best Picture: *The Best Years of Our Lives*. **Best Actor:** Fredric March in *The Best Years of Our Lives*. **Best Actress:** Olivia de Havilland in *To Each His Own*. **Best Supporting Actor:** Harold Russell in *The Best Years of Our Lives*. **Best Supporting Actress:** Anne Baxter in *The Razor's Edge*. **Best Director:** William Wyler for *The Best Years of Our Lives*.

TWENTIETH YEAR   1947

Best Picture: *Gentleman's Agreement*. **Best Actor:** Ronald Colman in *A Double Life*. **Best Actress:** Loretta Young in *The Farmer's Daughter*. **Best Supporting Actor:** Edmund Gwenn in *Miracle on 34th Street*. **Best Supporting Actress:** Celeste Holm in *Gentleman's Agreement*. **Best Director:** Elia Kazan for *Gentleman's Agreement*.

TWENTY-FIRST YEAR 1948

Best Picture: *Hamlet.* **Best Actor:** Laurence Olivier in *Hamlet.* **Best Actress:** Jane Wyman in *Johnny Belinda.* **Best Supporting Actor:** Walter Huston in *The Treasure of Sierra Madre.* **Best Supporting Actress:** Claire Trevor in *Key Largo.* **Best Director:** John Huston for *The Treasure of Sierra Madre.*

TWENTY-SECOND YEAR 1949

Best Picture: *All the King's Men.* **Best Actor:** Broderick Crawford in *All the King's Men.* **Best Actress:** Olivia de Havilland in *The Heiress.* **Best Supporting Actor:** Dean Jagger in *Twelve O'Clock High.* **Best Supporting Actress:** Mercedes McCambridge in *All the King's Men.* **Best Director:** Joseph L. Mankiewicz for *A Letter to Three Wives.*

TWENTY-THIRD YEAR 1950

Best Picture: *All About Eve.* **Best Actor:** José Ferrer in *Cyrano de Bergerac.* **Best Actress:** Judy Holliday in *Born Yesterday.* **Best Supporting Actor:** George Sanders in *All About Eve.* **Best Supporting Actress:** Josephine Hull in *Harvey.* **Best Director:** Joseph L. Mankiewicz for *All About Eve.*

TWENTY-FOURTH YEAR 1951

Best Picture: *An American in Paris.* **Best Actor:** Humphrey Bogart in *The African Queen.* **Best Actress:** Vivien Leigh in *A Streetcar Named Desire.* **Best Supporting Actor:** Karl Malden in *A Streetcar Named Desire.* **Best Supporting Actress:** Kim Hunter in *A Streetcar Named Desire.* **Best Director:** George Stevens for *A Place in the Sun.*

TWENTY-FIFTH YEAR 1952

Best Picture: *The Greatest Show on Earth.* **Best Actor:** Gary Cooper in *High Noon.* **Best Actress:** Shirley Booth in *Come Back, Little Sheba.* **Best Supporting Actor:** Anthony Quinn in *Viva Zapata!* **Best Supporting Actress:** Gloria Grahame in *The Bad and the Beautiful.* **Best Director:** John Ford for *The Quiet Man.*

TWENTY-SIXTH YEAR 1953

Best Picture: *From Here to Eternity.* **Best Actor:** William Holden in *Stalag 17.* **Best Actress:** Audrey Hepburn in *Roman Holiday.* **Best Supporting Actor:** Frank Sinatra in *From Here to Eternity.* **Best Supporting Actress:** Donna Reed in *From Here to Eternity.* **Best Director:** Fred Zinnemann for *From Here to Eternity.*

TWENTY-SEVENTH YEAR 1954

Best Picture: *On the Waterfront.* **Best Actor:** Marlon Brando in *On the Waterfront.* **Best Actress:** Grace Kelly in *The Country Girl.* **Best Supporting Actor:** Edmond O'Brien in *The Barefoot Contessa.* **Best Supporting Actress:** Eva Marie Saint in *On the Waterfront.* **Best Director:** Elia Kazan for *On the Waterfront.*

TWENTY-EIGHTH YEAR 1955

Best Picture: *Marty.* **Best Actor:** Ernest Borgnine in *Marty.* **Best Actress:** Anna Magnani in the *The Rose Tattoo.* **Best Supporting Actor:** Jack Lemmon in *Mister Roberts.* **Best Supporting Actress:** Jo Van Fleet in *East of Eden.* **Best Director:** Delbert Mann for *Marty.*

TWENTY-NINTH YEAR 1956

Best Picture: *Around the World in 80 Days.* **Best Actor:** Yul Brynner in *Anastasia.* **Best Actress:** Ingrid Bergman in *Anastasia.* **Best Supporting Actor:** Anthony Quinn in *Lust for Life.* **Best Supporting Actress:** Dorothy Malone in *Written on the Wind.* **Best Director:** George Stevens for *Giant.*

THIRTIETH YEAR 1957

Best Picture: *The Bridge on the River Kwai.* **Best Actor:** Alec Guinness in *The Bridge on the River Kwai.* **Best Actress:** Joanne Woodward in *The Three Faces of Eve.* **Best Supporting Actor:** Red Buttons in *Sayonara.* **Best Supporting Actress:** Miyoshi Umeki in *Sayonara.* **Best Director:** David Lean for *The Bridge on the River Kwai.*

THIRTY-FIRST YEAR 1958

Best Picture: *Gigi.* **Best Actor:** David Niven in *Separate Tables.* **Best Actress:** Susan Hayward in *I Want to Live.* **Best Supporting Actor:** Burl Ives in *The Big Country.* **Best Supporting Actress:** Wendy Hiller in *Separate Tables.* **Best Director:** Vincente Minnelli for *Gigi.*

THIRTY-SECOND YEAR 1959

Best Picture: *Ben-Hur.* **Best Actor:** Charlton Heston in *Ben-Hur.* **Best Actress:** Simone Signoret in *Room at the Top.* **Best Supporting Actor:** Hugh Griffith in *Ben-Hur.* **Best Supporting Actress:** Shelley Winters in *The Diary of Anne Frank.* **Best Director:** William Wyler for *Ben-Hur.*

THIRTY-THIRD YEAR   1960

Best Picture: *The Apartment*. **Best Actor:** Burt Lancaster in *Elmer Gantry*. **Best Actress:** Elizabeth Taylor in *Butterfield 8*. **Best Supporting Actor:** Peter Ustinov in *Spartacus*. **Best Supporting Actress:** Shirley Jones in *Elmer Gantry*. **Best Director:** Billy Wilder for *The Apartment*.

THIRTY-FOURTH YEAR   1961

Best Picture: *West Side Story*. **Best Actor:** Maximilian Schell in *Judgment at Nuremberg*. **Best Actress:** Sophia Loren in *Two Women*. **Best Supporting Actor:** George Chakiris in *West Side Story*. **Best Supporting Actress:** Rita Moreno in *West Side Story*. **Best Directors:** Robert Wise, Jerome Robbins for *West Side Story*.

THIRTY-FIFTH YEAR   1962

Best Picture: *Lawrence of Arabia*. **Best Actor:** Gregory Peck in *To Kill a Mockingbird*. **Best Actress:** Anne Bancroft in *The Miracle Worker*. **Best Supporting Actor:** Ed Begley in *Sweet Bird of Youth*. **Best Supporting Actress:** Patty Duke in *The Miracle Worker*. **Best Director:** David Lean for *Lawrence of Arabia*.

THIRTY-SIXTH YEAR   1963

Best Picture: *Tom Jones*. **Best Actor:** Sidney Poitier in *Lilies of the Field*. **Best Actress:** Patricia Neal in *Hud*. **Best Supporting Actor:** Melvyn Douglas in *Hud*. **Best Supporting Actress:** Margaret Rutherford in *The V.I.P.s*. **Best Director:** Tony Richardson for *Tom Jones*.

THIRTY-SEVENTH YEAR   1964

Best Picture: *My Fair Lady*. **Best Actor:** Rex Harrison in *My Fair Lady*. **Best Actress:** Julie Andrews in *Mary Poppins*. **Best Supporting Actor:** Peter Ustinov in *Topkapi*. **Best Supporting Actress:** Lila Kedrova in *Zorba the Greek*. **Best Director:** George Cukor for *My Fair Lady*.

THIRTY-EIGHTH YEAR   1965

Best Picture: *The Sound of Music*. **Best Actor:** Lee Marvin in *Cat Ballou*. **Best Actress:** Julie Christie in *Darling*. **Best Supporting Actor:** Martin Balsam in *A Thousand Clowns*. **Best Supporting Actress:** Shelley Winters in *A Patch of Blue*. **Best Director:** Robert Wise for *The Sound of Music*.

THIRTY-NINTH YEAR   1966

Best Picture: *A Man for All Seasons*. **Best Actor:** Paul Scofield in *A Man for All Seasons*. **Best Actress:** Elizabeth Taylor in *Who's Afraid of Virginia Woolf?* **Best Supporting Actor:** Walter Matthau in *The Fortune Cookie*. **Best Supporting Actress:** Sandy Dennis in *Who's Afraid of Virginia Woolf?* **Best Director:** Fred Zinnemann for *A Man for All Seasons*.

FORTIETH YEAR   1967

Best Picture: *In the Heat of the Night*. **Best Actor:** Rod Steiger in *In the Heat of the Night*. **Best Actress:** Katharine Hepburn in *Guess Who's Coming to Dinner*. **Best Supporting Actor:** George Kennedy in *Cool Hand Luke*. **Best Supporting Actress:** Estelle Parsons in *Bonnie and Clyde*. **Best Director:** Mike Nichols for *The Graduate*.

FORTY-FIRST YEAR   1968

Best Picture: *Oliver*. **Best Actor:** Cliff Robertson in *Charly*. **Best Actress:** Katharine Hepburn in *The Lion in Winter*. **Best Supporting Actor:** Jack Albertson in *The Subject Was Roses*. **Best Supporting Actress:** Ruth Gordon in *Rosemary's Baby*. **Best Director:** Carol Reed for *Oliver*.

FORTY-SECOND YEAR   1969

Best Picture: *Midnight Cowboy*. **Best Actor:** John Wayne in *True Grit*. **Best Actress:** Maggie Smith in *The Prime of Miss Jean Brodie*. **Best Supporting Actor:** Gig Young in *They Shoot Horses, Don't They?* **Best Supporting Actress:** Goldie Hawn in *Cactus Flower*. **Best Director:** John Schlesinger for *Midnight Cowboy*.

FORTY-THIRD YEAR   1970

Best Picture: *Patton*. **Best Actor:** George C. Scott in *Patton*. **Best Actress:** Glenda Jackson in *Women in Love*. **Best Supporting Actor:** John Mills in *Ryan's Daughter*. **Best Supporting Actress:** Helen Hayes in *Airport*. **Best Director:** Franklin J. Schaffner for *Patton*.

FORTY-FOURTH YEAR   1971

Best Picture: *The French Connection*. **Best Actor:** Gene Hackman in *The French Connection*. **Best Actress:** Jane Fonda in *Klute*. **Best Supporting Actor:** Ben Johnson in *The Last Picture Show*. **Best Supporting Actress:** Cloris Leachman in *The Last Picture Show*. **Best Director:** William Friedkin for *The French Connection*.

FORTY-FIFTH YEAR 1972

Best Picture: *The Godfather*. **Best Actor:** Marlon Brando in *The Godfather*. **Best Actress:** Liza Minnelli in *Cabaret*. **Best Supporting Actor:** Joel Grey in *Cabaret*. **Best Supporting Actress:** Eileen Heckart in *Butterflies Are Free*. **Best Director:** Bob Fosse for *Cabaret*.

FORTY-SIXTH YEAR 1973

Best Picture: *The Sting*. **Best Actor:** Jack Lemmon in *Save the Tiger*. **Best Actress:** Glenda Jackson in *A Touch of Class*. **Best Supporting Actor:** John Houseman in *The Paper Chase*. **Best Supporting Actress:** Tatum O'Neal in *Paper Moon*. **Best Director:** George Roy Hill for *The Sting*.

FORTY-SEVENTH YEAR 1974

Best Picture: *The Godfather, Part II*. **Best Actor:** Art Carney for *Harry and Tonto*. **Best Actress:** Ellen Burstyn in *Alice Doesn't Live Here Anymore*. **Best Supporting Actor:** Robert De Niro in *The Godfather, Part II*. **Best Supporting Actress:** Ingrid Bergman in *Murder on the Orient Express*. **Best Director:** Francis Ford Coppola for *The Godfather, Part II*.

FORTY-EIGHTH YEAR 1975

Best Picture: *One Flew Over the Cuckoo's Nest*. **Best Actor:** Jack Nicholson in *One Flew Over the Cuckoo's Nest*. **Best Actress:** Louise Fletcher in *One Flew Over the Cuckoo's Nest*. **Best Supporting Actor:** George Burns in *The Sunshine Boys*. **Best Supporting Actress:** Lee Grant in *Shampoo*. **Best Director:** Milos Forman for *One Flew Over the Cuckoo's Nest*.

FORTY-NINTH YEAR 1976

Best Picture: *Rocky*. **Best Actor:** Peter Finch in *Network*. **Best Actress:** Faye Dunaway in *Network*. **Best Supporting Actor:** Jason Robards in *All the President's Men*. **Best Supporting Actress:** Beatrice Straight in *Network*. **Best Director:** John G. Avildsen for *Rocky*.

FIFTIETH YEAR 1977

Best Picture: *Annie Hall*. **Best Actor:** Richard Dreyfuss in *The Goodbye Girl*. **Best Actress:** Diane Keaton in *Annie Hall*. **Best Supporting Actor:** Jason Robards in *Julia*. **Best Supporting Actress:** Vanessa Redgrave in *Julia*. **Best Director:** Woody Allen for *Annie Hall*.

FIFTY-FIRST YEAR 1978

Best Picture: *The Deer Hunter*. **Best Actor:** Jon Voight in *Coming Home*. **Best Actress:** Jane Fonda in *Coming Home*. **Best Supporting Actor:** Christopher Walken in *The Deer Hunter*. **Best Supporting Actress:** Maggie Smith in *California Suite*. **Best Director:** Michael Cimino for *The Deer Hunter*.

BIBLIOGRAPHY

Academy of Motion Picture Arts and Sciences, Research Council. *Motion Picture Sound Engineering*. New York: Van Nostrand, 1938.

Agee, James. *Agee on Film: Five Film Scripts*. Boston: Beacon, 1964.

Alicoate, Charles, ed. *Film Daily Year Book of Motion Pictures*. New York: *Film Daily* Annual.

Arliss, George. *My Ten Years in the Studios*. Boston: Little, Brown & Co., 1940.

Arnheim, Rudolf. *Film as Art*. Berkeley: University of California Press, 1957.

Bardeche, Maurice, and Brasillach, Robert. *The History of Motion Pictures*. New York: Norton, 1938.

Benoit-Levy, Jean. *The Art of the Motion Picture*. New York: Coward-McCann, 1946.

Bluestone, George. *Novels into Films*. Baltimore: Johns Hopkins Press, 1957.

Callenbach, Ernest. *Our Modern Art, the Movies*. Chicago: Center for Study of Liberal Education for Adults, 1955.

Catalog of Copyright Entries, cumulative series. Motion Pictures, 1912–1939. Washington, D.C.: Copyright Office, Library of Congress, 1951.

Catalog of Copyright Entries, cumulative series. Motion Pictures, 1940–1949. Washington, D.C.: Copyright Office, Library of Congress, 1953.

Catalog of Copyright Entries, cumulative series. Motion Pictures, 1950–1959. Washington, D.C.: Copyright Office. Library of Congress, 1963.

Catalog of Copyright Entries: Motion Pictures. Washington, D.C.: Copyright Office, Library of Congress. Semi-annual.

Ceram, C. W. *Archaeology of the Cinema*. New York: Harcourt, 1965.

Clason, W. E. *Dictionary of Cinema, Sound and Music*. New York: Van Nostrand, 1956.

Cogley, John. *Report on Blacklisting*. v. 1, Movies. New York: Fund for the Republic, 1956.

Conant, Michael. *Antitrust in the Motion Picture Industry*. Berkeley and Los Angeles: University of California Press, 1960.

Cooke, David C. *Behind the Scenes in Motion Pictures*. New York: Dodd, 1960.

Crowther, Bosley. *Hollywood Rajah: The Life and Times of Louis B. Mayer*. New York: Holt, 1960.

Crowther, Bosley. Lion's Share: *The Story of an Entertainment Empire*. New York: Dutton, 1957.

Dale, Edgar. *The Content of Motion Pictures*. New York: Macmillan, 1935.

Dale, Edgar, and Morrison, John. *Motion Picture Discrimination. An Annotated Bibliography*. Columbus, Ohio: Bureau of Educational Research, Ohio State University, 1951.

Dimmitt, Richard B. *A Title Guide to the Talkies: A Comprehensive Listing of 16,000 Feature-length Films from October 27, 1927, until December 1963*. 2 vols. New York: Scarecrow, 1965.

Dixon, Campbell, ed. *International Film Annual*, No. 1, 1957. New York: Doubleday.

Doyle, G. R. *Twenty-five Years of Films*. London: Mitre Press, 1936.

Everson, William K. *The American Movies*. New York: Atheneum, 1963.

Fenin, George N., and Everson, William K. *The Western: From Silents to Cinerama*. New York: Orion Press, 1962.

Field, Robert D. *The Art of Walt Disney*. New York: Macmillan, 1942.

Franklin, Harold B. *Sound Motion Pictures: From the Laboratory to Their Presentation*. New York: Doubleday, Doran & Co., 1929.

Fulton, A. R. *Motion Pictures: The Development of an Art from Silent Films to the Age of Television*. Norman: University of Oklahoma Press, 1960.

Goldwyn, Samuel. *Behind the Screen*. New York: Doran, 1923.

Green, Abel, and Laurie, Joe, Jr. *Show Biz, from Vaude to Video*. New York: Henry Holt & Co. 1951.

Griffith, Richard, and Mayer, Arthur. *The Movies*. New York: Simon and Schuster, 1957.

Hampton, Benjamin B. *A History of the Movies*. New York: Covici-Friede, 1931.

Handel, Leo A. *Hollywood Looks at Its Audience*. Urbana: University of Illinois Press, 1950.

Hays, Will H. *See and Hear: A Brief History of Motion Pictures and the Development of Sound*. New York: Motion Picture Producers and Distributors of America, 1929.

Holaday, Perry W., and Stoddard, George D. *Getting Ideas from the Movies*. New York: Macmillan, 1933.

Huaco, George A. *The Sociology of Film Art*. New York: Basic Books, 1965.

Hughes, Elinor. *Famous Stars of Filmdom*. Boston: L. C. Page & Co., 1932.

Inglis, Ruth A. *Freedom of the Movies: A Report on Self-regulation from the Commission on Freedom of the Press*. Chicago: University of Chicago Press, 1947.

International Film Guide. London: Tantivy Press. Annual.

Jacobs, Lewis. *The Rise of the American Film: A Critical History*. New York: Harcourt, Brace & Co., 1939.

Jacobs, Lewis, ed. *Introduction to the Art of the Movies: An Anthology of Ideas on the Nature of Movie Art*. New York: Noonday Press, 1960.

Kael, Pauline. *I Lost It at the Movies*. Boston: Atlantic-Little, 1965.

Kiesling, Barrett C. *Talking Pictures: How They Are Made, How to Appreciate Them*. New York: Johnson Pub. Co., 1937.

Knight, Arthur. *Liveliest Art: A Panoramic History of the Movies*. New York: Macmillan, 1957.

Lee, Norman. *Film Is Born: How 40 Film Fathers Bring a Modern Talking Picture into Being*. London: Jordan & Sons, 1945.

LeRoy, Mervyn. *It Takes More Than Talent*, as told to Alyce Canfield. New York: Alfred A. Knopf, 1953.

McAnany, Emile G. *The Film Viewer's Handbook*. Glen Rock: Paulist Press, 1965.

Mayer, Arthur. *Merely Colossal*. New York: Simon and Schuster, 1953.

Michael, Paul. *The Academy Awards: A Pictorial History*. Indianapolis: Bobbs-Merrill, 1964.

Michael, Paul. *Humphrey Bogart: The Man and His Films*. Indianapolis: Bobbs-Merrill, 1965.

Miller, Diane Disney. *The Story of Walt Disney*. New York: Holt, 1957.

New York City. Works Progress Administration. *The Film Index, a Bibliography*. New York: Museum of Modern Art Film Library, 1941.

Pitkin, Walter B., and Marston, William M. *The Art of Sound Pictures*. New York: Appleton, 1930.
Rideout, Eric H. *The American Film*. London: Mitre Press, 1937.

Sadoul, Georges. *Histoire Generale du Cinema*. 2 vols. Paris: Denocl., 1947. *1888–1949: A Pictorial Survey of World Cinema*, new enl. ed. London: Studio Publications, 1950.

Schary, Dore. *Case History of a Movie*. New York: Random House, 1950.

Schickel, Richard. *Movies: The History of an Art and an Institution*. New York: Basic Books, 1964.

Speed, F. M. *Movie Cavalcade: The Story of the Cinema, Its Stars, Studios and Producers*. London: Raven Books, 1944.

Talbot, Daniel, ed. and comp. *Film: An Anthology*. New York: Simon and Schuster, 1959.

Taylor, John R. *Cinema Eye, Cinema Ear: Some Key Film-Makers of the Sixties*. New York: Hill & Wang, 1964.

Thrasher, Frederic, ed. *Okay for Sound: How the Screen Found Its Voice*. New York: Duell, Sloan & Pearce, 1946.

Tyler, Parker. *Magic and Myth of the Movies*. New York: Henry Holt & Co., 1947.

Wagenknecht, Edward. *The Movies in the Age of Innocence*. Norman: University of Oklahoma Press, 1962.

Warshow, Robert. *The Immediate Experience: Movies, Comics, Theatre, and Other Aspects of Popular Culture*. Garden City: Doubleday, 1964.

Winchester's Screen Encyclopedia. London: Winchester Pub., 1948.

Zinsser, William K. *Seen Any Good Movies Lately?* New York: Doubleday, 1958.

Zukor, Adolph. *The Public Is Never Wrong: The Autobiography of Adolph Zukor*, with Dale Kramer. New York: G. P. Putnam's Sons, 1953.

INDEX

Page numbers in **boldface** indicate photographs

337

Post, Ted, 170
Potter, H.C., 77, 186
Preminger, Otto, 10, 41, 75, 84, 153, 174, 184, 220

Quine, Richard, 257, 320

Rafelson, Bob, 80
Raffill, Stewart, 3
Rapper, Irving, 54, 175, 200, 204, 230
Ray, Nicholas, 142, 149, 228
Reed, Carol, 4, 296, 329
Reed, Luther, 231
Regan, Frank, 118
Reiner, Carl, 202
Reinhardt, Max, 180
Reis, Irving, 18
Reisner, Charles F., 122
Reitherman, Wolfgang, 229
Renoir, Jean, 262
Richardson, Tony, 329
Ritchie, Michael, 19
Ritt, Martin, 128, 163, 262
Robbins, Jerome, 311, 329
Roberts, Bill, 77
Robson, Mark, 34, 45, 71, 123, 133, 215, 297, 304, 306
Rosenberg, Stewart, 54
Ross, Herbert, 90, 101, 220, 276, 299
Rossen, Robert, 8, 129, 136
Rouse, Russell, 286
Ruggles, Wesley, 48, 130, 244, 254, 259
Russell, Ken, 294

Russell, William D., 60

Saks, Gene, 20, 38, 201
Sandrich, Mark, 83, 93, 117, 121, 247, 261, 295
Santell, Alfred, 57, 317
Satterfield, Paul, 77
Saville, Victor, 107, 148
Schaffner, Franklin J., 213, 214, 219, 329
Schlesinger, John, 175, 179, 329
Schoedsack, Ernest G., 148, 260
Schultz, Michael, 42
Scorcese, Martin, 8, 280
Seaton, George, 5, 14, 55, 182
Seiler, Lewis, 107
Seiter, William A., 234, 251
Seitz, George B., 156, 166
Selwyn, Edgar, 255
Shavelson, Melville, 80, 125, 246
Shear, Barry, 315
Sherman, Lowell, 184, 249
Sherman, Vincent, 112, 187
Shumlin, Herman, 309
Sidney, George, 11, 13, 38, 43, 73, 113, 211, 251, 289, 290, 306
Siegel, Don, 46, 54, 65
Silverstein, Elliott, 43
Simon, S. Sylvan, 89
Siodmak, Robert, 142
Sirk, Douglas, 170, 321
Smight, Jack, 5, 112
Spielberg, Steven, 50, 139

Stahl, John M., 18, 131, 146, 154
Stevens, Art, 229
Stevens, George, 7, 64, 94, 105, 109, 136, 184, 218, 248, 278, 279, 319, 328
Stevenson, Robert, 2, 117, 165, 177, 183, 260
Sturges, John, 19, 105, 108, 245
Sturges, Preston, 110, 151, 181
Sutherland, Edward, 213
Szwarc, Jeannot, 139

Tashlin, Frank, 261
Taurog, Norman, 29, 32, 94, 95, 230, 322, 326
Thompson, J. Lee, 109
Thorpe, Richard, 58, 104, 137, 139, 196, 290
Tokar, Norman, 83
Tourneur, Jacques, 44, 81
Tuttle, Frank, 213, 235, 287, 307

Van Dyke, W.S., 4, 144, 173, 175, 195, 223, 236, 240, 278, 280, 286, 296
Vidor, Charles, 56, 95, 111, 143, 167, 260
Vidor, King, 45, 71, 111, 198, 258, 273, 309
von Sternberg, Joseph, 184, 248

Wadleigh, Michael, 320
Waggner, George, 208
Walker, Hal, 16, 71, 231, 233, 238

Walsh, Raoul, 22, 50, 119, 133, 233, 272, 285
Walters, Charles, 20, 69, 72, 119, 157, 220, 274, 302
Wayne, John, 6, 106
Webb, Jack, 70, 215
Webb, Robert D., 167
Welles, Orson, 48, 169
Wellman, William A., 22, 118, 210, 224, 267, 270
Werker, Alfred, 125
West, Roland, 7
Whale, James, 33, 87, 144, 250
Whorf, Richard, 292
Wicki, Bernhard, 161
Wilcox, Fred M., 152
Wilder, Billy, 14, 69, 84, 164, 170, 206, 238, 246, 259, 264, 266, 276, 318, 327, 329
Winner, Michael, 61
Wise, Robert, 75, 138, 258, 262, 311, 329
Wood, Sam, 52, 59, 85, 102, 150, 196, 209, 222, 241, 272
Wyler, William, 23, 24, 25, 51, 60, 63, 68, 88, 90, 115, 141, 155, 159, 187, 235, 284, 311, 321, 327, 328

Yates, Peter, 36, 61
Young, Terence, 67, 88, 291, 303, 307

Zinnemann, Fred, 88, 114, 119, 145, 179, 200, 202, 243, 275, 328, 329

PRODUCERS

Abbott, George, 211
Adler, Buddy, 10, 37, 88, 114, 115, 133, 166, 238, 263
Adler, Lou, 302
Aldrich, Robert, 129, 312
Allen, Irwin, 220, 296
Altman, Robert, 193
Arkoff, Samuel Z., 315
Arthur, Robert, 1, 40, 51, 86, 162, 208, 249
Asher, E.M., 18
Asher, Irving, 25, 29
Axelrod, George, 172

Bacher, William A., 154
Backlar, Marshall, 221
Bart, Peter, 91
Bassler, Robert, 111, 256, 292
Beatty, Warren, 30, 114, 248
Beck, John, 113, 254
Beckerman, Sidney, 175
Berman, Pandro S., 7, 27, 37, 78, 83, 93, 109, 124, 128, 137, 138, 163, 184, 194, 201, 234, 247, 259, 265, 278, 281, 290, 295, 317, 325
Bernhard, Harvey, 203
Bill, Tony, 270
Bischoff, Sam, 11, 45
Black, Noel, 221
Blanke, Harry, 3, 200, 297
Blatty, William Peter, 76
Blaustein, Julian, 35
Blumenthal, Richard M., 287
Bogdanovich, Peter, 212, 312
Boorman, John, 62
Borzage, Frank, 82
Brabourne, John, 188
Brackett, Charles, 84, 148, 164, 195, 276, 282, 292
Bregman, Martin, 69, 245
Bresler, Jerry, 305
Briskin, Mort, 308, 316
Briskin, Samuel J., 143, 271
Broccoli, Albert R., 63, 67, 88, 100, 160, 174, 206, 264, 324
Bronston, Samuel, 73, 149
Brooks, Joseph, 323
Brooks, Mel, 118
Brooks, Richard, 132, 223
Brower, Mitchell, 94
Brown, Clarence, 128, 135
Brown, David, 139

Brown, Harry Joe, 40, 44, 57
Buchman, Sidney, 143
Buckner, Robert, 34, 98, 157, 239
Butcher, Edward, 134

Cacoyannis, Michael, 325
Camp, Joe, 24
Capra, Frank, 120, 137, 164, 178, 186, 187, 269, 322
Carr, Allan, 103
Carroll, Gordon, 54
Castle, William, 236
Chaplin, Charles, 104, 158
Chartoff, Robert, 234, 285
Chertok, Jack, 54
Cimino, Michael, 61
Coblenz, Walter, 9
Coe, Fred, 182
Cohn, Harry, 136, 205
Considine, John W., Jr., 32, 35, 142
Cooper, Merian C., 85, 224, 243, 250
Coppola, Francis Ford, 9, 97
Corman, Roger, 315
Cowan, Lester, 53, 191, 270
Cramer, Joe, 298
Crouse, Russell, 16
Cummings, Irving, 191
Cummings, Jack, 31, 73, 134, 194, 245, 272, 281, 290, 306

Da Costa, Morton, 188
Daley, Robert, 74, 75, 92, 170
D'Antoni, Philip, 36, 87
Dare, Daniel, 190, 232, 304
Dassin, Jules, 296
Daves, Delmer, 213, 274
David, Saul, 77, 209, 306
Deeley, Michael, 61
de Grunwald, Anatole, 305
De Laurentis, Dino, 149, 303, 309
De Mille, Cecil B., 35, 49, 56, 105, 198, 218, 227, 239, 252, 270, 281, 301, 302
Derr, E. B., 121
Diamond, I. A. L., 14
Disney, Walt, 2, 30, 77, 83, 177, 183, 247, 257, 300
Dolan, Robert Emmett, 313
Donen, Stanley, 45, 132, 211
Dorfman, Robert, 213
Douglas, Michael, 204
Dubs, Arthur R., 3

Edelman, Louis F., 36, 208, 260
Edens, Roger, 90
Edington, Harry E., 150
Edwards, Blake, 217, 229, 230, 250
Elfand, Martin, 69
Emerson, John, 240
Engel, Samuel G., 52, 172, 189
Engelberg, Mort, 256
Epstein, Mel, 32, 313
Epstein, Philip G., 187
Evans, Robert, 47, 175

Feldman, Charles K., 246, 272, 312
Feldman, Edward S., 209
Feldman, Phil, 315
Fellows, Robert, 123
Ferrer, Mel, 307
Ferry, Christian, 29
Feuer, Cy, 38
Fields, Freddie, 164
Fineman, B. P., 144
Finklekoffe, Fred F., 16
Fonda, Henry, 299
Fonda, Peter, 72
Ford, John, 85, 152, 250, 285
Foreman, Carl, 109, 305
Foreman, John, 37
Foster, David, 94
Foy, Bryan, 107, 126
Frank, Melvin, 2, 91, 186
Frankenheimer, John, 172
Franklin, Sidney, 52, 168, 185, 187, 226, 314, 322
Frankovich, Mike J., 38
Freed, Arthur, 10, 13, 18, 20, 50, 72, 95, 113, 178, 207, 251, 254, 279, 292, 324
Freeman, Joel, 247
Frenke, Eugene, 115
Friedman, Stephen, 153, 255
Frye, William, 5, 6

Garnett, Tay, 206
Gershwin, Jerry, 112
Gil, David, 141
Ginsberg, Henry, 94
Glazer, Benjamin, 230, 249
Glucksman, Ernest D., 201
Goetz, William, 152, 242
Golden, Edward A., 120
Goldwyn, Samuel, 15, 24, 27, 36, 60, 68, 100, 111, 128, 147, 159, 210,

220, 222, 235, 243, 273, 284, 311, 314, 320, 321
Goodwin, Richard, 188
Gordon, Leon, 148
Gordon, Max, 1
Gottfried, Howard, 195
Gottlieb, Alex, 122
Grainger, Edmund, 123, 240, 307
Greene, Clarence, 286
Greshler, Abner J., 16
Griffith, D. W., 2
Grossberg, Jack, 255
Gruskoff, Michael, 323
Guber, Peter, 61

Haight, George, 244
Hakim, Robert, 262
Haley, Jack, Jr., 283
Harmon, Sidney, 98
Harrison, Doane, 14
Hathaway, Henry, 198
Havelock-Allan, Anthony, 238
Hawks, Howard, 25, 114, 229, 231, 293
Hayward, Leland, 183, 264
Hecht, Harold, 14, 27, 43, 81, 176, 244
Heller, Paul M., 58, 74
Hellinger, Mark, 147, 192, 282
Hellman, Jerome, 52, 179
Hempstead, David, 150, 186, 197
Herman, Norman T., 66
Hertzberg, Michael, 28, 252
Hibler, Winston, 83
Higgins, Colin, 112
Hill, James, 296, 304
Hitchcock, Alfred, 27, 63, 173, 197, 199, 223, 227, 266, 271, 293
Hoffman, Herman, 19
Hornblow, Arthur, 120, 307, 318
Hornblow, Arthur, Jr., 16, 43, 92, 127, 138, 170, 181, 202, 237, 278, 310
Houseman, John, 18, 75, 146, 168
Hughes, Howard, 89, 116, 210, 242
Hulburd, Merritt, 51
Hunter, Ross, 5, 170, 217, 288
Huston, John, 183, 185
Hyman, H. Bernard, 39, 226, 240, 241
Hyman, Kenneth, 65

Jackson, Felix, 118
Jacobs, Arthur P., 219, 220
Jaffe, Stanley R., 19, 101
Jessel, George, 69, 313

341